Group Dynamics

Third Edition

Donelson R. Forsyth

Virginia Commonwealth University

Brooks/Cole • Wadsworth

I(T)P® An International Thomson Publishing Company

Belmont • Albany • Bonn • Boston • Cincinnati • Detroit • Johannesburg • London
Madrid • Melbourne • Mexico City • New York • Pacific Grove • Paris
Singapore • Tokyo • Toronto • Washington

To David and Rachel

Sponsoring Editor: *Marianne Taflinger*
Marketing Team: *Margaret Parks, Alicia Barelli*
Editorial Assistant: *Rachael Bruckman*
Advertising Communications: *Donna Shore*
Ancillary Editor: *Jennifer Wilkinson*
Production Editor: *Tom Novack*
Permissions: *The Permissions Group*
Interior Design: *Hespenheide Design*
Cover Design: *Roger Knox*

Design Coordinator: *Gary Hespenheide*
Art Editor: *Jennifer Mackres*
Project Management: *Hespenheide Design*
Typesetting: *Omegatype Typography, Inc.*
Cover Printing: *R. R. Donnelley & Sons Co./Crawfordsville*
Printing and Binding: *R. R. Donnelley & Sons Co./Crawfordsville*

For more information, contact:

WADSWORTH PUBLISHING COMPANY
10 Davis Drive
Belmont, CA 94002
USA

International Thomson Publishing Europe
Berkshire House 168-173
High Holborn
London WC1V 7AA
England

Thomas Nelson Australia
102 Dodds Street
South Melbourne, 3205
Victoria, Australia

Nelson Canada
1120 Birchmount Road
Scarborough, Ontario
Canada M1K 5G4

International Thomson Editores
Seneca 53
Col. Polanco
11560 México, D. F., México

International Thomson Publishing GmbH
Königswinterer Strasse 418
53227 Bonn
Germany

International Thomson Publishing Asia
60 Albert Street
#15-01 Albert Complex
Singapore 189969

International Thomson Publishing Japan
Hirakawacho Kyowa Building, 3F
2-2-1 Hirakawacho
Chiyoda-ku, Tokyo 102
Japan

Printed in the United States of America
10 9 8 7 6 5 4 3

Library of Congress Cataloging-in-Publication Data

Forsyth, Donelson R., 1953–
    Group dynamics / Donelson R. Forsyth.—3rd ed.
        p.   cm.
    Includes bibliographical references and index.
    ISBN (invalid) 0-534-26147-5
    1. Social groups.   I. Title.
HM131.F685   1998
302.3'4—dc21
                                        98-43023
                                        CIP

Brief Contents and Cases

1 **THE SCIENCE OF GROUP DYNAMICS** 1

2 **STUDYING GROUPS** 27

3 **THE INDIVIDUAL AND THE GROUP** 57
C. P. Ellis: From Klan Member to Enlightened Humanitarian 58

4 **JOINING AND LEAVING GROUPS** 89
The Impressionists: The Group that Redefined Beauty 90

5 **STRUCTURE** 119
Andes Survivors: One Group's Triumph over Extraordinary Adversity 120

6 **COHESION AND DEVELOPMENT** 147
Disney Studios: The Team that Walt Built 148

7 **INFLUENCE** 173
The Corona Trial Jury: The Group as Arbiter of Justice 174

8 **POWER** 207
The People's Temple: The Metamorphic Effects of Power 208

9 **CONFLICT** 235
Jobs versus Sculley: When Group Members Turn Against Each Other 236

10 **PERFORMANCE** 267
The Relay Test Room: Enhancing Productivity Through Teamwork 268

11 **DECISION MAKING** 305
Kennedy's Advisory Committee: Collective Errors and Disastrous Decisions 306

12 **LEADERSHIP** 339
Grace Pastiak of Tellabs, Inc.: Transforming People and Groups Through Leadership 340

13 **INTERGROUP RELATIONS** 375
The Rattlers and the Eagles: Group Against Group 376

14 **THE GROUP ENVIRONMENT** 409
Sealab: Living and Working in an Extraordinary Group Environment 410

15 **CROWDS AND COLLECTIVE BEHAVIOR** 441
The Who Concert Stampede: A Crowd Gone Mad? 442

16 **GROUPS AND CHANGE** 471
The Therapy Group: Groups as Interpersonal Resources 472

Contents

1 THE SCIENCE OF GROUP DYNAMICS
1

THE NATURE OF GROUPS 2
What Is a Group? Some Examples 2
What Is a Group? A Definition 5
What Is a Group? Properties
   and Processes 7
Groups Are Dynamic 11

THE NATURE OF GROUP DYNAMICS 11
The Discovery of Groups 12
Are Groups Real? 13
Contemporary Group Dynamics 18
Group Dynamics Is Dynamic 22

SUMMARY 23
FOR MORE INFORMATION 24
ACTIVITIES 25
1–1 What Is a Group? 25
1–2 Do Groups Play an Influential
     Role in Your Life? 25

2 STUDYING GROUPS
27

MEASUREMENT IN
GROUP DYNAMICS 28
Observational Techniques 29
Self-Report Measures 35

RESEARCH DESIGNS
IN GROUP DYNAMICS 39
Case Studies 39

Experimentation 40
Correlational Designs 42
Selecting a Research Design 44

THEORIES IN GROUP DYNAMICS 45
Motivational Models 46
Behavioral Approaches 46
Systems Theories 47
Cognitive Approaches 48
Biological Models 50
Selecting a Theory 51

SUMMARY 51
FOR MORE INFORMATION 52
ACTIVITIES 53
2–1 What Do Groups *Do?* 53
2–2 Can Group Discussions Be
     Measured Objectively? 54

3 THE INDIVIDUAL AND THE GROUP
57

C. P. Ellis: From Klan Member to
Enlightened Humanitarian 58

FROM ISOLATION TO BELONGING 58
The Replacement Hypothesis 59
The Belongingness Hypothesis 59
Groups and Society 64
The Value of Groups 66

FROM INDIVIDUALITY
TO COLLECTIVITY 69
Groups and Identity 69

Which Self? The Two Sides to Identity   75
Social Identity and Self-Worth   79
Turning Against the Group:
    Seeking Individuality   83

SUMMARY   84
FOR MORE INFORMATION   85
ACTIVITIES   86
3–1   How Much Is Your Sense
      of Self Based on Your Groups?   86
3–2   What Is Your Collective
      Self-Esteem?   86

**4 JOINING AND LEAVING GROUPS
89**

**The Impressionists: The Group
that Redefined Beauty   90**

BECOMING A GROUP MEMBER   90
Introversion and Extraversion   91
Social Motivation   91
Social Anxiety, Shyness, and Groups   93
Men, Women, and Groups   94

GROUP FORMATION   95
Affiliation, Ambiguity,
    and Social Comparison   95
Stress and Social Support   100
Groups and Collective Endeavors   101
Proximity and Social Integration   102
Interpersonal Attraction   103
The Economics of Membership   108

GROUP SOCIALIZATION   110
Costs and Commitment   110
Stages of Socialization   112
The End of Membership   115

SUMMARY   116
FOR MORE INFORMATION   117
ACTIVITIES   118
4–1   How Does Interpersonal
      Attraction Develop in Groups?   118
4–2   What Are the Rewards and
      Costs of Group Membership?   118

**5 STRUCTURE
119**

**Andes Survivors: One Group's
Triumph over Extraordinary
Adversity   120**

NORMS   120
The Development of Norms   121
The Transmission of Norms   123

ROLES   124
Role Differentiation   124
Role Stress   128

INTERMEMBER RELATIONS   130
Status Hierarchies   130
Social Standing   136
Communication Networks   139
The Ties that Bind   142

SUMMARY   143
FOR MORE INFORMATION   144
ACTIVITIES   145
5–1   What Is Group Structure?   145
5–2   What Is Sociometry?   145

**6 COHESION AND DEVELOPMENT
147**

**Disney Studios: The Team
that Walt Built   148**

THE NATURE OF GROUP COHESION   149
What Is Group Cohesion?   149
Measuring Group Cohesion   152

DEVELOPING GROUP COHESION   154
Stages of Group Development   154
Cycles of Group Development   159

CONSEQUENCES OF COHESION   160
Member Satisfaction and Adjustment   160
Group Dynamics and Influence   161
Group Performance   162

APPLICATION: WORK TEAMS   164
What Is a Work Team?   165
Team Building   165
Are Teams Effective?   167

SUMMARY   168
FOR MORE INFORMATION   169
ACTIVITIES   170
6–1 In What Ways Do Groups
      Change Over Time?   170
6–2 What Is a Team?   171

7 INFLUENCE
173

**The Corona Trial Jury: The Group
as Arbiter of Justice**   **174**

MAJORITY INFLUENCE:
THE POWER OF THE MANY   175
Asch and Majority Influence   175
Limits to Majority Influence   181

MINORITY INFLUENCE:
THE POWER OF THE FEW   184
Moscovici and Minority Influence   184
Influence as Social Impact   187

SOURCES OF GROUP INFLUENCE   190
Informational Influence   190
Normative Influence   192
Interpersonal Influence   193

APPLICATION:
UNDERSTANDING JURIES   197
Jury Dynamics   197
How Effective Are Juries?   199
Improving Juries   200

SUMMARY   202
FOR MORE INFORMATION   204
ACTIVITIES   205
7–1 What Does Social Influence
      Look Like?   205
7–2 Are You a Conformist?   205

8 POWER
207

**The People's Temple:
The Metamorphic Effects of Power 208**

OBEDIENCE TO AUTHORITY   208
The Milgram Experiments   209

Milgram's Findings   210

SOURCES OF POWER   213
Power Bases   214
Power Tactics   218
The Dynamics of Authority   221
The Roots of Obedience   224

THE METAMORPHIC EFFECTS
OF POWER   225
Compliance and Conversion   225
Resistance to Influence   226
Changes in the Powerholder   228
Question Authority   231

SUMMARY   231
FOR MORE INFORMATION   232
ACTIVITIES   233
8–1 Do People Underestimate
      the Power of Groups?   233
8–2 Who Has the Power in
      the Group?   234

9 CONFLICT
235

**Jobs versus Sculley: When Group
Members Turn Against Each Other 236**

THE ROOTS OF CONFLICT   237
Disaffection and Disagreement   238
Substantive Conflicts   239
Procedural Conflicts   241
Competition and Conflict   241
Social Dilemmas   247

CONFRONTATION AND ESCALATION   251
Uncertainty → Commitment   251
Perception → Misperception   252
Weak Tactics → Stronger Tactics   253
Reciprocity → Upward Conflict Spiral   255
Few → Many   256
Irritation → Anger   256

CONFLICT RESOLUTION   257
Commitment → Negotiation   257
Misperception → Understanding   259
Strong Tactics → Cooperative Tactics   259

Upward → Downward Conflict Spirals   261
Many → One   262
Anger → Composure   263
The Value of Conflict   263

SUMMARY   264
FOR MORE INFORMATION   265
ACTIVITIES   265
9–1   How Do You Manage Conflict
      in Groups?   265
9–2   What Are the Causes of
      Everyday Conflict?   266

**10 PERFORMANCE
     267**

**The Relay Test Room: Enhancing
Productivity Through Teamwork   268**

SOCIAL FACILITATION   268
When Does Social Facilitation Occur? 269
Why Does Social Facilitation Occur?   272
Social Facilitation: Conclusions
    and Applications   275

SOCIAL COMBINATION   277
Composition: Who Is in the Group?   277
Task Demands: What Is to Be Done?   280
Two Heads Are Better, Sometimes   285

SOCIAL MOTIVATION   286
Productivity Losses in Groups   286
Causes of Social Loafing   288
Increasing Social Motivation   291
When Coordination and Motivation
    Losses Combine: Brainstorming   294

SUMMARY   299
FOR MORE INFORMATION   300
ACTIVITIES   301
10–1 Types of Tasks   301
10–2 Brainstorming   302

**11 DECISION MAKING
     305**

**Kennedy's Advisory Committee:
Collective Errors and
Disastrous Decisions   306**

GROUPS AS DECISION MAKERS   307
Remembering Information   307
Processing Information   309

GROUPS AS IMPERFECT
DECISION MAKERS   315
Sharing Information   315
Group Discussion: Boon or Bane?   318
Cognitive Limitations   319
Group Polarization   320

VICTIMS OF GROUPTHINK   324
Symptoms of Groupthink   325
Causes of Groupthink   328
Predicting the Emergence of
    Groupthink   330
Preventing Groupthink   332

SUMMARY   334
FOR MORE INFORMATION   336
ACTIVITIES   337
11–1 Making Decisions In Groups   337
11–2 Observe a Group Decision   338

**12 LEADERSHIP
     339**

**Grace Pastiak of Tellabs, Inc.:
Transforming People and Groups
Through Leadership   340**

THE NATURE OF LEADERSHIP   340
Questions about Leadership   340
Leadership: A Conceptual Definition 343
Leadership: A Behavioral Definition 344

LEADERSHIP EMERGENCE   347
Personal Qualities of Leaders   348
Who Will Lead? A Cognitive
    Explanation   353

LEADER EFFECTIVENESS   355
Fiedler's Contingency Model   355
"Style" Theories   359
Participation Theories   361
Leader-Member Exchange Theory   367
Transformational Leadership   368
Women and Men as Leaders   369
What Is the Key to Leadership?   370

Contents

SUMMARY 371
FOR MORE INFORMATION 372
ACTIVITIES 373
12–1 What Is Your Leadership Style? 373
12–2 Leadership Interviews 374

13 INTERGROUP RELATIONS
375

The Rattlers and the Eagles:
Group Against Group 376

COMPETITION AND CONFLICT:
US VERSUS THEM 378
Competition and Mutual Distrust 379
Escalation of Conflict 381

SOCIAL CATEGORIZATION:
PERCEIVING US AND THEM 385
The Ingroup/Outgroup Bias 386
Cognitive Consequences
of Categorization 389
Does Categorization Cause Conflict? 393

RESOLVING INTERGROUP CONFLICT:
UNITING US AND THEM 396
Intergroup Contact 396
Beyond Contact: Promoting
Intergroup Cooperation 397
Cognitive Cures for Conflict 401
Conflict Management 403
Resolving Conflict: Conclusions 405

SUMMARY 405
FOR MORE INFORMATION 407
ACTIVITIES 407
13–1 Experiencing Intergroup Conflict 407
13–2 Intergroup Relations in the News 408

14 THE GROUP ENVIRONMENT
409

Sealab: Living and Working in
an Extraordinary Group
Environment 410

GROUPS IN CONTEXT 411
Temperature 411

Noise 412
Environmental Load 413
Staffing 415
Dangerous Places 418

GROUP SPACES 419
Personal Space 419
Reactions to Spatial Invasion 421
Seating Arrangements 424

GROUP PLACES 427
Group Territories 428
Territoriality Within Groups 432
Groups in Spaces and Places:
Beyond Sealab 437

SUMMARY 437
FOR MORE INFORMATION 438
ACTIVITIES 439
14–1 Territoriality 439
14–2 Group Synomorphy 440

15 CROWDS AND COLLECTIVE
BEHAVIOR
441

The Who Concert Stampede:
A Crowd Gone Mad? 442

KINDS OF COLLECTIVES 443
Crowds 444
Collective Movements 449

COLLECTIVE DYNAMICS 453
Le Bon's Crowd Psychology 453
Convergence Theories 455
Emergent Norm Theory 456
Deindividuation Theory 457
Self-Awareness and Deindividuation 462
Collectives and Identity 464

POSTSCRIPT: COLLECTIVES
ARE GROUPS 466

SUMMARY 468
FOR MORE INFORMATION 468
ACTIVITIES 469
15–1 Observing Crowds 469
15–2 Experiencing Collective
Behavior 470

16 GROUPS AND CHANGE
471

**The Therapy Group: Groups
as Interpersonal Resources** 472

GROUP APPROACHES TO CHANGE 472
Group Psychotherapy 473
Interpersonal Learning Groups 477
Self-Help Groups 480

SOURCES OF CHANGE IN GROUPS 481
Universality and Hope 482
Social Learning 483
Group Cohesion 486
Disclosure and Catharsis 487
Altruism 488
Insight 488

THE EFFECTIVENESS OF GROUPS 489
Perceptions Versus Behaviors 490
Evidence of Negative Effects 490
Types of Groups and Effectiveness 491

The Value of Groups 492
SUMMARY 493
FOR MORE INFORMATION 494
ACTIVITIES 495
16–1 Self-Disclosure in Groups 495
16–2 Visit a Change-Promoting Group 496

REFERENCES
497

NAME INDEX
587

SUBJECT INDEX
608

CREDITS
620

Preface

Why study groups? Why learn about the processes that unfold in interacting, dynamic groups? Why study theories that explain these processes? Why extend these theories to explain more and more about groups?

The answer is not complicated: Because groups are important. They are important, at the *psychological* level, for individuals' actions, thoughts, and emotions can't be understood without taking into consideration the groups they belong to and the groups that surround them. Human behavior is more often than not group behavior, so people can't be understood when cut apart from their groups (including their families, friendship cliques, work groups). Groups also have a profound impact on individuals; groups shape actions, thoughts, and feelings.

Groups are important at the *sociological* level. The dictionary that defines a society as an "organized system of individuals living as members of a community" is mistaken. A society is an organization of groups rather than individuals. All kinds of societies—hunting/gathering, horticultural, pastoral, industrial, and postindustrial—are defined by the characteristics of the small groups that comprise them. Societal forces, such as traditions, values, and norms, don't reach directly to individuals, but instead work through the groups to which each individual belongs.

Groups are also important for *practical* reasons. Much of the world's work is done by groups, so by understanding them we move toward making them more efficient. If we want to improve productivity in a factory, problem-solving in a boardroom, or learning in the classroom we must understand groups. Groups, too, hold the key to solving such societal problems as racism, sexism, and international conflict. Because groups are the building blocks of society any attempt to change society will succeed only if the groups within that society change.

Last, groups are *personally* important. You spend your entire life surrounded by and embedded in groups. Through membership in groups you define and confirm your values and beliefs and take on or refine a social identity. When you face uncertain situations, in groups you gain reassuring information about your problems and security in companionship. In groups you learn about relations with others, the type of impressions you make on others, and the way you can relate with others more effectively. Groups influence you in consequential ways, so you ignore their influence at your own risk. The corrolary to the maxim "The unexamined life is not worth living" may well be "The unexamined group interaction is not worth repeating."

OVERVIEW

This book does not review exhaustively the extensive field of group dynamics, but serves instead as an introduction to the theories, studies, and empirical findings pertinent to groups. As a primer rather than an encyclopedia, *Group Dynamics* seeks one basic goal: To inventory the results of scientific explorations of the nature of groups. It achieves this goal by integrating, whenever possible, theory and research, basic science and application, classic and contemporary work, and psychological and sociological analyses of groups.

Theory and Research. The text takes a scientific approach to groups. Hundreds of empirical studies of group processes are described and summarized, but most are those that extend our theoretical understanding of groups. This emphasis on theory-grounded knowledge sometimes means that less central, though nonetheless interesting, topics are sometimes slighted, but when possible the curious reader is referred to other sources for additional information.

Basic and Applied Science. Group dynamics appeals to theoretically minded basic research scientists and applications-oriented individuals who work with groups in industrial, organizational, educational, judiciary, and therapeutic contexts. We take as given, however, Kurt Lewin's dictum: There is nothing so practical as a good theory. Lewin argued against the traditional distinction between basic and applied science by suggesting that scientific understanding will occur most rapidly if researchers and individuals with applied interests work together to understand groups. This text also embraces this unified approach to the study of groups.

Traditional and Contemporary Topics. Our current understanding of groups was shaped by the work of Kurt Lewin and many other scholars of the 19th and 20th century. The text concentrates on topics that lie at the heart of contemporary group dynamics, but classic analyses of groups are integrated with current topics to achieve an historically grounded overview.

Psychology, Sociology, and Other Social Sciences. No one discipline holds the exclusive rights to the study of groups. Scientists in such fields as psychology, sociology, social psychology, anthropology, speech and communication, political science, business, education, and psychiatry examine the nature of groups, and whenever possible the text integrates these perspectives to build an interdisciplinary analysis of group behavior.

FEATURES

Every attempt has been made to create a textbook that teaches group dynamics rather than one that simply exposes the student to basic principles and research findings. The 16 chapters progress from basic issues and processes to the analysis of more specialized topics, but this order is somewhat arbitrary and many may prefer a different sequence.

Terms, Glossary, and Names. Key terms are presented in boldface type, and they are defined at the bottom of the page where they are first mentioned. Citations are given in the style of the American Psychological Association, and usually include investigators' last names and the date of the publication of the research report or book. When named in the text their first and last names are included.

Outlines, Summaries, and Readings. The first page of each chapter asks several questions examined in that chapter, and also outlines the chapter's contents. Each chapter uses three levels of headings. The primary headings are printed in all capitals, the secondary headings are printed in boldface type, and the tertiary headings begin individual paragraphs. Each chapter also ends with a concise summary, which answers the questions posed at the beginning of the chapter and list of sources to consult for more information.

Activities. Each chapter includes two suggestions for activities that can be completed either in classroom groups or outside the class. For example, students are urged to conduct observations of groups, assess the structure of a group through sociometry, estimate a group's cohesiveness, document the phases of group development for a group to which they belong, solve problems and make decisions in groups, interview people to identify common assumptions about leadership, and attend a public meeting of a support group.

Cases. Chapters 3 to 16 use case studies to illustrate and integrate the chapter's contents. The chapter on group formation, for example, focuses on the impressionists, and the chapter dealing with conformity highlights a jury in a murder trial. All the cases are or were real groups rather than hypothetical ones, and the incidents described are documented events that occurred within the group.

CHANGES FROM THE SECOND EDITION

The third edition of Group Dynamics retains many of the features of the earlier editions. Each chapter uses a case study of a real group, rather than a vignette of a hypothetical group, to engage the reader and provide continuity within each chapter. The book's 2,500 references to research reports, theoretically based articles, books, and chapters in edited volumes provide a comprehensive, empirically driven perspective on groups. As with previous editions, the chapters are written to stand alone, so they can be read in any order.

So what is new? The most essential change is in coverage: The review of theory and research has been updated to reflect advances of the last 10 years. Researchers continue to gain new insights into groups, and the text reviews and summarizes these advances. Specific changes include:

Chapter 1, The Science of Groups, reviews the nature of groups and the nature of group dynamics. The "defining features of groups" list has been amended to include social identity, and the section dealing with group goals presents McGrath's taxonomy of group tasks. The analysis of the question "Are groups real?" reviews the supervening qualities of groups.

Chapter 2, Studying Groups, describes basic measurement methods and designs researchers use to test their hypotheses about groups. New to this edition is an extensive treatment of theories that explain group processes.

Chapter 3, The Individual and the Group, is a new chapter. After asking the basic question, "Why groups?," it reviews the impact of the group on individuals' social identity. This chapter examines a number of current topics in group research, including individualism-collectivism, cross-cultural aspects of group behavior, social categorization, social identity theory, and the belongingness hypothesis. The chapter's case considers the way C. P. Ellis's life changed as he joined new groups and left others behind.

Chapter 4, Joining and Leaving Groups, explores three basic questions: "Who joins groups?," "When do groups form?," and "When do groups disband?" The coverage of individual differences in tendencies to join groups (introversion-extraversion, sex differences) is expanded, and social exchange theory and group socialization theory provide the guiding theoretical frameworks for integrating the empirical evidence. This material provides insights into the situational and personal factors that contributed to the formation of one of the most influential artists circle of all time: the impressionists.

Chapter 5, Structure, describes the tendency for relationships among the group members to become organized and predictable. In addition to the analysis of roles and intermember relations (status, attraction, and communication), the third major structural feature of groups, norms, is discussed in this chapter, rather than in the chapter dealing with conformity. The case study examines the developmental of norms, roles, and intermember relations in a group of young men stranded in the Andes.

Chapter 6, Cohesion and Development, is a new chapter for this edition. Analyses of group development, which were previously examined in a separate chapter, are now reviewed within the context of a group's evolution from a collection of separate individuals into a cohesive unit. The concept of cohesion is reviewed in much more detail and is used to explain how teams can be created and used to improve group performance. The development of teamwork in a work group is illustrated in the chapter's case: the Disney Studios during the creation of the movie *Snow White*.

Chapter 7, Influence, examines how group processes can change individual members' thoughts, feelings, and behaviors. Both sides of social influence—minority influence and majority influence—are reviewed, along with the classic experimental paradigms developed by Solomon Asch and Serge Moscovici. Dynamic social impact theory and cognitive foundations of influence are covered in more detail, and the chapter's case—the jury in the murder trial of Juan Corona—provides a backdrop for the analysis of decision-making in juries.

Chapter 8, Power, explores the reasons behind more dramatic forms of social influence, particularly the power of an authority over subordinates. Stanley Milgram's studies of obedience provide the central focus for this chapter, and such concepts as power bases, power tactics, the metamorphic effects of power are used to explain the roots of the obedience he documented. Informational power, diffusion of responsibility, and compliance tactics are a few of the concepts considered in more detail in this edition, and the chapter's case study is the People's Temple: a religious group that obeyed a leader's order to commit suicide.

Chapter 9, Conflict, is an extensively revised analysis of intragroup disputes. This chapter begins by considering basic types of conflict within groups, including personality, substantive, and procedural conflicts, as well as conflicts rooted in competition. A section that explains why conflicts tend to escalate in groups is complemented by a section that explains how conflicts can be controlled. The material on coalition formation has been drastically reduced, whereas coverage of the Prisoner's Dilemma and styles of conflict management have been expanded. An organizational conflict, the rivalry between two corporate executives in a major U.S. company, provides the case material for this chapter.

Chapter 10, Performance, reviews three basic aspects of group performance: social facilitation, social combination, and social motivation. Classic analyses of these processes, such as Robert Zajonc's analyses of social influence, Ivan Steiner's model of group combination, and Max Ringelmann's work on performance decrements are integrated with recent studies of electronic-performance monitoring, team diversity, team motivation, and team-member coordination. The chapter's case study examines how a manufacturing plant used a team to increase worker productivity.

Chapter 11, Decision Making, updates the insights provided by Irving Janis's theory of groupthink and studies of polarization in groups with more recent studies of groups-as-information-processors. The cognitive foundations of group decision making are reviewed more thoroughly, as is the tendency for groups to oversample shared information during discussions. The group that planned the ill-fated Bay of Pigs invasion provides considerable insight into the limitations of groups.

Chapter 12, Leadership, provides an updated analysis of leadership and management processes in groups. Questions of leadership emergence and effectiveness are considered in detail in this chapter, which now follows the chapters on group performance to reflect the greater emphasis on the leader's impact on productivity rather than as a source of social influence. Leader-member exchange theory and transformational leadership theory are new additions to this chapter, which returns frequently to questions of sex differences and sex biases in the leadership process. A woman executive in a major U.S. company serves as the chapter's case study.

Chapter 13, Intergroup Relations, considers the causes and consequences of disputes between groups. The roots of intergroup conflict, particularly the group discontinuity effect and categorization-based biases, are reviewed in more detail, as are cognitive methods for minimizing conflict (such as decategorization and recategorization). The Robbers Cave experiment serves as the chapter's case.

Chapter 14, The Group Environment, reviews the impact of the environment—temperature, noise, space, and territoriality—on the group and its members. Coverage of basic ambient features, such as noise and staffing, is expanded, and the analysis of territoriality and crowding has been streamlined. Sealab, a military project in which men lived in a cramped underseas habitat for over two weeks, provides the backdrop for the analysis.

Chapter 15, Crowds and Collective Behavior, considers larger groups and more geographically dispersed aggregates, such as social movements. This chapter now stresses the relative normalcy of such groups, and the presentation of theoretical perspectives on crowds and collectives reduces the emphasis on deindividuation theory but adds a social identity theory analysis of crowds. The case: a large crowd of people that panicked waiting for a rock concert.

Chapter 16, Groups and Change, thoroughly reviews various means of achieving personal change through membership in groups, including psychotherapy groups and self-help groups. The analysis of curative factors in groups has been expanded, and the material on effectiveness is now considered as a postscript to the chapter. An interpersonal psychotherapy group provides the case study for the chapter.

ACKNOWLEDGMENTS

Most things in this world are accomplished by groups rather than by single individuals working alone. This book is no exception. Although I am personally responsible for the ideas presented in this book, many colleagues also provided me with indispensible comments and suggestions, including:

Scott Allison, University of Richmond;
Wynona Elder, formerly of Southwestern Baptist Theological Seminary;
Wendy Harrod, Iowa State University;
Jesse Jordan, Francis Marion University;
Steve Karau, University of Southern Illinois;
Arthur Kemp, Central Missouri State University;
Mark Leary, Wake Forest University;
Glenn Littlepage, Middle Tennessee University;
Michael Lovaglia, University of Iowa;
Robart Mauro, University of Oregon;
Richard Moreland, University of Pittsburgh;
Janet Sigal, Fairleigh Dickinson University;
Mark Stasson, Virginia Commonwealth University;
Stanley Strong, Virginia Commonwealth University; and
Sue Szczesny, Wayne State University;
Kipling Williams, University of New South Wales.

But groups, as well as individuals, helped with the project. My classes provided me with the opportunity to refine my presentation of the materials, for my students were all too eager to give me feedback about ambiguities and weaknesses. The graduate students and faculty of the Social Psychology Division of Virginia Commonwealth University provided me with many opportunities to share my conceptualizations about groups and their processes through classes, colloquia, and informal discussions. The members of the production teams at Brooks/Cole and Hespenheide Design also deserve special thanks for their capable efforts, and they include Marianne Taflinger, Gary Hespenheide, Tom Novack, Marjorie Sanders, Jennifer Wilkinson, Rachael Bruckman, and Margaret Parks.

Last, but certainly not least, my most important group—my family—deserves special acknowledgment. They never read a single word of the book, but then again they never criticized a single word in the book either. Moreover, they provided the emotional and interpersonal antidote to the long nights spent researching, reading, and writing. Thank you, Claire, David, and Rachel.

Donelson R. Forsyth

1

The Science of Group Dynamics

Group dynamics are the potent interpersonal processes that take place in groups. The tendency to join with others in groups is perhaps the most important single characteristic of humans, and these groups leave an indelible imprint on their members and society. To understand people, we must understand their groups.

- What is a group, and what characteristics do most groups possess?
- When did researchers begin studying groups scientifically?
- Are groups real in the sense that they are more than the sum total of the individuals who belong to them?
- What assumptions guide contemporary researchers' studies of groups and their processes?

CONTENTS

THE NATURE OF GROUPS

What Is a Group? Some Examples

What Is a Group? A Definition

What Is a Group? Properties and Processes

Groups Are Dynamic

THE NATURE OF GROUP DYNAMICS

The Discovery of Groups

Are Groups Real?

Contemporary Group Dynamics

Group Dynamics Is Dynamic

SUMMARY

FOR MORE INFORMATION

ACTIVITIES

Groups are and always will be essential to human life. Our primal ancestors protected themselves from dangerous animals, human enemies, and natural disasters by joining together in groups. Teams of workers in ancient civilizations combined their efforts to build dams, irrigation systems, and colossal monuments. Merchants and craftspeople formed guilds to organize business practices as early as 300 B.C. The Romans used groups extensively, organizing their complex society by means of military tribunes, legislative bodies, and trade associations. Religious rites, too, have traditionally been group activities (Zander, 1985).

Groups remain the context for most social activities. Of the billions of people populating the world, all but an occasional recluse or exile belong to a group. We find groups everywhere we turn: audiences, boards of directors, committees, dance troupes, families, gangs, juries, orchestras, sororities, support groups, teams, and on and on. The world is teeming with groups. Most of us belong to several groups, and the number of groups in the world probably reaches well beyond 5 billion.

The impact of these groups on individuals, their communities, and their cultures is enormous. Thus, to understand individuals, we must necessarily understand their groups. Virtually all of the activities of our lives—working, learning, worshiping, relaxing, playing, and even sleeping—occur when we are in groups rather than isolated from others. Groups are the basic building blocks of society. Cultural forces do not reach directly to the individual, but instead work through the groups to which the individual belongs. Understanding groups, then, is the key to understanding ourselves, other people, and society.

Yet, groups remain something of a mystery: unstudied at best, misunderstood at worst. So here we unravel some of their mysteries by examining their basic nature, their processes, and their impact on our lives. We begin by considering two fundamental questions. First, what do we mean by the word *group?* What is a group, what are the key characteristics of groups, and what kinds of group processes will we be studying? Second, what do we mean by *group dynamics?* What assumptions will we embrace as we describe, analyze, and compare the various groups that populate the planet? What approach will we take, as scientists, to the study of groups?

THE NATURE OF GROUPS

Centuries ago, Cicero wrote, "A man does not wonder at what he sees frequently, even though he be ignorant of the cause." Could the commonness of groups inhibit our understanding of them? We live in and around groups and become so accustomed to them that we do not notice their influence. So we will begin our scientific analysis of groups by defining the term *group* and delineating the key elements of most groups.

What Is a Group? Some Examples

When scientific researchers encounter intriguing phenomena—a rarely seen species of spider, an illness unlike any other, a particle emitting atypical radiation—they often initiate their study by gathering as much circumstantial information as possible. Here we consider some commonplace groups and some extraordinary ones before offering a definition of the word *group*.

The Artists. The classicists dominated the world of art in 19th-century France. They favored religious and historical images and they belittled any painter who offered a contrasting perspective on artistic form and content. But a dedicated band of radical painters and artists eventually overwhelmed the classicists. Two founding members of the movement, Claude Monet and Camille Pissarro, met in 1860 and immediately became friends. Two years later, Edouard Manet and Edgar Degas joined them in their search for alternative forms of artistic expression. Later that year, Monet met Pierre-Auguste Renoir, Alfred Sisley, and Frédéric Bazille and persuaded them to join the clique.

The young artists worked together to develop a new approach to painting, often journeying into the countryside to paint landscapes. They sometimes painted side by side and patiently critiqued one another's work. They also met in cafés in Paris to discuss technique, subject matter, and artistic philosophies. Art critics rejected their approach for years, and the artists scarcely earned enough money to survive. But in time they were recognized by the art community as a new school of painting—the impressionists—and their paintings are now revered and worth millions of dollars (Farrell, 1982).

The Survivors. The rugby team's chartered plane crashed in clear weather on a snow-covered peak deep in the Andes Mountains. The crash survivors banded together, pooling their resources and skills to survive in the subzero temperatures. Each one was responsible for performing certain tasks. Some cleaned their sleeping quarters, some tended the injured, and others melted snow into drinking water. The captain of the team coordinated these activities until an avalanche killed him. Three cousins then stepped forward to take on the business of running the group's activities.

The group lived for weeks by eating the bodies of those who had died in the crash and avalanche, but when starvation seemed imminent, they sent two men down the mountain to seek help. The two walked for 14 days before they reached a small farm on the edge of the great mountain range. Their sudden appearance after 70 days was followed by a rescue operation that lifted the remaining 14 from the crash site. Those who had managed to stay alive later pointed out that "it was their combined efforts which saved their lives" (Read, 1974, p. 310).

The Jury. The 12 men and women began deliberating the case of *California v. Juan Corona* on January 11, 1973. The jurors spent considerable time discussing the evidence in general and clarifying among themselves the judge's instructions. The group moved painstakingly, reviewing each bit of evidence and insisting that all members state their views openly. Each day, too, as they left the courthouse for dinner and their hotel rooms, they passed by a crowd that supported the defendant. They also had to face his four young children, who were strategically placed where each juror would see them.

The jurors who believed that Corona was guilty gradually began to dominate the group's discussion. After spending hours examining evidence found at one particular grave, the jury concluded that Corona must have been the one who dug the grave. Receipts bearing Corona's name had been found in the grave, and one juror persuasively argued that since Corona never threw away receipts and the receipts had been still folded together when found, they must have fallen from his pocket when he was digging the hole. After eight days of argument, discussion, and debate, the group reached its conclusion: guilty (Villaseñor, 1977).

The Congregation.   Jim Jones was a leader. His teaching influenced many, and membership in his church, The People's Temple Full Gospel Church, eventually swelled to 8000. Rumors of improprieties began circulating, however. Former members reported that at some meetings, those who had displeased Jones were severely beaten before the whole congregation, with microphones used to amplify their screams. Jones, some said, insisted on being called Father, and he demanded absolute dedication and obedience from his followers. Many members donated all their property to the church, and one couple even turned over their 6-year-old son on demand.

Jones moved the group to Guyana, in South America, where he established Jonestown. Press releases described the settlement as a utopian community, but rumors still circulated. Was Jonestown a utopia or a prison? Then disaster struck when church members attacked and killed members of a delegation from the United States. Jones, fearing the dismantling of his empire, ordered his followers to take their own lives. Authorities who first reached the settlement were met by a scene of unbelievable ghastliness. On Jones's orders, more than 900 men, women, and children had killed themselves. Jones's body lay near his chair, where he sat beneath the motto "Those who do not remember the past are condemned to repeat it" (Krause, 1978).

The Committee.   President John F. Kennedy created the group because the issues at hand were so complex that they would have overwhelmed a single individual. He was reviewing the Central Intelligence Agency's plan to back an invasion of Cuba by 1400 anti-Castro exiles, but he didn't want to want to make the decision by himself. So the president gathered an elite group of political figures with years of experience in making important government decisions. The group met for many hours, and a strong feeling of mutual respect soon welded the group into a cohesive unit.

The group decided to approve the invasion, and they personally chose the site for the landing: an inlet on the southern side of Cuba called Bahía de Cochinos, the Bay of Pigs. But on the day of the invasion, little went according to plan. The committee had assumed that the Cuban army would be disorganized, ill equipped, and small, but in less than 24 hours, 200 men in the landing force had been killed, and the remaining 1200 were captured quickly. The attack that had been so carefully planned by the committee ended in complete disaster, and the committee members spent the following months wondering at their shortsightedness and cataloging all the blunders they had made (Janis, 1972, 1982, 1983).

The Therapy Group.   The seven members of the group were outpatients at a university clinic. All seven reported problems in relating to other people, to the extent that they could not establish meaningful interpersonal relationships. The two psycho-therapists who led the group during the weekly meetings encouraged the members to share problems from their daily lives and give one another support. They also asked the members to disclose information about themselves to others and gave them feedback that helped them acquire useful social skills.

Despite the fact that the group was composed entirely of people who had never been able to maintain friendships or intimate relationships, it became remarkably unified. The members rarely missed a session, and they grew more confident whenever they disclosed some previously unmentioned aspect of themselves. The therapists felt that the group seemed to plod at times, but the clients themselves were excited by their ability to interact successfully. The group lasted for 30 months, after which clinical testing indicated that the members "did extraordinarily well and underwent substantial characterologic changes as well as complete symptomatic remission" (Yalom, 1985, p. 267).

What Is a Group? A Definition

A loosely organized band of outcasts from the art community struggling to refine the way they created beauty. A sports team surviving against all odds in a frozen environment. Twelve men and women deciding the fate of an accused serial killer. A powerful religious leader and his followers committing suicide in the utopia they called Jonestown. Military and political experts planning an ill-fated invasion. Seven troubled individuals working to overcome their psychological problems.

Each of these collections of people may seem unique, but each possesses that one critical element that defines a group: *interdependence among the members* (Lewin, 1948). We understand intuitively that three persons seated in separate rooms working on unrelated tasks can hardly be considered a social group, for they cannot influence one another in any way. If, however, we create the potential for interdependence by letting at least one person influence or be influenced by the others, these three individuals can be considered a rudimentary group. The impressionists, for example, lived and worked together, influencing one another's ideas and techniques. Stranded in the Andes, the survivors helped one another overcome the many hardships they faced. The members of the therapy group provided one another with encouragement and support. In all these examples, and in most other groups, members "have relationships to one another that make them interdependent to some significant degree" (Cartwright & Zander, 1968, p. 46). A **group,** then, is two or more interdependent individuals who influence one another through social interaction.

This definition, although consistent with many theoretical perspectives on groups, is but one definition among many. As Table 1–1 reveals, many theorists stress interdependence when describing groups, while others highlight other properties, such as communication, influence, identity, and structure. The definition also sets no size restrictions on groups. It assumes that very small collectives, such as dyads (two

Group: Two or more interdependent individuals who influence one another through social interaction.

TABLE 1–1   A SAMPLING OF DEFINITIONS OF *GROUP*

Central Feature	Definition
Communication	"We mean by a group a number of persons who communicate with one another, often over a span of time, and who are few enough so that each person is able to communicate with all the others, not at second hand, through other people, but face-to-face" (Homans, 1950, p. 1).
Influence	"Two or more persons who are interacting with one another in such a manner that each person influences and is influenced by each other person" (Shaw, 1981, p. 454).
Interaction	"A group is a social system involving regular interaction among members and a common group identity. This means that groups have a sense of "weness" that enables members to identify themselves as belonging to a distinct entity" (Johnson, 1995, p. 125).
Interdependence	"A group is a collection of individuals who have relations to one another that make them interdependent to some significant degree" (Cartwright & Zander, 1968, p. 46).
Interrelations	"A group is an aggregation of two or more people who are to some degree in dynamic interrelation with one another" (McGrath, 1984, p. 8).
Psychological significance	"Descriptively speaking, a psychological group is defined as one that is psychologically significant for the members, to which they relate themselves subjectively for social comparison and the acquisition of norms and values, . . . that they privately accept membership in, and which influences their attitudes and behavior" (Turner, 1987, pp. 1–2).
Shared identity	"A group exists when two or more people define themselves as members of it and when its existence is recognized by at least one other" (Brown, 1988, pp. 2–3).
Structure	"A group is a social unit which consists of a number of individuals who stand in (more or less) definite status and role relationships to one another and which possesses a set of values or norms of its own regulating the behavior of individual members, at least in matters of consequences to the group" (Sherif & Sherif, 1956, p. 144).

members) and triads (three members), and very large collectives are all groups (Simmel, 1902). But dyads possess many unique characteristics simply because they include only two members. The dyad is, by definition, the only group that dissolves when one member leaves and the only group that can never be broken down into subgroups (or coalitions). Very large collectives, such as mobs, crowds, or congregations like the People's Temple, also have unique qualities. In a very large group, for example, individual members can never influence every other member; as a result, interdependence is minimal. As groups increase in size, they tend to become more complex and more formally structured (Hare, 1976). By definition, however, all are considered groups, even though size may influence the group in many ways.

But when does a collection of people change from a nongroup into a group? groups—the jury, the committee, the survivors—clearly meet the definition's requirement of mutual influence among members. Others do not. The People's Temple, for example, was so large that only the potential for influence existed. Similarly, people waiting for a bus may not seem to fit the definition of a group, but they may become a group when one passenger asks the others if they can change a dollar bill.

The definition is also limited by its brevity. It defines the barest requirements of a group, but leaves unanswered other questions about groups. If we want to understand a group—for example, people stranded on a mountainside, political decision makers, or a therapy group—we need to ask many more questions: What do the people do in the group? Does the group have a leader? How unified is the group? How has the group changed over time? Deciding that a collection of people qualifies as a group is only the beginning of understanding that group.

What Is a Group? Properties and Processes

Every group is unique in some ways. A band of artists like the impressionists will never exist again, for the painters in the group were unique in their artistry and outlook. The players from the stranded rugby team, in its struggle to survive, did something that few other groups ever do: They ate the corpses of those who died in the crash. Some religious groups perform strange rituals, but the People's Temple outstripped them all by committing mass suicide.

These groups, despite their distinctive characteristics, also possessed properties and dynamics that are common to all groups. At their café conversations, the artists bickered over who was right and who was wrong, as so many groups do. The rugby team set goals, as do many work teams. The People's Temple became remarkably cohesive. When we study a group, we must go beyond its unique qualities by considering characteristics common to most groups, including interaction, structure, cohesiveness, social identity, and goals (Borgatta, Cottrell, & Meyer, 1956; DeLamater, 1974; Hare, 1976; Mullen, 1987a, 1990; Turner, 1985).

Interaction. Group members *do* things to and with each other. If you had watched the French artists, you would have seen them offering one another advice, exchanging stories about their own hardships, and asking for reactions to their work. Observing the final day of the Jonestown group would have revealed a very different form of interaction, with Jones demanding and winning obedience from all the church members. Regardless of the group setting, group membership generally implies some form of social interaction among the members (Bonner, 1959; Homans, 1950; Stogdill, 1959).

Group interaction comes in many guises, but much of the interaction revolves around the *tasks* the group must accomplish. In most groups, members must coordinate their various skills, resources, and motivations so that the group can make a decision, generate a product, or achieve a victory. When the jury reviewed each bit of testimony, when the committee argued over the best place for the invasion, and when the therapist asked members to pick a time to meet the following week, the group's interaction was task focused.

spring from the interpersonal, or *socioemotional,* side of group
_ists faltered or needed financial support, the others would buoy
_words or money. When one of the jurors disagreed with the others,
criticized and made to feel foolish. When one of the clients wore a
other members of the therapy group would notice it and compliment
_ood taste. Such actions do not help the group accomplish its designated
_hey do sustain the emotional bonds linking the members to one another
_ie group (Bales, 1950).

_ture. Group members' interactions are organized and interconnected. Among
_ Andes survivors, for example, three of the young men became the group's leaders, and they regularly made decisions for the rest of the group. Among the artists,
discussions of art were always influenced by their friendships, for artists who disliked
each other argued more than artists who liked each other. Similarly, Kennedy's advisory committee gradually accepted the idea of an invasion and with it the unspoken
rule "Don't argue with President Kennedy."

These regularities reflect **group structure:** the stable pattern of relationships among
members. **Roles,** for example, specify the general behaviors expected of people who
occupy different positions within the group. The roles of leader and follower are fundamental ones in many groups, but other roles—the information seeker, information
giver, elaborator, procedural technician, encourager, compromiser, harmonizer—may
emerge in any group (Benne & Sheats, 1948; Mudrack & Farrell, 1995; Salazar,
1996). Group members' actions and interactions are also shaped by their group's
norms: consensual standards that describe what behaviors should and should not be
performed in a given context (Forsyth, 1995).

Roles, norms, and other structural aspects of groups, although unseen and often
unnoticed, lie at the heart of its most dynamic processes. When people first join a
group, they spend much of their time initially trying to come to terms with the requirements of their role. If they cannot meet the role's demand, they might not remain a
member for long. Norms within a group are defined and renegotiated over time, and
conflicts often emerge as people violate norms. In group meetings, the opinions of
those with higher status carry more weight than those of the rank-and-file members.
When several members form a subgroup within the larger group, they exert more influence on the rest of the group. And when people manage to place themselves at the
hub of the group's information exchange patterns, their influence over others also increases. If you had to choose only one aspect of a group to study, you would probably
learn the most by studying its structure.

Group structure: A stable pattern of relationships among the members of a group.
Roles: The behaviors expected of people in specific positions within a group; the parts played by
different members of a group.
Norms: Implicit standards that describe what behaviors should and should not be performed in a
given context; consensual guidelines that prescribe the socially appropriate, or "normal," course
of action.

Group Cohesion.   Many people condemned the Andes survivors for eating passengers who had died when the plane crashed. But the group members themselves never wavered from their decision or their commitment to the group itself. They responded by stressing the importance of their group, crediting the group with saving their lives. The jury, in contrast, disbanded immediately after the verdict was reached, and some individual members criticized the group's final decision.

The strength of the bonds linking members to one another and to their group— it's **group cohesion**—defines its unity, oneness, and solidarity. Groups vary in their level of cohesiveness. The jury was clearly less cohesive than the Andes survivors. However, all groups require some modicum of cohesiveness, or else the group would disintegrate and cease to exist as a group (Dion, 1990). Increases in cohesiveness generally go hand in hand with increases in the group's capacity to retain its members. At the individual level, cohesiveness derives from each member's attraction to other group members, whether this attraction is based on liking, respect, or trust. And at the group level, cohesiveness reflects that "we-feeling" that joins people together to form a single unit. Thus, cohesiveness "contributes to a group's potency and vitality; it increases the significance of membership for those who belong to the group" (Cartwright, 1968, p. 91).

Social Identity.   Only rarely are people unwitting members of groups. Rather, they realize that their group exists, and that they are members, and they recognize other members of their group (Merton, 1957). This **social identity** amounts to a shared perception of themselves as members of the same group or social category. Social identity (also called *collective identity*) includes all self-conceptions that arise from membership in all kinds of social groups, including clubs, cliques, communities, and religions. The collective self also includes membership in demographic groups (e.g., "I am a man" or "I am an American") if individuals consider these qualities important and relevant to their self-concept (Tajfel, 1981; Turner, 1982; Turner, Hogg, Oakes, Reicher, & Wetherell, 1987).

The artists, for example, eventually recognized that they were members of a new movement in the world of art, but this sense of solidarity took time to evolve. Initially they felt that they were only developing their own personal talents and that they were working independently of the others. But the Parisian art world repeatedly criticized them all for inaccurately depicting the scenes and people they painted. The painters, in time, took on this label themselves and came to think of themselves as a group distinct from other groups of artists working in Paris at that time. They were no longer just individuals named Monet, Pissarro, Manet, Degas. Instead, they were individuals who were also impressionists (Turner, Oakes, Haslam, & McGarty, 1994).

Group cohesion: The strength of the bonds linking group members to the group, the unity (or weness) of a group, feelings of attraction for specific group members and the group itself, and the degree to which the group members coordinate their efforts to achieve goals.
Social identity: That part of the self-concept that derives from one's membership in social groups and categories; self-conceptions shared by members of the same group or category.

Goals.   Groups usually exist for a reason. The artists wanted recognition for their work. The Andes team wanted to live. The jury was convened to make a decision about guilt or innocence. The members of the People's Temple were seeking religious and spiritual enlightenment. In each case, the members of the group united in their pursuit of common goals. In groups, we solve problems, create products, create standards, communicate knowledge, have fun, perform arts, create institutions, and even ensure our safety from attacks by other groups. Put simply, groups make it easier to attain our goals. For this reason, much of the world's work is done by groups rather than by individuals.

Groups do so many things that their activities can be classified in a variety of ways. Joseph E. McGrath's circumplex of group tasks, for example, distinguishes among four basic group goals: Generating, Choosing, Negotiating, and Executing. As Figure 1–1 indicates, each of these basic categories can be further subdivided,

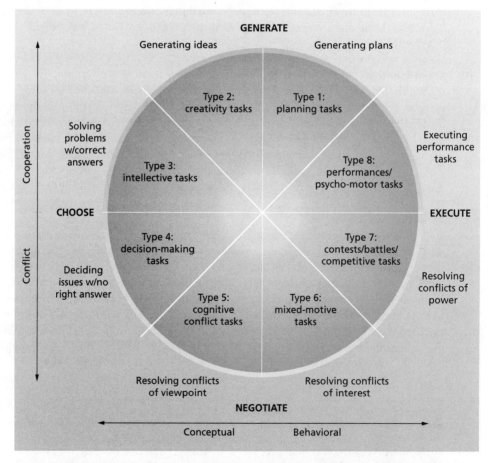

FIGURE 1–1   What do groups *do?* Joseph E. McGrath's task circumplex identifies 8 basic activities undertaken by groups: planning, creating, solving problems, making decisions, forming judgments, resolving conflicts, competing, and performing.

yielding a total of 8 basic tasks. When groups work at *generating* tasks they strive to concoct the strategies they will use to accomplish their goals (planning tasks) or create altogether new ideas and approaches to their problems (creativity tasks). When *choosing*, groups make decisions about issues that have correct solutions (intellective tasks) or problems that can be answered in many ways (decision-making tasks). When groups are *negotiating* they must resolve differences of opinion among the members of the group regarding their goals or their decisions (cognitive-conflict tasks) or resolve competitive disputes among members (mixed-motive tasks). The most behaviorally oriented groups actually do things. *Executing* groups compete against other groups (contest/battles) and perform (performances). Some groups perform tasks from nearly all of McGrath's categories, whereas others concentrate on only one subset of goals (Arrow & McGrath, 1995; McGrath, 1984).

Groups Are Dynamic

If you were limited to a single word, how would you describe the processes that take place in groups? What word illuminates the interdependence of people in groups? And what word adequately summarizes a group's capacity to promote social interaction, create patterned interrelationships among its members, bind members together to form a single unit, and accomplish its goals?

Kurt Lewin (1943, 1948, 1951), who many argue is the founder of the movement to study groups scientifically, chose the word *dynamic*. Groups tend to be powerful rather than weak, active rather than passive, fluid rather than static, and catalyzing rather than reifying. Lewin used the term **group dynamics** to stress the powerful impact of these complex social processes on group members. Although Lewin died unexpectedly of a heart attack just as group dynamics was beginning to develop more fully, his students and colleagues carried on the Lewinian tradition in their theory, research, and applications (Back, 1992; Bargal, Gold, & Lewin, 1992; Marrow, 1969; White, 1990, 1992).

THE NATURE OF GROUP DYNAMICS

When Kurt Lewin (1951) described the way groups and individuals act and react to changing circumstances, he named these processes group dynamics. But Lewin also used the phrase to describe the scientific discipline devoted to the study of these dynamics. Later, Dorwin Cartwright and Alvin Zander, two of the most prolific researchers in the field, supplied a formal definition, calling it a "field of inquiry dedicated to advancing knowledge about the nature of groups, the laws of their development, and their interrelations with individuals, other groups, and larger institutions" (1968, p. 7).

Cartwright and Zander also pointed out what group dynamics is not. It is not, for example, a therapeutic perspective holding that psychological well-being can be ensured through participation in small groups guided by a skilled therapist. Nor is it the communication of certain rules or guidelines that enable individuals to develop

---

Group dynamics: The scientific study of groups; also a general term for group processes.

the skills needed for smooth and satisfying social interactions. Finally, group dynamics does not refer to a loose collection of maxims concerning how groups should be organized—emphasizing, for example, such niceties as equal participation by all group members, democratic leadership, and high levels of member satisfaction. Rather, group dynamics is an attempt to subject the many aspects of groups to scientific analysis through the construction of theories and the rigorous testing of these theories through empirical research.

Group dynamics is not even a century old. Although ancient scholars pondered the nature of groups, the first scientific studies of groups were not carried out until the 1900s. Cartwright and Zander (1968), in their review of the origins of group dynamics, suggest that its slow development stemmed in part from several unfounded assumptions about groups. For example, many people felt that the dynamics of groups was a private affair, not something that scientists should lay open to public scrutiny. Others felt that human behavior was too complex to be studied scientifically and that this complexity was magnified enormously when groups of interacting individuals became the objects of interest. Still others believed that the causes of group behavior were so obvious that they were unworthy of scientific attention.

The field also developed slowly because group dynamicists disagreed among themselves on many basic issues. Group dynamics was not established by a single theorist or researcher who laid down a set of clear-cut assumptions and principles. Rather, group dynamics developed gradually as theorists debated basic issues and researchers developed new methods for studying groups. Because these early efforts form the foundation of contemporary group dynamics, the remainder of the chapter briefly examines the history of the field. (McGrath, 1997, Newcomb, 1978, Pepitone, 1981, and Steiner, 1986, also detail the development of group dynamics.)

The Discovery of Groups

Group dynamics emerged during the 50-year period from 1890 to 1940 as researchers from psychology, sociology, and related fields became increasingly interested in groups. Near the turn of the century, sociologists and psychologists "discovered" groups almost simultaneously (Steiner, 1974). Sociologists, trying to explain how religious, political, economic, and educational systems function to sustain society, highlighted the role played by groups in maintaining social order (Shotola, 1992). Émile Durkheim (1897/1966), for example, argued that individuals who aren't members of friendship, family, or religious groups can lose their sense of identity and as a result are more likely to commit suicide. Similarly, Charles Horton Cooley (1909, p. 23) stressed the importance of **primary groups**—small groups characterized by face-to-face interaction, interdependency, and strong group identification. Cooley felt that primary groups, such as families, children's play groups, and emotionally close peers, "are fundamental in forming the social nature and ideas of the individual."

At the same time, psychologists began studying how individuals react in group settings. In 1895, the French psychologist Gustave Le Bon published his book *Psych-*

Primary groups: Small, influential groups (e.g., families or friendship cliques) characterized by face-to-face interaction, interdependency, and strong group identification.

ologie des Foules (Psychology of Crowds), which describes how individuals are transformed when they join a group: "Under certain circumstances, and only under those circumstances, an agglomeration of men presents new characteristics very different from those of the individuals composing" the group (1895/1960, p. 23). Although Le Bon's work was speculative, Norman Triplett's 1898 laboratory study of competition confirmed that other people, by their mere presence, can change us. He arranged for 40 children to play a game that involved turning a small reel as quickly as possible. He found that those who played the game in pairs turned the reel faster than those who were alone, experimentally verifying the impact of one person on another.

These early studies of groups, viewed in retrospect, achieved two goals. First, they suggested that if sociologists and psychologists are to understand society and the individuals in that society, they must understand groups. Second, these early theoretical and empirical studies provided examples of the way questions about groups could be answered through scientific analysis. These early studies did not, however, provide a definitive answer to a very fundamental question that continued to separate the sociological and the psychological view on groups: Are groups real, or are they merely social mirages—illusions created by perceptual processes that prompt us to see unity where none exists?

Are Groups Real?

The roots of group dynamics in both sociology and psychology produced two different orientations to the study of groups. One approach was group oriented; it assumed that each person is "an element in a larger system, a group, organization, or society. And what he does is presumed to reflect the state of the larger system and the events occurring in it" (Steiner, 1974, p. 96). The alternative orientation was more individualistic, focusing on the individual in the group. Researchers who took this approach sought to explain the behavior of each group member, and they ultimately wanted to know if such psychological processes as attitudes, motivations, or personality were the true determinants of social behavior. Sociological researchers tended to adopt the group-oriented perspective, and psychological researchers favored the individualistic orientation (Steiner, 1974, 1983, 1986).

Group-oriented and individualistic researchers answered the question, "Are groups real?" differently. Group-oriented researchers felt that groups, and the processes that occurred within them, were scientifically authentic. Durkheim (1897/1966) argued that his studies of suicide provided clear evidence of the reality of groups, for it revealed that a very personal act—ending one's life—can be predicted by considering the individual's links to social groups. Durkheim was also impressed by the work of Le Bon and other crowd psychologists and went so far as to suggest that large groups of people sometimes acted with a single mind. He felt that such groups, rather than being mere collections of individuals in a fixed pattern of relationships with one another, were linked by a unifying **groupmind,** or collective conscious. Durkheim believed that

---

Groupmind: A hypothetical unifying mental force linking group members together; also called collective conscious.

this force was sometimes so strong that the will of the group could dominate the will of the individual.

Many psychologists interested in group phenomena rejected the reality of such concepts as groupmind or collective conscious. Floyd A. Allport, the foremost representative of this perspective, argued that such terms were unscientific, since they referred to phenomena that simply did not exist. In his 1924 text *Social Psychology*, he wrote that "nervous systems are possessed by individuals; but there is no nervous system of the crowd" (p. 5). He added, "Only through social psychology as a science of the individual can we avoid the superficialities of the crowdmind and collective mind theories" (p. 8). Taking the individualistic perspective to the extreme, Allport concluded that groups should never be studied by psychologists, since they did not exist as scientifically valid phenomena. Because Allport believed that "the actions of all are nothing more than the sum of the actions of each taken separately" (p. 5), he felt that a full understanding of the behavior of individuals in groups could be achieved by studying the psychology of the group members. Groups, according to Allport, were not real entities.

Allport's reluctance to accept such dubious concepts as groupmind into social psychology helped ensure the field's scientific status. His hard-nosed attitude also forced researchers to back up their claims about groups. Many group-oriented theorists believed in the reality of groups; they were certain that a group could not be understood by only studying its individual members. Allport's skepticism, however, spurred them to identify the characteristics of groups that set them apart from mere aggregations of individuals (Sandelands & St. Clair, 1993).

Groups Are Greater Than Their Parts.   Is a group more than just a collection of individuals? Kurt Lewin (1951) relied on his formal theory of human behavior, *field theory*, to provide an answer. Field theory assumes that the behavior of people in groups is determined by aspects of the person and aspects of the environment. The formula $B = f(P, E)$ summarizes this assumption. In a group context, this formula implies that the behavior of group members (B) is a function (f) of the interaction of their personal characteristics (P) with environmental factors (E), which include features of the group, the group members, and the situation. According to Lewin, whenever a group comes into existence, it becomes a unified system with emergent properties that cannot be fully understood by piecemeal examination. Lewin applied the Gestalt dictum "The whole is greater than the sum of the parts" to groups.

Many group phenomena lend support to Lewin's belief that a group is more than the sum of the individual members. A group's cohesiveness, for example, goes beyond the mere attraction of each individual member for one another (Hogg, 1992). Individuals may not like each other a great deal, and yet when they join together, they experience powerful feelings of unity and esprit de corps. Groups sometimes perform tasks far better—and far worse—than might be expected, given the talents of their

---

$B = f$ (P, E): Lewin's interactionism formula, which assumes that each person's behavior (B) is a function of his or her personal qualities (P), the social environment (E), *and* the interaction of these personal qualities with factors present in the social setting.

individual members. When individuals combine synergistically in a group, they some-times accomplish incredible feats and make horrible decisions that no single individ-ual could ever conceive (Hackman, 1987; Janis, 1983). Such groups seem to possess *supervening qualities* "that cannot be reduced to or described as qualities of its par-ticipants" (Sandelands & St. Clair, 1993, p. 443).

Muzafer Sherif (1936) was one of the first researchers to document one of these group-level qualities—a social norm—in a laboratory setting. Sherif created norms by asking groups of men to state aloud their estimates of the distance a dot of light had moved. He found that over time, the men accepted a standard estimate in place of their own idiosyncratic judgments. Subsequent studies found evidence of change in both the individual and the group when a single individual who made extreme judg-ments was placed in the group. This individual deflected the rest of the group mem-bers' judgments so that a more extreme norm guided the group members' judgments. Once this arbitrary standard had been created, the individual was removed from the group and replaced by a fresh member. The remaining group members retained the large-distance norm, however, and the newest group member gradually adapted to the higher standard. Old members were removed from the group and replaced with naive subjects, but the new initiates continued to shift their estimates in the direction of the group norm. The arbitrary group norm eventually disappeared, but not before the group memberships had been changed five or six times (MacNeil & Sherif, 1976). This norm, then, did not exist only in the minds of the individual mem-bers, but was a part of the group's structure that existed apart from each member.

Groups Are Living Systems.   A group, in a very real sense, is alive: It acquires energy and resources from its environment, maintains its structure, and grows over time. Some groups are so stable that their basic processes and structures remain unchanged for days, weeks, or even years, but such groups are rare. Bruce W. Tuckman's theory of **group development,** for example, assumes that most groups move through the five stages summarized in Figure 1–2 (Tuckman, 1965; Tuckman & Jensen, 1977). In the *forming* phase, the group members become oriented toward one another. In the *storming* phase, conflicts surface in the group as members vie for status and the group sets its goals. These conflicts subside when the group becomes more structured and standards emerge in the *norming* phase. In the *performing* phase, the group moves beyond disagreement and organizational matters to concentrate on the work to be done. The group continues to function at this stage until it reaches the *adjourning* stage, when it disbands. Groups also tend to cycle repeatedly through some of these stages as group members strive to maintain a balance between task-oriented actions and emotionally expressive behaviors (Bales, 1965).

Groups Are Seen as Real by Perceivers.   The controversy over the reality of groups lost much of its intensity when researchers stopped asking the question, "Are groups real?" and began asking, "When do people think that groups are real?" The basic prin-ciple here is that if people "define situations as real, they are real in their consequences"

Group development: Patterns of growth and change that emerge over the group's life span.

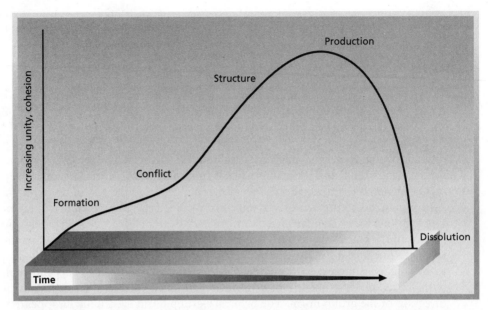

FIGURE 1–2   How do groups change over time? Tuckman's theory of group development argues that nearly all groups pass through five stages during their development: formation (forming), conflict (storming), structure (norming), production (performing), and dissolution (adjourning).

(Thomas, 1928). Even if groups aren't real, they may nonetheless have important interpersonal consequences if people define them to be real.

Donald T. Campbell's (1958a) analysis of entitativity explains why some groups are considered real groups, whereas others are thought to be mere aggregates of individuals. Campbell based his analysis on the work of Gestalt psychologists, who had wondered how the human mind decides whether something perceived is a Gestalt or a random collection of unrelated elements. Coining the term **entitativity** to describe the extent to which something seems to be a unified entity, Campbell suggested that people rely on certain perceptual cues as they intuitively determine which aggregations of individuals are groups and which ones are not. For example, the spectators at a football game may seem to be a disorganized mass of individuals who happen to be in the same place at the same time. But the tendency for the spectators to shout the same cheer, express similar emotions, and move together to create the wave gives the fans entitativity.

What cues do we rely on to make our judgments about entitativity? Campbell emphasized three:

- common fate: the extent to which individuals in the aggregate seem to experience the same, or interrelated, outcomes
- similarity: the extent to which the individuals display the same behaviors or resemble one another
- proximity: the distance between individuals in the aggregate

Entitativity: The quality of being an entity; perceived groupness.

Consider, for example, four people silently sharing a table at the library. They could be four close friends studying together, or they could be four strangers. To answer the question, "Is this a group?" you must consider common fate, similarity, and proximity. The principle of common fate predicts that the degree of "groupness" you attribute to the cluster would increase if, for example, all the members got up and left the room together or began laughing together. Your confidence that this cluster was a real group would also be bolstered if you noticed that all four were reading from the same textbook or were wearing the same fraternity shirt. Finally, if the members moved closer to one another, you would become even more certain that you were watching a group.

Research supports Campbell's analysis of entitativity, for the factors he identified have been shown to influence both members' and nonmembers' perceptions of a group's unity (Hamilton & Sherman, 1996). People identify more closely with their group when all the members share a common fate—for example, if they all fail together or succeed together (Deutsch, 1949a). People recruited for newly formed groups, if told their group members share many similarities, are more likely to respond as a unified group in comparison to people who are led to believe that their group includes dissimilar individuals (Knowles & Brickner, 1981; Schachter, Ellertson, McBride, & Gregory, 1951). When researchers repeatedly told women working in isolation that they were nonetheless members of a group, the women accepted this label and later rated themselves more negatively after their "group" failed (Zander, Stotland, & Wolfe, 1960). Proximity also influences entitativity, for people display more group-level reactions when they meet face-to-face in a single location than when they meet across long distances in telephone conference calls or through computer-mediated discussions (Kraut, Egido, & Galegher, 1990; Lea & Spears, 1991).

Groups Influence Individuals.   Allport challenged the existence of groups, but even he could not deny that people sometimes act differently when in groups (Allport, 1962). Some of these changes are subtle ones. Moving from isolation to a group context can reduce our sense of uniqueness, but at the same time it can enhance our ability to perform simple tasks rapidly (Triplett, 1898). Interacting with other people can also prompt us to gradually change our attitudes and values as we come to agree with the overall consensus of the group (Newcomb, 1943). When group members identify with the groups they belong to, their sense of self changes to include a collective component as well as an individual component (Turner et al., 1987). Our behavioral profiles also tend to change, depending on the group we are in. Carline may act extraverted and friendly when she is playing a team sport, but at the office she may display a different behavioral profile. Indeed, researchers found that people generally agreed when rating a fellow group member on such qualities as friendliness and achievement orientation, but only if the raters and ratee all belonged to the same group. Because Mark and Audrey play on the same softball team with Carline, they often agree when rating Carline; but they probably wouldn't agree so much if Mark knew Carline from the office and Audrey knew Carline from the softball team. Behavioral consistency is high within groups, but not across different groups, suggesting that groups change the way members act (Malloy, Albright, Kenny, Agatstein, & Winquist, 1997).

Groups also change people more dramatically. Le Bon (1895/1960) suggested that members of a group can be transformed into an unthinking, impulsive mob that will follow almost any order. Stanley Milgram (1963), in the early 1960s, found that a wide variety of people, if placed in a powerful group situation, would bend to the will of a malevolent authority and harm another person. More recently, researchers have verified the *discontinuity effect,* which holds that people are much more competitive as groups responding to other groups than as individuals responding to other individuals (Pemberton, Insko, & Schopler, 1996). Groups may just be collections of individuals, but these collections change their members.

Groups Are Real.   These theoretical and empirical analyses offer a way out of the troubling "Are groups real?" conundrum. Not all collections of individuals are groups, but the perceiver will consider an aggregate with qualities of unity to be a group. Moreover, once a group is judged to be real perceptually, this classification leads to a host of perceptual and interpersonal consequences. People who think they are part of a group respond differently than people who do not think they are in a group, and observers' impressions of people differ when they think that the people they are watching are members of a unified group. Labeling an aggregate a "group," then, is not just a matter of semantics. Designating a group real makes it real in its consequences.

Contemporary Group Dynamics

The work of early pioneers, such as Lewin, set the foundation for the emerging field of group dynamics. In time, most psychologists abandoned their prejudices against groups as objects of scientific analysis, and Allport himself amended his initial position on the issue by eventually acknowledging the reality of groups (1961, 1962).

By the 1950s, the field was ready to move from its childhood into its adulthood. Armed with new theories of group behavior and a set of increasingly sophisticated research methods, investigators began to examine many more aspects of groups and their dynamics. The field also grew beyond its roots in psychology and sociology to become more interdisciplinary, and many of these new researchers studied more practical aspects of groups. These developments, which we review briefly here, shaped the content, assumptions, and methods of contemporary group dynamics.

Interdisciplinary Approach.   Group dynamics was founded by sociologists and psychologists, but its roots have spread to many other branches of the social sciences. The relevance of groups to topics studied in many academic and applied disciplines gives group dynamics an interdisciplinary character. For example, researchers who prefer to study individuals may find themselves wondering what impact group participation will have on the individual's cognitions, attitudes, and behavior. Those who study organizations may find that these larger social entities actually depend on the dynamics of small subgroups within the organization. Indeed, social scientists examining such global issues as the development and maintenance of culture may find themselves turning their attention toward small groups as the unit of cultural transmission.

Table 1–2 summarizes this interdisciplinary breadth. The overall aims of these disciplines may be quite different, but groups are relevant to nearly all the social sci-

TABLE 1–2   GROUP DYNAMICS: AN INTERDISCIPLINARY FIELD

Discipline	Some Relevant Topics
Psychology	Personality and group behavior, problem solving, perceptions of other people, motivation, conflict
Sociology	Self and society, influence of norms on behavior, role relations, deviance
Anthropology	Groups in cross-cultural contexts, societal change, social and collective identities
Political science	Leadership, intergroup and international relations, political influence, power
Speech and communication	Information transmission in groups, problems in communication, networks
Business and industry	Work motivation, productivity, team building, goal setting, focus groups
Social work	Team approaches to treatment, family counseling, groups and adjustment
Education	Classroom groups, team teaching, class composition and educational outcomes
Clinical/counseling psychology	Therapeutic change through groups, sensitivity training, training groups, self-help groups, group psychotherapy
Criminal justice	Organization of law enforcement agencies, gangs, jury deliberations
Sports and recreation	Team performance, effects of victory and failure, cohesion and performance

ences. Psychologists tend to focus on the behavior of individuals in groups; sociologists, in contrast, focus more on the group and its relation to society. Anthropologists find that group processes are relevant to understanding many of the common features of various societies; political scientists examine the principles of group relations and leadership; and communication researchers focus more specifically on the communication relations in groups. Although this listing of disciplines is far from complete, it does convey the idea that the study of groups is not limited to any one field. As A. Paul Hare and his colleagues once noted, "This field of research does not 'belong' to any one of the recognized social sciences alone. It is the common property of all" (Hare, Borgatta, & Bales, 1955, p. vi).

Applications.   Groups are also relevant to many applied areas, as Table 1–2 shows. The study of groups in the work setting has long occupied business-oriented researchers concerned with the effective organization of people. Although early discussions of business administration and personnel management tended to overlook the importance of groups, the 1930s witnessed a tremendous growth in management-oriented group research (e.g., Barnard, 1938; Mayo, 1933). People in organizations ranging from businesses to hospitals to the armed forces began to take notice of the critical role that interpersonal relations played in their own organizations, and soon principles of group behavior became an integral part of most philosophies of effective administrative practices. This interest in groups in organizational settings continues to this day, and many group psychologists are also organizational psychologists (Sanna & Parks, 1997). Social workers frequently found themselves dealing with such groups as social clubs, gangs, neighborhoods, and family clusters, and an awareness of group processes helped crystalize their understanding of group life. Educators were also influenced by group research, as were many of the medical fields that dealt with patients on a group basis. Many methods of helping people change rely on group principles (Stewart, Stewart, & Gazda, 1997).

The application of group dynamics to practical problems is consistent with Lewin's call for **action research.** Lewin argued in favor of the intertwining of basic and applied research, for he firmly believed that there "is no hope of creating a better world without a deeper scientific insight into the function of leadership and culture, and of other essentials of group life" (1943, p. 113). To achieve this goal, he assured practitioners that in many instances "there is nothing so practical as a good theory" (1951, p. 169) while charging basic researchers with the task of developing theories that can be applied to important social problems (Cartwright, 1978; Lewin, 1946, 1947).

Topics.   Throughout the history of group dynamics, some approaches that initially seemed promising have been abandoned after they contributed relatively little or failed to stimulate consistent lines of research. The idea of groupmind, for example, was discarded when researchers identified more likely causes of crowd behavior. Similarly, such concepts as syntality, groupality, and lifespace initially attracted considerable interest but stimulated little research (see Cattell, 1948, Bogardus, 1954, and Lewin, 1951, respectively). In contrast, researchers have studied other topics continuously since they were first broached (Hare, Blumberg, Davies, & Kent, 1994; Levine & Moreland, 1990, 1995, 1998; McGrath, 1997).

Table 1–3 samples the topics that currently interest group dynamicists, and it foreshadows the topics considered in the remainder of this book. Chapters 1, 2, and 3 explore the foundations of the field by reviewing the group dynamics perspective (Chapter 1) and the methods and theories of the field (Chapter 2). This introductory section ends by asking and answering two fundamental questions about people and their groups (Chapter 3): Why are human beings such social, group-oriented animals? And what are the consequences of a social, rather than an asocial, existence?

Chapters 4, 5, and 6 focus on group development: how groups change and evolve over time. In Chapter 4, we probe group formation: Who joins groups, when do groups form, and when do people leave groups? In Chapter 5, we turn to the topic of group structure—how groups develop systems of roles and intermember relationships—before we turn to the factors that transform a group of unrelated individuals into a cohesive, unified group (Chapter 6).

A group is a complex social system, a microcosm of powerful interpersonal forces that significantly shape members' actions. Chapters 7, 8, and 9 examine the flow of

---

Action research: Lewin's term for scientific inquiry that not only expands basic theoretical knowledge, but also yields solutions to significant social problems.

TABLE 1–3 TOPICS STUDIED BY GROUP DYNAMICISTS

Category and Topic	Issues
Foundations	
1 Introduction to group dynamics	What is a group? What are the most common characteristics of a group? How did the field of group dynamics develop? Are groups real, scientifically speaking? What aspects of groups should be investigated?
2 Research methods	How do researchers measure group phenomena? How can observers of groups remain objective? What are the advantages of experimental and nonexperimental methods? What are the dominant theoretical perspectives in the field?
3 Individuals and groups	Why do individuals join groups? Are human beings instinctively drawn to groups? What psychological needs are met by groups? How do people change when they become members of groups? Do their identities change?
Development	
4 Joining and leaving groups	What personality characteristics predispose people to join groups? When do people join groups rather than remain alone? Why do people leave groups?
5 Structure	In what ways does a group become organized over time? What types of roles typically exist in a group? How do status, attraction, and communication networks develop in groups?
6 Cohesion	Why are some groups more unified than others? Do groups go through a predictable sequence of stages as they mature from a new group to a mature group? When does a group become a team?
Influence and Interaction	
7 Conformity and influence	When will people conform to a group's standard, and when will they remain independent? How do norms develop, and why do people obey them? Do nonconformists ever succeed in influencing the rest of the group?
8 Power	Why are some members of groups more powerful than others? What types of power tactics are most effective in influencing others? Does power corrupt? Why do people obey authorities?
9 Conflict	What causes disputes between group members? When will a small disagreement escalate into a conflict? How can disputes in groups be resolved?
Group Performance	
10 Performance	Do people perform tasks more effectively in groups or when they are alone? Why do people sometimes expend so little effort when they are in a group? When does a group outperform an individual?
11 Decision making	What are the basic steps that groups usually follow when making decisions? Why do some highly cohesive groups make disastrous decisions? Why do groups sometimes make riskier decisions than individuals?

continued

TABLE 1–3   CONTINUED

Category and Topic	Issues
12 Leadership	What is leadership? If a group forms without a leader, which person will eventually step forward to become the leader? Should a leader be task focused or relationship focused? Is democratic leadership superior to autocratic leadership?
Issues and Applications	
13 Intergroup relations	What causes disputes between groups? What changes take place as a consequence of intergroup conflict? What factors exacerbate conflict? How can intergroup conflict be resolved?
14 Group environment	What impact does the physical setting have on an interacting group? Are groups territorial? What happens when groups do not have sufficient space available to them? How do groups cope with severe environments?
15 Crowds and collective behavior	What types of crowds are common? Why do crowds and collectives form? Do people lose their sense of self when they join a crowd? When is a crowd likely to become unruly?
16 Groups and change	How can groups be used to improve personal adjustment and health? What is the difference between a therapy group and a self-help group? Are group approaches to treatment effective? Why do they work?

influence and interaction in groups. Chapter 7 looks at the way group members sometimes change their opinions, judgments, or actions so that they match the opinions, judgments, or actions of the rest of the group (conformity). Chapter 8 extends this topic by considering how group members make use of social power to influence others and how people respond to such influence. Chapter 9 analyzes the conflicts that sometimes erupt within groups.

The next several chapters turn to questions of group performance. Groups are performance machines. Much of the world's work is done by people working together rather than individuals working alone. Investigators have identified a host of factors that influence a group's productivity (Chapter 10), and their studies suggest ways to minimize inefficiency and errors when working in groups. We study processes and problems in decision-making groups in Chapter 11 and leadership in Chapter 12.

The final chapters of the book deal with specific issues and applications. Chapter 13, for example, considers the processes that unfold when two groups come into conflict, and Chapter 14 reviews the impact of environmental factors on group processes. In Chapter 15, we shift our focus from smaller groups to larger ones: mobs, crowds, and social movements. These larger groups are, in many respects, no more than specific cases of groups, but sometimes their members act in extreme, atypical ways. Chapter 16 concludes this section by considering therapeutic uses of groups.

Group Dynamics Is Dynamic

The field of group dynamics emerged in the 1940s as theorists and researchers concluded that groups are real and that they should be subjected to scientific analysis. In the 1950s and 1960s, the field grew rapidly as theorists and researchers studied more and more topics, the field became more interdisciplinary, and the accumulated knowledge was applied to practical problems.

This rapid expansion slowed once the study of groups gained acceptance in both sociology and psychology, but even today the field remains vibrant. Groups are studied by a range of investigators in a host of different disciplines. Although these researchers have very different goals, pursuits, and paradigms, they all recognize that groups are essential to human life. Through membership in groups, we define and confirm our values and beliefs and take on or refine our social identity. When we face uncertain situations, we join groups to gain reassuring information about our problems and security in companionship. Even though we must sometimes bend to the will of a group and its leaders, through groups we can reach goals that would elude us if we attempted them as individuals. Our groups are sometimes filled with conflict; but by resolving this conflict, we learn how to relate with others more effectively. Groups are a fundamental to social lives, and we must accept the charge of understanding them.

SUMMARY

What is a group, and what characteristics do most groups possess?

1. No two groups are identical, but all *groups,* by definition, include two or more interdependent individuals who influence one another through social interaction.

2. Groups share certain common features:
   - interaction, including activities that focus on the task at hand and activities that concern the interpersonal relations linking group members
   - *group structure,* including *roles, norms,* and interpersonal relations
   - *cohesiveness,* which determines the unity of the group
   - *social identity,* or collective identity, which is a shared recognition that one is a member of a group
   - goals

When did researchers begin studying groups scientifically?

The term *group dynamics* refers to both the group processes and the field.

1. Lewin first used the term to describe the powerful processes that take place in groups, but group dynamics also refers to the scientific study of groups.

2. This relatively young science has roots in both sociology and psychology. Sociologists have long recognized that *primary groups* are the bridges that link individuals to society, and psychologists have studied how people act when they are in groups rather than alone.

3. This interdisciplinary heritage gives group dynamics a broad conceptual foundation, but it also generated debates over the scientific value of such concepts as *groupmind* (collective conscious) and the reality of groups themselves.

Are groups real?

Allport and other early investigators suggested that groups are no more than the sum of the individual members. In time, however, researchers answered the question, "Are groups real?" by concluding:

1. Groups are greater than the sum of their parts, for groups often possess characteristics that cannot be deduced

from the individual members' characteristics. This conclusion is consistent with Lewin's (1951) field theory, which maintains that behavior is a function of the person and the environment, or $B = f(P, E)$.

2. Groups are living systems. Tuckman's theory of *group development,* for example, assumes that most groups move through the five stages of forming, storming, norming, performing, and adjourning over time.

3. Groups are seen as real by perceivers. As the concept of *entitativity* also suggests, when groups are perceived to be real, they yield real interpersonal consequences.

4. Groups influence individuals. Groups alter members' attitudes, values, and perceptions and in some cases cause radical alterations in personality and actions.

What assumptions guide contemporary researchers' studies of groups and their processes?

The period from 1950 to 1970 was marked by rapid growth in the field, as theorists and researchers expanded the range of topics and orientations.

1. Researchers have examined a wide variety of group processes, including group development, structure, influence, power, performance, and conflict.

2. The field is an interdisciplinary one, including many researchers outside of sociology and psychology.

3. Many researchers carry out *action research* by utilizing scientific methods to identify solutions to practical problems.

4. Group dynamics retains its designation as the "field of inquiry dedicated to advancing knowledge about the nature of groups" (Cartwright & Zander, 1968, p. 7).

FOR MORE INFORMATION

Group Dynamics, edited by Dorwin Cartwright and Alvin Zander (1968), is a classic in the scientific field of groups, with chapters dealing with group membership, conformity, power, leadership, and motivation.

"Group Processes," a chapter by John M. Levine and Richard L. Moreland (1995) provides an excellent introduction to the study of groups, with specific sections dealing with the ecology, composition, structure, and performance of small groups.

"The Heritage of Kurt Lewin: Theory, Research, and Practice," edited by David Bargal, Martin Gold, and Miriam Lewin (1992), is a special issue of the *Journal of Social Issues* devoted to the contributions of group dynamics founder Kurt Lewin.

The Marshall Cavendish Encyclopedia of Personal Relationships: Human Behavior, How Groups Work (Vol. 15) edited by Rupert Brown (1990), is an introduction to groups, with chapters on teamwork, morale, intergroup conflict, and leadership.

Small Group Research: A Handbook, by A. Paul Hare, Herbert H. Blumberg, Martin F. Davies, and M. Valerie Kent (1994), is a massive compilation of research publications in the field of groups.

"Small Group Research, That Once and Future Field: An Interpretation of the Past with an Eye to the Future," by Joseph E. McGrath (1997), comprehensively summarizes the history of the field of group dynamics and offers penetrating proposals for the future of the field.

ACTIVITY 1-1 WHAT IS A GROUP?

Humans are social animals, for we naturally gravitate away from isolation into groups. But what, precisely, is a group?

1. Which collections of people listed below are groups, and which ones are not? Label each one as **G**roup, **A**ggregate, or **?** if you aren't certain.
   _____ the spectators at a college football game
   _____ a man and a woman flirting with each other, having just met each other for the first time in a singles club
   _____ a secretary talking to the boss by telephone
   _____ five students at a university working together on a classroom assignment in a group dynamics class
   _____ a mob of rioters burning stores in the inner city
   _____ five people talking to each other on-line in a computer "chat room"
   _____ a committee deciding the best way to handle a production problem
   _____ five adolescent males who hang out together skateboarding on a city corner
   _____ the Rolling Stones fan club
   _____ six employees wearing sound-muffling headphones working on an assembly line
   _____ individuals waiting in silence at a bus stop
   _____ the Smith family of New York (Mr. Smith, Mrs. Smith, and Jane Smith, their daughter) dining together
   _____ all the women with blue eyes who live in Japan
   _____ all the faculty in the department of political science on a Sunday afternoon
   _____ all people who think of themselves as Germans
2. Rank these groups from the "most grouplike" (1) to the "least grouplike" (15).
3. If you were writing a dictionary, how would you define the word *group?*

ACTIVITY 1–2 DO GROUPS PLAY AN INFLUENTIAL ROLE IN YOUR LIFE?

Almost all of our time is spent interacting in groups. We are educated in groups, we work in groups, we worship in groups, and we play in groups. But even though we live our lives in groups, we often take them for granted. Consider their influence on you by naming the groups to which you belong, as well as others that influence you.

1. Make a list of all the groups you belong to now. List as many as possible. Don't forget family, clubs, sports teams, classes, social groups, cliques of friends, work teams, and social categories that are meaningful to you (e.g., American).
2. Do any of the groups you belong to transform its members into a unit that is greater than the sum of its parts? Does the group have supervening qualities?
3. Which group has changed the most over time? Describe this change briefly.

(continued)

ACTIVITY 1–2 **CONTINUED**

4. Which group is highest in entitativity (others perceive it to be real)?
5. Which group has influenced you, as an individual, the most? Explain the group's influence on you briefly.
6. Identify five groups that you do not belong to but that influence you in some way. Of these groups, which one influences you—your behaviors, your emotions, or your outcomes —the most?

2

Studying Groups

Just as scientists use exacting procedures to study aspects of the physical and natural environment, so do group dynamicists use scientific methods to further their understanding of groups. Through research, group dynamicists separate fact from fiction and truth from myth.

- How do researchers measure the way groups, and the individuals in those groups, feel, think, and behave?
- How do researchers search for and test their hypotheses about groups rigorously?
- What are the strengths and weaknesses of the various research strategies used by group dynamicists?
- What general theoretical perspectives guide researchers as they explore groups and the people in them?

CONTENTS

MEASUREMENT IN GROUP DYNAMICS
Observational Techniques
Self-Report Measures
RESEARCH DESIGNS IN GROUP DYNAMICS
Case Studies
Experimentation
Correlational Designs
Selecting a Research Design
THEORIES IN GROUP DYNAMICS
Motivational Models
Behavioral Approaches
Systems Theories
Cognitive Approaches
Biological Models
Selecting a Theory
SUMMARY
FOR MORE INFORMATION
ACTIVITIES

Down through the ages, scholars and sages have offered insights into groups. Ralph Waldo Emerson believed that a group is only as effective as its weakest link: "There need be but one wise man in a company and all are wise, so a blockhead makes a blockhead of his companions." Cicero felt that people in mobs act rashly: "A mob has no judgment, no discretion, no direction, no discrimination, no consistency." Aristotle believed that leadership is an innate talent: "Men are marked out from the moment of birth to rule or be ruled." Neitzche questioned the rationality of groups when he wrote, "Madness is the exception in individuals but the rule in groups."

These savants may be correct. Perhaps one person with meager abilities can ruin a group and one gifted person ensure its success. Maybe people immersed in large crowds respond impulsively. But these scholars' analyses of the nature of groups are limited in one important way: All are untested. Can we predict a group's performance by taking into account the skills of its best member and worst member? How do people behave in crowds? Are leaders born rather than made? Are groups intellectually inferior to individuals? Without scientific analysis, we cannot be certain.

What makes a discipline a science? According to sociologist George Caspar Homans, "When the test of the truth of a relationship lies finally in the data themselves, and the data are not wholly manufactured—when nature, however stretched out on the rack, still has a chance to say 'No!'—then the subject is a science" (1967, p. 4). This definition suggests that researchers must "stretch nature out on the rack"; that is, they must measure the processes and phenomena they study. Homans's definition also tells researchers to test "the truth of the relationship" in some way. We may think that putting a poor performer in a group may undermine the group's product or that personality characteristics present at birth determine one's leadership potential, but how can we test these hypotheses?

This chapter examines these two aspects of science—measurement and research design—before turning to a third: theory. Scientists don't just test and measure. They also create conceptual frameworks to organize their findings. Homans (1950, p. 5) recognized that "nothing is more lost than a loose fact" and urged the development of theories to "give one general form in which the results of observations of many particular groups may be expressed" (p. 21). We consider current conceptualizations about groups in the chapter's final section.

MEASUREMENT IN GROUP DYNAMICS

Progress in science often depends on the development of tools for conducting research. Biologists made dozens of discoveries when they perfected the compound microscope. Astronomers refined their theories of celestial phenomena with the invention of the telescope. Similarly, to understand groups, researchers needed to find ways to assess group members' interpersonal actions and psychological reactions. Here we trace the growth and impact of two important measurement tools—observational strategies and self-report measures—that gave group dynamics a foothold in the scientific tradition.

Observational Techniques

Researchers turned to **observational measures** when they first examined groups. Historians, philosophers, and writers had used observational techniques for centuries, so the idea of answering questions about groups by watching them seemed both reasonable and efficient (Cartwright & Zander, 1968). Over the years, researchers have developed various approaches to observation, but the essence of the method has remained the same: Watch and record the actions taken by group members, including verbal behaviors (such as conversation among members) and nonverbal behaviors (such as gestures and movements).

William Foote Whyte (1943) relied on observational measures in his ethnographic study of Italian American gangs in the heart of Boston. He rented a room from an Italian family who lived in the inner city and joined the Nortons, a group of young men who gathered at a particular corner on Norton Street. He also participated in a club known as the Italian Community Club. Whyte observed and recorded these groups for 3½ years, gradually developing a detailed portrait of this community and its groups.

Whyte's study underscored the strong link between the individual member and the group. It also illustrated some key features of observational measures. Whyte not only joined the groups he studied, but also revealed his identity to them: The group members knew that he was a student at Harvard writing a book about their community. These decisions all had a great impact on his study and its conclusions.

Participant Observation. Whyte actually joined the groups he studied. This method of **participant observation** is "a process in which the observer's presence in a social situation is maintained for the purpose of scientific investigation. The observer is in a face-to-face relationship with the observed, and, by participating with them in their natural life setting, he gathers data" (Schwartz & Schwartz, 1955, p. 344; see also Schwartz & Jacobs, 1979; Whyte, 1991). Whyte, as a participant observer, gained access to information that would have been hidden from an external observer. His techniques also gave him a very detailed understanding of the gang. Unfortunately, his presence in the group may have changed the group itself. He went bowling with the Nortons, gambled with them, and even lent money to some of the members. His presence in the group undoubtedly modified its structure, and therefore the group he describes is not a typical corner gang, but rather a corner gang with a researcher in it (see Figure 2–1).

Overt and Covert Observation. Whyte was an overt observer of the group; the Nortons knew that he was a social scientist and that he was recording their behavior.

Observational measures: Measurement methods that involve watching and recording individual and group actions.
Participant observation: Watching and recording interpersonal behavior while taking part in the social process.

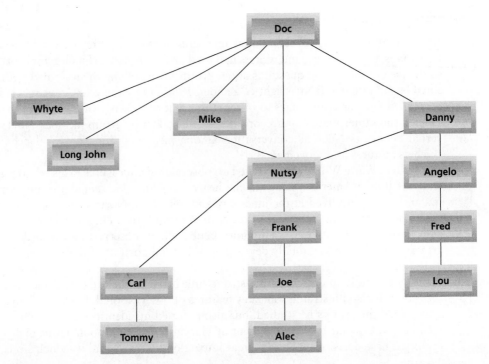

FIGURE 2-1   How were the Nortons organized? Lines between each member indicate inter-dependence, and members who are placed above others in the chart had more influence than those in the lower positions. Doc was the recognized leader of the group, and Mike and Danny were second in terms of status. Whyte, the researcher, was connected to the group through Doc.

(*Source:* Whyte, 1955.)

Such openness meant that he did not have to mislead the group in any way, but by revealing his purpose, he may have indirectly influenced the gang's behavior. As one corner boy once remarked, "You've slowed me down plenty since you've been down here. Now, when I do something, I have to think what Bill Whyte would want to know about it and how I can explain it. Before I used to do things by instinct" (p. 301).

The tendency for individuals to act differently when they know they are being observed is called the **Hawthorne effect,** after research conducted by Elton Mayo and his research associates at the Hawthorne Plant of the Western Electric Company (Landsberger, 1958; Mayo, 1945; Roethlisberger & Dickson, 1939). These researchers studied productivity in the workplace by systematically varying a number of features while measuring the workers' output. They moved one group of women to a separate room and monitored their performance carefully. Next, they manipulated features of

---

Hawthorne effect: A change in behavior that occurs when individuals know they are being studied by researchers.

the work situation, such as the lighting in the room and the duration of rest periods. They were surprised when all the changes led to improved worker output. Dim lights, for example, raised efficiency, but so did bright lights. The Mayo researchers, to their credit, realized that the group members were working harder because they were being observed and also because they felt that the company was taking a special interest in them. (Varying views on these studies are presented by Bramel & Friend, 1981, Franke, 1979, and Franke & Kaul, 1978.)

Mayo's work underscored the importance of considering interpersonal factors in the work setting, but at the same time it warned investigators of a serious research problem: Group members act differently when they believe they are being observed by social scientists interested in their behavior (Barnard, 1938; McGregor, 1960). Because the Hawthorne effect can limit the generalizability of research findings, some researchers prefer to use **covert observation,** whereby the observer records the group's activities without the group's knowledge. Such methods are commendable methodologically, but researchers face ethical issues if their observations invade the privacy of the people they are watching. Nondeceptive methods avoid these moral quagmires but at the price of less accurate information (Humphreys, 1975; Sieber, 1992; Steininger, Newell, & Garcia, 1984).

Structuring Observations. Whyte decided to observe the Nortons each day, but he postponed organizing his observations. He took extensive notes and only later integrated them to form an overall picture of the group. Some researchers feel that such an open approach to observation minimizes the impact of the researcher's preconceptions on the study (Barton & Lazarfeld, 1969; Glaser & Strauss, 1967; Schwartz & Jacobs, 1979). Others, however, argue that such openness puts too much trust in the observational powers of the researchers: They may let initial, though implicit, expectations shape their records (Mitroff & Kilmann, 1978; Rosnow & Rosenthal, 1997; Weick, 1985).

Albert H. Hastorf and Hadley Cantril (1954) demonstrated just such a perceptual bias in their classic "They Saw a Game" experiment. They asked college students to watch a film of two teams playing a football game. They selected a game between Dartmouth and Princeton that featured extremely rough play and many penalties against both teams. Indeed, both quarterbacks were injured in the game. When Hastorf and Cantril asked Dartmouth and Princeton students to record the number and severity of the infractions that had been committed by the two teams, the Princeton students weren't very accurate. Dartmouth students saw the Princeton Tigers commit about the same number of infractions as the Dartmouth players. Princeton students, however, disagreed with the Dartmouth observers; they saw the Dartmouth team commit more than twice as many infractions as the Princeton team. Apparently, the Princeton observers' preference for their own team distorted their perceptions of the group interaction.

Covert observation: A measurement method that records group members' actions without the subjects' knowledge.

Structured observational measures offer one possible solution to the lack of objectivity in observations. Like biologists who classify living organisms under such categories as phylum, subphylum, class, and order or psychologists who classify people into various personality groupings or types, researchers who use a structured observational method classify each group behavior into an objectively definable category. They achieve this goal by first deciding which behaviors in the group are of interest and which are not. Next, they set up the categories to be used in the coding system. The researchers then note the occurrence and frequency of these targeted behaviors (Weick, 1985; Weingart, 1997).

Researchers can now choose from a wide assortment of structured observational systems; indeed, one researcher has actually developed a structured coding system for classifying types of coding systems (Trujillo, 1986). Robert Freed Bales's method, shown in Table 2–1, has proved particularly useful (Bales, 1950, 1970, 1980). Bales called his first coding system **Interaction Process Analysis (IPA)**. Researchers who use IPA can classify each bit of behavior performed by a group member into 1 of 12 categories. Six of these categories (1–3 and 10–12) pertain to *socioemotional activities* that sustain or weaken interpersonal relationships within the group. Complimenting another person is an example of a positive socioemotional behavior, whereas insulting a group member reflects negative socioemotional behavior. The other six categories pertain to *task activity,* or behavior that focuses on the problem the group is trying to solve. Giving and asking for information, opinions, and suggestions related to the problem the group faces are all examples of task-oriented activity.

To use IPA, observers must learn to identify the 12 types of behavior defined by Bales (see Table 2–1). Observers must listen to the group discussion, break the verbal content down into the meaningful units, and then classify each behavior using a profile form containing the categories listed in Table 2–1. If Sophia, for example, begins the group discussion by asking "Should we introduce ourselves?" and Barbara answers, "Yes," the observers write "Sophia–Group" beside Category 8 (Sophia asks for opinion from whole group) and "Barbara–Sophia" beside Category 5 (Barbara gives opinion to Sophia). If later in the interaction Stephan angrily tells the entire group, "This group is a boring waste of time," the coders write "Stephan–Group" beside Category 12 (Stephan seems unfriendly to entire group).

If observers are well trained, a structured coding system such as IPA will yield data that are both reliable and valid. **Reliability** is determined by a measure's consistency across time, components, and raters. If a rater, when she hears the statement "This group is a boring waste of time," always classifies it as a Category 12 behavior, then the rating is reliable. The measure has *interrater reliability* if different raters, work-

---

Structured observational measures: Methods of measurement that involve classifying (coding) the subject's actions under clearly defined categories. Bales's Interaction Process Analysis (IPA) and SYMLOG are examples of such coding systems.

Interaction Process Analysis (IPA): A structured coding system developed by Bales that can be used to classify group behavior into socioemotional and task-oriented categories.

Reliability: The degree to which a measurement technique consistently yields the same conclusion at different times. For measurement techniques with two or more components, reliability is also the degree to which these various components all yield similar conclusions.

**TABLE 2-1   THE CATEGORIES OF THE ORIGINAL AND
THE REVISED INTERACTION PROCESS ANALYSIS SYSTEM**

General Categories	1950 IPA Categories	1970 IPA Categories
A. Positive (and mixed) actions	1. Shows solidarity	1. Seems friendly
	2. Shows tension release	2. Dramatizes
	3. Agrees	3. Agrees
B. Attempted answers	4. Gives suggestion	4. Gives suggestion
	5. Gives opinion	5. Gives opinion
	6. Gives orientation	6. Gives information
C. Questions	7. Asks for orientation	7. Asks for information
	8. Asks for opinion	8. Asks for opinion
	9. Asks for suggestion	9. Asks for suggestion
D. Negative (and mixed) actions	10. Disagrees	10. Disagrees
	11. Shows tension	11. Shows tension
	12. Shows antagonism	12. Seems unfriendly

Source: Bales, 1970.

ing independently, all think that the phrase belongs in Category 12. **Validity** describes the extent to which the technique measures what it is supposed to measure. Interaction process analysis is valid if it actually measures the amount of socioemotional and task-oriented activity in the group. If the observers are incorrect in their coding or the categories do not accurately reflect the socioemotional and task-oriented aspects of a group, the scores are not valid (Kellehear, 1993).

Interaction process analysis is useful because it records the number of times a particular type of behavior has occurred and makes possible comparison across categories, group members, and even different groups. Bales has also improved both the reliability and validity of his coding system over the years. As Table 2–1 indicates, Bales revised the categories in 1970, and even more recently he proposed a further elaboration of the entire system. This newest version is called **SYMLOG**, which stands for **System of Multiple Level Observation of Groups** (Bales, 1980, 1988; Polley, 1991). SYMLOG is based on three dimensions: dominance/submission, friendly/unfriendly, and instrumentally controlled/emotionally expressive. A SYMLOG-trained observer can watch a group interact and then rate each member on each of the 26 categories shown in Table 2–2. The group's leader, for example, might get high

---

Validity: The degree to which an assessment technique measures what it was designed to measure.
SYMLOG (System of Multiple Level Observation of Groups): A three-dimensional theory and observational system developed by Bales for studying group behavior.

TABLE 2–2   CATEGORIES IDENTIFIED IN THE SYMLOG GROUP OBSERVATION SYSTEM

Label	General Behavior Description	Values
U	Active, dominant, talks a lot	Material success and power
UP	Extravert, outgoing, positive	Popularity and social success
UPF	A purposeful democratic task leader	Social solidarity and progress
UF	An assertive businesslike manager	Strong effective management
UNF	Authoritarian, controlling, disapproving	A powerful authority, law and order
UN	Domineering, tough-minded, powerful	Tough-minded assertiveness
UNB	Provocative, egocentric, shows off	Rugged individualism, self-gratification
UB	Jokes around, expressive, dramatic	Having a good time, self-expression
UPB	Entertaining, sociable, smiling, warm	Making others feel happy
P	Friendly, egalitarian	Egalitarianism, democratic participation
PF	Works cooperatively with others	Altruism, idealism, cooperation
F	Analytical, task oriented, problem solving	Established social beliefs and values
NF	Legalistic, has to be right	Value-determined restraint of desires
N	Unfriendly, negativistic	Individual dissent, self-sufficiency
NB	Irritable, cynical, won't cooperate	Social nonconformity
B	Shows feelings and emotions	Unconventional beliefs and values
PB	Affectionate, likable, fun to be with	Friendship, liberalism, sharing
DP	looks up to others, appreciative, trustful	Trust in the goodness of others
DPF	Gentle, willing to accept responsibility	Love, faithfulness, loyalty
DF	Obedient, works submissively	Hard work, self-knowledge, subjectivity
DNF	Self-punishing, works too hard	Suffering
DN	Depressed, sad, resentful, rejecting	Rejection of popularity
DNB	Alienated, quits, withdraws	Admission of failure, withdrawal
DB	Afraid to try, doubts own ability	Noncooperation with authority
DPB	Quietly happy just to be with others	Quiet contentment, taking it easy
D	Passive, introverted, says little	Giving up all selfish desires

Note: U = up (dominant), D = down (submissive), P = positive (friendly), N = negative (unfriendly), F = forward (instrumentally controlled), and B = backward (emotionally expressive).

Source: Bales, 1980.

ratings for "active, dominant, talks a lot" but low ratings on "passive, introverted, says little." A disillusioned group member, in contrast, might get high scores for "irritable, cynical, won't cooperate." These 26 ratings can then be combined to yield scores for each person on three fundamental dimensions: dominance–submission (up–down), friendly–unfriendly (positive–negative), and instrumentally controlled–emotionally expressive (forward–backward). The observer can then create a graphic representation of the group like the one shown in Figure 2–2. This fictitious group was charted by asking people to complete SYMLOG ratings of such well-known people as Jesus, Hitler, Groucho Marx, and Henry Ford (Isenberg & Ennis, 1981). The investigators discovered that the three dimensions of SYMLOG neatly summarized these ratings and that the classifications of these stimulus persons followed predictable patterns. For example, Hitler was viewed as UNF (up, negative, forward), Jesus was PF (positive, forward), and Groucho was UPB (up, positive, backward). The investigators cautiously suggest that other dimensions not measured by SYMLOG may also be important (Breiger & Ennis, 1979; Hare, 1985; Polley, 1984, 1986, 1987, 1989; Polley, Hare, & Stone, 1988).

Given the greater reliability and validity of structured observations, why did Whyte take an unstructured approach? Whyte was more interested in gaining an understanding of the entire community and its citizenry, so a structured coding system's narrow focus on specific behaviors would have yielded an unduly narrow analysis. At the time he conducted his study, very few researchers had studied community groups, so Whyte did not know which behaviors he should scrutinize if he wanted to understand the group. Whyte was also unfamiliar with the groups he studied, so he chose to immerse himself in fieldwork. His research was more exploratory, designed to develop theory first and validate hypotheses second, so he used an unstructured observational approach. If he had been testing a hypothesis by measuring specific aspects of a group, then the rigor and objectivity of a structured approach would have been preferable (Latour, Garnier, & Ferraris, 1993).

Self-Report Measures

Whyte did not just watch Doc, Mike, Danny, and the others as they interacted with one another and others in the community. Time and again, Whyte supplemented his observations by questioning the group members. Whenever he was curious about their thoughts, perceptions, and emotions, he would ask them, as indirectly as possible, to describe their inner reactions.

Self-report measures are based on the idea that if you want to know how group members feel about something or why they performed a particular behavior, ask them to tell you. How you go about asking can vary; you can administer carefully constructed personality tests, distribute attitude questionnaires, or conduct face-to-face interviews. But these self-report measures are all alike in that they involve asking a question and recording the answer (Dawes & Smith, 1985).

Jacob L. Moreno used self-report methods to study young women living in 14 adjacent cottages of an institution. The women were neighbors, but they weren't very neighborly. Discipline problems were rampant, and disputes continually arose among the groups and among members of the same group who were sharing a cottage. Moreno felt that the tensions would abate if he could regroup the women into more compatible clusters and put the greatest physical distance between hostile groups. So

---

Self-report measures: Assessment devices, such as questionnaires, tests, or interviews, that ask respondents to describe their feelings, attitudes, or beliefs.

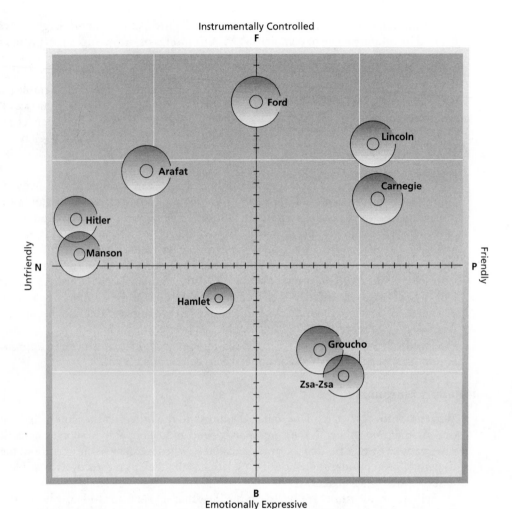

FIGURE 2–2   What three dimensions should observers note when describing the groups they study? SYMLOG measures the extent to which each member behaves in a dominant or submissive (up–down), friendly or unfriendly (positive-negative), and instrumentally controlled or emotionally expressive (forward-backward) way. Each individual's location in the group relative to the others can then be determined. Researchers used SYMLOG in this study by asking observers to rate historical and contemporary figures, including Abraham Lincoln in a meeting of his cabinet, actress Zsa-Zsa Gabor at a party, Hamlet talking with the gravedigger, Groucho Marx on a TV show, Charles Manson talking to his cult, Yassir Arafat talking with the PLO, Dale Carnegie at a dinner meeting, and business leader Henry Ford at a board meeting. Hitler, for example, was rated as somewhat instrumentally controlled, very unfriendly, but very dominant (the size of the circle indicates dominance–submission score). Groucho Marx was viewed as dominant also, but was considered by observers in this study to be emotionally expressive and friendly.

(*Source:* Isenberg & Ennis, 1981.)

he asked the women to indicate who they liked the most on a confidential question-naire. Moreno then used these responses to construct more harmonious groups, and his efforts were rewarded when the overall level of antagonism in the community dwindled (Moreno, 1934/1953).

Moreno called this technique for measuring the relations between group members **sociometry.** A researcher begins a sociometric study by asking group members one or more questions about the other members. To measure attraction, the researcher might ask, "Whom do you most like in this group?" but such questions as "Whom in the group would you like to work with the most?" or "Whom do you like the least?" can also be used. Researchers often limit the number of choices participants can make.

In the second phase, the researcher summarizes these choices by drawing a **sociogram,** a diagram of the relationships among group members. The researcher first draws a circle to represent each member. Next, the researcher draws in the feelings of each group member about the others, using arrows to indicate the direction of relationships. Next, as depicted in Figure 2–3, the researcher draws the diagram again to organize it into a more meaningful pattern. For example, those individuals who are frequently chosen as most liked by others could be put in the center of the diagram, and the least frequently chosen people could be placed about the periphery.

In the final stage, the researcher identifies the configurations of the group and the positions of each member. This step often includes the identification of (1) "populars," or "stars," the highly popular group members; (2) "rejected" individuals, who are disliked by many group members; (3) "isolates," who are infrequently chosen; (4) "pairs," two people who, by listing each other as their first choice, have reciprocal bonds; and (5) "clusters" of individuals within the group, who make up a subgroup, or clique. The researcher can also use the responses to calculate various indices of attraction, including (1) the number of times a person is chosen by the other group members (choice status); (2) the number of times a person is rejected by others (rejection status); (3) the relative number of mutual pairs in a group (group cohesion); and (4) the relative number of isolates (group integration). The researcher can also use more elaborate statistical methods, depending on the type of data available (Iacobucci, 1990; Kenny & Judd, 1996; Maassen, Akkermans, & Van der Linden, 1996; Norma & Smith, 1985; Terry & Coie, 1991).

Self-report methods, such as sociometry, have both weaknesses and strengths. They depend very much on knowing what questions to ask the group members. A maze of technical questions also confronts researchers designing questionnaires. If respondents do not answer the questions consistently—if, for example, Jos indicates that he likes Gerard the most on Monday but on Tuesday changes his choice to Claire—then the

---

Sociometry: A measurement technique developed by Moreno that summarizes graphically and mathematically patterns of intermember relations.
Sociogram: A graphic representation of the patterns of intermember relations created through sociometry.

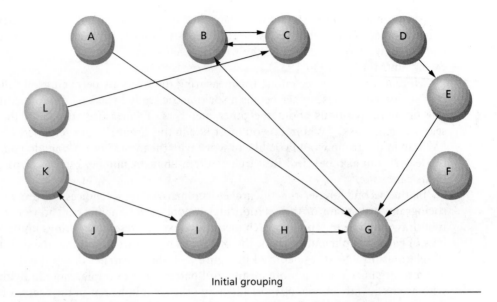

Initial grouping

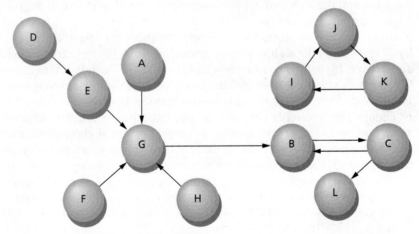

FIGURE 2–3   How can the structure of a group be measured? A sociogram charts group structure by identifying relationships among the members. In this sociogram of a 12-person group, A–L are all group members, but G is a star, L and D are isolates, B and C are a pair, and I, J, and K form a cluster.

responses will be unreliable. Also, if questions are not worded properly, the instrument will lack validity, since respondents may misinterpret what is being asked. Validity is also a problem if group members are unwilling to disclose their personal attitudes, feelings, and perceptions or are unaware of these internal processes (Whitley, 1996).

Despite these limitations, self-report methods tell us much about group phenomena, but from the perspective of the participant rather than the observer. When researchers are primarily interested in personal processes such as perceptions, feelings, and beliefs, self-report methods may be the only means of assessing these private processes. But if participants are biased, their self-reports may not be as accurate as we would like. In such cases, researchers should use observational techniques.

RESEARCH DESIGNS IN GROUP DYNAMICS

Good measurement does not guarantee good science. Researchers who watch groups and ask group members questions can develop a detailed description of a group, but they must go beyond description if they are to *explain* groups. Measurement "stretches nature out on the rack," but once researchers collect their data, they must use the information to test hypotheses about group phenomena. Researchers use many techniques to check the adequacy of their suppositions about groups, but the three most common approaches are (1) case studies of single groups, (2) experimental studies that manipulate aspects of the group situation, and (3) correlational analyses of the relationship between various aspects of groups.

Case Studies

One of the best ways to understand groups in general is to understand one group in particular. This approach has a long and venerable tradition in all the sciences, with some of the greatest advances in thinking coming from the **case study**—an in-depth examination of a single group. If the group has not yet disbanded, the researcher may decide to observe it as it carries out its functions. Alternatively, investigators may cull facts about the group from interviews with members, descriptions of the group written by journalists, or members' biographical writings. Researchers then use this information to construct an overall picture of the group and estimate the extent to which the examined case supports their hypothesis (Cahill, Fine, & Grant, 1995; Yin, 1993, 1994).

Researchers have done case studies of cults, naval personnel living in Sealab, government leaders at an international summit, religious communes, rock-and-roll bands, crisis intervention teams in psychiatric hospitals, families coping with an alcoholic member, focus groups used to study children's understanding of AIDS, and adolescent peer groups (see Festinger, Riecken, & Schachter, 1956; Radloff & Helmreich, 1968; Hare & Naveh, 1986; Stones, 1982; Bennett, 1980; Murphy & Keating, 1995; Carvalho & Brito, 1995; Hoppe, Wells, Morrison, & Gillmore, 1995; Adler & Adler, 1995, respectively). Irving Janis, for example, used this method to study the poor decision-making strategies used by groups responsible for such fiascoes as the Bay of Pigs invasion, the defense of Pearl Harbor before its attack in World War II, and the escalation of the Vietnam War. Relying on archival methods, Janis sought out

---

Case study: A research technique that involves examining, in as much detail as possible, the dynamics of a single group or individual.

available information about several such bumbling groups and then looked for their similarities. He examined historical documents, minutes of the meetings, diaries, letters, group members' memoirs, and their public statements before concluding that these groups were victims of **groupthink**—"a deterioration of mental efficiency, reality testing, and moral judgment that results from in-group pressures" (1972, p. 9). Janis specified the major determinants and symptoms of groupthink and suggested steps to avoid it. (Chapter 11 examines Janis's theory in more detail.)

All research designs offer both advantages and disadvantages, and case studies are no exception. By focusing on a limited number of cases, researchers often provide richly detailed descriptions that make fascinating reading. When researchers use archival methods, such as examining public records pertaining to the group, then the study does not disrupt or alter naturally occurring group processes. Janis, for example, studied groups that had already disbanded, so he did not need to worry about altering the phenomenon under study. At a more pragmatic level, researchers can carry out case studies relatively easily.

Case studies, however, yield only limited information about groups in general. Researchers who use the method must bear in mind that the group studied may be so unique that it tells us little about other groups. Also, researchers rarely use objective measures of group processes when conducting case studies, so their interpretations can be influenced by their own assumptions and biases. Even worse, the materials themselves may be inaccurate or unavailable to the researcher. Janis, for example, was forced to "rely mainly on the contemporary and retrospective accounts by the group members themselves, . . . many of which are likely to have been written with an eye to the author's own place in history" (1972, p. v). Finally, case studies only imply, but rarely establish, causal relationships among important variables in the group under study. Janis felt that groupthink was causing the poor decisions in the groups he studied, but some other unnoticed factor could actually have been the prime causal agent.

Experimentation

Between 1937 and 1940, Kurt Lewin, Ronald Lippitt, and Ralph White studied the way a leader can radically change the behaviors of the group members (Lewin, Lippitt, & White, 1939; White, 1990; White & Lippitt, 1968). They arranged for 10- and 11-year-old boys to meet after school in five-member groups to work on hobbies such as woodworking and painting. An adult led each group by adopting one of three styles of leadership: autocratic, democratic, or laissez-faire. The autocratic leader made all the decisions for the group, never asking for input from the boys. The autocratic leader gave orders, criticized the boys, and remained aloof. The democratic leader explained long-term goals and steps to be taken to reach the goals, but the boys themselves made all the group's decisions. Democratic leaders rarely gave orders and commands, and the criticism they did give group members was deserved. The final type of leader was labeled laissez-faire, for this leader gave the group members very little guid-

---

Groupthink: A strong concurrence-seeking tendency that interferes with effective group decision making.

ance. These leaders never participated in group interactions, allowing the boys to work in whichever way they wished. The laissez-faire leaders provided information if asked, but rarely offered information, criticism, or guidance spontaneously.

The researchers observed the groups as they worked with each type of leader, measuring group productivity and aggressiveness. When they reviewed their findings, they discovered that the autocratic groups spent more time working (74%) than the democratic groups (50%), which in turn spent more time working than the laissez-faire groups (33%). Although these results argue in favor of the efficiency of an autocratic leadership style, the observers also noted that when the leader left the room for any length of time, the democratically led groups kept right on working, whereas the boys in the autocratic groups stopped working. Lewin, Lippitt, and White also discovered a relationship between leadership style and the level of aggression displayed by group members. Observers noted high rates of hostility in the autocratically led groups, as well as more demands for attention, more destructiveness, and a greater tendency to single out one group member to serve as the target of almost continual verbal abuse. The researchers felt that this target for criticism and hostility, or scapegoat, provided members with an outlet for pent-up hostilities that could not be acted out against the powerful group leader.

The Characteristics of Experiments.   Lewin, Lippitt, and White's study of leadership styles possesses the three key features of an **experiment.** First, the researchers selected a variable that they believed caused changes in group processes. This variable, termed the **independent variable,** was manipulated by the researchers by giving groups different types of leaders (autocratic, democratic, or laissez-faire). Second, the researchers assessed the effects of the independent variable by measuring such factors as productivity and aggressiveness. The variables that researchers measure are called **dependent variables** because their magnitude depends on the strength and nature of the independent variable. Lewin, Lippitt, and White hypothesized that group leadership style would influence productivity and aggressiveness, so they tested this hypothesis by manipulating the independent variable (style) and measuring the dependent variables (productivity and aggressiveness).

Third, the experimenters tried to maintain control over other variables that might hamper interpretation of their results. The researchers never assumed that the only determinant of productivity and aggressiveness was leadership style; they knew that other variables, such as the personality characteristics and abilities of the group members, could influence the dependent variables. In the experiment, however, the researchers were not interested in these other variables. Their hypotheses were specifically focused on the relationship among leadership style, productivity, and aggressiveness. Therefore,

---

Experiment: A research design in which the investigator manipulates at least one variable by randomly assigning participants to two or more different conditions while measuring at least one other variable.

Independent variables: Those aspects of the situation manipulated by the researcher in an experimental study; the causal variables in a cause-effect relationship.

Dependent variables: The responses of the subject measured by the researcher; the effect variables in a cause-and-effect relationship.

they made certain that these other variables were controlled in the experimental situation. For example, they took pains to ensure that the groups they created were "roughly equated on patterns of interpersonal relationships, intellectual, physical, and socioeconomic status, and personality characteristics" (White & Lippitt, 1968, p. 318). The groups were also assigned at random to the experimental conditions. Because no two groups were identical, these variations could have resulted in some groups working harder than others. The researchers used random assignment of groups to even out these initial inequalities. They hoped that any differences found on the dependent measure would be due to the independent variable rather than uncontrolled differences among the participating groups.

The key characteristics of an experiment, then, are the manipulation of the independent variable, the systematic assessment of the dependent variables, and the control of other possible contaminating factors. When the experiment is properly designed and conducted, researchers can assume that any differences among the conditions on the dependent variables are produced by the variable that is manipulated and not by some other variable they forgot to control.

Advantages and Disadvantages.   Why do group dynamicists so frequently rely on experimentation to test their hypotheses about groups? This preference derives, in part, from the inferential power of experimentation. Researchers who design their experiments carefully can make inferences about the causal relationships linking variables. If the investigators keep all variables constant except for the independent variable and the dependent variable changes, then they can cautiously conclude that the independent variable caused the dependent variable to change. Experiments, if properly conducted, can be used to detect causal relationships among variables.

Experiments offer an excellent means of testing hypotheses about the causes of group behavior, but they are not without their logistical, methodological, and ethical problems. Researchers cannot always control the situation sufficiently to manipulate the independent variable or keep other variables constant. Moreover, to maintain control over the conditions of an experiment, researchers may end up studying closely monitored but artificial group situations. Experimenters often work in laboratories with ad hoc groups that are created just for the research, and these groups may differ in important ways from naturally occurring groups. Although an experimenter can heighten the impact of the situation by withholding information about the study, such deception can be challenged on ethical grounds. Of course, experiments can be conducted in the field using already existing groups, but they will almost necessarily involve the sacrifice of some degree of control and will reduce the strength of the researchers' conclusions. Hence, the major advantage of experimentation, the ability to draw causal inferences, can be offset by the major disadvantage of experimentation, basing conclusions on contrived situations that say little about the behavior of groups in more naturalistic settings. (These issues are discussed in more detail by Anderson & Bushman, 1997, and Driskell & Salas, 1992.)

Correlational Designs

When Theodore Newcomb joined the faculty at Bennington College in the mid-1930s, he was struck by the divergence in attitudes between the first-year students, the more advanced students, and the students' families. Most Bennington students came from well-to-do New England families whose strong conservatism was indicated by their presidential preferences. In the 1936 presidential elections, the majority of the families of the students favored Alfred M. Landon, the Republican candidate, rather than Franklin D. Roosevelt, the Democratic (and eventually victorious) candidate. First-year students shared the attitudes of their families, but students and families gradually divaricated over time (Newcomb, 1943).

Newcomb believed that the students' attitudes changed as their reference groups changed. **Reference groups** provide us with guidelines or standards for evaluating ourselves, our attitudes, and our beliefs (Hyman, 1942). Any group that plays a significant role in our life, such as our family, a friendship clique, colleagues at work, or even a group in which we would like to claim membership, can become a reference group for us (Singer, 1990). When students first enrolled at Bennington, their families served as their reference group, so their attitudes matched their families' attitudes. The longer students remained at Bennington, however, the more their attitudes changed to match the attitudes of their new reference group, the rest of the college population. Their families had conservative attitudes, but the college community supported mainly liberal attitudes, and Newcomb hypothesized that many Bennington women shifted their attitudes in response to this reference-group pressure.

Newcomb tested this reference-group hypothesis by administering questionnaires and interviews to an entire class of Bennington students from their entrance in 1935 to their graduation in 1939. He found a consistent trend toward liberalism in many of the students and reasoned that this change resulted from peer-group pressure because it was more pronounced among the popular students. Those who endorsed nonconservative attitudes were (1) "both capable and desirous of cordial relations with the fellow community members" (1943, p. 149), (2) more frequently chosen by others as friendly, and (3) a more cohesive subgroup than the conservative students. Individuals who did not become more liberal tended to be isolated from the college's social life or they were very family oriented. These reference groups changed the students permanently, for the students who changed in college were still liberals when Newcomb measured their political beliefs some 25 years later (Newcomb, Koenig, Flacks, & Warwick, 1967).

Characteristics of Correlational Studies.   Newcomb's Bennington study was a **correlational study;** he examined the naturally occurring relationships among several variables without manipulating any of them. Newcomb felt, for example, that as students came to identify more closely with other students, their attitudes and values changed to match those of their peers. Therefore, he assessed students' popularity, their dependence on their families, and changes in their political attitudes. Then he examined the relationships among these variables by carrying out several statistical tests. At no point did he try to manipulate the group situation.

Reference groups: Groups that provide individuals with a reference point for defining their own personal attitudes, beliefs, and social worth.
Correlational study: A nonexperimental research technique that uses statistical procedures to examine the nature of the relationship between variables of interest.

Correlational studies take their name from the statistic **correlation coefficient,** which in mathematical notation is written as *r*. This statistic summarizes the strength and direction of the relationship between two variables. It ranges from +1 to –1, with the distance from zero (0), the neutral point, indicating the strength of the relationship. If Newcomb had found that the correlation between students' popularity and liberal attitudes was close to 0, for example, he would have concluded that the two variables were unrelated to each other. If the correlation was significantly different from 0—in either a positive or negative direction—his study would have shown that these two variables were related to each other. The sign of the correlation (+ or –) indicates the direction of the relationship. If, for example, the correlation between popularity and attitudes was +.68, this positive correlation would indicate that both variables increased and decreased together; the more popular the student, the more liberal her attitude. A negative correlation, such as –.57, would indicate that the variables were inversely related; more popular students tended to have less liberal attitudes. Thus, a correlation is a handy way of summarizing a great deal of information about the relationship between two variables.

Advantages and Disadvantages.   Researchers use correlational designs whenever they wish to know more about the relationship between variables. Are group leaders usually older than their followers? Do groups become more centralized as they become larger? Do people who are more committed to their group tend to express attitudes that match their group's position? These are all questions that researchers might ask concerning the relationship between variables. When coupled with accurate measurement techniques, correlational studies offer a means of clearly describing these relationships without disrupting or manipulating any aspect of the group.

Correlational studies, however, yield only limited information about the causal relationship between variables because no variables are manipulated by the researcher. Newcomb's data, for example, indicated that the attitude changes he measured were related to reference-group pressures, but he could not rule out other possible causes. Perhaps, unknown to Newcomb, the most popular women on campus all read the same books, which contained arguments that persuaded them to give up their conservative attitudes. Newcomb also could not be certain about the *direction* of the relationship he documented. He believed that individuals who joined the liberal reference group became more liberal themselves, but the causal relationship may have been just the opposite: People who expressed more liberal attitudes may have been asked to join more liberal reference groups. Although these alternative explanations seem implausible, they cannot be eliminated, given the methods used by Newcomb.

Selecting a Research Design

Researchers use a variety of empirical procedures to study groups. Some observe group processes and then perform a qualitative analysis of their observations, whereas others insist on quantitative measurement methods and elaborate controlled experiments.

Correlation coefficient: A statistic that measures the strength and direction of a relationship between two variables. Often symbolized by *r*, correlations can range from –1.0 to +1.0.

Some researchers conduct their studies in field situations using naturally occurring groups, whereas others bring groups into the laboratory or even create ad hoc groups for the research. Some researchers undertake exploratory studies with no clear idea of what results to expect, whereas other research is designed to test hypotheses carefully derived from a specific theory. Some researchers study group phenomena by asking volunteers to role-play group members, and others simulate group interaction with computers.

This diversity of research methods doesn't reflect group dynamicists' uncertainty about which technique is best. Rather, the diversity stems from the unique advantages and disadvantages offered by each method. Case studies limit the researcher's ability to draw conclusions, to quantify results, and to make objective interpretations. But some topics, such as groupthink, are difficult to study by any other method. As Janis himself points out, it would be difficult to examine groups that make decisions about national policies, including war and civil defense, through correlational studies or experimentation. But the real forte of the case study approach is its power to provide grist for the theoretician's mill, enabling the investigator to formulate hypotheses that set the stage for other research methods.

Such stimulation of theory is also frequently a consequence of correlational research. These studies are limited in causal power, but they yield precise estimates of the strength of the relationships among variables. And compared with experimentation, they are usually more ethical. Experimentation provides the firmest test of causal hypotheses, predicting that variable X will cause such and such a change in variable Y. In the properly designed and conducted experiment, the researcher can test several hypotheses about groups, making the method both rigorous and efficient. But where an artificial setting would yield meaningless results, where the independent variable cannot be manipulated, or where too little is known about the topic even to suggest what variables are causal, some other approach would be preferable. The solution, then, is to use multiple methods for studying groups. As Joseph E. McGrath explains, "All methods have inherent flaws—though each has certain advantages. These flaws cannot be avoided. But what the researcher can do is to bring more than one approach, more than one method, to bear on each aspect of a problem" (1984, p. 30).

THEORIES IN GROUP DYNAMICS

Successful researchers don't just develop ingenious methods for measuring group processes and test their hypotheses. They also develop compelling theoretical explanations for group phenomena. Science, more than any other approach to gaining knowledge, advocates the long-term goal of increasing and systematizing our knowledge about the subject matter. Theories provide the means of organizing known facts about groups and so create orderly knowledge out of discrete bits of information. Theories also yield suggestions for future research. When researchers extend existing theories into new areas, they discover new information about groups while simultaneously testing the strength of their theories.

We will review some of the basic approaches to the study of groups with the caveat that these approaches are not necessarily mutually exclusive. Most theories embrace assumptions from one or more of the motivational, behavioral, systems, cognitive, and biological perspectives.

Motivational Models

Why do some people vie for leadership in their groups, whereas others remain content with less prominent roles? Why do some groups struggle against adversity, whereas others give up after the first setback? Why do some people shy away from groups, whereas others join dozens? Many theorists offer answers that stress the role played by group members' **motivations**. Habits, goals, instincts, expectations, and drives prompt group members to take action (Geen, 1995). Indeed, the word *motivation* comes from the verb "to move."

Kurt Lewin's **level-of-aspiration theory** is, at core, a motivational model, for it explains how people set goals for themselves and their groups (Lewin, Dembo, Festinger, & Sears, 1944). The theory assumes that people enter achievement situations with an ideal outcome in mind—for example, earning an A in the course, winning the game, or making a specific amount of money. Over time, however, people may revise their expectations as they repeatedly fail or succeed in reaching their ideals. Lewin used the term *level of aspiration (LOA)* to describe this compromise between ideal goals and more realistic expectations.

Alvin Zander (1971/1996) applied LOA theory to groups by studying how individual members set goals for their groups and how they revise their goals after each group success or failure. When group members complete a task, they expend considerable mental energy reviewing their efforts and outcomes. They gather and weigh information about their performance and determine if they met the group's standards. They review the strategies they used to accomplish their task and determine if these strategies require revision. They also plan their future undertakings, ever mindful of the long-term goals they have set for themselves.

Zander found that a group's LOA often slightly exceeds individual members' LOA. In one study, he arranged for boys to play a simple skills game in groups. After each failure, the boys lowered their LOA, and after each success, they raised it; but their group LOA was slightly more optimistic than a strict forecast based on past performance would predict. The boys, when discussing their performance, exchanged encouraging suggestions, and this advice may have increased their optimism. Zander also found that groups raise their LOA more after success than they lower it after failure and that some groups set themselves up for failure by setting overly optimistic goals. Difficult goals challenge members to work harder to improve performance, but groups that fail consistently have low group morale and high turnover in membership (Zander, 1971/1996).

Behavioral Approaches

Many theories of group behavior are consistent with B. F. Skinner's (1953, 1971) **behaviorism**. Skinner believed that psychological processes, such as motives and drives,

---

Motivations: Wants, needs, and other psychological processes that energize certain responses, prompting people to respond in one way rather than another.
Level-of-aspiration theory: A theoretical perspective developed by Lewin that explains how people set goals for themselves and their groups.
Behaviorism: A theoretical orientation that describes the way behaviors are learned through such conditioning processes as stimulus-response associations and reinforcement.

may shape people's reactions in groups, but he also believed that such psychological processes are too difficult to index accurately. So Skinner recommended studying the things that people actually do rather than the psychological states that may have instigated the action. And actions, Skinner believed, tend to be consistent with the *law of effect;* that is, behaviors that are followed by positive consequences, such as rewards, will occur more frequently, whereas behaviors that are followed by negative consequences will become rarer (e.g., Blau, 1964; Foa & Foa, 1971; Homans, 1974; La Gaipa, 1977).

John Thibaut and Harold Kelley's (1959) **social exchange theory** extended Skinner's behaviorism to groups. They agreed that individuals hedonistically strive to maximize their rewards and minimize their costs. But when individuals join groups, they no longer control their outcomes. Groups create interdependence among members, so that the actions of each group member potentially influence the outcomes and actions of every other group member. Mara, for example, can spend several days working on a project, struggling to complete it successfully. But what if Mara collaborates with Steven on the project? When Mara works alone, she determines her own success. But when she works with Steven, his actions partially shape her outcomes. Mara may enjoy certain aspects of her interaction with Steven, but she may also find some of the things he does irritating. Thibaut and Kelley assume that Mara and Steven will negotiate throughout their interaction to secure greater personal rewards while minimizing costs.

Systems Theories

Researchers in a variety of fields, including engineering, biology, and medicine, have repeatedly found that unique results are obtained when a system is formed by creating dependency among formerly independent components. Systems, whether they are bridges, ecological niches, or organisms, synthesize several parts or subsystems to form a unified whole. These systems, because they are based on interrelated parts, can change to an extraordinary degree when one of their constituent components changes.

A **systems theory** approach assumes that groups are systems of interacting individuals. Indeed, this definition of a system could easily serve as a definition of a group:

> [A system is] a set of interacting units with relationships among them. The word "set" implies that the units have some common properties. These common properties are essential if the units are to interact or have relationships. The state of each unit is constrained by, conditioned by, or dependent on the state of other units. The units are coupled. Moreover, there is at least one measure of the sum of its units which is larger than the sum of that measure of its units. [Miller, 1978, p. 16]

Just as a system receives inputs from the environment, processes this information through internal communication, and then outputs its products, groups gather information, review that information, and generate products. Groups are also capable of

Social exchange theory: An economic model of interpersonal relationships that argues that individuals seek out relationships that offer them many rewards while exacting few costs.
Systems theory: A general theoretical approach that assumes that groups are systems—collections of individual units that combine to form an integrated, complex whole.

formulating goals and working toward these goals through united action, and group members are responsive to environmental feedback concerning the efficacy of their actions. The communication of information—a key concept in systems theory—similarly plays a central role in groups that must analyze inputs, provide feedback to members, and formulate decisions regarding group action. Indeed, larger groups may be built on a number of smaller subsystems, all of which are integrated into an overall Gestalt.

Systems theory provides a model for understanding a range of group-level processes, including group development, productivity, and interpersonal conflict (Tubbs, 1995). Figure 2–4, for example, explains group productivity by identifying *inputs* that feed into the group setting, *processes* that take place within the group as it works on the task, and *outputs* generated by the system. Inputs include any factors that are present in the situation when the group begins its work on the task. Many of these inputs are related to the characteristics of the individual members. A group whose individuals are skilled at the task or very interested in doing well will likely perform better than a group comprised of unskilled, uninterested members. Group-level factors, such as group structure and cohesiveness, may also determine how the group carries out its work, as will environment-level factors. For example, groups working on complex tasks under the mandate of an external authority will likely perform differently than groups working on simple tasks that won't be evaluated outside the group (Hackman, 1987; Hackman & Morris, 1975; Littlepage, Schmidt, Whisler, & Frost, 1995; McGrath, 1964, 1997).

These input factors all influence the processes that take place within the group as members work together to complete the task. How will group members communicate information with one another? Will they select strategies to help them reach their goals, and will they revise these strategies if they don't seem to be working well? What if two members disagree about procedures or solutions? How will this conflict be handled by the group? Who will lead the group, and who will follow? Communication, planning, conflict, and leadership are just a few of the internal processes that will transform inputs into outputs. These outputs include aspects of the group's performance (e.g., products, decisions, errors) and changes in the factors that serve as inputs to the system. If the group performs poorly, for example, it may become less cohesive or it may seek out new members. Members of successful groups, in contrast, may become more satisfied with their group and take steps to make sure that the group uses the same procedures to solve the next problem.

Cognitive Approaches

A group's dynamics, in many cases, becomes understandable only when we consider the **cognitive processes** that occur within each individual in the group. When people join a group for the first time, they immediately begin to form an impression of the group. This perceptual work prompts them to search for information about the other group members, rapidly identifying those who are outgoing, shy, and intelligent

---

Cognitive processes: Mental processes that acquire, organize, and integrate information. Cognitive processes include memory systems that store data and the psychological mechanisms that process this information.

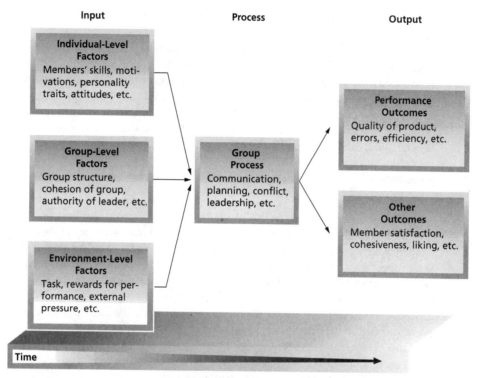

FIGURE 2–4   What are the most important determinants of a group's efficiency in performing a task? A systems approach to group productivity assumes that the multiple components of a group interact with one another over time. The model identifies those factors that act as inputs to the group, the group processes that respond to those inputs, and the outputs generated by those processes.

(*Source:* McGrath, 1964.)

(Albright, Kenny, & Malloy, 1988). Group members also search their memories for stored information about the group and the tasks it must face, and they must retrieve that information before they can use it. A group member must also take note of the actions of others and try to understand what caused the other person to act in this way. Thus, group members are busy perceiving, judging, reasoning, and remembering, and all these mental activities influence their understanding of one another, the group, and themselves (Fiske & Goodwin, 1994; Nye, 1994).

Joseph Berger and his colleagues offer a cognitive analysis of who will rise to the top of a group's status hierarchy and who will fall to the bottom. Their **expectation-states theory** assumes that group members, while interacting with one another, intuitively take note of two types of cues as they allocate status within the group. *Specific-status*

Expectation-states theory: An explanation of status differentiation in groups that assumes that group members allocate status to group members who display positively valued, rather than negatively valued, status characteristics.

characteristics are qualities that attest to each individual's level of ability to perform the specific task at hand. *Diffuse-status characteristics* are general qualities that group members think are relevant to ability and evaluation. Any characteristic—sex, age, ethnicity, and so on—can serve as a diffuse-status characteristic if people associate that quality with certain skills. Those who possess numerous status-earning characteristics are implicitly identified and then permitted to perform more numerous and varied group actions, to provide greater input and guidance for the group, to influence others by evaluating their ideas, and to reject the influence attempts of others (Berger, Wagner, & Zelditch, 1992; Wagner & Berger, 1993).

Biological Models

Group members can solve complex problems, communicate with one another using spoken and written language, build and operate massive machines, and plan their group's future. But group members are also living creatures whose responses are often shaped by biological, biochemical, and genetic characteristics. When conflict arises in the group, heart rates escalate and other body changes occur to help members cope with the stress (Blascovich, Nash, & Ginsburg, 1978). When groups are trapped in confining, cramped spaces, members often become physiologically aroused, and this arousal can interfere with their work (Evans & Cohen, 1987). When others encroach on our territories, we instinctively respond to defend our turf.

One biological perspective, **evolutionary theory,** or **sociobiology,** argues that these group behaviors may be genetically determined. This perspective argues that in the last 15 million years, the human species has evolved socially as well as physically. Through the process of natural selection, individuals who were even slightly predisposed to engage in adaptive social behaviors tended to survive longer and to be more successful in passing their genes along to future generations. Over countless generations, this selection process weeded out individuals who lacked these predispositions, while those who possessed them prospered. Even though these tendencies may not enhance our fitness in today's world, aeons spent in harsher environments have left us genetically predisposed to perform certain social behaviors when situational cues evoke ancient instincts (Buss & Schmitt, 1993; Buss and Kenrick, 1998).

Evolutionary theory offers insight into a range of group processes, including affiliation, intergroup conflict, and aggression. For example, its explanation of the tendency for many groups to struggle to maintain control over specific geographical areas—territoriality—is intriguing. Most modern groups no longer need to defend their turf against outsiders, yet groups and group members retain their territorial ways. Why? Evolutionary psychology suggests that our ancestors lived in tribes that gathered nuts, berries, and other foods from the land as they foraged. These tribes, like the !Kung and the Mescalero Apaches of today, built no permanent dwellings, but they did establish control over certain geographical areas (Altman & Chemers, 1980). By marking their areas and attacking intruders, they gained an evolutionary edge over others, and their

Evolutionary theory (sociobiology): A biological approach to understanding behavior that assumes that recurring patterns of behavior in animals ultimately stem from evolutionary pressures that increase the likelihood of adaptive social actions while extinguishing nonadaptive practices.

offspring were more likely to survive. Natural selection thus favored individuals who were members of territorial groups, with the result that today's groups are driven by an instinctive need to defend their territories against encroachment by others (Kaplan & Kaplan, 1989; Rushton, 1989).

Selecting a Theory

Group dynamics, with its roots in both psychology and sociology, is rich with theory. Some of these theories trace group processes back to psychological processes: the motivations of the individual members, the mental processes that sustain their conception of their social environment, and even their instinctive urges and proclivities. Other theories focus more on the group as a social system that is integrated in the surrounding community and society.

These different theoretical perspectives, however, are not mutually exclusive paradigms struggling for the distinction as *the* explanation of group behavior. Some researchers test hypotheses derived from only one theory; others draw on several perspectives as they strive to describe, predict, control, and explain groups and their members. Just as the questions "How should I measure this aspect of the group?" and "How should I test my hypothesis about groups?" can be answered in more than one way, no one solution can be offered in response to the question, "What theory explains group behavior?" Many of the greatest advances in understanding groups have occurred, not when one theory has been pitted against another, but when two or more theories have been synthesized to form a new, more encompassing theoretical perspective. In Homans's (1950, p. 4) words, "We have a great deal of fact to work with, [and] we also have a great deal of theory. The elements of a synthesis are on hand."

SUMMARY

How do researchers measure the way groups, and the individuals in those groups, feel, think, and behave?

Two basic measurement methods are observation of behavior and self-report.

1. *Observational measures* involve observing and recording events transpiring in groups. Some researchers, such as William F. Whyte, prefer *participant observation;* Whyte studied a corner gang by joining it. Others remain outside the group under study and guard against the biasing influences of the *Hawthorne effect* by keeping their research agenda a secret from the group members they are watching (*covert observation*).

2. Researchers use various *structured observational measures* in their studies, for such systems yield a more objective record of group members' actions. Bales's *Interaction Process Analysis* (IPA) with its categories pertaining to task and socioemotional behaviors, and his *SYMLOG* approach are examples of structured observational systems.

3. *Reliability* and *validity* are essential qualities in any measure, for it must be consistent and it must measure what it is designed to measure.

4. *Self-report measures* ask group members to describe their own perceptions and experiences. Moreno's *sociometry,* for example, involves asking members to report whom they like the most. The researcher can then use this information

to generate a *sociogram,* a visual image of the interpersonal relations in the group.

How do researchers search for and test their hypotheses about groups rigorously?

1. Janis utilized a *case study* approach in searching for the symptoms and causes of *groupthink* in government decision-making groups.
2. Lewin, Lippitt, and White studied the impact of autocratic, democratic, and laissez-faire leaders on groups by conducting an *experiment.* They manipulated the *independent variable* (leadership style), assessed several *dependent variables* (aggressiveness, productivity, etc.), and limited the influence of other possible causal factors by controlling the situation and assigning groups to experimental conditions at random.
3. Newcomb investigated how *reference groups* can influence their members' attitudes and political beliefs by carrying out a *correlational study.* Rather than manipulating aspects of the situation, he gauged the strength of the naturally occurring relationships between such variables as political preferences and popularity. Often, such information is summarized in the form of a *correlation coefficient.*

What are the strengths and weaknesses of these research methods?

1. The conclusions drawn from case studies can be highly subjective, but they stimulate theory and provide detailed information about particular groups.
2. Groups studied in experimental settings may not display the dynamics of naturally occurring groups, but experi-

mentation provides the clearest test of cause-and-effect hypotheses.
3. Correlational studies provide only limited information about causality, but they yield precise estimates of the strength of the relationship between two variables and raise fewer moral questions for researchers.

What general theoretical perspectives guide researchers as they explore groups and the people in them?

1. Motivational models stress members' *motivations,* as illustrated by Lewin's *level-of-aspiration theory.*
2. Theories based on *behaviorism,* such as Thibaut and Kelley's *social exchange theory,* assume that individuals act to maximize their rewards and minimize their costs.
3. A systems theory approach assumes that groups are *systems.* An input-process-output model of group performance exemplifies the systems approach.
4. Berger's *expectation-states theory* is a *cognitive processes* approach, for it assumes that group members' perceptual, judgmental, and cognitive activities shape their responses.
5. Biological perspectives, such as *evolutionary theory,* or *sociobiology,* argue that some group behaviors, such as territoriality, may be rooted in group members' biological heritage.

FOR MORE INFORMATION

Applications of Case Study Research, by R. K. Yin (1993), provides a detailed analysis of the strengths and weaknesses of case study methods.

"Can You Study Real Teams in Contrived Settings?," a chapter by James E. Driskell and

Eduardo Salas (1992) in *Teams: Their Training and Performance*, analyzes validity issues that face researchers who study groups in laboratory settings.

Motives and Goals in Groups, by Alvin Zander (1971/1996), is a classic analysis of how the qualities and effectiveness of working groups are determined by the motives and goals of the group members.

People Studying People: Artifacts and Ethics in Behavioral Research, by Ralph L. Rosnow and Robert Rosenthal (1997), is an intriguing overview of the many technical and ethical problems that researchers encounter when they subject human behavior to scientific scrutiny.

Street Corner Society, by William Foote Whyte (1943), remains one of the best examples of applying the case study method to understanding a group's dynamics.

Theoretical Research Programs: Studies in the Growth of Theory, edited by Joseph Berger and Morris Zelditch, Jr. (1993), offers insights into the way theorists develop their conceptual models by conducting systematic programs of research.

ACTIVITY 2–1 WHAT DO GROUPS *DO?*

Find an aggregate of individuals in some public place. Observe the grouping of people for at least 20 minutes, and be sure to take notes. Answer the following questions.

1. Where did you find your group?
2. What were the characteristics of the people in the group?
3. How were the people arranged in the physical environment? (You may include a diagram if you wish.)
4. What were the characteristics of the *group* (rather than the people in the group)?
a. Interaction: How were the members interacting with each other?
b. Structure: Could you discern the group's norms, roles, status hierarchy, or communication patterns?
c. Cohesiveness: Did the group seem unified?
d. Identity: Do you think the members shared a sense of identity with one another?
e. Goals: What was the group's purpose?
5. Was the aggregate you observed a "group" in the text's sense of the word? Was it high in entitativity, or perceived groupness, or was it a loose conglomeration?
6. Critique your study of the group from a measurement standpoint. How could you have increased the scientific accuracy and value of your observations?
7. Did anything about the group puzzle or surprise you? Did your observation raise questions that could be answered through research?

ACTIVITY 2–2 CAN GROUP DISCUSSIONS BE MEASURED OBJECTIVELY?

The purpose of this activity is to measure the patterns of communication among members of a group or study the content of a group's discussion. Find a group to observe, such as a class discussing a topic (but not a class listening to a lecture), a meeting of a government group, a meeting at your place of work, or even a group featured in a television program or movie. Next, study the group's communication patterns and the content of the discussion.

1. *Communication analysis.* Document who speaks to whom, using a chart like the one shown in Figure 2–5 to help you keep track of the information flow. When, for example, Erick speaks to Kelley, record the interaction in the Erick-to- Kelley box. At the end of the meeting, compute the percentage of contributions of each member and general speaking patterns. If the communication rate is not too great, you can also record how long each member speaks and turn-taking exchanges (who speaks after whom). Use the data you collect to draw conclusions about the group's structure and process.

From	To						
	Audrey	Erick	Jon	Pat	Kelley	Group	Total
Audrey	—					11	2
Erick	HHT 1	—	111		111	HHT	17
Jon	11	HHT	—		11	1	10
Pat				—		1	1
Kelley	1	HHT 1	111		—	1111	14
Total	9	11	6	0	5	13	44

FIGURE 2–5   Who speaks to whom in the group? When observing a group, develop a chart like this one to keep track of the group discussion. Each time a member speaks to another member, make a note of it in the appropriate box. You can then use the information to identify the group's discussion leader as well as other members who were more or less active in the discussion.

2. *Content analysis.* Analyze the content of the discussion by classifying each remark using a structured coding system, such as Bales's Interaction Process Analysis (IPA), SYMLOG (Bales, Cohen, & Williamson, 1979), or a system that you personally devise. The categories of IPA appear in Table 2–1. To use this system, develop a chart like the one shown in Figure 2–6. Each time an individual makes a remark, classify it into one of the IPA categories and record who said it by marking the appropriate box. If, for example, Erick says, "I don't think that is such a good idea," then mark the "Gives opinion" box for Erick. Use the data you collect to draw conclusions about the group's structure and process.

IPA	Member					
Behaviors	Audrey	Erick	Jon	Pat	Kelley	Total
Seems friendly	I		I I			3
Dramatizes	I	I	I I	I I		6
Agrees			I			1
Gives suggestion		I I I				3
Gives opinion		I I				2
Gives information	I	I I I			I I	6
Asks for information					I	1
Asks for opinion			I I		I I I	5
Asks for suggestion			I		I	2
Disagrees				I I I	LHT	8
Shows tension				I I		2
Seems unfriendly				I I		2
Total	3	9	8	9	12	41

FIGURE 2–6 What kinds of information did members exchange in their group? This sample chart is based on the Interaction Process Analysis (IPA) categories. Each time a member speaks, classify the remark into one of the 12 categories shown in the left-hand column and indicate who said it. You can then use the information to identify the overall content of the group's discussion.

3

The Individual and the Group

When people choose group membership over independence from others, they retain their personal qualities—their motives, emotions, and outlooks—but add to them a social identity: a sense of self that incorporates their collective, rather than their individualistic, characteristics. Groups blur the boundary between the personal and the interpersonal.

- Why do people sacrifice their independence to become members of groups?
- In what ways does membership in a group change a person's self-concept and social identity?
- Is self-esteem shaped by the personal qualities we possess, the value of the groups to which we belong, or both our personal and collective qualities?

CONTENTS

C. P. Ellis: From Klan Member to Enlightened Humanitarian

FROM ISOLATION TO BELONGING

The Replacement Hypothesis

The Belongingness Hypothesis

Groups and Society

The Value of Groups

FROM INDIVIDUALITY TO COLLECTIVITY

Groups and Identity

Which Self? The Two Sides to Identity

Social Identity and Self-Worth

Turning Against the Group: Seeking Individuality

SUMMARY

FOR MORE INFORMATION

ACTIVITIES

C. P. Ellis: From Klan Member to Enlightened Humanitarian

Claiborne P. Ellis was a man like any other. He grew up in North Carolina, in the southern United States. He never finished school, but always found work: pumping gas, cleaning offices, driving a bread truck. He married, raised his children, and worked overtime to get by. He believed in America, he went to church every Sunday, and he obeyed the law. Everyone called him C. P. (Terkel, 1980).

C. P. was an individualist. He worked hard, held firm to his personal beliefs when others disputed them, and looked to no one for favors. But C. P. was also a member of many groups, and these groups exerted an inexorable impact on C. P. Ellis the individual. He quit school with only an eighth-grade education when his father died and his family needed him to earn money. In the 1950s, he became a member of a group that opposed racial equality—the Ku Klux Klan (KKK)—and eventually became his chapter's president. In the 1960s, he denounced the Klan's racist values and joined the Durham Human Relations Council. In the 1970s, he served on the local school board and joined the labor movement. The union members eventually elected him chief steward.

C. P. illustrates the intricate relationship between the individual and the group. The notion of individualism is a cornerstone of Western thought, but this doctrine ignores the inseparable connection between the person and the group. A life of independence, free of restrictions imposed by others, sounds alluring, but as social beings we seek connections with others. No one, as John Donne wrote, is an island. Why do people usually prefer membership in a group over the freedom of independence?

C. P.'s case also reveals the many things that happen to people when they stop being individuals and start being group members. When people create groups, new social entities are born, and these social entities are the catalyst for changes in the individual members. We assume that our personal qualities and characteristics are formed by slow-moving psychological processes, yet when we move from one group to another, we change as individuals: The C. P. who was a Klan member isn't the same C. P. who is manager of a union. How do people change when they choose association over isolation?

FROM ISOLATION TO BELONGING

C. P. did not set out to join the KKK, but he was curious about a group of young white men who congregated near the gasoline station where he worked: "They said they were with the Klan and have meetings close-by. Would I be interested? Boy, that was an opportunity I really looked forward to! To be part of somethin'" (quoted in Terkel, 1980, p. 202).

Aristotle proclaimed that a human being is "by nature a social animal, and an individual who is unsocial naturally and not accidentally is either beneath our notice or more than human." But what prompts us to join together with other members of our species? C. P. Ellis, like most people, took pride in his independence from others; and yet, like most people, he sought out and accepted memberships in groups. Do we seek membership in groups because we are searching for security and intimacy? Are groups the bridge between the individual and society at large? Are we herd animals destined by genetics to seek out others?

The Replacement Hypothesis

Sigmund Freud is best known for his insightful, if controversial, analyses of personality and adjustment. His psychodynamic model argued that deep-seated psychological processes—sexual impulses, conflicts between desires and ideals, and cravings created by early childhood experiences—shape behavior, even though people aren't aware of their influence. But Freud (1922) also studied groups. In *Group Psychology and the Analysis of Ego,* he explained people's willingness to submit to the authority of a leader with the *replacement hypothesis.* According to this hypothesis, groups provide a replacement for our first, and most fulfilling, group: the family.

Freud based his analysis on two key concepts—identification and transference. Freud argued that very young children are totally self-centered and cannot bond with their parents. As they mature, however, *identification* prompts them to imitate their parents, and they shift from self-love to parental love. When they bond with their parents, they find satisfaction through a sense of belonging, dependency on another, protection from external threats, and enhanced self-development. Freud also used his concept of *transference* to explain how groups come to take the place of childhood families as we reach adulthood. Freud observed that some of his patients reacted to him the way they had reacted to their parents when they were children. They *transferred* their feelings for the parents to Freud, making him an authority figure for them. Freud theorized that a similar transference occurs in groups when individuals accept leaders as authority figures. This transference leads to identification with the leader, and other group members come to take the place of siblings. Group membership may be an unconscious means of regaining the security of the family, and the emotional ties that bind members to their groups are like the ties that bind children to their family (Kohut, 1984).

Freud's replacement hypothesis is speculative. Researchers have not confirmed its key concepts, including identification and transference. Yet, some members of long-term, emotionally intense groups—therapeutic groups, support groups, and combat units, for example—respond to leaders as if they were parents, treat one another like siblings, and show pronounced grief and withdrawal when someone leaves the "family" (Janis, 1963; Wrong, 1994). They react as if their group has become a family for them. Freud's concept of the unconscious also explains why people cannot always explain their reasons for taking part in a group's activities. Most people avoid isolation and seek out social interaction, but they may not be able to articulate the reasons for their group-seeking tendencies because their motivations are unconscious ones.

The Belongingness Hypothesis

Freud believed that adults need to be in groups because in groups they can recapture the sense of security that they felt with a nurturing parent and form sound relations with others, just as they bonded with their brothers and sisters (Lee & Robbins, 1995). This supposition is consistent with Roy F. Baumeister and Mark R. Leary's

(1995) **belongingness hypothesis.** They assume that all people need to belong to social groups: All "human beings have a pervasive drive to form and maintain at least a minimum quantity of lasting, positive, and impactful interpersonal relationships" (p. 497). They liken the need to belong to other basic needs, such as hunger or thirst. A person who hasn't eaten will feel hungry, but a person who has little contact with other people will feel unhappy and lonely. Baumeister and Leary believe that group membership fulfills a generic need to establish positive, enduring relationships with other people (Rook 1984; Shaver & Buhrmester, 1983).

The Effects of Isolation.   Just as an inadequate diet can undermine one's health, so isolation from other people can lead to pronounced psychological discomfort. The diaries of individuals who have been isolated from others for long periods of time—stranded explorers, scientists working in seclusion, and prisoners in solitary confinement— describe psychological suffering that was more disturbing than the physical deprivations. Like the stranded Robinson Crusoe, they complain of **loneliness:** "I am singled out and separated, as it were, from all the world, to be miserable. I am divided from mankind, a solitary; one banished from human society. I have no soul to speak to or to relieve me" (Defoe, 1908, p. 51). As their isolation wears on, they also report fear, insomnia, memory lapses, depression, fatigue, and general confusion. Prolonged periods of isolation are also marked by hallucinations and delusions, as when one solo sailor at sea was startled when he thought he saw a pirate steering his life raft (Bone, 1957; Burney, 1961).

The negative consequences of isolation are rarely seen when people voluntarily seek solitude or make good use of their time alone to engage in self-reflection. Some thinkers, writers, and artists have even reached the apex of their creativity during times of isolation, when they weren't distracted by contact with other people (Storr, 1988; Suedfeld, 1997). But forced, long-term solitude, such as solitary confinement in a prison, is often disturbing. Some cultures consider solitary confinement a form of torture.

Loneliness and Inclusion.   How do isolated people feel? Whereas starving people call their discomfort hunger, isolated people call their distress **loneliness.** Loneliness is a negative experience, for it creates such feelings as sadness, depression, helplessness, shame, and self-pity (Rubenstein & Shaver, 1982).

Loneliness can take one of two forms: social loneliness and emotional loneliness. *Social loneliness* occurs when people do not belong to any groups that provide members with opportunities for interaction. People who have moved to a new city or changed school often experience social loneliness because they are no longer embedded in a network of friends and acquaintances. *Emotional loneliness,* in contrast, occurs when a person desires but cannot establish a meaningful, intimate relation-

---

Belongingness hypothesis: The supposition that all people are motivated to seek out and join with other humans and that those who are deprived of this contact will experience discomfort and loneliness.
Loneliness: Feelings of desperation, boredom, self-deprecation, and depression experienced when individuals feel that their personal relationships are too few or unsatisfying.

ship with another person. Divorce or the loss of a lover often sets the stage for emotional loneliness (DiTommaso & Spinner, 1997; Russell, Cutrona, Rose, & Yurko, 1984; Weiss, 1973). Both forms of loneliness create such feelings as sadness, depression, helplessness, shame, and self-pity (Rubenstein & Shaver, 1982).

Transitory, impersonal groups—audiences in a darkened movie theater, passengers on a bus, people waiting in a queue—do little to ease either social or emotional loneliness. Sitting with other people in a theater or striking up a conversation with a stranger on a bus creates a connection momentarily, but the need to belong is best slaked by stable, personally involving relationships (Baumeister & Leary, 1995; Jones & Carver, 1991). As Figure 3–1 suggests, playing on an amateur athletic team,

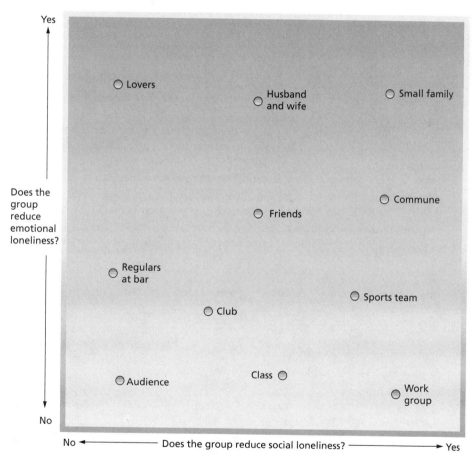

FIGURE 3–1 Can groups prevent feelings of emotional and social loneliness? In emotionally intimate groups, such as romantic dyads or families, members are linked by emotionally strong bonds: they might describe themselves as best friends, as buddies, or as lovers. Other groups may not provide an antidote to emotional loneliness, but may prevent social loneliness by linking members in a network of stable relations.

(*Source:* Shaver & Buhrmester, 1983.)

working each day with the same group of associates, or frequenting a neighborhood bar may be sufficient to prevent social loneliness. A tight-knit group of friends or a family, in contrast, may be so emotionally involving that members never feel the lack of a dyadic love relationship. Indeed, a poll of Americans indicated that those who belonged to more groups and organizations were less lonely than those who kept to themselves (Rubenstein & Shaver, 1980). College students who belonged to a cohesive, satisfying group reported much less loneliness than students who belonged to poorly integrated groups (Anderson & Martin, 1995; Schmidt & Sermat, 1983). Membership in groups with extensive interconnections among all the members has also been linked to reduced loneliness (Kraus, Davis, Bazzini, Church, & Kirchman, 1993; Stokes, 1985). People who belong to groups that provide them with social support are healthier than individuals who have few ties to other people, for they suffer fewer psychological problems and physical illnesses (Harlow & Cantor, 1996; Stroebe, Stroebe, Abakoumkin, & Schut, 1996). They even live longer than lonely loners (Stroebe, 1994; Sugisawa, Liang, & Liu, 1994).

Inclusion and Ostracism.   The belongingness hypothesis argues that people who are isolated from others, like hungry or thirsty people, will experience discomfort. The theory also argues that just as people avoid feeling hungry and thirsty, so people strive to be included in groups and avoid being excluded from them (Buss, 1983; Leary, 1990). As Figure 3–2 indicates, we are satisfied when a group takes us in, but a group that actively seeks us out provides maximal inclusion. In contrast, we respond negatively when a group ignores or avoids us, but maximal exclusion—the group rejects, ostracizes, abandons, or banishes us—is particularly punishing (Williams & Sommer, 1997). The KKK, for example, recruited C. P. for membership and cheered him during the induction ceremony: "After I had taken my oath, there was loud applause goin' throughout the buildin', musta been at least four hundred people. For this one

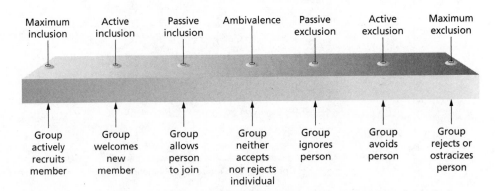

FIGURE 3–2   Is inclusion an all-or-none process or a continuum ranging from maximal inclusion to maximal exclusion? When groups actively seek us out, we experience maximal inclusion, and when they actively ostracize us, we experience maximal exclusion.

(*Source:* Leary, 1990.)

little ol' person. It was a thrilling moment" (quoted in Terkel, 1980, p. 203). Other groups, though, deliberately excluded him.

Because people seek inclusion and avoid exclusion, they often remain members of groups that have long since lost their value to them (Baumeister & Tice, 1990; Leary, 1990). People also monitor their acceptance by others, and if other people show signs of excluding them, they modify their behaviors to regain acceptance (Leary, Tambor, Terdal, & Downs, 1995; Williams & Sommer, 1997). One pair of researchers created ostracism by scheduling two confederates and one subject for each session. When the experimenter left the room, the confederates began to bounce a ball back and forth between them. In some cases, the confederates included the subject in their game, but in other cases, they stopped bouncing the ball to the subject after about a minute. The subjects, when later asked how much they liked the other two group members, rated their partners more negatively when they had been ostracized. Women who had been ostracized, however, worked harder on a subsequent collective task, apparently to regain acceptance by the rest of the group. Women were also more likely to blame themselves for their ostracism (e.g., "I have trouble making a good impression with others"). Men, in contrast, did not compensate by working harder or take the blame for their rejection (Williams & Sommer, 1997).

Exclusion also influences self-esteem: one's feelings of personal worth. Leary and his colleagues examined the impact of exclusion on self-esteem by asking sets of five individuals to interact briefly and exchange some sample essays. Participants then rated each other privately on a questionnaire, indicating with whom they would most want to work. The researchers, after examining the questionnaires, told three of the subjects that they would be part of a group for the remainder of the research and told the other two that they would be working alone. In half the sessions, the researchers announced that people who were ranked negatively by the other group members would be the isolates, but in other sessions, they said that the group-versus-individual decision was determined by a random drawing (Leary et al., 1995).

The individuals who thought they had been excluded from the group reacted the most negatively to their rejection, particularly if they thought the other subjects, and not the experimenters' random choice, caused them to be excluded. They reported feeling less competent, adequate, useful, smart, and valuable than did the included group members. The rejected members were also more negative than accepted members when they rated their coparticipants, and they also rationalized their exclusion when asked, "How much did you want to be selected for the three-person 'central' group?" Individuals who were rejected said they didn't really want to be in the group, after all (Leary et al., 1995).

These findings support Leary's *sociometer model* of self-esteem. This theory suggests that people intuitively keep track of their inclusion and exclusion in groups, and a drop in self-esteem is an internal signal that warns of possible exclusion. Like a gauge that indicates how much fuel is left in the tank, self-esteem is a gauge that indicates the extent to which the person is included in groups. If the gauge drops, then exclusion is likely. So when we experience a dip in our self-esteem, we search for and correct characteristics and qualities that have put us at risk for social exclusion. The sociometer model concludes that most people have high self-esteem not because they think well of themselves, but because they are careful to maintain inclusion in social groups (Haupt & Leary, 1997; Leary et al., 1995).

Groups and Society

Psychologists tend to explain group behavior by examining personality or qualities of the person ("In the beginning, there is the person"). Sociologists usually explain behavior "from the standpoint of units of interaction comprised of multiple persons (in the beginning, there is society . . .)" (Stryker, 1997, p. 316). To a sociologist, groups form because they are a natural consequence of a social existence. All human beings face similar demands in terms of securing food, shelter, and safety and producing off-spring, but they cannot attain these goals by themselves. So they establish relation-ships with others to facilitate the attainment of these goals. These relationships become, in time, so customary that they become part of the society's **social structure**: stable patterns of interactions among individuals. The individual who lives apart from others, never marries, and works a job that requires no interaction with others is a rarity in a world ordered, routinized, and regulated by groups (Schooler, 1994).

Primary Groups.   Society is sustained by a variety of groups, but most can be classi-fied into one of two broad categories: primary groups and secondary groups (or complex groups). *Primary groups,* so labeled by sociologist Charles Horton Cooley (1909) are small, close-knit groups, such as families, friendship cliques, and neigh-borhoods (see Chapter 1, p. 12). Individuals become part of primary groups, in many cases, by necessity: Most are born into a family, which provides for their well-being until they can join other social groups. Other primary groups form when people interact in significant, meaningful ways for a prolonged period of time.

Primary groups provide a number of basic functions for individual members: They protect them from harm, care for them when they are ill, and provide them with shel-ter and sustenance (see Table 3–1). But Cooley (1909, pp. 26–27) believed that their most important function was in creating a bridge between the individual and society at large:

> Primary groups are primary in the sense that they give the individual his earli-est and completest experience of social unity, and also in the sense that they do not change in the same degree as more elaborate relations, but form a com-paratively permanent source out of which the latter are ever springing.

Cooley felt that individuals learn to become social animals through interaction in their primary groups. Individuals who never experience life within an organized network of interpersonal relations never develop their capacity to relate to others satisfactorily.

Societies also socialize their members through such groups. In primary groups, individuals acquire their attitudes, values, and identities, learn the skills needed to

---

Social structure: Stable patterns of interactions among individuals and groups.

TABLE 3-1   CHARACTERISTICS OF PRIMARY AND SECONDARY GROUPS

Attribute	Primary Groups	Secondary Groups
Size	Small number of members who meet face-to-face; all members know one another	Large number of members; members do not necessarily interact with or know one another
Duration	Long-term, with membership enduring for prolonged periods	Group may form and disband quickly; membership is fluid
Unity	High in cohesiveness and solidarity; members identify with the group and are emotionally connected to each other	Connections among members are formal and impersonal; members do not know one another well
Organization	Group acts as a whole, with behavior dictated by personal qualities of individual members	Group is patterned by the roles and statuses of members; individuals enact roles
Examples	Play group, family, neighborhood elders, long-term work unit	Professional association, union, business, congregation

contribute to the group, discover and internalize the rules that govern social behavior, and become practiced at modifying their behavior in response to social norms and others' requirements. C. P. Ellis, for example, learned his attitudes, values, and ethics in his family group. He never considered going to college because no one in his family ever completed high school. He went to church and worked hard because his father went to church and worked hard. His family also taught him to be prejudiced. It was his father who told him that Blacks, Jews, and Catholics were bad: "Don't have anything to do with 'em" (quoted in Terkel, 1980, p. 205).

Peers are another influential primary group. Children willingly amend their actions and preferences to match the norms of their play groups (Berndt, 1992, 1996). Even very young children imitate the way their playmates dress, talk, and act (Adler, Kless, & Adler, 1992). Children who do not like broccoli will eat it if they are having lunch with a group of broccoli-loving children (Birch, 1987). When anti-achievement norms develop in classrooms, students soon learn to disrupt class and fail tests (Ball, 1981), but teenagers who are part of the "brainy" clique value high academic achievement (Brown, Mounts, Lamborn, & Steinberg, 1993). Indeed, as children grow older, the peer group becomes the primary source of social values, replacing the influence of the family (Harris, 1995). Twins who have the same friends are more similar to one another in terms of personality and academic achievement than twins who are treated similarly by their parents (Loehlin, 1997).

Secondary Groups.   In earlier times, individuals belonged only to primary groups. They could live out their entire lives without leaving their small, close-knit families, tribes, or communities. As societies became more complex, however, so did their social structures and their groups (Toennies, 1887). Legal and political systems developed to coordinate actions and make community-level decisions. Organized religions provided answers to questions of values, morality, and meaning. Educational systems took over some of the teaching duties previously assigned to the family. Economic systems developed to regulate production and the attainment of financial goals.

These more complex social structures are called **secondary groups.** As Table 3–1 indicates, such groups are larger and more formally organized than primary groups, and they tend to be shorter in duration and less emotionally involving. However, secondary groups continue to define the individual's place in the social structure of society (Parsons, Bales, & Shils, 1953). Religious groups provide a prime example. Individuals often endorse a specific religion, such as Christianity or Islam, but their connection to their religion occurs in smaller groups known as congregations. These secondary groups are formally structured and led by a religious authority, yet they provide members with a sense of membership, reaffirm the values and norms of the group, and strengthen bonds among members (Finke & Stark, 1992).

Secondary groups became more influential in C. P.'s life as he grew older. When a member of the Klan, his attitudes and values reflected that group's policies and declarations. As he became more aware of civil injustice, however, he quit the KKK and began working closely with the Human Relations Council. This group changed him fundamentally. He was selected to lead the group, and he worked closely with Ann Atwater, a leader in the African American community. In time he realized, "Here we are, two people from the far ends of the fence, havin' identical problems, except her bein' black and me bein' white." He felt that "the whole world was openin' up, and I was learnin' new truths that I had never learned before" (Terkel, 1980, pp. 207–208, 209).

The Value of Groups

Why do people respond so negatively when others exclude them? Why do people avoid isolation, monitor their acceptance in groups, and question their self-worth when others shun them? Why are most societies organized around small, face-to-face groups?

A *functional perspective* assumes that the profound tendency for humans to gather in groups reflects the usefulness of groups to their members. Individuals in groups can secure advantages and avoid disadvantages that would plague the lone individual (Mackie & Goethals, 1987; Moreland, 1987; Stroebe & Stroebe, 1996; Zander, 1985). Although the list of functions that groups fulfill for members is very long, most of them fall into one of the categories summarized in Table 3–2 (Forsyth, 1996). For aeons, humans have survived by hunting and gathering food in groups, by joining together when threatened by harsh circumstances, and by turning back

---

Secondary groups: Large, often formally organized groups and organizations that structure members' social relations.

TABLE 3-2 WHAT DO GROUPS DO FOR THEIR MEMBERS?

Function	Description
Belonging	Groups meet the human need to be included in an interpersonal network. They promote contact between people, regulate relations with others, and increase the quality and duration of social interaction. They provide members with a sense of inclusion and security.
Intimacy	Groups, and cohesive groups in particular, provide the opportunity for warm, supportive, loving relationships with others.
Generativity	Groups do things and so help members increase their productivity, accomplish their personal and shared goals, and complete tasks that individuals could not accomplish if working alone.
Support	Groups help members cope with minor and major life crises by providing them with emotional and tangible resources. Group members compliment and encourage one another, provide mutual assistance, and share needed resources.
Influence	Groups are often the arena for the exercise and application of social power and influence. Groups offer individuals the means to influence greater numbers of individuals.
Exploration	Groups provide members with information, new ideas, and new experiences. They provide instruction and opportunities for learning through communication and other social learning processes.

Source: Forsyth, 1996.

predators through mutual defense. Group members also help one another. They care for others who are sick, injured, or too young to take care of themselves. When they take us into their midst, they satisfy our need to belong, providing us with a replacement for our original family.

So groups are functional. By joining with others, C. P. secured advantages and avoided disadvantages that would have plagued him had he remained alone. He joined the KKK because he believed that the group would help him achieve his political goals. He joined with community leaders to improve his city's educational system. He eventually joined the union so that he could earn better wages. He took no handouts, but he certainly used groups to achieve his goals.

Some theorists, impressed by the benefits of living in groups, suggest that the preference for group life over solitude is a manifestation of an instinctive drive that is common in many species. The idea of a "herd instinct" in humans is not a new one (Edman, 1919; McDougall, 1908). William McDougall (1908), for example, argued that humans are inexorably drawn to "the vast human herd," which "exerts a baneful attraction on those outside it" (p. 303). Recent advances in evolutionary psychology, however, have sparked new interest in the instinctive bases of group behavior. Evolutionary psychology, which was discussed briefly in Chapter 2, draws from Charles Darwin's original theorizing, as well as more recent revisions of evolutionary theory offered by sociobiologists. Darwin set forth the basic tenets of the approach in his concepts of natural selection and survival of the fittest. He maintained that given the natural variation among individual members of a species, some will have more of the qualities needed for survival than others. These individuals, on the whole, will likely produce more offspring, and these offspring will have their parents' useful characteristics. Over time, then, nature will selectively favor individuals with the qualities that match the demands of the environment.

Darwin dealt primarily with biological and anatomical fitness, but sociobiology assumes that recurring patterns of social behaviors also stem from evolutionary processes that increase adaptive actions while extinguishing nonadaptive practices (Wilson, 1975). Nature did not just encourage the development of webbed feet on ducks or a keen sense of smell in dogs, but also such social tendencies as banding together to ward off intruders and preferred methods for establishing dominance hierarchies. Sociobiology also expanded Darwin's concept of **fitness.** For Darwin, fitness was determined by reproductive success: Individuals with characteristics that increased their reproductive success were the fittest because they were more likely to pass their genes along to the next generation. Sociobiologists, however, recognized the value of **inclusive fitness:** enhancing the survival of one's relatives and their offspring. Because copies of our own genes are present in our sisters, brothers, and other relatives, when we help them survive and reproduce, we are indirectly encouraging the survival of our own genes in future generations (Hamilton, 1964). Evolutionary psychology draws on these concepts to suggest that our propensity to gather in groups is determined, in large part, by our genetic endowment. In ancient times, our genetic ancestors left the protection of the trees of the rain forests to become ground dwellers. In this harsh environment, those who were predisposed to join groups were much more likely to survive and breed than people who avoided social contacts (and likely became prey). Those who joined with others in an organized band to hunt large animals were likely more successful than individuals who remained alone. Relatives who lived in close proximity to one another could sustain and nurture children who carried copies of their genes. Because groups increased our ancestors' fitness, over countless generations, genes that promoted solitude seeking were weeded out of the gene pool, whereas genes that encouraged group joining prospered.

In the modern world, the advantages of group life over solitude are not so clear. People who buy their food in grocery stores and live in houses with dead bolts on the doors don't need to worry much about effective food-gathering strategies or protection from predation. These modern conditions, however, cannot undo the effects of millions of years of natural selection. Gregariousness remains a part of the biological makeup of humans (Barash, 1982; Buss, 1996; Levine, 1996).

Are humans driven by a herd instinct? Perhaps. Anthropologists have documented the great diversity of human societies, but across all these variations, they find one constancy: People live in groups rather than alone (Coon, 1946). People

---

Fitness: A species member's reproductive success.
Inclusive fitness: A species member's ability to ensure the survival of its genes in future generations, often by enhancing the survival of relatives and their offspring.

seem to be naturally predisposed to identify those who are in their own group. And with no justification, they treat members of their own group more positively than members of other groups (Rushton, 1989). Studies indicate that infants seem to be predisposed to form strong attachments to others and that babies who are deprived of close human contact have higher mortality rates (Ainsworth, 1979; Bowlby, 1980). Evidence suggests that cooperative group life is a more stable strategy in evolutionary terms than competition and individualism (Axelrod & Hamilton, 1981).

Evolutionary explanations of social behavior remain controversial, however. Researchers are only now subjecting the theory to close scrutiny, so its assumptions should be considered skeptically. The theory is difficult to test experimentally, and its basic premise—that characteristics that enhance our fitness have a genetic basis—is arguable. Just because groups are useful doesn't mean that we are instinctively drawn to them (Quadagno, 1979). Moreover, even if we are gregarious instinctively, other factors also play a role in determining our decision to join or leave a group. Early childhood experiences, for example, may determine the extent to which we prefer solitude or the company of others (Harlow & Harlow, 1966). Nonetheless, the approach offers a compelling answer to the question, "Why do people seek out other people?" We instinctively value the contribution a group can make to our genetic destiny.

FROM INDIVIDUALITY TO COLLECTIVITY

C. P. Ellis, like most people, chose sociality over individuality; he joined groups rather than remaining alone. In choosing interdependence over independence, he availed himself of the many benefits that groups provide their members. His choice, however, also set in motion interpersonal processes that gradually reshaped his attitudes, beliefs, and identity. His private, personal qualities—his interests, beliefs, attitudes, and so on—changed as his new groups resocialized him. His self-concept also changed as he began to take on new social roles and memberships.

When C. P. quit the KKK, he no longer thought of himself as a klansman, and he was no longer a racist. And when he joined the mixed-race Human Relations Council, his sense of self-worth soared: He was proud to say that he was a member of the group. As C. P. the group member moved from one group to another, C. P. the individual changed.

Groups and Identity

Scholars have struggled to understand the connection between the individual and the group for centuries. Some view people as autonomous, self-reliant creatures who only reluctantly join groups. Others put the group at the center of their analysis, emphasizing interconnections between people and the relative interchangeability of each individual within the overall system. Indeed, some consider the integration of these two opposing perspectives to be social psychology's "master problem" (Allport, 1924).

Individuals, however, do not appear to be troubled by the "master problem," for most succeed in integrating both the individual and the group in their own identities and self-definitions. Unique, individualistic qualities—traits, beliefs, skills, and so on—constitute the **personal identity**. The collective self, or **social identity**, includes all those qualities that spring from membership in a vast array of social groups, including families, cliques, work groups, neighborhoods, tribes, cities, regions, and countries (Caporael & Brewer, 1995; Turner et al., 1987). Our personal identity describes our unique, idiosyncratic qualities; it is the "me" component of the self. Our social identity describes our connection to other people, to groups, and to society; it is the "we" component of the self.

Researchers, by asking people to describe themselves in detail, have identified the kinds of characteristics most commonly contained in the social identity (see Table 3–3). *Social roles,* such as spouse, lover, parent, stepparent, care-giver, and worker, define one's position in groups and social networks. C. P. was a father, a husband, a union organizer, and the cochair of the Humans Relations Council. *Memberships* include participation in specific social groups, such as car pools, clubs, or church groups, as well as identification with larger social categories based on ethnicity, age, religion, or some other widely shared characteristic. C. P. was a member of the Human Relations Council, a church, a union, and the Ellis family. He was also a White man, an American, a middle-aged person, a southerner, and a Christian. Because C. P. did not identify closely with most southerners or other people his age, these social categories were not included in his social identity. He did, however, consider himself a White person and an American, so these category memberships defined his social identity. Social identities also often include information based on *relations,* or interpersonal bonds, with other people (Brewer & Gardner, 1996). When C. P. thought of his close friendship with Human Relations Council cochair Ann Atwater or his feelings for his son Tim, then his relational social identity was activated (Brewer & Gardner, 1996). This distinction has also been described as a common bond versus a common identity (Prentice, Miller, & Lightdale, 1994).

Some of these characteristics are more collectivistic than others. When participants in one study compared 64 different collectivist characteristics (e.g., son, woman, bookworm, scientist, athlete, smoker, Catholic, and African American), they distinguished between ones based on relationships, vocations and avocations, political affiliation, stigmatized groups, and social categories. Yet, even within these broad categories, specific identities differed from one another in important ways. The uncle and the daughter roles were viewed as relatively similar, but the uncle role was considered to be passive and less relational than the daughter role. The lover role, like the daughter role, was considered to be an active role, but it was perceived to be achieved later in life rather than ascribed early in life (Deaux, Reid, Mizrahi, & Ethier, 1996). Ethnic and religious identities, too, were viewed as more collectivistic than roles associated with occupational categories (Brown et al., 1992).

Personal identity: That part of the self-concept that derives from individualistic qualities such as traits, beliefs, and skills.

Social identity: That part of the self-concept that derives from one's membership in social groups and categories; self-conceptions shared by members of the same group or category.

TABLE 3-3   CATEGORIES OF INFORMATION IN THE SOCIAL, OR COLLECTIVE, IDENTITY

Component	Examples
Roles	Athlete, care-giver, churchgoer, community volunteer, daughter, friend, group member, neighbor, parent, relative, secretary, son, spouse, stepparent, student, worker
Group memberships	Book club, class, clique, club, committee, department, executive board, fraternity, gang, neighborhood association, research group, rock band, sorority, sports team, squad, work team
Category memberships	Alcoholic, athlete, Christian, deaf person, Democrat, earthling, feminist, gardener, gay, Hispanic, retired person, Republican, salesperson, scientist, smoker, southerner, welfare recipient
Relations	Friend to others, in love, close to other people, helpful to others in need, involved in social causes

Sources: Brewer & Gardner, 1966; Gecas & Burke, 1995; Rhee, Uleman, Lee, & Roman, 1995; Thoits, 1992.

Individualism and Collectivism.   How much of the self is personal and how much is interpersonal? The answer depends, in part, on culture, personality, and ethnicity (Baumeister, 1986; Triandis, 1990). Indeed, the idea that individuals are independent entities is peculiar to societies founded on **individualism.** As Table 3-4 indicates, Western countries such as the United States and Great Britain stress the rights of the individual over the group. The individual is the center of such societies, and their rights to private property, to express themselves, and to engage in actions for their own personal gain are protected and even encouraged (MacFarlane, 1978). Many Asian, African, and South American societies, in contrast, stress **collectivism.** They emphasize the unity of all people rather than each person's individuality. Members of such societies do not consider themselves unique, autonomous people who exist separately from other people. The Gahuku-Gama of Highland New Guinea, for example, do not recognize individuals apart from their roles as father, mother, chief, and so on. They do not even grasp the concept of friendship, for such a concept requires liking between two individuals (Read, 1986). The Akaramas of Peru paint their bodies so elaborately that individuals are unrecognizable. Tribes sleep in same-sex groups of 10 or 12, and when individuals die, their passing goes unnoticed (Schneebaum, 1969). In Japan, the word for self, *jibun,* means "one's portion of the shared space" (Hamaguchi, 1985). To them, "the concept of a self completely independent

Individualism: An ideology or personal orientation that places greater emphasis on the individual, including his or her rights, independence, and relationships with other individuals, and less emphasis on the rights of the group.
Collectivism: An ideology or personal orientation that emphasizes the similarity of all members of a group rather than each person's individuality.

TABLE 3-4   INDIVIDUALISM AND COLLECTIVISM IN 30 COUNTRIES AND REGIONS, RANKED FROM THE MOST INDIVIDUALISTIC (1) TO THE MOST COLLECTIVISTIC (30)

Rank	Country	Rank	Country
1	United States	16	Iran
2	Australia	17	Jamaica
3	Great Britain	18	Brazil
4	Canada	19	Turkey
5	Netherlands	20	Greece
6	Italy	21	Mexico
7	Belgium	22	Africa (eastern nations)
8	France	23	Hong Kong
9	Ireland	24	Chile
10	South Africa	25	Africa (western nations)
11	Finland	26	El Salvador
12	Austria	27	Taiwan
13	Israel	28	Costa Rica
14	India	29	Venezuela
15	Japan	30	Panama

Source: Adapted from Hofstede, 1980.

from the environment is very foreign," as people are not perceived apart from the existing social context (Azuma, 1984, p. 973).

People who live in collectivistic cultures think of themselves as group members first and individuals second, whereas people who live in individualistic cultures are egocentric rather than sociocentric. Harry C. Triandis and his colleagues illustrated this difference by asking people from various countries to describe themselves. As they expected, these self-descriptions contained more references to social identities—membership in groups, roles in society, ethnicity—when people were from collectivistic countries (e.g., Japan, China). Indeed, some individuals from the People's Republic of China described themselves exclusively in interpersonal terms. And some U.S. residents used only personal descriptors: They had no elements of a collective identity (Triandis, McCusker, & Hui, 1990). Other research suggests that people from collectivistic countries resist describing their qualities if the social context is not specified. Japanese people, for example, described themselves differently when they were with different people and in different social situations. Americans, in contrast, described themselves similarly across different situations (Cousins, 1989). Students in the United States, more than students in China, assume that people's behaviors are caused by personality traits rather than factors in the situation (Chiu, Hong, & Dweck, 1997).

Groups, and people's relations within their groups, also differ in collectivistic versus individualistic cultures. Roles and responsibilities tend to be more tightly defined and followed in collectivistic cultures. Many collectivistic cultures stress respect for those who hold positions of authority and avoid disagreement or dissent (Schwartz, 1994). They more frequently follow the dictates of social norms when making choices and selecting a course of action, whereas people in individualistic cultures rely on their personal attitudes and preferences (Triandis, 1996). In collectivistic cultures, people are more likely to consider the consequences of their actions for others and are more diligent in making sure others' needs are met (Miller, 1994). Competition between individuals is greater in individualistic countries, whereas cooperation and communalism is greater in collectivistic ones. People in individualistic societies have more interactions with other people, but these interactions tend to be one-on-one. People in collectivistic cultures have fewer one-on-one interactions with a smaller range of people, but they have more interactions in groups (Wheeler, Reis, & Bond, 1989). People from individualistic and collectivistic cultures even insult one another differently. Personal insults, such as "You are stupid," characterize conflicts in individualistic cultures, whereas remarks about one's family and group typify disputes between two collectivists (Semin & Rubini, 1990).

These generalities are not without exception. Some collectivistic societies, for example, tolerate considerable conflict within their groups. Members of Israeli kibbutzes, for example, often engage in heated debates, whereas Koreans strive for harmony and avoid discord. Both cultures are relatively collectivistic, yet their approaches to resolving disputes differ substantially (Triandis, 1995, 1996). Indeed, the tendency to classify people into two groups—individualistic and collectivistic—on the basis of their nationality may reflect the cultural biases of the Western theorists who first proposed this distinction (Gaines et al., 1997).

Individual Differences in Collectivism.   Just as cultures differ in how much they stress the individual versus the group, individuals within any given culture differ in the emphasis they put on their individuality versus their group memberships. Some people, termed **interdependents** (or allocentrics) put their groups' goals and needs above their own (Markus, Kitayama, & Heiman, 1996; Triandis, 1995). They are respectful of other members of their groups, and they value their memberships in groups, their friendships, and tradition. They would likely agree with the following statements:

- "The well-being of my co-workers is important to me." (Triandis, 1995, p. 207)
- "I think it is more important to give priority to group interests rather than to personal ones." (Kashima et al., 1995, p. 928)
- "It is important for me to maintain harmony within my group." (Singelis, 1994, p. 585)
- "I like to live close to my good friends." (Triandis et al., 1990, p. 1013)
- "I consider myself to be a team player." (Gaines et al., 1997, p. 1466)

Interdependents (allocentrics): Individuals who are dispositionally predisposed to put their groups' goals and needs above their own.

Independents (or idiocentrics), in contrast, are emotionally detached from their groups; they put their own personal goals above the goals of the groups (Markus et al., 1996; Triandis, 1995). They value equality, social justice, and self-reliance, and they would likely agree with these statements:

- "One should live one's life independently of others as much as possible." (Triandis et al., 1990, p. 1013)
- "I often do 'my own thing.' " (Triandis, 1995, p. 207)
- "I often do what I feel like doing without paying attention to others' feelings." (Kashima et al., 1995, p. 928)
- "I am the same person at home that I am at school." (Singelis, 1994, p. 585)
- "I feel that I'm master of my own fate." (Gaines et al., 1997, p. 1466)

Interdependents seek out groups and become more interconnected with their groups than independents (Cheek, 1989). People who stress their personal, independent identity tend to play sports that require little interaction with other people. They tend to exercise by jogging or swimming, and they say that they exercise because it gives them a feeling of self-satisfaction. People who stress their interdependence, in contrast, more frequently play team sports such as volleyball or soccer, and they do so because they "enjoy competing or exercising with other people" (Leary, Wheeler, & Jenkins, 1986, p. 16). Interdependents seek jobs that will enhance the quality of their relationships with other people, and their satisfaction with their work depends on the quality of their relationships with their co-workers. Independents choose jobs that are personally fulfilling and that offer them opportunities for advancement (Leary et al., 1986). Interdependents may also be more loyal to their groups. A high degree of interdependence is associated with patriotism and pride in one's country (Kowalski & Wolfe, 1994).

Individuals who are more independent than interdependent also tend to stress their unique, unusual qualities. One measure of the tendency to set oneself apart from other people, the Individuation Scale, asks people to indicate their willingness to engage in attention-getting behaviors, such as self-disclosure and nonconformity (Maslach, Stapp, & Santee, 1985). People who score high on the individuation scale report a greater frequency of owning distinctive possessions (such as a special kind of car), having a unique self-expressive symbol (such as a nickname), expressing unique opinions, criticizing someone in front of others, making controversial statements, and looking directly into someone's eyes while talking to him or her. People scoring low on the scale reported a greater frequency of wearing the kind of clothes that others wear, owning standard possessions, avoiding distinctive nicknames, avoiding accessories or colors that get attention, controlling distracting gestures, expressing popular opinions, agreeing with other people, not criticizing others, remaining quiet in a group, and avoiding eye contact. They are more likely to engage in conventional behaviors and seek social acceptance.

Independents (idiocentrics): Individuals who are dispositionally predisposed to put their own personal interests and motivations above their groups' interests and goals.

Ethnicity, Gender, and Identity.   People's readiness to connect to groups and to put the group's interests above their own also varies across racial, ethnic, and gender categories. African Americans, Latinos, and Asian Americans, for example, are more collectivistic than Anglos (Gaines et al., 1997). Their greater collectivism stems, in part, from long-held cultural traditions that put greater emphasis on family ties and mutual help. Ethnic identities also reflect these groups' minority status within the majority-Anglo culture (Phinney, 1996). Members of ethnic groups living in societies where they are in the minority sometimes identify with the majority; but in other cases, their identities are defined by their ethnicity. One three-stage model of African American ethnic identity, for example, argues that individuals in the first stage of identity development either do not characterize people, including themselves, on the basis of ethnicity (diffusion) or they accept other people's definition of their ethnicity without question (foreclosure). This *unexamined identity stage* ends when individuals begin exploring the meaning of their ethnicity. This *exploration stage* is characterized by immersion in one's ethnic culture and in some cases adamant rejection of the values of the majority. The final stage, *identity achievement,* occurs when individuals internalize their ethnicity in their sense of self (Phinney, 1989, 1996).

Men and women also differ in their collectivistic orientation. In Western cultures, at least, women more often stress connections with other people, whereas men stress independence and autonomy (Cross & Madson, 1997; Josephs, Markus, & Tafarodi, 1992). Investigators cleverly illustrated this difference by asking men and women to provide them with as many as 20 photographs that "describe how you see yourself . . . [and] . . . tell something about who you are" (Dollinger, Preston, O'Brien, & DiLalla, 1996, p. 1270). As Figure 3–3 indicates, women included more pictures of interpersonal situations—people touching, people smiling, themselves with other people, and groups—than men. Although the magnitude of this difference between the sexes is a matter of considerable debate, some evidence suggests that it stems from women's greater emotional relatedness to other people rather than their greater sociability per se (Kashima et al., 1995).

Which Self? The Two Sides to Identity

When C. P. quit the KKK and joined the Human Relations Council, he did not just change his group allegiance: He changed his identity. Because groups embed themselves in our identities, most people consider themselves to be both individuals and group members. But when did C. P. think of himself as "we" rather than "me"?

Henri Tajfel, John Turner, and their colleagues's **social identity theory** explains how C. P.'s identity—his answer to the question, "Who am I?"—was shaped by his group memberships (Tajfel, 1981; Turner, 1982, 1985). The theory assumes that a sense of identity begins with *categorization*, which occurs when we intuitively classify

---

Social identity theory: A theoretical analysis of group processes and intergroup relations that assumes that a group influences its members' self-concepts and self-esteem, particularly when individuals categorize themselves as group members and identify strongly with the group.

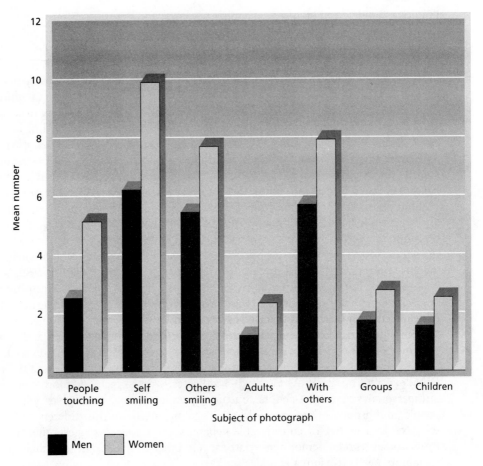

FIGURE 3–3 Are women more closely connected to other people than are men? When researchers asked men and women to provide them with a photo essay that described "who they are," women's essays included more photographs of people than men's.

(*Source:* Dollinger, Preston, O'Brien, & DiLalla, 1996.)

objects and individuals into inclusive categories. Without much thought, C. P. placed people into categories: man or woman; child, adult, or elder; Anglo, Hispanic, Black, Asian; introvert or extravert. C. P. also categorized himself, and then, through *identification,* he came to incorporate portions of the groups he belonged to in his self-concept. Instead of just thinking of himself as "me" or "I," he considered himself to be an "us" and "we." Through identification, members also come to recognize how similar they are to other members of the group.

Categorization in Groups.   When C. P. first met Howard Clements, he assigned him to the categories "man" and "African American." When he met Terry Sanford, he thought of him as "White," "man," and "leader." Such categories ignore each individual's unique qualities, but they are useful summaries of vast amounts of information about people in general. As Gordon Allport (1954, p. 19) explained: "The human mind must think with the aid of categories. Once formed, categories are the basis for normal prejudgment. We cannot possibly avoid this process. Orderly living depends upon it."

We do not just categorize other people; we also classify ourselves into various groups and categories. We have vast amounts of information pertaining to the self stored in our memories, but much of this information describes our group-level qualities rather than our personal attributes (Greenwald & Pratkanis, 1984). Our self-definition at any given moment can therefore shift from "me" to "we" if something in the situation prompts us to categorize ourself as a group member (Abrams & Hogg, 1990; Turner, 1985; Turner et al., 1987). Individuals who find that they are the only representative of a particular ethnic or gender group may suddenly become very aware of that aspect of themselves (McGuire & McGuire, 1988). People who feel that they are being scrutinized by other people are more likely to think of themselves as individuals rather than as group members (Mullen, Rozell, & Johnson, 1996).

Just thinking about links to other people can trigger categorization. Researchers examined such categorization by asking college students to think, for 2 minutes, about the ways they were similar to or different from their family and friends. When the subjects later described themselves in their own words, they mentioned more of their individual qualities when they had thought about their dissimilarities and more of their group memberships after they thought about their similarities to others (Trafimow, Triandis, & Goto, 1991).

Categorization is an automatic rather than controlled cognitive process. Controlled cognitive processes are initiated, monitored, and terminated at will. Automatic processes, in contrast, are rapid, autonomous, effortless, and involuntary, and they take place outside of awareness (Bargh, 1990). Hence, even though people may not notice the activation of their social identities, these identities may influence them nonetheless. This automaticity was illustrated by researchers who used a very subtle procedure to activate individuals' group-level identities (Brewer & Gardner, 1996, Experiment 3). They asked participants to circle all the pronouns in a story, and they primed the collective self by manipulating the kinds of pronouns people read. In some cases, most of the pronouns focused on "we" or "us"; for others the pronouns referred to "them" and "they"; and for subjects in the control condition, the pronouns referred to "it." When the subjects finished their task, they described themselves in their own words. As predicted, people who had searched for "we" pronouns included more collectivistic components in their self-descriptions than did individuals who had searched for "they" or "it." This effect was particularly pronounced when the story containing the pronouns described a large group activity (a football game) rather than a small group activity (an automobile trip).

Researchers are continuing to investigate precisely how individualistic and collectivistic information is stored in memory. Some investigators stress the qualitatively distinct nature of these two types of information, but others argue that social and personal identities are intermingled in our memories (Abrams, 1994; Deaux, 1996; Reid & Deaux, 1996).

Identification with Groups.   C. P., when he first joined the Human Relations Council, recognized that he was a member of the group. But he did not identify with the group, for it stood for many ideas that he rejected. Only over time did he abandon his older allegiances and embrace fully his membership in the Human Relations Council. He stopped proclaiming "I'm in the KKK" and began explaining "I'm the chair of the Human Relations Council."

When C. P. identified with the Human Relations Council, he incorporated this group into his social identity, "together with the value and emotional significance attached to that membership" (Tajfel, 1981, p. 255). Just as Freud (1922) believed that identification causes children to bond with and imitate their parents, identification with the group prompts members to bond with and take on the characteristics of the group. People who identify with their group don't just think, "I am a member of this group." They experience a strong sense of belonging to their group and take pride in their membership. They are more involved in the group's activities, as indicated by their participation at meetings, their acceptance of group norms, and their willingness to help the group meet its goals (Abrams, 1992; Deaux, 1996).

People who identify with a group also feel that they are similar to the other members of the group. Once C. P. identified with the Human Relations Council, he noticed that all the members were concerned with improving social conditions. They were also targets of discrimination, and economically exploited, just as he was. With the increased sense of similarity comes the tendency to engage in **self-stereotyping:** the integration of stereotypes pertaining to the group in one's own self-descriptions (Biernat, Vescio, & Green, 1996). Medical students, for example, do not define themselves as physicians until their training is nearly complete. But by graduation, their selves include the component "physician," and they describe themselves in ways that are consistent with stereotypes about physicians (Preiss, 1968). Individuals who join nudist colonies, as their social identities shift, begin to match the typical nudist's values: They describe themselves as very friendly, liberal, free of social constraints, and so on (Weinberg, 1966).

Identification cements individuals to their own group, or *ingroup,* but it widens the gap between individuals and all other groups—*outgroups.* Once people begin to think in terms of "we" and "us," they also begin to recognize "them" and "they." When C. P.'s identification with the Human Relations Council was complete, he came to value the group's work while at the same time distrusting the motives and goals of people who were not members of the Human Relations Council. Social identity theory, as we will see in Chapter 13, argues that the conflicts that erupt between groups have their seed in the categorization and identification processes that magnify the disparity between the ingroup and the outgroup (Tajfel, 1981; Turner, 1982).

Social identification also impacts group members' sense of self-worth. Because identification blurs the boundary between the individual and the group, when the groups we identify with succeed, we succeed as well. But when they fail, their failure

---

Self-stereotyping: Accepting socially shared generalizations about people who are members of our group as self-descriptive.

can provoke negative feelings about ourselves. We consider this integral relationship between group membership and self-esteem in the closing section of this chapter.

Social Identity and Self-Worth

C. P. Ellis felt shame when he was a child, particularly when he compared his tattered shirts and pants with the new clothes his classmates wore to school. But when he joined the KKK, his shame melted away, replaced by self-confidence (Terkel, 1980, p. 203): "I was led into a large meeting room, and this was the time of my life! It was thrilling. Here's a guy who's worked all his life and struggled all his life to be something, and here's the moment to be something." When C. P. joined this group, he didn't just acquire a new identity; he also acquired self-worth.

The evaluative side of the self-concept is known as **self-esteem.** Your self-esteem is shaped, in part, by your appraisal of your personal, individualistic qualities. People who fail to achieve personally important goals or feel that they possess negative, unattractive qualities have lower self-esteem than people who are successful and manifest appealing personal qualities (Bracken, 1996). But because the self-concept has both individualistic and collectivistic components, self-esteem is not determined only by personal qualities. When individuals join groups, their self-concept becomes connected to that group, and the value of that group comes to influence their feelings about their personal worth.

People who belong to prestigious groups tend to have higher self-esteem than those who belong to stigmatized groups (Rosenberg, 1979). High school students, for example, often seek out membership in one of the school's "in crowds." Those who are members of the most prestigious groups generally report feeling very satisfied with themselves and their group. Those students who want to be a part of an in crowd but aren't accepted by this clique are the most dissatisfied (Brown & Lohr, 1987). People who were members of prestigious or satisfying groups in high school have higher levels of self-esteem later in life (Wright & Forsyth, 1997). Sports fans' moods swing up and down as their favorite team wins and looses. After a loss, they feel depressed and rate themselves more negatively; but after a win, they feel elated and rate themselves more positively (Hirt, Zillmann, Erickson, & Kennedy, 1992).

Jennifer Crocker, Riia Luhtanen, and their colleagues examined the relationship between people's self-esteem and their feelings about their groups by developing a measure of **collective self-esteem** (Crocker & Luhtanen, 1990; Crocker, Luhtanen, Blaine, & Broadnax, 1994; Luhtanen & Crocker, 1992). Instead of asking people if they felt good or bad about themselves, Crocker and Luhtanen asked individuals to evaluate the groups to which they belonged. Drawing on prior work on social

---

Self-esteem: A person's overall assessment of his or her worth; the evaluative component of the self.

Collective self-esteem: A person's overall assessment of that portion of his or her self-concept that is based on membership in social groups, including families, cliques, neighborhoods, tribes, cities, regions, and countries.

TABLE 3–5   ITEMS FROM THE COLLECTIVE SELF-ESTEEM INVENTORY

Subscale	Issue	Example Item
Membership	Am I a valuable or ineffective member of the groups I belong to?	I am a worthy member of the social groups I belong to.
Private	Do I evaluate the groups I belong to positively or negatively?	I feel good about the social groups I belong to.
Public	Do other people evaluate the groups I belong to positively or negatively?	In general, others respect the social groups that I am a member of.
Identity	Are the groups I belong to an important or unimportant part of my identity?	In general, belonging to social groups is an important part of my self-image.

Source: Adapted from Luhtanen & Crocker, 1992.

identity and esteem, they developed items that tap four basic issues: membership esteem, private collective self-esteem, public collective self-esteem, and importance to identity (see Table 3–5). When they compared scores on the collective self-esteem scale to more traditional measures of self-esteem, they found that people with high membership, public, and private collective esteem scores had higher personal self-esteem, suggesting that membership in groups contributes to feelings of self-worth.

The strength of this group → member self-esteem connection should not be overstated, however. Members' self-esteem and their group's worth are often related, but membership in a stigmatized or objectively worthless group does not invariably drive down members' self-esteem (Crocker & Major, 1989). Retarded adolescents, even though they know they belong to the negatively stereotyped social category "special education students," do not necessarily have lower self-esteem (Stager, Chassin, & Young, 1983). African Americans, despite living in a culture where stereotypes about their group are negative, do not have lower self-esteem than Anglo Americans. Members of groups that fail do not always feel like personal failures (Leary & Forsyth, 1987). When C. P. joined the Human Relations Council, his friends condemned the group as too liberal, but C. P.'s self-esteem rose. But just how do group members insulate themselves from the esteem-damaging implications of their membership in less-than-prestigious groups?

Rejecting the Negative.   The group → member self-esteem connection can be broken by refuting or denying the negative reputation attached to one's group. C. P.'s friends called him when he joined the Human Relations Council, saying things like, "C. P., what the hell is wrong with you? You're selling out" (quoted in Terkel, 1980, p. 207). His boss, however, told him that membership in the Human Relations Council was an honor and even gave him some time off (with pay) to attend its meetings. C. P. sided with his boss to conclude that the Human Relations Council was an outstanding group.

Just as individuals may be skeptical when they are given negative feedback about themselves or their performance, group members are selective when it comes to accepting information about the value of their groups. In one study, researchers arranged for groups with between four and seven members to work together on a series of communication and decision-making tasks. They then told some groups that they had performed very well and other groups that they had performed very poorly before giving the groups 5 minutes to talk about their performance. The failure groups spent much of their time rejecting the feedback: claiming it was unfair, criticizing the criteria used, and blaming the researchers. The success groups rarely questioned the validity of the feedback (Norvell and Forsyth, 1984).

Members of stigmatized groups and minority groups similarly protect their personal appraisals of their groups from the unfair negative stereotypes about their groups held by nonmembers. Retarded adolescents who do not rate the social category "special education students" negatively have higher self-esteem than retarded adolescents who self-stereotype (Stager et al., 1983). Incarcerated delinquents who believe that delinquents, as a group, have offensive characteristics have lower self-esteem than delinquents who do not hold negative stereotypes about their group (Chassin & Stager, 1984). Crocker, Luhtanen, and their colleagues (1994) also found that members of racial minorities who reject the majority's stereotypes about their group do not display low self-esteem. They measured people's perceptions of the value of their racial group memberships using a version of the private collective self-esteem scale as well as people's perceptions of others' evaluation of their group using the public collective self-esteem scale (see Table 3–5). They discovered that African Americans were more positive about being Black than Anglo Americans were about being White. However, African Americans were much less likely to agree that "others respect African Americans as a group." For African Americans, however, only private collective self-esteem scores were correlated with their self-esteem ($r = .37$); public collective self-esteem was not. So long as individuals believe that the groups they belong to are valuable, then they will experience a heightened sense of personal self-esteem.

Comparison Between Groups. Leon Festinger (1950, 1954) suggests that in many cases, people seek out others because they require information about themselves and the environment, and this needed information is only available from other people. Although in some instances physical reality provides an objective standard for the validation of personal opinions, beliefs, or attitudes, in other cases individuals must turn to social reality to test their validity. People engage in **social comparison** to determine if their beliefs, opinions, or attitudes are consistent with the interpretations of appropriate others. Although Festinger felt that social comparison is usually guided by the need for accurate information, researchers now believe that people engage in social comparison for a variety of different reasons: to evaluate their own qualities, to set personal goals, to help other people, or to (they hope) discover that they are superior to the people around them (Helgeson & Mickelson, 1995; Wood, 1996).

Social identity theory focuses on the self-enhancing side of social comparison (Hogg, Terry, & White, 1995; McGarty, Haslam, Hutchinson, & Turner, 1994). Social identity theorists assume that people strive to maintain or enhance their feelings

Social comparison: Evaluating the accuracy of personal beliefs and attitudes by comparing oneself to others.

of self-worth. Moreover, because our social identities are linked to our groups, our feelings of self-worth can be enhanced by stressing the relative superiority of our groups to other groups. The tendency to view our own groups more positively than other groups is called the **ingroup–outgroup bias.** Gang members view their group more positively than a rival gang. Teammates praise their own players and derogate players on the other team. If Group A and Group B are working side by side on laboratory tasks, members of A will rate Group A as better than B, but members of B will rate Group B more favorably than A. Chapter 13 examines this bias in more detail, for some theorists believe that it plays a major role in creating conflict between groups (Brewer, 1979; Luhtanen & Crocker, 1991).

But what if our groups are relatively inferior to other groups? What if we belong to a team that loses all the games it plays? Social identity theory suggests that such situations call for *social creativity:* Group members compare the ingroup to the out-group on some new dimension. One researcher illustrated such social creativity by asking members of a last-place ice hockey team (1 win and 21 losses) to rate their team and their opponents on four key attributes: aggressive, dirty, skilled, and moti-vated (Lalonde, 1992). The players admitted that their opponents were more skilled, but they also argued that their opponents were more aggressive and that they played dirty.

The Group-Serving Bias.   The groups we belong to and identify with do not always prosper. A group may formulate an effective plan for dealing with a problem, but another may create a plan that ends in disaster. The committee may strive to consider all issues, but it may make a terrible decision. The Human Relations Council pro-posal was rejected flatly by the school board. For every team that triumphs, there is a team that is triumphed over.

How do group members protect their sense of self-worth after a group failure? Past research suggests that group members often display a **group-serving bias** (socio-centric bias), with group members emphasizing the group's responsibility after success and the group's blamelessness after failure (Forsyth, Berger, & Mitchell, 1981). After success, members may praise the entire group for its good work with such comments as "We all did well" or "Our hard work really paid off." Similarly, after failure, mem-bers may join together in blaming outside forces and absolving one another of blame. Indeed, some studies have shown that members of successful groups attribute more responsibility to the "average" member and the group as a whole than do members of failing groups (Forsyth & Schlenker, 1977; Schlenker, Soraci, & McCarthy, 1976). In addition, the more positive the group's performance on the task, the more likely the group members will express commitment to the group, emphasize their membership in the group, accurately recall their group's score, and exaggerate the degree of con-sensus present in the group (Leary & Forsyth, 1987).

Ingroup–outgroup bias: The tendency to view the ingroup, its members, and products more positively than other groups, their members, and their products.
Group-serving bias (sociocentric bias): The general tendency to attribute positive outcomes to the group and its members but negative outcomes to external factors.

In most cases, the need to enhance personal self-esteem and collective self-esteem are complementary, for our personal self-worth usually prospers when our collective self-worth increases. But when the collective and personal selves collide, members may protect their personal self-esteem at the expense of their social identity. Instead of a group-serving bias, members display a **self-serving bias:** They attribute positive outcomes to internal, personal factors while blaming negative outcomes on external, situational factors—including other group members (Leary & Forsyth, 1987). When trying to recall a turning point in a team sport, athletes usually point to something they did rather than the contributions of others (Brawley, 1984). Students who work closely with a professor on a joint project give, on average, over 80% of the credit to themselves rather than their mentor (Ross & Sicoly, 1979). In organizations, subordinates blame negative performance appraisals on their boss, the poor working conditions, or unfair standards, but credit their own hard work when they receive a positive review (Giola & Sims, 1985). Members of failing groups also claim that they exercised less influence over other group members than subjects in successful groups (Leary & Forsyth, 1987). People are more likely to deny their connections to a group after it fails in a process called cutting off reflected failure (or CORFing) (Snyder, Lassegard, & Ford, 1986).

By derogating and distancing themselves from the group, individuals manage to protect their personal self-esteem while sacrificing collective self-esteem. In consequence, self-serving biases occur more frequently in individualistic cultures, whereas group-serving biases characterize collectivistic cultures (Heine & Lehman, 1997; Kitayama, Markus, Matsumoto, & Norasakkunkit, 1997).

Turning Against the Group: Seeking Individuality

People protect their collective esteem as actively as they protect their personal self-esteem. They deny that their groups possess negative qualities. They consider their groups to be superior to alternative groups. They give their groups credit for their successes, but blame outside influences when their groups fail. But there are limits to what individuals will tolerate, and if a group is a threat to members' esteem, then in time they will turn against it. C. P. was an active member of the KKK for many years, and when others condemned the group, he defended it. Eventually, however, he withdrew from the group, and in so doing limited its influence on his identity and self-esteem.

Members do not sacrifice their individuality for the group. When people can choose the groups they belong to or identify with, they often shift their allegiances, leaving groups that are lower in status or prone to failure and seeking membership in prestigious or successful ones (Crocker, Blaine, & Luhtanen, 1993; Ellemers, Wilke, & van Knippenberg, 1993). When C. P. could no longer deny the growing rift between his values and the KKK, he changed his affiliation. He resigned from the Klan and joined a more liberal, more egalitarian organization. Social identity theorists call this process *individual mobility* (Ellemers, Spears, & Doosje, 1997).

Self-serving bias: The general tendency to attribute positive outcomes to personal factors but negative outcomes to external factors—including the other members of the group.

People also take steps to accentuate their unique personal qualities if they feel that their individuality is being ignored by the group. As Marilyn Brewer's *optimal distinctiveness theory* suggests, most people have two fundamental needs: the need to be assimilated by the group and the need for differentiation from the group. Individuals are most satisfied if they achieve optimal distinctiveness: Their unique personal qualities are noted and appreciated, yet they feel similar to other group members in many respects (Brewer, 1991; Brewer, Manzi, & Shaw, 1993; Brewer & Weber, 1994). Achieving a feeling of uniqueness is as important as satisfying our need to belong (Goethals, Messick, & Allison, 1991; Snyder & Fromkin, 1980).

When C. P. left the KKK, he put his individual needs above his group's. He sympathized with the Klan members, but he could no longer accept the group's goals and values. So he joined the Human Relations Council, and that reshaped his attitudes, values, and beliefs. In time, he abandoned his prejudiced ways of thinking, earned a high school education, and became a leader in his community. In describing the experience, he writes:

> It was almost like bein' born again. It was a new life. I didn't have these sleepless nights I used to have when I was active in the Klan and slippin' around at night. I could sleep at night and feel good about it. . . . My whole life had changed. [Quoted in Terkel, 1980, p. 209]

SUMMARY

Why do people sacrifice their independence to become members of groups?

1. Freud's replacement hypothesis suggests that members unconsciously replace their childhood family with other groups.

2. Baumeister and Leary's *belongingness hypothesis* likens the need to join a group to such basic needs as hunger and thirst. Isolation from others can be distressing, particularly if involuntary, and if prolonged can result in social and emotional *loneliness*. The sociometer model argues that self-esteem tracks the degree to which one maintains inclusion in groups and avoids exclusion from them.

3. Groups are *social structures*. Both close-knit, intimate *primary groups*, such as families, friendship cliques, and neighborhoods, and larger and more formally structured *secondary groups* socialize individuals and connect them to society at large.

4. A functional perspective highlights the survival, psychological, interpersonal, and practical advantages of group membership. Evolutionary psychology suggests that groups offered protection against environmental dangers that threatened the survival of humans, thus enhancing group members' *fitness* and *inclusive fitness*. As a result, individuals are instinctively drawn to other humans.

In what ways does membership in a group change a person's self-concept and social identity?
Individual qualities define one's *personal identity*, whereas social roles (e.g., spouse, lover, parent), membership in groups (e.g., club member, churchgoer), membership in social categories (e.g., American, teenager), and relations with other people define one's *social identity* (or collective identity).

1. The social identity component is more substantial in cultures that stress *collectivism* rather than *individualism*, among individuals who are *interdependents* (allocentrics) rather than *independents* (idiocentrics), among individuals who are members of certain ethnic groups or minorities, and among women rather than men.

2. *Social identity theory* traces the development of a collective identity back to two key processes: categorization and identification.
   - Through categorization, individuals automatically classify people, including themselves, into groups.
   - Through identification, individuals come to bond with and take on the characteristics of their groups (*self-stereotyping*). Identification also creates ingroup favoritism and outgroup rejection.

Is self-esteem shaped by the personal qualities we possess, the value of the groups to which we belong, or both our personal and collective qualities? Social identity processes directly influence group members' *self-esteem*.

1. Those who join prestigious groups often have higher *collective self-esteem* than those who belong to less positively valued groups. However, individuals who are members of stigmatized groups, failing groups, or groups that are derogated by nonmembers often protect their collective self-esteem through
   - rejection of negative information about their groups
   - biased *social comparisons* that stress the relative superiority of their own groups to other groups (the *ingroup-outgroup bias*)
   - social creativity
   - *group-serving biases*

2. In some cases, individuals will choose to promote their own personal interests over their groups through
   - *self-serving biases* that reduce their personal responsibility for negative group outcomes
   - denial of connections to groups that are performing poorly (cutting off reflected failure)
   - resignation from the group (individual mobility)

3. Overall, people strive to maintain an optimal balance between their personal identity and their collective identity.

FOR MORE INFORMATION

"C. P. Ellis," a chapter in Studs Terkel's book *American Dreams: Lost and Found,* (1980), describes Ellis's transformation from a prejudiced member of a hate group to an advocate of civil rights.

"Culture and 'Basic' Psychological Principles," a chapter by Hazel Rose Markus, Shinobu Kitayama, and Rachel J. Heiman (1996), surveys the developing integration of social psychology with cultural analyses of individuals and groups.

Individualism and Collectivism, by Harry C. Triandis (1995), examines recent theory and research dealing with the two sides of the self: the collective and the personal.

"The Need to Belong: Desire for Interpersonal Attachments as a Fundamental Human Motivation," by Roy F. Baumeister and Mark R. Leary (1995), marshalls evidence in support of their belongingness hypothesis.

Social Comparison, edited by Jerry Suls and Thomas Ashby Wills (1991), contains updated reviews, theoretical analyses, and new insights into group members' tendency to compare themselves to other people.

"Social Identification," a chapter by Kay Deaux (1996) examines the psychological mechanisms involved in identification and the consequences of such identification for identity.

Social Identity Theory, edited by Dominic Abrams and Michael A. Hogg (1990), provides a clear overview of social identity theory as well as chapters dealing with applications of that perspective to such topics as intergroup conflict, language development, and social stereotypes.

ACTIVITY 3–1 HOW MUCH IS YOUR SENSE OF SELF BASED ON YOUR GROUPS?

How much of your self is personal and how much is interpersonal? Explore your sense of self by taking the "Who Am I?" 20 statements test (Kuhn & McPartland, 1954; Watkins, Yau, Dahlin, & Wondimu, 1997).

1. Number the lines on a sheet of paper from 1 to 20. On each line, complete the statement "I am . . ." with whatever aspect of yourself comes to mind. Answer as if you were talking to yourself, not to somebody else. Write the answers in the order they occur to you, and don't worry if they aren't logical or factual. Do not continue reading about this activity until *after* you finish making your list!

2. Read each statement and then classify it into one of two categories. Collectivistic qualities are any descriptions that refer to the self in relationship to others. It includes roles ("I am a student,"), family relations ("I am a mother,"), ethnicity, race, gender, and origins ("I am an African American," "I am from the States"), and religion. Individualistic qualities are qualities that apply to you personally, such as traits, attitudes, habits, and mood ("I am intelligent," "I like to play soccer").

3. Summarize your self-concept by computing the percentage of your self that is individualistic versus collectivistic.
   a. Is your self-concept more individualistic or collectivistic?
   b. Did you tend to list collectivistic qualities earlier in the list than individualistic ones?
   c. Was it difficult to classify the self-descriptions as either individualistic or collectivistic?
   d. Which qualities are more central to your identity: the collectivistic components or the individualistic components?

ACTIVITY 3–2 WHAT IS YOUR COLLECTIVE SELF-ESTEEM?

Your evaluation of yourself—your self-esteem—depends on the value you put on your individual qualities as well as the value you put on your collective ones.

1. Select one social group or category that you belong to and with which you identify strongly. The group can be an actual social group, such as a team, a church congregation, or your university. It can also be a social category that reflects your race, gender, religion, or ethnicity.

(continued)

ACTIVITY 3–2 CONTINUED

2. Describe the importance of this group for your identity.
   a. Do you frequently characterize people, including yourself, as inside or outside this group?
   b. Have you listened to other people's discussions of what it means to belong to this group?
   c. Have you explored what membership in this group means to you personally?
   d. Has your connection to this group changed over time?
3. Explore your collective self-esteem by answering these four sets of questions about this group (based on Luhtanen & Crocker, 1992).
   a. Membership esteem: Do you feel that you are a valuable member of this group? Do you feel good about the contributions you make to it?
   b. Private esteem: Do you evaluate this group positively? Are you proud to be a part of this group?
   c. Public esteem: Do other people evaluate this group positively? Do nonmembers respect this group?
   d. Identity esteem: Is this group an important part of your identity?

4

Joining and Leaving Groups

When do people join with others to form groups? In part, the motivation to join a group comes from within: Some people are drawn to groups, just as others prefer solitude. The too-human tendency to join groups also comes from without: The situations people face can be so novel, ambiguous, or frightening that they prefer to face them with others rather than alone. Moreover, just as a host of personal and situational factors conspire to create groups, so they also contribute to their dissolution.

- Who joins groups?
- When and why do people create new groups and join existing groups?
- When and why do people leave their groups?

CONTENTS

The Impressionists: The Group that Redefined Beauty

BECOMING A GROUP MEMBER

Introversion and Extraversion

Social Motivation

Social Anxiety, Shyness, and Groups

Men, Women, and Groups

GROUP FORMATION

Affiliation, Ambiguity, and Social Comparison

Stress and Social Support

Groups and Collective Endeavors

Proximity and Social Integration

Interpersonal Attraction

The Economics of Membership

GROUP SOCIALIZATION

Costs and Commitment

Stages of Socialization

The End of Membership

SUMMARY

FOR MORE INFORMATION

ACTIVITIES

The Impressionists: The Group that Redefined Beauty

The group that changed the world's opinion about beauty was born in Paris, France, in 1860, when several disgruntled painters met by happenstance. These artists—among them Manet, Monet, Degas, Cézanne, Pissarro, and Morisot—were united by their opposition to the conservatism of the Academy of Fine Arts. The academy's standards determined which paintings and sculptures could be displayed at the national gallery, the Salon. Most artists acquiesced to the academy's guidelines, but this small group of renegade painters rebelled. They faced financial hardships, self-doubt, and harassment by the art community, but they labored on to develop alternative techniques. The group disbanded in time, but not before the world accepted its approach to art—impressionism (Farrell, 1982; Kapos, 1995).

We can ask many questions about the artists who founded impressionism. How did they settle the many conflicts that threatened their group? Why did Manet become the group's leader and Degas the malcontent? How did the group counter the constraints imposed by the academy? But one question—perhaps the most basic of all—concerns the group's origin. Why did it come into existence in the first place? In 1858, Manet, Monet, and the others were busy pursuing their careers independently. But by the mid-1860s, they had joined to form the most influential artists circle of all time. What were the circumstances that drove these individuals to combine their resources in a group that endured for over 30 years?

People seek solitude from time to time, but most of us spend our lives in groups. Nearly all human societies are organized around small groups, such as families, clans, communities, and tribes (Mann, 1988). As noted in Chapter 3, most people, when separated from their group for too long a time, experience anxiety and stress (Rofé, 1984). Even when a group we belong to dwindles in value, too often we maintain our membership rather than strike out on our own (Haupt & Leary, 1997). And those rare individuals who insist on living their lives apart from others, refusing to join any groups, are considered curiosities, eccentrics, or even mentally unsettled (Storr, 1988). Who joins groups and who remains aloof? When is a group most likely to form? How do people select groups to join, and when do they decide to leave them?

BECOMING A GROUP MEMBER

Claude Monet and Vincent van Gogh were both passionate about their art, and they experimented with techniques that went far beyond the conventions of their time. But whereas Monet joined with others whenever possible, making his work as much a result of group effort as an individual one, van Gogh kept to himself, interacting primarily with his brother and a few friends. Monet sought out membership but van Gogh kept to himself.

Not everyone who joins a group is a "joiner," and people who prefer independence over association are not necessarily "loners." But dispositional factors certainly separate the Monets and the van Goghs—those who seek out membership in groups and those who avoid it.

Introversion and Extraversion

People differ, at a psychological level, in their readiness to join together with other people. Psychologist Carl G. Jung (1924) called this dimension of personality introversion-extraversion. **Introverts,** he suggested, are bashful, withdrawn, quiet, reclusive, and shy; they remain detached, and even move away from others. **Extraverts,** in contrast, seek out contact with other people. They are sociable, outgoing, gregarious, and talkative. Extraverts, more than introverts, are likely to prefer the company of others, particularly in pleasant and enjoyable situations (Fox, 1984; Henry & Solano, 1983; Smernou & Lautenschlager, 1991; Von Dras & Siegler, 1997).

Most personality theorists agree that the tendency to move toward people or away from people is a basic component of personality (Horney, 1945). Researchers attempting to distill personality down to a small number of key elements generally agree on five basic dimensions (often referred to as the "Big Five"). The first dimension in most of these models is introversion-extraversion (Goldberg, 1993). Different cultures imbue introversion and extraversion with unique, culture-specific meaning, but researchers have identified this sociability dimension in dozens of countries. People the world over spontaneously appraise themselves and others in terms of their group-seeking tendencies (Digman, 1990; Yang & Bond, 1990).

Extraverts may seek out groups because such interactions are stimulating, and extraverts are more likely to seek out stimulating experiences than are introverts (Eysenck, 1990). Extraverts' greater involvement in groups may also reflect the recruitment preferences of those who are already in the group. Some qualities, like intelligence, morality, and friendliness, are difficult to judge during initial encounters, but we are particularly good at detecting extraversion in others (Albright, Kenny, & Malloy, 1988; Kenny, Horner, Kashy, & Chu, 1992). If a group is looking for people who will be sociable and connect easily with others, then they might recruit extraverts more actively than introverts. Groups that do not value extraversion in its members, however, would choose introverts. For example, gatherings of trekkies—devotees of the science fiction program *Star Trek*—tend to include primarily introverts because this group requires little contact among members (Stever, 1995).

Social Motivation

Why did Monet rely on other people rather than pursue his goals alone? Motivational theorists argue that *social motives*—such as the need for affiliation, intimacy, and power—guide the choices we make and the goals we seek (Geen, 1995; Murray, 1938).

Need for Affiliation. People who seek out contact with other people often have a high **need for affiliation (nAffiliation).** People with a high need for affiliation tend to join groups more frequently, spend more of their time in groups, communicate more

---

Introverts: Individuals who tend to withdraw from social contact.
Extraverts: Individuals who prefer contact with other people rather than isolation and solitude.
Need for affiliation (nAffiliation): The dispositional tendency to seek out others.

with other group members, and accept other group members more readily (McAdams & Constantian, 1983; McClelland, 1985; Smart, 1965). But they are also more anxious in social situations, perhaps because they are more fearful of rejection by others (Byrne, 1961; McAdams, 1982, 1995). When others treat them badly or reject them, they avoid people rather than seek them out (Hill, 1991).

Need for Intimacy. Individuals who have a high **need for intimacy** (*n*Intimacy), like those who have a high need for affiliation, prefer to join with others. Such individuals, however, seek close, warm relations and are more likely to express caring and concern for other people (McAdams, 1982, 1995). They do not fear rejection, but instead are more focused on friendship, camaraderie, reciprocity, and mutual help. In one study, researchers gave people electronic pagers for one week and asked them to write down what they were doing and how they felt each time they were beeped. People who had a high need for intimacy were more frequently interacting with other people when beeped. They were also happier than people with a low need for intimacy if they were with other people when they were beeped (McAdams & Constantian, 1983).

Need for Power. Because group interactions provide many opportunities to influence others, those with a high **need for power** (*n*Power) also tend to seek out groups (McAdams, 1982; Winter, 1973). Researchers studied college students' power needs by asking them to recall ten recent group interactions that lasted for at least 15 minutes. The students described what had happened in each episode, what had been discussed, and their role in the group. Those with a high power motive took part in relatively fewer dyadic interactions but more large-group interactions (more than four members). They also reported exercising more control in these groups by organizing and initiating activities, assuming responsibility, and attempting to persuade others. This relationship between the need for power and participation in groups was strongest for men (McAdams, Healy, & Krause, 1984).

FIRO. William C. Schutz (1958, 1992) integrates the need for affiliation, intimacy, and power in his **Fundamental Interpersonal Relations Orientation** theory, or **FIRO** (rhymes with *Cairo*). Schutz identifies three basic needs that can be satisfied when we are in groups. *Inclusion,* the desire to be part of a group and to be accepted by a group, is similar to *n*Affiliation. The second motive, *control,* corresponds to *n*Power, for it is the need to guide the group by organizing and maintaining the group's processes. *Affection,* or openness, is the desire to experience warm, positive relations with others. This need is similar to *n*Intimacy.

Schutz believes that these needs influence group behavior in two ways: They determine how we treat other people and how we want others to treat us. Inclusion

---

Need for intimacy (*n*Intimacy): The dispositional tendency to seek warm, positive relationships with others.

Need for power (*n*Power): The dispositional tendency to seek control over others.

Fundamental Interpersonal Relations Orientation (FIRO): Schutz's theory of group formation that emphasizes compatibility among three basic needs: inclusion, control, and affection.

involves our desire to join with other people and our need to be accepted by them. Control refers to our need to dominate others but also our willingness to let others dominate us. Affection includes a desire to like others as well as a desire to be liked by them. The FIRO-B, which Schutz developed, measures both the need to express and the need to receive inclusion, control, and affection (see Table 4–1).

Groups offer members a way to satisfy these basic needs. If, for example, Angela has a strong need to receive and express inclusion, she will probably prefer to do things in a group rather than to perform tasks individually. If she needs to express control, she may seek membership in a group that she can control. Or if she wishes to receive affection from others, she may seek out other people who seem warm and friendly. In general, then, the greater the intensity of these needs in any given individual, the more likely that person is to take steps to create, or seek out membership in, a group (Schutz, 1958, 1992).

Social Anxiety, Shyness, and Groups

Just as introversion-extraversion and social motives push people toward groups, other personal qualities may push them away. **Shyness**, for example, reduces the frequency and quality of one's group experiences. As early as age 2, some children begin to display fear or shyness when they encounter a person they do not recognize (Kagan, Snidman, & Arcus, 1992). Some grade school children consistently seek out other people, whereas others show signs of shyness and withdrawal when they are in groups (Asendorpf & Meier, 1993). Shy adults report feeling awkward, uncomfortable, and

TABLE 4–1   EXAMPLE ITEMS FROM FIRO-B

Dimension	Need to Express the Behavior	Need to Receive the Behavior from Others
Inclusion	I try to be with other people.	I like people to invite me to things.
	I join social groups.	I like people to include me in their activities.
Control	I try to take charge of things when I am with people.	I let other people decide what to do.
	I try to have other people do things I want done.	I let other people take charge of things.
Affection	I try to be friendly to people.	I like people to act friendly toward me.
	I try to have close relationships with people.	I like people to act close toward me.

Source: Schutz, 1958.

Shyness: The tendency to experience social anxiety across situations.

tense when interacting with people they do not know very well (Cheek & Buss, 1981). Shy people join groups less frequently than nonshy individuals (Zimbardo, 1977b).

Most people manage to cope with their shyness (Leary & Miller, 1986). In some cases, however, this discomfort escalates into **social anxiety**. Historical accounts of the troubled life of van Gogh, for example, comment on his anxiety over his failed relationships. He had some friends, and he tried to join his fellow artists, but he could not sustain these relationships.

Social anxiety sets in when people want to make a good impression, but they do not think that their attempts to establish relationships will succeed (Leary & Kowalski, 1995; Schlenker & Leary, 1982). Because of these pessimistic expectations, when these individuals interact with other people, they suffer troubling emotional, physiological, and behavioral side effects. They feel tense, awkward, uncomfortable, and scrutinized. They become physiologically aroused, to the point that their pulse races, they blush and perspire, and they feel "butterflies" in their stomach. This anxiety can cause them to *disaffiliate*—to "reduce the amount of social contact they have with others" (Leary & Kowalski, 1995, p. 157). Socially anxious people, even when they join groups, do not actively participate; they can be identified by their silence, downcast eyes, and low speaking voice. They may also engage in *innocuous sociability* (Leary, 1983). They merge into the group's background by indicating general interest in the group and agreement with the other group members while consistently minimizing their personal involvement in the group interaction.

Men, Women, and Groups

Nearly all the impressionists were men; Morisot and Cassatt were exceptions. Why? Are men more likely to join together with other men to accomplish their tasks, or are women the more social sex?

Studies of men and women find some differences in their tendency to join groups, but the differences are far from clear. When investigators sampled 800 adults in the United States, they found that men belonged to more professional groups, governing boards, political parties, and military organizations than women. Men had more friends than women, but women reported closer ties with members of their family and they spent more time in their groups than did men (Booth, 1972). Another survey found that women belonged to more religious and informal recreational groups than men and that women's associations were more intimate and caring (Umberson, Chen, House, Hopkins, & Slaten, 1996). Survey researchers also found that younger men (18- to 26-year-olds) visited with friends and attended parties more frequently than younger women and that women spent more time with their families. The sexes did not differ in time spent in solitary activities (Osgood, Wilson, O'Malley, Bachman, & Johnston, 1996). Studies of community action groups also find no consistent gender differences (Parkum & Parkum, 1980), and women are just as likely as men to join atypical groups, such as cults, satanic covens, and communes (Pittard-Payne, 1980).

Social anxiety: A feeling of apprehension and embarrassment experienced when anticipating or actually interacting with other people.

The differences that emerge, although subtle, indicate that women seek membership in smaller, informal, intimate groups, whereas men seek membership in larger, more formal, task-focused groups. These tendencies may reflect women's and men's differing interpersonal orientations. As noted in Chapter 3, men tend to define themselves as individuals separate and distinct from others, whereas women's self-definitions may be more interpersonal. They define themselves in terms of their memberships in groups and their relationships with other people (Cross & Madson, 1997). The differences may also reflect the emphasis that the two sexes put on achieving power and establishing connections with others (Basow, 1992; Maccoby, 1990). Both of these goals can best be achieved in groups, but they require membership in different types of groups. Men, seeking power and influence, join competitive, goal-oriented groups, where they can vie for status. Women, seeking intimate relationships, would be more likely to join small, supportive groups (Baumeister & Sommer, 1997). Indeed, women's groups tend to be more unified than men's groups (Booth, 1972; Hill & Stull, 1981; Winstead, 1986).

These sex differences are also entangled with role differences and cultural stereotypes. In cultures where men and women tend to enact different roles, the roles may shape opportunities for involvement in groups. If women are primarily responsible for domestic duties and childbearing, their opportunities for memberships in groups may be limited (Nielsen, 1990). Hence, as attitudes toward the role of women have changed in contemporary society, differences in social participation have also begun to diminish (Lal Goel, 1980; Smith, 1980). Sexist attitudes may also work to exclude women and men from certain types of groups. Women, for example, were until recently deliberately excluded from juries in the United States. (The United States' Supreme Court ruled that women could not be excused from jury duty because of their sex in 1975.) As sexist attitudes decline, differences in membership in various types of groups may also abate.

GROUP FORMATION

In the 1800s, France opened grand museums devoted to art, and the general public turned out in mass at each new exhibition. The cafés were filled with aspiring young artists who trained under the tutelage of the masters. Yet, among all these artists, only a handful joined together to form the hub of the impressionists. Why did these men and women join together to form a group?

Affiliation, Ambiguity, and Social Comparison

The impressionists, because they rejected conventional approaches to art, faced uncertainty each time they stood before a blank canvas. So they often painted together, exchanging ideas about colors and techniques, as they refined their approach to art. Their reliance on each other for information is consistent with social comparison theory (Festinger, 1950, 1954). As noted in Chapter 3, we often compare our personal viewpoint to the views expressed by others to determine if those views are "correct," "valid," or "proper" (Goethals & Darley, 1987; Wills, 1991).

Misery Loves Company.   Stanley Schachter (1959) examined social comparison theory by convincing people that they faced an ambiguous and possibly dangerous situation. When the women he recruited for his study arrived, the researcher introduced
himself as Dr. Gregor Zilstein from the Medical School's Departments of Neurology
and Psychiatry. In serious tones, he explained that he was studying the effects of electric shock on human beings. In one condition (low anxiety), the room contained no
electrical devices; the experimenter explained that the shocks would be so mild that
they would "resemble more a tickle or a tingle than anything unpleasant" (p. 14).
Subjects assigned to the high-anxiety condition, however, faced a vast collection of
electrical equipment and were informed, "These shocks will hurt, they will be painful
. . . but, of course, they will do no permanent damage" (p. 13). The researcher then
asked the subject if she wanted to wait for her turn alone or with others. Many more
of the women in the high-anxiety condition (63%) than in the low-anxiety condition
(33%) chose to wait with others. Schachter concluded that "misery loves company."

Misery Loves Miserable Company.   But did the subjects join the group so that they
could acquire information through social comparison? Maybe they were so frightened
that they didn't want to be alone. Schachter explored this possibility by replicating the
high-anxiety condition of his original experiment, complete with the shock equipment
and Dr. Zilstein. He held anxiety at a high level, but manipulated the amount of information that could be gained by affiliating with others. He told half of the women that
they could wait with other women who were about to receive shocks; they were similar to the subjects. He told the others that they could join women "waiting to talk to
their professors and advisors" (p. 22), the dissimilar condition. Schachter felt that if the
women believed that the others could not provide them with any social comparison
information, there would be no reason to join them. The findings confirmed his analysis: 60% of the women asked to wait with others if they all faced a similar situation,
but no one in the dissimilar condition expressed affiliative desires. We generally affiliate
with people who are similar to us in certain ways because these individuals provide us
with the most useful information (Gump & Kulik, 1997). As Schachter put it: "Misery
doesn't love just any kind of company, it loves only miserable company" (p. 24).

Misery Loves Reassuring Company.   Schachter believed that people affiliate to achieve
cognitive clarity: They use others to increase the accuracy of their interpretation of the
situations they face. Subsequent researchers, however, have extended Schachter's
work by finding a second important reason to join groups: to acquire reassuring, fear-
allaying information about the situation. Individuals awaiting surgery, for example,
preferred a roommate who was recovering from the operation they were about to
undergo rather than someone who was also waiting for the operation (Kulik & Mahler, 1989). They also reported talking with their roommate about the operation more
if their roommate had already had the operation and was recovering (Kulik, Mahler,
& Moore, 1996). In another study, when people who were told they would be given
shocks were asked if they wanted to wait with someone who seemed very fearful,
moderately fearful, or calm, they chose to wait with less fearful people (Rabbie, 1963).
Misery doesn't just seek miserable company; it sometimes seeks reassuring company
(Affleck & Tennen, 1991; Helgeson & Michelson, 1995).

Researchers confirmed both of these social comparison motives—the need for cognitive clarity and the need for reassurance—by watching the way group members reacted to three types of situations: frightening situations, ambiguous situations, and embarrassing situations. The investigators asked four to six strangers to meet in a room labeled with the sign "Sexual Attitudes—Please Wait Inside." In the fear-provoking condition, the room contained several electrical devices and information sheets that suggested that the study involved electric shock and sexual stimulation. In the ambiguous condition, the subjects found only two cardboard boxes filled with computer forms. In the anxiety-provoking (embarrassing) condition, the equipment and boxes were replaced by contraceptive devices, books on venereal disease, and color pictures of nude men and women. Observers behind a one-way mirror watched the group for 20 minutes, recording the five types of behavior shown in Figure 4–1: interaction

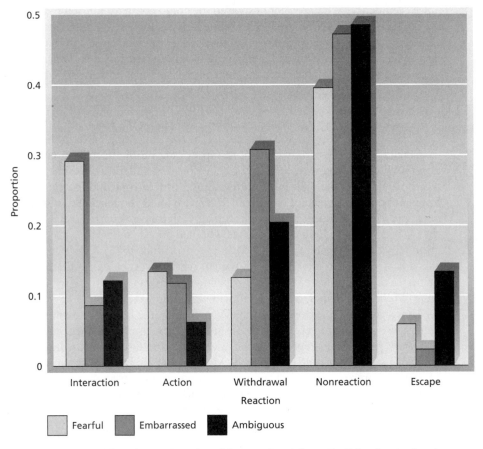

FIGURE 4–1 When do people seek social comparison information? People who faced an ambiguous situation did not talk among themselves as much as people who were fearful. People who were anxious and embarrassed interacted the least, and they often withdrew from the group.

(*Source:* Morris et al., 1976.)

(talking about the situation), action (e.g., examining the equipment), withdrawal (e.g., reading a book), controlled nonreaction (e.g., talking about something other than the experiment), and escape (Morris et al., 1976).

The observers discovered that the group members engaged in social comparison the most when they were fearful. As Figure 4–1 indicates, groups who faced the ambiguous situation spent about 12% of the time talking among themselves, but groups sitting in a room with the fear-inducing electrical equipment spent nearly 30% of the time gathering information through communication. Groups who thought that the study involved sexual behavior interacted the least, and they also showed more withdrawal. Their reactions are consistent with studies that indicate that people do not affiliate when they feel embarrassed (Buunk & Hoorens, 1992).

Misery Loves More Miserable Company (Sometimes).   Social comparison, in addition to providing information and reassurance, can also bolster self-esteem and inspire confidence. When Monet despaired, he could compare himself to Sisley, whose work received little acknowledgment while he was alive. And when Monet compared himself to the relatively successful Morisot, he reminded himself that he, too, could succeed as a painter. Monet was engaging in **downward social comparison** when he chose inferior people as targets for his comparison and **upward social comparison** when he compared himself with superior people.

Both downward and upward social comparisons help people cope with threatening, unpleasant circumstances (Collins, 1996; Major, Testa, & Bylsma, 1991). Downward social comparisons remind us that we are doing better than others. Our own plight often seems less bleak and our coping more effective in comparison to people who are doing worse than we are (Wood, 1989). Upward comparison, in contrast, provides people with information about how to cope and increases feelings of hope (Snyder, Cheavens, & Sympson, 1997; Taylor & Lobel, 1989). Groups of students just entering college and people coping with cancer reported feeling better when they listened to anecdotes about people who had coped effectively with the same situation (Taylor, Aspinwall, Guiliano, Dakof, & Reardon, 1993). Cancer patients, when asked if they want to interact with a patient who was doing worse than, the same as, or better than they were, preferred a partner who was slightly better off than they were (Molleman, Pruyn, & van Knippenberg, 1986).

Upward social comparison can leave us feeling like failures, however. When students were asked to keep track of the people they compared themselves to over a two-week period, they reported feeling depressed and discouraged when they associated with superior people (Wheeler & Miyake, 1992). These negative consequences of upward comparison appear to be greatest when comparisons involve attributes or skills that are central to our self-definitions. Imagine, for example, that you are a mediocre painter who wants to be a great painter. In this case, you will probably avoid joining a group of world-famous artists. If, however, you paint primarily for enjoy-

---

Downward social comparison: Comparing ourselves to others who are performing less effectively than we are.
Upward social comparison: Comparing ourselves to others who are performing more effectively than we are.

ment but take pride in your business successes, you may feel very comfortable associating with better artists (Lockwood & Kunda, 1997).

Abraham Tesser, Jennifer Campbell, and their associates have developed an intriguing model that explains why we associate with relatively superior people. Their **self-evaluation maintenance (SEM) model** assumes that the ideal comember or friend is someone who performs worse than we do on tasks that we think are important but very well on tasks that we do not think are important. Such associates provide us with targets for downward social comparison, and by drawing attention to our association with them, we can bask in the glory of their accomplishments in areas that do not interest us (Pilkington, Tesser, & Stephens, 1991; Tesser, 1988, 1991; Tesser & Campbell, 1983; Tesser, Campbell, & Smith, 1984).

Tesser and Campbell tested the model by giving elementary school students a list of activities (sports, art, music, math) and asking them to pick out ones that they considered important or unimportant. The students also identified their most and least preferred classmate. One week later, the students rated their ability, their close classmate's ability, and their distant classmate's ability in one area they felt was important and one they felt was unimportant. As Figure 4–2 indicates, if the students thought that the task was important, they judged their performance superior to their close friend's.

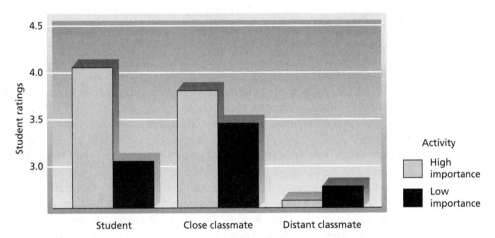

FIGURE 4–2 Do we like people who outperform us on tasks that we think are important? When students rated their own performance on a task they felt was important to them, they rated themselves as somewhat better than their close friend and much better than the distant classmate. But students rated their friend more positively than themselves when the task had no implications for their self-worth.

(*Source:* Tesser, Campbell, & Smith, 1984.)

Self-evaluation maintenance (SEM) model: A theory proposed by Tesser and Campbell that assumes that we maintain and enhance our self-esteem by associating with high-achieving individuals who excel in areas that are not relevant to our own self-esteem and avoiding association with high-achieving individuals who excel in areas that are important to our self-esteem.

If the task was not important to them personally, they felt that they had performed relatively worse. The performances of disliked classmates were derogated for both important and unimportant tasks (Tesser et al., 1984).

Stress and Social Support

Monet initially sought to change the art world singlehandedly, but he soon found that he needed help from others. Frequently penniless, he sold his work to other artists so he could buy food and pay for his lodging. He could not afford his own studio, so Bazille and Renoir invited him to share one with them. He journeyed with them to the countryside outside of Paris, where they painted scenes side by side and offered each other advice and encouragement. When Monet injured his leg, Bazille cared for him. Monet's group was an invaluable resource that helped him overcome barriers he could not surmount on his own.

When people find themselves in stressful, difficult circumstances, they often cope by forming or joining a group. In times of trouble, such as illness, divorce, or loss, people seek out friends and relatives (Dooley & Catalano, 1984). When students first go to college, they cope by forming extensive social networks of peers and friends (Hays & Oxley, 1986). People who have been diagnosed with serious illnesses often join small discussion groups with other patients (Jacobs & Goodman, 1989). People who have personal problems, such as a general feeling of unhappiness or dissatisfaction, prefer to get help from friends and relatives rather than mental-health professionals (Wills & DePaulo, 1991). Individuals experiencing work-related stress, such as layoffs, time pressures, or inadequate supervision, cope by joining with co-workers (Caplan, Vinokur, Price, & van Ryn, 1989; Cooper, 1981).

Groups counter stress by providing members with social comparison information (Wills, 1991). But groups also offer members **social support:** personal actions and resources that help members cope with minor aspects of everyday living, daily hassles, and more significant life crises (Coyne & Downey, 1991; Finch et al., 1997). As Table 4–2 indicates, group members provide *emotional support* when they compliment and encourage one another, express their friendship for others, and listen to others' problems without offering criticism or suggestions. They offer *informational support* when they give directions, offer advice, and make suggestions about how to solve a particular problem. They also offer *task support* and *tangible assistance* to one another when they help one another with their work or lend each other money. Last, most groups offer their members a sense of *belonging:* We are a part of something when we are members of a group (Sarason, Pierce, & Sarason, 1990).

Admittedly, some groups fail to deliver on their promise of support. They add stressors by stirring up conflicts, increasing responsibilities, and exposing members to criticism (Hays & Oxley, 1986; Seeman, Seeman, & Sayles, 1985). Overall, however, groups are more frequently supportive rather than burdensome. People who receive support from others tend to experience less stress in their lives, are less likely to suffer

---

Social support: Emotional support, advice, guidance, and tangible assistance given to others when they experience stress, daily hassles, and more significant life crises.

TABLE 4–2   SOME FORMS OF SOCIAL SUPPORT PROVIDED BY GROUPS

Type of Support	Example
Emotional support	• Complimenting and encouraging others • Showing respect for abilities or skills • Listening to others' problems without offering criticism or suggestions • Sharing feelings
Informational support	• Giving directions, advice, and suggestions • Demonstrating a way to perform a task • Explaining problems, approaches
Task support and tangible assistance	• Helping one another with work • Doing small favors • Lending money
Belonging	• Expressing acceptance of person • Expressing approval for entire group • Demonstrating inclusion in group

---

from depression and other psychological problems, and are physically healthier (Barrera, 1986; Herbert & Cohen, 1993; Uchino, Cacioppo, & Kiecolt-Glaser, 1996). Social support is particularly valuable when people find themselves in threatening circumstances: a divorce, a job change, a move, or the like. Stressful life circumstances leave us at risk for psychological and physical illness, but groups can serve as protective buffers against these negative consequences (Cohen & Wills, 1985; Wills & Cleary, 1996). Researchers verified this *buffering effect* in one study of individuals trying to recover from a devastating crisis (e.g., death of a spouse or child). People who were more firmly embedded in a social network of friends, relatives, and neighbors were less depressed than people who weren't integrated into groups (Norris & Murrell, 1990).

Groups and Collective Endeavors

Across a range of circumstances, groups are the means to achieve goals that would be beyond the reach of a single individual. Some tasks require a group because they require enormous amounts of time or strength: No one person could build the pyramids of Egypt or the Hoover Dam. Other goals can only be accomplished when several individuals pool their unique talents in a coordinated effort: Orchestra members and baseball players perform different tasks, which in combination create a group product. Other tasks could be accomplished by an individual, but a group is more efficient: One talented individual could build a car, but an assembly line of workers is more effective. Some tasks, too, are made more interesting when performed by a group: One can sew quilts or harvest grapes alone, but groups make these routine tasks more engaging. As Alvin Zander (1985, p. 33) explains, "Individuals create a group when they develop a purpose that collaboration can help them meet" (see Table 4–3).

TABLE 4-3   COLLECTIVE GOALS SOUGHT BY GROUPS

Purpose of the Group	Typical Groups
Protect members from physical harm	Neighborhood association, emergency squad, army platoon
Solve a problem for members or for those who created the group	Committee, commission, task force, research staff
Reduce costs for members	Buyers cooperative, trade association
Make resources available	Bank, rental agency
Accomplish heavy, arduous tasks	Construction crew, assembly line
Make jobs more tolerable	Quilting bee
Set standards for others to follow	Legislative body, ethics review board
Change the opinions of persons outside the group	Citizens action group, political party
Worship a deity	Religious body
Pay homage to ideas or objects	Patriotic society, veterans group
Heal members and nonmembers	Psychotherapy group, surgery team
Teach	Schools, tutoring agency
Discover new information	Research team, professional society
Make things for consumers	Factory, production line
Enrich leisure time of members	Hobby club, discussion group
Give advice to those who seek it	Consultation firm, support group
Render decisions on guilt	Jury, supreme court
Engage in the performing arts	Orchestra, dance company, drama troupe
Capture those who break the law	Police, posse, vigilantes
Administer an organization	Executive committee, trustees, regents

Source: Zander, 1985.

When are individuals likely to seek goals through collective action? Zander argues that one of the most important factors is degree of dissatisfaction with one's current outcomes. If a substantial number of individuals "realize that a situation is not what it might be and that something ought to be done" (p. 52), collective action becomes increasingly likely. A community group seeking lower taxes, the civil rights movement, and Mothers Against Drunk Driving (MADD) exemplify such groups (Miller, 1983). Culture, too, plays a role. As noted in Chapter 3, individuals who grow up in collectivistic cultures would be more likely to rely on groups to complete tasks and achieve their goals.

Proximity and Social Integration

Group members often assume that their groups result from rational planning or common interests. But in many instances, mere *proximity* is the more powerful determinant of a group's formation. When teachers assign students seats in classrooms, cliques of pupils in adjacent seats develop (Segal, 1974). People assigned to rooms in dorms or apartments at random are more likely to form friendships with people who occupy nearby rooms or apartments (Nahemow & Lawton, 1975; Newcomb, 1960). Couples who live in more centrally located apartments have more friends than those who live in secluded apartments, even assigned to apartments randomly (Festinger, Schachter, & Back, 1950). Monet, Manet, Degas, and many other impressionists lived in the same neighborhood in Paris. Their paths crossed, and crossed again, until eventually a group was formed.

Why do people tend to form groups with people who just happen to be nearby? As Richard Moreland (1987) notes in his social integration theory of group formation, groups emerge gradually over time as individuals find themselves interacting with the same subset of individuals with greater and greater frequency. Repeated interactions may foster a sense of groupness, as the interactants come to think of themselves as a group and people outside the group begin to treat them as a group (Arkin & Burger, 1980). Close proximity also sets the stage for **mere exposure.** We are likely to more frequently see people whose offices, homes, and desks are located near ours, and this frequent exposure may increase our liking for them (Bornstein, Leone, & Galley, 1987).

Other factors in addition to proximity can increase the opportunity for interaction and the likelihood that a group will grow. The impressionists frequented the same cafés in their neighborhood, and these shared locations promoted opportunities for discussions about art and political philosophies. Similarly, commuters who regularly use the same subway stops in New York City eventually gel into identifiable groups, as do students who patronize the same bars near college campuses (Milgram, 1992; Willsie & Riemer, 1980). Groups also form when otherwise unrelated individuals are drawn to a single individual who becomes the hub for gradually developing bonds among the various members (Redl, 1942). Indeed, any factor that promotes interaction among individuals, including proximity, a regularly used location, or a unifying leader, can contribute to the formation of groups by "strengthening the bonds among persons" (Moreland, 1987, p. 81).

Interpersonal Attraction

We do not form groups with people who happen to be nearby because we are shallow or indiscriminating. Rather, proximity increases interaction between people, and interaction cultivates attraction. Monet came into contact with many artists when he first began painting, but he only liked some of these artists: Pissarro, Cézanne, and Manet. He met them by chance, but their mutual attraction toward one another transformed them into a group.

Theodore Newcomb (1960, 1961, 1979, 1981) investigated the impact of attraction on group formation by offering 17 young men starting their studies at the University of Michigan free rent if they answered his questions each week. Newcomb

---

Mere exposure: The tendency to form a positive attitude toward stimuli that are encountered repeatedly.

(1981) found that many roommates ended up liking each other—strong evidence of the impact of proximity on group formation. He also found, however, that a clique of 7 men formed within the dormitory that went beyond propinquity. These 7 individuals, when asked to indicate who they liked in the total group, gave relatively high rankings to one another. The remaining members of the total group did not show the same level of mutual attraction as the smaller clique. Newcomb also discovered that the clique grew as friendship pairs expanded to include additional members (Moreland, 1987). The first groups to form were dyads; usually, roommates or people living in adjoining rooms became friends. Over time, these dyads expanded to include other individuals who were attracted to one or both of the original dyad members. This same kind of chaining process has been documented in other emerging groups, such as adolescents' peer-group associations, leisure groups, and social movements (Benford, 1992). Larry may decide to attend his first union meeting, alumni association gathering, or political action group because a friend, relative, or co-worker he likes invites him to come along. The impressionists' development into a group followed such a chaining pattern: Monet and Pissarro became friends first, with other artists bonding with either Monet or Pissarro.

Interpersonal attraction also influences the group's willingness to recruit and accept new members as well as the enthusiasm of potential members to join the group. In contrast to *closed groups,* the membership ranks of *open groups* change over time as members drop out and new members join (Ziller, 1964). Open groups may look for certain qualifications in potential new members, but in many cases, they extend invitations of membership to people who meet one fundamental criterion: The group likes them. Even business recruiters, who mindfully seek out employees with certain skills and aptitudes, tend to base their choices on attractiveness rather than expertise (Graves & Karren, 1996; Graves & Powell, 1988, 1995). When senior executives select lower-level managers for promotion into the executive group, they tend to select people who they believe they will be able to get along with (Hogan, Curphy, & Hogan, 1994). Job applicants, too, are more likely to accept an offer from a company whose recruiter behaved in a friendly rather than unfriendly way (Goltz & Giannantonio, 1995).

A number of factors, by increasing attraction between individuals, can thus contribute to group formation. Just as individuals are drawn to certain people—those who express similar attitudes and values, those who respond positively to them, and those who are physically attractive or competent—so do individuals seek out groups whose members possess these qualities. Let's consider some of these factors in more detail.

The Similarity Principle.   When Newcomb examined the subgroups that emerged spontaneously in his dormitory study, he noticed that subgroup members' values, beliefs, and interests were similar. One clique, for example, contained men who endorsed liberal political and religious attitudes, were all registered in the arts college, came from the same part of the country, and shared similar aesthetic, social, theoretical, economic, political, and religious values. Members of the second subgroup were all veterans, were majors in engineering, and shared similar religious, economic, and political values. A third subgroup differed from the first two cliques in that its members were all from small midwestern towns and were all Protestants. Lastly, men who did not belong to any subgroup displayed unique values and interests (Newcomb, 1960, 1961, 1963).

Newcomb had found strong evidence for the **similarity principle:** We like people who are similar to us in some way. This effect has been obtained in studies of several other groups, and it appears to be caused by a number of interrelated processes (Byrne, Ervin, & Lamberth, 1970; Curry & Emerson, 1970; Griffitt & Veitch, 1974; Hill & Stull, 1981; Kandel, 1978; Wright & Crawford, 1971, Study 4). First, people who adopt the same values and attitudes that we do reassure us that our beliefs are accurate (Festinger, 1954). We therefore find association with such people very rewarding (Byrne, 1971; Clore & Byrne, 1974). Second, similarity serves as a signal to suggest that future interactions will be free of conflict (Insko & Schopler, 1972). Third, once we discover that we are similar to another person, we tend to immediately feel a sense of unity with that person (Arkin & Burger, 1980). Two strangers chatting casually on an airplane, for example, feel united if they find that they share even the smallest similarity, such as the same middle name or a favorite TV program. Last, disliking a person who seems similar may prove to be psychologically distressing. After all, if a person is similar to us, it follows logically that he or she must be attractive (Festinger, 1957; Heider, 1958).

The Complementarity Principle.   The similarity principle exerts a powerful influence on groups, but sometimes we prefer the company of people who are dissimilar to us. If, for example, Claude enjoys leading groups, he will not be attracted to other individuals who also strive to take control of the group. Instead, he will respond more positively to those who accept his guidance. According to the **complementarity principle,** we are attracted to people who possess characteristics that complement our own personal characteristics (Kerckhoff & Davis, 1962; Levinger, Senn, & Jorgensen, 1970; Meyer & Pepper, 1977).

Which tendency is stronger, similarity or complementarity? Some investigators, working primarily with dyads, have found that similarity is much more common than complementarity (Levinger et al., 1970; Magaro & Ashbrook, 1985; Meyer & Pepper, 1977). Other researchers do not agree, however, for they find that the members of close-knit groups tend to possess compatible, and somewhat dissimilar, needs (Kerckhoff & Davis, 1962; O'Connor & Dyce, 1997).

In all likelihood, group members respond positively to both similarity and complementarity. We may, for example, be attacted to people whose qualities complement our own, yet we may nonetheless feel we are very similar to such people (Dryer & Horowitz, 1997). We may also prefer people who are similar to us in some ways, but who complement us in other ways. Schutz (1958), for example, distinguishes between

---

Similarity principle: The tendency for group members to like people who are similar to them in some way.
Complementarity principle: The tendency for group members to like people who are dissimilar to them in ways that complement their personal qualities.

interchange compatibility and *originator compatibility*. Interchange compatibility exists when group members have similar expectations about the group's intimacy, control, and inclusiveness. Interchange compatibility would be high if all the members expect that their group will be formally organized with minimal expressions of intimacy, but low if some think that they can share their innermost feelings while others want a more reserved exchange. Originator compatibility exists when people who wish to act on their needs for control, inclusion, and affection join in groups with people who wish to accept these expressions of control, inclusion, and affection. For example, originator compatibility would be high if a person with a high need to control the group joined a group whose members wanted a strong leader.

Schutz tested his theory by constructing groups of varying compatibility. He created originator compatibility by placing in each group one member with a high need for control, one member with a high need for inclusion, and three members with lower needs for control and inclusion. In addition, interchange compatibility was established by grouping people with similar needs for affection. All the groups in this set were compatible, but levels of affection were high in half of the groups and low in the other half. A set of incompatible groups was also created by including group members who varied significantly in their need for affection, ranging from high to low. As Schutz predicted, (1) cohesiveness was higher in the compatible groups than in the incompatible groups, and (2) the compatible groups worked on problems far more efficiently than the incompatible groups. He found similar results in studies of groups that form spontaneously—such as street gangs and friendship circles in fraternities (Schutz, 1958).

The Reciprocity Principle.   When Groucho Marx joked, "I wouldn't join a club that would want me as a member," he was denying the power of the **reciprocity principle:** liking tends to be met with liking in return. When we discover that someone else accepts and approves of us—they give friendly advice, compliment us, or declare their admiration for us—we usually respond by liking them in return (Jones, 1973; Shrauger, 1975). Newcomb (1979) found strong evidence of reciprocity, as have other investigators (Kandel, 1978; Segal, 1979; Wright, Ingraham, & Blackmer, 1984). Some group members, like Groucho, may not like to be liked, but these exceptions to the reciprocity principle are relatively rare.

Negative reciprocity also occurs in groups: We dislike those who seem to reject us. In one study, college students discussed controversial issues in groups. Unknown to the true subjects in the experiment, two of the three group members were confederates of the experimenter who either accepted or rejected the comments of the subject. Indeed, during a break between the discussion and the completion of a measure of attraction to the group, the rejecting confederates excluded the subject from their discussion by talking among themselves and giving the subject an occasional "dirty" look. Naturally, subjects were less attracted to their comembers when they had re-

---

Reciprocity principle: The tendency for liking to be met with liking in return; if A likes B, then B will tend to like A.

jected them. The rejection also served to lower subjects' opinions of themselves (Pepi-tone & Wilpinski, 1960).

The Minimax Principle. Social exchange theory argues that individuals' decisions to join groups will, in most cases, conform to the **minimax principle:** People will join groups and remain in groups that provide them with the maximum number of val-ued rewards while incurring the fewest number of possible costs (Kelly & Thibaut, 1978; Moreland & Levine, 1982; Thibaut & Kelley, 1959). Rewards include accep-tance by others, camaraderie, assistance in reaching personal goals, social support and comparison information, exposure to new ideas, and opportunities to interact with people who are interesting and attractive. But groups have costs as well: time, money, energy, and the like. Indeed, when researchers asked prospective group mem-bers to identify the rewards and costs they felt the group might create for them, 40% mentioned such social and personal rewards as meeting people, making new friends, developing new interests, or enhancing their self-esteem. They also mentioned such rewards as learning new skills, increased opportunities for networking, and fun. The members also anticipated costs, however. Over 30% expected to lose time and money by joining a group. Other frequently mentioned costs were social pressures, possible injury or illness, and excessive demands made by the group for their time. These prospective members, by the way, optimistically felt that the groups they were con-sidering joining would offer them far more rewards than costs (Brinthaupt, More-land, & Levine, 1991; Moreland, Levine, & Cini, 1993).

The group members themselves are also an important source of rewards and costs. Many of the impressionists, for example, considered having to interact with Degas a major cost of membership in the impressionists. In a letter to Pissarro, Gustave Caille-botte wrote: "Degas introduced disunity into our midst. It is unfortunate for him that he has such an unsatisfactory character. He spends his time haranguing at the Nouvelle-Athènes or in society. He would do much better to paint a little more" (quoted in Den-vir, 1993, p. 181).

People are usually attracted to groups whose members possess positively valued qualities and avoid groups of people with objectionable characteristics. We prefer to associate with people who are generous, enthusiastic, punctual, dependable, helpful, strong, truthful, and intelligent (Bonney, 1947; Thibaut & Kelley, 1959). We tend to dislike, and reject as potential group members, individuals who possess socially unat-tractive personal qualities—people who seem pushy, rude, or self-centered (Gilchrist, 1952; Iverson, 1964). People who complain too frequently are also viewed negatively (Kowalski, 1996), as are people who add little of interest to the group. Indeed, boring people are particularly unappealing when members of small groups. Such individuals tend to be passive in groups, but when they do take part in the interaction, they speak slowly, pause before making a point, and drag out the meeting. Bores also sidetrack the group unnecessarily, show little enthusiasm, and seem too serious and preoccupied

---

Minimax principle: The tendency to prefer relationships and group memberships that provide the maximum number of valued rewards and incur the fewest number of possible costs.

with themselves. Worst of all, boring group members complain about their own problems (negative egocentrism) and talk incessantly about trivial topics (banality).

If given the choice, people much prefer the company of interesting people to boring people. In one study, subjects listened to a tape recording of a conversation that included a boring group member (someone who displayed many of the behaviors listed in Table 4–4) or an interesting group member (someone who avoided these behaviors). When the subjects later rated the discussers, they felt that the interesting targets were more likeable, friendly, enthusiastic, popular, emotional, intelligent, personal, strong, and secure than the boring targets (Leary, Rogers, Canfield, & Coe, 1986).

The Economics of Membership

Why did such artists as Manet, Pissarro, and Bazille join with Monet to create an artists circle? As we have seen, the group offered the members a number of advantages over remaining alone. By joining Monet, the impressionists gained a sounding board for ideas, social support, help with tasks they could not accomplish alone, and friends. But the group also created costs for members, who had to spend time and personal resources before they could enjoy the benefits the group offered. The minimax principle argues that those who joined the group must have felt that the benefits outweighed the costs.

TABLE 4–4   THE COMPONENTS OF BORING BEHAVIOR

Dimension	Definition	Example Behaviors
Passivity	Participating at a low rate	Adds nothing to conversation; doesn't express opinions; doesn't hold up end of conversation
Tediousness	Communicating in a boring manner	Talks slowly; rambles; includes too much detail
Distraction	Interfering with the group's interaction	Talks about past too much; is excited by trivial things; is easily sidetracked
Low affectivity	Lacking emotion or expressiveness	Lacks enthusiasm; has monotonous voice; avoids eye contact
Boring ingratiation	Awkwardly trying to impress others	Tries hard to be funny; tries hard to be nice; tries to impress you
Seriousness	Maintaining a serious demeanor	Doesn't smile; is very serious
Negative egocentrism	Complaining about one's own problems	Is constantly complaining; acts bored
Self-preoccupation	Lacking interest in others	Talks about self; always talks about problems
Banality	Talking about trite and trivial things	Talks about trivial, superficial things; repeats stories and jokes

Source: Leary, Rogers, Canfield, & Coe, 1986.

Do we, then, join any group that promises us a favorable reward/cost ratio. Howard Kelley and John Thibaut argued that although we may be attracted to such groups, our decision to actually join is based on two factors: our comparison level and our comparison level for alternatives. **Comparison level (CL)** is the standard by which individuals evaluate the desirability of group membership. The CL derives from the average of all outcomes known to the individual and is usually strongly influenced by previous relationships. If, for example, Degas's prior group memberships yielded very positive rewards with very few costs, his CL should be higher than someone who has experienced fewer rewards and more costs through group membership. According to Thibaut and Kelley (1959, p. 21), groups that "fall above CL would be relatively 'satisfying' and attractive to the member; those entailing outcomes that fall below CL would be relatively 'unsatisfying' and unattractive" (see also Kelley & Thibaut, 1978).

Comparison level, however, only predicts when we will be satisfied with membership in a group. If we want to predict when people will join groups and leave them, we must also take into account the value of other, alternative groups. What if Degas could have joined several artists circles, all of which surpassed his CL? Which one would he then select? According to Thibaut and Kelley (1959), the group with the best reward/cost balance will determine Degas's **comparison level for alternatives**, or CL_{alt}. Thibaut and Kelley argue that "CL_{alt} can be defined informally as the lowest level of outcomes a member will accept in the light of available alternative opportunities" (1959, p. 21).

Entering and exiting groups is largely determined by CL_{alt}, whereas satisfaction with membership is determined by CL (see Table 4–5). For example, what if you are considering joining a group of students preparing for an examination? According to Thibaut and Kelley, you will estimate the positive and negative outcomes that will

TABLE 4–5   THE IMPACT OF COMPARISON LEVEL AND COMPARISON LEVEL FOR ALTERNATIVES ON SATISFACTION WITH GROUP MEMBERSHIP AND DECISION TO JOIN A GROUP

		Membership in-Group is	
		Above CL	**Below CL**
Membership in Group is	Above CL_{alt}	Membership is satisfying and will join group	Membership is dissatifying, but will join group
	Below CL_{alt}	Membership is satisfying, but will not join group	Membership is dissatisfying and will not join group

Source: Thibaut & Kelley, 1959.

Comparison level (CL): In Thibaut and Kelley's social exchange theory, the standard by which the individual evaluates the quality of any social relationship.
Comparison level for alternatives (CL_{alt}): In Thibaut and Kelley's social exchange theory, the standard by which the individual evaluates the quality of *other* groups that he or she may join.

_mbership in the group. Looking at rewards, you may believe that join-
.p will make learning easier, will lead to increased interaction with several
_ individuals, and will also yield an improved course grade. On the negative
_owever, the group might be boring. If these rewards and costs balance out
_e your CL, then you will be interested in membership. The value of alternative
_oups, however, also determines your decision, for the study group's value must
exceed your CL_{alt}. In fact, you might decide that remaining outside the study group
will yield a more favorable reward/cost ratio; in this instance, remaining alone estab-
lishes the lower limit of your CL_{alt}.

GROUP SOCIALIZATION

Cézanne, Morisot, Renoir, and others stopped exhibiting with the other impressionists when critics lambasted the group's works. Degas, in particular, became less interested in the group, and in time he distanced himself from the group through his
public declarations and through his art. Why do some people maintain their commitment to their groups, whereas others decide to end their membership?

Our understanding of membership dynamics owes much to the work of Richard
Moreland and John Levine (1982). Their theory of **group socialization** assumes that a
person's passage through a group depends on two processes: evaluation and commitment. *Evaluation* is determined, in large part, by the balance of rewards to costs—a
more favorable ratio translates into a more favorable evaluation (Kelley & Thibaut,
1978; Thibaut & Kelley, 1959). *Commitment* describes the "enduring adherence" of
the relationship between the individual and the group (Kelley, 1983, p. 313). An individual who is committed to a group "is expected to stay in that relationship" for a relatively long time (Kelley, 1983, p. 287).

These two processes are mutual ones, however. The individual member evaluates
the group and develops some degree of commitment to it, but the group also evaluates the individual and develops some degree of commitment to him or her. Degas,
for example, initially valued his membership in the impressionist group because he
appreciated the artistic and interpersonal rewards it offered. But when people began
buying his work Degas lost interest in his membership. The impressionists, also evaluated Degas. They initially accepted him as a colleague, but over time their evaluation became more negative as he made few contributions to the group. Thus,
individuals appraise their group, and the group appraises the individual member.

Costs and Commitment

Evaluation and commitment are often positively related: Individuals who evaluate
their group positively are committed to the group, and a group that evaluates a mem-

---

Group socialization: A pattern of change in the relationship between an individual and a group
that begins when an individual first considers joining the group and ends when he or she leaves it.

ber favorably tries to keep that individual in the group. Yet, a positive evaluation does not necessarily lead to commitment. One early member of the impressionists, Morisot, liked the group, but she wasn't committed to long-term membership. Conversely, Cézanne felt that membership during the later years was unrewarding, but he still felt a strong sense of commitment to the group.

Commitment to a group is in many cases determined by the availability of alternative groups—in the language of social exchange theory, by CL_{alt}. Members who feel that they have no alternative to remaining in the group are often the most committed. Members also become more committed to a group the more they put into it. Although putting time, energy, and personal resources into a group raises the costs associated with membership, everyday experience suggests that people sometimes become more favorable toward their group the more they invest in it. Many groups require new members to pass elaborate initiation tests on the premise that these personal investments strengthen the bond between the individual and the group. People who join emotionally involving groups such as fraternities, social movements, or cults sometimes become more and more committed to the movement each time they make a personal investment in it.

Festinger's (1957) cognitive dissonance theory offers an intriguing explanation for the relationship between investment and commitment. Dissonance theory suggests that increased commitment that follows personal investment results from members' attempts to reduce the conflict among their beliefs about their groups (Festinger et al., 1956). Because the two cognitions, "I have invested in the group" and "The group has some cost-creating characteristics" are dissonant, these beliefs cause the members psychological discomfort. Although people can reduce cognitive dissonance in many ways, one frequent method is to emphasize the rewarding features of the group while minimizing the costly characteristics. By thinking more about the positive features of the group, individuals can reduce their uncertainty about its value.

Festinger and his colleagues investigated this process in their classic study of an atypical group that formed around a psychic, Marion Keech. Keech convinced her followers that the world was coming to an end, but that the inhabitants of a planet named Clairon would rescue the group before the apocalypse. Many members of the group committed all their personal resources to the group or gave away their personal possessions in the weeks before the scheduled departure from the planet. Yet, the group did not disband even when the rescuers never arrived. Keech claimed that the dedication of the group had so impressed God that the earth had been spared, and many of the members responded by becoming even more committed to their group. Membership was costly, but each investment tied them more strongly to the group. (See, too, Atlas, 1990; Batson, 1975; Bliese, 1990; Hardyck & Braden, 1962.)

Other researchers have tested the impact of costs and commitment using more traditional research procedures (Aronson & Mills, 1959; Axsom, 1989; Gerard & Mathewson, 1966). Elliot Aronson and Judson Mills, for example, manipulated the investments that individuals made before joining a group discussing topics related to sexual behavior. They randomly assigned female college students to one of three experimental conditions: a severe initiation condition, a mild initiation condition, and a control condition. Subjects assigned to the severe initiation condition had to read aloud to the male experimenter a series of obscene words and two "vivid descriptions of sexual activity from contemporary novels." In the mild initiation condition, subjects read five sex-related but nonobscene words. In the control condition, subjects were not put through any kind of initiation whatsoever.

At this point, the subjects were told that their group was already meeting. The subjects could not interrupt the session, but they were given the opportunity to listen to the group discussion with headphones. What the subjects actually heard was a recorded group discussion that had been "deliberately designed to be as dull and banal as possible" (Aronson & Mills, 1959, p. 179). The participants discussed "dryly and haltingly" the sexual behavior of animals, mumbled frequently, uttered disjointed sentences, and lapsed into long silences. When the tape ended, the researchers asked the subjects to rate the group they listened to on a number of dimensions. When they totaled up these ratings, they found that the people who had worked hardest to join the boring group were more positive than those who had experienced a mild initiation or no initiation at all.

Aronson and Mills concluded that the initiation increased attraction by creating cognitive dissonance, but other factors may also account for the initiation-attraction relationship. Individuals may find strict, demanding groups attractive because stringent standards ensure that other group members will be highly involved in the group, too, so one's investments in the group will be matched by everyone else (Iannaccone, 1994). Their public expressions of liking for such groups may also stem more from a desire to save face after making a faulty decision than from the psychic discomfort of cognitive dissonance (Schlenker, 1975). Initiations also fail to heighten attraction if they frustrate new members or make them angry (Lodewijkx & Syroit, 1997).

Stages of Socialization

Moreland and Levine's model of group socialization assumes that individuals and groups change their evaluations of and commitment to one another over time. These changes create a predictable sequence of changes between the individual and the group, which is summarized in Figure 4–3. During each stage, the individual and the group evaluate each other, and commitment level increases and decreases as the individual progresses through the socialization process. When members reach the transition point at the end of a stage, they experience a role transition and move into the next stage.

Investigation.   The cautious search for information is the hallmark of the *investigation* phase. During this period, potential members engage in *reconnaissance;* they compare available groups with one another to determine which ones will best fulfill their needs. Groups, in turn, engage in *recruitment* as they try to estimate the value of each individual who is interested in joining them. In successful cases, this mutual investigation ends when the group asks the candidate to join and the prospective member accepts. This transition point is termed *entry* (see Figure 4–3).

One's assumptions about the value of groups in general influence the investigation phase. Consider new students entering college. Although some will decide to join an or-

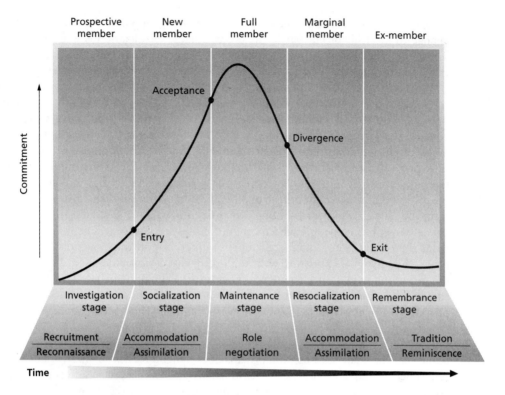

FIGURE 4-3 What stages mark our transition through a group? The Moreland and Levine model of group socialization identifies five stages of socialization, demarcated by four transition points. Roles are listed across the top of the figure, and individual-level and group-level processes are shown at the bottom. The curved line represents a hypothetical individual's history of commitment in a group, but other patterns are equally likely.

(*Source:* Moreland & Levine, 1982.)

ganization on campus, such as student government, a sorority, or a music club, others will avoid membership. Moreland and his colleagues found that students who had belonged to high school groups tried harder to find groups that would help them achieve their personal goals, provided those prior experiences had been positive. A student who was active in student government in high school, for example, was likely to investigate political parties on campus, but only if the high school experience had been rewarding (Pavelshak, Moreland, & Levine, 1986). Individuals with either little prior experience or negative experiences in groups avoided membership in groups (Bohrnstedt & Fisher, 1986; Gold & Yanof, 1985; Hanks & Eckland, 1978; Ickes, 1983; Ickes & Turner, 1983).

Socialization.   The individual's move from prospective member to new member initiates the *socialization* process. In the group's eyes, the initiate is a newcomer who must accept the group's culture. To the new member, the group must be flexible enough to change to meet his or her particular needs. Again, socialization is a mutual process: Through *assimilation,* the individual accepts the group's norms, values, and perspectives, and through *accommodation,* the group adapts to fit the newcomer's needs.

When this period of adjustment is completed, the *acceptance* transition point is reached, and the individual becomes a full member. This role transition point can be delayed, however, if the oldtimers react to the newcomer in negative ways. Newcomers, too, can prolong their assimilation into the group by remaining cautiously aloof or by misinterpreting other members' reactions. Moreland (1985) studied how people react when they think they are newcomers by arranging for groups of five unacquainted individuals to meet for several weeks to discuss various topics. He told two of the five that the group had been meeting for some time and that they were the only newcomers. Although the role of newcomer existed only in the minds of the two subjects, people who thought themselves newcomers behaved differently from the others. They interacted more frequently and more positively with each other, they were less satisfied with the group discussion, and their descriptions of the group made reference to members' seniority. Thus, the belief that one is a newcomer who will be treated differently by the oldtimers can act as a self-fulfilling prophecy: The newcomers may act in ways that slow their acceptance by the rest of the group.

Maintenance.   The socialization process does not end even when individuals become full-fledged group members. Even seasoned group members must adjust as the group adds new members, adopts new goals in place of old objectives, or modifies status and role relationships. Much of this *maintenance* phase is devoted to *role negotiation.* The group may, for example, require the services of a leader who can organize the group's activities and motivate members. The individual, in contrast, may wish instead to remain a follower who is responsible for relatively routine matters. During this phase, the group and the individual negotiate the nature and quantity of the member's expected contribution to the group.

Many group members remain in the maintenance period until their membership in the group reaches a scheduled conclusion. An employee who retires, a student who graduates from college, or an elected official whose term in office expires all leave the group after months or years of successful maintenance. In some cases, however, the maintenance process builds to a transition point that Moreland and Levine label *divergence.* The group may, for example, force individuals to take on roles that they do not find personally rewarding. Individuals, too, may fail to meet the group's expectations concerning appropriate behavior, and role negotiation may reach an impasse. When the divergence point is reached, the socialization process enters a new phase: resocialization.

Resocialization.   During resocialization, the former full member takes on the role of a marginal member whose future in the group is uncertain. The individual sometimes precipitates this crisis, often in response to increased costs and dwindling rewards, waning commitment to the group, and dissatisfaction with responsibilities and duties.

The group, too, can be the instigator, reacting to a group member who is not contributing or is working against the group's explicit and implicit purposes.

Moreland and Levine identify two possible outcomes of resocialization. The group and the individual, through accommodation and assimilation, can resolve their differences. In this instance, *convergence* occurs, and the individual once more becomes a full member of the group. Alternatively, resocialization efforts can fail (see Figure 4–3). The group may conclude that the individual is no longer acceptable as a member and move to expel him or her. Similarly, the individual may reevaluate his or her commitment to the group and decide to leave. As a result, the divergence between the group and individual becomes so great that a final role transition is reached: *exit*.

Remembrance.   When the individual and the group finally reach a parting of the ways, one final task remains: The ex-member and the remaining group members review their shared experience during a period of *remembrance*. Former members *reminisce* about their time spent in the group. They may review their entry into the group, weigh their contributions and the outcomes of their membership, and make sense of their recent departure from the group. The group members, meanwhile, discuss their former comembers by reviewing, for example, their commitment to the group, their contributions and actions while members of the group, and their reasons for leaving. If the group reaches a consensus on these issues, their conclusions become part of the group's *tradition*. This tradition often takes a negative tone, particularly when the individual's exit results from divergence during resocialization. This hostility toward individuals who leave the group may stem "from the threat to the group's values" that such individuals imply. The "ex-member is a living symbol of the inferiority imputed to the group's values" (Merton, 1957, p. 296), so the group tends to dismiss the contributions of such individuals.

The End of Membership

How can Degas's membership in the impressionists be described? As Moreland and Levine's model suggests, group members' reactions to their group at any particular time are based on their evaluation of the value of membership, their commitment to the group, and their role in relationship to the group. Degas, at the start of the investigation phase, admired the group and was committed to its goals. Over time, however, incompatibilities created a gap between him and the others that resocialization could not heal; when the divergence became too great, he left the group.

The rest of the impressionists, however, remained friends. They often exhibited their works individually and spent months in isolation, but they still provided each other with help as necessary. Indeed, for many years, they met regularly at the Café Riche, where they would discuss art, politics, and literature. And in time, they reached their goal of fame and fortune. By the turn of the century, most were invited, at last, to present in traditional shows, and collectors payed handsome prices for their work. They came to Paris to learn to paint as individuals, but they changed the world's definition of fine art as a group.

SUMMARY

Who joins groups? The tendency to join groups is partly determined by individuals' personal qualities, including traits, social motives, and gender.

1. *Introverts* are more likely to avoid groups, whereas *extraverts* seek out the stimulation that groups provide.
2. Some people are also more motivated than others to seek out groups, for groups offer a likely means of satisfying the *need for affiliation,* the *need for intimacy,* and the *need for power.* Schutz's *Fundamental Interpersonal Relations Orientation (FIRO)* theory explains how people use groups to satisfy their need to receive and express inclusion, control, and affection.
3. Those individuals who experience *shyness* and *social anxiety* are less likely to join groups.
4. Women seek membership in smaller, informal, intimate groups, whereas men seek membership in larger, formal, task-focused groups, but these sex differences are compounded with role differences and cultural stereotypes pertaining to men and women.

When and why do people create new groups and join existing groups? The group formation process is shaped by such interpersonal factors as social comparison, social support, proximity, and attraction.

1. Schachter found that people who face an ambiguous situation affiliate to acquire information through social comparison. However:
   • By choosing comparison targets who are performing poorly in the situation (*downward social comparison*), individuals bolster their own sense of competence, and by choosing superior

targets (*upward social comparison*), individuals refine their expectations.
   • The *self-evaluation maintenance (SEM) model* argues that people prefer to associate with individuals who do not outperform them in areas that are very relevant to their self-esteem.
2. Groups are an important source of *social support.* They work as a protective buffer that shields us from the harmful effects of stress.
3. Groups are useful on a practical level. People often face goals that they cannot attain working alone, so they join in a collaborative effort. Zander notes that people pursue goals in groups when they become dissatisfied with current outcomes.
4. Groups sometimes form when *mere exposure* creates a sense of recognition and attraction among people.
5. Newcomb, in his studies of the acquaintance process, found that people who like one another often bond together to form a group. Attraction patterns are generally consistent with the following principles:
   • *similarity principle:* People like those who are similar to them in some way.
   • *complementarity principle:* People like others whose qualities complement their own qualities.
   • *reciprocity principle:* Liking tends to be mutual.
   • *minimax principle:* Individuals are attracted to groups that offer them maximum rewards and minimal costs.
6. Social exchange theory maintains that satisfaction with group membership is primarily determined by *comparison level* (CL), whereas *comparison level for alternatives* (CL_{alt}) determines whether members will join, stay in, or leave a group.

When and why do people leave their groups?
Moreland and Levine's model of *group socialization* provides a comprehensive overview of how individuals pass through groups and how their passage changes their groups.

1. Like social exchange theory, their socialization model assumes that individuals and groups evaluate one another and that this evaluation is determined by the balance between rewards and costs and on one's assumptions about the value of groups in general.

2. Group socialization theory describes a general sequence of stages that typify the individual's movement through the group: investigation, socialization, maintenance, resocialization, and remembrance.

FOR MORE INFORMATION

Canvases and Careers: Institutional Change in the French Painting World, by Harrison C. White and Cynthia A. White (1993), comprehensively examines the sociological mechanisms that set the stage for the impressionists' success.

The Chronicle of Impressionism, by B. Denvir (1993), provides the time line for the development of the impressionists and includes reproductions of both their art and their personal correspondences.

"The Formation of Small Groups," by Richard L. Moreland (1987), provides an overall framework for understanding group formation by describing four ways individuals become integrated into a group: environmental integration, behavioral integration, affective integration, and cognitive integration.

The Psychology of Affiliation, by Stanley Schachter (1959), describes the exacting scientific methods he used to document when and why we seek out others.

Social Anxiety, by Mark R. Leary and Robin M. Kowalski (1995), is a highly informative discussion of the causes and consequences of social anxiety.

"Socialization in Small Groups: Temporal Changes in Individual-Group Relations," by Richard L. Moreland and John M. Levine (1982), is the definitive statement of the transition of individuals through their groups.

When Prophecy Fails: A Social and Psychological Study of a Modern Group That Predicted the Destruction of the World, by Leon Festinger, Henry W. Riecken, and Stanley Schachter (1956), is a theoretically guided case study of a doomsday group that remains relevant even today.

ACTIVITY 4–1 HOW DOES INTERPERSONAL ATTRACTION DEVELOP IN GROUPS?

Join together with other people in a classroom group and discuss an issue selected by the instructor. When the group meeting is over, reflect on the processes that unfolded as you got to know the other group members. Consider your feelings and experiences, and try to reason out the causes of your reactions, satisfactions, and emotions.

1. Describe your interpersonal behavior in the group. Did you act in a way that others would consider to be dominant? friendly? helpful? supportive? active? List the other people in the group, and describe them using adjectives or short phrases, such as "seemed interested," "took control," "helpful," and so on.
2. Was there anyone in the group whom you particularly liked? What was it about that person that attracted you?
3. Someone in the group probably impressed you less than everyone else. What was it about that person that caused you to react less positively?
4. How did you react to the group as a whole? Did you like being a member of the group?
5. How did the group react to you at the interpersonal level? Do you think the group liked and accepted you? Why or why not?

ACTIVITY 4–2 WHAT ARE THE REWARDS AND COSTS OF GROUP MEMBERSHIP?

What do your groups *do* for you? What rewards do they provide you that offset the costs they create for you?

1. Describe a group that you have been an active member of for at least three months.
2. What do you get out of membership in the group?
   a. Does the group accept you? Does it satisfy your need to belong?
   b. Is the group a source of interesting experiences or new ideas? Is it a source of useful information?
   c. Do you like the other people in the group? Do you enjoy being with them?
   d. Do you enjoy the group activities?
   e. Does the group help you accomplish tasks and reach goals that are important for you personally?
   f. Do you enjoy taking charge in the group?
   g. Does the group help you in various ways? Do members provide you with social support? with advice? with tangible assistance, such as money, food, or the like?
3. What kind of costs do you incur by belonging to the group?
   a. Does belonging to the group take time away from other activities?
   b. Is it monetarily expensive to belong to the group?
   c. Does the group pressure you into doing things you would rather avoid?
   d. Do you dislike some of the people in the group and dread certain group functions?
   e. Are you frequently bored by the group?
4. Overall, what is your evaluation of the group and your commitment to this group? Do you plan to remain a member for very long?

5

Structure

Each group is unique in many ways, but beneath the surface lie certain structures that are common to virtually all groups. All but the most ephemeral groups develop structure: norms, roles, and intermember relations.

- What are norms, and how do they structure interactions in groups?
- What are roles? Which roles occur most frequently in groups?
- How and why do status hierarchies develop in groups?
- What factors influence the group's sociometric structure?
- What are the interpersonal consequences of communication networks in groups?

CONTENTS

Andes Survivors: One Group's Triumph over Extraordinary Adversity

NORMS

The Development of Norms

The Transmission of Norms

ROLES

Role Differentiation

Role Stress

INTERMEMBER RELATIONS

Status Hierarchies

Social Standing

Communication Networks

The Ties That Bind

SUMMARY

FOR MORE INFORMATION

ACTIVITIES

Andes Survivors: One Group's Triumph over Extraordinary Adversity

The pilot of the chartered Fairchild F-227 made a fatal error. He misjudged his location and began his descent from cruising altitude too soon. By the time he realized his mistake, he could not keep the plane from crashing deep in the snow-covered Andes of South America.

Most of the crash survivors were players from a rugby team who were traveling from Uruguay to Chile for a match. They felt fortunate to have survived a crash that killed so many, but they faced hardships that would have broken even the hardest and most resolute. Their only shelter from the cold was the wrecked fuselage. Food was scarce. The mountain was so barren that they had little fuel for a fire. They spent hours just melting enough snow for drinking water. As the ordeal wore on, the survivors argued intensely over the likelihood of a rescue. Some insisted that searchers would soon find them. Others maintained that they must climb down from the mountain. Some became so apathetic that they didn't care. At night, the cries of the injured were often answered with anger rather than pity, for the severely cramped sleeping arrangements created continual conflict. And early one morning, as they were sleeping, an avalanche filled the cabin with snow, and many died before they could dig their way out.

The group escaped from the crash site after nearly three months. But the group that came down from the Andes was not the same group that began the chartered flight; the pattern of relationships among the group members—that is, the group's structure—had been altered. The survivors developed new standards and values that were unlike any of the rugby team's norms. The group began without a leader but ended up with "commanders," "lieutenants," and "explorers." Men who were at first afforded little respect or courtesy eventually earned considerable status within the group. Some who were well liked before the crash became outcasts, and some who hardly spoke to the others became active communicators within the group.

Any group, whether stranded in the Andes, sitting around a conference table, or working to manufacture new automobiles, can be better understood by studying its structure: the underlying pattern of stable relations among the group members. Just as physicists, when studying an unknown element, analyze its basic atomic structure rather than its superficial features, so group dynamicists look beyond the unique features of groups for evidence of these basic structures. Three of these key structural components—norms, roles, and relations—are examined in this chapter (see Lofland, 1995; Miller & Prentice, 1996; Scott & Scott, 1981, for reviews).

NORMS

The survivors of the crash needed to coordinate their actions if they were to survive. With food, water, and shelter severely limited, the group members were forced to interact with and rely on each other continually, and any errant action on the part of one person would disturb, and even endanger, several other people. So members soon began to follow a shared set of rules that defined how the group would sleep at night, what types of duties each healthy individual was expected to perform, and how food and water were to be apportioned.

The emergent consensual standards that regulate group members' behaviors are norms. Norms are a fundamental element of a group's structure, for they provide direction and motivation, organize social interactions, and make other people's responses predictable and meaningful. Each group member is restrained to a degree by norms, but each one also benefits from the order that norms provide. Norms define the socially appropriate way to respond in the group—the *normal* course of action— and the types of actions that should be avoided if at all possible (Sorrels & Kelley, 1984). Some norms are descriptive: They describe the kinds of behavior people *usually* perform. These **descriptive norms** define what most people would do, feel, or think in a particular situation. **Injunctive norms**, or **prescriptive norms**, are more evaluative: They describe the sorts of behaviors people *ought* to perform. People who do not comply with descriptive norms may be viewed as unusual, but people who violate injunctive norms are considered "bad" and are open to sanction by the other group members. In the Andes group, those who failed to do their fair share of work were criticized by the others, given distasteful chores, and sometimes even denied food and water (Cialdini, Kallgren, & Reno, 1991; Cialdini, Reno, & Kallgren, 1990; Miller & Prentice, 1996).

The Development of Norms

Groups sometimes write down and formally adopt norms as their group's rules, but most norms emerge gradually as members align their behaviors until they match certain standards. An example of this normative process is the Andes survivors' decision to eat the bodies of passengers who had died in the plane crash and avalanche. The survivors had nothing else to eat, and within days of the crash, they began feeling the effects of starvation. As early as the fourth day, one group member remarked that the only source of nourishment was the frozen bodies of the crash victims. Although the others took the remark to be a joke, by the tenth day, "the discussion spread as these boys cautiously mentioned it to their friends or those they thought would be sympathetic" (Read, 1974, p. 76). When the question was discussed by the entire group, a small subgroup of boys argued in favor of eating the corpses, but many others in the group claimed that they could not bring themselves to think of their dead friends as food. The next day, however, their hopes of rescue were crushed when they learned by radio that the air force had given up the search. The realization that help was not forthcoming forced most of the group members to consume a few pieces of meat, and in the end, cannibalism became the norm.

Descriptive norms: Shared expectations that define what most people would do, feel, or think in a particular situation; those who violate such norms are considered unusual or atypical.

Injunctive norms (prescriptive norms): Evaluative expectations that define what people should and should not do in a given situation; those who violate such norms are evaluated negatively.

According to Muzafer Sherif, this type of change reflects how people in groups over time come to develop standards that serve as frames of reference for behaviors and perceptions (M. Sherif, 1936, 1966; see, too, C. W. Sherif, 1976). Although a group facing an ambiguous problem or situation may start off with little internal consensus and great variability in behavior, members soon structure their experiences until they conform to a standard developed within the group. The group can turn to outside authorities or the traditions of society at large for their norms, but group norms often develop through reciprocal influence. In the Andes group, individuals did not actively try to conform to the judgments of others, but used the information contained in others' responses to revise their own opinions and beliefs. Writes Sherif (1966, pp. xii–xiii): "When the external surroundings lack stable, orderly reference points, the individuals caught in the ensuing experience of uncertainty mutually contribute to each other a mode of orderliness to establish their own orderly pattern."

As noted briefly in Chapter 1, Sherif studied the development of norms by taking advantage of the *autokinetic effect,* the illusory movement of a stationary pinpoint of light in a dark room. He asked individuals, dyads, and triads seated in a darkened room to make a judgment about how far a dot of light moved. After repeated trials, Sherif found that individuals making judgments by themselves established their own idiosyncratic average estimates, which varied from 1 to 10 inches. When people made their judgments in groups, however, their personal estimates blended with those of other group members until a consensus was reached. Figure 5–1 shows one group's shift from individual responding to normative responding. Before joining the group, individuals varied considerably in their estimates; one subject thought that the light moved an average of 7 inches on each trial, and the other two individuals' estimates averaged 1 inch and 2 inches. When these individuals were part of a group, however,

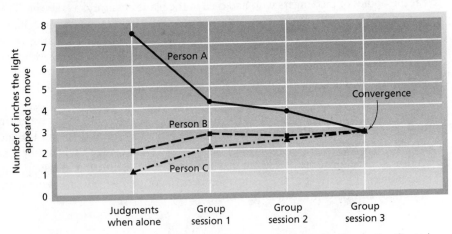

FIGURE 5–1 How do norms develop in groups? Subjects' judgments in Sherif's study converged over time. Their private, pregroup judgments differed markedly, but when they joined with others, their judgments converged.

(Data from M. Sherif, 1936.)

their judgments converged over time in what Sherif called a *funnel pattern;* by the final session, a norm of just over 2 inches had been formed.

The Transmission of Norms

Sherif concluded that new norms develop within groups whenever the context provides little information to guide actions or to enable members to formulate beliefs. He also concluded that people in the autokinetic situation were not simply changing their public estimations of distance, but were *internalizing* the group's consensus. When he again arranged for people to make their judgments alone, he found that they continued to base their estimates on the norm that emerged in the group that they belonged to previously (Sherif, 1966). They obeyed their group's norm even when there was no external pressure to do so, suggesting that they personally accepted the standard as their own (Kelman, 1961).

Groups, too, internalize norms by accepting them as legitimate standards for behavior. In one study, researchers put a confederate in each three-member group. The confederate steadfastly maintained that the dot of light was moving about 15 inches, clearly an excessive estimate, given that most estimates averaged about 3 to 4 inches. Once the confederate deflected the group's distance norm upward, he was removed from the group and replaced by a naive subject. The remaining group members, however, still retained the large distance norm, and the newest addition to the group gradually adapted to the higher standard. The researchers continued to replace group members with new subjects, but new members continued to shift their estimates in the direction of the group norm. Eventually, this arbitrary group norm disappeared as judgments of distance came back down to an average of 3.5 inches, but in most cases, the more reasonable norm did not develop until group membership had changed five or six times. Groups corrected themselves, but it took several generations before a more reasonable norm emerged (Jacobs & Campbell, 1961; MacNeil & Sherif, 1976; Pollis, Montgomery, & Smith, 1975).

A norm, once established, becomes a social fact—a part of the group's stable structure. Even though the individuals who originally fostered the norms are no longer present, their normative innovations remain a part of the organization's traditions, and newcomers must change to adopt that tradition. Newcomers to a group can sometimes influence their group's norms, but it is usually the individual who assimilates the group's norms, values, and perspectives (Moreland & Levine, 1982). Recall, for example, the results of Newcomb's 1943 study of political attitudes, discussed in Chapter 2. He discovered that students changed their attitudes until their political preferences matched the attitudes of their classmates and professors. More recently, Christian Crandall (1988) documented similar shifts in a study of bulimia, a pernicious cycle of binge eating followed by self-induced vomiting or other forms of purging. Certain social groups, such as cheerleading squads, dance troupes, sports teams, and sororities, tend to have strikingly high rates of eating disorders (Crago, Yates, Beutler, & Arizmendi, 1985; Garner & Garfinkel, 1980; Squire, 1983). In explanation, Crandall notes that such groups adopt norms that encourage binging and purging. Rather than viewing these actions as abnormal and a threat to health, the sororities that

Crandall studied accepted purging as a normal means of controlling one's weight. The women who were popular in such groups were the ones who binged at the rate established by the group's norms. Even worse, women who did not binge when they first joined the group often took up the practice the longer they remained in the group. Thus, even norms counter to society's general traditions can establish a life of their own in small subgroups within that society.

ROLES

On the day after the crash, Marcelo, the captain of the rugby team, organized the efforts of those who could work. Two young men and one of the women administered first aid to the injured. A subgroup of boys melted snow for drinking water, and another team cleaned the cabin of the airplane. These various positions in the group—leader, doctor, snow melter, cabin cleaner—are all examples of roles: sets of behaviors that are characteristic of persons in a particular social context (Biddle, 1979; Salazar, 1996).

Roles within a group are, in some respects, similar to roles in a play. For dramatists, roles describe the characters that the actors portray before the audience. To become Romeo in Shakespeare's *Romeo and Juliet,* for example, the actor must perform certain actions and recite his dialogue accordingly. Similarly, roles in groups structure behavior by dictating the "part" that members take as they interact. Once cast in a role such as leader, outcast, or questioner, the group member tends to perform certain actions and interact with other group members in a particular way. But members can, in many cases, negotiate within the group as they move in and out of different roles. Group members who want to influence others may seek the role of leader, and those who wish to maintain a low profile may seek out the follower's role (Callero, 1994).

Just as some variability is permitted in theatrical roles, roles do not structure group members' actions completely. An actor playing the role of Romeo must perform certain behaviors as part of his role; he wouldn't be Shakespeare's Romeo if he didn't fall in love with Juliet. He can, however, recite his lines in an original way, change his stage behaviors, and even ad lib. In social groups, too, people can fulfill the same role in somewhat different ways, and so long as they do not stray too far from the role's basic requirements, the group tolerates this variation. However, like the stage director who replaces an actor who presents an unsatisfactory Romeo, the group can replace members who repeatedly fail to play their part within the group. Indeed, the role often supersedes any particular group member. When the role occupant departs, the role itself remains and is filled by a new member (Hare, 1994; Stryker & Statham, 1985).

Role Differentiation

Sometimes people deliberately create roles. A group may decide to enhance its efficiency by organizing and so elects a chairperson, a secretary, and heads of subcommittees. Someone outside the group, such as the group's supervisor, may create roles within

the group by mandate. But even without a deliberate atter
group structure, the group will probably develop an *informal*
Members may initially consider themselves to be just memb
each other. But in time, roles will emerge as each group memb
specific range of actions and interact with other group members

This **role differentiation** process occurred rapidly among the
groups that face difficult problems or emergencies tend to (
rapidly than groups facing less stressful circumstances (Bales,
leader, doctor, and cleaner emerged first, soon followed by the "i
ated makeshift snowshoes, hammocks, and water-melting devices   ., who
was determined to hike down from the mountain; and "complaii.ei," "pessimist,"
"optimist," and "encourager."

Types of Roles.   What roles tend to emerge as a group becomes organized? Certainly,
the role of leader is a fundamental one in many groups, but other roles should not be
overlooked. Many of these roles, such as "expert," "secretary," and "organizer," are
similar in that they revolve around the task the group is tackling. People who fulfill
these **task roles** focus on the group's goals, its task, and members' attempts to support one another as they work. Marcelo, for example, was a task-oriented leader, for
he organized work squads and controlled the rationing of the group's meager food
supplies, and the rest of the members obeyed his orders. He did not, however, satisfy
the group members' interpersonal and emotional needs. By the ninth day of the ordeal, morale was sagging, and Marcelo began crying silently to himself at night. Yet,
as if to offset Marcelo's inability to cheer up the survivors, several group members
became more positive and friendly, actively trying to reduce conflicts and to keep
morale high. The woman in the group, Liliana Methol, provided a "unique source of
solace" for the young men she cared for, and she came to take the place of their absent mothers and sweethearts. One of the younger boys "called her his god-mother,
and she responded to him and the others with comforting words and gentle optimism" (Read, 1974, p. 74).

Methol filled a **socioemotional role** in the Andes group. A group may need to
accomplish its tasks, but it must also ensure that the interpersonal and emotional
needs of the members are met. Whereas the "coordinator" and "energizer" structure
the group's work, such roles as "supporter," "clown," and even "critic" help satisfy
the emotional needs of the group members.

The tendency for groups to develop both task roles and socioemotional roles is
consistent with Kenneth D. Benne and Paul Sheats's (1948) studies conducted at the
National Training Laboratories (NTL), an organization devoted to the improvement

---

Role differentiation: The development of distinct roles in a group, such as leader, follower, or
complainer.
Task roles: Positions in a group occupied by group members who perform goal-oriented, task-
focused behaviors.
Socioemotional roles: Positions in a group filled by group members who perform supportive,
interpersonally accommodative behaviors.

groups. Benne and Sheats concluded that a group, to survive, must meet two basic demands: The group must accomplish its tasks, and the relationships among members must be maintained. Table 5–1 lists the typical task roles that Benne and Sheats identified, including coordinator, elaborator, energizer, evaluator/critic, information giver, information seeker, and opinion giver. Table 5–1 also lists the socioemotional roles that most frequently emerge in groups, including compromiser, encourager, follower, and harmonizer. The task roles facilitate the group's attainment of its goals, and the socioemotional roles reduce interpersonal strains and stresses within the group. Benne and Sheats also identified a third set of roles: the individualistic roles. Like the malingerers in the Andes groups—several young men who did little work and demanded that others care for them—those who adopt individualistic roles emphasize their own needs over the group's needs.

Why Differentiation? Why do task roles and socioemotional roles emerge in so many different groups? One answer, proposed by Bales and his colleagues, suggests that very few individuals can simultaneously fulfill both the task and socioemotional needs of the group (Bales, 1955, 1958; Parsons et al., 1953). When task specialists try to move groups toward their goals, they must necessarily give orders to others, restrict the behavioral options of others, criticize other members, and prompt them into action. These actions may be necessary to reach the goal, but the group members may react negatively to the task specialists' prodding. Because most of the members believe the task specialist to be the source of the tension, "someone other than the task leader must assume a role aimed at the reduction of interpersonal hostilities and frustrations" (Burke, 1967, p. 380). The peacekeeper who intercedes and tries to maintain harmony is the socioemotional specialist. Task and socioemotional roles, then, are a natural consequence on these two partly conflicting demands.

Bales's research team identified these tendencies by tracking the emergence of task and socioemotional experts in decision-making groups across four sessions. Bales used his Interaction Process Analysis system to identify certain specific types of behavior within the groups. As noted in Chapter 2 (see Table 2–1), half of categories in IPA focus on task-oriented behaviors: either direct attempts to solve specific problems in the group or attempts to exchange information via questioning. The remaining six categories are reserved for positive socioemotional behavior (shows solidarity, tension release, agreement) or negative socioemotional behavior (disagrees, shows tension, shows antagonism). Bales found that individuals rarely performed both task and socioemotional behaviors: Most people gravitated toward either the task role or the socioemotional role. The task specialist (labeled the "idea man") tended to dominate in the problem-solving area by giving more suggestions and opinions and by providing more orientation than the socioemotional specialist (labeled the "best-liked man"). The latter, however, dominated in the interpersonal areas by showing more solidarity, more tension release, and greater agreement with other group members. The task specialist tended to elicit more questions, displays of tension, antagonism, and disagreement, whereas the socioemotional specialist received more demonstrations of solidarity, tension reduction, and solutions to problems. Moreover, this differentiation became more pronounced over time. During the first session, the same person was both the

TABLE 5–1   ROLES IN GROUPS

Role	Function
Task Roles	
Initiator/contributor	Recommends novel ideas about the problem at hand, new ways to approach the problem, or possible solutions not yet considered
Information seeker	Emphasizes getting the facts by calling for background information from others
Opinion seeker	Asks for more qualitative types of data, such as attitudes, values, and feelings
Information giver	Provides data for forming decisions, including facts that derive from expertise
Opinion giver	Provides opinions, values, and feelings
Elaborator	Gives additional information—examples, rephrasings, implications—about points made by others
Coordinator	Shows the relevance of each idea and its relationship to the overall problem
Orienter	Refocuses discussion on the topic whenever necessary
Evaluator/critic	Appraises the quality of the group's methods, logic, and results
Energizer	Stimulates the group to continue working when discussion flags
Procedural technician	Cares for operational details, such as the materials and machinery
Recorder	Takes notes and maintains records
Socioemotional Roles	
Encourager	Rewards others through agreement, warmth, and praise
Harmonizer	Mediates conflicts among group members
Compromiser	Shifts his or her own position on an issue to reduce conflict in the group
Gatekeeper and expediter	Smooths communication by setting up procedures and ensuring equal participation from members
Standard setter	Expresses, or calls for discussion of, standards for evaluating the quality of the group process
Group observer/ commentator	Points out the positive and negative aspects of the group's dynamics and calls for change if necessary
Follower	Accepts the ideas offered by others and serves as an audience for the group
Individual Roles	
Aggressor	Expresses disapproval of acts, ideas, feelings of others; attacks the group
Block	Negativistic; resists the group's influence; opposes group unnecessarily
Dominator	Asserts authority or superiority; manipulative
Evader and self-confessor	Expresses personal interests, feelings, opinions unrelated to group goals
Help seeker	Expresses insecurity, confusion, self-deprecation
Recognition seeker	Calls attention to him- or herself; self-aggrandizing
Playboy/girl	Uninvolved in the group; cynical, nonchalant
Special-interest pleader	Remains apart from the group by acting as a representative of another social group or category

Source: Benne & Sheats, 1948.

task specialist and the socioemotional specialist in 56.5% of the groups. By the fourth session, only 8.5% of the leaders occupied both roles. Indeed, in most cases, individuals dropped their role as task leader to ensconce themselves more securely in the role of socioemotional expert (Bales, 1953, 1958; Bales & Slater, 1955; Slater, 1955).

Not all individuals and not all groups separate the task and socioemotional roles (Turner & Colomy, 1988). Students in classroom groups, for example, when asked to rate their fellow group members on the Benne and Sheats (1948) roles listed in Table 5–1, often attributed task and socioemotional roles to the same individual. Indeed, the correlation between the two roles was .25. Groups with members who filled both roles were also more cohesive and performed more effectively (Mudrack & Farrell, 1995). Differentiation becomes more likely, however, when the group is experiencing conflict about its goals. In one study of such groups, the correlation between task and socioemotional behavior was minus .73 (Burke, 1967).

Role Stress

Some roles in a play are more complicated than others. Romeo appears in many scenes and recites line after line of dialogue, whereas the role of guard is much more limited in scope. Romeo is a lover, devoted son, and friend, but the guards are basically just guards. Variation in the complexity of roles also occurs in groups; members expect the occupants of some roles to perform only one type of behavior, but they expect people in other roles to exhibit a wide range of behaviors. Like the star of a play, those who enact complex roles often enjoy greater status in the group. Yet, complex roles can create considerable stress for the occupants, particularly when the behaviors associated with the role are ambiguously defined or they conflict with one another (Kahn, Wolfe, Quinn, Snoek, & Rosenthal, 1964).

Role Ambiguity.   Because roles often emerge as group members interact with one another over time, the responsibilities and expectations of any particular role are sometimes ill defined. In the Andes group, Marcelo emerged as the task leader, but the group never clearly defined his responsibilities, his rights, or his authority. Even when a group deliberately creates a role, such as executive assistant, technical support staff member, or even supervisor, neither the occupant of the role (the role taker) nor the rest of the group (the role senders) may clearly understand the responsibilities of the new role. In such cases, role takers will likely experience **role ambiguity.** They wonder if they are acting appropriately, they perform behaviors that others in the group should be carrying out, and they question their ability to fulfill their responsibilities. Role ambiguity is indexed by agreement with the following statements (House, Schuler, & Levanoni, 1983, p. 336):

- I don't know what is expected of me.
- I work under unclear policies and guidelines.

Role ambiguity: Unclear expectations about the behaviors to be performed by individuals who occupy particular positions within the group.

- The planned goals and objectives are not clear.
- I don't know how I will be evaluated for a raise or promotion.

Role Conflict.   In some instances, group members may find themselves occupying several roles at the same time, with the requirements of each role making demands on their time and abilities. If the multiple activities required by one role mesh with those required by the other, role takers experience few problems. If, however, the expectations that define the appropriate activities associated with these roles are incompatible, **role conflict** may occur (Brief, Schuler, & Van Sell, 1981; Graen, 1976; Van Sell, Brief, & Schuler, 1981). Role conflict can prompt these kinds of complaints (House et al., 1983, p. 336):

- I work with two or more groups who operate quite differently.
- I often get myself involved in situations with conflicting requirements.
- I'm often asked to do things that are against my better judgment.
- I do things that are likely to be accepted by one person and not by others.
- I receive incompatible requests from two or more people.

Researchers have identified many varieties of role conflict, but two of the more problematic types are interrole conflict and intrarole conflict. **Interrole conflict** occurs when role takers discover that the behaviors associated with one of their roles are incompatible with those associated with another one of their roles. Carline, who has been a member of a small production unit for several years, may experience role conflict when she is promoted to a supervisory position; the behaviors required of her as manager may clash with her role of friend and workmate. Similarly, Mark may find that his student role conflicts with another role he occupies, such as boyfriend, husband, or employee. If the student role requires spending every free moment in the library studying for exams, such roles as companion and friend will be neglected.

Intrarole conflict results from contradictory demands within a single role. A supervisor in a factory, for example, may be held responsible for overseeing the quality of production, training new personnel, and providing feedback or goal-orienting information. At another level, however, supervisors become the supervised, because they take directions from a higher level of management. Thus, the members of the team expect the manager to keep their secrets and support them in any disputes with the management, but the upper echelon expects obedience and loyalty (Katz & Kahn, 1978; Miles, 1976). Role conflict also arises when role takers and role senders have different expectations. The newly appointed supervisor may assume that leadership means giving orders, maintaining strict supervision, and criticizing incompetence. The work group, however, may feel that leadership entails eliciting cooperation in the group, providing support and guidance, and delivering rewards.

Role conflict: Intragroup and intraindividual conflict that results from incompatibility in role relations.
Interrole conflict: Incompatibility between two simultaneously enacted roles.
Intrarole conflict: Incompatibility among the behaviors that make up a single role, often resulting from inconsistent expectations on the part of the person who occupies the role and other members of the group.

Role Conflict and Group Performance.   Researchers have implicated both role ambiguity and role conflict as potential sources of low employee morale and job stress. In one study of accountants and hospital employees, role stress was linked to feelings of tension, decreased job satisfaction, and employee turnover (Kemery, Bedeian, Mossholder, & Touliatos, 1985). Indeed, when the results of dozens of studies of role ambiguity and conflict are synthesized, they suggest that role stress is detrimental to organizational success. The size of the relationship between role conflict and performance varied considerably across studies, but increases in role ambiguity and conflict were usually associated with an increased desire to leave the organization and with decreases in commitment to the organization, involvement, satisfaction, and participation in decision making (Brown, 1996; Fisher & Gitelson, 1983; Jackson & Schuler, 1995; King & King, 1990; Peterson, Smith, Akande, & Ayestaran, 1995).

What can organizations do to help their employees cope with role stress? One solution involves making role requirements explicit; managers should write job descriptions for each role within the organization and provide employees with feedback about the behaviors expected of them. The workplace can also be designed so that potentially incompatible roles are performed in different locations and at different times. In such cases, however, the individual must be careful to engage in behaviors appropriate to the specific role, because slipping into the wrong role at the wrong time can lead to considerable embarrassment (Gross & Stone, 1964). Some companies, too, develop explicit guidelines regarding when one role should be sacrificed so that another can be enacted, or they may prevent employees from occupying positions that can create role conflict (Brief et al., 1981; Sarbin & Allen, 1968; Van Sell et al., 1981).

INTERMEMBER RELATIONS

On the 17th day, an avalanche swept down on the sleeping survivors, filling their makeshift shelter with snow. Marcelo and Liliana Methol were killed, and so soon a new order emerged in the group. Instead of two leaders, three young men stepped forward to take over control of the group. Why these three? They were cousins, and their kinship bonds connected them to one another so securely that they formed the hub of the group's interpersonal relations.

Connections among the members of a group provide the basis for the third component of group structure: intermember relations. The Andes survivors were a group, but they were also many individuals who were connected to one another in different ways. Norms and roles describe the kinds of behaviors that group members perform when they occupy particular positions within the group, but they do not specify the linkages among the individual members. Which one of the three cousins had the most authority? Who in a group is most liked by others, and who is an isolate? How does information flow through a group from one person to the next? The answers depend on the group's intermember relations: patterns of status, attraction, and communication.

Status Hierarchies

The roles that emerged in the Andes group following the crash defined who would lead, explore, and care for the injured. The individuals who took on these roles, however, were not equal in terms of authority in the group. After the avalanche, Fito Strauch was more influential than the other group members; when he gave orders, most of the others obeyed. Also, the group's explorers were afforded more authority than the rank-and-file members. These stable variations in dominance, prestige, and control among the group members reflect the group's **status relations, or authority relations.**

Status patterns are often hierarchical and centralized. In the Andes group, as Figure 5–2 illustrates, Fito Strauch, E. Strauch, and Fernandez formed a coalition that controlled most of the group's activities. This triumvirate was supported by its "lieutenants": a group of three younger men who made certain that the leaders' orders were enforced and who also carried out certain minor duties. Their requests carried less force than those of Fito Strauch, but they still commanded a fair amount of respect.

Below the lieutenants we find a special class of group members called the explorers. These individuals were the fittest and strongest and had been chosen to hike down the mountain in search of help. In preparing for their journey, they were given special privileges, including better sleeping arrangements and more clothing, food,

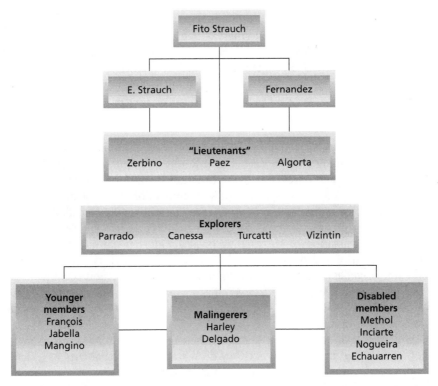

FIGURE 5–2 Did a chain of command exist in the Andes group? After the avalanche, the group developed a hierarchical, centralized authority structure.

Status relations (authority relations): Stable distributions of authority or prestige in the group; the "chain of command" or hierarchy of dominance.

and water. They were not leaders in the usual sense, but they could require lower echelon members to obey their orders. These lower ranking members fell into three clusters. The rank-and-file members included three men who, because of their youth and disposition, were considered childish and unstable. Their authority was equal to that of the four men who had received disabling injuries but somewhat greater than that of the two group members who were considered malingerers.

Figure 5–2 depicts the levels of authority that existed in the group. The power holders at the top of the hierarchy made more decisions, took more responsibility, and served as the foci for communication within the group. Below this top level was a second stratum of members who had less power than the leaders but more prestige than the occupants of lower echelons. As we move down the chain of command, authority diminishes and the number of occupants at each subordinate level increases. Hence, the lines of group authority formed a pyramid pattern like that of formally organized groups such as businesses and military organizations (Dale, 1952).

Status differences in groups violate our expectations of "equal treatment for all," but in the microsociety of the group, equality is the exception and inequality the rule. Initially, group members may start off on an equal footing. But over time, **status differentiation** takes place: Certain individuals acquire the authority to coordinate the activities of the group, providing others with guidance and relaying communications (Bales, 1950; Fisek & Ofshe, 1970). But who rises to the top of the heap and who remains at the bottom? The answer ultimately depends on the individual and the group. First, does the individual group member communicate his or her claim to higher status to the other group members? Second, do the other group members accept or reject this individual's claim to authority?

Claiming Status.   All social animals know how to communicate the message "I am in charge." Dominant chimpanzees chatter loudly at potential rivals, the leader of the wolf pack growls and bares his teeth at low-ranking wolves, and the ranking lioness in the pride swats another with her paw. Members of these social groups compete for status, for the individual at the top of the hierarchy—the so-called alpha male or female—enjoys greater access to the group's resources. These high-ranking members maintain their position by threatening or attacking low-ranking members, who in turn manage to avoid these attacks by performing behaviors that signal deference and submissiveness. This system of dominance and submission is called a "pecking order" because (at least in chickens) it determines who will do the pecking and who will be pecked. Sociobiologists argue that pecking orders limit conflict in groups and increase individual and group survival (Mazur, 1973; Wilson, 1975).

Humans, too, compete for status in their groups. Humans rarely snarl at one another to signal their status, but they do use such nonverbal cues as a firm handshake, an unwavering gaze, a relaxed but poised posture, or an unsmiling countenance to let others know that they should be respected (Leffler, Gillespie, & Conaty, 1982). In the boardroom, for example, a dark suit, an expensive watch, and a con-

---

Status differentiation: The development of authority relations within groups.

servative hairstyle connote power, but in a small group of friends, a more casual look may be more appropriate. Large, sweeping gestures using the hands and head, a relaxed but poised posture, an attentive (but unsmiling) expression, a direct gaze, and a firm handshake or touch are all actions that lay a claim to status. People also seek status by speaking clearly and loudly, whereas those who speak softly and pepper their comments with nervous giggles are afforded less authority (Berry & McArthur, 1986; Damhorst, 1990; Lee & Ofshe, 1981; Mazur, 1983; Mazur et al., 1980; Ofshe & Lee, 1981; Patterson, 1991).

People also use verbal communications to signal their status and authority. People who want others to respect them often initiate conversations and shift the discussion to their own areas of competence (Godfrey, Jones, & Lord, 1986). A person seeking high status would be more likely to (1) tell other people what they should do, (2) interpret other people's statements, (3) confirm or dispute other people's viewpoints, and (4) summarize or reflect on the discussion (Stiles, Orth, Scherwitz, Hennrikus, & Vallbona, 1984; Stiles et al., 1997). In a study group, for example, a high-status member may say, "I've studied this theory before," "I know this stuff backward and forward," or "I think it's more important to study the lecture notes than the text." A low-status individual, in contrast, may lament that "I always have trouble with this subject" or "I'm not sure I understand the material." Status seekers also use strong rather than weak tactics when they try to influence others (Kipnis, 1984), and they talk the most when they are in groups (Cappella, 1985; Dovidio, Brown, Heltman, Ellyson, & Keating, 1988).

Perceiving Status.   Individuals' status-seeking efforts will be for naught if the group rejects their claims. In the Andes group, one young man, to attain the high-status role of explorer, tried to impress others by undertaking risky physical adventures. The other group members, however, wanted explorers to be cautious rather than risk takers, and so they selected someone else for the role. He displayed characteristics and actions that he felt would earn him status, but because these claims did not match group members' intuitive beliefs about who deserves status, his bid for authority failed.

Expectation-states theory, developed by Joseph Berger and his colleagues, provides a detailed analysis of the impact of group members' expectations on the status-organizing process. As noted briefly in Chapter 2, this theory assumes that status differences are most likely to develop when members are working collectively on a task that they feel is important. Because the group hopes that it can successfully complete the project, group members intuitively take note of one another's *status characteristics*—personal qualities that they think are indicative of ability or prestige. Those who possess numerous status characteristics are implicitly identified and then permitted to perform more numerous and varied group actions, to provide greater input and guidance for the group, to influence others by evaluating their ideas, and to reject the influence attempts of others. (The basic propositions of the theory are discussed in Berger, Cohen, & Zelditch, 1972; Berger, Conner, & Fisek, 1974; Berger, Fisek, Norman, & Zelditch, 1977; Berger, Webster, Ridgeway, & Rosenholtz, 1986; Fisek, Berger, & Norman, 1995; Humphreys & Berger, 1981; Ridgeway, Berger, & Smith, 1985; Ridgeway & Walker, 1995; and Wagner & Berger, 1993.)

Expectation-states theorists believe that we generally take two types of cues into consideration when formulating expectations about ourselves and other group members. **Specific-status characteristics** are qualities that attest to each individual's level of ability at the task to be performed in the given situation. On a basketball team, for example, height may be a specific-status characteristic, whereas prior jury duty may determine status in a jury (Strodtbeck & Lipinski, 1985). In the Andes group, the higher-status explorers were chosen on the basis of several specific-status qualities: strength, determination, health, and maturity.

We also notice **diffuse-status characteristics:** general qualities of the person that the members think are relevant to ability and evaluation. Sex, age, wealth, ethnicity, status in other groups, or cultural background can serve as diffuse-status characteristics if people associate these qualities with certain skills, as did the members of the Andes group. Among the survivors, age was considered an important diffuse-status characteristic, with youth being negatively valued.

Researchers have largely confirmed expectations-states theory's prediction that individuals with positively evaluated specific-status and diffuse-status characteristics usually command more authority than those who lack status-linked qualities (Berger & Zelditch, 1985; Ridgeway & Walker, 1995; Wagner & Berger, 1993; Wilke, 1996). In police teams, officers with more work experience exercised more authority than less experienced partners (Gerber, 1996). Members of dyads working on a perceptual task deferred to their partner if he or she seemed more skilled at the task (Foddy & Smithson, 1996). People who are paid more are permitted to exert more influence over people who are paid less (Harrod, 1980; Stewart & Moore, 1992). When air force bomber crews work on nonmilitary tasks, higher ranking members are more influential (Torrance, 1954). Juries allocate more status to jurors who have served on juries previously or who have more prestigious occupations (Strodtbeck, James & Hawkins, 1957). The bulk of the research also confirms the following causal sequence in status allocation: (a) group member X displays specific- and diffuse-status characteristics, (b) group members form higher expectations about X's capabilities, and (c) group members allow X to influence them (Driskell & Mullen, 1990).

Incongruencies in Status Allocations.   Individuals who deserve status are not always afforded status by their groups (Schneider & Cook, 1995). Imagine, for example, a jury that includes these three individuals:

- Dr. Prof, a 40-year-old White woman who teaches in the School of Business and who has written several books on management.
- Mr. Black, a 35-year-old African American executive with outstanding credentials and long experience in a leadership position.
- Dr. White, a 58-year-old male physician who has an active general practice.

Specific-status characteristics: Specific behavioral and interpersonal characteristics that group members take as evidence of one's ability at the task to be performed in the given situation.
Diffuse-status characteristics: General qualities, such as sex and age, that group members use to allocate status in groups.

Considerable evidence suggests that a jury of middle-class White Americans, when selecting a foreman, would be biased against Dr. Prof and Mr. Black and biased in favor of Dr. White. Dr. Prof and Mr. Black, despite their specific-status credentials, may be disqualified from positions of status in the group by their diffuse- (and completely irrelevant) status characteristics. In contrast, Dr. White poses little incongruency for the group if the group members unfairly consider advanced age, white skin, and an M.D. degree to be positive features. This phenomenon is known as **status generalization:** Group members let general-status (diffuse-status) characteristics influence their expectations even though these characteristics are irrelevant in the given situation (Molm, 1986; Ridgeway & Balkwell, 1997).

Status generalization explains why women and African Americans are given less status and authority in groups than are Anglo Americans and men. Despite growing changes in sexist and racist attitudes in society, stereotypical biases still make gaining status in small groups a difficult task for women, African Americans, and other minorities (Nielsen, 1990). Women and African Americans report more dissatisfaction about how status is allocated in groups (Cohen, 1982; Crosbie, 1979; Hembroff, 1982; McCranie & Kimberly, 1973). Women and minorities must also put extra effort into their activities and reach higher performance standards just to remain on a par with the advantaged White men (Foschi, 1996; Pugh & Wahrman, 1983). Group performance, although often improved when groups become diverse, will suffer if the group overlooks the valuable contributions offered by members who are competent but not considered worthy of high status (Galen, 1994; Jackson, 1992; Kirchler & Davis, 1986).

These negative effects often fade over time as group members gain experience working together. Groups that initially allocate status unfairly revise their hierarchies as they recognize the skills and abilities of previously slighted members (Watson, Kumar, & Michaelsen, 1993). Given enough time, women and minorities find that they no longer need to continually prove themselves to the others (Hembroff & Myers, 1984; Markovsky, Smith, & Berger, 1984). Women and minorities who communicate their involvement in the group to the other members also tend to gain status more rapidly, as do those who act in a group-oriented manner rather than a self-oriented way (Freeze & Cohen, 1973; Martin & Sell, 1985; Pugh & Wahrman, 1983; Ridgeway, 1982). In one study, men and women deliberately adopted either a cooperative, friendly interaction style or an emotionally distant, self-absorbed style. The men, when they joined otherwise all-women groups, achieved high status no matter what style they exhibited. Women in otherwise all-male groups achieved high status only if they displayed a group-oriented motivation. External authorities can also undo unfair status generalizations by explicitly stressing the qualifications of women and minorities or by training group members to recognize their biases (Lundy, 1992; Ridgeway, 1989).

Status generalization: The tendency for irrelevant, diffuse-status characteristics to influence the status hierarchy in the group.

Social Standing

Some of the 19 Andes survivors rose to positions of authority, while others remained relatively powerless. Yet, to describe the group in just these terms would be to miss a vital part of the social structure. The individuals were not just leaders and followers, powerful and powerless; they were also friends and enemies.

Jacob Moreno, the developer of sociometry, maintains that the tendency to react to one another on a spontaneous, affective level imparts a unique quality to human groups. Our relationships with other group members take on many different shades—hate, condemnation, liking, friendship, love, and so on—but only rarely do we react neutrally to one another. Taken together, these relationships make up the group's **attraction relations**, or **sociometric structure** (Moreno, 1960).

Sociometric Differentiation. The sociometric structure of the Andes survivors changed gradually during the long ordeal. Figure 5–3 partially summarizes the results of this **sociometric differentiation** process by focusing on the relationship between the rank-and-file group members and the four explorers, Turcatti, Parrado, Vizintin, and Canessa. Nearly everyone admired Turcatti and Parrado; their warmth, optimism, and physical strength buoyed the sagging spirits of the others. Vizintin and Canessa, in contrast, "did not inspire the same affection" (Read, 1974, p. 141). They liked each other but had few other friends within the group. Mangino, one of the younger men, was an exception; he liked them both. Most of the others, however, quarreled with them constantly.

Attraction patterns like those in the Andes group are not a disorganized jumble of likes and dislikes but a network of stable social relationships (Doreian, 1986). Just as members of the group can be ranked from low to high in terms of status, so, too, can the members be ordered from least liked to most liked (Maassen, Akkermans, & van der Linden, 1996). *Popular* individuals (stars) receive the most positive sociometric nominations within the group; *rejected* group members (outcasts) get picked the most when group members identify whom they dislike; *neglected* group members (isolates) receive few nominations of any kind; and the *average* members are liked by several others in the group (Coie, Dodge, & Kupersmidt, 1990; Newcomb, Bukowski, & Pattee, 1993). In the Andes group, for example, Parrado was admired by all; he was, sociometrically, the star of the group. Delgado, in contrast, was the group's outcast; he had no friends in the group, and the young men ridiculed him constantly for not doing his share of the work.

Like sociometric relations in most groups, the Andes survivors' sociometric structure tended toward *reciprocity* and *transitivity*. Vizintin, for example, liked Canessa, and Canessa liked Vizintin in return. Such reciprocity of both liking and disliking is a powerful tendency in most settings; it has been documented repeatedly in a variety of groups, including football teams, police squads, psychotherapy groups, and classroom groups (Kandel, 1978; Newcomb, 1979; Segal, 1979; Wright, Ingraham, & Blackmer, 1984). Exceptions to reciprocity sometimes occur, and some forms of attraction tend to

---

Attraction relations (sociometric structure): Patterns of liking and disliking in a group.
Sociometric differentiation: The development of patterns of liking and disliking in a group.

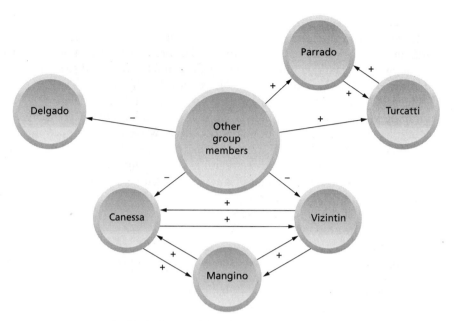

FIGURE 5-3 Who liked whom in the Andes group? Lines marked with a plus sign indicate liking, lines marked with a minus sign indicate disliking, and arrows indicate the direction of the effect.

be less reciprocal than other forms of attraction, but these exceptions to the reciprocity principle are relatively rare (Segal, 1979). The Andes group also showed signs of network transitivity: Canessa liked Mangino, Mangino liked Vizintin, and in confirmation of transitivity, Canessa liked Vizintin (A → B, B → C, so A → C).

Clusters, or *cliques,* also existed in the Andes group, for Vizintin, Canessa, and Mangino formed a unified coalition within the larger group. Others rarely hesitated to show their disdain for the members of this subgroup, but these three were joined by strong bonds of attraction. In many cases, subgroups display *homophily:* Members are more similar to one another than they are to the members of the total group. Members of the same racial category, for example, may join to form a coalition, or the group may separate naturally into all-male and all-female cliques (Hallinan, 1981; Schofield & Whitley, 1983; Thorne, 1993). Group members also often deliberately form and manipulate cliques within larger groups by systematically including some individuals and excluding others (Adler & Adler, 1995).

Maintaining Structural Balance. Why do most groups tend toward reciprocity, transitivity, and homophily? Fritz Heider's **balance theory** offers a possible answer.

Balance theory: A theoretical framework advanced by Heider that assumes that interpersonal relationships can be either balanced (integrated units with elements that fit together without stress) or unbalanced (inconsistent units with elements that conflict with one another). Heider believed that unbalanced relationships create an unpleasant tension that must be relieved by changing some element of the system.

According to Heider, attraction relations in groups are balanced when they fit together to form a coherent, unified whole. A dyad, for example, is balanced only if liking (or disliking) is mutual. If Vizintin liked Canessa but Canessa disliked Vizintin, the dyad would be unbalanced, and the result would be structural strain (Cartwright & Harary, 1956, 1970; Heider, 1958; Newcomb, 1963).

The sociometric structures of larger groups also tend to be balanced. The triad containing Vizintin, Canessa, and Mangino, for example, is balanced because everyone in it likes one another; all bonds are positive. What would happen, however, if Mangino came to dislike Canessa? According to Heider, this group would be unbalanced, since the product of the three relationships (Vizintin likes Canessa, Mangino likes Vizintin, and Mangino dislikes Canessa) is negative. In general, a group is balanced if (1) all the relationships are positive or (2) an even number of negative relationships occur in the group. Conversely, groups are unbalanced if they contain an odd number of negative relations.

Because unbalanced sociometric structures generate tension among group members, people are motivated to correct the imbalance and restore the group's equilibrium. Heider notes, however, that this restoration of balance can be achieved through either psychological changes in the individual members or interpersonal changes in the group. If Mangino initially likes only Vizintin and not Canessa, he may change his attitude toward Canessa when he recognizes the strong bond between Vizintin and Canessa. Alternatively, group members who are disliked by the other group members may be ostracized, as in the case of Delgado (Taylor, 1970). Lastly, because the occurrence of a single negative relationship within a group can cause the entire group to become unbalanced, large groups tend to include a number of smaller, better balanced cliques (Newcomb, 1981). The Andes group, for example, was somewhat unbalanced overall, but subgroups tended to be very harmonious (Cartwright & Harary, 1956, 1970; Mayer, 1975). As a result, the group was high in cohesiveness.

Determinants of Social Standing.   Why did Parrado gain social standing in the group, and why was Delgado held in disregard? One's popularity, in large part, is determined by the interpersonal factors reviewed in Chapter 4: Similarity, complementarity, reciprocity, personality qualities, and even physical attractiveness can influence one's sociometric ranking in a group. Parrado was similar to the others in age and background, and he possessed qualities that the others admired: He was optimistic, handsome, dependable, helpful, and strong. Delgado, unfortunately, did not possess such attributes. Interaction with Delgado incurred considerable costs and yielded very few interpersonal rewards (Thibaut & Kelley, 1959).

In another group, Delgado might have been well liked, for he was quite articulate and socially skilled. In the Andes group, however, the fit between his personal qualities and the group was poor. As Lewin's concept of interactionism emphasizes, popularity cannot be predicted solely on the basis of the group members' personal qualities. Different groups value different attributes; the qualities that earn a person popularity in a boardroom differ from those that predict sociometric standing on a baseball team or in a biker gang. Thus, predictions of social standing must take into account the person-group fit—the degree to which individuals' attributes match the qualities valued by the groups to which they belong.

The impact of person-group fit on social standing has been studied extensively in children's groups (Boivin, Dodge, & Coie, 1995; Wright, Giammarion, & Parad, 1986). Researchers in one study used sociometric methods to identify popular, rejected, neglected, and average boys in elementary school classes. They also had trained observers rate each boy's behavior during several free-play periods, looking for evidence of aggressiveness, cooperation, and withdrawal. Supporting a "social misfit" hypothesis, the investigators found that in nonaggressive groups and socially active groups, the rejected boys engaged in the most aggressive behaviors or they too frequently played by themselves. It is interesting to note, however, that the popular boys in groups characterized by relatively high levels of hostility, fighting, and verbal abuse were not more aggressive in general, but they did display more emotional hostility when provoked by others. These results suggest that popularity in one group does not guarantee popularity in another group; a sociometric star in one group can become an outcast misfit in another.

Communication Networks

In the Andes group, the three leaders stayed in close communication, discussing any problems among themselves before relaying their interpretations to the other group members. The other members usually routed all information to the threesome, who then informed the rest of the group. In contrast, the injured members were virtually cut off from communication with the others during the day, and they occasionally complained that they were the last to know of any significant developments.

Regular patterns of information exchange among members of a group are called **communication networks.** Like other structural features of groups, communication networks are sometimes deliberately set in place when the group is organized. Many companies, for example, adopt a hierarchical communication network that prescribes how information is passed up to superiors, down to subordinates, and horizontally to one's equals. Even when no formal attempt is made to organize communication, an informal communication network will usually take shape over time. Moreover, this network tends to parallel status and attraction patterns. Take the Andes group as a case in point. Individuals who occupied high-status roles—the explorers, the food preparers, and the lieutenants—communicated at much higher rates and with more individuals than individuals who occupied the malingerer and injured roles (Aiken & Hage, 1968; Bacharach & Aiken, 1979; Jablin, 1979; Shaw, 1964).

Centralization and Performance.   Researchers at the Group Networks Laboratory at the Massachusetts Institute of Technology conducted some of the first studies of communication networks in the 1950s. Harold J. Leavitt (1951), for example, created different types of networks by seating men at a circular table but separating them by means of a partition. He then gave each person a card bearing five of the following symbols: ○ ▲ ☆ ❏ + ♦. Subjects were to identify the one symbol out of the six that was common to all the group members' cards.

Communication networks: Patterns of communication in a group that describe who speaks most frequently to whom (e.g., wheel, circle, or chain).

Subjects could easily solve the problem by comparing all the cards, but Leavitt restricted the flow of communication. He would open particular slots in the partitions separating the participants to create four types of networks: the wheel, the chain, the Y, and the circle (see Figure 5–4). In the wheel network, one person in the group communicated with everyone, but the others communicated only with the individual located at the hub position. People in a chain passed along information sequentially. In the Y, only one member could contact more than one other person. And in the circle, all members could interact with two other persons. Leavitt found that in all but the circle, group members tended to send information to the more central member, who integrated the data and sent back a solution. This summarizing of

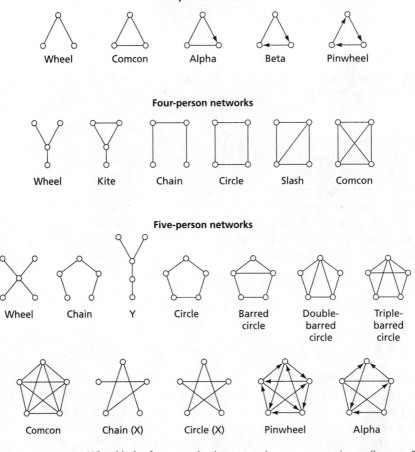

FIGURE 5–4   What kinds of communication networks are common in small groups? Researchers have studied the impact of various forms of networks by systematically opening and closing connections among individuals in small groups. Arrows indicate direction of communication, and lines without arrows are bidirectional. The X designation in the five-person groups indicates that members can communicate only with people seated across from them.

(*Source:* Shaw, 1964.)

the data was most easily accomplished in the wheel, as all members could interact directly with the central member, whereas in the Y and chain, the pooling process took longer (Bavelas, 1948, 1950; Bavelas & Barrett, 1951; Leavitt, 1951).

Leavitt's study, and subsequent research as well, has shown again and again that one of the most important features of a network is its degree of centralization (Shaw, 1964, 1978). With centralized networks, one of the positions is located at the "crossroads" of communications, as in the wheel and Y of Figure 5–4. As Leavitt's findings suggested, groups with this type of structure tend to use the hub position as the data-processing center, and its occupant typically collects information, synthesizes it, and then sends it back to others. In decentralized structures, like the circle or comcon (a network in which all individuals can communicate with one another), the number of channels at each position is roughly equal, so no one position is more central than another. These groups tend to use a variety of organizational structures when solving their problems, including the so-called each-to-all pattern, in which everyone sends messages in all directions until someone gets the correct answer. Centralization can also be more precisely indexed by considering the relative number of links joining the positions in the network (Bavelas, 1948, 1950; Freeman, 1977; Grofman & Own, 1982; Moxley & Moxley, 1974).

The early MIT studies suggested that a centralized network was more efficient than a decentralized network. Leavitt, for example, found that individual and group error rates were lower in the centralized Y and wheel than in the more decentralized chain and circle. Other studies tended to support this conclusion, as centralized groups outscored decentralized groups in time taken to find a solution, number of messages sent, finding and correcting errors, and improvement with practice (Shaw, 1964, 1978). The only exceptions occurred when the simple tasks like that used by Leavitt were replaced with more complicated ones: arithmetic, sentence construction, problem solving, and discussion. When the task was more complex, the decentralized networks outperformed the centralized ones.

These contradictory results led Marvin E. Shaw to propose that network efficiency is related to information saturation. When a group is working on a problem, exchanging information, and making a decision, the central position in the network can best manage the inputs and interactions of the group. As work progresses and the number of communications being routed through the central member increases, however, a saturation point can be reached at which the individual can no longer efficiently monitor, collate, or route incoming and outgoing messages. Shaw notes that saturation can occur in a decentralized network, but it becomes more likely when a group with a centralized structure is working on complex problems. Because the "greater the saturation the less efficient the group's performance" (Shaw, 1964, p. 126), Shaw predicts that when the task is simple, centralized networks are more efficient than decentralized networks; when the task is complex, decentralized networks are superior.

Positional Effects.   In the Andes group, the malingerers, the younger men, and the injured often complained about the food, their living conditions, and their leadership. Their morale was low, but the rest of the group hardly noticed because they so rarely communicated with them directly. These peripheral members' reactions are typical of people who find themselves in the outlying positions in centralized communication networks. In such networks, most of the group's actions are controlled by whoever is in the central position, and that person can arbitrarily open and close channels of communication. Whereas central-position occupants typically report that they are very much satisfied with the group structure, the more peripheral members emphasize their dissatisfaction. Indeed, the more removed the position is from the center of the network, the less satisfied is the occupant (Eisenberg, Monge, & Miller, 1983; Krackhardt & Porter, 1986; Lovaglia & Houser, 1996). Shaw (1964) notes that since the number of peripheral positions in a centralized network exceeds the number of central positions, the overall level of satisfaction in a centralized group is lower than the level of satisfaction in a decentralized group.

Position is linked not only to satisfaction and enjoyment but also to role allocation. In Leavitt's study, for example, participants completed a questionnaire at the close of the session that included the item "Did your group have a leader? If so, who?" The responses to this query concerning leadership indicated that the individual in the most central position of the network was chosen to be the leader by 100% of the group members in the wheel, by 85% of the group members in the Y, and by 67% of the group members in the chain. In contrast, leadership choices in the egalitarian circle were approximately equally divided across all the different positions (Freeman, 1979).

Communication in Hierarchical Networks.   For reasons of efficiency and control, many organizations adopt hierarchical communication networks (Goetsch & McFarland, 1980). In such networks, information can pass either horizontally, among members on the same rung of the communication ladder, or vertically, up and down from followers to leaders and back (Jablin, 1979). Evidence indicates that upward communications are strikingly different from downward communications (Browning, 1978; Sias & Jablin, 1995). What type of information passes downward from superior to subordinate? Explanations of actions to be taken, the reasons for actions, suggestions to act in a certain manner, and feedback concerning performance are examples. Upward communications from subordinates to superiors, in contrast, include information on performance, insinuations about a peer's performance, requests for information, expressions of distrust, factual information, or grievances concerning the group's policies. These upward communications, moreover, tend to be fewer in number, briefer, and more guarded than downward communications. Indeed, in larger organizations, the upward flow of information may be much impeded by the mechanics of the transferral process and by the low-status members' reluctance to send information that might reflect unfavorably on their performance, abilities, and skills (Bradley, 1978; Browning, 1978; Manis, Cornell, & Moore, 1974). The reticence of low-status members means that good news travels quickly up the hierarchy, whereas the top of the ladder will be the last to learn bad news (see Jablin, 1979, 1982, for a detailed review of communication in hierarchical organizations).

The Ties That Bind

On December 21, 1972, the radio announcer told Uruguay and the world the news: Two of the passengers from the missing airplane, Fernando Parrado and Roberto Canessa, had been found in a place called Los Maitenes on the River Azufre. The two explorers had hiked for 10 days until, running low on food and supplies, they had stumbled into a farmer tending his cattle. Parrado himself guided the rescue helicopters back to the crash site, and by Christmas Day the men were back in civilization. All of them, when asked how they survived, credited the group: "the unity of the sixteen" is what saved them (Read, 1974, p. 310). And when they read the book that described their ordeal on the mountainside, they complained of only one inaccuracy. They felt that author Piers Paul Read failed to capture the "faith and friendship which inspired them" for 70 days.

SUMMARY

What are norms, and how do they *structure* interactions in groups?

1. *Norms* set the standards for group behavior.
   - *Descriptive norms* define what most people do, feel, or think in the group.
   - *Injunctive norms* differentiate between desirable and undesirable actions.
2. Sherif's work showed that norms are consensual standards that develop over time as members personally accept the group's standards and transmit them to others.

What are roles? Which roles occur most frequently in groups? *Roles* specify the types of behaviors expected of individuals who occupy particular positions within the group.

1. Roles develop as group members interact with one another (*role differentiation*), but most fall under one of two categories: *task roles* and *socioemotional roles*.
2. The same person rarely holds both the task role and the socioemotional role in the group.
3. *Role ambiguity* occurs when the behaviors associated with a role are poorly defined, whereas *role conflict* occurs when group members occupy two or

more roles that call for incompatible behaviors (*interrole conflict*) or when the demands of a single role are contradictory (*intrarole conflict*).

How and why do status hierarchies develop in groups? Most groups develop a stable pattern of variations in *status relations* (or *authority relations*) through a *status differentiation* process.

1. In some instances, people compete with one another for status in groups. Individuals who speak rapidly without hesitating, advise others what to do, and confirm others' statements are often more influential than individuals who display cues that signal submissiveness.
2. Group members' perceptions of one another also determine status. *Expectation-states theory* argues that group members allocate status by considering
   - *specific-status characteristics:* skills and aptitudes that will facilitate the group's performance in a given context
   - *diffuse-status characteristics:* general personal qualities that the group members think indicate ability or prestige
3. When *status generalization* occurs, group members unfairly allow irrelevant characteristics such as race, age, or ethnic background to influence the allocation of prestige.

What factors influence the group's sociometric structure? A group's *attraction relations* (*sociometric structure*) develop through a *sociometric differentiation* process that orders group members from least liked to most liked.

1. Attraction relations tend to be reciprocal and transitive, and clusters or coalitions often exist within the group that are higher in homophily than the group as a whole.

2. As Heider's *balance theory* suggests, sociometric structures also tend to be balanced: They fit together to form a coherent, unified whole.

3. Sociometric differentiation generally favors individuals who possess socially attractive qualities, such as cooperativeness or physical appeal, but social standing also depends on the degree to which the individual's attributes match the qualities valued by the group (person-group fit).

What are the interpersonal consequences of communication networks in groups? A group's *communication network* may parallel formally established paths, but most groups also have an informal network that defines who speaks to whom most frequently.

1. A group's network, in addition to structuring communication, influences a variety of group and individual outcomes, including performance, effectiveness, and members' level of satisfaction.

2. Centralized networks are most efficient for simple tasks. Peripheral members are often dissatisfied in such networks.

3. More information generally flows downward in hierarchical networks than flows upward, and the information that is sent upward is often unrealistically positive.

FOR MORE INFORMATION

Alive, by Piers Paul Read (1974), is the best-selling account of the young men who crashed in the Andes and survived by creating a potent group.

"Conceptualizing Structure in Social Psychology," a special issue of *Social Psychology Quarterly* edited by Cecilia L. Ridgeway (1994), offers advanced theoretical and empirical analyses of social structure and its impact on individuals.

"The Construction of Social Norms and Standards," by Dale T. Miller and Deborah A. Prentice (1996), examines the nature of social norms, with particular emphasis on their impact on perceptions and social judgments.

"Dynamics of Inclusion and Exclusion in Preadolescent Cliques," by Patricia A. Adler and Peter Adler (1995), is a fascinating qualitative study of how children deliberately create small groups by selectively including and excluding classmates.

"Role Conflict and Role Ambiguity: A Critical Assessment of Construct Validity," by Lynda A. King and Daniel W. King (1990), summarizes past research dealing with role stress and offers a compelling assessment of the validity of such concepts as role conflict and role ambiguity.

Status, Rewards, and Influence, edited by Joseph Berger and Morris Zelditch, Jr. (1985), is a vast compendium of in-depth analyses of various aspects of status structures in groups.

ACTIVITY 5–1: **WHAT IS GROUP STRUCTURE?**

Take a moment to reflect on the structure of a group to which you belong. This group can be one that meets regularly in a work or social setting, or it can be a subgroup of the students within a class. (You can even consider your family's structure!) Describe the group's structure in terms of roles, norms, and intermember relations.

1. List the members of your group by first name.
2. Describe each person's behavior with three or more adjectives and a role label such as leader, follower, Mr. Friendly, deviate, joker, silent member, conformist, high talker, or brains.
3. List some of the norms that exist in your group. Are any of these norms relatively unique or unusual? Does anyone violate any norms and need censuring by the group?
4. Draw a diagram of the authority relations in the group, placing the leader at the top, followed by those next in status, and so on.
5. Draw a sociogram (see Chapter 2, pp. 37–38) of your group that reflects patterns of attraction. Use your best judgment to determine who likes and dislikes whom.
6. Graph the communication network in your group. How efficient is the organization? How can it be changed to be more effective?

ACTIVITY 5–2: **WHAT IS SOCIOMETRY?**

Group dynamicist Jacob L. Moreno found that he could reduce the amount of conflict in groups if he grouped together people who liked one another. He developed sociometry to help him accurately measure social relationships.

1. Find a group of people who are willing to answer a few questions about the group. Once they agree to help you, ask each member three questions: Whom do you respect the most? Whom do you like the most? Whom do you communicate with the most?
2. Summarize these choices by drawing a sociogram. Draw circles to represent each group member, then use lines capped with arrows to indicate respect, liking, and communication. If the group is large, you may need to draw three separate graphs, one for each type of relationship.
3. Redraw the diagram, putting people who are frequently chosen in the center and those who are not at the periphery. You may need to try several arrangements to find one that gives you a clear diagram of the group.
4. In several sentences, draw some conclusions about the group based on the sociogram. Identify
   • stars: highly popular members
   • isolates: infrequently chosen individuals
   • pairs: reciprocal partners
   • clusters: subgroups or cliques

6

Cohesion and Development

Groups, like all living things, develop over time. The group may begin as a collection of strangers, but before long, uncertainty gives way to conflict, which in turn gives way to cohesion as members become bound to their group by strong social bonds.

- What is group cohesion?
- What stages do groups typically pass through as they develop over time?
- What are the positive and negative consequences of cohesion?
- Does team building enhance group productivity?

CONTENTS

Disney Studios: The Team that Walt Built

THE NATURE OF GROUP COHESION

What Is Group Cohesion?

Measuring Group Cohesion

DEVELOPING GROUP COHESION

Stages of Group Development

Cycles of Group Development

CONSEQUENCES OF COHESION

Member Satisfaction and Adjustment

Group Dynamics and Influence

Group Performance

APPLICATION: WORK TEAMS

What Is a Work Team?

Team Building

Are Teams Effective?

SUMMARY

FOR MORE INFORMATION

ACTIVITIES

Disney Studios: The Team that Walt Built

Walt Disney probably came up with the idea sitting in a darkened theater in Paris. Parisians so loved his cartoons that theaters showed dozens of Mickey Mouse's adventures back-to-back with no feature film. Disney, watching the audience's delight, envisioned a full-length animated film. On the way back to his California studio, he decided he would base the movie on a fairy tale about a princess named Snow White.

Disney spent four years making the movie. Along the way, he also created an extraordinary group at Disney Studios. He began with a core of animators who were the best in the field. Many of them prided themselves on their own accomplishments, but Disney demanded collaboration; they worked, not as lone individuals, but in teams. Disney met regularly with small groups of artists, animators, writers, and musicians as they developed the story line for the movie, wrote the dialogue and music, and turned 250,000 drawings into a finished product. Conflicts often erupted at Disney Studios as the company ran short of assets, but the teams became incredibly cohesive. They proved wrong the Hollywood skeptics who called their project "Walt's Folly." When *Snow White* was released in 1937, it was hailed as a major achievement in filmmaking.

Groups like Disney Studios are both mysterious and alluring. They are mysterious because their unity often develops unexpectedly and without an obvious source. In some cases, individuals who seem well matched never jell into a team; yet, in other groups, the unlikeliest of allies become so interlocked that they seem to fit together like pieces of a jigsaw puzzle. Do they owe their cohesiveness to some kind of unseen social "chemistry" that transforms the members into a team, leaving us to wonder why so many of the groups we belong to lack this mysterious unity? Cohesive groups are also alluring, for they seem to offer their members advantages that no humdrum, uninvolving group can.

This chapter offers some insight into the mystery of **group cohesion.** Although the idea of cohesion is appealing, we must remain skeptical of the scientific worth of the concept until we can answer some basic questions: How can cohesion be defined? Can it be measured? What are the personal and interpersonal consequences of cohesiveness? And as we demystify group cohesion by specifying its nature, causes, and consequences, we must also reconsider the allure of such groups. Are cohesive groups always better than ones that are not cohesive? Do cohesive groups impose costs on their members as well as providing them with valued rewards? Should we strive to transform all our groups into cohesive teams?

Group cohesion: The strength of the bonds linking group members to the group, the unity (or we-ness) of a group, feelings of attraction for specific group members and the group itself, and the degree to which the group members coordinate their efforts to achieve goals.

THE NATURE OF GROUP COHESION

The Disney group had many noteworthy qualities. Members were extremely motivated, their leader pursued excellence doggedly, and the group managed to overcome incredible obstacles to achieve its goal. But perhaps its most unique feature was its cohesiveness. Although some groups achieve only the barest traces of solidarity, the Disney group became so cohesive that it seemed to function as a single whole. But what does it mean to say that a group is cohesive?

What Is Group Cohesion?

Intuitively, we know the difference between cohesive groups and groups that are not cohesive. Cohesive groups are unified. An esprit de corps permeates the group and morale is high. Members enjoy interacting with one another, and they remain in the group for prolonged periods of time. But what about the group where all the members like one another—they are close friends—but they have no commitment to the group as a whole? Or the case where members no longer feel emotionally connected to one another but still feel a strong sense of commitment to their group? Are these groups cohesive, too? It all depends on how you define it (Dion, 1990; Dion & Evans, 1992; Hogg, 1993; Keyton, 1992; Mudrack, 1989).

Cohesion Is a Binding Force. Most scholars trace the concept of cohesion back to the theoretical efforts of Kurt Lewin, Leon Festinger, and their colleagues at the Research Center for Group Dynamics, originally located at the Massachusetts Institute of Technology (MIT) but later moved to the Institute for Social Research at the University of Michigan (Hogg, 1992; Zander, 1979b). Lewin, as early as 1943, used the term *cohesion* to describe the forces that keep groups intact by pushing members together and countering forces that push them apart. Festinger and his colleagues, in their studies of groups that spring up spontaneously in housing complexes, formally defined cohesion as "the total field of forces which act on members to remain in the group" (Festinger, Schachter, & Back, 1950, p. 164).

This conceptualization draws on the concept of cohesion in physics, where it is defined as the strength of the molecular attraction that holds particles of matter together. Applied to groups, then, cohesion is the strength of the bonds linking individual members to one another and to their group as a whole. People in cohesive groups "stick together," whereas the members of groups that lack cohesion drift away from one another. Indeed, all groups must be somewhat cohesive to exist. If the ties that bind members to the group never form, then the group will exist only momentarily and may be more accurately labeled an "aggregate of individuals" rather than a "group" (Carron, 1982; Donnelly, Carron, & Chelladurai, 1978).

Cohesion Is Group Unity. The people who worked on *Snow White* felt as if they were members of the best animation studio in the world, and they were certain that they would achieve their goals. They described the group with words like *family,* *team,* and *community.* It was "as if we were all members of the same class at West Point," one reminisced (quoted in Schickel, 1968, p. 184).

Many theorists feel that this "belongingness," or "we-ness," is the essence of group cohesion (Bollen & Hoyle, 1990; Dion, 1990; Fine & Holyfield, 1996; Owen, 1985). Members of cohesive groups share a heightened sense of belonging to the group as a whole, and they recognize their similarity with other group members. They also show signs of a shared social identity, for as "we-ness" emerges members tend to categorize themselves as group members and define themselves in terms of their group membership (Hogg, 1992). Individuals who are members of cohesive groups—with cohesion defined as a strong sense of belonging to an integrated community—are more actively involved in their groups, are more enthusiastic about their groups, and even suffer from fewer social and interpersonal problems (Hoyle & Crawford, 1994). They will even sacrifice their own individual desires for the good of the group (Prapavessis & Carron, 1997).

Cohesion Is Attraction.   Some theorists consider cohesion a special kind of interpersonal attraction (Lott & Lott, 1965). At the individual level, members of cohesive groups like one another. The Disney Studios workers, for example, became close friends, and in time they had few connections outside the group. Indeed, Walt Disney intervened when he felt that people were being *too* friendly: He banned any kind of romantic relationships between co-workers in his studio. At the group level, members are attracted to the group itself rather than any specific member. Members may not be friends, but they are very positive about the group (Carron, Widmeyer, & Brawley, 1988; Dion, 1990).

Michael Hogg and his colleagues extend this distinction between individual- and group-level attraction in their analysis of personal versus social attraction. Hogg argues that while members of cohesive groups usually like one another, this *personal attraction* isn't group cohesion. Rather, group cohesion corresponds to *social attraction:* a liking of other group members that is based on their status as typical group members. Unlike personal attraction, which is grounded on personal relationships between specific members, social attraction is depersonalized; it reflects our tendency to admire individuals who possess the kinds of qualities that typify our group. Hogg finds that any factor that increases members' tendency to categorize themselves as group members (e.g., conflict with other groups, the presence of an outgroup, or activities that focus members' attention on their group identity) will reduce personal attraction but increase depersonalized, social attraction (Hogg, Cooper-Shaw, & Holzworth, 1993; Hogg & Hains, 1996; Hogg & Hardie, 1991; Hogg, Hardie, & Reynolds, 1995).

These two types of attraction may influence a group's cohesion in different ways. Although cohesive groups tend to retain their members for longer periods of time than noncohesive groups, this connection between cohesion and membership stability is strongest when cohesion is based on the members' attraction to the group as a unit rather than their attraction toward individual members (Mobley, Griffeth, Hand, & Meglino, 1979).

Cohesion Is Teamwork.   Many theorists believe that cohesion has more to do with members' willingness to work together to accomplish their objectives than it does with positive interpersonal relations or feelings of unity. Studies of sports teams, for example, find that most players, when asked to describe their team's cohesiveness, stress the quality of their teamwork (Carron, 1982; Yukelson, Weinberg, & Jackson, 1984). Task-oriented groups, such as military squads or flight crews, are unified by members' shared drive to accomplish their goals (Guzzo, 1995). Much of the unity of the Disney group, for example, was based on "a passionate commitment to the new art on the part of many of the employees that far exceeded the kind of loyalty most companies can command" (quoted in Schickel, 1968, p. 184). Indeed, groups that are cohesive— in the sense that they pursue their chosen goals with great intensity—are characterized by considerable interdependence of members, stability of membership, feelings of responsibility for the group's outcomes, reduced absenteeism, and resistance to disruptions (Widmeyer, Brawley, & Carron, 1992).

Cohesion Is Multidimensional.   As Table 6–1 indicates, different group dynamicists have conceptualized cohesiveness in different ways. Some, dismayed by this diversity, have suggested that the concept should be discarded as too ambiguous to be useful (Mudrack, 1989). Others, however, note that this diversity reflects the complexity inherent in the concept itself. Kenneth Dion and his colleagues, for example, believe that cohesiveness is a multidimensional construct. Binding social forces, a sense of unity, attraction to individual members and the group itself, and the group's ability to work as a team are all components of cohesiveness, but a cohesive group may not exhibit all of these qualities. As a result, there is no such thing as a typical cohesive group. One group might be cohesive because the members are all good friends. Another group may become cohesive because its members work closely with one another in an integrated, well-coordinated manner. Another group might be cohesive because all the members feel a strong sense of belonging to the group (Cota, Dion, & Evans, 1993; Cota, Evans, Dion, Kilik, & Longman, 1995; Dion, 1990; Dion & Evans, 1992).

TABLE 6–1   COHESION: A MULTIDIMENSIONAL CONSTRUCT

Dimension	Definition
Social force	"The total field of forces that act on members to remain in the group" (Festinger, Schachter, & Back, 1950, p. 164)
Group unity	"A synthesis of individuals' sense of belonging to a group and their sense of morale associated with membership in the group" (Hoyle & Crawford, 1994, pp. 477–478)
Attraction	"That group property that is inferred from the number and strength of mutual positive attitudes among the members of a group" (Lott & Lott, 1965, p. 259)
Teamwork	"A dynamic process that is reflected in the tendency for a group to stick together and remain united in pursuit of its goals and objectives" (Carron, 1982, p. 124)

Measuring Group Cohesion

An **operational definition** describes the way a construct, such as leadership, cohesiveness, or power, can be measured (Hempel, 1966). Just as theorists have defined cohesiveness in many different ways conceptually, so researchers have developed many different ways to measure cohesiveness empirically. (Hogg, 1992, provides a comprehensive review of methods used to assess cohesion.)

Observing Cohesion.   The cohesiveness of the Disney group was palpable. Observers, watching the men and women go about their day's work, were drawn to one inevitable conclusion: This group is cohesive.

Observational strategies have been used to index group cohesion with considerable success. George Caspar Homans (1950), for example, used observational methods in his studies of work teams. He monitored interpersonal relations among members, noting instances of conflict or tension and how smoothly the group worked together as a unit. Researchers have used observation to index the cohesiveness of adolescent peer groups (Adler & Adler, 1995), therapy groups (Budman, Soldz, Demby, Davis, & Merry, 1993), leisure groups (Fine & Holyfield, 1996), work squads (Kidder, 1981), and gangs (Davis, 1982).

Some investigators have sought to increase the precision of observational methods by using structured coding systems, such as Robert Bales's Interaction Process Analysis (IPA) or his System of Multiple Level Observation of Groups (SYMLOG; Bales, 1980, 1988). As noted in Chapter 2, SYMLOG lets observers identify the location of each group member within the overall structure of the group. People who are similar in terms of their friendliness, for example, would be placed next to one another in the SYMLOG chart, whereas a member who is very task oriented and a member who is more emotionally expressive would be located far apart. Bales assesses the unity of the group by considering how many of the members are clumped together by observers. He can also see if the group includes marginal members or subgroups that stand in opposition to the others in the group (Bales, 1988; Kelly & Duran, 1985; Keyton & Springston, 1990).

Other investigators have used observational methods to indirectly assess cohesion. To gauge the cohesiveness of therapy groups, researchers timed the length of the session-ending "group hug" (Kirshner, Dies, & Brown, 1978). Some researchers have recorded how close together group members stand and whether or not they position themselves to prevent nonmembers from intruding on the group's space (Knowles & Brickner, 1981). Investigators have tracked cohesion and identification with a group by recording how many people wear apparel that connects them with a group or organization and by counting the number of plural pronouns used by group members. If group members say, "We won that game" or "We got the job done" rather than "They lost that game" or "I got the job done," researchers assume that the group is cohesive (Cialdini et al., 1976, Experiment 1; Snyder, Lassegard, & Ford, 1986).

Operational definition: The specific measurement operation that a researcher uses to quantify a theoretical concept.

Self-Report Approaches. Self-report methods offer yet another means of operationally defining cohesiveness. Leon Festinger and his colleagues used sociometry in their study of groups of people living in the same court of housing projects (Festinger, Schachter, & Back, 1950). After the residents supplied the names of all their good friends, the investigators calculated the ratio of in-court choices to outside-court choices. The greater the ratio, the greater was the cohesiveness of the court (Lott & Lott, 1965).

A second self-report approach assumes that group members can describe the unity of their group accurately. Investigators have used a variety of questions to tap into cohesion, including: "Do you want to remain a member of this group?" "How did you like your team?" and "How strong a sense of belonging do you feel you have to the people you work with?" (Schachter, 1951; Schachter, Ellertson, McBride, & Gregory, 1951; and Indik, 1965, respectively). Researchers also use multi-item scales that include many questions that can be combined to yield a single index of cohesiveness. For example:

1. The *Group Environment Scale (GES)* measures cohesiveness by asking for yes/no answers to items such as "There is a feeling of unity and cohesion in this group" and "Members put a lot of energy into this group" (Moos & Humphrey, 1974; Moos, Insel, & Humphrey, 1974).
2. The *Group Attitude Scale (GAS)* assesses members' "desire to identify with and be an accepted member of the group" (Evans & Jarvis, 1986, p. 204) by asking them to indicate how much they want to remain a member of the group, like it, and feel included in it.
3. The *Group Environment Questionnaire (GEQ)* asks two kinds of questions. One set focuses on *group integration:* Do members feel that the group is working as a unit to accomplish its task-oriented and social goals? Another set concerns *attraction to the group:* Do members like the group, its members, and the way it goes about accomplishing its tasks? Because integration and attraction can refer to either the social activities of the group or the task activities of the group, the GEQ has four subscales: Attraction to the Group—Social (liking for the group), Attraction to the Group—Task (attitude toward the way the group members work together), Group Integration—Social (perceptions of the group's social unity), and Group Integration—Task (perceptions of the group's unity when working on tasks). (For more information, see Widmeyer, Brawley, & Carron, 1985, 1992).
4. The *Perceived Cohesion Scale (PCS;* Bollen & Hoyle, 1990) asks group members to comment directly on their feelings of belonging to the group (e.g., "I feel a sense of belonging to my group") and their enthusiasm for the group (e.g., "I am happy to belong to this group").

Selecting a Measure. This plethora of operational definitions can create challenges for researchers. When they measure cohesiveness in different ways, they often report differing conclusions. A study using a self-report measure of cohesion might find that cohesive groups outproduce groups that are not cohesive, but other investigators may not replicate this finding when they use an observational method to operationalize cohesiveness (Mullen, Anthony, Salas, & Driskell, 1994). Moreover, some operational definitions may correspond more closely to the theoretical definition than others. A measure that focuses only on group members' perceptions of their group's cohesiveness, for example, may be assessing something very different than a measure that focuses on the actual strength of the relationships linking individuals to their group.

These drawbacks, however, are offset by the advantages that multiple operationalizations afford. Investigators, depending on the constraints of the research setting, can choose the measure that best suits their needs. Variations in measuring cohesiveness have also enriched the theoretical meaning of the term. Different measurement methods often yield very different kinds of information, and researchers have concluded that cohesiveness has multiple components and that different operations may measure different components. Cohesiveness may also be based on very different criteria in different kinds of groups: What unifies the members of a work group may not unify the members of a religious congregation (Ridgeway, 1983). These dynamics may go unnoticed if researchers use only one measure of cohesiveness (Evans & Dion, 1991; Hogg, 1992; Keyton, 1991, 1992; Mudrack, 1989).

DEVELOPING GROUP COHESION

Disney Studios was, without question, cohesive: Strong forces kept the group together (perhaps the most powerful force was Walt Disney himself), the studio was extraordinarily unified, most of the members liked one another, and they worked diligently to create *Snow White*. But the group did not become cohesive all at once. When Disney first described the project to his core animators, many were skeptical; no one had ever managed to accomplish the goal Disney sought. Disney then went about hiring many new employees, and as each new face appeared at the drafting tables, the group was forced to adjust. The work was demanding, and many had difficulty reaching Disney's high standards.

The Disney group, like all groups, changed over time. Initial uncertainties gave way to stable patterns of interaction; tensions between members waxed and waned; old members were replaced by new ones; and members abandoned old roles to take on new ones. As a result of this group development, the studio grew from a collection of talented individuals into an organized system of interdependent teams.

Stages of Group Development

The group dynamicist William Fawcett Hill was at one time so intrigued by developmental processes in groups that he diligently filed away each theory that he found on that subject. Over the years, his collection grew and grew, until finally the number of theories reached 100. At that moment, Hill notes, the "collecting bug was exterminated, as the object of the quest had lost its rarity" (Hill & Gruner, 1973, p. 355; see also Hare, 1982; Lacoursiere, 1980).

The morass of theoretical models dealing with development, though daunting, is not altogether irremediable. Theoreticians are at variance on many points, but most agree that groups pass through several phases, or stages, as they develop. Just as humans mature from infancy to childhood, adolescence, adulthood, and old age, stage models of group development theorize that groups move from one stage to the next in a predictable, sequential fashion. Disney Studios, for example, became unified, but only after earlier stages marked by confusion, conflict, and growing group structure.

What stages typify the developmental progression of groups? The number and names of the stages vary among theorists. Many models, however, highlight certain interpersonal outcomes that must be achieved in any group that exists for a prolonged period. Members of most groups must, for example, discover who the other members are, achieve a degree of interdependence, and deal with conflict (Hare, 1982; Lacoursiere, 1980; Wheelan, 1994). Therefore, most models include the basic stages shown in Table 6–2. Initially, the group members must become oriented toward one another. Next, they often find themselves in conflict, and some solution is sought to improve the group environment. In the third phase, norms and roles develop that regulate behavior, and the group achieves greater unity. In the fourth phase, the group can perform as a unit to achieve desired goals. And the final stage ends the sequence of development with the group's adjournment. Bruce W. Tuckman (Tuckman, 1965; Tuckman & Jensen, 1977) labeled these five stages forming (orientation), storming (conflict), norming (structure), performing (work) and adjourning (dissolution).

Forming: The Orientation Stage.   When the group is forming, members often suffer through an *orientation stage* marked by mild tension and guarded interchanges. Because they know little about one another, members of a new group carefully monitor

TABLE 6–2   FIVE STAGES OF GROUP DEVELOPMENT

Stage	Major Processes	Characteristics
1. Orientation (forming)	Members becoming familiar with one another and the group; dependency and inclusion issues; acceptance of leader and group consensus	Tentative, polite communications; concern over ambiguity, group's goals; active leader; compliant members
2. Conflict (storming)	Disagreement over procedures; expression of dissatisfaction; tension among members; antagonism toward leader	Criticism of ideas; poor attendance; hostility; polarization and coalition formation
3. Structure (norming)	Growth of cohesiveness and unity; establishment of roles, standards, and relationships; increased trust, communication	Agreement on procedures; reduction in role ambiguity; increased "we-ness"
4. Work (performing)	Goal achievement; high task orientation; emphasis on performance and production	Decision making; problem solving; mutual cooperation
5. Dissolution (adjourning)	Termination of roles; completion of tasks; reduction of dependency	Disintegration and withdrawal; increased independence and emotionality; regret

their behavior to make certain that they avoid any embarrassing lapses of social poise. Feeling uncomfortable and constrained, they may be reluctant to discuss their personal views and values with people they know so little about. This ambiguous situation is further complicated by the absence of any specific norms regarding the regulation of interaction and goal attainment as well as uncertainty about their role in the group. This tension can be so uncomfortable that people who believe that they lack the social skills necessary to cope with the situation actively avoid group membership (Cook, 1977; Leary & Kowalski, 1995).

With time, tension is dispelled as the ice is broken and group members become better acquainted (Thibaut and Kelley, 1959). After the initial inhibitions subside, group members typically begin exchanging information about themselves and their goals. To better understand and relate to the group, individual members gather information about their comembers by formulating attributions concerning their personality characteristics, interests, and attitudes (Heider, 1958). In addition, through self-disclosure of their own characteristics, group members reveal enough information about themselves to enable others to get to know them better (Jourard, 1971). In time, a level of familiarity is reached, but not before the group members have made considerable investments of personal effort and time.

Storming: The Conflict Stage.   As the tension caused by the newness of the Disney group waned, tension over goals, procedures, and authority waxed. Walt Disney had firm ideas about how his employees should act—he banned profanity, alcohol consumption, and office romances—and his staff often grumbled about his restrictive policies. Conflict came to a head when several members protested by animating an X-rated sequence featuring Mickey and Minnie Mouse. Walt Disney, unamused, fired them (Eliot, 1993).

Many groups go through a *conflict stage* as members struggle to define their group's goals, their relations with one another, and the roles that members will play in the group. In large groups like the Disney group, this conflict often centers around relationships between the leader and the rest of the group. In the orientation stage, members accept the leader's guidance with few questions, but as the group matures, leader-member conflicts disrupt the group's functioning. Members may oscillate between "fight and flight": Some may openly challenge the leader's policies and decisions (fight), whereas others may respond by minimizing contact with the leader (flight). In groups that have no formally appointed leader, conflicts erupt as members vie for status and roles within the group. Once stable patterns of authority, attraction, and communication develop, conflicts subside, but until then, group members jockey for authority and power (Bennis & Shepard, 1956; Wheelan & McKeage, 1993).

Despite its negative connotations, conflict in groups is as common as group harmony. As sociology's conflict theory suggests, the dynamic nature of the group ensures continual change, but along with change come stresses and strains that surface in the form of conflict. In rare instances, group members may avoid all conflict because their actions are perfectly coordinated; but in most groups, the push and pull of interpersonal forces inevitably exerts its influence (Dahrendorf, 1958, 1959). Low levels of conflict in a group can be an indication of remarkably positive interpersonal

relations, but it is more likely that the group members are simply u̱
tivated, and bored (Fisher, 1980).

But conflict is not just unavoidable; it may actually be a requir͏
creating group cohesion. If conflict escalates out of control, it can a
But more often, conflict has positive consequences. Members of cohesi
understand one another's perspectives, and such understanding canno
hostility has surfaced, been confronted, and been resolved (Bennis & Sh
Deutsch, 1969). Conflicts "serve to 'sew the social system together' b   ͏lling
each other out, thus preventing disintegration along one primary line of cleavage"
(Coser, 1956, p. 801). Conflicts also help groups clarify their goals by forcing members to make choices that reflect the group's negotiated preferences. Conflict even
provides a means of venting personal hostilities. If hostilities are never expressed,
they may build up to a point where the group can no longer continue as a unit.

Norming: The Structure Stage.   With each crisis overcome, the Disney Studios became more stable, more organized, and more cohesive. Disney created formal chains
of command and clear administrative responsibilities. The "secretary-manager of
animators," for example, was specifically and formally charged with monitoring the
work of the animators, identifying the tasks they were to accomplish, adjusting their
compensation, and establishing routines, procedures, and deadlines. People complained from time to time about the rules, the work, and the salary, but they became
fiercely loyal to the project and to their co-workers.

Groups in the third stage of group development, the *structure stage,* become both
unified and organized. Whereas groups in the orientation and conflict stages are characterized by low levels of intimacy, friendship, and unity, the group becomes a unified
whole when it reaches the structure stage. Mutual trust and support increase, members
cooperate with each other more, and members try to reach decisions through consensus. The group becomes cohesive (Hare, 1976; Tuckman, 1965; Wheelan, 1994).

The group also becomes more organized. It resolves the problems that caused earlier conflicts—uncertainty about goals, roles, and authority—and prepares to get down
to the work at hand. Norms, those taken-for-granted rules that dictate how members
should behave, emerge more clearly and guide the group members as they interact with
one another. Differences of opinion still arise, but now they are dealt with through constructive discussion and negotiation. Members communicate openly with one another
about personal and group concerns, in part because members know one another better. At Disney, employees did not always agree with one another, or with the boss, but
they changed the way they dealt with disagreement. Instead of hinting at problems or
arguing, they negotiated their way to agreements that benefited everyone. When Walt
Disney offhandedly asked one animator, "How are things going?" the unhappy animator felt secure enough to say, "Just terrible." So Disney let him switch to a different
team, where his performance improved dramatically.

Performing: The Work Stage.   Few groups are productive immediately; instead, productivity must usually wait until the group matures. A. Paul Hare, after studying historical records of the Camp David conference of 1978 that brought together delegates

from Egypt, Israel, and the United States, concluded that most of the positive outcomes were achieved during a two-day period near the end of the conference (Hare & Naveh, 1984). He reports a similar shift in performance in a group of factory workers assembling relay units, workshop participants, and the members of an anthropological expedition (Hare, 1967, 1982). Robert Bales, too, after systematically coding the types of behaviors exhibited by group members, concluded that task-focused actions occur more frequently later in the group's life (Bales & Strodtbeck, 1951; Borgatta & Bales, 1953; Heinicke & Bales, 1953).

Disney Studios reached this *work stage* by 1935. Visitors to Disney Studios said that it reminded them of a beehive. People were working elbow to elbow in crowded offices, holding informal conferences in hallways, arguing the merits of a particular technique over lunch, and staying late to go to art classes taught by senior animators. They were getting the job of creating *Snow White* done.

Not all groups reach this productive stage, unfortunately. If you have never been a member of a group that failed to produce, you are a rare individual indeed. In a study of neighborhood action committees, only 1 of 12 groups reached the productivity stage; all the others were bogged down at the conflict or cohesion stages (Zurcher, 1969). An early investigation of combat units found that out of 63 squads, 13 could be clearly classified as effective performance units (Goodacre, 1953). An analysis of 18 personal growth groups concluded that only 5 managed to reach the task performance stage (Kuypers, Davies, & Hazewinkel, 1986; see also Kuypers, Davies, & Glaser, 1986). These studies and others suggest that time is needed to develop a working relationship, but time alone is no guarantee that the group will be productive (Gabarro, 1987).

Adjourning: The Dissolution Stage.   Much of the camaraderie and work ethic of Disney Studios in the mid-1930s faded when *Snow White* was completed. The studio turned to other projects, but the enthusiasm and novelty of that first animated feature could never be recaptured. Many of Disney's employees remained utterly loyal to him, but others increasingly questioned his methods. Disney Studios, although still successful, productive, and creative, lost much of its unity. In 1941, the golden age of Disney Studios ended when many of the animators went out on strike.

A group's entry into the *dissolution stage* can be either planned or spontaneous. Planned dissolution takes place when the group accomplishes its prescribed goals or exhausts its time and resources. A baseball team playing the last game of the season, a wilderness expedition at the end of its journey, a jury delivering its verdict, and an ad hoc committee filing its report are all examples of groups that are ending as scheduled. Spontaneous dissolution, in contrast, results when an unanticipated problem arises that makes continued group interaction impossible. When groups fail repeatedly, their members or some outside power may decide that maintaining the group is a waste of time and resources. If the group fails to satisfy its members' social and interpersonal needs, members may abandon the group en masse and join other organizations. As social exchange theory maintains, when the number of rewards provided by group membership decreases and the costly aspects of membership escalate, group members become dissatisfied. If the members feel that they have no alternatives or that they have put too much into the group to abandon it, then they may remain in the group even though they are dissatisfied. If, however, group members feel that other groups are available or that nonparticipation is preferable to participation in such a costly group, they will be more likely to let their current group die (Rusbult, 1983, 1987; Rusbult & Martz, 1995; Rusbult, Zembrodt, & Gunn, 1982).

The dissolution stage can be stressful for members (Johnson, 1974; Mayadas & Glasser, 1985; Sarri & Galinsky, 1985). When dissolution is unplanned, the final sessions may be filled with conflict-laden exchanges among members, growing apathy and animosity, or repeated failures at the group's task. And even when it is planned, the members may feel distressed: Their work in the group may be over, but they still mourn for the group and suffer from a lack of personal support. When the Disney animators went out on strike, they probably experienced a wide range of negative feelings about the entire process: anxiety, feelings of inequity, and anger toward the company. Members of disbanding partnerships also tend to blame one another for the end of the group (Kushnir, 1984).

Cycles of Group Development

Tuckman's model, which can be operationalized using items like those in Table 6–3, is a *successive-stage theory;* it specifies the usual order of the phases of group development. Sometimes, however, development takes a different course. Although interpersonal exploration is often a prerequisite for other interpersonal outcomes, and cohesion and conflict often precede effective performance, this pattern is not universal. Some groups manage to avoid particular stages, others move through the stages but in a unique order, and still others seem to develop in ways that cannot be described by Tuckman's five stages (Seeger, 1983). Also, the demarcation between stages is not clear-cut. When group conflict is waning, for example, feelings of cohesion may be

---

TABLE 6–3 SAMPLE ITEMS FROM THE GROUP DEVELOPMENT QUESTIONNAIRE (GDQ)

Stage	Sample Items
Orientation	Members tend to go along with whatever the leader suggests.
	There is very little conflict expressed in the group.
Conflict	People seem to have very different views about how things should be done in this group.
	Members challenge the leader's ideas.
Structure	The group is spending its time planning how it will get its work done.
	We can rely on each other. We work as a team.
Work	The group gets, gives, and uses feedback about its effectiveness and productivity.
	The group encourages high performance and quality work.

Source: Wheelan & Hochberger, 1996.

increasing, but these time-dependent changes do not occur in a discontinuous, step-like sequence (Arrow, 1997).

Many theorists also believe that groups repeatedly cycle through stages during their lifetime, rather than just moving through each stage once (Arrow, 1997; Hill & Gruner, 1973; Mennecke, Hoffer, Wynne, 1992; Shambaugh, 1978). These *cyclical models* agree that certain issues tend to dominate group interaction during the various phases of a group's development, but they add that these issues can recur later in the life of the group. For example, Bales's **equilibrium model of group development** is based on the premise that group members strive to maintain a balance between accomplishing the task and enhancing the quality of the interpersonal relationships within the group (Bales, 1965). The group tends to oscillate between these two concerns, sometimes achieving high social cohesiveness but then shifting toward a more work-centered cohesiveness. A group such as Disney Studios, after working diligently on their tasks for days on end, would likely find that interpersonal bonds among members are strained. In response, the group shifts its focus from its main task—completing *Snow White*—to the interpersonal side of the group.

Bales thus argues that mature groups tend to cycle back and forth between what Tuckman calls the norming and performing stages: a period of prolonged group effort must be followed by a period of cohesion-creating interpersonal activity (Bales, 1963; Bales & Cohen, with Williamson, 1979). *Punctuated equilibrium* theories agree with Bales's view, but add that groups often go through periods of relatively rapid change. These changes may be precipitated by some internal crisis, such as the loss of a leader, or by changes in the type of task the group is attempting. The halfway point in the group's life, too, can trigger dramatic changes in the group as members realize that the time they have available to them is dwindling (Arrow, 1997; Gersick 1989).

CONSEQUENCES OF COHESION

Cohesion is something of a "purr word." Most of us, if asked to choose between two groups—one that is "cohesive" and another that "lacks unity"—would likely pick the cohesive group. But cohesiveness has its drawbacks. A cohesive group is an intense group, and this intensity affects the members, the group's dynamics, and the group's performance in both positive and negative ways. Cohesion leads to a range of consequences—not all of them desirable.

Member Satisfaction and Adjustment

Many of the men and women of Disney Studios, years later, would say 1932 to 1940 was a special time in their lives. People are usually much more satisfied with their groups when the group is cohesive rather than noncohesive. Across a range of groups

---

Equilibrium model of group development: Bales's assumption that groups, over time, maintain a balance between task demands and interpersonal demands.

in industrial, athletic, and educational settings, people who are members of highly compatible, cohesive subgroups report more satisfaction and enjoyment than members of noncohesive groups (Hackman, 1992; Hare, 1976; Hogg, 1992; Roy, 1973). One investigator studied teams of masons and carpenters working on a housing development. For the first five months of the project, the men worked at various assignments in groups formed by the supervisor. This period gave the men a chance to get to know virtually everyone working on the project, and natural likes and dislikes soon surfaced. The researcher then established cohesive groups by making certain that the teams only contained people who liked each other. As anticipated, the masons and carpenters were much more satisfied when they worked in cohesive groups. As one explained, "Seems as though everything flows a lot smoother. . . . The work is more interesting when you've got a buddy working with you. You certainly like it a lot better anyway" (Van Zelst, 1952, p. 183).

A cohesive group creates a healthier workplace, at least at the psychological level. Because people in cohesive groups respond to one another in a more positive fashion than the members of noncohesive groups, people experience less anxiety and tension in such groups (Myers, 1962; Shaw & Shaw, 1962). In studies conducted in industrial work groups, for example, employees reported less anxiety and nervousness when they worked in cohesive groups (Seashore, 1954). Investigations of therapeutic groups routinely find that the members improve their overall level of adjustment when their group is cohesive (Yalom, 1995). People also cope more effectively with stress when they are in cohesive groups (Bowers, Weaver, & Morgan, 1996; Zaccaro, Gualtieri, & Minionis, 1995).

Membership in a cohesive group can prove problematic for members, however, if they become too dependent on them. Irving Janis (1963), for example, describes how the formation of strong emotional ties in combat groups can result in maladaptive behavior when the group's composition is altered. Although the cohesiveness of the unit initially provides psychological support for the individual, the loss of comrades during battle causes severe distress. Furthermore, when the unit is reinforced with replacements, the original group members are reluctant to establish emotional ties with the newcomers, partly in fear of the pain produced by separation. Hence, they begin restricting their interactions, and a coalition of old versus new begins to evolve. In time, the group members can become completely detached from the group, and the group's development becomes arrested (Gruner, 1984).

Group Dynamics and Influence

As cohesion increases, the internal dynamics of the group intensify. People in cohesive groups more readily accept the group's goals, decisions, and norms. Furthermore, pressures to conform are greater in cohesive groups, and individuals' resistance to these pressures is weaker. One researcher directly manipulated cohesiveness by telling dyads either that they would enjoy being in the group, since care had been taken in assembling highly compatible teams, or that the group would not be cohesive, since the members were incompatible (Back, 1951). When members of cohesive groups later discovered that they disagreed with their partner's interpretations of three ambiguous stimuli, they tried to exert greater influence over their partner than did the members of noncohesive groups. Partners also conformed more in cohesive dyads, perhaps because they wanted to avoid confrontation. When the group norms emphasize the value of cooperation and agreement among members, members of highly cohesive groups avoid disagreement more than members of noncohesive groups (Courtright, 1978).

Other evidence suggests that members of cohesive groups sometimes react very negatively when a group member goes against the group consensus, and they take harsh measures to bring dissenters into line. Stanley Schachter (1951), for example, found that when cohesive groups discussed a topic that was relevant to the group's goals, members united against any dissenters, pressuring them to comply with the majority's position. If a dissenter refused to yield, members psychologically excluded the individual from the group, and the frequency of communications directed to the dissenter dropped dramatically. Cohesion can also increase negative group processes, including hostility and scapegoating (French, 1941; Pepitone & Reichling, 1955). In one study, cohesive and noncohesive groups worked on a series of insolvable problems. Although all the groups seemed frustrated, coalitions tended to form in noncohesive groups, whereas cohesive groups vented their frustrations through interpersonal aggression: overt hostility, joking hostility, scapegoating, and domination of subordinate members. The level of hostility became so intense in one group that observers lost track of how many offensive remarks were made; they estimated that the number surpassed 600 comments during the 45-minute work period (French, 1941).

Group Performance

Warren Bennis and Patricia Ward Biederman (1997), in their book *Organizing Genius,* label Disney Studios a "great group": one of only seven they hold up as sterling examples of what groups can accomplish. Bennis and Biederman found these great groups in all kinds of places—politics, business, universities, and the military—but despite their differences in orientation and goals, these groups shared many common features: Members were driven to achieve excellence, all had extraordinary leaders, and all were cohesive.

Brian Mullen and Carolyn Copper (1994) confirmed the link between cohesion and performance by carrying out a meta-analytic review: a review and synthesis of previous research that uses statistical procedures to combine the findings from multiple studies. They combed the research literature looking for studies that measured or manipulated group cohesiveness and group performance. Their search yielded 49 studies of 8702 members of a variety of groups: sports teams, work groups in business settings, expeditions, military squads, and laboratory groups. They then combined the results of these studies to answer three key questions.

Do cohesive groups outperform less unified groups? Mullen and Copper identified a number of studies that did not confirm the relationship between cohesion and performance, but when they surveyed all the available literature, they concluded that the "cohesion-performance effect does, in fact, exist to a highly significant degree" (p. 222). The relationship was stronger in nonlaboratory groups, such as military units and sports teams, then in laboratory groups, and in small groups rather than large ones.

Are cohesion and performance causally connected? Mullen and Copper examined the cohesion → performance hypothesis by comparing experimental studies that manipulated cohesion with studies that used correlational designs. Because the cohesion-performance relationship emerged in both types of studies, they concluded that cohesion causes improved performance. But the relationship between cohesion and performance is stronger in correlational studies. This disparity suggests that performance also causes changes in cohesiveness. Groups that succeed tend to become more cohesive, and groups that fail tend to become less cohesive. Hence, cohesion and performance are correlated because cohesion → performance and performance → cohesion.

What is it about cohesive groups that makes them more effective? Mullen and Copper explored this question by distinguishing between three components of cohesion: attraction, unity (group pride), and commitment to the task. They found that the cohesion-performance relationship was strongest when group cohesion was based on commitment to the task rather than attraction or group pride. Cohesion also counts more when the group's task requires high levels of interaction and interdependence (Gully, Devine, & Whitney, 1995).

These findings explain why some groups, even though they are cohesive, are not productive: The members are not committed to the group's performance goals. A major survey of 5871 factory workers in 228 groups found that the more cohesive the group, the less the productivity levels varied among members; members of cohesive groups produced nearly equivalent amounts, but individuals in noncohesive groups varied considerably more in their productivity. Furthermore, fairly low standards of performance had developed within some of the highly cohesive groups; thus, productivity was uniformly low among these groups. In contrast, in cohesive groups with relatively high performance goals, members were extremely productive (Seashore, 1954). In sum, so long as group norms encourage high productivity, cohesiveness and productivity are positively related: The more cohesive the group, the greater

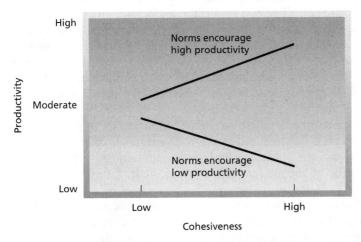

FIGURE 6-1 Do cohesive groups always outperform less cohesive groups? If the group's norms encourage productivity, cohesiveness and productivity will be positively correlated. If the group standards for performance are low, cohesiveness will actually undermine productivity.

its productivity. If group norms encourage low productivity, however, the relationship is negative (see Figure 6–1).

Schachter and his colleagues confirmed this hypothesis in an experimental study of female college students working in three-person teams on an assembly-line project (Schachter et al., 1951). First, half of the subjects were led to believe that they were members of cohesive groups, and the other subjects were convinced that their groups were noncohesive. Second, during the task, messages were ostensibly sent from one worker to another to establish performance norms. In some instances, the messages called for increased production (positive messages), but in other instances, the messages requested a slowdown (negative messages). As expected, the impact of the messages was significantly greater in the cohesive groups than in the noncohesive groups. Furthermore, the decreases in productivity brought about by the negative messages were greater than the increases brought about by the positive messages.

APPLICATION: WORK TEAMS

How should businesses, governments, hospitals, and military units be designed to maximize productivity? For many years, the experts concentrated on organizational efficiency. They assumed that people do not like to work and must be prodded into action by the promise of financial incentives, close supervision, and clear goals that they can attain with little effort. The experts considered workers mere "adjuncts to machines," and they designed workplaces in which employees did not waste time talking to one another (Taylor, 1923).

This view was shaken by the Hawthorne studies of group productivity conducted in the 1920s (Landsberger, 1958; Mayo, 1945; Roethlisberger & Dickson, 1939). The research team initially assumed that physical characteristics of the workplace determine productivity, so they tested different conditions with a small group of workers in an experimental test room. The environmental changes—lighting, temperature, frequency of breaks, and so on—all influenced performance, but their impact was mediated by the group's dynamics. People weren't working harder because the room was being changed, but because they were part of a small group that responded positively and productively to their special treatment. (Chapter 2 examines the methodological implications of the Hawthorne studies, and Chapter 10 uses one of the Hawthorne groups as an example of group productivity.)

The group-level approach to organizational productivity implied by the Hawthorne studies has been fully realized in the widespread use of **work teams** in business, industry, government, education, and health care settings today. Indeed, groups lie at the foundation of the modern organization. Half the workers in the United States belong to at least one team at work. Groups are used by as many as 80% of all larger organizations in the United States, and in countries like Sweden and Japan, their use approaches 100% (Applebaum & Blatt, 1994; Gordon, 1992). Because most large organizations rely on groups to accomplish their goals, the effectiveness of these groups plays a major role in determining the effectiveness of the overall organization.

Work teams: Cohesive production units.

Even though Disney Studios had a visionary leader and talented artists, its success was determined by group dynamics rather than individual abilities.

What Is a Work Team?

Teams possess the basic qualities of all groups: interaction, structure, cohesiveness, social identity, and goals. But the nature and magnitude of their group dynamics set them apart from other kinds of groups.

- *Interaction:* Team members' interactions are cooperative and coordinated. Members work together, combining their individual inputs in a deliberate way.
- *Structure:* Teams are structured groups. Group norms, members' specific roles in the group, and communication patterns are often explicitly stated.
- *Cohesiveness:* Teams are typically cohesive, particularly in the sense that members are united in their efforts to pursue a common goal.
- *Social identity:* Team members recognize their membership in the group and feel that the group is greater than the sum of the individual members.
- *Goals:* Teams are goal oriented. Teammates' interdependence is based on coordination of actions in pursuit of a common goal.

Teams also tend to be part of a larger organization, and the tasks that they work on and decisions they make impact larger projects (Salas, Bowers, & Cannon-Bowers, 1995). Specific team members usually have specialized knowledge, skills, and abilities that they contribute to the group, and the group's success depends on combining these individual inputs effectively (Blickensderfer, Cannon-Bowers, & Salas, 1997). Teams also often work under some kind of pressure, such as heavy workload, limited time, or competition with other groups (Dyer, 1984; Stout, Salas, & Fowlkes, 1997).

Teams perform a wide range of tasks in organizations. *Management and advisory groups,* such as administrative units, review panels, focus groups, committees, and advisory councils, identify and solve problems, make decisions about day-to-day operations and production, and set the goals for the organization's future. Small, autonomous *production groups,* including assembly lines, manufacturing teams, and maintenance crews, create the organization's products or deliver its services. *Project groups* composed of engineers, researchers, architects, and computer programmers develop innovative products and identify new solutions to existing problems. Many organizations use *action groups;* sports teams, surgery teams, police squads, military units, and orchestras are specialized groups that accomplish their goals through highly coordinated actions (Hackman, 1990; Sundstrom, De Meuse, & Futrell, 1990).

Team Building

Organizational experts often turn to group dynamics to identify ways to design, develop, and improve work groups. **Team building** begins with the assumption that

Team building: A general label for a wide variety of interventions designed to assess current level of group development, clarify and prioritize goals, increase group cohesiveness, and increase productivity in groups.

success in work groups results from a collaborative interdependence that develops through practice (Guzzo & Dickson, 1996; Swezey & Salas, 1992; Tjosvold, 1991). In many ways, team training in the workplace parallels team building in sports. Just as members of a team playing basketball or field hockey must learn how to pool their individual abilities and energies to maximize the team's performance, work group members must learn to coordinate their efforts with those of the other group members. Group goals must be set, work patterns structured, and a sense of group identity developed. Individual members must learn how to coordinate their actions, and any strains and stresses in interpersonal relations need to be identified and resolved (Katzenbach & Smith, 1993; Swezey & Salas, 1992).

How can organizations build better teams? Consultants and human resource management experts offer a range of suggestions and interventions for turning groups into teams.

Goal Setting.   Teams are, at core, goal-seeking groups, and they will function more effectively if their goals are clear to members. If a group has lost sight of its overall purpose, a team builder might recommend that the group develop a mission or vision statement. Once the overall purpose of the team is clarified—ideally through a consensus-building process—the group should identify the tasks that must be completed to achieve the group's overarching goals. In general, groups function more effectively when goals are explicit and members regularly receive feedback about their progress toward those goals (Locke & Latham, 1990; Weingart & Weldon, 1991).

Role Definition.   Teams tend to work more efficiently when the members understand the requirements of their roles. During team development, members may identify sources of role stress, which can occur when their responsibilities are ambiguous or when other people in the group misunderstand the duties associated with their role (see Chapter 5). In a smooth-functioning team, members know their own responsibilities, but they also know the roles that others perform. Teams also tend to have less centralized leadership structures, and so team builders must often teach groups to develop as autonomous production units.

Interpersonal Process Analysis.   Just as athletes must learn how to pool their individual abilities and energies to maximize the team's performance, employees must learn to coordinate their efforts with those of the other group members. Team members may complete exercises or take part in discussions that help them develop insight into the nature of their group's processes and their company's organizational dynamics. Members study the group's patterns of communication and attraction, decision-making procedures, sources of power, informal social norms, and varieties of intermember conflict. Team builders also make use of **process consultation** to help group members develop insight into the nature of their group's "work culture" (Schein,

---

Process consultation: Training group members to identify group processes (leadership, conflict) within the organization through didactic instruction, role playing, structured process analysis, and training in observational methods.

1971). A process consultation begins when an expert observes the unit at work and takes note of patterns of communication and attraction, decision-making procedures, sources of power, informal social norms, the potency of in-group pressures, and varieties of intermember conflict. Once the consultant understands how the group is working, he or she discusses these observations with the unit. Through didactic instruction, role playing, and training in observational methods, the consultant and group members develop ways to improve the group's dynamics.

Cohesion Building.   In most team sports, players must practice continually until they function as a single unit, and the desire for personal success must be transformed into a desire for group success. The team's coaches may create situations designed to foster a sense of team spirit, and they may encourage the players to formulate group goals, identify weaknesses in the team, and strive for cooperation and integration. Similarly, during team building in the work setting, the manager/consultant acts as the coach by helping the group develop a sense of team unity. Team building strengthens the group's morale by encouraging interpersonal trust, cooperation, and the development of a group identity.

Problem Solving.   Team members learn to use effective decisional methods to identify problems and their solution (Cooley, 1994). Many work teams, for example, are based on the **quality circle** model (Deming, 1975). Quality circles are small, employee-centered groups that are given decision-making authority by upper management. These teams meet to discuss problems in the workplace that are undermining productivity, efficiency, quality, or job satisfaction. Once the causes of these problems are identified, the group implements corrective changes. Should these changes prove ineffective, the problem-solving process begins again.

Are Teams Effective?

Organizational experts of the 1980s recommended using groups to accomplish goals, but today's experts go one step further: They recommend using *teams* to achieve organizational excellence. No matter what system the experts propose—quality circles, total quality management (TQM), job enrichment, self-managing teams, or management by objectives (MBO)—most will tout the benefits of using teams to get work done.

But is a team approach always the best approach (Dion, 1990)? Even though team building doesn't work in all cases, across many different types of organizations and job settings, absenteeism, turnover, and employee complaints decrease after a group-focused intervention (De Meuse & Liebowitz, 1981; Sundstrom et al., 1990; Woodman & Sherwood, 1980). Case studies of organizations also confirm the effectiveness of teams (Applebaum & Blatt, 1994). Texas Instruments, for example,

---

Quality circle: Small self-regulated group of employees charged with identifying ways to improve product quality.

increased productivity when it organized the employees into small groups whenever possible, took steps to build up team cohesiveness, and went to great lengths to establish clear goals based on realistic levels of aspiration (Bass & Ryterband, 1979). When a manufacturer in the United States shifted to work groups, supportive supervision, participant leadership, organizational overlap among groups, and intensity of group interaction, employee satisfaction increased and turnover decreased (Seashore & Bowers, 1970). Nonexperimental field studies of organizational development also support the wisdom of relying on teams. When researchers, through meta-analysis, examined the link between organizational change and performance, they found that companies that made multiple changes usually improved their performance and that group-level interventions were more closely linked to productivity than individual-level interventions (Macy & Izumi, 1993).

A team approach does not, however, ensure success. Cohesive groups, as noted earlier, can be strikingly unproductive if the group's norms do not call for high productivity. Also, some kinds of team-building interventions appear to be more useful than others. Interventions that increase group members' control over and involvement in work, for example, are more powerful than interventions that focus on morale boosting or envisioning goals (Cotton, 1993; Levine & D'Andrea Tyson, 1990).

Work teams are only one of the many areas where group dynamics overlaps with the field of organizational behavior. Because most work is carried out in groups, the influence of group processes is inevitable. When managers wonder how they should intervene to help their group become more productive, they are raising questions of leadership (Hollander & Offermann, 1990). Management teams that routinely make faulty decisions after spending months reviewing the issues may be suffering from groupthink. If productivity drops when members who once worked individually now pool their efforts in a communal project, the problem may be traced to social motivation problems. The study of organizations raises questions that are imminently practical, yet they are also ones that can be answered by drawing on theory and research in group dynamics.

SUMMARY

What is group cohesion?

1. Different groups achieve cohesiveness in different ways, for *group cohesion* reflects
   - the strength of the bonds linking group members to the group
   - the unity, or "we-ness," of a group
   - feelings of attraction for specific group members and the group itself
   - the degree to which the group members coordinate their efforts to achieve goals (teamwork)
2. Researchers have developed a number of *operational definitions* for cohesion, including observation, structured observation, and self-report methods.

What stages do groups typically pass through as they develop over time? Cohesion is, in most cases, the consequence of a period of *group development:* patterns of growth and change across the group's life span.

1. Many theorists agree with Tuckman's five-stage model:
   - Orientation (forming) stage: Members experience tentative interactions, tension, concern over ambiguity, growing interdependence, and attempts to identify the nature of the situation.
   - Conflict (storming) stage: Members express dissatisfaction with the group, respond emotionally, criticize one another, and form coalitions.
   - Structure (norming) stage: Unity increases, membership stabilizes, members report increased satisfaction, and the group's internal dynamics intensify.
   - Task performance (work) stage: Focus shifts to performance of tasks and goal attainment. Not all groups reach this stage, for even highly cohesive groups are not necessarily productive.
   - Dissolution (adjourning) stage: The group disbands. A group's entry into the dissolution stage can be either planned or spontaneous, but even planned dissolution can create problems for members as they work to reduce their dependence on the group.
2. Tuckman's model is a successive-stage theory; it specifies the usual order of the phases of group development. Cyclical models, such as Bales's *equilibrium model,* maintain that groups cycle through various stages repeatedly.

What are the positive and negative consequences of cohesion?

1. In most instances, cohesion is associated with increases in member satisfaction and decreases in turnover and stress.
2. Cohesion intensifies group processes. Dependence, pressure to conform, and acceptance of influence are greater in cohesive groups.
3. Even though cohesive groups usually outperform less cohesive groups, this relationship between cohesion and performance is strongest when members are committed to the group's tasks. Indeed, if group norms do not encourage high productivity, cohesiveness and productivity are not positively related.

Does team building enhance group productivity?

1. Teams are specialized types of performance groups. They stress cooperation among members, higher levels of structure and coordination, cohesion and identity, and goal attainment.
2. Examples of teams in business and industry include management and advisory groups, production groups, project groups, and action groups.
3. *Team building* uses a variety of methods to increase the effectiveness of *work teams,* including
   - clarifying goals and roles
   - training members to identify and control group processes
   - *process consultation* (observing, documenting, and analyzing the group's processes)
   - building cohesion
   - implementing structured approaches to decision making, such as *quality circles*
4. Team approaches do not ensure success, but they appear to increase effectiveness and member satisfaction.

....
FOR MORE INFORMATION
....

The Disney Version: The Life, Times, Art and Commerce of Walt Disney, by Richard Schickel (1968), describes the group that created *Snow White.*

Group Process: A Developmental Perspective,
by Susan A. Wheelan (1994), provides an
extensive analysis of each stage that marks
the maturation of most groups.

*The Social Psychology of Group
Cohesiveness: From Attraction to Social
Identity,* by Michael A. Hogg (1992), thoroughly reviews conceptual analyses of the
concept of cohesion and bases its integrative theoretical reinterpretation on social
identity theory.

*Team Effectiveness and Decision Making in
Organizations,* by Richard A. Guzzo,
Eduardo Salas, and associates (1995),
includes advanced chapters written by
leading researchers in the field of organizational dynamics and group effectiveness.

"Teams in Organizations: Recent Research on
Performance and Effectiveness," by
Richard A. Guzzo and Marcus W. Dickson
(*Annual Review of Psychology,* 1996) is a
succinct, up-to-date analysis of the use of
teams in organizational settings.

*Teamwork: What Must Go Right/What Can
Go Wrong,* by Carl E. Larson and Frank
M. J. Lafasto (1989), proffers eight basic
suggestions for creating successful, productive teams in organizations, including clear
goals, norms that encourage productivity,
and principled leadership.

ACTIVITY 6–1 IN WHAT WAYS DO GROUPS CHANGE OVER TIME?

Study the long-term development of a group to which you currently belong or once
belonged. Select a group that has a history that you can document, rather than one that
has only recently formed. Classes that meet for a semester before they disband, sports
teams, project teams at work, and informal friendship cliques are just a few of the types of
groups you can examine.

1. Begin by describing the group in detail as it existed when it first formed. Give examples
   and anecdotal evidence when appropriate.
2. Describe any changes that took place in the group over time. Make note of the extent to
   which the group experienced (a) an orientation stage, (b) conflict, (c) increased cohesion
   and changes in structure, and (d) a period of high performance. Which of the two theories discussed in the book—Tuckman's stage model or Bales's equilibrium model—best
   describes your group?
3. Discuss group socialization processes, focusing on yourself. Has your evaluation of, commitment toward, and role in the group changed over time? Has the group changed in its
   evaluation of and commitment to you?

ACTIVITY 6–2 WHAT IS A TEAM?

Teams are groups, but what makes them unique? Their unity? Their focus on group goals? The interdependence among members? Explore these questions by interviewing at least two members of a team. A work group in a business setting, a sports team, a policy or military squad, and a surgical team are all examples of the kinds of groups to investigate. Ask members five sets of questions, and record their answers before drawing general conclusions.

1. Interdependence questions:
   - Do the members of the group work well together?
   - Are there any problems coordinating the group's activities?
   - Do people work together, or do they primarily work on their own projects?
   - What happens when a group member doesn't perform up to the group's standards?
2. Structure questions:
   - How organized is the group?
   - Is it clear who is supposed to do what?
   - Are there conflicts about who is in charge?
3. Cohesiveness questions:
   - Would you say that your group is a cohesive, tight-knit one?
   - Do people like each other?
   - Does the group have much turnover?
4. Social identity questions:
   - Does the group have a name?
   - Are group members proud to say that they are members of this group?
   - Do the group members share a sense of identity with one another?
5. Goal questions:
   - Do members of your group put the group's goal above their own individual goals?
   - Do members work hard to reach the group's goals?
   - Does the group have a specific mission or goal?

7

Influence

Ancient peoples believed that an ethereal fluid—influentia—flowed down from the stars and planets and affected human actions. Group dynamicists agree that subtle, powerful forces leave their mark on people's personalities and behaviors, but they trace these forces to *social* influence: interpersonal processes that change group members' thoughts, feelings, and behaviors.

- When do people change their opinions, judgments, or actions to match the group's opinions, judgments, or actions?
- When do people resist the group's influence and instead change the majority's opinions, judgments, or actions?
- Why do people conform?
- Do social influence processes shape juries' verdicts?

CONTENTS

The Corona Trial Jury: The Group as Arbiter of Justice

MAJORITY INFLUENCE: THE POWER OF THE MANY

Asch and Majority Influence

Limits to Majority Influence

MINORITY INFLUENCE: THE POWER OF THE FEW

Moscovici and Minority Influence

Influence as Social Impact

SOURCES OF GROUP INFLUENCE

Informational Influence

Normative Influence

Interpersonal Influence

APPLICATION: UNDERSTANDING JURIES

Jury Dynamics

How Effective Are Juries?

Improving Juries

SUMMARY

FOR MORE INFORMATION

ACTIVITIES

The Corona Trial Jury: The Group as Arbiter of Justice

Do you solemnly swear that you will take this jury to some secret place and that you will not converse with them about the case, nor allow anyone else to do so, and when they have reached a verdict you will return them into court by order of the Court, so help you God?

With these words, the judge charged the jury in the trial of Juan Corona. Corona, a Mexican citizen and labor contractor, was on trial for the murders of 25 California men. Police discovered the bodies of the men in shallow graves in a lonely orchard outside Yuba City. The police traced receipts for supplies found in one of the graves back to Corona, and the prosecutor built his case on hundreds of bits of evidence that implicated Corona and no one else. But was Corona guilty of one of the largest mass murders in U.S. history?

After five months of trial, this question was put to a jury of Corona's peers: men and women, strangers to one another, chosen at random from the community, unschooled in legal principles, and unpracticed in group decision making (see Table 7–1). Ac-

TABLE 7–1   THE CORONA TRIAL JURORS

Juror	Age	Occupation	Characteristics
Faye Blazek	66	Retired teacher	Well educated; spoke with precision; backed up points with compelling arguments
Rick Bremen	26	Welder	Defended his points vehemently, often to the irritation of the other jurors
Frank Broksell	58	Retired toolmaker	Skeptical of the legal process; contributed only rarely
Larry Gallipeo	41	Ship construction	Quiet; maintained a casual, relaxed attitude during the deliberations
Matt Johnson	54	Retired sergeant	Easygoing, active contributor who diffused tension through laughter
Victor Lorenzo	45	Grocer	Reserved; contributed only when knowledgeable on the subject
George Muller	43	Employee at air base	Enthusiastic and outgoing; moderately involved in the discussion
Jim Owen	39	Shipyard inspector	Thoughtful contributor; offered appropriate and provocative insights
Ernie Phillips	53	Retired sergeant	Foreman of the jury; talkative and task oriented; accepted by jurors
Donald Rogers	60	Retired machinist	Smoked a cigar; irritated others by speaking loudly, brusquely
Naomi Underwood	61	Retired clerk	Prior experience in jury duty; high-strung; raised issues that others felt were irrelevant
Calvin Williams	51	School janitor	Only African American on the jury; frequent participant; guided the group and maintained discussion norms

Source: Villasenor, 1977.

cording to Victor Villaseñor's (1977) account of the Corona trial, the jurors took their work very seriously. They met at a large table hour after hour, reviewing the evidence, sharing their own interpretations of that evidence, pointing out inconsistencies in one another's reasoning, and from time to time voting by secret ballot. For eight days, this jury reviewed the evidence, debated points of law, separated fact from innuendo, and argued over ethics. For eight days, the jurors grappled with their charge, searching for agreement among themselves. When the deliberations ended, all the group members agreed: Corona was guilty.

How did the jury reach its verdict? The answer lies in **social influence:** interpersonal processes that change group members' thoughts, feelings, and behaviors. Much of this influence flows from the group to the individual. This *majority influence* pushes the group members together, toward consensus and stability. Social influence, however, sometimes flows from the individual to the group. If the group is to endure, its members must sacrifice some of their autonomy for the sake of the group's unity. But if the group is to meet new challenges and improve over time, it must recognize and accept ideas that conflict with the status quo. In the Corona jury, the majority prevailed, but the minority influenced the outcome, too. No one wanted to make a mistake, and so the jury spent time considering the arguments offered by jurors who did not think Corona was guilty. Whereas majority influence increases consensus within the group, *minority influence* sustains individuality and innovation. Here we consider the nature of this give-and-take between majorities and minorities and the implications of this influence process for understanding how juries make their decisions.

MAJORITY INFLUENCE: THE POWER OF THE MANY

The lone individual is free to think and act as he or she chooses, but group members must abandon some of their independence. The 12 jurors, once they walked into the jury room, had to coordinate their actions with the activities of the other group members. Each one strived to change the group to suit his or her personal inclinations, but at the same time, the group influenced each individual member: It swayed their judgments, favored one interpretation of reality over another, and encouraged certain behaviors while discouraging others. Four of the jurors walked into the jury room convinced that Corona was innocent, but one by one, they all changed their votes to guilty.

Asch and Majority Influence

Groups influence their members. This principle lies at the heart of group dynamics. Early researchers, such as M. Sherif (1936) and Newcomb (1943), confirmed this principle when they discovered that people's attitudes and outlooks shift when the group's attitudes and outlooks shift. (Their work is discussed in Chapters 2 and 5.) But it was Solomon Asch's studies of conformity that offered the most convincing evidence of the power of a group (Asch, 1952, 1955, 1957). The men he studied

---

Social influence: Interpersonal processes that change the thoughts, feelings, or behaviors of another person.

thought they were taking a visual acuity test. They sat in a semicircle facing Asch's experimenter, who explained that on each of 18 trials, he would show the group two cards. One card bore a single line that was to serve as the standard. The second card contained three numbered test lines (see Figure 7–1). The group's task: to pick the line that matched the standard line in length. One test line was always the same length as the standard line, so the correct answer was obvious. Few people made mistakes when making such judgments alone.

On each trial, the experimenter displayed the two cards and asked the subjects to state their answers aloud, starting at the left side of the semicircle. On the first trial, everyone in the group picked the correct answer. This agreement held for the second

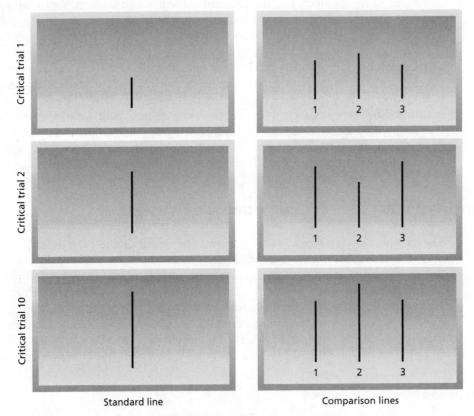

FIGURE 7–1 Will people agree with their group, even when the group is making an obvious mistake on a simple task? Asch asked groups to judge the length of lines, but all the group members except one were confederates who picked the wrong answer on 12 of the 18 problems. On the first of these 12 critical trials, the standard line was 3 inches long, and Comparison Line 3 was the correct answer. However, the group chose Line 1, which was actually 3¾ inches long. On the second critical trial, the correct answer was 1, but the group unanimously answered with 2. The lines used in the tenth critical trial are also shown; the correct answer in this case was 2, but the group suggested 1.

(*Source:* Asch, 1957.)

trial as well. But on the third trial, the first subject picked Line 1 even though Line 3 was a closer match to the stimulus. Then, as the other group members reported, each one followed the first subject's lead by selecting Line 1 as the correct answer. By the time the study was completed, the group had made mistakes on 12 of the 18 trials.

These mistakes were planned. Only one group member was an actual subject. All the others were trained confederates who deliberately made errors to see if the subject would conform to a unanimous majority's judgments. When the subject arrived, he was seated so that he answered after most of the other subjects did. He would study the lines, identify the correct answer, but hear everyone else make a different selection. When his turn came, he could disagree with the other subjects' judgments, or he could conform to the group's wrong answer.

How did Asch's subjects react? Many conformed, changing their answer to match the answer given by the other group members. In fact, 76.4% of 123 men made at least one conforming response. On average, a subject gave the correct answer on about two-thirds of the test trials but conformed on 36.8% of the trials (4.4 out of 12).

Asch himself was surprised by his findings (Gleitman, Rozin, & Sabini, 1997). He fully expected that his subjects would resist the pressure to conform and speak out against the incorrect majority's view. Yet they did not. In search of an explanation, Asch and other researchers looked more closely at the innocuous, but complex, situation that Asch's subjects faced. Although the task was easy, subjects made their judgments in public rather than in private. They were also the only members of the group who disagreed with the majority, and the majority was numerically substantial. In retrospect, Asch realized that these features of the group setting greatly increased the power of the majority.

Unanimity and Conformity.   On the sixth day of deliberations, the jury was split 9 to 3 favoring guilt. Naomi Underwood looked around the table, wondering who else had voted not guilty and hoping that others would swing that way, too. But when the jury voted again later that day, the tally was 11 to 1. Naomi now realized that she was the only person who thought that Corona was innocent of the murders, and on the next ballot, she changed her vote to guilty.

Like Naomi, Asch's subjects had no partner; all the other members of the group agreed among themselves, so each subject faced a unanimous majority. Whereas the lone person stands little chance of resisting the influence of the majority, a minority coalition, even if it contains only two individuals, is more likely to withstand the majority's attempts at influence. Asch demonstrated this effect by telling one of the confederates to agree with the subject on some trials. As predicted, when someone else disagreed with the majority, conformity rates were cut to one-fourth their previous levels. Even an inaccurate ally helped subjects withstand conformity pressures. In yet another variation, Asch arranged for some confederates to disagree with the majority but still give an incorrect answer. Subjects did not agree with the erroneous nonconformist, but his dissent made it easier for them to express their own viewpoint (Asch, 1955).

Why are members of a minority coalition able to resist conformity pressures that would overwhelm them were they alone? First, the power of the majority is weakened when its unanimity is broken. A single dissenter's arguments can be dismissed as personal idiosyncrasies or biases, but several dissenters cast doubt on the majority's view (Morris & Miller, 1975). Most subjects realize that the group will think that their nonconforming answer is strange and irrational. After all, "the correct judgment appeared so obvious that only perceptual incompetents, fools, or madmen could err" (Ross, Bierbrauer, & Hoffman, 1976, p. 149). A partner, however, makes their answer, and they themselves, seem more reasonable. Second, when people face the majority without a single ally, they bear the brunt of all the group's pressure; the influence pressures that are put on a single dissenter are just too great (Asch, 1955). Third, the larger the size of the minority coalition, the smaller the majority's coalition. A majority of five united against one is far stronger than a majority of four united against two (Clark, 1990).

Strength in Numbers.   When the subject in the Asch situation heard the first person name the incorrect line as the best match, he probably thought little of it. But when the second person agreed with the first, he must have started to wonder. Then a third, a fourth, and a fifth person: all agreeing with one another, all selecting the wrong answer. What should he do?

When it comes to social influence, size makes a difference. As the number of individuals in a unanimous majority increases, social influence increases—up to a point. When Asch replicated his procedures with groups ranging in size from 2 to 17 members, few people conformed when one other person disagreed with their judgments. When subjects faced two opponents (2 against 1), conformity increased to 13.6% and 3 against 1 increased conformity to 31.8%. Adding even more people generated a little more conformity (conformity peaked at 37.1% in the 7-person groups), but even 16 against 1 did not raise conformity appreciably above the 31.8% level achieved with 3 against 1 (Asch, 1952, 1955).

The positive relationship between majority size and conformity has been confirmed in many studies using both laboratory and field methods. However, the precise nature of the relationship between size and conformity is still much debated. Some theorists, such as Bibb Latané (1981) and Brian Mullen (1983, 1986b, 1987b), predict that the first person who opposes the lone minority has the greatest social impact. Each additional person adds to the majority's impact, but the gain in impact decreases as the majority grows larger and larger. Computer simulations of groups making decisions, including juries, confirm these predictions, with one important exception. As Figure 7–2 indicates, conformity is relatively rare when one person faces one other person, but it increases substantially in the case of one against two and one against three. The increase beyond a majority of four is negligible (Nowak & Latané, 1994; Tanford & Penrod, 1984; Tindale, Davis, Vollrath, Nagao, & Hinsz, 1990).

A host of situational and interpersonal factors, including anonymity of responses, the group's cohesiveness and longevity, and concern for accuracy, influence the shape of the conformity curve shown in Figure 7–2. Majorities, for example, become more influential when group members think that each person in the majority is acting independently of the others. People who were trying to make a decision about a court case, when given information about others' judgments, responded differently if they thought that these other people reached their conclusions independently of one an

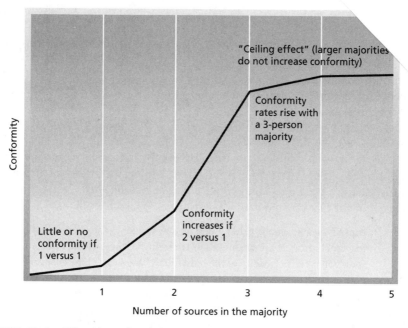

FIGURE 7-2 When do conformity pressures reach their peak in groups? Studies conducted in a number of settings suggest that conformity increases when one person disagrees with two people and again when one person disagrees with three people. Adding more people to the majority beyond three does not appreciably increase conformity. Note that any process that increases up to a point but then holds steady is called a "ceiling effect."

other. When the information was apparently coming from a single social entity—for example, a group of individuals working together—the magnitude of conformity was the same whether the group contained two members or six members. However, when the number of discrete social entities was increased (e.g., from two independent individuals to six independent individuals or from 1 four-person group to 2 two-person groups), a ceiling effect became evident when the number of entities reached three (Wilder, 1977, Experiment 2; see Jackson, 1987, and Wolf, 1987, for reviews).

Conformity and Compliance. When people respond to group influence by changing their stated position, one of at least two different processes may be occurring. **Compliance** occurs when group members privately disagree with the group, but publicly express an opinion that matches the opinions expressed by the majority of the group. Corona juror Naomi Underwood, for example, never accepted the guilty verdict. But as the deliberations wore on and she became exhausted, she decided to go

---

Compliance: Change that occurs when the targets of social influence publicly accept the influencer's position, but privately continue to maintain their original beliefs.

along with the majority even though she privately disagreed. **Conversion, or private acceptance,** in contrast, occurs when group members actually change their minds and come to agree with the group's position. On the Corona jury, for example, Calvin Williams initially voted not guilty because he did not know if general circumstantial evidence, such as bloodstains in Corona's truck, should be considered as evidence of particular murders. He changed his vote when this point was clarified during the deliberations (Allen, 1965; Kiesler & Kiesler, 1976; Levine & Russo, 1987; Nail, 1986; Nail & Van Leeuwen, 1993; Stricker, Messick, & Jackson, 1970; Willis, 1963).

Some of Asch's subjects conformed because of conversion: They thought they were mistaken in their personal judgment and decided that the group was correct. Most, though, were only complying: They went along with the majority, even though they thought that the majority was mistaken. As Asch explains:

> Among the extremely yielding persons we found a group who quickly reached the conclusion: "I am wrong, they are right." Others yielded in order "not to spoil your results." Many of the individuals who went along suspected that the majority were "sheep" following the first responder, or that the majority were victims of an optical illusion; nevertheless, these suspicions failed to free them at the moment of decision. [1955, p. 33]

Asch, by creating a situation in which group members stated their opinions publicly, increased pressure to comply. Had he let his subjects use secret ballots, fewer would have gone along with the majority. This conclusion is supported by studies of conformity in the so-called Crutchfield apparatus. Asch ingeniously captured the essentials of many group decision settings in his studies, but his procedure was inefficient: Many confederates were required to study just one subject. Richard S. Crutchfield (1955) solved this problem by leaving out the confederates. In Crutchfield's laboratory, the subjects made their judgments while seated in individual cubicles (see Figure 7–3). They flipped a small switch on a response panel to report their judgments to the researcher, and their answers would supposedly light up on the other group members' panels as well. Crutchfield told each person in the group that he or she was to answer last, and he himself simulated the majority's judgments from a master control box. During the critical trials, Crutchfield would lead subjects to think that all the other subjects were giving erroneous answers.

Crutchfield's method sacrifices the face-to-face interaction between the subject and confederates, but it is efficient: Five or more subjects participate in a single session, and no confederate is needed. Moreover, unlike the Asch situation, group members' responses are anonymous. Hence, fewer people agree with the majority in a Crutchfield situation relative to an Asch situation (Bond & Smith, 1996). Indeed, the change that takes place in such groups may reflect conversion rather than a temporary compliance that disappears when the individual is away from the group and its influence.

Conversion (private acceptance): Change that occurs when group members personally accept the influencer's position.

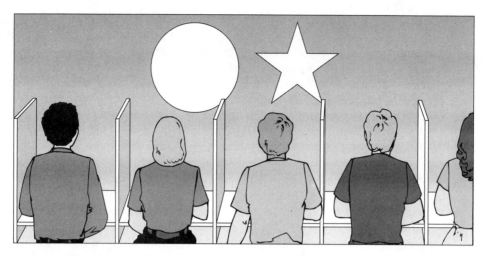

FIGURE 7–3   What is the Crutchfield apparatus? Richard Crutchfield studied conformity by seating subjects in individual booths and gathering their responses electronically. Subjects, when asked a question such as "Which one of the figures has a greater area, the star or the circle?" answered by flipping the appropriate switch in their booth. They thought that their answers were being transmitted to the experimenter and the other subjects, but in actuality, the experimenter was simulating the majority's judgment from a master control panel.

(*Source:* Wrightsman, 1977.)

Limits to Majority Influence

Asch studied young men making public judgments about relatively inconsequential matters. All lived in the United States at a time when their culture was politically conservative. Would his findings hold at other times, with other kinds of people, in other cultures? (See Allen, 1975; Bond & Smith, 1996; Hare, 1976; Kiesler & Kiesler, 1976.)

Conformity Across Cultures and Eras.   In the years since Asch first published his findings, other researchers have carried out his basic procedure in more than a dozen countries, including the United States, Britain, Belgium, Fiji, Holland, Kuwait, Portugal, and Zimbabwe. When Rod Bond and Peter B. Smith (1996) recently surveyed these studies, they concluded that Asch's study may have *underestimated* conformity by studying people living in a relatively individualistic culture. As noted in Chapter 3, individualistic cultures typical of Western societies place the individual above the collective. Collectivistic societies, which are more prevalent in Asia, Africa, and South America, stress shared goals and interdependence. As a result, people tend to conform more in collectivistic cultures, especially when the source of influence is family members or friends rather than strangers (Frager, 1970).

Bond and Smith also checked for changes in conformity during the period from 1952 to 1994 to determine if conformity rates fluctuated as society's tolerance of dissent waxed and waned. When Asch carried out his work, social norms stressed respect for authority and traditional values, whereas the late 1960s were marked by student activism and social disobedience. This period of rebelliousness was followed by a prolonged period of social stability. Do entire generations of people become more or less conforming, depending on the sociopolitical climate of the times in which they live? Bond and Smith discovered that conformity rates have indeed dropped since the 1950s, but they found no support for the idea that conformity is a "child of its time." Conformity is decreasing, but this decline was not sharper in the 1960s or more gradual in the relatively placid 1970s and 1980s (Larsen, 1982; Perrin & Spencer, 1980, 1981).

Conformity Across the Sexes.   What if Asch had tested women? Would they have conformed more than or less than the men? Alice H. Eagly and her colleagues reviewed dozens of studies before concluding that women conform more than men —but only when group members are sitting face-to-face and they must state their opinions aloud. In more anonymous, low-surveillance situations, such as that developed by Crutchfield, differences between men and women are almost nonexistent (Cooper, 1979; Eagly & Carli, 1981; cf. Bond & Smith, 1996).

Why do women only conform more than men in face-to-face groups? Eagly suggests that despite changes in stereotypes about women and men, groups traditionally reward men for acting in dominant, nonconforming ways and women for acting in cooperative, communal ways. If women feel that they should behave in a traditional way, they may conform more than men (Eagly, Wood, & Feshbaugh, 1981). But women who do not accept the traditional role of women do not conform more than men (Bem, 1975, 1985). Women, too, may agree with other group members for interpersonal reasons (Eagly et al., 1981). Whereas men tend to use disagreement to separate themselves from the rest of the group, women may use agreement to create consensus and cohesion (Maslach, Santee, & Wade, 1987; Santee & Jackson, 1982; Santee & Maslach, 1982). Sexist attitudes, too, may prevent women from expressing their dissent in groups. Studies of status allocation reviewed in Chapter 5, for example, indicate that women are often accorded less status than men in groups. This sexist bias against women undermines their resistance to influence and weakens their power to influence others (Eagly, 1987).

Conformity Across People.   The young men that Asch studied varied, to some extent, in their reaction to the majority's influence. The majority of them conformed, but only 6 (5%) agreed with every single error made by the majority. And 23.6% never conformed at all.

Different group members respond to influence in different ways. Some tend to conform more than others, and these variations often reflect differences in age, personality, and expertise. Conformists are often authoritarians: Their conventionality, conservative values, and unwillingness to confront authority increase their willingness to accept the majority's opinion (see Table 7–2). Conformists also tend to let the situation and other people influence their perceptions, opinions, and outlooks. Nonconformists, in contrast, are lower in their need for social approval and more self-confident. Noncon-

TABLE 7–2   A SAMPLING OF PERSONALITY CHARACTERISTICS THAT ARE
RELIABLY ASSOCIATED WITH CONFORMITY AND NONCONFORMITY

Characteristic	Reaction to Influence
Authoritarianism	Authoritarians respect and obey authorities and social conventions; they maintain the status quo (Altemeyer, 1988).
Dependency	People who are high in dependency display heightened compliance, conformity, and suggestibility as well as sensitivity to interpersonal cues (Bornstein, 1992).
Gender identity	Masculine and androgynous individuals conform less on gender-neutral tasks than feminine individuals (Bem, 1975).
Individuation	People who are high in the desire to publicly differentiate themselves from others (high individuators) are more willing to express dissenting opinions and contribute more to group discussions (Whitney, Sagrestano, Maslach, 1994).
Intelligence	Less intelligent people and individuals who are uncertain of their abilities conform more (conformity and intelligence are negatively correlated, $r = -.63$; Crutchfield, 1955).
Self-blame	Adolescents who tend to blame themselves for negative outcomes conform more than individuals who are low in self-blame (Costanzo, 1970).
Self-esteem	Low-self-esteem individuals conform more than moderate- and high-self-esteem individuals (Berkowitz & Lundy, 1957).
Self-monitoring	High self-monitors, because of higher self-presentational tendencies, conform more when striving to make a positive impression (Chen, Shechter, & Chaiken, 1996).

formists, too, are in some cases **counterconformists,** or **anticonformists:** people who tend to refuse to conform to any majority, apparently because they resist all forms of authority and influence, regardless of the source (Schein, 1956).

Conformity Across Tasks and Settings.   Asch studied conformity in newly formed groups working on a very simple task that was not particularly consequential. Would his findings have varied if he had used a task that had dramatic consequences?

Robert Baron and his colleagues (1996) examined these issues by replacing Asch's line-judgment task with the "identify the suspect" task. They showed subjects slides of a suspect and then asked them to identify the suspect in a slide showing four people standing in a police lineup. The researchers made the task easier for some subjects by showing them the slides for a total of 15 seconds and harder for others by cutting the viewing time down to only 1.5 seconds. They also told some subjects to be as accurate in their judgments as possible, but downplayed the need for accuracy for others. When the task was a very easy one, subjects conformed to the incorrect

Counterconformists (anticonformists): People who publicly express ideas, beliefs, and judgments that conflict with the group's standards simply to disagree with the group.

judgments of two confederates on 33% of the critical trials when the task was unimportant, but on only 16% of the critical trials when the researchers stressed the importance of accuracy. Increasing the difficulty of the task reversed this effect, for conformity jumped from 35% in the low-importance condition to 54% in the high-importance condition (Baron, Vandello, & Brunsman, 1996; Campbell, Tesser, & Fairey, 1986; Di Vesta, 1959).

Baron's work illustrates the situational specificity of conformity. Groups vary in size, structure, cohesiveness, and goals, and their tasks vary in complexity, ambiguity, and importance. When these aspects of the group situation shift, so do conformity pressures. A key corollary to the premise that groups influence their members is the notion that the strength of that influence depends on the nature of the group situation.

MINORITY INFLUENCE: THE POWER OF THE FEW

Galileo, despite pressure from religious authorities, insisted that the planets revolve around the sun rather than the earth. Mohandas K. Gandhi, the leader of the Indian nationalist movement, suffered repeated imprisonment and abuses when he refused to submit to the colonial authority. Martin Luther King, Jr., was brutalized and demeaned for advocating racial equality, yet he continued his efforts until his death. The composer Igor Stravinsky was denounced as a musical heretic when *The Rite of Spring* was first performed, but he refused to change a note.

These historical examples offer a counterpoint to Asch's findings, for they demonstrate that the majority does not always overwhelm the minority; sometimes, the dissenter, despite all the majority's pressure, stands firm. Indeed, in all these cases, the minority actually changed the majority. The minority sometimes becomes the influencer, and the majority changes in response to that influence (Crano, 1994; Nemeth, 1994; Moscovici, 1994; Witte, 1994).

Moscovici and Minority Influence

Serge Moscovici and his colleagues have demonstrated the power of the minority by reversing the traditional Asch situation. Instead of placing a single subject in a group of confederates, Moscovici tests the reaction of two or more subjects to the disagreeing judgments of one or two confederates. In one experiment, Moscovici and his colleagues asked six-person groups to judge the color and brightness of a series of color slides. All the slides were blue, but Moscovici's confederates consistently argued they were green. When making their judgments, 8.4% of the subjects shifted their judgments from blue to green—not as much influence as found in the Asch study, but a significant amount of influence nonetheless (Moscovici, Lage, & Naffrechoux, 1969; see, too, Moscovici, 1985, 1994; Moscovici & Faucheux, 1972; Moscovici & Lage, 1976; Moscovici & Nemeth, 1974; Moscovici & Personnaz, 1980; Nemeth, 1985).

Subsequent research, conducted in many cases in research laboratories in Europe rather than the United States, confirmed and extended Moscovici's findings. Many of these studies suggest that minorities are the most influential when they adopt a consistent behavioral style—when they unwaveringly argue their position. Such behavioral consistency is particularly influential when the majority interprets the consistency positively. Groups will listen more to consistent minorities whose dissent is taken to be a sign of their confidence and perspicacity rather than their rigidity and closed-mindedness (Wood, Lundgren, Ouellette, Busceme, & Blackstone, 1994). Hence:

- Minorities who offer compelling arguments that contradict the majority are more influential than minorities who fail to refute the majority's position (Clark, 1990).
- Minorities are more influential when the majority is uncertain about the correctness of its position (Witte, 1994).
- Minorities who explain their dissent by saying, "I think it's important that you cooperate with me; I know what I'm doing," are more influential than minorities who adopt a more subdued style *if* their solutions to the group's problems are correct (Shackelford, Wood, & Worchel, 1996, Experiment 2).
- Minorities who are so confident that they deliberately choose to sit at the head of the table are more influential than minorities who sit at a side chair (Nemeth & Wachtler, 1974).
- Flexible minorities who grant minor concessions to the majority are more influential than rigid minorities (Mungy, 1982; Mungy & Pérez, 1991; Pérez & Mungy, 1996).

In general, the greater the perceived competency and group-centered motivation of the individual, the more influential the minority (Levine & Russo, 1987). Minorities become less influential when the other members of the group redefine the boundaries of the group so that the minority is thought to be a member of the outgroup (Alvaro & Crano, 1997).

Status and Minority Influence.   Minorities who consistently disagree influence the majority, but so do minority members who preface their dissent with conformity. Edwin P. Hollander (1971) studied the impact of early conformity in five-man groups working on a complex decisional task. Hollander's confederate systematically violated certain rules of procedure during the early phases of problem solving or later in the session. Hollander found that the confederate's influence over the others tended to increase over time but that a confederate who prefaced his nonconformity with conformity exerted somewhat more influence than an early nonconformist. Similar findings were reported when children with well-developed leadership skills were placed in new groups (Merei, 1958). Those who tried to take over and change the group immediately were rejected, whereas those who worked within the group for a time before attempting innovations became successful influencers.

Hollander (1971) developed the concept of **idiosyncrasy credits** to explain the group's positive reaction to the minority who prefaces dissent with conformity. According to Hollander (1971, p. 573), idiosyncrasy credits are "the positive impressions

---

Idiosyncrasy credits: Interpersonal credits, or bonuses, earned by individuals each time they make a contribution to their group.

of a person held by others, whether defined in the narrower terms of a small face-to-face group or a larger social entity such as an organization or even a total society." These credits accumulate during the course of interaction, typically as the member contributes to the progress of the group toward desired goals. Because high-status members have usually contributed more in the past and possess more valued personal characteristics, they have more idiosyncrasy credits. Therefore, if they do not conform, their actions are more tolerable to the other members. The low-status members' balance of credits is, in comparison, very low; hence, they are permitted a smaller latitude for nonconformity. The idiosyncrasy model suggests that influence levels in a group are increased by careful conformity to group norms during the early phases of group formation, followed by dissent when a sufficient balance of credit has been established (Hollander, 1958, 1960, 1961, 1971, 1981).

Hollander's advice about early conformity contrasts, to some extent, with Moscovici's recommendations concerning consistent nonconformity. Hollander warns that dissenters who challenge the majority without first earning high status in the group will probably be overruled by the majority, but Moscovici argues that consistent nonconformity will lead to innovation and change. Both tactics, however, may prove effective. Researchers compared the two in group discussions of three issues. One minority built up idiosyncrasy credits by agreeing on the first two issues the group discussed, but then disagreeing on the third. The second minority built up consistency by disagreeing with the group on all three issues. Both minorities were influential, although the minority who built up idiosyncrasy credits was more influential in all-male groups (Bray, Johnson, & Chilstrom, 1982).

Compliance Versus Conversion.   Moscovici believes that minorities and majorities influence in two different ways. Majorities influence members directly; they create compliance as individuals compare their judgments with other group members' judgments. Minorities, in contrast, influence members indirectly; they create *conversion* to the minority's position as individuals struggle to validate their judgments. Many of the Corona jurors, for example, expressed misgivings after they filed their final decision. Naomi Underwood, in particular, regretted her decision to side with those who favored guilt; she had complied, but she had not converted (Moscovici, 1994; see, too, Maass, West, & Cialdini, 1987; Nemeth, 1986).

Moscovici theorizes that this indirect influence of minorities occurs at a latent level, becoming evident only when the group has completed its initial deliberations and moved on to another task. Researchers demonstrated this tendency in one study by asking five-person groups to make an award in a simulated personal-injury case. One of the five group members was a confederate who consistently argued for an award of $3000, which was substantially below the $15,000 award favored by the majority. On the final vote, the majority's position was unchanged, but when the subjects turned to a second case, they gave significantly smaller awards than subjects who had never been exposed to the minority (Nemeth & Wachtler, 1974).

Thus, when behavior is measured directly, the majority prevails. When an indirect measure is taken, however, the minority may prevail (Maass & Clark, 1984). The indirect impact of the minority may also extend to the level of perception. Moscovici and Bernard Personnaz exposed female subjects to a series of blue slides that were consistently labeled green by a confederate. On each trial, the subject reported her judgment of the color (the direct measure) but was also asked to look at a blank white screen and report the color of the slide's afterimage (the indirect measure). Unknown to the subjects, the afterimage of blue is yellow/orange, and the afterimage of green is red/purple. Subjects' judgments of the color of the slides were not influenced by the minority, as Moscovici predicted. But their judgments of the afterimage did change; they saw more red/purple (Moscovici & Personnaz, 1980).

These findings are provocative and have generated considerable debate (Doms & Van Averinaet, 1980; Sorrentino, King, & Leo, 1980). When combined with other evidence, however, they suggest that "minorities tend to produce profound and lasting changes in attitudes and perceptions that generalize to new settings and over time . . . whereas majorities are more likely to elicit compliance that is confined to the original influence setting" (Maass et al., 1987, pp. 56–57). Minorities, then, are a source of *innovation* in groups, for they shake the confidence of the majority and force the group to seek out new information about the situation. In one series of studies, when people worked on problems in groups, they often accepted the majority's solutions, even if those solutions were flawed. If, however, a minority argued for a non-obvious solution, the group members abandoned the flawed solutions and sought solutions that were both novel and correct. They did not accept the minority's proposal, as they had the majority's, but they did reevaluate their original answer (Nemeth, 1994; Nemeth & Wachtler, 1983).

Influence as Social Impact

Influence in groups is two-sided. From the majority's perspective, change takes place when the minority abandons its radical ideas and conforms. From the minority's perspective, change takes place when the majority reexamines and possibly revises its position. But change in groups is actually a mutual process; the majority influences the minority, and the minority influences the majority (Latané, 1997; Spitzer & Davis, 1978; Tanford & Penrod, 1984).

Bibb Latané's **social impact theory** explains this dynamic tension between majorities and minorities in groups. He illustrates his theory by likening people to light bulbs. When a single lamp in an otherwise dark room is switched on, the room is filled with brightness. But the amount of light in the room depends on the strength of the bulb in the lamp: A 25-watt bulb gives just enough light to see by; a 100-watt bulb reaches every corner. The lamp's location is also important. A lamp in one corner may leave the opposite corner of the room in shadows. Also, if we want more light, we can always turn on more lamps. Eventually, though, the room will become so bright that adding another light will make no difference.

In an analogous fashion, the impact of group members on one another depends on their *strength,* or status in the group. People who are new to a group, for example,

Social impact theory: An analysis of social influence processes that proposes that the impact of any source of influence depends on the strength, immediacy, and number of influencers involved. Symbolically, $I = f(SIN)$.

may have little status and so cannot influence the group. They are 25-watt bulbs surrounded by 100-watt bulbs. People who are physically present or nearby—whether they are members of the minority or the majority—are higher in *immediacy* and so more influential. The *number* of individuals in the majority and the minority also determines the magnitude of social impact. As with light bulbs, the more people, the greater their impact—up to a point. The first light you turn on in a dark room has a greater impact than the hundredth light you turn on. Similarly, the first person who disagrees with you has more impact than the hundredth person added to a majority that disagrees with you. Thus, conformity pressures increase, but at a gradually decreasing rate (Latané, 1981, 1996, 1997; Latané & Wolf, 1981).

Latané sums up this theorizing with the *law of social impact*: Impact is a function of the strength (S), immediacy (I), and number (N) of the people (or, more precisely, sources) present, or $I = f(SIN)$. As this law predicts, factors that increase the strength of a source of influence—occupation, age, expertise, status, or authority—increase the source's impact on others (Mullen, 1985). When individuals identify the people who have the most impact on them, they are far more likely to identify people who work or live in close proximity to them, as the concept of immediacy suggests (Latané, Liu, Nowak, Bonevento, & Zheng, 1995). And, as noted earlier in the chapter, both majorities and minorities become more influential as they increase in size (Latané & Wolf, 1981; Wolf & Latané, 1983).

Latané and his colleagues, in their more recent analyses, use the basic model to describe the way social influence processes change groups over time. Some groups, like those studied by Asch and Moscovici, only meet once, discuss issues, and then disband. Others, like the Corona jury, revisit their decision again and again as the majority pushes for consensus and conformity and the minority stresses divergence and doubt. Can we predict how opinions change in such groups?

Latané's revised model, **dynamic social impact theory,** assumes that groups are dynamic, complex systems rather than static, simple systems. Simple systems can usually be understood once the laws underlying the behavior of the system are identified. Complex systems, in contrast, follow an intricate, unstable pattern that is governed by many interlinked components that act, in some cases, as random influences on the system. Complex systems appear to be ever-changing, aperiodic, and utterly unpredictable, but closer examination reveals an order to this apparent chaos. When Latané studied groups discussing issues repeatedly, he identified four tendencies: consolidation, clustering, correlation, and continuing diversity (Latané, 1996, 1997; Latané & Bourgeois, 1996; Latané & L'Herrou, 1996; Latané & Liu, 1996; Latané & Nowak, 1994; Nowak, Szamrej, & Latané, 1990).

1. *Consolidation.* Over time, the majority grows in size and the minority dwindles in size. Just as the Corona jury converged on the guilty verdict, groups become more unified in their opinions over time.

Dynamic social impact theory: An extension of social impact theory that examines consolidation, clustering, correlation, and continuing diversity in groups that are spatially distributed and interacting repeatedly over time.

2. *Clustering.* As the law of social impact suggests, people are more influenced by their closest neighbors, and so clusters of group members with similar opinions emerge in groups. Clustering is more likely when group members communicate more frequently with members who are close by and less frequently with more distant group members. Clustering can also occur, however, if group members can move around within the group. In the Corona trial, the jurors who voted not guilty moved so that they could sit together.

3. *Correlation.* Over time, the group members' opinions on other issues—even ones that are not discussed in the group—converge, so that their opinions on a variety of matters are correlated. In the Corona jury, for example, members of the majority might find that they also agree on when to break for lunch or what program to watch on television. Members of the minority also agree with one another, but they disagree with the majority's choices on these unrelated matters.

4. *Continuing diversity.* Because of clustering, members of minorities are often shielded from the influence attempts of the majority, and their beliefs continue on within the group. Diversity drops if the majority is very large and the members of the minority are physically isolated from one another, but diversity continues when the minority members who communicate with the majority resist the majority's influence attempts.

Latané and his colleagues identified all four patterns in a study of classroom groups (Harton, Green, Jackson, & Latané, 1998). They asked students to answer several multiple-choice questions twice: once on their own, and once after talking about the questions with the two people sitting on either side of them. Consolidation occurred on several of the questions. On one, 17 of the 30 students favored an incorrect alternative before discussion. After discussion, 5 more students changed their answers and sided with the incorrect majority—including 3 students who had initially answered the question correctly! The majority increased from 57% to 73%. Clustering was also apparent; 11 students disagreed with both of their neighbors initially, but after discussion, only 5 students disagreed with both neighbors—indeed, two large clusters of 6 and 13 students who all agreed with one another emerged. Students within clusters also tended to give the same answers as one another on other items (correlation), and some individuals refused to change their answers, even though no one else agreed with them (continuing diversity).

These four patterns vary, depending on how many times the group holds its discussion, the dispersion of the group members, the group's communication network, the status of particular individuals, group members' desire to reach agreement, and other aspects of the situation (Kameda, 1996; Kameda & Sugimori, 1995; Latané, 1997). The four tendencies are robust, however, and answer some key questions about influence in groups. Do most groups eventually converge on a single opinion that represents the average across all members? Dynamic social impact theory says no; groups tend to become polarized on issues as clusters form within the group. Does social pressure eventually force all those who disagree with the minority to conform? Again, dynamic social impact theory suggests that minorities, particularly in spatially distributed groups, are protected from influence. So long as minorities can cluster together, then diversity in groups is ensured.

SOURCES OF GROUP INFLUENCE

At the beginning of the trial, the 12 members of the Corona jury differed in their opinions about politics, the law, and the defendant's guilt. But when their deliberations ended, the group had reached consensus on a single verdict. Why did the group members who initially believed that Corona was innocent change their vote to guilty?

Many people think of conformity in a negative way. They assume that the jurors who changed their vote yielded to the group's pressure and so failed to stand up for their personal beliefs. This pejorative view underestimates the complexity of social influence. Individuals in any group, including the Corona jury, change their behavior for a variety of reasons (Deutsch & Gerard, 1955; Kelley, 1952). Through *informational influence,* the group provides members with information that they can use to make decisions and form opinions. When *normative influence* occurs, group members tailor their actions to fit the group's standards and conventions. *Interpersonal influence,* in contrast, occurs when the group uses verbal and nonverbal influence tactics to induce change. These factors, which we will now consider, combine to create change.

Informational Influence

Why did Calvin Williams, who initially believed that Corona was innocent, eventually convert to the majority's side? Because of **informational influence:** social influence that results from discovering new information about a situation by observing others' responses. Calvin Williams did not mindlessly go along with the majority's verdict. Rather, when Calvin learned that most of the jury believed that Corona was guilty, he wondered, "Why did so many of the jurors draw different conclusions about the case than I did?" and "Am I correct in my interpretation of the evidence?" Calvin changed his mind because he reconsidered his position.

Social Comparison. Social comparison theory assumes that group members, as active information processors, treat other people's responses as data when formulating their own opinions and making decisions (see Chapter 4). People construct meaningful and coherent definitions of social situations and validate their conclusions by comparing themselves to others (Fazio, 1979). In some cases, groups deliberately gather information about members' opinions. The Corona trial jurors, for example, took a vote before they had done very much deliberation, because they were "anxious to know where everyone else stood before expressing their own views" (Villaseñor, 1977 p. 63). In most cases, however, information about others' views is gathered during routine discussion (Gerard & Orive, 1987; Orive, 1988a, 1988b). Interestingly, this intuitive surveying of others' opinions tends to be a biased one. Members of the majority often underestimate the size of their own group, whereas minority members overestimate the degree to which others agree with them. This tendency, called the

---

Informational influence: Social influence that results from discovering new information about a situation by observing others' responses.

false consensus effect, leaves minority members thinking that there is more support for their position than there actually is (Gross & Miller, 1997; Krueger & Clement, 1997; Mullen & Hu, 1988).

Systematic Processing of Information.   How did Calvin, who favored a not-guilty verdict, respond when he heard so many other groups members take the prosecutor's side? Did he ignore their arguments? Did he argue against their claims, generating even more ideas that supported his preferred view? Or did he accept the majority's decision without thinking too much about the implications?

Diane Mackie (1987) suggests that individuals who discover that they disagree with others undertake a systematic analysis of all available judgment-relevant information. Mackie led her subjects to believe that they were part of a small minority that disagreed with a majority on such matters as foreign policy and juvenile justice. After her subjects listened to members of both the minority and the majority argue their positions, Mackie asked them to record their thoughts and reactions. Analysis of these cognitive reactions indicated that subjects recalled more of the arguments offered by the majority, and they had more positive reactions to the majority's view after the discussion. Mackie also found that people who more extensively processed the majority's message also changed their opinions more than those who did not process the message (see, too, De Dreu & De Vries, 1996; Trost, Maass, & Kenrick, 1992).

Minorities, too, stimulate cognitive elaboration of decision-relevant information. As Moscovici argued, minorities influence majorities by creating "cognitive conflicts" that challenge the status quo of the group by calling for a reevaluation of issues at hand. Such a minority undermines the majority's certainty and forces the group to seek out new information about the situation. When a minority is present, groups take longer to reach their conclusions and are more likely to consider multiple perspectives when drawing conclusions (Peterson & Nemeth, 1996). If the majority considers the minority members to be part of the ingroup, it will think positively rather than negatively about the minority position (Alvaro & Crano, 1997). Minorities also prompt group members to use more varied strategies in solving problems and to devise more creative solutions (Nemeth, 1986; Nemeth & Kwan, 1985, 1987; Nemeth, Mosier, & Chiles, 1992). In some cases, group members remember information presented by the minority better than information presented by the majority (Nemeth, Mayseless, Sherman, & Brown, 1990).

Exposure to others' positions, in addition to providing additional information and prompting a more thorough analysis of that information, can also cause group members to reinterpret, or cognitively restructure, key aspects of the issue (Allen & Wilder, 1980; Tindale, Smith, Thomas, Filkins, & Sheffey, 1996; Wood, Pool, Leck, & Purvis, 1996). Researchers documented restructuring in one study by asking subjects to respond to a number of opinion items while seated in standard Crutchfield testing booths (Allen & Wilder, 1980). Although each statement was accompanied by information about the opinions of a previous group of participants, the subjects

---

False consensus effect: Perceivers' tendency to assume that their personal qualities and characteristics are common in the general population.

were not asked to give their opinions on the items. Rather, they were asked to define certain phrases in the statements. The subjects were shown an item such as "I would never go out of my way to help another person," and then they learned that a four-person group had unanimously agreed with the statement, clearly an unexpected and unpopular response (Allen & Wilder, 1980, p. 1118). When the subjects were asked what the phrase "go out of my way" meant in the sentence, they reinterpreted it to mean "risk my life" rather than "be inconvenienced."

Heuristic Thought and Influence.   Informational influence also capitalizes on group members' willingness to make use of **heuristics** when they make decisions. Dual-process models of social cognition suggest that individuals do not always systematically process information when they form their judgments. When their cognitive resources are limited or they are not motivated to do the cognitive work necessary to weigh the information available to them, people rely on heuristics: simplifying inferential principles or rules of thumb that generate decisions efficiently and rapidly (Baker & Petty, 1994; Peterson & Nemeth, 1996; Wood et al., 1996). If individuals base their responses on such heuristics as "Don't make waves," "The majority rules," or "To get along, go along," they will be more likely to accept the majority's viewpoint (Chen, Shechter, & Chaiken, 1996). Indeed, people's postdecision explanations for their choices may just be after-the-fact justifications for choices driven by heuristic thought rather than systematic thought (Buehler & Griffin, 1994; Griffin & Buehler, 1993).

Normative Influence

The jurors did not change simply because they acquired relevant information from the other jurors. Rather, they changed because the group's norms changed. Just as Sherif's (1936) subjects eventually agreed on how much a pinpoint of light in an otherwise dark room moved, the jury eventually settled on a verdict (see Chapter 5). The group waffled from guilt to innocence for a week, but on the eighth day, a new norm emerged: Corona is guilty. When the judge later asked each one of the group to give his or her personal decision on each count, every single juror said "guilty."

Normative influence causes us to feel, think, and act in ways that are consistent with our group's norms (Aronson, 1980; Deutsch & Gerard, 1955; Kelley, 1952). At an interpersonal level, people feel compelled to act in accordance with norms because a variety of negative consequences could result from nonconformity. People who consistently violate their group's norms are often reminded of their duty and told to change their ways. They are often disliked, assigned lower status jobs, and in some cases dismissed from the group (Schachter, 1951). Normative influence, however, also has a per-

---

Heuristics: Inferential principles or rules of thumb that people use to reach conclusions when the amount of available information is limited, ambiguous, or contradictory.
Normative influence: Social influence that results from personal and interpersonal pressures to conform to group norms.

sonal component, for people obey norms to fulfill their own expectations about proper behavior. Norms are not simply external constraints but internalized standards; people feel duty bound to adhere to norms because, as responsible members of their groups, they accept the legitimacy of the established norms and recognize the importance of supporting these norms. Thus, people obey norms not only because they fear the negative interpersonal consequences—ostracism, ridicule, punishment—that their nonconformity may produce, but also because they feel personally compelled to live up to their own expectations.

Stanley Milgram (1992) documented the personal consequences of violating norms. His student researchers broke the "first-come, first-served" norm of subway seating by asking subway riders in New York City to give up their seats. Many people turned over their seats to the students, but Milgram was more interested in how the students felt. The students were volunteers who were deliberately breaking the situational norms in the name of research, but all "felt anxious, tense, and embarrassed. Frequently, they were unable to vocalize the request for a seat and had to withdraw" (Milgram, 1992, p. 42). Milgram, who also performed the norm violation task, described the experience as wrenching and concluded that there is an "enormous inhibitory anxiety that ordinarily prevents us from breaching social norms" (p. xxiv).

Normative influence accounts for many empirical relations evident in research. If normative pressures are weakened, perhaps because the majority cannot reach unanimous agreement on the correct responses (Allen, 1975; Morris & Miller, 1975), majority influence declines. But if these normative pressures are heightened—perhaps by increasing the cohesiveness of the group (Festinger, Schachter, & Back, 1950), creating an expectation of future interaction (Lewis, Langan, & Hollander, 1972), or emphasizing the importance of maintaining a congenial group atmosphere (Reckman & Goethals, 1973)—conformity tends to increase. Lastly, the concept of normative social influence also explains why certain people, such as those with a high need for social approval, conform more than others (Bornstein, 1992).

Interpersonal Influence

Just before a key vote by the jurors, Naomi interrupted the proceedings (Villaseñor, 1977, p. 149):

> "Wait. I got one thing to say. If Corona is so guilty, then why didn't the sheriff come and tell us that he knows Corona is guilty?"
>
> Everyone looked at Naomi. Victor and Matt, almost in unison, pushed back their chairs and lowered their heads, trying not to laugh. Frank and Larry looked at each other. Rogers yelled:
>
> "Because that's not evidence! That would be hearsay! Dammit, why don't you ask why God doesn't come down here and tell us everything about everybody, then we don't even need the jury system and we can all go home!"

More is going on here than informational or normative influence. The jurors have detected a nonconformist in their midst, and they are deliberately trying to change her behavior through **interpersonal influence.** Instead of providing Naomi with information or reiterating the group's norms, the jurors are using verbal and nonverbal tactics—complaining, demanding, threatening, pleading, negotiating, pressuring, manipulating, rejecting, and so on—to induce change.

Stanley Schachter (1951) documented interpersonal influence by planting three kinds of confederates in a number of all-male discussion "clubs." The *deviant* always disagreed with the majority. The *slider* disagreed initially, but conformed over the course of the discussion. The *mode* served as a control: He consistently agreed with the majority. Schachter also manipulated the groups' cohesiveness by putting some of the subjects in clubs that interested them and others in clubs that did not interest them. He assumed that people with common interests would be more cohesive than those with disparate interests. In addition, the groups discussed a topic that was either relevant or irrelevant to the group's stated purpose.

Schachter was interested in how group members would pressure the deviant during the course of the discussion, so he kept track of each comment directed to the deviant, slider, and mode by the other group members. He predicted that the group would initially communicate with the mode, deviant, and slider at equal rates. But once the group became aware of the deviant and slider's disagreement, group members would concentrate on these two participants. Schachter believed that communication would continue at a high rate until the dissenter capitulated to the majority opinion (as in the case of the slider) or the majority concluded that the deviant would not budge from his position (as in the case of the nonchanging deviant), but that this reaction would be exacerbated by the group's cohesiveness, the relevance of the task, and group members' dislike for the deviant.

Influence and Ostracism. Figure 7–4 summarizes Schachter's findings. In most cases, the groups communicated with the slider and the mode at a relatively low rate throughout the session, whereas communications with the deviant increased during the first 35 minutes of discussion. At the 35-minute mark, however, some groups seem to have rejected the deviant. These groups were cohesive ones working on a task that was relevant to the group's goals and whose members also developed a negative attitude toward the deviant. If the group liked the deviant, communication increased all the way up to the final minute. But if the group disliked the deviant, communication dropped precipitously.

Schachter's findings highlight the difference between inclusive and exclusive reactions to minorities (Berkowitz, 1971; Emerson, 1954; Mills, 1962; Mucchi-Faina, 1994; Orcutt, 1973). Most of his groups displayed an *inclusive reaction* to the deviant: Communication between the majority and the minority was intensive and hostile, but the minority was still perceived to be a member of the ingroup. If an *exclusive reaction* occurred, however, communication with the deviant dwindled along with overt hostility, and the deviant was perceptually removed from the group by the majority members. An exclusive reaction becomes more likely when group members think that their group is very heterogeneous (Festinger, Pepitone, & Newcomb, 1952; Festinger & Thi-

---

Interpersonal influence: Social influence that results from other group members selectively encouraging conformity while discouraging or even punishing nonconformity.

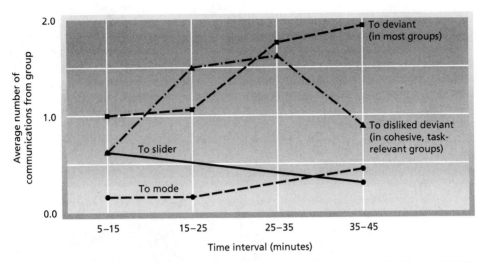

FIGURE 7-4   How does a group react to a dissenter who refuses to conform? Schachter (1951) found that the person who disagreed with the others usually received the most communication throughout the discussion period. The only exception occurred in cohesive groups working on a relevant task when the group disliked the deviant. In this case, communications tapered off. The average number of communications addressed to the mode increased slightly over the session, while communication with the slider decreased.

(*Source:* Adapted from Schachter, 1951.)

baut, 1951). Highly cohesive groups, too, will sometimes "redefine the group's boundary" if the dissenter is inflexible and the issue is important (Gerard, 1953). So-called *double minorities*—individuals who disagree with the group and possess one (or more) other unique qualities that distinguish them from the rest of the group—are also more likely to face exclusion (Sampson, 1971; Sampson & Brandon, 1964).

Interpersonal Rejection.   The group members did not just argue with the deviate: They also rejected the deviate. When Schachter's subjects rated each other on likability, the deviant was voted the sociometric outcast, whereas the mode was liked the most. The deviate was also saddled with the secretarial chores of the group; the mode and slider were assigned more desirable positions. This rejection was more pronounced in the more cohesive groups.

Subsequent studies have replicated this relationship between rejection and nonconformity, although these later studies frequently note that certain situational factors increase the magnitude of this relationship (Tata et al., 1996). Task relevance, cohesiveness, interdependency, behavior extremity, and the degree of threat posed by the dissenter all work to increase rejection. The deviate's contribution to the task, apologies for deviation, group norms that encourage deviation and innovation, and a history of previous conformity reduce the likelihood of rejection. Overall, however, the general relationship between nonconformity and rejection appears to be a robust one. (See Levine, 1980, for a comprehensive review.)

Schachter also found that the slider, who disagreed with the majority only briefly, was not as well liked as the mode. John Levine and his associates have confirmed this tendency, for they find that a little dissent often leads to a little rejection. In one study, subjects voted on an issue five times, and the experimenters manipulated these responses to create six experimental conditions. Subjects in the control condition believed that the group was unanimous in its opinions on the issue. The rest of the subjects, in contrast, received information indicating that one of the group members was a nonconformist. In the neutral → agree condition, this individual initially expressed a neutral opinion but agreed with the majority by Vote 5. In the neutral → disagree condition, just the reverse occurred: The nonconformist shifted from neutral to disagreement during the sessions. Other variations are shown in Figure 7–5 (Le-

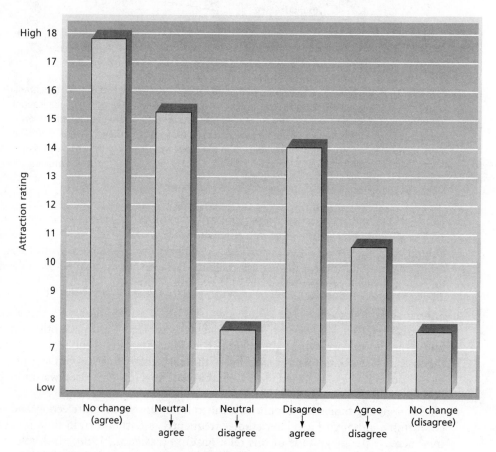

FIGURE 7–5 Do groups like members who disagree with the majority? The unchanging conformist (no change) and the slider who moved from neutrality to agreement (neutral → agree) were the best liked. The slider who shifted all the way from nearly complete disagreement to nearly complete agreement (disagree → agree) and the slider who actually moved away from the majority opinion (agree → disagree) were rated as somewhat attractive. The slider who moved from neutrality to disagreement and the constant dissenter were the most negatively evaluated of all members.

(*Source:* Levine, Saxe, and Harris, 1976.)

vine, Saxe, & Harris, 1976; see, too, Levine, 1980; Levine & Ranelli, 1978; Levine & Ruback, 1980; Levine, Sroka, & Snyder, 1977).

The subjects then described their opinion of the nonconformist. These ratings, which are shown in Figure 7–5, suggest that a slider who eventually agrees with the majority's opinion will be liked slightly less than a conformist. Demonstrating initial conformity and subsequently disagreeing also garnered less attraction, suggesting that individuals who save their complaints for the end of a group's discussion will be particularly disliked (Kruglanski & Webster, 1991). The constant nonconformist, however, was also disliked, suggesting that subjects interpreted refusal to yield as a sign of closed-mindedness rather than independence (Thameling & Andrews, 1992). These reactions to the dissenter likely reflect group members' tendencies to like people who are similar to them in some way (Pendell, 1990). They also support the strategy of yea-saying: "To get along, go along."

APPLICATION: UNDERSTANDING JURIES

Groups have served as the final arbiter of guilt and innocence for centuries. As far back as the 11th century, the neighbors of those accused of wrongdoing were asked both to provide information about the actions of the accused and to weigh the evidence. Witnesses and experts now provide the evidence, but the jury remains responsible for weighing the testimony of each person before rendering a verdict. More than 300,000 juries convene each year in American courtrooms. (Hyman & Tarrant, 1975, and Moore, 1973, discuss the history of juries.)

Jury Dynamics

The jury situation is designed to foster careful decision making and tolerance for all viewpoints, but juries are, at core, groups. The jury's final decision depends not only on the evidence presented in the trial, the attorneys' arguments, and the judge's instructions, but also on social influence.

Verdict-Driven and Evidence-Driven Juries.   Reid Hastie, Steven Penrod, and Nancy Pennington (1983), in their book *Inside the Jury,* describe the processes that typically unfold once the jury is sequestered in the jury room. Most juries begin by electing a leader and deciding if balloting will be secret or public. Some juries immediately take a straw poll of their initial preferences, and over 30% reach complete consensus on that first ballot (Penrod & Hastie, 1980). But when members disagree, they initiate a consensus-seeking process. During this phase of the deliberation, the group may ask the judge for instructions and request additional information concerning the evidence. The group spends most of its time, however, discussing points favoring the two possible verdicts.

The jury's approach to the deliberations depends, in part, on how it structures the task. Hastie, Penrod, and Pennington note that jurors generally approach the decision in one of two ways. Some jurors appear to be *verdict driven.* They reach a decision about the verdict before deliberation and cognitively organize the evidence into two categories: evidence that favors a verdict of guilt and evidence that favors a verdict of innocence. *Evidence-driven* jurors, in contrast, resist making a final decision on the verdict until they have reviewed all the available evidence; then they generate a "story" that organizes the evidence (Hastie, Penrod, & Pennington, 1983; Pennington & Hastie, 1986, 1992). When juries contain both verdict-driven and evidence-driven jurors, the approach preferred by the majority of the jurors is generally used to structure the deliberations. When researchers created mock three-person juries containing two members who shared the same type of cognitive orientation, this cognitive majority dominated the deliberations, and in most cases the individual with the alternative viewpoint restructured his or her approach so that it matched the majority's approach (Kameda, 1994).

Minority Influence and Verdicts.   The drama *Twelve Angry Men* captures the frustrations of a jury trying to reach a verdict in a murder trial. Eleven jurors agree in the first straw poll that the defendant is guilty. The majority attacks the lone holdout's position. The holdout, however, stands firm, and one by one, the rest of the group members change their minds. The jury eventually returns a verdict of not guilty.

This plot is dramatic but unrealistic; in juries, the minority rarely influences the majority. When 7 to 11 jurors (a majority) favor guilt on the first ballot, in 90% of the cases, the jury returns a verdict of guilty. If 7 or more jurors vote not guilty on the first ballot, the verdict is not guilty in 86% of the cases (Kalven & Zeisel, 1966). Most jurors implicitly adopt the norm (or social decision rule): If a significant majority of the members (say, two-thirds) favor a verdict, then everyone in the group should agree with that verdict (Davis, Bray, & Holt, 1977; Davis, Kameda, Parks, Stasson, & Zimmerman, 1989; Davis, Stasson, Ono, & Zimmerman, 1988).

Even though the majority tends to prevail in juries, the statistics in Table 7–3 show that staunch minorities can sometimes hang a jury or even persuade the majority to adopt its viewpoint. In the famous Mitchell/Stans Watergate conspiracy trial, for example, the first vote favored guilt, 8 to 4. One of the four, however, was a wealthy vice

TABLE 7–3   MINORITY AND MAJORITY INFLUENCE IN JURIES

The Outcome of the Deliberation	Percentage
Now many juries agree on a verdict on the first ballot?	31.0
How many juries, after deliberation, adopt the verdict initially favored by a majority of jurors?	56.5
How many juries, after deliberation, adopt the verdict initially favored by a minority of jurors?	2.5
How many juries cannot reach a verdict ("hung jury")?	5.6
How many juries are split 6 to 6 on the first ballot (and so they have no minority or majority)?	4.4

Source: Penrod and Hastie, 1980.

president of a bank who had achieved a position of high status in the group. During the deliberation, he enlarged the size of the minority coalition until the jury shifted to acquittal (Wrightsman, Nietzel, & Fortune, 1994). He was successful, in part, because of the substantial size of the minority. A lone dissenter will generally change his or her vote, but larger minorities are more influential. In fact, a computer model that simulates jury deliberations (DICE) assumes that a 3-person coalition in a standard 12-person jury will be relatively weak, but a 4- or 5-person coalition will be fairly influential (Hastie et al., 1983; Penrod & Hastie, 1980; Tanford & Penrod, 1983).

Status and Influence.   Some members of the Corona jury had higher status within the group than the other rank-and-file members: Ernie, the foreman, Faye, the retired teacher, and Jim, the shipyard inspector. Is it a coincidence that the verdict they favored was the final verdict of the jury?

Fairly or unfairly, people who have high prestige or status are more influential than low-status members. Fred L. Strodtbeck and his colleagues, in their studies of mock juries, carefully replicated all aspects of an actual trial. They selected sets of 12 individuals from a pool of eligible jurors, simulated the pretrial interview process designed to eliminate biased jurors (voir dire), and assembled the group in the courtroom. A bailiff then played a recording of a trial and asked the group to retire to a jury room to decide on a verdict. Except for the use of a recording, the groups were treated just like actual juries (Strodtbeck & Hook, 1961; Strodtbeck et al., 1957; Strodtbeck & Mann, 1956).

Consistent with expectation-states theory (see Chapters 2 and 5), juries favored people of higher socioeconomic status (proprietors and clerical workers) over those of lower socioeconomic status (blue-collar workers) when choosing a foreman, even though no mention of occupation was made (Strodtbeck & Lipinski, 1985). High-status members also participated more frequently in the jury's discussions, often by offering more suggestions and providing more orientation to the task. High-status members were also more successful in convincing the others that their judgments on the case were the most accurate. The correlation between private predeliberation opinion and the jury's final decision was .50 for proprietors, but it dropped all the way down to .02 for the laborers (Strodtbeck et al., 1957). Sex differences were also apparent, for women joined in the discussion less frequently than men (James, 1959; Strodtbeck et al., 1957). Furthermore, women's comments were more often socioemotional in nature, showing solidarity and agreement, whereas men's comments were more task focused (Strodtbeck & Mann, 1956; see, too, Nemeth, Endicott, & Wachtler, 1976).

How Effective Are Juries?

Given what we know about conformity and nonconformity in groups, should the jury system be modified? Asch's studies tell us that people often conform and that even a correct minority often loses to an incorrect majority. As we have seen, normative, informational, and interpersonal influence are powerful forces in groups, and they can quash individuals' freedom to speak their minds. Juries are a time-honored tradition, but are they effective?

Determining the effectiveness of juries as deciders of guilt or innocence is a complicated task, for we can never know when the jury has been correct or incorrect in condemning or freeing a defendant. If a clear criterion for determining guilt existed, juries would not be necessary in the first place. Several bits of evidence, however, provide partial support for the effectiveness of juries as decision makers. First, jurors seem to take their role very seriously. As Villaseñor's account of the Corona jury vividly illustrates, jurors strive to reach the fairest decision possible (Hastie et al., 1983). One jury expert, after studying the responses of more than 2000 jurors participating in a Chicago law project, concludes:

> The most consistent theme that emerged from listening to the deliberations was the seriousness with which the jurors approached their job and the extent to which they were concerned that the verdict they reached was consistent with the spirit of the law and with the facts of the case. [Simon, 1980, p. 521]

Second, juries do well when compared with judges' preferences. In a survey of nearly 8000 actual criminal and civil trials, judges and juries disagreed on only 20% of the cases; for criminal trials, the jury was somewhat more lenient than the judge, but for civil trials, the disagreements were evenly split for and against the defendant. Furthermore, 80% of these disagreements occurred when the weight of the evidence was so close that the judge admitted that the verdict could have gone either way. This concord between verdicts may explain why 77% of the judges surveyed felt that the jury system was satisfactory, 20% felt that it had disadvantages that should be corrected, but only 3% felt that the system was so unsatisfactory that its use should be curtailed (Kalven & Zeisel, 1966).

Lastly, jurors are hardly unbiased, rational weighers of evidence; the defendant's physical appearance, the lawyer's style of questioning, and the sequencing of evidence are just a few of the factors that bias jurors' decisions (Dane & Wrightsman, 1982; Hastie et al., 1983; Kaplan, 1982; Wrightsman, Nietzel, & Fortune, 1998). These biases are largely controlled, however, by relying on group decisions rather than individual decisions. Simulations of juries suggest that the lone juror's initial biases and preferences have very little impact on the group's final decision, no matter what the size of the jury (Kerr & Huang, 1986).

Improving Juries

The judicial system is long on tradition, but in recent years, several innovations have been suggested and even implemented (Saks, 1977). Many of these changes focus on juries and are designed to increase their effectiveness and efficiency. But do these changes make sense, given the findings of group dynamicists?

Jury Size. In 1970, the U.S. Supreme Court returned a landmark ruling in the case of *Williams v. Florida* (National Center for State Courts [NCSC], 1976). Williams sought to have his conviction overturned on the grounds that the deciding jury had included only six persons. The Supreme Court, however, found in favor of the State, ruling that a six-person jury is large enough to promote group deliberation, protect members from intimidation, fairly represent the community, and weigh the facts in the case (*Williams v. Florida,* 1970). Psychology and law expert Michael J. Saks, however, suggests that the Supreme Court should have taken group dynamics research into consideration before making its decision (Saks, 1977; Saks & Hastie, 1978). As he notes, modifying the size could influence

- *Group structure.* Members of smaller juries participate at more equal rates; smaller juries are more cohesive; and members of larger juries communicate more.
- *Representativeness.* Smaller groups are not as representative of the community as larger ones. For example, if a community was 10% Latino and 90% Anglo, in all probability, about 80% of the 12-person juries would include at least one Latino, but only 40% of the 6-person juries would contain Latinos.
- *Majority influence.* The majority's influence may be greater in smaller juries because the likelihood of finding a partner for one's minority coalition becomes smaller. The Supreme Court erred in assuming that a 5 to 1 vote in a 6-person jury was essentially the same as a 10 to 2 split in a 12-person group. With the 10 to 2 vote, one's opinion is buttressed by the presence of a dissenting partner, whereas in the 5 to 1 vote, one must face the majority alone. As a result, the likelihood of a hung jury is greater in larger juries (Kerr & MacCoun, 1985).

Saks also notes, however, that despite size-related changes in group dynamics, small and large juries do not appear to differ significantly in the types of verdicts reached (Padawer-Singer, Singer, & Singer, 1977; Saks, 1977).

Unanimity. In 1972, three men were convicted, in separate trials, of assault, grand larceny, and burglary by the court system of Oregon. They appealed to the U.S. Supreme Court on the grounds that their right to a fair trial had been violated because the votes of the juries had not been unanimous. To the defendants' dismay, the Supreme Court ruled in favor of Oregon (*Apodoca v. Oregon,* 1972), concluding that the Sixth Amendment to the U.S. Constitution guarantees only that a "substantial majority of the jury" must be convinced of the defendant's guilt. Later in the ruling, the Court suggested that 75% agreement constitutes an acceptable minimum for most juries.

The Court's conclusion is, for the most part, justified by the empirical evidence. The verdict preferred by the majority of the jurors on the first vote usually becomes the final verdict in a large percentage of the cases with or without a unanimity rule. The minority's opinion sometimes prevails, but in such cases, the minority is usually so substantial that a 9-out-of-12 majority would not have been reached anyway. Most juries implicitly operate according to either a basic two-thirds or a 10-out-of-12 rule (Davis, Kerr, Atkin, Holt, & Meek, 1975; Davis, Kerr, Stasser, Meek, & Holt, 1977; Stasser, Kerr, & Bray, 1982).

Relaxing the requirement for unanimity, however, changes the decision-making process in juries. Juries that do not have to reach a unanimous decision render their judgments twice as quickly and are far less likely to come to a stalemate (Foss, 1981; Kerr et al., 1976). Saks and Hastie (1978, pp. 84–85) fear that juries that do not deliberate to unanimity do not deliberate sufficiently and make more mistakes: "convictions when the correct decision is acquittal; acquittals when the correct decision is conviction."

Voir Dire. The courts select jury members from a pool of potential participants through a process known as voir dire. **Voir dire,** which means "to speak truly," calls for verbal or written questioning of prospective jurors to uncover any biases or prejudices that may stand in the way of fairness and impartiality (Hans & Vidmar, 1982).

Until the 1970s, voir dire was primarily left up to the judge's discretion; defense lawyers could submit questions, but judges were free to omit them if they desired. However, in light of certain Supreme Court rulings in which convictions were overturned because trial judges had disallowed defense participation in voir dire (e.g., *Ham v. S. Carolina*, 1973), courts began opening up the procedure to attorneys. Systematic jury selection, whereby lawyers carefully study the jurors in the pool and use voir dire to identify sympathetic and antagonistic jurors, is now a common practice in major trials.

Systematic jury selection is controversial. Proponents argue that in many political and criminal trials, biases produced by unfair publicity, regional prejudices, and unrepresentative jury rosters must be controlled if the defendant is to receive just treatment. Critics feel that systematic selection is tantamount to jury rigging, since it produces lenient rather than fair juries and works to exclude certain types of people from juries.

Lawrence Wrightsman, an expert on psychology and the law, argues that judges should limit the number of jurors that lawyers can challenge during voir dire. He also recommends stricter guidelines for lawyers, who sometimes use the voir dire process to influence the jurors in their favor. Wrightsman suggests that voir dire questioning be carried out carefully so that jurors will respond honestly and that judges supervise the process more closely. Voir dire is a useful way of identifying highly biased individuals, but it should not be a means of manipulating the composition of the jury (Wrightsman et al., 1998).

SUMMARY

When do people change their opinions, judgments, or actions to match the group's opinions, judgments, or actions?

1. Asch studied *social influence* (majority influence) by measuring people's decisions when the majority of their group's members made conspicuous errors in judgments.
   - Approximately one-third of the people that Asch studied conformed.
   - Conformity increased when the majority was large and unanimous, but increasing the majority beyond four did not significantly increase conformity.
   - When group members must respond in public, their conformity may result from *compliance* rather than *conversion* (*private acceptance*).
   - Fewer group members conform when they can respond anonymously via secret ballot or the so-called Crutchfield apparatus.
2. Conformity rates vary across time, cultures, the sexes, and group settings.
   - Group members in collectivistic societies yield to majority influence more than those in individualistic societies.

Voir dire: The oral or written questioning of prospective jurors by counsel.

- Conformity rates have dropped slightly from 1952 to 1994.
- Women conform more than men, albeit only in face-to-face groups. Women may use conformity to increase group harmony, whereas men use nonconformity to create the impression of independence.
- People who conform consistently in groups tend to be more authoritarian but seek social approval. Nonconformists are more self-confident, and *counterconformists* (*anticonformists*) actively resist majority influence.
- Majority influence varies in strength depending on the size, structure, cohesiveness, and goals of the group and the nature of its tasks.

When do people resist the group's influence and instead change the majority's opinions, judgments, or actions?

1. Moscovici studied minority influence by measuring people's reactions to one or more consistent dissenters.
   - Moscovici found that a minority, particularly if behaviorally consistent, can change the majority.
   - Minorities who are accorded high status in the group can also influence the majority, for their *idiosyncrasy credits* protect them from sanctions when they display nonconformity.
   - The minority's influence is also more indirect than the majority's, sometimes becoming evident only when the group has completed its initial deliberations and moved on to another task. Minorities therefore create more conversion and innovation, whereas majorities create compliance.
2. Latané's *social impact theory* argues that both minority and majority influences are a function of the strength (*S*),

immediacy (*I*), and number (*N*) of the people present, or $I = f(SIN)$. *Dynamic social impact theory* extends this model by explaining consolidation, clustering, correlation, and continuing diversity in groups that are spatially distributed and interacting repeatedly over time.

Why do people conform?

1. *Informational influence* takes place whenever group members look to others for information.
   - As social comparison theory notes, people are a valuable source of information, although individuals often misjudge the extent to which others agree with their viewpoint (the *false consensus effect*).
   - Influence occurs when group members review available information and use *heuristics,* such as "To get along, go along."
2. *Normative influence* prompts group members to feel, think, and act in ways that are consistent with their group's social standards.
3. *Interpersonal influence* includes verbal and nonverbal tactics—complaining, demanding, threatening, pleading, negotiating, pressuring, manipulating, rejecting, and so on—designed to induce change.
   - Schachter's analysis of group rejection indicates that a nonconformist is generally less liked by others in the group.
   - Communication with a disliked deviant eventually diminishes, at least when cohesive groups are working on relevant tasks.

Do social influence processes shape juries' verdicts?

1. The magnitude of social influence suggests that the decisions reached by

groups, including juries, are shaped by social processes rather than an unbiased weighing of evidence.

- The majority determines the type of deliberation strategy used by juries (verdict driven or evidence driven).
- The verdict favored by the majority of the members prior to deliberation (or on the first straw poll) is usually the jury's final verdict.
- Jurors who have higher status occupations tend to dominate the group's discussion.

2. Available evidence suggests that juries are satisfactory vehicles for making legal decisions and that reductions in the size of juries, the elimination of the unanimity rule, and extended *voir dire* procedures have not significantly altered conviction and acquittal rates.

FOR MORE INFORMATION

"Culture and Conformity: A Meta-Analysis of Studies Using Asch's (1952b, 1956) Line Judgment Task," by Rod Bond and Peter B. Smith (1996), is a scholarly analysis of nearly 50 years of research into conformity.

Inside the Jury, by Reid Hastie, Steven D. Penrod, and Nancy Pennington (1983),

presents a masterful social-psychological analysis of communication, influence, and decision making in juries.

Jury: The People vs. Juan Corona, by Victor Villaseñor (1977), offers a vivid case study of how juries make decisions, as carefully constructed by a journalist who interviewed all the jurors after the trial.

Minority Influence, edited by Serge Moscovici, Angelica Mucchi-Faina, and Anne Maass (1994), is a collection of insightful reviews and empirical studies of the direct and indirect impact of minorities on groups.

Psychology and the Legal System, by Lawrence S. Wrightsman, Michael T. Nietzel, and William H. Fortune (1998), in addition to providing a general introduction to psychology and the law, has several chapters that specifically examine juries.

"Strength from Weakness: The Fate of Opinion Minorities in Spatially Distributed Groups," by Bibb Latané (1996), is a short but lucid application of dynamic social impact theory to majority-minority influence processes. This chapter is one of many excellent papers in Erich Witte and James H. Davis's edited volume *Understanding Group Behavior.*

ACTIVITY 7–1 WHAT DOES SOCIAL INFLUENCE LOOK LIKE?

Carry out one of these studies of conformity in everyday life.

1. *Everyday conformity.* Look for conformity in such places as the lines at a fast-food restaurant, bus stops as people wait for a bus, or the library. (Do people conform to the posted rules, or do they conform to informal norms?) Or look at the students who pass by a particular point on campus, and make a note of their appearance and dress. Are they all individuals, or do they conform to an implicit dress code?
2. *Creating conformity.* Carry out a field study of influence. For example: Ask passersby to sign a petition, and in some cases have a friend model compliance just before the subject passes; arrange for groups ranging in size from two to ten people to stare up at the top of a building, and note how many passersby join in the staring; wearing a groundskeeper uniform or regular clothes, order people to get off the grass. (Before you carry out such studies—even informally—get approval from authorities. Do not carry out such studies alone or away from campus.)
3. *Experiencing nonconformity.* Violate norms of civility and observe people's reactions. On a crowded bus, hum loudly. Or, if you have more courage, sing out loud. Ask the staff at the fast-food restaurant, "What looks good on the menu today?" Try to barter for a small purchase at a fast-food store. When someone says, "Hi, how are you," ask them, "Do you mean physically, mentally, or financially?" Watch people's reactions.

ACTIVITY 7–2 ARE YOU A CONFORMIST?

If you meet regularly in a group, take a moment to reflect on its influence on you. Do you change your behavior when you are in this group? Has the group influenced you in some way, even when you are no longer in the group?

1. Describe the group briefly: its composition, structure, dynamics, and tasks. How long have you belonged to the group, and what is your role in the group?
2. Is the group an influential one for you, personally? To answer this question, briefly describe your basic personality in terms of these five qualities: extraversion/introversion (outgoing vs. reserved), agreeability (friendly vs. aloof), conscientiousness (responsible vs. uninvolved), stability (assured vs. nervous), and openness (open to ideas vs. conservative). Do your actions in the group reflect your personal qualities, or do you act in ways that are inconsistent with your personality in this group?
3. People differ in their tendency to conform in groups. Do you have any conformity-increasing qualities? Are you shy? Do you prefer to change your behavior to match the demands of situations in which you find yourself? Do you avoid attracting too much attention to yourself when you are in social settings? Are you generally uncertain about the validity of your opinions and conclusions? Are you more introverted than extraverted?

8

Power

Power is essential to group life. By exerting control over others, authorities coordinate members' activities and guide them toward their goals. Power, however, can be used against the group, for authorities sometimes demand actions that members would otherwise never consider. We would not be social beings if we were immune to the impact of power, but power can corrupt.

- What are the limits of an authority's power over group members?
- What are the sources of power in groups?
- What are the consequences of the exercise of power in groups?

CONTENTS

The People's Temple: The Metamorphic Effects of Power

OBEDIENCE TO AUTHORITY

The Milgram Experiments

Milgram's Findings

The Riddle of Obedience

SOURCES OF POWER

Power Bases

Power Tactics

The Dynamics of Authority

The Roots of Obedience

THE METAMORPHIC EFFECTS OF POWER

Compliance and Conversion

Resistance to Influence

Changes in the Powerholder

Question Authority

SUMMARY

FOR MORE INFORMATION

ACTIVITIES

The People's Temple: The Metamorphic Effects of Power

The Reverend Jim Jones called Jonestown the ideal community: a place where everyone found love, happiness, and well-being. But the men, women, and children who joined Jones in the small village nestled in the jungles of Guyana did not find contentment. They found, instead, a group that exercised incredible power over their destiny. Jones asked members to make great personal sacrifices for the group, and time and again they obeyed. They worked long hours in the field. They were given too little to eat. They could not communicate with their loved ones back in the United States. They even complied when Jones demanded their lives. More than 900 members of the People's Temple swallowed poison when Jones ordered them "to die with dignity."

Why did the group members obey his order when refusal could have had no worse consequences than obedience? What force is great enough to make parents give poison to their children? Many blamed Jim Jones—his persuasiveness, his charisma, his depravity. Others emphasized the kind of people who join such groups—their psychological instability, their willingness to identify with causes, and their religious fervor. Still others suggested more fantastic explanations: mass hypnosis, government plots, and even divine intervention.

Such explanations underestimate the **power** of groups and their leaders: their capacity to influence members, even when the members try to resist this influence (Cartwright, 1959). As Chapter 7 noted, groups influence the way their members feel, think, and act. But groups do more than create uniformity through subtle social influence; they also compel obedience among members who would otherwise resist the group's wishes. Here we consider the sources of that power and the consequences of power for those who wield it and those who are subjected to it.

OBEDIENCE TO AUTHORITY

Bertrand Russell concluded many years ago that "the fundamental concept in social science is Power, in the same sense in which Energy is the fundamental concept in physics" (1938, p. 10). Few interactions advance very far before elements of power and influence come into play. The coach demanding obedience from a player, the police officer asking the driver for the car's registration, the teacher scowling at the errant student, and the boss telling an employee to get back to work are all relying on social power as they influence others (Cartwright, 1959). A powerful person can control others' actions to promote his or her own goals "without their consent, against their will, or without their knowledge or understanding" (Buckley, 1967, p. 186). They can "produce intended and foreseen effects on others" (Wrong, 1979, p. 21), even when the others try to resist.

Power: The capacity to influence others, even when they try to resist this influence.

But can social power—a commonplace process that shapes nearly all group interactions—generate such a dramatic and disastrous outcome as the Jonestown suicide?
Can a member of a group be so bent to the will of an authority that he or she would
follow any order, no matter how nocuous? Stanley Milgram's laboratory studies of
obedience to an authority suggest that the answer to these questions is yes.

The Milgram Experiments

Stanley Milgram studied group members' obedience to an authority by creating small
groups in his laboratory at Yale University. The experimenter acted as the leader of the
groups. He set each group's agenda, assigned tasks to the other two group members,
and issued the orders. He was a White man, about 30 years of age, and he dressed in
a gray technician's coat. The other two group members were assigned specific tasks by
the experimenter. The subject acted as the teacher by reading a series of paired words
(*blue box, nice day, wild day*, etc.) to the learner, who was supposed to memorize the
pairings. The teacher would check the learner's ability to recall the pairs by later reading the first word in the pair and several possible answers (e.g., *blue: sky, ink, box,
lamp*). Failures would be punished by an electric shock. This learner, however, was in
reality a member of the research team. He looked to be in his late 40s, and he acted in
a friendly, nervous way.

The experimenter, after he assigned the subject and the confederate their duties,
took both group members into the next room. The subject then watched as the learner
was strapped into a chair that was designed "to prevent excessive movement during
the shock." The learner sat quietly while an electrode was attached to his wrist. At the
end of this carefully rehearsed interaction, the learner asked if the shocks were dangerous. "Oh, no," said the experimenter, "although the shocks can be extremely painful,
they cause no permanent tissue damage" (Milgram, 1974, p. 19). The confederate, of
course, did not actually receive shocks.

The experimenter then led the subject back to the other room and seated him at
the shock generator. This bogus machine, which Milgram himself fabricated, featured
a row of 30 electrical switches. Each switch, when depressed, would send a shock to
the learner. The shock level of the first switch on the left was 15 volts; the next switch
was 30, the next was 45, and so on, all the way up to 450 volts. Milgram also labeled
the voltage levels, from left to right, "Slight Shock," "Moderate Shock," "Strong
Shock," "Very Strong Shock," "Intense Shock," "Extreme Intensity Shock," and
"Danger: Severe Shock." The final two switches were marked "XXX." The rest of
the face of the shock generator was taken up by dials, lights, and meters that flickered
whenever a switch was pressed.

The experimenter administered a sample shock of 45 volts to each subject, supposedly to give him an idea of the punishment magnitude. The study then began in
earnest. Using a microphone to communicate with the learner, the teacher read the list
of word pairs and then began "testing" the learner's memory. Each time the teacher
read a word and the alternatives, the learner indicated his response by pushing one of
four numbered switches that were just within reach of his bound hand. His response
lit up on the subject's control panel. Subjects were to deliver one shock for each mistake and increase the voltage one step each time.

Milgram set the stage for the order-giving phase by having the learner make mistakes deliberately. Although subjects punished that first mistake with just a 15-volt jolt, each subsequent failure was followed by a stronger shock. At the 300-volt level, the learner also began to protest the shocks by pounding on the wall, and after the next shock of 315 volts he stopped responding altogether. Most subjects assumed that the session was over at this point, but the experimenter told them to treat a failure to respond as a wrong answer and to continue delivering the shocks. When subjects balked, the experimenter, who was seated at a separate desk near the teacher's, would use a sequence of prods to goad them into action (Milgram, 1974, p. 21):

Prod 1: "Please continue" or "Please go on."
Prod 2: "The experiment requires that you continue."
Prod 3: "It is absolutely essential that you continue."
Prod 4: "You have no other choice; you must go on."

The situation was extremely realistic and served as a laboratory analog to real-world groups where authorities give orders to subordinates. The experimenter acted with self-assurance and poise. He gave orders crisply, as if he never questioned the correctness of his own actions, and he seemed surprised that the teacher would try to terminate the shock sequence. Yet, from the subjects' point of view, this authority was requiring them to act in a way that might be harmful to another person. When they accepted the $4.50 payment, they implicitly agreed to carry out the experimenter's instructions, but they were torn between this duty and their desire to protect the learner from possible harm. Milgram designed his experiment to determine which side would win in this conflict.

Milgram's Findings

Milgram was certain that very few of his participants would carry out the experimenter's orders. He went so far as to purchase special equipment that would let him record precisely the duration of each shock administered, expecting that few would give more than four or five (Elms, 1995). He also polled a number of psychological researchers and psychiatrists on the subject, asking them to predict how people would react in his study. None felt that subjects would shock to the 450-volt level; they predicted that most would quit at the 150-volt level.

Milgram and the other experts, however, underestimated the power of the situation. Of the 40 individuals who served as teachers in the experiment, 26 (65%) administered the full 450 volts to the helpless learner. None broke off before the 300-volt level, and several of the eventually disobedient subjects gave one or two additional shocks before finally refusing to yield to the experimenter's prods. The comments made by the subjects during the shock procedure and their obvious psychological distress revealed that they were unwilling to go on but felt unable to resist the experimenter's demands for obedience.

Milgram studied nearly 1000 people in a series of replications and extensions of his original study. In these later studies, some of which are discussed here, different aspects of the setting were systematically manipulated, allowing him to assess their influence on obedience rates. Although he continued to search for the limits of obedience, again and again his subjects buckled under the pressure of the experimenter's power.

Harm and Obedience.   After reviewing the results of the first 40 people he studied, Milgram decided that they did not realize they were hurting the learner. All they heard was an ambiguous pounding on the wall, which the experimenter told them to ignore. To make the harm more obvious, Milgram added additional cues that clearly signaled the learner's suffering.

- *Voice-feedback condition.* The learner's shouts and pleas (tape-recorded and carefully rehearsed) could be heard through the wall. He grunted when shocked at levels below 120 volts and complained about the pain. At 150 volts, he cried out, "Experimenter, get me out of here! I won't be in the experiment any more! I refuse to go on!" (Milgram, 1974, p. 23). He continued screaming and demanding release until the 300-volt level, when he refused to answer any more questions. Still, 62.5% of the subjects obeyed to the 450-volt level.
- *Proximity condition.* The learner sat in the same room as the teacher, voicing the same complaints used in the voice-feedback condition and writhing with pain at each shock. Obedience dropped to 40%.
- *Touch-proximity condition.* The learner sat next to the teacher and received his shock when he put his hand on a shock plate. At the 150-volt level, he refused to put his hand down on the plate, so the experimenter gave the subject an insulated glove and told him to press the learner's hand down onto the plate as he depressed the shock switch. Still, 30% obeyed.
- *Heart condition.* The learner was once more seated in the adjoining room, but as the experimenter connected the wires to his arm, the learner mentioned that he had a heart condition and asked about complications. The experimenter said that the shocks would cause no permanent damage. During the shock phase, the learner's groans and shouts of protest could be heard through the wall, and he also repeatedly complained that his heart was bothering him. Even though he stopped responding after 330 volts, 65% of the subjects continued to administer shocks to the 450-volt level.

Limiting the Experimenter's Power.   When Milgram intensified the learner's complaints, the subjects must have known they were hurting the victim. Yet, many still obeyed. So Milgram searched for ways to limit the experimenter's power over the teacher by manipulating the experimenter's surveillance capabilities, prestige, expertise, and legitimacy.

To take away some of the experimenter's scientific credibility, Milgram moved the study away from prestigious Yale University. He set up the study in an office building located in a shopping area: "The laboratory was sparsely furnished, though clean, and marginally respectable in appearance. When subjects inquired about professional affiliations, they were informed only that we were a private firm conducting research for industry" (Milgram, 1974, pp. 68–69). Obedience dropped to 48%, still a surprisingly large figure given the questionable research setting.

Milgram reduced the experimenter's control over the subject by removing the authority from the room. The teacher could hear the learner, but the experimenter left the room after going over the instructions. He continued giving orders by telephone, but only 20% of the participants were obedient to the 450-volt level. In fact, many subjects assured the experimenter that they were administering increasingly large shocks with each mistake when they were actually delivering only 15 volts.

The authority's power was further diminished by adding a fourth member to the group. The experimenter explained the study, as in other conditions, but gave no instructions about shock levels before being called away. The new subject, who was actually a confederate, filled the role of the authority; he suggested that shocks be given in increasingly strong doses and ordered the subject to continue giving shocks when the learner started to complain. Obedience dropped to 20%. Once subjects refused to continue, the confederate left the experimenter's desk and began administering the shocks. Most of the subjects (68.75%) failed to intervene by stopping the confederate.

In a particularly creative episode, the experimenter agreed to take the role of the learner to supposedly convince a reluctant learner that the shocks weren't harmful. The experimenter tolerated the shocks up the 150-volt, but then he shouted, "That's enough gentlemen!" The confederate, who had been watching the procedure, then insisted, "Oh, no, let's go on. Oh, no, come on, I'm going to have to go through the whole thing. Let's go. Come on, let's keep going" (Milgram, 1974, p. 102). In all cases, the subject released the experimenter; obedience to the ordinary person's command to harm the authority was nil.

Group Effects.   Milgram also demonstrated some interesting effects of other group members' behaviors on the subject's obedience. In one variation, the subject merely recorded information and performed other ancillary tasks while an accomplice flipped the shock switches. In this variation, 92.5% obediently fulfilled their tasks without intervening. If, however, the accomplice refused to administer shocks and the experimenter told the subject to take over, only 10% of the subjects were maximally obedient. Also, if two experimenters ran the research but one demanded continued shocking while another argued for stopping the shocks, all the subjects obeyed the commands of the benevolent authority.

Australian researchers obtained similar findings when they examined obedience in groups with a chain of command (Kilham & Mann, 1974). Because orders are often passed down from superiors to subordinates through a chain of command, the basic Milgram experiment was modified to include a transmitter, who relayed orders, and an executant, who actually delivered the shocks. As predicted, transmitters were more obedient than executants (54% versus 28%). In this study, men were more obedient than women, but other studies find either no difference between men and women (Milgram, 1974) or heightened obedience among women (Sheridan & King, 1972).

The Riddle of Obedience.   Milgram's results sparked controversies that are unresolved even today (Miller, Collins, & Brief, 1995a). Some researchers believe that the subjects were not taken in by Milgram's subterfuge; they knew no shocks were being administered but played along so as not to ruin the study (Mixon, 1977; Orne &

Holland, 1968). Milgram's research team, however, carefully interviewed all the participants, and fewer than 20% challenged the reality of the situation (Elms, 1995). Moreover, if participants saw through the elaborate duplicity, then why did they become so upset? According to Milgram,

> Many subjects showed signs of nervousness in the experimental situation, and especially upon administering the more powerful shocks. In a large number of cases the degree of tension reached extremes that are rarely seen in sociopsychological laboratory studies. Subjects were observed to sweat, tremble, stutter, bite their lips, groan, and dig their fingernails into their flesh. [1963, p. 375]

Indeed, the distress of the subjects was so great that the publication of the study sparked a controversy over the ethics of social-psychological research (Baumrind, 1964; Forsyth, 1981; Milgram, 1964, 1977; Miller, 1986, 1995; Schlenker & Forsyth, 1977).

Others note that Milgram's subjects were mostly men, they were paid for their time, and they lived at a time when people trusted authorities more than they do now. Yet, replications of the study using different procedures and participants have generally confirmed Milgram's initial findings (Martin, Lobb, Chapman, & Spillane, 1976; Meeus & Raaijmakers, 1995; Miranda, Caballero, Gomez, & Zamorano, 1981; Schurz, 1985; Shanab & Yahya, 1977). Many believe that the level of obedience that Milgram documented in his laboratory matches levels found in military, educational, and organizational settings (Brief, Buttram, Elliott, Reizenstein, & McCline, 1995; Miller et al., 1995a).

A related explanation focuses on the subjects themselves: their personalities, their temperaments, their normality. Just as many people, when first hearing of the Guyana tragedy, wondered, "What strange people they must have been to be willing to kill themselves," when people are told about Milgram's findings, they react with the question, "What kind of evil, sadistic men did he recruit for his study?" Yet, by all accounts, Milgram's subjects were normal and well adjusted, and subsequent attempts to link obedience to personality traits have been relatively fruitless (see Blass, 1991, for an analysis).

If Milgram's studies are methodologically sound and the obedience he observed does not reflect his subjects' peculiarities, then why did so many obey the orders of the authority? "It is not so much the kind of person a man is as the kind of situation in which he finds himself that determines how he will act," explains Milgram (1974, p. 205). The subjects had no power in the setting. The experimenter gave the orders, and the subjects followed those orders. Maybe they wanted to resist the commands of the experimenter, but like the hapless members of the People's Temple, they could not. As we will see in the next section, those who control the bases of power in a situation influence others, and those who do not are the targets of that influence.

SOURCES OF POWER

Over 4000 members of the Unification Church married each other in a mass ceremony because their leader, Reverend Sun Myung Moon, told them to do so. The

Branch Davidians remained barricaded in their compound until their leader, David
Koresh, ordered them to set it on fire. Thirty-seven members of the religious group
Heaven's Gate took their own lives because their leader convinced them that they
were leaving their bodies to join extraterrestrials in a nearby spaceship. Members of the
People's Temple drank cyanide-laced punch and died. Sixty-five percent of Milgram's
subjects administered painful electric shocks to an innocent person as he begged them
to stop.

These groups and their leaders were extraordinarily powerful, but they were not
uniquely powerful. When the coach tells the player to sit on the bench, the player
obeys. The driver turns over her license when the police officer demands it. The student stops his conversation with his friend when the teacher says, "No talking."
When one person acts in a dominant fashion, others tend to become submissive. When
one person seems weak, the other person will become strong. People usually do what
authorities tell them to do. Milgram merely explored the fuller implications of this
tendency (Carson, 1969; Gifford & O'Connor, 1987; MacCoun, 1993; Tyler, 1990;
Tyler & Lind, 1992; Strong et al., 1988).

But even if we accept that people in groups will sometimes follow an authority's
order rather than refuse, we are still left with the task of explaining the source of this
power. Reverend Moon, Jim Jones, Milgram's experimenter, as well as coaches, police
officers, and teachers, extract obedience from others. But where does this remarkable
power come from?

Power Bases

John R. P. French and Bertram Raven (1959), in a brilliant analysis of the roots of
power in groups and organizations, identified the six key **power bases** shown in
Table 8–1. Group members who control these power bases—they can reward or
punish group members, they are liked and respected, they are accepted by the members as legitimate authorities, and they are experts who have some special skill and
information—are more influential than group members who fail to secure a base of
power.

Reward Power.   Jones was adept in offering members what they needed, whether it
be security, economic support, companionship, political reform, or religious inspira-
tion. His ability to mediate the distribution of positive or negative reinforcers lay at
the heart of his **reward power.**

Rewards can take many forms: gold stars for students, salaries for workers, social
approval for subjects in experiments, positive feedback for employees, food for the
starving poor, freedom for prisoners, and even suicide for those who are leading tor-

---

Power bases: Sources of social power over other people; includes the capacity to reward and to
punish, status, attraction, expertise, and information.
Reward power: The capability of controlling the distribution of rewards given or offered to the
other group members.

TABLE 8-1   FRENCH AND RAVEN'S SIX BASES OF POWER

Base	Definition
Reward power	The capability of controlling the distribution of rewards given or offered to the target
Coercive power	The capacity to threaten and punish those who do not comply with requests or demands
Legitimate power	Authority that derives from the powerholder's legitimate right to require and demand obedience
Referent power	Influence based on the target's identification with, attraction to, or respect for the powerholder
Expert power	Influence based on the target's belief that the powerholder possesses superior skills and abilities
Informational power	Influence based on the potential use of informational resources, including rational argument, persuasion, or factual data

tured lives. Social exchange theory, however, suggests that rewards heighten power when (1) the rewards are valued, (2) the group members depend on the powerholder for the resource, and (3) the powerholder's promises seem credible. Jones, for example, offered members rewards and outcomes that they valued, and by moving the group to Jonestown, he increased his followers' dependence on him. Most of the group members also believed that Jones would keep his promises to them, and when disbelief came, it was too late. By this time, he had managed to strengthen his position in the group by building his coercive power (Emerson, 1962, 1981).

Coercive Power.   Accounts of the development of the People's Temple vividly describe Jones's growing reliance on physical and psychological punishment as a means of exacting obedience from his followers. When members broke the rules or disobeyed his orders, he was quick to punish them with beatings, solitary confinement, denials of food and water, and long hours of labor in the fields.

   Coercive power derives from one's capacity to dispense punishments to those who do not comply with requests or demands. Examples of coercive influence abound: Countries threaten other countries with attacks and economic sanctions. Employers threaten employees with the loss of pay, a transfer to an undesirable job, or even firing. Teachers punish mischievous students with extra assignments, detention, or a scowl. Disagreeing friends insult and humiliate one another, gang members coerce other members through acts of physical violence, and religious leaders threaten members with loss of grace or ostracism. People also use coercion to influence other group

---

Coercive power: The ability to punish or threaten those who do not comply with requests or demands.

members, although most people prefer to use reward power rather than coercive power if both are available (Molm, 1987, 1988). When two parties in conflict are equal in coercive power, they learn over time to avoid the use of their power (Lawler, Ford, & Blegen, 1988; Lawler & Yoon, 1996).

Legitimate Power.   Individuals who have **legitimate power** have the recognized right to ask others to obey their orders. A police officer telling a bystander to move along, a drill sergeant ordering the squad to attention, the professor waiting for the class to become quiet before a lecture, and the minister interpreting the Gospel for the congregation are powerful because they have the right to command the target and the target person is obligated to obey.

Legitimate power springs from the group structure itself—roles, status, and norms —rather than from the delivery or withholding of valued resources. Jones, for example, was the legitimate head of the People's Temple. He was also an ordained minister, his work was commended by many political and religious leaders, and he received such honors as the Martin Luther King, Jr., Humanitarian Award. When individuals joined the People's Temple they tacitly agreed to follow Jones's orders. In fact, "Consent is the necessary condition of a stable system of power. Legitimacy is important because it gives rise to consent" (Zelditch & Walker, 1984, p. 1).

When individuals obey the commands of another because they hope to earn a reward or avoid a punishment, their obedience dwindles when the powerholder's control over the resources diminishes. Members obey legitimate authorities, however, because they personally accept the norms of the group; they voluntarily obey from an internalized sense of duty, loyalty, or moral obligation. Legitimate power also "minimizes the need for maintaining means of coercion in constant readiness, continual surveillance of the power subjects, and regular supplies of economic or non-economic rewards. For these reasons, naked (that is, coercive) power always seeks to clothe itself in the garments of legitimacy" (Wrong, 1979, p. 52).

Legitimate power may be achieved by a variety of means—appointment by a legitimizing agent, election by members of the group, qualification through possession of specified characteristics, and so on—provided that the method is supported by group norms as the appropriate means of gaining this position of authority. Legitimacy, however, is also a perceptual process, with group members assessing their leader's legitimacy based on their own personal experiences with the leader. People who have prospered under a particular leader—gained status, been rewarded, enjoyed membership in a successful group—tend to feel that their leader is more legitimate than those who have experienced negative outcomes with the leader. People's perceptions of how they have been treated by the leader also shape their perceptions of legitimacy. People are more likely to follow the directives of leaders who seem trustworthy, who distribute resources fairly, and who treat people with the respect they feel they deserve (Tyler, 1989, 1990, 1994, 1997; Tyler & Degoey, 1996).

Legitimate power: Power that stems from an authority's justifiable right to require and demand compliance.

Referent Power. Who is the best-liked member of the group? Who is the most respected? Is there someone in the group whom everyone wants to please? The individual with **referent power** lies at the interpersonal center of the group. Just as group members seek out membership in selective, desirable groups, so they identify with and seek close association with respected, attractive group members. The members of the People's Temple were devoted to Jones—to the point where they loved, admired, and identified with him. Many made tremendous financial and emotional sacrifices in the hope of pleasing him. As one observer commented, "To his followers, Jones was a god whose power they could take into themselves merely by obeying him" (Allen, 1978, p. 121).

The concept of referent power explains how **charismatic leaders** manage to exert so much control over their groups. It was sociologist Max Weber who first used the term *charisma* to account for the almost irrational devotion that followers exhibit for their leaders. Charisma originally described a special power given by God to certain individuals. These individuals were capable of performing extraordinary, miraculous feats, and they were regarded as God's representatives on earth (Weber, 1921/1946). Weber argued that charismatic individuals do not have unique, wondrous powers, but they succeed because their followers *think* they have unique, wondrous powers. Weber himself was struck by the charismatic leader's power to demand actions that contradict established social norms: "Every charismatic authority . . . preaches, creates, or demands new obligations" (1921/1946, p. 243; see also Cavalli, 1986; Lepsius, 1986; Lindholm, 1990).

People sometimes use the term *charisma* to refer to a charming, dynamic leader, as in "Kennedy's good looks and warm smile made him a charismatic leader" (Bradley, 1987; Conger & Kanungo, 1987). Weber, however, reserved the term to describe the tremendous referent and legitimate power of the "savior-leader." Charismatic leaders such as Jones usually appear on the scene when a large group of people are dissatisfied or face a distressful situation. The leader offers these people a way to escape their problems, and the masses react with intense loyalty. In the vivid words of social critic Eric Hoffer (1951, p. 105), the charismatic leader

> personifies the certitude of the creed and justifies the resentment dammed up in the souls of the frustrated. He kindles the vision of a breathtaking future so as to justify the sacrifice of a transitory present. He stages the world of make-believe so indispensable for the realization of self-sacrifice and united action. He evokes the enthusiasm of communion—the sense of liberation from a petty and meaningless individual existence.

Expert Power. Group members often defer to, and take the advice of, those who seem to possess superior skills and abilities. A physician interpreting a patient's symptoms,

---

Referent power: Influence that is based on subordinates' identification with, attraction to, or respect for the powerholder.
Charismatic leaders: Powerful group authorities who extract high levels of commitment from their followers by relying primarily on referent and legitimate power.

a local resident giving directions to an out-of-towner, a teacher dictating the correct spelling of a word for a student, and a computer technician giving advice to a PC user can all transform their special knowledge into **expert power.** As with most of the power bases identified by French and Raven, a person does not actually need to be an expert to acquire expert power. The person must only be *perceived* by others to be an expert (Kaplowitz, 1978; Littlepage & Mueller, 1997). Researchers demonstrated the impact of perceived expertise on influence by arranging for dyads to work on a series of problems. Half of the subjects were led to believe that their partner's ability on the task was superior to their own, and the rest were told that their partner possessed inferior ability. As the concept of expert power suggests, individuals who thought that their partners were experts accepted their recommendations an average of 68% of the time, whereas subjects paired with partners perceived as inferior accepted their recommendation only 42% of the time (Foschi, Warriner, and Hart, 1985; see also Schopler & Layton, 1972a, 1972b).

Informational Power.   In 1965, Raven amended his original list of five power bases by adding **informational power:** the potential to use informational resources, including rational argument, persuasion, and factual data, to influence others (Raven, 1992). Jones was, by all accounts, a persuasive speaker. He offered the devoted a clear path to salvation, and they needed only to study his teachings and obey his orders to be saved. The strength of his personality, the simplicity of his ideology, and his willingness to act on his beliefs inspired a sincere trust among his followers, who eventually accepted him as the final source of truth and knowledge.

Power Tactics

French and Raven argued that people draw power from six key sources; Jones was powerful because he controlled all six bases, and his followers were weak because they lacked a power base (French & Raven, 1959; Raven, 1965, 1992). These six bases, however, are not the only means of influencing others. When people must influence others, they often report using promises, rewards, threats, punishment, expertise, and information. But they often supplement these tactics with other tactics. Table 8–2 samples these tactics, which vary in terms of directness, rationality, and bilaterality (Falbo, 1977; Falbo & Peplau, 1980; Kipnis, 1984).

- *Directness.* Direct tactics are explicit, overt methods of influence; threats, demands, and faits accomplis (simply going ahead and doing what you want to do despite objections) are all direct methods. Indirect tactics, in contrast, involve covert manipulation and indirect influence. When we drop hints, use ingratiation, or evade the issue, we are using indirect methods. David Kipnis (1984) uses the terms *strong* and *weak* rather than *direct* and *indirect.*

Expert power: Influence that derives from subordinates' assumption that the powerholder possesses superior skills and abilities.
Informational power: Influence based on the potential use of informational resources, including rational argument, persuasion, and factual data.

TABLE 8-2   SOME OF THE MANY TACTICS PEOPLE USE TO INFLUENCE OTHERS IN EVERYDAY SITUATIONS

Tactic	Examples	Tactic	Examples
Bully	• I yell at him. • I criticize her work. • I push him around.	Join forces	• I get the boss to agree with me. • I turn the group against her. • I get others to take my side.
Claim expertise	• I let her know I'm an expert. • I bury them in technical details. • I rely on my experience.	Manipulate	• I lie. • I get him to think it's his idea. • I leave out important details.
Complain	• I gripe about all the work I have to do. • I grumble about having to study. • I complain about my headache.	Negotiate	• I offer her a bargain. • I work out a compromise. • I wheel and deal.
Criticize	• I point out her limitations. • I tell him what I don't like about him. • I find fault with their work.	Persist	• I don't take no for an answer. • I reiterate my point. • I nag until he agrees.
Demand	• I insist that he stop. • I demand that the problem be solved. • I order her to continue.	Persuade	• I coax her into it. • I convert him to my side. • I present all the evidence.
Discuss	• I give him supporting reasons. • I explain why I favor the plan. • We talk about it.	Promise	• I promise to never do it again. • I offer her a bonus. • I offer to do some of his work.
Disengage	• I break up with her. • I give him the cold shoulder. • I stop talking to her.	Punish	• I fire her. • I slap him. • I take away her toys.
Evade	• I keep it from him. • I change the subject when it comes up. • I skip the meeting.	Put down	• I insult him. • I make him look like an idiot. • I make fun of her in front of her friends.
Fait accompli	• I just do it. • I don't get anyone's permission. • I avoid going through channels.	Request	• I say what I want. • I ask him to do me a favor. • I tell her what I expect.
Humor	• I try to make a joke out of it. • I tell a funny story. • I tease him about it.	Reward	• I increase his pay. • I give her a present. • I fix dinner for him.
Ingratiate	• I flatter her. • I try to be seductive. • I compliment him on the way he looks.	Supplicate	• I plead. • I cry. • I beg humbly for permission.
Inspire	• I appeal to her sense of fair play. • I cheer him on. • I remind her of her many good qualities.	Threaten	• I tell her that I'm going to leave her. • I threaten legal action. • I tell him that he might get fired.
Instruct	• I teach him how to do it. • I explain it in simple terms. • I set an example.		

Source: Drawn from various studies of influence, including Belk et al., 1988; Buss, Gomes, Higgins, & Lauterbach, 1987; Caldwell & Burger, 1997; Cowan, Drinkard, & MacGavin, 1984; Dillard & Fitzpatrick, 1985; Falbo, 1977; Falbo & Peplau, 1980; Howard, Blumstein, & Schwartz, 1986; Instone, Major, & Bunker, 1983; Kipnis, 1984; Kipnis & Consentino, 1969; Littlepage, Nixon, & Gibson, 1992; Marwell & Schmitt, 1967; Offermann & Schrier, 1985; Stets, 1997; Schriesheim & Hinkin, 1990; Wheeless, Barraclough, & Stewart, 1983; Wilkinson & Kipnis, 1978; Wiseman & Schenck-Hamlin, 1981; Yukl, Guinan, & Sottolano, 1995.

- *Rationality.* Tactics that emphasize reasoning, logic, and good judgment are the rational tactics; bargaining and persuasion are examples. Tactics such as ingratiation and evasion are nonrational tactics of influence, because they rely on emotionality and misinformation.
- *Bilaterality.* Some tactics are interactive, involving give-and-take on the part of both the influencer and the target of the influence. Such bilateral tactics include persuasion, discussion, and negotiation. Unilateral tactics, in contrast, can be enacted without the cooperation of the target of influence. Such tactics include demands, faits accomplis, evasion, and disengagement.

People choose different power tactics, depending on the nature of the group situation (Yukl, Falbe, & Joo, 1993; Yukl, Guinan, & Sottolano, 1995). A person who has high status in a group that is already rife with conflict will use different tactics than an individual who is low in status and wants to minimize conflict (e.g., Ansari & Kapoor, 1987; Canary, Cody, & Marston, 1986; Cheng, 1983; Holtgraves & Yang, 1992). Kipnis and his colleagues, for example, report that managers use a variety of strong and weak methods to influence subordinates, but when dealing with superiors, they rely heavily on rational methods such as persuasion and discussion. Kipnis also finds that those who are higher in status or authority in the group are more likely to use direct (strong) power tactics, whereas those who are low in status rely on indirect (weak) power tactics (Kipnis, 1984; Kipnis, Schmidt, Swaffin-Smith, & Wilkinson, 1984). A little boy, for example, may use relatively weak methods when trying to influence his father but stronger methods when interacting with his peers (Cowan, Drinkard, & MacGavin, 1984). Also, the more the target of the influence resists, the greater the likelihood that the influencer will shift from a weak tactic to a strong tactic (Gavin, Green, & Fairhurst, 1995; Kipnis, 1984; Michener & Burt, 1975a).

People also show personal preferences in their choice of tactics. Toni Falbo (1977) investigated these tendencies by asking people to write a short essay on the topic "How I Get My Way." She discovered that people who were very concerned with being accepted and liked by the other group members reported using indirect/rational tactics rather than direct/nonrational ones. In contrast, those who espoused a Machiavellian, manipulative philosophy when dealing with others tended to use indirect/nonrational tactics as opposed to direct/rational ones. Those with a proclivity to conform to the group's judgments reported using rational methods more than nonrational ones. Other researchers have found that extraverts use a greater variety of tactics than introverts (Caldwell & Burger, 1997).

Men and women also differ somewhat in their choice of power tactics. Men and women who supervised an ineffective employee used both rewards and criticism, but women intervened less frequently and with a more limited range of tactics. They promised fewer pay raises and threatened more pay deductions than men, and they were more likely to criticize subordinates (Instone, Major, & Bunker, 1983). The sexes also differ in their use of power in more intimate relationships, for men tend to use bilateral and direct tactics, whereas women report using unilateral and indirect methods (Belk et al., 1988; Falbo & Peplau, 1980). Women also use negative methods of influencing their partners more frequently than men, although this tendency may reflect their diminished status relative to men (Stets, 1997). Overall, people partnered with men—whether heterosexual or gay—tend to rely on relatively weak influence tactics, including manipulation and supplication (Howard, Blumstein, & Schwartz, 1986; cf. Koberg, 1985).

The Dynamics of Authority

Milgram's experimenter, like Jim Jones, derived his power from several bases. His power to reward was high, because he gave out the payment and also because he was an important source of positive evaluations; subjects wanted to win a favorable appraisal from this figure of authority. He also used coercive prods: "The experiment requires that you continue" and "You have no other choice, you must go on" warn of possible negative consequences for disobedience. Many subjects also assumed that the experimenter had a legitimate right to control their actions and that the learner had no right to quit the study. The subjects also respected Yale and recognized the importance of scientific research, so the experimenter had referent power. Very few knew much about electricity, either, and so they considered the experimenter an expert. He also persuaded them to continue by telling them that the study was important and that its findings would answer questions about how people learn. Milgram succeeded in constructing a situation in which the authority boasted all six forms of power: reward, coercive, legitimate, referent, expert, and informational.

The situation, however, also included powerful authority-subordinate dynamics. When individuals become part of a hierarchically organized group, they are no longer in control of their actions. They enter what Milgram calls the **agentic state;** they become agents of a higher authority (Milgram, 1974). In the obedience research, their role as teacher required them to pay attention to instructions, carefully monitor their own actions, and try to carry out the orders of the authority. Although they questioned the punishment of the learner, most accepted the authority's definition of the situation as a nonharmful one. Also, they felt little responsibility for what was happening to the learner, because they were only following orders. Disobedience, if it comes, arises only when the effects of obedience become so negative that inner beliefs about the value of human life overwhelm the external pressures of the situation. In the agentic state, obedience is easy; disobedience, in contrast, is achieved only with great difficulty and at a considerable psychological cost (Milgram, 1974; see Hamilton, 1986; Silver & Geller, 1978; Staub, 1985).

Responsibility and Obedience.   Responsibility for a group's goals and activities is not evenly distributed among all the members of a group. Those who occupy positions of authority within the group—leaders, executives, managers, and bosses—are generally viewed as more accountable than those who occupy such low-status positions as subordinate and employee (Blass, 1995, 1996; Hamilton & Sanders, 1995). In some cases,

---

Agentic state: The loss of autonomy that individuals experience when they become the agent of a higher authority.

this concentration of responsibility can become so great that subordinates in hierarchically organized groups no longer feel personally responsible for their own actions. They feel "responsibility *to* the authority" but "no responsibility *for* the content of the actions that the authority prescribes" (Milgram 1974, pp. 145–146).

Milgram believes that individuals who no longer feel morally or legally responsible for their own actions are more likely to obey an authority's orders. He documented this link between responsibility and obedience by asking his subjects to allocate responsibility for the situation among the three participants—the experimenter, the teacher, and the learner. Obedient subjects gave more responsibility to the experimenter than they gave to themselves. They also gave twice as much responsibility to the victim as did disobedient subjects. These disobedient subjects, in contrast, took more responsibility than they attributed to the experimenter (Mantell & Panzarella, 1976; Meeus & Raaijmakers, 1995; West, Gunn, & Chernicky, 1975).

Milgram's analysis of responsibility is also consistent with studies of **diffusion of responsibility:** People feel less personally responsible when they are in groups than when they are alone. Bibb Latané and John Darley (1970) used this concept to explain why no one intervened to help Kitty Genovese when she was murdered in Queens, New York. Latané and Darley, rather than attributing the bystanders' failure to help to apathy or heartlessness, concluded that each observer felt that someone else should take responsibility in the situation. Indeed, people who witnessed an emergency were more likely to report having thought that they were not responsible if they were in a group. People who were alone, in contrast, later claimed that they had spontaneously thought about their obligation to help (Schwartz & Gottlieb, 1976, 1980). Other negative group behaviors, including reductions in collective effort, conflict, mob behaviors, and vandalism, have all been attributed to the reduction in perceived responsibility that occurs in groups (Leary & Forsyth, 1987).

The Power of Roles.   When subjects arrived for the Milgram experiment, they were carefully cast into the role of teacher. The duties of that role were made clear to them, and it was not until the shock sequence progressed that they realized the demands that their role would put on them. Their role required their actions.

Philip Zimbardo's Stanford Prison Study underscores the power of roles. He selected two dozen healthy, intelligent, and psychologically normal men to serve as either prisoners or guards in a simulated prison. The prisoners were "arrested" by uniformed police, booked, and transported to a mock prison that Zimbardo and his colleagues had constructed in the basement of the psychology building at Stanford University. They were sprayed with a deodorant, searched, issued an identification number, and outfitted in a dresslike shirt, heavy ankle chain, and stocking cap. Guards were issued khaki uniforms, billy clubs, whistles, and reflective sunglasses. The guards were told to maintain security and order in the prison (Haney, Banks, & Zimbardo, 1973; Zimbardo, 1975).

Diffusion of responsibility: A reduction of personal responsibility that sometimes occurs when people are members of a group.

The study was scheduled to run for 2 weeks, but was terminated after only 6 days. Why? According to Zimbardo, the subjects became too immersed in the social situation. The prisoners seemed literally to become prisoners; although some rebelled, the majority became withdrawn and depressed. The guards also changed as the study progressed; many became increasingly tyrannical and arbitrary in their control of the prisoners. They woke the prisoners in the middle of the night and forced them to stand at attention for hours, locked them in a closet, required them to clean toilets with their bare hands, strictly enforced pointless rules, and censored prisoners' mail. Zimbardo confesses that he even found himself sinking too deeply into the role of warden, worrying over possible "prison breaks" and autocratically controlling visiting procedures.

Why did the prisoners respond so obediently and the guards so autocratically? Zimbardo believes that the participants felt compelled to act consistently with their roles. All of the subjects had a general idea of what it meant to act like a prisoner or like a guard. As the study progressed, they became more and more comfortable in their roles. Eventually, to be a guard meant controlling all aspects of the prison and protecting this control with force if necessary. Prisoners, on the other hand, were supposed to accept this control and try to get through the experience as easily as possible by obeying all the prison's rules. Subjects who refused to obey these norms were pressured by the other subjects to bring their behavior back in line; nonconformity was not tolerated.

Commitment and Obedience. Jim Jones's order to commit suicide did not surprise his followers. Even before the People's Temple moved to Guyana, Jones would talk about suicide with the group. On more than one occasion, Jones told the congregation that he had poisoned the sacramental wine and that all would be dead within the hour. He went so far as to plant confederates in the audience who feigned convulsions and death. Once in Jonestown, he repeated this ceremony, calling it the White Night. After enough repetitions, the thought of suicide, so alien to most people, became commonplace in the group.

Jones's White Night tactic illustrates the power of behavioral commitment. Jones did not suddenly order his followers to commit suicide. Instead, he prefaced his request with months of demands that increased in their intensity. Similarly, Milgram did not ask subjects to push a lever that would deliver 450 volts to the learner at the outset of the study. Instead, he asked them to only give the learner a mild shock if he answered incorrectly. No one refused. Over time, however, the demands escalated, and participants were unable to extricate themselves from the situation. Once they began, they could not stop (Gilbert, 1981; Modigliani & Rochat, 1995).

Studies of the influence tactics used by salespeople, fundraisers, authorities, and even panhandlers confirm the power of gradually escalating demands (Cialdini, 1993). The **foot-in-the-door technique,** for example, works by prefacing a major request with

---

Foot-in-the-door technique: A method of influence in which influencers first make a very small request that the target will probably agree to. Once the target agrees to the minor request, influencers then make the more important request.

a minor one that is so inconsequential that few people would refuse to comply. In-vestigators demonstrated the strength of this technique by asking homeowners to post a large, unattractive sign in their yards. Nearly all refused unless this major request had been preceded by a smaller request (Freedman & Fraser, 1966). Similar studies have also found that the two requests called for by the foot-in-the-door technique are superior to a single request for many types of behaviors, although such factors as the sex of the influencer and the amount of time that elapses between the two requests moderate the power of the foot-in-the-door method (Beaman, Cole, Preston, Klentz, & Steblay, 1983; Dillard, 1991).

The Chinese incorporated the foot-in-the-door tactic in the so-called "brainwash-ing" indoctrination methods that they used with U.S. prisoners captured during the Korean War. They began by subjecting the POWs to physical hardships and stressful psychological pressures. The men were often fatigued from forced marches, and their sleep was disrupted. Their captors broke down the chain of command in these units by promoting nonranking soldiers to positions of authority, and friendships among the men were systematically discouraged.

Although the Chinese relied heavily on traditional methods of influence, such as persuasion, indirect techniques proved more effective. The prisoners were initially asked to perform inconsequential actions, such as copying an essay out of a notebook or answering some questions about life in the United States. Once the men agreed to a minor request, a more significant request followed. They might be asked to write their own essays about communism or discuss the problems with capitalism. Each small concession led to a slightly larger one until the men found themselves collaborating with the Chinese. The Chinese rarely succeeded in permanently changing the men's atti-tudes and values, but they did extract obedience to their authority: Morale within the prison was poor, and the men rarely tried to escape (Schein, 1961; Segal, 1954).

The Roots of Obedience

A church member obediently swallowing poison. A soldier executing innocent civil-ians. A worker installing substandard building materials. A subject in an experiment giving an innocent victim painful shocks. Upon first hearing about such events, people often fall prey to the **fundamental attribution error (FAE)**: They blame the per-sonalities of the individuals rather than the powerful group processes at work that forced them to obey (Vorauer & Miller, 1997; West et al., 1975). Indeed, in extreme instances when a powerholder inflicts tremendous suffering and misfortune on people, the group members blame themselves for their misery. The members of the People's Temple may have felt so deserving of their fate that they chose to suffer rather than es-cape suffering. These feelings of self-condemnation may account for their willingness to take their own lives (Clark, 1971; Fanon, 1963; Gamson, 1968).

Yet, obedience is not a reflection of the nature of the individuals in the group, but an indication of the power of the group itself. By controlling key bases of power, using

Fundamental attribution error (FAE): The tendency to overestimate the causal influence of dis-positional factors while underemphasizing the causal influence of situational factors.

power tactics, exploiting the nature of the subordinate-authority relationship, and prefacing large demands with minor ones, authorities exert great influence on group members. As John Darley explains, "Many evil actions are not the volitional products of individual evil-doers. Instead, they are in some sense societal products, in which a complex series of social forces interact to cause individuals to commit multiple acts of stunning evil" (Darley, 1992, p. 204).

THE METAMORPHIC EFFECTS OF POWER

Once power is used, its side effects reverberate through the group, creating changes in both those it influences and those who exercise the influence (Kipnis, 1974, 1984). Some of the members of the People's Temple, when first subjected to Jones's coercive influence, became so angry that they left the group. Others accepted their punishment passively or even joined with Jones to inflict harm on others. And Jones himself changed as his influence in the group grew, morphing from an inspirational religious leader into a tyrant.

Compliance and Conversion

Both Milgram's subjects and the People's Temple members did as they were told, but the two groups differed in one crucial respect. Most of Milgram's subjects struggled to withstand the authority's pressure, for they believed that the learner should not be harmed. Many of Jones's followers, in contrast, zealously followed his orders. They did not strain against his authority; they had converted to his way of thinking (Darley, 1995; Lutsky, 1995; Staub, 1989, 1996).

Herbert Kelman (1958, 1961) identified three basic reactions that people display in response to coercive influence (see Table 8–3). In some cases, the powerholder only produces *compliance:* The group members do what they are told to do, but only because the powerholder demands it. Privately they do not agree with the powerholder, but publicly they yield to the pressure. Like Milgram's subjects, they obey

---

TABLE 8–3   KELMAN'S THREE-STAGE THEORY OF CONVERSION

Stage	Description
Compliance	The individual complies with the authority's demands, but does not personally agree with them. If the authority is not present, the target disobeys.
Identification	The individual's compliance with actual or anticipated demands of an authority is motivated by a desire to imitate and please the authority. The individual adopts the authority's actions, characteristics, and attitudes.
Internalization	The individual complies with the authority's demands because those demands are congruent with his or her own personal beliefs, goals, and values. The individual will perform the required actions even if not monitored by the authority.

Source: Kelman, 1958.

only when the powerholder maintains surveillance. *Identification* occurs when the target of the influence admires and therefore imitates the powerholder. When group members identify with the powerholder, their self-image changes as they take on the behaviors, characteristics, and roles of the person with power. Many members of the People's Temple admired Jones and wanted to achieve his level of religious intensity. They obeyed his orders because they identified with him.

Identification, if prolonged and unrelenting, can lead to the final stage: *internalization*. When internalization occurs, the individual "adopts the induced behavior because it is congruent with his value system" (Kelman, 1958, p. 53). The group members are no longer merely carrying out the powerholder's orders. Instead, their actions reflect their own personal beliefs, opinions, and goals. Even if the powerholder is not present, the group members will still undertake the required actions. Extreme obedience—such as occurred with Jonestown, the murder of millions of Jews by the Nazis during World War II, the My Lai massacre, and the Heaven's Gate group—often requires internalization. The group members' actions reflect their private acceptance of the authority's value system (Kelman & Hamilton, 1989).

Kelman's three-step model of conversion explains how groups convert recruits into fervent members over time. Cults, for example, insist that the members adopt the group's ideology, but in the early stages of membership, they only require compliance. New recruits are invited to pleasant group functions, where they are treated in a warm, positive way. Once they agree to join the group for a longer visit, the veteran members disorient them by depriving them of sleep, altering their diet, and persuading them to join into physically exhilarating activities. The recruits are usually isolated from friends and family to prevent any lapses in influence, subjected to lectures, and asked to take part in group discussions. Compliance with these small requests is followed by greater demands, as was the case with the Korean POWs. Eventually, the recruits freely agree to make personal sacrifices for the group, and these sacrifices prompt a further consolidation of their attitudes (Baron, Kerr, & Miller, 1992). Once they reach the consolidation stage, they have fully internalized the group's ideology and goals.

Resistance to Influence

Authorities do not always succeed. Sometimes the targets of influence do not obey, but instead escape the powerholder's region of control or apply influence in return. They may, for example, form a **revolutionary coalition** that opposes the powerholder's demands (Lawler, 1975; Lawler & Thompson, 1978, 1979). In one analysis of this process, subjects worked in three-person groups under the direction of a leader who was appointed to that post because he or she had outscored them on a bogus test of ability. The leader then proceeded to keep over half of the money earned by the work, giving each subject less than one-fourth. When the leader had personally decided how to apportion payment, 58% of the subjects rebelled by forming a coalition with the other

---

Revolutionary coalition: A subgroup formed within the larger group that seeks to overthrow the current group leader.

low-status subject. When the leader was not responsible for the payment scheme, only 25% revolted (Lawler & Thompson, 1978).

Counterconformity, discussed in Chapter 7, also becomes more likely when the authority lacks referent power, relies on nonrational influence methods, and asks the group members to carry out unpleasant assignments (Yukl, Kim, Falbe, 1996). Such conditions can generate **reactance** in group members. When reactance occurs, individuals strive to reassert their sense of freedom by reaffirming their autonomy (Brehm, 1976; Brehm & Brehm, 1981). In one study in which teammates had to make a choice between two alternatives marked 1-A and 1-B, 73% chose 1-A if the partner said, "I prefer 1-A," but only 40% chose 1-A if the partner demanded, "I think we should both do 1-A" (Brehm & Sensenig, 1966). In another study, 83% of the group members refused to go along with a group participant who said, "I think it's pretty obvious all of us are going to work on task A" (Worchel & Brehm, 1971).

The likelihood of conflict within the group also increases with the use of certain types of influence. Coercive influence tactics, such as threats and punishments, are tolerated by group members when the group is successful (Michener & Lawler, 1975), the leader is trusted (Friedland, 1976), and the use of such tactics is justified by the group's norms (Michener & Burt, 1975b). Coercive methods are also more effective when they are applied frequently and consistently to punish prohibited actions (Molm, 1994).

Coercive tactics can, however, generate anger and hostility (Johnson & Ewens, 1971; Mulder, Van Kijk, Soutenkijk, Stelwagen, & Verhagen, 1964). Studies of reciprocity in groups indicate that when people are rewarded by a powerholder, they tend to reciprocate with cooperation; if, in contrast, powerholders employ coercion, they provoke animosity (Schlenker, Nacci, Helm, & Tedeschi, 1976). Moreover, even when mildly coercive methods are used, such as threats, people often overreact and respond with even stronger threats. This escalating pattern sets in motion an upward spiral of conflict (Youngs, 1986). Hence, although coercive powerholders may be successful in initial encounters, influence becomes more difficult in successive meetings as the target's anger and resistance to pressure grow. Coercive and reward power can also cause group members to lose interest in their work. Supervisors who create feelings of autonomy sustain their subordinates' intrinsic interest in their work, whereas those who use coercive or rewarding methods find that productivity dwindles when they are not monitoring the group (Deci, Nezlek, & Sheinman, 1981; Pelletier & Vallerand, 1996). Indeed, organizational experts advocate *sharing power* with subordinates by delegating responsibilities, empowering workers, and making use of self-directed work teams (Hollander & Offermann, 1990).

The conflict created by coercive influence can disrupt the entire group's functioning. Studies of classrooms, for example, indicate that many teachers rely more heavily on coercion, but that these methods cause rather than solve disciplinary problems (Kounin, 1970). Coercive tactics such as physical punishment, displays of anger, and

---

Reactance: A complex emotional and cognitive reaction that occurs when individuals feel that their freedom to make choices has been threatened or eliminated.

shouting not only fail to change the target student's behavior but also lead to negative changes in the classroom's atmosphere (Kounin & Gump, 1958). When misbehaving students are severely reprimanded, other students often become more disruptive and uninterested in their schoolwork, and negative, inappropriate social activity spreads from the trouble spot throughout the classroom. This disruptive contagion, or **ripple effect,** is especially strong when the reprimanded students are powerful members of the classroom authority structure or when commands by teachers are vague and ambiguous. On the basis of these findings, the researchers suggested that teachers avoid the ripple effect by relying on other influence bases, including reward power, referent power, and expert power.

Reliance on direct, irrational influence methods can also undermine the quality of the relationship between the powerholder and the target. When Falbo (1977) arranged for people to meet in same-sex groups of three to five persons, she found that people who relied on discussion, persuasion, and expertise were most favorably evaluated, whereas those who emphasized manipulation, evasion, and threat received the most negative evaluations. Moreover, people who used (or at least reported using) indirect/rational strategies such as persuasion or ingratiation were rated as more considerate and friendlier than people who used direct/nonrational strategies such as threats and faits accomplis.

Other researchers have confirmed these findings, using a variety of research methods (Caldwell & Burger, 1997; French, Morrison, & Levinger, 1960; Litman-Adizes, Fontaine, & Raven, 1978; Pandey & Singh, 1987; Shaw & Condelli, 1986). When, for example, people rated the attractiveness of a manager who used either coercive, reward, legitimate, referent, expert, or informational power to influence a subordinate, the coercive powerholder was viewed as the least attractive (see Figure 8–1; Shaw & Condelli, 1986; see Podsakoff & Schriescheim, 1985, and Raven, 1992, for reviews).

Changes in the Powerholder

The metamorphic effects of power have long fascinated observers of the human condition (Kipnis, 1974). In their tragedies, the Greeks dramatized the fall of heroes who, swollen by past accomplishments, conceitedly compared themselves to the gods. Myth and folklore is replete with tales of temptations to seek too much power, as in the case of Icarus, whose elation at the power of flight caused his death. In our own century, we find examples of political thinkers who, like Jones, began their careers envisioning utopian societies but became cruel and inhuman dictators when they achieved positions of power. As Lord Acton warned, "Power tends to corrupt, and absolute power corrupts absolutely."

Power Corrupts.   When individuals acquire power, they tend to make use of it to influence others. Kipnis (1972) arranged for advanced business students to participate as managers in a simulated manufacturing company after telling them that their per-

---

Ripple effect: The contagious spread of negative, inappropriate social activity in groups and classrooms.

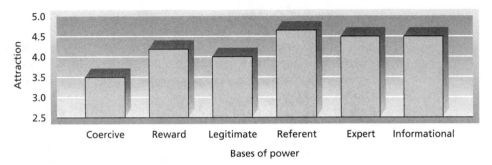

FIGURE 8-1 Whom do group members like best: the coercive, rewarding, legitimate, referent, expert, or informational leader? People rated the authority who used coercive methods the most negatively, and the referent, expert, and informational leaders the most positively.

(*Source:* Shaw & Condelli, 1986.)

formance would be a good indicator of their leadership potential in other executive situations. In one condition, the subjects were given a good deal of reward power and coercive power over their subordinates: They could award bonuses, cut pay, threaten and actually carry out transfers to other jobs, give additional instructions, and even fire a worker. The subjects in the second condition could use only persuasion or extra instructions to influence their subordinates.

The procedure was designed so that the managers could not actually see their workers but were kept informed of their production levels by an assistant, who brought in the finished products from the four workers. This arrangement was chosen so that Kipnis could control the level of productivity of the fictitious workers (all performed adequately) and also provide a reason for the use of an intercom system in giving orders to subordinates. These communications were surreptitiously recorded, and subsequent analyses revealed that the powerful managers initiated roughly twice as many attempts at influence as the nonpowerful managers and that the difference between the two types of managers became more apparent as the sessions progressed. In addition, the powerful and nonpowerful managers used different power tactics: The powerless ones relied on persuasion, whereas the powerful ones coerced or rewarded their workers. Other studies have yielded similar support for the idea that people with power tend to make use of it (Deutsch, 1973; Kipnis & Consentino, 1969), but they also suggest that the magnitude of this effect depends on many other factors (Bedell & Sistrunk, 1973; Black & Higbee, 1973; Goodstadt & Hjelle, 1973; Michener & Burt, 1975a).

Once power has been used to influence others, changes in powerholders' perceptions of themselves and of the target of influence may also take place. In many instances, the successful use of power as a means of controlling others leads to self-satisfaction, unrealistically positive self-evaluations, and overestimations of interpersonal power (Erez, Rim, & Keider, 1986; Kipnis, 1974; Raven & Kruglanski, 1970; Sorokin & Lundin, 1959). In the Kipnis simulation described here, for example, subjects were asked if their subordinates were performing well because of the workers' high self-motivation levels, their manager's comments and suggestions, or their desire for money. Analyses showed that the high-power managers felt that their workers were only in it for the money (which the manager could control), whereas the low-power managers felt that the workers were "highly motivated." In fact, in the powerful-manager condition, the correlation between the number of messages sent to the workers and the manager's agreement with the statement "My orders and influence caused the workers to perform effectively" was quite strong ($r = .65$; Kipnis, 1974). Other studies have also revealed this tendency for powerful individuals to assume that they themselves are the prime cause of other people's behavior (Kipnis, Castell, Gergen, & Mauch, 1976).

Devaluation of the target of the influence attempt also tends to covary with increased feelings of control over people. In a classic study of power dynamics in a mental hospital, Alvin Zander and his colleagues found that psychiatrists tended to underestimate the abilities of the psychologists they supervised (Zander, Cohen, & Stotland, 1959). Although the psychologists believed themselves to be capable of developing diagnoses and conducting therapy, the psychiatrists considered them qualified only to conduct psychological testing. Evidence also suggests that powerholders tend to (1) increase the social distance between themselves and the nonpowerful, (2) believe that the nonpowerful are untrustworthy and in need of close supervision, and (3) devalue the work and ability of the less powerful (Kipnis, 1972; Sampson, 1965; Strickland, 1958; Strickland, Barefoot, & Hockenstein, 1976). Powerful individuals also spend less time gathering and processing information about their subordinates, and as a result they are more likely to perceive them in a stereotypical fashion (Fiske, 1993a). This tendency to derogate the target person while simultaneously evaluating oneself more positively widens the gap between group members who have varying degrees of power.

The Mandate Phenomenon.   Individuals who acquire the power to influence others tend to use that power, and they tend to subsequently alter their perceptions of the people they influence. Too much power, however, can also prompt them to overstep the bounds of their authority. In 1937, for example, Franklin D. Roosevelt was elected president of the United States by an overwhelming majority and subsequently went about increasing the powers of the presidency beyond those specified in the U.S. Constitution. This reaction to increased power brought on by overwhelming support from the group has been labeled the **mandate phenomenon** (Clark & Sechrest, 1976).

Researchers confirmed this phenomenon by asking groups of college students to work on problems in a bad-smelling room. The researchers explained that various odors were used in the research, ranging from ones that cause nausea in 10% of the population to ones that cause nausea in 90% of the population. Groups elected a leader who was to pick the smell the group would be exposed to, but they were promised that the fouler the odor, the more money they would receive. In the *mandate condition*, leaders were told they had been unanimously selected to be the leader. Leaders in the *majority condition* thought they had won over 50% of the votes. Leaders

---

Mandate phenomenon: A tendency for leaders to overstep the bounds of their authority when they feel they have the overwhelming support of the group.

in the *control condition* were told they had been selected at random. Consistent with mandate phenomenon predictions, individuals who felt that they had the overwhelming support of their group selected more noxious odors than either the leaders elected by simple majority or the subjects in the control condition.

The Iron Law of Oligarchy.   Some people are power hungry. They seek it, not because they can use it to achieve their goals, but because they value power per se (Cartwright & Zander, 1968). Hence, once people attain power, they take steps to protect their sources of influence. This protective aspect of power translates into a small-group version of Michels's (1915/1959) iron law of oligarchy: Individuals in power tend to remain in power. Eventually, too, powerholders may become preoccupied with seeking power, driven by a strong motivation to acquire greater and greater levels of interpersonal influence (McClelland, 1975, 1985; Winter, 1973). This need for power, which was described in Chapter 4, is a prominent personality characteristic in individuals who rise to positions of authority in organizations and politics. Evidence also indicates, however, that when those with a high power motivation cannot exercise that power, they experience increased tension and stress (McClelland, 1985). Under such conditions, they also exaggerate the amount of conflict that exists in the group and overlook group members' efforts at cooperation (Fodor, 1984, 1985).

Question Authority

In 1976, Jones fought for the improvement of housing and for progressive political change in the San Francisco area, and his followers worked diligently toward the goals outlined by their leader. In 1978, he was accused of human rights violations, physical assault, and illicit sexual practices. Power changed all the members of the People's Temple, including Jones himself.

Authority is essential to group life. Without its organizing guidance, group members could not coordinate their efforts and achieve their goals. Yet, authorities that overstep their boundaries can undermine members' motivation, create conflict, and break the bonds between members. Authorities, too, must be wary of their own power, for power is easily misused. Who should question authority? Those who have it and those who are controlled by it.

SUMMARY

What are the limits of an authority's power over group members?

Power is the capacity to influence others, even when these others try to resist this influence.

1. Milgram tested people's ability to resist a powerful authority who ordered them to give painful and potentially harmful electric shocks to a confederate.

2. Sixty-five percent of Milgram's subjects obeyed, apparently because they felt powerless to refuse the orders of the authority. Changes in the setting influenced rates of obedience.

3. Critics noted methodological flaws of the procedures and suggested that the personal characteristics of Milgram's

subjects prompted them to obey, but
Milgram argued that his studies underscore the power of authorities.

What are the sources of power in groups?

1. French and Raven's analysis of *power
   bases* emphasizes *reward, coercive,
   legitimate, referent, expert,* and *informational power* (see Table 8–1). *Charismatic leaders,* for example, exert
   their influence by relying on legitimate
   and referent power.
2. People also use more specific tactics
   when they influence others.
   • These tactics, which include promises,
     threats, persuasion, manipulation,
     evasion, and disengagement, differ
     from one another in terms of direct-
     ness (or strength), rationality, and
     bilaterality.
   • Which tactic we use to influence oth-
     ers depends on both the nature of the
     setting (e.g., our status relative to the
     target's and the target's prior compli-
     ance) and our personal qualities
     (e.g., personality traits and gender).
3. Milgram's theory of the *agentic state*
   traces obedience back to the nature of
   the authority-subordinate relationship.
   When individuals become part of an
   organized hierarchy, they tacitly agree
   to follow the leader's orders. They also
   experience a reduction of responsibility, which is exacerbated by the tendency for people to feel less responsible
   when in groups rather than alone (*diffusion of responsibility*).
4. Individuals feel compelled to comply
   with the requirements of the role they
   occupy within the group, as Zimbardo's
   simulated prison study confirms.
5. Powerholders extract obedience from
   group members by taking advantage of
   the *foot-in-the-door technique:* They
   preface major demands with minor,
   inconsequential ones.

6. An explanation that traces obedience
   to the individuals in the situation may
   reflect the *fundamental attribution
   error (FAE),* which underestimates the
   power of group-level processes.

**What are the consequences of the exercise of
power in groups?**

1. Targets of influence may begin by
   merely complying with the authority's
   request, but over time they may experience identification and internalization.
   When group members identify with the
   authority or internalize the authority's
   demands, their obedience reflects their
   personal beliefs, rather than the constraints of the situation.
2. Coercive methods have also been
   linked to a number of dysfunctional
   group processes, including
   • *revolutionary coalitions*
   • *reactance*
   • shifts in the level of conflict as more
     group members rebel against the
     authority (the *ripple effect*)
   • disrupted interpersonal relations
3. Kipnis's studies of the metamorphic
   effects of power find that people who
   are given coercive power will use this
   power and that once it is used, the
   powerholders tend to overestimate
   their control over others and devalue
   these targets.
4. Powerholders who are very secure in
   this position may also overstep the
   bounds of their authority in a process
   termed the *mandate phenomenon,* or
   they may become so enamored of
   power that they are preoccupied with
   gaining it and using it.

FOR MORE INFORMATION

*Crimes of Obedience, Toward a Social Psy-
chology of Authority and Responsibility* by
Herbert C. Kelman and V. Lee Hamilton

(1989), analyzes the factors that sustain obedience in contemporary society.

Guyana Massacre: The Eyewitness Account, by Charles A. Krause (1978), provides a factual analysis of the demise of the People's Temple, as well as commentaries on cults in general.

Influence: Science and Practice, by Robert B. Cialdini (1993), is an exceptionally well written excursus on the techniques that "compliance professionals"—salespersons, advertisers, charity workers, and panhandlers—use to influence us in our daily lives.

Obedience to Authority, by Stanley Milgram (1974), describes his classic obedience studies in graphic detail.

"Power and Leadership in Organizations: Relationships in Transition," by Edwin P. Hollander and Lynn R. Offermann (1990), is an insightful and concise analysis of power and leadership in organizational settings.

Perspectives on Obedience to Authority: The Legacy of the Milgram Experiments, edited by Arthur G. Miller, Barry E. Collins, and Diana E. Brief (1995b), is a special issue of the *Journal of Social Issues* devoted to the study that some feel is "one of the best carried out in this generation" (Etzioni, 1968, pp. 278–280).

"The Social Psychology of Stanley Milgram," by Thomas Blass (1992), explores the variations in rates of obedience in Milgram's experiment and identifies personality characteristics that may elevate rates of compliance.

ACTIVITY 8–1 DO PEOPLE UNDERESTIMATE THE POWER OF GROUPS?

People often overlook social determinants of actions, but they overestimate the causal role played by internal, personal factors. When we read about Milgram's subjects or the members of radical religious groups, we assume that they were weak, gullible people who were easily influenced. Yet, these individuals' actions were largely a consequence of the powerful situations in which they found themselves.

1. Talk to people about the Milgram experiment. Ask them if they are familiar with the research, and if necessary, clarify the procedure and findings for them. Ask them:
   - Why do you think so many people obeyed the experimenter?
   - If you had been a subject in the study, would you have obeyed the experimenter?
2. Talk to people about radical religious groups, generally called cults. Ask them:
   - Why do people join such groups?
   - Do the leaders of cults wield special psychological powers over the members?
   - If, by some chance, you found yourself at a meeting of a cultlike group, what would you do?
3. Do people's comments about the Milgram experiment and cults reveal the fundamental attribution error? Do they blame the individuals for their actions and underestimate the power of the group?

ACTIVITY 8–2 WHO HAS THE POWER IN THE GROUP?

Objectively examine the power structures of a group to which you belong. This group can be one that meets regularly in a work or social setting, a subgroup of the students within a class, or even an entire class.

1. Describe the group briefly: its composition, structure, dynamics, and tasks. Who is influential in the group, and who is not?
2. Is power based on experience, age, position, and so on? Is power fairly distributed? Are some people who should be influential slighted by the group?
3. Trace the power in the group back to French and Raven's bases of power: coercive, reward, referent, legitimate, expert, and informational.
4. How do you typically influence other people in this group? Do you prefer to use rational methods? Irrational ones? Do you rely on some methods more than others? Review the list in Table 8–2 and identify your favorite and least favorite tactics.

9

Conflict

The word *conflict* implies disagreement, discord, and friction in the group; interaction where words, emotions, and actions produce disruptive effects. Yet, conflict is an unavoidable outgrowth of group life, for by entering into relations with others, we must negotiate and renegotiate our undertakings and our outcomes.

- What is conflict?
- What are the sources of conflict in groups?
- Why does conflict escalate?
- How can group members manage their conflict?

CONTENTS

Jobs versus Sculley: When Group Members Turn Against Each Other

THE ROOTS OF CONFLICT

Disaffection and Disagreement

Substantive Conflicts

Procedural Conflicts

Competition and Conflict

Social Dilemmas

CONFRONTATION AND ESCALATION

Uncertainty → Commitment

Perception → Misperception

Weak Tactics → Stronger Tactics

Reciprocity → Upward Conflict Spiral

Few → Many

Irritation → Anger

CONFLICT RESOLUTION

Commitment → Negotiation

Misperception → Understanding

Strong Tactics → Cooperative Tactics

Upward → Downward Conflict Spirals

Many → One

Anger → Composure

The Value of Conflict

SUMMARY

FOR MORE INFORMATION

ACTIVITIES

Jobs versus Sculley: When Group Members Turn Against Each Other

John Sculley, chief executive officer (CEO) of Apple Computer, Inc., heard the rumor just before his scheduled trip to China in May of 1985. His subordinates reported that Steve Jobs, one of the founders of the company, was planning a corporate coup once Sculley was out of the country. Sculley canceled his trip and called a board meeting. He opened the meeting by confronting Jobs:

"It's come to my attention that you'd like to throw me out of the company, and I'd like to ask if that's true."

Jobs's answer: "I think you're bad for Apple and I think you're the wrong person to run this company. . . . You really should leave this company. . . . You don't know how manufacturing works. You're not close to the company. The middle managers don't respect you."

Sculley, voice rising in anger, replied, "I made a mistake in treating you with high esteem. . . . I don't trust you, and I won't tolerate a lack of trust."

Sculley then polled the board members. Did they support Sculley or Jobs? All of them declared great admiration for Jobs, but they felt that the company needed Sculley's experience and leadership. Jobs then rose from the table and said, "I guess I know where things stand," before bolting from the room. Sculley transferred Jobs to a development position. Jobs later resigned from the company he had founded (Sculley, 1987, pp. 251–252).

Jobs versus Sculley was one of corporate America's most spectacular conflicts, but it was no anomaly. Rare is the group that avoids all **conflict.** When conflict occurs in a group, the actions or beliefs of one or more members of the group are unacceptable to and resisted by one or more of the other group members. The word *conflict* itself implies disagreement, discord, and friction among members of a group, for it comes from the Latin *conflictus:* "striking together with force." During group conflict, words, emotions, and actions "strike together" to produce disruptive effects. When conflicts inundate a group, the members stand against each other rather than in support of each other (Boardman & Horowitz, 1994; Fink, 1968).

Why do allies in a group sometimes turn into adversaries? This chapter answers this question by tracing the course of conflict in groups (Peterson, 1983). (Thus, this chapter focuses on conflicts that occur *within* groups—**intragroup conflict.** Chapter 13 considers the causes and consequences of conflict *between* groups—**intergroup conflict.**) As Figure 9–1 suggests, the process begins with an initial *conflict:* differences in opinion, disagreements over who should lead the group, individuals competing with each other for scarce resources, and the like. Whatever the cause of the initial disunity,

Conflict: Disagreement, discord, and friction that occur when the actions or beliefs of one or more members of the group are unacceptable to and resisted by one or more of the other group members.
Intragroup conflict: Disagreement, discord, and friction between members of the same group.
Intergroup conflict: Disagreement, discord, and friction between the members of two or more groups.

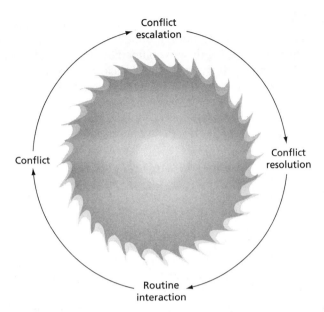

FIGURE 9–1 What is the course of conflict in groups? The typical conflict cycle begins when routine group interaction is disrupted by disagreement, discord, and friction among the members. This conflict often escalates as the group members become more involved in the dispute, but in time it abates as problems are resolved.

the group spends more and more time discussing the issue, and so the conflict grows. Persuasion gives way to arguing, emotions take the place of logic, and the once unified group splits into factions and coalitions. This period of *conflict escalation* is, in most cases, followed by a reduction in conflict and, ideally, *conflict resolution*. The board of directors at Apple Computer, for example, settled their conflict by backing Sculley and demoting Jobs—a rather severe means of resolving the dispute.

THE ROOTS OF CONFLICT

Conflict is everywhere. Members of 71 groups met for a semester in a college class. When asked, "Did your group experience any conflict?" they identified 424 instances of interpersonal irritation (Wall & Nolan, 1987). When Robert Bales and his colleagues used Interaction Process Analysis to record group interactions, some of the groups they observed spent as much as 20% of their time making hostile or negative comments (Bales & Hare, 1965). When researchers asked group members to work together on a frustrating, impossible-to-solve task, the researchers were startled by the intensity of the conflict that overtook the groups. In one particularly hostile group, members averaged 13.5 antagonistic comments per *minute* (French, 1941).

Most people, if given the choice, avoid situations that are rife with conflict (Witteman, 1991). Yet, conflict is an unavoidable consequence of life in groups. When people are sequestered away from other people, their ambitions, goals, and perspectives are their own concern. But a group, by its very nature, creates interdependence among its members, raising the possibility that members' likes and dislikes, their opinions and perspectives, their motives and their goals will clash. (See Fraser & Hipel, 1984; Levine & Thompson, 1996; Rubin, Pruitt, & Kim, 1994; Tjosvold, 1986 for reviews.)

Disaffection and Disagreement

Personal conflict, also called *affective conflict* (Guetzkow & Gyr, 1954), *personality conflict* (Wall & Nolan, 1987), or *emotional conflict* (Jehn, 1995), is rooted in individuals' antipathy for other group members. Personal likes and dislikes do not always translate into group conflict, but people often mention their disaffection for another group member when they air their complaints about their groups (Alicke et al., 1992; Kelley, 1979; Wall & Nolan, 1987). An interview study of high-level corporate executives, for example, revealed that these professionals argued with each other over company matters and they struggled for power, but in over 40% of the cases, their dispute was rooted in "individual enmity between the principals without specific reference to other issues." Disputants questioned each others' moral values, the way they treated their spouses, and their politics. They complained about the way their adversaries acted at meetings, the way they dressed at work and at social gatherings, their hobbies and recreational pursuits, and their personality traits. They just did not like each other very much (Morrill, 1995, p. 69).

Just as any factor that creates a positive bond between people can increase a group's cohesion, so any factor that creates disaffection can increase conflict. In many cases, people explain their conflicts by blaming the other person's negative personal qualities, such as moodiness, compulsivity, incompetence, communication difficulties, and sloppiness (Kelley, 1979). People usually dislike others who evaluate them negatively, so criticism—even when deserved—can generate conflict (Ilgen, Mitchell, & Fredrickson, 1981). Group members who treat others unfairly or impolitely engender more conflict than those who behave politely (Ohbuchi, Chiba, & Fukushima, 1996). People who have agreeable personalities are usually better liked by others, and they also exert a calming influence on their groups. In a study of dyads that included people who were either high or low in their agreeableness, dyads with two highly agreeable individuals displayed the least conflict, whereas dyads that contained two individuals who were low in agreeableness displayed the most conflict (Graziano, Jensen-Campbell, & Hair, 1996). Agreeable people also respond more negatively to conflict overall. When people described their day-to-day activities and their daily moods, conflict and bad moods covaried. People reported feeling unhappy, tense, irritated, and anxious on days when they experienced conflicts—especially if they were, by nature, agreeable people (Suls, Martin, & David, 1998).

Personal conflict: Interpersonal discord that occurs when group members dislike one another.

The relationship between disaffection and conflict explains why groups with greater diversity sometimes display more conflict than homogeneous groups. Just as similarity among members increases interpersonal attraction, dissimilarity tends to increase disaffection and conflict (Rosenbaum, 1986). Groups whose members had dissimilar personalities (e.g., differences in authoritarianism, cognitive complexity, and temperament) did not get along as well as groups composed of people whose personalities were more similar (Haythorn, Couch, Haefner, Langham, & Carter, 1956; Shaw, 1981). Heterogeneous teams developing new information technologies were better than homogeneous teams when identifying their goals and gathering information from other groups, but their overall level of performance was inferior because they could not work well together (Ancona & Caldwell, 1992). When group members were led to believe that they were similar to one another, cohesiveness increased and conflict decreased (Back, 1951). Groups whose members vary in terms of ability, experience, opinions, values, race, personality, ethnicity and so on, can capitalize on their members' wider range of resources and viewpoints, but these groups often suffer high levels of conflict (Moreland, Levine, & Wingert, 1996).

Heider's balance theory (see Chapter 5) goes so far as to suggest that arguing and fighting with someone we dislike is cognitively "harmonious"; the elements of the situation all "fit together without stress" (Heider, 1958, p. 180). If Steve likes John but the two do not agree on important issues facing the group, John will experience psychological stress, which he will reduce by changing his opinion of Steve, changing his opinion on the issues so that he agrees with Steve, or avoiding situations where the disagreement will surface.

Howard F. Taylor (1970) tested these predictions by arranging for male college students to discuss an issue with a confederate of the researcher whom they disliked or liked. This confederate either agreed with the subject or argued against him. Taylor coded the 30-minute discussion, searching for evidence of conflict, including tension (nervousness, stammering, blushing, expressions of frustration, and withdrawal), tension release (giggling, joking, cheerfulness, silliness), and antagonism (anger, hostility, taunting, and defensiveness).

Figure 9–2 partly summarizes Taylor's findings. As balance theory suggests, tension was greatest in the unbalanced pairs: when disagreeing people liked each other and when people who disliked each other agreed. The greatest amount of antagonism, however, occurred in pairs where discussants both disagreed and disliked each other. Taylor concludes that the most harmonious groups are ones where members like each other and find themselves in agreement. The least harmonious ones are balanced, but by negative rather than positive forces: Members dislike each other and they disagree. Taylor suspects that such groups would not endure for long outside the confines of the laboratory.

Substantive Conflicts

When IBM developed a personal computer and Apple Computer's profits dwindled, Sculley and Jobs began arguing over production, pricing, and marketing. Before long,

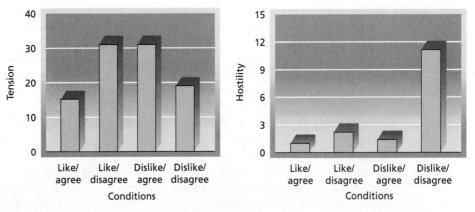

FIGURE 9–2 What happens when we argue with someone we like? When people who disagreed or agreed on an issue *and* either liked or disliked each other talked for 30 minutes, tension was greatest in pairs of disagreeing people who liked each other and agreeing people who disliked each other. The greatest amount of antagonism, however, occurred in pairs where discussants both disagreed and disliked each other.

(*Source:* Taylor, 1970.)

Sculley began to question Jobs's motives, and Jobs wondered if Sculley knew enough about the computer industry. Their working relationship dissolved.

When people discuss their problems and plans, they sometimes disagree with one another's analyses. These **substantive conflicts,** however, are integrally related to the group's work. They do not stem from personal disagreements between individuals, but from disagreements about issues that are relevant to the group's real goals and outcomes. Groups and organizations use such conflicts to make plans, increase creativity, solve problems, decide issues, and resolve conflicts of viewpoint (McGrath, 1984). Sculley and Jobs, as the leaders of Apple Computer, were *supposed* to argue and debate.

Even though substantive conflicts help groups reach their goals, these impersonal conflicts can turn into personal conflicts. People who disagree with the group, even when their position is a reasonable one, often provoke considerable animosity within the group. The dissenter who refuses to accept others' views is liked less, assigned low-status tasks, and sometimes ostracized (see Chapter 7). As the group struggles to reach consensus on the substantive issues at hand, it responds negatively to those group members who slow down this process (Kruglanski & Webster, 1991). In one study, groups of men who were supposed to reach a unanimous decision were hindered by one of the group members. This individual, who was a member of the research team, deliberately slowed the group down with persistent interruptions and questions. In some groups, he explained that he had a hearing problem, but other groups were

---

Substantive conflicts: Disagreements over issues that are relevant to the group's real goals and outcomes.

given no explanation for the member's frustrating behavior. At the end of the study, when given the opportunity to eliminate one person from the group, 100% of the group members chose the individual who interrupted the group without any excuse (Burnstein & Worchel, 1962).

Procedural Conflicts

Substantive conflicts occur when ideas, opinions, and interpretations clash. **Procedural conflicts** occur when strategies, policies, and methods clash. Group members may find themselves uncertain about how to resolve a problem, with some championing continued discussion and others favoring a vote. The leader of the group may make decisions and initiate actions without consulting the group; but the group may become irritated if denied an opportunity to participate in decision making (Smoke & Zajonc, 1962). During procedural conflicts, groups don't just disagree: They disagree on how to disagree.

Many groups minimize procedural ambiguities by adopting formal rules—bylaws, constitutions, statements of policies, or mission and procedures statements—that specify goals, decisional processes, and responsibilities (Houle, 1989). Many decision-making groups also rely on specific rules to regulate their discussions. The best-known set of rules was developed by Henry M. Robert, an engineer who was irritated by the conflict that characterized many of the meetings he attended. Robert's Rules of Order, which he first published in 1876, explicate not only "methods of organizing and conducting meetings, the duties of officers, and the names of ordinary motions," but also such technicalities as how motions should be stated, amended, debated, postponed, voted on, and passed (Robert, 1915/1971). No less than 7 pages are used to describe how the group member "obtains the floor," including suggestions for proper phrasings of the request, appropriate posture, and timing. More complex issues, such as the intricacies of voting, require as many as 20 pages of discussion. Robert purposely designed his rules to "restrain the individual somewhat," for he assumed that "the right of any individual, in any community, to do what he pleases, is incompatible with the interests of the whole" (1915/ 1971, p. 13). In consequence, the rules promote a formal, technically precise form of interaction, sometimes at the expense of openness, vivacity, and directness. Additionally, the rules emphasize the use of voting procedures to resolve differences, rather than discussion to consensus.

Competition and Conflict

Conflict is far more likely when group members, instead of working with one another to reach common goals, compete against each other for such resources as money, power, time, prestige, or materials. When Jobs diverted much of the company's resources into the Macintosh project, Sculley resisted. Jobs refused to back down, and

---

Procedural conflicts: Disagreements over the methods the group should use to complete its basic tasks.

the two stopped working together. They became competitors: For Sculley to succeed, Jobs would have to fail, and for Jobs to succeed, Sculley would have to fail.

Many social situations promote competition between people. When two people play backgammon, one must win and the other must lose. When two rivals in a business go after the same account, one will succeed and the other will fail. In a footrace, only one runner will end up in first place. As Morton Deutsch explains, such situations involve **competition**: The success of any one person means that someone else must fail. Deutsch (1949b) calls this form of interaction "contrient interdependence." Other situations, in contrast, are based on **cooperation**: The success of any one member of the group will improve the chances of success for the other members. Deutsch calls this form of interaction "promotive interdependence" (Deutsch, 1949b).

Competition is a powerful motivator of behavior. When individuals compete against one another, they sometimes expend greater effort, express more interest and satisfaction in their work, and set their personal goals higher. But competition promotes conflict between individuals. When people compete, they must look out for their own interests instead of the group's interests or their comember's interests. They cannot take pride in other group members' accomplishments, for each time someone else in the group excels, their own outcomes shrink. In cooperative groups, members enhance their outcomes by helping other members achieve success, but in competitive groups, members profit from others' errors. Because competing group members can only succeed if others fail, they may even sabotage others' work, criticize it, and withhold information and materials that others might need (Franken & Brown, 1995; Franken & Prpich, 1996; Steers & Porter, 1991; Tjosvold, 1995).

Deutsch studied these side effects of competition by creating two different grading systems in his college classes. Deutsch pitted some of his students against each other by telling them that their personal ranking in their group would determine their course grade. The individual who did the best in the group would get the highest grade, whereas the individual who did the worst would get the lowest grade. Deutsch created cooperative groups, as well. These students worked together to learn the material, and everyone in the group received the same grade. As Deutsch predicted, conflict was much more pronounced in the competitive groups. Members reported less dependency on others, less desire to win the respect of others, and greater interpersonal animosity. Members of cooperative groups, in contrast, acted friendlier during the meetings, were more encouraging and supportive, and communicated more frequently (Deutsch, 1949a, 1949b, 1973, 1980, 1985, 1994).

Other researchers, too, have found that cooperative situations tend to be friendly, intimate, and involving, whereas competitive situations are viewed as unfriendly, nonintimate, and uninvolving (Graziano, Hair, & Finch, 1997; King & Sorrentino, 1983). Work units with high levels of cooperation have fewer latent tensions, personality conflicts, and verbal confrontations (Tjosvold, 1995). Students in classrooms that

---

Competition: A performance situation structured in such a way that any one member of the group will succeed only if another member of the group fails.
Cooperation: A performance situation structured in such a way that the success of any one member of the group improves the chances of other members succeeding.

stress cooperation rather than individualism or competition work harder, show greater academic gains, and display better psychological adjustment (Johnson & Johnson, 1989; Johnson, Maruyama, Johnson, Nelson, & Skon, 1981; cf. Cotton & Cook, 1982). Sports teams, too, tend to be more cohesive and—depending on the demands of the particular sport—more successful when coaches instill a desire for team success rather than individual success (Zander, 1977; see Johnson & Johnson, 1994, and Schmitt, 1981, for detailed reviews).

Mixed-motive Conflict.　　Few situations involve pure cooperation or pure competition; the motive to compete is often mixed with the motive to cooperate. Sculley wanted to gain control over the Mac division, but he needed Jobs's help with product development. Jobs valued Sculley's organizational expertise, but he felt that Sculley misunderstood the company's goals. The men found themselves in a **mixed-motive situation:** They were tempted to compete and cooperate at the same time.

Social psychologists use a specialized laboratory technique known as the **prisoner's dilemma game,** or **PDG,** to study conflict in mixed-motive situations. This procedure takes its name from a quandary that ensnares two hypothetical prisoners. The two imaginary criminals, John and Steve, are being interrogated by police detectives in separate rooms. The police are certain that the two committed a crime, but they need a confession to be sure of a conviction. So they try to turn the two into competitors by telling them that the other is about to confess. Their choices are shown in Figure 9–3:

1. If John confesses and Steve does not, John will get no sentence at all, but Steve will get ten years.
2. If Steve confesses but John does not, Steve will be set free, but John will be locked away for ten years.
3. If both confess, a five-year sentence will be arranged.
4. If neither confesses, both will be tried on a minor charge that carries the light sentence of one year.

Steve and John, as partners in crime, want to cooperate with each other and resist the demands of the police. However, by competing with each other (and cooperating with the police), they will end up with either no sentence or a lighter sentence. Should John and Steve remain silent or give in to the pressure and confess (Luce & Raiffa, 1957)?

When researchers use the prisoner's dilemma to study conflict, the subjects play for points or money (see Figure 9–4). The two participants must individually pick one of two options labeled A and B. Option A is the cooperative choice. If both players pick A, then both will earn money. Option B is the competitive choice. If only one of the two players picks B, that player will make money and the other will lose money.

Mixed-motive situation: Performance settings in which the interdependence among interactants involves both competitive and cooperative goal structures.
Prisoner's dilemma game (PDG): A laboratory procedure in which players must make either cooperative or competitive choices to earn points or money; used in the study of cooperation, competition, and the development of mutual trust.

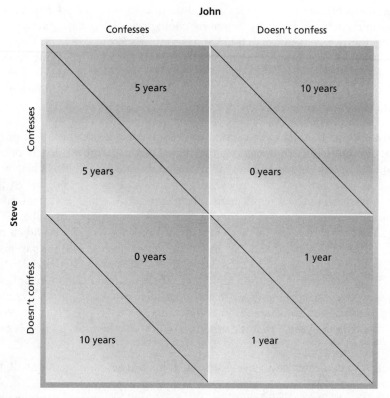

John

FIGURE 9–3   What is the "prisoner's dilemma?" This chart, or matrix, summarizes the problem that the two imaginary prisoners face. Each prisoner has two choices: Confess or don't confess. These choices are shown along the sides of the matrix. The numbers within each cell of the matrix correspond to the outcomes that the two prisoners can receive. In each cell, John's outcomes are shown above the diagonal line, and Steve's outcomes are shown below the diagonal. For example, if John confesses but Steve does not, John will go free, but Steve will receive ten years.

But if both pick B, both will lose money. Figure 9–4 is a *payoff matrix* that summarizes how much money the two will win or lose in the four possible situations:

1. If John chooses A and Steve chooses A, both earn 25¢.
2. If John chooses A and Steve chooses B, John loses 25¢ and Steve wins 50¢.
3. If John chooses B and Steve chooses A, John wins 50¢ and Steve loses 25¢.
4. If John chooses B and Steve chooses B, both lose 10¢.

The PDG captures the essence of a mixed-motive situation (Rapoport, 1985; Schlenker & Bonoma, 1978; Wrightsman, O'Connor, & Baker, 1972). Players want to maximize their earnings, so they are tempted to pick Option B. But most people realize that their partner wants to maximize his or her profit, and if both select B, then they will both lose money. So they are drawn to Option A, but are wary that their partner may pick B. Players usually cannot communicate with each other, and they must make their choices at the same time. They cannot wait to pick until after they

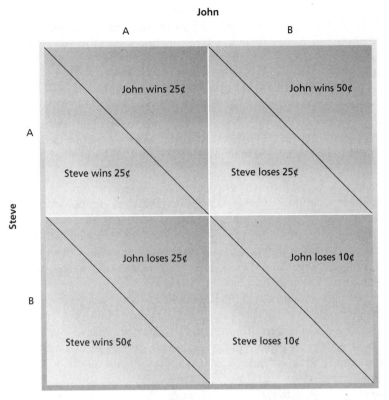

FIGURE 9–4 What should Steve do if he thinks that his partner, John, will compete with him? People who are given the chance to play the prisoner's dilemma for money or points are asked to select one of two options labeled A and B. In each cell, John's outcomes are shown above the diagonal line, and Steve's outcomes are shown below. For example, if Steve thinks that John will pick B—the competitive choice—then he will lose 25¢ if he picks A and 10¢ if he picks B.

learn their partner's choice. In most cases, players also make their choices several times. Each pair of choices between alternatives A and B is termed a *trial*.

Many people choose to compete rather than cooperate, although the proportion varies, depending on the value of the rewards offered, players' personality traits, the relative advantages of each strategy, and a variety of other factors (Deutsch, 1973; Komorita, 1987; Mori, 1996; Parks, Henager, & Scamahorn, 1996; Rapoport, 1988; Vinacke, 1971). When female college students seated in individual cubicles played the game using the same payoff matrix shown in Figure 9–4, 56% competed on the first trial (Messé & Sivacek, 1979). But in another study where men and women sat face-to-face before making their choices, only 20% competed. Competitiveness, however, jumped to 68% when they were partnered with a computer with humanlike features (Kiesler, Sproull, & Waters, 1996).

But what happens when people play the PDG for several trials? Significantly, people's choices are substantially influenced by their partner's choices. When people play the PDG with a partner who consistently makes cooperative choices, they themselves tend to cooperate. Those who encounter competitors, however, soon adopt this strategy, and they, too, begin to compete. As the **norm of reciprocity** suggests, cooperation begets cooperation, and competition begets competition. Negative reciprocity, however, is stronger than positive reciprocity: A cooperative person who runs into a competitive partner is likely to begin to compete *before* the competitive person begins to cooperate (Kelley & Stahelski, 1970a, 1970b, 1970c). Negative reciprocity is kept in check if cooperatively oriented individuals have the opportunity to withdraw from the interaction or can communicate their "good" intentions to their partners (Garner & Deutsch, 1974; Miller & Holmes, 1975), but in most situations, a partner turns into an opponent faster than an opponent turns into an ally (Carroll, 1987; Schlenker & Goldman, 1978).

Who Competes?   Both Jobs and Sculley were tough-minded entrepreneurs who sought to maximize their gains whenever possible. Did their personalities contribute to the conflict? Studies of group members' **social values** suggest that some people are natural competitors, whereas others are more cooperative or individualistic (Kelley, 1997; McClintock, Messick, Kuhlman, & Campos, 1973; Swap & Rubin, 1983). As Table 9–1 indicates, *competitors* view group disagreements as win-lose situations and find satisfaction in forcing their ideas on the others. Concessions and compromise, they believe, are only for losers. A competitor believes that "each person should get the most he can" and plays to win, even when playing a game with a child (Brenner & Vinacke, 1979, p. 291). *Cooperators,* in contrast, value accommodative interpersonal strategies. A cooperator would argue that "when people deal with each other, it's better when everyone comes out even" and if playing a game with a child would "try to arrange it so that no one really wins or loses" (Brenner & Vinacke, 1979, p. 291). *Individualists* are concerned only with their own outcomes. They make decisions based on what they think they personally will achieve, with no concern for others' outcomes. They neither interfere with nor assist others' attempts to reach their goals.

Individuals with competitive value orientations are more likely to find themselves in conflicts. The competitor's style is abrasive, spurring cooperative members to react with criticism and requests for fairer treatment. Competitors, however, rarely modify their behavior in response to these complaints, because they are relatively unconcerned with maintaining smooth interpersonal relations. Hence, competitors try to overwhelm cooperators, who sometimes respond by becoming competitive themselves. Also, when two competitors meet, the result is an intense conflict like that seen at Apple Computer. When the interaction is complete and one of the individuals has won, the loser often withdraws from the group altogether (Cummings, Harnett, & Stevens, 1971; Harnett, Cummings, & Hamner, 1973; Shure & Meeker, 1967).

These differences in social values orientations have been linked to other personal qualities, including agreeableness, achievement orientation, interpersonal orientation, and trust in others (Graziano et al., 1997; Swap & Rubin, 1983; Yamagishi, 1986).

Norm of reciprocity: A societal standard that enjoins individuals to pay back in kind what they receive from others.
Social values: The dispositional tendency to respond to conflict settings in a particular way; cooperators, for example, are predisposed to make choices that benefit both parties in a conflict, whereas competitors act to maximize their own outcomes and undermine others' outcomes.

TABLE 9-1 THREE BASIC SOCIAL VALUES ORIENTATIONS: COOPERATION, COMPETITION, AND INDIVIDUALISM

Orientation	Attributes
Competitor	Motivated to maximize own outcomes and minimize others' outcomes; views disagreements as win-lose situations
Cooperator	Motivated to maximize joint outcomes (seeks to maximize own outcomes and others' outcomes); seeks win-win solutions to disagreements
Individualist	Motivated to maximize own outcomes only; helps or harms others if these actions increase own outcomes; seeks own goals

Social values vary systematically across cultures. Many Western societies, for example, openly value competition. Their economic systems are based on competition, schools teach children the importance of surpassing others' achievements, and popular games and sports have winners and losers. More cooperative—and more peaceful—societies, in contrast, condemn competition, devalue individual achievement, and avoid any kind of competitive games (Bonta, 1997; Fry & Björkqvist, 1997; Van Lange, De Bruin, Otten, & Joireman, 1997).

Men, Women, and Competition.   What if John Sculley was Joanna Sculley: a woman, rather than a man? Would she and Jobs have battled as fiercely? Or would Joanna have used other, less competitive methods for settling the dispute?

Common sex role stereotypes generally assume that men are more competitive than women. Stories of executives conjure up images of individuals who are driven, ruthless, self-seeking, and male. Yet, experimental studies of cooperation and competition suggest that women are just as competitive as men (Sell, 1997; Sell, Griffith, & Wilson, 1993). One review of previous work found that in 21 experiments, women were more competitive, but 27 other studies suggested that women were less competitive (Rubin & Brown, 1975). Both men and women use more contentious influence methods when they are paired with a man rather than a woman, perhaps because they anticipate more conflict (Carli, 1989). When it comes to social values orientations, however, more women are cooperators and more men are competitors (Knight & Dubro, 1984). Women also tend to base their choices in conflict situations on factors other than the rewards they stand to gain. If, for example, their partner is attractive, women make more cooperative choices. If they do not like their partner, they are likely to compete (Kahn, Hottes, & Davis, 1971).

Social Dilemmas

Groups, by their very nature, create **social dilemmas** for their members. The members, as individuals, are motivated to maximize their own rewards and minimize their costs.

Social dilemmas: Interpersonal situations where individuals must choose between maximizing their personal outcomes and maximizing their group's outcomes.

They strive to extract all they can from the group, while minimizing the amount of time and energy it takes from them. Yet, as group members, they also wish to contribute to the group, for they realize that their selfishness can destroy the group. Conflicts arise when individualistic motives trump group-oriented motives and the collective intervenes to redress the imbalance.

Dividing Resources.   When Sculley and Jobs each insisted that he be given the authority to make critical decisions, the board of directors at Apple Computer only supported Sculley. Jobs believed that he had earned the right, through years of constant work, to control the company's direction, but the board disagreed.

Because most groups have limited resources, they must develop a fair means of doling them out to members. But what is fair or unfair is often open to debate. The **equity norm** prescribes basing members' outcomes on their inputs. An individual who has invested a good deal of time, energy, money, or other type of input in the group should receive more from the group than individuals who have contributed little. The **equality norm,** in contrast, recommends that all group members, irrespective of their inputs, be given an equal share of the payoff. Even though a person contributes only 20% of the group's resources, he or she should receive as much as the person who contributes 80%. Other norms, such as the power norm ("to the victor go the spoils") and the need norm ("the greatest good to those with the greatest needs"), can shape the way the group allocates its resources (Deutsch, 1975; Kerr, 1995).

Conflicts arise when group members disagree about which norm to use in making allocations or when the standards are not applied fairly (Allison & Messick, 1990; Samuelson & Allison, 1994; Samuelson & Messick, 1995). Men who contribute less to the group often argue in favor of the equality norm, whereas those who contribute more favor the equity norm. Women prefer equality over equity even when they outperform their co-workers (Leventhal & Lane, 1970). Members of larger groups prefer to base allocations on equity, whereas members of smaller groups stress equality (Allison, McQueen, & Schaerfl, 1992). Members of groups working on tasks where one individual's contributions are critically important for success prefer equitable distributions over egalitarian ones (Elliott & Meeker, 1984; Miller & Komorita, 1995).

How do group members react when they don't think resources are being allocated fairly? Group members who feel that they are receiving too little for what they are giving (*negative inequity*) sometimes withdraw from the group, reduce their effort, and turn in work of lower quality. Group members who feel that they are receiving too much for what they are giving (*positive inequity*) sometimes increase their efforts (Adams & Rosenbaum, 1962; Dittrich & Carrell, 1979). Negative inequity, though, is a much more likely cause of conflict than the more personally favorable experience of positive inequity (Rivera & Tedeschi, 1976).

Equity norm: A social standard that encourages distributing rewards and resources to members in proportion to their inputs.
Equality norm: A social standard that encourages distributing rewards and resources equally among all members.

Resource Dilemmas. Consider the "tragedy of the commons." A group of shepherds all use a common grazing land. The land can support many sheep, so the system works smoothly. However, several selfish members of the community want to maximize their personal profit, so they add animals to their own flocks. Others notice the extra sheep, so they, too, add to their flocks. Soon the commons is overgrazed, and all the sheep die from starvation (Hardin, 1968).

This **social trap,** or **resource dilemma,** occurs when members share a common resource that they want to maintain for their group, but individual members are tempted to take more than their fair share. But if everyone acts selfishly, then the common resource will be destroyed. Members are tempted by the short-term gains of competition, but if they succumb, they will incur long-term losses as a collective (Allison, Beggan, & Midgley, 1996; Komorita & Parks, 1994; Shepperd, 1993).

To examine when people choose self-interest over group interest, researchers have simulated resource dilemmas, giving groups of four or five people the chance to draw as many tokens as they want from a pool of available tokens. The pool is a renewable resource, for after each round of harvesting, it regenerates in direct proportion to the number of tokens remaining in the pool. If members quickly draw out all the tokens, the pool is permanently exhausted; cautious removal of only a small number of tokens ensures replenishment of the resource. Nonetheless, group members tend to act in their own self-interest by drawing out all the tokens, even when they realize that the pool is quite small (Brewer & Kramer, 1986; Yamagishi, 1994).

How can groups escape this dilemma? Both experience with the situation and communication among members appear to be critical factors (Allison & Messick, 1985a; Edney & Bell, 1984). In one study, triads harvested from a large or small pool. Members of half of the groups could communicate with one another, but the rest could not. The differences between these groups were striking. Over 80% of the groups that could not communicate bankrupted their pool within a minute. Even when the pool was large, the noncommunicating groups still had problems with overharvesting. Many of these groups realized the long-term negative consequences of overharvesting, but they did not manage their resources as well as the communicating groups. These results suggest that groups can avoid traps if their members can plan a strategy for dealing with the situation through face-to-face communication (Brechner, 1977).

Contributing to the Group. When group members in a college class described the sources of conflicts in their project groups, over 35% of their comments targeted disputes over workload. People had much to say about the dedication of their comembers to the group's goals, for some did not put in as much time, effort, and resources as the others expected (Wall & Nolan, 1987).

Group members don't just take too much from their groups. They also fail to give enough to them. Many studies of groups working on collective tasks find that members

Resource dilemma (social trap): A situation that tempts individuals to act in ways that will benefit them initially but will prove detrimental, in the long run, both to them and the group as a whole.

do not work as hard as they do when they are working for themselves. Such **free riding,** which we will examine in Chapter 10, occurs most frequently when individuals' contributions are combined in a single product and those contributions aren't monitored. In such cases, group members coast along, letting others do their share of the work. They also contribute less because they don't want to be exploited by the other loafers in the group (the *sucker effect;* Kerr, 1983). At the community level, this failure to contribute creates a *public goods dilemma.* Individuals undercontribute to community causes because they can still use the resources that the community provides even if they don't contribute (Komorita & Parks, 1994; Orbell, Dawes, & van de Kragt, 1995).

Free riding can cause conflict in a group. When too many individuals reduce their input to the group, the quality of the group's product declines along with cohesiveness (Williams, Jackson, & Karau, 1995). Free riding transfers too much of the responsibility for the group's output to some group members, who may object to the added burden. Some groups respond to free riding by implementing negative sanctions to minimize inequities in contributions, by extracting promises of satisfactory contributions from members, and by subjecting free riders to verbal abuse. Some individual group members, to counter the inequity of working in a group with free riders, may reduce their own contributions or withdraw from the group (see Komorita & Parks, 1994, for a review).

Sharing Blame and Fame.   When a group completes its work, members often dispute who gets credit and who gets blame. The board of directors at Apple Computer blamed Jobs's devotion to the Mac for the company's economic misfortunes. Sculley credited his skilled marketing interventions for Apple Computer's prosperity in the years following Jobs's dismissal. Jobs blamed Sculley for ruining the company.

Just as individuals carry out extensive appraisals of their successes and failures, so do group members devote significant cognitive resources to the analysis and comprehension of collective endeavors. This appraisal, however, is complicated by the collaborative nature of group activities. Group members must identify the factors that contributed to each member's performance, assign credit and blame, and make decisions regarding rewards, power, and status (Forsyth & Kelley, 1996). As noted in Chapter 3, group members' postperformance reactions are often *group-serving* (or sociocentric). After success, members may praise the entire group for its good work with such comments as "We all did well" or "Our hard work really paid off." After failure, members may join together in blaming outside forces and absolving one another of blame. Too frequently, however, members are *self-serving* (or egocentric); they take undue personal credit for success and blame one another for the group's misfortunes (Forsyth, 1980; Forsyth & Schlenker, 1977; Norvell & Forsyth, 1984).

Group-serving tactics unite the group, whereas self-serving tactics contribute to conflict (Leary & Forsyth, 1987). In one study, two teams competed in a game situation (Shaw & Breed, 1970). Certain members of each team were confederates of the researcher, and they systematically blamed one of the actual subjects for the team's

---

Free riding: Contributing less to a collective task when one believes that other group members will compensate for this lack of effort.

losses. Unfairly accused group members, relative to others who had escaped blame, were less satisfied with their teams, belittled their teammates' abilities, and preferred to work with other groups on future tasks (Shaw & Breed, 1970).

CONFRONTATION AND ESCALATION

Early in 1985, Sculley and Jobs began moving toward a showdown, pushed into conflict by their incompatibilities, their marked differences of opinion about their company, the competitive nature of their interdependence, and their refusal to take less than they felt they were due. They tried to quell the tension, but by spring the men were trapped in an escalating conflict.

Conflicts escalate. Even though the parties to the conflict may hope to reach a solution to their dispute quickly, a host of psychological and interpersonal factors can frustrate their attempts to control the conflict. As Sculley continued to argue with Jobs, he became more committed to his own position, and his view of Jobs and his position became biased. Sculley used stronger influence tactics, and soon other members of Apple Computer were drawn into the fray. All these factors fed the conflict, changing it from a disagreement to a full-fledged corporate war. (Jeffrey Z. Rubin, Dean G. Pruitt, and Sung Hee Kim, 1994, provide a detailed analysis of these transformational factors.)

Uncertainty → Commitment

As conflicts escalate, group members often become *more* committed to their positions instead of more understanding of the positions taken by others. Sculley, for example, became more certain that his insights were correct, and his disagreements with Jobs only increased this commitment (Staw & Ross, 1987). When people try to persuade others, they search out supporting arguments. If this elaboration process yields further consistent information, they become even more committed to their initial position (Petty & Cacioppo, 1986). Moreover, people feel that once they commit to a position publicly, they must stick with it. They may realize that they are wrong, but to save face they continue to argue against their opponents (Wilson, 1992). People rationalize their choices once they have made them: They seek out information that supports their views, they reject information that conflicts with their stance, and they become entrenched in their original position (Ross & Ward, 1995). Finally, if other group members argue too strongly, reactance may set in (Brehm, 1976; Brehm & Brehm, 1981). As noted in Chapter 8, when reactance occurs, group members become even more committed to their original position.

Commitment, when extreme, becomes **entrapment:** a special form of escalation that occurs when the group expends "more of its time, energy, money, or other resources than seems justifiable by external standards" (Rubin et al., 1994, p. 112). Entrapment

---

Entrapment: A form of escalation in which the parties expend more of their resources in the conflict than seems appropriate or justifiable by external standards.

occurs when groups become so invested in bad decisions that they refuse to reverse their decisions (Brockner, 1995; Brockner & Rubin, 1985).

The "dollar auction" illustrates entrapment by adding one special rule to traditional auction procedures. Participants are given the chance to bid for a dollar bill. The highest bidder gets to keep the dollar bill, but the second highest bidder gets no money and must pay the amount he or she bid. Bids flow slowly at first, but soon the offers climb over 50¢ toward the $1 mark. As the stakes increase, however, quitting becomes costly. If a bidder who offers 50¢ for the $1 is bested by someone offering 60¢, the 50¢ bidder will lose 50¢. So he or she is tempted to beat the 60¢ bid. This cycle continues upward, well beyond the value of the dollar bill in some cases—on occasion players have spent as much as $20 for the $1 (Teger, 1980).

Perception → Misperception

Individuals' reactions during conflict are shaped, in fundamental ways, by their perception of the situation and the people in that situation. When group members argue, they must determine why they disagree. If they conclude that their disagreement stems merely from the group's attempts to make the right decision, the disagreement will probably not turn into true conflict. If, however, participants attribute the disagreement to others' incompetence, belligerence, or argumentativeness, a simple disagreement can escalate into conflict (Messé, Stollak, Larson, & Michaels, 1979; Ross & Ward, 1995).

If perceptions were always accurate, people would understand one another better. Unfortunately, perceptual biases regularly distort individuals' inferences. One bias, the *fundamental attribution error,* occurs when group members assume that other people's behavior is caused by personal (dispositional) rather than situational (environmental) factors (Ross, 1977). If Jobs was affected by this error, he may have blamed Sculley's personality, beliefs, attitudes, and values for the conflict rather than pressure from the board of directors, the shareholders, or Jobs's own actions.

Because of the fundamental attribution error, group members assume that people who give them critical feedback, argue with them, or mistreat them in some way do so deliberately and that their actions reflect basic flaws in their personalities (Baumeister, Stillwell, & Wotman, 1990; Cunningham, Starr, & Kanouse, 1979; Messé et al., 1979; Murata, 1982). One team of researchers verified this tendency by pairing people playing a PDG-like game with partners who used one of four possible strategies:

1. *Competition.* They maximized personal gains while minimizing their partners' gains.
2. *Cooperation.* They maximized joint gains, striving to increase their own and their partners' outcomes.
3. *Individualism.* They ignored their partners' gains but maximized personal gains.
4. *Altruism.* They ignored their own personal gains but maximized their partners' gains.

When describing their partner's motives, the players were most accurate when playing an individualistic or competitive person and least accurate in interpreting cooperation and altruism (Maki, Thorngate, & McClintock, 1979). Moreover, people with competitive social values orientations are the most inaccurate in their perceptions of cooperation. When cooperators play the PDG with other cooperators, their perceptions of their partner's strategy are inaccurate only 6% of the time. When competitors play the PDG with cooperators, however, they misinterpret their partner's strategy 47% of the time, mistakenly believing that the cooperators are competing (Kelley & Stahelski, 1970a, 1970b, 1970c; Sattler & Kerr, 1991).

Weak Tactics → Stronger Tactics

We can influence people in dozens of different ways. As noted in Chapter 8, we can promise, reward, threaten, punish, bully, discuss, instruct, negotiate, manipulate, supplicate, ingratiate, and on and on. Some of these tactics are stronger than others. Threats, punishment, and bullying are all strong, contentious tactics because they are direct, nonrational, and unilateral. People utilize the weaker tactics at the outset of a conflict, but as the conflict escalates, they shift to stronger and stronger tactics. Sculley gradually shifted from relatively mild methods of influence (discussion, negotiation) to stronger tactics (threats). Eventually, he demoted Jobs (Carnevale & Pruitt, 1992).

Researchers studied this escalation process by paying subjects to construct birthday cards using paper, colored markers, and ribbons. Subjects' efforts were frustrated by a confederate of the researchers who deliberately hoarded materials that the subjects needed. As the hour wore on, it became clear that the confederate was going to make far more money than the subjects, and subjects became more and more frustrated. They responded by using stronger and more contentious influence tactics. As Table 9–2 indicates, all the subjects tried to solve their problem initially with statements and requests. When those methods failed, they shifted to demands and complaints. When those methods failed, they tried problem solving and appeals to a third

TABLE 9-2   INFLUENCE METHODS USED IN GROUPS SHARING SCARCE RESOURCES

Behavior	Example	Percentage Using
Requests	May I use the glue?	100.0
Statements	We need the glue.	100.0
Demands	Give me the glue, now!	88.9
Complaints	What's wrong with you? Why don't you share?	79.2
Problem solving	You can use our stapler if you share the glue.	73.6
Third party	Make them share!	45.8
Angry	I'm mad now.	41.7
Threat	Give me the glue or else.	22.2
Harassment	I'm not giving you any more ribbon until you return the glue.	16.7
Abuse	You are a selfish swine.	9.7

Source: Mikolic, Parker, & Pruitt, 1997.

party (the experimenter). In the most extreme cases, they used threats, abuse, and anger to try to influence the irritating confederate (Mikolic, Parker, & Pruitt, 1997).

People who use stronger tactics often overwhelm their antagonists, but such methods intensify conflicts. Morton Deutsch and Robert Krauss (1960) examined this intensification process in their classic "trucking game" simulation. They asked pairs of women to role-play the owners of a trucking company. The two companies, Acme and Bolt, carried merchandise over the roads mapped in Figure 9–5. Acme and Bolt each earned 60¢ after each complete run, minus 1¢ for each second taken up by the trip.

The truck route set the stage for competition and conflict between Acme and Bolt. The shortest path from start to finish for Acme was Route 216 and for Bolt was Route 106, but these routes merged into a one-lane highway. When trucks encountered each other along this route, one player had to back up to her starting position to let the other through. Acme and Bolt could avoid this confrontation by taking the winding alternate route, but this path took longer.

All the pairs played the same basic game, but some were provided with the power to threaten their opponents, and others were not. In the *unilateral-threat condition*, Acme was told that a gate, which only she could open and close, was located at the fork in Route 216. When the gate was closed, neither truck could pass this point in the road, making control of the gate a considerable benefit to Acme. If Bolt attempted to use the

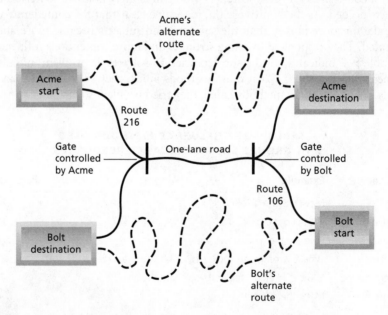

FIGURE 9–5   How did Deutsch and Krauss create conflict using their trucking game simulation? Players took the role of either Acme or Bolt and maneuvered their trucks along Route 216, Route 106, or the longer, alternative routes. In some cases, one or both players were given gates that they could close to bar access by their opponent.

(*Source:* Deutsch, 1973.)

main route, all Acme had to do was close the gate, forcing Bolt to back up and enabling Acme to reopen the gate and proceed quickly to her destination. Thus, when only Acme possessed the gate, Bolt's profits were greatly threatened. In the *bilateral-threat condition,* both sides had the use of gates located at the ends of the one-lane section of Route 216, and in the *control condition,* no gates were given to the players.

Deutsch and Krauss's control subjects soon learned to resolve the conflict over the one-lane road. Most of these pairs took turns using the main route, and on the average, each subject made a $1 profit. Winnings dwindled, however, when one of the players was given a gate. Subjects in the unilateral-threat condition lost an average of $2.03. Bolt's losses were twice as great as Acme's, but even Acme lost more than $1 at the game. Conflict was even worse when both Acme and Bolt had gates. In the bilateral-threat condition, both players usually took the longer route because the gates on the main route were kept closed, and losses in this condition averaged $4.38.

These findings convinced Deutsch and Krauss that the capacity to threaten others intensifies conflict. Indeed, if one party can or does threaten the other party, the threatened party will fare best if he or she *cannot* respond with a counterthreat (Borah, 1963; Deutsch & Lewicki, 1970; Froman & Cohen, 1969; Gallo, 1966). Equally powerful opponents, however, learn to avoid the use of their power if fear of retaliation is high (Lawler, Ford, & Blegen, 1988).

Reciprocity → Upward Conflict Spiral

Conflict-ridden groups may seem normless, with hostility and dissatisfaction spinning out of control. Yet, **conflict spirals** are in many cases sustained by the norm of reciprocity. Reciprocity suggests that when people who help you later need help, you are obligated to return the favor. However, the norm also implies that people who harm you are also deserving of harm themselves. The converse of "You scratch my back and I'll scratch yours" is "An eye for an eye, a tooth for a tooth" (e.g., Tedeschi, Gaes, & Rivera, 1977; Tedeschi, Smith, & Brown, 1974). If one group member criticizes the ideas, opinions, or characteristics of another, the victim of the attack will feel justified in counterattacking unless some situational factor legitimizes the hostility of the former.

If interactants followed the norm of reciprocity exactly, a mild threat would elicit a mild threat in return, and an attack would lead to a counterattack. But interactants tend to follow the norm of rough reciprocity: They give too much (overmatching) or give too little (undermatching) in return. In one study, women playing a PDG-like game against a confederate could send notes to their opponent and penalize her by taking points from her winnings. Reciprocity guided the player's actions, for the more often the confederate sent threats, the more often the subject sent threats; when the confederate's threats were large, the subject's threats were large; and confederates who exacted large fines triggered large fines from the subject. This reciprocity, however, was rough rather than exact. At low levels of conflict, the subjects overmatched threats and punishments, and at high levels of conflict, they undermatched their threats. The overmatching

---

Conflict spirals: Escalating patterns of conflict.

that occurs initially may serve as a strong warning, whereas the undermatching at high levels of conflict may be used to send a conciliatory gesture (Youngs, 1986).

Few → Many

When Jobs learned that Sculley was going to follow through with his threat to have him removed as the director of the Mac division, Jobs tried to persuade each member of the board to side with him in the dispute. His goal was to form a powerful coalition that would block Sculley's plans and swing the vote of the board in his favor.

Coalitions exist in most groups, but when conflict erupts, group members use them to shift the balance of power in their favor. Although the initial disagreement may involve only two group members, when conflicts intensify, group members often compel previously neutral members to identify with one faction or the other. Similarly, even when members initially express many different views, with time these multiparty conflicts are reduced to two-party blocs through coalition formation (Mack & Snyder, 1957). Coalitions often form between adversaries who decide to join forces temporarily to achieve a specific outcome (a mixed-motive situation). Although allies may wish to compete with one another, no single individual has enough power to succeed alone. Hence, while the coalition exists, the competitive motive must be stifled (Forsyth, 1990; Komorita & Parks, 1994).

Coalitions contribute to conflicts because they draw more members of the group into the fray. Coalitions are often viewed as contentious, heavy-handed influence tactics because individuals in the coalition work not only to ensure their own outcomes but also to worsen the outcomes of noncoalition members. Coalitions form with people and against other people (Thibaut & Kelley, 1959). In business settings, for example, the dominant coalition can control the organization, yet it works outside the bounds of the formal group structure (Pearce, Stevenson, & Porter, 1986; Stevenson, Pearce, & Porter, 1985). Those who are excluded from a coalition react with hostility to the coalition members and seek to regain power by forming their own coalitions. Thus, coalitions must be constantly maintained through strategic bargaining and negotiation (Murnighan, 1986).

Irritation → Anger

Few people can deal with conflicts dispassionately. When disputes arise, tempers flare, and this increase in negative emotions exacerbates the initial conflict. Most people, when asked to talk about a time when they became angry, said that they usually lost their temper when arguing with people they knew rather than with strangers (Averill, 1983). And many admitted that their anger increased the negativity of the conflict; 49% became verbally abusive when they were angered, and 10% said they became physically aggressive (Averill, 1983). Subjects in another study described a similar relationship between anger and aggression. Many people reported physically attacking someone or something, losing emotional control, or imagining violence against someone else when they were angry (Shaver, Schwartz, Kirson, & O'Connor, 1987). Even when group members begin by discussing their points calmly and dispassionately, as they become locked into their positions, emotional expression begins to replace logical discussion. As anxiety and tension increase, conflict escalates (Blascovich et al., 1978).

CONFLICT RESOLUTION

In one way or another, conflicts subside. Even when members are strongly committed to their own viewpoints, high levels of tension cannot be maintained indefinitely. In time, disputants regain control of their tempers and break the conflict spiral. When group members confront their problems and work toward a solution, conflict becomes a valued resource rather than a problem that must be eliminated. But how can group members change their group's hostility into harmony?

Commitment → Negotiation

Just as conflicts escalate when group members become firmly committed to a position and won't budge, conflicts de-escalate when group members are willing to negotiate with others to reach a solution that benefits all parties. **Negotiation** is a reciprocal communication process whereby two or more parties to a dispute examine specific issues, explain their positions, and exchange offers and counteroffers. Negotiation sometimes amounts to little more than simple bargaining or mutual compromise. In such *distributive negotiations,* both parties retain their competitive orientation and take turns making small concessions until some equally dissatisfying middle ground is reached. Haggling and bartering ("I'll give you $20 for it, and not a penny more!") illustrate this form of negotiation (for reviews, see Druckman, 1977, 1987; McKersie & Walton, 1992; Pruitt, 1981, 1987; Rubin, 1983; Thompson, 1990).

But *integrative negotiation* is not a competitive conflict management method (Rubin, 1994). As Roger Fisher and William Ury note, integrative negotiators work with other group members to achieve cooperative, integrative outcomes that benefit both sides. Fisher and Ury, drawing on studies and conferences conducted as part of the Harvard Negotiation Project, distinguish between the three types of negotiators shown in Table 9–3: soft negotiators, hard negotiators, and principled negotiators. Soft bargainers see negotiation as too close to competition, and they worry that the process will ruin the group's cohesiveness. So they choose a gentle style of negotiation: They make offers that are not in their best interests, they yield to others' demands, they avoid any confrontation, and they maintain their friendship. Hard bargainers, in contrast, use tough, competitive tactics during negotiations. They begin by taking an extreme position on the issue, and then they make small concessions only grudgingly. The hard bargainer uses contentious strategies of influence and says such things as "Take it or leave it," "This is my final offer," "This point is not open to negotiation," "My hands are tied," and "I'll see you in court" (Fisher, 1983).

Negotiation: A reciprocal communication process whereby two or more parties to a dispute examine specific issues, explain their positions, and exchange offers and counteroffers.

TABLE 9–3   THREE APPROACHES TO NEGOTIATION

The Soft Negotiator	The Hard Negotiator	The Principled Negotiator
Stress that the participants are friends.	Stress that the participants are adversaries.	Stress that the participants are problem solvers.
Make the goal agreement.	Make the goal victory.	Make the goal a wise outcome reached efficiently and amicably.
Make concessions to cultivate the relationship.	Demand concessions as a condition of the relationship.	Separate the people from the problem.
Be soft on the people and the problem.	Be hard on the problem and the people.	Be soft on the people, hard on the problem.
Trust others.	Distrust others.	Proceed independently of trust.
Change your position easily.	Dig in to your position.	Focus on interests, not positions.
Make offers.	Make threats.	Explore interests.
Disclose your bottom line.	Mislead as to your bottom line.	Avoid having a bottom line.
Accept one-sided losses to reach agreement.	Demand one-sided gains as a price of agreement.	Invent options for mutual gain.
Search for a single answer: the one they will accept.	Search for the single answer: the one you will accept.	Develop multiple options to choose from; decide later.
Insist on agreement.	Insist on your position.	Insist on using objective criteria.
Try to avoid a contest of will.	Try to win a contest of will.	Try to reach a result based on standards independent of will.
Yield to pressure.	Apply pressure.	Reason and be open to reason; yield to principle, not pressure.

Source: Fisher & Ury, 1981.

Principled negotiators, meanwhile, seek integrative solutions by side-stepping commitment to specific positions. Instead of risking entrapment, principled negotiators focus on the problem rather than the intentions, motives, and needs of the people involved. Positional bargaining, Fisher and Ury (1981, p. 5) argue, is too dangerous:

> When negotiators bargain over positions, they tend to lock themselves into those positions. The more you clarify your position and defend it against attack, the more committed you become to it. The more you try to convince the other side of the impossibility of changing your opening position, the more difficult it becomes to do so. Your ego becomes identified with your position.

Fisher and Ury recommend that negotiators explore a number of alternatives to the problems they face. During this phase, the negotiation is transformed into a group problem-solving session, with the different parties working together in search of creative solutions and new information that the group can use to evaluate these alternatives. Fisher and Ury's principled negotiators base their choice on objective criteria rather than power, pressure, self-interest, or an arbitrary decisional procedure. Such criteria can be drawn from moral standards, principles of fairness, objective indexes of market value, professional standards, tradition, and so on, but they should be recognized as fair by all parties.

Misperception → Understanding

Many conflicts are based on misperceptions. People often assume that others are competing with them, when in fact those other people only wish to cooperate. They think that people who criticize their ideas are criticizing them personally. They do not trust other people because they are convinced that their motives are selfish ones. They assume that their goals are incompatible, when in fact they seek the same outcomes (Thompson & Hrebec, 1996).

Group members must undo these perceptual misunderstandings by actively communicating information about their motives and goals through discussion. In one study, group members were given the opportunity to exchange information about their interests and goals, yet only about 20% did (Thompson, 1991). Those who did, however, were far more likely to discover shared goals and were able to reach solutions that benefited both parties to the conflict (Thompson, 1991; Weingart, Thompson, Bazerman, & Carroll, 1990). Other studies suggest that conflict declines when group members communicate their intentions in specific terms and make explicit references to trust, cooperation, and fairness (Bornstein, Rapoport, Kerpel, & Katz, 1989; Kerr & Kaufman-Gilliland, 1994; Lindskold, 1986; Swingle & Santi, 1972).

Communication is no cure-all for conflict, however. Group members can exchange information by communicating, but they can also create gross misunderstandings and deceptions. Communication offers group members the means to establish trust, but it can also fan the flames of group dispute by verbalizing feelings of hatred, disgust, or annoyance. For example, when Deutsch and Krauss (1960) let subjects in their trucking game study communicate with each other, messages typically emphasized threats and did little to reduce conflict (Deutsch, 1973). Communication is detrimental if these initial messages are inconsistent, hostile, and contentious (McClintock, Stech, & Keil, 1983; Pilisuk, Brandes, & van den Hove, 1976; Stech & McClintock, 1981). Communication can be beneficial, however, if interactants use it to create cooperative norms, if it increases trust among participants, and if it generates increased cohesion and unity in the group (Messick & Brewer, 1983).

Strong Tactics → Cooperative Tactics

Group members cope with conflict in many different ways. Some just overlook the problem and hope it goes away. Others discuss the problem, sometimes dispassionately and rationally, sometimes angrily and loudly. Others seek a neutral party to serve as a moderator. And some actually resort to physical violence (Morrill, 1995; Sternberg & Dobson, 1987.) Most of the tactics that people use to deal with conflict can be classified into one of four basic categories, as shown in Table 9–4.

TABLE 9–4   FOUR BASIC WAYS TO DEAL WITH CONFLICT

	Negative	Positive
Passive	**Avoiding:** Inaction, withdrawal, lose-lose, "wait-and-see" attitude, denial, evasion, exiting the group, minimizing own losses, low concern for self and for others.	**Yielding:** Acceptance, smoothing, accommodating, giving in, yielding-losing, maximizing others' outcomes; low concern for self and high concern for others
Active	**Fighting:** competing, forcing, dominating, contending, win-lose, maximizing own outcome and minimizing others' outcomes; high concern for self and low concern for others	**Cooperating:** sharing, collaborating, problem solving, win-win, synthesis, negotiation, maximizing joint outcomes; high concern for self and for others.

- *Avoiding.* Inaction is a favorite means of dealing with disputes. When students in small groups talked about their conflicts, they often said that they dealt with conflicts by adopting a "wait-and-see" attitude, hoping that they would eventually go away (Wall & Nolan, 1987). Many executives say that they "tolerate" conflicts, allowing them to simmer without doing anything to minimize them (Morrill, 1995). Rather than openly discussing disagreements, people who rely on avoidance change the subject, skip meetings, or even leave the group altogether.

- *Yielding.* People solve both large and small conflicts by giving in to the demands of others. Sometimes they yield because they have changed their opinion on the matter. Through discussion and negotiation, they realize that their position is in error, and so they agree with the viewpoint adopted by the others. In other cases, however, they may withdraw their demands without really being convinced that the other side is correct; for the sake of group unity or in the interest of time, they nonetheless withdraw all complaints. Thus, yielding can reflect either genuine conversion to the position taken by others or a temporary compliance resulting from interpersonal pressure.

- *Fighting.* Some people manage their disputes by trying to coerce others into accepting their view. They see the conflict as a win-lose situation and use competitive and powerful tactics to intimidate others. Fighting (forcing, dominating, or contending) can take many forms, including authoritative mandate, challenges, arguing, insults, accusations, complaining, vengeance, and even physical violence (Morrill, 1995). These conflict resolution methods are all contentious ones because they involve imposing one's solution on the other party.

- *Cooperating.* People who rely on cooperation to resolve disputes search for solutions that are acceptable to both sides in the conflict. Cooperating people do not try to battle it out, but instead strive to identify the issues underlying the dispute and then work together to identify a solution that is satisfying to both sides (Pruitt & Rubin, 1986). This orientation, which is also described as collaboration, problem solving, or a "win-win" orientation, entreats both sides in the dispute to consider their opponent's outcomes as well as their own.

These conflict management methods differ from one another in at least two important ways. First, some of the dispute resolution modes are negative rather than positive. The negative methods (avoidance and fighting) do not take into account others' outcomes (Pruitt, 1983), they intensify conflicts (Sternberg & Dobson, 1987), and they are viewed as more disagreeable (Jarboe & Witteman, 1996; van de Vliert & Euwema, 1994). The positive methods (yielding and cooperation) recognize and try to accommodate others' needs, mitigate conflict, and are viewed as more agreeable. Second, some of the methods are active, whereas others are more passive. Fighting and cooperating are both active approaches to coping with conflict, whereas yielding and avoidance are passive methods (Sternberg & Dodson, 1987; Sheppard, 1983; Thomas, 1992; van de Vliert & Euwema, 1994).

When conflict erupts, group members can use any or all of the basic modes of conflict resolution shown in Table 9–4, but only one of them—cooperation—offers an integrative solution to the group's problem. Avoidance, fighting, and yielding are often only temporary solutions, for they quell conflicts at the surface without considering the source. Cooperation, in contrast, is an active, positive method that yields both immediate and long-term benefits for the group (Deutsch, 1973; Thomas, 1992).

Upward → Downward Conflict Spirals

Consistent cooperation among people over a long period generally increases mutual trust. But when group members continually compete with each other, mutual trust becomes much more elusive (Haas & Deseran, 1981). When people cannot trust one another, they compete simply to defend their own best interests (Lindskold, 1978).

How can the upward spiral of competition and distrust, once initiated, be reversed? Robert Axelrod (1984; Axelrod & Hamilton, 1981) has explored this question by comparing a number of strategies in simulated competitions. After studying dozens of different strategies, ranging from always competing with a competitor to always cooperating with one, the most effective competition reverser to emerge is a strategy called **tit-for-tat**, or **TFT**. When using TFT, you begin bargaining by cooperating. If the other party cooperates, too, then you cooperate. But if the other party competes, then you compete as well. Each action by the other person is countered with the matching response: cooperation for cooperation, competition for competition. Axelrod feels that TFT works because it is both a provocable strategy and a forgiving strategy. It is provocable in the sense that it immediately retaliates against individuals who compete. It is forgiving, however, for it immediately reciprocates cooperation should the competitor respond cooperatively.

Individuals who follow a tit-for-tat strategy are viewed as "tough but fair"; those who cooperate with a competitor are viewed as weak; and those who consistently compete are considered unfair (McGillicuddy, Pruitt, & Syna, 1984). Because the effectiveness of TFT as a conflict reduction method is based on its provocability, any delay in responding to cooperation reduces the effectiveness of TFT. If a group member

---

Tit-for-tat (TFT): A bargaining strategy that begins with cooperation, but then imitates the other person's choice after that; cooperation is met with cooperation, competition with competition.

competes and this defection is not countered quickly with competition, TFT is less effective (Komorita, Hilty, Parks, 1991). TFT also loses some of its strength in "noisy" interactions, when behaviors cannot be clearly classified as competitive or cooperative (Wu & Axelrod, 1995). It is also less effective in larger groups, although this decline is minimized if individual members believe that a substantial subgroup within the total group is basing its choices on the TFT strategy (Komorita, Parks, & Hulbert, 1992; Parks & Komorita, 1997).

Many → One

Individuals who are not initially involved in the dispute should avoid "taking sides" in the emerging coalition formation process and should instead act as mediators. Although uninvolved group members may wish to stand back and let the disputants "battle it out," impasses, unflagging conflict escalation, or the combatants' entreaties may cause other group members or outside parties to help clarify the source of the problem and thus resolve the conflict (Hiltrop & Rubin, 1982).

Third parties, in general, facilitate conflict reduction by performing a number of important functions (Carnevale, 1986a, 1986b; Pruitt & Rubin, 1986; Raiffa, 1983; Rubin, 1980, 1986):

- Third parties reduce hostility and frustration by giving both sides an opportunity to express themselves while controlling contentiousness.
- If communication breaks down or the two disputants begin to misunderstand each other, the third party can correct the problem.
- Third parties help disputants save face by providing a graceful means of accepting concessions and by taking the blame for these concessions.
- Third parties can formulate and offer proposals for alternative solutions that both parties find acceptable.
- Third parties can manipulate aspects of the meeting, including its location, seating, formality of communication, time constraints, attendees, and agenda.
- Third parties can guide the disputants through the process of integrative problem solving described earlier.

However, if the disputants want to resolve the conflict on their own terms, third-party interventions are considered an unwanted intrusion (Rubin, 1980).

The effectiveness of third parties also depends on their power relative to the disputants. Go-betweens, moderators, facilitators, diplomats, advisers, mediators, or judges are all third-party intervenors, but they vary considerably in terms of power (LaTour, 1978; LaTour, Houlden, Walker, & Thibaut, 1976). In an *inquisitorial* procedure, the third party simply questions the two parties and then hands down a verdict that the two parties must accept. In *arbitration,* the disputants present their arguments to the third party, who then bases his or her decision on the information they provide. In a *moot,* the disputants and the third party discuss, in as open and informal a meeting as possible, the problems and possible solutions. Although moot third parties cannot make any binding decisions, they facilitate communication, make suggestions, and enforce standing rules. When the third party has no power to enforce participation or make recommendations, the intervention is known as *mediation*. Satisfaction with a third party depends on how well the intermediary fulfills these functions and also the intensity of the conflict. Mediational techniques such as arbitration that are effective when the conflict is subdued may not succeed when conflict intensity is high. Overall, most people prefer arbitration, followed by a moot, then mediation, and lastly inquisitorial procedures (LaTour et al., 1976; cf. Lind, Kurtz, Musante, Walker, & Thibaut, 1980).

Anger → Composure

When tempers flare, the group should encourage members to regain control over their emotions. "Count to ten" is a simple but effective recommendation for controlling conflict, as is the introduction of humor into the group discussion. Consistent with the idea that humor creates positive emotions that are not compatible with anger, individuals who were angry, when given the opportunity to retaliate, responded more positively if they had just been shown a series of amusing cartoons (Baron & Ball, 1974). Apologies, too, are effective means of reducing anger. When people are informed about mitigating causes—background factors that indicate that the insult is unintentional or unimportant—conflict is reduced (Betancourt & Blair, 1992; Ferguson & Rule, 1983). Groups can also control anger by developing norms that explicitly or implicitly prohibit shows of strong, negative emotion.

The Value of Conflict

Conflict is a natural consequence of joining a group. Groups bind their members and their members' outcomes together, and this interdependence can lead to conflict when members' qualities, ideas, goals, motivations, and outlooks clash. But this conflict is not always a pernicious process. Insofar as conflict is resolved successfully, it has stabilizing functions and becomes an integrating component of the group relationship. As noted in Chapter 6's analysis of group development, many groups pass through a period of conflict as they mature. This conflict phase expands the range of options, generates new alternatives, and enhances the group's unity by making explicit any latent hostilities and tensions. Conflict can make a group's goals more explicit and help members understand their role in the group (Bormann, 1975; Thibaut & Coules, 1952).

Conflict may also reshape the group in fundamental ways. In the case of Apple Computer, the conflict between Jobs and Sculley permanently changed the entire company. Before the conflict, Apple Computer was an unconventional, risk-taking builder of cutting-edge technology. After the conflict, the company focused on costs, increasing sales, and turning a profit. This change helped the company compete successfully against competitors, even though some of the original employees regretted the change. Sculley remained with Apple for nearly ten years before he moved on. Ironically, Steven Jobs rejoined Apple Computer in 1997 as chief executive officer. The conflict cycle continues.

SUMMARY

What is conflict? When *conflict* occurs in a group, the actions or beliefs of one or more members of the group are unacceptable to and resisted by one or more of the other group members.

1. *Intergroup conflict* involves two or more groups, and *intragroup conflict* occurs within a group.
2. Conflict follows a cycle from conflict to escalation to resolution.

What are the sources of conflict in groups?

1. *Personal conflict,* which arises when individual members do not like one another, is more prevalent in groups that are diverse.
2. *Substantive conflict* stems from disagreements about issues that are relevant to the group's goals and outcomes.
3. *Procedural conflicts* occur when members do not agree on group strategies, policies, and methods.
4. *Competition* creates conflict by pitting members against one another, whereas *cooperation* leads to mutual gain.
   - *Mixed-motive situations,* like the *prisoner's dilemma game (PDG),* stimulate conflict because they tempt individuals to compete rather than cooperate.
   - As the *norm of reciprocity* dictates, competition tends to provoke competition in return.
   - People who have competitive *social values* tend to compete more than cooperators and individualists, and men and women often respond to competitive and cooperative situations differently.
5. *Social dilemmas* stimulate conflict by tempting members to act in their own self-interest to the detriment of the group and its goals. Disputes arise

- when members disagree on how to divide up resources (the *equality norm* versus *the equity norm*)
- when one or more members exploit a shared resource (a *resource dilemma* or *social trap*)
- when members do not do their share in a public goods dilemma (*free riding*)
- when members avoid blame for group failure and take too much personal responsibility for group successes

Why does conflict escalate?
Once conflict begins, it often intensifies before it begins to abate.

1. When individuals defend their viewpoints in groups, their commitment can become overcommitment, and *entrapment* can occur.
2. Conflict is exacerbated by members' tendency to misperceive others and to assume that the other party's behavior is caused by personal (dispositional) rather than situational (environmental) factors. This fundamental attribution error is particularly strong during conflict, and individuals who are competitive by nature can fail to notice cooperation.
3. As conflicts worsen, members shift from weak to strong tactics. As Deutsch and Krauss's (1960) "trucking game" suggests, the use of contentious influence methods can lead to an upward *conflict spiral*.
4. Group members are more likely to form coalitions and become angry during conflict.

How can group members manage their conflict?

1. In many cases, members use *negotiation* (including integrative negotiation), to identify the issues underlying the dispute and then work together to identify a solution that is satisfying to both sides.
2. Of the four basic means of resolving conflicts—avoiding, yielding, fighting,

and cooperating—cooperating is more likely to promote group unity.

3. If a group member continues to compete, the *tit-for-tat* (*TFT*) strategy has proved useful as a conflict management strategy.

4. Third-party interventions, apologies, and the use of humor to diffuse anger are alternative means of managing conflict.

FOR MORE INFORMATION

"Conflict in Groups," a chapter by John M. Levine and Leigh Thompson, is a relatively high-level analysis of the causes, benefits, and liabilities of conflict in small groups.

Constructive Conflict Management: Managing to Make a Difference, by John Crawley (1994), is a superior "how-to" collection of pointers and suggestions for coping with various forms of conflict.

Social Conflict: Escalation, Stalemate, and Settlement (2nd ed.), by Jeffry Z. Rubin, Dean G. Pruitt, and Sung Hee Kim (1994) provides a thorough analysis of the causes and consequences of interpersonal conflict.

The Executive Way, by Calvin Morrill (1995), is a compelling analysis of the causes and consequences of conflict in the upper echelons of large corporations.

Getting to YES: Negotiating Agreement without Giving In (2nd ed.), by Roger Fisher, William Ury, and Bruce Patton (1991), describes a step-by-step strategy for resolving conflicts to the mutual benefit of both parties.

Odyssey: Pepsi to Apple . . . A Journal of Adventure, Ideas, and the Future, by John Sculley (with J. A. Byme, 1987), describes one side in the great *Jobs versus Sculley* confrontation.

The Resolution of Conflict: Constructive and Destructive Processes is Morton Deutsch's (1973) foundational, "must-read" analysis of conflict.

Social Dilemmas, by Samuel S. Komorita and Craig D. Parks (1994), reviews and organizes a wide array of problematic collaborative activities, including the prisoner's dilemma, public goods dilemmas, and social traps.

ACTIVITY 9–1 HOW DO YOU MANAGE CONFLICT IN GROUPS?

Think of a time when you experienced a group in conflict: when the actions or beliefs of one or more members of the group were unacceptable to and resisted by one or more of the other group members. The conflict need not have been intense or long-term, but it should have involved some type of disagreement among the members.

1. What started the disagreement? Was the conflict rooted in personal conflict, substantive conflict, procedural conflict, competition, or the group's inability to handle a social dilemma?
2. Did the conflict escalate? Did you notice any of these conflict intensifiers?
   - Commitment to positions instead of concern for issues
   - Misperceptions about the nature of the conflict
   - The use of contentious, too-strong tactics by members
   - Negative reciprocity (paybacks)
   - The formation of opposing coalitions
   - Strong emotions, such as anger
3. How did you respond in the situation? Which style of conflict resolution did you adopt?
4. What happened to the group? How was the conflict resolved? How did the experience change the group?

ACTIVITY 9–2 WHAT ARE THE CAUSES OF EVERYDAY CONFLICT?

Because few groups can avoid conflict altogether, we are frequently offered opportunities to observe the causes and consequences of conflict firsthand. Search out a group experiencing conflict, and carry out one of these activities.

1. Conflicts erupt frequently in corporate settings and are often rooted in personal dislikes and antipathies. Interview several members of the same company or organization, and ask them to talk about who they don't get along with and why. Is the conflict rooted in personality, substantive differences, or competition over resources?

2. If you belong to a group that discusses issues regularly, deliberately provoke a conflict by disagreeing with other members. Plan your disagreement carefully, and remain respectful of other people's positions. Watch, however, to see how the group responds and how you respond to the group. Be sure to take note of any conflict-intensifying reactions, such as commitment, misperceptions, and anger.

3. Watch individuals playing a competitive game, such as tennis, backgammon, or chess. Observe the way the competitors strive to overcome their opponent, but how they also try to minimize the harmful effects of competition to keep the situation friendly. Cautiously interfere with their interaction by asking the winner if he or she feels good about "crushing" his or her opponent.

4. Observe a group experiencing conflict. Try to follow the arguments offered by group members, and see if they use contentious influence tactics to overcome others. Watch for displays of anger, insulting remarks, threats, criticisms, nonverbal rejection, and the like. Or use a chart, like the one in Figure 2–6, to track the discussion. Each time a member speaks, classify the remark as positive or negative.

10

Performance

We turn to groups to get things done. Groups are the world's builders, decision makers, and problem solvers. When individuals combine their talents and energies in groups, they can accomplish goals that would overwhelm individuals. But even though groups often prevail, they do not always reach the goals they set for themselves.

- Do people work better when alone or in groups?
- What causes social facilitation?
- When are groups successful?
- Why do groups sometimes fail to reach their full potential?
- What steps can be taken to improve group performance?

CONTENTS

The Relay Test Room: Enhancing Productivity Through Teamwork

SOCIAL FACILITATION

When Does Social Facilitation Occur?

Why Does Social Facilitation Occur?

Social Facilitation: Conclusions and Applications

SOCIAL COMBINATION

Composition: Who Is in the Group?

Task Demands: What Is to Be Done?

Two Heads Are Better, Sometimes

SOCIAL MOTIVATION

Productivity Losses in Groups

Causes of Social Loafing

Increasing Social Motivation

When Coordination and Motivation Losses Combine: Brainstorming

SUMMARY

FOR MORE INFORMATION

ACTIVITIES

The Relay Test Room: Enhancing Productivity Through Teamwork

Nora, Helen, Dorothy, Olivia, and Flora all worked at the Hawthorne Plant of the Western Electric Company. Day after day, they sat at their workbenches, building the hardware needed for telecommunications relays out of an assortment of clamps, pins, screws, coils, and electronics parts. In May, their boss asked them if they would take part in an experiment. Management, he said, wanted to learn more about Western's employees, and so they had set up an observation room where a small subgroup could be studied for an extended period. The Relay Test Room group would consist of the five workers, one person to restock parts, an inspector, and at least one observer.

The Relay Test Room group spent the next five years turning out a total of 3.3 million small electronic components. During that period, researchers monitored the women's rates of production and observed their interactions. They expected that changes in the work setting—better lighting, fewer breaks, more vacations—would result in changes in the women's production rates. Their observations, however, prompted them to reach a different conclusion: Group processes, not aspects of the physical work setting, were the principal determinants of productivity (Hare, 1967; Mayo, 1933; Roethlisberger & Dickson, 1939; Whitehead, 1938).

Many people believe that the best way to get a job done is to form a group. Indeed, many of the billions of groups in the world exist to get a particular job done. People use groups to discuss problems, concoct plans, forge products, and make decisions. When a task would overwhelm a single person's time, energy, and resources, individuals turn to groups. Even when tasks can be accomplished by people working alone (such as assembling hardware for telecommunications systems), people often prefer to work in the company of others. Table 4–3 (p. 102) offers a sampling of various tasks accomplished by groups.

The world relies on groups to achieve its goals, but people sometimes challenge the wisdom of this custom. Although groups sometimes turn out excellent products, they often fall short of expectations. One task force may formulate an effective plan for dealing with a problem, whereas another may create a plan that ends in disaster. A team may practice diligently, but still play miserably during the big game. A group of women working together in a factory may assemble relays with incredible efficiency, but they may also spend so much time in conversation that their work suffers. Why do some groups perform impressively while others disappoint? This chapter answers this question by considering the processes that facilitate and inhibit productivity and performance in groups. Chapter 11 extends this analysis to groups formulating decisions.

SOCIAL FACILITATION

Building relays was essentially a one-person job. The women sat at their own benches and had all the necessary tools and materials within easy reach. The work was repetitive but called for a high degree of skill. Assemblers had to remember where each part went and cull faulty parts from their supplies when they ran across them. The task also demanded manual dexterity, for assembling a single relay required over 30 different movements of each hand. They did not need to talk to each other, although they often did (Whitehead, 1938).

Such situations are intriguing, for they lie at the boundary between nonsocial, purely individualistic settings and social, interpersonal settings. The women of the Relay Test Room were not interdependent, but neither were they lone individuals working in isolation. They did not work as a team, but they were all together in one place. Even though they did little to influence one another directly, the women—as social beings—responded to each other in predictable ways.

When Does Social Facilitation Occur?

Norman Triplett (1898) was one of the first researchers to ask the question, "What happens when individuals join together with other individuals?" Triplett, who was a bicycling enthusiast, noticed that cyclists performed better in races than they did when they were paced by motor-driven cycles or when they were timed riding the course alone. Triplett concocted a host of possible explanations for the improvement, which he tested by arranging for 40 children to perform a simple task in pairs or alone. As was the case with the cyclists, the children's times were better when they performed in pairs. Triplett's study documented **social facilitation:** the enhancement of performance when another person is present (Allport, 1920; Dashiell, 1930; Travis, 1925).

Coaction and Audiences.   Social facilitation occurs in both coaction settings and in audience settings. In Triplett's study, the children worked on the same task in the same room, but they did not interact with one another. This type of situation is a **coaction task.** Eating in a fast-food restaurant, taking a test in a classroom, riding a bicycle with a friend, or studying in the reading room of the library are everyday instances of coaction. An **audience task,** in contrast, involves an individual who performs a task in front of a spectator. One of the first scientific demonstrations of social facilitation in the presence of a passive spectator occurred in, of all places, an exercise laboratory. People who worked out lifting weights reached a fairly uniform level of performance, but when a researcher unexpectedly returned to the weight room one night, a subject whose performance had been constant for several days improved. The investigator concluded that the presence of a spectator was facilitating (Meumann, 1904).

After these promising initial confirmations of social facilitation for both coaction and audience tasks, researchers soon discovered exceptions to the general rule that working with others enhances performance. Floyd H. Allport's studies of what he called "co-working" or "co-feeling" groups, for example, did not always yield

---

Social facilitation: Improvement in task performance that occurs when people work in the presence of other people.
Coaction tasks: Performance situations where people are working on individual tasks in the presence of other people.
Audience tasks: Performance situations where people are working in front of one or more spectators.

evidence of social facilitation (Allport, 1920, p. 159). He arranged for his subjects to complete tasks twice, once while alone in a small testing cubicle and once with others at a table. To reduce competition, he cautioned his subjects not to compare their scores with one another, and he also told them that he himself would not be making comparisons. Allport found a slight but consistent improvement in the coacting condition as compared with the isolation condition. When, for example, subjects wrote down as many words as they could in response to words like *blue* or *game,* 14 of the 15 subjects generated more associates in the coaction condition. Moreover, when participants crossed out vowels in newspaper articles, performed multiplications, and thought up arguments to disprove points made in passages taken from philosophical works, people in groups produced more than people working in isolation—but their products were lower in quality. Likewise, other researchers sometimes reported gains in performance through coaction or when an audience was watching, but they also documented performance decrements as well (Burwitz & Newell, 1972; Carment, 1970; Martens & Landers, 1972; Travis, 1928; Weston & English, 1926).

Zajonc's Resolution.   These contradictory findings puzzled group dynamicists for many years, so much so that interest in social facilitation dwindled in the 1940s and 1950s. Then, in an article published in 1965, Robert B. Zajonc integrated the divergent results by drawing a distinction between dominant and nondominant responses. Zajonc noted that some behaviors are easier to learn and perform than others. These **dominant responses** are located at the top of the organism's response hierarchy, so they dominate all other potential responses. Behaviors that are part of the organism's behavioral repertoire but less likely to be performed are **nondominant responses.**

With the distinction between dominant and nondominant responses in mind, Zajonc turned to the other pieces of the puzzle. He pointed out that extensive studies of many organisms had repeatedly demonstrated that increases in arousal, activation, motivation, or drive level enhance the emission of dominant responses while impeding the performance of nondominant responses. He also reexamined prior studies of performance and noted that nearly all of the studies that documented social facilitation studied well-learned or instinctual responses, such as lifting weights, bicycling, or eating rapidly. He also noted that most researchers who reported negative effects of coaction or observation were studying novel, complicated, or unpracticed tasks, such as solving difficult math problems or writing poetry.

Putting these facts together, Zajonc concluded that the presence of others increases our tendency to perform dominant responses and decreases our tendency to perform nondominant responses. If the dominant response is the correct or most appropriate response in a particular situation, then social facilitation occurs; people will perform better when others are present than when they are alone. If the task calls for nondominant responses, however, then other people interfere with performance (see Figure 10–1). The

---

Dominant responses: Well-learned or instinctive behaviors that the organism has practiced and is primed to perform.
Nondominant responses: Novel, complicated, or untried behaviors that the organism has never performed before or has performed only infrequently.

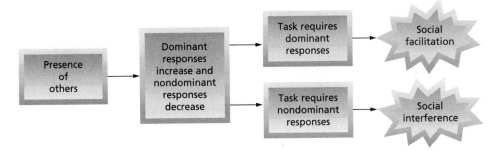

FIGURE 10-1   Do people work better when alone or in groups? Zajonc integrated previous research by noting that people display more dominant responses, and perform such behaviors more rapidly, when others are present. If the dominant response is appropriate in the situation, the presence of others is facilitating. If, however, the situation calls for a nondominant response, the presence of others will interfere with performance.

(*Source:* Zajonc, 1965.)

bulk of experimental studies of social facilitation fell into place when viewed from the parsimonious perspective suggested by Zajonc. Consider these examples.

- *Making speeches.* Allport found that people could generate words more rapidly when others were present, but when a second researcher replicated Allport's study, he discovered that people were less fluent when others watched. The studies used nearly identical procedures, but the participants in the second one stuttered when they spoke. For these people, verbal production was not a dominant response, and so the presence of an audience impeded their performance (Travis, 1928).
- *Running mazes.* Zajonc and his colleagues taught 32 female cockroaches (*Blatta orientalis*) to complete a maze or a simple runway task. Some roaches performed alone, others were part of a coacting pair, and still others were watched by other cockroaches (the cockroach spectators watched from their side of a plastic barrier). Both facilitating and inhibiting effects were obtained, just as Zajonc expected. As Table 10-1 indicates, an audience or coactor improved performance for the simple runway task. The audience or coactor impaired performance for the more complicated maze task (Zajonc, Heingartner, & Herman, 1969).
- *Playing games.* Researchers first surreptitiously watched people playing a game of pool to distinguish between skilled and unskilled players. Skilled players made at least two-thirds of their shots, and unskilled players missed at least two-thirds. Researchers then moved near the pool table and observed their play. Skilled players' performance improved 14% when they were observed, but unskilled players' performance dropped by over 30% (Michaels, Blommel, Brocato, Linkous, & Rowe, 1982).
- *Getting dressed.* Hazel Markus (1978) extended Zajonc's findings to humans by unobtrusively watching people take off their own shoes and socks and put on some unfamiliar articles of clothing. She discovered that people needed an average of 16.5 seconds to take off their own clothes when they were alone, but

**TABLE 10–1   MAZE-RUNNING SPEED
OF COCKROACHES WHEN COACTING AND ALONE**

Condition	Simple Maze	Complex Maze
Coacting	33.0 seconds	130.0 seconds
Alone	40.6 seconds	110.4 seconds

Source: Zajonc, Heingartner, & Herman, 1969.

they got the job done even faster if others were present. They needed just 13.5 seconds if someone was in the room with them—even if he sat with his back to them and never looked their way. If he watched them, then they needed only 11.7 to complete their change. The observer, though, slowed them up when they put on the unfamiliar clothes. They managed the unfamiliar task in 28.9 seconds when alone, but needed 32.7 and 33.9 seconds, respectively, when another person was present and when the other person was watching them.

In 1983, Charles Bond and Linda Titus examined 241 studies of social facilitation involving nearly 24,000 human subjects. When they combined the results of these studies statistically, they concluded that people work faster and produce more when others are present, but only when they work at simple tasks. The presence of others rarely enhances the *quality* of performance, and it decreases both quantity and quality of work on complex tasks. They also noted that the gains that occurred when people worked together on simple tasks were not as great as the losses that occurred when people worked on complex tasks. (For other reviews, see Baron, 1986; Geen, 1980, 1991; Geen & Gange, 1977; Guerin, 1986; Guerin & Innes, 1982; Suenaga, Andow, & Ohshima, 1981; Zajonc, 1980.)

Why Does Social Facilitation Occur?

Zajonc's analysis explains *when* social facilitation occurs. But *why* does the presence of others enhance dominant responses? Triplett (1898) offered a number of explanations for his observations of cyclists. Perhaps the pacing machine or lead rider creates a partial vacuum, and followers are pulled along with less effort. Maybe the lead rider or the pacing machine breaks the wind resistance and makes the follower's job easier. Also, the presence of other riders may buoy up the spirits of the competitors, encouraging them to expend greater effort. His laboratory study, however, eliminated most of these explanations and suggested, instead, that the presence of others is psychologically stimulating. But what is the source and nature of this mysterious "psychological stimulation"?

The Compresence Hypothesis.   Zajonc coined the word **compresence** to describe the state of responding in the presence of others. Compresence, he hypothesized, touches

---

Compresence: Responding when others are present.

off a basic arousal response in most social species (Zajonc, 1965, 1980). Because the presence or absence of co-species members is so important to such species, Zajonc believes that compresence arouses the individual "simply because one never knows, so to speak, what sorts of responses—perhaps even novel and unique—may be required in the next few seconds" (1980, p. 50). Zajonc believes that this arousal, and not some other higher order cognitive mechanism, such as fear of evaluation or competition, is what sustains social facilitation.

Zajonc's compresence hypothesis is consistent with studies that find that people who are "merely present" trigger social facilitation (Markus, 1978). In one study, for example, researchers cut off all forms of social interaction, communication, and evaluation between the observer and the subject, but social facilitation still occurred. When researchers blindfolded the observers and had him wear earplugs, his mere presence still enhanced performance on simple tasks and slowed performance on complex ones (Schmitt, Gilovich, Goore, & Joseph, 1986).

However, Zajonc's fundamental assumption—that the presence of others is physiologically arousing—has resisted confirmation. Some studies find evidence of increased heart rate and blood pressure, but the physiological effects of compresence are inconsistent (Cacioppo, Rourke, Marshall-Goodall, Tassinary, & Baron, 1990; Geen & Bushman, 1989). Humans do become physiologically aroused when others are nearby, but in many cases only when these others approach too closely (e.g., Middlemist, Knowles, & Matter, 1976) or when people feel that these others are evaluating them in some way (Seta & Seta, 1992). Moreover, the presence of certain people—such as close friends—can have a calming rather than arousing influence. When women performed a difficult math test with a friend who was merely present—the friend could touch the subject's wrist but was preoccupied with another task and was wearing a headset that blocked all sound—the subject's cardiovascular responses were lowered (Kamarck, Manuck, & Jennings, 1990).

Evaluation Apprehension.   Nickolas B. Cottrell (1972) rejects the idea that social animals are naturally aroused by the presence of other members of their species. He instead proposes that people learn, through experience, that other people are the source of most of the rewards and punishments they receive. Thus, individuals learn to associate social situations with evaluation and so feel apprehensive whenever other people are nearby. This **evaluation apprehension** enhances performance on simple tasks, but it become debilitating when people attempt more difficult projects. Cottrell thus believes that apprehension, and not the arousal response identified by Zajonc, is the source of social facilitation effects (Henchy & Glass, 1968; Weiss & Miller, 1971).

Studies of **self-presentation** in groups also underscore the motivational impact of evaluation apprehension (Goffman, 1959). Self-presentation theory assumes that group members actively control others' impressions of them by displaying social behaviors

---

Evaluation apprehension: An anxiety-creating concern to appear normal or competent.
Self-presentation: Influencing other people's social perceptions by selectively revealing personal information to them; includes both deliberate and unintentional attempts to establish, maintain, or refine the impression that others have.

that establish and maintain a particular social image, or *face*. Group members do not want the others to think that they possess negative, shameful qualities and characteristics, and so they strive to make a good impression (Goffman, 1959). Performance situations create self-presentational challenges for members, particularly when they feel they might fail. To avoid that potential embarrassment, group members redouble their efforts, particularly when self-presentational pressures are strong (Baumeister, 1986; Bond, 1982; Bond, Atoum, & VanLeeuwen, 1996).

The primary hypothesis that derives uniquely from Cottrell's theory—that any stimulus increasing the organism's apprehension over future rewards or punishments should increase drive levels—has received some support (Bond & Titus, 1983). When people find themselves in evaluative situations, they tend to perform dominant rather than nondominant responses (Cohen, 1979; Guerin, 1986; Seta, Crisson, Seta, & Wang, 1989). When, for example, individuals who were watched by an observer were explicitly told that the observer was evaluating them, their performance improved, but only when they were working on a simple task (Bartis, Szymanski, & Harkins, 1988; Geen, 1983). When people who have already failed once try the task a second time, they perform worse when others are present (Sanna & Shotland, 1990; Seta & Seta, 1995). Also, situational factors that decrease evaluation apprehension, such as allowing for private responses and unevaluative audiences, often eliminate social facilitation effects (Cottrell, Wack, Sekerak, & Rittle, 1968; Henchy & Glass, 1968; Martens & Landers, 1972; Sasfy & Okun, 1974). Finally, individuals who are highly confident perform better when evaluated by others, whereas those who doubt their ability to succeed perform better when alone (Sanna, 1992).

The presence of other people—even friends—also increases physiological reactivity if these friends are evaluative. As noted earlier, people were more relaxed when working on a task with a friend nearby. Their friend, however, was wearing earphones and could not evaluate the subject's performance (Kamarck et al., 1990). What would happen if the friend was a potential source of evaluation? When researchers replicated the study but had the friend watch the subject, the women were more physiologically aroused. Women were most relaxed, by the way, when they did the math in the presence of their pet dogs. The researchers suggest that the pets were an ideal source of social support, for they provided reassurance through their presence but could not evaluate their owner's performance (Allen, Blascovich, Tomaka, & Kelsey, 1991).

Other findings, though, do not support this emphasis on evaluation. Even when the companion refrains from attending to the individual in any way, social facilitation still occurs (Berger, 1981; Schmitt et al., 1986; Towler, 1986; Worringham & Messick, 1983). Animals that likely lack the capacity to feel nervous or embarrassed—puppies, chickens, mice, rats, monkeys, armadillos, ants, opossums, and even cockroaches—perform simple tasks better when other members of their species are present (Cottrell, 1972). Moreover, activities that involve little threat of evaluation—eating, drinking, getting dressed—still show social facilitation effects (Markus, 1978).

Cognitive Processes.   Zajonc stresses arousal, Cottrell underscores the importance of evaluation, but several cognitive models suggest that the presence of others changes our capacity to process information adequately. When people work in the presence of other people, they must split their attention between the task they are completing and the other person (Guerin, 1983; Guerin & Innes, 1982). The presence of an audience may also increase individuals' self-awareness, and as a result, they may focus their attention on themselves and fail to pay sufficient attention to the task (Carver & Scheier, 1981; Duval & Wicklund, 1972; Mullen & Baumeister, 1987).

Even though other people are a distraction, this distraction does not always translate into poorer performance. Distraction interferes with the attention given to the task, but these attention distractions can be overcome with effort. Therefore, on simple tasks, the interference effects are inconsequential compared with the improvement brought about by the conflict, and performance is thus facilitated. On more complex tasks, the increase in drive is insufficient to offset the effects of distraction, and performance is therefore impaired (Baron, 1986).

This *distraction-conflict theory* of social facilitation has been supported in several investigations (Baron, 1986; Groff, Baron, & Moore, 1983; Sanders, 1984; Sanders & Baron, 1975; Sanders, Baron, & Moore, 1978). As the model predicts, working with others appears to be somewhat distracting; people forget key aspects of the task when they complete it in the presence of others rather than alone (Gastorf, Suls, & Sanders, 1980; Sanders et al., 1978). Moreover, social facilitation effects tend to be stronger when subjects' attention is divided between the task and the other people who are present. If people are present but do not draw the subjects' attention, facilitation does not occur (Bond et al., 1996; Groff et al., 1983; Sanders et al., 1978).

Social Facilitation: Conclusions and Applications

Social facilitation occurs because human beings, as social animals, respond in predictable ways when joined by other members of their species (see Figure 10–2). Some of these reactions, as Zajonc suggested, are very basic ones, for human beings tend to become somewhat aroused when other humans are nearby (Cacioppo et al., 1990; Seta & Seta, 1992). But our arousal becomes more substantial when we realize that the people around us are evaluating our performance and may form the wrong impression of us if we perform badly. Cognitive mechanisms that govern how we process information and monitor our environment also come into play when we work in the presence of others (Bond & Titus, 1983; Geen, 1980, 1991; Geen & Bushman, 1987; Sanders, 1981).

These physiological, motivational, and cognitive processes, although relatively subtle, influence group members' reactions across a wide range of performance settings. Researcher John Aiello, for example, draws on studies of social facilitation in his analyses of *electronic performance monitoring,* or *EPM.* Many businesses can now track the performance of their employees throughout the workday with computer information networks. When workers use their computer to enter data, communicate with each, or search databases for stored information, their activity can be monitored automatically. Does EPM enhance performance, or does it create so much evaluation anxiety that performance suffers? Aiello finds that EPM may enhance employees' productivity, but in ways that are consistent with social facilitation effects. He studied people working on a data-entry task. Some were alone, some were working with others, and some were

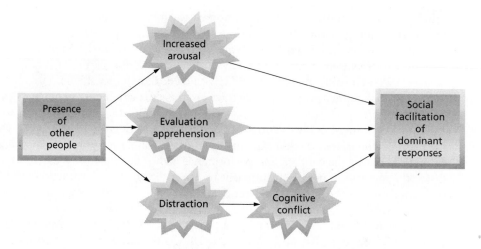

FIGURE 10-2   Why does social facilitation occur? Zajonc's arousal model assumes that the presence of others increases arousal. Cottrell's explanation of social facilitation argues that evaluation apprehension (and not arousal) is responsible for social facilitation when tasks are simple. Other theorists believe that other people are a distraction and that the attentional conflict that their presence creates can be motivating.

members of a cohesive group. Aiello discovered that EPM enhanced the performance of highly skilled workers, but it interfered with the performance of less skilled participants. Monitoring also increased workers' feeling of stress, except among those who were part of a cohesive work group (Aiello & Kolb, 1995).

Studies of social facilitation also raise questions about students' reliance on study groups when they prepare for examinations. Such groups offer members some advantages over studying alone. Some groups enhance members' motivation and help students stay focused on their academic goals (Dudley, Johnson, & Johnson, 1997; Finn & Rock, 1997). Moreover, if students receive useful instruction from other group members—clear explanations of concepts or practice in working problems that will appear on the test—then students who are members of study groups outperform students who do not study in groups (Webb, Troper, & Fall, 1995). Students who are committed to their groups and value the learning experiences they provide generally outperform students who react negatively to such groups (Freeman, 1996).

Study groups may, however, inhibit the acquisition of new concepts and skills. The presence of others can be distracting, and during the early phases of learning, this distraction can interfere with learning. The presence of other people also interferes with overt and covert practicing. When the subjects in one project needed to learn a list of words, they were too embarrassed to rehearse the material by saying it aloud, and as a result, their performance suffered (Berger et al., 1981). Indeed, studies of athletes acquiring new skills, of students learning a second language, and of clinicians developing their therapeutic skills indicate that learning proceeds more rapidly, at least initially, when students work alone rather than in groups (Berger, Carli, Garcia, & Brady, 1982; Ferris & Rowland, 1983; MacCracken & Stadulis, 1985; Schauer, Seymour, & Geen, 1985).

Once they have learned their skills, however, people should perform with others present if possible (Utman, 1997). Indeed, Zajonc recommends that the student

> study all alone, preferably in an isolated cubicle, and arrange to take his examinations in the company of many other students, on stage, and in the presence of a large audience. The results of his examination would be beyond his wildest expectations, provided, of course, he had learned his material quite thoroughly. [Zajonc, 1965, p. 274]

SOCIAL COMBINATION

The Relay Test Room group was a success. The women were experts, and so the presence of others enhanced their performance. Their output jumped by as much as 25% when they worked in the Relay Test Room.

The Relay Test Room, however, did more than just bring together individuals to work in a coaction or audience situation. Within a few weeks, the women changed from a collection of independent individuals into a work group. They developed a shared sense of identity and began to take pride in their group's productivity rates. Friendships formed within the group, and the observers quickly decided that "social sentiment and activity, so far from being one of the constants, was necessarily showing itself to be the dominating variable in the experiment" (Whitehead, 1938, p. 117). They were no longer single individuals working at a task, but members of an interacting group who combined their talents, skills, and energies to create the group's products.

When do interacting groups succeed at the tasks they are attempting, and when are they likely to fail? Ivan Steiner's (1972, 1976) **social combination theory** answers this question by breaking it into two simpler ones. He first asks, Does the group have the resources it needs to succeed? If the group members do not have the skills, talents, and energy needed to complete their tasks, then the group will likely fail. He then asks, Does the group combine its resources effectively? Even if members have the resources that the task requires, their group may nonetheless fail if they do not marshall these resources effectively. Performance, then, depends on the group's resources and the methods it uses to combine these resources to meet the demands of the tasks that face the group. (Gist, Locke, & Taylor, 1987; Gladstein, 1984; Goodman, Ravlin, & Schminke, 1987; Guzzo & Shea, 1992; Guzzo, Salas, and Associates, 1995; Hackman, 1990, 1992; Tjosvold, 1986; and Zander, 1971, 1977, 1982, 1985 also offer extensive analyses of group performance.)

Composition: Who Is in the Group?

Management did not pick the women of the Relay Test Room for their dedication to the company or special expertise as operators. Nora was productive, but she did not

---

Social combination theory: Steiner's theoretical analysis of group performance that assumes that productivity depends on the members' resources and the processes that determine how those resources are combined to create a group product.

take any special interest in the experiment. She was close to her family and fiancé, and considered only Helen to be a friend. Helen enjoyed the special attention received in the Relay Test Room, but she was not particularly motivated by it. She often rejected the influence attempts of her supervisor and the other group members. Dorothy was the most outgoing member of the group; she was "naturally gregarious, lively, and fond of a joke" (Whitehead, 1938, p. 155). Olivia came from a very cohesive family, and during the first years of the study, she kept to herself. Over time, however, she began to adjust to the situation, and she became good friends with Dorothy. Flora was a little older than the other workers. She wasn't as productive as some workers, but she "worked faithfully for her pay, she never showed petulance, and she thoroughly appreciated the real advantages of the Relay Test Room" (Whitehead, 1938, p. 156).

Group performance depends, in part, on who is in the group. When lone individuals work, solve problems, or make decisions, their performance depends on their personal talents, skills, and effort. When groups work, performance depends on the **composition** of the group: the qualities of the individuals who are members of the group. The Relay Test Room, for example, was a small group: only 5 members rather than 100. The members of the group were all women, and they were all experts at the task. But these women differed from one another in terms of age, personality, motivations, and attitudes, and these differences fundamentally influenced the group's performance (Moreland & Levine, 1992a; Moreland, Levine, & Wingert, 1996).

KSAs.   Some groups fail because they simply do not include people with the qualities and characteristics needed to get the job done. A group struggling to generate novel solutions to a problem may not have any creative people. And a soccer team made up of defensive fullbacks but no offensive goal scorers will likely lose. A group's performance depends, in part, on its members' knowledge, skills, and abilities, or **KSAs.**

What KSAs are important to groups? On the task side, groups whose members are more skilled at the work to be done outperform groups comprised of less skilled members. The Relay Test Room was productive because only highly skilled women were recruited for the group. Studies of sports teams find a direct relationship between the skill level of the players and the team performance: Better players equal better teams (Widmeyer, 1990). And the marvelously successful groups discussed by Warren Bennis and Particia Ward Biederman (1997) in their book *Organizing Genius* all contained individuals who were gifted in their fields. Bennis and Biederman attribute much of the success of these groups to the skill of the leaders who recruited these individuals. They write: "Recruiting the right genius for the job is the first step in building many great collaborations. Great Groups are inevitably forged by people unafraid of hiring people better than themselves" (p. 12).

On the interpersonal side, members must be able to work well with others on joint tasks. Communication skills, leadership ability, and a talent for managing conflicts are some of the qualities possessed by members of successful work teams (Bowers, Braun,

Composition: The number and type of people who make up the group.
KSAs: Acronym for knowledge, skills, abilities, and other characteristics that are needed to complete a job or task successfully.

& Morgan, 1997; Cannon-Bowers, Tannenbaum, Salas, & Volpe, 1995; Stout, Salas, & Fowlkes, 1997). In fact, two of the women in the original Relay Test Room were eventually removed from the group because of their interpersonal shortcomings. When Nora and Helen began ridiculing Dorothy and Olivia for working so rapidly, the researchers replaced them. Productivity skyrocketed (Whitehead, 1938).

Diversity.   The Relay Test Room was a relatively homogeneous group. Members were similar in terms of ethnicity, socioeconomic background, sex, and expertise. Would their performance have differed if some group members had unique personal qualities that distinguished them from the others? Do diverse, heterogeneous groups outperform homogeneous ones?

The value of diversity has been verified in a wide range of performance settings. Teams of researchers, for example, are more productive when they join with researchers from other disciplines (Pelz, 1956, 1967). Groups with individuals who have very different opinions generate more innovative solutions and detect errors in their group's decisions (Peterson & Nemeth, 1996). Management teams in banks that were diverse in terms of their educational histories and backgrounds were more innovative than teams that were homogeneous (Jackson, 1992). Groups that were solving math problems by drawing on group members' complementary bases of knowledge about mathematics performed better than even the most skilled member of the group (Stasson & Bradshaw, 1995). Groups that included Asian, African, Latino, and Anglo Americans outperformed groups that only included Anglos (McLeod, Lobel, & Cox, 1996).

Diversity does not, however, always help the group perform better. Much of the advantage of diverse groups occurs when members are all highly skilled but these skills do not overlap. Diversity in skill per se—some members of the group are competent but others are incompetent—does not appear to boost productivity (Tziner & Eden, 1985). Groups that bring together people with similar personalities tend to outperform groups whose members have dissimilar personalities (Shaw, 1981). Classroom groups performed best when they were composed of individuals whose personality characteristics were similar and focused on goal attainment (Bond & Shiu, 1997).

These conflicting findings attest to the mixed benefits and limitations offered by diversity in groups. Diverse groups may be better at coping with changing work conditions, because their wider range of talents and traits enhances their flexibility. Diversity should also help groups seek alternative solutions to problems and increase creativity and innovation. Diverse groups, however, may lack cohesion, because members may perceive each other as dissimilar. Moreover, as noted in Chapter 9, heterogeneity may increase conflict within the group (Jackson, May, & Whitney, 1995; Moreland et al., 1996).

Men and Women in Groups.   Would the Relay Test Room group have performed any differently if its members had been men or if the group had consisted of both men and women? Wendy Wood (1987), after reviewing 52 studies of sex differences in group performance, noted that some studies suggest that women outperform men, but other studies suggest that all-men groups are superior to all-women groups. She notes, though, that two factors covary with sex differences in group performance: task content and interaction style. First, in the studies that favored men, the content of the task was more consistent with the typical skills, interests, and abilities of men rather than women. Groups of men were better at tasks that required math or physical strength, whereas groups of women excelled on verbal tasks. Second, Wood suggests that sex differences in performance are influenced by the different interaction styles that men and women often adopt in groups. Men more frequently enact a task-oriented interaction style, whereas women enact an interpersonally oriented interaction style. Thus, men outperform women (to a small extent) when success is predicated on a high rate of task activity, and women outperform men when success depends on a high level of social activity (Wood, Polek, & Aiken, 1985).

These findings suggest that men would not have outperformed the women in the Relay Test Room. Although the task required manual dexterity, the women were all experts. Also, although men show a slight tendency to excel at tasks that require maximal productivity, positive social activities within the group were responsible for the high level of motivation maintained by the workers. If the group had become too task oriented, this source of motivational encouragement might have been lost (Eagly & Wood, 1991).

But what of heterogeneously gendered groups: groups that include both men and women? As noted earlier, studies of diversity suggest that groups that are more heterogeneous, whether based on abilities, skills, or sex, often outperform more homogeneous groups (Jackson, 1992; Wood, 1987). However, groups that achieve diversity by adding only one or two members of the social category, such as a group with one woman and many men or a group with several Anglos and a single Latino, may encounter more problems than homogeneous groups. When work groups include a single "token" woman, for example, co-workers are more likely to categorize each other in terms of their sex (Wilder, 1986b). Tokens are also scrutinized more than other group members, and this unwanted attention may make them so apprehensive that their performance suffers (Kanter, 1977). Tokens are more often targets of sexism and prejudice (Fiske, 1993b).

In many cases, tokens can minimize the harmful effects of their minority status by working effectively and expressing the commitment to the group (Eagly & Johnson, 1990; Ridgeway, 1982). Groups with tokens may outperform homogeneous groups, even when the groups attempt tasks that are traditionally reserved for homogeneously gendered groups. For example, one team of researchers watched groups working on a wilderness survival exercise—an activity that favors people who have knowledge of the outdoors. Groups of men generally outperformed women, but groups of men that included one woman performed best of all. The authors suggest that the addition of a woman in the otherwise all-male groups may have "calmed" the men's tendency to compete with one another and helped them to function as a team (Rogelberg & Rumery, 1996). These findings suggest that even a group that achieves heterogeneity by including a small number of dissimilar members may outperform a group with a more uniform membership.

Task Demands: What Is to Be Done?

No group can do everything. A group's prowess in one sphere may not generalize to other domains, for effectiveness is task specific. In some settings, the group must generate a physical product, but in other settings, the group makes judgments or solves problems (Hackman & Morris, 1975; Laughlin, 1980). As noted in Chapter 1, some groups generate products, but others make decisions, formulate strategies, and perform joint tasks (McGrath, 1984). Marvin E. Shaw (1963) identified six basic task dimensions: (1) the difficulty of the problem, (2) the number of acceptable solutions, (3) the intrinsic interest level of the task, (4) the amount of cooperation required among members, (5) the task's intellectual and/or manipulative requirements, and (6) the participants' familiarity with the task.

Steiner (1972), recognizing that a group may perform some tasks well but other tasks poorly, asks, "How are the group members' inputs combined to yield a group product?" A group that is assembling relays, for example, must combine members' products in ways that differ from the combination process used by a team playing baseball or workers mining coal. Steiner calls the combination processes dictated by the problem or group activity the **task demands.** These demands, he suggests, vary, depending on the divisibility of the task, the type of output desired, and the combination rules required to complete the task (see Table 10–2).

First, some tasks are *divisible*—they can be broken down into subtasks that can be assigned to different members—whereas other tasks are *unitary*. Building a house, planting a garden, or working a series of math problems by assigning one to each group member are all divisible tasks, because the entire task can be split into parts. Unitary tasks, however, cannot be divided: Only one painter is needed for a small closet in a house, only one gardener can plant a single seed, and only one person is needed to solve a simple math problem.

Second, some tasks call for a high rate of production (*maximization*), whereas others require a high-quality, correct outcome (*optimization*). With maximizing tasks, quantity is what counts. In a relay race, tug-of-war, or block-stacking problem, performance depends on sheer quantity; the emphasis is on maximal production. For optimizing tasks, a good performance is one that most closely matches a predetermined criterion. Examples of optimizing tasks include estimating the number of beans in a jar or coming up with the best solution to a problem.

Third, different tasks require groups to combine members' contributions in different ways. Additive tasks involve adding or summing individual inputs to yield a group product. Compensatory tasks require a "statisticized" group decision derived from the average of individual members' solutions. Disjunctive tasks require a single specific answer. Conjunctive tasks are completed only when all the group members perform some specific action. Lastly, on discretionary tasks, the group members are free to choose the method by which they will combine their inputs.

Additive Tasks.   **Additive tasks** are divisible and maximizing, for they require the summing together of individual group members' inputs to maximize the group product. In consequence, so long as each group member can perform the simple individualistic task required—such as pulling on a rope, cheering at a football game, clapping after a concert, or raking leaves in a yard—the productivity of the group will probably

---

Task demands: The combination processes dictated by the problem or group activity.
Additive tasks: Tasks that can be completed by adding together individual group members' inputs.

TABLE 10–2   A SUMMARY OF STEINER'S TYPOLOGY OF TASKS

Question	Answer	Task Type	Examples
Can the task be broken down into subcomponents?	Subtasks can be identified.	Divisible	Playing a football game, building a house, preparing a six-course meal
	No subtasks exist.	Unitary	Pulling on a rope, reading a book, solving a math problem
Which is more important, quantity produced or quality of performance?	Quantity	Maximizing	Generating many ideas, lifting the greatest weight, scoring the most runs
	Quality	Optimizing	Generating the best idea, getting the right answer, solving a math problem
How are individual inputs related to the group's product?	Individual inputs are added together.	Additive	Pulling a rope, stuffing envelopes, shoveling snow
	Group product is average of individual judgments.	Compensatory	Averaging individuals' estimates of the number of beans in a jar, weight of an object, room temperature
	Group selects the product from pool of individual members' judgments.	Disjunctive	Questions involving yes/no, either/or answers such as math problems, puzzles, and choices between options
	All group members must contribute to the product.	Conjunctive	Climbing a mountain, eating a meal, relay races, soldiers marching in file
	Group can decide how individual inputs relate to group product.	Discretionary	Deciding to shovel snow together, opting to vote on the best answer to a math problem, letting leader answer question

Source: Steiner, 1972, 1976.

exceed the productivity of the single individual. As we will see later in this chapter, people in groups do not always work hard at additive tasks; as the saying goes, "Many hands make light work." They still, however, outperform a solitary individual.

Compensatory Tasks.   When groups attempt **compensatory tasks,** the members must average their individual judgments or solutions together to yield the group's product (see Table 10–2). A group may not want to meet in a face-to-face meeting, for exam-

---

Compensatory tasks: Tasks that can be completed by averaging together individual group members' inputs.

ple, so members submit their votes to the chair, who tallies them up to reach a conclusion (Lorge, Fox, Davitz, & Brenner, 1958).

Marvin E. Shaw (1981), after a thorough review of existing research, concludes that groups that use compensatory methods make more accurate judgments than they would as individuals. Consider, for example, a group of people who were asked to estimate the temperature of their classroom (Knight, 1921). Naturally, some people overestimated the temperature, and others underestimated, and so the "group" judgment, which was an average of all the estimates offered, was more accurate than the judgments made by 80% of the individuals. Shaw also notes, however, that the increased accuracy of compensatory methods springs more from the use of multiple judgments than from the greater accuracy of groups per se. When single individuals make multiple estimates and their estimates are averaged, their judgments are also more accurate (Stoop, 1932).

Disjunctive Tasks.   When groups work at **disjunctive tasks,** they must generate a single solution that will stand as the group's product. Juries making decisions about guilt or innocence, several mechanics deciding which troublesome car problem to fix first, or the coaching staff setting the lineup for the day's game are all performing disjunctive tasks. Groups usually perform such tasks better than individuals do, but they rarely outperform their very best members. For example, in 1932, Marjorie E. Shaw studied four-person, same-sex groups working at various disjunctive puzzles. Her groups usually outscored individuals, but they took longer to finish and they rarely outperformed their best member. Indeed, sometimes they performed worse than their best member because the groups refused to accept the best member's answer as their own answer.

Subsequent studies explained the occasional failure of groups working on disjunctive tasks by contrasting the *truth-wins rule* with the *truth-supported wins rule*. In some cases, once someone in the group mentions the correct answer, the group adopts it as the group solution. Truth wins. But sometimes the group rejects the correct answer. Donna may be certain that the answer to the question "Who hit the game-winning home run in the 1960 World Series?" is Bill Mazeroski, but her team may not accept her solution because they doubt her skills or because someone of higher status may propose a different solution. Bill Mazeroski is the correct answer, but this truth will not win out over errors unless someone in the group supports Donna and her answer. Truth will win in such cases, but only if supported.

The truth-wins rule usually holds for groups working on Eureka-type problems, whereas the truth-supported wins rule holds for groups working on non-Eureka-type problems. When we are told the answer to a Eureka problem, we are very certain that the answer offered is correct. It fits so well, we react with an "Aha!" or "Eureka!" The answers to non-Eureka problems, in contrast, are not so satisfying. Even after arguing about them, we often wonder if the recommended

---

Disjunctive tasks: A task that is completed only when the group members reach agreement on a single answer that will stand as the group's product.

answer is the correct answer. Consider, for example, the famous horse-trading problem:

> A man bought a horse for $60 and sold it for $70. Then he bought it back for $80 and again sold it for $90. How much money did he make in the horse-trading business? [Maier & Solem, 1952]

When 67 groups discussed this problem, many included a member who knew the correct answer, but many of these groups nonetheless adopted the wrong solution. In this case, truth lost because knowledgeable members had a difficult time persuading the other members to adopt their solutions. In fact, some people later changed their answers to match the incorrect solution advocated by their groups (Maier & Solem, 1952). The answer, by the way, is $20. Thus, groups perform well at disjunctive tasks only if two critical conditions are met. First, someone in the group must suggest the correct answer. Second, the members of the group must adopt the answer as the group's solution (Davis, 1973; Littlepage, 1991; Lorge & Solomon, 1955; Smoke & Zajonc, 1962; Thomas & Fink, 1961).

Conjunctive Tasks.   The Relay Test Room did not use an assembly-line procedure to build its products. With an assembly line, workers repeatedly perform the same task, such as adding a particular part to a product as it passes by on the conveyor belt. Because such **conjunctive tasks** are not completed until all members of the group complete their portion of the job, the speed and quality of the work depends on the skill of the least skilled member. The speed of a group of mountain climbers moving up the slope is determined by the slowest member. The trucks in a convoy can move no faster than the slowest vehicle (Frank & Anderson, 1971; Steiner, 1972).

Groups often take steps to improve their proficiency on conjunctive tasks. In some cases, group members may urge their weakest members to work harder, and the members with less ability may respond with increased effort—the so-called **Köhler effect** (Köhler, 1926; Stroebe, Diehl, & Abakoumkin, 1996). If the conjunctive tasks are divisible, then the group can assign group members to the subcomponents that best match their skill levels. If the least competent member is matched with the easiest task, a more satisfying level of performance may be obtainable. If the least competent member is matched with a difficult subtask, performance will, of course, decline still further. (See Steiner, 1972, Chapter 3, for a detailed review of group performance on divisible tasks.)

Discretionary Tasks.   The final category of tasks identified by Steiner includes any task that group members can perform using their own preferred combination procedures. How, for example, would a group estimate the temperature of the room in which they were working? One simple method would involve averaging individual judgments. Alternatively, members could determine whether anyone in the group was particularly good at such judgments and then use this person's answer

---

Conjunctive tasks: Tasks that require input from all group members.
Köhler effect: An increase in performance by groups working on conjunctive tasks that occurs when the performance of less effective members improves.

as the group solution. In any case, judging the temperature of the room is a **discretionary task** because members themselves can choose the method for combining individual inputs.

Two Heads Are Better, Sometimes

Is a group more or less capable than a single individual? Steiner's social combination theory argues that a group's success depends, ultimately, on the resources that the group members contribute and the social combination rule used to combine their wisdom. As Table 10–3 indicates, groups clearly outperform the most skilled individual when the task is an additive one, and groups generally perform better than the average group member on many other kinds of tasks (compensatory, disjunctive, divisible conjunctive with matching, and discretionary).

Note, however, that these predictions describe the group's *potential* level of productivity. Groups working on additive tasks, in principle, will outperform an individual. Groups that include one person who knows the correct answer have the potential to solve a disjunctive problem. Groups do not always reach their full potential, however, because processes unfold within them that detract from their proficiency. These performance-inhibiting processes are examined in the next section and in Chapter 11 (Davis, 1973; Kerr, MacCoun, & Kramer, 1996b; Laughlin, 1996; Shiflett, 1979).

TABLE 10–3   A SUMMARY OF THE POTENTIAL PRODUCTIVITY OF GROUPS WORKING ON VARIOUS TASKS

Type of Task	Productivity Effect
Additive	*Better than the best:* The group exceeds the performance of even the best individual member.
Compensatory	*Better than most:* The group exceeds the performance of a substantial number of the individual members.
Disjunctive	*Equal to the best:* The group performs at the level of the most capable member, but only if the group accepts the most capable member's input as the group solution.
Conjunctive: unitary	*Equal to the worst:* Group performance equals the performance of the least capable member.
Conjunctive: divisible	*Better than the worst:* Performance will improve if subtasks match members' capabilities.
Discretionary	*Variable:* Performance depends on the combination rules adopted by the group.

Discretionary task: A relatively unstructured task that can be solved by using a variety of social combination procedures.

SOCIAL MOTIVATION

The members of the Relay Test Room were more productive than their co-workers in the main plant, but this high level of productivity did not mean that they were maximally productive. During any given week, some members of the groups would reach their usual levels of productivity, whereas others—especially Nora and Helen—would work below their maximum efficiency. As a result, the group produced more than individuals working in isolation, but the difference wasn't astonishing.

Why didn't the Relay Test Room women reach their full potential as a working group? Steiner (1972) draws on the concept of **process losses** to provide an answer. He notes that any prediction based only on task demands and member resources is optimistic, because it does not take into account group processes that detract from the group's proficiency. His "law" of group productivity predicts that

$$\frac{\text{Actual}}{\text{productivity}} = \frac{\text{Potential}}{\text{productivity}} - \frac{\text{Losses owing}}{\text{to faulty processes}}.$$

Thus, even when a group includes highly skilled members who possess all the resources they need to accomplish their tasks, faulty group processes may prevent them from succeeding. When process losses proliferate, the group's chances to become greater than the sum of its parts dwindle.

Productivity Losses in Groups

Max Ringelmann was a French agricultural engineer who, in the late 19th century, studied the productivity of horses, oxen, men, and machines in various agricultural applications. Should you plow a field with two horses or three? Can five men turn a mill crank faster than four? Ringelmann answered these questions by carrying out some of the first experimental studies in social psychology (Ringelmann, 1913). (Kravitz and Martin, 1986, present an excellent summary and interpretation of Ringelmann's work.)

One of Ringelmann's most startling discoveries pertained to the loss of productivity in groups working on additive tasks—projects that require the summing together of individual group members' inputs to yield a group product. Such tasks include competing in tugs-of-war, applauding at a concert, cheering at a sporting event, or teaming up to lift a heavy object. The work in the Relay Test Room was, in part, an additive task: Group productivity was determined by adding together the five workers' outputs.

Groups have an easy time with additive tasks, particularly when their performance is compared with that of individuals. A group of five persons making relays can easily outperform a single person, just as a team pulling a rope is stronger than a single opponent or an audience applauding makes more noise than an individual. Ringelmann found, however, that even though a group outperforms an individual, the group does

---

Process losses: Reductions in performance effectiveness or efficiency caused by faulty group processes, including motivational problems and coordination problems.

not usually work at maximum efficiency. When he had individuals and groups pull on a rope attached to a pressure gauge, groups performed below their capabilities (Moede, 1927). If two persons working alone could each pull 100 units, could they pull 200 units when they pooled their efforts? No, their output reached only 186. A three-person group did not produce 300 units, but only 255. An eight-person group managed only 392. Groups certainly outperformed individuals, but as more and more people were added, the group became increasingly inefficient (see Figure 10–3). The tendency for groups to become less efficient as group size increases is now known as the **Ringelmann effect** (Ingham, Levinger, Graves, & Peckham, 1974; Steiner, 1972).

Why might people working on an additive task fail to be as productive as they could be? First, **coordination losses** caused by "the lack of simultaneity of their efforts" interfere with performance (Ringlemann, 1913, p. 9). When working on additive tasks, individuals have difficulty combining their inputs in a maximally effective fashion. On a task such as rope pulling, for example, people tend to pull and pause at different times,

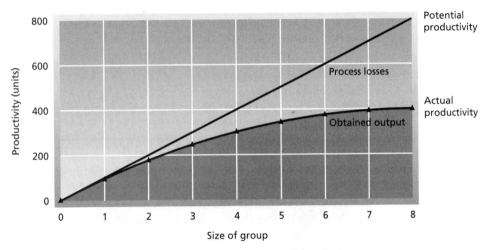

FIGURE 10–3 Do many hands make light work? Ringelmann (1913) recorded how much work single individuals did as well as the output of groups ranging in size from two to eight members. If a group's performance was based strictly on members' individual efforts, then a two-person group could produce 200 units, a three-person group could produce 300 units, and so on. Ringelmann found much less productivity. The means for his groups were 186, 255, 308, 350, 378, 392, and 392.

Ringelmann effect: The tendency for people to become less productive when they join a group; the larger the group, the more pronounced the loss of productivity.
Coordination losses: Inefficiency that results from group members' inability to combine their resources in a maximally productive fashion.

resulting in a failure to reach their full productive potential. New groups often cannot perform as well as more mature groups simply because members haven't learned to coordinate their efforts, and groups with many new members also suffer coordination losses, since coordination takes practice (Argote, Insko, Yovetich, & Romero, 1995; Arrow & McGrath, 1995; Wittenbaum & Stasser, 1996).

Second, Ringelmann speculated that people may not work so hard when they are in groups. After watching a group of prisoners turning the crank of a flour mill, he noted that their performance was "mediocre because after only a little while, each man, trusting in his neighbor to furnish the desired effort, contented himself by merely following the movement of the crank, and sometimes even let himself be carried along by it" (p. 10; translation from Kravitz & Martin, 1986, p. 938). This reduction of effort by individuals working in groups is called **social loafing** (Williams, Harkins, & Latané, 1981).

Ringelmann's insightful speculations have been confirmed experimentally. In one study, Bibb Latané, Kipling Williams, and Stephen Harkins told subjects that they were examining "the effects of sensory feedback on the production of sound in social groups" (1979, p. 824). So their job was to shout as loudly as they could while wearing blindfolds and headsets that played a stream of loud noise. Consistent with the Ringelmann effect, groups of subjects made more noise than individuals, but the group performance failed to reach its maximum. When the subjects were tested alone, they averaged a rousing 9.22 dynes/cm^2 (about as loud as a pneumatic drill). In dyads, each subject worked at only 66% of capacity, and in six-person groups, at 36%. This drop in productivity is charted in Figure 10–4 (Latané, Williams, & Harkins, 1979, Experiment 2, p. 826; see also Harkins, Latané, & Williams, 1980; Williams et al., 1981).

Latané and his colleagues separated out the relative impact of coordination losses and social loafing by testing noise production in "pseudogroups." In these conditions, subjects were led to believe that either one other subject or five other subjects were shouting with them, but in actuality, they were working alone (the blindfolds and headsets made this deception possible). Thus, any loss of production obtained in these conditions couldn't be due to coordination problems, because there weren't any other group members shouting. Instead, any decline in production could only be blamed on reduced effort brought about by social loafing. Figure 10–4 summarizes these findings. When subjects thought that one other person was working with them, they shouted only 82% as intensely, and if they thought that five other persons were shouting, they reached only 74% of their capacity. These findings suggest that even if work groups are so well organized that virtually all losses due to faulty coordination are eliminated, individual productivity might still be below par because of social loafing.

Causes of Social Loafing

Social loafing is not limited to groups that must exert physical effort. Loafing appears to be a pervasive aspect of groups, for it has been documented in groups working on

---

Social loafing: The reduction of individual effort exerted when people work in groups compared with when they work alone.

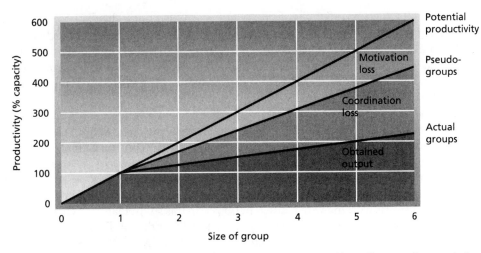

FIGURE 10-4 What causes the Ringelmann effect? Latané and his colleagues disentangled the two major causes of productivity losses in groups working on additive tasks by leading people to think that they were working in groups when they actually were not. The people in these "groups" (labeled "pseudogroups") suffered from motivation loss, but not from coordination loss, because they were actually working alone. The unshaded portion represents motivation loss (social loafing), and the lightly shaded portion represents coordination loss (experienced by the actual groups). They combine to create the Ringelmann effect.

(*Source:* Latané, Williams, & Harkins, 1979).

such diverse tasks as maze performance, vigilance exercises, creativity problems, job selection decisions, typing, swimming, and even brainstorming. The effect also seems to apply to men and women, to people of all ages, and to groups in many different cultures (Karau & Williams, 1993). But why do people loaf?

Anonymity and Evaluation Apprehension. Just as people performing simple tasks often work harder when an evaluative observer is watching, they often expend less effort when their contributions are hidden from others' evaluative scrutiny. Williams, Harkins, and Latané (1981, Experiment 1) studied the relationship between anonymity and social loafing by asking people to shout out loud when alone or in groups. In the pseudogroup condition, the subjects shouted alone but thought that others were shouting with them. In the group condition, subjects were part of groups that shouted at the same time. In a third condition, group members thought that others were shouting with them, but they also believed that their individual contributions would be identifiable. As in earlier studies, subjects in dyads and six-person groups worked at only 59% and 31% of their peak efficiency, respectively, and productivity remained low even when coordination losses were eliminated (69% for dyads and 61% for six-person groups). When output was identifiable, however, this loafing was virtually eliminated (Hardy & Latané, 1986; Kerr & Bruun, 1981; Sanna, 1992).

Why does identifiability decrease loafing? When our individual contributions are clearly known, evaluation apprehension sets in as we worry about how others will evaluate us. But when we are anonymous and our contributions are unidentified, the presence of others reduces evaluation apprehension, and social loafing becomes more likely (Harkins & Jackson, 1985; Harkins & Szymanski, 1987, 1988; Jackson & Latané, 1981; Szymanski & Harkins, 1987; Williams et al., 1981). Researchers illustrated the importance of evaluation by asking the members of a four-person group to generate as many ideas as possible for using a common object. The subjects did not discuss their task out loud but simply wrote their ideas on slips of paper. Some of the subjects thought that their ideas were individually identifiable, whereas others thought that their ideas were being collected in a common pool. In addition, some subjects believed that everyone was devising uses for the same object, but others thought that each group member was working with a different object. In this study, loafing occurred when ideas were pooled, but also when the subjects believed that their individual outputs were not comparable or could not be evaluated (Harkins & Jackson, 1985). Reduced evaluation apprehension, rather than anonymity per se, is a key cause of social loafing (Harkins, 1987; Szymanski & Harkins, 1993).

Collective Tasks Are Social Dilemmas.   A collective task can sometimes trap group members in a social dilemma. Group members may want to do their share to help the group reach its goals, but at the same time they are tempted to concentrate on their own personal goals. So they engage in *free riding:* They do less than their share of the work, yet still share equally in the group's rewards. People are most likely to free-ride when their contributions are combined in a single product and no one is monitoring the size of each person's contribution. Free riding also increases when group members worry that their co-workers are also holding back. Rather than look like a "sucker" by working harder than the others, group members reduce their efforts to match the level that they think other group members are expending (the "sucker effect").

Illusion of Productivity.   In a variety of work and interpersonal settings, the group's product is determined, in large part, by members' individual contributions to the collective goals. The nature of these contributions is rarely a matter of objective record, however, and so group members must intuitively gauge the quantity and quality of their group's product and their personal contributions to the endeavor. These estimates, however, are generally unrealistically positive, resulting in an **illusion of group productivity** (Homma, Tajima, & Hayashi, 1995; Stroebe, Diehl, & Abakoumkin, 1992). Members of groups working on collective tasks generally think that their group is more productive than most (Polzer, Kramer, & Neale, 1997). Nor do group members feel that they are doing less than their fair share. When members of a group trying to generate solutions to a problem were asked to estimate how many ideas they

---

Illusion of group productivity: The tendency for members to believe that their groups are performing effectively.

provided, each group member claimed an average of 36% of the ideas, when in reality they generated about 25% of the ideas (Paulus, Dzindolet, Poletes, & Camacho, 1993). Evidently, people aren't aware that they are loafing, or they are simply unwilling to admit it (Karau & Williams, 1993).

Increasing Social Motivation

Social loafing undermines group productivity. People carrying out all sorts of physical and mental tasks are individually less productive when they combine their efforts in a group situation. Even worse, loafing seems to go unrecognized by group members. Fortunately, steps can be taken to limit the deleterious consequences of collective action.

Increase Personal Involvement.   Social loafing can be undone by increasing each member's personal stake in the group's outcome. When individuals feel that a poor group performance will affect them personally, they do not loaf (Brickner, Harkins, & Ostrom, 1986). They also do not loaf if a high-quality performance will be rewarded (Shepperd, 1993, 1995; Shepperd & Wright, 1989). People are also less likely to loaf when they are working on interesting, involving, or challenging tasks (Brickner et al., 1986; Harkins & Petty, 1982; Zaccaro, 1984). Researchers tested the impact of involvement on loafing by asking college students to generate arguments either for or against a plan to make all seniors pass a comprehensive final examination before they were permitted to graduate. The researchers told some of the subjects that the plan was being considered for immediate implementation at their own university (high involvement), whereas others were told that the plan was being considered by another university (low involvement). As predicted, the only subjects who loafed were unidentifiable and uninvolved in the issue being discussed. If the plan pertained to them, they offered numerous thoughts, even when unidentified (Brickner et al., 1986).

Increased personal involvement in the group's tasks may prompt members to expend even more effort than they would if they were working alone. Kipling Williams and Steven Karau documented such motivational gains in groups by arranging for people to work on an additive task in groups. Some subjects were convinced that the task was a meaningful one; but the involvement of other subjects was systematically undermined by an experimenter who clearly considered the research topic boring. Subjects were also led to expect that their partners were skilled or unskilled at the task. Williams and Karau discovered that group members worked hardest when the task was meaningful and members believed that their co-worker's ability was minimal. The researchers described their results in terms of a **compensation effect:** Group members will work even harder at involving group tasks if they feel they must compensate for the shortcomings of other group members (Williams & Karau, 1991).

Compensation effect: An increase in performance by groups working on additive tasks that occurs when members work harder to compensate for the real or imagined shortcomings of the other members.

Minimize Free Riding.   Any factor that helps people escape from the social dilemma that collective endeavors pose will limit social loafing. When group members were convinced that their contributions were *indispensable*—their contribution was unique and essential for the group's success—they loafed less (Kerr & Bruun, 1983). Because free riding is less obvious in larger groups, loafing can be controlled by making groups smaller (Kameda, Stasson, Davis, Parks, & Zimmerman, 1992). Loafing also drops when group members believe that others in the group are both capable and willing to contribute to the group (Kerr, 1983). People who think that their co-workers will be expending maximum effort do not loaf, even when unidentifiable (Jackson & Harkins, 1985).

Clarify Group Goals.   Groups that set clear, attainable goals outperform groups whose members have lost sight of their objectives (Weldon & Weingart, 1993). For example, in one field investigation, truck drivers who hauled logs from the woods to the mill were initially told to "do their best" when loading the logs (Latham & Baldes, 1975). Unfortunately, with these vague instructions, the men only carried about 60% of what they could legally haul. When the drivers were later encouraged to reach a goal of 94% of the legal limit, they increased their efficiency and met this specific goal. And in a study of groups generating ideas, members loafed less when they had a clear standard by which to evaluate the quality of their own work and the group's work (Harkins & Szymanski, 1989). Other research suggests that clear goals stimulate a number of production-enhancing processes, including increases in effort, better planning, more accurate monitoring of the quality of the group's work, and increased commitment to the group (Weldon, Jehn, & Pradhan, 1991).

Set High Standards.   Are members inspired when they must struggle to achieve difficult goals, or would they prefer to set their goals low so that they can easily attain them? Kurt Lewin's level-of-aspiration theory, mentioned briefly in Chapter 2, explains how people set goals for themselves and their groups (Lewin et al., 1944). According to Lewin, people enter achievement situations with an ideal outcome in mind—for example, earning an A in the course, hitting a home run, turning out a given number of products, or making a specific amount of money. As they gain experience at the task, however, people revise these ideals to match more realistic expectations. For example, students entering a class may hope for a final grade of A, but if they fail the first two tests, they may have to revise their goals. Lewin used the term *level of aspiration (LOA)* to describe this compromise between ideal goals and more realistic expectations.

Groups also develop levels of aspiration. Although some groups select goals that are not consistent with their group's capabilities—some effective groups set their goals too low and ineffective groups optimistically expect success—most groups adopt LOAs that reflect their capabilities. Groups also tend to adjust their goals as they gain experience in the setting, with some evidence suggesting that groups are more sensitive than individuals to feedback. Whereas an individual who fails may continue to expect success, groups tend to revise their LOAs downward accordingly. People who occupy more central roles in the group tend to push their groups to set higher levels of aspiration, and cohesive groups are more optimistic than less cohesive groups (Medow & Zander, 1965; Zander & Medow, 1963, 195; Zander, Medow, & Efron, 1965).

Groups that set high goals tend to outproduce ones with lower LOAs (Harkins & Petty, 1982; Zander, 1971/1996). The Relay Test Room, for example, was not particularly impressive during the initial months. The women had been told "to cooperate with management and to work with a good will, but they were not to force output in any way" (Whitehead, 1938, p. 26). In fact, Nora and Helen repeatedly said "We were told to work like we feel, and we do" (p. 104), and they did not try to set any records. But when they were replaced, the norms changed. The group came to prize speed and productivity, and those who did not comply with this norm were constantly encouraged. As a result, the level of effort increased and productivity jumped.

Unrealistic goals can undermine motivation, however (Hinsz, 1995). Alvin Zander, in his studies of community groups, found that some set overly optimistic goals. Some of these groups had not reached their goals in more than four years, and this consistent history of failure adversely affected group morale, work enjoyment, and group efficiency. Thus, while the optimistic goal setting of successful groups challenged members to work harder and improve performance, the refusal to revise overly idealistic goals in unsuccessful groups set the stage for future failure (Zander, 1971/1996).

Increase Collective Efficacy.   Group performance is linked to members' expectations about their chances of success. Just as studies of self-efficacy indicate that people learn more, work harder, and achieve better outcomes when they believe that they have the skills required by the tasks they face, so groups with **collective efficacy** outperform groups that doubt their competence (Guzzo, Yost, Campbell, & Shea, 1993; Little & Madigan, 1997; Spink, 1990). In one study, men and women worked in triads building two model trucks out of Legos. After practicing the task, the group members were asked to indicate how rapidly they felt they could perform the task and their confidence in the group's ability to perform the task. Groups that were good at the task, as indicated by their performance during the practice period, outperformed less skilled groups. Collective efficacy, however, accounted for a significant portion of the variance in groups' performance beyond that accounted for by their performance on the practice test. Confident groups outperformed less confident groups, even when their overall level of ability was equal (Silver & Bufanio, 1996, 1997).

These findings are consistent with Karau and Williams's (1993) **collective effort model (CEM)**. Drawing on classic expectancy-value theories of motivation, they suggest that two factors determine group members' level of motivation: their expectations about reaching a goal and the value of that goal. Motivation is greatest when people think that the goal is within their reach (expectations are high) *and* they consider the goal to be valuable. Motivation diminishes if expectations are low *or* individuals do not

---

Collective efficacy: Group members' belief that their group can produce and regulate its outcomes.
Collective effort model (CEM): A theoretical explanation that traces losses of productivity in groups to diminished expectations about successful goal attainment and the diminished value of group goals.

value the goal. Working in a group, unfortunately, can diminish both our expectations about reaching our goal and the value that we place on that goal. In groups, the link between our effort and chances of success is ambiguous. Even if we work hard, others may not and the group may fail. Moreover, even if the group does succeed, we personally may not benefit much from the group's good performance. Earning a good grade on a project completed by a group may not be as satisfying as earning a good grade on a project that we completed working on our own. Karau and Williams tested the CEM's basic predictions in a meta-analysis. Their review of 78 studies indicates that loafing is reduced if individuals' expectations for success are high and they feel that the goal they are seeking is a valuable one.

Increase Unity.   People work harder for groups they value. The Relay Test Room, for example, became more productive as it became more important to its members. When the researchers presented them with weekly performance feedback, they took pleasure in discovering that the group was doing well. They came to think of themselves as group members first and as individuals second. As one member explained, "It isn't so much the money we care about as it is being considered the best and fastest group" (Whitehead, 1938, p. 134).

As Zander (1977) explains, group members typically have the choice of working for the group, for themselves, for both the group and themselves, or for neither and thus do not always choose to strive for group success. If, however, the members are united in pursuit of a common goal, then group-oriented motives should replace individualistic motives and the desire among members for group success should be strong (Wekselberg, Goggin, & Collings, 1997). In general, people who are more collectivistic loaf less than people who are more interested in pursuing individualistic goals (Erez & Somech, 1996). Women loaf less than men, and people from Eastern cultures loaf less than people from Western cultures (Karau & Williams, 1995). Cohesive groups also loaf less than noncohesive ones (Karau & Williams, 1997).

Increased unity, however, is no guarantee of good performance. As noted in Chapter 6, cohesive work groups are highly productive—but only if their norms emphasize productivity. In some extremely cohesive teams, the members may become so wrapped up in the social aspects of the group that interaction becomes the primary goal, while winning takes on secondary importance. Cohesiveness may have different effects, depending on whether the task calls for interaction between group members (Landers & Luschen, 1974). And some groups prosper in spite of their lack of unity. Studies of Olympic rowing teams found that the greater the internal conflict, the greater the group's effectiveness (Lenk, 1969). In one team, the conflicts were so intense that the members contemplated dissolution of the team, but managed to keep the group in existence by forming various coalitions. In spite of this animosity and disunity, the team won the Olympic gold that year (for reviews, see Carron, 1980; Cratty, 1981; Nixon, 1976).

When Coordination and Motivation Losses Combine: Brainstorming

Working in groups sets the stage for both social facilitation and social loafing. The presence of others motivates us and hence often improves our work on simple problems. But if our personal contributions to the total group effort cannot be identified and evaluated, social loafing can wipe out these gains.

Brainstorming groups provide a clear example of the detrimental, but often unrecognized, problems that groups face when working on collective tasks. **Brainstorming** is by far the best-known group technique for finding novel or creative solutions. Alex E. Osborn, an advertising executive, developed brainstorming to stimulate ideas via group discussion. He complained of constantly having to struggle for new ideas for his advertising campaigns, so he developed four basic rules to follow to ensure group creativity (Osborn, 1957):

1. *Expressiveness.* Express any idea that comes to mind, no matter how strange, wild, or fanciful. Don't be constrained or timid; freewheel whenever possible.
2. *Nonevaluation.* Don't evaluate any of the ideas in any way during the generation phase. All ideas are valuable.
3. *Quantity.* The more ideas, the better. Quantity is desired, for it increases the possibility of finding an excellent solution.
4. *Building.* Because all ideas belong to the group, members should try to modify and extend others' ideas whenever possible. Brainstorming is conducted in a group so that participants can draw from one another.

Brainstorming is a popular creativity technique, even though the bulk of the empirical evidence weighs against Osborn's method (Lamm & Trommsdorff, 1973; Mullen, Johnson, & Salas, 1991). Initial studies conducted in the late 1950s found positive effects of brainstorming, but these investigations "stacked the deck" against individuals; group members were told to follow Osborn's four basic brainstorming rules, whereas individuals weren't given any special rules concerning creativity (Cohen, Whitmyre, & Funk, 1960; Meadow, Parnes, & Reese, 1959). When individuals working alone were better informed about the purposes of the study and the need for highly creative responses, they tended to offer more solutions than individuals working in groups. In one study, for example, four-person groups came up with an average of 28 ideas in their session, whereas four individuals working alone suggested an average of 74.5 ideas when their ideas were pooled. The quality of ideas was also lower in groups; when the researchers rated each idea on creativity, they found that individuals had 79.2% of the good ideas. Groups also performed more poorly even when given more time to complete the task, as Figure 10–5 reveals (Diehl & Stroebe, 1987; see also Bouchard, Barsaloux, & Drauden, 1974; Bouchard, Drauden, & Barsaloux, 1974; Bouchard & Hare, 1970; Dunnette, Campbell, & Jaastad, 1963; Taylor, Berry, & Block, 1958).

The unimpressive yield offered by brainstorming groups cannot be blamed only on social loafing. While it is true that people striving to generate ideas do not work as hard as individuals working alone, other interpersonal and cognitive processes further

---

Brainstorming: A method for enhancing creativity in groups that calls for heightened expressiveness, inhibited evaluation, quantity rather than quality, and deliberate attempts to build on earlier ideas.

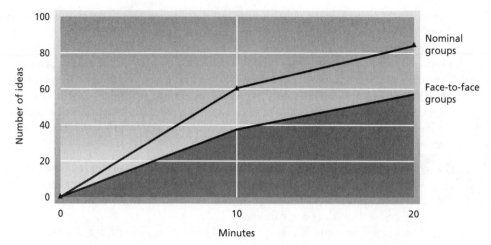

FIGURE 10–5 Is brainstorming an effective way to generate ideas? Despite the widespread popularity of brainstorming, people working individually (nominal groups) produce more ideas than people working in groups. Even when researchers gave people as much as 20 minutes to work, the groups still lagged behind the individuals. Groups given the chance to work for 40 minutes (not shown in graph) managed to finally produce as many ideas as individuals working for 20 minutes.

(*Source:* Diehl & Stroebe, 1991.)

compound the problem. The originators of the brainstorming concept thought that hearing others' ideas would stimulate the flow of ideas, but the clamor of creative voices instead results in a *blocking* effect. When people brainstorm in groups, they must wait their turn to get the floor and express their ideas, and during that wait, they forget their ideas or decide not to express them. Hearing others, too, is distracting and can interfere with their ability to do the cognitive work needed to generate ideas. Even when researchers tried to undo this blocking effect—by giving brainstormers note pads and organizing their speaking turns—groups still did not perform as well as individuals who were generating ideas alone (Diehl & Stroebe, 1987, 1991).

Evaluation apprehension can also limit the effectiveness of brainstorming groups, even though the "no evaluation" rule was designed to free members from such concerns (Diehl & Stroebe, 1987). Groups become even less effective when an authority watches them work—apparently because they worry that the authority may view their ideas negatively (Mullen et al., 1991). Individuals who are high in social anxiety are particularly unproductive brainstormers and report feeling more nervous, anxious, and worried compared to group members who are less anxiety prone (Camacho & Paulus, 1995).

Social comparison processes also conspire to lower standards of performance in brainstorming groups. Although undercontributors are challenged to reach the pace established by others, overcontributors tend to reduce their contributions to match the group's mediocre standards. This *social matching effect* tends to lower performance levels overall, but it can be minimized by increasing feelings of competition among members (Brown & Paulus, 1996; Paulus & Dzindolet, 1993; Seta, Seta, & Donaldson, 1991).

These studies offer a clear recommendation: Do not use face-to-face deliberative groups to generate ideas unless one or more of the following special precautions are taken:

1. Group members should be trained to follow brainstorming rules and be given feedback if they violate any of the basic principles. Groups that have not practiced brainstorming methods usually generate only mediocre ideas (Bouchard, 1972b; cf. Kramer, Kuo, & Dailey, 1997).
2. Group members who record their ideas individually, after the group session, may outperform more traditional brainstorming groups (Bouchard, 1972b; Philipsen, Mulac, & Dietrich, 1979).
3. Members should deliberately stop talking periodically to think in silence. Pauses and silences help members collect their thoughts and improve the results (Ruback, Dabbs, & Hopper, 1984).
4. Members should have plenty of time to complete the task. Groups that work under time pressure often produce more solutions, initially, but the quality of those solutions is lower than if they had spent more time on the task (Kelly, Futoran, & McGrath, 1990; Kelly & Karau, 1993).
5. Members should remind each other to stay focused on the task and to avoid telling stories, talking in pairs, or monopolizing the session (Paulus & Putman, 1996).
6. A skilled discussion leader can sometimes help the group reach high levels of creativity (Offner, Kramer, & Winter, 1996). A skilled leader can motivate members by urging them on ("We can do this!"), correcting mistakes in process ("Remember, the rules of brainstorming forbid criticism"), and providing them with a clear standard ("Let's reach 100 solutions!"). A facilitator can also record all ideas in full view of participants (Osborn, 1957; Rickards, 1974).

Researchers have also identified a number of methods that may offer alternatives to face-to-face brainstorming. One method, called **synectics,** involves identifying group members' goals, wishes, and frustrations; using analogies, metaphors, and fantasy; and using distracting activities and role-playing exercises. (See Gordon, 1961; Prince, 1970, 1975; and Ulschak, Nathanson, & Gillan, 1981, for a more detailed description of synectics.) Groups that use synectics are more effective than traditional brainstorming groups (Bouchard, 1972a; Bouchard et al., 1974).

Another approach, the **nominal-group technique** (NGT), minimizes blocking and loafing by reducing interdependence among members. André L. Delbecq and Andrew

---

Synectics: A technique for improving problem solving in groups that uses creativity-building exercises to enhance members' involvement and inventiveness.

Nominal-group technique (NGT): A group performance method that prefaces a face-to-face group session with a nominal-group phase, during which individuals work alone to generate ideas.

H. Van de Ven developed this method by integrating face-to-face groups and nominal groups: aggregates of noninteracting individuals that are groups "in name only" (Delbecq & Van de Ven, 1971; Delbecq, Van de Ven, & Gustafson, 1975; Van de Ven & Delbecq, 1971). NGT involves four basic phases:

Step 1. The group discussion leader introduces the problem or issue in a short statement that is written on a blackboard or flip chart. Once members understand the statement, they silently write ideas concerning the issue, usually working for 10 to 15 minutes.

Step 2. The members share their ideas with one another in a round-robin; each person states an idea, which is given an identification letter and written beneath the issue statement, and the next individual then adds his or her contribution.

Step 3. The group discusses each item, focusing primarily on clarification.

Step 4. The members rank the five solutions they most prefer, writing their choices on an index card. The leader then collects the cards, averages the rankings to yield a group decision, and informs the group of the outcome.

Delbecq and Van de Ven suggest that at this point, the group leader may wish to add two steps to further improve the procedure: a short discussion of the vote (optional Step 5) and a revoting (optional Step 6; Delbecq et al., 1975).

NGT is an effective alternative to traditional brainstorming (Gustafson, Shukla, Delbecq, & Walster, 1973; Van de Ven, 1974). Van de Ven (1974), for example, found that when groups discuss issues that tend to elicit highly emotional arguments, NGT groups produce more ideas and also report feeling more satisfied with the process than unstructured groups. The ranking/voting procedures also provide for an explicit mathematical solution that fairly weights all members' inputs and provides a balance between task concerns and socioemotional forces. By working alone during Step 1, members can generate many ideas without fear of sanctions by the other conferees. Then, in the interaction phase, the group is able to hash out differences and misunderstandings, all the while becoming committed to the final decision. The approach, however, is not without its drawbacks. Certain materials are needed, NGT meetings typically can focus on only one topic, and members sometimes feel uncomfortable in following the highly structured NGT format.

Electronic brainstorming, or **EBS,** offers certain advantages over face-to-face brainstorming groups. When groups brainstorm electronically, they use electronic mail, computer-based bulletin boards, and electronic conferencing (on-line discussions with shared information screens) to pool ideas over wide distances and at different times (Hollingshead & McGrath, 1995). Electronic communication offers a rapid way to disseminate ideas to the group and should increase participants' creativity by exposing them to a wide range of ideas. EBS also minimizes interpersonal pressures—particularly if brainstormers are not identified (Gallupe & Cooper, 1993; Roy, Gauvin, & Limayem, 1996).

Electronic brainstorming (EBS): Generating ideas and solving problems using computer-based communication methods rather than face-to-face group meetings.

EBS does not, however, erase problems of social coordination and motivation. Their effectiveness appears to depend, in part, on size. Because idea blocking grows worse as groups become larger, EBS groups that let several members respond at the same time outperform face-to-face groups when groups are larger than nine or ten members (Dennis & Valacich, 1993; Valacich, Dennis, & Connolly, 1994). Computer-mediated discussion can also provide members with too much stimulation, with the result that group members are overwhelmed by a flood of information to process (Nagasundaram & Dennis, 1993). Social matching also undermines productivity in EBS groups (Paulus, Larey, Putman, Leggett, & Roland, 1996). Researchers controlled how much information was exchanged among participants with three types of displays. Some subjects saw only their own ideas, others gained access to all the group's ideas at the end of the session, and still others were shown a continuously updated list of ideas generated by the group members. Group members who could monitor other people's idea production spontaneously matched each other's production rate, suppressing productivity (Roy et al., 1996). These mixed findings suggest that technology improves many aspects of group functioning but is no panacea for basic problems of social coordination and motivation that occur whenever people use groups to achieve goals.

SUMMARY

Do people work better when alone or in groups? Triplett's 1898 study of *social facilitation* suggests that people work more efficiently when other people are present.

1. Social facilitation occurs with both *coaction tasks* and *audience tasks*.
2. As Zajonc notes, social facilitation usually occurs only for simple tasks that require *dominant responses,* whereas social impairment occurs for complex tasks that require *nondominant responses.* Studies of a variety of species, including humans, support Zajonc's conclusion.

What causes social facilitation? Researchers have linked social facilitation to several personal and interpersonal processes, including arousal, evaluation apprehension, and distraction.

1. Zajonc's *compresence* hypothesis argues that the mere presence of a member of the same species raises the performer's arousal level by touching off a basic alertness response.
2. Cottrell's *evaluation apprehension* hypothesis proposes that the presence of others increases arousal only when individuals feel that they are being evaluated. *Self-presentation* theory suggests that this apprehension is greatest when performance may threaten the group member's public image.
3. The distraction-conflict theory emphasizes the mediational role played by distraction, attentional conflict, and increased motivation.
4. Theories of social facilitation predict when electronic performance monitoring and study groups will enhance performance.

When are groups successful? Steiner's *social combination theory* argues that group effectiveness depends, in large part, on the *composition* of the group and the type of task the group is attempting.

1. Performance depends on members' knowledge, skills, abilities, and other

characteristics (*KSAs*) and the diversity of the group, with heterogeneous groups generally outperforming homogeneous ones.

2. Sex differences in group performance are minimal.

3. *Task demands* depend on the task's divisibility (divisible versus unitary), the type of output desired (maximizing versus optimizing), and the social combination rule used to combine individual members' inputs.

   • Groups outperform individuals on *additive tasks* and *compensatory tasks*.

   • Groups perform well on *disjunctive tasks* if the group includes at least one individual who knows the correct solution.

   • Groups perform poorly on *conjunctive tasks* unless less skilled members increase their efforts (the *Köhler effect*) or the task can be subdivided.

   • The effectiveness of groups working on *discretionary tasks* covaries with the method chosen to combine individuals' inputs.

Why do groups sometimes fail to reach their full potential? Few groups reach their potential because negative group processes (*process losses*) place limits on their performance.

1. Groups become less productive as they increase in size. This *Ringelmann effect* is caused by *coordination losses* and by *social loafing,* the reduction of individual effort when people work in a group.

2. Latané and his colleagues identified the relative contributions of coordination losses and social loafing to the Ringelmann effect by studying groups and pseudogroups producing noise.

3. Social loafing is caused by anonymity, lack of identifiability, low evaluation apprehension, free riding, and group

members' inability to calibrate their group's effectiveness (the *illusion of productivity*).

What steps can be taken to improve group performance?

1. Group members work harder when they are personally interested in the group's task. When working on such tasks, they sometimes compensate for other group members by working harder (*compensation effect*).

2. Group members also exert more effort when they feel that their contributions to the group are indispensable, when they feel others will not free-ride, when the group's goals are clear and challenging, and when they are confident in their group's ability to reach its goals (*collective efficacy*).

3. Karau and Williams's *collective effort model* (*CEM*) assumes that motivation is related to group members' expectations about reaching a goal and the value of that goal.

4. *Brainstorming* groups often generate fewer ideas than individuals because of social loafing, blocking, and social matching. Other methods, including *synectics,* the *nominal-group technique* (*NGT*), and *electronic brainstorming* (*EBS*), offer advantages over traditional brainstorming.

FOR MORE INFORMATION

Group Process and Productivity, by Ivan D. Steiner (1972), is a timeless analysis of groups that includes entire chapters examining the relationship between composition, motivation, size, and performance.

Groups That Work (and Those That Don't), edited by J. Richard Hackman (1990), offers endless insights into group performance by documenting the causes and consequences of success and failure in over two dozen management groups, task forces, performing groups, and other assorted work groups.

The Industrial Worker, by Thomas North Whitehead (1938), provides a thorough analysis of early studies of industrial productivity, including the women of the Relay Test Room.

Motives and Goals in Groups, by Alvin Zander (1971, with a new introduction, 1996), systematically examines the intricate relationship between individual goals, group goals, and performance.

Organizing Genius: The Secrets of Creative Collaboration, by Warren Bennis and Patricia Ward Biederman (1997), offers a close look at seven of the most productive groups of the 20th century, including Disney Studios, Xerox's Palo Alto Research Center (PARC), and Lockheed's Skunk Works.

Team Performance Assessment and Measurement: Theory, Methods, and Applications, edited by Michael T. Brannick, Eduardo Salas, and Carolyn Prince (1997), is a compendium of cutting-edge instruments and techniques that can be used to measure a group's effectiveness.

ACTIVITY 10–1 **TYPES OF TASKS**

Join with other members of your class in small groups of three or four, and try to perform the following exercises. All of the questions, except the first one, should be solved through group discussion. Complete Question 1 before you join the group.

Problems

1. Without consulting with any of the group members, write down your answer to the following questions.
    a. What is the distance, in miles, between Paris, France, and Mexico City, Mexico?
    b. What is the exact population of the earth?
2. Once your group is seated together, each member should introduce himself or herself—even if you know each other well. Members should state their full name, their birthplace, and their most cherished possession.
3. What is the next letter in the following sequence? O T T F F S S
    a. I b. E c. D d. R e. L
4. How many cigars can a hobo make from 25 cigar butts if he needs 5 butts to make one cigar?
    a. 4 b. 5 c. 6 d. 7 e. 10
5. On one side of a river are three wives and three husbands. All of the men but none of the women can row. Get them all across the river by means of a boat carrying no more than three at one time. No man will allow his wife to be in the presence of another man unless he is also there.
6. Compute a group decision for Question 1 by averaging together everyone's judgments.
    a. What is the group's estimate of the distance between Paris and Mexico City?
    b. What is the group's estimate of the population of the earth?
7. On a separate sheet of paper, record as many uses as your group can think of for old tires.

ACTIVITY 10–1 **CONTINUED**

8. Rank-order the following animals in terms of how many hours a day the animal sleeps. Give the longest sleeper a 1 and the shortest sleeper an 8.

___ Bat	___ Elephant
___ Dolphin	___ Human
___ Sheep	___ Cat
___ Chimp	___ Mole

Classifying the Tasks

When your group finishes, check your solutions. Then answer these questions—either individually or as a group.

1. Which task was additive? How well did your group perform on this task? Were any of the variables that increased social loafing, such as free riding, social matching, and blocking, operating in your group?
2. Which task was compensatory? Was your group's score more accurate than your personal score? Would you recommend using groups to solve compensatory problems?
3. Which tasks were disjunctive? Describe, very briefly, the processes used by your group to solve the disjunctive tasks.
4. Which task was conjunctive? How rapidly did your group perform this task? If several groups worked on the problems, did your group finish before or after other groups?
5. Which task was discretionary? How did your group go about solving this task? Was this method successful? Were there any drawbacks to the method chosen by your group?

ACTIVITY 10–2 **BRAINSTORMING**

Paul B. Paulus and Vicky L. Putman (1996) offer a number of suggestions for carrying out a brainstorming session, including traditional group brainstorming and an adaptation they call "brainwriting."

Traditional Brainstorming

1. Form five-person groups and review the instructions for brainstorming found on page 295. Remember that criticism is not appropriate, and quantity of ideas is crucial. Radical ideas are welcome, and group members should try to expand on other people's suggestions.
2. Select one member of your group to act as the recorder of ideas. Recorders must not add any of their own ideas to the lists groups generate; they only write down others' ideas, and they should write down everything verbatim.
3. Work for 15 minutes on the following tourist problem: Each year, many Americans travel to Europe. But Americans also want to entice Europeans to come to America. What steps would you suggest to get more Europeans to visit America?
4. When the time allotted has expired, review the list and eliminate any redundant suggestions.

ACTIVITY 10–2 **CONTINUED**

Brainwriting
1. Form four-person groups and review the rules for brainstorming, as noted for traditional brainstorming above.
2. Instead of stating ideas aloud, one member of the group will begin by writing an idea on a sheet of paper. He or she then passes the paper on to the next member, who adds an idea. If a group member is slow in generating a new idea, the next group member can start a new sheet, which he or she can pass on to the next member.
3. Carry out Steps 3 and 4 given for the traditional brainstorming groups.

Post-Performance Review
1. How many ideas do you think you, as an individual, generated while brainstorming?
2. In general, do you believe that you would produce more ideas alone or by brainstorming in a group?
3. In general, do you believe that you would produce more *creative* ideas alone or by brainstorming in a group?
4. Evaluate the process your group used to generate its ideas.
   a. Did the production of ideas change over time?
   b. Did some individuals in the group produce more ideas than others?
   c. Did your group follow the rules of brainstorming?
5. Did any of the following coordination and motivational factors influence your group's performance?
   a. Social loafing
   b. Evaluation apprehension
   c. Blocking
   d. Social matching

Decision Making

When people must make important decisions, they turn to groups. Group decisions are often superior to an individual's, for groups can process more information more thoroughly. But groups do not always make good decisions. The strengths of groups are sometimes undermined by their liabilities, and group decisions are at times calamitous.

- Why make decisions in groups?
- What problems undermine the effectiveness of decision-making groups?
- Why do groups make riskier decisions than individuals?
- What is groupthink, and how can it be prevented?

CONTENTS

Kennedy's Advisory Committee: Collective Errors and Disastrous Decisions

GROUPS AS DECISION MAKERS

Remembering Information

Processing Information

GROUPS AS IMPERFECT DECISION MAKERS

Sharing Information

Group Discussion: Boon or Bane?

Cognitive Limitations

Group Polarization

VICTIMS OF GROUPTHINK

Symptoms of Groupthink

Causes of Groupthink

Predicting the Emergence of Groupthink

Preventing Groupthink

SUMMARY

FOR MORE INFORMATION

ACTIVITIES

Kennedy's Advisory Committee: Collective Errors and Disastrous Decisions

The date is April 4, 1961. President John F. Kennedy and his committee of advisers are contemplating invading Cuba. The committee's plan, which has been revised with the help of the Central Intelligence Agency, assumes that a squad of well-trained commandos can capture and defend a strip of land in the Bahía de Cochinos (Bay of Pigs) on the southern coast of Cuba. The commandos, once they control the Bay of Pigs, will then launch raids against Fidel Castro's army and encourage civilian revolt in Havana (see Figure 11–1).

The Bay of Pigs invasion takes place on April 17. The assault that Kennedy's committee spent hundreds of hours planning is a disaster. The entire attacking force is killed or captured within days, and the U.S. government must send food and supplies to Cuba to ransom them back. Group expert Irving Janis, after conducting a thorough analysis of the event, describes the decision as one of the "worst fiascoes ever perpetrated by a responsible government" (1972, p. 14).

Kennedy's committee was not unique. Like many other groups, it faced a problem needing a solution. Through discussion, the members pooled their expertise and information. They sought out information from all available sources, and then they thoroughly weighed alternatives and considered the ramifications of their actions (Hirokawa, 1990). When their alternatives were narrowed down to two—to invade or not invade—they made a decision as a group.

But the committee was typical in another way. Like so many other groups, it made the wrong decision. We owe much to groups: Groups put the first humans on the moon, built the Empire State Building, performed the first symphony, and invented the personal computer. But groups also planned the Watergate cover-up, marketed thalidomide, designed the O-rings that doomed the space shuttle *Challenger*, and piloted Air Florida's Flight 90 into Washington, DC's 14th Street Bridge. Groups have great strengths, but their limitations can only be ignored at great risk.

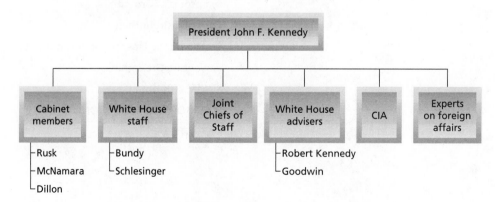

FIGURE 11–1 Who made the decision? The members of the committee that planned the Bay of Pigs invasion included many excellent individual decision makers. But when they approached the problem as a group, they failed to use their skills to examine the plan critically.

GROUPS AS DECISION MAKERS

People are not just social animals, but thinking, reasoning social animals. When obstacles prevent them from achieving their goals, they engage in problem solving to identify ways to overcome these barriers. They use their reasoning skills to draw conclusions from evidence. When making decisions, people must choose between alternatives, and by making judgments, they weigh the relative merits of opportunities that are available to them.

People often perform these cognitive activities as isolated individuals, but when the information to be processed is considerable or the potential consequences monumental, they do this cognitive work in groups. Indeed, a **collective information-processing model** of decision making assumes that groups, like individuals, seek out and process relevant information to perform tasks. Groups, however, seek and process information both cognitively and socially. Group members not only retrieve their personal memories, but also use one another as informational resources. Group members process information at the individual level by reviewing information, evaluating solutions, and generating alternative solutions, but they also process information at the group level through group discussion. Decision making, when a collaborative activity, involves generating information and processing that information through discussion (Hinsz, Tindale, & Vollrath, 1997; Kerr et al., 1996a, 1996b; Larson & Christensen, 1993).

Remembering Information

People often rely on groups to make decisions and solve problems because groups have better informational resources than individuals. A single person may know a great deal, but few of us can compete with the **collective memory** of a group of people (Clark, Stephenson, & Kniveton, 1990). The president's committee, for example, required a vast array of information about Cuba, Castro, the invasion force, the weapons to be used, and even the terrain of the beach where the commandos would land. These informational demands would have overwhelmed a lone individual, but the group's greater memory resources were sufficient for the task at hand.

Two heads are better than one because two heads can store more information. But two heads are also better because they can collaborate when creating the memory and when refreshing the memory from time to time. The committee, for example, established their memories about the morale of the invasion team during their initial briefing by the CIA. During that briefing, the group built a shared *mental model*, or *schema*, that they relied on throughout the rest of their meetings. Whenever they wondered if the troops would be able to capture the beachhead successfully, they recalled that the

---

Collective information-processing model: A general theoretical explanation of group decision making that assumes that groups combine information through group discussion and process that information to formulate decisions, choices, and judgments.
Collective memory: A group's combined memories, including each member's memories, the group's shared mental models, and transactive memory systems.

troops were (so they were told) well-trained freedom fighters and patriots who wanted to free their country from the grips of a dictator. In reality, the troops were poorly trained and disillusioned, but the committee's mental model was more positive. Like folklore, fable, and legends, groups develop collective memories that they review repeatedly and even pass on to new members (Fiske & Goodwin, 1996; Markus, Kitayama, & Heiman, 1996).

Cross-cuing also improves group memories. When group members discuss information, members may give each other cues that help them remember things that they would not recall if working alone. President Kennedy may not remember where the the force will land, but perhaps he will say, "I think it's a bay." This cue may trigger someone else's memories, so that the name Bay of Pigs is retrieved by the group even though none of the members could generate this name individually (Meudell, Hitch, & Boyle, 1995; Meudell, Hitch, & Kirby, 1992; Stasson & Bradshaw, 1995).

Groups also enhance their collective memories by creating **transactive memory systems** that effectively divide up information among the members. In the committee, for example, the CIA was recognized as the source of all information about the invasion force, and so other group members spent little effort deliberately storing information on that topic. When anyone needed to check a fact pertaining to commandos, they turned to the CIA and their memory stores (Clark & Stephenson, 1989; Wegner, 1987; Wegner, Giuliano, & Hertel, 1985).

But is collective memory more accurate and durable than individual memory? Researchers examined this question by testing the memories of both individuals and groups for words, images, and detailed textual material ("War of the Ghosts" from F. C. Bartlett, 1932). When researchers compared the memories of collaborative groups, nominal groups (groups of noninteracting individuals), and individuals, collaborative groups outperformed the average single individual and the best individual (see Figure 11–2). Collaborative groups did not, however, perform as well as nominal groups. Just as studies of brainstorming and social loafing, discussed in Chapter 10, would predict, recalling information in face-to-face groups resulted in *collective inhibition*. Interestingly, group memories also displayed many of the characteristics typically seen in individual memory. Individuals, for example, generally have better memory for information that they process more deeply and for pictures rather than words. Groups displayed these same tendencies when their memories were tested (Weldon & Bellinger, 1997).

The disappointing performance of collectives may have been due, in part, to these groups' inexperience working together. When groups first form, members are unable to determine which member can be counted on for what type of information. Over time, however, members become more proficient at recognizing, and taking advantage of, the strengths of each group member (Littlepage, Robison, & Reddington, 1997; Littlepage & Silbiger, 1992). Work groups typically improve their performance over time as

---

Transactive memory systems: A process by which information to be remembered is distributed to various members of the group, who can then be relied on to provide that information when it is needed.

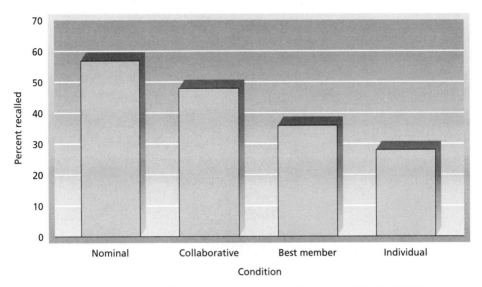

FIGURE 11–2   Who remembers more: groups, nominal groups, or individuals? When researchers tested groups' and individuals' memories, they discovered that collaborative groups outperformed the average individual and the best individual. Collaborative groups, though, could not remember as much information as nominal groups: aggregates of noninteracting individuals.

members learn to coordinate both their efforts and their informational resources (Goodman & Leyden, 1991). Training methods also influence transactive memories, for team members who are trained together rather than separately develop transactive memories more rapidly and so more accurately recall aspects of their training (Moreland, Argote, & Krishnan, 1996). These studies suggest that the committees's problems in managing information may have stemmed, in part, from the group's relative immaturity. The Bay of Pigs invasion was the first problem this group tried to solve (Wittenbaum, Vaughan, & Stasser, 1998).

Processing Information

Groups don't just have more information. They also process the information they have more thoroughly through discussion. The president's committee, for example, examined the invasion plan for several months. Even though the CIA argued that the invasion should be launched immediately, President Kennedy's group refused to move too quickly. The committee's deliberations over the next few months followed a pattern that is relatively common in decision-making groups. Although no two groups reach their decisions in precisely the same way, the stages shown in Figure 11–3 appear in many groups. During the initial *orientation stage,* the group identifies the problem to be solved, the choice that must be made, or the conflict that requires resolution. Next, during the *discussion stage,* the group gathers information about the situation and, if a decision must be made, identifies and considers options. In the *decision stage,* the group chooses its solution by reaching a consensus, bargaining, voting, or using some

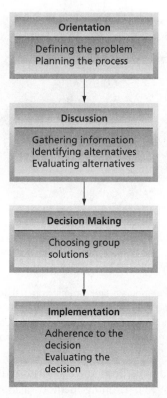

FIGURE 11-3 How does a group make a decision? Although no two groups reach their decisions in precisely the same way, many groups, after a brief orientation period, discuss the matter, make a decision, and then implement it.

other social decision process. Lastly, *implementation* must occur, and the impact of the decision is assessed (Dewey, 1910; Ellis & Fisher, 1994; Hirokawa, 1992).

Orientation.   How did the committee begin its work? Kennedy had just taken over the office of president, so his staff of advisers needed to take some time to develop an orientation to the group and to the problem. Members were introduced to one another, the problem facing the group was defined, and the steps to be taken in solving the problem were addressed (Moreland & Levine, 1992b).

As in most groups, this orientation period was very brief. Groups that spend time deliberately structuring their approach to their tasks generally outperform those who begin without first planning their activities, but group members rarely show much interest in process planning. When researchers listened to 100 groups working on projects, they discovered that many groups never even discussed strategies, and when someone did raise the issue, additional comments from other group members were unlikely to follow (Hackman & Morris, 1975). When groups are given a task, their first tendency is to begin their work rather than consider process-related issues

(Varela, 1971). Group members also believe that planning activities are less important than actual task activities, even when they are cautioned that proper planning is critical (Shure, Rogers, Larsen, & Tassone, 1962). This belief stems, in part, from the group members' willingness to apply whatever method they used in the past to current and future projects (Hackman & Morris, 1975).

Yet, controlling process by good planning generally has positive effects. When groups in one study worked on a role-playing problem involving survival on the moon, the only factor that distinguished successful groups from failing groups was the number of strategy-planning remarks made during the group discussion (Hirokawa, 1980). In a study of six conferences in which panels of experts evaluated new medical technologies, participants were more satisfied when the decisional procedures had been discussed in advance (Vinokur, Burnstein, Sechrest, & Wortman, 1985). Similarly, in a project that experimentally manipulated the use of process planning, groups were more productive when they were encouraged to discuss their performance strategies before working on a task requiring intermember coordination (Hackman, Brousseau, & Weiss, 1976). Process planning also leads to more positive ratings of group atmosphere, more verbal interaction, greater satisfaction with leadership, and flexibility in performing tasks (Hackman & Morris, 1975).

Discussion. During the discussion stage, the committee gathered and processed the information it needed to make its final decision. Members asked questions, and others offered answers. Group members criticized each others' ideas, when necessary, and offered corrections when they noted errors. The group members also monitored their work and intervened as necessary to bring the group back on task. The group's discussion, if like most discussions, probably also included an interpersonal element that complemented the focus on the work to be done (Bales, 1955, 1965). As Table 11–1 suggests, decision-making groups do more than share information, evaluate, monitor their progress, and plan. They also encourage each other, express commitment to the group, and help each other (Jehn & Shah, 1997; Weingart & Weldon, 1991; Weldon et al., 1991).

Just as the orientation period is essential to effective decision making, so time spent in active discussion increases the quality of the group's decision (Katz & Tushman, 1979). When researchers monitored group members' communications while working on a problem that could be solved only by properly sequencing individuals' responses, they found that the group's utilization of essential information through discussion proved to be the best predictor of success (Lanzetta & Roby, 1960). Moreover, project groups in a college class were more successful when members more actively discussed their task (Harper & Askling, 1980). Groups working on *collective induction problems* —tasks that require a cycle of hypothesis generation and testing—performed best when members discussed the problems actively and focused their analysis on evidence rather than hypotheses (Laughlin & Hollingshead, 1995). When researchers watching groups making a decision looked for each of the components of group discussion listed in Table 11–1, they discovered that 6 of the 7 were correlated with accuracy; only positive communication failed to covary with performance (Jehn & Shah, 1997).

TABLE 11–1   GROUP PROCESSES THAT INFLUENCE
THE EFFECTIVENESS OF A DISCUSSION GROUP'S PERFORMANCE

Component	Definition
Information sharing	Talking a great deal, willing to discuss; free expression of ideas, thoughts, and feelings
Planning	Formulating actions regarding time and function that will lead to specific goals
Critical evaluation	Critically evaluating each other's ideas or works; differences of opinion; disagreement on the decision made by group members; disagreements on who should do what or how something should be done
Positive communication	Encouraging better performance and positive reactions about a member's or a group's performance
Commitment to group	Attachment to the group; wanting to stay and do things with the group; tending to things; making sure everyone gets things done
Task monitoring	Assessing the performance and the likelihood that the group will reach its goal
Cooperation	Behavior that aids the performance of another group member or contributes to the ease with which group members coordinate their efforts; mutual helping

Source: Jehn & Shah, 1997.

Making the Decision.   By early April, the committee was ready to make its decision. The members had spent months examining the CIA's plan, and even though many questions remained unanswered, the group could delay no longer. Word of the plan had leaked to the press, and the group was worried that Castro would shore up his defenses if he suspected anything. They needed to make up their minds.

A **social decision scheme** is a group's method for combining individual members' inputs in a single group decision. In many cases, the social decision scheme is an implicit one. The *truth-wins rule,* noted in Chapter 10, is one such decision rule, as is the more frequently observed *majority-rules* model. This social decision scheme predicts that any decision favored by more than 50% of the group members will be selected by the group as its final decision, even in the absence of any explicit, formalized rule about how the final decision is to be made (Davis, 1996; Tindale, Smith, Thomas, Filkins, & Sheffey, 1996).

In other cases, though, the group may adopt an explicit social decision scheme that describes the procedures that the group must follow when making its decisions. Some common social decision schemes are delegation, averaging, voting, and discussion to unanimity (Davis, 1969; Wood, 1984).

Social decision scheme: The process by which individual inputs are combined to yield a group decision. A group that lets the leader make all decisions, for example, is relying on a "leader-decides" social decision scheme.

- *Delegating decisions.* An individual or subgroup within the group makes the decision for the entire group. Under a *dictatorship* scheme, the chairperson or some other authority makes the final decision with or without input from the group members. When an *oligarchy* operates in the group, a coalition of powerful individuals within the group speaks for the entire group. Other forms of delegation include asking an expert to provide an answer or forming a subcommittee made up of a few members to study the issue and reach a conclusion (Smoke & Zajonc, 1962).
- *Averaging individual inputs.* Groups make decisions individually (either before or after a group discussion), and these private recommendations are averaged together to yield an overall conclusion. For example, to choose among five possible candidates for a job opening, each member of the hiring committee could rank the candidates from 1 (the best) to 5, and the group could then average these rankings.
- *Voting.* Groups adopt the decision that a specified proportion of the group favors, such as the majority (more than 50%) or a two-thirds majority (66% or more).
- *Consensus.* The group discusses the issue until it reaches unanimous agreement without voting.

How the group makes its decision influences group members' satisfaction and willingness to act on the decision. Autocratic procedures, such as mandates from the group's leadership, may leave members feeling disenfranchised and ignored. When groups average individual members' inputs, all the group members' opinions are considered, and as noted in Chapter 10, this procedure often cancels out errors or extreme opinions. But a group that just averages without discussion may make an arbitrary decision that fails to satisfy any of the group members, all of whom may end up feeling little responsibility for implementing the decision. Still, autocratic and averaging methods save time, since the group need not hold a face-to-face meeting.

Voting, at least in most American and European groups, is by far the most frequently chosen method for reaching a decision. Voting offers the means of making a clear-cut decision, even on issues that deeply divide the group. This strength, however, is also a drawback, for when the vote is close, some members of the group may feel alienated and defeated. In consequence, they become dissatisfied with membership and are less likely to follow through on the decision (Castore & Murnighan, 1978). Voting can also lead to internal politics as members get together before meetings to apply pressure, form coalitions, and trade favors to ensure the passage of proposals that they favor. Also, if the vote is taken publicly, individuals may conform to previously stated opinions rather than expressing their personal views (Davis, Stasson, Ono, & Zimmerman, 1988).

Some groups avoid these drawbacks by relying on consensus to make decisions. Consensus decision schemes are involving and often lead to high levels of commitment to the decision and the group. Unfortunately, groups may not be able to reach consensus on all issues. Consensus building also takes a good deal of time, and if rushed, the strategy can misfire. In many cases, too, groups explicitly claim to be using the unanimity scheme, but the implicit goal may be something less than unanimity. When nine people on a jury all favor a verdict of guilty, for example, the three remaining jurors may hold back information that they believe would cause dissent within the group. As a result, in groups operating under a unanimity scheme, initial biases and errors are often perpetuated rather than corrected (Kameda & Sugimori, 1993). Thus, a consensus decision scheme is not necessarily superior to the other schemes (Hiro-kawa, 1984; Rawlins, 1984; Stumpf, Freedman, & Zand, 1979).

In general, groups prefer to reach a consensus on questions that require sensitive judgments, such as issues of morality; but on intellectual problem-solving tasks, a majority-rules voting scheme finds considerable acceptance (Kaplan & Miller, 1987). Members also prefer procedures that increase their sense of control over the discussion and outcome (Folger, 1993; Gilliland, 1994; Greenberg, 1994). People are more likely to regard a decision as a fair one if the decisional procedures are implemented "(a) consistently, (b) without self-interest, (c) on the basis of accurate information, (d) with opportunities to correct the decision, (e) with the interests of all concerned parties represented, and (f) following moral and ethical standards" (Brockner & Wiesenfeld, 1996, p. 189; Leventhal, Karuza, & Fry, 1980). Self-interest also plays a large role in shaping members' reactions to their group's decisions. When our group's decisions benefit us, we are quick to say that the decision is a just and wise one, even when unfair procedures were used. But if the decision harms us, we are far more likely to cry "foul" when the group used questionable methods to reach its decision (Brockner & Wiesenfeld, 1996). Even a dictator's judgment satisfies group members when it coincides with their own (Miller, Jackson, Mueller, & Scherching, 1987).

Implementation.   When the die is cast and the decision made, two significant pieces of work remain to be done. First, the decision must be implemented. If a union decides to strike, it must put its strike plan into effect. If a city planning commission decides that a new highway bypass is needed, it must take the steps necessary to begin construction. If an advisory committee approves an invasion plan, its members must mobilize the necessary military forces. Second, the quality of the decision must be evaluated. Was the strike necessary? Did we put the highway where it was needed the most? Was it really such a good idea to invade Cuba?

If the group's decision pertains to the group itself—its rules, its procedures, or its mission—implementation proceeds more smoothly when members had an active role in the decision-making process. Lester Coch and John R. P. French, Jr. (1948), documented this tendency in their classic analysis of procedural changes in a clothing mill. Management modified production methods frequently as a result of engineering advances and product alterations, and line workers reacted to each modification with protests. Turnover was high, productivity was down, and the amount of time needed for retraining after each production change was excessive.

Coch and French suspected that employees would be more willing to implement the recommended changes if they were involved more in planning them, and so they devised three different training programs. Employees in the *no-participation* program were not involved in the planning and implementation of the changes but were given an explanation for the innovations. Those in the *participation-through-representation* program attended group meetings where the need for change was discussed openly and an informal decision was reached. A subgroup was then chosen to become the "special" operators who would serve as the first training group. Employees in the third program, *total participation,* followed much the same procedures as those in the second method, but here all the employees, not a select group, were transferred to the training system.

Just as Coch and French predicted, the no-participation group improved very little; hostility, turnover, and inefficiency remained high. In fact, 17% of these workers quit rather than learn the new procedure, and those who remained never reached the goals set by management. The two participation conditions, in contrast, responded well. These workers learned their new tasks quickly, and their productivity soon surpassed prechange levels and management goals. Morale was high, only one hostile action was recorded, and none of the employees quit in the 40 days following the change. Furthermore, when the members of a control condition were run through a participation program several months later, they, too, reached appropriate production levels.

Quality circles, autonomous work groups, and *self-directed teams* are the modern-day counterparts to Coch and French's total-participation groups (Cascio, 1995). These groups usually include five to ten employees who perform similar jobs within the organization. They are often led by a supervisor who has been trained for the role, but participation is sometimes voluntary. These small groups identify problems in the workplace that are undermining productivity, efficiency, quality, or job satisfaction. Next, the group spends considerable time discussing the causes of the problems and suggesting possible solutions. Eventually, decisions are made about changes (usually by consensus), and these changes are implemented and evaluated. If the changes do not have the desired effect, the process is repeated. Quality circles, in particular, base their analyses on statistical data pertaining to productivity (Crocker, Chiu, & Charney, 1984; Deming, 1975).

These approaches tend to increase workers' level of satisfaction, and they may even increase productivity (Wagner, 1994). They are often relatively short-lived, however, particularly when they are not integrated into the organization's overall structure (Guzzo & Shea, 1992).

GROUPS AS IMPERFECT DECISION MAKERS

Rather than leave important decisions in the hands of one person, people frequently join together in groups to plan, decide, concoct, and judge. Yet, people often have harsh words to say about their groups. Members complain about time wasted in groups and swap jokes such as "An elephant is a mouse designed by a committee," "Trying to solve a problem through group discussion is like trying to clear up a traffic jam by honking your horn," and "Committees consist of the unfit appointed by the unwilling to do the unnecessary." When and why do groups make poor decisions?

Sharing Information

The committee spent much time talking about how U.S. citizens would react to the invasion and the incompetence of Castro's forces. They did not spend as much time talking about the weapons the troops would carry, the political climate in Cuba, the terrain of the area where the invasion would take place, or the type of communication system used by Cuban military forces. Only the CIA representatives knew that the morale of the invasion force was very low, but they never mentioned that information during the discussion. Joseph Newman, a journalist just back from visiting Cuba, met with President Kennedy privately and told him that the Cuban people would not rebel against Castro. Kennedy kept this information to himself during the group discussions.

The good news is that groups can pool their individual resources to make a decision that takes into account far more information than might any one individual's decision. The bad news is that groups spend too much of their discussion time examining shared information—details that two or more group members know in common —rather than unshared information (Stasser, 1992; Stasser, Talor, & Hanna, 1989; Wittenbaum & Stasser, 1996).

A group's tendency to spend more time discussing shared information does not always undermine the quality of the group's decision. Even though they may discuss shared information more thoroughly, members often base their final decision on pooled unshared information rather than on pooled shared information (Gigone & Hastie, 1993, 1997). Shared information influences judgments, but only because it shapes group members' prediscussion judgments and not because groups oversample that information during their discussions. Unshared information, although inadequately discussed, still influences judgments (Winquist & Larson, 1998). The harmful consequences of bias increase, though, when the group must have access to the unshared information if it is going to make a good decision. If a group is working on a problem where the shared information suggests that Alternative A is correct, but the unshared information favors Alternative B, then the group will only discover this so-called **hidden profile** if it pools the unshared information (Stasser & Titus, 1985).

Garold Stasser and William Titus (1985) examined just this type of problem by giving members of four-person groups 16 pieces of information about three candidates for student body president. Candidate A was the best choice for the post, for he possessed 8 positive qualities, 4 neutral qualities, and 4 negative qualities. The other two candidates had 4 positive qualities, 8 neutral qualities, and 4 negative qualities. When group members were given all the available information about the candidates, 83% of the groups favored Candidate A—a slight improvement over the 67% rate reported by the subjects before they joined their group. But groups did not fair so well when Stasser and Titus manipulated the distribution of the positive and negative information among the members to create a hidden profile. Candidate A still had 8 positive qualities, but Stasser and Titus made certain that each group member received information about only two of these qualities. Person 1, for example, knew that Candidate A had positive qualities P1 and P2; Person 2 knew that he had positive qualities P3 and P4; Person 3 knew that he had positive qualities P5 and P6; and Person 4 knew that he had positive qualities P7 and P8. But they all knew that Candidate A had negative qualities N1, N2,

---

Hidden profile: Problem where the best solution or decision will go unrecognized by group members if they fail to pool their unshared information effectively.

N3, and N4. Had they pooled their information carefully, they would have discovered that Candidate A had positive qualities P1 to P8 and only 4 negative qualities. But they oversampled the shared negative qualities and chose the less qualified candidate 76% of the time (Stasser & Titus, 1985, 1987).

Tasks and Sampling.   This tendency to oversample shared information reflects, in part, discussion's dual purpose. As a form of informational influence, discussions help individuals marshal the evidence and information they need to make good decisions. But as a form of normative influence, discussions give members the chance to influence each other's opinions on the issue. Discussing unshared information may be informationally useful, but discussing shared information helps the group reach consensus on the matter. Indeed, group members who anticipate a group discussion implicitly focus on information that they know others possess, instead of concentrating on information that only they possess (Wittenbaum, Stasser, & Merry, 1996). Group members also discuss shared information first, and only later get to unshared information (Larson, Foster-Fishman, & Keys, 1994).

Groups are therefore more likely to oversample shared information when working on judgmental tasks that do not have a demonstrably correct solution, but more likely to pool unshared information when they think that the task has a right or wrong answer (Laughlin, 1996). Indeed, even when groups are working on a task that can be solved, if members think that they do not have enough information, they are likely to oversample shared information and perform more poorly than if they think that they have the information they need to find the answer (Stasser & Stewart, 1992). When one member of the group had all the information and faced three other group members who had incomplete information, the minority was more influential—and groups performed best—when the group felt that the task had a demonstrably correct answer (Stewart & Stasser, 1998).

Leaders and Information Sharing.   James R. Larson, Jr. and his colleagues, in exploring some of the ways to eliminate the tendency to spend too much time talking about shared information, point to the role the leader can play in helping the group better manage its information. Rather than focusing the group on information that everyone already knows, an effective discussion leader can prompt members to reveal unshared information and can keep the group's attention focused on that information by repeating it during the discussion.

The researchers tested this hypothesis by giving three-person medical teams that included a resident, an intern, and a third-year medical student information about several cases. The residents, because of their greater expertise and higher pay, were the unofficial leaders of the groups, and they also tended to resist the tendency to oversample shared information. They repeated more shared information, but they also repeated more unshared information than the other group members. Moreover, as the discussion progressed, the residents were more and more likely to repeat unshared information that was mentioned during the session, evidence of their attempt to bring unshared information out through the discussion (Larson, Christensen, Abbott, & Franz, 1996).

Group Discussion: Boon or Bane?

Most experts on group communication agree that misunderstanding seems to be the rule in groups, with accurate understanding being the exception. Too many members simply lack the skills needed to express themselves clearly. They fail to make certain that their verbal and nonverbal messages are accurate and easily decipherable and thereby unintentionally mislead, confuse, or even insult other members (Gulley & Leathers, 1977). Inaccuracies also arise from both the simple information-processing limitations of human beings and their faulty listening habits. Listeners tend to *level* (simplify and shorten), *sharpen* (embellish distinctions made by the speaker), and *assimilate* (interpret messages so that they match personal expectations and beliefs) information offered by others during a discussion (Campbell, 1958b; Collins & Guetzkow, 1964).

Nor do all group members have the interpersonal skills a discussion demands. When researchers asked 569 full-time employees who worked jobs ranging from clerical positions to upper-level management to describe "in their own words what happens during a meeting that limits its effectiveness," they received nearly 2500 answers. The problems, which are summarized in Table 11–2, fall into seven basic categories: bad communication, egocentric behavior, nonparticipation, failure to stay focused (tendency to become sidetracked), interruptions, negative leadership behaviors, and negative attitudes and emotions. The participants in this research suggested that their

TABLE 11–2   PROBLEMS WHEN GROUPS MAKE DECISIONS

Problem (Frequency)	Description
Poor communication skills (10%)	Poor listening skills, ineffective voice, poor nonverbals, lack of effective visual aids, misunderstood or do not clearly identify topic, repetitive, jargon
Egocentric behavior (8%)	Dominating conversation and group; behaviors that are loud, overbearing; one-upmanship, show of power, manipulation, intimidation, filibustering; talk to hear self talk, followers or brownnosers, clowns and goof-offs
Nonparticipation (7%)	Not all participate; do not speak up, do not volunteer, are passive, lack discussion, silent starts
Sidetracked (6.5%)	Leave main topic
Interruptions (6%)	Members interrupt speaker, talk over others, socialize, allow phone calls, messages from customers/clients
Negative leader behavior (6%)	Unorganized and unfocused; not prepared; late, has no control, gets sidetracked, makes no decisions
Attitudes and emotions (5%)	Poor attitude, defensive or evasive, argumentative, personal accusations, no courtesy or respect, complain or gripe, lack of control of emotions

Source: DiSalvo, Nikkel, & Monroe, 1989.

groups fail more frequently than they succeed at solving problems (Di Salvo, Nikkel, & Monroe, 1989).

Groups also sometimes use discussion to *avoid* making a decision rather than *facilitate* making a decision. As Irving Janis and Leon Mann (1977) suggest, most people are reluctant decision makers, and so they use a variety of tactics during discussion to avoid having to face the decision. These tactics include the following:

- *Procrastination.* Rather than spending its time studying alternatives and arguing their relative merits, the group postpones the decision.
- *Bolstering.* The group quickly but arbitrarily formulates a decision without thinking things through completely and then bolsters the preferred solution by exaggerating the favorable consequences and minimizing the importance and likelihood of unfavorable consequences.
- *Avoiding responsibility.* The group denies responsibility by delegating the decision to a subcommittee or by diffusing accountability throughout the entire assemblage.
- *Ignoring alternatives.* The group engages in the fine art of muddling through (Lindblom, 1965) by considering "only a very narrow range of policy alternatives that differ to only a small degree from the existing policy" (Janis & Mann, 1977, p. 33).
- *"Satisficing."* Members accept as satisfactory any solution that meets only a minimal set of criteria instead of working to find the best solution. Although superior solutions to the problem may exist, the "satisficer" is content with any alternative that surpasses the minimal cutoff point.
- *Trivializing the discussion.* The group avoids dealing with larger issues by focusing on minor issues. In many cases, the law of triviality holds: The time a group spends discussing any issue will be in inverse proportion to the consequentiality of the issue (Parkinson, 1957, paraphrased from p. 24).

Cognitive Limitations

Groups generate decisions through processes that are both active and complex. Members formulate initial preferences, gather and share information about those preferences, and then combine their views in a single group choice. Although these tasks are relatively ordinary ones, they sometimes demand too much cognitive work from members. The president's committee, for example, wanted to weigh all the relevant factors carefully before making its choice, but the complexity of the problem outstripped the members' relatively meager cognitive capacity (Fiske & Taylor, 1991).

People's judgments in such cognitively demanding situations are often systematically distorted by cognitive and motivational biases. People often inappropriately use the information they have available to them, putting too much emphasis on vivid, interesting information while ignoring the implications of statistical information. People sometimes form conclusions very quickly and then don't sufficiently revise those conclusions once they acquire additional information. When people cannot easily imagine an outcome, they assume that such an outcome is less likely to occur than one that springs easily to mind. People overestimate their judgmental accuracy because they remember all the times their decisions were confirmed and forget the times their pre-dictions were disconfirmed. People make mistakes (Arkes, 1993; Plous, 1993).

Groups, unfortunately, are not immune from these judgmental biases. Just as indi-vidual jurors are influenced by information that is not relevant to the case (the extraevidentiary bias), so groups of jurors fail to discount irrelevant information when deliberating cases (MacCoun, 1990). Just as individuals tend to let initial invest-ments of resources in a project bias their decision to continue investing in the project (the sunk-cost effect), so groups will recommend pouring money into failing projects to justify their initial investment (Whyte, 1993). Indeed, considerable evidence sug-gests that groups may *accentuate* these judgmental errors. Far from protecting indi-viduals from these judgmental biases, groups are actually more error prone than individuals (Hinsz et al., 1997; Kerr et al., 1996a; Tindale, 1993).

Groups are also more likely to make mistakes when situational pressures interfere with group members' ability to properly process the information needed to make the correct decision. People become *cognitively busy,* for example, when they are trying to answer a phone call and track the course of the group's discussion or when a problem arises but they cannot stop to correct the difficulty. Flight crews, for example, rarely make errors as they perform the complex tasks required to pilot a plane successfully (Härtel & Härtel, 1997). During emergencies, however, the crew becomes cognitively busy, and their capacity to process information adequately can be overwhelmed. As a result, the crew members do not take advantage of group discussion to review their assumptions, and so important errors in judgment are not corrected by the group. These information-processing errors can have fatal consequences. Aviation experts often blame crashes on "human error," but the error usually lies with a group rather than individuals (Foushee, 1984; Ginnett, 1993; Helmreich & Foushee, 1993).

Group Polarization

Historians cannot say why President Kennedy decided to create a committee to help him explore the CIA's invasion plan, but he may have acted on the intuitively appealing notion that groups have a moderating impact on individuals. He may have assumed that a group, if faced with a choice between a risky alternative (such as "Invade Cuba") and a more moderate alternative (such as "Use diplomatic means to influence Cuba"), would prefer the moderate route. Unfortunately for Kennedy, for his advisers, and for the members of the attack force, groups' decisions actually tend to be more extreme than individuals' decisions. Groups do not urge restraint; instead, they polarize opinions.

The Risky-Shift Phenomenon.   At about the time that Kennedy's committee was grappling with the problems inherent in the invasion plan, group experts were initi-ating studies of the effects of group discussion on decision making. Although some researchers discovered that groups prefer more conservative solutions than individu-als (e.g., Atthowe, 1961; Hunt & Rowe, 1960), others found a surprising shift in the direction of greater risk (Stoner, 1961; Wallach, Kogan, & Bem, 1962). One group of researchers, for example, studied people's willingness to take risks by asking indi-viduals and groups to read over 12 hypothetical situations involving a choice between one of two possible courses of action (Wallach et al., 1962). In all the situations, the more rewarding outcome was also the riskier one, and subjects were asked, "What would the probability of success have to be before you would advise the character in the story to choose the riskier course of action?" The first item from this Choice-Dilemmas Questionnaire, along with the format used to measure subjects' responses, follows (Pruitt, 1971, p. 359):

> Mr. A, an electrical engineer, who is married and has one child, has been working for a large electronics corporation since graduating from college five years ago. He is assured of a lifetime job with a modest, though adequate, salary and liberal pension benefits upon retirement. On the other hand, it is very unlikely that his salary will increase much before he retires. While attending a convention, Mr. A is offered a job with a small, newly founded company which has a highly uncertain future. The new job would pay more to start and would offer the possibility of a share in the ownership if the company survived the competition of the larger firms.
>
> Imagine that you are advising Mr. A. Listed below are several probabilities or odds of the new company proving financially sound. Please check the lowest probability that you would consider acceptable to make it worthwhile for Mr. A to take the new job.
>
> ___ The chances are 1 in 10 that the company will prove financially sound.
>
> ___ The chances are 3 in 10 that the company will prove financially sound.
>
> ___ The chances are 5 in 10 that the company will prove financially sound.
>
> ___ The chances are 7 in 10 that the company will prove financially sound.
>
> ___ The chances are 9 in 10 that the company will prove financially sound.
>
> ___ Place a check here if you think Mr. A should not take the new job no matter what the probabilities.

These researchers documented an increase in risk taking when people made their choices in groups. When they added together choices from all 12 items, the investigators found that the mean of prediscussion individual decisions was 66.9 for men and 65.6 for women. The mean of the group's consensual decision, however, was 57.5 for men and 56.2 for women, a shift of 9.4 points in the direction of greater risk. This shift also occurred when individual judgments were collected after the group discussion and when the individual postdiscussion measures were delayed two to six weeks (the delayed posttests were collected from male subjects only). Participants in a control condition shifted very little.

The finding that groups seem to make riskier decisions than individuals was promptly dubbed the **risky-shift phenomenon,** and in the decade from 1960 to 1970, researchers discovered that discussion can intensify all sorts of attitudes, beliefs, values, judgments, and perceptions (Myers, 1982). Shifts were reliably demonstrated in many countries around the world, including Canada, the United States, England, France,

---

Risky-shift phenomenon: The tendency for groups to make riskier decisions than individuals would.

Germany, and New Zealand, and with many kinds of group participants (Pruitt, 1971). Although commentators sometimes wondered about the generality and significance of the phenomenon (Smith, 1972), laboratory findings were eventually bolstered by field studies (Lamm & Myers, 1978).

Polarizing Effects of Discussion.   During this research period, however, some investigators hinted at the possibility of the directly opposite process: a cautious shift. For example, when the early risky-shift researchers examined the amount of postdiscussion change revealed on each item of the Choice-Dilemmas Questionnaire, they frequently found that group members consistently advocated a less risky course of action than did individuals on one particular item (Wallach et al., 1962). Intrigued by this anomalous finding, subsequent researchers wrote additional choice dilemmas, and they, too, occasionally found evidence of a cautious shift. Then, in 1969, researchers reported evidence of individuals moving in both directions after a group discussion, suggesting that both cautious and risky shifts were possible (Doise, 1969; Moscovici & Zavalloni, 1969).

Somewhat belatedly, group dynamicists realized that risky shifts after group discussions were a part of a more general process. When people discuss issues in groups, there is a tendency for them to decide on a more extreme course of action than would be suggested by the average of their individual judgments, but the direction of this shift depends on what was initially the dominant point of view. David G. Myers and Helmut Lamm summarized this tendency with their **group polarization hypothesis:** The "average postgroup response will tend to be more extreme in the same direction as the average of the pregroup responses" (Myers & Lamm, 1976, p.603; see also Lamm & Myers, 1978).

Imagine two groups of four individuals whose opinions vary in terms of preference for risk. As Figure 11–4 indicates, when the average choice of the group members before discussion is closer to the risky pole of the continuum than to the cautious pole (as would be the case in a group composed of Persons A, B, C, and D), a risky shift will occur. If, in contrast, the group is composed of Persons C, D, E, and F, a cautious shift will take place, because the pregroup mean of 6.5 falls closer to the cautious pole. This example is, of course, something of an oversimplification, because the shift depends on distance from the psychological rather than the mathematical midpoint of the scale. As Myers and Lamm (1976) note, on choice dilemmas, an initial pregroup mean of 6 or smaller is usually sufficient to produce a risky shift, whereas a mean of 7 or greater is necessary to produce a cautious shift. If the pregroup mean falls between 6 and 7, shifting is unlikely.

What Causes Polarization?   Why do groups intensify individuals' reactions instead of moderating them? Early explanations that suggested that groups feel less responsible for their decisions and are overly influenced by risk-prone leaders gave way to

---

Group polarization hypothesis: An explanation of risky and cautious shifts in judgments following group discussion that assumes that judgments made after group discussion will be more extreme in the same direction as the average of individual judgments made prior to discussion.

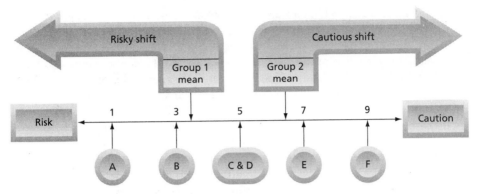

FIGURE 11-4 Why does group discussion polarize opinions? Imagine that Group 1 includes Person A (who chose 1), Person B (who chose 3), and Persons C and D (who both chose 5); the average of pregroup choices would be (1 + 3 + 5 + 5)/4, or 3.5. Because this mean is less than 5, a risky shift would probably occur in Group 1. If, in contrast, Group 2 contains Persons C, D, E, and F, their pregroup average would be (5 + 5 + 7 + 9)/4, or 6.5. Because this mean is closer to the caution pole, a conservative shift would probably occur in this group.

general acceptance of the *value hypothesis*. When individuals discuss their opinions in a group, they shift in the direction that they think is consistent with the values of their group or culture (Clark, 1971; Myers & Lamm, 1975, 1976). If they feel that taking risks is more acceptable than exercising caution, then they will become riskier after a discussion (Weigold & Schlenker, 1991). In France, where people generally like their government but dislike Americans, group discussion improved their attitude toward their government but exacerbated their negative opinions of Americans (Moscovici & Zavalloni, 1969). Similarly, prejudiced people who discussed racial issues with other prejudiced individuals became even more prejudiced. But when only mildly prejudiced persons discussed racial issues with other mildly prejudiced individuals, they became less prejudiced (Myers & Bishop, 1970).

Several processes likely sustain this shift in the direction of the culture's values. As social comparison theory suggests, group members are trying to accomplish two interrelated goals during discussions. First, they are attempting to evaluate the accuracy of their own position on the issue by comparing it with others. Second, they are trying to make a favorable impression within the group. When these two motives combine, the result is a tendency to describe one's own position in somewhat more extreme terms (Goethals & Zanna, 1979; Myers, 1978; Myers & Lamm, 1976; Sanders & Baron, 1977).

Persuasive-arguments theory, in contrast, stresses the information obtained during discussion. If discussion exposes the individual to persuasive arguments that favor Position A, the person will shift in that direction. If the discussion generates more anti-A arguments, however, the individual will shift in that direction (Burnstein &

Persuasive-arguments theory: An explanation of polarization in groups that assumes that group members shift in the direction of the more valued pole because they can generate more arguments favoring the more valued pole.

Vinokur, 1973, 1977; Vinokur & Burnstein, 1974, 1978). Indeed, researchers have found that the more frequently people restate their opinions during a group discussion, the more extreme those attitudes become. This polarization process becomes even stronger when group members repeat each other's arguments and incorporate them in their own publicly stated conclusions (Brauer, Judd, & Gliner, 1995).

Social decision theory offers yet a third explanation. As noted earlier, most groups adopt implicit rules about how they will make decisions about the issues they face (Davis, 1982). Interestingly, groups whose members are initially more risk prone than cautious seem to adopt a "risk-supported wins" scheme. If only one person favors a risky alternative, the group will not adopt it. But if two people throw their support behind a risky alternative, then the group often accepts the recommendation. Conversely, when the majority of the group members lean toward the cautious pole, the group seems to adopt a "caution-supported wins" scheme. If two people express support for a more conservative solution, then the group chooses that alternative (Davis, Kameda, & Stasson, 1992; Laughlin & Earley, 1982; Zuber, Crott, & Werner, 1992).

All three theories have been supported by researchers. For example, a number of studies have shown that polarization occurs when people have been exposed to others' positions but not to their arguments (Blascovich, Ginsburg, & Howe, 1975, 1976; Blascovich, Ginsburg, & Veach, 1975; Goethals & Zanna, 1979; Myers, 1978). These studies suggest that knowledge of group norms is sufficient to generate a shift. However, evidence also supports the persuasive-arguments and social combination theories. Studies indicate, for example, that the direction of polarization in a group depends on the preponderance of arguments for risk and caution possessed by individual members. If individuals can muster more arguments for risk, a risky shift occurs. If their discussion generates more arguments favoring caution, a cautious shift results (Burnstein & Vinokur, 1975; Kaplan & Miller, 1983; Vinokur & Burnstein, 1974, 1978).

The empirical success of these perspectives has prompted several theorists to suggest that the various processes combine to produce polarization (Isenberg, 1986; Kaplan & Miller, 1983). Social comparison theory, with its emphasis on self-presentational attempts to match or exceed the group norm, reflects the operation of normative influence in the group. Persuasive-arguments approaches and social decision theory, in contrast, emphasize informational influence processes (Kaplan & Miller, 1983). As noted in Chapter 7, normative and informational influence generally occur together, so it is likely that social comparison and persuasive argumentation also work together to create polarization.

VICTIMS OF GROUPTHINK

Irving Janis was intrigued by President Kennedy's committee. This group, like so many others, failed to make the best decision it could. The committee's failure, though, was so spectacular that Janis wondered if something more than such common group difficulties as faulty communication and judgmental biases was to blame (Aldag & Fuller, 1993).

Janis pursued this insight in a series of extensive case studies of groups like those described in Table 11–3. After studying these groups and their gross errors of judg-

TABLE 11–3 FIVE FIASCOES IN U.S. HISTORY: WAS GROUPTHINK TO BLAME?

Group	Fiasco
Senior advisers to Admiral H. E. Kimmel, including 20 captains, vice-admirals, and other executive naval officers	In 1941, this group concentrated on Pearl Harbor's importance as a training base to such an extent that the base was left unprotected.
President Truman's policy-making group, including the Joint Chiefs of Staff and members of the National Security Council	When this group authorized the crossing of the 38th parallel during the Korean War, China joined the conflagration.
President Kennedy's ad hoc advisory committee, including the secretaries of state and defense, Joint Chiefs of Staff, and top CIA officers	This group backed an ill-conceived plan to invade Cuba at the Bay of Pigs in 1961.
President Johnson's Tuesday Lunch Group, consisting of White House staff, the chairman of the Joint Chiefs of Staff, the CIA director, and several cabinet members	During lunch meetings held from 1965 to 1968, this group recommended the escalation of the Vietnam War.
President Nixon's White House Staff, including John Dean, John Ehrlichman, Charles E. Colson, and H. R. Haldeman	From 1971 to 1972, this group tried to cover up the activities surrounding the Watergate break-in by destroying evidence and bribing the burglars.

Source: Janis, 1982.

ment, he concluded that they suffered from **groupthink**: a distorted style of thinking that renders group members incapable of making a rational decision. According to Janis (1982, p. 9), groupthink is "a mode of thinking that people engage in when they are deeply involved in a cohesive ingroup, when the members' strivings for unanimity override their motivation to realistically appraise alternative courses of actions." During groupthink, members try so hard to agree with one another that they make mistakes and commit errors that could easily be avoided.

Symptoms of Groupthink

To Janis, groupthink is a disease that infects healthy groups, rendering them inefficient and unproductive. And like the physician who searches for symptoms that signal the onset of the illness, Janis has identified a number of symptoms that occur in group-think situations (Janis, 1972, 1982, 1983, 1985, 1989; Janis & Mann, 1977; Longley & Pruitt, 1980; Wheeler & Janis, 1980).

Interpersonal Pressure.   The struggle for consensus is an essential and unavoidable aspect of life in groups, but in groupthink situations interpersonal pressures make

---

Groupthink: A strong concurrence-seeking tendency that interferes with effective group decision making.

agreeing too easy and disagreeing too difficult. Tolerance for any sort of nonconformity seems virtually nil, and groups may use harsh measures to bring those who dissent into line. In the president's committee, criticism was taboo, and members who broke this norm were pressured to conform.

Self-Censorship.   Much of the unanimity seen in the committee stemmed not from group pressure, but from each individual's self-censorship. Many of the members of the group privately felt uncertain about the plan, but they kept their doubts to themselves. Some even sent private memorandums to the president before or after a meeting, but when the group convened, the doubting Thomases sat in silence. As Schlesinger (1965, p. 225) later wrote:

> In the months after the Bay of Pigs I bitterly reproached myself for having kept so silent during those crucial discussions in the Cabinet Room, though my feelings of guilt were tempered by the knowledge that a course of objection would have accomplished little save to gain me a name as a nuisance. I can only explain my failure to do more than raise a few timid questions by reporting that one's impulse to blow the whistle on this nonsense was simply undone by the circumstances of the discussion.

Mindguards.   Janis coined the term *mindguard* to refer to self-appointed vigilantes who protect group members from information that they think will disrupt the group. The mindguard diverts controversial information away from the group by losing it, forgetting to mention it, or deeming it irrelevant and thus unworthy of the group's attention. Alternatively, the mindguard may take dissenting members aside and pressure them to keep silent. The mindguard may use a variety of strategies to achieve this pressure: requesting the change as a personal favor, pointing out the damage that might be done to the group, or informing the dissenter that in the long run, disagreement would damage his or her position in the group (Uris, 1978). But whatever the method, the overall goal is the same: to contain dissent before it reaches the level of group awareness.

President Kennedy, Rusk, and the president's brother, Robert, all acted as mindguards. Kennedy, for example, withheld memorandums condemning the plan from both Schlesinger and Fulbright. Rusk suppressed information that his own staff had given him. One extreme example of this mindguarding occurred when Rusk, unable to attend a meeting, sent Undersecretary of State Chester Bowles. Although Bowles was "horrified" by the plan under discussion, President Kennedy never gave him the opportunity to speak during the meeting. Bowles followed bureaucratic channels to voice his critical misgivings, but his superior, Rusk, did not transmit those concerns to the committee, and he told Bowles that the plan had been revised. Ironically, Bowles was fired several weeks after the Bay of Pigs defeat.

Apparent Unanimity.   The committee's discussion of the plan was marked by apparent unanimity: The members seemed to agree that the basic plan presented by the CIA was the only solution to the problem and in later discussions appeared to just be "going through the motions" of debate. Retrospective accounts revealed that many of the group's members objected to the plan, but these objections never surfaced during the meetings. Instead, a "curious atmosphere of assumed consensus" (Schlesinger, 1965, p. 250) characterized discussion, as each person wrongly concluded that everyone else liked the plan. As Janis (1972, p. 39) explains, the group members played up "areas of convergence in their thinking, at the expense of fully exploring divergences that might disrupt the apparent unity of the group." Apparently, the members felt that it would be "better to share a pleasant, balmy group atmosphere than be battered in a storm."

Illusions of Invulnerability.   The committee, like many groups, suffered from the illusion of productivity: Members felt that they were performing well, even though they were not. This illusory thinking, although commonplace, becomes so extreme during groupthink that Janis has called it an *illusion of invulnerability*. Feelings of assurance and confidence engulfed the group. The members felt that their plan was virtually infallible and that their committee could not make major errors in judgment. Such feelings of confidence and power may help athletic teams or combat units reach their objectives, but the feeling that all obstacles can be easily overcome through power and good luck tends to cut short clear, analytic thinking in decision-making groups (Silver and Bufanio, 1996).

Illusions of Morality.   Although groups are capable of reaching admirable levels of moral thought, this capability is unrealized during groupthink (McGraw & Bloomfield, 1987). The plan to invade Cuba could unsympathetically be described as an unprovoked sneak attack by a major world power on a virtually defenseless country. But the decision makers, suffering from illusions of morality, seemed to lose their principles in the group's desire to bravely end Castro's regime. Although the means used to defeat the spread of communism may have been considered questionable, the group felt that the ends certainly justified them; the cause of democracy was offered as justification enough for the planned attack. These illusions are commonplace in such groups, particularly those that fail. When Phillip Tetlock reviewed the public statements of politicians who had served on committees that made poor decisions, he found that the faulty decision makers tended to make relatively more positive statements about their own country and causes (Tetlock, 1979).

Biased Perceptions of the Outgroup.   The members of the committee shared an inaccurate and negative opinion of Castro and his political ideology, and they often expressed these biased perceptions of the outgroup during group discussions. Castro was depicted as a weak leader, an evil communist, and a man too stupid to realize that his country was about to be attacked. His ability to maintain an air force was discredited, as was his control over his troops and the citizenry. The group participants' underestimation of their enemy was so pronounced that they sent a force of 1400 men to fight a force of 200,000 and expected an easy success. The group wanted to believe that Castro was an ineffectual leader and military officer, but this oversimplified picture of the dictator turned out to be merely wishful thinking.

Although Tetlock found little evidence of this devaluation of the outgroup in his work, a study of one groupthink crisis, the decision to escalate the Vietnam war, found a consistent theme in American justifications for U.S. intervention. In many of President Lyndon B. Johnson's speeches on the subject, he depicted the North Vietnamese as "savages" who were driven by an irrational desire to subjugate others by military force (Ivie, 1980).

Defective Decision-Making Strategies.   The decisions made in groupthink situations can be described in many different ways, but none of them is complimentary. Words like *fiasco, blunder, failure, error,* and *debacle* are fair descriptors, for groupthink leads to decisions that are so inadequate that they seem to ask disaster to strike.

Janis notes that these fiascoes are a logical outgrowth of the defective decision-making strategies so symptomatic of groupthink. The committee, for example, discussed two extreme alternatives—either endorse the Bay of Pigs invasion plan or abandon Cuba to communism—while ignoring all other potential alternatives. In addition, the group lost sight of its overall objectives as it became caught up in the minor details of the invasion plan, and it failed to develop contingency plans. Lastly, the group actively avoided any information that pointed to limitations in its plans while seeking out facts and opinions that buttressed its initial preferences. The group members didn't make a few small errors. They committed dozens of blunders.

Causes of Groupthink

Did these conformity pressures, illusions, misperceptions, and faulty decision-making strategies cause the group's error? Janis suggests that these faulty processes undoubtedly contributed to the faulty judgments (Janis, 1989), but he labelled them *symptoms* of the problem rather than actual *causes*. The causes of groupthink, which we consider here, include cohesiveness, isolation of the group, leadership style, and stress on the group to reach a good decision (Janis, 1972; Janis & Mann, 1977).

Cohesiveness.   The members of the president's committee felt fortunate to belong to a group that boasted such high morale and esprit de corps. Problems could be handled without too much internal bickering, personality clashes were rare, the atmosphere of each meeting was congenial, and replacements were never needed, because no one ever left the group. However, these benefits of cohesiveness did not offset one fatal consequence of a closely knit group: group pressures so strong that critical thinking degenerated into groupthink.

Of the many factors that contribute to the rise of groupthink, Janis emphasizes cohesiveness above all others. He admits that cohesive groups are not necessarily doomed to be victims of groupthink, but he points out that a "high degree of group cohesiveness is conducive to a high frequency of symptoms of groupthink, which, in turn, are conducive to a high frequency of defects in decision-making" (Janis, 1972, p. 199). Cohesiveness, when it reaches high levels, limits the amount of dissent in the group to the point that internal disagreements—so necessary for good decision making—disappear. In fact, evidence indicates that when someone does manage to disagree with the rest of the group, he or she is likely to be ostracized when group cohesiveness is high (Cartwright, 1968; Schachter, 1951). Certainly, noncohesive groups can also make terrible decisions—"especially if the members are engaging in internal warfare"—but they cannot experience groupthink (Janis, 1982, p. 176). Only in a cohesive group do the members refrain from speaking out against decisions, avoid arguing with others, and strive to maintain friendly, cordial relations at all costs.

Measures of cohesiveness were, of course, never collected for the president's committee. But many signs point to the group's unity. The committee members were all men, and they were in many cases close personal friends. These men, when describing the group in their memoirs, lauded the group, suggesting that attitudes toward the group were exceptionally positive. The members also identified with the group and its goals; all proudly proclaimed their membership in such an elite body. Robert Kennedy's remarks, peppered with frequent use of the words *we* and *us,* betray the magnitude of this identification (quoted in Guthman, 1971, p. 88; italics added):

> It seemed that with John Kennedy leading *us* and with all the talent he had assembled, nothing could stop *us. We* believed that if *we* faced up to the nation's problems and applied bold, new ideas with common sense and hard work, *we* would overcome whatever challenged *us.*

The group also retained all its members for the duration of the decision-making process, testimony to the strength of the forces working to keep members from leaving the group.

Isolation. The president's committee carried out its discussions in secret under the belief that the fewer people who knew of the plan, the better. The committee did not need to report its conclusions to anyone, including Congress, so there was no final review of the decision before putting the plan into action. This isolation also meant that very few outsiders ever came into the group to participate in the discussion; thus, the committee was virtually insulated from criticisms. Therefore, although many experts on military questions and Cuban affairs were available and, if contacted, could have warned the group about the limitations of the plan, the committee closed itself off from these valuable resources.

Leadership. President Kennedy's style of leadership in conducting the problem-solving sessions also contributed to groupthink. By tradition, the committee meetings, like cabinet meetings, were very formal affairs that followed a rigid protocol. The president could completely control the group discussion by raising only certain questions and asking for input from particular conferees. Open, free-wheeling discussion was possible only at the suggestion of the president, but since he tended to follow traditions while also suppressing any dissenting opinions, the group really never got down to the essential issues. His tendency to make his opinion clear at the outset of each meeting also stultified discussion. Also, his procedures for requiring a voice vote by individuals without prior group discussion paralleled quite closely the methods used by Asch (1952) to heighten conformity pressures in discussion groups.

Decisional Stress. Janis notes that our tendency to make use of coping mechanisms such as procrastination or bolstering actually becomes stronger when we must make major decisions. The insecurity of each individual can be minimized if the group quickly chooses a plan of action with little argument or dissension. Then, through collective discussion, the group members can rationalize their choice by exaggerating the positive consequences, minimizing the possibility of negative outcomes, and concentrating on minor details while overlooking larger issues. Naturally, these stress reduction tactics increase the likelihood of groupthink (Callaway, Marriott, & Esser, 1985).

Predicting the Emergence of Groupthink

Janis maintains that group members needn't worry too much if only one of the causes of groupthink is operating in their group. For example, if a group is highly cohesive but its meetings are held in public, are run by an impartial leader, and have low decisional stress, groupthink probably won't occur. If two or more groupthink causes are present, however, the likelihood of groupthink becomes much greater.

This model of groupthink has been supported in a number of case studies and archival analyses (Hensley & Griffin, 1986; Janis, 1985; Manz & Sims, 1982; Moorhead, Ference, & Neck, 1991; Schafer & Crichlow, 1996; Tetlock, 1979; Tetlock, Peterson, McGuire, Chang, & Feld, 1992; 't Hart, 1991). Janis and his colleagues, for example, identified 19 international crises that were initiated or resolved by top-level U.S. leaders. Next, using an elaborate content analysis system, they calculated the number of symptoms evidenced by each group. As predicted, the higher the number of symptoms, the more unfavorable the outcome of the group's deliberations ($r = .62$) (Herek, Janis, & Huth, 1987, 1989; Welch, 1989).

Experimental evidence, although limited, also supports the model (Callaway & Esser, 1984; Moorhead, 1982; Moorhead & Montanari, 1986; Neck & Moorhead, 1995; Street, 1997). In one study, John A. Courtright (1978) manipulated both cohesiveness in the group and the degree to which the group's discussion was constrained. He increased cohesiveness in some groups by giving members more time to interact with one another before considering the issue and by telling them that they would be extremely compatible. To manipulate decisional stress, he told groups in the *limiting condition* that little time was left for discussion and that "the best solutions usually come when one good idea cooperatively evolves from a small number of initial ideas" (p. 233). Courtright told groups in the *freeing condition* that sufficient time was available to fully discuss the issue and that "the best solutions usually come from vigorous competition among a large number of incompatible ideas" (p. 233). A *control condition* received no special instructions. Courtright found that groups in the freeing condition made better decisions when they were cohesive, but that cohesive groups in the limiting condition tended to disagree less with one another (see Figure 11–5).

Researchers have also clarified *why* cohesion may inhibit group performance. Janis believes that conformity pressures are so great in cohesive groups that members cannot engage in critical debate, and cohesion also increases members' desire to protect the group from threats. As a social identity approach suggests, members of cohesive groups are overly concerned with projecting a positive image of their group (and themselves) to others (Turner, Pratkanis, Probasco, & Leve, 1992). However, not all forms of cohesiveness are detrimental. Groups that derived their cohesiveness from members' com-

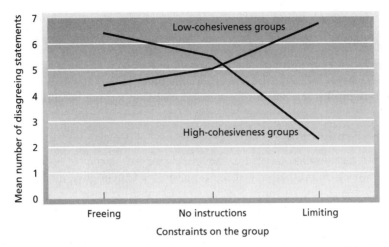

FIGURE 11-5   Is disagreement the rule or the exception in cohesive groups? In this study, cohesive group members disagreed the most in the freeing condition, less in the control (no-instruction) condition, and least in the limiting condition—the very condition that, theoretically, should have suffered from groupthink. Furthermore, these relationships tended to reverse in the low-cohesiveness condition, although the overall differences were not as pronounced.

(*Source:* Courtright, 1978.)

mitment to the task rather than from their friendship with other group members displayed significantly fewer symptoms of groupthink, whereas groups that were interpersonally cohesive displayed more symptoms (Bernthal & Insko, 1993). Researchers also note that cohesion even increases decision-making effectiveness in many cases. When researchers combined the results of seven different studies involving over 1000 subjects in a meta-analysis, they found that cohesive groups made poorer decisions—but only when other potential causes of groupthink were present in the group. If these other causes of groupthink, such as decisional stress or isolation, were absent, then cohesive groups tended to make better decisions (Mullen, Anthony, Salas, & Driskell, 1994).

Evidence also suggests that the leader's style may play a larger role in creating groupthink than Janis initially proposed (Chen, Lawson, Gordon, & McIntosh, 1996; Flowers, 1977; Hodson & Sorrentino, 1997; Moorhead, 1982). In one project, group members discussed evidence pertaining to a civil trial. Researchers told some of the groups' assigned leaders to adopt a *closed style* of leadership: They were to announce their opinions on the case prior to discussion. *Open style* leaders were told to withhold their own opinions until later in the discussion. Groups led by a leader who adopted a closed style were more biased in their judgments, particularly when many of the group members had a high need for certainty (Hodson & Sorrentino, 1997). Other evidence, however, suggests that leaders who are highly directive improve their group's decisions, provided that they limit their control to the group's decisional processes rather than the group's decisional outcomes (Peterson, 1997).

These findings provide some support for the adequacy of Janis's predictions, but several qualifications apply. Janis's distinction between symptoms and causes has not been confirmed empirically (Aldag & Fuller, 1993; Longley & Pruitt, 1980; McCauley, 1989; Moorhead & Montanari, 1986; Neck & Moorhead, 1992, 1995; Park, 1990; Tetlock et al., 1992). Janis also overlooks some factors that may cause faulty decisions, such as the group's stage of development, and he overemphasizes others (e.g., cohesiveness). His model, however, highlights how the information-processing limitations of groups can prevent them from reaching their full potential.

Preventing Groupthink

For 13 days in October 1962, the world swayed on the brink of nuclear holocaust. The Soviet Union, perhaps at the request of a Cuban government frightened by the misguided Bay of Pigs invasion, was rapidly constructing a missile base in Cuba. To resolve this crisis, President Kennedy once again called together his top advisers to form the Executive Committee of the National Security Council. Though it was somewhat larger than the original committee, many of the same individuals attended its meetings. For five days, these men considered the issues, debated possible solutions, and disagreed over strategies. They finally recommended a plan that involved a naval blockade of all Cuban ports. The strategy worked and the Russians agreed to dismantle the launching sites.

Why did the new executive committee succeed where the Bay of Pigs committee failed? The same people meeting in the same room and guided by the same leader worked equally hard under similar pressures. Both crises occurred in the same area of the world, involved the same foreign powers, and could have led to equally serious consequences. Yet, the executive committee worked with admirable precision and effectiveness. Members thoroughly analyzed a wide range of alternative courses of action, deliberately considered and then reconsidered the potential effects of their actions, consulted experts, and made detailed contingency plans in case the blockade failed to stop the Russians. This group, Janis (1982) believes, avoided groupthink by limiting a premature seeking of concurrence, correcting group members' misperceptions, and utilizing effective decision techniques.

Limiting Premature Seeking of Concurrence.   Kennedy did not take his Bay of Pigs failure lightly. In the months following the defeat, he explored and corrected the causes of his group's poor decision. As a result, his new group was prepared to deal with the Cuban missile crisis. No norm of conformity was given the slightest opportunity to develop, and each person in the group was able to express doubts and worries openly. Rules of discussion were suspended, agendas were avoided, and new ideas were welcomed. Although pressures to conform surfaced from time to time during the discussion, the members felt so comfortable in their role as skeptical critical thinkers that they were able to resist the temptation to go along with the consensus. In fact, the group never did reach 100% agreement on the decision to turn back Soviet ships.

The atmosphere of open inquiry can be credited to changes designed and implemented by Kennedy. Essentially, he dropped his closed style of leadership to become an open leader as he (1) carefully refused to state his personal beliefs at the beginning of the session, instead waiting until others had let their views be known; (2) required a full, unbiased discussion of the pros and cons of each possible course of action; (3) convinced his subordinates that he would welcome healthy criticism and condemn "yea-saying"; (4) arranged for the group to meet without him on several occasions; and (5) encouraged specific members of the group to take the role of dissenter, or "devil's advocate," during the group discussions.

Kennedy also arranged for this committee to meet separately in two subgroups. The committee members had practiced this approach on other policy issue decisions, and they were satisfied that it yielded many benefits: Arbitrary agreement with the views of the other subgroup was impossible, the lower level staff members felt more at ease expressing their viewpoints in the smaller meetings, and the presence of two coalitions in the subsequent combined meetings virtually guaranteed a spirited debate (Wheeler & Janis, 1980).

Correcting Misperceptions and Biases. Janis's image of people as reluctant decision makers does not quite match the executive committee members. The participants fully realized that *some* course of action had to be taken, and they resigned themselves to their difficult task. Their decisional conflict was fanned by doubts and worries over questions that they could not answer, and at times they must have been tempted to ease their discomfort by overestimating American superiority, belittling the Russians, and denying the magnitude of the dangers. Yet, through vigilant information processing, they succeeded in avoiding these misperceptions, illusions, and errors.

No trace of the air of confidence and superiority that permeated the planning sessions of the Bay of Pigs invasion was in evidence during the executive committee meetings. The men knew that they and their decision were imperfect and that wishful thinking would not improve the situation. President Kennedy repeatedly told the group that there was no room for error, miscalculation, or oversight in their plans, and at every meeting the members openly admitted the tremendous risks and dangers involved in taking coercive steps against the Russians. Each solution was assumed to be flawed, and even when the blockade had been painstakingly arranged, the members developed contingency plans in case it failed.

Members also admitted their personal inadequacies and ignorance and therefore willingly consulted experts who were not members of the group. No group member's statements were taken as fact until independently verified, and the ideas of younger, low-level staff members were solicited at each discussion. Participants also discussed the group's activities with their own staffs and entered each meeting armed with the misgivings and criticisms of these unbiased outsiders.

Lastly, instead of assuming that the Russians' actions justified any response (including full-scale invasion of Cuba), the committee discussed the ethics of the situation and the proposed solutions. For example, although some members felt that the Russians had left themselves open to any violent response the Americans deemed appropriate, the majority argued that a final course of action had to be consistent with "America's humanitarian heritage and ideals" (Janis, 1972, p. 157). Illusions of morality and invulnerability were successfully minimized along with biased perceptions of the outgroup.

Using Effective Decision Techniques. The executive committee is not an example of an effective decision-making body simply because its solution to the missile crisis worked. Rather, just as the decision methods used by the Bay of Pigs committee ensured their failure, the executive committee's use of effective, time-proven decision-making techniques increased its chances of success. Many initially favored military intervention, but the majority of the group members insisted that other alternatives be explored. This demand led to an expanded search for alternatives, and soon the following list emerged:

1. Do nothing.
2. Exert pressure on the Soviet Union through the United Nations.
3. Arrange a summit meeting between the two nations' leaders.
4. Secretly negotiate with Castro.
5. Initiate a low-level naval action involving a blockade of Cuban ports.
6. Bombard the sites with small pellets, rendering the missiles inoperable.
7. Launch an air strike against the sites with advance warning to reduce loss of life.
8. Launch an air strike without advance warning.
9. Carry out a series of air attacks against all Cuban military installations.
10. Invade Cuba.

Once this list was complete, the men focused on each course of action before moving on to the next. They considered the pros and cons, fleshed out unanticipated drawbacks, and estimated the likelihood of success. During this process, outside experts were consulted to give the members a better handle on the problem, and contingency plans were briefly explored. Even those alternatives that had initially been rejected were resurrected and discussed, and the group invested considerable effort in trying to find any overlooked detail. When a consensus on the blockade plan finally developed, the group went back over this alternative, reconsidered its problematic aspects, and meticulously reviewed the steps required to implement it. Messages were sent to the Russians, military strategies were worked out to prevent any slip-ups that would escalate the conflict, and a graded series of actions was developed to be undertaken should the blockade fail. Allies were contacted and told of the U.S. intentions, the legal basis of the intervention was established by arranging for a hemisphere blockade sanctioned by the Organization of American States, and African countries with airports that could have been used by Russia to circumvent the naval blockade were warned not to cooperate. To quote Robert Kennedy, "Nothing, whether a weighty matter or a small detail, was overlooked" (1969, p. 60).

SUMMARY

Why make decisions in groups? A *collective information-processing model* assumes that groups gather information and process that information to generate decisions and judgments.

1. A group's *collective memory* includes the combined memories of all individual memories. Mental models, cross-cuing, and *transactive memory systems* all work to enhance group memory, although research suggests that collective inhibition often occurs when groups try to remember information collectively.

2. Groups process information in four or more stages appearing consistently in many groups.
   - Orientation stage: The group identifies the problem to be solved and plans the process to be used in reaching the decision.

- Discussion stage: The group gathers information about the situation, identifies and weighs options, and tests its assumptions.
- Decision stage: The group relies on an implicit or explicit *social decision scheme* to combine individual preferences into a collective decision. Common schemes include delegating, averaging inputs, voting with various proportions needed for a decision, and consensus.
- Implementation stage: The group carries out the decision and assesses its impact. Members are more likely to implement decisions when they were actively involved in the decision-making process.

What problems undermine the effectiveness of decision-making groups?

1. Groups spend too much of their discussion time examining shared information—details that two or more of the group members know in common—rather than unshared information. Oversampling shared information leads to poorer decisions when a *hidden profile* would be revealed by considering the unshared information more closely.
2. Oversampling of shared information increases when tasks have no demonstrably correct solution and when group leaders do not actively draw out unshared information.
3. The usefulness of group discussion is limited, in part, by members' inability to express themselves clearly and their limited listening skills. Groups sometimes use discussion to avoid making decisions.
4. Judgment errors that cause people to overlook important information and overutilize unimportant information are often exacerbated in groups. These errors occur more frequently when group members are cognitively busy.

Why do groups make riskier decisions than individuals?

1. Common sense suggests that groups are more cautious than individuals, but early studies carried out using the Choice-Dilemmas Questionnaire found that group discussion generates a shift in the direction of the more risky alternative (the *risky-shift phenomenon*).
2. When researchers later found evidence of cautious shifts as well as risky ones, they concluded that the responses of groups tend to be more extreme than individual members' responses (the *group polarization hypothesis*).
3. Polarization is sustained by the desire to evaluate one's own opinions by comparing them to others' (social comparison theory), by exposure to other members' pro-risk or pro-caution arguments (*persuasive-arguments theory*), and by groups' implicit reliance on a "risk-supported wins" social decision scheme.

What is groupthink, and how can it be prevented?

1. Janis argues that fiascoes and blunders such as the decision to invade Cuba at the Bay of Pigs occur when group members strive for solidarity and cohesiveness to such an extent that any questions or topics that could lead to disputes are avoided. Janis calls this process *groupthink*.
2. Groupthink has multiple symptoms, including interpersonal pressure, self-censorship, mindguards, apparent unanimity, illusions of invulnerability, illusions of morality, biased perceptions of the outgroup, and defective decision-making strategies.

3. Janis identifies four major causes of groupthink: cohesiveness, isolation, closed leadership, and decisional stress.

4. Researchers have confirmed many of Janis's hypotheses regarding decision making in groups, particularly those dealing with cohesiveness and leadership style.

5. Janis notes that groups need not sacrifice cohesiveness to avoid the pitfall of groupthink. Rather, he recommends limiting premature seeking of concurrence, correcting misperceptions and errors, and improving the group's decisional methods.

FOR MORE INFORMATION

"The Emerging Conceptualization of Groups as Information Processors," by Verlin B. Hinsz, R. Scott Tindale, and David A. Vollrath (1997), is a wide-ranging synthesis of how such cognitive mechanisms as attention, encoding, storage, retrieval, processing, and learning shape group decisions.

Group Performance, by James H. Davis (1969), is a brief but seminal analysis of decision making in groups, with chapters examining social facilitation, group tasks, social transition schemes, composition, and communication networks.

Groupthink: Psychological Studies of Policy Decisions and Fiascos, by Irving Janis (1982), takes a sobering look at the pitfalls of group decision making, while recommending many ways to avoid groupthink. Excellent reading for anyone who regularly takes part in groups that make important decisions. *Crucial Decisions,* also written by Janis (1989), provides a more general analysis of decision making.

Small Group Decision Making, by Donald G. Ellis and B. Aubrey Fisher (4th ed, 1994), provides a detailed analysis of the communication processes that shape group decisions.

Understanding Group Behavior, edited by Erich H. Witte and James H. Davis (1996), offers readers an insider's look into the cognitive mechanisms that operate in decision-making and performing groups. The analyses are both theoretically sophisticated and intellectually challenging.

What's Social About Social Cognition? Research on Socially Shared Cognition in Small Groups, edited by Judith L. Nye and Aaron M. Brower (1996), offers a dozen chapters that explore the cognitive foundations of group behavior, including information sharing, transactive memory, heuristic-based biases in judgments, and categorization processes.

ACTIVITY 11–1 MAKING DECISIONS IN GROUPS

The following questions measure your ideas concerning people and events. Answer all of the items, even if you must guess. Then, join with others in a group and discuss the issues as a group. Reach a unanimous opinion on each.

1. A panel of psychologists has interviewed and administered personality tests to 30 engineers and 70 lawyers, all successful in their respective fields. The psychologists have written a description for each of these individuals. The one that follows was chosen at random from the 100 available descriptions. [Jack is a 45-year-old man. He is married and has four children. He is generally conservative, careful, and ambitious. He shows little interest in political and social issues and spends much of his free time on his many hobbies, which include home carpentry, sailing, and mathematical puzzles.] The chances that Jack is an engineer are
   a. less than 2 out of 10
   b. between 2 and 4 out of 10
   c. 50/50: 4 to 6 out of 10
   d. between 6 and 8 out of 10
   e. greater than 8 out of 10

2. A roulette wheel can indicate either black (B) or red (R). After the sequence B R B B B B, the next outcome will probably be
   a. B
   b. R
   c. Both are equally likely.

3. Linda is 31 years old, single, outspoken, and very bright. She majored in philosophy. As a student, she was deeply concerned with issues of discrimination and social injustice and also participated in antinuclear demonstrations. Check the most likely alternative.
   a. Linda is a bank teller.
   b. Linda is a bank teller and is active in the feminist movement.

4. How likely is it that a person in the United States will die from the following causes? Rank them from most prevalent to least prevalent (with 1 being the most prevalent and 18 the least).

____ poisoning by vitamins	____ suicide
____ fireworks accidents	____ breast cancer
____ venomous bite or sting	____ auto accident
____ flood	____ lung cancer
____ pregnancy/birth complications	____ stomach cancer
____ infectious hepatitis	____ accident (all types)
____ appendicitis	____ stroke
____ fire	____ cancer (all types)
____ drowning	____ heart disease

Score your answers by comparing your individual answers to your group's answers. Did you perform better than your group? What methods did your group use to solve the problems?

ACTIVITY 11–2 OBSERVE A GROUP DECISION

Find and observe a group that must make a decision. You might consider a televised city council meeting, a public committee meeting discussing some issue facing the community, a business group discussing a problem or strategy, a charitable board or foundation in its monthly meeting, or a university committee. Take notes on the group, and then answer the following questions:

1. What issues did the group members examine during the meeting? Did the group preface its discussion with an analysis of the procedures it would use to reach its decision?
2. Did the group use any methods to structure its discussion, such as an agenda, rules of order, a chairperson or leader, or voting procedures?
3. What procedures did the group use to reach its decision? Did it vote? Did it discuss matters to consensus?
4. Did the group become polarized as it discussed the problem? In other words, did the group rally rapidly behind a solution once several of the group members expressed their views publicly?
5. Were any of the symptoms of groupthink present in the group?
6. Were any of the causes of groupthink (identified by Janis) present in the group (e.g., cohesiveness, time pressure, stronger leader)? Could these factors have interfered with the group's decision-making capabilities.
7. In your opinion, was this group effective?

12

Leadership

Leaders are as universal as the groups they lead, but their ubiquity has not robbed them of their mystery. Leadership binds the leader to the led, the coach to the team, the executive to the staff, and the president to the citizenry in an interface that, in many cases, fundamentally shapes the group's future. If asked, "What one thing would you change to turn an inept group into a productive one?" most people would answer, "the leader."

- What is leadership?
- Who will lead?
- Why do some leaders succeed and others fail?

CONTENTS

Grace Pastiak of Tellabs, Inc.: Transforming People and Groups Through Leadership

THE NATURE OF LEADERSHIP

Questions About Leadership

Leadership: A Conceptual Definition

Leadership: A Behavioral Definition

LEADERSHIP EMERGENCE

Personal Qualities of Leaders

Who Will Lead? A Cognitive Explanation

LEADER EFFECTIVENESS

Fiedler's Contingency Model

"Style" Theories

Participation Theories

Leader-Member Exchange Theory

Transformational Leadership

Women and Men as Leaders

What Is the Key to Leadership?

SUMMARY

FOR MORE INFORMATION

ACTIVITIES

Grace Pastiak of Tellabs, Inc.: Transforming People and Groups Through Leadership

Tellabs, Inc., since opening its doors in 1975, has grown into a global supplier of high-end technology systems for telephone companies, long-distance carriers, wireless service providers, and cable operators. Their sales reached over $1.2 billion last year, up 38.5% from the previous year's record.

Tellabs traces its success back to its excellent employees and their equally excellent leaders. Consider, for example, Grace Pastiak. Pastiak has been with Tellabs for 20 years, first as a manager, then as Director of Manufacturing, and more recently as Director of Network Systems. Each position has brought Pastiak more work and responsibility, but also new opportunities to do what she does best: to lead people. She trains employees, helping them develop the skills they need for their work. She gathers information she needs to make decisions and set priorities, develops strategies for reaching goals, and implements solutions. She helps people work together effectively by dealing with conflicts, identifying shared and unshared responsibilities, and facilitating team-based procedures. Pastiak does not build the equipment Tellabs sells, but instead creates and manages the groups that build Tellabs's products.

Pastiak's successes, and the successes of others like her, raise many questions about the complicated and intricate interpersonal process we call leadership. First, what did Pastiak do to motivate her employees, ensure the smooth functioning of her teams, and solve problems in production? What do leaders do? Second, why did executives at Tellabs choose Pastiak to be a leader? Was she just the next in line for promotion, or did she emerge as the leader because of her special characteristics? And third, why did she succeed where others might have failed?

THE NATURE OF LEADERSHIP

People have probably been puzzling over leadership since the first cave dweller told the rest of the group, "We're doing this all wrong. Let's get organized." Leadership is an inevitable element of life in groups, a necessary prerequisite for coordinating the behavior of group members in pursuit of common goals. Indeed, leadership may be one of the few universals of human behavior (Mann, 1980). Ancient epics, such as *Beowolf, Song of Roland,* and the *Odyssey,* are filled with the exploits of leaders of small bands of adventurers. Egyptian hieroglyphics written 5000 years ago include the terms *leader* and *leadership* (Bass, 1990). Anthropological evidence indicates that "there are no known societies without leadership in at least some aspects of their social life" (Lewis, 1974, p. 4). But what is leadership?

Questions About Leadership

The political scientist James McGregor Burns (1978, p. 2) asserts that leadership is "one of the most observed and least understood phenomena on earth." Other experts have also expressed dismay at the prevalence of misunderstanding about leadership, complaining, for example, that most people "don't have the faintest concept of what leadership is all about" (Bennis, 1975, p. 1), that "the nature of leadership in our society is very imperfectly understood," and that the "many public statements about it are utter nonsense" (Gardner, 1965, pp. 3, 12). Scholars and laypeople are constantly offering prescriptive suggestions to leaders, but they often base their recommendations on some questionable assumptions (Bass, 1990; Northouse, 1997; Yukl, 1994).

Is Leadership Power?   Many people, including some prominent political leaders, assume that good leaders are capable of manipulating, controlling, and forcing their followers into obedience. Hitler, for example, defined leadership as the ability to move the masses, whether through persuasion or violence, and Ho Chi Minh once said that a good leader must learn to mold, shape, and change the people just as a woodworker must learn to use wood (see Table 12–1). But people who use domination and coercion

TABLE 12-1   POLITICAL EXPERTS' OPINIONS ON THE NATURE OF LEADERSHIP

Expert	Commentary
Benjamin Disraeli	"I must follow the people. Am I not their leader?"
Dwight D. Eisenhower	"Leadership is the ability to decide what is to be done, and then to get others to want to do it."
Adolf Hitler	"To be a leader means to be able to move masses."
John F. Kennedy	"I want to be a President who is a Chief Executive in every sense of the word—who responds to a problem, not by hoping his subordinates will act, but by directing them to act."
Ho Chi Minh	"To use people is like using wood. A skilled worker can make use of all kinds of wood, whether it is big or small, straight or curved."
Richard M. Nixon	A leader "implants noble ideals and principles with practical accomplishments."
Vance Packard	"Leadership appears to be the art of getting others to want to do something you are convinced should be done."
H. Ross Perot	"People cannot be managed. Inventories can be managed, but people must be led."
Theodore Roosevelt	"The best executive is the one who has the sense enough to pick good men to do what he wants done, and self-restraint enough to keep from meddling with them while they do it."
Margaret Thatcher	"Being powerful is like being a lady. If you have to tell people you are, you aren't."
Harry S Truman	"A leader is a man who has the ability to get other people to do what they don't want to do, and like it."
Lao Tzu	"A leader is best when people barely know that he exists, not so good when people acclaim him, worst when they despise him."

to influence others—whether they are kings, presidents, bosses, or managers—are not leaders. The term *leader* should be reserved for those who act in the best interests of a group with the consent of that group. Leadership is a form of power, but power *with* people rather than *over* people—a reciprocal relationship between the leader and the led. Nor do leaders hoard their power. A leader may control the sources of power within the group, but he or she distributes this power to other members (Hollander & Offermann, 1990; Sankowsky, 1995).

Are Leaders Born or Made?   Henry Ford, the founder of a major automotive empire, once remarked that asking "Who ought to be boss?" is like asking "Who ought to be the tenor in the quartet?" Obviously, the man who can sing tenor. Ford was suggesting that the ability to lead stems from a collection of natural qualities within the person. Leadership, he believed, was a talent that existed in some people but not in others. Because this talent derives from inborn characteristics, the "born follower" cannot develop this skill. Ford's view of leadership is widely shared, for many people assume that people with the "right stuff" rise to positions of authority. But studies of leadership emergence and effectiveness, which we will examine later in this chapter, suggest that leadership is as much an acquired skill as an inborn personal attribute. Certain personality variables are associated with effective leadership, but for the most part, leadership "is an achievement, not a birthright or happy accident of heredity" (Cribbin, 1972, p. 14).

Do Leaders Make a Difference?   What would have happened if Pastiak had taken a job with IBM or NYNEX instead of Tellabs? Would the company be as successful today? Studies suggest that people attribute too much influence to leaders. When experts analyze the causes of a company's success, they tend to concentrate on the cleverness of the corporate leaders rather than favorable markets or changes in the economy (Meindl, 1995; Meindl, Ehrlich, & Dukerich, 1985; Shamir, 1992). When a team fails, those in charge often decide to replace the group's leaders, for they assume that a different leader could have rescued the failing team (Gamson & Scotch, 1964). When people give all the credit for a group's success to the leader or blame him or her for a failure, they are overlooking the contributions of the other group members (Meindl et al., 1985). Leaders *do* influence their groups. Studies of leaders in all kinds of group situations— flight crews, politics, schools, military units, and religious groups—all suggest that some groups prosper when guided by good leaders (Bass, 1990; Cannella & Rowe, 1995). But few leaders deserve all the blame for their group's failures, and fewer still are heros who can fairly claim the lion's share of their group's achievements.

Do All Groups Have Leaders?   Not every group has a leader, but when tasks become complicated and the need for coordination grows, groups usually turn to leaders for guidance. As John K. Hemphill (1950) explains, larger groups encounter problems of coordination, administration, and communication that can be ameliorated by a leader. Therefore, members of large groups are more open to attempts by possible candidates to gain leadership. When Hemphill (1950) tested this hypothesis by comparing the behaviors of large-group leaders with those of small-group leaders, he found evidence of a greater reliance in the larger groups on the leader to make rules clear, keep members informed, and make group decisions. Hemphill (1961) also suggests that leaders appear in groups when (1) members feel that success on the group task is within their reach, (2) the rewards for success are valued, (3) the task requires group rather than individual effort, and (4) an individual with previous experience in the leadership role is present in the group. A group that is facing a stressful situation—such as a potential failure or danger—is also likely to embrace a leader's guidance (Hamblin, 1958; Helmreich & Collins, 1967; Moreland, 1997; Mulder & Stemerding, 1963; Pillai, 1996).

Do Followers Resist Leaders?   Some laypersons and experts suggest that groups function best without leaders—that reliance on a central authority figure weakens the group and robs members of their self-reliance. Some, too, note that groups chafe under the control of a leader, for they begrudge the authority and power of the leader (Gemmill, 1986; Heifetz, 1994). Yet, most people prefer to be led rather than be leaderless. Even when people set out to make a group a leaderless one, an informal leadership hierarchy eventually develops (see Chapter 5). Group members are usually more satisfied and productive when their groups have leaders (Berkowitz, 1953). Group members often complain about the quality of their leaders, but they seek out better ones rather than avoiding them altogether (Hogan, Curphy, & Hogan, 1994). Most people don't just accept the need for a leader, but appreciate the contribution the leader makes to the group and its outcomes (Friedman & Saul, 1991; Stewart & Manz, 1995).

Leadership: A Conceptual Definition

Pointing out what leadership is not is easier than pointing out what it is. Leadership is not the power to coerce others, an inborn trait, or a mysterious capacity to heal sick groups. But what is leadership? As Bernard Bass (1990, p. 11) writes, "There are as many different definitions of leadership as there are persons who have attempted to define it" (Barker, 1997).

Most definers agree, however, that **leadership** is a specialized form of social interaction: a reciprocal, transactional, and sometimes transformational process in which cooperating individuals are permitted to influence and motivate others to promote the attainment of group and individual goals. This definition is cumbersome, but it emphasizes several features noted by many previous definers.

1. Leadership is a *reciprocal* process involving the leader, the followers, and the group situation. The leader does not just influence the group members; rather,

---

Leadership: A reciprocal, transactional, and sometimes transformational process in which cooperating individuals are permitted to influence and motivate others to promote the attainment of group and individual goals.

the leader-follower relationship is mutual. An interactional view assumes that leadership cannot be understood independently of followership: the skills and qualities displayed by nonleaders (Barrow, 1977; Hollander, 1985, 1993; Hollander & Offermann, 1990).

2. Leadership is a *transactional,* social exchange process. Leaders and members work together, exchanging their time, energies, and skills to increase their joint rewards (Graen & Uhl-Bien, 1991; Hollander & Julian, 1969; Pigors, 1935).

3. Leadership is often a *transformational* process. The transformational leader heightens group members' motivation, confidence, and satisfaction by uniting members and changing their beliefs, values, and needs (Bass, 1985a, 1985b, 1997; Bass, Avolio, & Goldheim, 1987).

4. Leadership is a *cooperative* process of legitimate influence rather than sheer power (Grimes, 1978). In a small group, for example, the individual who influences others the most is often designated the leader (Hollander, 1985). The right to lead is, in most instances, voluntarily conferred on the leader by some or all members of the group (Kochan, Schmidt, & DeCotiis, 1975).

5. Leadership is an adaptive, *goal-seeking* process, for it organizes and motivates group members' attempts to attain personal and group goals (Katz & Kahn, 1978).

Pastiak, by this definition, is clearly a leader. She directs the efforts of her subordinates, but she always responds to their concerns. Indeed, she created a feedback system through which employees could give suggestions, which, when implemented, identified some important money-saving changes in production processes. She also provides help to her subordinates in exchange for their time and energy. As she explains, "Whenever someone has asked me for assistance, I've always tried to be of service" (quoted in Glasser & Smalley, 1995, p. 259). She also transforms her work groups into teams where members enjoy their work and their interactions. Clearly, Pastiak believes that "the real value of a manager at any level comes in bringing the best out of everybody on the team" (quoted in Glasser & Smalley, 1995, p. 52). For Pastiak, leadership is reciprocal, transactional, transformational, cooperative, and efficient.

Leadership: A Behavioral Definition

Pastiak was hired to lead the production unit at Tellabs, and the sign on her door read "Director." But what did Pastiak *do* as leader? What behaviors define the role of leader?

A work group demands different things of a leader than does a discussion group or a recreational group, but some similarities in leadership behavior emerge in a wide variety of groups. In the Ohio State University Leadership Studies, for example, investigators first developed a list of nine types of behavior observed in military and organizational leaders—behaviors that included initiating new practices, interacting informally with subordinates, representing the group, and integrating group action (Hemphill, 1950). They then asked members of various groups to indicate how many of these behaviors their leaders displayed. They then used a statistical technique known as factor analysis to eliminate overlapping and irrelevant behaviors, and they narrowed down the original nine types of behaviors to four: consideration, initiating structure, production emphasis, and sensitivity (Halpin & Winer, 1952). Of these four factors, the first two were the most important, accounting for over 80% of the variation in followers' ratings of their leaders.

Other researchers using many different procedures, studying many different types of groups, and working in various countries around the world have confirmed Ohio State's basic findings. Although the labels vary—supportive versus work-facilitative (Bowers & Seashore, 1966), employee-centered versus production-centered (Likert, 1967), relations-skilled versus administratively skilled (Mann, 1965), group maintenance versus goal achievement (Cartwright & Zander, 1968), and maintenance versus performance (Misumi, 1995)—two basic clusters usually emerge. One cluster pertains to interpersonal relations within the group (see Table 12–2). These **relationship behaviors** address the feelings, attitudes, and satisfactions of the members of the group and so correspond to the interpersonal, socioemotional side of the group (see Chapter 5). Even in groups that exist to complete tasks or solve problems, leaders must often take steps to meet the members' personal needs. Boosting morale, increasing cohesiveness, reducing interpersonal conflict, establishing rapport, and illustrating one's concern and consideration for group members all go into relationship leadership (Lord, 1977).

TABLE 12–2   LEADERSHIP BEHAVIOR: TASKS AND RELATIONSHIPS

Conceptual Labels	Definition	Sample Behaviors
Relationship Leadership		
-Relationship oriented -Socioemotional -Supportive -Employee centered -Relations-skilled -Group maintenance	Involves actions that maintain positive interpersonal relations in the group; entails friendliness, mutual trust, openness, and willingness to explain decisions	-Listens to group members -Is easy to understand -Is friendly and approachable -Treats group members as equals -Is willing to make changes
Task Leadership		
-Task oriented -Goal oriented -Work-faciliative -Production centered -Administratively skilled -Goal achievement	Involves actions that promote task completion; entails regulating behavior, monitoring communication, and reducing goal ambiguity	-Assigns tasks to members -Makes attitudes clear to the group -Is critical of poor work -Sees to it that the group is working to capacity -Coordinates activity

Relationship behaviors: Actions performed by group members or the group leader that improve interpersonal relations within the group; include consideration, supportiveness, and socioemotionality.

The second cluster of leadership behaviors is more goal oriented. These **task behaviors** pertain to the problem at hand rather than the personal satisfactions of the group members. Leaders must sustain their group, but they must also guide the group in the direction of successful goal attainment. Defining problems for the group, establishing communication networks, providing evaluative feedback, planning, motivating action, coordinating members' actions, and facilitating goal attainment by proposing solutions and removing barriers are critically important aspects of task leadership (Lord, 1977).

The Ohio State researchers built these two basic dimensions into their *Leader Behavior Description Questionnaire,* or *LBDQ* (Kerr, Schriesheim, Murphy, & Stogdill, 1974; Schriesheim & Eisenbach, 1995). Group members complete this measure by rating their leader on items like those presented in the right-hand column of Table 12–2. The totals from the two separate subscales index the two dimensions of leadership. These two elements of leadership also emerge when leaders talk about their work. As Pastiak explains, much of her work requires establishing rapport with her subordinates: She listens to them, deals with conflicts, and is concerned about their well-being and morale. But she is also task oriented. As she remarks, "My style has always been, 'We *are* going to do this. Now, if you have a better idea, I'm willing to listen. But if you don't, move over. Because I've got to get this done' " (quoted in Glasser & Smalley, 1995, p. 16). Indeed, her co-workers have two nicknames for Pastiak: Amazing Grace and Iron Butterfly.

Although Pastiak has displayed both task and relationship behaviors as a Tellabs leader, some leaders lean toward one or the other type of leadership. Robert Bales (1958), for example, called the leader who concentrates most of his or her efforts on the group's work the *task specialist.* The *socioemotional specialist,* in contrast, is more concerned with personal relations in the group. Different situations also require more or less of each type of leadership. As Figure 12–1 suggests, when a group is composed of competent individuals with a great need for independence, a sense of professional identity, and a disdain for the rewards that their work supervisors can offer, both relationship and task leadership are neutralized. In contrast, task leadership only becomes unnecessary when the group members can work on problems that are unambiguous, routine, and can clearly be evaluated. Lastly, formal, inflexible, and unambiguous group structures tend to neutralize task-oriented leadership, whereas group cohesiveness, low reward power, and spatial distance make both types of leadership unnecessary. These aspects of the situation serve as **leadership substitutes:** They "negate the leader's ability to either improve or impair subordinate satisfaction and performance" (Kerr & Jermier, 1978, p. 377). When a number of these substitutes are in evidence in a situation, leadership is both unnecessary and unlikely (Childers, Dubinsky, & Gencturk, 1986; Podsakoff & MacKenzie, 1997; Podsakoff, MacKenzie, & Bommer, 1996a, 1996b).

Task behaviors: Actions performed by group members or the group leader that are relevant to the group's tasks; include initiating structure, providing task-related feedback, and setting goals.
Leadership substitutes: Aspects of the group members, the task, and the group or organization that reduce or eliminate the need for a task leader, a relationship leader, or both a task and relationship leader.

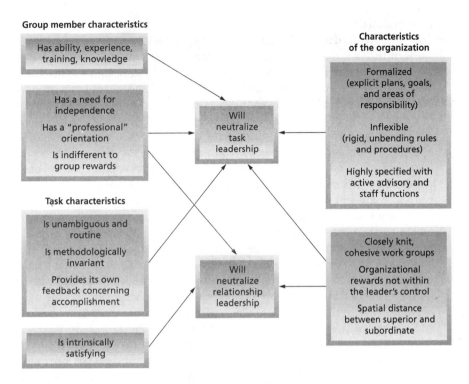

Group member characteristics

Has ability, experience, training, knowledge

Has a need for independence

Has a "professional" orientation

Is indifferent to group rewards

Task characteristics

Is unambiguous and routine

Is methodologically invariant

Provides its own feedback concerning accomplishment

Is intrinsically satisfying

Will neutralize task leadership

Will neutralize relationship leadership

Characteristics of the organization

Formalized (explicit plans, goals, and areas of responsibility)

Inflexible (rigid, unbending rules and procedures)

Highly specified with active advisory and staff functions

Closely knit, cohesive work groups

Organizational rewards not within the leader's control

Spatial distance between superior and subordinate

Group Dynamics 3rd ed. F12.01

FIGURE 12–1   When can groups work without a task or relationship leader? Studies of leadership substitutes suggest that different features of the group members, the task, and the organization can sometimes take the place of a leader.

(*Source:* Kerr & Jermier, 1978.)

LEADERSHIP EMERGENCE

Manet was the leader of the impressionist painters. Fito Strauch took control of the day-to-day activities of the Andes survivors. Jim Jones was the charismatic leader of the People's Temple. John F. Kennedy was elected president of the United States. Pastiak is the Director of Network Systems at Tellabs. But why Manet and not Degas? Why Strauch and not Canessa? Why Kennedy and not Nixon? Who will lead, and who will follow?

Scholars have debated this question for centuries. In the 19th century, for example, the historian Thomas Carlyle offered up his great-leader theory of history (Carlyle called it the "great-man" theory). He asserted that leaders do not achieve their positions by accident or twist of fate. Rather, these individuals possess certain characteristics that mark them for greatness. Carlyle believed that leaders are different from followers, so history could be best studied by considering the contributions of the few great men and women. The Russian novelist Leo Tolstoy took a contrasting viewpoint by emphasizing the role that situational factors play in determining history. To Tolstoy, such leaders as Alexander and Napoleon came to prominence because the spirit of the times—the *zeitgeist*—was propitious for the dominance of a single individual, and the qualities of the person were largely irrelevant to this rise to power. Tolstoy thus concluded that the conquests and losses of military leaders such as Napoleon were caused not by their decisions and skills but by uncontrollable aspects of the historical situation (Carlyle, 1841; Tolstoy, 1869/1952).

These two perspectives—Carlyle's great-leader theory and Tolstoy's *zeitgeist* approach—continue to shape our understanding of **leadership emergence.** The great-leader theory is consistent with *trait models,* which assume that leaders possess certain personality traits and qualities and that followers do not possess these traits. Tolstoy's *zeitgeist* view, in contrast, is consistent with *situational models,* which suggest that leadership is determined by a host of variables operating in the leadership situation, including the needs of the group members, the availability of resources, and, most importantly, the type of task to be performed (Simonton, 1980, 1987).

Interactional models of leadership, however, reconcile these two models by asserting that traits and situations interact to determine who will lead and who will not. If a group is about to disintegrate because of heated conflicts among the members, for example, the effective leader will be someone who can improve the group's interpersonal relations (Katz, 1977). Similarly, if individuals possess skills that facilitate performance on task x but undermine performance on task y, then they are likely to emerge as effective leaders only if the group is working on task x (Stogdill, 1974). Lewin's $B = f(P, E)$ formula, applied to leadership, suggests a leader's behavior is a function of the characteristics of the person *and* the characteristics of the group environment (Fiedler, 1996; House & Aditya, 1997).

Personal Qualities of Leaders

Pastiak, as an individual, possesses qualities that set her apart from others. She has seniority at Tellabs, for she has worked there for 20 years. She is extremely intelligent and articulate. She is, by nature, outgoing, friendly, and achievement oriented. Pastiak is also a woman. Are these the qualities we expect to find in a leader?

Height, Weight, and Age.   Leaders tend to differ physically from their subordinates. They are often older, taller, and heavier than the average group member. As Ralph Stogdill (1948, 1974) noted in his comprehensive reviews of leadership, the correlation between height and leadership varies from −.13 to +.71, but the average is about .30. Group members seem to associate height with power, but the relationship is not so strong that height is a prerequisite for leadership. History is filled with Napoleons who have managed to reach positions of leadership despite being short.

Stogdill found that the link between age and leadership emergence is more complicated. Leaders in informal discussion groups vary in age, whereas political and business

---

Leadership emergence: The process by which an individual becomes the leader of a formerly leaderless group.

leaders are often older than their subordinates. Stogdill suggests that in organizations and political settings, the climb up the ladder of leadership takes time. Fewer than 0.1% of the corporate executives listed in the *Register of Corporations, Directors, and Executives* are under 30 years of age (Stanton & Poors, 1967), and 74% are 50 or older. As Stogdill notes, "Organizations tend to rely upon administrative knowledge and demonstration of success that comes with experience and age" (1974, p. 76). Further, if group members assume that age is an indicator of wisdom, experience, and sagacity, they are likely to prefer a leader who is older rather than younger (Lawrence, 1996; Zajac & Westphal, 1996).

Intelligence. Stogdill (1948, 1974) cites 48 studies of the link between intellectual ability and leadership. Although the average correlation is small, on the order of .25 to .30, small-group and managerial leaders tend to score higher than average on standard intelligence tests, make superior judgments with greater decisiveness, be more knowledgeable, and speak more fluently. Leaders typically do not, however, exceed their followers in intellectual prowess by a wide margin (Simonton, 1985). Groups appear to prefer leaders who are more intelligent than the average group member, but too great a discrepancy introduces problems in communication, trust, and social sensitivity. Although highly intelligent individuals may be extremely capable and efficient leaders, their groups may feel that large differences in intellectual abilities translate into large differences in interests, attitudes, and values. Hence, although high intelligence may mean skilled leadership, a group prefers to be "ill-governed by people it can understand" (Gibb, 1969, p. 218).

Gender. Pastiak, as both a woman and a leader, is something of an exception, for even though the gender gap in leadership has narrowed in recent years, it has not closed. Labor is still divided by sex, with men more likely to work outside the home. Their overrepresentation in organizations and business settings provides them with far more leadership opportunities than are available to women. Moreover, even though the number of women working in managerial roles has risen steadily over the years, men hold a near monopoly on high-level leadership positions (Roos, 1985). In one study, more female managers than male managers felt excluded from career-related and informal interactions with senior managers (Cianni & Romberger, 1995), and some also expressed less confidence in their leadership abilities (Watson & Hoffman, 1996). A *glass ceiling* seems to block women's rise into top management positions. Women make up about 5% of middle management and only 1% of top management. A survey of corporate heads located 15 female chief executive officers and 2500 male CEOs (Nielsen, 1990).

This gender difference also shapes men and women's actions in small-group settings (Bass, 1990). Men are five times more likely to enact leadership behaviors than women in small, mixed-sex leaderless groups (Walker, Ilardi, McMahon, & Fennell, 1996) and so are more likely to emerge as leaders (Bartol & Martin, 1986; Eagly, 1987). Both leaders and subordinates perceive female leaders to be less dominant than male leaders (Snodgrass & Rosenthal, 1984). The lone man in an otherwise all-female group often becomes the leader, whereas the lone woman in an otherwise all-male group has little influence (Crocker & McGraw, 1984). The tendency for men to dominate women in informal discussion groups was obtained even when the men and women were all deemed to be androgynous (Porter, Geis, Cooper, & Newman, 1985), when group members were personally committed to equality for men and women (Sapp, Harrod, Zhao, 1996), and when the women in the group were more dominant, dispositionally, than the men (Megargee, 1969; Nyquist & Spence, 1986). When researchers paired together a person who tended to be interpersonally powerful and one who was more submissive, the dispositionally dominant person emerged as the leader in 73% of the same-sex dyads. But in mixed-sex dyads, the dominant man became the leader 90% of the time, but the dominant woman became the leader only 35% of the time (Nyquist & Spence, 1986).

Ethnic Diversity.   Leaders emerge all over the world, no matter what the culture, ethnicity, or race of the group members (Hunt & Peterson, 1997). Leadership may even be more common in cultures and subcultures that stress collectivistic, group-centered values. African American groups, for example, are often centered around strong leaders, even though Afrocentric groups stress harmony and unity more than Euro-American groups (Warfield-Coppock, 1995). The role of leader is also firmly embedded in the traditions of Latin American, Asian American, and Native American groups (Smith & Bond, 1993; Zamarripa & Krueger, 1983).

But how do the members of a subculture fare in groups where they are outnumbered by members of another group? First, minorities tend to be less influential in heterogeneous small groups and as a result are less likely to emerge as leaders (Bass, 1990; Mai-Dalton, 1993). For example, when Mexican American and Anglo American women interacted in groups, the Mexican American women exerted less influence relative to the Anglo American women (Roll, McClelland, & Abel, 1996). In a study conducted in Australia that paired Chinese students with Australian students, the Chinese students were less influential than the Australian students (Jones, Gallois, Callan, & Barker, 1995). Second, minorities tend to be underrepresented in leadership roles in business and organizational settings (Bass, 1990). African Americans in U.S. organizations and military groups, for example, are typically denied leadership positions in racially diverse groups, even if their qualities and experiences qualify them for that role (Molm, 1986; Webster & Driskell, 1983). When senior managers review the leadership potential of lower level managers, they give higher marks to Whites than to African American and Asian Americans (Landau, 1995). Asian Americans, despite their success in scientific and technical fields, are less likely than Whites and African Americans to achieve positions of leadership in those fields (Tang, 1997). Ethnic and racial minorities, like women, are underrepresented in the leadership world (Hooijberg & DiTomaso, 1996; Scandura & Lankau, 1996).

Personality.   Early leadership researchers believed that leaders possess certain personality traits that set them apart from others. This trait view, which in its strongest form assumed that some people were natural-born leaders, faded in popularity as researchers reported a series of failures to find any consistent impact of personality on behavior across a wide variety of situations. After conducting hundreds of studies, several reviewers concluded that the correlation between personality traits and leadership was too small to serve much predictive purpose (Mann, 1959; Stogdill, 1948).

In retrospect, this rejection of the trait model was premature. After painstakingly reviewing 163 studies in 1970, Stogdill concluded that leaders, relative to followers, were higher in ascendancy and energy level, sociability, achievement orientation, responsibility taking, adaptability, and self-confidence. When Robert Lord and his colleagues used meta-analytic methods to pool the results of dozens of studies of leadership emergence, they found that dominance, masculinity/femininity, and intelligence were all significantly related to leadership perceptions (Lord, De Vader, & Alliger, 1986). In general, the pattern of relationships is consistent with the so-called **big five dimensions of personality** identified by dozens of different researchers (Digman, 1990):

- *extraversion:* outgoing, sociable, interpersonal, expressive, gregarious
- *agreeableness:* friendly, warm, likable, generous, kind
- *conscientiousness:* responsible, achievement oriented, dependable, self-controlled
- *stability:* emotionally controlled, assured, not anxious, balanced
- *intelligence:* intellectually able, open to new ideas and experiences, cultured

Leaders tend to have elevated personality scores on all five of these dimensions, with extraversion, conscientiousness, and intelligence emerging as particularly consistent indicators in a number of studies conducted in organizational settings (Barrick & Mount, 1994; Hogan et al., 1994; Kirkpatrick & Locke, 1991; Ones, Mount, Barrick, & Hunter, 1994).

Going beyond traditional personality traits, Stephen Zaccaro and his colleagues believe that leaders also tend to be higher in *social intelligence:* the ability to perceive the needs and goals of the group members and then adjust to meet these varying situational demands (Kenny & Zaccaro, 1983; Zaccaro, 1995; Zaccaro, Foti, & Kenny, 1991; Zaccaro, Gilbert, Thor, & Mumford, 1991). Zaccaro and his colleagues repeatedly changed the membership composition of several groups as they worked on different tasks. Some of the tasks, such as group discussions of controversial topics, called for a leader who was good with people. Other tasks, in contrast, called for a leader who was task oriented. Even though the researchers dissolved the groups and re-formed them before assigning new tasks to each group, the same individuals tended to emerge as leaders in each newly reformulated group. Later analysis indicated that these individuals were able to alter their behaviors to fit the demands of the situation. If their group was working on a task that required good "people skills," they became more interpersonally oriented. But when the group needed a directive, task-oriented leader, these individuals stressed the task. These findings suggest that flexibility may be one of the most important qualities to look for in an effective leader (Zaccaro et al., 1991; see, too, Borgatta, Couch, & Bales, 1954).

Expertise.   When groups work collectively on tasks, individuals with more expertise usually rise higher in the group's leadership hierarchy. In a review of 52 studies of characteristics typically ascribed to the leader, Stogdill (1974) found that technical,

Big five dimensions of personality: Five fundamental aspects of personality, including extraversion, agreeableness (friendliness), conscientiousness (dependability), emotional stability, and intelligence. Perceivers tend to base their impressions of other people on these five factors.

task-relevant skills are mentioned in 35% of the studies. Groups are more accepting of leaders who have previously demonstrated task ability (Goldman & Fraas, 1965) and are more willing to follow the directions of a task-competent person than those of an incompetent person (Hollander, 1965). Furthermore, although high task ability facilitates leadership, low task ability seems to be an even more powerful factor in disqualifying individuals from consideration as leaders (Palmer, 1962). Given enough experience working together, most group members can distinguish between the skilled and the unskilled (Littlepage, Robison, & Reddington, 1997; Littlepage & Silbiger, 1992).

Field studies of leadership in organizational and military settings also suggest that individuals who possess valued skills are more often recognized as leaders. The successful head of the accounting department, for example, is usually recognized as a better accountant than his or her subordinates or other, less highly regarded managers (Tsui, 1984). Studies of ratings of military leadership ability also find that physical ability and task performance skills are highly correlated with leadership emergence (Rice, Instone, & Adams, 1984). Pastiak's emergence as a leader was probably due to her general leadership skills, however, rather than her skills in technology. As she herself admits, "The teams I'm working with right now—I'm *not* the subject matter expert" (quoted in Glasser & Smalley, 1995, p. 52).

Participation.   The relationship between expertise and leadership is heartening, for it suggests that groups tend to favor leaders who are qualified for that role. Studies of participation rates and leadership, though, offer an important qualification, for they suggest that the person who talks the most in the group is the most likely to emerge as leader (Burke, 1974; Stein & Heller, 1979, 1983). The data are surprising: The correlation between leadership emergence and most personal characteristics usually averages in the low .20s, but the correlation between participation rate and leadership ranges from .61 to .72 (Littlepage & Mueller, 1997; Malloy & Janowski, 1992; Stein & Heller, 1979).

Nor does it matter *what* the leader says. Supporting the so-called *babble effect*, people who make many useless remarks are more likely to emerge as leaders than individuals who make relatively few useful remarks. When researchers manipulated both the quantity and quality of the statements of a trained confederate in a problem-solving group, quantity overpowered quality (Sorrentino & Boutillier, 1975). The researchers created four-person groups and set them to work, but one of the group members was a confederate who systematically offered either many comments or few comments that were either high in quality (they promoted success on the tasks) or low in quality (they promoted failure on the tasks). When the subjects later rated, on 5-point scales, the confederate's confidence, interest in the problem, competence, influence over others, and contributions to solving the task, only his quantity of comments significantly influenced his ratings of confidence and interest. Furthermore, although the subjects viewed the confederate as more competent and more influential when he interjected high-quality rather than low-quality comments, the effects due to quantity were still stronger.

Why pick leaders based on the sheer quantity of their remarks? This tendency may stem from our assumption that the individual who is actively involved in the group discussion is interested in the group and is willing to take responsibility for its performance. Low participation rates, in contrast, imply that the individual has little interest in the group or its problems: "Quality is not positively related to leadership unless the competent person demonstrates his willingness to share his resources with the group members and is perceived as seriously trying to contribute to the group's goals" (Sorrentino & Boutillier, 1975, p. 411). These perceptions can apparently be best fostered by participating at high levels (Mullen, Salas, & Driskell, 1989; Sorrentino & Field, 1986).

Who Will Lead? A Cognitive Explanation

Does this maze of relationships between leadership emergence and such qualities as age, personality traits, and gender follow any discernible pattern? A number of leadership experts believe that **leader categorization theory** best accounts for these results. Are leaders intelligent or unintelligent, outgoing or introverted, understanding or insensitive, cooperative or inflexible, strict or undisciplined? Group members readily answer these questions by drawing on their intuitive beliefs about leaders. These cognitive structures are termed **implicit leadership theories** (Lord et al., 1986) or **leader prototypes** (Foti, Fraser, & Lord, 1982). Although each group member may have a unique conception of leadership, most people's leadership theories include task skills—the leader should be active, determined, influential, and in command—and people skills—the leader should be caring, interested, truthful, and open to others' ideas (Kenney, Schwartz-Kenney, & Blascovich, 1996). Group members also expect their leaders to be prototypical of their group. Groups that prize intellectual prowess and analytic ability and groups that stress action and adventure should have different implicit leadership theories (Fielding & Hogg, 1997; Hogg, 1996).

Members rely on their implicit leadership theories to sort group members into one of two categories: leader or follower. They intuitively note the actions and characteristics of the individuals in their group, compare them to their implicit leadership theories, and favor as leader the individual who matches that prototype of a leader (Lord, Foti, & De Vader, 1984; Lord & Maher, 1991). Implicit leadership theories also guide subordinates' evaluations of their leaders (Ilgen & Fujii, 1976; Lord, Binning, Rush, & Thomas, 1978; Rush, Thomas, & Lord, 1977). If members believe that leaders should be dominant, for example, they may only remember their leader acting dominantly and forget the times when their leader engaged in submissive behavior (Cronshaw & Lord, 1987; Lord, 1985; Lord & Alliger, 1985; Lord et al., 1984). Lord and his colleagues illustrated the biasing effects of implicit leadership theories in one study by arranging for raters to watch a videotape of a group interaction. After the tape, they asked the

---

Leader categorization theory: An information-processing model that assumes that group members rely on their implicit theories of leadership to intuitively classify other group members into the categories "leader" and "nonleader."
Implicit leadership theories: Each group member's personal assumptions about the naturally occurring relationship between leadership ability and various traits and attributes.
Leader prototypes: An abstract set of qualities and characteristics expected in a leader.

observers to identify behaviors that the leader had or had not performed. Lord found that the raters were less accurate, were less confident, and took longer to respond when trying to judge behaviors that were part of their leadership theories but had not been performed by the leader they had watched. He also found that the raters were less accurate but more confident when rating the leader on traits that were not part of their leadership theories (Foti & Lord, 1987).

Lord also believes that when researchers ask subordinates to describe their leaders, these ratings reflect the subordinates' implicit leadership theories more than their leaders' actions (Lord, 1985; Phillips & Lord, 1986). Why, asks Lord, do so many studies indicate that leadership has two sides, one focusing on relationships and one focusing on the task? Because, he answers, followers' implicit leadership theories include these two components. Lord and his colleagues have found that the implicit leadership theories adopted by laypeople match the explicit leadership theories developed by group dynamicists, and he worries that the distinction between task and relationship may rest more in group members' minds than in leaders' actual behaviors (Lord & Maher, 1991).

Categorization processes play a role in creating two sex differences in leadership: (1) Leaders tend to be men rather than women, and (2) male leaders are generally perceived to be more effective than female leaders. Although studies of men and women in positions of leadership reveal little evidence of male superiority (e.g., Eagly, Karau, & Makhijani, 1995), these evaluative and perceptual biases among group members persist (Eagly, Makhijani, & Klonsky, 1992; Rojahn & Willemsen, 1994; Shackelford, Wood, & Worchel, 1996). Both men and women, when surveyed, express a preference for male bosses (e.g., Rubner, 1991). As noted earlier in the chapter, men, more than women, gradually emerge as leaders in small, unstructured discussion groups (Eagly & Karau, 1991). Women receive lower evaluations and fewer promotions than men, even when actual performance data or behaviors are held constant (Geis, Boston, & Hoffman, 1985; Heilman, Block, & Martell, 1995). When a woman exerts influence in a group, members tend to frown and tighten their facial muscles; but when a man takes charge, members are more likely to nod in agreement (Butler & Geis, 1990). Despite changes in the public's overall attitude toward women as leaders, group members continue to be biased against female leaders (Gallup, 1990).

Leadership categorization theory suggests that these biases result from discrepancies between individuals' stereotypes about women and their implicit prototypes of leaders. Although gender stereotypes vary across time and place, people in virtually all cultures, when asked to describe women, spoke of their *expressive* qualities, including nurturance, emotionality, and warmth. They expected a "she" to be sentimental, affectionate, sympathetic, soft-hearted, talkative, gentle, and feminine. When describing men, they stressed their *instrumental* qualities, including productivity, energy, and strength (Williams & Best, 1990). Although successful leadership depends on both expressive and instrumental skills, many group members overemphasize the instrumental side of leadership (Dodge, Gilroy, & Fenzel, 1995; Forsyth, Schlenker, Leary, & McCown, 1985; Nye & Forsyth, 1991). Because women are considered the socioemotional experts rather than the task experts, their basic leadership skills are undervalued. Subordinates may also react negatively to female leaders because they are acting in ways that violate common stereotypes about how women should behave. Hence, people with liberal attitudes regarding women's roles respond positively to female leaders, whereas those with more traditional values do not (Forsyth, Heiney, & Wright, 1997). People also tend to respond more positively to women who adopt a more interpersonal, socioemotional style rather than a stronger, more dominating style (Cooper, 1997; Eagly et al., 1995; cf. Luthar, 1996).

LEADER EFFECTIVENESS

Alexander the Great controlled a huge empire without any modern means of transportation or communication. General George Patton inspired those under his command by displaying high levels of personal confidence, sureness, and an immense strength of character. Grace Pastiak has held high-level management positions in new business development, manufacturing operations, production and inventory control, and engineering operations. When the company decided to try to upgrade at least 10% of Tellabs's manufacturing procedures in a six-month period, Pastiak managed to convert 55% of the company's manufacturing methods during that time. Alexander, Patton, and Pastiak aren't simply leaders. They are effective leaders. But what is the key to their effectiveness?

Fiedler's Contingency Model

Fred Fiedler called his theory of leadership a **contingency model** because he assumed that leadership effectiveness was contingent on both the personal characteristics of the leader and the nature of the group situation (Fiedler, 1978, 1981). He developed his theory by studying groups that worked as teams and that had an appointed, elected, or emergent leader. He focused his attention on groups that generated products and performances that could be evaluated, and he measured aspects of the group settings and the leaders to see what combinations consistently led to good results. His basic conclusion: Effectiveness depends on the leader's motivational style and the favorability of the situation.

Motivational Style. Fiedler, like many other researchers, draws a distinction between *relationship-motivated leaders,* who try to find acceptance within their groups, and *task-motivated leaders,* who concentrate on completing the task. Fiedler measures these leadership styles with the **Least Preferred Co-Worker Scale (LPC Scale).** Respondents

---

Contingency model: Any model predicting that leadership depends on the interaction of the personal characteristics of the leader and the nature of the group situation; usually used in reference to Fiedler's (1981) theory that the effectiveness of a task- or relationship-oriented leader depends on the favorability of the group situation.
Least Preferred Co-Worker Scale (LPC Scale): A self-report method for assessing leadership style developed by Fiedler. Individuals who give relatively high ratings to their least preferred co-worker tend to adopt a relationship-oriented leadership style, whereas those who give low ratings to their least preferred co-worker tend to adopt a task-oriented style.

first think of the one individual with whom they have had the most difficulty working at some time. They then rate this person, dubbed the least preferred co-worker,
on bipolar adjective scales such as "pleasant-unpleasant," "friendly-unfriendly," and
"tense-relaxed." People who get high scores on the LPC are assumed to be relationship oriented; after all, they even rate the person they don't like to work with positively. Low LPC scorers are assumed to be task oriented.

Situational Control.   Just as leadership style is the key *personal* variable in Fiedler's
theory, control is the key *situational* factor in the model. If leaders can control the situation, they can be certain that decisions, actions, and suggestions will be carried out
by the group members. Leaders who have trouble gaining control, in contrast, cannot
be certain that the group members will carry out their assigned duties. What factors
determine control? Fiedler highlights leader-member relations, task structure, and position power.

- *Leader-member relations.* What is the quality of the relationship between the
  leader and the group? If the group is highly cohesive and relatively conflict free,
  the leader will be less concerned with peacekeeping and monitoring behavior.
- *Task structure.* Do group members clearly understand what is expected of
  them? When task structure is high, the group's tasks are straightforward and
  have only one right solution, whose correctness is easily checked. Tasks that are
  unstructured, in contrast, are ambiguous, admit to many correct solutions, and
  offer no "right" way of reaching the goal.
- *Position power.* How much authority does the leader possess? Leaders with high
  position power can control rewards, punishments, salaries, hiring, evaluation,
  and task assignment. In some groups, the leader may have relatively little power.

Figure 12–2 summarizes the relationship between these three variables and favorability of the leadership situations. Octant I in the chart is the most favorable setting:
leader-member relations are good, the task is structured, and the leader's power is
strong. Octant VIII is the least favorable situation, for all three variables combine in
a group that is difficult for the leader to control.

Predicting Leadership Effectiveness.   Fiedler does not believe that either type of leader
—task motivated or relationship motivated—is better overall. Instead, he predicts
that task leaders (low LPC) are most effective in situations that are either highly
favorable or unfavorable, whereas relationship leaders (high LPC) will be most effective in the middle-range situations. Assume, for example, that Pastiak is a low-LPC
leader: task rather than relationship motivated. When will the groups she leads perform the best? According to Figure 12–2, Pastiak will get the most out of groups in
Octants I, II, and III, where situational favorability is high, and groups in Octant
VIII—the least favorable situation. If she is a high-LPC leader, her groups will perform best in the middle-range situations: Octants IV to VI.

Why do relationship leaders prosper in the middle-range situations, whereas task
leaders perform best in more extreme group settings? Fiedler believes that the level of
stress experienced by the leader varies with situational control and that relationship

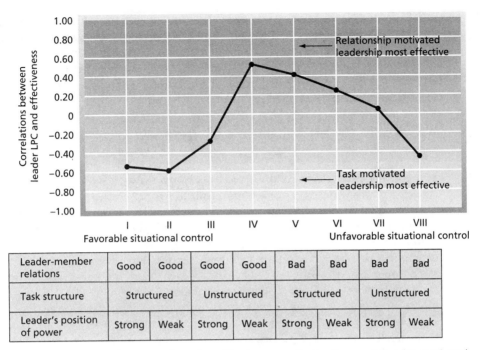

Leader-member relations	Good	Good	Good	Good	Bad	Bad	Bad	Bad
Task structure	Structured		Unstructured		Structured		Unstructured	
Leader's position of power	Strong	Weak	Strong	Weak	Strong	Weak	Strong	Weak

FIGURE 12–2 When is a task-motivated leader more effective than a relationship-motivated leader? Fiedler's contingency model argues that effectiveness depends on three aspects of the group situation: leader-member relations, task structure, and leader's position of power. Octant I corresponds to the most controllable and favorable situation, and Octant VIII corresponds to the least controllable and least favorable setting. The vertical axis indicates the predicted relationship between LPC scores and task performance. If the correlation is greater than 0 (positive), effectiveness is positively related to LPC; that is, relationship-motivated leaders are more effective. If the correlation is smaller than 0 (negative), effectiveness is negatively related to LPC; task-motivated leaders are more effective. The graph suggests that when the situation is favorable for the leader (Octants I, II, and III) or unfavorable (Octant VIII), a task-motivated leader is most effective.

and task leaders respond to that stress differently (Fiedler, 1993). When leaders are stressed by their lack of control in a situation (or by other factors, such as time pressures or a hostile boss), they rely too exclusively on their basic style. Therefore, the task leader concentrates on driving the group forward to complete its task and does not waste time worrying about the group members' need for positive interpersonal relations. The relationship leader, in contrast, spends too much time repairing relations in an irretrievably negative group (Bons & Fiedler, 1976).

But what about the success of the task leaders in favorable situations? Fiedler also believes that leaders, when they find themselves in less stressful (favorable) situations, expand their leadership behaviors, with the result that the task leader becomes more interpersonal, but the relationship leader becomes more concerned with the task. This strategy on the part of the relationship leader backfires, for group members rebel when their formerly personable leader becomes inconsiderate and directive. Martin Chemers

(1969) confirmed this tendency by giving both task and relationship leaders leadership training and then evaluating their actions in a favorable leadership setting. Task leaders became more considerate and enjoyed more positive leader-member relations after their training, but relationship leaders became less considerate after they were trained, and their relations with their subordinates deteriorated (Fiedler, 1978, 1986, 1993; Fielder & Chemers, 1974; Fiedler & Garcia, 1987).

Questions and Conclusions.   Like any theory, Fiedler's contingency model possesses both strengths and weaknesses. On the positive side, the contingency model takes into account both personal factors (LPC score) and situational factors (situational control) in predicting effectiveness, and the model is supported by a wealth of empirical data collected from a wide variety of groups (Fiedler, 1967, 1971a, 1971b, 1978, 1993). For example, when Fiedler (1964) studied antiaircraft artillery crews, he measured both the commander's leadership style (high or low LPC) and the favorability of the situation. In most crews, the leaders enjoyed a strong position power because their authority was determined by rank. In addition, task structure was high in most crews because the same sequence of decisions had to be made for each target. In some crews, however, the commander was well liked, whereas in other crews, the commander was disliked. As Figure 12–2 indicates, some crews were located in Octant I because leader-member relations were good, the task was structured, and position power was strong. Others, though, fell into Octant V because the leader-member relations were poor. Thus, a low LPC should be more effective for Octant I crews, but groups in Octant V should perform better with a high LPC leader. Supporting this prediction, Fiedler (1955) found that LPC scores were negatively correlated with effectiveness for artillery squads in Octant I ($r = -.34$), but positively correlated with effectiveness in Octant V ($r = .49$).

The effectiveness of a leadership training program derived from the theory, called Leader Match, also supports the theory. Although many different programs and techniques have been developed to train leaders, the results of these procedures are typically disappointing (Stogdill, 1974). Fiedler, however, suggests that these programs fail because they place too much emphasis on changing the leaders: making them more supportive, more decisive, more democratic, and so on. He suggests instead that the situation should be engineered to fit the leader's particular motivational style. He calls his training program Leader Match because he teaches conferees to modify their group situation until it matches their personal motivational style (Fiedler, Chemers, & Mahar, 1976). Studies of the effectiveness of this innovative training program suggest that trained leaders outperform untrained leaders (Burke & Day, 1986; Csoka & Bons, 1978; Fiedler, 1978).

Limitations of the model should not be discounted, however. Despite years of research, experts are divided on the model's validity, with some arguing that evidence supports the model and others arguing against it (Nathan, Hass, & Nathan, 1987; Peters, Hartke, & Pohlmann, 1985; Schriesheim, Tepper, & Tetrault, 1994; Strube & Garcia, 1981, 1983; Vecchio, 1983). Although many of the experimental studies support the model (e.g., Chemers & Skrzypek, 1972), others do not (Graen, Orris, Alvares, 1971; Vecchio, 1977). Also, whereas some experts in the area feel that the model's predictions are accurate in all eight of the octants (Strube & Garcia, 1981, 1983), others feel that predictions hold only in certain octants (Nathan et al., 1987; Peters et al., 1985; Vecchio, 1983). Indeed, several critics have argued that the correlations obtained by Fiedler should be interpreted cautiously because they do not reach conventional levels of statistical significance (Ashour, 1973a, 1973b; McMahon, 1972; Nathan et al., 1987; Schriesheim & Hosking, 1978). Many experts have also challenged the LPC Scale's validity (Schriesheim, Bannister, & Money, 1979; Schriesheim & Kerr, 1977; Stewart & Latham, 1986).

Given these conflicting appraisals of the model's adequacy, no immutable conclusions can be offered. The contingency model continues to be modified as new research findings come to light, and evidence suggests that much progress is being made (Chemers, 1983, 1987; Chemers, Hays, Rhodewalt, & Wysocki, 1985; Fiedler, 1993; Rice, 1978a, 1978b, 1979).

"Style" Theories

Fiedler's contingency model assumes that leaders have a preferred "style" of leading: Some tend to be relationship leaders, while others are task leaders. Many other leadership theories accept this basic premise, but add that some leaders deal effectively with *both* task and relationship demands. The style theories argue that effective leaders balance these two basic ingredients in the groups they lead (e.g., Bowers & Seashore, 1966; Hersey & Blanchard, 1977; House, 1971; Kerr et al., 1974; Likert, 1967; Misumi, 1985; Reddin, 1970).

The Leadership Grid.   Robert Blake and Jane Mouton, drawing on the Ohio State University Leadership Studies, hypothesize that leadership style depends on how one answers two basic questions: How important is the production of results by the group and how important are the feelings of people? To some leaders, their key goal is achieving results. For others, positive feelings in the group are so important that they emphasize teamwork and personal satisfaction. Others may feel that both these goals are important (Blake & McCanse, 1991; Blake & Mouton, 1964, 1978, 1980).

Blake and Mouton summarize these differences in leadership style in their **Leadership Grid** (formerly called the Managerial Grid), which is presented in Figure 12–3. Both dimensions, concern for people and concern for results, are represented as 9-point scales ranging from "low concern" to "high concern." Although in theory a person's orientation could fall at any of 81 possible positions on the grid, Blake and Mouton emphasize five orientations: those located at the four corner positions and one in the very center. An apathetic, impoverished 1,1 leader is hardly a leader, for he or she isn't interested in either subordinates' feelings or the production of results. The 9,1 individual (high on concern for production, low on concern for people, located in the lower right corner of the grid) is a taskmaster who seeks productivity at any cost. The 1,9 leader, in contrast, adopts a "country-club" approach that makes subordinates feel

---

Leadership Grid: A typology of leadership styles, proposed by Blake and Mouton, that assumes that people vary in their concern for people and results and that individuals who are high on both dimensions (9,9) make the best leaders.

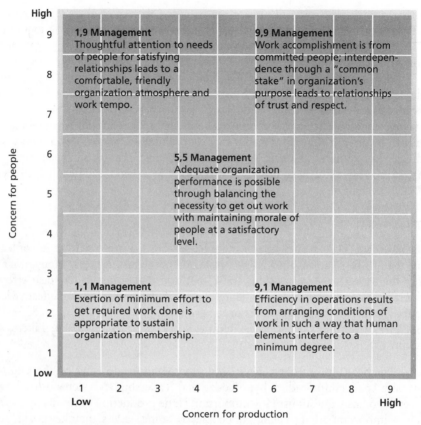

FIGURE 12–3 What is the one *best* style to use when leading people? The Leadership Grid (formerly called the Managerial Grid) distinguishes between five basic leadership styles and recommends the 9,9 style above all others.

(*Source:* Blake & McCanse, 1991.)

comfortable and relaxed while in the group. The "middle-of-the-roader," located at 5,5, tries to balance both performance and morale but sometimes sacrifices both when results and individuals' feelings come into conflict. Finally, the 9,9 leader values both people and products highly and therefore tackles organizational goals through team-work: "a high degree of shared responsibility, coupled with high participation, involve-ment, and commitment" (Blake & Mouton, 1982, p. 41).

Blake and Mouton are not contingency theorists; they feel that the 9,9 leadership style is the "one best style" to use when leading people (1982). In their initial studies, they found that managers who adopted the 9,9 style were far more successful in their careers than managers who adopted other methods (1964). They also note that studies conducted in educational, industrial, and medical organizations support the utility of the 9,9 leadership style, as do the favorable results of their management training system (Blake & Mouton, 1980, 1982, 1985, 1986). These results are impressive, but many experts still question their strong claim that the 9,9 style works in all situations (Kerr et al., 1974; Larson, Hunt, & Osborn, 1976; Nystrom, 1978; Quinn & McGrath, 1982).

Situational Leadership Theory. Paul Hersey and Kenneth Blanchard also describe leadership in terms of the relationship and task dimensions. Unlike Blake and Mouton's grid, however, their **situational leadership theory** suggests that effective leaders vary the extent to which they combine supportive behaviors with directive behaviors over time (Blanchard, Zigarmi, & Zigarmi, 1985; Hersey & Blanchard, 1976, 1977, 1982).

The amount of direction and support that a leader should provide depends, in large part, on the developmental level of the group or subordinate. Development has little to do with age; what counts is the group members' commitment to the group and its goals and their competence. Group members who are committed are usually confident, self-assured, and highly motivated. Competent members possess the skills and knowledge needed to perform their assigned tasks, perhaps because they have been trained or because they have experience (Blanchard et al., 1985).

Figure 12–4 describes the model's predictions. When group members are low in both commitment and competence, they work most effectively with a *directing* leader who is not supportive (S1). As the group develops and gains experience on the task and commitment to the group's goals, the leader can increase relationship behavior and adopt a *coaching* style (S2: high direction and support). Still later in the group's development, the leader can ease off on both types of leadership, starting first with direction. In moderately mature groups, the *supporting* leader is most effective (S3), and in fully mature groups, a *delegating* style is best (S4). Thus, an effective leader must display four different leadership styles as the group moves through its life cycle: directing, coaching, supporting, and delegating (Blanchard et al., 1985).

Some critics argue that the situational model puts too much emphasis on matching the maturity of the members; these experts call for a careful balancing of task and relationship orientation at all developmental levels (Nicholls, 1985). But the initial results are promising. In one investigation, newly hired employees needed and appreciated greater task structuring from their manager than did veteran employees (Vecchio, 1987). Also, several measures of leadership flexibility, such as the Leader Behavior Analysis II, function well as methods of assessing rigidity in leadership style (Graeff, 1983; Hersey, 1985; Lueder, 1985a, 1985b). Lastly, the training model based on the approach has become extremely popular, and it forms the basis for the "one-minute management" approach to leadership in organizational settings (Blanchard & Johnson, 1981; Blanchard, Zigarmi, & Nelson, 1993; Carew, Parisi-Carew, & Blanchard, 1986).

Participation Theories

The chief executive officer asks the board of directors for input before making a final judgment. Factory workers elect representatives who negotiate with the factory owners over a wage increase. A group of college students get together with their professor and vote on the topic they will research in the coming semester. Grace Pastiak does not make decisions without consulting the members of her team. Indeed, she doesn't just have an "open-door policy"—she doesn't even have a door on her office. She works at one end

---

Situational leadership theory: Hersey and Blanchard's theory of leadership that suggests that groups benefit from leadership that meshes with the stage of development of the group.

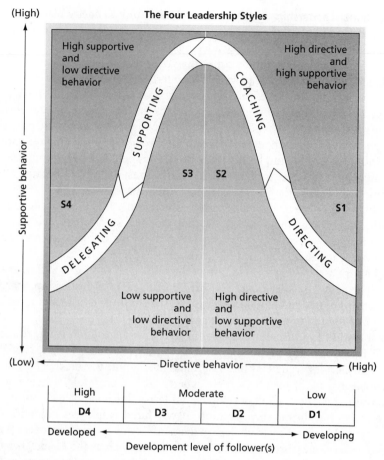

FIGURE 12–4 Which style of leadership works best across the life cycle of the group? The Hersey and Blanchard situational theory of leadership assumes that leaders must be flexible. When the group forms, they must use a directing behavior (S1); but over time, as the group develops, they should shift to other styles.

(*Source:* Blanchard, Zigarmi, & Zigarmi, 1985.)

of a large open area, surrounded by other employees, and when a problem arises, she calls her staff together to work out the solution. She believes that her staff gets more done because they feel responsible for the outcome.

Participation theories of leadership assume that group performance depends, in part, on the extent to which leaders share or retain their decision-making authority. At one

---

Participation theories: Leadership models that distinguish between various types of leadership strategies by assessing the extent to which the leader retains control over group decision or shares control with the group.

end of the participation continuum, the group members decide the issues in question. At the other end of the continuum, the leader alone weighs the available information and makes the decision. Between these two extremes are instances in which the leader makes the decision after receiving various amounts of information from the other group members. The question the leader must ask in each situation is clear: What point along this continuum is the most effective in terms of productivity and satisfaction?

The Lewin-Lippitt-White Study.   Kurt Lewin, Ronald Lippitt, and Ralph White studied this question in their classic comparison of authoritarian, democratic, and laissez-faire leadership (Lewin, Lippitt, & White, 1939; White & Lippitt, 1960, 1968). As noted briefly in Chapter 2, these researchers arranged for groups of 10- and 11-year-old boys to meet after school to work on various hobbies. In addition to the boys, each group included a man who adopted one of three leadership styles.

- The *authoritarian, or autocratic, leader* took no input from the members in making decisions about group activities, did not discuss the long-range goals of the group, emphasized his authority, dictated who would work on specific projects, and arbitrarily paired the boys with their work partners.
- The *democratic leader* made certain that all activities were first discussed by the entire group. He allowed the group members to make their own decisions about work projects or partners and encouraged the development of an egalitarian atmosphere.
- The *laissez-faire leader* rarely intervened in the group activities. Groups with this type of atmosphere made all decisions on their own without any supervision, and their so-called leader functioned primarily as a source of technical information.

In some cases, the boys were rotated to a different experimental condition so that they could experience all three types of participation.

The three types of leadership resulted in differences in efficiency, satisfaction, and aggressiveness. The autocratic groups spent as much time working on their hobbies as the democratic groups, but the laissez-faire groups worked considerably less (see Figure 12–5). When the leader left the room, however, work dropped off dramatically in the autocratically led groups, remained unchanged in the democratic groups, and actually increased in the laissez-faire groups. Furthermore, members of groups with an autocratic leader displayed greater reliance on the leader, expressed more critical discontent, and made more aggressive demands for attention. Democratic groups tended to be friendlier and more group oriented. Overall, the boys preferred democratic leaders to the other two varieties.

Although these findings seem to recommend democratic leadership over the two alternatives, the findings of Lewin, Lippitt, and White were not as clear-cut as Figure 12–5 implies. Several of the groups reacted to the autocratic leader with hostility, negativity, and scapegoating, but others responded very passively to their authoritarian leaders. In these latter groups, productivity was quite high (74%) when the leader was present, but it dropped to 29% when he left the room. Aggression, very apparent in some of the autocratically led groups, was replaced in these others by apathy and

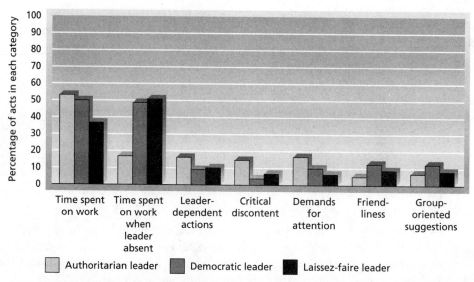

FIGURE 12–5   How do group members react to authoritarian, democratic, and laissez-faire leaders? Lewin, Lippitt, and White (1939) answered the question by recording a variety of behaviors of group members working under the direction of one of three types of leaders. Groups with either authoritarian or democratic leaders were more productive than the laissez-faire groups, but the autocratic groups were less productive when the leader left the room. Other findings suggest that the democratic groups were more cohesive.

(*Source:* White & Lippitt, 1960.)

acceptance of the situation. Although the group became aggressive if the autocratic leader was replaced with a more permissive one, when he was present, the group members worked hard, demanded little attention, only rarely engaged in horseplay, and closely followed his recommendations.

The relationship between participation and effectiveness is not a simple one. Indeed, Stogdill (1974), after reviewing more than 40 studies of various leadership methods that ranged along the participation continuum, concluded that no single participatory technique was more frequently associated with increases in productivity than another. Stogdill notes that satisfaction with the group seems to be highest in democratic groups as opposed to autocratic and laissez-faire groups, but even this conclusion fails to hold when groups expect an autocratic leader (Foa, 1957) or when the group is very large (Vroom & Mann, 1960).

Vroom's Normative Model.   Victor Vroom's **normative model** explains the relationship between participation and effectiveness by distinguishing between the five key

---

Normative model: A theory of leadership developed by Vroom that predicts the effectiveness of group-centered, consultative, and autocratic leaders across a number of group settings.

types of leaders shown in Figure 12–6 (Vroom, 1973, 1974, 1976; Vroom & Yetton, 1973). Although leaders can fall anywhere along the leader-centered, authoritarian to group-centered, democratic continuum, Vroom stresses these five basic types (paraphrased from Vroom & Yetton, 1973, p. 13):

- *Autocratic I (AI).* The leader solves the problem or makes the decision, using information available to him or her at that time.
- *Autocratic II (AII).* The leader obtains necessary information from members and then decides on the solution to the problem. In getting the information, the leader may choose not to tell the group members what the problem is. The role played by the members is one of providing information rather than suggesting or evaluating alternative solutions.
- *Consultative I (CI).* The leader shares the problem with relevant group members individually, getting their ideas and suggestions without bringing them together as a group. Then the leader makes the decision, which may not reflect the group members' influence.
- *Consultative II (CII).* The leader discusses the problem with the members as a group, collectively obtaining their ideas and suggestions. Then the leader makes the decision, which may not reflect the group members' influences.
- *Group II (GII).* The leader discusses the problem with the members as a group. Together, the leader and members devise and evaluate alternatives and attempt

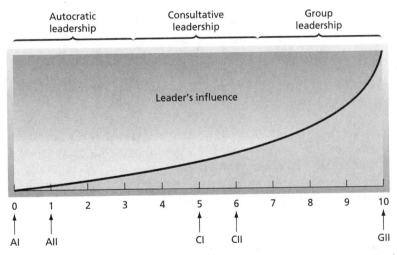

FIGURE 12–6 Should leaders share their decision-making authority with group members? Victor Vroom and his colleagues' normative model of leadership argues that leaders range from those who retain all control (autocratic leaders, AI) to leaders who share all decisions with the group (group leadership, GII). Leaders can fall anywhere along the authoritarian to democratic continuum, but Vroom focuses primarily on two autocratic methods (AI and AII), two consultative methods (CI and CII), and one group method (GII).

(*Source:* Vroom & Yetton, 1973.)

to reach agreement (consensus) on a solution. The leader's role is much like that of the chairperson of a committee. The leader does not try to influence the group to adopt a particular solution and is willing to accept and carry out any solution that is supported by the entire group.

Vroom's normative model, like Fiedler's model, is a contingency theory; it argues that no single leadership method will be best in all situations. In general, leaders should probably meet with the group whenever a major decision is to be made, but in some situations, this democratic approach may prove ineffective, time consuming, and dissatisfying to members. In these instances, a more autocratic type of leadership may be the most successful approach. To guide leaders in their choice of leadership method, Vroom and his colleagues list a number of rules of thumb to follow when selecting a leadership method (Vroom, 1976; Vroom & Jago; 1978; Vroom & Yetton, 1973). Some of these rules are designed to protect the quality of the decision the group is making, whereas others are designed to ensure the acceptance of the decision by the group. They include the following rules (paraphrased from Vroom & Jago, 1978, pp. 151–162):

- *Leader-information rule.* Do not use AI if the quality of the decision is important and if you do not have enough information or expertise to solve the problem alone.
- *Goal-congruence rule.* Do not use GII if the quality of the decision is important and if subordinates are not likely to pursue the organizational goals in their efforts to solve this problem.
- *Unstructured-problem rule.* Do not use AI, AII, or CI if finding a high-quality decision is important, if you lack sufficient information to solve the problem alone, and if the problem is unstructured. In such situations, input is needed from the group.
- *Acceptance rule.* Do not use autocratic methods (AI or AII) if acceptance of the decision by subordinates is critical to effective implementation and if it is not certain that an autocratic decision will be accepted.
- *Conflict rule.* Do not use AI, AII, or CI when the conditions noted by the acceptance rule hold and disagreement among subordinates is likely. In such instances, methods that require the resolution of differences should be used.
- *Fairness rule.* Do not use autocratic or consultative methods when the quality of the decision is unimportant but acceptance of the decision is critical and not certain to result from an autocratic decision.
- *Acceptance-priority rule.* Do not use autocratic or consultative methods if acceptance is critical but not likely to result from an autocratic decision and if subordinates are motivated to pursue organizational goals.

Does the normative model work? Available evidence, although scant, is supportive. Vroom and his colleagues, for example, report that when expert managers read a case study of a leadership decision and then make a recommendation about an appropriate leadership method, their suggestions coincide with the predictions of the normative model (Hill & Schmitt, 1977; Jago, 1978; Vroom & Yetton, 1973). More research, however, is needed to examine the impact of each of the five key methods in each situation specified by Vroom (Field, 1979; Field & House, 1990; Hill & Schmitt, 1977; Vroom & Jago, 1978).

Leader-Member Exchange Theory

Most leadership theories focus on the leader's style or strategy and how the group responds as a whole to various interventions. **Leader-member exchange theory (LMX theory)**, in contrast, traces satisfaction and performance back to the quality of the relationship between leaders and followers. LMX theory (and its predecessor, vertical dyad linkage theory) notes that leaders have dyadic relationships with each group member and that these dyadic relationships within the total group may be substantially different. In some cases, the member and leader may work well together. The leader may be satisfied with the member's work and provide him or her with extra responsibilities and rewards. The follower, in turn, may extend his or her role and express higher levels of satisfaction with the group. Other group members, though, may not respond as positively to the leader, and so their responses are defined by their role and their fixed responsibilities (Dansereau, Graen, & Haga, 1975; Graen & Cashman, 1975; Graen & Uhl-Bien, 1995).

LMX theory suggests that group members tend to cleave into subgroups within the overall group. One group, the ingroup or inner group, includes those individuals with positive linkages to the leader. Leaders spend more time working with these members, value their inputs more, and also provide them with more resources. These group members respond by working harder for the group, taking on additional role responsibilities, and declaring their loyalty to the leader and the group. The second group, the outgroup or outer group, includes individuals with less satisfying linkages to the leader. These individuals do their work, but do not contribute as much to the group. They also express less loyalty and support for the leader (Dienesch & Liden, 1986).

LMX theory's basic assumptions have been verified empirically (Gerstner & Day, 1997). Individuals who feel that they have a good working relationship with their leader are less likely to leave the group and more likely to earn higher performance evaluations, get promoted more rapidly, express more commitment to the organization, voice more positive attitudes about their work and the group, and garner more attention and support from their leader. They often view their relationship with their boss as a "partnership." Individuals who are not satisfied with their relationship think of their boss as an "overseer" who monitors their work but is otherwise uninterested in them as individuals (Duchon, Green, & Taber, 1986; Graen & Uhl-Bien, 1995). Researchers have also documented the natural tendency for subgroups to develop within groups and for disparities in performance to exist between these two cliques (Bass, 1990). Indeed, recognizing the substantial benefits to be gained by improving leader-member exchange

---

Leader-member exchange (LMX) theory: A dyadic, rather than group, approach to leadership that focuses on how the quality of one-to-one leader-member exchanges define members' roles and their relationship to the group and the leader.

encourages leaders to establish only inner-group relations—or at least minimize the number of people in the outer group (Graen & Uhl-Bien, 1991).

LMX theory's dyadic approach—stressing the relationship between each member and the leader—also provides an additional way of looking at leadership in general. Researchers have returned to other leadership theories, such as Fiedler's contingency model, and have begun to explore the type of leadership style leaders use with each group member. These dyadic-level approaches add a second layer of information about leadership to the more common group-level analysis (Ayman, Chemers, & Fiedler, 1995; Dansereau, Yammarino, & Markham, 1995; Hall & Lord, 1995; Schriesheim, Cogliser, & Neider, 1995; Yammarino & Bass, 1991).

Transformational Leadership

Some leaders do more than guide their groups from Point A to Point B. Some, "by the force of their personal abilities are capable of having profound and extraordinary effects on followers" (House & Baetz, 1979, p. 399). Max Weber (1921/1946), as noted in Chapter 8, called these leaders *charismatic leaders*. Such leaders, he believed, derived their power from their followers' devotion to them. Charismatic leaders are often inspirational speakers, expressing ideas that are both appealing and easily understood. Group members often express great affection for such leaders and accept their pronouncements on faith. Members also tend to become emotionally involved with the group and willingly sacrifice their own interests for the good of the group (Burns, 1978; House & Baetz, 1979).

Bernard Bass's (1997) theory of **transformational leadership** identifies the processes that charismatic leaders use to influence their followers. Bass (1997) believes that most leaders are transactional rather than transformational. They treat their relationship with their followers as a transaction: They define expectations, offer rewards, "formulate mutually satisfactory agreements, negotiate for resources, exchange assistance for effort, and provide commendations for successful follower performance" (Bass, 1997, p. 134). They also, in too many cases, lead by pointing out members' failings or by just ignoring problems until they become dire. Transformational leaders, however, go beyond rewards and punishments. These leaders tend to be self-confident and determined, and their communications with their followers are usually eloquent and enthusiastic (Waldman, Bass, & Yammarino, 1990; Yammarino & Bass, 1990).

Bass, in seeking the source of such leaders' social power, has identified four components of transformational leadership: idealized influence (or charisma), inspirational motivation, intellectual stimulation, and individualized consideration (paraphrased from Bass, 1997, p. 133):

- *Idealized influence.* Leaders express their conviction clearly and emphasize the importance of trust; they take stands on difficult issues and urge members to

---

Transformational leadership: A form of leadership whereby a charismatic individual inspires members to expend great energy and effort in the pursuit of their goals.

adopt their values; they emphasize the importance of purpose, commitment, and the ethical consequences of decisions.

- *Inspirational motivation.* Leaders articulate an appealing vision of the future; they challenge followers with high standards, talk optimistically with enthusiasm, and provide encouragement and meaning for what needs to be done.
- *Intellectual stimulation.* Leaders question old assumptions, traditions, and beliefs; they stimulate in others new perspectives and ways of doing things and encourage the expression of ideas and reasons.
- *Individualized consideration.* Leaders deal with others as individuals; they consider individual needs, abilities, and aspirations; they listen attentively and further individual members' development; they advise, teach, and coach.

Bass's transformational model offers a valuable counterpoint to theories that stress more routine, if more ubiquitous, forms of leadership. Even though most leaders are transactional, people recognize the ideal of the charismatic, transformational leader (Offerman, Kennedy, & Wirtz, 1994). Bass and his colleagues, by identifying the four components of transformational leadership, offer leaders clear suggestions for improving their motivational impact on members (Bass & Avolio, 1994; Lowe, Kroeck, & Sivasubramaniam, 1996; Yammarino, Spangler, & Bass, 1993). Additional research is needed, however, to explain cases when groups led by charismatic leaders engage in atypical and destructive behavior (O'Connor, Mumford, Clifton, Gessner, & Connelly, 1995).

Women and Men as Leaders

When it comes to leadership, do the sexes differ? Although this was once a moot question, because females were traditionally denied access to positions of leadership, changes in the role of women in contemporary society have resulted in an increasing number of female leaders. The number of Pastiaks in the world is rising.

How do these female leaders differ from their male counterparts in terms of effectiveness, style, and acceptance by subordinates? First, available evidence finds that men and women are equally effective as leaders (Brown, 1979; Eagly et al., 1995; Smith, 1997). For example, one review of 32 empirical studies found that in some laboratory studies, male leaders outperformed female leaders, but studies conducted in actual managerial settings generally found no gender differences (Brown, 1979). Some evidence suggests that women outperform men when the leadership setting demands relationship skills and teamwork rather than independence, but the overall sex differences in leadership skills are slight (Giannantonio, Olian, & Carroll, 1996; Klenke, 1996; Maher, 1997).

Second, do men and women adopt different leadership styles? As early as 1956, researchers suggested that men in groups tended to provide orientation, opinions, and directions designed to lead the group toward goal attainment, whereas women emphasized group solidarity, reduction of group tension, and avoidance of antagonism (Strodtbeck & Mann, 1956). Despite the many changes in perceptions of women and men during the years since that study, men still tend to be task oriented, whereas women are still friendlier and more interpersonally oriented (Leary, Robertson, Barnes,

& Miller, 1986; Wood, 1987). These sex differences in group behavior, however, may not translate into sex differences in leadership style. Men tend to be task oriented, but when they become leaders, they may add relationship-oriented actions to their behavioral repertoires. Similarly, when women become leaders, they may become more task oriented.

Alice Eagly and Blair Johnson (1990) explored this hypothesis by reviewing over 150 studies that compared the leadership styles adopted by men and women. As they expected, relative to men, women performed more relationship-oriented actions in laboratory groups and also described themselves as more relationship oriented on questionnaires. The sexes did not differ, however, in studies conducted in organizational settings (Dobbins & Platz, 1986). Indeed, as managers, women tended to be both task and relationship oriented, whereas men were primarily task oriented (Stratham, 1987). The only difference between men and women that emerged consistently across studies concerned participation: Women used a democratic style, whereas men were more autocratic.

Lastly, do people prefer to work for men rather than women? As noted earlier in this chapter, many individuals express a preference for male bosses. Recent studies of these biases, however, are also encouraging. A field study conducted with cadets at the U.S. Military Academy found no male favoritism (Rice et al., 1984), nor did surveys conducted in managerial settings (Kushell & Newton, 1986; Tsui & Gutek, 1984). Subordinates are often more satisfied when their leader adopts a democratic style or a relationship-oriented style, but gender per se has little impact on evaluations (Kushell & Newton, 1986). In addition, evidence suggests that group members' perceptual biases are minimized when they know how effectively the group and the leader have performed in the past (Dobbins, Stuart, Pence, & Sgro, 1985; Izraeli, Izraeli, & Eden, 1985; Nye & Simonetta, 1996; Wood & Karten, 1986).

What Is the Key to Leadership?

The question "What made Grace Pastiak such an effective leader?" has been answered by different theorists in different ways. Fiedler's model, noting Pastiak's favorable work situation, would predict that her task-motivated management style matched the situation she faced. Alternatively, the leadership style theorists might suggest that she is a master at providing her staff with clear goals and objectives while also maintaining positive relationships. Vroom's normative model would suggest that she also knows when to include others in the decision-making process and when to make decisions on her own. And Bass's model suggests that she is a charismatic, transformation leader.

These explanations of leadership, while stressing different processes, are similar in many respects. Virtually all explicitly consider the interaction between the leader's characteristics and the nature of the leadership situation. They may emphasize different leader characteristics (e.g., the leader's motivation, style, or method) and different features of the situation (such as situational control, group maturity, or attributes of the problem), but all take note of the interaction among leaders, members, and settings when predicting effectiveness. Leadership, as Lewin would conclude, is a function of the leaders, the led, and the group situation.

SUMMARY

What Is Leadership?

1. Specifying what leadership is *not* is easier than specifying what it is. It is not necessarily power to manipulate or control others, nor is it an inborn talent, a skill that can be learned by following a few guidelines, or the key to group success.
2. An interactional approach defines *leadership* as a reciprocal, transactional, and transformational process in which individuals are permitted to influence and motivate others to promote the attaining of group and individual goals.
3. A behavioral approach highlights two fundamental clusters of leadership behaviors: *relationship behaviors* and *task behaviors*. The Leader Behavior Description Questionnaire (LBDQ) assesses both components.
4. *Leadership substitutes* are features of the situation that fulfill critical interpersonal and task functions and so reduce the need for a leader.

Who Will Lead?

1. Early theories of *leadership emergence* adopted either a trait model or a situational model, but most modern theories are interactional models that base predictions on the reciprocal relationships among the leader, the followers, and the nature of the group situation.
2. Emergence is related to the leader's personal qualities, including physical characteristics such as height, weight, age, and gender; intelligence; personality traits; task abilities; and participation rates.
3. The *big five dimensions of personality* models argue that leaders tend to be extraverted, agreeable, conscientious, stable, and intelligent.

4. The *leader categorization theory* of leadership emergence suggests that individuals who act in ways that match the group members' *implicit leadership theories* or *leader prototypes* are likely to emerge as leaders.
5. Groups are sometimes unfairly biased against women as leaders.

Why Do Some Leaders Succeed and Others Fail?

1. Fiedler's *contingency model* bases its predictions on the leader's particular motivation style—task motivated or relationship motivated—as measured by the *Least Preferred Co-Worker Scale* (LPC Scale). By taking into consideration the leader-member relations, the task structure, and the leader's power, Fiedler's theory predicts that task-motivated (low-LPC) leaders are most effective in situations that are either extremely unfavorable or extremely favorable, whereas relationship-motivated leaders are most effective in intermediate situations.
2. Leadership style theorists assume that effectiveness depends on the leader's task and relationship behaviors.
   • The *leadership grid* proposed by Blake and Mouton assumes that people vary in their concern for others and in their concern for results and that individuals who are high on both dimensions (9,9) are the best leaders.
   • *Situational leadership theory*, as proposed by Hersey and Blanchard, suggests that groups benefit from leadership that meshes with the developmental stage of the group.
3. *Participation theories* of leadership extend the early findings of Lewin, Lippitt, and White regarding the effects of autocratic, democratic, and

laissez-faire leaders. Vroom's *norma-tive model* compares the effectiveness of autocratic, consultative, and group-centered leaders in many situations.

4. *Leader-member exchange (LMX) the-ory* focuses on the dyadic relationship linking the leader to each member of the group and notes that in many cases, two subgroups of linkages exist (the inner group and the outer group). Groups with more inner-group mem-bers are more productive.

5. Bass's *transformational leadership* the-ory identifies the processes that charis-matic leaders use to influence their followers. Bass emphasizes four compo-nents of transformational (rather than transactional) leadership: idealized influence (or charisma), inspirational motivation, intellectual stimulation, and individualized consideration.

FOR MORE INFORMATION

Bass and Stogdill's Handbook of Leadership: Theory, Research, and Managerial Applications, by Bernard M. Bass (1990, 3rd ed.), is the definitive reference for research into leadership. Its 1000 pages and 7500 references provide insight into virtu-ally all aspects of the leadership process.

Discovering the Leader Within: Running Small Groups Successfully, by Randy Fujishin (1997), is filled with behaviorally specific how-to suggestions for leading work groups and discussion.

Leadership: Theory and Practice, by Peter G. Northouse (1997), reviews all major theo-ries of leadership by focusing on the theo-retical and conceptual underpinnings of the theories (rather than efforts to test the models empirically).

Swim with the Dolphins: How Women Can Succeed in Corporate America on Their Own Terms, by Connie Glasser and Barbara Steinberg Smalley (1995), is the source of the Grace Pastiak case discussed in this chapter and uses interviews with successful women to develop a set of clear suggestions for effective leadership in busi-ness settings.

"What We Know about Leadership Effec-tiveness and Personality," by Robert Hogan, Gordon J. Curphy, and Joyce Hogan (1994), answers nine basic questions that come up when people talk about leaders and leadership, including "How should leaders be evalu-ated?" and "Why do we choose so many flawed leaders?"

Women and Leadership: A Contextual Perspective, by Karin Klenke (1996), is a multidisciplinary analysis of women as leaders, with chapters on female leaders in history, the media, popular literature, politics, and the workplace.

ACTIVITY 12–1 WHAT IS YOUR LEADERSHIP STYLE?

Most leadership theories argue that people consistently use a particular set of methods and techniques whenever they find themselves in charge of a group. Different theorists describe these leadership styles differently, but most highlight two key aspects: focus on the task and focus on the relationships among the members.

1. Complete Fred Fiedler's (1978) Least Preferred Co-Worker Scale to assess your own leadership style. Think of a person with whom you work least well. He or she may be someone you work with now or someone you knew in the past. This co-worker does not have to be the person you like least but should be the person with whom you had the most difficulty in getting a job done. Describe this person by circling one of the numbers between each pair of adjectives:

Pleasant	: 8 7 6 5 4 3 2 1 :	Unpleasant
Friendly	: 8 7 6 5 4 3 2 1 :	Unfriendly
Rejecting	: 1 2 3 4 5 6 7 8 :	Accepting
Tense	: 1 2 3 4 5 6 7 8 :	Relaxed
Distant	: 1 2 3 4 5 6 7 8 :	Close
Cold	: 1 2 3 4 5 6 7 8 :	Warm
Supportive	: 8 7 6 5 4 3 2 1 :	Hostile
Boring	: 1 2 3 4 5 6 7 8 :	Interesting
Quarrelsome	: 1 2 3 4 5 6 7 8 :	Harmonious
Gloomy	: 1 2 3 4 5 6 7 8 :	Cheerful
Open	: 8 7 6 5 4 3 2 1 :	Guarded
Backbiting	: 1 2 3 4 5 6 7 8 :	Loyal
Untrustworthy	: 1 2 3 4 5 6 7 8 :	Trustworthy
Considerate	: 8 7 6 5 4 3 2 1 :	Inconsiderate
Nasty	: 1 2 3 4 5 6 7 8 :	Nice
Agreeable	: 8 7 6 5 4 3 2 1 :	Disagreeable
Insincere	: 1 2 3 4 5 6 7 8 :	Sincere
Kind	: 8 7 6 5 4 3 2 1 :	Unkind

2. Add up the 18 numbers you circled to get a total between 18 and 144. According to Fiedler, if you scored 56 or less, you have a task-oriented style of leadership. A score of 63 or higher indicates a relationship-oriented style of leadership. If you scored between 56 and 63 you cannot be classified in either category.
3. Given your responses to the questionnaire, are you relationship or task oriented? Do the results of the LPC Scale match your own intuitions about what type of leader you are?
4. According to Fiedler, what type of group would be the "best" type of group for you to lead? Which would be the "worst"?
5. Think about the last time you acted as a leader in a group. Describe the nature of the interaction as the group worked on the task. What was the value of the three situational factors specified by Fiedler? Does his theory explain your relationship to the group?
6. How might you consider changing your leadership style or the situation to be more effective?

ACTIVITY 12-2 **LEADERSHIP INTERVIEWS**

People have strong opinions and assumptions about leadership, which are not always consistent with the findings generated by theories and researchers. Explore these intuitive leadership theories by locating two respondents (one man, one woman) and asking them for a few minutes of their time. Roommates, friends, attachment figures are perfectly appropriate interviewees. Ask them the following questions and any others you think are important to add. Record their answers in writing.

1. Can you name two or three people whom you feel were or are great leaders?
2. Is leadership an inborn talent or a learned skill?
3. Are leaders powerful people who can impose their will on others?
4. Do people like to work in groups that have leaders or ingroups that are leaderless?
5. Who makes a better leader, a woman or a man?
6. Have you ever been in a group where the leader failed to carry out his or her duties properly?
7. Have you ever been in a group led by a skilled leader?
8. If you were appointed the leader of a group—such as a jury or a group of employees in a place of business—what would be your most important duties?

13

Intergroup Relations

As a social species, humans strive to establish close ties with one another. Yet, the same species that seeks out connections with others also metes out enmity and rejection when it confronts members of another group. Intergroup relations tend toward conflict rather than harmony.

- What interpersonal factors disrupt relations between groups?
- What are the cognitive foundations of conflict between groups?
- How can intergroup relations be improved?

CONTENTS

The Rattlers and the Eagles: Group Against Group

COMPETITION AND CONFLICT: US VERSUS THEM

Competition and Mutual Distrust

Escalation of Conflict

SOCIAL CATEGORIZATION: PERCEIVING US AND THEM

The Ingroup/Outgroup Bias

Cognitive Consequences of Categorization

Does Categorization Cause Conflict?

RESOLVING INTERGROUP CONFLICT: UNITING US AND THEM

Intergroup Contact

Beyond Contact: Promoting Intergroup Cooperation

Cognitive Cures for Conflict

Conflict Management

Resolving Conflict: Conclusions

SUMMARY

FOR MORE INFORMATION

ACTIVITIES

The Rattlers and the Eagles: Group Against Group

On two midsummer days in 1954, a bus drove through Oklahoma City picking up excited 11-year-old boys to take them off to camp. They were "normal, well-adjusted boys of the same age, educational level, from similar sociocultural backgrounds and with no unusual features in their personal backgrounds" (Sherif, Harvey, White, Hood, & Sherif, 1961, p. 59). Their parents had paid a $25 fee, signed some consent forms, and packed them off to a camp situated in Robbers Cave State Park, which legend claimed was once a hideout for desperadoes.

Robbers Cave, however, was not your everyday summer camp. All of the boys had been hand picked by a research team that included Muzafer Sherif, O. J. Harvey, Jack White, William Hood, and Carolyn Sherif. The Sherifs and their colleagues had spent more than 300 hours interviewing the boys' teachers, studying their academic records, reviewing their family backgrounds, and unobtrusively recording their behavior in school and on the playground. The parents knew that the camp was actually part of a group dynamics research project, but the boys themselves had no idea that they were subjects in the **Robbers Cave Experiment.**

The staff brought the children to camp in two separate trips and kept them apart for a week. The boys spent the week camping, hiking, swimming, and playing sports, and both groups developed norms, roles, and structure. Some boys were designated leaders, others became followers, and both groups established territories within the park (see Figure 13–1). The boys named their groups the Rattlers and the Eagles and stenciled these names on their shirts and painted them onto flags. The staff members, who were also observers collecting data, noted clear increases in group-oriented behaviors, cohesiveness, and positive group attitudes. For example:

> At the hideout, Everett (a non-swimmer when camp started) began to swim a little. He was praised by all and for the first time the others called him by his preferred nickname. Simpson yelled, "Come on, dive off the board!" All members in the water formed a large protective circle into which Everett dived after a full 2 minutes of hesitation and reassurance from the others. [Sherif et al., p. 79]

When each group realized another group was camping nearby, references to "those guys," "they," and "outsiders" became increasingly frequent. Both teams wanted to compete with the other group and asked the staff to set up a tournament. Of course, a series of competitions between the two groups was exactly what the staff had in mind, so they held a tournament that included baseball games, tugs-of-war, tent-pitching competitions, cabin inspections, and a (rigged) treasure hunt.

As the competition wore on, tempers flared. When the Eagles lost a game, they retaliated by stealing the Rattlers' flag and burning it. The Rattlers raided the Eagles' cabin during the night, tearing out mosquito netting, overturning beds, and carrying

---

Robbers Cave Experiment: A field study performed by the Sherifs and their colleagues (1961) in an attempt to better understand the causes and consequences of intergroup conflict; the study derives its name from the state park that served as the site for the research.

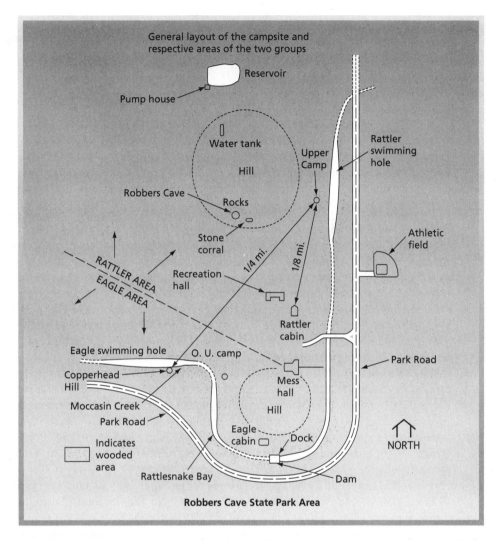

FIGURE 13–1 How did the Sherifs and their colleagues create intergroup conflict? Instead of observing conflict between naturally occurring groups, the Sherifs created groups at a summer camp in the Robbers Cave State Park in Oklahoma and then recorded the conflict that unfolded over time.

(*Source:* Sherif, Harvey, White, Hood, & Sherif, 1961.)

off personal belongings. When the Eagles won the overall tournament, the Rattlers absconded with the prizes. When fist fights broke out between the groups, the staff had to intervene to prevent the boys from seriously injuring one another. They moved the two groups to different parts of the camp, amid shouts of "poor losers," "bums," "sissies," "cowards," and "little babies."

Groups are everywhere, and so are conflicts between them. Intergroup conflict occurs at all levels of social organization—fights between gangs, organized disputes in industrial settings, race riots, and even conflicts between nations. Groups provide us with the means to achieve our most lofty goals, but when groups oppose each other, they are sources of hostility, abuse, and aggression. Although conflict between groups is one of the most complicated phenomena studied by social scientists, the goal of greater understanding and the promise of reduced tension remain enticing. Here we consider the nature of intergroup relations, with a focus on the sources of intergroup conflict and the ways such conflicts can be resolved.

COMPETITION AND CONFLICT: US VERSUS THEM

On the ninth day of the Robbers Cave Experiment, the Rattlers and the Eagles saw the tournament prizes for the first time: the shining trophy, medals for each boy, and—best of all—four-blade camping knives. The boys *wanted* these prizes, and nothing was going to stand in their way. From then on, all group activities revolved around the ultimate goal of winning the tournament. Unfortunately, although both groups aspired to win the prizes, success for one group meant failure for the other. Each group now saw the other as an enemy that had to be overcome if the prizes were to be won.

Realistic conflict theory maintains that intergroup conflict is caused by competition among groups over limited resources. This theory notes that the things that people value, including food, territory, wealth, power, natural resources, and energy, are so limited that if the members of one group manage to acquire a scarce commodity, the members of another group will go without it. Naturally, groups would prefer to be "haves" rather than "have-nots," so they take steps to achieve two interrelated outcomes: attaining the desired resources and preventing the other group from reaching its goals (Campbell, 1965; LeVine & Campbell, 1972). Theorists have implicated competition as the primary cause of class struggles (Marx & Engels, 1947), rebellions (Gurr, 1970), international warfare (Streufert & Streufert, 1986), racism (Gaines & Reed, 1995), religious persecutions (Clark, 1998), tribal rivalries in East Africa (Brewer & Campbell, 1976), police use of lethal force against citizens (Jacobs & O'Brien, 1998), and even the development of culture and social structure (Simmel, 1955; Sumner, 1906).

Robert Blake and Jane Mouton documented the close connection between competition and conflict in their work with business executives. They assigned participants in a two-week management training program to small groups that worked on a series of problem-solving tasks. Blake and Mouton never explicitly mentioned competition, but the participants knew that a group of experts would decide which group had produced the most adequate solution. Many viewed the project as a contest to see who was best, and they wholeheartedly accepted the importance of winning. Leaders who helped the group beat the opponent became influential, whereas leaders

---

Realistic conflict theory: A conceptual framework that argues that conflict between groups stems from competition for scarce resources, including food, territory, wealth, power, natural resources, and energy.

of losing groups were replaced. The groups bonded tightly during work and coffee breaks, and only rarely did any participant show liking for a member of another group. In some cases, hostility between the two groups became so intense that the "experiment had to be discontinued" and special steps taken to restore order, tempers, and "some basis of mutual respect" (Blake & Mouton, 1984, 1986, p. 72; Blake, Shepard, & Mouton, 1964). These findings and others suggest that competition— even competition that is only anticipated—can spark intergroup hostility (Bornstein, Budescu, & Zamir, 1997; Horwitz & Rabbie, 1982; Polzer, 1996; Rabbie, Benoist, Oosterbaan, & Visser, 1974; Rabbie & Horwitz, 1969; Rapoport & Bornstein, 1987; van Oostrum & Rabbie, 1995).

Competition and Mutual Distrust

Competition has been implicated as the cause of both intergroup conflict and intragroup conflict. Just as Chapter 9 concluded that many conflicts in groups occur when group members compete with each other, realistic conflict theory argues that relations between groups deteriorate when groups compete against each other for money, power, time, prestige, or materials. The competition-conflict relationship is particularly robust, however, at the group level. Indeed, Chester Insko, John Schopler, and their colleagues call the tendency for groups to respond more competitively than individuals the **discontinuity effect,** because the competitiveness of groups is out of proportion to the competitiveness displayed by individuals in groups. Even though individual group members may prefer to cooperate, when they join groups, this cooperative orientation is replaced by a competitive one (Hoyle, Pinkley, & Insko, 1989; Insko et al., 1987, 1988, 1992, 1993, 1994; Insko, Schopler, Hoyle, Dardis, & Graetz, 1990; Insko, Schopler, & Sedikides, 1998; McCallum et al., 1985; Schopler & Insko, 1992; Schopler et al., 1993, 1994, 1995; Schopler, Insko, Graetz, Drigotas, & Smith, 1991).

Insko, Schopler, and their colleagues documented this discontinuity effect by asking individuals and groups to play the prisoner's dilemma game (PDG). This mixed-motive game offers the two participating parties a choice between cooperative responding and competitive responding, and competition yields the highest rewards only if one of the two parties cooperates. When the Insko-Schopler research team had two individuals play the game, they averaged only 6.6% competitive responses over the course of the game. Competition was also rare when three independent, noninteracting individuals played three other independent individuals (7.5%). But when an interacting triad played another interacting triad, 36.2% of their choices were competitive ones, and when triads played triads but communicated their choices through representatives selected from within the group, competition rose to 53.5% (Insko et al., 1987).

This discontinuity between individuals and groups is not confined to laboratory groups playing a structured conflict game. When researchers examined everyday social interactions, they found that group activities were marked by more competition

---

Discontinuity effect: The markedly greater competitiveness of groups when interacting with groups, relative to the competitiveness of individuals interacting with individuals.

than one-on-one activities. Participants diligently recorded their interpersonal activities for an entire week, classifying them into one of five categories:

- One-on-one interactions: playing chess, walking to class with another person, and so on
- Within-group interactions: interactions with members of the same group, such as a club meeting or a classroom discussion
- One-on-group interactions: the individual subject interacting with a group, such as a student meeting with a panel of faculty for career information
- Group-on-one interactions: the individual is part of a group that interacts with a single individual, such as the subject and his friend Erick talking to Jonathan
- Group-on-group interactions: a soccer game, a joint session of two classes, and the like

As Figure 13–2 indicates, the proportion of competitive interactions within each type of interaction climbed steadily as people moved from one-on-one interactions to group interactions. These effects also emerged when sports activities, which could have exacerbated the competitiveness of groups, were eliminated from the analysis (Pemberton, Insko, & Schopler, 1996).

The discontinuity effect may result from group polarization: group members may shift toward greater competitiveness when they discover that others in the group also

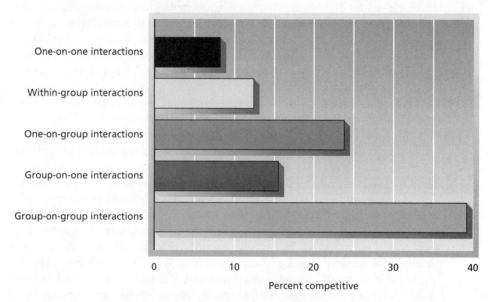

FIGURE 13–2 Are groups more competitive than individuals? Pemberton, Insko, and Schopler (1996) asked people to identify which of their week's interactions were competitive and which were cooperative. More of the interactions that involved groups rather than one-on-one dyadic interactions were considered competitive rather than cooperative.

(*Source:* Pemberton, Insko, & Schopler, 1996.)

favor the competitive, group-centered choice. Groups may also provide greater anonymity for members, so they feel less responsible for their competitive actions. But discontinuity is also likely produced by people's fundamental distrust of groups. When individuals play the PDG, their choices reflect their beliefs about their opponent's personality and preferences. When groups play the PDG against groups, their reactions are regulated by their expectations about how groups act when given the choice between cooperating and competing. And these expectations are usually negative (Insko & Schopler, 1998; Kramer & Messick, 1998).

Do people distrust groups? Insko, Schopler, and their colleagues examined this question by asking people to describe the types of traits and behaviors they expect to see in people as individuals and people who are part of a group. People were more wary of groups, describing them as more abrasive (competitive, aggressive, proud) and less agreeable (cooperative, trustworthy, helpful) than individuals. This pessimistic outlook also colored their expectations about specific group interactions, for people who were about to play the PDG against a group felt that the experience would be more abrasive than did individuals about to play the game as individuals (Hoyle, Pinkley, & Insko, 1989).

This lack of trust between groups also surfaces when members talk about their choices and plan their strategies. Members of groups expecting to play the PDG against another group question the motives of their opponents and refer to the likelihood that the other group will try to exploit them (Insko et al., 1994; Schopler et al., 1995). And if people are given a third option in the PDG—withdrawing instead of either competing or cooperating—they choose this safe, defensive option more frequently when playing in groups rather than as individuals (Insko et al., 1990, 1993; Schopler et al., 1993, 1995). Moreover, when individuals playing the PDG can communicate with one another, they often become more cooperative, but giving groups the chance to communicate with each other does not increase their cooperativeness (Insko et al., 1993). Indeed, groups were more likely to say such things as "We don't trust you" and "You better not cheat us" to their opponents (Insko et al., 1994).

Escalation of Conflict

The Rattlers and the Eagles did not immediately fall into conflict with each other. Before the games began, several members expressed curiosity about the other group, even suggesting that they might want to make friends with them. And during the first two days of the tournament, they refrained from excessive name-calling, and winners showed their good sportsmanship by cheering for the loser. But by the end of the tournament, the two groups of boys had to be physically restrained from hurting each other.

Conflict takes time to develop. Groups that have limited interaction do not become enemies, whereas groups whose paths cross repeatedly are more likely to end up locked in conflict. A study of professional ice hockey teams documented this fact by tracking the number of times that teams played each other and the number of penalties charged to the players for aggressive play—fighting, roughing, cross checking, high sticking, elbowing, slashing, and charging. The more frequently the teams met, the more likely the players played aggressively (Widmeyer & McGuire, 1997). Similarly, the teams at the Robbers Cave initially kept their hostilities in check, but as one competitive encounter followed after another, the conflict spiraled.

Conflict and Reciprocity.   Groups, like individuals, tend to follow the *norm of reciprocity:* They answer threats with threats, insults with insults, and aggression with aggression. The infamous Hatfield-McCoy feud, for example, began with the theft of some hogs by Floyd Hatfield (O. K. Rice, 1978). The McCoys countered by stealing hogs from another member of the Hatfield clan, and soon members of the two families began taking potshots at one another. By 1890, more then ten men and women had lost their lives as a direct result of interfamily violence. Likewise, studies of gangs indicate that many street fights stem from some initial negative action that, in reality, may pose little threat to the offended group. The target of the negative action, however, responds to the threat with a counterthreat, and the conflict spirals. Battles resulting in the death of gang members have begun over an ethnic insult, the intrusion of one group into an area controlled by another group, or the theft of one gang's property by another gang (Gannon, 1966; Yablonsky, 1959). Large-scale intergroup conflicts, such as race riots and warfare between countries, have also been caused by gradually escalating hostile exchanges (Goldberg, 1968; Holsti & North, 1965; North, Brody, & Holsti, 1964; Myers, 1997).

A spiral model of conflict intensification accurately describes the unfolding of violence at Robbers Cave. The conflict began with minor irritations and annoyances but built in intensity. The mildest form of rejection—verbal abuse—began when the groups met for the tournament. Insults were exchanged, members of the opposing team were given demeaning names, and verbal abuse ran high. Next, the groups began to actively avoid contact with each other, and intergroup discrimination also developed. The groups isolated themselves from each other at meals, and the boys expressed the belief that it was wrong for the other team to use the camp facilities or be given an equal amount of food. Last came the acts of physical violence—the raids, thefts, and fistfights. Thus, the conflict at Robbers Cave built in a series of progressively more dangerous stages from verbal abuse to avoidance to discrimination and finally to physical assault (Allport, 1954; Streufert & Streufert, 1986).

Power and Exploitation.   The Robbers Cave conflict did not end when the tournament concluded. Even though the formal competition was over, the Rattlers did not accept their defeat. They refused to admit their domination by the Eagles, and so they stole the prizes and attacked the Eagles. The Rattlers went so far as to tell the Eagles that "if they would get down on their bellies and crawl, they would return the prize knives and medals they had taken" (Sherif et al., 1961, p. 110), but the Eagles refused.

In many cases, intergroup conflicts, even though initially rooted in competition for scarce resources, can escalate into intergroup exploitation as one group tries to dominate the other. Not only do the groups wish to control the scarce resources, but they also wish to gain control over the other group as well. In some cases, this domination is purely economic. By manufacturing desirable goods or performing valuable services, the group can become the center of a developing trade system (Service, 1975). But domination can also occur through force and coercion (Carneiro, 1970).

Intergroup conflicts become particularly intense when one group tries to subdue and exploit another and that target group resists being dominated.

Insko and his colleagues examined the relationship between exploitation and conflict by creating a miniature social system in his laboratory. His microsocieties included three interdependent groups, multiple generations of members, a communication network, products, and a trading system. Each group had four members, but membership was always in flux because Insko replaced the senior member of each group with a new member every 20 minutes. The groups created a product (they folded paper into shapes of birds, boxes, boats, and hats) that they could trade to other groups. The groups communicated through an elected representative who exchanged messages and traded products with the other groups. Insko also stimulated trading by paying the groups more money if they sold him sets of paper shapes that included products made by other groups (Inkso et al., 1980, 1983).

The research team created two experimental conditions to examine the impact of coercive, exploitive power on productivity and intergroup relations. In one condition, which can be termed the economic-power condition, one of the groups was advantaged economically because it could make two types of shapes instead of only one: Group A made birds, Group C made boxes, but Group B made both boats and hats. Thus, Group B was the center of all bargaining and trading efforts. In a second condition, Group B was even more powerful, for it had the right to confiscate any products it desired from the other groups. In addition, in this condition the subjects were led to believe that the members of Group B were better problem solvers than the members of the other groups. This second condition can be called the coercive-power condition. (Insko referred to these conditions as the Service condition and the Carneiro condition, respectively.)

These differences in power had a dramatic effect on productivity and intergroup relations. When Group B had only economic power, all three groups reached very high levels of productivity. Group B, with its superior products, turned out nearly 100 products during the final generation of the experiment, and Groups A and C weren't far behind, with an average of about 70 products. But when Group B had coercive power, performance dropped. Even though Group B could confiscate products from the other groups and make more valuable sets, the other groups reacted very negatively to this exploitation. As time passed and Group B continued to steal their work, the members of the other groups held strikes and work slowdowns and sabotaged their products. By the final generation, production dropped by about 20% for Group B and by nearly 50% in groups A and C. Men, in particular, were more likely to strike back against the oppressive Group B members. Eventually, so little was left that Group B could not confiscate enough products to make much profit. The Group B members also sabotaged themselves. As the "idle-rich" hypothesis suggests, Group B members spent less time working when they could confiscate others' work. These results suggest that as with intragroup conflict, one sure way to create conflict is to give one group more coercive power than the other (Deutsch & Krauss, 1960). Apparently, when it comes to power, more is not always better.

Scapegoating and Conflict.   When the Eagles lost several games in the tournament, they felt frustrated and angrily blamed the Rattlers for their misfortunes. Later they would vent their anger by burning the Rattler flag. But what would have happened if the Eagles had been unable to attack the Rattlers? What if the Eagles were too fearful of retaliation to attack openly?

In most instances, if a group interferes with another group, the injured party would retaliate. If, however, the aggressor is extremely powerful, too distant, or difficult to locate, then the injured party may respond by turning its aggression onto another group. This third group, although not involved in the conflict in any way, would nonetheless be blamed and thereby become the target of aggressive actions. The third group, in this case, would be the scapegoat—a label derived from the biblical guilt-transference ritual. Anger originally aroused by one group becomes displaced upon another, more defenseless group. Attacking the guiltless group provides an outlet for pent-up angers and frustrations, and the aggressive group may then feel satisfied that justice has been done.

The **scapegoat theory** of intergroup conflict argues that tensions build up in people when they experience frustration, and these tensions must eventually find release. When group members are frustrated and dissatisfied, they sometimes respond by attacking groups that had nothing to do with their situation. The scapegoat theory explains why frustrating economic conditions often stimulate increases in prejudice and violence. Studies of anti-Black violence in southern areas of the United States between 1882 and 1930 indicate that outbreaks of violence tended to occur whenever the economy of that region worsened (Hovland & Sears, 1940). Indeed, the correlation between the price of cotton (the main product of that area at the time) and the number of lynchings of Black men by Whites ranged from –0.63 to –0.72, suggesting that when Whites were frustrated by the economy, they took out these frustrations by attacking Blacks (see also Hepworth & West, 1988, for a more sophisticated analysis of the Hovland-Sears data).

Scapegoating can also prompt oppressed groups to lash out at other oppressed groups. Even though the minority group is victimized by the majority group, the group responds by turning against another minority group rather than the more powerful majority (Harding, Proshansky, Kutner, & Chein, 1969; Myers, 1997). In a laboratory analog of this social process, researchers assigned subjects to one of three groups that worked at four tasks. All the subjects were led to believe that two of the groups, including theirs, had been assigned to work under adverse conditions; the third group's work conditions were designed to optimize their performance. The experimenters also gave the subjects feedback about each group's performance. The researchers told all the subjects that their group was performing only adequately, whereas the advantaged group was performing very well. The researchers also told some of the subjects that the other disadvantaged group's performance was similar to theirs, worse than theirs, or better than theirs. When the researchers gave the subjects the opportunity to harm the other groups' chances to earn a bonus, subjects treated the other disadvantaged group more positively if it was performing even worse than they were. But if the disadvantaged group performed as well as or even better than the ingroup, subjects inflicted more harm on the outgroup (see Figure 13–3). In contrast, subjects punished the advantaged group

---

Scapegoat theory: An explanation of intergroup conflict that argues that hostility caused by frustrating environmental circumstances is sometimes released by taking hostile actions against members of other social groups.

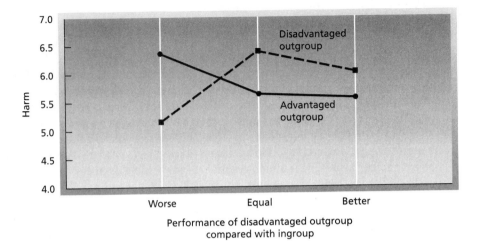

FIGURE 13-3 When will one disadvantaged group inflict harm on another disadvantaged group? When will a disadvantaged group attack another, more advantaged group? Rothgerber and Worchel (1997) discovered that disadvantaged groups were more aggressive if they felt that the other disadvantaged group was performing equal to or better than they were.

(*Source:* Rothgerber & Worchel, 1997.)

more when the other disadvantaged group was performing poorly (Rothgerber & Worchel, 1997).

SOCIAL CATEGORIZATION: PERCEIVING US AND THEM

The boys at Robbers Cave displayed antipathy toward the other group even before the idea of a competitive tournament was mentioned. Indeed, the Rattlers and Eagles had not even seen each other when they began to refer to "those guys" in a derogatory way (Sherif et al., 1961, p. 94):

> When the ingroup began to be clearly delineated, there was a tendency to consider all others as outgroup. . . . The Rattlers didn't know another group existed in the camp until they heard the Eagles on the ball diamond; but from that time on the outgroup figured prominently in their lives. Hill (Rattler) said "They better not be in our swimming hole." The next day Simpson heard tourists on the trail just outside of camp and was convinced that "those guys" were down at "our diamond" again.

The Sherifs suggested that the conflict between the two groups resulted from their competitions, but this explanation cannot fully account for the almost automatic rejection of members of the other group. Group members reject members of other groups not because they fear them or because they must compete with them, but simply because they belong to a *different* group.

The Ingroup/Outgroup Bias

People are classifiers. Young Mills, a Rattler, could tell at a glance each type of tree that grew at the Robbers Cave campsite. He could distinguish between the types of balls needed to play different sports and the type of weather that would be best for hiking rather than swimming. But he also engaged in *social categorization,* for he classified people into categories: man or woman; child, adult, or elder; staff member or camper; introvert or extravert. And even though Mills recognized a wide range of possible categories for classifying people, two of his most basic social categorizations were *ingroup member* and *outgroup member* (Jones, 1983; Wilder, 1986a, 1986b).

Social categorization plays a fundamental role in helping us understand the world around us (Allport, 1954). We do not, however, simply segment people into the categories "member of my group" and "member of another group" and then stop. Once people are categorized, we view people in our group (ingroup members) more favorably than those outside our group (outgroup members). At the group level, this tendency is called the **ingroup/outgroup bias;** among larger social groups, such as tribes, ethnic groups, or nations, the bias is termed **ethnocentrism** (Sumner, 1906).

Categorization and Friendships.   The Sherifs documented the ingroup/outgroup bias in all their field studies of intergroup conflict. Although the Robbers Cave Experiment is the best known of these studies, the Sherifs and their colleagues conducted similar projects at other camps. The first experiment, conducted in 1949 in a camp in northern Connecticut, roughly followed the procedures of the Robbers Cave study (Sherif & Sherif, 1953). The teams in that study called themselves the Red Devils and the Bull Dogs, and conflict was dispelled by (1) breaking up the two groups during meals and other camp activities and (2) staging a softball game between the entire camp and a team from another camp. A 1953 study (Sherif, White, & Harvey, 1955) was designed to test hypotheses concerning status and estimates of task performance but had to be aborted when the two groups, the Panthers and the Pythons, realized that the camp administration was creating the intergroup friction.

All three studies provide evidence of ingroup/outgroup bias, but the findings obtained in the Red Devils–Bull Dogs study are particularly striking (Sherif & Sherif, 1953). Unlike the campers at Robbers Cave, the boys were not separated into groups until a full week of campwide activities had been held. During that time, friendships formed, and the researchers deliberately placed friends in different groups during the second week. Thus, when groups were formed, many of the Red Devils had friends on the Bull Dogs team, and many Bull Dogs accepted Red Devils as friends.

Categorization, however, virtually obliterated these original friendships. Boys who continued to interact with members of the outgroup were branded traitors and threatened with bodily harm unless they broke off their friendships. One member of the Bull

---

Ingroup/outgroup bias: The tendency to view the ingroup, its members, and products more positively than the outgroup, its members, and its products. Ingroup favoritism is more common than outgroup rejection.
Ethnocentrism: The belief that one's own tribe, region, or country is superior to other tribes, regions, or countries.

Dogs who did not completely identify with the group was partially ostracized, and eventually, his parents had to remove him from the camp. A Red Devil who suggested that the two groups get together for a party was punished by the Red Devil's leader. This observational evidence was buttressed by the sociometric-choice data collected before and after the groups were formed. Before intergroup conflict, over 60% of the boys reported that their best friends were members of what would eventually become the outgroup. Later, after the groups were separated, cross-group friendships dwindled down to 10%.

Outgroup Rejection. The ingroup/outgroup bias is really two biases combined: a tendency to favor our own group, its members, and its products and a tendency to derogate another group, its members, and its products (Brewer, 1979; Coser, 1956; Hinkle & Schopler, 1986). At Robbers Cave, ingroup favoritism went hand in hand with outgroup rejection. When asked to name their friends, 92.5% of the Eagles' choices were Eagles, and 93.6% of the Rattlers' choices were fellow Rattlers. When asked to pick the one person they disliked the most, 95% of the Eagles selected a Rattler, and 75% of the Rattlers identified an Eagle.

These biases in ingroup/outgroup attraction have been confirmed in a number of other studies, but many suggest that ingroup favoritism is stronger than outgroup rejection. Lewis Coser (1956), for example, points out that outgroup hostility is not a necessary consequence of conflict. Rejection helps the group carry out aggressive actions against the opposing group, but outgroup hatred, rejection, and contempt do not always covary with ingroup cohesion, acceptance, and attraction. Marilynn Brewer agrees with Coser's conclusions: Conflict creates "the perception that one's own group is better, although the outgroup is not necessarily deprecated" (Brewer, 1979, p. 322; see also Brewer, 1986; Brewer & Brown, 1998).

Brewer suggests that the expression of outgroup hostility depends on a number of situational factors, including the similarity of ingroup and outgroup members, anticipated future interactions, the type of evaluation being made, and the competitive or cooperative nature of the intergroup situation. Groups that fail during intergroup contests, for example, are more likely to derogate the other group than are groups that win. Stephen Worchel and his colleagues (Worchel, Andreoli, & Folger, 1977) documented this tendency, convincing pairs of groups that they were competing, cooperating, or working independently. He then told half of the groups that they failed to earn prize money or succeeded in earning the money. All the subjects then indicated their liking for members of the other group on a 31-point scale. As expected, the subjects rated their own group more favorably; the average was about 25 on the 31-point scale. The ratings of the outgroup were lower, between 19 and 20, when the two groups were cooperating or working independently, and considerably lower (the average was 15) when the groups were competing. This outgroup rejection was even more pronounced if the groups later experienced a second failure. Winners in intergroup contests aren't as hostile toward the outgroup as are losers (Kahn & Ryen, 1972; Wilson & Miller, 1961).

Categorization and Cohesion. Coser (1956), in addition to noting that the pro–ingroup bias is stronger than the anti–outgroup bias, recognized that intergroup conflict has one useful side effect: It triggers a rapid rise in cohesion (1956, p. 87). At Robbers Cave, for example, as the competitions progressed, the two groups became more tightly organized. The attitudes of each group toward the other became more and more negative, but the cohesiveness of each unit became increasingly stronger. Although every defeat was associated with initial dejection and internal bickering, the groups channeled this animosity in the direction of the opponent. As time passed, the groups became better organized, and the group structure solidified.

Intergroup conflict does not invariably lead to increased cohesion (Tyerman & Spencer, 1983), nor is intergroup conflict a prerequisite for intragroup cohesion (Goldman, Stockbauer, & McAuliffe, 1977). In general, however, Coser's speculations concerning the solidifying effects of cohesion have been confirmed empirically: Rises in intergroup conflict tend to go hand in hand with increases in intragroup cohesion (Dion, 1973, 1979; Worchel, Lind, & Kaufman, 1975).

Differentiation.   Coser also suggested that "conflict serves to establish and maintain the identity and boundary lines of groups" (1956, p. 38). As the conflict between the Eagles and the Rattlers escalated, each group tended to emphasize the major distinctions between the two groups of combatants. The groups began to isolate themselves from each other and asked that they be allowed to eat separately. Unique group norms also began to develop, and if one group adopted a style of action, this behavior was soundly rejected by the other group. For example, the Rattlers cursed frequently; to distinguish themselves from those "bad cussers," the Eagles adopted the norm of no profanity. Later, their leader decided that the Rattlers were such poor sports that "the Eagles should not even talk to them anymore" (p. 106). Proprietary orientations toward certain portions of the camp also developed, along with mottoes, uniforms, and secret passwords.

Such differentiation is typical during intergroup conflict. Rather than noting shared similarities, the groups tend to emphasize their differences (Sherif, 1966). Competing groups also distance themselves from one another, whereas cooperating groups minimize distances (Ryen & Kahn, 1975). Members of competing groups even take pains to display nonverbal postures that are different from those displayed by members of the other group (LaFrance, 1985) or try to speak differently from the outgroup members. When people from different cultures find themselves in conflict, they often adopt a dialect, accent, or language form that is unique to their ingroup and foreign to the outgroup (Giles, 1977; Giles & Johnson, 1981; Krauss & Chiu, 1998).

Double-Standard Thinking.   Groups tend to use a double standard when evaluating their own actions and those of another group. When we refuse to yield to threats (which the other side calls requests), we are courageous, though they consider us stubborn. Pride in our own group is nationalism, though the other group takes it as evidence of ethnocentrism. We offer them concessions, but they interpret them as ploys. Examining such perceptual differences in Arabs' and Israelis' attributions concerning the cause of the major Middle East wars of 1948, 1956, 1967, and 1973, Ralph K. White (1977, p. 205) found that both sides believed the other side to have been the aggressor in all four wars. In two of these wars (1956, 1967), the Arabs believed that Israel had simply attacked without provocation. In the remaining two (1948, 1973), the Arabs admitted that they had initiated hostilities, but believed that they had been forced to do so by the expansionistic policies of Israel. Conversely, the Israelis felt that the 1948 and 1973 wars were "instances of naked, obvious Arab aggression" and that the 1956 and 1967 battles had been indirectly caused by the threats and malevolent intentions of the Arabs (White, 1965, 1966, 1969, 1977). Similar biases have been found when students in the United States are asked to evaluate actions performed by their country and by the Soviet Union (Oskamp & Hartry, 1968) and when Whites' and Blacks' judgments of ambiguously aggressive actions committed by either a Black or a White are compared (Sagar & Schofield, 1980). People judge actions that their own group performs positively, but they negatively evaluate these same actions when they are performed by the outgroup.

Cognitive Consequences of Categorization

Categorization is, in all likelihood, an automatic cognitive process; without much thought, people rapidly pigeonhole other people into categories. But once an individual is recognized as a member of our group or some other group, we rush to make generalizations about their qualities, their interests, and their unseen attributes. These generalizations, however, are often overgeneralizations that are driven more by the categorization process than by the evidence of our senses.

Outgroup Homogeneity Bias.   Most group members are quick to point out the many characteristics that distinguish them from the other members of their group ("Why, I'm not like them at all!"), but when they evaluate members of outgroups, they underestimate their variability ("They all look the same to me"). If you were an Eagle, for example, you would describe the Rattlers as poor sports who cheated whenever possible. When describing the Eagles, in contrast, you might admit that a few of the members were sissies and that maybe one Eagle liked to bend the rules, but you would probably argue that the Eagles were so heterogeneous that sweeping statements about their typical qualities couldn't be formulated (Quattrone, 1986). Studies of a variety of ingroups and outgroups—women versus men, physics majors versus dance majors, Sorority A versus Sorority B, Princeton students versus Rutgers students, Canadians versus Native Americans, and Blacks versus Whites—have documented this so-called **outgroup homogeneity bias**: the tendency for people to assume that the outgroup is much more homogeneous than the ingroup (Judd & Park, 1988; Linville & Fisher, 1998; Ostrom & Sedikides, 1992). The homogeneity bias is complemented by the **ingroup differentiation bias**. Group members' conceptualizations of other groups are

---

Outgroup homogeneity bias: The perceptual tendency to assume that the members of other groups are very similar to each other, whereas the membership of our own group is more heterogeneous.

Ingroup differentiation bias: The perceptual tendency to assume that our own group is diverse and heterogeneous, with members possessing distinctive qualities that differentiate them from each other.

simplistic and undifferentiated, but when they turn their eye to their own group, they note its diversity and complexity (Linville, 1982; Linville, Fischer, & Salovey, 1989; Linville, Fischer, & Yoon, 1996; Park & Rothbart, 1982).

The outgroup homogeneity bias does not emerge across all intergroup settings. Indeed, in many cases, the bias reverses entirely, with group members describing all the members of the ingroup as very similar and the outgroup as highly differentiated (Haslam & Oakes, 1995; Simon, Pantaleo, & Mummendey, 1995). This **ingroup homogeneity bias** usually occurs when the ingroup is threatened in some way. When psychology majors, for example, were told that an outgroup (business majors) was more intelligent, the psychology students who strongly identified with their major viewed all psychology majors as relatively similar (Doosje, Ellemers, & Spears, 1995). Indeed, under conditions of extreme conflict, both tendencies may emerge, prompting group members to assume that "none of us deserve this treatment" and "they have harmed us; they must all be punished" (Rothgerber, 1997).

Judgmental Biases.   The two sides of ingroup/outgroup bias are also evident when group members judge the quality of their group products. A rock band not only thinks that its music is very good, but also considers a rival group's music inferior. One ethnic group prides itself on its traditions and also views other groups' traditions with disdain. One team of researchers thinks that its theory explains intergroup conflict while criticizing other researchers' theories as inadequate.

The Sherifs illustrated the bias in evaluations of intergroup performance by asking the Eagles and Rattlers to judge the products of ingroup and outgroup members. After a bean-collecting game, the Sherifs asked the campers to estimate the number of beans each boy collected. The boys' estimates were very biased. Rattlers overestimated the number of beans collected by Rattlers and slightly underestimated the number of beans supposedly collected by Eagles. The estimates provided by the Eagles were inflated for both ingroup and outgroup members, but the error was much greater for ingroup evaluations. Subsequent laboratory studies have found similar biases in groups evaluating their own and others' products, but they also suggest that the magnitude of the bias depends on a host of situational factors, including the group's outcomes, the way evaluations are measured, and ambiguity about performance standards (Hinkle & Schopler, 1986).

The **linguistic intergroup bias** is more subtle than the blatant favoritism displayed by the Rattlers and the Eagles. Instead of exaggerating the quality of a product or action, the group members describe the action differently, depending on who performed it. If an ingroup member engages in a negative behavior, such as crying during a game, then members would describe that behavior very concretely—Elliott shed some tears. If the

---

Ingroup homogeneity bias: The tendency for group members to assume that their own group is homogeneous, with group members sharing many similar qualities; the opposite of the ingroup-differentiation bias.

Linguistic intergroup bias: The tendency to communicate positive ingroup and negative outgroup behaviors more abstractly than negative ingroup and positive outgroup behaviors.

outgroup member performed the same behavior, they would describe the action more abstractly—Elliott acted like a baby. Positive behaviors, in contrast, are described in abstract terms when attributed to an ingroup member but in very concrete terms when performed by an outgroup member (Maass, Ceccarelli, & Rudin, 1996; Maass, Milesi, Zabbini, & Stahlberg, 1995).

Group Attribution Error.   Group members tend to make sweeping statements about the entire outgroup after observing one or two of the group's members. If an African American employee is victimized by a European American boss, the victim may tend to assume that all Whites are racists. Similarly, a visitor to another country who is treated rudely by a passerby may leap to the conclusion that everyone who lives in that country is discourteous. Individuals in intergroup situations tend to fall prey to the *law of small numbers:* They assume that the behavior of a large number of people can be accurately inferred from the behavior of a few people (Quattrone & Jones, 1980).

The opposite process—assuming that the characteristics of a single individual in a group can be inferred from the general characteristics of the whole group—can also lead us astray. If we know our group's position on an issue, we are reluctant to assume that any one of us agrees with that position. When we know another group's position, however, we are much more willing to assume that each and every person in that group agrees with that position. Scott Allison and his colleagues studied the **group attribution error** by telling their college-student subjects that an election had recently been held at their college or at another college to determine how much funding should be given to the college's athletics programs. They then told the students the results of the vote and asked them to estimate the opinion of the "typical student" at the college where the vote was taken. When the students thought that the vote had been taken at their own college, they didn't want to assume that the individual's opinion would match the group's opinion. But when they thought that the vote was taken at another college, they were much more confident that the individual's opinions would match the group's opinions (Allison & Messick, 1985b; Allison, Worth, & King, 1990).

Stereotypes.   Social categorization makes it possible for us to distinguish between the members of our group and the members of other groups. When an Eagle met another Eagle on the trail, he probably expected the boy to be friendly, helpful, and brave. But if he encountered a Rattler, he expected the boy to be unfriendly, aggressive, and deceitful.

These expectations are based on **stereotypes:** cognitive generalizations about the qualities and characteristics of the members of a particular group or social category. In many ways, stereotypes function as cognitive labor-saving devices by helping us make rapid judgments about people based on their category memberships (McCauley,

---

Group attribution error: The tendency for perceivers to assume that individual group members' beliefs and characteristics can be inferred from their group's decisions and general characteristics.
Stereotypes: Socially shared generalizations about the people who are members of a particular group or social category.

Stitt, & Segal, 1980; Miller, 1982). And because they are widely adopted by most of the ingroup, they are shared social beliefs rather than individualistic expectations (Simon, Glaessner-Bayerl, & Stratenwerth, 1991). But stereotypes tend to be exaggerated rather than accurate, negative rather than positive, and resistant to revision even when we encounter individuals who directly disconfirm them (Linville, 1982; Stephan & Rosenfield, 1982). People also tend to cling to stereotypes so resolutely that they become unreasonable beliefs rather than honest misconceptions. Allport (1954, p. 8) writes: "Prejudgments become prejudices only if they are not reversible when exposed to new knowledge."

If stereotypes have all these perceptual and cognitive limitations, why do they persist? Walter Lippmann (1922), who first used the word *stereotype* to describe our intuitive assumptions about people, argued that the stereotype resists disconfirmation because "it stamps itself upon the evidence in the very act of securing the evidence." When we see people through eyes clouded by stereotypes, we misperceive and misremember people and events. Yet, only rarely do we notice these errors, for our stereotypes are protected by confirmatory biases that serve to affirm their validity.

We sometimes interpret ambiguous information so that it matches our expectations. Prejudiced White people, for example, when asked to make up a story about a picture of a Black person interacting with a White person, usually assumed that the White and Black individuals were arguing with one another, and they usually blamed the Black for starting the dispute (Allport & Postman, 1947). White college students who observed a staged argument between a Black and a White in which one person shoved the other described the push as "violent" when the perpetrator was Black, but "playing" or "dramatizing" when the perpetrator was White (Duncan, 1976). Junior high school boys described the actions committed by a Black male in a drawing as "meaner" and more threatening than the identical behavior performed by a White male (Sagar & Schofield, 1980). Stereotypes resist disconfirmation because we reinterpret the evidence until we see what we expect.

Stereotypes also influence what we remember and forget, for our recall of information that is consistent with our stereotypes is often superior to our recall of stereotype-inconsistent information. If we think that Rattlers are vulgar, for example, we are more likely to remember the time that one swore during the baseball game rather than the time that one said a prayer. If we think that Eagles are poor sports, we will forget the times that they cheered for us after one of the games. Myron Rothbart and his associates have examined these memory biases experimentally in a number of studies (Howard & Rothbart, 1980; Park & Rothbart, 1982; Rothbart, Davis-Stitt, & Hill, 1997; Rothbart, Evans, & Fulero, 1979; Rothbart, Fulero, Jensen, Howard, & Birrell, 1978; Rothbart, Sriram, & Davis-Stitt, 1996). In one, they gave subjects a bogus test before assigning them to either the underestimator or overestimator group. The subjects then read a series of self-descriptive statements supposedly written by underestimators and overestimators. Some of the behaviors were positive ("I took two disadvantaged kids on a one-week vacation" or "I saved enough money to spend a year traveling in Europe") and some were negative ("I had two brief affairs with other people while I was married" and "I spread rumors that my roommate was dishonest"). These statements were written on separate cards that were organized into two decks of

48. One deck was labeled overestimators, and the other was labeled underestimators. Ten minutes later, the subjects tried to sort the shuffled deck into the two original piles. Although memories for positive behaviors committed by the ingroup and outgroup members were equal and unbiased, memories for negative behaviors were distorted. Subjects remembered more of the negative behaviors associated with the outgroup and fewer of the negative behaviors associated with the ingroup (Howard & Rothbart, 1980).

This memory bias may explain **illusory correlations:** the tendency to overestimate the strength of the relationship between unrelated characteristics in the outgroup (McArthur & Friedman, 1980). Because we expect outgroup members to engage in negative behavior and we remember the times that they acted negatively rather than positively, we feel vindicated in thinking that membership in the outgroup and negative behaviors are correlated (Hamilton & Sherman, 1989).

Does Categorization Cause Conflict?

Categorization, although an essential cognitive tool for understanding ourselves and others, limits the veridicality of our perceptions. When we formulate impressions of others by relying on stereotypes and expectations, we underestimate the complexity of the outgroup, overlook information that is inconsistent with our expectations, and formulate judgments that are more extreme than they should be (Dovidio & Gaertner, 1993; Stephan, 1985). But does social categorization, in and of itself, cause conflict? Does the mere existence of identifiable groups within society, and the cognitive biases generated by these perceived groups, inevitably push groups into conflict?

Henri Tajfel, John Turner, and their colleagues have examined this question in their studies of the **minimal intergroup situation.** They began by randomly assigning participants to one of two groups, but told the participants that the division was based on some irrelevant characteristic, such as art preference. Next, the subjects read over a series of booklets asking them to decide how a certain amount of money should be allocated to other participants in the experiment. The names of the individuals were not given in the booklets, but the subject could tell which group a person belonged to by looking at his or her code number. The groups were minimal ones, for (1) members of the same group never interacted in a face-to-face situation, (2) the identities of ingroup and outgroup members were unknown, and (3) no one gained personally by granting more or less money to any particular person. The groups were "purely cognitive"; they existed only in the minds of the subjects themselves.

Tajfel and Turner's research revealed a systematic ingroup bias even in this minimal intergroup situation. Participants did not know one another, they would not be

---

Illusory correlations: Assumed relationships between two variables that are not actually related to one another; also, overestimations of the strength of the relationship between unrelated characteristics possessed by the members of a particular group.
Minimal intergroup situation: A research procedure used to study intergroup conflict that creates temporary groupings of anonymous people whose interdependence is virtually nil.

working together in the future, and their membership in the so-called group had absolutely no personal or interpersonal implications. Yet the subjects not only awarded more money to members of their own group, but they seemed to keep money from members of the other group. Indeed, the ingroup bias persisted even when the researcher went to great lengths to make it clear that assignment to a group was being done on a random basis and that giving money to the outgroup would not cause any monetary loss for any ingroup member. Tajfel and Turner concluded that the "mere perception of belonging to two distinct groups—that is, social categorization per se—is sufficient to trigger intergroup discrimination favoring the ingroup" (1986, p. 13; see also Billig & Tajfel, 1973; Tajfel, 1978a, 1978b, 1978c, 1981, 1982; Turner, 1981, 1982, 1983; Turner et al., 1987; compare with Berkowitz, 1994).

Social Identity and Categorization.   Tajfel and his colleagues turned to social identity theory to explain the biases they documented in the minimal group situation. This theory, as noted in Chapter 3, assumes that membership in groups can substantially influence members' sense of self. When the boys joined the Robbers Cave Experiment and became firmly embedded in their groups, their identities changed: They came to think of themselves as Rattlers or Eagles, and they accepted the group's characteristics as their own. The theory also suggests that as the boys came to identify with their group, their own self-worth became more closely tied to the worth of the group. If a Rattler dedicated himself to the group and the Rattlers failed, then the boy would likely experience a distressing reduction in his own self-esteem. Group members therefore stress the value of their own groups relative to others as a means of indirectly enhancing their own personal worth (Tajfel & Turner, 1986).

Researchers have confirmed some, but not all, of social identity theory's assumptions about the source of the ingroup/outgroup bias (Aschenbrenner & Schaefer, 1980; Brewer, 1979; Duckitt & Mphuthing, 1998; Mummendey, 1995). When individuals feel that the value of their group is being questioned, they respond by underscoring the distinctiveness of their own group and derogating others (Grant, 1993; Spears, Doosje, & Ellemers, 1997). Individuals who experience a threat to their self-esteem do indeed tend to discriminate more against outgroups, and low-status, peripheral members of the group are often the most zealous in their defense of their group and the rejection of the outgroup (Hogg & Sunderland, 1991; Noel, Wann, & Branscombe, 1995). Individuals are also more likely to draw comparisons between their group and other groups in areas where the comparison favors the ingroup. The Rattlers, for example, lost the tournament and so they admitted that the Eagles were better than the Rattlers at sports. But the Rattlers could stress their superiority in other spheres unrelated to the games, such as toughness or endurance (Mullen, Brown, & Smith, 1992; Reichl, 1997).

But does condemning other groups raise one's self-esteem? The effectiveness of this technique for sustaining self-esteem has not been confirmed consistently by researchers. In some cases, derogating outgroup members raises certain forms of self-esteem, but praising the ingroup tends to bolster self-esteem more than condemning the outgroup (Branscombe & Wann, 1994; Hogg & Sunderland, 1991; Hunter, Platow, Bell, Kypri, & Lewis, 1997; Hunter, Platow, Howard, & Stringer, 1996; Jetten, Spears, & Manstead, 1996). Also, even though people are quick to praise their ingroup, they still think that they, as individuals, are superior to the members of all groups—including their own (Lindeman, 1997).

Conflict and Exclusion.   The Rattlers, by condemning the Eagles, may have indirectly bolstered their own sense of self-worth, as social identity theory suggests. This disparagement of the outgroup, however, may have also helped them justify their mistreatment of the Eagles. Inflicting harm on other people, even members of another group, is inconsistent with universally shared principles of fairness and compassion. Yet, the Rattlers ruined the Eagles' possessions and attacked them physically. How did they deal with their feelings of shame about acting so aggressively?

They may have explained away their actions by blaming their victims. The Sherifs report no evidence suggesting that the boys at Robbers Cave ever considered their aggressions against the other team to be "wrong." Poor sports etiquette, verbal derision, destruction of others' property, theft, vandalism, and physical violence were all condoned as actions taken against the enemy. The boys felt that their own group had the right to seek victory at all costs and that the home group's actions were somehow more moral than those of the other team. The Eagles even held prayer meetings before each contest to ask for God's help in vanquishing their foe; several boys were certain that their success was the result of divine intervention.

Researchers identified similar group-protective strategies when they asked people to rate their own religious group and the members of another religious group. As expected, these people attributed far more positive qualities to their own group and more negative qualities to the outgroup, consistent with other studies of the ingroup/outgroup bias. This bias, however, was not a powerful predictor of individuals' aggressiveness toward members of the outgroup. Instead, their tendency to dehumanize the other group and reject its values mediated the relationship between conflicts of interest and aggression. These researchers concluded that ingroup/outgroup biases are a consequence, rather than a cause, of intergroup conflict (Struch & Schwartz, 1989).

This tendency to rationalize the harming of members of other groups has been variously termed *dehumanization, delegitimization,* and *moral exclusion* (Bandura, 1990; Bar-Tal, 1990; Staub, 1990). Ervin Staub (1989, 1990), for example, uses the concept of moral exclusion to explain cases of extreme violence perpetrated by one group against another: European Americans enslaving Africans; Nazi Germany's attempted genocide of Jews; "ethnic cleansing" in Croatia and Serbia; and the continuing warfare between Israelis and Arabs. Staub believes that in all these cases, aggressors denigrate the outgroup so completely that the outsiders are excluded from moral concern, for "it is difficult to harm people intensely whom one evaluates positively or strongly identifies with (Staub, 1990, p. 53). Groups that have a history of devaluing segments of their society are more likely to engage in moral exclusion, as are groups whose norms stress respect for authority and obedience. These groups, when they anticipate conflict with others groups, rapidly revise their opinions of their opponents so that they can take hostile actions against them.

The Evolution of Bias.   Sociobiology offers yet another explanation for the built-in biases that accompany social categorization. The tendency to categorize people is so pervasive—reaching across virtually all cultures and all times in human history—that some experts believe that it may have a genetic basis. As noted in Chapter 3, evolutionary psychologists believe that human beings are "herd animals" because groups provided individuals with survival advantages. In harsher environments, lone individuals survived only rarely, whereas those who banded with others in groups were more likely to survive and procreate.

This natural selection for sociality, however, may apply only to members of one's own small group or tribe (Insko, Schopler, & Sedikides, 1998). In all likelihood, early humans lived in small tribes comprised of people who were genetically similar. Therefore, by helping members of one's own group, one was also helping to protect copies of one's genes that were present in these other people. Because members of other groups were less genetically similar and less likely to be available to reciprocate any help if help was given them, human beings favored their own group over the outgroup. The outgroup, too, likely competed with the ingroup for land, food, water, and shelter and may have attempted to mate with the women of the ingroup through coercion. As E. O. Wilson (1975, p. 572) writes, "The spread of genes has always been of paramount importance." Because outsiders were a danger, people with the ability to recognize and avoid them tended to survive, while the less cautious tended to die off. After aeons of this natural selection process, the earth was populated primarily by human beings with a built-in readiness to respond positively to the ingroup and negatively to the outgroup (Caporael & Brewer, 1991; Gould, 1991; Rushton, 1989).

RESOLVING INTERGROUP CONFLICT: UNITING US AND THEM

The Robbers Cave researchers were left with a problem. The manipulations of the first two phases of the experiment had worked very well, for the Rattlers-Eagles war yielded a gold mine of data about intergroup conflict. Unfortunately, the two groups now despised each other. As conscientious social scientists, the Sherifs and their colleagues felt compelled to try to undo some of the negative effects of the study—to seek a method through which harmony and friendship could be restored at the Robbers Cave campsite.

Intergroup Contact

The Robbers Cave researchers first tried to reduce the conflict by uniting the groups in shared activities. They based their intervention on the **contact hypothesis**, which assumes that ingroup/outgroup biases will fade if people interact with members of the outgroup regularly. So the Sherifs arranged for the Rattlers and Eagles to join in seven pleasant activities, such as eating, playing games, viewing films, and shooting off firecrackers. Unfortunately, contact had little impact on the hostilities. During all these events, the lines between the two groups never broke, and antilocution, discrimination,

---

Contact hypothesis: The prediction that equal-status contact between the members of different groups will reduce intergroup conflict.

and physical assault continued unabated. When contact occurred during meals, "food fights" were particularly prevalent:

> After eating for a while, someone threw something, and the fight was on. The fight consisted of throwing rolls, napkins rolled in a ball, mashed potatoes, etc. accompanied by yelling the standardized, unflattering words at each other. The throwing continued for about 8–10 minutes, then the cook announced that cake and ice cream were ready for them. Some members of each group went after their dessert, but most of them continued throwing things a while longer. As soon as each gobbled his dessert, he resumed throwing. [Sherif et al., 1961, p. 158]

Contact lies at the heart of such social policies as school integration, foreign-student exchange programs, and the Olympics, but contact leaves much to be desired as a means of reducing intergroup conflict. Contact between racial groups at desegregated schools, for example, rarely reduces prejudice (Gerard, 1983; Schofield, 1978). When units of an organization that clash on a regular basis are relocated in neighboring offices, the conflicts remain (Brown, Condor, Matthews, Wade, & Williams, 1986). College students studying in foreign countries become increasingly negative toward their host countries the longer they remain in them (Stangor, Jonas, Stroebe, & Hewstone, 1996; Stroebe, Lenkert, & Jonas, 1988). Competing groups in laboratory studies remain adversaries if the only step taken to unite them is mere contact (Stephan, 1987; Worchel, 1986). Indeed, even before they initiated the contact, the Sherifs predicted that a "contact phase in itself will not produce marked decreases in the existing state of tension between groups" (Sherif et al., 1961, p. 51).

Beyond Contact: Promoting Intergroup Cooperation

When simple contact between the group members failed to ease their animosity, the Sherifs took the contact situation one step further: They would force the boys to work for **superordinate goals**. Because superordinate goals can be achieved only if two groups work together, the Sherifs assumed that they would foster intergroup cooperation. Hence, like feuding neighbors who unite when a severe thunderstorm threatens to flood their homes or like warring nations (in a recurring science fiction theme) that pool their technological skills to prevent the collision of the earth with an asteroid, the Rattlers and the Eagles might be reunited if they sought goals that could not be achieved by a single group working alone.

The staff created these superordinate goals by staging a series of crises. They secretly sabotaged the water supply and then asked the boys to find the source of the problem by tracing the water pipe from the camp back to the main water tank, located about 3/4 mile away. The boys became quite thirsty during their search and worked together to try to correct the problem. Eventually, they discovered that the main water valve had been turned off by "vandals," and they cheered when the problem was repaired. Later in this

---

Superordinate goals: Goals that can only be attained if the members of two or more groups work together by pooling their efforts and resources.

stage, the boys pooled their monetary resources to rent a movie that they all wanted to see, worked together to pull a broken-down truck, prepared meals together, exchanged tent materials, and took a rather hot and dusty truck ride together. After six days of cooperation, the tensions between the groups had been fairly well wiped out.

Why did contact between the Rattlers and the Eagles fail to unite the groups, whereas creating superordinate goals cured the conflict? The Robbers Cave groups had been competitors for the preceding week, and no explicit attempt was made to change the norms from a situation emphasizing competition to one calling for cooperation. Indeed, little payoff was afforded those group members who did try to work with outgroup members, for they earned no special rewards and were usually criticized by their fellow group members (Bodenhausen, Gaelick, & Wyer, 1987; Riordan & Riggiero, 1980). But when the Sherifs created superordinate goals, they redefined the nature of the situation. The emergencies forced the groups to cooperate. The staff stressed the importance of joint teamwork and treated the boys as equals. The situations also forced the boys to work with individual members of the outgroup for substantial periods of time. These changes combated the boys' ingroup/outgroup biases and effectively restored their unity.

Building Intergroup Cooperation.   Contact is much more likely to lead to a reduction in intergroup conflict when the prerequisites listed in Table 13–1 are satisfied. Consider, for example, Stuart W. Cook's (1985) study of European Americans who were prejudiced against African Americans. Cook carefully constructed a situation that included all of Table 13–1's ingredients. The prejudiced White women cooperated with a Black woman in a work setting. Both women were equal in status, and the work forced them to interact extensively with each other. The work situation was very egalitarian, and Cook's confederates frequently discussed topics dealing with racial equality and desegregation. The group also performed its responsibilities well and were paid for their work. Cook found that 40% of the women in the experimental condition showed a significant reduction in prejudice in comparison with only 12% in the control group.

Other researchers have confirmed the importance of each of the components in Table 13–1. Stephen Wright and his colleagues (1997), for example, have tested what they call the *extended contact hypothesis:* When group members learn that one or more members of their group have a friend in the outgroup, they express more positive intergroup attitudes. They conceptually replicated the Robbers Cave Experiment with college students who spent an entire day working in one of two groups on a variety of tasks. Groups first developed a sense of cohesiveness by designing a logo for their team and sharing personal information. The groups then competed against each other, and during lunch they watched as each group was given prizes and awards for defeating the other group. Later in the day, the groups worked on solitary tasks, except for two individuals who met together—supposedly to take part in an unrelated study. This meeting, however, was designed to create a friendly relationship between these two individuals, who then returned to their groups just before a final competition.

Wright discovered that the two group members who were turned into friends were more positive toward the outgroup. More importantly, however, this positivity generalized throughout the rest of the group. Even though the other group members had not

TABLE 13–1   NECESSARY INGREDIENTS
FOR CONFLICT-REDUCING CONTACT SITUATIONS

Cooperation	The situation should encourage individuals to work together in the pursuit of common goals rather than intergroup competition.
Status	The individuals who interact in the contact situation must be equal rather than different in authority or ability.
Personal interaction	The situation should encourage involving, affectively positive interactions among individuals rather than superficial contacts.
Norms	The norms in the social situation must encourage friendly, helpful, egalitarian attitudes and condemn ingroup/outgroup comparisons.
Positive outcomes	The joint activities undertaken by the groups should result in success rather than failure.

themselves developed friendships with members of the outgroup, the knowledge that someone in their group considered an outgroup member to be likable moderated the ingroup/outgroup bias (Wright, Aron, McLaughlin-Volpe, & Ropp, 1997).

Repeated contact may also be needed before intergroup hostilities begin to fade. In the Robbers Cave research, a whole series of superordinate goals was required to reduce animosity. Similarly, when students from two colleges worked together on problems, students from different schools accepted members from the outgroup only when they worked together twice. Students who worked with the outgroup just once or not at all rated the members of the outgroup more negatively than students who worked with the outgroup twice (Wilder & Thompson, 1980). Similar findings have been obtained in studies of desegregated schools. A long period of favorable intergroup contact may reduce prejudice, but if this favorable contact is followed by an equally long period in which contact is not encouraged, groups inevitably drift apart once again (Schofield & Sagar, 1977).

Intergroup experiences that lead to successes, too, are more effective than intergroup experiences that lead to negative outcomes. As a reinforcement position would suggest, when cooperating groups manage to succeed, the "warm glow of success" may generalize to the outgroup and create greater intergroup attraction. If the group fails, however, the negative effect associated with a poor performance will spread to the outgroup. In addition, if the cooperative encounter ends in failure, each group may blame the other for the misfortune, and intergroup relations may further erode (Worchel, 1986). The problem of failure was aptly demonstrated in one study in which groups that had previously competed were asked to work together to solve a problem (Worchel et al., 1977). Half the groups failed during the cooperative phase, and the other half succeeded. As predicted, when the intergroup cooperation ended in failure, outgroup members were still rejected. Other studies have replicated this effect and indicate that unless some excuse for the failure exists, a disastrous performance during cooperation will only serve to further alienate groups (Blanchard, Adelman, & Cook, 1975; Blanchard & Cook, 1976; Blanchard, Weigel, & Cook, 1975; Cook 1978, 1984; Mumpower & Cook, 1978; Weigel & Cook, 1975; Worchel & Norvell, 1980).

Cooperative Learning Groups.   The Sherifs discovered that contact that does not dispel interactants' expectations, stereotypes, and negative emotions can exacerbate the conflict. Similarly, studies of U.S. public schools suggest that desegregation often fails to eliminate racial and ethnic prejudices. Although integrated schools bring students from various groups into contact, they rarely promote cooperation between these groups (Amir, 1969, 1976; Cook, 1985; Schofield, 1978; Worchel, 1986). Instead of including the necessary ingredients for positive intergroup relations shown in Table 13–1, many school systems fail to encourage interaction among the members of various subgroups, and staff openly express hostile attitudes toward outgroup members (Brewer & Miller, 1984). Some schools, too, group students on the basis of prior academic experiences; as a result, educationally deprived students are segregated from students with stronger academic backgrounds (Schofield, 1978).

Desegregation will reduce prejudice only when supplemented by educational programs that encourage cooperation among members of different racial and ethnic groups. One technique that has yielded promising results involves forming racially mixed teams within the classroom. In the **jigsaw method,** for example, students from different racial or ethnic groups are assigned to a single learning group. These groups are then given an assignment that can be completed only if each individual member contributes his or her share. Study units are broken down into various subareas, and each member of a group must become an expert on one subject and teach that subject to other members of the group. In a class studying government, for example, the teacher might separate the pupils into three-person groups, with each member of the group being assigned one of the following topics: the judiciary system (the Supreme Court of the United States), the duties and powers of the executive branch (the president's office), and the functions of the legislative branch (Congress). Students can, however, leave their three-person groups and meet with their counterparts from other groups. Thus, everyone assigned to study one particular topic, such as the Supreme Court, would meet to discuss it, answer questions, and decide how to teach the material to others. Once they had learned their material, these students would then rejoin their original groups and teach the other members of their group what they had learned. Thus, the jigsaw class utilizes both group-learning and student-teaching techniques (Aronson, Stephan, Sikes, Blaney, & Snapp, 1978).

Studies of classrooms that use cooperative learning groups show some promising results. When reviewers combined the results of 31 separate studies statistically, they found that ingroup/outgroup hostility was reduced in cooperative classrooms (Johnson, Johnson, & Maruyama, 1984). These programs can be made even more effective by structuring the task so that each group member makes a contribution, randomly assigning students to roles within the group, and making certain that all groups contain an equal number of representatives from the group being merged. The procedures used to assign grades—either giving the entire group the same grade or giving grades to indi-

---

Jigsaw method: A team-learning technique that involves assigning topics to each group member, allowing students with the same topics to study together, and then requiring these students to teach their topics to the other members of their group.

viduals in the group—had little impact on the success of the intervention, nor did the degree to which each individual's contribution was made public (Miller & Davidson-Podgorny, 1987).

Cognitive Cures for Conflict

Cooperative contact does more than just promote positive interactions between people who were once antagonists. When individuals cooperate with the outgroup, their "us versus them" thinking fades, along with ingroup favoritism, outgroup rejection, and stereotyping (Brewer & Brown, 1998; Brewer & Miller, 1984; Miller & Brewer, 1986a, 1986b).

Decategorization.   During the waning days at the Robbers Cave, the boys began to abandon their collective identities. Some boys became less likely to think of themselves as Rattlers, but instead viewed themselves as individuals with specific interests, skills, and abilities. This **decategorization,** or individuation, of group members reduces intergroup conflict by reminding group members to think of outgroup members as individuals rather than as typical group members (Brewer & Brown, 1998). Researchers personalized the outgroup in one study by merging two distinct groups and giving them problems to solve. Some of the groups were urged to focus on the task, but others were encouraged to get to know one another. This manipulation decreased the magnitude of the ingroup/outgroup bias, although it did not eliminate it completely (Bettencourt, Brewer, Croak, & Miller, 1992). Individuation can also be increased by changing the perceived heterogeneity of the outgroup. When group members were told that one member of the outgroup strongly disagreed with his or her group during an episode of intergroup conflict, ingroup/outgroup biases were muted (Wilder, 1986b). The subjects looked at the outgroup and saw a collection of individuals rather than a unified group (Wilder, Simon, & Faith, 1996).

Recategorization.   Ingroup/outgroup biases can also be controlled by collapsing groups in conflict into a single group. Instead of stressing the individuality of group members, facilitators would stress their shared membership in a superordinate group or category (Dovidio, Gaertner, Isen, Rust, & Guerra, 1998; Gaertner, Dovidio, Anastasio, Bachman, & Rust, 1993; Gaertner, Rust, Dovidio, Bachman, & Anastasio, 1994). **Recategorization** can also be achieved by systematically manipulating the perceptual cues that people use to define groupness. In one study, researchers provided the members of competing groups with a single name, minimized spatial distance between the members, and created cooperative interdependence among the members. These cues increased the perceived unity, or entitativity, of the group members, and

---

Decategorization: Reducing social categorization tendencies by minimizing the salience of group memberships and stressing the individuality of each person in the group.
Recategorization: Reducing social categorization tendencies, by collapsing groups in conflict into a single group or category.

ingroup/outgroup biases diminished. Intergroup conflict can also be reduced more directly by making salient similarities between the ingroup and the outgroup and downplaying dissimilarities (Worchel, Axsom, Ferris, Samaha, & Schweitzer, 1978).

The Sherifs made use of recategorization in their 1949 study by pitting a softball team made up of members from both groups against an outside camp (Sherif & Sherif, 1953). This common-enemy approach was partially successful in that during the game, the boys cheered one another on and, when the home team won, congratulated themselves without paying heed to group loyalties. By introducing the third party, the common-enemy approach forced the boys to redefine themselves in terms of a single shared group identity. The Sherifs point out, however, that although combining groups in opposition to a common enemy works for a short time (during the actual competition or crisis), once the enemy is removed, the groups tend to return to the status quo.

Cross-Categorization. Ingroup/outgroup biases are also minimized when group members' other classifications—in addition to their group identity that is the focus of the conflict—are made salient to them. **Cross-categorization,** instead of uniting all individuals in a single group or breaking down groups altogether, decreases the power of the problematic group identity by shifting attention to alternative memberships that are less likely to provide ingroup/outgroup tensions. The Sherifs, if they had implemented this strategy at the Robbers Cave, would have introduced at least one other category and split the Rattlers and the Eagles into two new groups. The boys, for example, were drawn from both the north and the south side of Oklahoma City, so the Sherifs could have separated them into these two groups and introduced activities that would have made these identities salient. The Sherifs could have also reduced the boys' "cognitive load" in the situation so that they would not fall back on the older, better known Eagles-Rattlers distinction, and introduced the cross-categorizations at times when the boys were in positive rather than negative moods (Miller, Urban, & Vanman, 1998).

Controlling Stereotyped Thinking. Rather than attacking the categorization process, Patricia Devine (1989) recommends controlling the impact of stereotypes on perceptions. Stereotypes are automatically activated whenever one encounters a member of another group or is merely reminded of that other group by some symbol or other meaningful stimulus. The color of a person's skin, hair length, an accent, or a style of shoes may be enough to trigger a stereotype, which, once activated, may then influence responses. Even cues that are so subtle that we do not consciously recognize them may nonetheless prime our stereotypes.

Even though we may not be able to avoid the activation of stereotypes, we can control our subsequent thoughts to inhibit ingroup/outgroup biases (see Figure 13–4). Devine found that the Whites she studied could easily list the contents of their culture's stereotype about African Americans. She also found that Whites who were low in prejudice could describe the stereotype as accurately as those who were high in

---

Cross-categorization: Reducing the impact of social categorization on perceptions by making salient individuals' memberships in two or more social groups or categories that are not related to the categories generating ingroup/outgroup tensions.

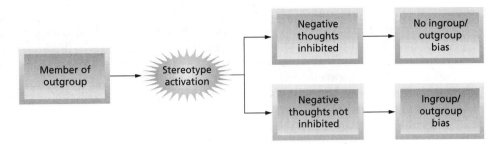

FIGURE 13–4 Are ingroup/outgroup biases inevitable? Devine's work (1995) suggests that social categorization automatically activates stereotypical beliefs about members of the outgroup, but that individual perceivers can inhibit the impact of these stereotypes on their thoughts, feelings, and actions. Prejudiced individuals cannot or do not inhibit their stereotypes.

prejudice. The unprejudiced Whites, however, could control their thoughts after the stereotypes were activated. When asked to list their thoughts about Black Americans, the unprejudiced subjects listed such things as "Blacks and Whites are equal" and "It's unfair to judge people by their color—they are individuals." Prejudiced people, in contrast, listed negative, stereotypical thoughts. Devine and her colleagues have also found that unprejudiced Whites feel guilty when they find themselves responding to African Americans in stereotypical ways, whereas prejudiced Whites do not (Devine, 1995; Devine, Monteith, Zuwerink, & Elliot, 1991).

Conflict Management

People often try to resolve intergroup conflicts through bargaining and negotiation. Such methods, as noted in Chapter 9, involve meetings where all parties to the dispute can discuss their grievances and recommend solutions. Both sides draw up a list of problems that are sources of dissatisfaction. Next, the two groups together consider each issue and seek a solution that is satisfying to both sides. When one issue is solved, the negotiations proceed to the next item on the agenda.

Unfortunately, few people have the necessary skills to manage intergroup conflict effectively. Negotiation, for most people, is only competition disguised as cooperation. The two parties refuse to accept each other's arguments, insist on maximizing their own interests, and use contentious bargaining tactics. These tactics, instead of quelling the conflict, intensify it (Fisher, 1994; Rubin, 1994). Indeed, in the Sherifs' 1949 study, an informal attempt by one of the Bull Dogs' leaders to negotiate with the Red Devils ended in increased antagonism:

> Hall . . . was chosen to make a peace mission. He joined into the spirit, shouting to the Bull Dogs, "Keep your big mouths shut. I'm going to see if we can make peace. We want peace."
>
> Hall went to the Red Devil cabin. The door was shut in his face. He called up that the Bull Dogs had only taken their own [belongings] . . . and they wanted peace. His explanation was rejected, and his peaceful intentions were derided. He ran from the bunkhouse in a hail of green apples. [Sherif & Sherif, 1953, p. 283]

Conflict experts, such as Herbert Kelman (1992), recommend training people to be more effective managers of intergroup conflict. Kelman and his colleagues have met repeatedly with high-ranking representatives from countries in the Middle East to solve problems in that region of the world. Kelman carefully structures the workshops so that participants can speak freely, and he intervenes only as necessary to facilitate the communication process. The workshops are completely confidential, discussion is open but focused on the conflict, and expectations are realistic. The workshops are not designed to resolve the conflict, but to give participants the behavioral skills needed to solve conflicts themselves (Rouhana & Kelman, 1994).

David and Roger Johnson (1994) have also created a conflict management program, but for students rather than international leaders. Johnson and Johnson design their program to achieve three major goals: to decrease the amount of tension between groups in schools and colleges; to increase students' ability to solve problems without turning to authorities; and to give students skills that they can use when they become adults. The program itself teaches students a five-step approach to resolving conflicts: Define the conflict; exchange information about the nature of the conflict; view the situation from multiple perspectives; generate solutions to the conflict; select a solution that benefits all parties. Johnson and Johnson, in evaluations of the program, report substantial reductions in discipline problems after training, as well as increases in academic achievement (Johnson & Johnson, 1994).

A third training model, Svenn Lindskold's (1978, 1979, 1986) **Graduated and Reciprocal Initiative in Tension Reduction (GRIT),** prescribes conflict management methods needed in extremely hostile intergroup conflict situations. When disputants have a prolonged history of conflict, misunderstandings, misperceptions, and hostility, attempts at cooperation are often misinterpreted by the opponents as attacks. Lindskold therefore focuses on developing mutual trust by teaching group members to communicate their desire to cooperate, engage in behaviors that are consistent with cooperative intentions, and initiate cooperative responses even in the face of competition.

The first three stages of GRIT call for adequate communication between the groups in the hope of establishing the "rules of the game." The next three stages are designed to increase trust between the two groups as the consistency in each group's responses demonstrates credibility and honesty. Lindskold suggests that these phases are crucial to overwhelm the skepticism of the opponents as well as the tendency for other parties to assume that the concessions are merely "smokescreens" or propaganda tactics. The final four steps are necessary only in extremely intense conflict situations in which the breakdown of intergroup relations implies a danger for the group members. In the case of military conflict, for example, the failure to stem the conflict could have disastrous consequences. Hence, each side must make concessions at a fixed rate while at the same time maintaining retaliatory capability.

The GRIT model clarifies the difficulties inherent in establishing mutual trust between parties that have been involved in a prolonged conflict. Although some of the stages are not applicable to all conflicts, the importance of clearly announcing inten-

---

Graduated and Reciprocal Initiative in Tension Reduction (GRIT): A ten-step system for reducing intergroup conflict by increasing trust and cooperation.

tions, making promised concessions, and matching reciprocation are relevant to all but the most transitory conflicts. Furthermore, case studies (Etzioni, 1967), simulations (Crow, 1963), and experiments (Lindskold, 1986; Lindskold & Aronoff, 1980) have lent considerable support to the recommendations of the GRIT model for inducing cooperation. At minimum, the model offers a good deal of promise as a guide for better relationships between groups.

Resolving Conflict: Conclusions

In his classic treatise *The Nature of Prejudice,* Gordon W. Allport (1954, p. 996) writes that "conflict is like a note on an organ. It sets all prejudices that are attuned to it into simultaneous vibration. The listener can scarcely distinguish the pure note from the surrounding jangle."

The Sherifs and their colleagues created just such a "jangle" at the Robbers Cave. The Rattlers and the Eagles were only young boys camping, but their conflict followed patterns seen in disputes between races, between regions, and between countries. But just as the Robbers Cave Experiment is a sobering commentary on the pervasiveness of conflict, so the resolution of that conflict is cause for optimism. The Sherif's created conflict, but they also resolved it. When it came time to return to Oklahoma City, several of the group members asked if everyone could go in the same bus:

> When they asked if this might be done and received an affirmative answer from the staff, some of them actually cheered. When the bus pulled out, the seating arrangement did not follow group lines. Many boys looked back at the camp, and Wilson (E) cried because camp was over. [Sherif et al., 1961, p. 182]

If the Robbers Cave conflict can end peacefully, others can as well.

SUMMARY

What interpersonal factors disrupt relations between groups? The *Robbers Cave Experiment,* a field study of intergroup conflict conducted by Muzafer and Carolyn Sherif and their colleagues, sheds considerable light on the interpersonal roots of conflict between groups.

1. As *realistic conflict theory* maintains, competition contributed significantly to the conflict.

2. When groups and individuals play the prisoner's dilemma game, groups respond much more competitively than individuals. This *discontinuity effect* is likely caused by individuals' distrust of groups.

3. Intergroup conflict, like intragroup conflict, tends to escalate over time. Both the norm of reciprocity and the use of contentious influence tactics stimulate conflict spirals.

4. The *scapegoat theory* explains why groups that experience setbacks sometimes fight other, more defenseless groups.

What are the cognitive foundations of conflict between groups?

1. *Social categorization* leads perceivers to classify people into two mutually exclusive groups: the ingroup and the outgroup.

2. Groups tend to favor the ingroup over the outgroup (the *ingroup/outgroup bias*). This bias, when applied to larger groups such as tribes or nations, is called *ethnocentrism*.

3. Ingroup favoritism tends to be stronger than outgroup rejection, but both forms of ingroup/outgroup bias emerged at Robbers Cave. Over time, the groups became more cohesive; more clearly differentiated; more favorable toward the ingroup, its members, and its products; and more negative toward the other group, its members, and its products.

4. During intergroup conflict, group members' judgments are often distorted by the following biases:
   - *Outgroup homogeneity bias:* The outgroup is assumed to be much more homogeneous than the ingroup.
   - *Ingroup differentiation bias:* Members assume their own group is diverse and heterogeneous.
   - *Ingroup homogeneity bias:* Members, particularly when their group is threatened, exaggerate the similarity of everyone in their group.
   - *Linguistic intergroup bias:* Actions performed by the ingroup are described differently than actions performed by the outgroup.
   - *Law of small numbers:* The behaviors and characteristics exhibited by a small number of outgroup members are generalized to all members of the outgroup.
   - *Group attribution error:* Group decisions are assumed to reflect individual group members' attitudes, irrespective of the particular procedures used in making the decisions.
   - *Stereotypes:* Cognitive generalizations are made about the qualities and characteristics of the members of a particular group or social category.

- *Illusory correlations:* There is a tendency to overestimate the strength of the relationship between unrelated characteristics in the outgroup.

5. People in Tajfel and Turner's *minimal intergroup situation* display the ingroup/outgroup bias, leading researchers to conclude that social categorization may be sufficient to create conflict.

6. Social identity process, exclusionary processes, and evolutionary processes are three possible mediators of the categorization-conflict relationship.

How can intergroup relations be improved?

1. The Sherifs' first, relatively unsuccessful attempt to reduce conflict was based on the *contact hypothesis*.

2. The Sherifs successfully reduced conflict in the camp by prompting the boys to work toward *superordinate goals*. Contact is effective only when it creates cooperation between the groups, participants are equal in status, interaction is intimate enough to sustain the development of friendships across the groups, norms encourage cooperation, and the groups succeed.

3. The *jigsaw method* is one of several cooperation-based educational interventions; it reduces conflict by assigning students from different racial or ethnic groups to a single learning group.

4. Cognitive approaches to conflict reduction focus on reducing categorization-based biases or their negative consequences. These methods include *decategorization, recategorization,* and *cross-categorization*.

5. Conflict management methods, such as the *Graduated and Reciprocal Initiative in Tension Reduction* (GRIT), reduce conflict by teaching group members the skills they need to resolve

interpersonal disputes through negotiation and mediation.

FOR MORE INFORMATION

Constructive Conflict Management: An Answer to Critical Social Problems? an issue of the *Journal of Social Issues* edited by Susan K. Boardman and Sandra V. Horowitz (1994), offers research-based recommendations for managing interpersonal, intergroup, and international conflicts.

Intergroup Cognition and Intergroup Behavior, edited by Constantine Sedikides, John Schopler, and Chester A. Insko (1998), draws together the theoretical and empirical work dealing with the cognitive foundations of intergroup conflict.

Intergroup Conflict and Cooperation: The Robbers Cave Experiment, by Muzafer Sherif, O. J. Harvey, B. Jack White, William R. Hood, and Carolyn W. Sherif (1961), describes in detail the well-known study of conflict between two groups of boys at a summer camp.

"Intergroup Relations," by Marilynn B. Brewer and Rupert J. Brown (1998), is a theoretically sophisticated review of the theory and research pertaining to intergroup processes.

Theories of Intergroup Relations, by Donald M. Taylor and Fathali M. Moghaddam (1994, 2nd ed.), systematically reviews all major theoretical perspectives on intergroup processes, including realistic conflict theory and social identity theory.

ACTIVITY 13-1 **EXPERIENCING INTERGROUP CONFLICT**

Think of a time when you experienced intergroup conflict—when you belonged to a group that had a rival group. It may be a group from your past, but you can probably consider one of your current groups, for who does not belong to a group that sometimes opposes another group? The group may also be a categorical one, where membership is based on similarity of members in terms of some demographic quality (e.g., race, ethnicity), or a dynamic group in which members interact with one another on a regular basis (Wilder & Simon, 1998).

1. Briefly describe the two groups (your group and the opposing group). What are the structural characteristics of the two groups (size, organization, goals) and the overall values of the groups?
2. What are members of the two groups like, as individuals and as group members?
3. What caused conflict between the groups? Can the conflict be traced back to a precipitating event or issue?
4. Do the members of the two groups categorize each other? That is, do they display such tendencies as the ingroup/outgroup bias, stereotyping, and double standards?
5. How did you personally respond in the situation?
6. Was the conflict resolved? Can you think of any better way you could have handled the situation?

ACTIVITY 13–2 INTERGROUP RELATIONS IN THE NEWS

Conflict between groups is such a pervasive aspect of our daily lives that we sometimes fail to notice it. Refocus your attention on groups, instead of the individuals in the groups, by reviewing the articles published in your local newspaper. Review each page of the newspaper, looking for descriptions of groups and evidence of conflict between those groups.

1. International news: What groups and nationalities are in the news? Are these groups described in positive or pejorative ways?
2. Local news: Are some of the issues facing your region of the country intergroup conflicts?
3. Letters to the editor: Do the editorials and letters to the editor describe grievances and complaints about a particular group? What groups do the writers belong to and what groups are they criticizing? Do their complaints reflect any of the perceptual biases listed in the summary, such as the outgroup homogeneity bias, the ingroup differentiation bias, and so on?
4. Sports and leisure: How are the sections dealing with sports, recreation, and leisure influenced by groups?
5. Advertisements: Don't overlook the advertisements, which are often designed to appeal to subgroups of the overall population. Do they reveal negative stereotypes about groups depicted?

14

The Group Environment

Because groups have altered the environment so substantially—erecting cities, leveling mountains, building comfortable homes and efficient workplaces—we assume that groups shape their spaces and places. But in many cases, it's the place that shapes the group. Groups exist in specific environments, and these environments determine the group's dynamics.

- How do basic features of the environment, such as temperature and noise, influence groups and their dynamics?
- What group processes are influenced by the distances that people maintain between themselves and other group members?
- What are the causes and consequences of a group's tendency to establish territories?

CONTENTS

Sealab: Living and Working in an Extraordinary Group Environment

GROUPS IN CONTEXT

Temperature

Noise

Environmental Load

Staffing

Dangerous Places

GROUP SPACES

Personal Space

Reactions to Spatial Invasion

Seating Arrangements

GROUP PLACES

Group Territories

Territoriality Within Groups

Groups in Spaces and Places: Beyond Sealab

SUMMARY

FOR MORE INFORMATION

ACTIVITIES

Sealab: Living and Working in an Extraordinary Group Environment

I n 1965, a group of ten volunteers lived for 15 days in a 12 by 57-foot steel cylinder on the floor of the Pacific Ocean. As willing guinea pigs in a U.S. Navy project called Sealab II, they tested the limits of human endurance by carrying out salvage operations and tests of equipment 200 feet beneath the ocean's surface. Visibility was only 10 to 20 feet, and on warm days the water temperature reached only 50°F. When outside of the cylinder, they performed difficult and time-consuming tasks while trying to avoid the attacks of scorpion fish. Inside the capsule, they found relief from the cold and danger, but even there they had to cope with discomfort, noise, and the inevitable irritation produced when ten men live in a space about the size of a trailer. Sealab is diagrammed in Figure 14–1.

Roland Radloff and Robert Helmreich (1968) kept detailed records of the men's daily interactions, and these records reveal the intricate relationship between the group's dynamics and its unique environment. The group's structure reflected where each man slept, his locker assignment, and his interpersonal skills. Men who were fatigued by the stress of the difficult living conditions became withdrawn and moody. Every task, from food preparation to communicating with the surface, required close coordination among the men. When one man was irritable, the other divers could not escape his mood. The men couldn't even carry on a normal conversation, because the equipment inside the habitat was so noisy.

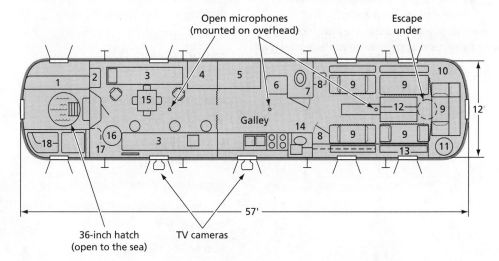

FIGURE 14–1   What was the physical layout of the space where the Sealab divers lived? Because the pressure inside the cylinder equaled the water pressure, the hatch remained open at all times. 1. Stowage area for dive gear. 2. Television. 3. Lab bench. 4. Fan housing. 5. Electrical equipment. 6. Refrigerator. 7. Toilet. 8. Locker. 9. Berths. 10. Stowage area. 11. Carbon dioxide can. 12. Table. 13. Bench. 14. Lavatory. 15. Table and chairs. 16. Water heater. 17. Storage. 18. Shower.

(*Source:* Radloff & Helmreich, 1968.)

Many disciplines, including environmental psychology, ethology, human ecology, demography, and ecological psychology, affirm the important impact of environmental variables on human behavior (Bell, Fisher, Baum, & Green, 1990; Darley & Gilbert, 1985; Stokols & Altman, 1987; Sundstrom, Bell, Busby, & Asmus, 1996). The steel cylinder was little more than a "hole in the ocean," but it was the group's workplace, home, and habitat. All the group's actions and interactions occurred within Sealab and the ocean surrounding it, and the qualities of that ambient environment shaped the group's dynamics. As Kurt Lewin's formula, $B = f(P, E)$, reminds us, behavior is a function of both the person (P) and the environment (E). Environmental components include the physical characteristics of the place the group occupies, the space available to the group, and the group's control over its territory.

GROUPS IN CONTEXT

Groups can be found in both the natural and built environment. At a post office, workers sort mail in noisy rooms bathed in fluorescent light. Hikers trek through the woods, taking care to leave no evidence of their passing. Rows of college students sit in a classroom listening to a lecturer drone. Members of a gang stand on and around a picnic bench in a park, harassing passersby. In a corporate conference room, executives sit in leather chairs at a massive mahogany table. The men of the Sealab moved between the natural environment and the built environment throughout the day as they worked in the ocean but rested inside the habitat.

In some cases, people report feeling rejuvenated and energized by the places their groups occupy (Hartig, Mang, & Evans, 1991; Herzog & Bosley, 1992). People also report benefits from spending time in places they feel attached to, including their homes, their rooms, or even cubicles in an office (Altman & Churchman, 1994; Carlopio, 1996). Environments, however, are more often a source of **stress**: strain caused by environmental circumstances that threaten one's sense of well-being and safety. Groups do not exist in neutral, passive voids but in fluctuating environments that are sometimes too hot, too cold, too impersonal, too intimate, too big, too little, too noisy, too quiet, too restrictive, or too open—but rarely just right (Baum, Singer, & Baum, 1982; Evans & Cohen, 1987; Halpern, 1995).

Temperature

One of the minor miseries of life occurs when people must work in a room that is either too hot or too cold. Although group members generally rate temperatures from the mid-60s to the mid-80s as "comfortable," temperatures that fall outside this range cause discomfort, irritability, and reduced productivity (Baron, 1978; Bell, 1981, 1992; Bell & Greene, 1982). When groups were assigned to work in a room at normal temperature

---

Stress: Negative physiological, emotional, cognitive, and/or behavioral responses to circumstances that threaten, or are thought to threaten, one's sense of well-being and safety.

(72.4°F) or in a hot room (93.5°F), the overheated group members reported feelings of fatigue, sadness, and discomfort, whereas subjects in the normal-temperature room reported feeling more elated, vigorous, and comfortable (Griffitt & Veitch, 1971). Studies also suggest that extremes in temperature can reduce interpersonal attraction (Griffitt, 1970) and interfere with successful task performance (Parsons, 1976). Also, one of the concomitants of high temperatures in groups is exposure to others' body odors, an experience that most people find objectionable (McBurney, Levine, & Cavanaugh, 1977).

Groups tend to be more aggressive when they are hot, as colloquialisms like "hot under the collar" and "flaring tempers" suggest. Mobs' violence is seasonal, with more riots occurring in the summer than the winter (Anderson, 1987, 1989; Anderson & Bushman, 1997; Anderson, Bushman, & Groom, 1997; Anderson & DeNeve, 1992). Groups may also disband when the environment they occupy becomes unpleasantly warm. In one study, researchers measured people's aggressiveness in a comfortable room versus a hot room. Instead of acting more aggressively in the hot room, the participants responded as rapidly as possible so that they could escape the noxious environmental setting. Thus, the heat-stressed subjects were angry, but they were so uncomfortable that their primary concern was to finish the experiment as quickly as possible (Baron, 1972; Baron & Bell, 1975, 1976; Bell, 1992).

Extreme temperatures are also physically harmful (Folk, 1974). When temperatures are high, people are more likely to suffer from exhaustion, stroke, and heart attacks. Extreme cold, meanwhile, can lead to hypothermia and death. The divers, for example, were constantly struggling to maintain their body heat at healthy levels when they worked in the frigid waters surrounding the habitat. Accounts of groups struggling in extremely cold natural environments, such as teams wintering over in Antarctica or mountain climbers, document the lethal effects of exposure to extremely cold temperatures. Jon Krakauer's (1997) vivid account of a deadly expedition to the top of Mount Everest describes the deaths of a group of climbers killed by exposure to extreme cold rather than from falls from the mountain.

Noise

Sealab was a noisy place. An air-filtering system ran for several hours each day and virtually obliterated all conversation. The cylinder also contained a variety of machinery and communication devices and was constantly filled with the sound of air tanks being loaded and unloaded. For technical reasons, the air inside the habitat had a high helium content. As anyone who has ever sucked the helium out of a balloon and then tried to talk knows, helium changes the tone and pitch of the voice. Hence, the men sounded like chipmunks.

Noise is any sound that is unwanted. Sounds in the range of 0 to 50 decibels (dB) are very soft and generally produce little irritation for the listener. Sounds over 80 dB, in contrast, may be bothersome enough to be called noise. In general, the louder the noise, the more likely it will produce distraction, irritation, and psychological stress

---

Noise: Unwanted sound.

(Cohen & Weinstein, 1981). Group communication becomes impossible in such environments, so members have problems coordinating their efforts. Coping with chronic noise also exacts a psychological toll. Groups in noisy places—people who work in noisy offices, families living in homes near airports, and children on playgrounds located near major highways—generally find that the noise has a disruptive impact on their social behaviors. People are less likely to interact with other people when in noisy places, and they also tend to be less helpful (Appleyard & Lintell, 1972; Mathews, Canon, & Alexander, 1974; Veitch, 1990).

Groups can cope with noise for short periods of time. When researchers bombarded people working on both simple and complex tasks with tape-recorded noise, the subjects quickly became so inured to the stimulus that they no longer noticed it (Glass & Singer, 1972; Glass, Singer, & Pennebaker, 1977). Groups cannot, however, cope for long periods of time with noise. As "individuals expend 'psychic energy' in the course of the adaptive process," they become "less able to cope with subsequent environmental demands and frustrations" (Glass et al., 1977, p. 134). These aversive aftereffects of chronic exposure to noise include physical illness (headaches, heart disease, allergies, and digestive disorders), infant and adult mortality rates, mental illness, interpersonal conflict, and even impotence (Cohen, 1980). Noise may even be partly responsible for differences in school performance displayed by children attending schools in urban rather than rural settings. Children attending a school located near an airport were routinely bombarded by 95 dB of noise. These children had higher blood pressure and were more likely to give up when working on a difficult task than children who attended a school in a quieter neighborhood. Even when the noise was reduced, children who were exposed for prolonged periods to the noise exhibited performance deficits (Cohen, Evans, Stokols, & Krantz, 1986; Cohen, Glass, & Singer, 1973; Evans, Hygge, & Bullinger, 1995).

Environmental Load

Picture the inside of Sealab at about 4 p.m. As the videocameras look on, some of the men inside are talking, others are readying their diving gear, others may be calculating data for reports, and someone is probably preparing the evening meal. The intercom sounds intermittently, giving announcements and orders for the following day. A school of fish appears in one of the viewing ports, and the men crowd around to catch a glimpse before the school flashes away into the murky water. The smell of the ocean emanating from the open hatch is strong, but it cannot mask the cooking odors and the smell of the men who have labored all day underwater.

At least two basic dimensions define the emotional impact of a place on its occupants. A group environment that is orderly, tastefully decorated, clean, and spacious would usually prompt a more favorable reaction than one that is shabby, unkempt, and odorous. People also respond to their environment by implicitly considering its intensity. Whereas some places are relaxing, others are so stimulating that they arouse occupants rather than relax them. Figure 14-2 demonstrates how these two dimensions —pleasantness and intensity—combine to describe the "feeling" people get when they occupy a given space. Most of the divers at Sealab, for example, responded positively to their highly arousing habitat, and so they considered it an exhilarating place. Some

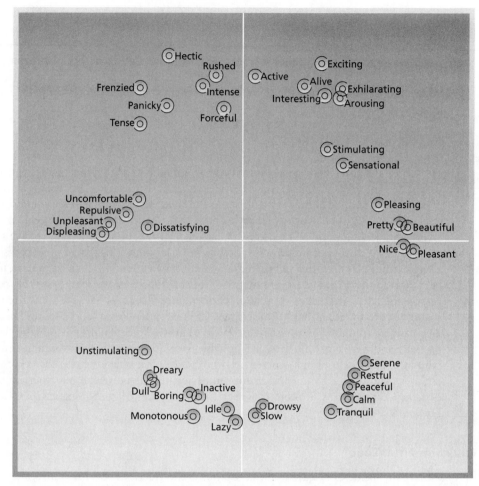

FIGURE 14–2   How do people appraise their environments? A two-dimensional model of affective appraisals suggests that people's perceptions of their natural and built environments reflect two basic questions: How pleasant is the place (positive versus negative), and how intense is the place (exciting versus relaxing)?

(*Source:* Russell & Lanius, 1984.)

divers, though, reacted negatively to Sealab, for they considered it stressful and tense. Few considered it boring or tranquil (Mehrabian & Russell, 1974, 1975; Russell & Lanius, 1984; Russell & Mehrabian, 1975).

Groups generally respond best, in terms of performance and satisfaction, in positive, stimulating environments. Studies of manufacturing teams, for example, find that they respond better when working in attractive spaces that are visually interesting rather than drab. Studies of groups living in harsh circumstances, such as teams stationed at Antarctica and explorers traveling for months on end in a confined space, complain more about the monotony of the environment than about the danger, discomfort, or isolation (Stuster, 1996). As one officer aboard a research ship wintering in the Arctic wrote: "Monotony was our enemy, and to kill time our endeavor; hardship there was none. . . . Monotony, as I again repeat, was the only disagreeable part of our wintering" (quoted in Mowat, 1977, p. 272). Such groups strive to make their environments more interesting, often by decorating common areas extensively.

An attractive environment is not always the best environment. Many successful groups, such as the Disney Studios group discussed in Chapter 6 and the team that invented the technology used in most modern personal computers, worked in relatively shabby settings (Bennis & Biederman, 1997). Too much stimulation can actually contribute to **overload;** that is, complex, stimulating environments can overwhelm group members. When members experience overload, they usually compensate by reducing the stimulation or leaving the situation itself. An overloaded Sealab diver, for example, might have compensated by reducing his contact with others, limiting the amount of information he received, avoiding conversations, staying in his bunk, or simply ignoring certain types of inputs (Baum, Calesnick, Davis, & Gatchel, 1982; Greenberg & Firestone, 1977; Milgram, 1970; Saegert, 1978).

These coping strategies are often effective. Students living in high-density dormitories who used screening strategies to limit their contact with other people, for example, were better adjusted than those who did not (Baum et al., 1982). In other cases, though, these strategies may not reduce members' stress. Men who coped with environmental stress by withdrawing from the very people who could have helped them cope with the situation (friends and loved ones), for example, were more maladjusted than men who did not withdraw (Evans, Palsane, Lepore, & Martin, 1989; Lepore, Evans, & Schneider, 1991). Similarly, when researchers masked the sounds of a busy office, performance improved, but workers experienced heightened arousal (Loewen & Suedfeld, 1992).

Staffing

Ecological psychologist Roger Barker argues that individual and group behavior can be best understood when viewed in context. Instead of focusing on the people in the place, Barker studies the place itself: the **behavior setting.** The checkout line at a store, an automobile repair shop, a bench in a park, a synagogue, and Sealab are all examples of behavior settings, for they are physically bounded places where people's actions are determined by the features and functions of the situation.

In many cases, the fit between the people and the behavior setting is so seamless that interactants don't even notice the influence of the place on their actions. A fast-food restaurant may use a system of guide chains and multiple cash registers to handle large numbers of customers efficiently. A high-use highway may have reversible lanes and computer-controlled traffic lights. In other behavior settings, though, the people do

---

Overload: An excessive number of inputs that come so rapidly that the information cannot be processed effectively.
Behavior setting: Ecological psychology's concept of a physically and temporally bounded social situation that determines the actions of the individuals in the setting.

not fit the place. When too many people are waiting to check out or the number of commuters on the highway grows so large that traffic is snarled, the behavior setting becomes a source of stress. Barker uses the word **synomorphy** to describe the fit between the setting and its human occupants (Barker, 1968, 1987, 1990; Barker et al., 1978).

Allan Wicker's **staffing theory** draws on the concept of synomorphy to explain group performance (Wicker, 1979, 1987). To choose a common example, consider workers in an office in a small business, university, or government agency who are responsible for typing papers and reports, answering the telephone, duplicating materials, and preparing paperwork on budgets, schedules, appointments, and so on. If the number of people working in the office is sufficient to handle all these activities, then the setting is synomorphic, or *optimally staffed*. But if telephones are ringing unanswered, reports are days late, and the photocopy machine is broken and no one knows how to fix it, then the office lacks "enough people to carry out smoothly the essential program and maintenance tasks" and is understaffed (Wicker, 1979, p. 71). On the other hand, if the number of group members exceeds that needed in the situation, the group is overstaffed (Sundstrom, 1987).

Table 14–1 summarizes staffing theory's prediction about the relationship between staffing and performance. Overstaffed groups may perform adequately—after all, so many extra people are available to carry out the basic functions—but overstaffing can

TABLE 14–1   GROUP MEMBERS' RESPONSES TO INADEQUATELY STAFFED WORK SETTINGS

Members of understaffed groups will tend to:	Members of overstaffed groups will tend to:
Show strong, frequent, and varied actions in carrying out goal-related behavior	Perform tasks in a perfunctory, lackadaisical manner
Act to correct inadequate behavior of others	Show a high degree of task specialization
Be reluctant to reject group members whose behavior is inadequate	Demonstrate little concern for the quality of the group product
Feel important, responsible, and versatile as a result of their participation	Exert little effort in helping others in the group
Be concerned about the continued maintenance of the group	Feel cynical about the group and its functions
Be less sensitive to and evaluative of individual differences among group members	Evidence low self-esteem, with little sense of competence and versatility
Think of themselves and other group members in terms of the jobs they do rather than in terms of personality characteristics	Focus on personalities and idiosyncrasies of people in the group rather than on task-related matters

Source: Wicker, 1979.

Synomorphy: Ecological psychology's term describing the quality of the fit between the human occupants and the physical situation.
Staffing theory: An ecological analysis of behavior settings that argues that both understaffing (not enough people) and overstaffing (too many people) can be detrimental.

lead to dissatisfaction with task-related activities and heightened rejection of other group members. Understaffed groups, in contrast, often respond positively to the challenging workload. Instead of complaining about the situation, understaffed groups sometimes display heightened involvement in their work and contribute more to the group's goals (Arnold & Greenberg, 1980; Wicker & August, 1995). Four-man groups, for example, when placed in an overstaffed situation (too few tasks to keep all members active), reported feeling less important, less involved in their work, less concerned with performance, and less needed. These effects were reversed in the understaffed groups (Wicker, Kirmeyer, Hanson, & Alexander, 1976). In another study, increased workload brought on by understaffing increased professionals' and long-term employees' involvement in their work, but understaffing led to decreased commitment among new employees and blue-collar workers. Understaffing was also associated with more negative attitudes toward the group (Wicker & August, 1995). Staffing theory also explains why individuals who are part of smaller groups and organizations get more involved in their groups; even though a large school offers more opportunities for involvement in small-group activities, the proportion of students who join school-based groups is higher in smaller schools (Gump, 1990).

How do groups cope with staffing problems? When researchers asked leaders of student groups this question, nearly 75% recommended recruiting more members or reorganizing the group as the best ways to deal with understaffing. Other solutions included working with other groups and adopting more modest group goals (see Figure 14–3). These leaders offered a wider range of solutions for overstaffing, including encouraging members to remain active in the group (often by assigning them specific

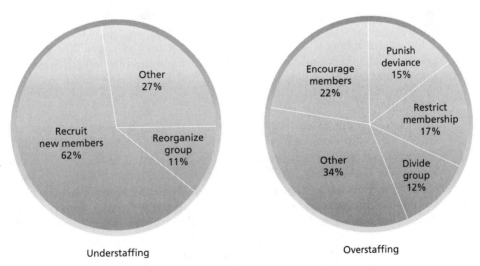

Understaffing   Overstaffing

FIGURE 14–3   How do groups cope with staffing problems? Leaders of student groups recommended dealing with understaffing by recruiting more members or by reorganizing so the group worked more efficiently. They frequently mentioned encouraging members and dividing the group as methods for dealing with overstaffing.

(*Source:* Cini, Moreland, & Levine, 1993.)

duties), enforcing rules about participation, dividing the group, taking in fewer members, changing the group's structure to include more positions, and adopting more ambitious goals (Cini, Moreland, & Levine, 1993).

Dangerous Places

The divers dreaded the end of their 15 days, not just because the interesting project was over, but also because it meant that they had to enter the personnel transfer capsule (PTC). In Radloff and Helmreich's words (1968, p. 77):

> The PTC was barely large enough to accommodate the ten men. Conditions inside it were very cramped. Once the men were all in, and had put on their football helmets and tightened their seat belts (used in order to reduce the possibility of head injuries should the capsule suddenly lurch), the hatch was sealed. It was then hauled to the surface on a cable dangling from the end of a crane on the support vessel. . . . During these operations, when the PTC was in the air swinging free, it could have collided with the support vessel or its structures, the cable could have failed, or the tackle might have slipped, dropping the PTC onto the deck or back into the sea.

If the PTC had sprung open during this operation, all the men would have died from decompression.

Groups sometimes find themselves in dangerous places. In some cases, these hazards are unavoidable and unpredictable. Some natural calamity, such as a flood, earthquake, or blizzard, may overtake a group. Some groups, too, work jobs that are riskier than most: Miners, ship crews, police officers, and military units often live and work in circumstances that can be life-threatening. The group, too, may occupy an inhospitable environment. The divers of the Sealab, for example, lived 200 feet below the surface of the ocean, and had they surfaced, they would have died. Similarly, some people live in neighborhoods where violence and aggression are so commonplace that their lives are often at risk.

Groups generally cope with danger by taking precautions designed to make the situation safer. Groups of explorers, for example, often cope with their dangerous situation by increasing the reliance on a chain of command, by stressing cooperation among members, and by monitoring each individual's connection to the group (Harrison & Connors, 1984; Suedfeld, 1987). Teamwork becomes more important in such situations, as one Sealab diver explained: "Maybe we were all welded together a little bit by the fact that it was a dangerous situation and maybe that makes men better friends" (Radloff & Helmreich, 1968, p. 108). Indeed, the failure of some groups to survive dangers can, in some cases, be traced back to failed teamwork. One climber who survived an expedition to Mount Everest that claimed five other lives traced the tragedy to a lack of teamwork and the harsh climate:

> The roar of the wind made it impossible to communicate from one tent to the next. In this godforsaken place, I felt disconnected from the climbers around me—emotionally, spiritually, physically—to a degree I hadn't experienced on any previous expedition. We were a team in name only, I'd sadly come to real-

ize. Although in a few hours we would leave camp as a group, we would ascend as individuals, linked to one another by neither rope nor any deep sense of loyalty. [Krakauer, 1997, p. 163]

GROUP SPACES

Anthropologist Edward T. Hall (1966) argues that much of our behavior is shaped by a "hidden dimension." In Sealab, this dimension determined where the divers sat during their meals. It placed limits on how many men could work on their equipment in the area around the diving hatch. This dimension even influenced the divers as they swam side by side in the murky water outside the habitat. What is this hidden dimension? Space.

Personal Space

People prefer to keep some space between themselves and others. This **personal space** provides a boundary that limits the amount of physical contact between people. This boundary extends farther in the front of the person than behind, but the individual is always near the center of this invisible buffer. Personal space is portable, but actively maintained and defended. When someone violates our personal space, we tend to take steps to correct this problem (Aiello, 1987). The term *personal space* is something of a misnomer, since the process actually refers to distances that people maintain between one another. Hence, it is an *interpersonal space* (Patterson, 1975). Some people seem to require more space than others, but as we will see, our spatial processes operate across a broad range of people and situations. (Aiello, 1987; Altman, 1975; Altman & Chemers, 1980; Evans & Howard, 1973; Hayduk, 1978, 1983; and Knowles, 1980, provide detailed reviews of the literature on personal space.)

Interpersonal Zones. Different group activities require different amounts of personal space. Hall, in describing these variations, proposes four **interpersonal zones** (see Table 14–2). The *intimate zone* is appropriate for only the most involving and personal behaviors, such as arm wrestling and whispering. The *personal zone,* in contrast, is reserved for a wide range of small-group experiences, such as discussions with friends, interaction with acquaintances, and conversation. More routine transactions are conducted in the *social zone*. Meetings held over large desks, formal dining, and professional presentations to small groups generally take place in this zone. The *public zone* is reserved for even more formal meetings, such as stage presentations, lectures, or addresses. Table 14–2 adds a fifth zone to those described by Hall. In the years since Hall proposed his taxonomy of interpersonal zones, groups have begun to meet more frequently in the *remote zone*. In this zone, group members are physically separated

Personal space: The area that individuals maintain around themselves into which others cannot intrude without arousing discomfort.
Interpersonal zones: Situationally determined interpersonal distances, including intimate, personal, social, public, and remote zones.

TABLE 14–2   INTERPERSONAL ZONES

Zone	Distance	Activities	Zone Characteristics
Intimate	Touching to 18 inches	Procreation, massage, comforting, accidental jostling, handshake, slow dancing	Sensory information concerning other is detailed and diverse; stimulus person dominates perceptual field.
Personal	18 inches to 4 feet	Friendly discussions, conversations, car travel, watching television	Other person can be touched if desired, but also avoided; gaze can be directed away from the other person with ease.
Social	4 feet to 12 feet	Dining, meetings with business colleagues, interacting with a receptionist	Visual inputs begin to dominate other senses; voice levels are normal; appropriate distance for many informal social gatherings.
Public	12 feet or more	Lectures, addresses, plays, dance recitals	All sensory inputs beginning to become less effective; voice may require amplification; facial expressions unclear.
Remote	Different locations	Electronic discussions, conference calls, telephone voice mail, e-mail	Primarily verbal inputs; facial and other behavioral nonverbal cues unavailable.

Source: Hall, 1966.

from each other but communicating with each other through such technologies as radio, telephone, and computers.

As Hall's theory of interpersonal zones suggests, small distances tend to be associated with friendlier, more intimate interpersonal activities. As a result, cohesive groups occupy smaller spaces than noncohesive gatherings (Evans & Howard, 1973); extraverted people maintain smaller distances from others than do introverts (Patterson & Sechrest, 1970); people who wish to create a friendly, positive impression usually choose smaller distances than less friendly people (Evans & Howard, 1973); and groups of friends tend to stand closer to one another than groups of strangers (Edney & Grundmann, 1979). Physical distance has little impact on remote groups, although individuals communicating via computer respond differently when their interface includes facial information as well as verbal information (Kiesler, Sproull, & Waters, 1996).

Why does distance influence so many group processes? One explanation, based on an **equilibrium model** of interpersonal communication, suggests that personal space, body orientation, and eye contact define the level of intimacy of any interaction. If group members feel that a low level of intimacy is appropriate, they may sit far apart, make

---

Equilibrium model: An explanation of distancing behavior in interpersonal settings that argues that the amount of eye contact, the intimacy of the topic, and smiling influence the amount of personal space required by interactants.

little eye contact, and assume a relatively formal posture. If, in contrast, the members are relaxing and discussing personal topics, they may move close together, make more eye contact, and adopt more relaxed postures (Argyle & Dean, 1965; Patterson, 1996). By continually adjusting their nonverbal and verbal behavior, group members can thereby keep the intimacy of their interactions at the level they desire (Burgoon, 1983; Kaplan, Firestone, Klein, & Sodikoff, 1983).

Men, Women, and Space. Would the amount of personal space maintained by the divers in Sealab have differed if they had been women? Probably, for studies suggest that women's personal spaces tend to be smaller than men's (Hayduk, 1983). Relative to men, women allow others to get closer to them, and they approach other people more closely. Women also take up less space by sitting with arms close to their sides and by crossing their legs, whereas men enlarge their personal space by assuming expansive, open positions (Edwards, 1972; Heshka & Nelson, 1971; Mehrabian, 1972).

Status. The type of relationship linking interactants plays a particularly significant role in determining personal space. A study of 562 U.S. Navy personnel, for example, found that subordinates conversing with superiors required more space than when conversing with peers (Dean, Willis, & Hewitt, 1975). In addition, many studies suggest that when we are with friends rather than strangers or mere acquaintants, our personal-space needs become relatively small. This effect occurs in both same-sex and mixed-sex dyads, although the effect is sometimes seen only in women (Hayduk, 1983).

Culture. Hall (1966) argues that cultures differ in their use of space. People socialized in *contact cultures* of the Mediterranean, the Middle East, and Latin America prefer strong sensory involvement with others and so they seek direct social contact whenever possible. In contrast, residents in such *noncontact countries* as the United States, England, and Germany try to limit their spatial openness with others. Given that all the divers in Sealab had been reared in the United States, they shared similar norms about how much distance should be maintained. If, however, the dive teams had included members from different cultural backgrounds, misunderstandings might have further complicated life in Sealab (Remland, Jones, & Brinkman, 1995).

Reactions to Spatial Invasion

Individuals cannot always protect their personal space from intrusion by others. In some cases, group members may find themselves in places where the available space is so limited that people cannot maintain appropriate distances between one another. In other instances, the group may have sufficient space, but for some reason, a member approaches so closely that he or she seems "too close for comfort."

How do group members react to such intrusions? High density does not always lead to feelings of crowding and other negative interpersonal outcomes. As Daniel Stokols (1972, 1978) notes, **density** refers to a characteristic of the environment—literally, the

---

Density: The number of individuals per unit of space.

number of people per unit of space. **Crowding,** in contrast, refers to a psychological, experiential state that occurs when people feel that they do not have enough space. Although the density of a given situation, such as a party, a rock concert, or Sealab, may be very high, interactants may not feel crowded at all. Yet, two persons sitting in a large room may still report that they feel crowded if they expected to be alone, are engaged in some private activity, or dislike each other intensely.

Arousal and Attributions.   Physiologically speaking, what happens to people when they find themselves in high-density situations? In many cases, they become aroused: Their heart rate and blood pressure increase, they breathe faster, and they sometimes perspire more (Evans, 1979). Indeed, this link between personal-space violations and arousal was confirmed in study of men micturating in a public restroom (Middlemist, Knowles, & Matter, 1976). Reasoning that arousal would lead to a general muscular contraction that would delay micturation and reduce its duration, the researchers set up a situation in which men using wall-mounted urinals were joined by a confederate who used either the next receptacle (near condition) or one located farther down the wall (far condition). When onset times and duration for men in the near and far condition were compared with those same times for men in a no-confederate control condition, the researchers found that personal-space invasion significantly increased general arousal.

This arousal is not always stressful, however. If the intruder is a close friend, a relative, or an extremely attractive stranger, closeness can be a plus (Willis, 1966). Similarly, if we believe that the other person needs help or is attempting to initiate a friendly relationship, we tend to react positively rather than negatively (Murphy-Berman & Berman, 1978). These findings suggest that the label that individuals use to interpret their arousal determines the consequences of crowding. If people attribute the arousal to others standing too close, then they will conclude "I feel crowded." If, in contrast, they explain the arousal in some other way—"I'm fearful," "I drank too much coffee," "I'm in love," and so on—they will not feel crowded.

Steven Worchel and his colleagues tested this attributional model of crowding by seating five-person groups in chairs placed either 20 inches apart or touching at the legs. These researchers told the groups that an inaudible noise would be played in the room as they worked on several tasks. They told some groups that the noise was detectable subconsciously and would lead to stressful, discomforting effects. They told other groups that the noise would have relaxing and calming effects, or they gave no explanation for the noise at all. The groups weren't actually exposed to any noise, but as Worchel predicted, crowded groups who thought that the noise would arouse them felt less crowded. Why? Because they attributed the arousal caused by crowding to the noise rather than to other people (Worchel & Yohai, 1979; see, too, Worchel & Teddlie, 1976).

Crowding: A psychological reaction that occurs when individuals feel that the amount of space available to them is insufficient for their needs.

Intensity.   Jonathan Freedman also argues that high-density situations aren't always aversive situations. His **density-intensity hypothesis** suggests that high density merely intensifies whatever is already occurring in the group situation (Freedman, 1975, 1979). If something in the situation makes the group interaction unpleasant, high density will make the situation seem even more unpleasant. If the situation is a very pleasant one, however, high density will make the good situation even better. Freedman tested this notion by placing groups of people in large or small rooms and then manipulating some aspect of the group interaction to create unpleasantness or pleasantness. In one investigation, groups of six to ten high school students sat on the floor of either a large room or a small room. Each delivered a speech and then received feedback from the other group members. Freedman made certain that in some groups, the feedback was always positive, whereas in other groups, the feedback was always negative. When the subjects later rated the room and their group, Freedman discovered that crowding intensified the effects of the feedback: People liked their group the most when they received positive feedback under high-density conditions and liked their group the least when they got negative feedback when crowded. Furthermore, Freedman found that these effects were clearest for all-female groups as opposed to all-male or mixed-sex groups (see also Storms & Thomas, 1977).

Controllability.   Crowded situations are unsettling because they undermine group members' control over their experiences. Crowded situations bring people into contact with others they would prefer to avoid, and if working groups cannot cope with the constraints of their environment, they may fail at their tasks. Group members can therefore cope with crowding by increasing their sense of control over the situation. Just as a sense of high personal control helps people cope with a range of negative life events, including failure, divorce, illness, and accidents, people are less stressed by environmental threats when they feel they can control their circumstances (Evans & Lepore, 1992; Rodin, 1976; Rodin & Baum, 1978; Schmidt & Keating, 1979; Sherrod & Cohen, 1979).

Researchers tested the benefits of controllability by asking groups of six men to work on tasks in either a small laboratory room or a large one. One problem was a 15-minute discussion of censorship, and the second involved blindfolding members one at a time and letting them wander about within a circle formed by the rest of the group. To manipulate control, one of the subjects was designated the *coordinator;* he was responsible for organizing the group, dealing with questions concerning procedures, and blindfolding members for the second task. A second subject, the *terminator,* was given control over ending the discussion and regulating each member's turn in the center of the circle. Significantly, group members who could control the group tasks through coordination or termination were not as bothered by the high-density situation as the four group members who were given no control over the situation (Rodin, Solomon, & Metcalf, 1978).

Density-intensity hypothesis: An explanation of crowding, predicting that high density makes unpleasant situations more unpleasant but pleasant situations more pleasant.

Interference.   Crowding is particularly troublesome when it interferes with the group's work. The Sealab crew, for example, did not react negatively to their high-density living conditions so long as the crowding did not undermine their group's effectiveness. Similarly, studies that find no ill effects of crowding generally study groups working on coaction problems that require little interaction. Studies that require the participants to complete interactive tasks, in contrast, tend to find negative effects of crowding (e.g., Heller, Groff, & Solomon, 1977; Paulus, Annis, Seta, Schkade, & Matthews, 1976).

Researchers demonstrated the importance of interference by deliberately manipulating both density and interaction. All-male groups worked in either a small laboratory room or a large one collating eight-page booklets. The order of the pages was not constant, however, but was determined by first selecting a card that had the order of pages listed in a random sequence. In the low-interaction condition, each person had all eight stacks of pages and a set of sequence cards. In the high-interaction condition, the stacks were located at points around the room, so subjects had to walk around the room in unpredictable patterns. In fact, the subjects often bumped into one another while trying to move from one stack to another. The interference created in the high-interaction condition led to decrements in task performance—provided density was high (Heller et al., 1977; see, too, McCallum, Rusbult, Hong, Walden, & Schopler, 1979; Morasch, Groner, & Keating, 1979; Paulus et al., 1976; Sundstrom, 1975).

Seating Arrangements

Group members can be found in all sorts of spatial configurations, including densely packed clusters, single-file lines, irregularly shaped circles, and disorganized clumps. These configurations, however, are often determined by the seating arrangements available to the group. In Sealab, for example, when four divers ate a meal at the table, they sat equidistant from one another at the four sides of the table. When conversing, they often sat side by side on the lab benches. When they were resting, distance from one another was determined by the location of the berths. As Robert Sommer (1967) notes, seating arrangements play a large role in creating a "small-group ecology." Although often unrecognized or simply taken for granted, seating pattern influences interaction, communication, and leadership in groups.

Seating Patterns and Social Interaction.   Groups behave very differently if their seating pattern is sociopetal rather than sociofugal. **Sociopetal** patterns promote interaction among group members by heightening eye contact, encouraging verbal communication, and facilitating the development of intimacy. **Sociofugal** arrangements, in contrast, discourage interaction among group members and can even drive participants out of the situation altogether. A secluded booth in a quiet restaurant, a park bench, or five chairs placed in a tight circle are sociopetal environments, whereas classrooms organized in rows, movie theaters, waiting rooms, and airport waiting areas are sociofugal. Sommer

---

Sociopetal: Referring to environmental conditions, including seating arrangements, that promote interaction among group members.
Sociofugal: Referring to environmental conditions that discourage or prevent interaction among group members.

feels that airport seating is deliberately designed to disrupt interaction. He notes that even people seated side by side on airport chairs cannot converse comfortably:

> The chairs are either bolted together and arranged in rows theater-style facing the ticket counters, or arranged back-to-back, and even if they face one another they are at such distances that comfortable conversation is impossible. The motive for the sociofugal arrangement appears the same as that in hotels and other commercial places—to drive people out of the waiting areas into cafes, bars, and shops where they will spend money. [1969, pp. 121–122]

Group members generally prefer sociopetal arrangements (Batchelor & Goethals, 1972; Giesen & McClaren, 1976). This preference, however, depends in part on the type of task undertaken in the situation (Ryen & Kahn, 1975; Sommer, 1969). Sommer found, for example, that college students' preferences varied when they were conversing, cooperating on some task, competing, or coacting on individual tasks. As Figure 14–4 shows, corner-to-corner and face-to-face arrangements were preferred for conversation, and side-to-side seating was selected for cooperation. Competing pairs either took a direct, face-to-face orientation (apparently to stimulate competition) or tried to

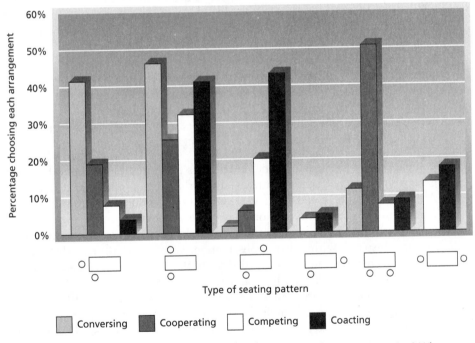

FIGURE 14–4 How do different chair arrangements influence group interaction? When Sommer compared six different kinds of seating arrangements, he discovered that corner-to-corner and face-to-face arrangements were preferred for conversation, and side-to-side seating was selected for cooperation. No one chose the arrangement where both interactants sit at the ends of the table when cooperating or conversing.

(*Source:* Sommer, 1969.)

increase interpersonal distance, whereas coacting pairs preferred arrangements that involved a visual separation. As one student stated, such an arrangement "allows staring into space and not into my neighbor's face" (Sommer, 1969, p. 63). Similar choices were found with round tables.

Groups in sociopetal environments act differently than groups in sociofugal spaces. In one study, dyads whose members sat facing each other seemed more relaxed, but dyads whose members sat at a 90° angle to each other were more affiliative (Mehrabian & Diamond, 1971). When researchers compared circle seating with L-shaped seating, the circle was associated with feelings of confinement but fostered greater interpersonal attraction (Patterson, Kelley, Kondracki, & Wulf, 1979; Patterson, Roth, & Schenk, 1979). People seated in the L-shaped groups, on the other hand, engaged in more self-manipulative behaviors and fidgeting, and they paused more during group discussions. Overall, the positive effects of the circle arrangement relative to the L arrangement were stronger in female groups than in male groups.

Men, Women, and Seating Preferences.   Women and men diverge, to a degree, in their preferences for seating arrangements; men prefer to position themselves across from those they like, and women prefer adjacent seating positions (Sommer, 1959). Obversely, men prefer that strangers sit by their side, whereas women feel that strangers should sit across from them. Researchers studied the confusion that this difference can cause by sending confederates to sit at the same table as solitary women and men working at a library. After a brief and uneventful period, the confederate left. When a second researcher then asked the subject some questions about the confederate and the library, the researchers discovered that men were the least favorably disposed toward the stranger who sat across from them but that women reacted more negatively to the stranger who sat next to them (Fisher & Byrne, 1975). Clearly, group members should be sensitive to the possibility that their spatial behaviors will be misinterpreted by others and should be willing to make certain that any possible misunderstandings will be short-lived.

Communication Patterns.   Bernard Steinzor's early studies of face-to-face discussion groups indicate that spatial patterns also influence communication rates in groups. Although at first he could find few significant relationships between seat location and participation in the discussion, one day while watching a group, he noticed a participant change his seat to sit opposite someone he had argued with during the previous meeting. Inspired by this chance observation, Steinzor (1950) reanalyzed his findings and discovered that individuals tended to speak after the person seated opposite them spoke. He reasoned that we have an easier time observing and listening to the statements of people who are seated in a position central to our visual field, so that their remarks serve as stronger stimuli for our own ideas and statements. The tendency for members of a group to comment immediately after the person sitting opposite them is now termed the **Steinzor effect.** The phenomenon appears to occur primarily in leaderless discussion groups, for later research suggests that when a strong leader is present, group members direct more comments to their closest neighbor (Hearne, 1957).

Steinzor effect: The tendency for members of a group to comment immediately after the person sitting opposite them.

Head-of-the-Table Effect. Where should the leader sit: at the head of the table or in one of the side chairs? With great consistency, leaders seek out the head of the table. Sommer (1969), for example, found that people appointed to lead small discussion groups tended to select seats at the head of the table. Those who move to this position of authority also tend to possess more dominant personalities (Hare & Bales, 1963), talk more frequently, and often exercise greater amounts of interpersonal influence (Strodtbeck & Hook, 1961).

Sommer suggests two basic explanations for this intriguing **head-of-the-table effect:** perceptual prominence and the social meaning associated with sitting at the head of the table. Looking first at prominence, Sommer suggests that in many groups, the chair at the end of the table is the most salient position in the group and that the occupant of this space can therefore easily maintain greater amounts of eye contact with more of the group members, can move to the center of the communication network, and (as the Steinzor effect suggests) can comment more frequently. Moreover, in Western cultures, where most studies of leadership have been conducted, the head chair at a table has been virtually defined as *the* most appropriate place for the leader to sit. Sommer is careful to note that this norm may not hold in other societies, but in most Western cultures, leadership and the head of the table go hand in hand.

Both factors play a role in the head-of-the-table effect. Investigators manipulated salience by having two persons sit on one side of the table and three on the other side. Although no one sat in the end seat, those seated on the two-person side of the table could maintain eye contact with three of the group members, but those on the three-person side could best focus their attention on only two members. Therefore, group members on the two-person side should be able to influence others more and hence be the more likely leaders. As predicted, 70% of the leaders came from the two-person side, and only 30% came from the three-person side (Howells & Becker, 1962).

In another study, the tendency for people to automatically associate the head of the table with leadership was examined by arranging for confederates to voluntarily choose or be assigned to the end position or some other position around a table (Nemeth & Wachtler, 1974). These confederates then went about systematically disagreeing with the majority of the group members on the topic under discussion, and the extent to which the subjects altered their opinions to agree with the deviant was assessed. Interestingly, the deviants succeeded in influencing the others only when they had freely chosen to sit in the head chair. Apparently, disagreeing group members sitting at the "normal" locations around the table were viewed as "deviants," whereas those who had the confidence to select the end chair were viewed more as "leaders" (Riess, 1982; Riess & Rosenfeld, 1980).

GROUP PLACES

When the men first swam through the Sealab's access hatch to begin their two-week stay, they entered an empty cylinder filled with equipment and supplies. But within days this

Head-of-the-table effect: The tendency for group members to associate the leadership role with the chair located at the head of the table.

physical space was transformed into the group's territory. The men chose bunks and stowed their personal gear in their lockers. They explored the waters outside the habitat, and soon a trip outside seemed like a "walk across the street." They also put up signs reading "Welcome to the Tiltin' Hilton" (the floor of the cylinder was tilted). By the end of the 15 days, the men felt at home in the capsule. As one diver explained, "You know that the Pacific Ocean is a mighty big place and you got a 36-inch hole that's home" (Radloff & Helmreich, 1968, p. 1). They also reacted negatively when another team of divers came to take their place: "When those guys came down there for the third team, I thought they were intruding. And I hated to see them come in because I realized that was the end" (p. 113).

Like so many animals—birds, wolves, lions, seals, geese, and even seahorses—human beings develop proprietary orientations toward certain geographical locations and defend these areas against intrusion by others. A person's home, a preferred seat in a classroom, a clubhouse, a football field, and the Sealab are all **territories**: specific areas that an individual or group claims, marks, and defends against intrusion by others.

When people establish a territory, they generally try to control who is permitted access. As Irwin Altman notes, however, the degree of control depends on the type of territory (see Table 14–3). Control is highest for **primary territories**: areas that are maintained and "used exclusively by individuals or groups . . . on a relatively permanent basis" (Altman, 1975, p. 112). Individuals maintain only a moderate amount of control over their **secondary territories**. These areas are not owned by the group members, but because members use such an area regularly, they come to consider it "theirs." The divers, for example, did not own Sealab, but they became so accustomed to it that it seemed like home to them. Similarly, college students often become very territorial about their seats in a class (Haber, 1980, 1982). Control over **public territories** is even more limited. Occupants can prevent intrusion while physically present, but they relinquish all claims when they leave. A bathroom stall or a spot on the beach can be claimed when occupied, but when the occupant leaves, another person can step in and claim the space. (Brown, 1987, thoroughly reviews much of the work on human territoriality.)

Group Territories

Territoriality is, in many cases, a group-level process. Instead of an individual claiming an area and defending it against other individuals, a group will lay claim to its turf and prevent other groups from using it. South American howler monkeys, for example, live together in bands of up to 20 individuals, and these groups forage within a fairly well defined region. The bands themselves are cohesive and free of internal strife, but when

---

Territories: Specific geographical areas that individuals or groups claim, mark, and defend against intrusion by others.
Primary territories: Well-controlled areas that are possessed on a long-term basis.
Secondary territories: Areas that are controlled on a regular basis, even though the individual has no exclusive claim to the space.
Public territories: Areas that the occupants control only when physically present in the situation; no expectation of future use exists.

TABLE 14-3   THREE TYPES OF TERRITORIES

Type of Territory	Examples	Degree of Control and Use by Occupants	Duration of User's Claim to Space
Primary	A family's home, a club-house, a bedroom, a dorm room, a study	*High:* Occupants control access and are very likely to actively defend this space.	*Long-term:* Individuals maintain control over the space on a relatively perma-nent basis; ownership is often involved.
Secondary	A table in a bar, a seat in a classroom, a regularly used parking space, the sidewalk in front of your home	*Moderate:* Individuals who habitually use a space come to consider it "theirs." Reaction to intrusions is milder.	*Temporary but recurrent:* Others may use the space, but must vacate area if occupant requests.
Public	Elevator, beach, telephone booth, playground, park, bathroom stall, restaurant counter	*Low:* Although occupant may prevent intrusion while present, no expec-tation of future use exists.	*None:* The individual or group uses the space on only the most temporary basis and leaves behind no markers.

Source: Altman, 1976.

another group of howlers is encountered during the day's wandering, a fight begins. Among howlers, this territorial defense takes the form of a "shouting match" in which the members of the two bands simply howl at the opposing group until one band, usu-ally the invading band, retreats. Indeed, boundaries are rarely violated, because each morning and night, the monkeys raise their voices in a communal and far-carrying howling session (Carpenter, 1958).

Human groups have also been known to territorialize areas. Classic sociological analyses of gangs, for example, often highlighted the tendency for young men to join forces in defense of a few city blocks that they considered to be their turf (Thrasher, 1927; Whyte, 1943; Yablonsky, 1962). Many gangs took their names from a street or park located at the very core of their claimed sphere of influence and sought to control areas around this base. Contemporary gangs, despite changes in size, violence, and involvement in crime, continue to be rooted to specific locations. Gangs in San Diego, California, for example, can be traced to specific geographical origins: the Red Steps and the Crips to Logan Heights, and the Sidros to San Ysidro (Sanders, 1994).

Gangs mark their territories through the placement of graffiti, or "tags," and also attack intruders. Philadelphia researchers found that the number of graffiti mentioning the local gang's name increased as one moved closer and closer to the home base, sug-gesting that the graffiti served as territorial markers warning intruders of the dangers of encroachment. This marking, however, was not entirely successful, for neighboring gangs would occasionally invade a rival's territory to spraypaint their own names over the territorial marker of the home gang or, at least, to append a choice obscenity. In fact, the frequency of graffiti attributable to outside groups provided an index of group power and prestige, for the more graffiti written by opposing gangs in one's territory, the weaker was the home gang (Ley & Cybriwsky, 1974b).

Human groups also maintain secondary and public territories. People at the beach, for example, generally stake out their claim by using beach towels, coolers, chairs, and other personal objects (Edney & Jordan-Edney, 1974). These temporary territories tend to be circular, and larger groups command bigger territories than smaller groups. Groups also create territories when they interact in public places, for in most cases, nonmembers are reluctant to break through group boundaries. Just as individuals are protected from unwanted social contact by their invisible bubble of personal space, so groups seem to be surrounded by a sort of "shell," or "membrane," that forms an invisible boundary for group interaction. Various labels have been used to describe this public territory, including *group space* (Edney & Grundmann, 1979; Minami & Tanaka, 1995), *interactional territory* (Lyman & Scott, 1967), *temporary group territory* (Edney & Jordan-Edney, 1974), *jurisdiction* (Roos, 1968), and *group personal space* (Altman, 1975). No matter what it is called, evidence indicates that this boundary often effectively serves to repel intruders.

Eric Knowles examined the impermeability of groups by placing two or four confederates in a hallway (Knowles, 1973). Subjects who wished to move through this space were forced either to walk between the interactants or to squeeze through the approximately 2½-foot space between the group and the hallway wall. Knowles found that 75% of the passersby chose to avoid walking through the group, but this figure dropped to about 25% in a control condition in which the interacting individuals were replaced by waste barrels. Knowles and his colleagues (Knowles, Kreuser, Haas, Hyde, & Schuchart, 1976) also discovered that when passing by an alcove that was occupied by a group, people would shift their path to increase the distance between themselves and the group. People begin invading a group's public territory if the distance between interactants becomes large (Cheyne & Efran, 1972) or if the group is perceived to be a crowd rather than a single entity (Knowles & Bassett, 1976). Furthermore, mixed-sex groups whose members are conversing with one another seem to have stronger boundaries (Cheyne & Efran, 1972), as do groups whose members are exhibiting strong emotions (Lindskold, Albert, Baer, & Moore, 1976).

Benefits of Territories.   Studies of territoriality in prisons (Glaser, 1964), naval ships (Heffron, 1972; Roos, 1968), neighborhoods (Newman, 1972), and dormitories (Baum & Valins, 1977) suggest that people feel far more comfortable when their groups can territorialize their living areas. The Sealab divers, for example, became more satisfied with their work and interpersonal relations as their feelings of territoriality increased. Similarly, an experimental study of groups that territorialize the rooms in which they work with signs and decorations found that members felt that the rooms belonged to the group, considered the rooms more pleasant, reported less arousal, and assumed that the rooms could hold fewer people than unclaimed rooms (Edney & Uhlig, 1977).

Andrew Baum, Stuart Valins, and their associates confirmed the benefits of territories in their studies of college students who were randomly assigned to one of two types of dormitories. Many lived in the more traditionally designed corridor-style dorm, which featured 17 double-occupancy rooms per floor. These residents could only claim the bedrooms they shared with their roommates as their territories. In contrast, students who lived in the suite-style dorms controlled a fairly well defined territory that included a private space shared with a roommate as well as the bathroom and lounge shared with several suitemates (Baum & Davis, 1980; Baum, Davis, & Valins, 1979; Baum, Harpin, & Valins, 1976).

Even though nearly equal numbers of individuals lived on any floor in the two types of designs, students in the corridor-style dormitories reported feeling more crowded, complained of their inability to control their social interactions with others, and emphasized their unfulfilled needs for privacy. Suite-style residents, on the other hand, developed deeper friendships with their suitemates, worked with one another more effectively, and even seemed more sociable when interacting with people outside the dormitory. Baum and Valins concluded that these differences stemmed from the corridor-style residents' inability to territorialize areas that they had to use repeatedly.

Territories and Intergroup Conflict.   Group members often feel more comfortable when they can establish a territory for their group, but territoriality can be a source of conflict between groups. Altman (1975), for example, describes a neighborhood in New York City that contained both Jewish and Irish Catholic residents. These two groups maintained relatively exclusive territories except during certain sanctioned times. The location of the parochial and public schools necessitated travel across the other group's territory twice a day, so during these times, the usual territorial rules were suspended. Altman notes, however, that even though passage through the rival territory was permissible during the specified times, the neighborhood children typically seemed ill at ease and circumspect as long as they were off their own turf.

All kinds of intergroup conflicts—from disputes between neighbors, to drive-by gang shootings, to civil wars, to wars between nations—are rooted in disputes over territories (Ardry, 1970). Such conflicts may be based on ancient group traditions. Because most human cultures live off the animals and plants that live and grow on the land around them, most cultures establish control over certain geographical areas (Altman & Chemers, 1980). Because these territories are important resources, groups compete for them, and conflict ensues (see Chapter 13). Territories are also defended for symbolic reasons. A group's power is often defined by the quality and size of the space it controls, so groups protect their turf as a means of protecting their reputations. An urban gang, for example, must be ready to attack intruding gangs because "a gang cannot lay any legitimate claim to public areas otherwise" (Sanders, 1994, p. 18). Most drive-by shootings are territorial disputes, occurring when the members of one gang deliberately enter an area controlled by a rival gang and shoot a member of that gang.

The Home Advantage.   Territorial disputes, curiously enough, usually end with the defender of the territory vanquishing the intruder. Case studies of street gangs indicate that defending groups usually succeed in repelling invading groups, apparently because they are more familiar with the physical layout of the area and have access to necessary resources (Whyte, 1943). One member of a gang in New York explained that his group never lost a fight ("rally") so long as it took place on his group's turf:

> Once a couple of fellows in our gang tried to make a couple of girls on Main Street. The boy friends of these girls chased our fellows back to Norton Street. Then we got together and chased the boy friends back to where they came

from. They turned around and got all Garden Street, Swift Street, and Main Street to go after us. . . . It usually started this way. Some kid would get beaten up by one of our boys. Then he would go back to his street and get his gang. They would come over to our street, and we would rally them. . . . I don't remember that we ever really lost a rally. Don't get the idea that we never ran away. We ran sometimes. We ran like hell. They would come over to our street and charge us. We might scatter, up roofs, down cellars, anywhere. We'd get ammunition there. . . . Then we would charge them—we had a good charge. They might break up, and then we would go back to our end of the street and wait for them to get together again. . . . It always ended up by us chasing them back to their street. We didn't rally them there. We never went looking for trouble. We only rallied on our own street, but we always won there. (Whyte, 1943, p. 51)

Groups seem to gain strength and resolve when the dispute takes place on their home territory, even if they are encountering an opponent who is physically stronger or more socially dominant.

This **home advantage** also influences the outcome of sporting events, for the home team is more frequently the victor rather than the loser (Schlenker, Phillips, Boniecki, & Schlenker, 1995a). When a basketball team must travel to the rival team's home court to play, they often make more errors, score fewer points, and end up the losers rather than the winners of the contest (Schwartz & Barsky, 1977). This advantage becomes even greater when the visiting team must travel longer distances and the fans watching the game support the home team and boo the opponent (Courneya & Carron, 1991; Greer, 1983). Playing at home can become something of a disadvantage in rare circumstances. When athletes play must-win games on their home field and they fear that they will fail, the pressure to win may become too great. And when a team is playing a series of games and it loses an early game at home, then, too, it may lose its home advantage to the emboldened adversary. Overall, however, groups tend to win at home (see, for more details, Baumeister, 1984, 1985, 1995; Baumeister & Showers, 1986; Schlenker et al., 1995a, 1995b).

Territoriality Within Groups

Territoriality also operates at the level of each individual in the group. Although the divers, as a group, claimed Sealab as home, each member of the team had his own bunk and his own locker within the steel cylinder. Such individual territories help group members maintain their *privacy* by providing them with a means of reducing contact with others. As Altman (1975) notes, depending on the situation, people prefer a certain amount of contact with others, and interaction in excess of this level produces feelings of crowding and invasion of privacy. The student in the classroom who is distracted by a jabbering neighbor, employees who are unable to concentrate on their jobs

---

Home advantage: The tendency for individuals and groups to gain an advantage over others when interacting in their home territory.

because of their noisy officemates' antics, and the wife who cannot enjoy reading a novel because her husband is playing the stereo too loud are all receiving excessive inputs from another group member. If they moderated their accessibility by successfully establishing and regulating a territorial boundary, they could achieve a more satisfying balance between contact with others and solitude.

Territories also work as *organizers* of group members' relationships (Edney, 1976). Once we know the location of others' territories, we can find or avoid them with greater success. Furthermore, because we often grow to like people we interact with on a regular basis, people with contiguous territories tend to like one another (Moreland, 1987). Territories also work to regularize certain group activities—such as preparing and eating food, sleeping, or studying—by providing a place for these activities. Lastly, territories define what belongs to whom; without a sense of territory, the concept of stealing would be difficult to define, because one could not be certain that the objects carried off actually belonged to someone else.

Territories also help individual group members define and express a sense of personal *identity*. Office walls often display posters, diplomas, crude drawings produced by small children, pictures of loved ones, or little signs with trite slogans, even when company regulations specifically forbid such personalizing markings. Although such decorations may seem insignificant to the chance visitor, to the occupant of the space, they have personal meaning and help turn a drab, barren environment into home.

Researchers studied personal territories by photographing the walls over the beds of students living in campus dormitories. As an incidental finding, they discovered that most of these decorations fit into one of the categories listed in Table 14–4. More importantly, however, they also found that students who eventually dropped out of school seemed to mark their walls more extensively—particularly in the categories of personal relations and music and theater—than students who stayed in school. Although "stay-ins" used fewer markers, their decorations revealed greater diversity, cutting across several categories. Whereas a dropout's wall would feature dozens of skiing posters or high school memorabilia, the stay-in's decorations might include syllabi, posters, wall hangings, plants, and family photos. The researchers concluded that the wall decorations of dropouts "reflected less imagination or diversity of interests and an absence of commitment to the new university environment" (Hansen & Altman, 1976; Vinsel, Brown, Altman, & Foss, 1980, p. 1114).

Territory and Status. The size and quality of an individual's territory within a group is, in many cases, a reflection of his or her social status within the group. In undifferentiated societies, people rarely divide up space into "yours," "mine," and "ours." The Basarawa of Africa, for example, do not make distinctions between people on the basis of age, sex, or prestige. Nor do they establish primary territories or build permanent structures (Kent, 1991). But stratified societies with leaders, status hierarchies, and classes are territorial. Moreover, the size and quality of the territories held by individuals tend to correspond to their status within society. The political and social elite in the community live in large, fine homes rather than small, run-down shacks (Cherulnik & Wilderman, 1986). Executives with large offices hold a higher, more prestigious position with the company than executives with small offices (Durand, 1977). Prison

TABLE 14–4   CATEGORIES FOR WALL DECORATIONS
IN DORMITORY ROOMS

Category	Decorations
Entertainment or equipment	Bicycles, skis, radios, stereos or components, climbing gear, tennis rackets
Personal relations	Pictures of friends and family, flowers, snapshots of vacations, letters, drawings by siblings
Values	Religious or political posters, bumper stickers, ecology signs, flags, sorority signs
Abstract	Prints or posters of flowers, kittens, landscapes; art reproductions
Reference items	Schedules, syllabi, calendars, maps
Music or theater	Posters of ballet, rock, or musical groups; theater posters
Sports	Ski posters, pictures of athletes, motorcycle races, magazine covers, mountain-climbing or hiking posters
Idiosyncratic	Handmade items (macramé, wall hangings, paintings), plants, unique items (stolen road signs, bearskins)

Source: Vinsel, Brown, Altman, & Foss, 1980.

inmates who control the most desirable portions of the exercise yard enjoy higher status than individuals who cannot establish a territory (Esser, 1973). As one informal observer has noted, in many large corporations, the entire top floor of a company's headquarters is reserved for the offices of the upper-echelon executives and can only be reached by a private elevator (Korda, 1975). Furthermore, within this executive area, offices swell in size and become more lavishly decorated as the occupant's position in the company increases. Substantiating these informal observations, a study of a large chemical company headquarters, a university, and a government agency found a clear link between office size and status (Durand, 1977). The correlation between size of territory and position in each group's organization chart was .81 for the company, .79 for the agency, and .29 for the university.

The link between territory and dominance in small groups tends to be more variable. Several studies suggest that territory size *increases* as status increases (Esser, 1973; Sundstrom & Altman, 1974). Other studies, however, indicate that territory size seems to *decrease* as status in the group increases (Esser, 1968; Esser, Chamberlain, Chapple, & Kline, 1965). Eric Sundstrom and Irwin Altman (1974) suggest that these contradictory results occur because territorial boundaries are more fluid in small groups. In one study that they conducted at a boys' rehabilitation center, they asked each subject to rank the other boys in terms of ability to influence others. In addition, an observer passed through the residence bedrooms, lounge, TV area, and bathrooms regularly and recorded territorial behaviors. The boys evaluated each area to determine which territories were more desirable than others.

Sundstrom and Altman found evidence of the territory-dominance relation, but the strength of this relation varied over time. During the first phase of the project, the high-status boys maintained clear control over more desirable areas, but when two of the most dominant boys were removed from the group, the remaining boys competed with one another for both status and space. By the end of the tenth week, however, the group had quieted back down, although certain highly dominant members continued to be disruptive. When formal observations were finally terminated, available evidence suggested that the group's territorial structures were once more beginning to stabilize.

These findings suggest that dominance-territory relations, like most group processes, are dynamic. In many small groups, the higher status members possess larger and more aesthetically pleasing territories, but chaotic intermember relations or abrupt changes in membership can create discontinuities in territorial behavior. In addition, the hostility that surfaced in the group when spatial claims were disputed suggests that territories can work as tension reducers by clarifying the nature of the social situation and increasing opportunities for maintaining privacy.

Territory and Stress in Isolated Groups.   During the International Geophysical Year (1957–1958), several countries sent small groups of military and civilian personnel to outposts in Antarctica. These groups were responsible for collecting various data concerning that largely unknown continent, but the violent weather forced the staff to remain indoors most of the time. Equipment malfunctioned regularly, radio contact was limited, and water rationing restricted bathing and laundering. As months went by and these conditions remained, interpersonal friction often surfaced, and the group members found themselves arguing over trivial issues. The members summarized their group malaise with the term *antarcticitis:* lethargy, low morale, grouchiness, and boredom brought on by their unique living conditions (Gunderson, 1973; see, too, Carrere & Evans, 1994; Stuster, 1996).

These Antarctic groups are by no means unique, for accounts of sailors confined in submarines (Weybrew, 1963), the divers living in Sealab (Helmreich, 1974; Radloff & Helmreich, 1968), astronauts in a spacecraft (Sandal, Vaernes, Bergan, Warncke, & Ursin, 1996), work teams on large naval ships (Luria, 1990), and crews on space stations (Stuster, 1996) report evidence of stress produced by these environmental circumstances of isolation. Although technological innovations make survival in even the most hostile environments possible, groups living in these space-age settings must learn to cope with age-old problems of interpersonal adjustment. Leaders must make certain that group members remain active and busy, and conflicts must be handled quickly and decisively. Groups that achieve high levels of teamwork tend to be more successful than ones with well-defined chains of command. Attention to spatial concerns, however, are also critical, for groups that develop individual and group territories tend to prosper, whereas those that fail to territorialize their spaces founder (Harrison, Clearwater, & McKay, 1991; Harrison & Connors, 1984; Leon, 1991; Palinkas, 1991).

Altman, William Haythorn, and their colleagues at the Naval Medical Research Institute in Bethesda, Maryland, studied territoriality in isolated groups by confining pairs of volunteers to a 12-by-12-foot room equipped with beds, a toilet cabinet, and a table and chairs (see Altman, 1973, 1977, and Haythorn, 1973, for summaries). The groups worked for several hours each day at various tasks, but were left to amuse themselves with card games and reading the rest of the time. The men in the isolation condition never left their room during the ten days of the experiment; matched pairs in a control condition were permitted to eat their meals at the base mess and sleep in their regular barracks.

The members of isolated groups quickly claimed particular bunks as theirs. Furthermore, this territorial behavior increased as the experiment progressed, with the isolated pairs extending their territories to include specific chairs and certain positions around the table. Not all of the groups, however, benefited by establishing territories. In some of the groups, territories structured the group dynamics and eased the stress of the situation, but in other dyads, these territories worked as barricades to social interaction and exacerbated the strain of isolation. Overall, withdrawal and time spent sleeping increased across the ten days of the study, whereas time spent in social interaction decreased. Other measures revealed worsened task performance and heightened interpersonal conflicts, anxiety, and emotionality for isolates who drew a "psychological and spatial 'cocoon' around themselves, gradually doing more things alone and in their own part of the room" (Altman & Haythorn, 1967, p. 174).

Altman and his colleagues followed up these provocative findings in a second experiment by manipulating three aspects of the group environment: (1) availability of privacy (half of the groups lived and worked in a single room, and the remaining groups had small adjoining rooms for sleeping, napping, reading, etc.); (2) expected duration of the isolation (pairs expected the study to last either 4 days or 20 days); and (3) amount of communication with the "outside world." Although the study was to last for eight days for all the pairs, more than half terminated their participation early. Altman explains this high attrition rate by suggesting that the aborting groups tended to "misread the demands of the situation and did not undertake effective group formation processes necessary to cope with the situation" (1973, p. 249). On the first day of the study, these men tended to keep to themselves, never bothering to work out any plans for coping with what would become a stressful situation. Then, as the study wore on, they reacted to increased stress by significantly strengthening their territorial behavior, laying increased claim to particular areas of the room. They also began spending more time in their beds, but they seemed simultaneously to be increasingly restless. Access to a private room and an expectation of prolonged isolation only added to the stress of the situation and created additional withdrawal, maladaptation, and eventual termination (Altman, Taylor, & Wheeler, 1971).

Groups that lasted the entire eight days seemed to use territoriality to their advantage in structuring their isolation. On the first day, they defined their territories, set up schedules of activities, and agreed on their plan of action for getting through the study. Furthermore, the successful groups tended to relax territorial restraints in the later stages of the project, thereby displaying a greater degree of positive interaction. As described by Altman (1977, p. 310):

> The epitome of a successful group was one in which the members, on the first or second day, laid out an eating, exercise, and recreation schedule; constructed a deck of playing cards, a chess set, and a Monopoly game out of paper. . . .

In essence, the men who adapted "decided how they would structure their lives over the expected lengthy period of isolation" (1977, p. 310). Although territorial behavior worked to the benefit of some of the groups, the last-minute attempts of some of the faltering groups to organize their spatial relations failed to improve their inadequate adaptation to the isolation.

Groups in Spaces and Places: Beyond Sealab

The Sealab divers were not the first group of people to spend time confined to a small living area, isolated from contact with the outside world. For centuries, explorers have hiked, sailed, flown, and rocketed from their homes to distant lands and planets, and many of these groups have endured very long periods of isolation in harsh climates.

These groups survived and achieved their goals because they did not overlook the impact of the environment on their groups. Whereas harsh environments and circumstances overwhelm lone individuals, groups are capable of overcoming the limiting conditions created by these environmental stressors. Some groups may not survive in a hostile environment, but others respond to stress by becoming better groups: more organized, more cohesive, and more efficient. In the words of the divers themselves (Radloff & Helmreich, 1968):

> If we hadn't had a real compatible group there might have been a lot of hard feelings. Everybody was cooperative. They all worked and helped each other as much as possible. I think it was a real good group. [p. 821]

> That was the hardest I have ever worked in my life. And it is the busiest I have ever been. I would go back right now. [p. 79]

SUMMARY

How do basic features of the environment, such as temperature and noise, influence groups and their dynamics? Features of the natural environment and built environment, such as extremes in temperature and noise, information overload, and dangerousness, can engender *stress* in groups and undermine performance.

1. High temperatures are linked to loss of attention as well as a number of other unpleasant consequences, including discomfort, aggression, and reduced productivity.
2. Group members can cope with exposure to *noise* for a short duration, but prolonged exposure is associated with psychological and physical difficulties.
3. People prefer positive, stimulating environments, but excessive stimulation can lead to cognitive *overload*.
4. Ecological psychologists maintain that *behavior settings* that lack *synomor-*

phy are inefficient and distressing. *Staffing theory* describes the causes and consequences of understaffing and overstaffing.

What group processes are influenced by the distances that people maintain between themselves and other group members? Studies of *personal space* suggest that group members prefer to keep a certain distance between themselves and others.

1. Smaller spaces are associated with greater intimacy, so space requirements tend to increase as the situation becomes less intimate. The five *interpersonal zones* are the intimate, personal, social, public, and remote zones.
2. The *equilibrium model* predicts that individuals will moderate their distances to achieve the desired level of intimacy, but researchers have also found that variations in space are linked to the gender, status, and cultural background of the interactants.

3. *Density* describes the number of people per unit of space, whereas *crowding* is a psychological reaction to high physical density.

4. Crowding is exacerbated by a number of factors, including cognitive processes that prompt individuals to make attributions about the causes of their arousal, group members' overall evaluation of the high-density setting (the *density-intensity hypothesis*), perceptions of control, and the degree to which others interfere with task performance.

5. Seating arrangements make up an important part of the ecology of a small group. *Sociopetal* spaces tend to encourage interaction, whereas *sociofugal* seating patterns discourage interaction. People generally prefer interaction-promoting sociopetal patterns, but these preferences vary with the type of task being attempted and the gender of the interactants.

6. Seating arrangements significantly influence patterns of attraction, communication, and leadership. For example, in many groups, individuals tend to speak immediately after the person seated opposite them (the *Steinzor effect*), and leadership is closely associated with sitting at the end of the table (the *head-of-the-table effect*).

What are the causes and consequences of groups' tendency to establish territories? Like many other animals, humans establish *territories*: geographical locations that an individual or group defends against intrusion by others.

1. Altman distinguishes between *primary territories, secondary territories,* and *public territories.* Studies of group space suggest that groups seem to be surrounded by a sort of shell that forms an invisible boundary for group interaction.

2. Territories promote adjustment and reduce stress, but they also promote intergroup conflict, as in the case of gang-related territoriality. Groups with a *home advantage* tend to outperform groups that are outside their territories.

3. Individuals' territories within a group also influence group dynamics, for they fulfill important privacy, organizing, and identity functions within the group. Territoriality also influences dominance and members' ability to cope with periods of prolonged isolation.

FOR MORE INFORMATION

Bold Endeavors: Lessons from Polar and Space Exploration, by Jack Stuster (1996), draws on interviews, historical documentation, and empirical research to develop a comprehensive, detailed analysis of the dynamics of groups that live and work in atypical environments, such as bases in Antarctica and space stations.

Gangbangs and Drive-bys: Grounded Culture and Juvenile Gang Violence, by William B. Sanders (1994), explains the development of gang activity in terms of territoriality, self-presentation, and grounded values.

Environmental Psychology, by Francis T. McAndrew (1993), offers a concise appraisal of environmental psychology, with compact chapters dealing with such topics as territoriality, interpersonal distance, and work, learning, and home environments.

Groups Under Stress: Psychological Research in SEALAB II, by R. Radloff and R. Helmreich (1968), is the source of the case study of the Sealab group, which lived for two weeks in a restrictive environment on the ocean floor.

Handbook of Environmental Psychology, edited by Daniel Stokols and Irwin Altman

(1987), contains chapters written by leading researchers and theorists in the field of person-environment relations. The 22 chapters in Volume One focus on basic processes, and the 21 chapters in Volume

Two consider applications and cross-cultural implications.

Personal Space, by Robert Sommer (1969), takes an entertaining look at interpersonal distancing processes.

ACTIVITY 14–1 TERRITORIALITY

Members of groups often develop a proprietary orientation toward specific areas of the group's space; for example, family members have their own rooms, faculty have their offices, and students in classes often sit at the same desk week after week. Study the territory of a professor at a university or a colleague where you work by first getting the consent of the occupant. Then, spend about 15 minutes in the individual's territory, taking notes and sketching its layout. Consider the following aspects of the space:

1. Who's territory did you observe? Give a thumbnail sketch of the individual's personality, focusing on introversion, achievement orientation, friendliness, emotionality, and intellectual prowess. What is the status of the occupant?
2. How large is the space? What is the actual measurement of the room? Does it seem large enough, or small and cluttered? What is your subjective appraisal of the size?
3. Where is the office located? Is it hidden away in an obscure part of the building or in a high-traffic area? What other rooms/offices are located nearby?
4. What is the overall quality of the space? Is it clean, freshly painted, in need of repair, modern, etc.?
5. Diagram the way the furniture is arranged, paying attention to desk, chairs, windows, and doorway.
6. What sort of markings are in the office or near the office? Are grades posted nearby? Is the room marked with a nameplate?
7. What types of territorial displays are present in the office itself (see Table 14–4)?
Entertainment or equipment (bicycles, skis, radios, tennis rackets)
Personal relations (pictures of friends, letters, drawings)
Values (religious or political posters, bumper stickers)
Abstract (prints, art, statues)
Reference items (schedules, syllabi, calendars)
Music/theater (posters of rock groups, ballet troupes)
Sports (pictures of athletes, magazines)
Idiosyncratic (crafts, wall hangings, plants)
8. Given your observations, would you consider the space you observed to be a territory?

ACTIVITY 14–2 GROUP SYNOMORPHY

The concept of synomorphy assumes that the shape and design of the places where group members interact inevitably shape their dynamics, for good and for worse. Study synomorphy by locating a complex behavior setting occupied by people. You might want to observe a crowded place, such as a high-density classroom, a fast-food restaurant, or an airport terminal. You could also consider a cafeteria serving area, the checkout desk in the library, the entrance to a high-use building, or a busy street corner. Just be certain that the place you observe is one that involves relatively complex interactions between the individuals and the setting they occupy.

1. Describe, in detail, the place that you are observing. Give its general characteristics, including dimensions.
2. Is the space available appropriate given the number of people present and their actions? Is overcrowding a problem? Is understaffing a problem?
3. Consider the way people enter into and move in the space. For example, are the doorways and halls sufficient to handle the flow of traffic? Is the area easy to reach from an outside location? Are the stairs or aisles conveniently located and adequate? Is the space barrier-free?
4. Describe how the people in the space react to it. Do they seem to like it or dislike it? Does it seem to be stressful for them? Does it influence the nature of their interactions?
5. Critique the space, concentrating on synomorphy. Does the form fit function? Does the space fit the tasks to be done? Is it too noisy, crowded, or ugly?

15

Crowds and Collective Behavior

Groups are not always small, intimate, and stable. Large groups, such as crowds of people that exist only temporarily, and even larger groups, such as social movements, are similar to smaller groups in many respects. Yet, these collectives possess unique features as well. We expect individuals and small groups to act rationally, but who is surprised when a crowd, mob, or movement acts in odd and unusual ways?

- When does a group become a collective?
- What theories explain collective behavior?
- How different are collectives from other types of groups?

CONTENTS

The Who Concert Stampede: A Crowd Gone Mad?

KINDS OF COLLECTIVES

Crowds

Collective Movements

COLLECTIVE DYNAMICS

Le Bon's Crowd Psychology

Convergence Theories

Emergent Norm Theory

Deindividuation Theory

Self-Awareness and Deindividuation

Collectives and Identity

POSTSCRIPT: COLLECTIVES ARE GROUPS

SUMMARY

FOR MORE INFORMATION

ACTIVITIES

The Who Concert Stampede: A Crowd Gone Mad?

Dusk is turning into darkness on December 3, 1979. Nearly 8000 people are waiting to get into Cincinnati's Riverfront Coliseum to hear a concert by one of rock's most successful bands, the Who. Seating isn't reserved, and the most dedicated fans arrived early in the afternoon so that they could get seats down near the stage. But they've been joined now by thousands of others, and the throng is packed so tightly that whenever someone near the fringe pushes forward, ripples spread through the rest of the group. Pranksters move about the perimeter, shoving at its edges and laughing as the shove passes like a wave through the group (see Figure 15–1).

The doors open at 7:30, and the eager crowd surges forward. A crowd of 8000 is loud, but above the din the concertgoers hear the band warming up. As those on the periphery push forward, people near the doors are picked up off the ground and borne along by the tide of other human beings. The ticket takers work as fast as they can, but the back of the group is moving faster than the front, and the flow jams. People near the clogged doors are pushed together, forcefully. Some lose consciousness

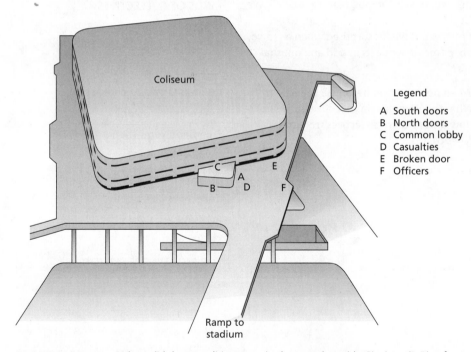

Legend

A South doors
B North doors
C Common lobby
D Casualties
E Broken door
F Officers

FIGURE 15–1. Where did the casualities occur in the crowd outside Cincinnati's Riverfront Coliseum? An estimated 8000 people were in the area leading from the ramp to the doors, and density was very high outside the south doors. When individuals fell outside these doors, concertgoers behind them were pushed over them by the crowd.

(*Source:* Johnson, 1987.)

and fall to the concrete floor. Those around them try to pull them back to their feet, but the rest of the crowd sees the open doors and hears only the music. They push forward relentlessly, and the helpers fall or are pushed past those who have fallen.

Eleven people die in the crowd, and many others are injured. An emergency room supervisor comments that "the bodies were marked with multiple contusions, bruises and the victims had suffered hemorrhages" ("The Who," 1979, p. A-19). Survivors' descriptions reported by the news media revealed the gruesome details:

- "People were hitting other people, and a girl fell down in front of me. I helped her up finally."
- "All of a sudden, I went down. . . .I couldn't see anything."
- "My face was being pressed to the floor. I felt I was smothering."
- "I saw people's heads being stepped on. I fell and couldn't get up. People kept pushing me down."
- "People just didn't seem to care. I couldn't believe it. They could see all the people piled up and they still tried to climb over them just to get in" ("The Who," 1979, p. A-19).

This tragedy is a grim example of **collective behavior:** the actions of a large group of people who are responding in a similar way to an event or situation (McPhail, 1991). Many of the concertgoers were enthusiastic; police described them as "rowdy." When the doors opened, many pushed forward, stepping over the injured. Some tried to help, but many did not seem to be concerned about the injured. Indeed, they acted extraordinarily, displaying emotions and making choices that could not be predicted from their individual characteristics. In this chapter, we consider the many types of social aggregates that fall under the category "collective"—crowds, mobs, riots, and social movements—before considering the qualities they share with most groups and the qualities that make them unique.

KINDS OF COLLECTIVES

The term *collective,* if taken literally, would describe any aggregate of two or more individuals and hence would be synonymous with the term *group* (Blumer, 1951). Most theorists, however, reserve the term for larger, more spontaneous social groups. A baseball team, a company's board of directors, and a family at a meal are all groups, but we typically would not call them collectives because they are too small, too organized, and too stable. Collectives, in contrast, tend to be larger and less deliberately organized. As Table 15–1 suggests, many collectives spring up spontaneously, exist only briefly, and then fade away as members go their separate ways. A list of collectives, then, would include various types of *crowds,* such as an audience at a movie, a street throng watching a building burn, a line of people (queue) waiting to purchase

---

Collective behavior: Similar and sometimes unusual actions performed by individuals in a large group.

TABLE 15–1   CHARACTERISTICS OF COLLECTIVES

Quality	Description
Size and proximity	Collectives tend to be large (more than 20 members); in some cases, all the members "can monitor each other by being visible to or within earshot of one another" (Snow & Oliver, 1995, p. 572).
Joint action	Members of collectives display "common or concerted" forms of behavior (McPhail, 1991, p. 159). Group members may move in the same direction or perform the same general types of behaviors.
Ephemeral	Collectives sometimes (but not always) form and disband rapidly.
Unplanned	Collectives tend to form spontaneously in response to a situation or event. They often have no standards for defining membership and do not adopt operational strategies. Collectives that exist beyond the formative period tend to develop more traditional organizational structures.
Unconventional	Collectives exist outside of traditional forms of social structures and institutions. Members also sometimes engage in atypical, aberrant behaviors.

tickets, a lynch mob, and a panicked group fleeing from danger. But the list would also include *collective movements* of individuals who, although dispersed over a wide area, display common shifts in opinion or actions (Blumer, 1951; McPhail, 1991; Turner & Killian, 1987).

Crowds

The throng of concertgoers massed outside the Riverfront Coliseum was a **crowd:** an aggregate of individuals sharing a common focus and concentrated in a single location. Individuals who are sitting on benches and blankets in a park or walking along a city block occupy a common location, but they don't become a crowd unless something happens—a fire, a car collision, or a mugging, for example—to create a common focus of attention (Milgram & Toch, 1969).

Crowds come in all shapes, sizes, and types (Blumer, 1946; Brown, 1954; Milgram & Toch, 1969). Whereas some are hostile, others are fearful, greedy, or even joyful; some remain stationary, whereas others move about collectively; some watch events passively, whereas others take part actively (see Figure 15–2). Although "no taxonomy seems fully adequate to the task of naming all crowd phenomena," the types of crowds examined here are among the most common: casual crowds, audiences, queues, mobs, and crowds that panic (Milgram & Toch, 1969, p. 515).

Casual Crowds.   Shoppers in a mall are just individuals until a woman spanks her small child when he cries too loudly. Suddenly, the hundred pairs of eyes of an instantly

---

Crowd: A gathering of people who share a common focus and who occupy a single location.

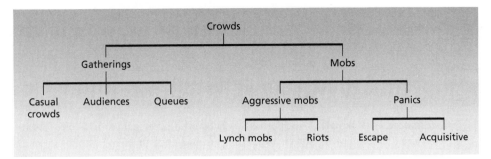

FIGURE 15–2   When does a group become a crowd? Crowds are so diverse that they cannot be easily categorized. Many of the more common crowds, however, fit into two basic clusters: gatherings and mobs.

(*Source:* Brown, 1954; Lofland, 1981; McPhail, 1991.)

formed crowd focus on the woman, who hurries out the door. A **casual crowd,** or *street crowd,* is a group of otherwise unrelated individuals who, while going about their own personal business, end up in the same general vicinity and share a common experience (Blumer, 1946; Brown, 1954). Although such crowds are often short-lived, even these fleeting collectives possess boundaries that limit their size and extent. These boundaries are relatively permeable at the edges of the crowd, where individuals are allowed to enter and exit freely, but permeability diminishes as one moves nearer the center of the crowd. Also, roles, status hierarchies, and other group structures may not be very evident within such crowds, but close probing usually reveals some underlying structure. Casual crowds, for example, often form around *crowd crystals:* one or more individuals who, by drawing attention to themselves or some event, prompt others to join them (Canetti, 1962). Subgroups also exist in these crowds, for in many cases, the people who populate public places are part of small groups rather than lone individuals. At the Who concert, for example, groups of friends waited together for the concert to begin, and these subgroups remained intact even during the fatal crush at the entrance doors. Evidence also indicates that those who occupy central positions in casual crowds are likely to be more actively involved in the experience than those who are content to remain on the fringes (Milgram & Toch, 1969).

Stanley Milgram and his colleagues examined the formation of casual crowds by watching 1424 pedestrians walking along a busy New York City sidewalk. As the pedestrians passed by one section of the sidewalk, they encountered one or more confederates who were gazing at the sixth floor of a nearby building. These confederates acted as crowd crystals by watching the building for 1 minute before gradually dispersing. Meanwhile, a camera filmed the passersby to determine how many looked up at the building or stopped and joined this casual crowd. If we define

Casual crowd: A group of otherwise unrelated individuals who, while going about their own personal business, end up in the same general vicinity and share a common focus.

crowd membership as (1) occupying the same vicinity and (2) sharing the same focus of attention, the results in Figure 15–3 indicate that even a small group of three persons was sufficient to trigger the formation of a casual crowd. If, in contrast, we require that passersby actually stop walking and stand with the confederates before we consider them part of the crowd, then the larger the crowd, the greater the likelihood that others will join it (Milgram, Bickman, & Berkowitz, 1969).

Audiences.   A crowd of individuals who deliberately gather in a particular area to observe some event or activity is called an **audience** or conventional crowd. Unlike the members of a casual crowd, individuals in an audience join the crowd deliberately, and they are also bound more by social conventions that dictate their location and movements (Blumer, 1946). They enter the area via aisles or pathways and occupy locations that are determined by seating arrangements or by custom. While observing, they may perform a variety of behaviors, including clapping, cheering, shouting, or questioning, but these actions are usually in accord with the norms of the particular setting. Moreover, when the event or performance has ended, the crowd disperses in an orderly fashion (Hollingworth, 1935).

Lines.   The waiting line, or **queue,** is a very special type of crowd. Like the casual crowd, the queue includes strangers who will probably never meet again. But like the

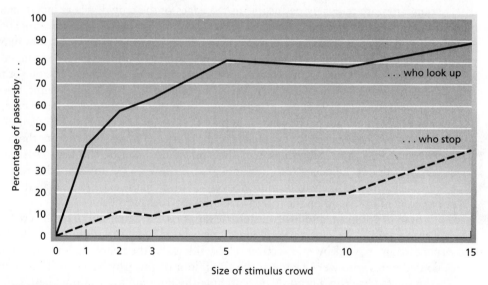

FIGURE 15–3   How many people, when they passed by one or more people who were looking up at a building, looked in the same direction as the starers or actually stopped walking and stood with the starers?

(*Source:* Milgram, Bickman, & Berkowitz, 1969.)

Audience: Individuals who deliberately gather in a particular area to observe some event or activity.
Queue: People waiting in a line for some event or service.

members of an audience, those in this group have joined deliberately to achieve a particular goal, and as members of the crowd, they are bound by certain norms of behavior (Mann, 1969, 1970). Queues are an interference, for they prevent us from immediately achieving our goal of purchasing tickets, services, or other commodities, but they also protect us from late-arriving competitors for these commodities. As Milgram and his colleagues note (Milgram, Liberty, Toledo, & Wackenhut, 1986, p. 683):

> As in the case of most social arrangements, people defer to the restraints of the form, but they are also its beneficiary. The queue thus constitutes a classic illustration of how individuals create social order, on the basis of a rudimentary principle of equity, in a situation that could otherwise degenerate into chaos.

But what prevents the queue from breaking down into a disorderly crowd? Milgram notes that in addition to environmental supports, such as ushers, rails, and ropes, queues are also protected by norms of civility. People in many cultures implicitly obey norms concerning queues and are ready to challenge those who try to violate the norm.

Milgram studied queues by having both male and female accomplices break into 129 lines waiting outside ticket offices and the like in New York City. Working either alone or in pairs, the accomplices would simply say, "Excuse me, I'd like to get in here," and then insert themselves in the line. In an attempt to determine who is most likely to enforce the norm, Milgram also included either one or two passive confederates in some of the queues he studied. These individuals, who were planted in the line in advance, stood directly behind the point of intrusion (Milgram et al., 1986).

Objections occurred in nearly half of the lines studied. In a few cases (10.1%), queuers used physical action, such as a tap on the shoulder or a push. In 21.7% of the lines, the reaction was verbal, such as "No way! The line's back there. We've all been waiting and have trains to catch" and "Excuse me, it's a line." In another 14.7% of the lines, queuers used dirty looks, staring, and hostile gestures to object to the intrusion nonverbally. Objections were also more prevalent when two persons broke into the line rather than one, and they were least prevalent when two confederates separated the intruders from the other queuers. Overall, 73.3% of the complaints came from people standing behind the point of intrusion rather than from people standing in front of the intrusion. Other investigators found that line-breakers encountered less hostility when they appeared to be joining someone they knew and when they only broke in near the very end of the line (Schmitt, Dubé, & Leclerc, 1992). These findings suggest that self-interest, as well as the normative force of the queue's rules, mediated reactions to the queue-breakers' actions.

Mobs. An emotionally charged crowd is a **mob.** Mobs tend to form when some event, such as a crime, a catastrophe, or a controversial action, evokes the same kind of affect and action in a substantial number of people. The hallmark of the mob is its emotion (Lofland, 1981). Indeed, early accounts of mobs argued that individuals in mobs were so overwhelmed by their emotions that they could no longer control their

Mob: An emotionally charged crowd.

actions. Unless the situation is diffused, the mob becomes volatile, unpredictable, and capable of violent action. In mobs, impulse replaces reason. Leonard Doob puts it very strongly, calling a mob "a device for going crazy together" (1952, pp. 292–293). He adds that "after a mob disbands, many of the participants may report that they 'lost their heads.' In the light of 'pure reason' they may be shocked by the ways in which they behaved."

Mobs, even though they stimulate members' emotions, are not necessarily irrational; nor are they necessarily violent. When sports fans celebrate a victory, when partiers parade New Orleans streets during Mardi Gras, or when patriots celebrate the end of a conflict, the members share positive emotions: joy, jubilation, and exhilaration. Their aggressive counterparts, however, tend to be more common—or at least they receive more attention in the media (Milgram & Toch, 1969). *Lynch mobs* terrorized Black men in the southern United States until only recently. The first documented lynch mob occurred in the United States in 1882, but by 1950, lynch mobs had killed thousands. Virtually all the victims were Black, and many of the killings were savagely brutal (Mullen, 1986a; Tolnay & Beck, 1996). *Hooliganism* is common in Europe. Large numbers of football (soccer) fans, often intoxicated, spill into the streets around the stadiums, fighting among themselves and with fans who support the opposing team (Dunning, Murphy, & Williams, 1986; Oyserman & Saltz, 1993). The abuse of low-status group members by groups of bullies, which is sometimes termed *mobbing,* is a regular occurrence in both school and work settings (Schuster, 1996; Whitney & Smith, 1993).

Riots can be construed as mobs on a grander scale. In 1969, when the police force of Montreal went on strike for 17 hours, riots broke out all over the city. As expected, professional crimes skyrocketed, but the noncriminal population also ran amok. A heterogeneous crowd of the impoverished, the rich, and the middle class rampaged along the central business corridor, looting and vandalizing. Fires were set, 156 stores were looted, $300,000 worth of glass was shattered, 2 people were killed, and 49 were wounded. Despite the violence, observers commented that the entire incident seemed "carnival-like" (Clark, 1969).

Crowds That Panic. Other crowds are charged with a different emotion: fear. During catastrophes, such as fires, floods, or earthquakes, crowds of people sometimes seek escape en masse from the dangerous situation. If the situation is seen as so dangerous that the only safe course of action is escape, but the escape routes are very limited, a crowd **panic** can occur (Strauss, 1944). Members, fearing personal harm or injury, struggle to escape from the situation and from the crowd itself (Canetti, 1962, pp. 26–27):

> The individual breaks away and wants to escape from it because the crowd, as a whole, is endangered. But because he is still stuck in it, he must attack it. . . . The more fiercely each man "fights for his life" the clearer it becomes he is fighting

---

Panic: A feeling of fear and of being threatened; a group of people who are seeking escape en masse from a dangerous situation.

against all the others who hem him in. They stand there like chairs, balustrades, closed doors, but different from these in that they are alive and hostile.

Panics often result in a staggering loss of life. In 1903, for example, a panic at Chicago's Iroquois Theater killed nearly 600 people. When a small fire broke out backstage, the management tried to calm the audience. But when the lights shorted out and fire was visible behind the stage, the crowd stampeded for the exits. Some were burned, and others died by jumping from the fire escapes to the pavement, but many more were killed as fleeing patrons trampled them. One observer described the panic this way:

> In places on the stairways, particularly where a turn caused a jam, bodies were piled seven or eight feet deep. Firemen and police confronted a sickening task in disentangling them. An occasional living person was found in the heaps, but most of these were terribly injured. The heel prints on the dead faces mutely testified to the cruel fact that human animals stricken in terror are as mad and ruthless as stampeding cattle. Many bodies had the clothes torn from them, and some had the flesh trodden from their bones. (Foy & Harlow, 1928/1956).

Experimental simulations of panicked crowds suggest that individuals who must take turns exiting from a dangerous situation are most likely to panic when they believe that the time available to escape is very limited and they are very fearful of the consequences of a failure to escape (Kelley, Contry, Dahlke, & Hill, 1965; Mintz, 1951). Larger groups, even if given more time to effect their escape, are also more likely to panic than smaller ones (Chertkoff, Kushigian, & McCool, 1996). These simulations also illustrate the difference between *escape panics* and *acquisitive panics*. In acquisitive panics, individuals are working under time pressure, and often in competition against others, to acquire scarce commodities. In escape panics, the crowd is trying to flee from an aversive situation.

The crowd at the Who concert, from all objective reports, was an escape panic rather than an aggressive mob or acquisitive panic. Although the news media described the crowd as a drugged-crazed stampede bent on storming into the concert, police interviews with survivors indicate that the crowd members in the center of the crush were trying to flee *from* the dangerous overcrowding rather than *to* the concert. Also, although some individuals in the crowd were clearly fighting to get out of the danger, Good Samaritans in the crowd helped others to safety (Johnson, 1987).

Collective Movements

Not all collective phenomena transpire at close distances. In some cases, individuals who are physically dispersed may still be similarly influenced and act in similar and often atypical ways. Such curious phenomena are variously termed **collective movements,** mass movements, or dispersed collective behavior, although this terminology

---

Collective movements: Mass phenomena in which individuals who are physically dispersed are similarly influenced and act in similar and sometimes unusual ways.

is by no means formalized or universally recognized (Genevie, 1978; Smelser, 1962). But like crowds, collective phenomena come in many varieties, including fads, crazes, fashions, rumors, and social movements.

Fads, Crazes, and Fashions.   In 1929, as the United States plunged into the Great Depression, people had little time or money to spend playing golf. But several entrepreneurs set up "miniature golf courses" in cities, and the idea took hold of the nation with a vengeance. Miniature golf spread over the entire country, and some people were predicting that the game would replace all other sports as the country's favorite form of recreation. The craze died out within six months (LaPiere, 1938).

A **fad** is an abrupt, but short-lived, change in the opinions, behaviors, or lifestyles of a large number of widely dispersed individuals. Fads are remarkable both because they influence so many people so rapidly and because they disappear without leaving any lasting impact on society. Hula Hoops, the Twist, discos, breakdancing, and baby beanies captured the imagination of many Americans, but within months their popularity dwindled. **Crazes** are similar to fads in most respects, except that they are just a bit more irrational, expensive, or widespread. Streaking (running naked) on college campuses, the rapid proliferation of cellular telephones, and the widespread use of cocaine all qualify as crazes. Last, fads that pertain to styles of dress or manners are generally termed **fashions.** Clamdiggers gave way to hiphuggers, which were supplanted by bellbottoms, which lost out to blue jeans. Ties and lapels expand and contract, women's hemlines move up and down, and last season's color takes a backseat to this season's shade (Ragone, 1981).

Rumors and Mass Hysteria.   In 1954, rumors that windshields were being damaged by nuclear fallout began circulating in the Seattle area. The rumors escalated into a mild form of mass hysteria as reporters devoted much attention to the issue, residents jammed police telephone lines reporting damage, and civic groups demanded government intervention. Subsequent investigation revealed that no damage at all had occurred (Medalia & Larsen, 1958).

Rumors play an integral part in a variety of collective phenomena, including riots, panics, and crazes. Future rioters, for example, often mill about for hours swapping stories about injustices before taking any aggressive actions. Panics and crazes, too, are often sustained by rumors, particularly when the mass media perpetuate hearsay in news reports and announcements (Allport & Postman, 1947; Milgram & Toch, 1969). A recent epidemic of koro (a rare delusion characterized by the fear that one's sex organs will disappear) that swept through the Han region of China, for example, was traced to exposure to rumors about the fictitious malady (Cheng, 1997).

Ralph L. Rosnow (1980) argues that two conditions tend to influence the spread of rumor: the degree of anxiety that individuals are experiencing and their uncertainty

---

Fad: An abrupt, but usually short-lived, change in the opinions, behaviors, or lifestyles of a large number of widely dispersed individuals.
Crazes: Irrational, costly, or widespread fads.
Fashions: Fads that pertain to styles of dress or manners.

about the true nature of the situation. He argues that just as individuals often affiliate with others in threatening situations, "ambiguous or chaotic" situations tend to generate rumors. By passing rumors, individuals convey information (albeit false) about the situation. Rumors also reduce anxiety by providing, in most cases, reassuring reinterpretations of the ambiguous event (Walker & Berkerle, 1987). After the Three Mile Island nuclear power plant accident, for example, rumors circulated so rampantly that a rumor control center had to be opened to supply more accurate information. Rosnow, after studying this incident, maintains that even though many of the rumors were preposterous, they gave people a sense of security in a time of great anxiety (Rosnow & Kimmel, 1979; Rosnow, Yost, & Esposito, 1986).

Rumors also provide the basis for **mass hysteria:** the spontaneous outbreak of atypical thoughts, feelings, or actions in a group or aggregate, including psychogenic illness, common hallucinations, and bizarre actions (Pennebaker, 1982; Phoon, 1982). One well-known case of mass hysteria occurred on Halloween night in 1938 when Orson Welles broadcast the radio play *The War of the Worlds*. General panic prevailed as listeners, taking the dramatization at face value, reacted by warning relatives, taking defensive precautions, contemplating suicide, and fleeing from the "invaded areas" (Cantril, 1940).

Sometimes, the panic is confined to a specific geographical area, institution, or organization. For example, in June 1962, workers at a garment factory began complaining of nausea, pain, disorientation, and muscular weakness; some actually collapsed at their jobs or lost consciousness. Rumors spread rapidly that the illness was caused by "some kind of insect" that had infested one of the shipments of cloth from overseas, and the owners began making efforts to eradicate the bug. No bug was ever discovered, however, and experts eventually concluded that the "June Bug incident" had been caused by mass hysteria (Kerckhoff & Back, 1968; Kerckhoff, Back, & Miller, 1965).

These outbreaks of a contagious psychogenic illness are not that rare. Researchers can never definitively determine which cases of widespread illness are socially produced rather than biologically produced, but one study of work groups identified 23 separate cases that involved large numbers of individuals afflicted with "physical symptoms . . . in the absence of an identifiable pathogen" (Colligan & Murphy, 1982, p. 35). Over 1200 people were affected by these outbreaks, with most reporting symptoms that included headaches, nausea, dizziness, and weakness. Many were women working in relatively repetitive, routinized jobs, and the illness often spread through friendship networks. Similarly, studies of pupils in school often conclude that many epidemics, such as outbreaks of fainting or nausea, are caused by hysterical contagion (Bartholomew, 1997; Bartholomew & Sirois, 1996; Lee, Leung, Fung, & Low, 1996). Some experts believe that as many as 75% of the epidemics that are blamed on the presence of irritants in buildings—the so-called *sick building syndrome*—are actually cases of mass hysteria (Rothman & Weintraub, 1995).

Mass hysteria: The spontaneous outbreak of atypical thoughts, feelings, and/or actions in a group or aggregate, including psychogenic illness, common hallucinations, and bizarre actions.

How can group-level delusions be controlled? Some experts suggest that as soon as the possibility of a physical cause is eliminated, medical experts should tell workers that their problems are caused by stress rather than physical illness. A second means of limiting the spread of such delusions involves altering the setting. In some instances, the outbreaks occur when employees have been told to increase their productivity or when they have been working overtime. Poor labor-management relations have also been implicated, as have negative environmental factors, such as noise, poor lighting, and exposure to dust, foul odors, or chemicals. These findings suggest that psychogenic outbreaks can be reduced by improving working conditions and reducing situational stressors (Colligan, Pennebaker, & Murphy, 1982).

Social Movements.   In 1096, thousands upon thousands of Europeans, urged on by Pope Urban II, marched to Jerusalem to "free the Holy Land from the pagans." In 1789, large bands of French citizens fought government forces and eventually overthrew the government. In December of 1955, Dr. Martin Luther King and a dozen other ministers founded the Montgomery Improvement Association, which succeeded in dismantling the segregated bus system in Montgomery, Alabama. In 1976, David Moore joined a group of young people who were interested in personal development, religion, and space travel. Some 20 years later, David and 38 other members of a group called Heaven's Gate committed suicide.

A **social movement** is a deliberate, relatively organized attempt to achieve a change or resist a change in a social system (see Table 15–2). Social movements, like other forms of collective behavior, often arise spontaneously in response to some problem, such as unfair government policies, societal ills, or threats to personal values. Social movements are not short-lived, however. Over time, social movements tend to gain new members, set goals, and develop leadership structures, until eventually they change from spontaneous gatherings of people into *social movement organizations,* or SMOs. SMOs have all the structural characteristics of any organization, including clearly defined goals, rational planning, and bureaucratic leadership structures (Zald & Ash, 1966; see Gamson, 1992, McAdam, McCarthy, & Zald, 1988, and Snow & Oliver, 1995, for detailed reviews of social movements.)

Social movements, like crowds, vary in their longevity and their goals (Appelbaum & Chambliss, 1995; Cameron, 1966). *Reformist movements* seek to improve existing institutions, often through civil disobedience and demonstrations. The U.S. civil rights movement, for example, sought to change existing laws that gave unfair power to Whites, although the movement did not challenge the basic democratic principles of the country. *Revolutionary movements,* in contrast, seek more sweeping changes in existing social institutions. The revolts in France in the late 1700s, for example, were revolutionary movements, for the protestors sought to overthrow the monarchy and replace it with a democracy. *Reactionary movements,* instead of trying to achieve change, seek to slow it or even to reinstate extinct social systems. The Ku Klux Klan

---

Social movement: A deliberate, relatively organized attempt to achieve a change or resist a change in a social system.

TABLE 15-2 VARIOUS TYPES OF COLLECTIVES

Type of Collective	Defining characteristics
Crowd	A temporary gathering of individuals who share a common focus of interest
Audience	Spectators at an exhibition, performance, or event
Queue	A waiting line or file of individuals
Panic	A threatened crowd, seeking either escape from danger or competing for a scarce commodity
Mob	An acting crowd, often aggressive in character
Riot	A large, less localized and less organized mob
Craze, fad, or fashion	An abrupt but short-lived change in the opinions, behaviors, life-styles, or dress of a large number of widely dispersed individuals
Mass hysteria and rumors	The spontaneous outbreak of atypical thoughts, feelings, and/or actions in a group or aggregate, including psychogenic illness, common hallucinations, and bizarre actions
Social movement	A deliberate, organized attempt to achieve a change or resist a change in a social system

is one such movement, as are many militia groups and groups that argue against alternative lifestyles. *Communitarian movements* strive to create more ideal living conditions than currently exist in modern society, often by withdrawing from contact with nonmembers. Communes of the 1960s were communitarian movements, as are many so-called religious cults, like the Heaven's Gate group.

COLLECTIVE DYNAMICS

Groups that undertake extreme actions—crowds, mobs, riots, cults, and the like—are social-psychological mysteries that fascinate both layperson and researcher alike. Although groups are so commonplace that they usually go unnoticed and unscrutinized, atypical groups and their members invite speculation, raising questions such as these: What unseen forces control people when they are part of an extraordinary group? Why do crowds sometimes turn into violent mobs? Do human beings lose their rationality when they are immersed in mobs (Miller, 1985; McPhail & Wohlstein, 1983; Turner & Killian, 1987)?

Le Bon's Crowd Psychology

Gustave Le Bon published his classic analysis of mobs and movements, *The Crowd*, in 1895. Le Bon was fascinated by large groups, but he also feared their tendency to erupt into violence. Perhaps because of these biases, he concluded that a crowd of people could, in certain instances, become a unified entity that acted as if guided by a single collective mind. Writes Le Bon (1895/1960, p. 27):

> Whoever be the individuals that compose it, however like or unlike be their mode of life, their occupations, their character, or their intelligence, the fact that they have been transformed into a crowd puts them in possession of a sort of collective mind which makes them feel, think, and act in a manner quite different from that in which each individual of them would feel, think, and act were he in a state of isolation.

Le Bon believed that no matter what the individual qualities of the people in the group, the crowd would transform them, changing them from rational, thoughtful individuals into impulsive, unreasonable, and extreme followers. Once people fall under the "law of the mental unity of crowds," they act as the collective mind dictates (1895/1960, p. 24).

Le Bon was a physician, and so he viewed the collective mind as a kind of disease that infected one part of the group and then spread throughout the rest of the crowd. After observing many crowds firsthand, Le Bon concluded that emotions and behaviors could be transmitted from one person to another just as germs can be passed along, and he felt that this process of **contagion** accounted for the tendency for group members to behave in very similar ways (Wheeler, 1966).

The occurrence of contagion in groups is quite common. One person laughing in an audience will stimulate laughter in others. Question-and-answer sessions after a lecture usually begin very slowly but soon snowball as more and more questioners begin raising their hands. Le Bon believed that such contagion processes reflected the heightened suggestibility of crowd members, but other processes may be at work as well. Because many crowd settings are ambiguous, social comparison processes may prompt members to rely heavily on other members' reactions when they interpret the situation (Singer, Baum, Baum, & Thew, 1982). Contagion may also arise in crowds through imitation, social facilitation, or conformity (Chapman, 1973; Freedman & Perlick, 1979; Nosanchuk & Lightstone, 1974; Tarde, 1903).

Herbert Blumer combines these various processes when he argues that contagion involves *circular reactions* rather than *interpretative reactions* (Blumer, 1946, 1951, 1957). During interpretative interactions, group members carefully reflect on the meaning of others' behavior and try to formulate valid interpretations before making any kind of comment or embarking on a line of action. During circular reactions, however, the group's members fail to examine the meaning of others' actions cautiously and carefully and therefore tend to misunderstand the situation. When they act on the basis of such misunderstandings, the others in the group also begin to interpret the situation incorrectly, and a circular process is thus initiated that eventually culminates in full-blown behavioral contagion.

Contagion: The transmission of behaviors and emotions from one member of a collective to another.

Convergence Theories

What could the members of such widely disparate and internally heterogeneous collectives as the following possibly have in common: rioters in Los Angeles, zealots eagerly confessing their sins during a religious crusade, shoppers rampaging through a department store searching for bargains, and Korean students throwing rocks at soldiers during a protest rally? According to **convergence theory,** a great deal, because in all these instances, individuals join the group because they possess particular personal characteristics. Although these predisposing features may be latent or virtually unrecognizable, they are the true causes of the formation of both large and small collectives. Such aggregates are not merely haphazard gatherings of dissimilar strangers; rather, they represent the convergence of people with compatible needs, desires, motivations, and emotions. By joining in the group, the individual makes possible the satisfaction of these needs, and the crowd situation serves as a trigger for the spontaneous release of previously controlled behaviors. As Eric Hoffer (1951, p. 9) writes, "All movements, however different in doctrine and aspiration, draw their early adherents from the same types of humanity; they all appeal to the same types of mind."

But what "types of mind" are likely to join a crowd or movement? Are crowd members "joiners"? Are people who seek out membership in collective movements different, in terms of their personalities and values, than people who do not join such groups? Early conceptions of crowds, which portrayed members as less intelligent, more easily influenced, more impulsive, and more violent, have not been confirmed empirically (Martin, 1920; Meerloo, 1950). People who join radical religious groups are usually teenagers or young adults, and although they tend to be more idealistic and open to new experience and also higher in psychological dependency, they show no signs of psychological disturbance (Bromley, 1985; Levine, 1984; Walsh, Russell, & Wells, 1995). People who join social movements do tend to be higher in "personal efficacy": They believe that through their personal involvement, they can make a difference (Snow & Oliver, 1995). Self-confidence, achievement orientation, need for autonomy, dominance, self-acceptance, and maturity are also positively correlated with social activism (Werner, 1978).

People who are particularly frustrated by their economic or social situation are also more likely to take part in social movements. As the concept of **relative deprivation** suggests, people who are suffering the most—those who are most impoverished, persecuted, or endangered—are not necessarily the most likely to join revolutionary social movements. Rather, those who join social movements tend to be people who have higher expectations but who have not succeeded in realizing these expectations. Consider, for example, the Black Power movement of the 1960s. African Americans who joined this collective were often individuals who had succeeded in escaping from

---

Convergence theory: An explanation of collective behavior that assumes that individuals with similar needs, values, or goals tend to converge to form a single group.
Relative deprivation: The psychological state that occurs when individuals feel that their personal attainments (egoistic deprivation) or their group's attainments (fraternalistic deprivation) are below their expectations.

poverty, crime, and discrimination. These gains, however, served to raise their expectations, which remained largely unfulfilled. These individuals thus experienced greater frustration and anger than African Americans who experienced even more intense privations but expected little better. They responded by taking part in change-promoting groups (Caplan, 1970; Crosby, 1976).

The tendency to take part in social movements appears to be more closely linked to fraternalistic deprivation rather than to egoistic deprivation. Egoistic deprivation occurs when individuals are dissatisfied with the gains they have personally achieved. Fraternal deprivation occurs when one is a member of a group that does not enjoy the same level of prosperity as other groups (Runcimann, 1966). Individuals who are active in revolutionary social movements, such as the national separatist movement in Quebec and Ireland, for example, are more likely to be dissatisfied with their group's outcomes rather than their own personal outcomes (Abrams, 1990; Guimond & Dubé-Simard, 1983).

Emergent Norm Theory

Ralph Turner and Lewis Killian's **emergent norm theory** questions the idea that unusual social processes operate in crowds and collectives (Turner, 1964; Turner & Killian, 1972). Indeed, Turner and Killian reject one of the fundamental assumptions of most collective behavior theories—that crowds are extremely homogeneous—and conclude that the "mental unity of crowds" is primarily an illusion. Crowds, mobs, and other collectives only seem to be unanimous in emotions and actions because the members all adhere to norms that are relevant in the given situation. Granted, these emergent norms may be unique and sharply contrary to more general societal standards, but as they emerge in the group situation, they exert a powerful influence on behavior.

Turner and Killian base their analysis on Sherif's (1936) classic analysis of the gradual alignment of action in groups. As noted in Chapter 5, norms emerge gradually in ambiguous situations as members align their actions. Individuals do not actively try to conform to the judgments of others, but instead use the group consensus when making their own behavioral choices. In most cases, the group's norms are consistent with more general social norms pertaining to work, family, relations, and civility. In other cases, however, norms emerge in groups that are odd, atypical, or unexpected.

A normative approach partly explains *baiting crowds:* groups that form below a person who is threatening to commit suicide by jumping from a building, bridge, or tower (Mann, 1981). These crowds, rather than merely watching, often begin to bait the jumper who fails to act swiftly. When Leon Mann studied such crowds, he was unable to determine whether the baiters in a crowd possessed any identifying personality or demographic characteristics (as convergence theory would suggest); he did

---

Emergent norm theory: An explanation of collective behavior that suggests that the uniformity in behavior often observed in collectives is caused by members' conformity to unique normative standards that develop spontaneously in those groups.

note, however, that baiting became more likely as crowd size increased. Mann suggested that larger crowds are more likely to include at least one person who introduces the baiting norm into the group: "In a large crowd at least one stupid or sadistic person will be found who is prepared to cry 'Jump!' and thereby provide a model suggestible for others to follow" (Mann, 1981, p. 707). Mann reports evidence of the baiting norm in several of the crowds in which members not only encouraged the victim to "end it all" but also jeered and booed as rescuers attempted to intervene.

Emergent norm theory, in contrast to other analyses of crowds and collectives, argues that collectives are not out of control or normless. Rather, behavior is socially structured, but by an unusual, temporary norm rather than by more traditional social standards. For example, cults, such as Heaven's Gate, condone mass suicide (Forsyth, 1997). Adolescent peer cliques pressure members to take drugs and commit illegal acts (Corsaro & Eder, 1995). Groups of women, such as sororities, can develop norms that promote unhealthy actions, such as binge eating and purging (Crandall, 1988). Urban gangs accept norms that emphasize toughness, physical strength, and the use of drugs (Jankowski, 1991). Groups of hooligans at British soccer matches consider violence a normal part of the event, and the mass media sustain this view (Dunning et al., 1986; Mann, 1979). Although these actions—when viewed from a more objective perspective—may seem out of control and very strange, for the group members they are consistent with the emergent norms.

Deindividuation Theory

Leon Festinger, Albert Pepitone, and Theodore Newcomb (1952) coined the term **deindividuation** to describe how individuals can become so "submerged in the group" that they feel as though they no longer stand out as individuals. This feeling, they argued, can create a "reduction of inner restraints" and, in the extreme, atypical actions. Although several other researchers explored these initial ideas (e.g., Singer, Brush, & Lublin, 1965; Ziller, 1964), much of the subsequent research has been stimulated by Philip Zimbardo's process model of deindividuation. This model, summarized in Figure 15–4, assumes that anonymity, reduced responsibility, and other situational features can create a deindividuated state: a subjective experience in which the individual group members experience "a lowered threshold of normally restrained behavior" (1969, p. 251). Unlike emergent norm theory, which suggests that people are following the group's norms, Zimbardo suggests that people escape normative regulation when deindividuated (Zimbardo, 1969, 1975, 1977a).

Anonymity.   Zimbardo felt that *anonymity* was a variable of paramount importance in the deindividuation process. Group members achieve anonymity in many ways—wearing disguises, using an alias, avoiding acquaintances, or joining a group whose members are very similar to one another. These methods are equivalent in that

---

Deindividuation: An experiential state, caused by input factors such as group membership and anonymity, that is characterized by the loss of self-awareness, altered experiencing, and atypical behavior.

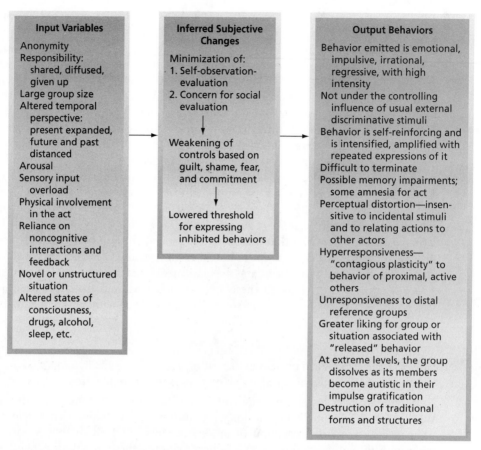

Input Variables	Inferred Subjective Changes	Output Behaviors

Anonymity
Responsibility:
    shared, diffused,
    given up
Large group size
Altered temporal
    perspective:
    present expanded,
    future and past
    distanced
Arousal
Sensory input
    overload
Physical involvement
    in the act
Reliance on
    noncognitive
    interactions and
    feedback
Novel or unstructured
    situation
Altered states of
    consciousness,
    drugs, alcohol,
    sleep, etc.
	Minimization of:
	1. Self-observation-
	    evaluation
	2. Concern for social
	    evaluation
	
	↓
	
	Weakening of
	controls based on
	guilt, shame, fear,
	and commitment
	
	↓
	
	Lowered threshold
	for expressing
	inhibited behaviors
		Behavior emitted is emotional,
		    impulsive, irrational,
		    regressive, with high
		    intensity
		Not under the controlling
		    influence of usual external
		    discriminative stimuli
		Behavior is self-reinforcing and
		    is intensified, amplified with
		    repeated expressions of it
		Difficult to terminate
		Possible memory impairments;
		    some amnesia for act
		Perceptual distortion—insen-
		    sitive to incidental stimuli
		    and to relating actions to
		    other actors
		Hyperresponsiveness—
		    "contagious plasticity" to
		    behavior of proximal, active
		    others
		Unresponsiveness to distal
		    reference groups
		Greater liking for group or
		    situation associated with
		    "released" behavior
		At extreme levels, the group
		    dissolves as its members
		    become autistic in their
		    impulse gratification
		Destruction of traditional
		    forms and structures

FIGURE 15–4   What is deindividuation? Zimbardo's model specifies the conditions of deindividuation, such as anonymity and reduced responsibility, that stimulate the onset of the process. These features lead to the deindividuated state, which in turn generates a series of deindividuated behaviors that represent the outputs of the process.

(*Source:* Zimbardo, 1969.)

they prevent identification: "Others can't identify or single you out, they can't eval-uate, criticize, judge, or punish you" (Zimbardo, 1969, p. 255). If people conform to norms only because they fear legal reprisals, anonymity eases the likelihood that those in authority will locate and punish them for engaging in strange or illegal activities (Dodd, 1985; Ley & Cybriwsky, 1974a). In such cases, anonymity and atypical action go hand in hand. Mann (1981), in his study of baiting crowds, found that most of these crowds gather at night, when anonymity is easier. Studies of people communicating by computer find that these anonymous users often engage in a prac-tice called *flaming;* they express their ideas and opinions far more strongly than is appropriate (Kiesler, Siegel, & McGuire, 1984; McGuire, Kiesler, & Siegel, 1987). According to anthropological evidence, in 92.3% (12 out of 13) of the most highly aggressive cultures—ones known to practice headhunting and torture captives—warriors disguised their appearance prior to battle, whereas only 30% (3 out of 10) of the low-aggression cultures featured similar rituals (Watson, 1973). Even groups assembled in classroom and laboratory settings behave more inappropriately when members are anonymous: They use obscene language, break conventional norms governing conversation, express themselves in extreme ways, criticize one another, and perform embarrassing behaviors (Cannavale, Scarr, & Pepitone, 1970; Lindskold & Finch, 1982; Mathes & Guest, 1976; Singer et al., 1965).

Research also suggests that anonymity increases aggression (Donnerstein, Donnerstein, Simon, & Ditrichs, 1972; Mann, Newton, & Innes, 1982; Mathes & Kahn, 1975; Page & Moss, 1976). Zimbardo (1969), under an elaborate pretense, asked all-female groups to give 20 electric shocks to two women. Anonymous women wore large lab coats (size 44) and hoods over their heads, and they were not permitted to use their names. Women who were identifiable were greeted by name and wore large name tags, and the experimenter emphasized their uniqueness and individuality. Although identifiability was unrelated to the number of shocks given (the average was 17 of 20), the unidentifiable subjects held their switches down nearly twice as long as the identifiable subjects (0.90 second versus 0.47 second).

Zimbardo's decision to dress his subjects in hoods, the garb of lynch mobs and other criminals, may have exaggerated the relationship between anonymity and aggression (Johnson & Downing, 1979). His subjects might have responded to the experimenter's orders to deliver the shock differently if prosocial cues, rather than antisocial cues, had been present in the setting. Researchers verified this tendency, giving the White women who acted as subjects costumes to wear under the guise of masking individual characteristics. In the prosocial-cues condition, nurses' gowns were used; the experimenter explained that "I was fortunate the recovery room let me borrow these nurses' gowns." In the antisocial-cues conditions, the costumes resembled Ku Klux Klan outfits: "I'm not much of a seamstress; this thing came out looking kind of Ku Klux Klannish" (p. 1534). Anonymity polarized the groups, making them more prosocial or more antisocial, depending on the valence of the situational cues.

Anonymity also had a positive effect on groups that were sitting in a well lit or totally darkened room. All the subjects in this study were escorted to and from the room and were assured that the other subjects would not be told their identities (Gergen, Gergen, & Barton, 1973, p. 129). Those individuals in the dark room reported feeling aroused, but in no case did the anonymous (and possibly deindividuated) group members exhibit hostility, aggressiveness, or violence. Rather, nearly all became more intimately involved with one another in a positive fashion. In the words of one participant, a "group of us sat closely together, touching, feeling a sense of friendship and loss as a group member left. I left with a feeling that it had been fun and nice." Apparently, the situation helped people express feelings that they would have otherwise kept hidden, but these feelings were those of affection rather than aggression (see Figure 15–5).

Responsibility.   As Le Bon argued so many years ago, the crowd is "anonymous, and in consequence irresponsible" (1895/1960, p. 30). When individuals are part of

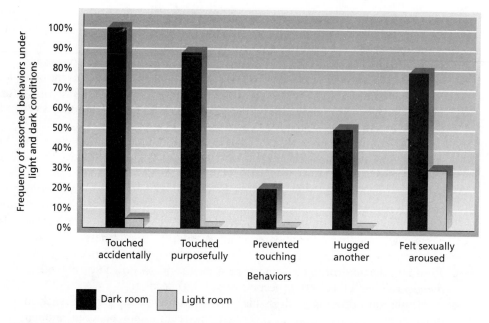

FIGURE 15–5 What would a group of people do if they found themselves in a totally darkened room with strangers? Groups in a darkened room engaged in many behaviors that, under more usual circumstances, would have been odd.

(*Source:* Gergen, Gergen, & Barton, 1973.)

a group, they tend to feel less responsible. This *diffusion of responsibility* has been verified in dozens of studies of people who faced various emergencies alone or in a group. Of the nearly 6000 people studied, about 75% helped when alone, but only 53% helped when in a group (Latané & Nida, 1981). Members of groups may also experience a reduction in responsibility if an authority who demands compliance is present (Milgram, 1974). In addition, if the consequences are somehow separated from the act itself—as when a bombardier presses a bomb-release switch, a technician in an underground bunker launches a missile aimed at a site 1000 miles away, or the person you are shocking remains unseen and unheard—a sense of responsibility for the negative consequences is lessened. Zimbardo (1969) gives examples of groups that actually take steps to ensure the diffusion of responsibility, as when murderers pass around their weapons from hand to hand so that responsibility for the crime is distributed through the entire group rather than concentrated in the one person who pulls the trigger or wields the knife.

Group Membership.   Solo individuals sometimes feel anonymous and free of responsibility for their actions, but these individuals are not deindividuated, for deindividuation is a group process. Edward Diener and his associates compared groups with individuals by taking advantage of a unique tradition: Halloween trick-or-treating

(Diener, Fraser, Beaman, & Kelem, 1976). Their subjects were 1352 children from the Seattle area who visited one of the 27 experimental homes scattered throughout the city. An observer hidden behind a decorative panel recorded the number of extra candy bars and money (pennies and nickels) taken by the trick-or-treaters, who were told to take one candy bar each. The children came to the house alone or in small groups (exceedingly large groups were not included in the study, nor were groups that included an adult). An experimenter manipulated anonymity by asking some children to give their names and addresses. As expected, the children took more money and candy in groups rather than alone and when they were anonymous rather than identified. The effects of anonymity on solitary children were not very pronounced, however, whereas in the group conditions, the impact of anonymity was enhanced (see Figure 15–6). These findings, which have been supported in other investigations, suggest that the term *deindividuation* is used most appropriately in reference to people who perform atypical behavior while members of a group (Cannavale, Scarr, & Pepitone, 1970; Mathes & Guest, 1976; Mathes & Kahn, 1975).

Group Size.   Are larger groups more likely to act in unusual ways? Mann's (1981) study of baiting crowds found that large crowds (more than 300 members) baited more than small crowds. Mann also discovered that people are more likely to respond to religious messages when they are part of a larger rather than smaller group (Newton & Mann, 1980). At the end of many religious meetings, audience members are invited to become "inquirers" by coming forward and declaring their dedication to Christ. In 57 religious meetings, the correlation between crowd size

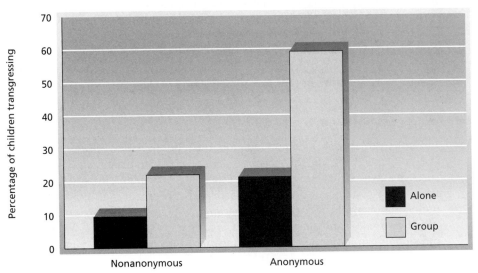

FIGURE 15–6   What are the combined effects of anonymity and group membership on counternormative behavior? Both anonymity and group membership contributed to transgression, but anonymity combined with group membership produced a substantial increase in transgression.

(*Source:* Diener, Fraser, Beaman, & Kelem, 1976.)

and the proportion of people who moved down to the stage to become inquirers was .43. Indeed, on Sundays the correlation rose to .78. Larger lynch mobs are also more violent than smaller ones. When Brian Mullen (1986a) examined the records of 60 lynchings in which the number of victims ranged from one to four and the size of the mob ranged from 4 to 15,000, he found that as the ratio of victims to mob size decreased, atrocities increased.

Arousal. Zimbardo lists a number of other variables that stimulate deindividuated action, including altered temporal perspective, sensory overload, heightened involvement, lack of situational structure, and the use of drugs. Many of these factors, he suggests, function by arousing group members. He contends that arousal "increases the likelihood that gross, agitated behavior will be released, and that cues in the situation that might inhibit responding will not be noticed." Continuing, he proposes that "extreme arousal appears to be a necessary condition for achieving a true state of 'ecstasy'—literally, a stepping out of one's self" (1969, p. 257). Zimbardo even suggests that certain war rituals, such as war dances and group singing, are actually designed to arouse participants and enable them to be deindividuated when the fighting starts: "Among cannibals, like the Cenis or certain Maori and Nigerian tribes, the activity of ritual bonfire dance which precedes eating the flesh of another human being is always more prolonged and intense when the victim is to be eaten alive or uncooked" (1969, p. 257).

Research has shown that reactions are intensified when group members are physiologically aroused. Arousal produced by anger or frustration has been repeatedly linked to increases in aggressive responses in humans, particularly when cues that are associated with aggression are present in the situation (Berkowitz, 1990, 1993; Ferguson & Rule, 1983). Evidence also indicates that emotionally neutral activities such as exercise and physical exertion can create a state of general physiological arousal that in certain situations is misinterpreted as excitement, anger, and hostility (Zillmann, 1983). Aroused individuals, too, are more likely to ignore inhibitory situational cues (Zillmann, Bryant, Cantor, & Day, 1975).

Self-Awareness and Deindividuation

In Zimbardo's theory of deindividuation, the input variables create certain changes in the group members, and these changes are the most immediate causes of the abnormal social behaviors that are eventually observed. Although Zimbardo describes these intervening psychological changes briefly, Edward Diener (1979, 1980) proposes a multicomponent theory of deindividuation involving two discrete components: a loss of self-awareness and altered experiencing. First, as studies of **self-awareness** suggest, individuals can focus their attention outward, onto other group members or environ-

---

Self-awareness: The psychological state in which one's attention is focused on the self, personal standards, or inner experiences.

mental objects, or inward, onto the self. When this focus is on the self, people become more self-aware and are more likely to attend to their emotional and cognitive states, carefully consider their behavioral options, and monitor their actions closely. When this focus is on features of the situation that are external to the person, people fail to monitor their actions and may therefore overlook any discrepancies between moral and social standards and their behavior (Carver & Scheier, 1981, 1983, 1984; Wicklund, 1980). In consequence, "deindividuated persons do not have the capacity for self-regulation and the ability to plan for the future. Thus, prevented from self-attention and self-monitoring by the group situation, they become more reactive to immediate stimuli and emotions and are unresponsive to norms and the long-term consequences of behavior" (Diener, 1980, p. 210).

When individuals do not feel self-aware, they are more likely to misconstrue the nature of the situation (Scheier, Carver, & Gibbons, 1979), fail to help others who are in need (Wegner & Schaefer, 1978), and perform more counternormative actions (Beaman, Klentz, Diener, & Svanum, 1979; Carver, 1975). Reductions in self-awareness may also lead to other cognitive and emotional changes, including disturbances in concentration and judgment, the feeling that time is moving slowly or rapidly, extreme emotions, a sense of unreality, and perceptual distortions. This altered experiential state may even be intensely pleasant. As Zimbardo notes, members of mobs, even when engaged in intensely violent and aggressive actions such as lynchings and rioting, often appear joyous, boisterous, and happy (Diener, 1979; Mann, Newton, & Innes, 1982).

Do people who are immersed in a crowd experience reduced self-awareness and altered experiential states? Diener (1979) examined this question by creating eight-person groups. Six of the group members were Diener's accomplices, trained to facilitate or inhibit the development of deindividuation. In the *self-aware condition*, the confederates seemed restless and fidgety. Everyone wore name tags as they worked on tasks designed to heighten self-awareness, such as providing personal responses to questions, sharing their opinions on topics, and disclosing personal information about themselves. In the *non-self-aware condition*, Diener shifted the subjects' focus of attention outward by having them perform a series of mildly distracting tasks. The problems were not difficult, but they required a good deal of concentration and creativity. In the *deindividuation condition*, Diener tried to foster feelings of group cohesiveness, unanimity, and anonymity by treating the members as interchangeable and by putting the groups through a variety of arousing activities.

When Diener asked the subjects to describe how they felt during the study, he identified the two clusters, or factors, shown in Table 15–3. The first factor, self-awareness, encompasses a lack of self-consciousness, little planning of action, high group unity, and uninhibited action. The second dimension, altered experiencing, is also consistent with the theory in that it ties together a number of related processes, such as "unusual" experiences, altered perceptions, and a loss of individual identity. When Diener compared the responses of subjects in the three conditions of his experiment, he discovered that (1) deindividuated subjects displayed a greater loss of self-awareness than both the non-self-aware and the self-aware subjects and (2) deindividuated subjects reported more extreme altered experiencing than the self-aware subjects.

TABLE 15–3   THE NATURE OF DEINDIVIDUATION

Factor	Typical Characteristics
Loss of self-awareness	• Minimal self-consciousness
	• Lack of conscious planning as behavior becomes spontaneous
	• Lack of concern for what others think of you
	• Subjective feeling that time is passing quickly
	• Liking for the group and feelings of group unity
	• Uninhibited speech
	• Performing uninhibited tasks
Altered experiencing	• Unusual experiences, such as hallucinations
	• Altered states of consciousness
	• Subjective loss of individual identity
	• Feelings of anonymity
	• Liking for the group and feelings of group unity

Source: Diener, 1979.

Steven Prentice-Dunn and Ronald W. Rogers (1982) extended these findings by manipulating both self-awareness and the group members' accountability for their actions. Half of the subjects were led through a series of experiences that focused their attention on the situation, whereas the others were frequently reminded to pay attention to their personal feelings. Also, to manipulate accountability, some subjects were told that their actions would be carefully monitored, whereas others were led to believe that their actions were not going to be linked to them personally. The subjects, who participated in four-man groups, were then given the opportunity to deliver ostensible electric shocks to a confederate.

The results of the study supported the two-factor model of deindividuation on three counts. First, the subjects who were prompted to focus on the situation were lower in private self-awareness, and they tended to behave more aggressively. Second, analysis of the subjects' questionnaire responses revealed the two components emphasized by Diener: low self-awareness and altered experiencing. Third, using a statistical procedure known as path analysis, Prentice-Dunn and Rogers found that both of these components mediated the relationship between the variables they manipulated and subjects' aggressive response (Prentice-Dunn & Rogers, 1980, 1982, 1983; Prentice-Dunn & Spivey, 1986; Rogers & Prentice-Dunn, 1981).

Collectives and Identity

Deindividuation theory assumes that when individuals in collectives lose their sense of identity, they are more likely to act in unusual ways. Yet, in many cases, collectives *sustain* rather than undermine individuals' identities. The act of joining a social movement, for example, can be one of self-definition: The alcoholic who joins Alcoholics Anonymous proclaims, "I am an alcoholic," just as the man who joins Promise Keepers lays public claim to his religiosity and masculinity (Melucci, 1989). Collectives are also intergroup settings, so when individuals join them, their personal and social identities change (Reicher & Levine, 1994; Reicher, Spears, & Postmes, 1995).

Social Identity and Intergroup Conflict. Mobs, riots, and gangs are often intergroup phenomena. Riots in inner cities, for example, usually occur when inner-city residents contend against another group: the police (Goldberg, 1968). Violence during athletic competitions often occurs when the fans on one team attack, en masse, the fans or players from another team (Leonard, 1980). Protests on college campuses pit students against the university administration (Lipset & Wolin, 1965). Inner-city gangs vie for turf against other gangs (Sanders, 1994). Militia groups rise up to confront civil and judicial authorities (Flynn & Gerhardt, 1989). A lone collective is a rarity, for in most cases, collectives emerge in opposition to other collectives.

Collectives, as intergroup phenomena, provide members with an enlarged view of the self, based not just on individual qualities but also on collectivistic qualities. Such collectives do not lead to deindividuation, but to a depersonalized sense of self that reflects group-level qualities rather than individual ones. The presence of an outgroup increases the salience of the collective identity, and members begin to perceive themselves and the situation in ways that reflect the *ingroup/outgroup bias:* Other members of the ingroup are viewed positively, as are their actions, whereas outgroup members and their actions are denigrated (see Chapter 13).

S. D. Reicher's (1984, 1987, 1996) analyses of rioters' social identities are consistent with social identity theory. One riot occurred when members of the National Union of Students organized a demonstration in London. The leaders of the group planned to march to the Houses of Parliament, but when the police blocked their path, conflict erupted. As the tension between the groups escalated, the students became more unified. When one member of the group was arrested by the police, students attacked the police unit as a group. They also felt that the police were behaving violently and that they themselves only responded in self-defense. As one student put it: "To some extent there was a feeling of there was the students and there was the police and you knew which side you were on so you had to be up in the front with students, you know. And there was a lot of crowd empathy" (quoted in Reicher, 1996, p. 126).

Individuation. A paradox permeates analyses of individuality and collectives. On the one hand, many theorists assume that submersion in a group results in the attainment of power and an escape from societal inhibitions; hence, group members seek and try to maintain the experience of deindividuation. In contrast, many psychologists believe that people can enjoy psychological well-being only when they are able to establish and maintain their own unique identities. In the words of R. D. Laing (1960, p. 44), "A firm sense of one's own autonomous identity is required in order that one may be related as one human being to another. Otherwise, any and every relationship threatens the individual with loss of identity" (Dipboye, 1977; Fromm, 1965; Laing, 1960; Maslow, 1968).

An identity affirmation approach to collective behavior suggests that group members who feel "lost" in a group will try to reestablish their individual identities. People in large crowds, for example, may act oddly to regain a sense of individuality, and not because they feel anonymous. Individuals who take part in riots may do so not to protest their group's unfair treatment, but to reaffirm their individual identities. As one resident of the riot-torn community of Watts (in Los Angeles) explained, "I don't believe in burning, stealing, or killing, but I can see why the boys did what they did. They just wanted to be noticed, to let the world know the seriousness of their state of life" (Milgram & Toch, 1969, p. 576). Similarly, members of large groups, such as industrial workers, students in large classrooms, people working in bureaucratic organizations, and employees in companies with high turnover rates, may perform atypical actions just to stand apart from the "crowd."

Christina Maslach (1972) examined this individuation process by making two people in a four-person group feel individuated; she referred to them by name, made more personal comments to them, and maintained a significant amount of eye contact. She made the other two feel deindividuated by avoiding close contact with them and addressing them impersonally. When these individuals were later given the opportunity to engage in a free-response group discussion and complete some questionnaires, the deindividuated subjects evidenced various identity-seeking reactions. Some attempted to make themselves seem as different as possible from the other group members by giving more unusual answers to the questions, making longer comments, joining in the discussion more frequently, and attempting to capture the attention of the experimenter. Other subjects seemed to redefine their identities by revealing more intimate details of their personalities and beliefs through longer and more unusual self-descriptions.

POSTSCRIPT: COLLECTIVES ARE GROUPS

For well over a century, most theorists and researchers have assumed that crowds are unique social aggregates, a "perversion of human potential," where impulse and chaos replace reason and order (Zimbardo, 1969). Le Bon argued that crowds develop a collective mind that leaves individual members unable to think for themselves. Convergence theories assume that atypical groups are staffed by atypical people. Groups often develop odd, unusual norms, and members may forget who they are when they sink too deeply into their groups. This belief in the "madness of crowds" is so deeply ingrained in our conception of collectives that some individuals who commit violent crimes in groups face reduced sentences. Deindividuated and driven to conform to their group's usual norms, they are not held personally responsible for their actions (Colman, 1991).

Yet, collectives are, at core, groups, and so the processes that shape group behavior are likely to also shape collective behaviors. Many contemporary theorists, rather than assuming that collectives are atypical groups that require special theories that include novel or even mysterious processes, argue that the "madding crowd" is more myth than reality. Collective behavior is not bizarre, but instead a rational attempt by a number of individuals to seek change through united action. These groups form, change, and disband following the same patterns that govern other groups, and the internal structures and processes of a collective and a group are more similar than different (Lofland, 1981; McPhail, 1991; Snow & Oliver, 1995).

Clark McPhail (1991) elaborates this viewpoint in his book *The Myth of the Madding Crowd*. McPhail maintains that early theorists were too biased by their preconceived belief that crowds are crazed. He himself carried out extensive field studies of actual collective movements over a ten-year period so that he could determine, firsthand, what such groups do. His conclusions are threefold:

> First, individuals are not driven mad by crowds; they do not lose cognitive control! Second, individuals are not compelled to participate by some madness-in-common, or any other sovereign psychological attribute, cognitive style, or predisposition that distinguishes them from nonparticipants. Third, the majority of behaviors in which members of these crowds engaged are neither mutually inclusive nor extraordinary, let alone mad. (McPhail, 1991, p. xxii)

One hundred years of theory and research is a stalwart legacy that cannot be easily dismissed. Yet, the available evidence favors the crowd-is-a-group view. Le Bon's (1895/1960) crowd psychology and Zimbardo's (1969) theory of deindividuation make dire predictions about crowds and mobs, but when researchers combined the results of 60 independent experimental studies they found that dramatic changes in self-control and inappropriate behavior are rare. They concluded that the conditions that exist in mobs, such as membership in a large crowd, anonymity, and a decline in self-awareness, prompt group members to conform to situation-specific group norms, but that these norms are rarely inconsistent with general social norms (Postmes & Spears, 1998).

Field observations of crowds and collectives also attest to these groups' rationality and normality rather than their irrationality and impulsivity. McPhail (1991), for example, concludes that violence is very rare in crowds. In most cases, individuals in the groups are committed to particular goals, and like any performing group, they do their share of the work to increase the group's chances for success. Moreover, when violence does occur, it takes the form of intergroup conflict rather than mindless savagery. Even the group at the Who concert did not behave badly. Many experts condemned the crowd, calling it a stampede, but when Cincinnati sociologist Norris R. Johnson looked more closely at the evidence, he concluded that the crowd did not "stampede" or engage in selfish, destructive behavior. Indeed, the amount of helping shown by the people in the crowd exceeded what we would normally expect to find among a group of bystanders.

The crowd-as-mad and the crowd-as-group views must be reconciled in a more complete understanding of collective behavior. Crowds do, on occasion, perpetrate great wrongs—wrongs that seem more malevolent than any one individual's capacity for evil. Yet, people in crowds usually act in ways that are unremarkable. Indeed, crowds are groups, and collective dynamics are, for the most part, group dynamics. Hence, the next time you hear of a crowd behaving oddly, do not dismiss its actions as one more illustration of a group gone wrong.

SUMMARY

When does a group become a collective?
Collectives are relatively large, ephemeral, spontaneous collections of people who tend to display similar—and sometimes unusual—forms of behavior (see Table 15–2).

1. *Collective behavior* refers to the actions of both *crowds* and *collective movements.*
2. Crowds include gatherings (*casual crowds, audiences,* and *queues*) and *mobs* (aggressive mobs and *panics*). In general, members of gatherings conform to social norms, whereas members of mobs and crowds in panic display hostile and fearful actions, respectively.
3. Individuals need not be concentrated in a single location to display convergence in action, for such collective movements as *fads, crazes, fashions,* rumors, *mass hysteria,* and *social movements* can influence widely dispersed individuals.

What theories explain collective behavior?

1. Le Bon proposed that crowds seem to be governed by a collective mind and that *contagion* causes crowd members to experience similar thoughts and emotions.
2. *Convergence theories* propose that the individuals who join groups often possess similar needs and personal characteristics. Studies of *relative deprivation,* for example, suggest that people whose attainments fall below their expectations are more likely to join social movements.
3. Turner and Killian's *emergent norm theory* posits that crowds often develop unique standards for behavior and that

these atypical norms exert a powerful influence on behavior.

4. Zimbardo's deindividuation theory traces collective phenomena back to *deindividuation,* which can be broken down into three components: inputs, internal changes, and behavioral outcomes. Inputs, or causes of deindividuation, include feelings of anonymity, reduced responsibility (diffusion of responsibility), membership in large groups, and a heightened state of physiological arousal.
5. The deindividuated state itself appears to involve two basic components: reduced *self-awareness* (minimal self-consciousness, lack of conscious planning, uninhibited speech, and performance of uninhibited tasks) and altered experiencing (disturbances in concentration and judgment, the feeling that time is moving slowly or rapidly, extreme emotions, a sense of unreality, and perceptual distortions).
6. Social identity theory notes that collective behavior is often intergroup behavior, and so (a) collectives sustain rather than undermine individuals' identities and (b) collective behavior in some cases represents an attempt to reestablish a sense of individuality.

How different are collectives from other types of groups? Recent analyses of crowds and collectives have questioned the "crowd-as-mad" assumption. Collectives differ from more routine groups in degree rather than in kind.

FOR MORE INFORMATION

"Collective Behavior: Crowds and Social Movements," by Stanley Milgram and Hans Toch (1969), although written 30 years ago, offers fundamental insights into collective behavior.

The Crowd (translation of *Psychologie des foules*), by Gustave Le Bon (1895/1960), has been described as one of the most influential books dealing with social behavior ever written.

"The Human Choice: Individuation, Reason, and Order Versus Deindividuation, Impulse, and Chaos," by Phillip G. Zimbardo (1969), is a wide-ranging analysis of the causes and consequences of the loss of identity that sometimes occurs in groups.

The Myth of the Madding Crowd, by Clark McPhail (1991), expertly synthesizes prior theoretical work on crowds with McPhail's field studies of actual crowds to dispel many absurd myths about crowds and replace them with data-based propositions.

"Panic at 'The Who Concert Stampede': An Empirical Assessment," by Norris R. Johnson (1987), provides considerable background information and theoretical analysis of the crowd that pushed through the doors at Cincinnati's Riverfront Coliseum in 1979.

"Social Movements and Collective Behavior: Social Psychological Dimensions and Considerations," by David A. Snow and Pamela E. Oliver (1995), reviews recent theory and research dealing with the factors that prompt people to join social movements.

ACTIVITY 15–1 **OBSERVING CROWDS**

Locate and observe a crowd for at least 15 minutes. Do not watch an organized crowd, but instead find one that has formed spontaneously in a public place: people at a mall, people watching an unscheduled event (such as a street mime), and people loitering in a park are all possibilities. If you have no luck finding a crowd, then study an audience instead (so long as it is not a classroom audience).

1. Describe the general characteristics of the crowd. Give an estimate of its size, dimensions, movement, and life span, and indicate if subgroups exist within the overall crowd.
2. Search for evidence of a structure within the crowd. Try to identify individuals at the center of the crowd or the general focus of attention of the crowd as a unit.
3. What are the members of the crowd doing? (Are they walking, sitting, speaking, applauding, etc.?) Estimate the proportion of crowd members acting similarly.
4. Explain the dynamics of the crowd by considering these basic questions:
   a. Are the individuals in the crowd acting in unusual or unexpected ways?
   b. What is the emotional climate of the crowd?
   c. In what ways are the members of the crowd similar to each other?
   d. Are the members of the crowd conforming to norms that traditionally apply in this setting, or are they acting counternormatively?
   e. Does the crowd oppose some other group or organization?
5. Which theory of crowds offers the most insight into the crowd you observed? Why?

ACTIVITY 15–2 EXPERIENCING COLLECTIVE BEHAVIOR

Recall a time, within the last six months, when you were part of a large crowd or collective. Have you, for example, recently attended a sporting event, concert, or demonstration? A large gathering of a religious group or a street festival? Watched a parade or attended a political rally? (If you haven't been part of a large collective recently, then interview someone who has.)

1. How large was the crowd, and what were the circumstances that led you to join the group?
2. What kinds of actions did the group members perform? What did you do in the group?
3. How did you feel during the group experience: happy, sad, guilty, joyful, angry, upset, excited?
4. Did you feel self-conscious? Did you feel as though you were being singled out for observation, or did you feel as though you were relatively unidentifiable?
5. Are memories of the event clear? Are you unable to remember with certainty what happened at some points during the event?
6. Did you act in ways that are consistent or inconsistent with how you normally act?

Groups and Change

People often rely on groups to improve their psychological adjustment and social relations. Groups, by their very nature, provide members with information, support, and guidance, and so many personal and interpersonal problems can be resolved when confronted in a group rather than alone.

- What are some of the ways that groups are used to help members change?
- How do groups promote change?
- How effective are groups in bringing about change?

CONTENTS

The Therapy Group: Groups as Interpersonal Resources

GROUP APPROACHES TO CHANGE

Group Psychotherapy

Interpersonal Learning Groups

Self-Help Groups

SOURCES OF CHANGE IN GROUPS

Universality and Hope

Social Learning

Group Cohesion

Disclosure and Catharsis

Altruism

Insight

THE EFFECTIVENESS OF GROUPS

Perceptions Versus Behaviors

Evidence of Negative Effects

Types of Groups and Effectiveness

The Value of Groups

SUMMARY

FOR MORE INFORMATION

ACTIVITIES

The Therapy Group: Groups as Interpersonal Resources

Dr. R. and Dr. M., the group's leaders, began the session by introducing themselves and asking each member to do the same. The members, one at time, muttered something about themselves, but no one said much more than "I teach school for a living" or "I moved to Palo Alto when I was six." Several could barely bring themselves to speak to the group, and most stared at the floor rather than make eye contact with anyone. They did not even speak when the leaders asked them direct questions about their feelings or thoughts. The hour passed slowly.

The members of this group were very different from one another in many ways, but they did share one quality: In interviews with psychologists at the Stanford University clinic, each one complained of severe problems developing and sustaining relationships with other people. All had a history of loneliness and interpersonal isolation, and some were so withdrawn that they were diagnosed as schizoid personalities. They had been placed together in a therapeutic group to help them solve their problems in social adjustment. The group met each week for two years, in sessions designed to help the members change the way they related to other people.

The idea that a group can be used as a change-promoting agent is not a new one. Throughout history, personal change has often been achieved through social mechanisms rather than individualistic, asocial processes. As early as 1905, a Boston physician arranged for patients who were suffering from tuberculosis to meet in groups to ward off feelings of depression and to discuss ways to overcome their disease (Pratt, 1922). Jacob L. Moreno (1934), who developed sociometry, also advocated acting out troubling relationships and feelings in groups. Sigmund Freud (1922) presented a cogent analysis of group processes that provided the foundation for conducting psychoanalysis in groups, and Kurt Lewin (1936) was an outspoken champion of group approaches to achieving social and personal change. Indeed, it was Lewin who stated the basic "law" of change in groups: "It is easier to change individuals formed into a group than to change any of them separately" (1951, p. 228).

This chapter asks three basic questions about groups and change. First, what are some of the ways that groups are used to achieve change in individual members? Second, how do groups help members change? (What change-evoking and change-maintaining processes operate in most groups?) And third, are groups effective means of bringing about change? The group led by Dr. R. and Dr. M. benefited the members tremendously, but do groups sometimes do more harm than good?

GROUP APPROACHES TO CHANGE

People join groups to solve many different kinds of problems. Some want to get rid of something: weight, sadness, irrational thoughts, or overwhelming feelings of worthlessness and despair. Others are seeking new skills and outlooks: insight into their own characteristics, a better sense of how others see them, or a new repertoire of behaviors they can use to improve their relationships with others. And still others seek the strength they need to resist an addiction or obsession: the temptation to drink alcohol, use drugs, or batter their spouse.

The variety of change-promoting groups reflects the variety of individuals' goals. The early group formats devised by Moreno, Freud, and Lewin have evolved into today's jogging and fitness clubs; consciousness-raising groups; support groups for parents, children, grandparents, and ex-spouses; workshops and leadership seminars; marriage and family counseling groups; religious retreats; self-help groups; psychotherapy groups; and on and on. These groups, despite their many varieties, all help individuals achieve goals that they cannot reach on their own. Moreover, most fit one of the three basic categories shown in Table 16–1. **Group psychotherapy** helps people overcome troublesome psychological problems. **Interpersonal learning groups** help individuals gain self-understanding and improve their relationships with others. **Self-help groups,** or mutual-support groups, are voluntarily formed groups of people who help one another cope with or overcome a common problem.

Group Psychotherapy

Dr. R. and Dr. M. were both psychologists, trained to help people overcome troublesome psychological and personal problems. Both of them frequently worked with clients in one-on-one psychotherapy sessions, but they also treated some of their clients in group sessions. These psychotherapy sessions involved treating individuals

TABLE 16–1 SOME BASIC APPROACHES TO USING GROUPS AS AGENTS OF PERSONAL AND INTERPERSONAL CHANGE

Type	Basic Goal	Leader	Examples
Group psychotherapy	Improve psychological functioning and adjustment of individual members	Mental-health professional: psychologist, psychiatrist, clinical social worker	Psychoanalytic and Gestalt groups, psychodrama, interpersonal, cognitive-behavioral group therapy
Interpersonal learning group	Help members gain self-understanding and improve their interpersonal skills	Varies; trained and licensed professionals to untrained amateurs	T-groups, encounter groups, seminars and workshops
Self-help group	Help members cope with or overcome specific problems or life crises	Usually a volunteer layperson; many groups do not include a leadership position	Alcoholics Anonymous, Weight Watchers, support groups for care-givers

Group psychotherapy: The treatment of psychological problems in a group context.
Interpersonal learning groups: A group intervention designed to help relatively well adjusted individuals extend their self-understanding and improve their relationships with others.
Self-help groups: Groups of people who meet regularly to help one another cope with or overcome a problem they have in common; also called mutual-support groups.

"in groups, with the group itself constituting an important element in the therapeutic process" (Slavson, 1950, p. 42). When such groups were initially proposed, skeptics questioned the wisdom of putting people who are suffering from psychological problems together in one group. How, they asked, could troubled individuals be expected to cope in a group when they had failed individually? And how could the therapist guide the therapeutic process in a group, given the subtle nuances that pervade one-to-one therapies? History, however, has proved the skeptics wrong. Groups are currently used to treat all types of psychiatric problems, including addictions, thought disorders, depression, eating disorders, and personality disorders (Kaplan & Sadock, 1993; Long, 1998; Spira, 1997). The sample we consider here includes psychoanalytic groups, Gestalt groups, interpersonal therapy groups, and behavior therapy groups.

Psychoanalytic Groups.   Freud's approach to therapy, *psychoanalysis,* assumes that most psychological problems are caused by inner conflicts. Freud was convinced that most people avoid confronting these conflicts by repressing them, so during therapy he asked his patients to talk about their memories, fantasies, dreams, and fears in the hope that they would gain insight into their unconscious mind. As necessary, Freud also offered *interpretations* of his patients' free associations to help them identify the sources of their motivations and emotions, and he took advantage of *transference,* the tendency for patients to transfer the emotions they feel for their parents or siblings to the therapist. By capitalizing on transference, Freud succeeded in helping his patients work through unresolved conflicts.

These methods, although used primarily with individual patients, form the basis of **psychoanalytic group therapy.** Freud himself, some suggest, practiced group psychoanalysis when he and his students met to discuss his theories and cases (Kanzer, 1983; Roth, 1993). In such groups, the therapist is very much the leader, for he or she directs the group's discussion during the session, offers interpretations, and summarizes the group's efforts. Most psychoanalytic groups adhere to the *principle of shifting attention,* whereby therapists shift their focus from one patient to the next during the course of a single group session. This shifting of attention means that group members change roles during the session, sometimes acting as the patient seeking help, sometimes the observer of others' problems, and on occasion the helper who gives counsel to a fellow group member. This rotation gives patients an opportunity to develop empathic listening skills, and it also gives them time to reflect on the information uncovered during the session. The group setting also offers more opportunities to work through problems that result from early family conflicts. Individual therapy usually stimulates parental transference, but during group psychoanalysis, sibling transference also occurs. Members may find themselves reacting to one another inappropriately, but their actions, when examined more closely, may parallel the way they treated a brother or sister when they were young (Day, 1981; Kutash & Wolf, 1993; Rutan & Stone, 1993).

Psychoanalytic group therapy: An approach to group therapy that uses Freud's methods of interpretation and transference to help members gain insight into their unconscious conflicts, motives, and defenses.

Gestalt Groups.   Frederick ("Fritz") S. Perls is generally recognized as the founder of Gestalt therapy. Perls drew his theoretical principles from Gestalt psychologists, who argue that perception requires the active integration of perceptual information. The word *Gestalt,* which means "whole" or "form," suggests that we perceive the world as unified, continuous, and organized. Like Freud, Perls assumed that people often repress their emotions to the point that unresolved interpersonal conflicts turn into "unfinished business." Perls, however, believed that people are capable of self-regulation and great emotional awareness, and he used therapy to help patients reach their potential (Perls, 1969; Perls, Hefferline, & Goodman, 1951).

In some cases, **Gestalt group therapy** is one-to-one Gestalt therapy conducted in a group setting. Group members observe one another's "work," but they do not interact. More frequently, however, interaction takes place among group members, with the therapist actively orchestrating the events. Therapists often rely on *experiments,* which are experiential exercises designed to stimulate emotional understanding. When using the *hot seat,* one person in the group sits in the center of the room and publicly works through his or her emotional experiences. The *empty-chair* method involves imagining that another person or a part of oneself is sitting in an empty chair and then carrying on a dialogue with the person. These techniques are quite powerful, and individuals often become very emotional during the session. Also, because of the difficulties inherent in trying to understand the emotional experiences of another person, Gestalt therapists resist offering interpretations to their patients (Goulding & Goulding, 1979; Greve, 1993).

Psychodrama, developed by Jacob Moreno (1953), also makes use of exercises to stimulate emotional experiences in group members. During psychodrama sessions, the group members reenact specific turbulent episodes from group members' lives or events that happened within the group. Moreno believed that psychodrama's emphasis on physical action is more involving than passive discussion and that the drama itself helps members overcome their reluctance to discuss critical issues (Kipper, 1978; Sacks, 1993).

Interpersonal Group Psychotherapy.   An interpersonal approach to psychological disturbances assumes that many psychological problems, such as depression, anxiety, and personality disorders, can be traced back to social sources—particularly, interactions with friends, relatives, and acquaintances. Rather than searching for psychodynamic causes, interpersonal theorists assume that maladaptive behavior results from "an individual's failure to attend to and correct the self-defeating, interpersonally unsuccessful aspects of his or her interpersonal acts" (Kiesler, 1991, pp. 442–443).

Many group therapists, recognizing the interpersonal bases of psychological problems, use the group setting to help members examine their interpersonal behavior. Irvin

---

Gestalt group therapy: An approach to group therapy in which clients are taught to understand the unity of their emotions and cognitions through a leader-guided analysis of their behavior in the group situation.
Psychodrama: A therapeutic tool developed by Moreno that stimulates active involvement in the group session through role playing.

Yalom's (1995) **interpersonal group psychotherapy** (also called interactive group psychotherapy), for example, uses the group as a "social microcosm" where members respond to one another in ways that are characteristic of their interpersonal tendencies outside of the group. Therapy groups, as groups, display a full array of group dynamics, including social influence, structure, conflict, and development. The therapist takes advantage of the group's dynamics to help members learn about how they influence others and how others influence them. Members do not discuss problems they are facing at home or at work, but instead focus on interpersonal experiences within the group: the *here and now* rather than the *then and there*. When, for example, two members begin criticizing each other, a client uses powerful influence tactics, or another refuses to get involved in the group's meetings, therapists prompt group members to examine and explain the members' interaction (Yalom, 1995).

Cognitive-Behavioral Therapy Groups.   Some therapists, rather than searching for the cause of the problematic behavior in unseen unconscious conflicts or interpersonal transactions, take a behavioral approach to mental health. This approach assumes that problematic thoughts and behaviors are acquired through experience. Thus, interventions are based on principles derived from learning theories (Skinner, 1953, 1971). The goals of behavior therapy are defined in terms of desirable cognitions and behaviors that will be encouraged (e.g., expressing positive emotions with one's spouse) and undesirable cognitions and behaviors that will be extinguished (e.g., drinking alcohol).

   Cognitive-behavioral therapy groups use these principles with two or more individuals (Flowers, 1979; Hollander & Kazaoka, 1988; Rose, 1993). If Drs. M. and R. were cognitive-behavioral therapists, they would follow a series of standard procedures before, during, and after the group intervention. Prior to treatment, they would measure their patients' social skills using behavioral rating methods. They would also review with each patient the purpose of the therapy and, in some cases, ask the patient to watch videotaped examples of group therapy sessions. Such pretherapy reviews not only create change-enhancing expectancies, but also help members identify the specific goals of the therapeutic intervention (Higginbotham, West, & Forsyth, 1988). At this point, the therapists might also ask the patients to sign a *behavioral contract* that describes in objective terms the goals the group members are trying to achieve.

   During the therapy itself, Drs. M. and R. would rely on a number of behavioral methods, including modeling, rehearsal, and feedback. *Modeling* involves demonstrating particular behaviors while the group members observe (Bandura, 1977). The group leaders may engage in 1-minute conversation with each other, videotape the interaction, and then play it back to the group while identifying the nonverbal and verbal behaviors that made the conversation flow smoothly. During *rehearsal,* group

---

Interpersonal group psychotherapy: An approach to group therapy that uses the group situation to help members learn about themselves and their interpersonal tendencies.
Cognitive-behavioral therapy groups: The treatment of interpersonal and psychological problems through the application of behavioral principles in a group setting.

members practice particular skills themselves, either with one another or through role-playing exercises. These practice sessions can be videotaped and played back to the group so that the participants can see precisely what they are doing correctly and what aspects of their behavior need improvement. This feedback phase involves not only reassurance and praise from the leaders but also support from the other group members (Bellack & Hersen, 1979; Curran, 1977; Galassi & Galassi, 1979).

Interpersonal Learning Groups

Humanistic psychologists are united in their belief that the human race too frequently fails to reach its full potential. Although our relationships with others should be rich and satisfying, they are more often than not superficial and limiting. Also, although we are capable of profound self-understanding and acceptance, most of us do not understand ourselves very well. These limitations are not so severe that we seek treatment from a psychotherapist, but our lives would be richer if we could overcome them.

Lewin was one of the first to suggest using small groups for teaching people interpersonal skills. Lewin believed that groups and organizations often fail because their members aren't trained in human relations. He therefore recommended close examination of group experiences to give people a deeper understanding of themselves and their groups' dynamics. Other theorists expanded on this basic idea, and by 1965, the *human potential movement* was in high gear (Back, 1973; Gazda & Brooks, 1985; Lakin, 1972).

Training Groups (T-Groups).

How can people learn about group dynamics? Members could learn the facts about effective interpersonal relations by attending lectures or by reading books about group dynamics, but Lewin argued that good group skills are most easily acquired by actually experiencing human relations. Hence, he developed specialized **training groups,** or **T-groups.** As one advocate of group training explained, "The training laboratory is a special environment in which [group members] learn new things about themselves. . . . It is a kind of emotional re-education" (Marrow, 1964, p. 25).

Lewin discovered the utility of such groups when he arranged for his students to observe and later discuss the dynamics of work groups. These discussions were usually held in private. One evening a few of the work-group members asked if they could listen to the students' interpretations. Lewin agreed to their request, and sure enough, the participants confirmed Lewin's expectations by sometimes vehemently disagreeing with the observations and interpretations offered by Lewin's students. However, the animated discussion that followed proved to be highly educational, and Lewin realized that everyone in the group was benefiting enormously from the analysis of the group's processes and dynamics (Benne, 1964).

Training groups (T-groups): Skill-development groups in which individuals interact in unstructured group settings and then analyze the dynamics of that interaction.

One of the most noteworthy aspects of T-groups is their lack of structure. Although from time to time the conferees might meet in large groups to hear lectures or presentations, most learning takes place in small groups. Even though the group includes a designated leader, often called a *facilitator* or trainer, this individual acts primarily as a catalyst for discussion rather than as director of the group. Indeed, during the first few days of a T-group's existence, group members usually complain about the lack of structure and the situational ambiguity, blaming the trainer for their discomfort. This ambiguity is intentional, however, for it shifts responsibility for structuring, understanding, and controlling the group's activities to the participants themselves. As the group grapples with problems of organization, agenda, goals, and structure, the members reveal their preferred interaction styles to others. They also learn to disclose their feelings honestly, gain conflict reduction skills, and find enjoyment from working in collaborative relationships.

After Lewin's death in 1947, his colleagues organized the National Training Laboratory (NTL). The laboratory was jointly sponsored by the National Education Association, the Research Center for Group Dynamics, and the Office of Naval Research (ONR). Researchers and teachers at the center further developed the concept of training groups in special workshops, or "laboratories," and during the last 50 years, thousands of educators, executives, and leaders have participated in programs offered by NTL and other training centers. Although the long-term effectiveness of T-groups is still being debated, training groups continue to play a key role in many organization development interventions (Bednar & Kaul, 1979; Burke & Day, 1986; Kaplan, 1979).

Growth Groups.   The T-group was a precursor of group techniques designed to enhance spontaneity, increase personal growth, and maximize members' sensitivity to others. As the purpose of the group experience shifted from training in group dynamics to increasing sensitivity, the name changed from T-group to **sensitivity-training group,** or **encounter group** (Johnson, 1988; Lieberman, 1994).

The humanistic therapist Carl Rogers (1970) was a leader in the development of encounter groups. Rogers believed that most of us lose sight of our basic goodness because our needs for approval and love are rarely satisfied. We reject many aspects of ourselves, deny our failings, and hold our feelings in when interacting with other people. Rogers felt that the encounter group helps us restore our trust in our own feelings, our acceptance of our most personal qualities, and our openness when interacting with others. If Rogers had been leading the Stanford University group of socially isolated individuals, he would have encouraged the members to "open up" to one another by displaying their inner emotions, thoughts, and worries. Recognizing that the group members probably felt insecure about their social competencies, Rogers would have given each one unconditional positive regard and helped

---

Sensitivity-training group: An unstructured group experience designed to enhance spontaneity, increase personal awareness, and maximize members' sensitivity to others.
Encounter group: A form of sensitivity training that provides individuals with the opportunity to gain deep interpersonal intimacy with other group members.

them express their feelings by repeating any statements they made. Rogers would also have used role playing and other exercises to encourage them to experience and express intense feelings of anger, caring, loneliness, and helplessness. Stripped of defensiveness and facades, Rogers believed, group members would encounter each other "authentically."

Structured Learning Groups.   Both T-groups and encounter groups are open-ended, *unstructured* approaches to interpersonal learning. Members of such groups follow no agenda, examine events that unfold spontaneously within the confines of the group itself, and give one another feedback about their interpersonal effectiveness when appropriate. **Structured learning groups,** in contrast, are planned interventions that focus on a specific interpersonal problem or skill. Integrating behavioral therapies with experiential learning, the group leaders identify specific learning outcomes before the sessions. They then develop behaviorally focused exercises that will help members practice these targeted skills. In a session on nonverbal communication, group members may be assigned a partner and then be asked to communicate a series of feelings without using spoken language. During assertiveness training, group members might practice saying no to one another's requests. In a leadership training seminar, group members may be asked to role-play various leadership styles in a small group. These exercises are similar in that they actively involve the group members in the learning process.

Thousands of local and national institutes use structured learning groups in their seminars and workshops. Although the formats for these structured experiences differ substantially, most include the components summarized in Table 16–2. The leader begins with a brief *orientation* session, in which he or she reviews the critical issues and focuses members on the exercise's goals. Next the group members *experience* the event or situation by carrying out a structured group exercise. When they have completed the exercise, the members engage in a general *discussion* of their experiences within the group. This phase can be open-ended, focusing on feelings and subjective

---

TABLE 16–2   BASIC STEPS IN MANY EXPERIENTIAL INTERPERSONAL LEARNING GROUPS

Component	Typical Characteristics
Orientation	Didactic overview of the goals of the exercise
Experience	Interaction within the group, including role-playing, simulations, discussion tasks
Discussion	Summarizing the experience, sharing personal reactions and interpretations
Analysis	Making sense of the experience, formulating meaning, drawing conclusions
Application	Identifying implications, proposing changes to make outside of the group setting

---

Structured learning groups: Planned interventions, such as workshops, seminars, or retreats, that focus on a specific interpersonal problem or skill.

interpretations, or it, too, can be structured through the use of questioning, information exchange procedures, or videotape recording. This discussion phase should blend into a period of *analysis*, during which the consultant helps group members identify consistencies in their behavior and the behaviors of others. In many cases, the consultant guides the group's analysis of underlying group dynamics and offers a conceptual analysis that gives meaning to the event. The interpersonal learning cycle ends with *application* as the group members use their new-found knowledge to enhance their relationships at work and at home.

Self-Help Groups

Instead of seeking help from a mental-health professional, the men and women in the Stanford University therapy group could have joined a self-help group, a voluntary group whose members share a common problem and meet for the purpose of exchanging social support. Self-help groups, also known as mutual-support groups, exist for nearly every major medical, psychological, or stress-related problem. There are groups for sufferers of heart disease, cancer, liver disease, and AIDs; groups for people who provide care for those suffering from chronic disease, illness, and disability; groups to help people overcome addictions to alcohol and other substances; groups for children of parents overcome by addictions to alcohol and other substances; and groups for a wide variety of life problems, including groups to help people manage money or time (see Table 16–3).

These groups differ from each other in many ways, but most are self-governing, with members rather than experts or mental-health professionals determining activities. They also tend to stress the importance of treating all members fairly and giving everyone an opportunity to express their viewpoints. The members face a common predicament, problem, or concern, so they are "psychologically bonded by the compelling similarity of member concerns" (Jacobs & Goodman, 1989, p. 537). These

TABLE 16–3   VARIETIES OF SELF-HELP GROUPS

Type of Group	Examples
Anti-addiction	Alcoholics Anonymous, Gamblers Anonymous, Take Off Pounds Sensibly (TOPS), Weight Watchers
Family support	In Touch (for parents of children with mental handicaps), Adult Children of Alcoholics, Al-Anon
Medical and rehabilitation	National Bell's Palsy Online Support Group, CARE (Cancer Aftercare and Rehabilitation Society), Recovery, Inc. (for recovering psychotherapy patients), Reach to Recovery (for breast cancer patients)
Social rights	Campaign for Homosexual Equality, local chapters of the National Organization for Women, the Gay Activists' Alliance
General social support	Association of the Childless and Childfree, Parents Without Partners, Singles Anonymous

groups all stress the importance of reciprocal helping, for members are supposed to both give help to others as well as receive it from others. Self-help groups usually charge little in the way of fees.

Alcoholics Anonymous (AA) is an example of a mutual-support group. AA was founded by Bill Wilson in 1935. Wilson had tried to quit drinking for years, but no matter what he tried, he always returned to his addiction. After a fourth hospital stay for acute alcoholism, Wilson experienced a profound, almost mystical experience that convinced him that he could overcome his drinking problem. Together with his friend, physician, and fellow alcoholic William D. Silkworth, Wilson developed a series of guidelines for maintaining abstinence. Wilson's program formed the basis of Alcoholics Anonymous, which grew to be an international organization with millions of members. Despite AA's size, change is still achieved through local chapters of alcoholics who meet regularly to review their success in maintaining their sobriety. AA meetings emphasize testimonials, mutual self-help, and adherence to the 12-stage program (the "12 steps") described by the AA doctrine. These steps include admitting one's powerlessness over alcohol; surrendering one's fate to a greater power; taking an inventory of personal strengths, weaknesses, and moral failings; and helping others fight their addiction (Flores, 1997).

The variety of self-help groups is enormous. Like AA, many such groups form because the members' needs are not being met by existing educational, social, or health agencies. Self-help groups are growing in terms of numbers and members, with perhaps as many as 8 million people in the United States alone belonging to such groups (Goodman & Jacobs, 1994; Jacobs & Goodman, 1989).

SOURCES OF CHANGE IN GROUPS

The members of the group conducted by Dr. R. and Dr. M. changed slowly over the course of their treatment. Members who had been so socially anxious that they became tongue-tied whenever they tried to carry on a conversation identified the causes of this anxiety and overcame it. People who had never been able to converse openly about their feelings practiced disclosing this kind of personal information. Group members learned how to understand and interpret other people's feelings and to respond to those feelings appropriately. Despite their many previous failures at maintaining any type of relationship, the members' bonds with one another became very strong. The therapists felt that the group seemed dull at times, but the clients themselves were very satisfied with their group, and they rarely missed a session.

Drs. R. and M.'s group was a successful one, for the members changed in ways they desired. After two years of weekly sessions, the group members felt that their problems relating to other people had been corrected. But what was the source of the group's therapeutic power? What **curative factors** (or therapeutic factors) operate in groups?

Curative factors: Elements present in group settings that aid and promote personal growth and adjustment; includes such factors as the installation of hope, universality, imparting of information, altruism, and interpersonal learning.

e 16–4 and Butler & Fuhriman, 1983a; Crouch, Bloch, & Wanlass, 1994; ٬n, 1978; Sherry & Hurley, 1976; Yalom, 1995; Yalom & Vinogradov, 1993.)

ality and Hope

Some individuals have problems coping with the negative events that overtake them. Some blame themselves for accidents and misfortunes that no one could have foreseen. Others spend so much time wondering "Why me?" that they fail to identify ways to overcome their problems. Some sink into a depression that saps their motivation, and they end up convinced that their situation is hopeless (Bulman & Wortman, 1977; Burns & Seligman, 1991; Lowery, Jacobsen, & DuCette, 1993).

Groups help members deal with feelings of failure, uniqueness, and hopelessness. When group members first join their groups, they often feel that their problems are unique ones, but by comparing themselves with others in the group, they come to recognize the *universality* of the problems they face. Self-help groups, in particular, create a sense of shared suffering among members (Lieberman, 1993). Everyone at an AA

TABLE 16–4 FACTORS THAT PROMOTE CHANGE IN GROUPS

Factor	Definition	Meaning to Member
Universality	Recognition of shared problems, reduced sense of uniqueness	We all have problems.
Hope	Increased sense of optimism from seeing others improve	If other members can change, so can I.
Vicarious learning	Developing social skills by watching others	Seeing others talk about their problems inspired me to talk, too.
Interpersonal learning	Developing social skills by interacting with others	I'm learning to get along better with other people.
Guidance	Accepting advice and suggestions from the group members	People in the group give me good suggestions.
Cohesion	Feeling accepted by others	The group accepts me and understands me.
Self-disclosure	Revealing personal information to others	I feel better for sharing things I've kept secret for too long.
Catharsis	Releasing pent-up emotions	It feels good to get things off my chest.
Altruism	Increased sense of efficacy from helping others	Helping other people has given me more self-respect.
Insight	Gaining a deeper understanding of oneself	I've learned a lot about myself.

Sources: Bloch, Reibstein, Crouch, Holroyd, & Themen, 1979; Mahrer & Nadler, 1986; Shaughnessy & Kivlighan, 1995; Yalom, 1975, 1985).

meeting, for example, publicly states, "I am an alcoholic," and this ri.
the other participants that their problem is shared by others.

Social Comparison and Adjustment.   Groups set the stage for heath-pron.
comparison processes. When individuals feel threatened or confused, they ,
iate with others. Schachter's (1959) classic study of women waiting to receiv
shocks, for example, confirmed the tendency to seek out group membership ,
of stress (see Chapter 4). Through affiliation, people secure social support, bu
can also acquire information about their condition from other group memoers.
Indeed, when people are with others who face similar problems or troubling events,
they feel better, in terms of self-esteem and mood, than when they are with dissimilar
people (Frable, Platt, & Hoey, 1998).

But group members are not unbiased seekers of information. When given a choice,
they make comparisons that will provide them with reassuring information as well as
accurate information. As noted in Chapter 4, when selecting a target for social comparisons, people often prefer someone who is experiencing even more severe hardships or someone who is not coping with their problems effectively. This tendency to
engage in *downward social comparison* minimizes members' sense of victimization
and raises their overall sense of self-esteem (Gibbons & Gerrard, 1989; Wood, Taylor,
& Lichtman, 1985). But they also compare themselves with people who are coping
effectively with their problems. This *upward social comparison* helps members identify ways to improve their own situation (Buunk, 1995; Taylor & Lobel, 1989).
Although such "supercopers" may threaten members by drawing their attention to
their own limitations, they also reassure members that their problems can be overcome. In general, contact with such people is reassuring; direct *comparison* with them
is not (Taylor & Lobel, 1989).

Collective Hope.   C. R. Snyder and his colleagues (1997) believe that people's sense of
hope is one of the best predictors of their mental health and adjustment. Individuals
who are hopeful can identify many ways to reach their goals, and they are also relatively confident that they can carry out the actions that are necessary to reach their
goals (Snyder, Cheavens, & Sympson, 1997). Everett Worthington and his colleagues
(1997) verified the value of raising group members' sense of hope in a study of marital
enrichment programs. These researchers, to offset the pessimism felt by many married
people about their chances of avoiding divorce, developed a hope-enrichment therapy
that stressed the components of Snyder's hope model. Clients were encouraged to take
the initiative in improving their relationship, and they were taught specific behaviors
they could use to accomplish this goal. Trained couples had higher relationship satisfaction and better interaction skills than couples in a control condition.

Social Learning

Many theorists have underscored the value of groups as arenas for interpersonal
learning (Lieberman, 1980; Yalom, 1975). By participating in a group, individuals
gain information about themselves, their problems, and their social relationships with

others. Within the social microcosm of the small group, individuals "become aware of the significant aspects of their interpersonal behavior: their strengths, their limitations, their parataxic distortions, and their maladaptive behavior that elicits unwanted responses from others" (Yalom, 1975, p. 40). Of the 10 curative factors in Table 16–4, vicarious learning, interpersonal learning, and guidance (direct instruction) are most closely related to social learning processes.

Vicarious Learning.   Social learning theory maintains that people can acquire new attitudes and behaviors by observing others' actions (Bandura, 1977). When two members who were once enemies reach an accord by discussing their differences, observing group members learn how they can resolve interpersonal conflicts. Group leaders can also model desirable behaviors by treating the group members in positive ways and avoiding behaviors that are undesirable (Dies, 1994). In one study, the coleaders of therapy groups modeled social interactions that the group members considered difficult or anxiety provoking. The leaders then helped the group members perform these same behaviors through role playing. Groups that used explicit modeling methods showed greater improvement than groups that only discussed the problematic behaviors (Falloon, Lindley, McDonald, & Marks, 1977).

Interpersonal Learning.   What would Drs. R. and M.'s clients have learned about themselves by interacting with others in a supportive group setting? First, they would have received direct feedback from the other group members about their qualities. The individual who is lonely because he alienates everyone by acting rudely may be told, "You should try to be more sensitive" or "You are always so judgmental, it makes me sick." Some groups exchange so much evaluative information that members withdraw from the group rather than face the barrage of negative feedback (Scheuble, Dixon, Levy, & Kagan-Moore, 1987). Most group leaders, however, are careful to monitor the exchange of information between members so that individuals receive the information they need in positive ways.

Interpersonal learning also occurs indirectly as group members implicitly monitor their impact on the other people within their group and draw conclusions about their own qualities from others' reactions to them. The other group members become, metaphorically, a mirror that members use to understand themselves (Cooley, 1902). A group member may begin to think that she has good social skills if the group always responds positively each time she contributes to the group discussion. Another member may decide that he is irritating if his comments are always met with anger and hostility. This indirect feedback helps members perceive themselves more accurately. Individuals who are socially withdrawn, for example, tend to evaluate their social skills negatively even though the other group members view them positively (Christensen & Kashy, 1998). Individuals also tend to rate themselves as more anxious than others tend to perceive them as being (Marcus & Wilson, 1996). Extended contact with others in a group setting should repair these negative perceptions.

Interpersonal learning also occurs as members observe themselves in the group setting. As self-perception theory suggests, people often "come to 'know' their own attitudes, emotions, and other internal states partially by inferring them from observations of their own over behavior and/or the circumstances in which this behavior occurs" (Bem, 1972, p. 2). If individuals observe themselves acting in ways that suggest that they are socially skilled—for example, disclosing information about themselves appropriately and maintaining a conversation—then they may infer that they *are* socially skilled.

Guidance. When people join groups, they become recipients, willing or not, of the advice and guidance of the leader and the other group members. When researchers analyzed recordings of therapy sessions, they discovered that therapists respond to clients at several levels. They provide information and guidance, ask a variety of questions, repeat and paraphrase the client's statements, confront the client's interpretations of problems, offer their own interpretation of the causes of the client's problems, and express their approval of and support for the client (Hill et al., 1988).

Although most would agree that the therapist should guide the group, experts disagree when discussing *how much* guidance a leader should provide. Many clinicians advocate the leader-centered approaches typical of psychoanalytic, Gestalt, and behavioral groups. In such groups, the leader is the central figure. He or she guides the course of the interaction, assigns various tasks to the group members, and occupies the center of the centralized communication network. In some instances, the group members may not even communicate with one another but only with the group leader. Other therapists, however, advocate a nondirective style of leadership in which all group members communicate with one another. These group-oriented approaches, which are typified by encounters or T-groups, encourage the analysis of the group's processes, with the therapist/leader sometimes facilitating the process but at other times providing no direction whatsoever.

Studies of groups indicate that both directive and nondirective leaders are effective agents of change so long as they are caring, and they help members interpret the cause of their problems, keep the group on course, and meet the members' socioemotional needs (Lieberman, Yalom, & Miles, 1973). Moreover, just as effective leaders in organizational settings sometimes vary their interventions to fit the situation, so effective leaders in therapeutic settings shift their methods as the group matures. During the early stages of treatment, members may respond better to a task-oriented leader, whereas in the later stages, a socioemotional leader may be more helpful (Kivlighan, 1997).

Several studies suggest that groups with two leaders are more effective than groups with only one leader. **Coleadership** eases the burdens put on the group's leader. The two leaders can lend support to each other and can also offer the group members their combined knowledge, insight, and experience. Also, male/female teams may be particularly beneficial, since they offer a fuller perspective on gender issues and serve as models of positive but nonromantic heterosexual relationships. The advantages of coleadership, however, are lost if the leaders are unequal in status or engage in power struggles during group sessions (Thune, Manderscheid, & Silbergeld, 1981).

Coleadership: Installing two equal-status leaders within a single group, a practice often used in therapeutic groups.

Group Cohesion

Cohesion may not be a sufficient condition for effective groups, but it may be a necessary one (Yalom, 1985). Without cohesion, feedback would not be accepted, norms would never develop, and groups could not retain their members. In emphasizing the value of highly cohesive groups, Yalom and his colleagues join a long line of researchers who have reached similar conclusions. As early as 1951, Dorwin Cartwright suggested that if groups were to be used as change agents, the members should have a strong sense of group identity and belonging; otherwise, the group would not exert sufficient influence over its members. Others, too, have noted that the "cotherapeutic influence of peers" in the therapy group requires group cohesion (Bach, 1954, p. 348; Frank, 1957; Goldstein, Heller, & Sechrest, 1966).

A group's cohesiveness fluctuates over time, depending on its longevity and stage of development. Even when the group's task is a therapeutic one, time is needed to achieve cohesiveness. In one study, investigators observed and coded the behaviors displayed by adolescents in a program of behavioral change. These groups did not immediately start to work on self-development issues, nor did the group members try to help one another. Rather, the groups first moved through orientation, conflict, and cohesion-building stages before they began to make therapeutic progress (Hill & Gruner, 1973).

Other studies also suggest that the success of the group depends to a large extent on its movement through stages of development. Although the stages receive various labels from various theorists, many accept the five emphasized by Bruce Tuckman (1965): forming, storming, norming, performing, and adjourning. As noted in Chapter 6, during the forming stage, individual members are seeking to understand their relationship to the newly formed group and strive to establish clear intermember relations. During the storming stage, group members often find themselves in conflict over status and group goals; consequently, hostility, disruption, and uncertainty dominate group discussions. During the next phase, norming, the group strives to develop a group structure that increases cohesiveness and harmony. The performing stage is typified by a focus on group productivity and decision making. Lastly, when the group fulfills its goals, it reaches its final stage of development, adjourning. If a group does not move through these stages, its members will not be able to benefit from the experience (MacKenzie, 1994, 1997; Yalom, 1995).

Dennis Kivlighan and his colleagues illustrated the important impact of group development on therapeutic outcomes by matching interventions to the developmental "maturity" of the group. Group members were given structured help in expressing either anger or intimacy before either the fourth or ninth group session of their therapy. The information dealing with anger clarified the value of anger as a natural part of group participation and provided suggestions for communicating it. The information dealing with intimacy clarified the value of intimacy in groups and provided suggestions for its appropriate expression toward others. As anticipated, when the interventions were matched to the most appropriate developmental stage—for example, when group members received the information on anger during the storming phase (session 4) and the information on intimacy during the norming phase (session 9)—the subjects displayed more comfort in dealing with intimacy, more appropriate expressions of intimacy and anger, fewer inappropriate expressions of intimacy, and more congruence between self-ratings and other ratings of interpersonal style (Kivlighan, McGovern, & Corazzini, 1984).

Disclosure and Catharsis

Groups become more unified the more the members engage in **self-disclosure:** the sharing of personal, intimate information with others (Corey & Corey, 1992; Leichtentritt & Shechtman, 1998). When groups first convene, members usually focus on superficial topics and avoid saying anything too personal or provocative. In this *orientation stage,* members try to form a general impression of each other and possibly to make a good impression themselves. In the *exploratory affective stage,* members discuss their personal attitudes and opinions, but avoid intimate topics. This stage is often followed by the *affective stage,* when a few topics still remain taboo. When the group reaches the final stage, *stable exchange,* all personal feelings are shared (Altman & Taylor, 1973).

Self-disclosure can be something of a challenge for some individuals. Individuals experiencing personality and psychological disturbances, for example, often disclose the wrong sorts of information at the wrong time (McGuire & Leak, 1980). Men and boys, too, are generally more reserved in their rate of self-disclosure (Brooks, 1996; Kilmartin, 1994; Shechtman, 1994). Thus, therapists must sometimes take special steps to induce the male members of therapy groups to share personal information about themselves, including modeling disclosure and incorporating disclosure rituals in the group (Horne, Jolliff, & Roth, 1996).

Self-disclosure and cohesion are reciprocally related. Each new self-disclosure deepens the group's intimacy, and this increased closeness then makes further self-disclosures possible (Kaul & Bednar, 1986; Roark & Sharah, 1989; Tschuschke & Dies, 1994). By sharing information about themselves, members are expressing their trust in the group and signaling their commitment to the therapeutic process (Rempel, Holmes, & Zanna, 1985). Disclosing troubling, worrisome thoughts also reduces the discloser's level of tension and stress. Individuals who keep their problems secret but continually ruminate about them display signs of physiological and psychological distress, whereas individuals who have the opportunity to disclose these troubling thoughts are healthier and happier (Pennebaker, 1990).

Members can also vent strong emotions in groups, although the value of such emotional venting continues to be debated by researchers. Some side with Freud's initial analysis of emotions and tension. Freud believed that strong emotions can build up, like steam in a boiler. If this psychological steam isn't vented from time to time, the strain on the system can cause psychological disorders. Therefore, healthy people discharge these emotions in a process he called **catharsis.** Others, however, suggest that "blowing off steam" is rarely helpful, for in the extreme, venting heightens members' psychological distress and upset (Ormont, 1984).

Self-disclosure: The process of revealing personal, intimate information about oneself to others.
Catharsis: The release of emotional tensions.

Altruism

The group's leader is not the only source of help available to group members. Other group members can sometimes draw on their own experiences to offer insights and advice to one another. This mutual assistance provides benefits for both parties. Even though the group's leader is the official expert in the group, people are often more willing to accept help from people who are similar to themselves (Wills & DePaulo, 1991). The helper, too, "feels a sense of being needed and helpful; can forget self in favor of another group member; and recognizes the desire to do something for another group member" (Crouch et al., 1994, p. 285). Mutual assistance teaches group members the social skills that are essential to psychological well-being (Ferencik, 1992).

Mutual assistance is particularly important in self-help groups. Mended Hearts, a support group that deals with the psychological consequences of open-heart surgery, tells members that "you are not completely mended until you help mend others" (Lieberman, 1993, p. 297). AA groups formalize and structure helping in the 12-step procedures. Newcomers to the group are paired with sponsors, who meet regularly with the new member outside of the regular group meetings.

Insight

Individuals' perceptions of their personal qualities are generally accurate. Individuals who think of themselves as assertive tend to be viewed that way by others, just as warm, outgoing individuals are viewed as friendly and approachable (Kenny, Kieffer, Smith, Ceplenski, & Kulo, 1996; Levesque, 1997). In some cases, however, individuals' self-perceptions are inaccurate (Andersen, 1984). An individual may believe that he is attractive, socially skilled, and friendly, when in fact he is unattractive, interpersonally incompetent, and hostile.

Groups promote self-understanding by exposing us to the unknown areas of ourselves. Although we are not particularly open to feedback about our own attributes, when several individuals provide us with the same feedback, we are more likely to internalize this information (Jacobs, 1974; Kivlighan, 1985). Also, when the feedback is given in the context of a long-term, reciprocal relationship, it cannot be so easily dismissed as biased or subjective. Group leaders, too, often reward members for accepting rather than rejecting feedback, and the setting itself works to intensify self-awareness. In a supportive, accepting group, we can reveal hidden aspects of ourselves, and we therefore feel more open and honest in our relationships. Lastly, even qualities that are unknown to others and to ourselves can emerge and be recognized during group interactions (Luft, 1984).

Studies of group members' evaluations of the therapeutic experience also attest to the importance of insight. When participants in therapeutic groups were asked to identify events that took place in their groups that helped them the most, they stressed universality, interpersonal learning, cohesion (belonging), and insight (see Figure 16–1). During later sessions, they stressed interpersonal learning even more, but universality became less important (Kivlighan & Mullison, 1988; Kivlighan, Multon, & Brossart, 1996). In other studies that asked group members to rank or rate the importance of these curative factors, the group members emphasized self-understanding, interpersonal learning, and catharsis (Butler & Fuhriman, 1983a; Markovitz & Smith, 1983;

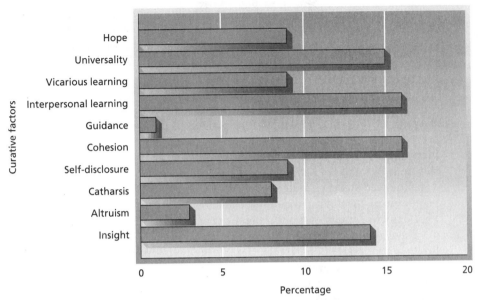

FIGURE 16–1 Which group experiences do members of therapeutic groups value the most? Participants in therapeutic groups stressed universality, interpersonal learning, cohesion (belonging), and insight when identifying events that were most important to them personally. During later sessions, they stressed interpersonal learning even more, but universality became less important.

(*Source:* Kivlighan & Mullison, 1988.)

Maxmen, 1973, 1978; Rohrbaugh & Bartels, 1975; Rugel & Meyer, 1984). In general, individuals who stress the value of self-understanding tend to benefit the most from participation in a therapeutic group (Butler & Fuhriman, 1983b).

THE EFFECTIVENESS OF GROUPS

What would you do if you were bothered by some personal problem? Perhaps, like the men and women in the therapy group led by Drs. R. and M., you have trouble making friends. Or maybe you are having problems adjusting to a new job or wish that you could be more productive when you are at work. Perhaps you have finally resolved to stop smoking or drinking or you just can't seem to get over the depression that has enveloped you since your mother passed away last year. Whatever the problem, you have not succeeded in changing on your own. So you decide to join a change-promoting group.

Would this group really help you achieve the changes you desire? Researchers and therapists have been debating this question for many years. Reviewers, after sifting through hundreds of studies evaluating the effectiveness of group interventions, rejected many as so methodologically flawed that they yielded no information whatsoever (Bednar & Kaul, 1978, 1979, 1994; Burlingame, Kircher, & Taylor, 1994; Fuhriman & Burlingame, 1994a; Kaul & Bednar, 1986). Those studies that did use valid methods, however, generally weighed in favor of group-level interventions. Addie Fuhriman and Gary M. Burlingame (1994a), after reviewing 700 group therapy studies and seven meta-analytic reviews of prior research, concluded that group methods are effective treatments for a wide variety of psychological problems. Burlingame and his colleagues, in a meta-analytic review of 23 studies that directly compared individual and group treatment methods, concluded that both approaches were effective, but that neither was superior to the other (McRoberts, Burlingame, & Hoag, 1998). A study of 7000 individuals who responded to a *Consumer Reports* questionnaire reached similar conclusions: All forms of psychological treatment, including group interventions, were effective. Indeed, AA received particularly positive evaluations in this study (Seligman, 1995, 1996; see, too, Christensen & Jacobson, 1994). In sum, the "accumulated evidence indicates that group treatments have been more effective than no treatment, than placebo or nonspecific treatments, or than other recognized psychological treatments, at least under some circumstances" (Bednar & Kaul, 1994, p. 632).

These positive conclusions, however, require some qualification. First, the changes brought about by group experiences are often more perceptual than behavioral. Second, in some cases, groups can do more harm than good for participants. Third, all groups are not created equal: Some may be more effective in promoting change than others. These issues are examined next.

Perceptions Versus Behaviors

Richard Bednar and Theodore J. Kaul (1979), after culling the studies of change that were methodologically flawed, concluded that most studies had reported changes only on self-report data, rather than on behavioral data. Reviews of experiential groups, for example, generally find stronger evidence of perceptual changes than of behavioral changes (Bates & Goodman, 1986; Berman & Zimpfer, 1980; Budman, Demby, Feldstein, & Gold, 1984; Ware, Barr, & Boone, 1982). One review, for example, identified 26 controlled studies of personal growth groups that (1) used both pretest and posttest measures, (2) met for at least 10 hours, and (3) had a long-term follow-up (at least one month after termination). Summarizing these methodologically superior studies, the reviewers concluded that group treatments did result in enduring positive changes, particularly at the self-report level (Berman & Zimpfer, 1980). These and other findings suggest that groups are most useful in promoting changes in the "ability to manage feelings, directionality of motivation, attitudes towards the self, attitudes towards others, and interdependence" but that behavior changes are slight (Gibb, 1970, p. 2114; Shaw, 1981).

Evidence of Negative Effects

Of the seven men and women who began their therapy with Drs. R. and M., only five completed the experience successfully. One dropped out of the group to join the armed forces. Another, however, quit the group after only a few months. She complained that the experience was too stressful and that it was causing her more harm than good.

Bednar and Kaul note that groups can fail in two distinct ways. First, a participant may decide to leave the group before he or she has benefited in any way; such an individual is usually labeled a **premature termination,** or dropout (Holmes, 1983). A **casualty,** in contrast, is significantly harmed by the group experience. A casualty might, for example, commit suicide as a result of the group experience, require individual therapy to correct harm caused by the group, or report continued deteriorations in adjustment over the course of the group experience. The number of casualties reported in studies has ranged from none among 94 participants in a human relations training lab followed up after five months (Smith, 1975, 1980) to a high of 8% of the participants in a study of 17 encounter groups (Lieberman et al., 1973). A relatively high casualty rate (18%) was obtained in one study of 50 married couples who participated in marathon encounter groups, but this rate was inflated by the problems the couples were experiencing before entering the group (Doherty, Lester, & Leigh, 1986). No evidence is available concerning the rate of casualties in self-help groups, but statistics maintained by the NTL indicate that 25 individuals who participated in the program prior to 1974 experienced a severe psychological reaction (Back, 1974). This number is less than 0.2% of the participants.

Bednar and Kaul (1978) note that most premature terminations result from failed expectations about the purposes of the group or an inadequate match between the group member's goals and the leader's methods. Casualties, in contrast, can most often be traced to a particularly negative event in the group. In one study, for example, an individual sought psychiatric treatment immediately after the group attacked her for being overweight:

> She stated that the group was an extremely destructive one for her. The group operated by everybody "ganging up on one another, thirteen to one, and bulldozing them until they were left on the ground panting." She was bitterly attacked by the group and finally dropped out after an attack on her in which she was labeled "a fat Italian mama with a big shiny nose." She was also told that she probably had "a hell of a time getting any man to look at her." (Lieberman et al., 1973, p. 189)

Given these potential problems, group therapists, trainers, facilitators, and members themselves are urged to use care when interacting in their groups. Casualties can be minimized by limiting conflict during sessions and making certain that the group atmosphere is supportive, nonevaluative, and nonthreatening (Mitchell & Mitchell, 1984; Scheuble et al., 1987).

Types of Groups and Effectiveness

Groups conform to no single set of procedures: Some groups are leader centered (psychoanalytic or Gestalt groups), whereas others are group focused (encounter groups

---

Premature termination: The withdrawal of a participant from a change-promoting group before the individual has benefited in any way.
Casualty: An individual who is significantly harmed by his or her experiences in a change-promoting group.

and T-groups), and the group's activities can range from the highly structured (inter-personal learning groups) to the unstructured (encounter groups). In some groups, the members themselves are responsible for running the meeting (self-help groups), whereas in other situations, the facilitator runs the session (structured groups). Group practitioners also vary greatly in their orientations and techniques: Some focus on emo-tions with Gestalt exercises, others concentrate on the here and now of the group's interpersonal processes, and still others train members to perform certain behaviors through videotaped feedback, behavioral rehearsal, and systematic reinforcement.

Given this diversity of purposes and procedures, one might expect some types of groups to emerge as more effective than others. Yet, differences in treatment effective-ness are relatively rare. Morton Lieberman, Irvin Yalom, and Matthew Miles (1973), for example, investigated the overall impact of a 12-week experiential group on mem-bers' adjustment. They began by assigning 206 Stanford University students to 1 of 18 therapy groups representing ten theoretical orientations: Gestalt, transactional analy-sis, NTL T-groups, Synanon, Esalen, psychoanalysis, marathon, psychodrama, en-counter, and encounter with tape-recorded instructions. Trained observers coded the groups' interactions, with particular attention to leadership style. Before, during, immediately after, and six months following the participation, they administered a battery of items assessing group members' self-esteem, attitudes, self-satisfaction, val-ues, satisfaction with friendships, and so on. Measures were also completed by the comembers, the leaders, and by group members' acquaintances.

Somewhat unexpectedly, the project discovered that no one theoretical approach had a monopoly on effectiveness. For example, two separate Gestalt groups with dif-ferent leaders were included in the design, but the members of these two groups evi-denced widely discrepant gains. One of the Gestalt groups ranked among the most successful in stimulating participant growth, but the other group yielded fewer bene-fits than all of the other groups.

A number of factors could account for this apparent equivalence of therapies (Stiles, Shapiro, & Elliott, 1986). First, the various group therapies may be differentially effec-tive, but researchers' measures may not be sensitive enough to detect these variations. Second, a group's effectiveness may depend as much on who is in the group and who leads the group as on the methods used. The question isn't "Is Therapy X more effective than Therapy Y?" but "What type of group run by which therapist is effective for this individual with this type of problem?" (Paul, 1967). Third, although group interven-tions are based on widely divergent theoretical assumptions, these assumptions may not lead to differences in practice. A leader of a Gestalt group and the leader of a psychody-namic group, for example, may explain their goals and methods in very different theo-retical terms, but they may nonetheless rely on identical methods when in their groups. Fourth, as the concept of curative factors suggests, despite their heterogeneity in pur-poses and procedures, therapeutic groups have certain characteristics in common, and these common aspects of groups and their dynamics account for their therapeutic effects.

The Value of Groups

Groups are not all benefit with no cost. Groups can demand great investment of time and energy from their members. While groups provide social support, they are also the source of considerable stress for their members. Groups, too, can socialize members in ways that are not healthy and set social identity processes in motion that increase conflict between groups (Forsyth & Elliott, in press).

Their checkered impact in no way, however, detracts from their significance in shaping mental health. Groups are essential to human life. Groups help their members define and confirm their values, beliefs, and identities. When individuals are beset by problems and uncertainties, groups offer reassurance, security, support, and assistance. Groups are places where people can learn new social skills and discover things about themselves and others. Groups, too, can produce changes in members when other approaches have failed. Both researchers and mental-health professionals who understand groups agree with Lewin's law: "It is easier to change individuals formed into a group than individuals who are alone" (1951, p. 228).

SUMMARY

What are some of the ways that groups are used to help members change? Most change-oriented groups focus either on therapeutic adjustment (*group psychotherapy*), interpersonal and emotional growth (*interpersonal learning groups*), or overcoming addictions or other life stresses (*self-help groups*).

1. Group psychotherapy sessions, conducted by a mental-health professional, focus on psychological problems.

   - In *psychoanalytic group therapy* the therapist helps members gain insight into their problems by offering interpretations and working through sibling and parental transference effects.
   - In *Gestalt group therapy,* the therapist promotes emotional growth by using experiments, avoiding interpretations, and, in some cases, extensive role-playing methods (*psychodrama*).
   - In *interpersonal group psychotherapy,* the leader takes advantage of the group's dynamics to help members learn about how they influence others and how others influence them.

   - In *cognitive-behavioral therapy groups,* the therapist uses principles derived from learning theory to encourage specific behaviors while extinguishing others. This approach makes use of a number of behavioral methods, including behavioral contracts, modeling, behavior rehearsal, and feedback.

2. Interpersonal learning groups involve attempts to help relatively well adjusted individuals improve their self-understanding and relationships with others.

   - In *training groups,* or *T-groups,* members are encouraged to actively confront and resolve interpersonal issues through unstructured discussions.
   - In *sensitivity-training groups* or *encounter groups,* individuals are urged to disclose personal aspects of themselves to others and to provide other members with positive feedback.
   - In *structured learning groups,* members take part in planned exercises that focus on a specific interpersonal problem or skill. Most of these interventions involve a learning cycle that begins with an orienting

overview and then moves from experience to discussion to analysis and to application.

3. Self-help groups often form spontaneously when people combine their energies and efforts in an attempt to cope with or overcome a common problem. These groups, such as Alcoholics Anonymous (AA), tend to use inspirational testimonials, mutual help, shared similarities, and collective encouragement.

How do groups promote change? A number of *curative factors* (therapeutic factors) operate in groups to promote change.

1. Groups, by providing opportunities to engage in social comparison and mutual support, convince members of the universality of their problems and give them hope.
2. Groups facilitate social learning, including vicarious learning (model of behaviors), interpersonal feedback, and guidance (direct instruction). Much of this social learning occurs at the member-to-member level, but leaders and *coleaders* are also significant sources of feedback and guidance.
3. Cohesive groups offer individuals the opportunity to help others and to be helped by them, and they serve as buffers against stress. Therapeutic groups, like all groups, generally become more cohesive over time.
4. Groups become more intimate as members reveal private information about themselves (*self-disclosure*). When group members vent strong emotions, the resulting *catharsis* may reduce their stress.
5. Group members also benefit from increased self-confidence produced by helping others and by gaining insight about their personal qualities from other group members.

How effective are groups in bringing about change? Most group approaches are effective methods for helping individuals change their thoughts, emotions, and actions.

1. Changes fostered by group experiences are often more perceptual than behavioral.
2. Participation in groups can also lead to a number of negative consequences, although every *premature termination* from a group is not necessarily a psychological *casualty.*
3. Group methods, despite their diversity, tend to be equally effective.

FOR MORE INFORMATION

Basics of Group Psychotherapy, edited by Harold S. Bernard and K. Roy MacKenzie (1994), includes chapters that are genuinely practical, for they focus on topics that clinicians must deal with as they study ways to use group psychotherapy in their practices.

Group Counseling: Strategies and Skills, by E. Jacobs, Robert L. Masson, and Riley L. Harvill (1998), is a straightforward analysis of the skills, tools, and ideas that novice leaders can use to facilitate change-promoting groups.

Group Psychotherapy with Addicted Populations: An Integration of Twelve Step and Psychodynamic Theory, by Philip J. Flores (1997), examines the interpersonal and intrapersonal processes that operate in both "12-step programs" (such as Alcoholics Anonymous) and therapeutic groups.

Handbook of Group Psychotherapy: An Empirical and Clinical Synthesis, edited by Addie Fuhriman and Gary M. Burlingame (1994b), is a comprehensive synthesis of research studies that have investigated the nature and efficacy of group psychotherapy.

"Psychology and Self-help Groups: Predictions on a Partnership," by Marion K.

Jacobs and Gerald Goodman (1989), provides an overview of self-help groups. *The Theory and Practice of Group Psychotherapy* (4th ed.), by Irvin D. Yalom (1995), sets forth Yalom's basic principles of interpersonal group therapy, which stresses the basic curative factors common to all group approaches to change.

ACTIVITY 16–1 SELF-DISCLOSURE IN GROUPS

Practice disclosing information about yourself with other members of the class or with friends or loved ones.

1. *Confidentiality.* Before the group disclosure session, group members should first agree that what is said should not be repeated outside the group.
2. *Orientation.* Begin self-disclosing information focusing on relatively factual information about yourself. Everyone in the group should mention something about themselves, answering such questions as:
   - Where is your birthplace?
   - How many brothers and sisters do you have?
   - What is your occupation or major in college?
3. *Attitudes and Interests.* Group members, once they have disclosed some basic information about themselves, should discuss more personal topics, including:
   - What are your views on such topics as politics, government, or religion?
   - What are your hobbies and preferred pastimes?
   - What are your favorite foods or preferences in music?
4. *Personal Strengths and Weaknesses.* If members become more comfortable disclosing personal information, the group can move beyond attitudes and interests to more confidential topics, including:
   - What do you most enjoy about school (or work)?
   - What are your shortcomings that prevent you from being as successful as you would like to be?
   - How much money do you make?
   - What aspects of your personality do you dislike?
   - Are you satisfied with your ability to make friends and maintain relationships?
5. *Intimate Disclosures.* If all the members of the group are comfortable discussing intimate personal information, members may want to turn to such questions as:
   - What things have you done in the past that you are ashamed of?
   - How satisfying is your sex life?
   - Has anyone hurt your feelings deeply?

After the exercise, spend time reviewing the self-disclosure process. Did the group move from less intimate to more intimate topics as it practiced self-disclosure? Did the group become more cohesive as more members self-disclosed? How did you feel during and after the exercise?

ACTIVITY 16–2 VISIT A CHANGE-PROMOTING GROUP

Visit a support group or an anti-addiction meeting and note its dynamics. A wide variety of such groups, including Alcoholics Anonymous, Narcotics Anonymous, and CoDependents Anonymous hold public meetings regularly. Most groups have no objection to people watching, so long as they do not violate the group's norms regarding anonymity and turn taking. You should take notes after the meeting, but not during the meeting.

1. Arrive a few minutes early and watch as people come to the meeting. What is the composition of the group, in terms of number of people, age, sex, ethnicity, and so on?
2. Describe the beginning of the group's meeting. For example, does the group recite a prayer or state its goals?
3. Does the group provide members with advice and information on how to deal with their problems?
4. Describe how the group provides motivational and emotional support to its members. Do group members encourage each other, and do some members provide positive examples?
5. From your observation, does the group take advantage of any of the curative factors identified in Table 16–4?
6. Give your overall analysis of the group's effectiveness.

References

Abrams, D. (1990). *Political identity: Relative deprivation, social identity, and the case of Scottish nationalism.* London: Economic and Social Research Council.

Abrams, D. (1992). Processes of social identification. In G. M. Breakwell (Ed.), *Social psychology of identity and self-concept* (pp. 57–99). New York: Surrey University Press.

Abrams, D. (1994). Social self-regulation. *Personality and Social Psychology Bulletin, 20,* 473–483.

Abrams, D., & Hogg, M. A. (Eds.). (1990). *Social identity theory, constructive and critical advances.* New York: Springer-Verlag, 1990.

Adams, J. S., & Rosenbaum, W. B. (1962). The relationship of worker productivity to cognitive dissonance about wage inequities. *Journal of Applied Psychology, 46,* 161–164.

Adler, P. A., & Adler, P. (1995). Dynamics of inclusion and exclusion in preadolescent cliques. *Social Psychology Quarterly, 58,* 145–162.

Adler, P. A., Kless, S. J., & Adler, P. (1992). Socialization to gender roles: Popularity among elementary school boys and girls. *Sociology of Education, 65,* 169–187.

Affleck, G., & Tennen, H. (1991). Social comparison and coping with major medical problems. In J. Suls & T. A. Wills (Eds.), *Social comparison: Contemporary theory and research* (pp. 369–394). Hillsdale, NJ: Erlbaum.

Aiello, J. R. (1987). Human spatial behavior. In D. Stokols & I. Altman (Eds.), *Handbook of environmental psychology* (Vol. 1, pp. 389–504). New York: Wiley.

Aiello, J. R., & Kolb, K. J. (1995). Electronic performance monitoring and social context: Impact on productivity and stress. *Journal of Applied Psychology, 80,* 339–353.

Aiken, M., & Hage, J. (1968). Organizational interdependence and intraorganizational structure. *American Sociological Review, 33,* 912–930.

Ainsworth, M. D. S. (1979). Infant-mother attachment. *American Psychologist, 34,* 932–937.

Albright, L., Kenny, D. A., & Malloy, T. E. (1988). Consensus in personality judgments at zero acquaintance. *Journal of Personality and Social Psychology, 55,* 387–395.

Aldag, R. J., & Fuller, S. R. (1993). Beyond fiasco: A reappraisal of the groupthink phenomenon and a new model of group decision processes. *Psychological Bulletin, 113,* 533–552.

Alicke, M. D., Braun, J. C., Glor, J. E., Klotz, M. L., Magee, J., Sederholm, H., & Siegel, R. (1992). Complaining behavior in social interaction. *Personality and Social Psychology Bulletin, 18,* 286–295.

Allen, H. (1978). Cults: The battle for the mind. In C. A. Krause, *Guyana massacre: The eyewitness account* (pp. 111–121). New York: Berkley Publishing Corporation.

Allen, K. M., Blascovich, J., Tomaka, J., & Kelsey, R. M. (1991). Presence of human friends and pet dogs as moderators of autonomic responses to stress in women. *Journal of Personality and Social Psychology, 61,* 582–589.

Allen, V. L. (1965). Situational factors in conformity. *Advances in Experimental Social Psychology, 2,* 133–175.

Allen, V. L. (1975). Social support for nonconformity. *Advances in Experimental Social Psychology, 8,* 2–43.

Allen, V. L., & Wilder, D. A. (1980). Impact of group consensus and social support on stimulus meaning: Mediation of conformity by cognitive restructuring. *Journal of Personality and Social Psychology, 39,* 1116–1124.

Allison, S. T., Beggan, J. K., & Midgley, E. H. (1996). The quest for "similar instances" and "simultaneous possibilities": Metaphors in social dilemma research. *Journal of Personality and Social Psychology, 71,* 479–497.

Allison, S. T., McQueen, L. R., & Schaerfl, L. M. (1992). Social decision making processes and the equal partitionment of shared resources. *Journal of Experimental Social Psychology, 28,* 23–42.

Allison, S. T., & Messick, D. M. (1985a). Effects of experience on performance in a replenishable resource trap. *Journal of Personality and Social Psychology, 49,* 943–948.

Allison, S. T., & Messick, D. M. (1985b). The group attribution error. *Journal of Experimental Social Psychology, 21,* 563–579.

Allison, S. T., & Messick, D. M. (1990). Social decision heuristics in the use of shared resources. *Journal of Behavioral Decision Making, 3,* 195–204.

Allison, S. T., Worth, L. T., & King, M. C. (1990). Group decisions as social inference heuristics. *Journal of Personality and Social Psychology, 58,* 801–811.

Allport, F. H. (1920). The influence of the group upon association and thought. *Journal of Experimental Psychology, 3,* 159–182.

Allport, F. H. (1924). *Social psychology.* Boston: Houghton Mifflin.

Allport, F. H. (1961). The contemporary appraisal of an old problem. *Contemporary Psychology, 6,* 195–197.

Allport, F. H. (1962). A structuronomic conception of behavior: Individual and collective. I. Structural theory and the master problem of social psychology. *Journal of Abnormal and Social Psychology, 64,* 3–30.

Allport, G. W. (1954). *The nature of prejudice.* Reading, MA: Addison-Wesley.

Allport, G. W., & Postman, L. J. (1947). *The psychology of rumor.* New York: Holt.

Altemeyer, B. (1988). *Enemies of freedom: Understanding right-wing authoritarianism.* San Francisco: Jossey-Bass.

Altman, I. (1973). An ecological approach to the functioning of socially isolated groups. In J. E. Rasmussen (Ed.), *Man in isolation and confinement* (p. 241–269). Chicago: Aldine.

Altman, I. (1975). *The environment and social behavior.* Pacific Grove, CA: Brooks/Cole.

Altman, I. (1977). Research on environment and behavior: A personal statement of strategy. In D.

Stokols (Ed.), *Perspectives on environment and behavior* (pp. 303–324). New York: Plenum.

Altman, I., & Chemers, M. M. (1980). *Culture and environment.* Pacific Grove, CA: Brooks/Cole.

Altman, I., & Churchman, A. S. (Eds.). (1994). *Human behavior and the environment: Advances in theory and research, place attachment* (Vol. 12). New York: Plenum.

Altman, I., & Haythorn, W. W. (1967). The ecology of isolated groups. *Behavioral Science, 12,* 169–182.

Altman, I., & Taylor, D. A. (1973). *Social penetration: The development of interpersonal relationships.* New York: Holt, Rinehart & Winston.

Altman, I., Taylor, D. A., & Wheeler, L. (1971). Ecological aspects of group behavior in social isolation. *Journal of Applied Social Psychology, 1,* 76–100.

Alvaro, E. M., & Crano, W. D. (1997). Indirect minority influence: Evidence for leniency in source evaluation and counterargumentation. *Journal of Personality and Social Psychology, 72,* 949–964.

Amir, Y. (1969). Contact hypothesis in ethnic relations. *Psychological Bulletin, 71,* 319–342.

Amir, Y. (1976). The role of intergroup contact in change of prejudice and ethnic relations. In P. A. Katz (Ed.), *Towards the elimination of racism.* New York: Pergamon.

Ancona, D. G., & Caldwell, D. F. (1992). Demography and design: Predictors of new product team performance. *Organization Science, 3,* 321–341.

Andersen, S. M. (1984). Self-knowledge and social inference: II. The diagnosticity of cognitive/affective and behavioral data. *Journal of Personality and Social Psychology, 46,* 294–307.

Anderson, C. A. (1987). Temperature and aggression: Effects on quarterly, yearly, and city rates of violent and nonviolent crime. *Journal of Personality and Social Psychology, 49,* 91–97.

Anderson, C. A. (1989). Temperature and aggression: Ubiquitous effects of heat on occurrences of human violence. *Psychological Bulletin, 106,* 74–96.

Anderson, C. A., & Bushman, B. J. (1997). External validity of "trivial" experiments: The case of laboratory aggression. *Review of General Psychology, 1,* 19–41.

Anderson, C. A., Bushman, B. J., & Groom, R. W. (1997). Hot years and serious and deadly assault: Empirical tests of the heat hypothesis. *Journal of Personality and Social Psychology, 73,* 1213–1223.

Anderson, C. A., & DeNeve, K. M. (1992). Temperature, aggression, and the negative affect escape model. *Psychological Bulletin, 111,* 347–351.

Anderson, C. M., & Martin, M. M. (1995). The effects of communication motives, interaction involvement, and loneliness on satisfaction: A model of small groups. *Small Group Research, 26,* 118–137.

Ansari, M. A., & Kapoor, A. (1987). Organizational context and upward influence tactics. *Organizational Behavior and Human Decision Processes, 40,* 39–49.

Apodoca v. Oregon, 406 U.S. 404 (1972).

Appelbaum, R. P., & Chambliss, W. J. (1995). *Sociology.* New York: HarperCollins.

Applebaum, E., & Blatt, R. (1994). *The new American workplace.* Ithaca, NY: ILR.

Appleyard, D., & Lintell, M. (1972). The environment quality of city streets: The resident's viewpoint. *Journal of the American Institute of Planners, 38,* 84–101.

Ardry, R. (1970). *The territorial imperative: A personal inquiry into the animal origins of property and nations.* New York: Atheneum.

Argote, L., Insko, C. A., Yovetich, N., & Romero, A. A. (1995). Group learning curves: The effects of turnover and task complexity on group performance. *Journal of Applied Social Psychology, 25,* 512–529.

Argyle, M., & Dean, J. (1965). Eye-contact, distance, and affiliation. *Sociometry, 28,* 289–304.

Arkes, H. R. (1993). Some practical judgment and decision-making research. In N. J. Castellan, Jr. (Ed.), *Individual and group decision making: Current issues* (pp. 3–18). Hillsdale, NJ: Erlbaum.

Arkin, R. M., & Burger, J. M. (1980). Effects of unit relation tendencies on interpersonal attraction. *Social Psychology Quarterly, 43,* 380–391.

Arnold, D. W., & Greenberg, C. I. (1980). Deviate rejection within differentially manned groups. *Social Psychology Quarterly, 43,* 419–424.

Aronson, E. (1980). *The social animal* (3rd ed.). San Francisco: Freeman.

Aronson, E., & Mills, J. (1959). The effects of severity of initiation on liking for a group. *Journal of Abnormal and Social Psychology, 59,* 177–181.

Aronson, E., Stephan, C., Sikes, J., Blaney, N., & Snapp, M. (1978). *The Jigsaw classroom.* Newbury Park, CA: Sage.

Arrow, H. (1997). Stability, bistability, and instability in small group influence patterns. *Journal of Personality and Social Psychology, 72,* 75–85.

Arrow, H., & McGrath, J. E. (1995). Membership dynamics in groups at work: A theoretical framework. *Research in Organizational Behavior, 17,* 373–411.

Asch, S. E. (1952). *Social psychology.* Englewood Cliffs, NJ: Prentice Hall.

Asch, S. E. (1955). Opinions and social pressures. *Scientific American, 193(5),* 31–35.

Asch, S. E. (1957, April). An experimental investigation of group influence. In *Symposium on preventive and social psychiatry.* Symposium conducted at the Walter Reed Army Institute of Research. Washington, DC: U.S. Government Printing Office.

Aschenbrenner, K. M., & Schaefer, R. E. (1980). Minimal group situations: Comments on a mathematical model and on the research paradigm. *European Journal of Social Psychology, 10,* 389–398.

Asendorpf, J. B., & Meier, G. H. (1993). Personality effects on children's speech in everyday life: Sociability-mediated exposure and shyness-mediated reactivity in social situations. *Journal of Personality and Social Psychology, 64,* 1072–1083.

Ashour, A. S. (1973a). Further discussion of Fiedler's contingency model of leadership effectiveness. *Organizational Behavior and Human Performance, 9,* 369–376.

Ashour, A. S. (1973b). The contingency model of leadership effectiveness: An evaluation. *Organizational Behavior and Human Performance, 9,* 339–355.

Atlas, J. (1990). A psychohistorical view of crusade origins. *Journal of Psychohistory, 17,* 412–415.

Atthowe, J. M., Jr. (1961). Interpersonal decision making: The resolution of a dyadic conflict. *Journal of Abnormal and Social Psychology, 62,* 114–119.

Averill, J. R. (1983). Studies on anger and aggression: Implications for theories of emotion. *American Psychologist, 38,* 1145–1160.

Axelrod, R. (1984). *The evolution of cooperation.* New York: Basic Books.

Axelrod, R., & Hamilton, W. D. (1981). The evolution of cooperation. *Science, 211,* 1390–1396.

Axsom, D. (1989). Cognitive dissonance and behavior change in psychotherapy. *Journal of Experimental Social Psychology, 25,* 234–252.

Ayman, R., Chemers, M. M., & Fiedler, F. (1995). The contingency model of leadership effectiveness: Its levels of analysis. *Leadership Quarterly, 6,* 147–167.

Azuma, H. (1984). Secondary control as a heterogeneous category. *American Psychologist, 39,* 970–971.

Bach, G. R. (1954). *Intensive group psychotherapy.* New York: Ronald Press.

Bacharach, S. B., & Aiken, M. (1979). The impact of alienation, meaninglessness, and meritocracy on supervisor and subordinate satisfaction. *Social Forces, 57,* 853–870.

Back, K. W. (1951). Influence through social communication. *Journal of Abnormal and Social Psychology, 46,* 9–23.

Back, K. W. (1973). *Beyond words: The story of sensitivity training and the encounter movement.* Baltimore: Penguin Books.

Back, K. W. (1974). Intervention techniques: Small groups. *Annual Review of Psychology, 25,* 367–387.

Back, K. W. (1992). This business of topology. *Journal of Social Issues, 48(2),* 51–66.

Baker, S. M., & Petty, R. E. (1994). Majority and minority influence: Source-position imbalance as a determinant of message scrutiny. *Journal of Personality and Social Psychology, 67,* 5–19.

Bales, R. F. (1950). *Interaction process analysis: A method for the study of small groups.* Reading, MA: Addison-Wesley.

Bales, R. F. (1953). The equilibrium problem in small groups. In T. Parsons, R. F. Bales, & E. A. Shils (Eds.), *Working papers in the theory of action* (pp. 111–161). Glencoe, IL: The Free Press.

Bales, R. F. (1955). How people interact in conferences. *Scientific American, 192(3),* 31–35.

Bales, R. F. (1958). Task roles and social roles in problem-solving groups. In E. E. Maccoby, T. M. Newcomb, & E. L. Hartley (Eds.), *Readings in social psychology.* New York: Holt, Rinehart & Winston.

Bales, R. F. (1965). The equilibrium problem in small groups. In A. P. Hare, E. F. Borgatta, & R. F. Bales (Eds.), *Small groups: Studies in social interaction.* New York: Knopf.

Bales, R. F. (1970). *Personality and interpersonal behavior.* New York: Holt, Rinehart & Winston.

Bales, R. F. (1980). *SYMLOG case study kit.* New York: The Free Press.

Bales, R. F. (1988). A new overview of the SYMLOG system: Measuring and changing behavior in groups. In R. B. Polley, A. P. Hare, & P. J. Stone (Eds.), *The SYMLOG practitioner: Applications of small group research* (pp. 319–344). New York: Praeger.

Bales, R. F., & Cohen, S. P. with Williamson, S. A. (1979). *SYMLOG: A system for the multiple level observation of groups.* New York: The Free Press.

Bales, R. F., & Hare, A. P. (1965). Diagnostic use of the interaction profile. *Journal of Social Psychology, 67,* 239–258.

Bales, R. F., & Slater, P. E. (1955). Role differentiation in small decision-making groups. In T. Parsons and R. F. Bales (Eds.), *Family, socialization, and interaction process* (pp. 259–306). Glencoe, IL: The Free Press.

Bales, R. F., & Strodtbeck, F. L. (1951). Phases in group problem solving. *Journal of Abnormal and Social Psychology, 46,* 485–495.

Ball, S. J. (1981). *Beachside comprehensive: A case study of secondary schooling.* New York: Cambridge University Press.

Bandura, A. (1977). *Social-learning theory.* Englewood Cliffs, NJ: Prentice Hall.

Bandura, A. (1990). Selective activation and disengagement of moral control. *Journal of Social Issues, 46(1),* 27–46.

Barash, D. P. (1982). *Sociobiology and behavior* (2nd ed.). New York: Elsevier.

Bargal, D., Gold, M., & Lewin, M. (Eds.). (1992). *Journal of Social Issues, 48(2).*

Bargh, J. A. (1990). Auto-motives: Preconscious determinants of social interaction. In E. T. Higgins & R. M. Sorrentino (Eds.), *Handbook of motivation and cognition: Foundations of social behavior* (Vol. 2, pp. 93–130). New York: Guilford Press.

Barker, R. A. (1997). How can we train leaders if we do not know what leadership is? *Human Relations, 50,* 343–362.

Barker, R. G. (1968). *Ecological psychology.* Stanford, CA: Stanford University Press.

Barker, R. G. (1987). Prospecting in ecological psychology: Oskaloosa revisited. In D. Stokols & I. Altman (Eds.), *Handbook of environmental psychology* (Vol. 2, pp. 1413–1432). New York: Wiley.

Barker, R. G. (1990). Recollections of the Midwest Psychological Field Station. *Environment and Behavior, 22,* 503–513.

Barker, R. G., & Associates. (1978). *Habitats, environments, and human behavior: Studies in ecological psychology and eco-behavioral sciences from the Midwest Psychological Field Station, 1947–1972.* San Francisco: Jossey-Bass.

Barnard, C. I. (1938). *The functions of the executive.* Cambridge, MA: Harvard University Press.

Baron, R. A. (1972). Aggression as a function of ambient temperature and prior anger arousal. *Journal of Personality and Social Psychology, 21,* 183–189.

Baron, R. A. (1978). Aggression and heat: The "long hot summer" revisited. In A. Baum, J. E. Singer, & S. Valins (Eds.), *Advances in environmental psy-*

chology (Vol. 1, pp. 57–84). Hillsdale, NJ: Erlbaum.

Baron, R. A., & Ball, R. L. (1974). The aggression-inhibiting influence of nonhostile humor. *Journal of Experimental Social Psychology, 10,* 23–33.

Baron, R. A., & Bell, P. A. (1975). Aggression and heat: Mediating effects of prior provocation and exposure to an aggressive model. *Journal of Personality and Social Psychology, 31,* 825–832.

Baron, R. A., & Bell, P. A. (1976). Aggression and heat: The influence of ambient temperature, negative affect, and a cooling drink on physical aggression. *Journal of Personality and Social Psychology, 33,* 245–255.

Baron, R. S. (1986). Distraction-conflict theory: Progress and problems. *Advances in Experimental Social Psychology, 19,* 1–40.

Baron, R. S., Kerr, N. L., & Miller, N. (1992). *Group process, group decision, group action.* Pacific Grove, CA: Brooks/Cole.

Baron, R. S., Vandello, J. A., & Brunsman, B. (1996). The forgotten variable in conformity research: Impact of task importance on social influence. *Journal of Personality and Social Psychology, 71,* 915–927.

Barrera, M., Jr. (1986). Distinctions between social support concepts, measures, and models. *American Journal of Community Psychology, 14,* 413–422.

Barrick, M. R., & Mount, M. K. (1991). The Big Five personality dimensions and job performance: A meta-analysis. *Personnel Psychology, 44,* 1–26.

Barrow, J. C. (1977). The variables of leadership: A review and conceptual framework. *Academy of Management Review, 2,* 231–251.

Bar-Tal, D. (1990). Causes and consequences of delegitimization: Models of conflict and ethnocentrism. *Journal of Social Issues, 46(1),* 65–81.

Bartholomew, R. E. (1997). Mass hysteria. *British Journal of Psychiatry, 170,* 387–388.

Bartholomew, R. E., & Sirois, F. (1996). Epidemic hysteria in schools: An international and historical overview. *Educational Studies, 22,* 285–311.

Bartis, S., Szymanski, K., & Harkins, S. G. (1988). Evaluation and performance: A two-edged knife. *Personality and Social Psychology Bulletin, 14,* 242–251.

Bartlett, F. C. (1932). *A study in experimental and social psychology.* New York: Cambridge University Press.

Bartol, K. M., & Martin, D. C. (1986). Women and men in task groups. In R. D. Ashmore & F. K. DelBoca (Eds.), *The social psychology of female-male relations* (pp. 259–310). New York: Academic Press.

Barton, A. H., & Lazarfeld, P. H. (1969). Some functions of qualitative analysis in social research. In G. J. McCall & J. L. Simmons (Eds.), *Issues in participant observation* (pp. 163–196). Reading, MA: Addison-Wesley.

Basow, S. A. (1992). *Gender: Stereotypes and roles* (3rd ed.). Pacific Grove, CA: Brooks/Cole.

Bass, B. M. (1985a). Good, better, best. *Organizational Dynamics, 13,* 26–40.

Bass, B. M. (1985b). *Leadership and performance beyond expectations.* New York: The Free Press.

Bass, B. M. (1990). *Bass and Stogdill's handbook of leadership: Theory, research, and managerial applications* (3rd ed.). New York: The Free Press.

Bass, B. M. (1997). Does the transactional-transformational leadership paradigm transcend organizational and national boundaries? *American Psychologist, 52,* 130–139.

Bass, B. M., & Avolio, B. J. (1994). *Improving organizational effectiveness through transformational leadership.* Thousand Oaks, CA: Sage.

Bass, B. M., Avolio, B. J., & Goldheim, L. (1987). Biography and the assessment of transformational leadership at the world-class level. *Journal of Management, 13,* 7–19.

Bass, B. M., & Ryterband, E. C. (1979). *Organizational psychology* (2nd ed.). Boston: Allyn & Bacon.

Batchelor, J. P., & Goethals, G. R. (1972). Spatial arrangements in freely formed groups. *Sociometry, 35,* 270–279.

Bates, B., & Goodman, A. (1986). The effectiveness of encounter groups: Implications of research for counselling practice. *British Journal of Guidance and Counselling, 14,* 240–251.

Batson, C. D. (1975). Rational processing or rationalization? The effect of disconfirming information on a state religious belief. *Journal of Personality and Social Psychology, 32,* 176–184.

Baum, A., Calesnick, L. E., Davis, G. E., & Gatchel, R. J. (1982). Individual differences in coping with crowding: Stimulus screening and social overload. *Journal of Personality and Social Psychology, 43,* 821–830.

Baum, A., & Davis, G. E. (1980). Reducing the stress of high-density living: An architectural intervention. *Journal of Personality and Social Psychology, 38,* 471–481.

Baum, A., Davis, G. E., & Valins, S. (1979). Generating behavioral data for the design process. In J. R.

Aiello & A. Baum (Eds.), *Residential crowding and design* (pp. 175–196). New York: Plenum.

Baum, A., Harpin, R. E., & Valins, S. (1976). The role of group phenomena in the experience of crowding. In S. Saegert (Ed.), *Crowding in real environments.* Newbury Park, CA: Sage.

Baum, A., Singer, J., & Baum, C. (1982). Stress and the environment. *Journal of Social Issues, 37(1),* 4–35.

Baum, A., & Valins, S. (1977). *Architecture and social behavior: Psychological studies of social density.* Hillsdale, NJ: Erlbaum.

Baumeister, R. F. (1984). Choking under pressure: Self-consciousness and paradoxical effects of incentives on skillful performance. *Journal of Personality and Social Psychology, 46,* 610–620.

Baumeister, R. F. (1985). The championship choke. *Psychology Today, 19(4),* 48–52.

Baumeister, R. F. (1986). *Public self and private self.* New York: Springer-Verlag.

Baumeister, R. F. (1995). Disputing the effects of championship pressures and home audiences. *Journal of Personality and Social Psychology, 68,* 644–648.

Baumeister, R. F., & Leary, M. R. (1995). The need to belong: Desire for interpersonal attachments as a fundamental human motivation. *Psychological Bulletin, 117,* 497–529.

Baumeister, R. F., & Showers, C. J. (1986). A review of paradoxical performance effects: Choking under pressure in sports and mental tests. *European Journal of Social Psychology, 16,* 361–383.

Baumeister, R. F., & Sommer, K. L. (1997). What do men want? Gender differences and two spheres of belongingness. *Psychological Bulletin, 122,* 38–44

Baumeister, R. F., Stillwell, A., & Wotman, S. R. (1990). Victim and perpetrator accounts of interpersonal conflict: Autobiographical narratives about anger. *Journal of Personality and Social Psychology, 59,* 994–1005.

Baumeister, R. F., & Tice, D. M. (1990). Anxiety and social exclusion. *Journal of Social and Clinical Psychology, 9,* 165–195.

Baumrind, D. (1964). Some thoughts on ethics of research: After reading Milgram's "Behavioral study of obedience." *American Psychologist, 19,* 421–423.

Bavelas, A. (1948). A mathematical model for group structures. *Applied Anthropology, 7,* 16–30.

Bavelas, A. (1950). Communication patterns in task-oriented groups. *Journal of the Acoustical Society of America, 22,* 725–730.

Bavelas, A., & Barrett, D. (1951). An experimental approach to organization communication. *Personnel, 27,* 367–371.

Beaman, A. L., Cole, C. M., Preston, M., Klentz, B., & Steblay, N. M. (1983). Fifteen years of foot-in-the-door research: A meta-analysis. *Personality and Social Psychology Bulletin, 9,* 181–196.

Beaman, A. L., Klentz, B., Diener, E., & Svanum, S. (1979). Objective self-awareness and transgression in children: A field study. *Journal of Personality and Social Psychology, 37,* 1835–1846.

Bedell, J., & Sistrunk, F. (1973). Power, opportunity, costs, and sex in a mixed-motive game. *Journal of Personality and Social Psychology, 25,* 219–226.

Bednar, R. L., & Kaul, T. (1978). Experiential group research: Current perspectives. In S. L. Garfield and A. E. Bergin (Eds.), *Handbook of psychotherapy and behavior change* (2nd ed., pp. 769–815). New York: Wiley.

Bednar, R. L., & Kaul, T. (1979). Experiential group research: What never happened. *Journal of Applied Behavioral Science, 15,* 311–319.

Bednar, R. L., & Kaul, T. (1994). Experiential group research: Can the canon fire? In S. L. Garfield and A. E. Bergin (Eds.), *Handbook of psychotherapy and behavior change* (4th ed., pp. 631–663). New York: Wiley.

Belk, S. S., Snell, W. E., Jr., Garcia-Falconi, R., Hernandez-Sanchez, J. E., Hargrove, L., & Holtzman, W. H., Jr. (1988). Power strategy use in the intimate relationships of women and men from Mexico and the United States. *Personality and Social Psychology Bulletin, 14,* 439–447.

Bell, P. A. (1981). Physiological, comfort, performance, and social effects of heat stress. *Journal of Social Issues, 37,* 71–94.

Bell, P. A. (1992). In defense of the negative affect escape model of heat and aggression. *Psychological Bulletin, 111,* 342–346.

Bell, P. A., Fisher, J. D., Baum, A., & Greene, T. E. (1990). *Environmental psychology* (4th ed.). Fort Worth, TX: Holt, Rinehart & Winston.

Bell, P. A., & Greene, T. C. (1982). Thermal stress: Physiological, comfort, performance, and social effects of hot and cold environments. In G. W. Evans (Ed.), *Environmental stress.* London: Cambridge University Press.

Bellack, A., & Hersen, M. (1979). *Research and practice in social skills training.* New York: Plenum.

Bem, D. J. (1972). Self-perception theory. *Advances in Experimental Social Psychology, 6,* 2–62.

Bem, S. L. (1975). Sex role adaptability: One consequence of psychological androgyny. *Journal of Personality and Social Psychology, 31,* 634–643.

Bem, S. L. (1985). Androgyny and gender schema theory: A conceptual and empirical integration. *Nebraska Symposium on Motivation, 32,* 179–226.

Benford, R. D. (1992). Social movements. In E. F. Borgatta & M. L. Borgatta (Eds.), *Encyclopedia of Sociology* (Vol. 4, pp. 1880–1887). New York: MacMillan.

Benne, K. D. (1964). History of the T-group in the laboratory setting. In L. P. Bradford, J. R.. Gibb, & K. D. Benne (Eds.), *T-group theory and laboratory method: Innovation in re-education* (pp. 80–135). New York: Wiley.

Benne, K. D., & Sheats, P. (1948). Functional roles of group members. *Journal of Social Issues, 4(2),* 41–49.

Bennett, H. S. (1980). *On becoming a rock musician.* Amherst: University of Massachusetts Press.

Bennis, W., & Biederman, P. W. (1997). *Organizing genius: The secrets of creative collaboration.* Reading, MA: Addison-Wesley.

Bennis, W. G. (1975). *Where have all the leaders gone?* Washington, DC: Federal Executive Institute.

Bennis, W. G., & Shepard, H. A. (1956). A theory of group development. *Human Relations, 9,* 415–437.

Berger, J., Cohen, B. P., & Zelditch, M., Jr. (1972). Status characteristics and social interaction. *American Sociological Review, 37,* 241–255.

Berger, J., Conner, T. L., & Fisek, M. H. (Eds.). (1974). *Expectation states theory: A theoretical research program.* Cambridge, MA: Winthrop.

Berger, J., Fisek, M. H., Norman, R. Z., & Zelditch, M., Jr. (1977). *Status characteristics and social interaction.* New York: Elsevier.

Berger, J., Wagner, D. G., & Zelditch, M., Jr. (1992). A working strategy for constructing theories: State organizing processes. In G. Ritzer (Ed.), *Studies in metatheorizing in sociology* (pp. 107–123). Thousand Oaks, CA: Sage.

Berger, J., Webster, M., Jr., Ridgeway, C., & Rosenholtz, S. J. (1986). Status cues, expectations, and behavior. *Advances in Group Processes, 3,* 1–22.

Berger, J., & Zelditch, M., Jr. (Eds.). (1985). *Status, rewards, and influence.* San Francisco: Jossey-Bass.

Berger, J., & Zelditch, M., Jr. (Eds.). (1993). *Theoretical research programs: Studies in the growth of theory.* Stanford, CA: Stanford University Press.

Berger, R. E. (1981). *Heart rate, arousal, and the "mere presence" hypothesis of social facilitation.*

Unpublished doctoral dissertation, Virginia Commonwealth University, Richmond, VA.

Berger, S. M., Carli, L. C., Garcia, R., & Brady, J. J., Jr. (1982). Audience effects in anticipatory learning: A comparison of drive and practice-inhibition analyses. *Journal of Personality and Social Psychology, 42,* 478–486.

Berger, S. M., Hampton, K. L., Carli, L. L., Grandmaison, P. S., Sadow, J. S., Donath, C. H., & Herschlag, L. R. (1981). Audience-induced inhibition of overt practice during learning. *Journal of Personality and Social Psychology, 40,* 479–491.

Berkowitz, L. (1953). Sharing leadership in small, decision-making groups. *Journal of Abnormal and Social Psychology, 48,* 231–238.

Berkowitz, L. (1971). Reporting an experiment: A case study in leveling, sharpening, and assimilation. *Journal of Experimental Social Psychology, 7,* 237–243.

Berkowitz, L. (1990). On the formation and regulation of anger and aggression: A cognitive-neoassociationistic analysis. *American Psychologist, 45,* 494–503.

Berkowitz, L. (1993). Aggression: Its causes, consequences, and control. New York: McGraw-Hill.

Berkowitz, L., & Lundy, R. M. (1957). Personality characteristics related to susceptibility to influence by peers or authority figures. *Journal of Personality, 25,* 306–316.

Berkowitz, N. H. (1994). Evidence that subjects' expectancies confound intergroup bias in Tajfel's minimal group paradigm. *Personality and Social Psychology Bulletin, 20,* 184–195.

Berman, J. J., & Zimpfer, D. G. (1980). Growth groups: Do the outcomes really last? *Review of Educational Research, 50,* 505–524.

Bernard, H. S., & MacKenzie, K. R. (1994). *Basics of group psychotherapy.* New York: Guilford Press.

Berndt, T. J. (1992). Friends and friends' influence in adolescence. *Current Directions in Psychological Science, 1,* 156–159.

Berndt, T. J. (1996). Friendships in adolescence. In N. Vanzetti & S. Duck (Eds.), *A lifetime of relationships* (pp. 182–212). Pacific Grove, CA: Brooks/Cole.

Bernthal, P. R., & Insko, C. A. (1993). Cohesiveness without groupthink: The interactive effects of social and task cohesion. *Group and Organizational Management, 18,* 66–87.

Berry, D. S., & McArthur, L. Z. (1986). Perceiving character in faces: The impact of age-related craniofacial changes on social perception. *Psychological Bulletin, 100,* 3–18.

Betancourt, H., & Blair, I. (1992). A cognition (attribution)-emotion model of violence in conflict situations. *Personality and Social Psychology Bulletin, 18,* 343–350.

Bettencourt, B. A., Brewer, M. B., Croak, M. R., & Miller, N. (1992). Cooperation and the reduction of intergroup bias: The role of reward structure and social orientation. *Journal of Experimental Social Psychology, 28,* 301–309.

Biddle, B. J. (1979). *Role theory: Expectations, identities, and behavior.* New York: Academic Press.

Biernat, M., Vescio, T. K., & Green, M. L. (1996). Selective self-stereotyping. *Journal of Personality and Social Psychology, 71,* 1194–1209.

Billig, M. G., & Tajfel, H. (1973). Social categorization and similarity in intergroup behavior. *European Journal of Social Psychology, 3,* 27–52.

Birch, L. L. (1987). Children's food preferences: Developmental patterns and environmental influences. *Annals of Child Development, 4,* 171–208.

Black, T. E., & Higbee, K. L. (1973). Effects of power, threat, and sex on exploitation. *Journal of Personality and Social Psychology, 27,* 382–388.

Blake, R. R., & McCanse, A. A. (1991). *Leadership dilemmas? Grid solutions.* Houston, TX: Gulf.

Blake, R. R., & Mouton, J. S. (1964). *The managerial grid.* Houston, TX: Gulf.

Blake, R. R., & Mouton, J. S. (1978). *The new managerial grid.* Houston, TX: Gulf.

Blake, R. R., & Mouton, J. S. (1980). *The versatile manager: A Grid profile.* Homewood, IL: Dow Jones/Irwin.

Blake, R. R., & Mouton, J. S. (1982). How to choose a leadership style. *Training and Development Journal, 36,* 39–46.

Blake, R. R., & Mouton, J. S. (1984). *Solving costly organizational conflicts: Achieving intergroup trust, cooperation, and teamwork.* San Francisco: Jossey-Bass.

Blake, R. R., & Mouton, J. S. (1985). Presidential (Grid) styles. *Training and Development Journal, 39,* 30–34.

Blake, R. R., & Mouton, J. S. (1986). From theory to practice in interface problem solving. In S. Worchel & W. G. Austin (Eds.), *Psychology of intergroup relations* (2nd ed., pp. 67–87). Chicago: Nelson-Hall.

Blake, R. R., Shepard, H. A., & Mouton, J. S. (1964). *Managing intergroup conflict in industry.* Houston, TX: Gulf.

Blanchard, F. A., Adelman, L., & Cook, S. W. (1975). Effect of group success and failure upon interpersonal attraction in cooperating interracial groups. *Journal of Personality and Social Psychology, 31,* 1020–1030.

Blanchard, F. A., & Cook, S. W. (1976). Effects of helping a less competent member of a cooperating interracial group on the development of interpersonal attraction. *Journal of Personality and Social Psychology, 34,* 1245–1255.

Blanchard, F. A., Weigel, R. H., & Cook, S. W. (1975). The effect of relative competence of group members upon interpersonal attraction in cooperating interracial groups. *Journal of Personality and Social Psychology, 32,* 519–530.

Blanchard, K., & Johnson, S. (1981). *The one minute manager.* New York: Berkley Books.

Blanchard, K., Zigarmi, D., & Nelson, R. (1993). Situational leadership after 25 years: A retrospective. *The Journal of Leadership Studies, 1,* 22–36.

Blanchard, K., Zigarmi, P., & Zigarmi, D. (1985). *Leadership and the one minute manager.* New York: Morrow.

Blascovich, J., Ginsburg, G. P., & Howe, R. C. (1975). Blackjack and the risky shift, II: Monetary stakes. *Journal of Experimental Social Psychology, 11,* 224–232.

Blascovich, J., Ginsburg, G. P., & Veach, T. L. (1975). A pluralistic explanation of choice shifts on the risk dimension. *Journal of Personality and Social Psychology, 31,* 422–429.

Blascovich, J., Nash, R. F., & Ginsburg, G. P. (1978). Heart rate and competitive decision making. *Personality and Social Psychology Bulletin, 4,* 115–118.

Blass, T. (1991). Understanding behavior in the Milgram obedience experiment: The role of personality, situations, and their interactions. *Journal of Personality and Social Psychology, 60,* 398–413.

Blass, T. (1992). The social psychology of Stanley Milgram. *Advances in Experimental Social Psychology, 25,* 277–329.

Blass, T. (1995). Right-wing authoritarianism and role as predictors of attributions about obedience to authority. *Personality and Individual Differences, 19,* 99–100.

Blass, T. (1996). Attribution of responsibility and trust in the Milgram obedience experiment. *Journal of Applied Social Psychology, 26,* 1529–1535.

Blau, P. M. (1964). *Exchange and power in social life.* New York: Wiley.

505

Blickensderfer, E., Cannon-Bowers, J. A., & Salas, E. (1997). *Training teams to self-correct: An empirical investigation.* Paper presented at the 12th Annual Meeting of the Society for Industrial and Organizational Psychology, St. Louis, MO.

Bliese, J. R. (1990). The motives of the First Crusaders: A social psychological analysis. *Journal of Psychohistory, 17,* 393–411.

Bloch, S., Reibstein, J., Crouch, E., Holroyd, P., & Themen, J. (1979). A method for the study of therapeutic factors in group psychotherapy, *British Journal of Psychiatry, 40,* 477–493.

Blumberg, H. H., Hare, A. P., Kent, V., & Davies, M. F. (Eds.). (1983). *Small groups and social interaction* (Vols. 1 and 2). New York: Wiley.

Blumer, H. (1946). Collective behavior. In A. M. Lee (Ed.), *New outline of the principles of sociology.* New York: Barnes & Noble.

Blumer, H. (1951). Collective behavior. In A. M. Lee (Ed.), *Principles of sociology.* New York: Barnes & Noble.

Blumer, H. (1957). Collective behavior. In J. B. Gittler (Ed.), *Review of sociology: Analysis of a decade.* New York: Wiley.

Boardman, S. K., & Horowitz, S. V. (Eds.). (1994). Constructive conflict management: An answer to critical social problems? *Journal of Social Issues, 50(1).*

Bodenhausen, G. V., Gaelick, L., & Wyer, R. S., Jr. (1987). Affective and cognitive factors in intragroup and intergroup communication. *Review of Personality and Social Psychology, 9,* 137–166.

Bogardus, E. S. (1954). Group behavior and groupality. *Sociology and Social Research, 38,* 401–403.

Bohrnstedt, G. W., & Fisher, G. A. (1986). The effects of recalled childhood and adolescent relationships compared to current role performances on young adults' affective functioning. *Social Psychology Quarterly, 49,* 19–32.

Boivin, M., Dodge, K. A., & Coie, J. D. (1995). Individual-group behavioral similarity and peer status in experimental play groups of boys: The social misfit revisited. *Journal of Personality and Social Psychology, 69,* 269–279.

Bollen, K. A., & Hoyle, R. H. (1990). Perceived cohesion: A conceptual and empirical examination. *Social Forces, 69,* 479–504.

Bond, C. F., Jr. (1982). Social facilitation: A self-presentational view. *Journal of Personality and Social Psychology, 42,* 1042–1050.

Bond, C. F., Jr., Atoum, A. O., & VanLeeuwen, M. D. (1996). Social impairment of complex learning in the wake of public embarrassment. *Basic and Applied Social Psychology, 18,* 31–44.

Bond, C. F., Jr., & Titus, L. J. (1983). Social facilitation: A meta-analysis of 241 studies. *Psychological Bulletin, 94,* 265–292.

Bond, M. H., & Shiu, W. Y. (1997). The relationship between a group's personality resources and the two dimensions of its group process. *Small Group Research, 28,* 194–217.

Bond, R., & Smith, P. B. (1996). Culture and conformity: A meta-analysis of studies using Asch's (1952b, 1956) line judgment task. *Psychological Bulletin, 119,* 111–137.

Bone, E. (1957). *Seven years solitary.* London: McMillan.

Bonner, H. (1959). Group dynamics: Principles and applications. New York: Ronald.

Bonney, M. E. (1947). Popular and unpopular children: A sociometric study. *Sociometry Monographs,* No. 99, A80.

Bons, P. M., & Fiedler, F. E. (1976). Changes in organizational leadership and the behavior of relationship- and task-motivated leaders. *Administrative Science Quarterly, 21,* 433–472.

Bonta, B. D. (1997). Cooperation and competition in peaceful societies. *Psychological Bulletin, 121,* 299–320.

Booth, A. (1972). Sex and social participation. *American Sociological Review, 37,* 183–193.

Borah, L. A., Jr. (1963). The effects of threat in bargaining: Critical and experimental analysis. *Journal of Abnormal and Social Psychology, 66,* 37–44.

Borgatta, E. F., & Bales, R. F. (1953). Task and accumulation of experience as factors in the interaction of small groups. *Sociometry, 16,* 239–252.

Borgatta, E. F., Cottrell, L. S., Jr., & Meyer, H. J. (1956). On the dimensions of group behavior. *Sociometry, 19,* 223–240.

Borgatta, E. F., Couch, A. S., & Bales, R. F. (1954). Some findings relevant to the great man theory of leadership. *American Sociological Review, 19,* 755–759.

Bormann, E. G. (1975). *Discussion and group methods: Theory and practices* (2nd ed.). New York: Harper & Row.

Bornstein, G., Budescu, D., & Zamir, S. (1997). Cooperation in intergroup, N-person, and two-person games of chicken. *Journal of Conflict Resolution, 41,* 384–406.

Bornstein, G., Rapoport, A., Kerpel, L., & Katz, T. (1989). Within- and between-group communication in intergroup competition for public goods. *Journal of Experimental Social Psychology, 25,* 422–436.

Bornstein, R. F. (1992). The dependent personality: Developmental, social, and clinical perspectives. *Psychological Bulletin, 112,* 3–23.

Bornstein, R. F., Leone, D. R., & Galley, D. J. (1987). The generalizability of subliminal mere exposure effects: Influence of stimuli perceived without awareness on social behavior. *Journal of Personality and Social Psychology, 53,* 1070–1079.

Bouchard, T. J. (1972a). A comparison of two group brainstorming procedures. *Journal of Applied Psychology, 56,* 418–421.

Bouchard, T. J. (1972b). Training, motivation, and personality as determinants of the effectiveness of brainstorming groups and individuals. *Journal of Applied Psychology, 56,* 324–331.

Bouchard, T. J., Barsaloux, J., & Drauden, G. (1974). Brainstorming procedure, group size, and sex as determinants of the problem-solving effectiveness of groups and individuals. *Journal of Applied Psychology, 59,* 135–138.

Bouchard, T. J., Drauden, G., & Barsaloux, J. (1974). A comparison of individual, subgroup, and total group methods of problem solving. *Journal of Applied Psychology, 59,* 226–227.

Bouchard, T. J., & Hare, M. (1970). Size, performance, and potential in brainstorming groups. *Journal of Applied Psychology, 54,* 51–55.

Bowers, C. A., Braun, C. C., & Morgan, B. B., Jr. (1997). Team workload: Its meaning and measurement. In M. T. Brannick, E. Salas, & C. Prince (Eds.), *Team performance assessment and measurement: Theory, methods, and applications* (pp. 85–108). Mahwah, NJ: Erlbaum.

Bowers, C. A., Weaver, J. L., & Morgan, B. B., Jr. (1996). Moderating the performance effects of stressors. In J. E. Driskell & E. Salas (Eds.), *Stress and human performance* (pp. 163–192). Mahwah, NJ: Erlbaum.

Bowers, D. G., & Seashore, S. E. (1966). Predicting organizational effectiveness with a four-factor theory of leadership. *Administrative Science Quarterly, 11,* 238–263.

Bowlby, J. (1980). *Attachment and loss* (Vol. 1). London: Hogarth.

Bracken, B. A. (Ed.). (1996). *Handbook of self-concept: Developmental, social, and clinical considerations.* New York: Wiley.

Bradley, P. H. (1978). Power, status, and upward communication in small decision-making groups. *Communication Monographs, 45,* 33–43.

Bramel, D., & Friend, R. (1981). Hawthorne, the myth of the docile worker, and class bias in psychology. *American Psychologist, 36,* 867–878.

Brannick, M. T., Salas, E., & Prince, C. (Eds.). (1997). *Team performance assessment and measurement: Theory, methods, and applications.* Mahwah, NJ: Erlbaum.

Branscombe, N. R., & Wann, D. L. (1994). Collective self-esteem consequences of outgroup derogation when a valued social identity is on trial. *European Journal of Social Psychology, 24,* 641–657.

Brauer, M., Judd, C. M., & Gliner, M. D. (1995). The effects of repeated expressions on attitude polarization during group discussions. *Journal of Personality and Social Psychology, 68,* 1014–1029.

Brawley, L. R. (1984). Unintentional egocentric biases in attributions. *Journal of Sport Psychology, 6,* 264–278.

Bray, R. M., Johnson, D., & Chilstrom, J. T., Jr. (1982). Social influence by group members with minority opinions: A comparison of Hollander & Moscovici. *Journal of Personality and Social Psychology, 43,* 78–88.

Brechner, K. C. (1977). An experimental analysis of social traps. *Journal of Experimental Social Psychology, 13,* 552–564.

Brehm, J. W. (1976). Responses to loss of freedom: A theory of psychological reactance. In J. W. Thibaut, J. T. Spence, & R. C. Carson (Eds.), *Contemporary topics in social psychology* (pp. 51–78). Morristown, NJ: General Learning Press.

Brehm, J. W., & Sensenig, J. (1966). Social influence as a function of attempted and implied usurpation of choice. *Journal of Personality and Social Psychology, 4,* 703–707.

Brehm, S. S., & Brehm, J. W. (1981). *Psychological reactance: A theory of freedom and control.* New York: Academic Press.

Breiger, R. L., & Ennis, J. G. (1979). Personae and social roles: The network structure of personality types in small groups. *Social Psychology Quarterly, 42,* 262–270.

Brenner, O. C., & Vinacke, W. E. (1979). Accommodative and exploitative behavior of males versus females and managers versus nonmanagers as measured by the Test of Strategy. *Social Psychology Quarterly, 42,* 289–293.

Brewer, M. B. (1979). In-group bias in the minimal intergroup situation: A cognitive-motivational analysis. *Psychological Bulletin, 86,* 307–324.

Brewer, M. B. (1986). The role of ethnocentrism in intergroup conflict. In S. Worchel & W. G. Austin (Eds.), *Psychology of intergroup relations* (2nd ed., pp. 88–102). Chicago: Nelson-Hall.

Brewer, M. B. (1991). The social self: On being the same and different at the same time. *Personality and Social Psychology Bulletin, 17,* 475–782.

Brewer, M. B., & Brown, R. J. (1998). Intergroup relations. In D. T. Gilbert, S. T. Fiske, & G. Lindzey (Eds.), *The handbook of social psychology* (4th ed., Vol. 2, pp. 554–594). New York: McGraw-Hill.

Brewer, M. B., & Campbell, D. T. (1976). *Ethnocentrism and intergroup attitudes: East African evidence.* New York: Halsted Press.

Brewer, M. B., & Gardner, W. (1996). Who is this "We"? Levels of collective identity and self representations. *Journal of Personality and Social Psychology, 71,* 83–93.

Brewer, M. B., & Kramer, R. M. (1986). Choice behavior in social dilemmas: Effects of social identity, group size, and decision framing. *Journal of Personality and Social Psychology, 50,* 543–549.

Brewer, M. B., Manzi, J. M., & Shaw, J. S. (1993). In-group identification as a function of depersonalization, distinctiveness, and status. *Psychological Science, 4,* 88–92.

Brewer, M. B., & Miller, N. (1984). Beyond the contact hypothesis: Theoretical perspectives on desegregation. In N. Miller & M. Brewer (Eds.), *Groups in contact: The psychology of desegregation* (pp. 281–302). New York: Academic Press.

Brewer, M. B., & Weber, J. G. (1994). Self-evaluation effects of interpersonal versus intergroup social comparison. *Journal of Personality and Social Psychology, 66,* 268–275.

Brickner, M. A., Harkins, S. G., & Ostrom, T. M. (1986). Effects of personal involvement: Thought-provoking implications for social loafing. *Journal of Personality and Social Psychology, 51,* 763–770.

Brief, A. P., Buttram, R. T., Elliott, J. D., Reizenstein, R. M., & McCline, R. L. (1995). Releasing the beast: A study of compliance with orders to use race as a selection criterion. *Journal of Social Issues, 51(3),* 177–193.

Brief, A. P., Schuler, R. S., & Van Sell, M. (1981). *Managing job stress.* Boston: Little, Brown.

Brinthaupt, T. M., Moreland, R. L., & Levine, J. M. (1991). Sources of optimism among prospective group members. *Personality and Social Psychology Bulletin, 17,* 36–43.

Brockner, J. (1995). How to stop throwing good money after bad: Using theory to guide practice. In D. A. Schroeder (Ed.), *Social dilemmas: Perspectives on individuals and groups* (pp. 163–182). Westport, CT: Praeger.

Brockner, J., & Rubin, J. Z. (1985). *The social psychology of conflict escalation and entrapment.* New York: Springer-Verlag.

Brockner, J., & Wiesenfeld, B. M. (1996). An integrative framework for explaining reactions to decisions: Interactive effects of outcomes and procedures. *Psychological Bulletin, 120,* 189–208.

Bromley, D. G. (1985). Cult facts and fiction. *VCU Magazine, 14(2),* 10–15.

Brooks, G. R. (1996). Treatment for therapy-resistant men. In M. P. Andronico (Ed.), *Men in groups: Insights, interventions, and psychoeducational work* (pp. 7–19). Washington, DC: American Psychological Association.

Brown, B. B. (1987). Territoriality. In D. Stokols & I. Altman (Eds.), *Handbook of environmental psychology* (Vol. 1, pp. 505–531). New York: Wiley.

Brown, B. B., & Lohr, N. (1987). Peer group affiliation and adolescent self-esteem: An integration of ego-identity and symbolic-interaction theories. *Journal of Personality and Social Psychology, 52,* 47–55.

Brown, B. B., Mounts, N., Lamborn, S. D. & Steinberg, L. (1993). Parenting practices and peer group affiliation in adolescence. *Child Development, 64,* 467–482.

Brown, R. (1988). *Group processes: Dynamics within and between groups.* New York: Blackwell.

Brown, R. (Ed.). (1990). *The Marshall Cavendish encyclopedia of personal relationships: Human behavior, How groups work* (Vol. 15). Oxford: Cavendish.

Brown, R., Condor, S., Matthews, A., Wade, G., & Williams, J. A. (1986). Explaining intergroup differentiation in an industrial organization. *Journal of Occupational Psychology, 59,* 273–286.

Brown, R., Hinkle, S., Ely, P. G., Fox-Cardamone, L., Maras, P., & Taylor, L. A. (1992). Recognizing group diversity: Individualist-collectivist and autonomous-relational social orientations and their implications for intergroup processes. *British Journal of Social Psychology, 31,* 327–342.

Brown, R. W. (1954). Mass phenomena. In G. Lindzey (Ed.), *Handbook of social psychology*

(Vol. 2, pp. 833–876). Cambridge, MA: Addison-Wesley.

Brown, S. M. (1979). Male versus female leaders: A comparison of empirical studies. *Sex Roles, 5,* 595–611.

Brown, S. P. (1996). A meta-analysis and review of organizational research on job involvement. *Psychological Bulletin, 120,* 235–255.

Brown, V., & Paulus, P. B. (1996). A simple dynamic model of social factors in group brainstorming. *Small Group Research, 27,* 91–114.

Browning, L. (1978). A grounded organizational communication theory derived from qualitative data. *Communication Monographs, 45,* 93–109.

Buckley, W. (1967). *Sociology and modern systems theory.* Englewood Cliffs, NJ: Prentice Hall.

Budman, S. H., Demby, A., Feldstein, M., & Gold, M. (1984). The effects of time-limited group psychotherapy: A controlled study. *International Journal of Group Psychotherapy, 34,* 587–603.

Budman, S. H., Soldz, S., Demby, A., Davis, M., & Merry, J. (1993). What is cohesiveness? An empirical investigation. *Small Group Research, 24,* 199–216.

Buehler, R., & Griffin, D. (1994). Change-of-meaning effects in conformity and dissent: Observing construal processes over time. *Journal of Personality and Social Psychology, 67,* 984–996.

Bulman, R. J., & Wortman, C. B. (1977). Attributions of blame and coping in the "real world": Severe accident victims react to their lot. *Journal of Personality and Social Psychology, 35,* 351–363.

Burgoon, J. K. (1983). Nonverbal violations of expectations. In J. M. Wiemann & R. P. Harrison (Eds.), *Sage annual reviews of communication: Nonverbal interaction* (Vol. 11). Newbury Park, CA: Sage.

Burke, M. J., & Day, R. R. (1986). A cumulative study of the effectiveness of managerial training. *Journal of Applied Psychology, 71,* 232–245.

Burke, P. J. (1967). The development of task and social-emotional role differentiation. *Sociometry, 30,* 379–392.

Burke, P. J. (1974). Participation and leadership in small groups. *American Sociological Review, 39,* 832–842.

Burlingame, G. M., Kircher, J. C., & Taylor, S. (1994). Methodological considerations in group psychotherapy research: Past, present, and future practices. In A. Fuhriman & G. M. Burlingame (Eds.), *Handbook of group psychotherapy: An empirical*

and clinical synthesis. (pp. 41–82). New York: Wiley.

Burney, C. (1961). *Solitary confinement* (2nd ed.). New York, St. Martin's Press.

Burns, J. M. (1978). *Leadership.* New York: Harper.

Burns, M. O., & Seligman, M. E. P. (1991). Explanatory style, helplessness, and depression. In C. R. Snyder and D. R. Forsyth (Eds.), *Handbook of social and clinical psychology: The health perspective* (pp. 267–284). New York: Pergamon.

Burnstein, E., & Vinokur, A. (1973). Testing two classes of theories about group-induced shifts in individual choice. *Journal of Experimental Social Psychology, 9,* 123–137.

Burnstein, E., & Vinokur, A. (1975). What a person thinks upon learning he has chosen differently from others: Nice evidence for the persuasive-arguments explanation of choice shifts. *Journal of Experimental Social Psychology, 11,* 412–426.

Burnstein, E., & Vinokur, A. (1977). Persuasive arguments and social comparison as determinants of attitude polarization. *Journal of Experimental Social Psychology, 13,* 315–332.

Burnstein, E., & Worchel, P. (1962). Arbitrariness of frustration and its consequences for aggression in a social situation. *Journal of Personality, 30,* 528–540.

Burwitz, L., & Newell, K. M. (1972). The effects of the mere presence of coactors on learning a motor skill. *Journal of Motor Behavior, 4,* 99–102.

Buss, A. H. (1983). Social rewards and personality. *Journal of Personality and Social Psychology, 44,* 553–563.

Buss, D. M. (1996). The evolutionary psychology of human social strategies. In E. T. Higgins & A. W. Kruglanski (Eds.), *Social psychology: Handbook of basic principles* (pp. 3–38). New York: Guilford Press.

Buss, D. M., Gomes, M., Higgins, D. S., & Lauterbach, K. (1987). Tactics of manipulation. *Journal of Personality and Social Psychology, 52,* 1219–1229.

Buss, D. M., & Kenrick, D. T. (1998). Evolutionary social psychology. In D. T. Gilbert, S. T. Fiske, & G. Lindzey (Eds.), *The handbook of social psychology* (4th ed., Vol. 2, pp. 982–1026). Boston, MA: McGraw-Hill.

Buss, D. M., & Schmitt, D. P. (1993). Sexual strategies theory: An evolutionary perspective on human mating. *Psychological Bulletin, 100,* 204–232.

Butler, D., & Geis, F. L. (1990). Nonverbal affect responses to male and female leaders: Implications for leadership evaluations. *Journal of Personality and Social Psychology, 58,* 48–59.

Butler, T., & Fuhriman, A. (1983a). Curative factors in group therapy: A review of the recent literature. *Small Group Behavior, 14,* 131–142.

Butler, T., & Fuhriman, A. (1983b). Level of functioning and length of time in treatment variables influencing patients' therapeutic experience in group psychotherapy. *International Journal of Group Psychotherapy, 33,* 489–505.

Buunk, B. P. (1995). Comparison direction and comparison dimension among disabled individuals: Toward a refined conceptualization of social comparison under stress. *Personality and Social Psychology Bulletin, 21,* 316–330.

Buunk, B. P., & Hoorens, V. (1992). Social support and stress: The role of social comparison and social exchange processes. *British Journal of Clinical Psychology, 31,* 445–457.

Byrne, D. (1961). Anxiety and the experimental arousal of affiliation need. *Journal of Abnormal and Social Psychology, 63,* 660–662.

Byrne, D. (1971). *The attraction paradigm.* New York: Academic Press.

Byrne, D., Ervin, C. F., & Lamberth, J. (1970). Continuity between the experimental study of attraction and real-life computer dating. *Journal of Personality and Social Psychology, 16,* 157–165.

Cacioppo, J. T., Rourke, P. A., Marshall-Goodall, B. S., Tassinary, L. G., & Baron, R. S. (1990). Rudimentary physiological effects of mere observation. *Psychophysiology, 27,* 177–186.

Cahill, S., Fine, G. A., & Grant, L. (1995). Dimensions of qualitative research. In K. S. Cook, G. A. Fine, & House, J. S. (Eds.), *Sociological perspectives on social psychology* (pp. 605–628). Boston: Allyn & Bacon.

Caldwell, D. F., & Burger, J. M. (1997). Personality and social influence strategies in the workplace. *Personality and Social Psychology Bulletin, 23,* 1003–1012.

Callaway, M. R., & Esser, J. K. (1984). Groupthink: Effects of cohesiveness and problem-solving procedures on group decision making. *Social Behavior and Personality, 12,* 157–164.

Callaway, M. R., Marriott, R. G., & Esser, J. K. (1985). Effects of dominance on group decision making: Toward a stress-reduction explanation of groupthink. *Journal of Personality and Social Psychology, 49,* 949–952.

Callero, P. L. (1994). From role-playing to role-using: Understanding role as resource. Special issue: Conceptualizing structure in social psychology. *Social Psychology Quarterly, 57,* 228–243.

Camacho, L. M., & Paulus, P. B. (1995). The role of social anxiousness in group brainstorming. *Journal of Personality and Social Psychology, 68,* 1071–1080.

Cameron, W. B. (1966). *Modern social movements: A sociological outline.* New York: Random House.

Campbell, D. T. (1958a). Common fate, similarity, and other indices of the status of aggregates of persons as social entities. *Behavioral Science, 3,* 14–25.

Campbell, D. T. (1958b). Systematic error on the part of human links in communication systems. *Information and Control, 1,* 334–369.

Campbell, D. T. (1965). Ethnocentric and other altruistic motives. In D. Levine (Ed.), *Nebraska symposium on motivation* (Vol. 13). Lincoln: University of Nebraska Press.

Campbell, J. D., Tesser, A., & Fairey, P. J. (1986). Conformity and attention to the stimulus: Some temporal and contextual dynamics. *Journal of Personality and Social Psychology, 51,* 315–324.

Canary, D. J., Cody, M. J., & Marston, P. J. (1986). Goal types, compliance-gaining, and locus of control. *Journal of Language and Social Psychology, 5,* 249–269.

Canetti, E. (1962). *Crowds and power.* London: Gollancz.

Cannavale, F. J., Scarr, H. A., & Pepitone, A. (1970). Deindividuation in the small group: Further evidence. *Journal of Personality and Social Psychology, 16,* 141–147.

Cannella, A. A., & Rowe, W. G. (1995). Leader capabilities, succession, and competitive context: A study of professional baseball teams. *Leadership Quarterly, 6,* 69–88.

Cannon-Bowers, J. A., Tannenbaum, S. I., Salas, E., & Volpe, C. E. (1995). Defining team competencies and establishing team training requirements. In R. Guzzo, E. Salas, & Associates, *Team effectiveness and decision making in organizations* (pp. 333–380). San Francisco: Jossey-Bass.

Cantril, H. (1940). *The invasion from Mars.* Princeton: Princeton University Press.

Caplan, N. (1970). The new ghetto man: A review of recent empirical studies. *Journal of Social Issues, 26(1),* 59–73.

Caplan, R. D., Vinokur, A. D., Price, R. H., & Van Ryn, M. (1989). Job seeking, reemployment, and mental health: A randomized field experiment in coping with job loss. *Journal of Applied Psychology, 74,* 759–769.

Caporael, L. R., & Brewer, M. B. (1991). The quest for human nature: Social and scientific issues in evolutionary psychology. *Journal of Social Issues, 47(3),* 1–10.

Caporael, L. R., & Brewer, M. B. (1995). Hierarchical evolutionary theory: There is an alternative, and it's not creationism. *Psychological Inquiry, 6,* 31–34.

Cappella, J. N. (1985). Controlling the floor in conversation. In A. W. Siegman & S. Feldstein (Eds.), *Multichannel integrations of nonverbal behavior* (pp. 69–103). Hillsdale, NJ: Erlbaum.

Carew, D. K., Parisi-Carew, E., & Blanchard, K. H. (1986). Group development and situational leadership: A model for managing groups. *Training and Development Journal, 40(6),* 46–50.

Carli, L. L. (1989). Gender differences in interaction style and influence. *Journal of Personality and Social Psychology, 56,* 565–576.

Carlopio, J. R. (1996). Construct validity of a physical work environment satisfaction questionnaire. *Journal of Occupational Health Psychology, 1,* 330–344.

Carlyle, T. (1841). *On heroes, hero-worship, and the heroic.* London: Fraser.

Carment, D. W. (1970). Rate of simple motor responding as a function of coaction, competition, and sex of the participants. *Psychonomic Science, 19,* 340–341.

Carneiro, R. L. (1970). A theory of the origin of the state. *Science, 169,* 239–249.

Carnevale, P. J. D. (1986a). Mediating disputes and decisions in organizations. *Research on Negotiation in Organizations, 1,* 251–269.

Carnevale, P. J. D. (1986b). Strategic choice in mediation. *Negotiation Journal, 2,* 41–56.

Carnevale, P. J., & Pruitt, D. G. (1992). Negotiation and mediation. *Annual Review of Psychology, 43,* 531–582.

Carpenter, C. R. (1958). Territoriality: A review of concepts and problems. In A. Roe & G. G. Simpson (Eds.), *Behavior and evolution.* New Haven: Yale University Press.

Carrere, S., & Evans, G. W. (1994). Life in an isolated and confined environment: A qualitative study of the role of the designed environment. *Environment and Behavior, 26,* 707–741.

Carroll, J. W. (1987). Indefinite terminating points and the iterated Prisoner's Dilemma. *Theory and Decision, 22,* 247–256.

Carron, A. V. (1980). *Social psychology of sport.* Ithaca, NY: Mouvement Publications.

Carron, A. V. (1982). Cohesiveness in sports groups: Interpretations and considerations. *Journal of Sport Psychology, 4,* 123–128.

Carron, A. V., Widmeyer, W. N., & Brawley, L. R. (1988). Group cohesion and individual adherence to physical activity. *Journal of Sport and Exercise Psychology, 10,* 127–138.

Carson, R. C. (1969). *Interaction concepts of personality.* Chicago: Aldine.

Cartwright, D. (1951). Achieving change in people: Some applications of group dynamics theory. *Human Relations, 4,* 381–392.

Cartwright, D. (1959). A field theoretical conception of power. In D. Cartwright (Ed.), *Studies in social power.* Ann Arbor, MI: Institute for Social Research.

Cartwright, D. (1968). The nature of group cohesiveness. In D. Cartwright & A. Zander (Eds.), *Group dynamics: Research and theory* (3rd ed., pp. 91–109). New York: Harper & Row.

Cartwright, D. (1978). Theory and practice. *Journal of Social Issues, 34(4),* 168–175.

Cartwright, D., & Harary, F. (1956). Structural balance: A generalization of Heider's theory. *Psychological Review, 63,* 277–293.

Cartwright, D., & Harary, F. (1970). Ambivalence and indifference in generalizations of structural balance. *Behavioral Science, 14,* 497–513.

Cartwright, D., & Zander, A. (Eds.). (1968). *Group dynamics: Research and theory* (3rd ed.). New York: Harper & Row.

Carvalho, E. R., & Brito, V. C. A. (1995). Sociometric intervention in family therapy: A case study. *Journal of Group Psychotherapy, Psychodrama and Sociometry, 47,* 147–164.

Carver, C. S. (1975). Physical aggression as a function of objective self-awareness and attitudes toward punishment. *Journal of Experimental Social Psychology, 11,* 510–519.

Carver, C. S., & Scheier, M. F. (1981). Attention and self-regulation: A control-theory approach to human behavior. New York: Springer-Verlag.

Carver, C. S., & Scheier, M. F. (1983). Two sides of the self: One for you and one for me. In J. Suls & A. G. Greenwald (Eds.), *Psychological perspectives on the self* (Vol. 2). Hillsdale, NJ: Erlbaum.

Carver, C. S., & Scheier, M. F. (1984). Self-focused attention in test anxiety: A general theory applied to a specific phenomenon. In H. van der Ploeg, R. Schwarzer, & C. D. Spielberger (Eds.), *Advances in test anxiety research* (Vol. 3). Hillsdale, NJ: Erlbaum.

Cascio, W. F. (1995). Whither industrial and organizational psychology in a changing world of work? *American Psychologist, 50,* 928–939.

Castore, C. H., & Murnighan, J. K. (1978). Determinants of support for group decisions. *Organizational Behavior and Human Performance, 22,* 75–92.

Cattell, R. B. (1948). Concepts and methods in the measurement of group syntality. *Psychological Review, 55,* 48–63.

Cavalli, L. (1986). Charismatic domination, totalitarian dictatorship, and plebiscitary democracy in the twentieth century. In C. F. Graumann & S. Moscovici (Eds.), *Changing conceptions of leadership* (pp. 67–81). New York: Springer-Verlag.

Chapman, A. J. (1973). Funniness of jokes, canned laughter, and recall performance. *Sociometry, 36,* 569–578.

Chassin, L., & Stager, S. F. (1984). Determinants of self-esteem among incarcerated delinquents. *Social Psychology Quarterly, 47,* 382–390.

Cheek, J. M. (1989). Identity orientations and self-interpretation. In D. M. Buss & N. Cantor (Eds.), *Personality psychology* (pp. 275–285). New York: Springer-Verlag.

Cheek, J. M., & Buss, A. H. (1981). Shyness and sociability. *Journal of Personality and Social Psychology, 41,* 330–339.

Chemers, M. M. (1969). Cross-cultural training as a means of improving situational favorableness. *Human Relations, 22,* 531–546.

Chemers, M. M. (1983). Leadership theory and research: A systems-process integration. In P. B. Paulus (Ed.), *Basic group processes* (pp. 9–39). New York: Springer-Verlag.

Chemers, M. M. (1987). Leadership processes: Intrapersonal, interpersonal, and societal influences. *Review of Personality and Social Psychology, 8,* 252–277.

Chemers, M. M., Hays, R. B., Rhodewalt, F., & Wysocki, J. (1985). A person-environment analysis of job stress: A contingency model explanation. *Journal of Personality and Social Psychology, 49,* 628–635.

Chemers, M. M., & Skrzypek, G. J. (1972). Experimental test of the contingency model of leadership effectiveness. *Journal of Personality and Social Psychology, 24,* 173–177.

Chen, S., Shechter, D., & Chaiken, S. (1996). Getting at the truth or getting along: Accuracy- versus impression-motivated heuristic and systematic processing. *Journal of Personality and Social Psychology, 71,* 262–275.

Chen, Z., Lawson, R. B., Gordon, L. R., & McIntosh, B. (1996). Groupthink: Deciding with the leader and the devil. *Psychological Record, 46,* 581–590.

Cheng, J. L. (1983). Organizational context and upward influence: An experimental study of the use of power tactics. *Group and Organization Studies, 8,* 337–355.

Cheng, S. (1997). Epidemic genital retraction syndrome: Environmental and personal risk factors in southern China. *Journal of Psychology and Human Sexuality, 9,* 57–70.

Chertkoff, J. M., Kushigian, R. H., & McCool, M. A., Jr. (1996). Interdependent exiting: The effects of group size, time limit, and gender on the coordination of exiting. *Journal of Environmental Psychology, 16,* 109–121.

Cherulnik, P., & Wilderman, S. (1986). Symbols of status in urban neighborhoods. *Environment and Behavior, 18,* 604–622.

Cheyne, J. A., & Efran, M. G. (1972). The effect of spatial and interpersonal variables on the invasion of group controlled territories. *Sociometry, 35,* 477–487.

Childers, T. L., Dubinsky, A. J., & Gencturk, E. (1986). On the psychometric properties of a scale to measure leadership substitutes. *Psychological Reports, 59,* 1215–1226.

Chiu, C., Hong, Y., & Dweck, C. S. (1997). Lay dispositionism and implicit theories of personality. *Journal of Personality and Social Psychology, 73,* 19–30.

Christensen, A., & Jacobson, N. S. (1994). Who (or what) can do psychotherapy: The status and challenge of nonprofessional therapies. *Psychological Science, 5,* 8–12.

Christensen, P. N., & Kashy, D. A. (1998). Perceptions of and by lonely people in initial social interaction. *Personality and Social Psychology Bulletin, 24,* 322–329.

Cialdini, R. B. (1993). *Influence: Science and practice* (3rd ed.). New York: HarperCollins.

Cialdini, R. B., Borden, R., Thorne, A., Walker, M., Freeman, S., & Sloane, L. R. (1976). Basking in reflected glory: Three (football) field studies.

Journal of Personality and Social Psychology, 34, 366–375.

Cialdini, R. B., Kallgren, C. A., & Reno, R. R. (1991). A focus theory of normative conduct: A theoretical refinement and reevaluation of the role of norms in human behavior. *Advances in Experimental Social Psychology, 24,* 201–234.

Cialdini, R. B., Reno, R. R., & Kallgren, C. A. (1990). A focus theory of normative conduct: Recycling the concept of norms to reduce littering in public places. *Journal of Personality and Social Psychology, 58,* 1015–1026.

Cianni, M., & Romberger, B. (1995). Interactions with senior managers: Perceived differences by race/ethnicity and by gender. *Sex Roles, 32,* 353–373.

Cini, M. A., Moreland, R. L., & Levine, J. M. (1993). Group staffing levels and responses to prospective and new group members. *Journal of Personality and Social Psychology, 65,* 723–734.

Clark, G. (1969, November). What happens when the police strike? *New York Times Magazine,* p. 45.

Clark, K. B. (1971). The pathos of power. *American Psychologist, 26,* 1047–1057.

Clark, N. K., & Stephenson, G. M. (1989). Group remembering. In P. Paulus (Ed.), *Psychology of group influence* (2nd ed., pp. 357–391). Hillsdale, NJ: Erlbaum.

Clark, N. K., Stephenson, G. M., & Kniveton, B. (1990). Social remembering: Quantitative aspects of individual and collaborative remembering by police officers and students. *British Journal of Psychology, 81,* 73–94.

Clark, R. D., III. (1971). Group-induced shift toward risk: A critical appraisal. *Psychological Bulletin, 76,* 251–270.

Clark, R. D., III. (1990). Minority influence: The role of argument refutation on the majority position and social support for the minority position. *European Journal of Social Psychology, 20,* 489–497.

Clark, R. D., III, & Sechrest, L. B. (1976). The mandate phenomenon. *Journal of Personality and Social Psychology, 34,* 1057–1061.

Clark, S. (1998). International competition and the treatment of minorities: Seventeenth-century cases and general propositions. *American Journal of Sociology, 103,* 1267–1308.

Clore, G. L., & Byrne, D. (1974). A reinforcement-affect model of attraction. In T. Huston (Ed.), *Foundations of interpersonal attraction.* New York: Academic Press.

Coch, L., & French, J. R. P., Jr. (1948). Overcoming resistance to change. *Human Relations, 1,* 512–532.

Cohen, D. J., Whitmyre, J. W., & Funk, W. H. (1960). Effect of group cohesiveness and training upon group thinking. *Journal of Applied Psychology, 44,* 319–322.

Cohen, E. G. (1982). Expectation states and interracial interaction in school settings. *Annual Review of Sociology, 8,* 209–235.

Cohen, J. L. (1979). Social facilitation: Increased evaluation apprehension through permanency of record. *Motivation and Emotion, 3,* 19–33.

Cohen, S. (1980). Aftereffects of stress on human performance and social behavior: A review of research and theory. *Psychological Bulletin, 88,* 82–108.

Cohen, S., Evans, G. W., Stokols, D., & Krantz, D. (1986). *Behavior, health, and environmental stress.* New York: Plenum.

Cohen, S., Glass, D. C., & Singer, J. E. (1973). Apartment noise, auditory discrimination, and reading ability in children. *Journal of Experimental Social Psychology, 9,* 407–422.

Cohen, S., & Weinstein, N. (1981). Nonauditory effects of noise on behavior and health. *Journal of Social Issues, 37(1),* 36–70.

Cohen, S., & Wills, T. A. (1985). Stress, social support, and the buffering hypothesis. *Psychological Bulletin, 98,* 310–357.

Coie, J. D., Dodge, K. A., & Kupersmidt, J. B. (1990). Peer group behavior and social status. In S. R. Asher & J. D. Coie (Eds.), *Peer rejection in childhood* (pp. 17–59). New York: Cambridge University Press.

Colligan, M. J., & Murphy, L. R. (1982). A review of mass psychogenic illness in work settings. In M. J. Colligan, J. W. Pennebaker, & L. R. Murphy (Eds.), *Mass psychogenic illness: A social psychological analysis* (pp. 33–52). Hillsdale, NJ: Erlbaum.

Colligan, M. J., Pennebaker, J. W., & Murphy, L. R. (Eds.). (1982). *Mass psychogenic illness: A social psychological analysis.* Hillsdale, NJ: Erlbaum.

Collins, B. E., & Guetzkow, H. (1964). *A social psychology of group processes for decision-making.* New York: Wiley.

Collins, R. L. (1996). For better or worse: The impact of upward social comparison on self-evaluations. *Psychological Bulletin, 119,* 51–69.

Colman, A. M. (1991). Crowd psychology in South African murder trials. *American Psychologist, 46,* 1071–1079.

Conger, J. A., & Kanungo, R. N. (1987). Toward a behavioral theory of charismatic leadership in organizational settings. *Academy of Management Review, 12,* 637–647.

Cook, M. (1977). The social skill model and interpersonal attraction. In S. Duck (Ed.), *Theory and practice in interpersonal attraction.* New York: Academic Press.

Cook, S. W. (1978). Interpersonal and attitudinal outcomes in cooperating interracial groups. *Journal of Research and Development in Education, 12,* 97–113.

Cook, S. W. (1984). The 1954 social science statement and school desegregation: A reply to Gerard. *American Psychologist, 39,* 819–832.

Cook, S. W. (1985). Experimenting on social issues: the case of school desegregation. *American Psychologist, 40,* 452–460.

Cooley, C. H. (1902). *Human nature and the social order.* New York: Scribners.

Cooley, C. H. (1909). *Social organization.* New York: Scribner.

Cooley, E. (1994). Training an interdisciplinary team in communication and decision-making skills. *Small Group Research, 25,* 5–25.

Coon, C. S. (1946). The universality of natural groupings in human societies. *Journal of Educational Sociology, 20,* 163–168.

Cooper, C. L. (1981). Social support at work and stress management. *Small Group Behavior, 12,* 285–297.

Cooper, H. M. (1979). Statistically combining independent studies: A meta-analysis of sex differences in conformity research. *Journal of Personality and Social Psychology, 37,* 131–146.

Cooper, V. W. (1997). Homophily or the Queen Bee Syndrome: Female evaluation of female leadership. *Small Group Research, 28,* 483–499.

Corey, M., & Corey, G. (1992). *Groups: Process and practice* (4th ed.). Pacific Grove, CA: Brooks/Cole.

Corsaro, W. A., & Eder, D. (1995). Development and socialization of children and adolescents. In K. S. Cook, G. A. Fine, & J. S. House (Eds.), *Sociological perspectives on social psychology* (pp. 421–451). Needham Heights, MA: Allyn & Bacon.

Coser, L. A. (1956). *The functions of social conflict.* Glencoe, IL: The Free Press.

Costanzo, P. R. (1970). Conformity development as a function of self-blame. *Journal of Personality and Social Psychology, 14,* 366–374.

Cota, A. A., Dion, K. L., & Evans, C. R. (1993). A reexamination of the structure of the Gross Cohesiveness Scale. *Educational and Psychological Measurement, 53,* 499–506.

Cota, A. A., Evans, C. R., Dion, K. L., Kilik, L., & Longman, R. S. (1995). The structure of group cohesion. *Personality and Social Psychology Bulletin, 21,* 572–580.

Cotton, J. L. (1993). *Employee involvement.* Newbury Park, CA: Sage.

Cotton, J. L., & Cook, M. S. (1982). Meta-analyses and the effects of various reward systems: Some different conclusions from Johnson et al. *Psychological Bulletin, 92,* 176–183.

Cottrell, N. B. (1972). Social facilitation. In C. G. McClintock (Ed.), *Experimental social psychology* (pp. 185–236). New York: Holt, Rinehart & Winston.

Cottrell, N. B., Wack, D. L., Sekerak, G. J., & Rittle, R. H. (1968). Social facilitation of dominant responses by the presence of an audience and the mere presence of others. *Journal of Personality and Social Psychology, 9,* 245–250.

Courneya, K. S., & Carron, A. V. (1991). Effects of travel and length of home stand/road trip on the home advantage. *Journal of Sport and Exercise Psychology, 13,* 42–49.

Courtright, J. A. (1978). A laboratory investigation of groupthink. *Communication Monographs, 43,* 229–246.

Cousins, S. D. (1989). Culture and self-perception in Japan and the United States. *Journal of Personality and Social Psychology, 56,* 124–131.

Cowan, G., Drinkard, J., & MacGavin, L. (1984). The effects of target, age, and gender on use of power strategies. *Journal of Personality and Social Psychology, 47,* 1391–1398.

Coyne, J. C., & Downey, G. (1991). Social factors and psychopathology: Stress, social support, and coping processes. *Annual Review of Psychology, 42,* 401–425.

Crago, M., Yates, A., Beutler, L. E., & Arizmendi, T. G. (1985). Height-weight ratios among female athletes: Are collegiate athletics the precursors to an anorexic syndrome? *International Journal of Eating Disorders, 4,* 79–87.

Crandall, C. S. (1988). Social contagion of binge eating. *Journal of Personality and Social Psychology, 55,* 588–598.

Crano, W. D. (1994). Context, comparison, and change: Methodological and theoretical contributions to a theory of minority (and majority) influence. In S. Moscovici, A. Mucchi-Faina, & Anne

Maass (Eds.), *Minority influence* (pp. 17–46). Chicago: Nelson-Hall.

Cratty, B. J. (1981). *Social psychology in athletics.* Englewood Cliffs, NJ: Prentice Hall.

Crawley, J. (1994). *Constructive conflict management: Managing to make a difference.* San Diego: Pfeiffer.

Cribbin, J. J. (1972). *Effective managerial leadership.* New York: American Management Association.

Crocker, J., Blaine, B., & Luhtanen, R. (1993). Self-esteem: Cognitive and motivational consequences for prejudice and intergroup behavior. In M. A. Hogg & D. Abrams (Eds.), *Group motivation: social psychological perspectives* (pp. 52–67). London: Harvester Wheatsheaf.

Crocker, J., & Luhtanen, R. (1990). Collective self-esteem and ingroup bias. *Journal of Personality and Social Psychology, 58,* 60–67.

Crocker, J., Luhtanen, R., Blaine, B., & Broadnax S. (1994). Collective self-esteem and psychological well-being among White, Black, and Asian college students. *Personality and Social Psychology Bulletin, 20,* 503–513.

Crocker, J., & Major, B. (1989). Social stigma and self-esteem: The self-protective properties of stigma. *Psychological Review, 96,* 608–630.

Crocker, J., & McGraw, K. M. (1984). What's good for the goose is not good for the gander: Solo status as an obstacle to occupational achievement for males and females. *American Behavioral Scientist, 27,* 357–369.

Crocker, O. L., Chiu, J. S. L., & Charney, C. (1984). *Quality circles.* Ontario, Canada: Methuen.

Cronshaw, S. F., & Lord, R. G. (1987). Effects of categorization, attribution, and encoding processes on leadership perceptions. *Journal of Applied Psychology, 72,* 97–106.

Crosbie, P. V. (1979). Effects of status inconsistency: Negative evidence from small groups. *Social Psychology Quarterly, 42,* 110–125.

Crosby, F. (1976). A model of egoistical relative deprivation. *Psychological Review, 83,* 85–113.

Cross, S. E., & Madson, L. (1997). Models of the self: Self-construals and gender. *Psychological Bulletin, 122,* 5–37.

Crouch, E. C., Bloch, S., & Wanlass, J. (1994). Therapeutic factors: Interpersonal and intrapersonal mechanisms. In A. Fuhriman & G. M. Burlingame (Eds.), *Handbook of group psychotherapy: An empirical and clinical synthesis* (pp. 269–315). New York: Wiley.

Crow, W. J. (1963). A study of strategic doctrines using the Inter-Nation Simulation. *Journal of Conflict Resolution, 7,* 580–589.

Crutchfield, R. S. (1955). Conformity and character. *American Psychologist, 10,* 191–198.

Csoka, L. S., & Bons, P. M. (1978). Manipulating the situation to fit the leader's style? Two validation studies of Leader Match. *Journal of Applied Psychology, 63,* 295–300.

Cummings, L. L., Harnett, D. L., & Stevens, O. J. (1971). Risk, fate, conciliation and trust: An international study of attitudinal differences among executives. *Academy of Management Journal, 14,* 285–304.

Cunningham, J. D., Starr, P. A., & Kanouse, D. E. (1979). Self as actor, active observer, and passive observer: Implications for causal attributions. *Journal of Personality and Social Psychology, 37,* 1146–1152.

Curran, J. P. (1977). Skills training as an approach to the treatment of heterosexual-social anxiety: A review. *Psychological Bulletin, 84,* 140–157.

Curry, T. J., & Emerson, R. M. (1970). Balance theory: A theory of interpersonal attraction? *Sociometry, 33,* 216–238.

Dahrendorf, R. (1958). Toward a theory of social conflict. *Journal of Conflict Resolution, 2,* 170–183.

Dahrendorf, R. (1959). *Class and class conflict in industrial society.* Palo Alto, CA: Stanford University Press.

Dale, R. (1952). *Planning and developing the company organization structure.* New York: American Management Association.

Damhorst, M. L. (1990). In search of a common thread: Classification of information communicated through dress. *Clothing and Textiles Research Journal, 8(2),* 1–12.

Dane, F. C., & Wrightsman, L. S. (1982). Effects of defendants' and victims' characteristics on jurors' verdicts. In N. L. Kerr & R. M. Bray (Eds.), *Psychology of the courtroom* (pp. 83–115). New York: Academic Press.

Dansereau, F., Graen, G. C., & Haga, W. (1975). A vertical dyad linkage approach to leadership in formal organizations. *Organizational Behavior and Human Performance, 13,* 46–78.

Dansereau, F., Yammarino, F. J., & Markham, S. E. (1995). Leadership: The multiple-level approaches. *Leadership Quarterly, 6,* 251–263.

Darley, J. (1992). Social organization for the production of evil. *Psychological Inquiry, 3,* 199–218.

Darley, J. M. (1995). Constructive and destructive obedience: A taxonomy of principal-agent relationships. *Journal of Social Issues, 51(3)*, 125–154.

Darley, J. M., & Gilbert, D. T. (1985). Social psychological aspects of environmental psychology. In G. Lindzey & E. Aronson (Eds.), *Handbook of social psychology* (3rd ed., Vol. 2, pp. 949–991). New York: Random House.

Dashiell, J. F. (1930). An experimental analysis of some group effects. *Journal of Abnormal and Social Psychology, 25*, 190–199.

Davis, J. H. (1969). *Group performance.* Reading, MA: Addison-Wesley.

Davis, J. H. (1973). Group decision and social interaction: A theory of social decision schemes. *Psychological Review, 80*, 97–125.

Davis, J. H. (1982). Social interaction as a combinatorial process in group decision. In H. Brandstätter, J. H. Davis, & G. Stocker–Kreichgauer (Eds.), *Group decision making* (pp. 27–58). London: Academic Press.

Davis, J. H. (1996). Group decision making and quantitative judgments: A consensus model. In E. H. Witte & J. H. Davis (Eds.), *Understanding group behavior: Consensual action by small groups* (Vol. 1, pp. 35–60). Hillsdale, NJ: Erlbaum.

Davis, J. H., Bray, R. M., & Holt, R. W. (1977). The empirical study of decision processes in juries: A critical review. In J. L. Tapp & F. J. Levine (Eds.), *Law, justice, and the individual in society.* New York: Holt, Rinehart & Winston.

Davis, J. H., Kameda, T., Parks, C., Stasson, M., & Zimmerman, S. (1989). Some social mechanics of group decision making: The distribution of opinion, polling sequence, and implications for consensus. *Journal of Personality and Social Psychology, 57*, 1000–1012.

Davis, J. H., Kameda, T., & Stasson, M. (1992). Group risk taking: Selected topics. In J. F. Yates (Ed.), *Risk-taking behavior* (pp. 63–199). Chichester: Wiley.

Davis, J. H., Kerr, N. L., Atkin, R. S., Holt, R., & Meek, D. (1975). The decision processes of 6- and 12-person juries assigned unanimous and ²⁄₃ majority rules. *Journal of Personality and Social Psychology, 32*, 1–14.

Davis, J. H., Kerr, N. L., Stasser, G., Meek, D., & Holt, R. (1977). Victim consequences, sentence severity, and decision processes in mock juries.

Organizational Behavior and Human Performance, 18, 346–365.

Davis, J. H., Stasson, M., Ono, K., & Zimmerman, S. (1988). Effects of straw polls on group decision making: Sequential voting pattern, timing, and local majorities. *Journal of Personality and Social Psychology, 55*, 918–926.

Davis, J. R. (1982). *Street gangs: Youth, biker, and prison groups.* Dubuque, IA: Kendall/Hunt.

Dawes, R. M., & Smith, T. L. (1985). Attitude and opinion measurement. In G. Lindzey & E. Aronson (Eds.), *Handbook of social psychology* (3rd ed., Vol. 1, pp. 509–566). New York: Random House.

Day, M. (1981). Psychoanalytic group therapy in clinic and private practice. *American Journal of Psychiatry, 138*, 64–69.

De Dreu, C. K. W., & De Vries, N. K. (1996). Differential processing and attitude change following majority versus minority arguments. *British Journal of Social Psychology, 35*, 77–90.

De Meuse, K. P., & Liebowitz, S. J. (1981). An empirical analysis of team-building research. *Group and Organizational Studies, 6*, 357–378.

Dean, L. M., Willis, F. N., & Hewitt, J. (1975). Initial interaction distance among individuals equal and unequal in military rank. *Journal of Personality and Social Psychology, 32*, 294–299.

Deaux, K. (1996). Social identification. In E. T. Higgins & A. W. Kruglanski (Eds.), *Social psychology: Handbook of basic principles* (pp. 777–798). New York: Guilford Press.

Deaux, K., Reid, A., Mizrahi, K., Ethier, K. A. (1996). Parameters of social identity. *Journal of Personality and Social Psychology, 68*, 280–291.

Deci, E. L., Nezlek, J., & Sheinman, L. (1981). Characteristics of the rewarder and intrinsic motivation of the rewardee. *Journal of Personality and Social Psychology, 40*, 1–10.

Defoe, D. (1908). The life and strange surprising adventures of Robinson Crusoe, of York, mariner, as related by himself. Philadelphia: Altemus.

DeLamater, J. A. (1974). A definition of "group." *Small Group Behavior, 5*, 30–44.

Delbecq, A. L., & Van de Ven, A. H. (1971). A group process model for problem identification and program planning. *Journal of Applied Behavioral Science, 7*, 466–492.

Delbecq, A. L., Van de Ven, A. H., & Gustafson, D. H. (1975). *Group techniques for program planning.* Glenview, IL: Scott, Foresman.

Deming, W. E. (1975). On some statistical aids towards economic production. *Interfaces, 5,* 1–15.

Dennis, A. R., & Valacich, J. S. (1993). Computer brainstorms: More heads are better than one. *Journal of Applied Psychology, 78,* 531–537.

Denvir, B. (1993). *The chronicle of impressionism.* New York: Little, Brown.

Deutsch, M. (1949a). An experimental study of the effects of cooperation and competition upon group process. *Human Relations, 2,* 199–231.

Deutsch, M. (1949b). A theory of cooperation and competition. *Human Relations, 2,* 129–152.

Deutsch, M. (1969). Socially relevant science: Reflections on some studies of interpersonal conflict. *American Psychologist, 24,* 1076–1092.

Deutsch, M. (1973). *The resolution of conflict: Constructive and destructive processes.* New Haven, CT: Yale University Press.

Deutsch, M. (1975). Equity, equality, and need: What determines which value will be used as the basis of distributive justice? *Journal of Social Issues, 31(3),* 137–149.

Deutsch, M. (1980). Fifty years of conflict. In L. Festinger (Ed.), *Retrospections on social psychology* (pp. 46–77). New York: Oxford University Press.

Deutsch, M. (1985). *Distributive justice: A social psychological perspective.* New Haven, CT: Yale University Press.

Deutsch, M. (1994). Constructive conflict resolution: Principles, training, and research. *Journal of Social Issues, 50(1),* 13–32.

Deutsch, M., & Gerard, H. B. (1955). A study of normative and informational social influences upon individual judgment. *Journal of Abnormal and Social Psychology, 51,* 629–636.

Deutsch, M., & Krauss, R. M. (1960). The effect of threat upon interpersonal bargaining. *Journal of Abnormal and Social Psychology, 61,* 181–189.

Deutsch, M., & Lewicki, R. J. (1970). "Locking in" effects during a game of Chicken. *Journal of Conflict Resolution, 14,* 367–378.

Devine, P. G. (1989). Stereotypes and prejudice: Their automatic and controlled components. *Journal of Personality and Social Psychology, 56,* 5–18.

Devine, P. G. (1995). Prejudice and out-group perception. In A. Tesser (Ed.), *Advanced social psychology* (pp. 467–524). New York: McGraw-Hill.

Devine, P. G., Monteith, M. J., Zuwerink, J. R., & Elliot, A. J. (1991). Prejudice with and without compunction. *Journal of Personality and Social Psychology, 60,* 817–830.

Dewey, J. (1910). *How we think.* New York: Heath.

Di Salvo, V. S., Nikkel, E., & Monroe, C. (1989). Theory and practice: A field investigation and identification of group members' perceptions of problems facing natural work groups. *Small Group Behavior, 20,* 551–567.

Di Vesta, F. J. (1959). Effects of confidence and motivation on susceptibility to informational social influence. *Journal of Abnormal and Social Psychology, 59,* 204–209.

Diehl, M., & Stroebe, W. (1987). Productivity loss in brainstorming groups: Toward the solution of a riddle. *Journal of Personality and Social Psychology, 53,* 497–509.

Diehl, M., & Stroebe, W. (1991). Productivity loss in idea-generating groups: Tracking down the blocking effect. *Journal of Personality and Social Psychology, 61,* 392–403.

Diener, E. (1979). Deindividuation, self-awareness, and disinhibition. *Journal of Personality and Social Psychology, 37,* 1160–1171.

Diener, E. (1980). Deindividuation: The absence of self-awareness and self-regulation in group members. In P. B. Paulus (Ed.), *Psychology of group influence* (pp. 209–242). Hillsdale, NJ: Erlbaum.

Diener, E., Fraser, S. C., Beaman, A. L., & Kelem, R. T. (1976). Effects of deindividuating variables on stealing by Halloween trick-or-treaters. *Journal of Personality and Social Psychology, 33,* 178–183.

Dienesch, R. M., & Liden, R. C. (1986). Leader/member exchange model of leadership: A critique and further development. *Academy of Management Review, 11,* 618–634.

Dies, R. R. (1994). Therapist variables in group psychotherapy research. In A. Fuhriman & G. M. Burlingame (Eds.), *Handbook of group psychotherapy: An empirical and clinical synthesis* (pp. 114–154). New York: Wiley.

Digman, J. M. (1990). Personality structure: Emergence of the five-factor model. *Annual Review of Psychology, 41,* 417–440.

Dillard, J. P. (1991). The current status of research on sequential-request compliance techniques. *Personality and Social Psychology Bulletin, 17,* 283–288.

Dillard, J. P., & Fitzpatrick, M. A. (1985). Compliance-gaining in marital interaction. *Personality and Social Psychology Bulletin, 11,* 419–433.

Dion, K. L. (1973). Cohesiveness as a determinant of ingroup-outgroup bias. *Journal of Personality and Social Psychology, 28,* 163–171.

Dion, K. L. (1979). Intergroup conflict and intragroup cohesiveness. In W. G. Austin & S. Worchel (Eds.), *The social psychology of intergroup relations* (pp. 211–224). Pacific Grove, CA: Brooks/Cole.

Dion, K. L. (1990). Group morale. In R. Brown (Ed.), *The Marshall Cavendish encyclopedia of personal relationships: Human behavior, How groups work* (Vol. 15, pp. 1854–1861). Oxford: Cavendish.

Dion, K. L., & Evans, C. R. (1992). On cohesiveness: Reply to Keyton and other critics of the construct. *Small Group Research, 23,* 242–250.

Dipboye, R. L. (1977). Alternative approaches to deindividuation. *Psychological Bulletin, 84,* 1057–1075.

DiTommaso, E., & Spinner, B. (1997). Social and emotional loneliness: A re-examination of Weiss' typology of loneliness. *Personality and Individual Differences, 22,* 417–427.

Dittrich, J. E., & Carrell, M. R. (1979). Organization equity perceptions, employee job satisfaction, and departmental absence and turnover rates. *Organizational Behavior and Human Performance, 24,* 29–40.

Dobbins, G. H., & Platz, S. J. (1986). Sex differences in leadership: How real are they? *Academy of Management Review, 11,* 118–127.

Dobbins, G. H., Stuart, C., Pence, E. C., & Sgro, J. A. (1985). Cognitive mechanisms mediating the biasing effects of leader sex on ratings of leader behavior. *Sex Roles, 12,* 549–560.

Dodd, D. K. (1985). Robbers in the classroom: A deindividuation exercise. *Teaching of Psychology, 12,* 89–91.

Dodge, K. A., & Crick, N. R. (1990). Social information-processing bases of aggressive behavior in children. *Personality and Social Psychology Bulletin, 16,* 8–22.

Dodge, K. A., Gilroy, F. D., & Fenzel, L. M. (1995). Requisite management characteristics revisited: Two decades later. *Journal of Social Behavior and Personality, 10,* 253–264.

Doherty, W. J., Lester, M. E., & Leigh, G. K. (1986). Marriage encounter weekends: Couples who win and couples who lose. *Journal of Marital and Family Therapy, 12,* 49–61.

Doise, W. (1969). Intergroup relations and polarization of individual and collective judgments. *Journal of Personality and Social Psychology, 12,* 136–143.

Dollinger, S. J., Preston, L. A., O'Brien, S. P., & DiLalla, D. L. (1996). Individuality and relatedness of the self: An autophotographic study. *Journal of Personality and Social Psychology, 71,* 1268–1278.

Doms, M., & Van Avermaet, E. (1980). Majority influence, minority influence, and conversion behavior: A replication. *Journal of Experimental Social Psychology, 16,* 283–292.

Donnelly, P., Carron, A. V., Chelladurai, P. (1978). *Group cohesion and sport.* Ottawa: CAHPER.

Donnerstein, E., Donnerstein, M., Simon, S., & Ditrichs, R. (1972). Variables in interracial aggression: Anonymity, expected retaliation, and a riot. *Journal of Personality and Social Psychology, 22,* 236–245.

Doob, L. (1952). *Social psychology.* New York: Holt.

Dooley, D., & Catalano, R. (1984). The epidemiology of economic stress. *American Journal of Community Psychology, 12,* 387–409.

Doosje, B., Ellemers, N., & Spears, R. (1995). Perceived intragroup variability as a function of group status and identification. *Journal of Experimental Social Psychology, 31,* 410–436.

Doreian, P. (1986). Measuring relative standing in small groups and bounded social networks. *Social Psychology Quarterly, 49,* 247–259.

Dovidio, J. F., Brown, C. E., Heltman, K., Ellyson, S. L., & Keating, C. F. (1988). Power displays between women and men in discussions of gender-linked tasks: A multichannel study. *Journal of Personality and Social Psychology, 55,* 580–587.

Dovidio, J. F., & Gaertner, S. L. (1993). Stereotypes and evaluative intergroup bias. In D. M. Mackie & David L. Hamilton (Eds.), *Affect, cognition, and stereotyping: Interactive processes in group perception* (pp. 167–193). New York: Academic Press.

Dovidio, J. F., Gaertner, S. L., Isen, A. M., Rust, M., & Guerra, P. (1998). Positive affect, cognition, and the reduction of intergroup bias. In C. Sedikides, J. Schopler, & C. A. Insko (Eds.), *Intergroup cognition and intergroup behavior* (pp. 337–366). Mahwah, NJ: Erlbaum.

Driskell, J. E., & Mullen, B. (1990). Status, expectations, and behavior: A meta-analytic review and test of theory. *Personality and Social Psychology Bulletin, 16,* 541–553.

Driskell, J. E., & Salas, E. (1992). Can you study real teams in contrived settings? The value of small group research to understanding teams. In R. W. Swezey & E. Salas (Eds.), *Teams: Their training and performance* (pp. 101–124). Norwood, NJ: Ablex.

Druckman, D. (Ed.). (1977). *Negotiations.* Newbury Park, CA: Sage.

Druckman, D. (1987). New directions for a social psychology of conflict. In D. J. D. Sandole & I. Sandole-Staroste (Eds.), *Conflict management and problem solving: Interpersonal to international applications* (pp. 50–56). London: Frances Pinter.

Dryer, D. C., & Horowitz, L. M. (1997). When do opposites attract? Interpersonal complementarity versus similarity. *Journal of Personality and Social Psychology, 72,* 592–603.

Duchon, D., Green, S. G., & Taber, T. D. (1986). Vertical dyad linkage: A longitudinal assessment of antecedents, measures, and consequences. *Journal of Applied Psychology, 71,* 56–60.

Duckitt, J., & Mphuthing, T. (1998). Group identification and intergroup attitudes: A longitudinal analysis in South Africa. *Journal of Personality and Social Psychology, 74,* 80–85.

Dudley, B. S., Johnson, D. W., & Johnson, R. T. (1997). Using cooperative learning to enhance the academic and social experiences of freshman student athletes. *Journal of Social Psychology, 137,* 449–459.

Duncan, B. L. (1976). Differential social perception and attribution of intergroup violence: Testing the lower limits of stereotyping of blacks. *Journal of Personality and Social Psychology, 34,* 590–598.

Dunnette, M. D., Campbell, J., & Jaastad, K. (1963). The effect of group participation on brainstorming effectiveness for two industrial samples. *Journal of Applied Psychology, 47,* 30–37.

Dunning, E. G., Murphy, P. J., & Williams, J. M. (1986). Spectator violence at football matches: Towards a sociological explanation. *British Journal of Sociology, 37,* 221–244.

Durand, D. E. (1977). Power as a function of office space and physiognomy: Two studies of influence. *Psychological Reports, 40,* 755–760.

Durkheim, É. (1897/1966). *Suicide.* New York: The Free Press.

Duval, S., & Wicklund, R. A. (1972). *A theory of objective self-awareness.* New York: Academic Press.

Dyer, J. L. (1984). Team research and team training: A state-of-the-art review. In F. A. Muckler (Ed.), *Human factors review: 1984* (pp. 285–323). Santa Monica, CA: Human Factors Society.

Eagly, A. H. (1987). *Sex differences in social behavior: A social-role interpretation.* Hillsdale, NJ: Erlbaum.

Eagly, A. H., & Carli, L. L. (1981). Sex of researchers and sex-typed communications as determinants of sex differences in influenceability: A meta-analysis of social influence studies. *Psychological Bulletin, 90,* 1–20.

Eagly, A. H., & Johnson, B. T. (1990). Gender and leadership style: A meta-analysis. *Psychological Bulletin, 108,* 233–256.

Eagly, A. H., & Karau, S. J. (1991). Gender and the emergence of leaders: A meta-analysis. *Journal of Personality and Social Psychology, 60,* 685–710.

Eagly, A. H., Karau, S. J., & Makhijani, M. (1995). Gender and the effectiveness of leaders: A meta-analysis. *Journal of Personality and Social Psychology, 117,* 125–145.

Eagly, A. H., Makhijani, M. G., & Klonsky, B. G. (1992). Gender and the evaluation of leaders: A meta-analysis. *Psychological Bulletin, 111,* 3–22.

Eagly, A. H., & Wood, W. (1991). Explaining sex differences in social behavior: A meta-analytic perspective. *Personality and Social Psychology Bulletin, 17,* 306–315.

Eagly, A. H., Wood, W., & Fishbaugh, L. (1981). Sex differences in conformity: Surveillance by the group as a determinant of male nonconformity. *Journal of Personality and Social Psychology, 40,* 384–394.

Edman, I. (1919). *Human traits and their social significance.* New York: Houghton Mifflin.

Edney, J. J. (1976). Human territories: Comment on functional properties. *Environment and Behavior, 8,* 31–48.

Edney, J. J., & Bell, P. A. (1984). Sharing scarce resources: Group-outcome orientation, external disaster, and stealing in a simulated commons. *Small Group Behavior, 15,* 87–108.

Edney, J. J., & Grundmann, M. J. (1979). Friendship, group size, and boundary size: Small group spaces. *Small Group Behavior, 10,* 124–135.

Edney, J. J., & Jordan-Edney, N. L. (1974). Territorial spacing on a beach. *Sociometry, 37,* 92–104.

Edney, J. J., & Uhlig, S. R. (1977). Individual and small group territories. *Small Group Behavior, 8,* 457–468.

Edwards, D. J. A. (1972). Approaching the unfamiliar: A study of human interaction distances. *Journal of Behavioral Science, 1,* 249–250.

Eisenberg, E. M., Monge, P. R., & Miller, K. I. (1983). Involvement in communication networks as a predictor of organizational commitment. *Human Communication Research, 10,* 179–201.

Eliot, M. (1993). *Walt Disney: Hollywood's dark prince: A biography.* Secaucus, NJ: Carol Publishing Group.

Ellemers, N., Spears, R., & Doosje, B. (1997). Sticking together or falling apart: In-group identification as a psychological determinant of group commitment versus individual mobility. *Journal of Personality and Social Psychology, 72,* 617–626.

Ellemers, N., Wilke, H., & van Knippenberg, A. (1993). Effects of the legitimacy of low group or individual status on individual and collective status-enhancement strategies. *Journal of Personality and Social Psychology, 64,* 766–778.

Elliott, G. C., & Meeker, B. F. (1984). Modifiers of the equity effect: Group outcome and causes for individual performance. *Journal of Personality and Social Psychology, 46,* 586–597.

Ellis, D. G., & Fisher, M. (1994). *Small group decision making* (4th ed.). New York: McGraw-Hill.

Elms, A. C. (1995). Obedience in retrospect. *Journal of Social Issues, 51(3),* 21–31.

Emerson, R. M. (1954). Deviation and rejection: An experimental replication. *American Sociological Review, 19,* 688–693.

Emerson, R. M. (1962). Power-dependence relations. *American Sociological Review, 27,* 31–40.

Emerson, R. M. (1981). Social exchange theory. In M. Rosenberg & R. H. Turner (Eds.), *Social psychology: Sociological perspectives* (pp. 30–65). New York: Basic Books.

Erez, M., Rim, Y., & Keider, I. (1986). The two sides of the tactics of influence: Agent vs. target. *Journal of Occupational Psychology, 59,* 25–39.

Erez, M., & Somech, A. (1996). Is group productivity loss the rule or the exception? Effects of culture and group-based motivation. *Academy of Management Journal, 39,* 1513–1537.

Esser, A. H. (1968). Dominance hierarchy and clinical course of psychiatrically hospitalized boys. *Child Development, 39,* 147–157.

Esser, A. H. (1973). Cottage Fourteen: Dominance and territoriality in a group of institutionalized boys. Small Group Behavior, 4, 131–146.

Esser, A. H., Chamberlain, A. S., Chapple, E. D., & Kline, N. S. (1965). Territoriality of patients on a research ward. In J. Wortis (Ed.), *Recent advances in biological psychiatry.* New York: Plenum.

Etzioni, A. (1967). The Kennedy experiment. *The Western Political Quarterly, 20,* 361–380.

Etzioni, A. (1968). A model of significant research. *International Journal of Psychiatry, 6,* 278–280.

Evans, C. R., & Dion, K. L. (1991). Group cohesion and performance: A meta-analysis. *Small Group Research, 22,* 175–186.

Evans, G. W. (1979). Behavioral and physiological consequences of crowding in humans. *Journal of Applied Social Psychology, 9,* 27–46.

Evans, G. W., & Cohen, S. (1987). Environmental stress. In D. Stokols & I. Altman (Eds.), *Handbook of environmental psychology* (Vol. 1, pp. 571–610). New York: Wiley.

Evans, G. W., & Howard, R. B. (1973). Personal space. *Psychological Bulletin, 80,* 334–344.

Evans, G. W., Hygge, S., & Bullinger, M. (1995). Chronic noise and psychological stress. *Psychological Science, 6,* 333–338.

Evans, G. W., & Lepore, S. J. (1992). Conceptual and analytic issues in crowding research. *Journal of Environmental Psychology, 12,* 163–173.

Evans, G. W., Palsane, M. N., Lepore, S. J., & Martin, J. (1989). Residential density and psychological health: The mediating effects of social support. *Journal of Personality and Social Psychology, 57,* 994–999.

Evans, N. J., & Jarvis, P. A. (1986). The Group Attitude Scale: A measure of attraction to group. *Small Group Behavior, 17,* 203–216.

Eysenck, H. (1990). Biological dimensions of personality. In L. A. Pervin (Ed.), *Handbook of personality: Theory and research* (pp. 244–276). New York: Guilford Press.

Falbo, T. (1977). The multidimensional scaling of power strategies. *Journal of Personality and Social Psychology, 35,* 537–548.

Falbo, T., & Peplau, L. A. (1980). Power strategies in intimate relationships. *Journal of Personality and Social Psychology, 38,* 618–628.

Falloon, I. R. H., Lindley, P., McDonald, R., & Marks, I. M. (1977). Social skills training of outpatient groups: A controlled study of rehearsal and homework. *British Journal of Psychiatry, 131,* 599–609.

Fanon, F. (1963). *The wretched of the earth.* New York: Grove.

Farrell, M. P. (1982). Artists' circles and the development of artists. *Small Group Behavior, 13,* 451–474.

Fazio, R. H. (1979). Motives for social comparison: The construction-validation distinction. *Journal of Personality and Social Psychology, 37,* 1683–1698.

Ferencik, B. M. (1992). The helping process in group therapy: A review and discussion. *Group, 16,* 113–124.

Ferguson, T. J., & Rule, B. G. (1983). An attributional analysis of anger and aggression. In R. G. Geen &

E. I. Donnerstein (Eds.), *Aggression: Theoretical and empirical reviews* (Vol. 1). New York: Academic Press.

Ferris, G. R., & Rowland, K. M. (1983). Social facilitation effects on behavioral and perceptual task performance measures: Implications for work behavior. *Group and Organization Studies, 8,* 421–438.

Festinger, L. (1950). Informal social communication. *Psychological Review, 57,* 271–282.

Festinger, L. (1954). A theory of social comparison processes. *Human Relations, 7,* 117–140.

Festinger, L. (1957). *A theory of cognitive dissonance.* Stanford, CA: Stanford University Press.

Festinger, L., Pepitone, A., & Newcomb, T. (1952). Some consequences of deindividuation in a group. *Journal of Abnormal and Social Psychology, 47,* 382–389.

Festinger, L., Riecken, H. W., & Schachter, S. (1956). *When prophecy fails.* Minneapolis: University of Minnesota Press.

Festinger, L., Schachter, S., & Back, K. (1950). *Social pressures in informal groups.* New York: Harper.

Festinger, L., & Thibaut, J. (1951). Interpersonal communication in small groups. *Journal of Abnormal and Social Psychology, 46,* 92–99.

Fiedler, F. E. (1955). The influence of leader-keyman relations on combat crew effectiveness. *Journal of Abnormal and Social Psychology, 51,* 227–235.

Fiedler, F. E. (1964). A contingency model of leadership effectiveness. *Advances in Experimental Social Psychology, 1,* 150–190.

Fiedler, F. E. (1967). *A theory of leadership effectiveness.* New York: McGraw-Hill.

Fiedler, F. E. (1971a). *Leadership.* Morristown, NJ: General Learning Press.

Fiedler, F. E. (1971b). Note on the methodology of Graen, Orris, and Alvarez studies testing the contingency model. *Journal of Applied Psychology, 55,* 202–204.

Fiedler, F. E. (1978). The contingency model and the dynamics of the leadership process. *Advances in Experimental Social Psychology, 12,* 59–112.

Fiedler, F. E. (1981). Leadership effectiveness. *American Behavioral Scientist, 24,* 619–632.

Fiedler, F. E. (1986). The contribution of cognitive resources to leadership performance. *Journal of Applied Social Psychology, 16,* 532–548.

Fiedler, F. E. (1993). The leadership situation and the black box in contingency theories. In M. M. Chemers & R. Ayman (Eds.), *Leadership theory and research: Perspectives and directions* (pp. 1–28). San Diego: Academic Press.

Fiedler, F. E. (1996). Research on leadership selection and training: One view of the future. *Administrative Science Quarterly, 41,* 241–250.

Fiedler, F. E., & Chemers, M. M. (1974). *Leadership and effective management.* Glenview, IL: Scott, Foresman.

Fiedler, F. E., Chemers, M. M., & Mahar, L. (1976). *Improving leadership effectiveness: The Leader Match concept.* New York: Wiley.

Fiedler, F. E., & Garcia, J. E. (1987). New approaches to leadership: Cognitive resources and organizational performance. New York: Wiley.

Field, R. H. G. (1979). A critique of the Vroom-Yetton contingency model of leadership behavior. *Academy of Management Review, 4,* 249–257.

Field, R. H. G., & House, R. J. (1990). A test of the Vroom-Yetton model using manager and subordinate reports. *Journal of Applied Psychology, 75,* 362–366.

Fielding, K. S., & Hogg, M. A. (1997). Social identity, self-categorization, and leadership: A field study of small interactive groups. *Group Dynamics: Theory, Research, and Practice, 1,* 39–51.

Finch, J. F., Barrera, M., Jr., Okun, M. A., Bryant, W. H., Pool, G. J., & Snow-Turek, A. L. (1997). The factor structure of received social support: Dimensionality and the prediction of depression and life satisfaction. *Journal of Social and Clinical Psychology, 16,* 323–342.

Fine, G. A., & Holyfield, L. (1996). Secrecy, trust, and dangerous leisure: Generating group cohesion in voluntary organizations. *Social Psychology Quarterly, 59,* 22–38.

Fink, C. F. (1968). Some conceptual difficulties in the theory of social conflict. *Journal of Conflict Resolution, 12,* 412–460.

Finke, R., & Stark, R. (1992). The churching of America, 1776–1990: Winners and losers in our religious economy. New Brunswick, NJ: Rutgers University Press.

Finn, J. D., & Rock, D. A. (1997). Academic success among students at risk for school failure. *Journal of Applied Psychology, 82,* 221–234.

Fisek, M. H., Berger, J., & Norman, R. Z. (1995). Evaluations and the formation of expectations. *American Journal of Sociology, 101,* 731–746.

Fisek, M. H., & Ofshe, R. (1970). The process of status evolution. *Sociometry, 33,* 327–346.

Fisher, B. A. (1980). *Small group decision making* (2nd ed.). New York: McGraw-Hill.

Fisher, C. D., & Gitelson, R. (1983). A meta-analysis of the correlates of role conflict and ambiguity. *Journal of Applied Psychology, 68,* 320–333.

Fisher, J. D., & Byrne, D. (1975). Too close for comfort: Sex differences in response to invasions of personal space. *Journal of Personality and Social Psychology, 32,* 15–21.

Fisher, R. (1983). Negotiating power. *American Behavioral Science, 27,* 149–166.

Fisher, R., & Ury, W. (with B. Patton, Ed.). (1981). *Getting to YES: Negotiating agreement without giving in.* Boston: Houghton-Mifflin.

Fisher, R., Ury, W., & Patton, B. (1991). *Getting to YES: Negotiating agreement without giving in* (2nd ed.). New York: Penguin Books.

Fisher, R. J. (1994). Generic principles for resolving intergroup conflict. *Journal of Social Issues, 50(1),* 47–66.

Fiske, S. T. (1993a). Controlling other people: The impact of power on stereotyping. *American Psychologist, 48,* 621–628.

Fiske, S. T. (1993b). Social cognition and social perception. *Annual Review of Psychology, 44,* 155–194.

Fiske, S. T., & Goodwin, S. A. (1994). Social cognition research and small group research, a West Side Story or . . . ? Special issue: Social cognition in small groups. *Small Group Research, 25,* 147–171.

Fiske, S. T., & Goodwin, S. A. (1996). Social cognition research and small group research, a West Side Story or. . . . In J. L. Nye & A. M. Brower (Eds.), *What's social about social cognition? Research on socially shared cognitions in small groups* (pp. xiii–xxxiii). Thousand Oaks, CA: Sage.

Fiske, S. T., & Taylor, S. E. (1991). *Social cognition* (2nd ed.). New York: McGraw-Hill.

Flores, P. J. (1997). Group psychotherapy with addicted populations: An integration of twelve step and psychodynamic theory. Binghamton, NY: Haworth.

Flowers, J. (1979). Behavioral analysis of group therapy and a model for behavioral group therapy. In D. Upper & S. Ross (Eds.), *Behavioral group therapy, 1979: An annual review.* Champaign, IL: Research Press.

Flowers, M. L. (1977). A laboratory test of some implications of Janis' groupthink hypothesis. *Journal of Personality and Social Psychology, 35,* 888–896.

Flynn, K., & Gerhardt, G. (1989). *The silent brotherhood: Inside America's racist underground.* New York: Penguin.

Foa, U. G. (1957). Relation of worker's expectation to satisfaction with supervisor. *Personnel Psychology, 10,* 161–168.

Foa, U. G., & Foa, E. B. (1971). Resource exchange: Toward a structural theory of interpersonal relations. In A. W. Siegman & B. Pope (Eds.), *Studies in dyadic communication.* New York: Pergamon Press.

Foddy, M., & Smithson, M. (1996). Relative ability, paths of relevance, and influence in task-oriented groups. *Social Psychology Quarterly, 59,* 140–153.

Fodor, E. M. (1984). The power motive and reactivity to power stresses. *Journal of Personality and Social Psychology, 47,* 853–859.

Fodor, E. M. (1985). The power motive, group conflict, and physiological arousal. *Journal of Personality and Social Psychology, 49,* 1408–1415.

Folger, R. (1993). Reactions to mistreatment at work. In J. K. Murnighan (Ed.), *Social psychology in organizations: Advances in theory and research* (pp. 161–183). Englewood Cliffs, NJ: Prentice Hall.

Folk, G. E., Jr. (1974). *Textbook of environmental physiology.* Philadelphia: Lea & Febiger.

Forsyth, D. R. (1980). The functions of attributions. *Social Psychology Quarterly, 43,* 184–189.

Forsyth, D. R. (1981). A psychological perspective on ethical uncertainties in behavioral research. In A. J. Kimmel (Ed.), *New directions for methodology of social and behavioral science: Ethics of human subject research* (No. 10). San Francisco: Jossey-Bass.

Forsyth, D. R. (1990). *Group dynamics* (2nd ed.). Pacific Grove, CA: Brooks/Cole.

Forsyth, D. R. (1995). Norms. In A. S. R. Manstead & M. Hewstone (Eds.), *The Blackwell encyclopedia of social psychology* (pp. 412–417). Cambridge: Blackwell.

Forsyth, D. R. (1996). *The functions of groups.* Paper presented at the annual meetings of the American Psychological Association. Toronto, Canada.

Forsyth, D. R. (1997). *The paradoxes of Heaven's Gate* [Online]. Available: http://www.vcu.edu/hasweb/psy/psy633/hg.htm [1998, April 15].

Forsyth, D. R., Berger, R., & Mitchell, T. (1981). The effects of self-serving vs. other-serving claims of responsibility on attraction and attribution in groups. *Social Psychology Quarterly, 44,* 59–64.

Forsyth, D. R., & Elliott, T. R. (in press). Group dynamics and psychological well-being: The impact of groups on adjustment and dysfunction. In R. Kowalski & M. R. Leary (Eds.), *The social psychology of emotional and behavioral problems:*

Interfaces of social and clinical psychology. Washington, DC: American Psychological Association.

Forsyth, D. R., Heiney, M. M., & Wright, S. S. (1997). Biases in appraisals of women leaders. *Group Dynamics: Theory, Research, and Practice, 1,* 98–103.

Forsyth, D. R., & Kelley, K. N. (1996). Heuristic-based biases in estimations of personal contributions to collective endeavors. In J. L. Nye & A. M. Brower (Eds.), *What's social about social cognition? Research on socially shared cognitions in small groups* (pp. 106–123). Thousand Oaks, CA: Sage.

Forsyth, D. R., & Schlenker, B. R. (1977). Attributing the causes of group performance: Effects of performance quality, task importance, and future testing. *Journal of Personality, 45,* 220–236.

Forsyth, D. R., Schlenker, B. R., Leary, M. R., & McCown, N. E. (1985). Self-presentational determinants of sex differences in leadership behavior. *Small Group Behavior, 16,* 197–210.

Foschi, M. (1996). Double standards in the evaluation of men and women. *Social Psychology Quarterly, 59,* 237–254.

Foschi, M., Warriner, G. K., & Hart, S. D. (1985). Standards, expectations, and interpersonal influence. *Social Psychology Quarterly, 48,* 108–117.

Foss, R. D. (1981). Structural effects in simulated jury decision making. *Journal of Personality and Social Psychology, 40,* 1055–1062.

Foti, R. J., Fraser, S. L., & Lord, R. G. (1982). Effects of leadership labels and prototypes on perceptions of political leaders. *Journal of Applied Psychology, 67,* 326–333.

Foti, R. J., & Lord, R. G. (1987). Prototypes and scripts: The effects of alternative methods of processing information on rating accuracy. *Organizational Behavior and Human Decision Processes, 39,* 318–340.

Foushee, H. C. (1984). Dyads and triads at 35,000 feet: Factors affecting group process and aircrew performance. *American Psychologist, 39,* 886–893.

Fox, S. (1984). The sociability aspect of extraversion as a situation-specific dimension. *Social Behavior and Personality, 12,* 7–10.

Foy, E., & Harlow, A. F. (1928/1956). *Clowning through life.* New York: Dutton.

Frable, D. E. S., Platt, L., & Hoey, S. (1998).Concealable stigmas and positive self-perceptions: Feeling better around similar others. *Journal of Personality and Social Psychology, 74,* 909–922.

Frager, R. (1970). Conformity and anticonformity in Japan. *Journal of Personality and Social Psychology, 15,* 203–210.

Frank, F., & Anderson, L. R. (1971). Effects of task and group size upon group productivity and member satisfaction. *Sociometry, 34,* 135–149.

Frank, J. D. (1957). Some determinants, manifestations, and effects of cohesiveness in therapy groups. *International Journal of Group Psychotherapy, 7,* 53–63.

Franke, R. H. (1979). The Hawthorne experiments: Re-view. *American Sociological Review, 44,* 861–867.

Franke, R. H., & Kaul, J. D. (1978). The Hawthorne experiments: First statistical interpretation. *American Sociological Review, 43,* 623–643.

Franken, R. E., & Brown, D. J. (1995). Why do people like competition? The motivation for winning, putting forth effort, improving one's performance, performing well, being instrumental, and expressing forceful/aggressive behavior. *Personality and Individual Differences, 19,* 175–184.

Franken, R. E., & Prpich, W. (1996). Dislike of competition and the need to win: Self-image concerns, performance concerns, and the distraction of attention. *Journal of Social Behavior and Personality, 11,* 695–712.

Fraser, N. M., & Hipel, K. W. (1984). *Conflict analysis: Models and resolutions.* New York: North-Holland.

Freedman, J. L. (1975). *Crowding and behavior.* San Francisco: Freeman.

Freedman, J. L. (1979). Reconciling apparent differences between responses of humans and other animals to crowding. *Psychological Review, 86,* 80–85.

Freedman, J. L., & Fraser, S. C. (1966). Compliance without pressure: The foot-in-the-door technique. *Journal of Personality and Social Psychology, 4,* 195–202.

Freedman, J. L., & Perlick, D. (1979). Crowding, contagion, and laughter. *Journal of Experimental Social Psychology, 15,* 295–303.

Freeman, K. A. (1996). Attitudes toward work in project groups as predictors of academic performance. *Small Group Research, 27,* 265–282.

Freeman, L. C. (1977). A set of measures of centrality based on betweenness. *Sociometry, 40,* 35–41.

Freeman, L. C. (1979). Centrality in social networks: I. Conceptual clarification. *Social Networks, 1,* 215–239.

Freeze, L., & Cohen, B. P. (1973). Eliminating status generalization. *Sociometry, 36,* 177–193.

French, J. R. P., Jr. (1941). The disruption and cohesion of groups. *Journal of Abnormal and Social Psychology, 36,* 361–377.

French, J. R. P., Jr., Morrison, H., & Levinger, G. (1960). Coercive power and forces affecting conformity. *Journal of Abnormal and Social Psychology, 61,* 93–101.

French, J. R. P., Jr., & Raven, B. (1959). The bases of social power. In D. Cartwright (Ed.), *Studies in social power.* Ann Arbor, MI: Institute for Social Research.

Freud, S. (1922). *Group psychology and the analysis of ego.* London: Hogarth.

Friedland, N. (1976). Social influence via threats. *Journal of Experimental Social Psychology, 12,* 552–563.

Friedman, S. D., & Saul, K. (1991). A leader's wake: Organization member reactions to CEO succession. *Journal of Management, 17,* 619–642.

Froman, L. A., Jr., & Cohen, M. D. (1969). Threats and bargaining efficiency. *Behavioral Science, 14,* 147–153.

Fromm, E. (1965). *Escape from freedom.* New York: Holt, Rinehart & Winston.

Fry, D. P., & Björkqvist, K. (Eds.). (1997). *Cultural variation in conflict resolution: Alternatives to violence.* Mahwah, NJ: Erlbaum.

Fuhriman, A., & Burlingame, G. M. (1994a). Group psychotherapy: Research and practice. In A. Fuhriman & G. M. Burlingame (Eds.), *Handbook of group psychotherapy: An empirical and clinical synthesis.* (pp. 3–40). New York: Wiley.

Fuhriman, A., & Burlingame, G. M. (Eds.). (1994b). *Handbook of group psychotherapy: An empirical and clinical synthesis.* New York: Wiley.

Fujishin, R. (1997). *Discovering the leader within: Running small groups successfully.* San Francisco: Acada.

Gabarro, J. J. (1987). The development of working relationships. In J. W. Lorsch (Ed.), *Handbook of organizational behavior* (pp. 172–189). Englewood Cliffs, NJ: Prentice Hall.

Gaertner, S. L., Dovidio, J. F., Anastasio, P. A., Bachman, B. A., & Rust, M. C. (1993). The common ingroup identity model: Recategorization and the reduction of intergroup bias. *European Review of Social Psychology, 4,* 1–26.

Gaertner, S. L., Rust, M., Dovidio, J. F., Bachman, B. A., & Anastasio, P. (1994). The contact hypothesis: The role of a common ingroup identity on reducing intergroup bias. *Small Group Research, 25,* 224–249.

Gaines, S. O., Jr., Marelich, W. D., Bledsoe, K. L., Steers, W. N., Henderson, M. C., Granrose, C. S., Barájas, L., Hicks, D., Lyde, M., Takahashi, Y., Yum, N., Ríos, D. I., García, B. F., Farris, K. R., & Page, M. S. (1997). Links between race/ethnicity and cultural values as mediated by racial/ethnic identity and moderated by gender. *Journal of Personality and Social Psychology, 72,* 1460–1476.

Gaines, S. O., Jr., & Reed, E. S. (1995). Prejudice: From Allport to DuBois. *American Psychologist, 50,* 96–103.

Galassi, J. P., & Galassi, M. D. (1979). Modification of heterosocial skills deficits. In A. S. Bellack & M. Hersen (Eds.), *Research and practice in social skills training.* New York: Plenum.

Galen, M. (1994, January 31). White, male, and worried. *Business Week,* pp. 50–55.

Gallo, P. S., Jr. (1966). Effects of increased incentives upon the use of threat in bargaining. *Journal of Personality and Social Psychology, 4,* 14–20.

Gallup, G. H. (1990). *The Gallup poll.* Wilmington, DE: Scholarly Resources.

Gallupe, R. B., & Cooper, W. H. (1993). Brainstorming electronically. *Sloan Management Review, 35,* 27–36.

Gamson, W. A. (1968). *Power and discontent.* Belmont, CA: Wadsworth.

Gamson, W. A. (1992). The social psychology of collective action. In A. Morris & C. Mueller (Eds.), *Frontiers of social movement theory* (pp. 53–76). New Haven, CT: Yale University Press.

Gamson, W. A., & Scotch, N. (1964). Scapegoating in baseball. *American Journal of Sociology, 70,* 69–70.

Gannon, T. M. (1966). Emergence of the "defensive" group norm. *Federal Probation, 30(4),* 44–47.

Gardner, J. W. (1965). The antileadership vaccine. *Annual Report of the Carnegie Corporation.* New York: Carnegie Corporation.

Garner, D. M., & Garfinkel, P. E. (1980). Sociocultural factors in the development of anorexia nervosa. *Psychological Medicine, 10,* 647–656.

Garner, K., & Deutsch, M. (1974). Cooperative behavior in dyads: Effects of dissimilar goal orientations and differing expectations about the partner. *Journal of Conflict Resolution, 18,* 634–645.

Gastorf, J. W., Suls, J., & Sanders, G. S. (1980). Type A coronary-prone behavior pattern and social facilitation. *Journal of Personality and Social Psychology, 38,* 773–780.

Gavin, M. G., Green, S. G., & Fairhurst, G. T. (1995). Managerial control strategies for poor performance over time and the impact on subordinate reactions. *Organizational Behavior and Human Decision Processes, 63,* 207–221.

Gazda, G. M., & Brooks, D. K. (1985). The development of the social/life skills training movement. *Journal of Group Psychotherapy, Psychodrama and Sociometry, 38,* 1–10.

Gecas, V., & Burke, P. J. (1995). Self and identity. In K. S. Cook, G. A. Fine, & J. S. House (Eds.), *Sociological perspectives on social psychology* (pp. 41–67). Boston: Allyn & Bacon.

Geen, R. G. (1980). The effects of being observed on performance. In P. B. Paulus (Ed.), *Psychology of group influence* (pp. 61–97). Hillsdale, NJ: Erlbaum.

Geen, R. G. (1983). Evaluation apprehension and the social facilitation/inhibition of learning. *Motivation and Emotion, 7,* 203–212.

Geen, R. G. (1991). Social motivation. *Annual Review of Psychology, 42,* 377–399.

Geen, R. G. (1995). *Human motivation: A social psychological approach.* Pacific Grove, CA: Brooks/Cole.

Geen, R. G., & Bushman, B. J. (1987). Drive theory: Effects of socially engendered arousal. In B. Mullen & G. R. Goethals (Eds.), *Theories of group behavior* (pp. 89–109). New York: Springer-Verlag.

Geen, R. G., & Bushman, B. J. (1989). The arousing effects of social presence. In H. Wagner & A. Manstead (Eds.), *Handbook of social psychophysiology* (pp. 261–281). London: Wiley.

Geen, R. G., & Gange, J. J. (1977). Drive theory of social facilitation: Twelve years of theory and research. *Psychological Bulletin, 84,* 1267–1288.

Geis, R. G., Boston, M. B., & Hoffman, N. (1985). Sex of authority role models and achievement by men and women: Leadership performance and recognition. *Journal of Personality and Social Psychology, 49,* 636–653.

Gemmill, G. (1986). The mythology of the leader role in small groups. *Small Group Behavior, 17,* 41–50.

Genevie, L. E. (Ed.). (1978). *Collective behavior and social movements.* Itasca, IL: Peacock.

Gerard, H. B. (1953). The effect of different dimensions of disagreement on the communication process in small groups. *Human Relations, 6,* 249–271.

Gerard, H. B. (1983). School desegregation: The social science role. *American Psychologist, 38,* 869–877.

Gerard, H. B., & Mathewson, G. C. (1966). The effects of severity of initiation on liking for a group: A replication. *Journal of Experimental Social Psychology, 2,* 278–287.

Gerard, H. B., & Orive, R. (1987). The dynamics of opinion formation. *Advances in Experimental Social Psychology, 20,* 171–202.

Gerber, G. L. (1996). Status in same-gender and mixed-gender police dyads: Effects on personality attributions. *Social Psychology Quarterly, 59,* 350–363.

Gergen, K. J., Gergen, M. M., & Barton, W. H. (1973). Deviance in the dark. *Psychology Today, 10,* 129–130.

Gersick, C. J. G. (1989). Marking time: Predictable transitions in task groups. *Academy of Management Journal, 32,* 274–309.

Gerstner, C. R., & Day, D. V. (1997). Meta-analytic review of leader-member exchange theory: Correlates and construct issues. *Journal of Applied Psychology, 82,* 827–844.

Giannantonio, C. M., Olian, J. D., & Carroll, S. J. (1996). An experimental study of gender and situational effects in a performance evaluation of a manager. *Psychological Reports, 76,* 1004–1006.

Gibb, C. A. (1969). Leadership. In G. Lindzey & E. Aronson (Eds.), *The handbook of social psychology* (2nd ed., Vol. 4, pp. 205–282). Reading, MA: Addison-Wesley.

Gibb, J. R. (1970). Effects of human relations training. In A. E. Bergin & S. L. Garfield (Eds.), *Handbook of psychotherapy and behavior change.* New York: Wiley, 1971.

Gibbons, F. X., & Gerrard, M. (1989). Effects of upward and downward social comparison on mood states. *Journal of Social and Clinical Psychology, 8,* 14–31.

Giesen, M., & McClaren, H. A. (1976). Discussion, distance, and sex: Changes in impressions and attraction during small group interaction. *Sociometry, 39,* 60–70.

Gifford, R., & O'Connor, B. (1987). The interpersonal circumplex as a behavior map. *Journal of Personality and Social Psychology, 52,* 1019–1026.

Gigone, D., & Hastie, R. (1993). The common knowledge effect: Information sharing and group judgment. *Journal of Personality and Social Psychology, 65,* 959–974.

Gigone, D., & Hastie, R. (1997). Proper analysis of the accuracy of group judgments. *Psychological Bulletin, 121,* 149–167.

Gilbert, S. J. (1981). Another look at the Milgram obedience studies: The role of the graduated series of shocks. *Personality and Social Psychology Bulletin, 7,* 690–695.

Gilchrist, J. C. (1952). The formation of social groups under conditions of success and failure. *Journal of Abnormal and Social Psychology, 47,* 174–187.

Giles, H. (Ed.). (1977). *Language, ethnicity, and intergroup relations.* London: Academic Press.

Giles, H., & Johnson, P. (1981). The role of language in ethnic group relations. In J. C. Turner & H. Giles (Eds.), *Intergroup behavior* (pp. 199–272). Oxford: Blackwell.

Gilliland, S. W. (1994). Effects of procedural and distributive justice on reactions to a selection system. *Journal of Applied Psychology, 79,* 691–701.

Ginnett, R. C. (1993). Crews as groups: Their formation and their leadership. In E. L. Wiener, B. G. Kanki, & R. L. Helmreich (Eds.), *Cockpit resource management* (pp. 71–98). San Diego: Academic Press.

Giola, D. A., & Sims, H. P. (1985). Self-serving bias and actor-observer differences in organizations: An empirical analysis. Journal of Applied Social Psychology, *15,* 547–563.

Gist, M. E., Locke, E. A., & Taylor, M. S. (1987). Organizational behavior: Group structure, process, and effectiveness. *Journal of Management, 13,* 237–257.

Gladstein, D. L. (1984). Groups in context: A model of task group effectiveness. *Administrative Science Quarterly, 29,* 499–517.

Glaser, B. G., & Strauss, A. L. (1967). The discovery of grounded theory: Strategies for qualitative research. Chicago: Aldine.

Glaser, D. (1964). *The effectiveness of a prison and parole system.* Indianapolis: Bobbs-Merrill.

Glass, D. C., & Singer, J. E. (1972). *Urban stress.* New York: Academic Press.

Glass, D. C., Singer, J. E., & Pennebaker, J. W. (1977). Behavioral and physiological effects of uncontrollable environmental events. In D. Stokols (Ed.), *Perspectives on environment and behavior* (pp. 131–151). New York: Plenum.

Glasser, C., & Smalley, B. S. (1995). Swim with the dolphins: How women can succeed in corporate America on their own terms. New York: Warner.

Gleitman, H., Rozin, P., & Sabini, J. (1997). Solomon E. Asch (1907–1996). *American Psychologist, 52,* 984–985.

Godfrey, D. K., Jones, E. E., & Lord, C. G. (1986). Self-promotion is not ingratiating. *Journal of Personality and Social Psychology, 50,* 106–115.

Goethals, G. R., & Darley, J. M. (1987). Social comparison theory: Self-evaluation and group life. In B. Mullen & G. R. Goethals (Eds.), *Theories of group behavior* (pp. 21–47). New York: Springer-Verlag.

Goethals, G. R., Messick, D. M., & Allison, S. T. (1991). The uniqueness bias: Studies of constructive social comparison. In J. Suls & T. A. Wills (Eds.), *Social comparison: Contemporary theory and research* (pp. 149–176). Hillsdale, NJ: Erlbaum.

Goethals, G. R., & Zanna, M. P. (1979). The role of social comparison in choice shifts. *Journal of Personality and Social Psychology, 37,* 1469–1476.

Goetsch, G. G., & McFarland, D. D. (1980). Models of the distribution of acts in small discussion groups. *Social Psychology Quarterly, 43,* 173–183.

Goffman, E. (1959). *The presentation of self in everyday life.* Garden City, NY: Doubleday.

Gold, M., & Yanof, D. S. (1985). Mothers, daughters, and girlfriends. *Journal of Personality and Social Psychology, 49,* 654–659.

Goldberg, L. (1968). Ghetto riots and others: The faces of civil disorder in 1967. *Journal of Peace Research, 2,* 116–132.

Goldberg, L. R. (1993). The structure of phenotypic personality traits. *American Psychologist, 48,* 26–34.

Goldman, M., & Fraas, L. A. (1965). The effects of leader selection on group performance. *Sociometry, 28,* 82–88.

Goldman, M., Stockbauer, J. W., & McAuliffe, T. G. (1977). Intergroup and intragroup competition and cooperation. *Journal of Experimental Social Psychology, 13,* 81–88.

Goldstein, A. P., Heller, K., & Sechrest, L. B. (1966). *Psychotherapy and the psychology of behavior change.* New York: Wiley.

Goltz, S. M., & Giannantonio, C. M. (1995). Recruiter friendliness and attraction to the job: The mediating role of inferences about the organization. *Journal of Vocational Behavior, 46,* 109–118.

Goodacre, D. M. (1953). Group characteristics of good and poor performing combat units. *Sociometry, 16,* 168–178.

Goodman, G., & Jacobs, M. K. (1994). The self-help, mutual-support group. In A. Fuhriman & G. M. Burlingame (Eds.), *Handbook of group psychotherapy: An empirical and clinical synthesis* (pp. 489–526). New York: Wiley.

Goodman, P. S., & Leyden, D. P. (1991). Familiarity and group productivity. *Journal of Applied Psychology, 76,* 578–586.

Goodman, P. S., Ravlin, E., & Schminke, M. (1987). Understanding groups in organizations. *Research in Organizational Behavior, 9,* 121–173.

Goodstadt, B. E., & Hjelle, L. A. (1973). Power to the powerless: Locus of control and use of power. *Journal of Personality and Social Psychology, 27,* 190–196.

Gordon, J. (1992). Work teams? How far have they come? *Training, 29,* 59–65.

Gordon, W. (1961). Synectics: The development of creative capacity. New York: Harper & Row.

Gould, S. J. (1991). Exaptation: A crucial tool for an evolutionary psychology. *Journal of Social Issues, 47(3),* 43–65.

Goulding, R. L., & Goulding, M. M. (1979). *Changing lives through redecision therapy.* New York: Brunner/Mazel.

Graeff, C. L. (1983). The situational leadership theory: A critical view. *Academy of Management Review, 8,* 285–291.

Graen, G. B. (1976). Role-making processes within complex organizations. In M. D. Dunnette (Ed.), *Handbook of industrial organizational psychology.* Chicago: Rand McNally.

Graen, G. B., & Cashman, J. (1975). A role-making model of leadership in formal organizations: A developmental approach. In J. G. Hunt & L. L. Larson (Eds.), *Leadership frontiers* (pp. 143–166). Kent, OH: Kent State University Press.

Graen, G. B., Orris, J. B., & Alvares, K. M. (1971). Contingency model of leadership effectiveness: Some experimental results. *Journal of Applied Psychology, 55,* 196–201.

Graen, G. B., & Uhl-Bien, M. (1991). The transformation of professionals into self-managing and partially self-designing contributors: Toward a theory of leadership making. *Journal of Management Systems, 3(3),* 33–48.

Graen, G. B., & Uhl-Bien, M. (1995). Relationship-based approach to leadership: Development of leader-member exchange (LMX) theory of leadership over 25 years: Applying a multi-level multi-domain perspective. *Leadership Quarterly, 6,* 219–247.

Grant, P. R. (1993). Ethnocentrism in response to a threat to social identity. *Journal of Social Behavior and Personality, 8,* 143–154.

Graves, L. M., & Karren, R. J. (1996). The employee selection interview: A fresh look at an old problem. *Human Resource Management, 35(Summer),* 163–180.

Graves, L. M., & Powell, G. N. (1988). An investigation of sex discrimination in recruiters' evaluations of actual applicants. *Journal of Applied Psychology, 73,* 20–29.

Graves, L. M., & Powell, G. N. (1995). The effect of sex similarity on recruiters' evaluations of actual applicants: A test of the similarity-attraction paradigm. *Personnel Psychology, 48,* 85–98.

Graziano, W. G., Hair, E. C., & Finch, J. F. (1997). Competitiveness mediates the link between personality and group performance. *Journal of Personality and Social Psychology, 73,* 1394–1408.

Graziano, W. G., Jensen-Campbell, L. A., & Hair, E. C. (1996). Perceiving interpersonal conflict and reacting to it: The case for agreeableness. *Journal of Personality and Social Psychology, 70,* 820–835.

Greenberg, C. I., & Firestone, I. J. (1977). Compensatory responses to crowding: Effects of personal space intrusion and privacy reduction. *Journal of Personality and Social Psychology, 35,* 637–644.

Greenberg, J. (1994). Using socially fair treatment to promote acceptance of a work site smoking ban. *Journal of Applied Psychology, 79,* 288–297.

Greenwald, A. G., & Pratkanis, A. R. (1984). The self. In R. S. Wyer, Jr., & T. K. Srull (Eds.), *Handbook of social cognition* (Vol. 3). Hillsdale, NJ: Erlbaum.

Greer, D. L. (1983). Spectator booing and the home advantage: A study of social influence in the basketball arena. *Social Psychology Quarterly, 46,* 252–261.

Greve, D. W. (1993). Gestalt group psychotherapy. In H. I. Kaplan & M. J. Sadock (Eds.), *Comprehensive group psychotherapy* (3rd ed., pp. 228–235). Baltimore: Williams & Wilkins.

Griffin, D., & Buehler, R. (1993). Role of construal processes in conformity and dissent. *Journal of Personality and Social Psychology, 65,* 657–669.

Griffitt, W. (1970). Environmental effects on interpersonal affective behavior: Ambient effective temperature and attraction. *Journal of Personality and Social Psychology, 15,* 240–244.

Griffitt, W., & Veitch, R. (1971). Hot and crowded: Influence of population density and temperature on interpersonal affective behavior. *Journal of Personality and Social Psychology, 17,* 92–98.

Griffitt, W., & Veitch, R. (1974). Preacquaintance attitude similarity and attraction revisited: Ten days in a fall-out shelter. *Sociometry, 37,* 163–173.

Grimes, A. J. (1978). Authority, power, influence and social control: A theoretical synthesis. *Academy of Management Review, 3,* 724–737.

Groff, B. D., Baron, R. S., & Moore, D. L. (1983). Distraction, attentional conflict, and drivelike behavior. *Journal of Experimental Social Psychology, 19,* 359–380.

Grofman, B., & Owen, G. (1982). A game theoretic approach to measuring degree of centrality in social networks. *Social Networks, 4,* 213–224.

Gross, E., & Stone, G. P. (1964). Embarrassment and the analysis of role requirements. *American Journal of Sociology, 70,* 1–15.

Gross, S. R., & Miller, N. (1997). The "golden section" and bias in perceptions of social consensus. *Personality and Social Psychology Review, 1,* 241–271.

Gruner, L. (1984). Membership composition of open and closed therapeutic groups: A research note. *Small Group Behavior, 15,* 222–232.

Guerin, B. (1983). Social facilitation and social monitoring: A test of three models. *British Journal of Social Psychology, 22,* 203–214.

Guerin, B. (1986). Mere presence effects in humans: A review. *Journal of Experimental Social Psychology, 22,* 38–77.

Guerin, B., & Innes, J. M. (1982). Social facilitation and social monitoring: A new look at Zajonc's mere presence hypothesis. *British Journal of Social Psychology, 21,* 7–18.

Guetzkow, H., & Gyr, J. (1954). An analysis of conflict in decision-making groups. *Human Relations, 7,* 367–382.

Guimond, A., & Dubé-Simard, L. (1983). Relative deprivation theory and the Quebec nationalist movement: The cognitive-emotion distinction and the personal-group deprivation issue. *Journal of Personality and Social Psychology, 44,* 526–535.

Gulley, H. E., & Leathers, D. G. (1977). *Communication and group process.* New York: Holt, Rinehart & Winston.

Gully, S. M., Devine, D. J., & Whitney, D. J. (1995). A meta-analysis of cohesion and performance: Effects of level of analysis and task interdependence. *Small Group Research, 26,* 497–520.

Gump, B. G., & Kulik, J. A. (1997). Stress, affiliation, and emotional contagion. *Journal of Personality and Social Psychology, 72,* 305–319.

Gump, P. V. (1990). A short history of the Midwest Psychological Field Station. *Environment and Behavior, 22,* 436–457.

Gunderson, E. K. E. (1973). Individual behavior in confined or isolated groups. In J. E. Rasmussen (Ed.), *Man in isolation and confinement* (pp. 145–164). Chicago: Aldine.

Gurr, T. R. (1970). *Why men rebel.* Princeton, NJ: Princeton University Press.

Gustafson, D. H., Shukla, R. M., Delbecq, A. L., & Walster, G. W. (1973). A comparative study of differences in subjective likelihood estimates made by individuals, interacting groups, Delphi groups, and nominal groups. *Organizational Behavior and Human Performance, 9,* 280–291.

Guthman, E. (1971). *We band of brothers.* New York: Harper & Row.

Guzzo, R. A. (1995). Introduction: At the intersection of team effectiveness and decision making. In R. A. Guzzo, E. Salas, & Associates, *Team effectiveness and decision making in organizations* (pp. 1–8). San Francisco: Jossey-Bass.

Guzzo, R. A., & Dickson, M. W. (1996). Teams in organizations: Recent research on performance and effectiveness. *Annual Review of Psychology, 47,* 307–338.

Guzzo, R. A., Salas, E., & Associates (1995). *Team effectiveness and decision making in organizations.* San Francisco: Jossey-Bass.

Guzzo, R. A., & Shea, G. P. (1992). Group performance and intergroup relations in organizations. In M. D. Dunnette & L. M. Hough (Eds.), *Handbook of industrial and organizational psychology* (2nd ed., Vol. 3, pp. 269–313). Palo Alto, CA: Consulting Psychologists Press.

Guzzo, R. A., Yost, P. R., Campbell, R. J., & Shea, G. P. (1993). Potency in groups: Articulating a construct. *British Journal of Social Psychology, 32,* 87–106.

Haas, D. F., & Deseran, F. A. (1981). Trust and symbolic exchange. *Social Psychology Quarterly, 44,* 3–13.

Haber, G. M. (1980). Territorial invasion in the classroom: Invadee response. *Environment and Behavior, 12,* 17–31.

Haber, G. M. (1982). Spatial relations between dominants and marginals. *Social Psychology Quarterly, 45,* 219–228.

Hackman, J. R. (1987). The design of work teams. In J. W. Lorsch (Ed.), *Handbook of organizational behavior* (pp. 315–342). Englewood Cliffs, NJ: Prentice Hall.

Hackman, J. R. (Ed.). (1990). *Groups that work (and those that don't).* San Francisco: Jossey-Bass.

Hackman, J. R. (1992). Group influences on individuals in organizations. In M. D. Dunnette & L. M. Hough (Eds.), *Handbook of industrial and organizational psychology* (2nd ed., Vol. 3, pp. 199–267). Palo Alto, CA: Consulting Psychologists Press.

Hackman, J. R. (1998). Why teams don't work. In R. S. Tindale, L. Heath, J. Edwards, E. J. Posavac, F. B. Bryant, Y. Suarez-Balcazar, E. Henderson-King, & J. Myers (Eds.), *Theory and research on small groups* (pp. 245–267) New York, Plenum.

Hackman, J. R., Brousseau, K. R., & Weiss, J. A. (1976). The interaction of task design and group performance strategies in determining group effectiveness. *Organizational Behavior and Human Performance, 16,* 350–365.

Hackman, J. R., & Morris, C. G. (1975). Group tasks, group interaction process, and group performance effectiveness: A review and proposed integration. *Advances in Experimental Social Psychology, 8,* 47–99.

Hall, E. T. (1966). *The hidden dimension.* New York: Doubleday.

Hall, R. J., & Lord, R. G. (1995). Multi-level information processing explanations of followers' leadership perceptions. *Leadership Quarterly, 6,* 265–287.

Hallinan, M. T. (1981). Recent advances in sociometry. In S. R. Asher & J. M. Gottman (Eds.), *The development of children's friendships* (pp. 91–115). New York: Cambridge University Press.

Halpern, D. (1995). *Mental health and the built environment: More than bricks and mortar?* London: Taylor & Francis.

Halpin, A. W., & Winer, B. J. (1952). *The leadership behavior of the airplane commander.* Columbus, OH: Ohio State University Research Foundation.

Ham v. S. Carolina, 409 U.S. 524 (1973).

Hamaguchi, E. (1985). A contextual model of the Japanese: Toward a methodological innovation in Japanese studies. *Journal of Japanese Studies, 11,* 289–321.

Hamblin, R. L. (1958). Leadership and crises. *Sociometry, 21,* 322–335.

Hamilton, D. L., & Sherman, S. J. (1989). Illusory correlations: Implications for stereotype theory and research. In D. Bar-Tal, C. F. Graumann, A. W. Kruglanski, & W. Stroebe (Eds.), *Stereotyping and prejudice: Changing conceptions* (pp. 59–82). New York: Springer-Verlag.

Hamilton, D. L., & Sherman, S. J. (1996). Perceiving persons and groups. *Psychological Review, 103,* 336–355.

Hamilton, V. L. (1986). Chains of command: Responsibility attribution in hierarchies. *Journal of Applied Social Psychology, 16,* 118–138.

Hamilton, V. L., & Sanders, J. (1995). Crimes of obedience and conformity in the workplace: Surveys of Americans, Russians, and Japanese. *Journal of Social Issues, 51(3),* 67–88.

Hamilton, W. D. (1964). The genetic evolution of social behavior: I and II. *Journal of Theoretical Biology, 7,* 1–52.

Haney, C., Banks, C., & Zimbardo, P. (1973). Interpersonal dynamics in a simulated prison. *International Journal of Criminology and Psychology, 1,* 69–97.

Hanks, M., & Eckland, B. K. (1978). Adult voluntary associations and adolescent socialization. *Sociological Quarterly, 19,* 481–490.

Hans, V. P., & Vidmar, N. (1982). Jury selection. In N. L. Kerr & R. M. Bray (Eds.), *Psychology of the courtroom* (pp. 39–82). New York: Academic Press.

Hansen, W. B., & Altman, I. (1976). Decorating personal places: A descriptive analysis. *Environment and Behavior, 8,* 491–504.

Hardin, G. (1968). The tragedy of the commons. *Science, 162,* 1243–1248.

Harding, J., Proshansky, H., Kutner, B., & Chein, I. (1969). Prejudice and ethnic relations. In G. Lindzey & E. Aronson (Eds.), *The handbook of social psychology* (2nd ed., Vol. 5, pp. 1–76). Reading, MA: Addison-Wesley.

Hardy, C., & Latané, B. (1986). Social loafing on a cheering task. *Social Science, 71(2–3),* 165–172.

Hardyck, J. A., & Braden, M. (1962). Prophecy fails again: A report of a failure to replicate. *Journal of Abnormal and Social Psychology, 65,* 136–141.

Hare, A. P. (1967). Small group development in the relay assembly testroom. *Sociological Inquiry, 37,* 169–182.

Hare, A. P. (1976). *Handbook of small group research* (2nd ed.). New York: The Free Press.

Hare, A. P. (1982). *Creativity in small groups.* Newbury Park, CA: Sage.

Hare, A. P. (1985). The significance of SYMLOG in the study of group dynamics. *International Journal of Small Group Research, 1,* 38–50.

Hare, A. P. (1994). Types of roles in small groups: A bit of history and a current perspective. *Small Group Research, 25,* 433–448.

Hare, A. P., & Bales, R. F. (1963). Seating position and small group interaction. *Sociometry, 26,* 480–486.

Hare, A. P., Blumberg, H. H., Davies, M. F., & Kent, M. V. (1994). *Small group research: A handbook.* Norwood, NJ: Ablex.

Hare, A. P., Blumberg, H. H., Davies, M. F., & Kent, M. V. (1996). *Small groups: An introduction.* Westport, CT: Praeger.

Hare, A. P., Borgatta, E. F., & Bales, R. F. (1955). *Small groups: Studies in social interaction.* New York: Knopf.

Hare, A. P., & Naveh, D. (1986). Conformity and creativity: Camp David, 1978. *Small Group Behavior, 17,* 243–268.

Harkins, S. G. (1987). Social loafing and social facilitation. *Journal of Experimental Social Psychology, 23,* 1–18.

Harkins, S. G., & Jackson, J. M. (1985). The role of evaluation in eliminating social loafing. *Personality and Social Psychology Bulletin, 11,* 457–465.

Harkins, S. G., Latané, B., & Williams, K. (1980). Social loafing: Allocating effort or taking it easy. *Journal of Experimental Social Psychology, 16,* 457–465.

Harkins, S. G., & Petty, R. E. (1982). Effects of task difficulty and task uniqueness on social loafing. *Journal of Personality and Social Psychology, 43,* 1214–1229.

Harkins, S. G., & Szymanski, K. (1987). Social loafing and social facilitation: New wine in old bottles. *Review of Personality and Social Psychology, 9,* 167–188.

Harkins, S. G., & Szymanski, K. (1988). Social loafing and self-evaluation with an objective standard. *Journal of Experimental Social Psychology, 24,* 354–365.

Harkins, S. G., & Szymanski, K. (1989). Social loafing and group evaluation. *Journal of Personality and Social Psychology, 56,* 934–941.

Harlow, H. F., & Harlow, M. K. (1966). Learning to love. *American Scientist, 54,* 244–272.

Harlow, R. E., & Cantor, N. (1996). Still participating after all these years: A study of life task participation in later life. *Journal of Personality and Social Psychology, 71,* 1235–1249.

Harnett, D. L., Cummings, L. L., & Hamner, W. C. (1973). Personality, bargaining style, and payoff in bilateral monopoly bargaining among European managers. *Sociometry, 36,* 325–345.

Harper, N. L., & Askling, L. R. (1980). Group communication and quality of task solution in a media production organization. *Communication Monographs, 47,* 77–100.

Harris, J. R. (1995). Where is the child's environment? A group socialization theory of development. *Psychological Review, 102,* 458–489.

Harrison, A. A., Clearwater, Y. A., & McKay, C. P. (Eds.). (1991). *From Antarctica to outer space: Life in isolation and confinement.* New York: Springer-Verlag.

Harrison, A. A., & Connors, M. M. (1984). Groups in exotic environments. *Advances in Experimental Social Psychology, 18,* 50–87.

Harrod, W. J. (1980). Expectations from unequal rewards. *Social Psychology Quarterly, 43,* 126–130.

Härtel, C. E. J., & Härtel, G. F. (1997). SHAPE-assisted intuitive decision making and problem solving: Information-processing-based training for conditions of cognitive busyness. *Group Dynamics: Theory, Research, and Practice, 1,* 187–199.

Hartig, T., Mang, M., & Evans, G. W. (1991). Restorative effects of natural environment experience. *Environment and Behavior, 23,* 3–26.

Harton, H. C., Green, L. R., Jackson, C., & Latané, B. (1998). Demonstrating dynamic social impact: Consolidation, clustering, correlation, and (sometimes) the correct answer. *Teaching of Psychology, 25,* 31–35.

Haslam, A. S., & Oakes, P. J. (1995). How context-independent is the outgroup homogeneity effect? A response to Bartsch and Judd. *European Journal of Social Psychology, 12,* 469–475.

Hastie, R., Penrod, S. D., & Pennington, N. (1983). *Inside the jury.* Cambridge, MA: Harvard University Press.

Hastorf, A. H., & Cantril, H. (1954). They saw a game. *Journal of Abnormal and Social Psychology, 49,* 129–134.

Haupt, A. L., & Leary, M. R. (1997). The appeal of worthless groups: Moderating effects of trait self-esteem. *Group Dynamics: Theory, Research, and Practice, 1,* 124–132.

Hayduk, L. A. (1978). Personal space: An evaluative and orienting overview. *Psychological Bulletin, 85,* 117–134.

Hayduk, L. A. (1983). Personal space: Where we now stand. *Psychological Bulletin, 94,* 293–335.

Hays, R. B., & Oxley, D. (1986). Social network development and functioning during a life transition. *Journal of Personality and Social Psychology, 50,* 304–313.

Haythorn, W. W. (1973). The miniworld of isolation: Laboratory studies. In J. E. Rasmussen (Ed.), *Man in isolation and confinement* (pp. 219–239). Chicago: Aldine.

Haythorn, W., Couch, A. S., Haefner, D., Langham, P., & Carter, L. F. (1956). The effects of varying combinations of authoritarian and equalitarian leaders and followers. *Journal of Abnormal and Social Psychology, 53,* 210–219.

Hearne, G. (1957). Leadership and the spatial factor in small groups. *Journal of Abnormal and Social Psychology, 54,* 269–272.

Heffron, M. H. (1972). The naval ship as an urban design problem. *Naval Engineers Journal, 12,* 49–64.

Heider, F. (1958). *The psychology of interpersonal relations.* New York: Wiley.

Heifetz, R. A. (1994). Some strategic implications of William Clinton's strengths and weaknesses. *Political Psychology, 15,* 763–768.

Heilman, M. E., Block, C. J., & Martell, R. F. (1995). Sex stereotypes: Do they influence perceptions of managers? *Journal of Social Behavior and Personality, 10,* 237–252.

Heine, S. J., & Lehman, D. R. (1977). The cultural construction of self-enhancement: An examination of group-serving biases. *Journal of Personality and Social Psychology, 72,* 1268–1283.

Heinicke, C. M., & Bales, R. F. (1953). Developmental trends in the structure of small groups. *Sociometry, 16,* 7–38.

Helgeson, V. S., & Mickelson, K. D. (1995). Motives for social comparison. *Personality and Social Psychology Bulletin, 21,* 1200–1209.

Heller, J. F., Groff, B. D., & Solomon, S. H. (1977). Toward an understanding of crowding: The role of physical interaction. *Journal of Personality and Social Psychology, 35,* 183–190.

Helmreich, R. L. (1974). Evaluation of environments: Behavioral observations in an undersea habitat. In J. Lang, C. Burnette, W. Moleski, & D. Vachon (Eds.), *Designing for human behavior.* Stroudsburg, PA: Dowden, Hutchinson, & Ross.

Helmreich, R. L., & Collins, B. E. (1967). Situational determinants of affiliative preference under stress. *Journal of Personality and Social Psychology, 6,* 79–85.

Helmreich, R. L., & Foushee, H. C. (1993). Why crew resource management? Empirical and theoretical bases of human factors training in aviation. In E. L. Wiener, B. G. Kanki, & R. L. Helmreich (Eds.), *Cockpit resource management* (pp. 3–45). San Diego: Academic Press.

Hembroff, L. A. (1982). Resolving status inconsistency: An expectation states theory and test. *Social Forces, 61,* 183–205.

Hembroff, L. A., & Myers, D. E. (1984). Status characteristics: Degrees of task relevance and decision process. *Social Psychology Quarterly, 47,* 337–346.

Hempel, C. G. (1966). *Philosophy of natural science.* Englewood Cliffs, NJ: Prentice Hall.

Hemphill, J. K. (1950). Relations between the size of the group and the behavior of "superior" leaders. *Journal of Social Psychology, 32,* 11–22.

Hemphill, J. K. (1961). Why people attempt to lead. In L. Petrullo & B. M. Bass (Eds.), *Leadership and interpersonal behavior.* New York: Holt, Rinehart & Winston.

Henchy, T., & Glass, D. C. (1968). Evaluation apprehension and the social facilitation of dominant and subordinate responses. *Journal of Personality and Social Psychology, 10,* 446–454.

Henry, W. P., & Solano, C. H. (1983). Photographic style and personality: Developing a coding system for photographs. *Journal of Psychology, 115,* 79–87.

Hensley, T. R., & Griffin, G. W. (1986). Victims of groupthink: The Kent State University Board of Trustees and the 1977 gymnasium controversy. *Journal of Conflict Resolution, 30,* 497–531.

Hepworth, J. T., & West, S. G. (1988). Lynchings and the economy: A time-series reanalysis of Hovland and Sears (1940). *Journal of Personality and Social Psychology, 55,* 239–247.

Herbert, T. B., & Cohen S. (1993). Stress and immunity in humans: A meta-analytic review. *Psychosomatic Medicine, 55,* 364–379.

Herek, G. M., Janis, I. L., & Huth, P. (1987). Decision-making during international crises: Is quality of process related to outcome? *Journal of Conflict Resolution, 31,* 203–226.

Herek, G. M., Janis, I. L., & Huth, P. (1989). Quality of U.S. decision making during the Cuban missile crisis: Major errors in Welch's reassessment. *Journal of Conflict Resolution, 33,* 446–459.

Hersey, P. (1985). A letter to the author of "Don't be misled by LEAD." *Journal of Applied Behavioral Science, 21,* 152–153.

Hersey, P., & Blanchard, K. H. (1976). Leader effectiveness and adaptability description (LEAD). In J. W. Pfeiffer & J. E. Jones (Eds.), *The 1976 annual handbook for group facilitators* (Vol. 5). La Jolla, CA: University Associates.

Hersey, P., & Blanchard, K. H. (1977). *Management of organizational behavior: Utilizing human resources* (3rd ed.). Englewood Cliffs, NJ: Prentice Hall.

Hersey, P., & Blanchard, K. H. (1982). *Management of organizational behavior* (4th ed.). Englewood Cliffs, NJ: Prentice Hall.

Herzog, T. R., & Bosley, P. J. (1992). Tranquility and preference as affective qualities of natural environment. *Journal of Environmental Psychology, 12,* 115–127.

Heshka, S., & Nelson, Y. (1972). Interpersonal speaking distance as a function of age, sex, and relationship. *Sociometry, 25,* 491–498.

Higginbotham, H. N., West, S. G., & Forsyth, D. R. (1988). Psychotherapy and behavior change: Social, cultural, and methodological perspectives. New York: Pergamon.

Hill, C. A. (1991). Seeking emotional support: The influence of affiliative need and partner warmth. *Journal of Personality and Social Psychology, 60,* 112–121.

Hill, C. E., Helms, J. E., Tichenor, V., Spiegel, S. B., O'Grady, K. E., & Perry, E. S. (1988). Effects of therapist response modes in brief psychotherapy. *Journal of Counseling Psychology, 35,* 222–233.

Hill, C. T., & Stull, D. E. (1981). Sex differences in effects of social and value similarity in same-sex friendship. *Journal of Personality and Social Psychology, 41,* 488–502.

Hill, T. E., & Schmitt, N. (1977). Individual differences in leadership decision making. *Organizational Behavior and Human Performance, 19,* 353–367.

Hill, W. F., & Gruner, L. (1973). A study of development in open and closed groups. *Small Group Behavior, 4,* 355–381.

Hiltrop, J. M., & Rubin, J. Z. (1982). Effect of intervention mode and conflict of interest on dispute resolution. *Journal of Personality and Social Psychology, 42,* 665–672.

Hinkle, S., & Schopler, J. (1986). Bias in the evaluation of in-group and out-group performance. In S. Worchel & W. G. Austin (Eds.), *Psychology of intergroup relations* (2nd ed., pp. 196–212). Chicago: Nelson-Hall.

Hinsz, V. B. (1995). Goal setting by groups performing an additive task: A comparison with individual goal setting. *Journal of Applied Social Psychology, 25,* 965–990.

Hinsz, V. B., Tindale, R. S., & Vollrath, D. A. (1997). The emerging conceptualization of groups as information processors. *Psychological Bulletin, 121,* 43–64.

Hirokawa, R. Y. (1980). A comparative analysis of communication patterns within effective and ineffective decision-making groups. *Communication Monographs, 47,* 312–321.

Hirokawa, R. Y. (1984). Does consensus really result in higher quality group decisions? In G. M. Phillips & J. T. Wood (Eds.), *Emergent issues in human decision making* (pp. 40–49). Carbondale, IL: Southern Illinois University Press.

Hirokawa, R. Y. (1990). The role of communication in group decision-making efficacy. *Small Group Research, 21,* 190–204.

Hirokawa, R. Y. (1992). Communication and group decision-making efficacy. In R. S. Cathcart & L. A. Samovar (Eds.), *Small group communication: A reader* (6th ed., pp. 165–177). Dubuque, IA: Brown.

Hirt, E. R., Zillmann, D., Erickson, G. A., & Kennedy, C. (1992). Costs and benefits of allegiance: Changes in fans' self-ascribed competencies after team victory versus defeat. *Journal of Personality and Social Psychology, 63,* 724–738.

Hodson, G., & Sorrentino, R. M. (1997). Groupthink and uncertainty orientation: Personality differences in reactivity to the group situation. *Group Dynamics: Theory, Research, and Practice, 1,* 144–155.

Hoffer, E. (1951). *The true believer.* New York: Harper & Row.

Hofstede, G. (1980). *Culture's consequences: International differences in work-related values.* Newbury Park, CA: Sage.

Hofstede, G. (1983). Dimensions of national cultures in fifty countries and three regions. In J. B. Deregowaki, S. Dziurawiec, & R. C. Annis (Eds.), *Explications in cross-cultural psychology* (pp. 335–355). Lisse, the Netherlands: Swets and Zeitlinger B. V.

Hogan, R., Curphy, G. J., & Hogan, J. (1994). What we know about leadership: Effectiveness and personality. *American Psychologist, 49,* 493–504.

Hogg, M. A. (1992). *The social psychology of group cohesiveness: From attraction to social identity.* New York: New York University Press.

Hogg, M. A. (1993). Group cohesiveness: A critical review and some new directions. *European Review of Social Psychology, 4,* 85–111.

Hogg, M. A. (1996). Intragroup processes, group structure and social identity. In W. P. Robinson (Ed.), *Social groups and identities: Developing the legacy of Henri Tajfel* (pp. 65–93). Oxford, England: Butterworth-Heinemann.

Hogg, M. A., Cooper-Shaw, L., & Holzworth, D. W. (1993). Group prototypicality and depersonalized attraction in small interactive groups. *Personality and Social Psychology Bulletin, 19,* 452–465.

Hogg, M. A., & Hains, S. C. (1996). Intergroup relations and group solidarity: Effects of group identification and social beliefs on depersonalized attraction. *Journal of Personality and Social Psychology, 70,* 295–309.

Hogg, M. A., & Hardie, E. A. (1991). Social attraction, personal attraction, and self-categorization. *Personality and Social Psychology Bulletin, 17,* 175–180.

Hogg, M. A., Hardie, E. A., & Reynolds, K. (1995). Prototypical similarity, self-categorization, and depersonalized attraction: A perspective on group cohesiveness. *European Journal of Social Psychology, 25,* 159–177.

Hogg, M. A., & Sunderland, J. (1991). Self-esteem and intergroup discrimination in the minimal group paradigm. *British Journal of Social Psychology, 30,* 51–62.

Hogg, M. A., Terry, D. J., & White, K. M. (1995). A tale of two theories: A critical comparison of identity theory with social identity theory. *Social Psychology Quarterly, 58,* 255–269.

Hollander, E. P. (1958). Conformity, status, and idiosyncrasy credit. *Psychological Review, 65,* 117–127.

Hollander, E. P. (1960). Competence and conformity in the acceptance of influence. *Journal of Abnormal and Social Psychology, 61,* 365–369.

Hollander, E. P. (1961). Some effects of perceived status on responses to innovative behavior. *Journal of Abnormal and Social Psychology, 63,* 247–250.

Hollander, E. P. (1965). Validity of peer nominations in predicting a distance performance criterion. *Journal of Applied Psychology, 49,* 434–438.

Hollander, E. P. (1971). *Principles and methods of social psychology* (2nd ed.). New York: Oxford University Press.

Hollander, E. P. (1981). *Principles and methods of social psychology* (3rd ed.). New York: Oxford University Press.

Hollander, E. P. (1985). Leadership and power. In G. Lindzey & E. Aronson (Eds.), *Handbook of social psychology* (3rd ed., Vol. 2, pp. 485–537). New York: Random House.

Hollander, E. P. (1993). Legitimacy, power, and influence: A perspective on relational features of leadership. In M. M. Chemers & R. Ayman (Eds.), *Leadership theory and research: Perspectives and directions* (pp. 29–47). San Diego: Academic Press.

Hollander, E. P., & Julian, J. W. (1969). Contemporary trends in the analysis of leadership processes. *Psychological Bulletin, 71,* 387–397.

Hollander, E. P., & Offermann, L. R. (1990). Power and leadership in organizations: Relationships in transition. *American Psychologist, 45,* 179–189.

Hollander, M., & Kazaoka, K. (1988). Behavior therapy groups. In S. Long (Ed.)., *Six group therapies* (pp. 257–326). New York: Plenum.

Hollingshead, A. B., & McGrath, J. E. (1995). Computer-assisted groups: A critical review of the empirical research. In R. A. Guzzo, E. Salas & Associates, *Team effectiveness and decision making in organizations* (pp. 46–78). San Francisco: Jossey-Bass.

Hollingworth, H. L. (1935). *The psychology of the audience.* New York: American Books.

Holmes, P. (1983). "Dropping out" from an adolescent therapeutic group: A study of factors in the patients and their parents which may influence this process. *Journal of Adolescence, 6,* 333–346.

Holsti, O. R., & North, R. (1965). The history of human conflict. In E. B. McNeil (Ed.), *The nature of human conflict.* Englewood Cliffs, NJ: Prentice Hall.

Holtgraves, T., & Yang, J. (1992). Interpersonal underpinnings of request strategies: General principles and differences due to culture and gender. *Journal of Personality and Social Psychology, 62,* 246–256.

Homans, G. C. (1950). *The human group.* New York: Harcourt, Brace, & World.

Homans, G. C. (1967). *The nature of social science.* New York: Harcourt, Brace & World.

Homans, G. C. (1974). *Social behavior: Its elementary forms.* San Diego: Harcourt Brace Jovanovich.

Homma, M., Tajima, K., & Hayashi, M. (1995). The effects of misperception of performance in brainstorming groups. *Japanese Journal of Experimental Social Psychology, 34,* 221–231.

Hooijberg, R., DiTomaso, N. (1996). Leadership in and of demographically diverse organizations. *Leadership Quarterly, 7,* 1–19.

Hoppe, M. J., Wells, E. A., Morrison, D. M., & Gillmore, M. R. (1995). Using focus groups to discuss sensitive topics with children. *Evaluation Review, 19,* 102–114.

Horne, A. M., Jolliff, D. L., & Roth, E. W. (1996). Men mentoring men in groups. In M. P. Andronico

(Ed.), *Men in groups: Insights, interventions, and psychoeducational work* (pp. 97–112). Washington, DC: American Psychological Association.

Horney, K. (1945). *Our inner conflicts.* New York: Norton.

Horwitz, M., & Rabbie, J. M. (1982). Individuality and membership in the intergroup system. In H. Tajfel (Ed.), *Social identity and intergroup relations* (pp. 241–274). New York: Cambridge University Press.

Houle, C. O. (1989). *Governing boards: Their nature and nurture.* San Francisco: Jossey-Bass.

House, R. J. (1971). A path goal theory of leader effectiveness. *Administrative Science Quarterly, 16,* 321–338.

House, R. J., & Aditya, R. N. (1997). The social scientific study of leadership: Quo vadis? *Journal of Management, 23,* 409–473.

House, R. J., Schuler, R. S., & Levanoni, E. (1983). Role conflict and ambiguous scales: Realities or artifacts? *Journal of Applied Psychology, 68,* 334–337.

House, R. L., & Baetz, M. L. (1979). Leadership: Some empirical generalizations and new research directions. *Research in Organizational Behavior, 1,* 341–423.

Hovland, C., & Sears, R. (1940). Minor studies of aggression: VI. Correlation of lynchings with economic indices. *Journal of Psychology, 9,* 301–310.

Howard, J. A., Blumstein, P., & Schwartz, P. (1986). Sex, power, and influence tactics in intimate relationships. *Journal of Personality and Social Psychology, 51,* 102–109.

Howard, J. W., & Rothbart, M. (1980). Social categorization and memory for in-group and out-group behavior. *Journal of Personality and Social Psychology, 38,* 301–310.

Howells, L. T., & Becker, S. W. (1962). Seating arrangement and leadership emergence. *Journal of Abnormal and Social Psychology, 64,* 148–150.

Hoyle, R. H., & Crawford, A. M. (1994). Use of individual-level data to investigate group phenomena: Issues and strategies. *Small Group Research, 25,* 464–485.

Hoyle R. H., Pinkley R. L., & Insko C. A. (1989). Perceptions of behavior: Evidence of differing expectations for interpersonal and intergroup interactions. *Personality and Social Psychology Bulletin, 15,* 365–376.

Humphreys, L. (1975). *Tearoom trade* (enlarged ed.). New York: Aldine.

Humphreys, P., & Berger, J. (1981). Theoretical consequences of the status characteristics formulation. *American Journal of Sociology, 86,* 953–983.

Hunt, E. B., & Rowe, R. R. (1960). Group and individual economic decision making in risk conditions. In D. W. Taylor (Ed.), *Experiments on decision making and other studies.* Arlington, VA: Armed Services Technical Information Agency.

Hunt, J. G., & Peterson, M. F. (1997). International perspectives on international leadership. *Leadership Quarterly, 8,* 203–231.

Hunter, J. A., Platow, M. J., Bell, L. M., Kypri, K., & Lewis, C. A. (1997). Intergroup bias and self-evaluation: Domain-specific self-esteem, threats to identity and dimensional importance. *British Journal of Social Psychology, 36,* 405–426.

Hunter, J. A., Platow, M. J., Howard, M. L., & Stringer, M. (1996). Social identity and intergroup evaluative bias: Realistic categories and domain specific self-esteem in a conflict setting. *European Journal of Social Psychology, 26,* 631–647.

Hyman, H. (1942). The psychology of status. *Archives of Psychology, 38* (269).

Hyman, H. M., & Tarrant, C. M. (1975). Aspects of American trial jury history. In R. J. Simon (Ed.), *The jury system in America.* Newbury Park, CA: Sage.

Iacobucci, D. (1990). Derivation of subgroups from dyadic interactions. *Psychological Bulletin, 107,* 114–132.

Iannaccone, L. R. (1994). Why strict churches are strong. *American Journal of Sociology, 99,* 1180–1211.

Ickes, W. (1983). Influences of past relationships on subsequent ones. In P. B. Paulus (Ed.), *Basic group processes* (pp. 315–337). New York: Springer-Verlag.

Ickes, W., & Turner, M. (1983). On the social advantages of having an older, opposite-sex sibling: Birth order influence in mixed-sex dyads. *Journal of Personality and Social Psychology, 45,* 210–222.

Ilgen, D. R., & Fujii, D. S. (1976). An investigation of the validity of leader behavior descriptions obtained from subordinates. *Journal of Applied Psychology, 61,* 642–651.

Ilgen, D. R., Mitchell, T. R., & Fredrickson, J. W. (1981). Poor performances: Supervisors' and subordinates' responses. *Organizational Behavior and Human Performance, 27,* 386–410.

Indik, B. P. (1965). Organization size and member participation: Some empirical tests of alternate explanations. *Human Relations, 15,* 339–350.

Ingham, A. G., Levinger, G., Graves, J., & Peckham, V. (1974). The Ringelmann effect: Studies of group size and group performance. *Journal of Personality and Social Psychology, 10,* 371–384.

Insko, C. A., Gilmore, R., Drenan, S., Lipsitz, A., Moehle, D., & Thibaut, J. (1983). Trade versus expropriation in open groups: A comparison of two types of social power. *Journal of Personality and Social Psychology, 44,* 977–999.

Insko C. A., Hoyle R. H., Pinkley R. L., Hong G., Slim R., Dalton, G., Lin, Y., Ruffin, P. P., Dardis, G. J., Bernthal, P. R., & Schopler, J. (1988). Individual-group discontinuity: The role of a consensus rule. *Journal of Experimental Social Psychology, 24,* 505–519.

Insko C. A., Pinkley, R. L., Hoyle, R. H., Dalton, B., Hong, G., Slim, R., Landry, P., Holton, B., Ruffin, P. F., & Thibaut, J. (1987). Individual-group discontinuity: The role of intergroup contact. *Journal of Experimental Social Psychology, 23,* 250–267.

Insko, C. A., & Schopler, J. (1972). *Experimental social psychology.* New York: Academic Press.

Insko, C. A., & Schopler, J. (1998). Differential distrust of groups and individuals. In C. Sedikides, J. Schopler, & C. A. Insko (Eds.), *Intergroup cognition and intergroup behavior* (pp. 75–107). Mahwah, NJ: Erlbaum.

Insko C. A., Schopler, J., Drigotas, S. M., Graetz, K., Kennedy, J., Cox, C., & Bornstein, G. (1993). The role of communication in interindividual-intergroup discontinuity. *Journal of Conflict Resolution, 37,* 108–138.

Insko, C. A., Schopler, J., Graetz, K. A., Drigotas, S. M., Currey, K. P., Smith, S. L., Brazil, D., & Bornstein, G. (1994). Interindividual-intergroup discontinuity in the Prisoner's Dilemma Game. *Journal of Conflict Resolution, 38,* 87–116.

Insko, C. A., Schopler, J., Hoyle, R. H., Dardis, G. J., & Graetz, K. A. (1990). Individual-group discontinuity as a function of fear and greed. *Journal of Personality and Social Psychology, 58,* 68–79.

Insko, C. A., Schopler, J., Kennedy, J. F., Dahl, K. R., Graetz, K. A., & Drigotas, S. M. (1992). Individual-group discontinuity from the differing perspectives of Campbell's realistic group conflict theory and Tajfel and Turner's social identity theory. *Social Psychology Quarterly, 55,* 272–291.

Insko, C. A., Schopler, J., & Sedikides, C. (1998). Personal control, entitativity, and evolution. In C. Sedikides, J. Schopler, & C. A. Insko (Eds.), *Inter-*

group cognition and intergroup behavior (pp. 109–120). Hillsdale, NJ: Erlbaum.

Inkso, C. A., Thibaut, J. W., Moehle, D., Wilson, M., Diamond, W. D., Gilmore, R., Solomon, M. R., & Lipsitz, A. (1980). Social evolution and the emergence of leadership. *Journal of Personality and Social Psychology, 39,* 431–448.

Instone, D., Major, B., & Bunker, B. B. (1983). Gender, self confidence, and social influence strategies: An organizational simulation. *Journal of Personality and Social Psychology, 44,* 322–333.

Isenberg, D. J. (1986). Group polarization: A critical review and meta-analysis. *Journal of Personality and Social Psychology, 50,* 1141–1151.

Isenberg, D. J., & Ennis, J. G. (1981). Perceiving group members: A comparison of derived and imposed dimensions. *Journal of Personality and Social Psychology, 41,* 293–305.

Iverson, M. A. (1964). Personality impressions of punitive stimulus persons of differential status. *Journal of Abnormal and Social Psychology, 68,* 617–626.

Ivie, R. L. (1980). Images of savagery in American justifications for war. *Communication Monographs, 47,* 279–294.

Izraeli, D. N., Izraeli, D., & Eden, D. (1985). Giving credit where credit is due: A case of no sex bias in attribution. *Journal of Applied Social Psychology, 15,* 516–530.

Jablin, F. M. (1979). Superior-subordinate communication: The state of the art. *Psychological Bulletin, 86,* 1201–1222.

Jablin, F. M. (1982). Formal structural characteristics of organizations and superior-subordinate communication. *Human Communication Research, 8,* 338–347.

Jackson, J. M. (1987). Social impact theory: A social forces model of influence. In B. Mullen & G. R. Goethals (Eds.), *Theories of group behavior* (pp. 112–124). New York: Springer-Verlag.

Jackson, J. M., & Harkins, S. G. (1985). Equity in effort: An explanation of the social loafing effect. *Journal of Personality and Social Psychology, 49,* 1199–1206.

Jackson, J. M., & Latané, B. (1981). All alone in front of all those people: Stage fright as a function of number and type of co-performances and audience. *Journal of Personality and Social Psychology, 40,* 73–85.

Jackson, S. E. (1992). Team composition in organizational settings; Issues in managing an increasingly diverse workforce. In S. Worchel, S. Wood, & J. A. Simpson (Eds.), *Group process and productivity* (pp. 138–172). Newbury Park, CA: Sage.

Jackson, S. E., May, K. E., & Whitney, K. (1995). Understanding the dynamics of diversity in decision-making teams. In R. A. Guzzo, E. Salas & Associates, *Team effectiveness and decision making in organizations* (pp. 204–261). San Francisco: Jossey-Bass.

Jackson, S. E., & Schuler, R. S. (1995). Understanding human resource management in the context of organizations and their environments. *Annual Review of Psychology, 46,* 237–264.

Jacobs, A. (1974). The use of feedback in groups. In A. Jacobs & W. W. Spradlin (Eds.), *Group as an agent of change.* New York: Behavioral Publications.

Jacobs, D., & O'Brien, R. M. (1998). The determinants of deadly force: A structural analysis of police violence. *American Journal of Sociology, 103,* 837–862.

Jacobs, E., Masson, R. L., Harvill, R. L. (1998). *Group counseling: Strategies and skills.* Pacific Grove, CA: Brooks/Cole.

Jacobs, M. K., & Goodman, G. (1989). Psychology and self-help groups: Predictions on a partnership. *American Psychologist, 44,* 536–545.

Jacobs, R. C., & Campbell, D. T. (1961). The perpetuation of an arbitrary tradition through several generations of a laboratory microculture. *Journal of Abnormal and Social Psychology, 62,* 649–658.

Jago, A. G. (1978). Configural cue utilization in implicit models of leader behavior. *Organizational Behavior and Human Performance, 22,* 474–496.

James, R. (1959). Status and competency of jurors. *American Journal of Sociology, 64,* 563–570.

Janis, I. L. (1963). Group identification under conditions of external danger. *British Journal of Medical Psychology, 36,* 227–238.

Janis, I. L. (1972). *Victims of groupthink.* Boston: Houghton-Mifflin.

Janis, I. L. (1982). *Groupthink: Psychological studies of policy decisions and fiascos* (2nd ed.). Boston: Houghton Mifflin.

Janis, I. L. (1983). Groupthink. In H. H. Blumberg, A. P. Hare, V. Kent, & M. F. Davis (Eds.), *Small groups and social interaction* (Vol. 2, pp. 39–46). New York: Wiley.

Janis, I. L. (1985). International crisis management in the nuclear age. *Applied Social Psychology Annual, 6,* 63–86.

Janis, I. L. (1989). *Crucial decisions: Leadership in policy making and crisis management.* New York: The Free Press.

Janis, I. L., & Mann, L. (1977). *Decision making: A psychological analysis of conflict, choice, and commitment.* New York: The Free Press.

Jankowski, M. S. (1991). *Islands in the street: Gangs and American urban society.* Berkeley: University of California Press.

Jarboe, S. C., & Witteman, H. R. (1996). Intragroup conflict management in task-oriented groups: The influence of problem sources and problem analyses. *Small Group Research, 27,* 316–338.

Jehn, K. A. (1995). A multimethod examination of the benefits and detriments of intragroup conflict. *Administrative Science Quarterly, 40,* 256–282.

Jehn, K. A., & Shaw, P. P. (1997). Interpersonal relationships and task performance: An examination of mediating processes in friendship and acquaintance groups. *Journal of Personality and Social Psychology, 72,* 775–790.

Jetten, J., Spears, R., & Manstead, A. S. R. (1996). Intergroup norms and intergroup discrimination: Distinctive self-categorization and social identity effects. *Journal of Personality and Social Psychology, 71,* 1222–1233.

Johnson, A. G. (1995). *The Blackwell dictionary of sociology: A user's guide to sociological language.* Cambridge, MA: Blackwell.

Johnson, C. (1974). Planning for termination of the group. In P. Glasser, R. Sarri, & R. Vinter (Eds.), *Individual change through small groups* (pp. 258–265). New York: The Free Press.

Johnson, D. W., & Johnson, R. (1989). *Cooperation and competition: Theory and research.* Edina, MN: Interaction Book Company.

Johnson, D. W., & Johnson, R. T. (1994). Constructive conflict in the schools. *Journal of Social Issues, 50(1),* 117–137.

Johnson, D. W., Johnson, R. T., & Maruyama, G. (1984). Goal interdependence and interpersonal attraction in heterogeneous classrooms: A meta-analysis. In N. Miller & M. Brewer (Eds.), *Groups in contact: The psychology of desegregation* (pp. 187–212). New York: Academic Press.

Johnson, D. W., Maruyama, G., Johnson, R., Nelson, D., & Skon, L. (1981). Effects of cooperative, competitive, and individualistic goal structures on achievement: A meta-analysis. *Psychological Bulletin, 89,* 47–62.

Johnson, F. (1988). Encounter group therapy. In S. Long (Ed.), *Six group therapies* (pp. 115–158). New York: Plenum.

Johnson, M. P., & Ewens, W. (1971). Power relations and affective style as determinants of confidence in impression formation in a game situation. *Journal of Experimental Social Psychology, 7,* 98–110.

Johnson, N. R. (1987). Panic at "The Who concert stampede": An empirical assessment. *Social Problems, 34,* 362–373.

Johnson, R. D., & Downing, L. L. (1979). Deindividuation and valence of cues: Effects on prosocial and antisocial behavior. *Journal of Personality and Social Psychology, 37,* 1532–1538.

Jones, E. S., Gallois, C., Callan, V. J., & Barker, M. (1995). Language and power in an academic context: The effects of status, ethnicity, and sex. *Journal of Language and Social Psychology, 14,* 434–461.

Jones, G. V. (1983). Identifying basic categories. *Psychological Bulletin, 94,* 423–428.

Jones, S. C. (1973). Self and interpersonal evaluations: Esteem theories versus consistency theories. *Psychological Bulletin, 79,* 185–199.

Jones, W. H., & Carver, M. D. (1991). Adjustment and coping implications of loneliness. In C. R. Snyder and D. R. Forsyth (Eds.), *Handbook of social and clinical psychology: The health perspective* (pp. 395–415). New York: Pergamon.

Josephs, R. A., Markus, H. R., & Tafarodi, R. W. (1992). Gender and self-esteem. *Journal of Personality and Social Psychology, 63,* 391–402.

Jourard, S. (1971). *Self-disclosure: An experimental analysis of the transparent self.* New York: Wiley.

Judd, C. M., & Park, B. (1988). Out-group homogeneity: Judgments of variability at the individual and group levels. *Journal of Personality and Social Psychology, 54,* 778–788.

Jung, C. G. (1924). *Psychological types, or the psychology of individuation.* (H. G. Baynes, Trans.). New York: Harcourt, Brace & World.

Kagan, J., Snidman, N., & Arcus, D. M. (1992). Initial reactions to unfamiliarity. *Current Directions in Psychological Science, 1,* 171–174.

Kahn, A., Hottes, J., & Davis, W. L. (1971). Cooperation and optimal responding in the Prisoner's Dilemma Game: Effects of sex and physical attractiveness. *Journal of Personality and Social Psychology, 17,* 267–279.

Kahn, A., & Ryen, A. H. (1972). Factors influencing the bias towards one's own group. *International Journal of Group Tensions, 2,* 33–50.

Kahn, R. L., Wolfe, D. M., Quinn, R. P., Snoek, J. D., & Rosenthal, R. A. (1964). *Organizational stress: Studies in role conflict and ambiguity.* New York: Wiley.

Kalven, H., Jr., & Zeisel, H. (1966). *The American jury.* Boston: Little, Brown.

Kamarck, T. W., Manuck, S. B., & Jennings, J. R. (1990). Social support reduces cardiovascular reactivity to psychological challenge: A laboratory model. *Psychosomatic Medicine, 52,* 42–58.

Kameda, T. (1994). Group decision making and social sharedness. *Japanese Psychological Review, 37,* 367–385.

Kameda, T. (1996). Procedural influence in consensus formation: Evaluating group decision making from a social choice perspective. In E. Witte & J. Davis (Eds.), *Understanding group behavior: Consensual action by small groups* (Vol. 1, pp. 137–161). Mahwah, NJ: Erlbaum.

Kameda, T., Stasson, M. F., Davis, J. H., Parks, C. D., & Zimmerman, S. K. (1992). Social dilemmas, subgroups, and motivation loss in task-oriented groups: In search of an "optimal" team size in division of work. *Social Psychology Quarterly, 55,* 47–56.

Kameda, T., & Sugimori, S. (1993). Psychological entrapment in group decision making: An assigned decision rule and a groupthink phenomenon. *Journal of Personality and Social Psychology, 65,* 282–292.

Kameda, T., & Sugimori, S. (1995). Procedural influence in two-step group decision making: Power of local majorities in consensus formation. *Journal of Personality and Social Psychology, 69,* 865–876.

Kandel, D. B. (1978). Similarity in real-life adolescent friendship pairs. *Journal of Personality and Social Psychology, 36,* 306–312.

Kanter, R. M. (1977). Some effects of proportions on group life: Skewed sex ratios and responses to token women. *American Journal of Sociology, 82,* 465–490.

Kanzer, M. (1983). Freud: The first psychoanalytic group leader. In H. I. Kaplan & B. J. Sadock (Eds.), *Comprehensive group psychotherapy* (2nd ed., pp. 8–14). Baltimore: Williams & Wilkins.

Kaplan, H. I., & Sadock, B. J. (Eds.). (1993). *Comprehensive group psychotherapy* (3rd ed.). Baltimore: Williams & Wilkins.

Kaplan, K. J., Firestone, I. J., Klein, K. W., & Sodikoff, C. (1983). Distancing in dyads: A comparison of four models. *Social Psychology Quarterly, 46,* 108–115.

Kaplan, M. F. (1982). Cognitive processes in the individual juror. In N. L. Kerr & R. M. Bray (Eds.), *Psychology of the courtroom* (pp. 197–220). New York: Academic Press.

Kaplan, M. F., & Miller, C. E. (1983). Group discussion and judgment. In P. B. Paulus (Ed.), *Basic group processes* (pp. 65–94). New York: Springer-Verlag.

Kaplan, M. F., & Miller, C. E. (1987). Group decision making and normative versus informational influence: Effects of type of issue and assigned decision rule. *Journal of Personality and Social Psychology, 53,* 306–313.

Kaplan, R., & Kaplan, S. (1989). *The experience of nature: A psychological perspective.* New York: Cambridge University Press.

Kaplan, R. E. (1979). The conspicuous absence of evidence that process consultation enhances task performance. *Journal of Applied Behavioral Science, 15,* 346–360.

Kaplowitz, S. A. (1978). Towards a systematic theory of power attribution. *Social Psychology, 41,* 131–148.

Kapos, M. (1995). *The impressionists and their legacy.* New York: Barnes & Noble.

Karau, S. J., & Williams, K. D. (1993). Social loafing: A meta-analytic review and theoretical integration. *Journal of Personality and Social Psychology, 65,* 681–706.

Karau, S. J., & Williams, K. D. (1995). Social loafing: Research findings, implications, and future directions. *Current Directions in Psychological Science, 5,* 134–140.

Karau, S. J., & Williams, K. D. (1997). The effects of group cohesiveness on social loafing and social compensation. *Group Dynamics: Theory, Research, and Practice, 1,* 156–168.

Kashima, Y., Yamaguchi, S., Kim, U., Choi, S., Gelgand, M. J., & Yuki, M. (1995). Culture, gender, and self: A perspective from individualism-collectivism research. *Journal of Personality and Social Psychology, 69,* 925–937.

Katz, D., & Kahn, R. L. (1978). *The social psychology of organizations* (2nd ed.). New York: Wiley.

Katz, R. (1977). The influence of group conflict on leadership effectiveness. *Organizational Behavior and Human Performance, 20,* 265–286.

Katz, R., & Tushman, M. (1979). Communication patterns, project performance, and task characteristics: An empirical evaluation and integration in an R & D setting. *Organization Behavior and Human Performance, 23,* 139–162.

Katzenbach, J. R., & Smith, D. K. (1993). The discipline of teams. *Harvard Business Review, 71,* 111–120.

Kaul, T. J., & Bednar, R. L. (1986). Experiential group research: Results, questions, and suggestions. In S. L. Garfield & A. E. Bergin (Eds.), *Handbook of psychotherapy and behavior change* (3rd ed., pp. 671–714). New York: Wiley.

Kellehear, A. (1993). *The unobtrusive researcher: A guide to methods.* New South Wales, Australia: Allen & Unwin.

Kelley, H. H. (1952). Two functions of reference groups. In G. E. Swanson, T. M. Newcomb, & E. L. Hartley (Eds.), *Readings in social psychology* (2nd ed.). New York: Holt.

Kelley, H. H. (1979). *Personal relationships: Their structures and processes.* Hillsdale, NJ: Erlbaum.

Kelley, H. H. (1983). Love and commitment. In H. H. Kelley, E. Berscheid, A. Christensen, J. H. Harvey, T. L. Huston, G. Levinger, E. McClintock, L. A. Peplau, & D. R. Peterson, *Close relationships* (pp. 265–314). New York: Freeman.

Kelley, H. H. (1997). Expanding the analysis of social orientations by reference to the sequential-temporal structure of situations. *European Journal of Social Psychology, 27,* 373–404.

Kelley, H. H., Contry, J. C., Dahlke, A. E., & Hill, A. H. (1965). Collective behavior in a simulated panic situation. *Journal of Experimental Social Psychology, 1,* 20–54.

Kelley, H. H., & Stahelski, A. J. (1970a). Errors in perceptions of intentions in a mixed-motive game. *Journal of Experimental Social Psychology, 6,* 379–400.

Kelley, H. H., & Stahelski, A. J. (1970b). Social interaction basis of cooperators' and competitors' beliefs about others. *Journal of Personality and Social Psychology, 16,* 66–91.

Kelley, H. H., & Stahelski, A. J. (1970c). The inference of intentions from moves in the Prisoner's Dilemma Game. *Journal of Experimental Social Psychology, 6,* 401–419.

Kelley, H. H., & Thibaut, J. W. (1978). *Interpersonal relations: A theory of interdependence.* New York: Wiley.

Kelly, J. R., Futoran, G. C., & McGrath, J. E. (1990). Capacity and capability: Seven studies of entrainment of task performance rates. *Small Group Research, 21,* 283–314.

Kelly, J. R., & Karau, S. J. (1993). Entrainment of creativity in small groups. *Small Group Research, 24,* 179–198.

Kelly, L., & Duran, R. L. (1985). Interactions and performance in small groups: A descriptive report. *International Journal of Small Group Research, 1,* 182–192.

Kelman, H. C. (1958). Compliance, identification, and internalization: Three processes of attitude change. *Journal of Conflict Resolution, 2,* 51–60.

Kelman, H. C. (1961). Processes of opinion change. *Public Opinion Quarterly, 25,* 57–78.

Kelman, H. C. (1992). Informal mediation by the scholar/practitioner. In J. Bercovitch & J. Rubin (Eds.), *Mediation in international relations: Multiple approaches to conflict management* (pp. 64–96). New York: St. Martin's Press.

Kelman, H. C., & Hamilton, V. L. (1989). *Crimes of obedience: Toward a social psychology of authority and responsibility.* New Haven, CT: Yale University Press.

Kemery, E. R., Bedeian, A. G., Mossholder, K. W., & Touliatos, J. (1985). Outcomes of role stress: A multisample constructive replication. *Academy of Management Review, 28,* 363–375.

Kennedy, R. F. (1969). *Thirteen days.* New York: Norton.

Kenney, R. A., Schwartz-Kenney, B. M., & Blascovich, J. (1996). Implicit leadership theories: Defining leaders described as worthy of influence. *Personality and Social Psychology Bulletin, 22,* 1128–1143.

Kenny, D. A., Horner, C., Kashy, D. A., & Chu, L. (1992). Consensus at zero acquaintance: Replication, behavioral cues, and stability. *Journal of Personality and Social Psychology, 62,* 88–97.

Kenny, D. A., & Judd, C. M. (1996). A general procedure for the estimation of interdependence. *Psychological Bulletin, 119,* 138–148.

Kenny, D. A., Kieffer, S. C., Smith, J. A., Ceplenski, P., & Kulo, J. (1996). Circumscribed accuracy among well-acquainted individuals. *Journal of Experimental Social Psychology, 32,* 1–12.

Kenny, D. A., & Zaccaro, S. J. (1983). An estimate of variance due to traits in leadership. *Journal of Applied Psychology, 68,* 678–685.

Kent, S. (1991). Partitioning space: Cross-cultural factors influencing domestic spatial segmentation. *Environment and Behavior, 23,* 438–473.

Kerckhoff, A. C., & Back, K. W. (1968). *The June Bug: A study of hysterical contagion.* New York: Appleton-Century-Crofts.

Kerckhoff, A. C., Back, K. W., & Miller, N. (1965). Sociometric patterns in hysterical contagion. *Sociometry, 28,* 2–15.

Kerckhoff, A. C., & Davis, K. E. (1962). Value consensus and need complementarity in mate selection. *American Sociological Review, 27,* 295–303.

Kerr, N. L. (1983). Motivation losses in small groups: A social dilemma analysis. *Journal of Personality and Social Psychology, 45,* 819–828.

Kerr, N. L. (1995). Norms in social dilemmas. In D. A. Schroeder (Ed.), *Social dilemmas: Perspectives on individuals and groups* (pp. 31–48). Westport, CT: Praeger.

Kerr, N. L., Aronoff, J., & Messé, L. A. (in press). Methods of small group research. In H. T. Reis & C. M. Judd (Eds.), *Handbook of research methods in social psychology.* New York: Cambridge University Press.

Kerr, N. L., Atkin, R. S., Stasser, G., Meek, D., Holt, R. W., & Davis, J. H. (1976). Guilt beyond a reasonable doubt: Effect of concept definition and assigned decision rule on the judgments of mock jurors. *Journal of Personality and Social Psychology, 34,* 282–294.

Kerr, N. L., & Bruun, S. E. (1981). Ringelmann revisited: Alternative explanations for the social loafing effect. *Personality and Social Psychology Bulletin, 7,* 224–231.

Kerr, N. L., & Bruun, S. E. (1983). Dispensability of member effort and group motivation losses: Free-rider effects. *Journal of Personality and Social Psychology, 44,* 78–94.

Kerr, N. L., & Huang, J. Y. (1986). Jury verdicts: How much difference does one juror make? *Personality and Social Psychology Bulletin, 12,* 325–343.

Kerr, N. L., & Kaufman-Gilliland, C. M. (1994). Communication, commitment, and cooperation in social dilemmas. *Journal of Personality and Social Psychology, 66,* 513–529.

Kerr, N. L., & MacCoun, R. J. (1985). The effects of jury size and polling method on the process and product of jury deliberation. *Journal of Personality and Social Psychology, 48,* 349–363.

Kerr, N. L., MacCoun, R. J., & Kramer, G. P. (1996a). Bias in judgment: Comparing individuals and groups. *Psychological Review, 103,* 687–719.

Kerr, N. L., MacCoun, R. J., & Kramer, G. P. (1996b). "When are N heads better (or worse) than one?": Biased judgment in individuals and groups. In E. H. Witte & J. H. Davis (Eds.), *Understanding* group behavior: Consensual action by small groups (Vol. 1, pp. 105–136). Hillsdale, NJ: Erlbaum.

Kerr, S., & Jermier, J. M. (1978). Substitutes for leadership: Their meaning and measurement. *Organizational Behavior and Human Performance, 22,* 375–403.

Kerr, S., Schriesheim, C. A., Murphy, C. J., & Stogdill, R. M. (1974). Toward a contingency theory of leadership based upon the consideration and initiating structure literature. *Organizational Behavior and Human Performance, 12,* 62–82.

Keyton, J. (1991). Evaluating individual group member satisfaction as a situational variable. *Small Group Research, 22,* 200–219.

Keyton, J. (1992). Comment on Evans and Dion: Still more on group cohesion. *Small Group Research, 23,* 237–241.

Keyton, J., & Springston, J. (1990). Redefining cohesiveness in groups. *Small Group Research, 21,* 234–254.

Kidder, T. (1981). *The soul of a new machine.* Boston: Little, Brown.

Kiesler, C. A., & Kiesler, S. B. (1976). *Conformity* (2nd ed.). Reading, MA: Addison-Wesley.

Kiesler, D. J. (1991). Interpersonal methods of assessment and diagnosis. In C. R. Snyder & D. R. Forsyth (Eds.), *Handbook of social and clinical psychology: The health perspective* (pp. 438–468). New York: Pergamon.

Kiesler, S., Siegel, J., & McGuire, T. W. (1984). Social psychological aspects of computer-mediated communication. *American Psychologist, 39,* 1123–1134.

Kiesler, S., Sproull, L., & Waters, K. (1996). A prisoner's dilemma experiment on cooperation with people and human-like computers. *Journal of Personality and Social Psychology, 70,* 47–65.

Kilham, W., & Mann, L. (1974). Level of destructive obedience as a function of transmitter and executant roles in the Milgram obedience paradigm. *Journal of Personality and Social Psychology, 29,* 696–702.

Kilmartin, C. T. (1994). *The masculine self.* New York: Macmillan.

King, G. A., & Sorrentino, R. M. (1983). Psychological dimensions of goal-oriented interpersonal situations. *Journal of Personality and Social Psychology, 44,* 140–162.

King, L. A., & King, D. W. (1990). Role conflict and role ambiguity: A critical assessment of construct validity. *Psychological Bulletin, 107,* 48–64.

Kipnis, D. (1972). Does power corrupt? *Journal of Personality and Social Psychology, 24,* 33–41.

Kipnis, D. (1974). *The powerholders.* Chicago: University of Chicago Press.

Kipnis, D. (1984). The use of power in organizations and in interpersonal settings. *Applied Social Psychology Annual, 5,* 179–210.

Kipnis, D., Castell, P. J., Gergen, M., & Mauch, D. (1976). Metamorphic effects of power. *Journal of Applied Psychology, 61,* 127–135.

Kipnis, D., & Consentino, J. (1969). Use of leadership powers in industry. *Journal of Applied Psychology, 53,* 460–466.

Kipnis, D., Schmidt, S. M., Swaffin-Smith, C., & Wilkinson, I. (1984). Patterns of managerial influence: Shotgun managers, tacticians, and bystanders. *Organizational Dynamics, 12(3),* 58–67.

Kipper, D. A. (1978). Trends in the research on the effectiveness of psychodrama: Retrospect and prospect. *Group Psychotherapy, 31,* 5–18.

Kirchler, E., & Davis, J. H. (1986). The influence of member status differences and task type on group consensus and member position change. *Journal of Personality and Social Psychology, 51,* 83–91.

Kirkpatrick, S. A., & Locke, E. A. (1991). Leadership: Do traits matter? *Academy of Management Executive, 5(2),* 48–60.

Kirshner, B. J., Dies, R. R., & Brown, R. A. (1978). Effects of experimental manipulation of self-disclosure on group cohesiveness. *Journal of Consulting and Clinical Psychology, 46,* 1171–1177.

Kitayama, S., Markus, H. R., Matsumoto, H., & Norasakkunkit, V. (1997). Individual and collective processes in the construction of the self: Self-enhancement in the United States and self-criticism in Japan. *Journal of Personality and Social Psychology, 72,* 1245–1267.

Kivlighan, D. M., Jr. (1985). Feedback in group psychotherapy: Review and implications. *Small Group Behavior, 16,* 373–386.

Kivlighan, D. M., Jr. (1997). Leader behavior and therapeutic gain: An application of situational leadership theory. *Group Dynamics: Theory, Research, and Practice, 1,* 32–38.

Kivlighan, D. M., Jr., McGovern, T. V., & Corazzini, J. G. (1984). Effects of content and timing of structuring interventions on group therapy process and outcome. *Journal of Counseling Psychology, 31,* 363–370.

Kivlighan, D. M., Jr., & Mullison, D. (1988). Participants' perception of therapeutic factors in group counseling: The role of interpersonal style and stage of group development. *Small Group Behavior, 19,* 452–468.

Kivlighan, D. M., Jr., Multon, K. D., & Brossart, D. F. (1996). Helpful impacts in group counseling: Development of a multidimensional rating system. *Journal of Counseling Psychology, 43,* 347–355.

Klenke, K. (1996). *Women and leadership: A contextual perspective.* NY: Springer.

Knight, G. P., & Dubro, A. F. (1984). Cooperative, competitive, and individualistic social values: An individualized regression and clustering approach. *Journal of Personality and Social Psychology, 46,* 98–105.

Knight, H. C. (1921). *A comparison of the reliability of group and individual judgment.* Unpublished master's thesis, Columbia University.

Knowles, E. S. (1973). Boundaries around group interaction: The effect of group size and member status on boundary permeability. *Journal of Personality and Social Psychology, 26,* 327–331.

Knowles, E. S. (1980). An affiliative conflict theory of personal and group spatial behavior. In P. B. Paulus (Ed.), *Psychology of group influence* (pp. 133–188). Hillsdale, NJ: Erlbaum.

Knowles, E. S., & Bassett, R. L. (1976). Groups and crowds as social entities: The effects of activity, size, and member similarity on nonmembers. *Journal of Personality and Social Psychology, 34,* 837–845.

Knowles, E. S., & Brickner, M. A. (1981). Social cohesion effects on spatial cohesion. *Personality and Social Psychology Bulletin, 7,* 309–313.

Knowles, E. S., Kreuser, B., Haas, S., Hyde, M., & Schuchart, G. E. (1976). Group size and the extension of social space boundaries. *Journal of Personality and Social Psychology, 33,* 647–654.

Koberg, C. S. (1985). Sex and situational influences on the use of power: A follow-up study. *Sex Roles, 13,* 625–639.

Kochan, T. A., Schmidt, S. M., & DeCotiis, T. A. (1975). Superior-subordinate relations: Leadership and headship. *Human Relations, 28,* 279–294.

Köhler, O. (1926). Kraftleistungen bei Einzel- und Gruppenarbeit. Industrielle Psychotechnik, *3,* 274–282.

Kohut, H. (1984). *How does analysis cure? Contributions to the psychology of the self* (A. Goldberg, Ed., with the collaboration of P. Stepansky). Chicago, University of Chicago Press.

Komorita, S. S. (1987). Cooperative choice in decomposed social dilemmas. *Personality and Social Psychology Bulletin, 13,* 53–63.

Komorita, S. S., Hilty, J. A., & Parks, C. D. (1991). Reciprocity and cooperation in social dilemmas. *Journal of Conflict Resolution, 35,* 494–518.

Komorita, S. S., & Parks, C. D. (1994). *Social dilemmas.* Dubuque, IA: Brown & Benchmark.

Komorita, S. S., Parks, C. D., & Hulbert, L. G. (1992). Reciprocity and the induction of cooperation in social dilemmas. *Journal of Personality and Social Psychology, 62,* 607–617.

Korda, M. (1975). *Power! How to get it, how to use it.* New York: Ballantine.

Kounin, J. S. (1970). *Discipline and group management in classrooms.* New York: Holt, Rinehart & Winston.

Kounin, J. S., & Gump, P. V. (1958). The ripple effect in discipline. *Elementary School Journal, 59,* 158–162.

Kowalski, R. M. (1996). Complaints and complaining: Functions, antecedents, and consequences. *Psychological Bulletin, 119,* 179–196.

Kowalski, R. M., & Wolfe, R. (1994). Collective identity orientation, patriotism, and reactions to national outcomes. *Personality and Social Psychology Bulletin, 20,* 533–540.

Krackhardt, D., & Porter, L. W. (1986). The snowball effect: Turnover embedded in communication networks. *Journal of Applied Psychology, 71,* 50–55.

Krakauer, J. (1997). *Into thin air.* New York: Random House.

Kramer, M. W., Kuo, C. L., & Dailey, J. C. (1997). The impact of brainstorming techniques on subsequent group processes: Beyond generating ideas. *Small Group Research, 28,* 218–242.

Kramer, R. M., & Messick, D. M. (1998). Getting by with a little help from our enemies: Collective paranoia and its role in intergroup relations. In C. Sedikides, J. Schopler, & C. A. Insko (Eds.), *Intergroup cognition and intergroup behavior* (pp. 233–256). Mahwah, NJ: Erlbaum.

Kraus, L. A., Davis, M. H., Bazzini, D. G., Church, M., & Kirchman, C. M. (1993). Personal and social influences on loneliness: The mediating effect of social provisions. *Social Psychology Quarterly, 56,* 37–53.

Krause, C. A. (1978). *Guyana massacre: The eyewitness account.* New York: Berkley Publishing Corporation.

Krauss, R. M., & Chiu, C. (1998). Language and social behavior. In D. T. Gilbert, S. T. Fiske, & G. Lindzey (Eds.), *The handbook of social psychology* (4th ed., Vol. 2, pp. 41–88). New York: McGraw-Hill.

Kraut, R. E., Egido, C., & Galegher, J. (1990). Patterns of contact and communication in scientific research collaboration. In J. Galegher, R. E. Kraut, & C. Egido (Eds.), *Intellectual teamwork: Social and technological foundations of cooperative work* (pp. 149–171). Hillsdale, NJ: Erlbaum.

Kravitz, D. A., & Martin, B. (1986). Ringelmann rediscovered: The original article. *Journal of Personality and Social Psychology, 50,* 936–941.

Krueger, J., & Clement, R. W. (1997). Estimates of social consensus by majorities and minorities: The case for social projection. *Personality and Social Psychology Review, 1,* 299–312.

Kruglanski, A. W., & Webster, D. M. (1991). Group members' reactions to opinion deviates and conformists at varying degrees of proximity to decision deadline and of environmental noise. *Journal of Personality and Social Psychology, 61,* 212–225.

Kuhn, M. H., & McPartland, T. S. (1954). An empirical investigation of self-attitudes. *American Sociological Review, 19,* 68–76.

Kulik, J. A., & Mahler, H. I. M. (1989). Stress and affiliation in a hospital setting: Preoperative roommate preference. *Personality and Social Psychology Bulletin, 15,* 183–193.

Kulik, J. A., Mahler, H. I. M., & Moore, P. J. (1996). Social comparison and affiliation under threat: Effects on recovery from major surgery. *Journal of Personality and Social Psychology, 71,* 967–979.

Kushell, E., & Newton, R. (1986). Gender, leadership style, and subordinate satisfaction: An experiment. *Sex Roles, 14,* 203–209.

Kushnir, T. (1984). Social psychological factors associated with the dissolution of dyadic business partnerships. *Journal of Social Psychology, 122,* 181–188.

Kutash, I. L., & Wolf, A. (1993). Psychoanalysis in groups. In H. I. Kaplan & M. J. Sadock (Eds.), *Comprehensive group psychotherapy* (3rd ed., pp. 126–138). Baltimore: Williams & Wilkins.

Kuypers, B. C., Davies, D., & Glaser, K. H. (1986). Developmental arrestations in self-analytic groups. *Small Group Behavior, 17,* 269–302.

Kuypers, B. C., Davies, D., & Hazewinkel, A. (1986). Developmental patterns in self-analytic groups. *Human Relations, 39,* 793–815.

La Gaipa, J. J. (1977). Interpersonal attraction and social exchange. In S. Duck (Ed.), *Theory and practice in interpersonal attraction.* New York: Academic Press.

Lacoursiere, R. B. (1980). *The life cycle of groups.* New York: Human Sciences Press.

LaFrance, M. (1985). Postural mirroring and intergroup relations. *Personality and Social Psychology Bulletin, 11,* 207–217.

Laing, R. D. (1960). *The divided self.* London: Tavistock.

Lakin, M. (1972). *Experiential groups: The uses of interpersonal encounter, psychotherapy groups, and sensitivity training.* Morristown, NJ: General Learning Press.

Lal Goel, M. (1980). Conventional political participation. In D. H. Smith, J. Macaulay, & Associates (Eds.), *Participation in social and political activities: A comprehensive analysis of political involvement, expressive leisure time, and helping behavior* (pp. 108–132). San Francisco: Jossey-Bass.

Lalonde, R. N. (1992). The dynamics of group differentiation in the face of defeat. *Personality and Social Psychology Bulletin, 18,* 336–342.

Lamm, H., & Myers, D. G. (1978). Group-induced polarization of attitudes and behavior. *Advances in Experimental Social Psychology, 11,* 145–195.

Lamm, H., & Trommsdorff, G. (1973). Group versus individual performance on tasks requiring ideational proficiency (brainstorming): A review. *European Journal of Social Psychology, 3,* 361–388.

Landau, J. (1995). The relationship of race and gender to managers' ratings of promotion potential. *Journal of Organizational Behavior, 16,* 391–401.

Landers, D. M., & Luschen, G. (1974). Team performance outcome and the cohesiveness of competitive coacting teams. *International Journal of Sport Sociology, 9,* 57–71.

Landsberger, H. A. (1958). *Hawthorne revisited.* Ithaca, NY: Cornell University Press.

Lanzetta, J. T., & Roby, T. B. (1960). The relationship between certain group process variables and group problem-solving efficiency. *Journal of Social Psychology, 52,* 135–148.

LaPiere, R. (1938). *Collective behavior.* New York: McGraw-Hill.

Larsen, K. S. (1982). Cultural conditions and conformity: The Asch effect. *Bulletin of the British Psychological Society, 35,* 347.

Larson, C. E., & Lafasto, F. M. J. (1989). *Teamwork: What must go right/what can go wrong.* Newbury Park, CA: Sage.

Larson, J. R., & Christensen, C. (1993). Groups as problem solving units: Toward a new meaning of social cognition. *British Journal of Social Psychology, 32,* 5–30.

Larson, J. R., Christensen, C., & Abbott, A. S., & Franz, T. M. (1996). Diagnosing groups: Charting the flow of information in medical decision-making teams. *Journal of Personality and Social Psychology, 71,* 315–330.

Larson, J. R., Foster-Fishman, P. G., & Keys, C. B. (1994). The discussion of shared and unshared information in decision-making groups. *Journal of Personality and Social Psychology, 67,* 446–461.

Larson, L. L., Hunt, J. G., & Osborn, R. N. (1976). The great Hi-Hi leader behavior myth: A lesson from Occam's Razor. *Academy of Management Journal, 19,* 628.

Latané, B. (1981). The psychology of social impact. *American Psychologist, 36,* 343–356.

Latané, B. (1996). Strength from weakness: The fate of opinion minorities in spatially distributed groups. In E. Witte & J. Davis (Eds.), *Understanding group behavior: Consensual action by small groups* (Vol. 1., pp. 193–219). Mahwah, NJ: Erlbaum.

Latané, B. (1997). Dynamic social impact: The societal consequences of human interaction. In C. McGarty & A. Haslam (Eds.), *The message of social psychology: Perspectives on mind and society* (pp. 200–220). Oxford, England: Blackwell.

Latané, B., & Bourgeois, M. J. (1996). Experimental evidence for dynamic social impact: The emergence of subcultures in electronic groups. *Journal of Communication, 46(4),* 35–47.

Latané, B., & Darley, J. M. (1970). *The unresponsive bystander: Why doesn't he help?* New York: Appleton-Century-Crofts.

Latané, B., & L'Herrou, T. (1996). Social clustering in the Conformity Game: Dynamic social impact in electronic groups. *Journal of Personality and Social Psychology, 70,* 1218–1230.

Latané, B., & Liu, J. H. (1996). The intersubjective geometry of social space: How physical distance structures social interaction. *Journal of Communication, 46(4),* 26–34.

Latané, B., Liu, J. H., Nowak, A., Bonevento, M., & Zheng, L. (1995). Distance matters: Physical space and social impact. *Personality and Social Psychology Bulletin, 21,* 795–805.

Latané, B., & Nida, S. (1981). Ten years of research on group size and helping. *Psychological Bulletin, 39,* 308–324.

Latané, B., & Nowak, A. (1994). Attitudes as catastrophes: From dimensions to categories with increasing involvement. In R. Vallacher & A.

Nowak (Eds.), *Dynamical systems in social psychology* (pp. 219–249). New York: Academic Press.

Latané, B., Williams, K., & Harkins, S. (1979). Many hands make light the work: The causes and consequences of social loafing. *Journal of Personality and Social Psychology, 37,* 822–832.

Latané, B., & Wolf, S. (1981). The social impact of majorities and minorities. *Psychological Review, 88,* 438–453.

Latham, G. P., & Baldes, J. J. (1975). The "practical significance" of Locke's theory of goal settings. *Journal of Applied Psychology, 60,* 122–124.

Latour, A., Garnier, C., & Ferraris, J. (1993). L'observation des processus de groupe: Difficultes methodologiques et perspectives. *Canadian Journal of Behavioural Science, 25,* 286–302.

LaTour, S. (1978). Determinants of participant and observer satisfaction with adversary and inquisitorial modes of adjudication. *Journal of Personality and Social Psychology, 36,* 1531–1545.

LaTour, S., Houlden, P., Walker, L., & Thibaut, J. (1976). Some determinants of preference for modes of conflict resolution. *Journal of Conflict Resolution, 20,* 319–356.

Laughlin, P. R. (1980). Social combination processes of cooperative problem solving groups on verbal intellective tasks. In M. Fishbein (Ed.), *Progress in social psychology.* Hillsdale, NJ: Erlbaum.

Laughlin, P. R. (1996). Group decision making and collective induction. In E. H. Witte & J. H. Davis (Eds.), *Understanding group behavior: Consensual action by small groups* (Vol. 1, pp. 61–80). Hillsdale, NJ: Erlbaum.

Laughlin, P. R., & Earley, P. C. (1982). Social combination models, persuasive arguments theory, social comparison theory, and choice shift. *Journal of Personality and Social Psychology, 42,* 273–280.

Laughlin, P. R., & Hollingshead, A. B. (1995). A theory of collective induction. *Organizational Behavior and Human Decision Processes, 61,* 94–107.

Lawler, E. J. (1975). An experimental study of factors affecting the mobilization of revolutionary coalitions. *Sociometry, 38,* 163–179.

Lawler, E. J., Ford, R. S., & Blegen, M. A. (1988). Coercive capability in conflict: A test of bilateral deterrence versus conflict spiral theory. *Social Psychology Quarterly, 51,* 93–107.

Lawler, E. J., & Thompson, M. E. (1978). Impact of a leader's responsibility for inequity on subordinate revolts. *Social Psychology Quarterly, 41,* 264–268.

Lawler, E. J., & Thompson, M. E. (1979). Subordinate response to a leader's cooptation strategy as a function of type of coalition power. *Representative Research in Social Psychology, 9,* 69–80.

Lawler, E. J., & Yoon, J. (1996). Commitment in exchange relations: Test of a theory of relational cohesion. *American Sociological Review, 61,* 89–108.

Lawrence, B. S. (1996). Organizational age norms: Why is it so hard to know one when you see one? *Gerontologist, 36,* 209–220.

Le Bon, G. (1960). *The crowd.* New York: The Viking Press. (Original work published in 1895)

Lea, M., & Spears, R. (1991). Computer-mediated communication, de-individuation, and group decision-making. In S. Greenberg (Ed.), *Computer-supported cooperative work and groupware* (pp. 155–174). New York: Harcourt Brace Jovanovich.

Leary, M. R. (1983). *Understanding social anxiety.* Thousand Oaks, CA: Sage.

Leary, M. R. (1990). Responses to social exclusion: Social anxiety, jealousy, loneliness, depression, and low self-esteem. *Journal of Social and Clinical Psychology, 9,* 221–229.

Leary, M. R., & Forsyth, D. R. (1987). Attributions of responsibility for collective endeavors. *Review of Personality and Social Psychology, 8,* 167–188.

Leary, M. R., & Kowalski, R. M. (1995). *Social anxiety.* New York: Guilford Press.

Leary, M. R., & Miller, R. S. (1986). Social psychology and dysfunctional behavior: Origins, diagnosis, and treatment. New York: Springer-Verlag.

Leary, M. R., Robertson, R. B., Barnes, B. D., & Miller, R. S. (1986). Self-presentations of small group leaders: Effects of role requirements and leadership orientation. *Journal of Personality and Social Psychology, 51,* 742–748.

Leary, M. R., Rogers, P. A., Canfield, R. W., & Coe, C. (1986). Boredom in interpersonal encounters: Antecedents and social implications. *Journal of Personality and Social Psychology, 51,* 968–975.

Leary, M. R., Tambor, E. S., Terdal, S. K., & Downs, D. L. (1995). Self-esteem as an interpersonal monitor: The sociometer hypothesis. *Journal of Personality and Social Psychology, 68,* 518–530.

Leary, M. R., Wheeler, D. S., Jenkins, T. B. (1986). Aspects of identity and behavioral preferences: Studies of occupational and recreational choice. *Social Psychology Quarterly, 49,* 11–18.

Leavitt, H. J. (1951). Some effects of certain communication patterns on group performance. *Journal of Abnormal and Social Psychology, 46,* 38–50.

Lee, M. T., & Ofshe, R. (1981). The impact of behavioral style and status characteristics on social influence: A test of two competing theories. *Social Psychology Quarterly, 44,* 73–82.

Lee, P. W. H., Leung, P. W. L., Fung, A. S. M., & Low, L. C. K. (1996). An episode of syncope attacks in adolescent schoolgirls: Investigations, intervention and outcome. *British Journal of Medical Psychology, 69,* 247–257.

Lee, R. M., Robbins, S. B. (1995). Measuring belongingness: The social connectedness and the social assurance scales. *Journal of Counseling Psychology, 42,* 232–241.

Leffler, A., Gillespie, D. L., & Conaty, J. C. (1982). The effects of status differentiation on nonverbal behavior. *Social Psychology Quarterly, 45,* 153–161.

Leichtentritt, J., & Shechtman, Z. (1998). Therapist, trainee, and child verbal response modes in child group therapy. *Group Dynamics: Theory, Research, and Practice, 2,* 36–47.

Lenk, H. (1969). Top performance despite internal conflict. In J. W. Loy & G. S. Kenyon (Eds.), *Sport, culture, and society.* New York: Macmillan.

Leon, G. R. (1991). Individual and group process characteristics of polar expedition teams. *Environment and Behavior, 23,* 723–748.

Leonard, W. M., II. (1980). *A sociological perspective on sport.* Minneapolis: Burgess.

Lepore, S. J., Evans, G. W., & Schneider, M. L. (1991). Dynamic role of social support in the link between chronic stress and psychological distress. *Journal of Personality and Social Psychology, 61,* 899–909.

Lepsius, M. R. (1986). Charismatic leadership: Max Weber's model and its applicability to the rule of Hitler. In C. F. Graumann & S. Moscovici (Eds.), *Changing conceptions of leadership* (pp. 53–66). New York: Springer-Verlag.

Leventhal, G. S., Karuza, J., & Fry, W. R. (1980). Beyond fairness: A theory of allocation preferences. In G. Mikula (Ed.), *Justice and social interaction* (pp. 167–218). New York: Springer-Verlag.

Leventhal, G. S., & Lane, D. W. (1970). Sex, age, and equity behavior. *Journal of Personality and Social Psychology, 15,* 312–316.

Levesque, M. J. (1997). Meta-accuracy among acquainted individuals: A social relations analysis of interpersonal perception and metaperception. *Journal of Personality and Social Psychology, 72,* 66–74.

Levine, D. I., & D'Andrea Tyson, L. (1990). Participation, productivity, and the firm's environment. In A. S. Blinder (Ed.), *Paying for productivity* (pp. 183–237). Washington, DC: Brookings Institute.

Levine, J. M. (1980). Reaction to opinion deviance in small groups. In P. B. Paulus (Ed.), *Psychology of group influence*. Hillsdale, NJ: Erlbaum.

Levine, J. M., & Moreland, R. L. (1990). Progress in small group research. *Annual Review of Psychology, 41,* 585–634.

Levine, J. M., & Moreland, R. L. (1995). Group processes. In A. Tesser (Ed.), *Advanced social psychology* (pp. 419–465). New York: McGraw-Hill.

Levine, J. M., & Moreland, R. L. (1998). Small groups. In D. T. Gilbert, S. T. Fiske, & G. Lindzey (Eds.), *The handbook of social psychology* (4th ed., Vol. 2, pp. 415–469). Boston, MA: McGraw-Hill.

Levine, J. M., & Ranelli, C. J. (1978). Majority reaction to shifting and stable attitudinal deviates. *European Journal of Social Psychology, 8,* 55–70.

Levine, J. M., & Ruback, R. B. (1980). Reaction to opinion deviance: Impact of a fence-straddler's rationale on majority evaluation. *Social Psychology Quarterly, 43,* 73–81.

Levine, J. M., & Russo, E. M. (1987). Majority and minority influence. *Review of personality and social psychology, 8,* 13–54.

Levine, J. M., Saxe, L., & Harris, H. J. (1976). Reaction to attitudinal deviance: Impact of deviate's direction and distance of movement. *Sociometry, 39,* 97–107.

Levine, J. M., Sroka, K. R., & Snyder, H. N. (1977). Group support and reaction to stable and shifting agreement/disagreement. *Sociometry, 40,* 214–224.

Levine, J. M., & Thompson, L. (1996). Conflict in groups. In E. T. Higgins, & A. W. Kruglanski (Eds.), *Social psychology: Handbook of basic principles* (pp. 745–776). New York: Guilford.

LeVine, R. A., & Campbell, D. T. (1972). *Ethnocentrism: Theories of conflict, ethnic attitudes, and group behavior.* New York: Wiley.

Levine, S. (1996, March). *The psychobiological consequences of social behavior.* Paper presented at the New York Academy of Sciences Conference on the Integrative Neurobiology of Affiliation, Washington, DC.

Levine, S. V. (1984). Radical departures. *Psychology Today, 18(8),* 21–27.

Levinger, G., Senn, D. J., & Jorgensen, B. W. (1970). Progress toward permanence in courtship: A test of the Kerckhoff-Davis hypothesis. *Sociometry, 33,* 427–433.

Lewin, K. (1936). *Principles of topological psychology.* New York: McGraw-Hill.

Lewin, K. (1943). Forces behind food habits and methods of change. *Bulletin of the National Research Council, 108,* 35–65.

Lewin, K. (1946). Action research and minority problems. *Journal of Social Issues, 2(4),* 34–46.

Lewin, K. (1947). Frontiers in group dynamics. *Human Relations, 1,* 143–153.

Lewin, K. (1948). *Resolving social conflicts: Selected papers on group dynamics.* New York: Harper.

Lewin, K. (1951). *Field theory in social science.* New York: Harper.

Lewin, K., Dembo, T., Festinger, L., & Sears, P. S. (1944). Level of aspiration. In J. M. Hunt (Ed.), *Personality and the behavior disorders.* New York: Ronald.

Lewin, K., Lippitt, R., & White, R. (1939). Patterns of aggressive behavior in experimentally created "social climates." *Journal of Social Psychology, 10,* 271–299.

Lewis, H. S. (1974). *Leaders and followers: Some anthropological perspectives.* Reading, MA: Addison-Wesley.

Lewis, S. A., Langan, C. J., & Hollander, E. P. (1972). Expectation of future interaction and the choice of less desirable alternatives in conformity. *Sociometry, 35,* 404–447.

Ley, D., & Cybriwsky, R. (1974a). The spatial ecology of stripped cars. *Environment and Behavior, 6,* 53–68.

Ley, D., & Cybriwsky, R. (1974b). Urban graffiti as territorial markers. *Annals of the Association of American Geographers, 64,* 491–505.

Lieberman, M. A. (1980). Group methods. In F. H. Kanfer & A. P. Goldstein (Eds.), *Helping people change.* New York: Pergamon.

Lieberman, M. A. (1993). Self-help groups. In H. I. Kaplan & M. J. Sadock (Eds.), *Comprehensive group psychotherapy* (3rd ed., pp. 292–304). Baltimore: Williams & Wilkins.

Lieberman, M. A. (1994). Growth groups in the 1980s: Mental Health Implications. In A. Fuhriman & G. M. Burlingame (Eds.), *Handbook of group psychotherapy: An empirical and clinical synthesis* (pp. 527–558). New York: Wiley.

Lieberman, M. A., Yalom, I., & Miles, M. (1973). *Encounter groups: First facts.* New York: Basic Books.

Likert, R. (1967). *The human organization.* New York: McGraw-Hill.

Lind, E. A., Kurtz, S., Musante, L., Walker, L., & Thibaut, J. W. (1980). Procedure and outcome effects on reactions to adjudicated resolution of conflicts of interest. *Journal of Personality and Social Psychology, 39,* 643–656.

Lindblom, C. E. (1965). *The intelligence of democracy.* New York: The Free Press.

Lindeman, M. (1997). Ingroup bias, self-enhancement and group identification. *European Journal of Social Psychology, 27,* 337–355.

Lindholm, C. (1990). *Charisma.* Cambridge, MA: Blackwell.

Lindskold, S. (1978). Trust development, the GRIT proposal, and the effects of conciliatory acts on conflict and cooperation. *Psychological Bulletin, 85,* 772–793.

Lindskold, S. (1979). Conciliation with simultaneous or sequential interaction. *Journal of Conflict Resolution, 23,* 704–714.

Lindskold, S. (1986). GRIT: Reducing distrust through carefully introduced conciliation. In S. Worchel & W. G. Austin (Eds.), *Psychology of intergroup relations* (2nd ed., pp. 305–322). Chicago: Nelson-Hall.

Lindskold, S., Albert, K. P., Baer, R., & Moore, W. C. (1976). Territorial boundaries of interacting groups and passive audiences. *Sociometry, 39,* 71–76.

Lindskold, S., & Aronoff, J. R. (1980). Conciliatory strategies and relative power. *Journal of Experimental Social Psychology, 16,* 187–198.

Lindskold, S., & Finch, M. L. (1982). Anonymity and the resolution of conflicting pressures from the experimenter and from peers. *Journal of Psychology, 112,* 79–86.

Linville, P. W. (1982). The complexity-extremity effect and age-based stereotyping. *Journal of Personality and Social Psychology, 42,* 193–211.

Linville, P. W., & Fischer, G. W. (1998). Group variability and covariation: Effects on intergroup judgment and behavior. In C. Sedikides, J. Schopler, & C. A. Insko (Eds.), *Intergroup cognition and intergroup behavior* (pp. 123–150). Mahwah, NJ: Erlbaum.

Linville, P. W., Fischer, G. W., & Salovey, P. (1989). Perceived distributions of the characteristics of ingroup and out-group members: Empirical evidence and a computer simulation. *Journal of Personality and Social Psychology, 57,* 165–188.

Linville, P. W., Fischer, G. W., & Yoon, C. (1996). Perceived covariation among the features of ingroup and outgroup members: The outgroup covariation effect. *Journal of Personality and Social Psychology, 70,* 421–436.

Lippmann, W. (1922). *Public opinion.* New York: Harcourt & Brace.

Lipset, S. M., & Wolin, S. S. (1965). *The Berkeley student revolt.* Garden City, NY: Anchor.

Litman-Adizes, T., Fontaine, G., & Raven, B. (1978). Consequences of social power and causal attribution for compliance as seen by powerholder and target. *Personality and Social Psychology Bulletin, 4,* 260–264.

Little, B. L., & Madigan, R. M. (1997). The relationship between collective efficacy and performance in manufacturing work teams. *Small Group Research, 28,* 517–534.

Littlepage, G. E. (1991). Effects of group size and task characteristics on group performance: A test of Steiner's model. *Personality and Social Psychology Bulletin, 17,* 449–456.

Littlepage, G. E., & Mueller, A. L. (1997). Recognition and utilization of expertise in problem-solving groups: Expert characteristics and behavior. *Group Dynamics: Theory, Research, and Practice, 1,* 324–328.

Littlepage, G. E., Nixon, C. T., & Gibson, C. R. (1992). Influence strategies used in meetings. *Journal of Social Behavior and Personality, 7,* 529–538.

Littlepage, G. E., Robison, W., & Reddington, K. (1997). Effects of task experience and group experience on group performance, member ability, and recognition of expertise. *Organizational Behavior and Human Decision Processes, 69,* 133–147.

Littlepage, G. E., Schmidt, G. W., Whisler, E. W., & Frost, A. G. (1995). An input-process-output analysis of influence and performance in problem-solving groups. *Journal of Personality and Social Psychology, 69,* 877–889.

Littlepage, G. E., & Silbiger, H. (1992). Recognition of expertise in decision-making groups: Effects of group size and participation patterns. *Small Group Research, 23,* 344–355.

Locke, E. A., & Latham, G. P. (1990). *A theory of goal-setting and task performance.* Englewood Cliffs, NJ: Prentice Hall.

Lockwood, P., & Kunda, Z. (1997). Superstars and me: Predicting the impact of role models on the self. *Journal of Personality and Social Psychology, 73,* 91–103.

Lodewijkx, H. F. M., & Syroit, J. E. M. M. (1997). Severity of initiation revisited: Does severity of initiation increase attractiveness in real groups? *European Journal of Social Psychology, 27,* 275–300.

Loehlin, J. C. (1997). A test of J. R. Harris's theory of peer influences on personality. *Journal of Personality and Social Psychology, 72,* 1197–1201.

Loewen, L. J., & Suedfeld, P. (1992). Cognitive and arousal effects of masking office noise. *Environment and Behavior, 24,* 381–395.

Lofland, J. (1981). Collective behavior: The elementary forms. In M. Rosenberg & R. H. Turner (Eds.), *Social psychology* (pp. 411–446). New York: Basic Books.

Lofland, L. H. (1995). Social interaction: Continuities and complexities in the study of nonintimate sociality. In K. S. Cook, G. A. Fine, & J. S. House (Eds.), *Sociological perspectives on social psychology* (pp. 176–202). Boston: Allyn & Bacon.

Long, S. (Ed.). (1988). *Six group therapies.* New York: Plenum.

Longley, J., & Pruitt, D. G. (1980). Groupthink: A critique of Janis's theory. In L. Wheeler (Ed.), *Review of personality and social psychology* (Vol. 1). Newbury Park, CA: Sage.

Lord, R. B., & Maher, K. J. (1991). *Leadership and information processing: Linking perceptions and performance.* Boston: Unwin Hyman.

Lord, R. G. (1977). Functional leadership behavior: Measurement and relation to social power and leadership perceptions. *Administrative Science Quarterly, 22,* 114–133.

Lord, R. G. (1985). An information processing approach to social perceptions, leadership, and behavioral measurement in organizations. *Research in Organizational Behavior, 7,* 87–128).

Lord, R. G., & Alliger, G. M. (1985). A comparison of four information processing models of leadership and social perception. *Human Relations, 38,* 47–65.

Lord, R. G., Binning, J. F., Rush, M. C., & Thomas, J. C. (1978). The effect of performance cues and leader behavior on questionnaire ratings of leadership behavior. *Organizational Behavior and Human Performance, 21,* 27–39.

Lord, R. G., De Vader, C. L., & Alliger, G. M. (1986). A meta-analysis of the relation between personality traits and leadership perceptions: An application of validity generalization procedures. *Journal of Applied Psychology, 71,* 402–410.

Lord, R. G., Foti, R. J., & De Vader, C. L. (1984). A test of leadership categorization theory: Internal structure, information processing, and leadership perceptions. *Organization Behavior and Human Performance, 34,* 343–378.

Lorge, I., Fox, D., Davitz, J., & Brenner, M. (1958). A survey of studies contrasting quality of group performance and individual performance, 1920–1957. *Psychological Bulletin, 55,* 337–372.

Lorge, I., & Solomon, H. (1955). Two models of group behavior in the solution of Eureka-type problems. *Psychometrika, 20,* 139–148.

Lott, A. J., & Lott, B. E. (1965). Group cohesiveness as interpersonal attraction: A review of relationships with antecedent and consequent variables. *Psychological Bulletin, 64,* 259–309.

Lovaglia, M. J., & Houser, J. A. (1996). Emotional reactions and status in groups. *American Sociological Review, 61,* 867–883.

Lowe, K. B., Kroeck, K. G., Sivasubramaniam, N. (1996). Effectiveness correlates of transformation and transactional leadership: A meta-analytic review of the MLQ literature. *Leadership Quarterly, 7,* 385–425.

Lowery, B. J., Jacobsen, B. S., & DuCette, J. (1993). Causal attribution, control, and adjustment to breast cancer. *Journal of Psychosocial Oncology, 10,* 37–53.

Luce, R. D., & Raiffa, H. (1957). *Games and decisions.* New York: Wiley.

Lueder, D. C. (1985a). Don't be mislead by LEAD. *Journal of Applied Behavioral Science, 21,* 143–151.

Lueder, D. C. (1985b). A rejoinder to Dr. Hersey. *Journal of Applied Behavioral Science, 21,* 154.

Luft, J. (1984). *Groups process: An introduction to group dynamics* (3rd ed.). Palo Alto, CA: Mayfield.

Luhtanen, R., & Crocker, J. (1991). Self-esteem and intergroup comparisons: Toward a theory of collective self-esteem. In J. Suls & T. A. Wills (Eds.), *Social comparison: Contemporary theory and research* (pp. 211–236). Hillsdale, NJ: Erlbaum.

Luhtanen, R., & Crocker, J. (1992). A collective self-esteem scale: Self-evaluation of one's social identity. *Personality and Social Psychology Bulletin, 18,* 302–318.

Lundy, J. L. (1992). Teams: How to develop peak performance teams for world-class results. Chicago: Dartnell.

Luria, S. M. (1990). More about psychology and the military. *American Psychologist, 45,* 296–297.

Luthar, H. K. (1996). Gender differences in evaluation of performance and leadership ability: Autocratic vs. democratic managers. *Sex Roles, 35,* 337–349.

Lutsky, N. (1995). When is "obedience" obedience? Conceptual and historical commentary. *Journal of Social Issues, 51(3),* 55–65.

Lyman, S. M., & Scott, M. B. (1967). Territoriality: A neglected sociological dimension. *Social Problems, 15,* 236–249.

Maass, A., Ceccarelli, R., & Rudin, S. (1996). Linguistic intergroup bias: Evidence for in-group-protective motivation. *Journal of Personality and Social Psychology, 71,* 512–526.

Maass, A., & Clark, R. D., III. (1984). Hidden impact of minorities: Fifteen years of minority influence research. *Psychological Bulletin, 95,* 428–450.

Maass, A., Milesi, A., Zabbini, S., & Stahlberg, D. (1995). Linguistic intergroup bias: Differential expectancies or in-group protection? *Journal of Personality and Social Psychology, 68,* 116–126.

Maass, A., West, S. G., & Cialdini, R. B. (1987). Minority influence and conversion. In C. Hendrick (Ed.), *Review of Personality and Social Psychology, 8,* 55–79.

Maassen, G. H., Akkermans, W., & Van der Linden, J. L. (1996). Two-dimensional sociometric status determination with rating scales. *Small Group Research, 27,* 56–78.

Maccoby, E. E. (1990). Gender and relationships: A developmental account. *American Psychologist, 45,* 513–520.

MacCoun, R. J. (1990). The emergence of extralegal bias during jury deliberation. *Criminal Justice and Behavior, 17,* 303–314.

MacCoun, R. J. (1993). Drugs and the law: A psychological analysis of drug prohibition. *Psychological Bulletin, 113,* 497–512.

MacCracken, M. J., & Stadulis, R. E. (1985). Social facilitation of young children's dynamic balance performance. *Journal of Sport Psychology, 7,* 150–165.

MacFarlane, A. (1978). The origins of English individualism: The family, property, and social transition. Oxford, England: Blackwell.

Mack, R. W., & Snyder, R. C. (1957). The analysis of social conflict? Toward an overview and synthesis. *Journal of Conflict Resolution, 1,* 212–248.

MacKenzie, K. R. (1994). Group development. In A. Fuhriman & G. M. Burlingame (Eds.), *Handbook of group psychotherapy: An empirical and clinical synthesis* (pp. 223–268). New York: Wiley.

MacKenzie, K. R. (1997). Clinical application of group development ideas. *Group Dynamics: Theory, Research, and Practice, 1,* 275–287.

Mackie, D. (1987). Systematic and nonsystematic processing of majority and minority persuasive communications. *Journal of Personality and Social Psychology, 53,* 41–52.

Mackie, D. M., & Goethals, G. R. (1987). Individual and group goals. *Review of Personality and Social Psychology, 8,* 144–166.

MacNeil, M. K., & Sherif, M. (1976). Norm change over subject generations as a function of arbitrariness of prescribed norm. *Journal of Personality and Social Psychology, 34,* 762–773.

Macy, B. A., & Izumi, H. (1993). Organizational change, design, and work innovation: A meta-analysis of 131 North American field studies? 1961–1991. *Research in Organizational Change and Development, 7,* 235–313.

Magaro, P. A., & Ashbrook, R. M. (1985). The personality of societal groups. *Journal of Personality and Social Psychology, 48,* 1479–1489.

Maher, K. J. (1997). Gender-related stereotypes of transformational and transactional leadership. *Sex Roles, 37,* 209–225.

Mahrer, A. R., & Nadler, W. P. (1986). Good moments in psychotherapy: A preliminary review, a list, and some promising research avenues. *Journal of Consulting and Clinical Psychology, 54,* 10–15.

Mai-Dalton, R. R. (1993). Managing cultural diversity on the individual, group, and organizational levels. In M. M. Chemers & R. Ayman (Eds.), *Leadership theory and research: Perspectives and directions* (pp. 189–215). San Diego: Academic Press.

Maier, N. R. F., & Solem, A. R. (1952). The contribution of a discussion leader to the quality of group thinking: The effective use of minority opinions. *Human Relations, 5,* 277–288.

Major, B., Testa, M., & Bylsma, W. H. (1991). Responses to upward and downward social comparisons: The impact of esteem-relevance and perceived control. In J. Suls & T. A. Wills (Eds.), *Social comparison: Contemporary theory and research* (pp. 237–260). Hillsdale, NJ: Erlbaum.

Maki, J. E., Thorngate, W. B., & McClintock, C. G. (1979). Prediction and perception of social motives. *Journal of Personality and Social Psychology, 37,* 203–220.

Malloy, T. E., Albright, L., Kenny, D. A., Agatstein, F., & Winquist, L. (1997). Interpersonal perception and metaperception in nonoverlapping social groups. *Journal of Personality and Social Psychology, 72,* 390–398.

Malloy, T. E., & Janowski, C. L. (1992). Perceptions and metaperceptions of leadership: Components, accuracy, and dispositional correlates. *Personality and Social Psychology Bulletin, 18,* 700–708.

Manis, M., Cornell, S. D., & Moore, J. C. (1974). Transmission of attitude-relevant information through a communication chain. *Journal of Personality and Social Psychology, 30,* 81–94.

Mann, F. C. (1965). Toward an understanding of the leadership role in formal organizations. In R. Dubin, G. C. Homans, F. C. Mann, & D. C. Miller (Eds.), *Leadership and productivity.* San Francisco: Chandler.

Mann, J. H. (1959). A review of the relationships between personality and performance in small groups. *Psychological Bulletin, 56,* 241–270.

Mann, L. (1969). Queue culture. The waiting line as a social system. *American Journal of Sociology, 75,* 340–354.

Mann, L. (1970). The psychology of waiting lines. *American Scientist, 58,* 390–398.

Mann, L. (1979). Sports crowds viewed from the perspective of collective behavior. In J. H. Goldstein (Ed.), *Sports, games, and play: Social and psychological viewpoints.* Hillsdale, NJ: Erlbaum.

Mann, L. (1980). Cross-cultural studies of small groups. In H. C. Triandis & R. W. Brislin (Eds.), *Handbook of cross-cultural psychology: Social psychology* (Vol. 5). Boston: Allyn & Bacon.

Mann, L. (1981). The baiting crowd in episodes of threatened suicide. *Journal of Personality and Social Psychology, 41,* 703–709.

Mann, L. (1988). Cultural influence on group processes. In M. H. Bond (Ed.), *The cross-cultural challenge to social psychology* (pp. 182–195). Thousand Oaks, CA: Sage.

Mann, L., Newton, J. W., & Innes, J. M. (1982). A test between deindividuation and emergent norm theories of crowd aggression. *Journal of Personality and Social Psychology, 42,* 260–272.

Mantell, D. M., & Panzarella, R. (1976). Obedience and responsibility. *British Journal of Social and Clinical Psychology, 15,* 239–245.

Manz, C. C., & Sims, H. P. (1982). The potential for "groupthink" in autonomous work groups. *Human Relations, 35,* 773–784.

Marcus, D. K., & Wilson, J. R. (1996). Interpersonal perception of social anxiety: A social relations analysis. *Journal of Social and Clinical Psychology, 15,* 471–487.

Markovitz, R. J., & Smith, J. E. (1983). Patients' perceptions of curative factors in short term group psychotherapy. *International Journal of Group Psychotherapy, 33,* 21–39.

Markovsky, B., Smith, L. F. & Berger, J. (1984). Do status interventions persist? *American Sociological Review, 49,* 373–382.

Markus, H. (1978). The effect of mere presence on social facilitation: An unobtrusive test. *Journal of Experimental Social Psychology, 14,* 389–397.

Markus, H. R., Kitayama, S., & Heiman, R. J. (1996). Culture and "basic" psychological principles. In E. T. Higgins & A. W. Kruglanski (Eds.), *Social psychology: Handbook of basic principles* (pp. 857–913). New York: Guilford.

Marrow, A. J. (1964). *Behind the executive mask.* New York: American Management Association.

Marrow, A. J. (1969). *The practical theorist: The life and work of Kurt Lewin.* New York: Basic Books.

Martens, R., & Landers, D. M. (1972). Evaluation potential as a determinant of coaction effects. *Journal of Experimental Social Psychology, 8,* 347–359.

Martin, E. D. (1920). *The behavior of crowds.* New York: Harper.

Martin, J., Lobb, B., Chapman, G. C., & Spillane, R. (1976). Obedience under conditions demanding self-immolation. *Human Relations, 29,* 345–356.

Martin, M. W., & Sell, J. (1985). The effect of equating status characteristics on the generalization process. *Social Psychology Quarterly, 48,* 178–182.

Marwell, G., & Schmitt, D. R. (1967). Dimensions of compliance-gaining behavior: An empirical analysis. *Sociometry, 30,* 350–364.

Marx, K., & Engels, F. (1947). *The German ideology.* New York: International Publishers.

Maslach, C. (1972). Social and personal bases of individuation. Proceedings of the 80th Annual Convention of the American Psychological Association, 7, 213–214.

Maslach, C., Santee, R. T., & Wade, C. (1987). Individuation, gender role, and dissent: Personality mediators of situational forces. *Journal of Personality and Social Psychology, 53,* 1088–1093.

Maslach, C., Stapp, J., & Santee, R. T. (1985). Individuation: Conceptual analysis and assessment. *Journal of Personality and Social Psychology, 49,* 729–738.

Maslow, A. H. (1968). *Toward a psychology of being.* New York: Van Nostrand Reinhold.

Mathes, E. W., & Guest, T. A. (1976). Anonymity and group antisocial behavior. *Journal of Social Psychology, 100,* 257–262.

Mathes, E. W., & Kahn, A. (1975). Diffusion of responsibility and extreme behavior. *Journal of Personality and Social Psychology, 5,* 881–886.

Mathews, E., Canon, L. K, & Alexander, K. R. (1974). The influence of level of empathy and ambient noise on body buffer zone. *Personality and Social Psychology Bulletin, 1,* 367–369.

Maxmen, J. (1973). Group therapy as viewed by hospitalized patients. *Archives of General Psychiatry, 28,* 404–408.

Maxmen, J. (1978). An educative model for in-patient group therapy. *International Journal of Group Psychotherapy, 28,* 321–338.

Mayadas, N., & Glasser, P. (1985). Termination: A neglected aspect of social group work. In M. Sundel, P. Glasser, R. Sarri, & R. Vinter (Eds.), *Individual change through small groups* (2nd ed., pp. 251–261). New York: The Free Press.

Mayer, T. (1975). *Mathematical models of group structure.* New York: Bobbs-Merrill.

Mayo, E. (1933). *The human problems of an industrial civilization.* Cambridge, MA: Harvard University Press.

Mayo, E. (1945). *The social problems of an industrial civilization.* Cambridge, MA: Harvard University Press.

Mazur, A. (1973). Cross-species comparison of status in established small groups. *American Sociological Review, 38,* 513–529.

Mazur, A. (1983). Hormones, aggression, and dominance in humans. In B. Svare (Ed.), *Hormones and aggressive behavior.* New York: Plenum.

Mazur, A., Rosa, E., Faupel, M., Heller, J., Leen, R., & Thurman, B. (1980). Physiological aspects of communication via mutual gaze. *American Journal of Sociology, 86,* 50–74.

McAdam, D., McCarthy, J. D., & Zald, M. N. (1988). Social movements. In N. J. Smelser (Ed.), *The handbook of sociology* (pp. 695–737). Newbury Park, CA: Sage.

McAdams, D. P. (1982). Experiences of intimacy and power: Relationships between social motives and autobiographical memory. *Journal of Personality and Social Psychology, 42,* 292–301.

McAdams, D. P. (1995). What do we know when we know a person? *Journal of Personality, 63,* 365–396.

McAdams, D. P., & Constantian, C. A. (1983). Intimacy and affiliation motives in daily living: An experience sampling analysis. *Journal of Personality and Social Psychology, 45,* 851–861.

McAdams, D. P., Healy, S., & Krause, S. (1984). Social motives and patterns of friendship. *Journal of Personality and Social Psychology, 47,* 828–838.

McAndrew, F. T. (1993). *Environmental psychology.* Pacific Grove: Brooks/Cole.

McArthur, L. Z., & Friedman, S. (1980). Illusory correlation in impression formation: Variations in the shared distinctiveness effect as a function of the distinctive person's age, race, and sex. *Journal of Personality and Social Psychology, 39,* 615–624.

McBurney, D. H., Levine, J. M., & Cavanaugh, P. H. (1977). Psychophysical and social ratings of human body odor. *Personality and Social Psychology Bulletin, 3,* 135–138.

McCallum, D. M., Harring, K., Gilmore, R., Drenan, S., Chase, J., Insko, C. A., & Thibaut, J. (1985). Competition between groups and between individuals. *Journal of Experimental Social Psychology, 21,* 301–320.

McCallum, R., Rusbult, C. E., Hong, G. K., Walden, T., & Schopler, J. (1979). Effects of resource availability and importance of behavior on the experience of crowding. *Journal of Personality and Social Psychology, 37,* 1304–1313.

McCauley, C. (1989). The nature of social influence in groupthink: Compliance and internalization. *Journal of Personality and Social Psychology, 57,* 250–260.

McCauley, C. C., Stitt, L., & Segal, M. (1980). Stereotyping: From prejudice to prediction. *Psychological Bulletin, 87,* 195–208.

McClelland, D. C. (1975). *Power: The inner experience.* New York: Irvington.

McClelland, D. C. (1985). How motives, skills, and values determine what people do. *American Psychologist, 40,* 812–825.

McClintock, C. G., Messick, D. M., Kuhlman, D. M., & Campos, F. T. (1973). Motivational bases of choice in three-choice decomposed games. *Journal of Experimental Social Psychology, 9,* 572–590.

McClintock, C. G., Stech, F. J., & Keil, L. J. (1983). The influence of communication on bargaining. In P. B. Paulus (Ed.), *Basic group processes* (pp. 205–233). New York: Springer-Verlag.

McCranie, E. W., & Kimberly, J. C. (1973). Rank inconsistency, conflicting expectations, and injustice. *Sociometry, 36,* 152–176.

McDougall, W. (1908). *An introduction to social psychology.* London: Methuen.

McGarty, C., Haslam, S. A., Hutchinson, K. J., & Turner, J. C. (1994). The effects of salient group memberships on persuasion. *Small Group Research, 25,* 267–293.

McGillicuddy, N. B., Pruitt, D. G., & Syna, H. (1984). Perceptions of firmness and strength in negotiation. *Personality and Social Psychology Bulletin, 10,* 402–409.

McGrath, J. E. (1964). *Social psychology: A brief introduction.* New York: Holt.

McGrath, J. E. (1984). *Groups: Interaction and performance.* Englewood Cliffs, NJ: Prentice Hall.

McGrath, J. E. (1997). Small group research, that once and future field: An interpretation of the past with an eye to the future. *Group Dynamics: Theory, Research, and Practice, 1,* 7–27.

McGraw, K. M., & Bloomfield, J. (1987). Social influence on group moral decisions: The interactive effects of moral reasoning and sex role orientation. *Journal of Personality and Social Psychology, 53,* 1080–1087.

McGregor, D. (1960). *The human side of enterprise.* New York: McGraw-Hill.

McGuire, J. P., Leak, G. K. (1980). Prediction of self-disclosure from objective personality assessment techniques. *Journal of Clinical Psychology, 36,* 201–204.

McGuire, T. W., Kiesler, S., & Siegel, J. (1987). Group and computer-mediated discussion effects in risk decision making. *Journal of Personality and Social Psychology, 52,* 917–930.

McGuire, W. J., & McGuire, C. V. (1988). Content and process in the experience of self. *Advances in Experimental Social Psychology, 21,* 97–144.

McKersie, R. B., & Walton, R. E. (1992). A retrospective on the Behavioral Theory of Labor Negotiations. Special issue: Conflict and negotiation in organizations: Historical and contemporary perspectives. *Journal of Organizational Behavior, 13,* 277–285.

McLeod, P. L., Lobel, S. A., & Cox, T. H. (1996). Ethnic diversity and creativity in small groups. *Small Group Research, 27,* 248–264.

McMahon, J. T. (1972). The contingency model: Logic and method revised. *Personnel Psychology, 25,* 697–710.

McPhail, C. (1991). *The myth of the madding crowd.* Hawthorne, NY: Aldine de Gruyter.

McPhail, C., & Wohlstein, R. R. (1983). Individual and collective behaviors within gatherings, demonstrations, and riots. *Annual Review of Sociology, 9,* 579–600.

McRoberts, C., Burlingame, G. M., & Hoag, M. J. (1998). Comparative efficacy of individual and group psychotherapy: A meta-analytic perspective. *Group Dynamics: Theory, Research, and Practice, 2,* 101–117.

Meadow, A., Parnes, S. J., & Reese, H. (1959). Influence of brainstorming instructions and problem sequence on a creative problem solving test. *Journal of Applied Psychology, 43,* 413–416.

Medalia, N. Z., & Larsen, O. N. (1958). Diffusion and belief in a collective delusion: The Seattle windshield pitting epidemic. *American Sociological Review, 23,* 180–186.

Medow, H., & Zander, A. (1965). Aspirations for the group chosen by central and peripheral members. *Journal of Personality and Social Psychology, 1,* 224–228.

Meerloo, J. A. (1950). *Patterns of panic.* New York: International Universities Press.

Meeus, W. H. J., & Raaijmakers, Q. A. W. (1995). Obedience in modern society: The Utrecht studies. *Journal of Social Issues, 51(3),* 155–175.

Megargee, E. I. (1969). Influence of sex roles on the manifestation of leadership. *Journal of Applied Psychology, 53,* 377–382.

Mehrabian, A. (1972). *Nonverbal communication.* Chicago: Aldine-Atherton.

Mehrabian, A., & Diamond, S. G. (1971). Effects of furniture arrangement, props, and personality on social interaction. *Journal of Personality and Social Psychology, 20,* 18–30.

Mehrabian, A., & Russell, J. A. (1974). A verbal measure of information rate for studies in environmental psychology. *Environment and Behavior, 6,* 233–252.

Mehrabian, A., & Russell, J. A. (1975). The basic emotional impact of environments. *Perceptual and Motor Skills, 38,* 283–301.

Meindl, J. R. (1995). The romance of leadership as a follower-centric theory: A social constructionist approach. *Leadership Quarterly, 6,* 329–341.

Meindl, J. R., Ehrlich, S. B., & Dukerich, J. M. (1985). The romance of leadership and the evaluation of organizational performance. *Academy of Management Journal, 30,* 90–109.

Melucci, A. (1989). *Nomads of the present: Social movements and individual needs in contemporary society* (J. Keanne & P. Mier, Eds.). Philadelphia: Temple University Press.

Mennecke, B. E., Hoffer, J. A., & Wynne, B. E. (1992). The implications of group development and history for group support system theory and practice. *Small Group Research, 23,* 524–572.

Merei, F. (1958). Group leadership and institutional-ization. In E. E. Maccoby, T. M. Newcomb, & E. L. Hartley (Eds.), *Readings in social psychology* (3rd ed.). New York: Holt, Rinehart & Winston.

Merton, R. K. (1957). *Social theory and social structure.* New York: The Free Press.

Messé, L. A., & Sivacek, J. M. (1979). Predictions of others' responses in a mixed-motive game: Self-justification or false consensus? *Journal of Personality and Social Psychology, 37,* 602–607.

Messé, L. A., Stollak, G. E., Larson, R. W., & Michaels, G. Y. (1979). Interpersonal consequences of person perception in two social contexts. *Journal of Personality and Social Psychology, 37,* 369–379.

Messick D. M., & Brewer, M. B. (1983). Solving social dilemmas: A review. *Review of Personality and Social Psychology, 4,* 11–44.

Meudell, P. R., Hitch, G. J., & Boyle, M. M. (1995). Collaboration in recall: Do pairs of people cross-cue each other to produce new memories? *Quarterly Journal of Experimental Psychology: Human Experimental Psychology, 48(A),* 141–152.

Meudell, P. R., Hitch, G. J., & Kirby, P. (1992). Are two heads better than one? Experimental investigations of the social facilitation of memory. *Applied Cognitive Psychology, 6,* 525–543.

Meumann, E. (1904). Haus- und Schularbeit: Experimente an Kindern der Volkschule. *Die Deutsche Schule, 8,* 278–303, 337–359, 416–431.

Meyer, J. P., & Pepper, S. (1977). Need compatibility and marital adjustment in young married couples. *Journal of Personality and Social Psychology, 35,* 331–342.

Michaels, J. W., Blommel, J. M., Brocato, R. M., Linkous, R. A., & Rowe, J. S. (1982). Social facilitation and inhibition in a natural setting. *Replications in Social Psychology, 2,* 21–24.

Michels, R. (1915/1959). Political parties: A sociological study of the oligarchical tendencies of modern democracy. New York: Dover.

Michener, H. A., & Burt, M. R. (1975a). Components of "authority" as determinants of compliance. *Journal of Personality and Social Psychology, 31,* 606–614.

Michener, H. A., & Burt, M. R. (1975b). Use of social influence under varying conditions of legitimacy. *Journal of Personality and Social Psychology, 32,* 398–407.

Michener, H. A., & Lawler, E. J. (1975). The endorsement of formal leaders: An integrative model. *Journal of Personality and Social Psychology, 31,* 216–223.

Middlemist, R. D., Knowles, E. S., & Matter, C. F. (1976). Personal space invasions in the lavatory: Suggestive evidence for arousal. *Journal of Personality and Social Psychology, 33,* 541–546.

Mikolic, J. M., Parker, J. C., & Pruitt, D. G. (1997). Escalation in response to persistent annoyance: Groups versus individuals and gender effects. *Journal of Personality and Social Psychology, 72,* 151–163.

Miles, R. H. (1976). A comparison of the relative impacts of role perceptions of ambiguity and conflict by role. *Academy of Management Journal, 19,* 25–35.

Milgram, S. (1963). Behavioral study of obedience. *Journal of Abnormal and Social Psychology, 67,* 371–378.

Milgram, S. (1964). Issues in the study of obedience: A reply to Baumrind. *American Psychologist, 19,* 848–852.

Milgram, S. (1970). *The experience of living in cities. Science, 167,* 1461–1468.

Milgram, S. (1974). *Obedience to authority.* New York: Harper & Row.

Milgram, S. (1977, October). Subject reaction: The neglected factor in the ethics of experimentation. *Hastings Center Report,* 19–23.

Milgram, S. (1992). *The individual in a social world: Essays and experiments* (2nd ed.). New York: McGraw-Hill.

Milgram, S., Bickman, L., & Berkowitz, L. (1969). Note on the drawing power of crowds of different size. *Journal of Personality and Social Psychology, 13,* 79–82.

Milgram, S., Liberty, H. J., Toledo, R., & Wackenhut, J. (1986). Response to intrusion into waiting lines. *Journal of Personality and Social Psychology, 51,* 683–689.

Milgram, S., & Toch, H. (1969). Collective behavior: Crowds and social movements. In G. Lindzey & E. Aronson (Eds.), *Handbook of social psychology* (2nd ed., Vol. 4, pp. 507–610). Reading, MA: Addison-Wesley.

Miller, A. G. (1982). Historical and contemporary perspectives on stereotyping. In A. G. Miller (Ed.), *In the eye of the beholder: Contemporary issues in stereotyping.* New York: Praeger.

Miller, A. G. (1986). *The obedience experiments.* New York: Praeger.

Miller, A. G. (1995). Constructions of the obedience experiments: A focus upon domains of relevance. *Journal of Social Issues, 51(3),* 33–53.

Miller, A. G., Collins, B. E., & Brief, D. E. (1995a). Perspectives on obedience to authority: The legacy of the Milgram experiments. *Journal of Social Issues, 51(3),* 1–19.

Miller, A. G., Collins, B. E., & Brief, D. E. (Eds.). (1995b). *Journal of Social Issues, 51(3).*

Miller, C. E., Jackson, P., Mueller, J., & Scherching, C. (1987). Some social psychological effects of group decision rules. *Journal of Personality and Social Psychology, 52,* 325–332.

Miller, C. E., & Komorita, S. S. (1995). Reward allocation in task-performing groups. *Journal of Personality and Social Psychology, 69,* 80–90.

Miller, D. L. (1985). *Introduction to collective behavior.* Belmont, CA: Wadsworth.

Miller, D. T., & Holmes, J. G. (1975). The role of situational restrictiveness on self-fulfilling prophecies: A theoretical and empirical extension of Kelley and Stahelski's triangle hypothesis. *Journal of Personality and Social Psychology, 31,* 661–673.

Miller, D. T., & Prentice, D. A. (1996). The construction of social norms and standards. In E. T. Higgins & A. W. Kruglanski (Eds.), *Social psychology: Handbook of basic principles* (pp. 799–829). New York: Guilford Press.

Miller, F. D. (1983). Group processes in successful community groups. In H. H. Blumberg, A. P. Hare, V. Kent, & M. F. Davies (Eds.), *Small groups and social interaction* (Vol. 2, pp. 329–335). New York: Wiley.

Miller, J. G. (1978). *Living systems.* New York: McGraw-Hill.

Miller, J. G. (1994). Cultural diversity in the morality of caring: Individually oriented versus duty-based interpersonal moral codes. *Cross-Cultural Research, 28,* 3–39.

Miller, N., & Brewer, M. B. (1986a). Categorization effects on ingroup and outgroup perception. In J. Dovidio & S. Gaertner (Eds.), *Prejudice, discrimination, and racism: Theory and research* (pp. 209–230). New York: Academic Press.

Miller, N., & Brewer, M. B. (1986b). Social categorization theory and team learning procedures. In R. S. Feldman (Ed.), *The social psychology of education* (pp. 172–198). New York: Cambridge University Press.

Miller, N., & Davidson-Podgorny, G. (1987). Theoretical models of intergroup relations and the use of cooperative teams as an intervention for desegregated settings. *Review of Personality and Social Psychology, 9,* 41–67.

Miller, N., Urban, L. M., & Vanman, E. J. (1998). A theoretical analysis of crossed social categorization effects. In C. Sedikides, J. Schopler, & C. A. Insko (Eds.), *Intergroup cognition and intergroup behavior* (pp. 393–422). Mahwah, NJ: Erlbaum.

Mills, T. M. (1962). A sleeper variable in small groups research: The experimenter. *Pacific Sociological Review, 5,* 21–28.

Minami, H., & Tanaka, K. (1995). Social and environmental psychology: Transaction between physical space and group-dynamic processes. *Environment and Behavior, 27,* 43–55.

Mintz, A. (1951). Non-adaptive group behavior. *Journal of Abnormal and Social Psychology, 46,* 150–159.

Miranda, F. S. B., Caballero, R. B., Gomez, M. N. G., & Zamorano, M. A. M. (1981). Obediencia a la autoridad [Obedience to authority]. *Psiquis: Revista de Psiquiatria, Psicolo, 2,* 212–221.

Misumi, J. (1985). *The behavioral science of leadership.* Ann Arbor: University of Michigan Press.

Misumi, J. (1995). The development in Japan of the performance-maintenance (PM) theory of leadership. *Journal of Social Issues, 51(1),* 213–228.

Mitchell, R. C., & Mitchell, R. R. (1984). Constructive management of conflict in groups. *Journal for Specialists in Group Work, 9,* 137–144.

Mitroff, I. I., & Kilmann, R. H. (1978). *Methodological approaches to social science.* San Francisco: Jossey-Bass.

Mixon, D. (1977). Why pretend to deceive? *Personality and Social Psychology Bulletin, 3,* 647–653.

Mobley, W. H., Griffeth, R. W., Hand, H. H., & Meglino, B. M. (1979). Review and conceptual analysis of employee turnover process. *Psychological Bulletin, 86,* 493–522.

Modigliani, A., & Rochat, F. (1995). The role of interaction sequences and the timing of resistance in shaping obedience and defiance to authority. *Journal of Social Issues, 51(3),* 107–123.

Moede, W. (1927). Die Richtlinien der Leistungs-Psychologie. *Industrielle Psychotechnik, 4,* 193–207.

Molleman, E., Pruyn, J., & van Knippenberg, A. (1986). Social comparison processes among cancer patients. *British Journal of Social Psychology, 25,* 1–13.

Molm, L. D. (1986). Gender, power, and legitimation: A test of three theories. *American Journal of Sociology, 91,* 1156–1186.

Molm, L. D. (1987). Extending power-dependence theory: Power processes and negative outcomes. *Advances in Group Processes, 4,* 171–198.

Molm, L. D. (1988). The structure and use of power: A comparison of reward and punishment power. *Social Psychology Quarterly, 51,* 108–122.

Molm, L. D. (1994). Is punishment effective? Coercive strategies in social exchange. *Social Psychology Quarterly, 57,* 75–94.

Moore, L. E. (1973). *The jury.* Cincinnati, OH: Anderson.

Moorhead, G. (1982). Groupthink: Hypothesis in need of testing. *Group and Organization Studies, 7,* 429–444.

Moorhead, G., Ference, R., & Neck, C. P. (1991). Group decision fiascoes continue: Space shuttle Challenger and a revised groupthink framework. *Human Relations, 44,* 539–550.

Moorhead, G., & Montanari, J. R. (1986). An empirical investigation of the groupthink phenomenon. *Human Relations, 39,* 399–410.

Moos, R. H., & Humphrey, B. (1974). *Group Environment Scale, Form R.* Palo Alto, CA: Consulting Psychologists Press.

Moos, R. H., Insel, P. M., & Humphrey, B. (1974). *Preliminary manual for Family Environment Scale, Work Environment Scale, and Group Environment Scale.* Palo Alto, CA: Consulting Psychologists Press.

Morasch, B., Groner, N., & Keating, J. (1979). Type of activity and failure as mediators of perceived crowding. *Personality and Social Psychology Bulletin, 5,* 223–226.

Moreland, R. L. (1985). Social categorization and the assimilation of "new" group members. *Journal of Personality and Social Psychology, 48,* 1173–1190.

Moreland, R. L. (1987). The formation of small groups. *Review of Personality and Social Psychology, 8,* 80–110.

Moreland, R. L. (1997). *Leadership in small groups: Expanding our analytical horizons.* Paper presented at the Interface of Leadership and Team Processes in Organizations: Implications for Understanding Work Effectiveness, Washington, DC.

Moreland, R. L., Argote, L., & Krishnan, R. (1996). Socially shared cognition at work: Transactive memory and group performance. In J. L. Nye & A. M. Brower (Eds.), *What's social about social cognition? Research on socially shared cognitions in small groups* (pp. 57–84). Thousand Oaks, CA: Sage.

Moreland, R. L., & Levine, J. M. (1982). Socialization in small groups: Temporal changes in individual-group relations. *Advances in Experimental Social Psychology, 15,* 137–192.

Moreland, R. L., & Levine, J. M. (1992a). The composition of small groups. *Advances in Group Processes, 9,* 237–280.

Moreland, R. L., & Levine, J. M. (1992b). Problem identification by groups. In S. Worchel, W. Wood, & J. A. Simpson (Eds.), *Group process and productivity* (pp. 17–47). Newbury Park, CA: Sage.

Moreland, R. L., Levine, J. M, & Cini, M. A. (1993). Group socialization: The role of commitment. In M. Hogg & D. Abrams (Eds.), *Group motivation: Social psychological perspectives* (pp. 105–129). London: Harvester Wheatsheaf.

Moreland, R. L., Levine, J. M., & Wingert, M. L. (1996). Creating the ideal group: Composition effects at work. In E. Witte & J. Davis (Eds.), *Understanding group behavior: Small group processes and interpersonal relations* (Vol. 2, pp. 11–35). Mahwah, NJ: Erlbaum.

Moreno, J. L. (1932/1953). *Who shall survive? Foundations of sociometry, group psychotherapy and sociodrama* (Rev. ed.). Beacon, NY: Beacon House.

Moreno, J. L. (Ed.). (1960). *The sociometry reader.* Glencoe, IL: The Free Press.

Mori, K. (1996). Effects of trust and communication on cooperative choice in a two-person prisoner's dilemma game. *Japanese Journal of Experimental Social Psychology, 35,* 324–336.

Morrill, C. (1995). *The executive way.* Chicago: University of Chicago Press.

Morris, W. N., & Miller, R. S. (1975). Impressions of dissenters and conformers: An attributional analysis. *Sociometry, 38,* 327–339.

Morris, W. N., Worchel, S., Bois, J. L., Pearson, J. A., Rountree, C. A., Samaha, G. M., Wachtler, J., & Wright, S. L. (1976). Collective coping with stress: Group reactions to fear, anxiety, and ambiguity. *Journal of Personality and Social Psychology, 33,* 674–679.

Moscovici, S. (1985). Social influence and conformity. In G. Lindzey & E. Aronson (Eds.), *Handbook of social psychology* (3rd ed., Vol. 2, pp. 347–412). New York: Random House.

Moscovici, S. (1994). Three concepts: Minority, conflict, and behavioral styles. In S. Moscovici, A. Mucchi-Faina, & Anne Maass (Eds.), *Minority influence* (pp. 233–251). Chicago: Nelson-Hall.

Moscovici, S., & Faucheux, C. (1972). Social influence, conformity bias, and the study of active minorities. *Advances in Experimental Social Psychology, 6,* 150–202.

Moscovici, S., & Lage, E. (1976). Studies in social influence. III. Majority versus minority influence in a group. *European Journal of Social Psychology, 6,* 149–174.

Moscovici, S., Lage, E., & Naffrechoux, M. (1969). Influence of a consistent minority on the responses of a majority in a color perception task. *Sociometry, 12,* 365–380.

Moscovici, S., Mucchi-Faina, A., & Maass, A. (Eds.). (1994). *Minority influence.* Chicago: Nelson-Hall.

Moscovici, S., & Nemeth, C. J. (1974). Minority influence. In C. J. Nemeth (Ed.), *Social psychology: Classic and contemporary integrations* (pp. 217–249). Chicago: Rand McNally.

Moscovici, S., & Personnaz, B. (1980). Studies in social influence. V. Minority influence and conversion behavior in a perceptual task. *Journal of Experimental Social Psychology, 16,* 270–282.

Moscovici, S., & Zavalloni, M. (1969). The group as a polarizer of attitudes. *Journal of Personality and Social Psychology, 12,* 125–135.

Mowat, F. (1977). *Ordeal by ice: The search for the Northwest Passage.* Toronto: McClelland & Steward.

Moxley, R. L., & Moxley, N. F. (1974). Determining point centrality in uncontrived social networks. *Sociometry, 37,* 122–130.

Mucchi-Faina, A. (1994). Theoretical perspectives on minority influence: Conversion versus divergence? In S. Moscovici, A. Mucchi-Faina, & Anne Maass (Eds.), *Minority influence* (pp. 115–133). Chicago: Nelson-Hall.

Mudrack, P. E. (1989). Defining group cohesiveness: A legacy of confusion? *Small Group Behavior, 20,* 37–49.

Mudrack, P. E., & Farrell, G. M. (1995). An examination of functional role behavior and its consequences for individuals in group settings. *Small Group Behavior, 26,* 542–571.

Mulder, M., & Stemerding, A. (1963). Threat, attraction to group, and need for strong leadership. *Human Relations, 16,* 317–334.

Mulder, M., Van Kijk, R., Soutenkijk, S., Stelwagen, T., & Verhagen, J. (1964). Non-instrumental liking tendencies toward powerful group members. *Acta Psychologica, 22,* 367–386.

Mullen, B. (1983). Operationalizing the effect of the group on the individual: A self-attention perspective. *Journal of Experimental Social Psychology, 19,* 295–322.

Mullen, B. (1985). Strength and immediacy of sources: A meta-analytic evaluation of the forgotten elements of social impact theory. *Journal of Personality and Social Psychology, 48,* 1458–1466.

Mullen, B. (1986a). Atrocity as a function of lynch mob composition: A self-attention perspective. *Personality and Social Psychology Bulletin, 12,* 187–197.

Mullen, B. (1986b). Effects of strength and immediacy in group contexts: Reply to Jackson. *Journal of Personality and Social Psychology, 50,* 514–516.

Mullen, B. (1987a). Introduction: The study of group behavior. In B. Mullen & G. R. Goethals (Eds.), *Theories of group behavior* (pp. 1–19). New York: Springer-Verlag.

Mullen, B. (1987b). Self-attention theory: The effects of group composition on the individual. In B. Mullen & G. R. Goethals (Eds.), *Theories of group behavior* (pp. 125–146). New York: Springer-Verlag.

Mullen, B. (1990). Why groups matter. In R. Brown (Ed.), *The Marshall Cavendish encyclopedia of personal relationships: Human behavior, How groups work* (Vol. 15, pp. 1800–1807). Oxford: Cavendish.

Mullen, B., Anthony, T., Salas, E., & Driskell, J. E. (1994). Group cohesiveness and quality of decision making: An integration of tests of the groupthink hypothesis. *Small Group Research, 25,* 189–204.

Mullen, B., & Baumeister, R. F. (1987). Group effects on self-attention and performance: social loafing, social facilitation, and social impairment. *Review of Personality and Social Psychology, 9,* 189–206.

Mullen, B., Brown, R., & Smith, C. (1992). Ingroup bias as a function of salience, relevance, and status: An integration. *European Journal of Social Psychology, 22,* 103–122.

Mullen, B., & Copper, C. (1994). The relation between group cohesiveness and performance: An integration. *Psychological Bulletin, 115,* 210–227.

Mullen, B., & Hu, L. (1988). Social projection as a function of cognitive mechanisms: Two meta-analytic integrations, *British Journal of Social Psychology, 27,* 333–356.

Mullen, B., Johnson, C. & Salas, E. (1991). Productivity loss in brainstorming groups: A meta-analytic review. *Basic and Applied Social Psychology, 12,* 3–23.

Mullen, B., Rozell, D., & Johnson, C. (1996). The phenomenology of being in a group: Complexity approaches to operationalizing cognitive representation. In J. L. Nye & A. M. Brower (Eds.), *What's social about social cognition? Research on socially shared cognitions in small groups* (pp. 205–229). Thousand Oaks, CA: Sage.

Mullen, B., Salas, E., & Driskell, J. (1989). Salience, motivation, and artifacts as contributors to the relationship between participation rate and leadership. *Journal of Experimental Social Psychology, 25*, 545–559.

Mummendey, A. (1995). Positive distinctiveness and social discrimination: An old couple living in divorce. *European Journal of Social Psychology, 25*, 657–670.

Mumpower, J. L., & Cook, S. W. (1978). The development of interpersonal attraction in cooperating interracial groups: The effects of success-failure, race and competence of groupmates, and helping a less competent groupmate. *International Journal of Group Tensions, 8*, 18–50.

Mungy, G. (1982). *The power of minorities.* London: Academic Press.

Mungy, G., & Pérez, J. A. (1991). *Social psychology of minority influence.* Oxford, England: Cambridge University Press.

Murata, K. (1982). Attribution processes in a mixed-motive interaction: The role of active observer's behavior. *Behaviormetrika, 12*, 47–61.

Murnighan, J. K. (1986). Organizational coalitions: Structural contingencies and the formation process. *Research on Negotiation in Organizations, 1*, 155–174.

Murphy, S. A., & Keating, J. P. (1995). Psychological assessment of postdisaster class action and personal injury litigants: A case study. *Journal of Traumatic Stress, 8*, 473–482.

Murphy-Berman, V., & Berman, J. (1978). Importance of choice and sex invasions of personal space. *Personality and Social Psychology Bulletin, 4*, 424–428.

Murray, H. A. (1938). *Explorations in personality.* New York: Oxford University Press.

Myers, A. E. (1962). Team competition, success, and the adjustment of group members. *Journal of Abnormal and Social Psychology, 65*, 325–332.

Myers, D. G. (1978). The polarizing effects of social comparison. *Journal of Experimental Social Psychology, 14*, 554–563.

Myers, D. G. (1982). Polarizing effects of social interaction. In H. Brandstätter, J. H. Davis, & G. Stocker-Kreichgauer (Eds.), *Group decision making.* New York: Academic Press.

Myers, D. G., & Bishop, G. D. (1970). Discussion effects on racial attitudes. *Science, 169*, 778–789.

Myers, D. G., & Lamm, H. (1975). The polarizing effect of group discussion. *American Scientist, 63*, 297–303.

Myers, D. G., & Lamm, H. (1976). The group polarization phenomenon. *Psychological Bulletin, 83*, 602–627.

Myers, D. J. (1997). Racial rioting in the 1960s: An event history analysis of local conditions. *American Sociological Review, 62*, 94–112.

Nagasundaram, M., & Dennis, A. R. (1993). When a group is not a group: The cognitive foundation of group idea generation. *Small Group Research, 24*, 463–489.

Nahemow, L., & Lawton, M. P. (1975). Similarity and propinquity in friendship formation. *Journal of Personality and Social Psychology, 32*, 205–213.

Nail, P. R. (1986). Toward an integration of some models and theories of social response. *Psychological Bulletin, 100*, 190–206.

Nail, P. R., & Van Leeuwen, M. D. (1993). An analysis and restructuring of the diamond model of social response. *Personality and Social Psychology Bulletin, 19*, 106–116.

Nathan, B. R., Hass, M. A., & Nathan, M. L. (1987, August). *Meta-analysis of Fiedler's leadership theory: A figure is worth a thousand words.* Paper presented at the Annual Meetings of the American Psychological Association, New York City.

National Center for State Courts [NCSC]. (1976). *Facets of the jury system: A survey.* Denver, CO: Research and Information Service, NCSC.

Neck, C. P., & Moorhead, G. (1992). Jury deliberations in the trial of U.S. v. John DeLorean: A case analysis of groupthink avoidance and an enhanced framework. *Human Relations, 45*, 1077–1091.

Neck, C. P., & Moorhead, G. (1995). Groupthink remodeled: The importance of leadership, time pressure, and methodical decision-making procedures. *Human Relations, 48*, 537–557.

Nemeth, C. (1985). Dissent, group process, and creativity: The contribution of minority influence. *Advances in Group Processes, 2*, 57–75.

Nemeth, C. J. (1986). Differential contributions of majority and minority influence. *Psychological Review, 93*, 23–32.

Nemeth, C. J. (1994). The value of minority dissent. In S. Moscovici, A. Mucchi-Faina, & Anne Maass (Eds.), *Minority influence* (pp. 3–15). Chicago: Nelson-Hall.

Nemeth, C. J., Endicott, J., & Wachtler, J. (1976). From the '50s to the '70s: Women in jury deliberations. *Sociometry, 39,* 293–304.

Nemeth, C. J., & Kwan, J. L. (1985). Originality of word associations as a function of majority vs. minority influence. *Social Psychology Quarterly, 48,* 277–282.

Nemeth, C. J., & Kwan, J. L. (1987). Minority influence, divergent thinking, and detection of correct solutions. *Journal of Applied Social Psychology, 17,* 788–799.

Nemeth, C. J., Mayseless, O., Sherman, J., & Brown, Y. (1990). Exposure to dissent and recall of information. *Journal of Personality and Social Psychology, 58,* 429–437.

Nemeth, C. J., Mosier, K., & Chiles, C. (1992). When convergent thought improves performance: Majority versus minority influence. *Personality and Social Psychology Bulletin, 18,* 139–144.

Nemeth, C. J., & Wachtler, J. (1974). Creating the perceptions of consistency and confidence: A necessary condition for minority influence. *Sociometry, 37,* 529–540.

Nemeth, C. J., & Wachtler, J. (1983). Creative problem solving as a result of majority vs. minority influence. *European Journal of Social Psychology, 13,* 45–55.

Newcomb, A. F., Bukowski, W. M., & Pattee, L. (1993). Children's peer relations: A meta-analytic review of popular, rejected, neglected, controversial, and average sociometric status. *Psychological Bulletin, 113,* 99–128.

Newcomb, T. M. (1943). *Personality and social change.* New York: Dryden.

Newcomb, T. M. (1960). Varieties of interpersonal attraction. In D. Cartwright and A. Zander (Eds.), *Group dynamics: Research and theory* (2nd ed.). Evanston, IL: Row, Peterson.

Newcomb, T. M. (1961). *The acquaintance process.* New York: Holt, Rinehart & Winston.

Newcomb, T. M. (1963). Stabilities underlying changes in interpersonal attraction. *Journal of Abnormal and Social Psychology, 66,* 376–386.

Newcomb, T. M. (1978). Individual and group. *American Behavioral Scientist, 5,* 631–650.

Newcomb, T. M. (1979). Reciprocity of interpersonal attraction: A nonconfirmation of a plausible hypothesis. *Social Psychology Quarterly, 42,* 299–306.

Newcomb, T. M. (1981). Heiderean balance as a group phenomenon. *Journal of Personality and Social Psychology, 40,* 862–867.

Newcomb, T. M., Koenig, K., Flacks, R., & Warwick, D. (1967). *Persistence and change: Bennington College and its students after 25 years.* New York: Wiley.

Newman, O. (1972). *Defensible space.* New York: Macmillan.

Newton, J. W., & Mann, L. (1980). Crowd size as a factor in the persuasion process: A study of religious crusade meetings. *Journal of Personality and Social Psychology, 39,* 874–883.

Nicholls, J. R. (1985). A new approach to situational leadership. *Leadership and Organization Development Journal, 6(4),* 2–7.

Nielsen, J. M. (1990). *Sex and gender in society: Perspectives on stratification.* Prospect Heights, IL: Waveland Press.

Nixon, H. L. (1976). *Sport and social organization.* Indianapolis, IN: Bobbs-Merrill.

Noel, J. G., Wann, D. L., & Branscombe, N. R. (1995). Peripheral ingroup membership status and public negativity toward outgroups. *Journal of Personality and Social Psychology, 68,* 127–137.

Norma, E., & Smith, D. R. (1985). Benchmark for the blocking of sociometric data. *Psychological Bulletin, 97,* 583–591.

Norris, F. H., & Murrell, S. A. (1990). Social support, life events, and stress as modifiers of adjustment to bereavement by older adults. *Psychology and Aging, 5,* 429–436.

North, R. C., Brody, R. A., & Holsti, O. R. (1964). Some empirical data on the conflict spiral. *Peace Research Society International Papers, 1,* 1–14.

Northouse, P. G. (1997). *Leadership: Theory and practice.* Thousand Oaks, CA: Sage.

Norvell, N., & Forsyth, D. R. (1984). The impact of inhibiting or facilitating causal factors on group members' reactions after success and failure. *Social Psychology Quarterly, 47,* 293–297.

Nosanchuk, T. A., & Lightstone, J. (1974). Canned laughter and public and private conformity. *Journal of Personality and Social Psychology, 29,* 153–156.

Nowak, A., & Latané, B. (1994). Simulating the emergence of social order from individual behavior. In N. Gilbert & J. Doran (Eds.), *Simulating societies: The computer simulation of social processes.* (pp. 63–84). London: University College London Press.

Nowak, A., Szamrej, J., & Latané, B. (1990). From private attitude to public opinion: A dynamic theory of social impact. *Psychological Review, 97,* 362–376.

Nye, J. L. (1994). Discussion: The social perceiver as a social being. Special issue: Social cognition in small groups. *Small Group Research, 25,* 316–322.

Nye, J. L., & Brower, A. M. (Eds.). (1996). What's social about social cognition? Research on socially shared cognitions in small groups. Thousand Oaks, CA: Sage.

Nye, J. L., & Forsyth, D. R. (1991). The effects of prototype-based biases on leadership appraisals: A test of leadership categorization theory. *Small Group Research, 22,* 360–379.

Nye, J. L., & Simonetta, L. G. (1996). Followers' perceptions of group leaders: The impact of recognition-based and inference-based processes. In J. L. Nye & A. M. Brower (Eds.), *What's social about social cognition? Research on socially shared cognitions in small groups* (pp. 124–153). Thousand Oaks, CA: Sage.

Nyquist, L. V., & Spence, J. T. (1986). Effects of dispositional dominance and sex role expectations on leadership behaviors. *Journal of Personality and Social Psychology, 50,* 87–93.

Nystrom, P. C. (1978). Managers and the Hi-Hi leader myth. *Academy of Management Journal, 21,* 325–331.

O'Connor, B. P., & Dyce, J. (1997). Interpersonal rigidity, hostility, and complementarity in musical bands. *Journal of Personality and Social Psychology, 72,* 362–372.

O'Connor, J., Mumford, M. D., Clifton, T. C., Gessner, T. L., & Connelly, M. S. (1995). Charismatic leaders and destructiveness: An historiometric study. *Leadership Quarterly, 6,* 529–555.

Offerman, L. R., Kennedy, J. K., & Wirtz, P. W. (1994). Implicit theories: Content, structure and generalizability. *Leadership Quarterly, 5,* 43–58.

Offermann, L. R., & Schrier, P. E. (1985). Social influence strategies: The impact of sex, role, and attitudes toward power. *Personality and Social Psychology Bulletin, 11,* 286–300.

Offner, A. K., Kramer, T. J., & Winter, J. P. (1996). The effects of facilitation, recording, and pauses on group brainstorming. *Small Group Research, 27,* 283–298.

Ofshe, R., & Lee, M. T. (1981). Reply to Greenstein. *Social Psychology Quarterly, 44,* 383–385.

Ohbuchi, K., Chiba, S., & Fukushima, O. (1996). Mitigation of interpersonal conflicts: Politeness and time pressure. *Personality and Social Psychology Bulletin, 22,* 1035–1042.

Ones, D. S., Mount, M. K., Barrick, M. R., & Hunter, J. E. (1994). Personality and job performance: A critique of the Tett, Jackson, and Rothstein (1991) meta-analysis. *Personnel Psychology, 47,* 147–156.

Orbell, J., Dawes, R., & van de Kragt, A. (1995). Cooperation under laissez faire and majority decision rules in group-level social dilemmas. In D. A. Schroeder (Ed.), *Social dilemmas: Perspectives on individuals and groups* (pp. 105–116). Westport, CT: Praeger.

Orcutt, J. D. (1973). Societal reaction and the response to deviation in small groups. *Social Forces, 52,* 261–267.

Orive, R. (1988a). Group consensus, action immediacy, and opinion confidence. *Personality and Social Psychology Bulletin, 14,* 573–577.

Orive, R. (1988b). Social projection and social comparison of opinions. *Journal of Personality and Social Psychology, 54,* 943–964.

Ormont, L. R. (1984). The leader's role in dealing with aggression in groups. *International Journal of Group Psychotherapy, 34,* 553–572.

Orne, M. T., & Holland, C. H. (1968). On the ecological validity of laboratory deceptions. *International Journal of Psychiatry, 6,* 282–293.

Osborn, A. F. (1957). *Applied imagination.* New York: Scribner.

Oskamp, S., & Hartry, A. (1968). A factor-analytic study of the double standard in attitudes toward U.S. and Russian actions. *Behavioral Science, 13,* 178–188.

Ostrom, T. M., & Sedikides, C. (1992). Out-group homogeneity effects in natural and minimal groups. *Psychological Bulletin, 112,* 536–552.

Owen, W. F. (1985). Metaphor analysis of cohesiveness in small discussion groups. *Small Group Behavior, 16,* 415–424.

Oyserman, D., & Saltz, E. (1993). Competence, delinquency, and attempts to attain possible selves. *Journal of Personality and Social Psychology, 65,* 360–374.

Padawer-Singer, A. M., Singer, A. N., & Singer, R. L. J. (1977). An experimental study of twelve vs. six member juries under unanimous vs. nonunanimous decisions. In B. D. Sales (Ed.), *Psychology in the legal process.* New York: Spectrum.

Page, R. A., & Moss, M. K. (1976). Environmental influences on aggression: The effects of darkness and proximity of victim. *Journal of Applied Social Psychology, 6,* 126–133.

Palinkas, L. A. (1991). Effects of physical and social environments on the health and well-being of Antarctic winter-over personnel. *Environment and Behavior, 23,* 782–799.

Palmer, G. J. (1962). Task ability and effective leadership. *Psychological Reports, 10,* 863–866.

Pandey, J., & Singh, P. (1987). Effects of machiavellianism, other-enhancement, and power-position on affect, power feeling, and evaluation of the ingratiator. *Journal of Psychology, 121,* 287–300.

Park, B., & Rothbart, M. (1982). Perception of outgroup homogeneity and levels of social categorization: Memory for the subordinate attributes of in-group and out-group members. *Journal of Personality and Social Psychology, 42,* 1051–1068.

Park, W. (1990). A review of research on groupthink. *Journal of Behavioral Decision Making, 3,* 229–245.

Parkinson, C. N. (1957). *Parkinson's law and other studies in administration.* Boston: Houghton Mifflin.

Parks, C. D., Henager, R. F., & Scamahorn, S. D. (1996). Trust and reactions to messages of intent in social dilemmas. *Journal of Conflict Resolution, 40,* 134–151.

Parks, C. D., & Komorita, S. S. (1997). Reciprocal strategies for large groups. *Personality and Social Psychology Review, 1,* 314–322.

Parkum, K. H., & Parkum, V. C. (1980). Citizen participation in community planning and decision making. In D. H. Smith, J. Macaulay, & Associates (Eds.), *Participation in social and political activities: A comprehensive analysis of political involvement, expressive leisure time, and helping behavior* (pp. 153–167). San Francisco: Jossey-Bass.

Parsons, H. M. (1976). Work environments. In I. Altman & J. Wohlwill (Eds.), *Human behavior and environment* (Vol. 1). New York: Plenum.

Parsons, T., Bales, R. F., & Shils, E. (1953). *Working papers in the theory of action.* New York: The Free Press.

Patterson, M. L. (1975). Personal space—Time to burst the bubble? *Man-Environment Systems, 5,* 67.

Patterson, M. L. (1991). A functional approach to nonverbal exchange. In R. S. Feldman & B. Rimé (Eds.), *Fundamentals of nonverbal behavior* (pp. 458–495). New York: Cambridge University Press.

Patterson, M. L. (1996). Social behavior and social cognition: A parallel process approach. In J. L. Nye & A. M. Brower (Eds.), *What's social about social cognition? Research on socially shared cognitions in small groups* (pp. 87–105). Thousand Oaks, CA: Sage.

Patterson, M. L., Kelley, C. E., Kondracki, B. A., & Wulf, L. J. (1979). Effects of seating arrangement on small group behavior. *Social Psychology Quarterly, 42,* 180–185.

Patterson, M. L., Roth, C. P., & Schenk, C. (1979). Seating arrangement, activity, and sex differences in small group crowding. *Personality and Social Psychology Bulletin, 5,* 100–103.

Patterson, M. L., & Sechrest, L. B. (1970). Interpersonal distance and impression formation. *Journal of Personality, 38,* 161–166.

Paul, G. L. (1967). Strategy of outcome research in psychotherapy. *Journal of Consulting Psychology, 31,* 109–118.

Paulus, P. B., Annis, A. B., Seta, J. J., Schkade, J. K., & Matthews, R. W. (1976). Density does affect task performance. *Journal of Personality and Social Psychology, 34,* 248–353.

Paulus, P. B., & Dzindolet, M. T. (1993). Social influence processes in group brainstorm. *Journal of Personality and Social Psychology, 64,* 575–586.

Paulus, P. B., Dzindolet, M. T., Poletes, G., & Camacho, L. M. (1993). Perception of performance in group brainstorming: The illusion of group productivity. *Personality and Social Psychology Bulletin, 19,* 78–89.

Paulus, P. B., Larey, T. S., Putman, V. L., Leggett, K. L., & Roland, E. J. (1996). Social influence processes in computer brainstorming. *Basic and Applied Social Psychology, 18,* 3–14.

Paulus, P., & Putman, V. (1996, November). *Demonstrating group brainstorming effects.* Paper presented at the Annual Conference of the Society of Southeastern Social Psychologists, Virginia Beach, VA.

Pavelshak, M. A., Moreland, R. L., & Levine, J. M. (1986). Effects of prior group memberships on subsequent reconnaissance activities. *Journal of Personality and Social Psychology, 50,* 56–66.

Pearce, J. L., Stevenson, W. B., & Porter, L. W. (1986). Coalitions in the organizational context. *Research on Negotiation in Organizations, 1,* 97–115.

Pelletier, L. G., & Vallerand, R. J. (1996). Supervisors' beliefs and subordinates' intrinsic motivation: A behavioral confirmation analysis. *Journal of Personality and Social Psychology, 71,* 331–340.

Pelz, D. C. (1956). Some social factors related to performance in a research organization. *Administrative Science Quarterly, 1,* 310–325.

Pelz, D. C. (1967). Creative tensions in the research and development climate. *Science, 157,* 160–165.

Pemberton, M. B., Insko, C. A., & Schopler, J. (1996). Memory for and experience of differential competitive behavior of individuals and groups. *Journal of Personality and Social Psychology, 71,* 953–966.

Pendell, S. D. (1990). Deviance and conflict in small group decision making: An exploratory study. *Small Group Research, 21,* 393–403.

Pennebaker, J. W. (1982). Social and perceptual factors affecting symptom reporting and mass psychogenic illness. In M. J. Colligan, J. W. Pennebaker, & L. R. Murphy (Eds.), *Mass psychogenic illness: A social psychological analysis* (pp. 139–153). Hillsdale, NJ: Erlbaum.

Pennebaker, J. W. (1990). *Opening up: The healing power of confiding in others.* New York: Morrow.

Pennington, N., & Hastie, R. (1986). Evidence evaluation in complex decision-making. *Journal of Personality and Social Psychology, 51,* 242–258.

Pennington, N., & Hastie, R. (1992). Explaining the evidence: Tests of the Story Model for juror decision making. *Journal of Personality and Social Psychology, 62,* 189–206.

Penrod, S., & Hastie, R. (1980). A computer simulation of jury decision making. *Psychological Review, 87,* 133–159.

Pepitone, A. (1981). Lessons from the history of social psychology. *American Psychologist, 36,* 972–985.

Pepitone, A., & Reichling, G. (1955). Group cohesiveness and the expression of hostility. *Human Relations, 8,* 327–337.

Pepitone, A., & Wilpinski, C. (1960). Some consequences of experimental rejection. *Journal of Abnormal and Social Psychology, 60,* 359–364.

Pérez, J. A., & Mungy, G. (1996). The conflict elaboration theory of social influence. In E. Witte & J. Davis (Eds.), *Understanding group behavior: Small group processes and interpersonal relations* (Vol. 2, pp. 191–210). Mahwah, NJ: Erlbaum.

Perls, F. (1969). *Gestalt therapy verbatim.* Lafayette, CA: Real People Press.

Perls, F., Hefferline, R., & Goodman, P. (1951). *Gestalt therapy: Excitement and growth in the human personality.* New York: Julian Press.

Perrin, S., & Spencer, C. P. (1980). The Asch effect? A child of its time? *Bulletin of the British Psychological Society, 32,* 405–406.

Perrin, S., & Spencer, C. P. (1981). Independence or conformity in the Asch experiment as a reflection of cultural and situational factors. *British Journal of Social Psychology, 20,* 205–210.

Peters, L. H., Hartke, D. D., & Pohlmann, J. T. (1985). Fiedler's contingency theory of leadership: An application of the meta-analytical procedures of Schmidt and Hunter. *Psychological Bulletin, 97,* 274–285.

Peterson, D. R. (1983). Conflict. In H. H. Kelley, E. Berscheid, A. Christensen, J. H. Harvey, T. L. Huston, G. Levinger, E. McClintock, L. A. Peplau, & D. R. Peterson, *Close relationships* (pp. 360–396). New York: Freeman.

Peterson, M. F., Smith, P. B., Akande, A., & Ayestaran, S. (1995). Role conflict, ambiguity, and overload: A 21-nation study. *Academy of Management Journal, 38,* 429–452.

Peterson, R. S. (1997). A directive leadership style in group decision making can be both virtue and vice: Evidence from elite and experimental groups. *Journal of Personality and Social Psychology 72,* 1107–1121.

Peterson, R. S., & Nemeth, C. J. (1996). Focus versus flexibility: Majority and minority influence can both improve performance. *Personality and Social Psychology Bulletin, 22,* 14–23.

Petty, R. E., & Cacioppo, J. T. (1986). The elaboration likelihood model of persuasion. *Advances in Experimental Social Psychology, 19,* 124–205.

Philipsen, G., Mulac, A., & Dietrich, D. (1979). The effects of social interaction on group idea generation. *Communication Monographs, 46,* 119–125.

Phillips, J. S., & Lord, R. G. (1986). Notes on the practical and theoretical consequences of implicit leadership theories for the future of leadership measurement. *Journal of Management, 12,* 31–41.

Phinney, J. S. (1989). Stages of ethnic identity development in minority group adolescents. *Journal of Early Adolescence, 9,* 34–49.

Phinney, J. S. (1996) When we talk about American ethnic groups, what do we mean? *American Psychologist, 51,* 918–927.

Phoon, W. H. (1982). Outbreaks of mass hysteria at workplaces in Singapore: Some patterns and modes of presentation. In M. J. Colligan, J. W. Pennebaker, & L. R. Murphy (Eds.), *Mass psychogenic illness: A social psychological analysis* (pp. 21–31). Hillsdale, NJ: Erlbaum.

Pigors, P. (1935). *Leadership or domination.* Boston: Houghton Mifflin.

Pilisuk, M., Brandes, B., & van den Hove, D. (1976). Deceptive sounds: Illicit communication in the laboratory. *Behavioral Science, 21,* 515–523.

Pilkington, C. J., Tesser, A., & Stephens, D. (1991). Complementarity in romantic relationships: A self-evaluation maintenance perspective. *Journal of Social and Personal Relationships, 8,* 481–504.

Pillai, R. (1996). Crisis and the emergence of charismatic leadership in groups: An experimental investigation. *Journal of Applied Social Psychology, 26,* 543–562.

Pittard-Payne, B. (1980). Nonassociational religious participation. In D. H. Smith, J. Macaulay, & Associates (Eds.), *Participation in social and political activities: A comprehensive analysis of political involvement, expressive leisure time, and helping behavior* (pp. 214–243). San Francisco: Jossey-Bass.

Plous, S. (1993). The psychology of judgment and decision making. New York: McGraw-Hill.

Podsakoff, P. M., & MacKenzie, S. B. (1997). Kerr and Jermier's substitutes for leadership model: Background, empirical assessment, and suggestions for future research. *Leadership Quarterly, 8,* 117–132.

Podsakoff, P. M., MacKenzie, S. B., & Bommer, W. H. (1996a). Meta-analysis of the relationships between Kerr and Jermier's substitutes for leadership and employee job attitudes, role perceptions, and performance. *Journal of Applied Psychology, 81,* 380–399.

Podsakoff, P. M., MacKenzie, S. B., & Bommer, W. H. (1996b). Transformational leader behaviors and substitutes for leadership as determinants of employee satisfaction, commitment, trust, and organizational citizenship behaviors. *Journal of Management, 22,* 259–298.

Podsakoff, P. M., & Schriescheim, C. A. (1985). Field studies of French and Raven's bases of power: Critique, reanalysis, and suggestions for future research. *Psychological Bulletin, 97,* 387–411.

Polley, R. B. (1984). Subjectivity in issue polarization. *Journal of Applied Social Psychology, 14,* 426–440.

Polley, R. B. (1986). Rethinking the third dimension. *International Journal of Small Group Research, 2,* 134–140.

Polley, R. B. (1987). The dimensions of social interaction: A method for improved rating scales. *Social Psychology Quarterly, 50,* 72–82.

Polley, R. B. (1989). On the dimensionality of interpersonal behavior: A reply to Lustig. *Small Group Behavior, 20,* 270–278.

Polley, R. B. (1991). Group process as diagnostic: An introduction. *Small Group Research, 22,* 92–98.

Polley, R. B., Hare, A. P., & Stone, P. J. (Eds.). (1988). *The SYMLOG practitioner: Applications of small group research.* New York: Praeger.

Pollis, N. P., Montgomery, R. L., & Smith, T. G. (1975). Autokinetic paradigms: A reply to Alexander, Zucker, and Brody. *Sociometry, 38,* 358–373.

Polzer, J. T. (1996). Intergroup negotiations: The effects of negotiating teams. *Journal of Conflict Resolution, 40,* 678–698.

Polzer, J. T., Kramer, R. M., & Neale, M. A. (1997). Positive illusions about oneself and one's group. *Small Group Research, 28,* 243–266.

Porter, N., Geis, F. L., Cooper, E., & Newman, E. (1985). Androgyny and leadership in mixed-sex groups. *Journal of Personality and Social Psychology, 49,* 808–823.

Posluszny, D. M., Hyman, K. B., & Baum, A. (1998). Group interventions in cancer: The benefits of social support and education on patient adjustment. In R. S. Tindale, L. Heath, J. Edwards, E. J. Posavac, F. B. Bryant, Y. Suarez-Balcazar, E. Henderson-King, & J. Myers (Eds.), *Theory and research on small groups* (pp. 87–105) New York, Plenum.

Postmes, T., & Spears, R. (1998). Deindividuation and antinormative behavior: A meta-analysis. *Psychological Bulletin, 123,* 238–259.

Prapavessis, H., & Carron, A. V. (1997). Sacrifice, cohesion, and conformity to norms in sport teams. *Group Dynamics: Theory, Research, and Practice, 1,* 231–240.

Pratt, J. H. (1922). The principle of class treatment and their application to various chronic diseases. *Hospital Social Services, 6,* 401–417.

Preiss, J. J. (1968). Self and role in medical education. In C. Gordon & K. J. Gergen (Eds.), *The self in social interaction* (pp. 207–218). New York: Wiley.

Prentice, D. A., Miller, P., & Lightdale, J. R. (1994). Asymmetries in attachments to groups and to their members: Distinguishing between common-identity and common-bond groups. *Personality and Social Psychology Bulletin, 20,* 484–493.

Prentice-Dunn, S., & Rogers, R. W. (1980). Effects of deindividuating situation cues and aggressive models on subjective deindividuation and aggression. *Journal of Personality and Social Psychology, 39,* 104–113.

Prentice-Dunn, S., & Rogers, R. W. (1982). Effects of public and private self-awareness on deindividuation and aggression. *Journal of Personality and Social Psychology, 43,* 503–513.

Prentice-Dunn, S., & Rogers, R. W. (1983). Deindividuation and aggression. In R. G. Geen & E. I. Donnerstein (Eds.), *Aggression: Theoretical and empirical reviews* (Vol. 1). New York: Academic Press.

Prentice-Dunn, S., & Spivey, R. W. (1986). Extreme deindividuation in the laboratory: Its magnitude and subjective components. *Personality and Social Psychology Bulletin, 12,* 206–215.

Prince, G. (1970). *The practice of creativity.* New York: Harper & Row.

Prince, G. (1975). The mind spring theory. *Journal of Creative Behavior, 9(3),* 159–181.

Pruitt, D. G. (1971). Choice shifts in group discussion: An introductory review. *Journal of Personality and Social Psychology, 20,* 339–360.

Pruitt, D. G. (1981). *Negotiation behavior.* New York: Academic Press.

Pruitt, D. G. (1983). Strategic choice in negotiation. *American Behavioral Science, 27,* 167–194.

Pruitt, D. G. (1987). Creative approaches to negotiation. In D. J. D. Sandole & I. Sandole-Staroste (Eds.), *Conflict management and problem solving: Interpersonal to international applications* (pp. 62–76). London: Frances Pinter.

Pruitt, D. G., & Rubin, J. Z. (1986). *Social conflict: Escalation, stalemate, and settlement.* New York: Random House.

Pugh, M. D., & Wahrman, R. (1983). Neutralizing sexism in mixed-sex groups: Do women have to be better than men? *American Journal of Sociology, 88,* 746–762.

Quadagno, J. S. (1979). Paradigms on evolutionary theory: The sociobiological model of natural selection. *American Sociological Review, 44,* 100–109.

Quattrone, G. A. (1986). On the perception of a group's variability. In S. Worchel & W. G. Austin (Eds.), *Psychology of intergroup relations* (2nd ed., pp. 25–48). Chicago: Nelson-Hall.

Quattrone, G. A., & Jones, E. E. (1980). The perception of variability within in-groups and out-groups: Implications for the law of small numbers. *Journal of Personality and Social Psychology, 38,* 141–152.

Quinn, R. E., & McGrath, M. R. (1982). Moving beyond the single solution perspective. *Journal of Applied Behavioral Science, 18,* 463–472.

Rabbie, J. (1963). Differential preference for companionship under stress. *Journal of Abnormal and Social Psychology, 67,* 643–648.

Rabbie, J. M., Benoist, F., Oosterbaan, H., & Visser, L. (1974). Differential power and effects of expected competitive and cooperative intergroup interaction upon intra- and outgroup attitudes. *Journal of Personality and Social Psychology, 30,* 46–56.

Rabbie, J. M., & Horwitz, M. (1969). Arousal of ingroup-outgroup bias by a chance win or loss. *Journal of Personality and Social Psychology, 13,* 269–277.

Radloff, R., & Helmreich, R. (1968). *Groups under stress: Psychological research in SEALAB II.* New York: Irvington.

Ragone, G. (1981). Fashion, "crazes," and collective behavior. *Communications, 7,* 249–268.

Raiffa, H. (1983). Mediation of conflicts. *American Behavioral Science, 27,* 195–210.

Rapoport, A. (1985). Provision of public goods and the MCS experimental paradigm. *American Political Science Review, 79,* 148–155.

Rapoport, A. (1988). Provision of step-level public goods: Effects of inequality in resources. *Journal of Personality and Social Psychology, 54,* 432–440.

Rapoport, A., & Bornstein, G. (1987). Intergroup competition for the provision of binary public goods. *Psychological Review, 94,* 291–299.

Raven, B. H. (1965). Social influence and power. In I. D. Steiner & M. Fishbein (Eds.), *Current studies in social psychology* (pp. 371–382). New York: Holt, Rinehart & Winston.

Raven, B. H. (1992). A power/interaction model of interpersonal influence: French and Raven thirty years later. *Journal of Social Behavior and Personality, 7,* 217–244.

Raven, B. H., & Kruglanski, A. W. (1970). Conflict and power. In P. Swingle (Ed.), *The structure of conflict.* New York: Academic Press.

Rawlins, W. K. (1984). Consensus in decision-making groups: A conceptual history. In G. M. Phillips & J. T. Wood (Eds.), *Emergent issues in human decision making* (pp. 19–39). Carbondale, IL: Southern Illinois University Press.

Read, K. E. (1986). *Return to the high valley: Coming full circle.* Berkeley, CA: University of California Press.

Read, P. P. (1974). *Alive.* New York: Avon.

Reckman, R. F., & Goethals, G. R. (1973). Deviancy and group orientation as determinants of group composition preferences. *Sociometry, 36,* 419–423.

Reddin, W. J. (1970). *Managerial effectiveness.* New York: McGraw-Hill.

Redl, F. (1942). Group emotion and leaders. *Psychiatry, 5,* 573–596.

Reicher, S. D. (1984). The St. Pauls riot: An explanation of the limits of crowd action in terms of a social identity model. *European Journal of Social Psychology, 14,* 1–21.

Reicher, S. D. (1987). Crowd behavior as social action. In J. C. Turner, M. A. Hogg, P. J. Oakes, S. D. Reicher, & M. S. Wetherell (Eds.), *Rediscovering the social group: A self-categorization* theory (pp. 171–202). Oxford: Blackwell.

Reicher, S. D. (1996). "The Battle of Westminster": Developing the social identity model of crowd behavior in order to explain the initiation and development of collective conflict. *European Journal of Social Psychology, 26,* 115–134.

Reicher, S. D., & Levine, M. (1994). Deindividuation, power relations between groups and the expression of social identity: The effects of visibility to the outgroup. *British Journal of Social Psychology, 33,* 145–163.

Reicher, S. D., Spears, R., & Postmes, T. (1995). A social identity model of deindividuated phenomena. *European Review of Social Psychology, 6,* 161–198.

Reichl, A. J. (1997). Ingroup favoritism and outgroup favoritism in low status minimal groups: Differential responses to status-related and status-unrelated measures. *European Journal of Social Psychology, 27,* 617–633.

Reid, A., & Deaux, K. (1996). Relationship between social and personal identities: Segregation or integration. *Journal of Personality and Social Psychology, 71,* 1084–1091.

Remland, M. S., Jones, T. S., & Brinkman, H. (1995). Interpersonal distance, body orientation, and touch: Effects of culture, gender, and age. *Journal of Social Psychology, 135,* 281–297.

Rempel, J. K., Holmes, J. G., & Zanna, M. P. (1985). Trust in close relationships. *Journal of Personality and Social Psychology, 49,* 95–112.

Rhee, E., Uleman, J. S., Lee, H. K., & Roman, R. J. (1995). Spontaneous self-descriptions and ethnic identities in individualistic and collectivistic cultures. *Journal of Personality and Social Psychology, 69,* 142–152.

Rice, O. K. (1978). *The Hatfields and the McCoys.* Lexington, KY: University Press of Kentucky.

Rice, R. W. (1978a). Psychometric properties of the esteem for Least Preferred Co-worker (LPC) Scale. *Academy of Management Review, 3,* 106–118.

Rice, R. W. (1978b). Construct validity of the Least Preferred Co-worker (LPC) score. *Psychological Bulletin, 85,* 1199–1237.

Rice, R. W. (1979). Reliability and validity of the LPC Scale: A reply. *Academy of Management Review, 4,* 291–294.

Rice, R. W., Instone, D., & Adams, J. (1984). Leader sex, leader success, and leadership process: Two field studies. *Journal of Applied Psychology, 69,* 12–31.

Rickards, T. (1974). *Problem solving through creative analysis.* London: Halsted Press.

Ridgeway, C. L. (1982). Status in groups: The importance of motivation. *American Sociological Review, 47,* 76–88.

Ridgeway, C. L. (1983). *The dynamics of small groups.* New York: St. Martin's Press.

Ridgeway, C. L. (1989). Understanding legitimation in informal status orders. In J. Berger, M. Zelditch, Jr., & B. Anderson (Eds.), *Sociological theories in progress: New formulations* (pp. 131–159). Newbury Park, CA: Sage.

Ridgeway, C. L. (Ed.). (1994). Conceptualizing structure in social psychology. *Social Psychology Quarterly, 57,* 161–273.

Ridgeway, C. L., & Balkwell, J. W. (1997). Group processes and the diffusion of status beliefs. *Social Psychology Quarterly, 60,* 14–31.

Ridgeway, C. L., Berger, J., & Smith, L. F. (1985). Nonverbal cues and status: An expectation states approach. *American Journal of Sociology, 90,* 955–978.

Ridgeway, C. L., & Walker, H. A. (1995). Status structures. In K. S. Cook, G. A. Fine, & J. S. House (Eds.), *Sociological perspectives on social psychology* (pp. 281–310). Boston: Allyn & Bacon.

Riess, M. (1982). Seating preferences as impression management: A literature review and theoretical integration. *Communication, 11,* 85–113.

Riess, M., & Rosenfeld, P. (1980). Seating preferences as nonverbal communication: A self-presentational analysis. *Journal of Applied Communications Research, 8,* 22–30.

Ringelmann, M. (1913). Research on animate sources of power: The work of man. *Annales de l'Institut National Agronomique, 2e série—tome XII,* 1–40.

Riordan, C., & Riggiero, J. (1980). Producing equal-status interracial interaction: A replication. *Social Psychology Quarterly, 43,* 131–136.

Rivera, A. N., & Tedeschi, J. T. (1976). Public versus private reactions to positive inequity. *Journal of Personality and Social Psychology, 34,* 895–900.

Roark, A. E., & Sharah, H. S. (1989). Factors related to group cohesiveness. *Small Group Behavior, 20,* 62–69.

Robert, H. M. (1915/1971). *Robert's rules of order* (Rev. ed.). New York: Morrow.

Rodin, J. (1976). Crowding, perceived choice, and response to controllable and uncontrollable outcomes. *Journal of Experimental Social Psychology, 12,* 564–578.

Rodin, J., & Baum, A. (1978). Crowding and helplessness: Potential consequences of density and loss of control. In A. Baum & Y. Epstein (Eds.), *Human responses to crowding.* Hillsdale, NJ: Erlbaum.

Rodin, J., Solomon, S. K., & Metcalf, J. (1978). Role of control in mediating perceptions of density. *Journal of Personality and Social Psychology, 36,* 988–999.

Roethlisberger, F. J., & Dickson, W. J. (1939). *Management and the worker.* Cambridge, MA: Harvard University Press.

Rofé, Y. (1984). Stress and affiliation: A utility theory. *Psychological Review, 91,* 235–250.

Rogelberg, S. G., & Rumery, S. M. (1996). Gender diversity, team decision quality, time on task, and interpersonal cohesion. *Small Group Research, 27,* 79–90.

Rogers, C. (1970). *Encounter groups.* New York: Harper & Row.

Rogers, R. W., & Prentice-Dunn, S. (1981). Deindividuation and anger-mediated interracial aggression: Unmasking regressive racism. *Journal of Personality and Social Psychology, 41,* 63–73.

Rohrbaugh, M., & Bartels, B. D. (1975). Participants' perceptions of curative factors in therapy and growth groups. *Small Group Behavior, 6,* 430–456.

Rojahn, K., & Willemsen, T. M. (1994). The evaluation of effectiveness and likability of gender-role congruent and gender-role incongruent leaders. *Sex Roles, 30,* 109–119.

Roll, S., McClelland, G., & Abel, T. (1996). Differences in susceptibility to influence in Mexican American and Anglo females. *Hispanic Journal of Behavioral Sciences, 18,* 13–20.

Rook, K. S. (1984). Promoting social bonding: Strategies for helping the lonely and socially isolated. *American Psychologist, 39,* 1389–1407.

Roos, P. A. (1985). *Gender and work: A comparative analysis of industrial societies.* New York: State University of New York Press.

Roos, P. D. (1968). Jurisdiction: An ecological concept. *Human Relations, 21,* 75–84.

Rose, S. D. (1993). Cognitive-behavioral group psychotherapy. In H. I. Kaplan & M. J. Sadock (Eds.), *Comprehensive group psychotherapy* (3rd ed., pp. 205–214). Baltimore: Williams & Wilkins.

Rosenbaum, M. E. (1986). The repulsion hypothesis: On the nondevelopment of relationships. *Journal of Personality and Social Psychology, 51,* 1156–1166.

Rosenberg, M. (1979). *Conceiving the self.* New York: Basic Books.

Rosnow, R. L. (1980). Psychology of rumor reconsidered. *Psychological Bulletin, 87,* 578–591.

Rosnow, R. L., & Kimmel, A. J. (1979). Lives of a rumor. *Psychology Today, 13(6),* 88–92.

Rosnow, R. L., & Rosenthal, R. (1997). People studying people: Artifacts and ethics in behavioral research. New York: Freeman.

Rosnow, R. L., Yost, J. H., & Esposito, J. L. (1986). Belief in rumor and likelihood of rumor transmission. *Language and Communication, 6,* 189–194.

Ross, L. (1977). The intuitive psychologist and his shortcomings: Distortions in the attribution process. *Advances in Experimental Social Psychology, 10,* 173–220.

Ross, L., Bierbrauer, G., & Hoffman, S. (1976). The role of attribution processes in conformity and dissent: Revisiting the Asch situation. *American Psychologist, 31,* 148–157.

Ross, L., & Ward, A. (1995). Psychological barriers to dispute resolution. *Advances in Experimental Social Psychology, 27,* 255–304.

Ross, M., & Sicoly, F. (1979). Egocentric biases in availability and attribution. *Journal of Personality and Social Psychology, 37,* 322–336.

Roth, B. E. (1993). Freud: The group psychologist and group leader. In H. I. Kaplan & M. J. Sadock (Eds.), *Comprehensive group psychotherapy* (3rd ed., pp. 10–21). Baltimore: Williams & Wilkins.

Rothbart, M., Davis-Stitt, C., & Hill, J. (1997). Effects of arbitrarily placed category boundaries on similarity judgments. *Journal of Experimental Social Psychology, 33,* 122–145.

Rothbart, M., Evans, M., & Fulero, S. (1979). Recall for confirming events: Memory processes and the maintenance of social stereotypes. *Journal of Experimental Social Psychology, 15,* 343–355.

Rothbart, M., Fulero, S., Jensen, C., Howard, J., & Birrell, P. (1978). From individual to group impressions: Availability heuristics in stereotype formation. *Journal of Experimental Social Psychology, 14*, 237–255.

Rothbart, M., Sriram, N., & Davis-Stitt, C. (1996). The retrieval of typical and atypical category members. *Journal of Experimental Social Psychology, 32*, 309–336.

Rothgerber, H. (1997). External intergroup threat as an antecedent to perceptions in in-group and out-group homogeneity. *Journal of Personality and Social Psychology, 73*, 1206–1212.

Rothgerber, H., & Worchel, S. (1997). The view from below: Intergroup relations from the perspective of the disadvantaged group. *Journal of Personality and Social Psychology, 73*, 1191–1205.

Rothman, A. L., & Weintraub, M. I. (1995). The sick building syndrome and mass hysteria. *Neurologic Clinics, 13*, 405–412.

Rouhana, N. N., & Kelman, H. C. (1994). Promoting joint thinking in international conflicts: An Israeli-Palestinian continuing workshop. *Journal of Social Issues, 50(1)*, 157–178.

Roy, D. F. (1973). "Banana time"—Job satisfaction and informal interaction. In W. G. Bennis, D. E. Berlew, E. H. Schein, & F. I. Steele (Eds.), *Interpersonal dynamics* (pp. 403–417). Homewood, IL: Dorsey.

Roy, M. C., Gauvin, S., & Limayem, M. (1996). Electronic group brainstorming: The role of feedback and productivity. *Small Group Research, 27*, 214–247.

Ruback, R. B., Dabbs, J. M., Jr., & Hopper, C. H. (1984). The process of brainstorming: An analysis with individual and group vocal parameters. *Journal of Personality and Social Psychology, 47*, 558–567.

Rubenstein, C. M., & Shaver, P. (1980). Loneliness in two northeastern cities. In J. Hartog & R. Audy (Eds.), *The anatomy of loneliness*. New York: International Universities Press.

Rubenstein, C. M., & Shaver, P. (1982). The experience of loneliness. In L. A. Peplau & D. Perlman (Eds.), *Loneliness: A sourcebook of current theory, research, and therapy*. New York: Wiley-Interscience.

Rubin, J. Z. (1980). Experimental research on third-party intervention in conflict: Toward some generalizations. *Psychological Bulletin, 87*, 379–391.

Rubin, J. Z. (1983). Negotiation. *American Behavioral Science, 27*, 135–147.

Rubin, J. Z. (1986). Third parties within organizations: A responsive commentary. *Research on negotiation in organizations, 1*, 271–283.

Rubin, J. Z. (1994). Models of conflict management. *Journal of Social Issues, 50(1)*, 33–46.

Rubin, J. Z., & Brown, B. R. (1975). *The social psychology of bargaining and negotiation*. New York: Academic Press.

Rubin, J. Z., Pruitt, D. G., & Kim, S. H. (1994). *Social conflict: Escalation, stalemate, and settlement* (2nd ed.). New York: McGraw-Hill.

Rubner, M. B. (1991). More workers prefer a man in charge. *American Demographics, 13*, 11.

Rugel, R. P., & Meyer, D. J. (1984). The Tavistock group: Empirical findings and implications for group therapy. *Small Group Behavior, 15*, 361–374.

Runcimann, W. G. (1966). *Relative deprivation and social justice*. London: Routledge & Kegan Paul.

Rusbult, C. E. (1983). A longitudinal test of the investment model: The development (and deterioration) of satisfaction and commitment in heterosexual involvements. *Journal of Personality and Social Psychology, 45*, 101–117.

Rusbult, C. E. (1987). Responses to dissatisfaction in close relationships: The exit-voice-loyalty-neglect model. In D. Perman & S. Duck (Eds.), *Intimate relationships: Development, dynamics, and deterioration* (pp. 209–237). Newbury Park, CA: Sage.

Rusbult, C. E., & Martz, J. M. (1995). Remaining in an abusive relationship: An investment model analysis of nonvoluntary dependence. *Personality and Social Psychology Bulletin, 21*, 558–571.

Rusbult, C. E., Zembrodt, I. M., & Gunn, L. K. (1982). Exit, voice, loyalty, and neglect: Responses to dissatisfaction in romantic involvements. *Journal of Personality and Social Psychology, 43*, 1230–1242.

Rush, M. C., Thomas, J. C., & Lord, R. G. (1977). Implicit leadership theory: A potential threat to the internal validity of the leader behavior questionnaires. *Organizational Behavior and Human Performance, 20*, 93–110.

Rushton, J. P. (1989). Genetic similarity, human altruism, and group selection. *Behavioral and Brain Sciences, 12*, 503–559.

Russell, B. (1938). *Power*. London: Allen & Unwyn.

Russell, D., Cutrona, C. E., Rose, J., & Yurko, K. (1984). Social and emotional loneliness: An examination of Weiss's typology of loneliness. *Journal of Personality and Social Psychology, 46*, 1313–1321.

Russell, J. A., & Lanius, U. F. (1984). Adaptation levels and the affective appraisal of environments. *Journal of Environmental Psychology, 4,* 119–135.

Russell, J. A., & Mehrabian, A. (1975). Task, setting, and personality variables affecting the desire to work. *Journal of Applied Psychology, 60,* 518–520.

Rutan, J. S., & Stone, W. (1993). *Psychodynamic group psychotherapy* (2nd ed.). New York: Guilford Press.

Ryen, A. H., & Kahn, A. (1975). The effects of intergroup orientation on group attitudes and proxemic behavior: A test of two models. *Journal of Personality and Social Psychology, 31,* 302–310.

Sacks, J. M. (1993). Psychodrama. In H. I. Kaplan & M. J. Sadock (Eds.), *Comprehensive group psychotherapy* (3rd ed., pp. 214–228). Baltimore: Williams & Wilkins.

Saegert, S. (1978). High-density environments: Their personal and social consequences. In A. Baum & Y. M. Epstein (Eds.), *Human response to crowding.* Hillsdale, NJ: Erlbaum.

Sagar, H. A., & Schofield, J. W. (1980). Racial and behavioral cues in black and white children's perceptions of ambiguously aggressive acts. *Journal of Personality and Social Psychology, 39,* 590–598.

Saks, M. J. (1977). *Jury verdicts.* Lexington, MA: Heath.

Saks, M. J., & Hastie, R. (1978). *Social psychology in court.* New York: Van Nostrand Reinhold.

Salas, E., Bowers, C., & Cannon-Bowers, J. A. (1995). Military team research: Ten years of progress. *Military Psychology, 7,* 55–75.

Salazar, A. J. (1996). An analysis of the development and evolution of roles in the small group. *Small Group Research, 27,* 475–503.

Sampson, E. E. (1971). *Social psychology and contemporary society.* New York: Wiley.

Sampson, E. E., & Brandon, A. C. (1964). The effects of role and opinion deviation on small group behavior. *Sociometry, 27,* 261–281.

Sampson, R. V. (1965). *Equality and power.* London: Heinemann.

Samuelson, C. D., & Allison, S. T. (1994). Cognitive factors affecting the use of social decision heuristics in resource-sharing tasks. *Organizational Behavior and Human Decision Processes, 58,* 1–27.

Samuelson, C. D., & Messick, D. M. (1995). When do people want to change the rules for allocating shared resources? In D. A. Schroeder (Ed.), *Social dilemmas: Perspectives on individuals and groups* (pp. 144–162). Westport, CT: Praeger.

Sandal, G. M., Vaernes, R., Bergan, T., Warncke, M., & Ursin, H. (1996). Psychological reactions during polar expeditions and isolation in hyperbaric chambers. *Aviation, Space, and Environmental Medicine, 67,* 227–234.

Sandelands, L., & St. Clair, L. (1993). Toward an empirical concept of group. *Journal for the Theory of Social Behavior, 23,* 423–458.

Sanders, G. S. (1981). Driven by distraction: An integrative review of social facilitation theory and research. *Journal of Experimental Social Psychology, 17,* 227–251.

Sanders, G. S. (1984). Self-presentation and drive in social facilitation. *Journal of Experimental Social Psychology, 20,* 312–322.

Sanders, G. S., & Baron, R. S. (1975). The motivating effects of distraction on task performance. *Journal of Personality and Social Psychology, 32,* 956–963.

Sanders, G. S., & Baron, R. S. (1977). Is social comparison irrelevant for producing choice shifts? *Journal of Experimental Social Psychology, 13,* 303–314.

Sanders, G. S., Baron, R. S., & Moore, D. L. (1978). Distraction and social comparison as mediators of social facilitation effects. *Journal of Experimental Social Psychology, 14,* 291–303.

Sanders, W. B. (1994). *Gangbangs and drive-bys: Grounded culture and juvenile gang violence.* New York: Aldine de Gruyter.

Sankowsky, D. (1995). Charismatic leader as narcissist: Understanding the abuse of power. *Organizational Dynamics, 23(4),* 57–71.

Sanna, L. J. (1992). Self-efficacy theory: Implications for social facilitation and social loafing. *Journal of Personality and Social Psychology, 62,* 774–786.

Sanna, L. J., & Parks, C. D. (1997). Group research trends in social and organizational psychology: Whatever happened to intragroup research? *Psychological Science, 8,* 261–267.

Sanna, L. J., & Shotland, R. L. (1990). Valence of anticipated evaluation and social facilitation. *Journal of Experimental Social Psychology, 26,* 82–92.

Santee, R. T., & Jackson, S. E. (1982). Sex differences in evaluative implications of conformity and dissent. *Social Psychology Quarterly, 45,* 121–125.

Santee, R. T., & Maslach, C. (1982). To agree or not to agree: Personal dissent amid social pressure to conform. *Journal of Personality and Social Psychology, 42,* 690–700.

Sapp, S. G., Harrod, W. J., & Zhao, L. (1996). Leadership emergence in task groups with egalitarian gender-role expectations. *Sex Roles, 34*, 65–83.

Sarason, I. G., Pierce, G. R., & Sarason, B. R. (1990). Social support and interactional processes: A triadic hypothesis. *Journal of Social and Personal Relationships, 7*, 495–506.

Sarbin, T. R., & Allen, V. L. (1968). Increasing participation in a natural group setting: A preliminary report. *Psychological Record, 18*, 1–7.

Sarri, R. C., & Galinsky, M. J. (1985). A conceptual framework for group development. In M. Sundel, P. Glasser, R. Sarri, & R. Vinter (Eds.), *Individual change through small groups* (2nd ed., pp. 70–86). New York: The Free Press.

Sasfy, J., & Okun, M. (1974). Form of evaluation and audience expertness as joint determinants of audience effects. *Journal of Experimental Social Psychology, 10*, 461–467.

Sattler, D. N., & Kerr, N. L. (1991). Might versus morality explored: Motivational and cognitive bases for social motives. *Journal of Personality and Social Psychology, 60*, 756–765.

Scandura, T. A., & Lankau, M. J. (1996). Developing diverse leaders: A leader-member exchange approach. *Leadership Quarterly, 7*, 243–263.

Schachter, S. (1951). Deviation, rejection, and communication. *Journal of Abnormal and Social Psychology, 46*, 190–207.

Schachter, S. (1959). *The psychology of affiliation.* Stanford, CA: Stanford University Press.

Schachter, S., Ellertson, N., McBride, D., & Gregory, D. (1951). An experimental study of cohesiveness and productivity. *Human Relations, 4*, 229–238.

Schafer, M., & Crichlow, S. (1996). Antecedents of groupthink: A quantitative study. *Journal of Conflict Resolution, 40*, 415–435.

Schauer, A. H., Seymour, W. R., & Geen, R. G. (1985). Effects of observation and evaluation on anxiety in beginning counselors: A social facilitation analysis. *Journal of Counseling and Development, 63*, 279–285.

Scheier, M. F., Carver, C. S., & Gibbons, F. X. (1979). Self-directed attention, awareness of bodily states, and suggestibility. *Journal of Personality and Social Psychology, 37*, 1576–1588.

Schein, E. H. (1956). The Chinese indoctrination program for prisoners of war: A study of attempted "brainwashing." *Psychiatry, 19*, 149–172.

Schein, E. H. (1961). *Coercive persuasion.* New York: Norton.

Schein, E. H. (1971). Process consultation: Its role in organization development. Reading, MA: Addison-Wesley.

Scheuble, K. J., Dixon, K. N., Levy, A. B., & Kagan-Moore, L. (1987). Premature termination: A risk in eating disorder groups. *Group, 11*, 85–93.

Schickel, R. (1968). The Disney version: The life, times, art and commerce of Walt Disney. New York: Simon & Schuster.

Schlenker, B. R. (1975). Liking for a group following an initiation: Impression management or dissonance reduction? *Sociometry, 38*, 99–118.

Schlenker, B. R., & Bonoma, T. V. (1978). Fun and games: The validity of games for the study of conflict. *Journal of Conflict Resolution, 22*, 7–37.

Schlenker, B. R., & Forsyth, D. R. (1977). On the ethics of psychological research. *Journal of Experimental Social Psychology, 13*, 369–396.

Schlenker, B. R., & Goldman, H. J. (1978). Cooperators and competitors in conflict: A test of the "triangle model." *Journal of Conflict Resolution, 22*, 393–410.

Schlenker, B. R., & Leary, M. R. (1982). Social anxiety and self presentation: A conceptualization and model. *Psychological Bulletin, 92*, 641–669.

Schlenker, B. R., Nacci, P., Helm, B., & Tedeschi, J. T. (1976). Reactions to coercive and reward power: The effects of switching influence modes on target compliance. *Sociometry, 39*, 316–323.

Schlenker, B. R., Phillips, S. T., Boniecki, K. A., & Schlenker, D. R. (1995a). Championship pressures: Choking or triumphing in one's own territory. *Journal of Personality and Social Psychology, 68*, 632–643.

Schlenker, B. R., Phillips, S. T., Boniecki, K. A., & Schlenker, D. R. (1995b). Where is the home choke? *Journal of Personality and Social Psychology, 68*, 649–652.

Schlenker, B. R., Soraci, S., & McCarthy, B. (1976). Self-esteem and group performance as determinants of egocentric perceptions in cooperative groups, *Human Relations, 29*, 1163–1176.

Schlesinger, A. M., Jr. (1965). *A thousand days.* Boston: Houghton Mifflin.

Schmidt, D. E., & Keating, J. P. (1979). Human crowding and personal control: An integration of the research. *Psychological Bulletin, 86*, 680–700.

Schmidt, N., & Sermat, V. (1983). Measuring loneliness in different relationships. *Journal of Personality and Social Psychology, 44*, 1038–1047.

Schmitt, B. H., Dubé, L., & Leclerc, F. (1992). Intrusions into waiting lines: Does the queue constitute a social system? *Journal of Personality and Social Psychology, 63,* 806–815.

Schmitt, B. H., Gilovich, T., Goore, N., & Joseph, L. (1986). Mere presence and social facilitation: One more time. *Journal of Experimental Social Psychology, 22,* 242–248.

Schmitt, D. R. (1981). Performance under cooperation or competition. *American Behavioral Scientist, 24,* 649–679.

Schneebaum, T. (1969). *Keep the river on your right.* New York: Grove Press.

Schneider, J., & Cook, K. (1995). Status inconsistency and gender: Combining revisited. Special issue: Extending interaction theory. *Small Group Research, 26,* 372–399.

Schofield, J. W. (1978). School desegregation and intergroup relations. In D. Bar-Tal & L. Saxe (Eds.), *The social psychology of education.* Washington, DC: Halstead.

Schofield, J. W., & Sagar, H. A. (1977). Peer interaction patterns in an integrated middle school. *Sociometry, 40,* 130–138.

Schofield, J. W., & Whitley, B. E., Jr. (1983). Peer nomination vs. rating scale measurement of children's peer preferences. *Social Psychology Quarterly, 46,* 242–251.

Schooler, C. (1994). A working conceptualization of social structure: Mertonian roots and psychological and sociocultural relationships. *Social Psychology Quarterly, 57,* 262–273.

Schopler, J., & Insko, C. A. (1992). The discontinuity effect in interpersonal and intergroup relations: Generality and mediation. *European Review of Social Psychology, 3,* 121–151.

Schopler, J., Insko, C. A., Currey, D., Smith, S., Brazil, D., Riggins, T., Gaertner, L., & Kilpatrick, S. (1994). The survival of a cooperative tradition in the intergroup discontinuity context. *Motivation and Emotion, 18,* 301–315.

Schopler, J., Insko, C. A., Drigotas, S. M., Wieselquist, J., Pemberton, M., & Cox, C. (1995). The role of identifiability in the reduction of interindividual-intergroup discontinuity. *Journal of Experimental Social Psychology, 31,* 553–574.

Schopler, J., Insko, C. A., Graetz, K. A., Drigotas, S. M., & Smith, V. A. (1991). The generality of the individual-group discontinuity effect: Variations in positivity-negativity of outcomes, players' relative power, and magnitude of outcomes. *Per-*

sonality and Social Psychology Bulletin, 17, 612–624.

Schopler, J., Insko, C. A., Graetz, K. A., Drigotas, S., Smith, V. A., & Dahl, K. (1993). Individual-group discontinuity: Further evidence for mediation by fear and greed. *Personality and Social Psychology Bulletin, 19,* 419–431.

Schopler, J., & Layton, B. D. (1972a). *Attributions of interpersonal influence and power.* Morristown, NJ: General Learning Press.

Schopler, J., & Layton, B. D. (1972b). Determinants of the self-attribution of having influenced another person. *Journal of Personality and Social Psychology, 22,* 326–332.

Schriesheim, C. A., Bannister, B. D., & Money, W. H. (1979). Psychometric properties of the LPC Scale: An extension of Rice's review. *Academy of Management Review, 4,* 287–290.

Schriesheim, C. A., Cogliser, C. C., & Neider, L. L. (1995). Is it "trustworthy"? A multiple-levels-of-analysis re-examination of an Ohio State leadership study, with implications for future research. *Leadership Quarterly, 6,* 111–145.

Schriesheim, C. A., & Eisenbach, R. J. (1995). An exploratory and confirmatory factor-analytic investigation of item wording effects on the obtained factor structures of survey questionnaire measures. *Journal of Management, 21,* 1177–1193.

Schriesheim, C. A., & Hinkin, T. R. (1990). Influence tactics used by subordinates: A theoretical and empirical analysis and refinement of the Kipnis, Schmidt, and Wilkinson subscales. *Journal of Applied Psychology, 75,* 246–257.

Schriesheim, C. A., & Hosking, D. (1978). Review essay of Fiedler, F. E., Chemers, M. M., & Mahar, L. Improving leadership effectiveness: The Leader Match concept. *Administrative Science Quarterly, 23,* 496–505.

Schriesheim, C. A., & Kerr, S. (1977). Theories and measures of leadership: A critical appraisal of current and future directions. In J. G. Hunt and L. L. Larson (Eds.), *Leadership: The cutting edge.* Carbondale, IL: Southern Illinois University Press.

Schriesheim, C. A., Tepper, B. J., & Tetrault, L. A. (1994). Least preferred co-worker score, situational control, and leadership effectiveness: A meta-analysis of contingency model performance predictions. *Journal of Applied Psychology, 79,* 561–573.

Schulenberg, J., Bachman, J. G., O'Malley, P. M., Bachman, J. G., & Johnston, L. D. (1996). High school educational success and subsequent substance use: A panel analysis following adolescents into young adulthood. *American Sociological Review, 61,* 635–655.

Schurz, G. (1985). Experimentelle Uberprufung des Zusammenhangs zwischen Personlichkeitsmerkmalen und der Bereitschaft zum destruktiven Gehorsam gegenuber Autoritaten [Experimental test of the relationship between personality characteristics and the readiness for destructive obedience authorities]. *Zeitschrift fur Experimentelle und Angew, 32,* 160–177.

Schuster, B. (1996). Mobbing, bullying, and peer rejection. *Psychological Science Agenda, 9(4),* 12–13.

Schutz, W. (1992). Beyond FIRO-B. Three new theory-driven measures—Element B: behavior, Element F: feelings, Element S: self. *Psychological Reports, 70,* 915–937.

Schutz, W. C. (1958). FIRO: A three-dimensional theory of interpersonal behavior. New York: Rinehart.

Schwartz, B., & Barsky, S. F. (1977). The home advantage. *Social Forces, 55,* 641–661.

Schwartz, H., & Jacobs, J. (1979). *Qualitative sociology: A method to the madness.* New York: The Free Press.

Schwartz, M. S., & Schwartz, C. G. (1955). Problems in participant observation. *American Journal of Sociology, 60,* 343–354.

Schwartz, S. H. (1994). Are there universal aspects in the structure and contents of human values? *Journal of Social Issues, 50(4),* 19–45.

Schwartz, S. H., & Gottlieb, A. (1976). Bystander reactions to a violent theft: Crime in Jerusalem. *Journal of Personality and Social Psychology, 34,* 1188–1199.

Schwartz, S. H., & Gottlieb, A. (1980). Bystander anonymity and reactions to emergencies. *Journal of Personality and Social Psychology, 39,* 418–430.

Scott, W. A., & Scott, R. (1981). Intercorrelations among structural properties of primary groups. *Journal of Personality and Social Psychology, 41,* 279–292.

Sculley, J. (with J. A. Byme). (1987). Odyssey: Pepsi to Apple . . . A journey of adventure, ideas, and the future. New York: Harper & Row.

Seashore, S. E. (1954). *Group cohesiveness in the industrial work group.* Ann Arbor, MI: Institute for Social Research.

Seashore, S. E., & Bowers, D. G. (1970). The durability of organizational change. *American Psychologist, 25,* 227–233.

Sedikides, C., Schopler, J., & Insko, C. A. (Eds.). (1998). *Intergroup cognition and intergroup behavior.* Mahwah, NJ: Erlbaum.

Seeger, J. A. (1983). No innate phases in group problem solving. *Academy of Management Review, 8,* 683–689.

Seeman, M., Seeman, T., & Sayles, M. (1985). Social networks and health status: A longitudinal analysis. *Social Psychology Quarterly, 48,* 237–248.

Segal, H. A. (1954). Initial psychiatric findings of recently repatriated prisoners of war. *American Journal of Psychiatry, 111,* 358–363.

Segal, M. W. (1974). Alphabet and attraction: An unobtrusive measure of the effect of propinquity in a field setting. *Journal of Personality and Social Psychology, 30,* 654–657.

Segal, M. W. (1979). Varieties of interpersonal attraction and their interrelationships in natural groups. *Social Psychology Quarterly, 42,* 253–261.

Seligman, M. E. P. (1995). The effectiveness of psychotherapy: The Consumer Reports study. *American Psychologist, 50,* 965–974.

Seligman, M. E. P. (1996). Science as an ally of practice. *American Psychologist, 51,* 1072–1079.

Sell, J. (1997). Gender, strategies, and contributions to public goods. *Social Psychology Quarterly, 60,* 252–265.

Sell, J., Griffith, W. I., & Wilson, R. K. (1993). Are women more cooperative than men in social dilemmas? *Social Psychology Quarterly, 56,* 211–222.

Semin, G. R., & Rubini, M. (1990). Unfolding the concept of person by verbal abuse. *European Journal of Social Psychology, 20,* 463–474.

Service, E. R. (1975). *Origins of the state and civilization.* New York: Norton.

Seta, C. E., & Seta, J. J. (1992). Increments and decrements in mean arterial pressure as a function of audience composition: An averaging and summation analysis. *Personality and Social Psychology Bulletin, 18,* 173–181.

Seta, C. E., & Seta, J. J. (1995). When audience presence is enjoyable: The influences of audience awareness of prior success on performance and task interest. *Basic and Applied Social Psychology, 16,* 95–108.

Seta, J. J., Crisson, J. E., Seta, C. E., & Wang, M. A. (1989). Task performance and perceptions of anxiety: Averaging and summation in an evaluative setting. *Journal of Personality and Social Psychology, 56,* 387–396.

Seta, J. J., Seta, C. E., & Donaldson, S. (1991). The impact of comparison processes on coactors' frustration and willingness to expend effort. *Personality and Social Psychology Bulletin, 17,* 560–568.

Shackelford, S., Wood, W., & Worchel, S. (1996). Behavioral styles and the influence of women in mixed-sex groups. *Social Psychology Quarterly, 59,* 284–293.

Shambaugh, P. W. (1978). The development of the small group. *Human Relations, 31,* 283–295.

Shamir, B. (1992). Attribution of influence and charisma to the leader: The romance of leadership revisited. *Journal of Applied Social Psychology, 22,* 386–407.

Shanab, M. E., & Yahya, K. A. (1977). A behavioral study of obedience in children. *Journal of Personality and Social Psychology, 35,* 530–536.

Shaughnessy, P., & Kivlighan, D. M., Jr. (1995). Using group participants' perceptions of therapeutic factors to form client typologies. *Small Group Research, 26,* 250–268.

Shaver, P., & Buhrmester, D. (1983). Loneliness, sex-role orientation, and group life: A social needs perspective. In P. B. Paulus (Ed.), *Basic group processes* (pp. 259–288). New York: Springer-Verlag.

Shaver, P., Schwartz, J., Kirson, D., & O'Connor, C. (1987). Emotion knowledge: Further exploration of a prototype approach. *Journal of Personality and Social Psychology, 52,* 1061–1086.

Shaw, J. I., & Condelli, L. (1986). Effects of compliance outcome and basis of power on the powerholder-target relationship. *Personality and Social Psychology Bulletin, 12,* 236–246.

Shaw, M. E. (1963). *Scaling group tasks: A method for dimensional analysis.* Technical Report No. 1, ONR contract NR 170–266, Nonr-580(11).

Shaw, M. E. (1964). Communication networks. *Advances in Experimental Social Psychology, 1,* 111–147.

Shaw, M. E. (1978). Communication networks fourteen years later. In L. Berkowitz (Ed.), *Group processes.* New York: Academic Press.

Shaw, M. E. (1981). *Group dynamics: The psychology of small group behavior* (3rd ed.). New York: McGraw-Hill.

Shaw, M. E., & Breed, G. R. (1970). Effects of attribution of responsibility for negative events on behavior in small groups. *Sociometry, 33,* 382–393.

Shaw, M. E., & Shaw, L. M. (1962). Some effects of sociometric grouping upon learning in a second grade classroom. *Journal of Social Psychology, 57,* 453–458.

Shechtman, Z. (1994). The effect of group psychotherapy on close same-gender friendships among boys and girls. *Sex Roles, 30,* 829–834.

Sheppard, B. H. (1983). Managers as inquisitors: Some lessons from the law. In H. Bazerman & R. J. Lewicki (Eds.), *Negotiating in organizations* (pp. 193–213). Beverly Hills, CA: Sage.

Shepperd, J. A. (1993). Productive loss in performance groups: A motivational analysis. *Psychological Bulletin, 113,* 67–81.

Shepperd, J. A. (1995). Remedying motivation and productivity loss in collective settings. *Current Directions in Psychological Science, 5,* 131–133.

Shepperd, J. A., & Wright, R. A. (1989). Individual contributions to a collective effort: An incentive analysis. *Personality and Social Psychology Bulletin, 15,* 141–149.

Sheridan, C. L., & King, R. G., Jr. (1972). Obedience to authority with an authentic victim. *Proceedings of the 80th Annual Convention of the American Psychological Association, 7,* 165–166.

Sherif, C. W. (1976). *Orientation in social psychology.* New York: Harper & Row.

Sherif, M. (1936). *The psychology of social norms.* New York: Harper & Row.

Sherif, M. (1966). *In common predicament: Social psychology of intergroup conflict and cooperation.* Boston: Houghton Mifflin.

Sherif, M., Harvey, O. J., White, B. J., Hood, W. R., & Sherif, C. W. (1961). *Intergroup conflict and cooperation. The Robbers Cave Experiment.* Norman, OK: Institute of Group Relations.

Sherif, M., & Sherif, C. W. (1953). *Groups in harmony and tension.* New York: Harper & Row.

Sherif, M., & Sherif, C. W. (1956). *An outline of social psychology* (rev. ed.). New York: Harper & Row.

Sherif, M., White, B. J., & Harvey, O. J. (1955). Status in experimentally produced groups. *American Journal of Sociology, 60,* 370–379.

Sherrod, D. R., & Cohen, S. (1979). Density, personal control, and design. In J. R. Aiello & A. Baum (Eds.), *Residential crowding and design* (pp. 217–227). New York: Plenum.

Sherry, P., & Hurley, J. R. (1976). Curative factors in psychotherapeutic and growth groups. *Journal of Clinical Psychology, 32,* 835–837.

Shiflett, S. (1979). Toward a general model of small group productivity. *Psychological Bulletin, 86,* 67–79.

Shotola, R. W. (1992). Small groups. In E. F. Borgatta & M. L. Borgatta (Eds.), *Encyclopedia of sociology* (Vol. 4, pp. 1796–1806). New York: Macmillan.

Shrauger, J. S. (1975). Responses to evaluation as a function of initial self-perceptions. *Psychological Bulletin, 82,* 581–596.

Shure, G. H., & Meeker, J. R. (1967). A personality/attitude scale for use in experimental bargaining studies. *Journal of Psychology, 65,* 233–252.

Shure, G. H., Rogers, M. S., Larsen, I. M., & Tassone, J. (1962). Group planning and task effectiveness. *Sociometry, 25,* 263–282.

Sias, P. M., & Jablin, F. M. (1995). Differential superior-subordinate relations, perceptions of fairness, and coworker communication. *Human Communication Research, 22,* 5–38.

Sieber, J. (1992). *Planning ethically responsible research.* Thousand Oaks, CA: Sage.

Silver, M., & Geller, D. (1978). On the irrelevance of evil: The organization and individual actions. *Journal of Social Issues, 34(4),* 125–135.

Silver, W. S., & Bufanio, K. A. (1996). The impact of group efficacy and group goals on group task performance. *Small Group Research, 27,* 347–349.

Silver, W. S., & Bufanio, K. A. (1997). Reciprocal relationships, causal influences, and group efficacy: A reply to Kaplan. *Small Group Research, 28,* 559–562.

Simmel, G. (1902). The number of members as determining the sociological form of the group. *American Journal of Sociology, 8,* 1–46, 158–196.

Simmel, G. (1955). *Conflict.* New York: The Free Press.

Simon, B., Glaessner-Bayerl, B., & Stratenwerth, I. (1991). Stereotyping and self-stereotyping in a natural intergroup context: The case of heterosexual and homosexual men. *Social Psychology Quarterly, 54,* 252–266.

Simon, B., Pantaleo, G., & Mummendey, A. (1995). Unique individual or interchangeable group member? The accentuation of intragroup differences versus similarities as an indicator of the individual self versus the collective self. *Journal of Personality and Social Psychology, 69,* 106–119.

Simon, R. J. (1980). *The jury: Its role in American society.* Lexington, MA: Heath.

Simonton, D. K. (1980). Land battles, generals, and armies: Individual and social determinants of victory and casualties. *Journal of Personality and Social Psychology, 38,* 110–119.

Simonton, D. K. (1985). Intelligence and personal influence in groups: Four nonlinear models. *Psychological Review, 92,* 532–547.

Simonton, D. K. (1987). *Why presidents succeed.* New Haven, CT: Yale University Press.

Singelis, T. M. (1994). The measurement of independent and interdependent self-construals. *Personality and Social Psychology Bulletin, 20,* 580–591.

Singer, E. (1990). Reference groups and social evaluations. In M. Rosenberg & R. H. Turner (Eds.), *Social psychology: Sociological perspectives* (pp. 66–93). New Brunswick, NJ: Transaction Publishers.

Singer, J. E., Baum, C. S., Baum, A., & Thew, B. D. (1982). Mass psychogenic illness: The case for social comparison. In M. J. Colligan, J. W. Pennebaker, & L. R. Murphy (Eds.), *Mass psychogenic illness: A social psychological analysis* (pp. 155–169). Hillsdale, NJ: Erlbaum.

Singer, J. E., Brush, C. A., & Lublin, S. C. (1965). Some aspects of deindividuation: Identification and conformity. *Journal of Experimental Social Psychology, 1,* 356–378.

Skinner, B. F. (1953). *Science and human behavior.* New York: Macmillan.

Skinner, B. F. (1971). *Beyond freedom and dignity.* New York: Knopf.

Slater, P. E. (1955). Role differentiation in small groups. *American Sociological Review, 20,* 300–310.

Slavson, S. R. (1950). Group psychotherapy. *Scientific American, 183(6),* 42–45.

Smart, R. (1965). Social-group membership, leadership, and birth order. *Journal of Social Psychology, 67,* 221–225.

Smelser, N. J. (1962). *Theory of collective behavior.* New York: The Free Press.

Smernou, L. E., & Lautenschlager, G. J. (1991). Autobiographical antecedents and correlates of neuroticism and extraversion. *Personality and Individual Differences, 12,* 49–59.

Smith, D. H. (1980). Participation in outdoor recreation and sports. In D. H. Smith, J. Macaulay, & Associates (Eds.), *Participation in social and political activities: A comprehensive analysis of political involvement, expressive leisure time, and helping behavior* (pp. 177–201). San Francisco: Jossey-Bass.

Smith, D. M. (1997). Women and leadership. In P. G. Northouse, *Leadership: Theory and practice* (pp. 204–238). Thousand Oaks, CA: Sage.

Smith, M. B. (1972). Is experimental social psychology advancing? *Journal of Experimental Social Psychology, 8,* 86–96.

Smith, P. (1975). Controlled studies of the outcome of sensitivity training. *Psychological Bulletin, 82,* 597–622.

Smith, P. B. (1980). The outcome of sensitivity training and encounter. In P. B. Smith (Ed.), *Small groups and personal change* (pp. 25–55). New York: Methuen.

Smith, P. B., & Bond, M. H. (1993). *Social psychology across cultures: Analysis and perspectives.* Boston: Allyn & Bacon.

Smoke, W. H., & Zajonc, R. B. (1962). On the reliability of group judgments and decisions. In J. H. Criswell, H. Solomon, & P. Suppes (Eds.), *Mathematical methods in small group processes.* Stanford, CA: Stanford University Press.

Snodgrass, S. E., & Rosenthal, R. (1984). Females in charge: Effects of sex of subordinate and romantic attachment status upon self-ratings of dominance. *Journal of Personality, 52,* 355–371.

Snow, D. A., & Oliver, P. E. (1995). Social movements and collective behavior: Social psychological dimensions and considerations. In K. S. Cook, G. A. Fine, & J. S. House (Eds.), *Sociological perspectives on social psychology* (pp. 571–599). Needham Heights, MA: Allyn & Bacon.

Snyder, C. R., Cheavens, J., & Sympson, S. C. (1997). Hope: An individual motive for social commerce. *Group Dynamics: Theory, Research, and Practice, 1,* 107–118.

Snyder, C. R., & Fromkin, H. L. (1980). *Uniqueness: The human pursuit of difference.* New York: Plenum.

Snyder, C. R., Lassegard, M., & Ford, C. E. (1986). Distancing after group success and failure: Basking in reflected glory and cutting off reflected failure. *Journal of Personality and Social Psychology, 51,* 382–388.

Sommer, R. (1959). Studies in personal space. *Sociometry, 22,* 247–260.

Sommer, R. (1967). Small group ecology. *Psychological Bulletin, 67,* 145–152.

Sommer, R. (1969). *Personal space.* Englewood Cliffs, NJ: Prentice Hall.

Sorokin, P. A., & Lundin, W. A. (1959). *Power and morality: Who shall guard the guardians?* Boston, MA: Sargent.

Sorrels, J. P., & Kelley, J. (1984). Conformity by omission. *Personality and Social Psychology Bulletin, 10,* 302–305.

Sorrentino, R. M., & Boutillier, R. G. (1975). The effect of quantity and quality of verbal interaction on ratings of leadership ability. *Journal of Experimental Social Psychology, 11,* 403–411.

Sorrentino, R. M., & Field, N. (1986). Emergent leadership over time: The functional value of positive motivation. *Journal of Personality and Social Psychology, 50,* 1091–1099.

Sorrentino, R. M., King, G., & Leo, G. (1980). The influence of the minority on perception: A note on a possible alternative explanation. *Journal of Experimental Social Psychology, 16,* 293–301.

Spears, R., Doosje, B., & Ellemers, N. (1997). Self-stereotyping in the face of threats to group status and distinctiveness: The role of group identification. *Personality and Social Psychology Bulletin, 23,* 538–553.

Spink, K. S. (1990). Collective efficacy in the sport setting. *International Journal of Sport Psychology, 21,* 380–395.

Spira, J. L. (1997). Understanding and developing psychotherapy groups for medically ill patients. In J. L. Spira (Ed.), *Group therapy for medically ill patients* (pp. 3–52). New York: Guilford Press.

Spitzer, C. E., & Davis, J. H. (1978). Mutual social influence in dynamic groups. *Social Psychology, 41,* 24–33.

Squire, S. (1983). *The slender balance.* New York: Pinnacle.

Stager, S. F., Chassin, L., & Young, R. D. (1983). Determinants of self-esteem among labeled adolescents. *Social Psychology Quarterly, 46,* 3–10.

Stangor, C., Jonas, K., Stroebe, W., & Hewstone, M. (1996). Influence of student exchange on national stereotypes, attitudes, and perceived group variability. *European Journal of Social Psychology, 26,* 663–675.

Stanton & Poors. (1967). *Register of corporations, directors, and executives.* New York: Stanton & Poors.

Stasser, G. (1992). Pooling of unshared information during group discussions. In S. Worchel, W. Wood, & J. A. Simpson (Eds.), *Group process and productivity* (pp. 48–67). Newbury Park, CA: Sage.

Stasser, G., Kerr, N. L., & Bray, R. M. (1982). The social psychology of jury deliberations: Structure, process, and product. In N. L. Kerr & R. M. Bray (Eds.), *Psychology of the courtroom* (pp. 221–256). New York: Academic Press.

Stasser, G., & Stewart, D. (1992). Discovery of hidden profiles by decision-making groups: Solving a problem versus making a judgment. *Journal of Personality and Social Psychology, 63,* 426–434.

Stasser, G., Taylor, L. A., & Hanna, C. (1989). Information sampling in structured and unstructured discussions of three- and six-person groups. *Journal of Personality and Social Psychology, 57,* 67–78.

Stasser, G., & Titus, W. (1985). Pooling of unshared information in group decision making: Biased information sampling during discussion. *Journal of Personality and Social Psychology, 48,* 1467–1478.

Stasser, G., & Titus, W. (1987). Effects of information load and percentage of shared information on the dissemination of unshared information during group discussion. *Journal of Personality and Social Psychology, 53,* 81–93.

Stasson, M. F., & Bradshaw, S. D. (1995). Explanations of individual-group performance differences: What sort of "bonus" can be gained through group interaction? *Small Group Research, 26,* 296–308.

Staub, E. (1985). The psychology of perpetrators and bystanders. *Political Psychology, 6,* 61–85.

Staub, E. (1989). *The roots of evil: The origins of genocide and other group violence.* New York: Cambridge University Press.

Staub, E. (1990). Moral exclusion, personal goal theory, and extreme destructiveness. *Journal of Social Issues, 46(1),* 47–64.

Staub, E. (1996). Cultural-societal roots of violence: The examples of genocidal violence and of contemporary youth violence in the United States. *American Psychologist, 51,* 117–132.

Staw, B. M., & Ross, J. (1987). Behavior in escalation situations: Antecedents, prototypes, and solutions. *Research in Organizational Behavior, 9,* 39–78.

Stech, F. J., & McClintock, C. G. (1981). Effects of communicating timing on duopoly bargaining outcomes. *Journal of Personality and Social Psychology, 40,* 664–674.

Steers, R. M., & Porter, L. W. (1991). *Motivation and work behavior* (4th ed.). New York: McGraw-Hill.

Stein, R. T., & Heller, T. (1979). An empirical analysis of the correlations between leadership status and participation rates reported in the literature. *Journal of Personality and Social Psychology, 37,* 1993–2002.

Stein, R. T., & Heller, T. (1983). The relationship of participation rates to leadership status: A meta-analysis. In H. H. Blumberg, A. P. Hare, V. Kent, & M. Davies (Eds.), *Small groups and social interaction* (Vol. 1, pp. 401–406). New York: Wiley.

Steiner, I. D. (1972). *Group process and productivity.* New York: Academic Press.

Steiner, I. D. (1974). Whatever happened to the group in social psychology? *Journal of Experimental Social Psychology, 10,* 94–108.

Steiner, I. D. (1976). Task-performing groups. In J. W. Thibaut, J. T. Spence, & R. C. Carson (Eds.), *Contemporary topics in social psychology* (pp. 393–422). Morristown, NJ: General Learning Press.

Steiner, I. D. (1983). What ever happened to the touted revival of the group? In H. Blumberg, A. Hare, V. Kent, & M. Davies (Eds.), *Small groups and social interaction* (Vol. 2, pp. 539–547). New York: Wiley.

Steiner, I. D. (1986). Paradigms and groups. *Advances in Experimental Social Psychology, 19,* 251–289.

Steininger, M., Newell, J. D., & Garcia, L. T. (1984). *Ethical issues in psychology.* Homewood, IL: Dorsey Press.

Steinzor, B. (1950). The spatial factor in face to face discussion groups. *Journal of Abnormal and Social Psychology, 45,* 552–555.

Stephan, W. G. (1985). Intergroup relations. In G. Lindzey & E. Aronson (Eds.), *Handbook of social psychology* (3rd ed., Vol. 2, pp. 599–658). New York: Random House.

Stephan, W. G. (1987). The contact hypothesis in intergroup relations. *Review of Personality and Social Psychology, 9,* 13–40.

Stephan, W. G., & Rosenfield, D. (1982). Racial and ethnic stereotypes. In A. G. Miller (Ed.), *In the eye of the beholder: Contemporary issues in stereotyping.* New York: Praeger.

Sternberg, R. J., & Dobson, D. M. (1987). Resolving interpersonal conflicts: An analysis of stylistic consistency. *Journal of Personality and Social Psychology, 52,* 794–812.

Stets, J. E. (1997). Status and identity in marital interaction. *Social Psychology Quarterly, 60,* 185–217.

Stevenson, W. B., Pearce, J. L., & Porter, L. W. (1985). The concept of "coalition" in organizational theory and research. *Academy of Management Review, 10,* 256–267.

Stever, G. S. (1995). Gender by type interaction effects in mass media subcultures. *Journal of Psychological Type, 32,* 3–22.

Stewart, A. E., Stewart, E. A., & Gazda, G. M. (1997). Assessing the need for a new group journal. *Group Dynamics: Theory, Research, and Practice, 1,* 75–85.

Stewart, D. D., & Stasser, G. (1998). The sampling of critical, unshared information in decision-making groups: The role of an informed minority. *European Journal of Social Psychology, 28,* 95–113.

Stewart, D. W., & Latham, D. R. (1986). On some psychometric properties of Fiedler's contingency model of leadership. *Small Group Behavior, 17,* 83–94.

Stewart, G. L., & Manz, C. C. (1995). Leadership for self-managing work teams: A typology and integrative model. *Human Relations, 48,* 747–770.

Stewart, P. A., & Moore, J. C. (1992). Wage disparities and performance expectations. *Social Psychology Quarterly, 55,* 78–85.

Stiles, W. B., Lyall, L. M., Knight, D. P., Ickes, W., Waung, M., Hall, C. L., & Primeau, B. E. (1997). Gender differences in verbal presumptuousness and attentiveness. *Personality and Social Psychology Bulletin, 23,* 759–772.

Stiles, W. B., Orth, J. E., Scherwitz, L., Hennrikus, D., & Vallbona, C. (1984). Role behaviors in routine medical interviews with hypertensive patients: A repertoire of verbal exchanges. *Social Psychology Quarterly, 47,* 244–254.

Stiles, W. B., Shapiro, D. A., & Elliott, R. (1986). "Are all psychotherapies equivalent?" *American Psychologist, 41,* 165–180.

Stogdill, R. M. (1948). Personal factors associated with leadership. *Journal of Psychology, 23,* 35–71.

Stogdill, R. M. (1959). *Individual behavior and group achievement.* New York: Oxford.

Stogdill, R. M. (1974). *Handbook of leadership.* New York: The Free Press.

Stokes, J. P. (1985). The relation of social network and individual difference variables to loneliness. *Journal of Personality and Social Psychology, 48,* 981–990.

Stokols, D. (1972). On the distinction between density and crowding: Some implications for future research. *Psychological Review, 79,* 275–278.

Stokols, D. (1978). In defense of the crowding construct. In A. Baum, J. E. Singer, & S. Valins (Eds.), *Advances in environmental psychology* (Vol. 1, pp. 111–130). Hillsdale, NJ: Erlbaum.

Stokols, D., & Altman, I. (Eds.). (1987). *Handbook of environmental psychology* (Vols. 1 & 2). New York: Wiley.

Stoner, J. A. F. (1961). *A comparison of individual and group decisions involving risk.* Unpublished

master's thesis, Massachusetts Institute of Technology.

Stones, C. R. (1982). A community of Jesus people in South Africa. *Small Group Behavior, 13,* 264–272.

Stoop, J. R. (1932). Is the judgment of the group better than that of the average member of the group? *Journal of Experimental Psychology, 15,* 550–562.

Storms, M. D., & Thomas, G. C. (1977). Reactions to physical closeness. *Journal of Personality and Social Psychology, 35,* 319–328.

Storr, A. (1988). *Solitude: A return to the self.* New York: The Free Press.

Stout, R. J., Salas, E., & Fowlkes, J. E. (1997). Enhancing teamwork in complex environments through team training. *Group Dynamics: Theory, Research, and Practice, 1,* 169–182.

Stratham, A. (1987). The gender model revisited: Differences in the management styles of men and women. *Sex Roles, 16,* 409–429.

Strauss, A. L. (1944). The literature on panic. *Journal of Abnormal and Social Psychology, 39,* 317–328.

Street, M. D. (1997). Groupthink: An examination of theoretical issues, implications, and future research suggestions. *Small Group Research, 28,* 72–93.

Streufert, S., & Streufert, S. C. (1986). The development of international conflict. In S. Worchel & W. G. Austin (Eds.), *Psychology of intergroup relations* (2nd ed., pp. 134–152). Chicago: Nelson-Hall.

Stricker, L. J., Messick, S., & Jackson, D. N. (1970). Conformity, anticonformity, and independence: Their dimensionality and generality. *Journal of Personality and Social Psychology, 16,* 494–507.

Strickland, L. H. (1958). Surveillance and trust. *Journal of Personality, 26,* 206–215.

Strickland, L. H., Barefoot, J. C., & Hockenstein, P. (1976). Monitoring behavior in the surveillance and trust paradigm. *Representative Research in Social Psychology, 7,* 51–57.

Strodtbeck, F. L., & Hook, L. H. (1961). The social dimensions of a twelve-man jury table. *Sociometry, 24,* 397–415.

Strodtbeck, F. L., James, R. M., & Hawkins, C. (1957). Social status in jury deliberations. *American Sociological Review, 22,* 713–719.

Strodtbeck, F. L., & Lipinski, R. M. (1985). Becoming first among equals: Moral considerations in jury foreman selection. *Journal of Personality and Social Psychology, 49,* 927–936.

Strodtbeck, F. L., & Mann, R. D. (1956). Sex role differentiation in jury deliberations. *Sociometry, 19,* 3–11.

Stroebe, M. S. (1994). The broken heart phenomenon: An examination of the mortality of bereavement. *Journal of Community and Applied Social Psychology, 4,* 47–61.

Stroebe, W., Diehl, M., & Abakoumkin, G. (1992). The illusion of group effectivity. *Personality and Social Psychology Bulletin, 18,* 643–650.

Stroebe, W., Diehl, M., & Abakoumkin, G. (1996). Social compensation and the Köhler effect: Toward a theoretical explanation of motivation gains in group productivity. In E. Witte & J. Davis (Eds.), *Understanding group behavior: Small group processes and interpersonal relations* (Vol. 2., pp. 37–65). Mahwah, NJ: Erlbaum.

Stroebe, W., Lenkert, A., & Jonas, K. (1988). Familiarity may breed contempt: The impact of student exchange on national stereotypes and attitudes. In W. Stroebe, A. W. Kruglanski, D. Bar-Tal, & M. Hewstone (Eds.), *The social psychology of intergroup conflict* (pp. 167–187). New York: Springer-Verlag.

Stroebe, W., & Stroebe, M. (1996). The social psychology of social support. In E. T. Higgins & A. W. Kruglanski (Eds.), *Social psychology: Handbook of basic principles* (pp. 597–621). New York: Guilford.

Stroebe, W., Stroebe, M. S., Abakoumkin, G., & Schut, H. (1996). The role of loneliness and social support in adjustment to loss: A test of attachment versus stress theory. *Journal of Personality and Social Psychology, 70,* 1241–1249.

Strong, S. R., Hills, H. I., Kilmartin, C. T., DeVries, H., Lanier, K., Nelson, B. N., Strickland, D., & Meyer, C. W., III. (1988). The dynamic relations among interpersonal behaviors: A test of complementarity and anticomplementarity. *Journal of Personality and Social Psychology, 54,* 798–810.

Strube, M. J., & Garcia, J. E. (1981). A meta-analytic investigation of Fiedler's contingency model of leadership effectiveness. *Psychological Bulletin, 90,* 307–321.

Strube, M. J., & Garcia, J. E. (1983). On the proper interpretation of empirical findings: Strube and Garcia (1981) revisited. *Psychological Bulletin, 93,* 600–603.

Struch, N., & Schwartz, S. H. (1989). Intergroup aggression: Its predictors and distinctness from ingroup bias. *Journal of Personality and Social Psychology, 56,* 364–373.

Stryker, S. (1997). "In the beginning there is society": Lessons from a sociological social psychology. In C. McGarty & S. A. Haslam (Eds.), *The message of social psychology: Perspectives on mind in society* (pp. 315–327). Cambridge, MA: Blackwell.

Stryker, S., & Statham, A. (1985). Symbolic interaction and role theory. In G. Lindzey & E. Aronson (Eds.), *Handbook of social psychology* (3rd ed., Vol. 1, pp. 311–378). New York: Random House.

Stumpf, S. A., Freedman, R. D., & Zand, D. E. (1979). Judgmental decisions: A study of interactions among group members, group functioning, and the decision situation. *Academy of Management Journal, 22,* 765–782.

Stuster, J. (1996). *Bold endeavors: Lessons from polar and space exploration.* Annapolis, MD: Naval Institute Press.

Suedfeld, P. (1987). Extreme and unusual environments. In D. Stokols & I. Altman (Eds.), *Handbook of environmental psychology* (Vol. 1, pp. 863–887). New York: Wiley.

Suedfeld, P. (1997). The social psychology of "invictus": Conceptual and methodological approaches to indomitability. In C. McGarty & S. A. Haslam (Eds.), *The message of social psychology: Perspectives on mind in society* (pp. 329–341). Cambridge, MA: Blackwell.

Suenaga, T., Andow, K., & Ohshima, T. (1981). Social facilitation: History, current studies, and future perspectives. *Japanese Psychological Review, 24,* 423–457.

Sugisawa, H., Liang, J., Liu, X. (1994). Social networks, social support, and mortality among older people in Japan. *Journals of Gerontology, 49,* S3-S13.

Suls, J., Martin, R., & David, J. P. (1998). Person-environment fit and its limits: Agreeableness, neuroticism, and emotional reactivity to interpersonal conflict. *Personality and Social Psychology Bulletin, 24,* 88–98.

Suls, J., & Wills, T. A. (Eds.). (1991). *Social comparison: Contemporary theory and research.* Hillsdale, NJ: Erlbaum.

Sumner, W. G. (1906). *Folkways.* New York: Ginn.

Sundstrom, E. (1975). An experimental study of crowding: Effects of room size, intrusion, and goal-blocking on nonverbal behavior, self-disclosure, and self-reported stress. *Journal of Personality and Social Psychology, 32,* 645–654.

Sundstrom, E. (1987). Work environments: Offices and factories. In D. Stokols & I. Altman (Eds.), *Handbook of environmental psychology* (Vol. 1, pp. 733–782). New York: Wiley.

Sundstrom, E. & Altman, I. (1974). Field study of dominance and territorial behavior. *Journal of Personality and Social Psychology, 30,* 115–125.

Sundstrom, E., Bell, P. A., Busby, P. L., & Asmus, C. (1996). Environmental psychology: 1989–1994. *Annual Review of Psychology, 47,* 485–512.

Sundstrom, E., De Meuse, K. P., & Futrell, D. (1990). Work teams: Applications and effectiveness. *American Psychologist, 45,* 120–133.

Swap, W. C., & Rubin, J. Z. (1983). Measurement of interpersonal orientation. *Journal of Personality and Social Psychology, 44,* 208–219.

Swezey, R. W., & Salas, E. (Eds.). (1992). *Teams: Their training and performance.* Norwood, NJ: Ablex.

Swingle, P. G., & Santi, A. (1972). Communication in non-zero sum games. *Journal of Personality and Social Psychology, 23,* 54–63.

Szymanski, K., & Harkins, S. G. (1987). Social loafing and self-evaluation with a social standard. *Journal of Personality and Social Psychology, 53,* 891–897.

Szymanski, K., & Harkins, S. G. (1993). The effect of experimenter evaluation on self-evaluation within the social loafing paradigm. *Journal of Experimental Social Psychology, 29,* 268–286.

't Hart, P. (1991). Irving L. Janis' *Victims of Groupthink. Political Psychology, 12,* 247–278.

Tajfel, H. (1978a). Interindividual behavior and intergroup behavior. In H. Tajfel (Ed.), *Differentiation between social groups.* New York: Academic Press.

Tajfel, H. (1978b). Social categorization, social identity, and social comparison. In H. Tajfel (Ed.), *Differentiation between social groups* (pp. 61–76). New York: Academic Press.

Tajfel, H. (1978c). The achievement of group differentiation. In H. Tajfel (Ed.), *Differentiation between social groups* (pp. 77–98). New York: Academic Press.

Tajfel, H. (1981). *Human groups and social categories.* New York: Cambridge University Press.

Tajfel, H. (1982). The social psychology of intergroup relations. *Annual Review of Psychology, 33,* 1–39.

Tajfel, H., & Turner, J. C. (1986). The social identity theory of intergroup behavior. In S. Worchel & W. G. Austin (Eds.), *Psychology of intergroup relations* (2nd ed., pp. 7–24). Chicago: Nelson-Hall.

Tanford, S., & Penrod, S. (1983). Computer modeling of influence in the jury: the role of the consistent juror. *Social Psychology Quarterly, 46,* 200–212.

Tanford, S., & Penrod, S. (1984). Social influence model: A formal integration of research on majority and minority influence processes. *Psychological Bulletin, 95,* 189–225.

Tang, J. (1997). The Model Minority thesis revisited: (Counter)evidence from the science and engineering fields. *Journal of Applied Behavioral Science, 33,* 291–314.

Tarde, G. (1903). *The laws of imitation.* New York: Holt.

Tata, J., Anthony, T., Hung-yu, L., Newman, B., Tang, S., Millson, M., & Sivakumar, K. (1996). Proportionate group size and rejection of the deviate: A meta-analytic integration. *Journal of Social Behavior and Personality, 11,* 739–752.

Taylor, D. M., & Moghaddam, F. M. (1994). *Theories of intergroup relations* (2nd ed.). Westport, CT: Praeger.

Taylor, D. W., Berry, P. C., & Block, C. H. (1958). Does group participation when using brainstorming facilitate or inhibit creative thinking? *Administrative Science Quarterly, 3,* 23–47.

Taylor, F. W. (1923). *The principles of scientific management.* New York: Harper.

Taylor, H. F. (1970). *Balance in small groups.* New York: Van Nostrand Reinhold.

Taylor, S. E., Aspinwall, L. G., Giuliano, T. A., Dakof, G. A., Reardon, K. (1993). Storytelling and coping with stressful events. *Journal of Applied Social Psychology, 23,* 703–733.

Taylor, S. E., & Lobel, M. (1989). Social comparison activity under threat: Downward evaluation and upward contacts. *Psychological Review, 96,* 569–575.

Tedeschi, J. T., Gaes, G. G., & Rivera, A. N. (1977). Aggression and the use of coercive power. *Journal of Social Issues, 33(1),* 101–125.

Tedeschi, J. T., Smith, R. B., III, & Brown, R. C. (1974). A reinterpretation of research on aggression. *Psychological Bulletin, 81,* 540–563.

Teger, A. (1980). *Too much invested to quit.* New York: Pergamon.

Terkel, S. (1980). *American dreams, lost and found.* New York: Ballantine.

Terry, R., & Coie, J. D. (1991). A comparison of methods for defining sociometric status among children. *Developmental Psychology, 27,* 867–880.

Tesser, A. (1988). Toward a self-evaluation maintenance model of social behavior. *Advances in Experimental Social Psychology, 21,* 181–227.

Tesser, A. (1991). Emotion in social comparison and reflection processes. In J. Suls & T. A. Wills (Eds.), *Social comparison: Contemporary theory and research* (pp. 117–148). Hillsdale, NJ: Erlbaum.

Tesser, A., & Campbell, J. (1983). Self-definition and self-evaluation maintenance. In J. Suls & A. G. Greenwald (Eds.), *Psychological perspectives on the self* (Vol. 2). Hillsdale, NJ: Erlbaum.

Tesser, A., Campbell, J., & Smith, M. (1984). Friendship choice and performance: Self-evaluation maintenance in children. *Journal of Personality and Social Psychology, 46,* 561–574.

Tetlock, P. E. (1979). Identifying victims of groupthink from public statements of decision makers. *Journal of Personality and Social Psychology, 37,* 1314–1324.

Tetlock, P. E., Peterson, R. S., McGuire, C., Chang, S., & Feld, P. (1992). Assessing political group dynamics: A test of the groupthink model. *Journal of Personality and Social Psychology, 63,* 403–425.

Thameling, C. L., & Andrews, P. H. (1992). Majority responses to opinion deviates: A communicative analysis. *Small Group Research, 23,* 475–502.

"The Who," the what, but why? (1979, December 5). *Richmond News Leader,* p. A19.

Thibaut, J. W., & Coules, J. (1952). The role of communication in the reduction of interpersonal hostility. *Journal of Abnormal and Social Psychology, 47,* 770–777.

Thibaut, J. W., & Kelley, H. H. (1959). *The social psychology of groups.* New York: Wiley.

Thoits, P. A. (1992). Identity structures and psychological well-being: Gender and marital status comparisons. *Social Psychology Quarterly, 55,* 236–256.

Thomas, E. J., & Fink, C. F. (1961). Models of group problem solving. *Journal of Abnormal and Social Psychology, 63,* 53–63.

Thomas, K. W. (1992). Conflict and negotiation processes in organizations. In M. D. Dunnette & L. M. Hough (Eds.), *Handbook of industrial and organizational psychology* (2nd ed., Vol. 3, pp. 651–717). Palo Alto, CA: Consulting Psychologists Press.

Thomas, W. I. (1928). *The child in America.* New York: Knopf.

Thompson, L. (1990). Negotiation behavior and outcomes: Empirical evidence and theoretical issues. *Psychological Bulletin, 108,* 515–532.

Thompson, L. (1991). Information exchange in negotiation. *Journal of Experimental Social Psychology, 27,* 161–179.

Thompson, L., & Hrebec, D. (1996). Lose-lose agreements in interdependent decision making. *Psychological Bulletin, 120,* 396–409.

Thorne, B. (1993). *Gender play.* New Brunswick, NJ: Rutgers University Press.

Thrasher, F. M. (1927). *The gang.* Chicago: University of Chicago Press.

Thune, E. S., Manderscheid, R. W., & Silbergeld, S. (1981). Sex, status, and cotherapy. *Small Group Behavior, 12,* 415–442.

Tindale, R. S. (1993). Decision errors made by individuals and groups. In N. J. Castellan (Ed.), *Individual and group decision making* (pp. 109–124). Hillsdale, NJ: Erlbaum.

Tindale, R. S., Davis, J. H., Vollrath, D. A., Nagao, D. H., & Hinsz, V. B. (1990). Asymmetrical social influence in freely interacting groups: A test of three models. *Journal of Personality and Social Psychology, 58,* 438–449.

Tindale, R. S., Smith, C. M., Thomas, L. S., Filkins, J., & Sheffey, S. (1996). Shared representations and asymmetric social influence processes in small groups. In E. H. Witte & J. H. Davis (Eds.), *Understanding group behavior: Consensual action by small groups* (Vol. 1, pp. 81–104). Hillsdale, NJ: Erlbaum.

Tjosvold, D. (1986). *Working together to get things done.* Lexington, MA: Lexington Books.

Tjosvold, D. (1991). Team organization: An enduring competitive advantage. New York: Wiley.

Tjosvold, D. (1995). Cooperation theory, constructive controversy, and effectiveness: Learning from crisis. In R. A. Guzzo, E. Salas, & Associates, *Team effectiveness and decision making in organizations* (pp. 79–112). San Francisco: Jossey-Bass.

Toennies, F. (1887/1963). *Community and society* [Gemeinscheaft and Gesellschaft]. NY: Harper & Row.

Tolnay, S. E., & Beck, E. M. (1996). Vicarious violence: Spatial effects on southern lynchings, 1890–1919. *American Journal of Sociology, 102,* 788–815.

Tolstoy, L. (1869/1952). *War and peace.* Chicago: Encyclopedia Britannica.

Torrance, E. P. (1954). The behavior of small groups under the stress conditions of "survival." *American Sociological Review, 19,* 751–755.

Towler, G. (1986). From zero to one hundred: Coaction in a natural setting. *Perceptual and Motor Skills, 62,* 377–378.

Trafimow, D., Triandis, H. C., & Goto, S. G. (1991). Some tests of the distinction between the private self and the collective self. *Journal of Personality and Social Psychology, 60,* 649–655.

Travis, L. E. (1925). The effect of a small audience upon eye-hand coordination. *Journal of Abnormal and Social Psychology, 20,* 142–146.

Travis, L. E. (1928). The influence of the group upon the stutterer's speed in free association. *Journal of Abnormal and Social Psychology, 23,* 45–51.

Triandis, H. C. (1990). Cross-cultural studies of individualism and collectivism. *Nebraska Symposium on Motivation, 1989, 39,* 41–133.

Triandis, H. C. (1995). *Individualism and collectivism.* Boulder, CO: Westview Press.

Triandis, H. C. (1996). The psychological measurement of cultural syndromes. *American Psychologist, 51,* 407–415.

Triandis, H. C., McCusker, C., & Hui, C. H. (1990). Multimethod probes of individualism and collectivism. *Journal of Personality and Social Psychology, 59,* 1006–1013.

Triplett, N. (1898). The dynamogenic factors in pacemaking and competition. *American Journal of Psychology, 9,* 507–533.

Trost, M. R., Maass, A., & Kenrick, D. T. (1992). Minority influence: Personal relevance biases cognitive processes and reverses private acceptance. *Journal of Experimental Social Psychology, 28,* 234–254.

Trujillo, N. (1986). Toward a taxonomy of small group interaction-coding systems. *Small Group Behavior, 17,* 371–394.

Tschuschke, V., & Dies, R. R. (1994). Intensive analysis of therapeutic factors and outcome in long-term inpatient groups. *International Journal of Group Psychotherapy, 44,* 185–208.

Tsui, A. S. (1984). A role-set analysis of managerial reputation. *Organizational Behavior and Human Performance, 34,* 64–96.

Tsui, A. S., & Gutek, B. A. (1984). A role set analysis of gender differences in performance, affective relationships, and career success of industrial middle managers. *Academy of Management Journal, 27,* 619–635.

Tubbs, S. L. (1995). *A systems approach to small group interaction* (5th ed.). New York: McGraw-Hill.

Tuckman, B. W. (1965). Developmental sequences in small groups. *Psychological Bulletin, 63,* 384–399.

Tuckman, B. W., & Jensen, M. A. C. (1977). Stages of small group development revisited. *Group and Organizational Studies, 2,* 419–427.

Turner, J. C. (1981). The experimental social psychology of intergroup behavior. In J. C. Turner & H. Giles (Eds.), *Intergroup behavior* (pp. 144–167). Oxford: Blackwell.

Turner, J. C. (1982). Towards a cognitive redefinition of the social group. In H. Tajfel (Ed.), *Social identity and intergroup relations* (pp. 15–40). Cambridge, England: Cambridge University Press.

Turner, J. C. (1983). Some comments on "The measurement of social orientations in the minimal group paradigm." *European Journal of Social Psychology, 13,* 351–367.

Turner, J. C. (1985). Social categorization and the self-concept: A social-cognitive theory of group behavior. *Advances in Group Processes, 2,* 77–122.

Turner, J. C., Hogg, M. A., Oakes, P. J., Reicher, S. D., & Wetherell, M. S. (1987). *Rediscovering the social group: A self-categorization theory.* New York: Blackwell.

Turner, J. C., Oakes, P. J., Haslam, S. A., & McGarty, C. (1994). Self and collective: Cognition and social context. *Personality and Social Psychology Bulletin, 20,* 454–463.

Turner, M. E., Pratkanis, A. R., Probasco, P., & Leve, C. (1992). Threat, cohesion, and group effectiveness: Testing a social identity maintenance perspective on groupthink. *Journal of Personality and Social Psychology, 63,* 781–796.

Turner, R. H. (1964). Collective behavior. In R. E. L. Faris (Ed.), *Handbook of modern sociology.* Chicago: Rand McNally.

Turner, R. H., & Colomy, P. (1988). Role differentiation: Orienting principles. *Advances in Group Processes, 5,* 1–27.

Turner, R. H., & Killian, L. M. (1972). *Collective behavior* (2nd ed.). Englewood Cliffs, NJ: Prentice Hall.

Turner, R. H., & Killian, L. M. (1987). *Collective behavior* (3rd ed.). Englewood Cliffs, NJ: Prentice Hall.

Tyerman, A., & Spencer, C. (1983). A critical test of the Sherifs' Robber's Cave Experiments: Intergroup competition and cooperation between groups of well-acquainted individuals. *Small Group Behavior, 14,* 515–531.

Tyler, T. R. (1989). The psychology of procedural justice: A test of the group-value model. *Journal of Personality and Social Psychology, 57,* 830–838.

Tyler, T. R. (1990). *Why people obey the law.* New Haven, CT: Yale University Press.

Tyler, T. R. (1994). Psychological models of the justice motive. *Journal of Personality and Social Psychology, 67,* 850–863.

Tyler, T. R. (1997). The psychology of legitimacy: A relational perspective on voluntary deference to authorities. *Personality and Social Psychology Review, 1,* 323–345.

Tyler, T. R., & Degoey, P. (1996). Trust in organizational authorities: The influence of motive attributions on willingness to accept decisions. In R. Kramer & T. R. Tyler (Eds.), *Trust in organizational authorities* (pp. 331–356). Thousand Oaks, CA: Sage.

Tyler, T. R., & Lind, E. A. (1992). A relational model of authority in groups. *Advances in Experimental Social Psychology, 25,* 115–191.

Tziner, A., & Eden, D. (1985). Effects of crew composition on crew performance: Does the whole equal the sum of its parts? *Journal of Applied Psychology, 70,* 85–93.

Uchino, B. N., Cacioppo, J. T., & Kiecolt-Glaser, J. K. (1996). The relationship between social support and physiological processes: A review with emphasis on underlying mechanisms and implications for health. *Psychological Bulletin, 119,* 488–531.

Ulschak, F. L., Nathanson, L., & Gillan, P. G. (1981). *Small group problem solving.* Reading, MA: Addison-Wesley.

Umberson, D., Chen, M. D., House, J. S., Hopkins, K., & Slaten, E. (1996). The effect of social relationships on psychological well-being: Are men and women really so different? *American Sociological Review, 61,* 837–857.

Uris, A. (1978). Executive dissent: How to say no and win. New York: AMACOM.

Utman, C. H. (1997). Performance effects of motivational state: A meta-analysis. *Personality and Social Psychology Review, 1,* 170–182.

Valacich, J. S., Dennis, A. R., & Connolly, T. (1994). Idea generation in computer-based groups: A new ending to an old story. *Organizational Behavior and Human Decision Making, 57,* 448–467.

Van de Ven, A. H. (1974). *Group decision-making effectiveness.* Kent, OH: Kent State University Center for Business and Economic Research Press.

Van de Ven, A. H., & Delbecq, A. L. (1971). Nominal versus interacting group process for committee decision making effectiveness. *Academy of Management Journal, 14,* 203–212.

van de Vliert, E., & Euwema, M. C. (1994). Agreeableness and activeness as components of conflict behaviors. *Journal of Personality and Social Psychology, 66,* 674–687.

Van Egeren, L. F. (1979). Cardiovascular changes during social competition in a mixed-motive game. *Journal of Personality and Social Psychology, 37,* 858–864.

Van Lange, P. A. M., De Bruin, E. M. N., Otten, W., & Joireman, J. A. (1997). Development of prosocial, individualistic, and competitive orientations: Theory and preliminary evidence. *Journal of Personality and Social Psychology, 73,* 733–746.

van Oostrum, J., & Rabbie, J. M. (1995). Intergroup competition and cooperation within autocratic and democratic management regimes. *Small Group Research, 26,* 269–295.

Van Sell, M., Brief, A. P., & Schuler, R. S. (1981). Role conflict and role ambiguity: Integration of the literature and directions for future research. *Human Relations, 34,* 43–71.

Van Zelst, R. H. (1952). Sociometrically selected work teams increase production. *Personnel Psychology, 5,* 175–185.

Varela, J. A. (1971). *Psychological solutions to social problems.* New York: Academic Press.

Vecchio, R. P. (1977). An empirical examination of the validity of Fiedler's model of leadership effectiveness. *Organizational Behavior and Human Performance, 19,* 180–206.

Vecchio, R. P. (1983). Assessing the validity of Fiedler's contingency model of leadership: A closer look at Strube and Garcia. *Psychological Bulletin, 93,* 404–408.

Vecchio, R. P. (1987). Situational leadership theory: An examination of a prescriptive theory. *Journal of Applied Psychology, 72,* 444–451.

Veitch, J. A. (1990). Office noise and illumination effects on reading comprehension. *Journal of Environmental Psychology, 10,* 209–217.

Villaseñor, V. (1977). *Jury: The people vs. Juan Corona.* Boston: Little, Brown.

Vinacke, W. E. (1971). Negotiations and decisions in a politics game. In B. Lieberman (Ed.), *Social choice.* New York: Gordon & Breach.

Vinokur, A., & Burnstein, E. (1974). The effects of partially shared persuasive arguments on group-induced shifts: A group-problem-solving approach. *Journal of Personality and Social Psychology, 29,* 305–315.

Vinokur, A., & Burnstein, E. (1978). Depolarization of attitudes in groups. *Journal of Personality and Social Psychology, 36,* 872–885.

Vinokur, A., Burnstein, E., Sechrest, L., & Wortman, P. M. (1985). Group decision making by experts: Field study of panels evaluating medical technologies. *Journal of Personality and Social Psychology, 49,* 70–84.

Vinsel, A., Brown, B. B., Altman, I., & Foss, C. (1980). Privacy regulation, territorial displays, and effectiveness of individual functioning. *Journal of Personality and Social Psychology, 39,* 1104–1115.

Von Dras, D. D., & Siegler, I. C. (1997). Stability in extraversion and aspects of social support at midlife. *Journal of Personality and Social Psychology, 72,* 233–241.

Vorauer, J. D., Miller, D. T. (1997). Failure to recognize the effect of implicit social influence on the presentation of self. *Journal of Personality and Social Psychology, 73,* 281–295.

Vroom, V. H. (1973). A new look at managerial decision making. *Organizational Dynamics, 1,* 66–80.

Vroom, V. H. (1974). Decision making and the leadership process. *Journal of Contemporary Business, 3,* 47–64.

Vroom, V. H. (1976). Leadership. In M. D. Dunnette (Ed.), *Handbook of industrial and organizational psychology.* Chicago: Rand McNally.

Vroom, V. H., & Jago, A. G. (1978). On the validity of the Vroom/Yetton model. *Journal of Applied Psychology, 63,* 151–162.

Vroom, V. H., & Mann, F. C. (1960). Leader authoritarianism and employee attitudes. *Personnel Psychology, 13,* 125–140.

Vroom, V. H., & Yetton, P. W. (1973). *Leadership and decision making.* Pittsburgh, PA: University of Pittsburgh Press.

Wagner, D. G., & Berger, J. (1993). Status characteristics theory: The growth of a program. In J. Berger & M. Zelditch, Jr. (Eds.), *Theoretical research programs: Studies in the growth of theory* (pp. 24–63). Stanford, CA: Stanford University Press.

Wagner, J. A. (1994). Participation effects on performance and satisfaction: A reconsideration of research evidence. *Academy of Management Review, 19,* 312–330.

Waldman, D. A., Bass, B. M., & Yammarino, F. J. (1990). Adding to contingent-reward behavior: The augmenting effect of charismatic leadership. *Group and Organization Studies, 15,* 381–394.

Walker, C. J., & Berkerle, C. A. (1987). The effect of state anxiety on rumor transmission. *Journal of Social Behavior and Personality, 2,* 353–360.

Walker, H. A., Ilardi, B. C., McMahon, A. M., & Fennell, M. L. (1996). Gender, interaction, and leadership. *Social Psychology Quarterly, 59,* 255–272.

Wall, V. D., Jr., & Nolan, L. L. (1987). Small group conflict: A look at equity, satisfaction, and styles of conflict management. *Small Group Behavior, 18,* 188–211.

Wallach, M. A., Kogan, N., & Bem, D. J. (1962). Group influence on individual risk taking. *Journal of Abnormal and Social Psychology, 65,* 75–86.

Walsh, Y., Russell, R. J. H., & Wells, P. A. (1995). The personality of ex-cult members. *Personality and Individual Differences, 19,* 339–344.

Ware, R., Barr, J. E., & Boone, M. (1982). Subjective changes in small group processes: An experimental investigation. *Small Group Behavior, 13,* 395–401.

Warfield-Coppock, N. (1995). Toward a theory of Afrocentric organizations. *Journal of Black Psychology, 21,* 30–48.

Watkins, D., Yau, J., Dahlin, B., & Wondimu, H. (1997). The Twenty Statements Test: Some measurement issues. *Journal of Cross-Cultural Psychology, 28,* 626–633.

Watson, C., & Hoffman, L. R. (1996). Managers as negotiators: A test of power versus gender as predictors of feelings, behavior, and outcomes. *Leadership Quarterly, 7,* 63–85.

Watson, R. I., Jr. (1973). Investigation into deindividuation using a cross-cultural survey technique. *Journal of Personality and Social Psychology, 25,* 342–345.

Watson, W. E., Kumar, K., & Michaelsen, L. K. (1993). Cultural diversity's impact on interaction process and performance: Comparing homogeneous and diverse task groups. *Academy of Management Journal, 36,* 590–602.

Webb, N. M., Troper, J. D., & Fall, R. (1995). Constructive activity and learning in collaborative small groups. *Journal of Educational Psychology, 87,* 406–423.

Weber, M. (1921/1946). The sociology of charismatic authority. In H. H. Gert & C. W. Mills (Trans. & Eds.), *From Max Weber: Essay in sociology* (pp. 245–252). New York: Oxford University Press.

Webster, M., Jr., & Driskell, J. E., Jr. (1983). Processes of status generalization. In H. H. Blumberg, A. P. Hare, V. Kent, & M. F. Davies (Eds.), *Small groups and social interaction* (Vol. 1, pp. 57–67). New York: Wiley.

Wegner, D. M. (1987). Transactive memory: A contemporary analysis of the group mind. In B. Mullen & G. R. Goethals (Eds.), *Theories of group behavior* (pp. 185–208). New York: Springer-Verlag.

Wegner, D. M., Giuliano, T., & Hertel, P. T. (1985). Cognitive interdependence in close relationships. In W. Ickes (Ed.), *Compatible and incompatible relationships* (pp. 253–276). New York: Springer-Verlag.

Wegner, D. M., & Schaefer, D. (1978). The concentration of responsibility: An objective self-awareness analysis of group size effects in helping situations. *Journal of Personality and Social Psychology, 36,* 147–155.

Weick, K. E. (1985). Systematic observational methods. In G. Lindzey & E. Aronson (Eds.), *Handbook of social psychology* (3rd ed., Vol. 1, pp. 567–634). New York: Random House.

Weigel, R. H., & Cook, S. W. (1975). Participation in decision-making: A determinant of interpersonal attraction in cooperating interracial groups. *International Journal of Group Tensions, 5,* 179–195.

Weigold, M. F., & Schlenker, B. R. (1991). Accountability and risk taking. *Personality and Social Psychology Bulletin, 17,* 25–29.

Weinberg, M. S. (1966). Becoming a nudist. *Psychiatry, 29,* 15–24.

Weingart. L. R. (1997). How did they do that? The ways and means of studying group process. *Research in Organizational Behavior, 19,* 189–239.

Weingart, L. R., Thompson, L. L., Bazerman, M. H., & Carroll, J. S. (1990). Tactical behavior and negotiation outcomes. *The International Journal of Conflict Management, 1,* 7–31.

Weingart, L. R., & Weldon, E. (1991). Processes that mediate the relationship between a group goal and group member performance. *Human Performance, 4,* 33–54.

Weiss, R. F., & Miller, F. G. (1971). The drive theory of social facilitation. *Psychological Review, 78,* 44–57.

Weiss, R. S. (1973). Loneliness: The experience of emotional and social isolation. Cambridge, MA: MIT Press.

Wekselberg, V., Goggin, W. C., & Collings, T. J. (1997). A multifaceted concept of group maturity and its measurement and relationship to group performance. *Small Group Research, 28,* 3–28.

Welch, D. A. (1989). Crisis decision making reconsidered. *Journal of Conflict Resolution, 33,* 430–445.

Weldon, E., Jehn, K. A., & Pradhan, P. (1991). Processes that mediate the relationship between a group goal and improved group performance. *Journal of Personality and Social Psychology, 61,* 555–569.

Weldon, E., & Weingart, L. R. (1993). Group goals and group performance. *British Journal of Social Psychology, 32,* 307–334.

Weldon, M. S., & Bellinger, K. D. (1997). Collective memory: Collaborative and individual processes in remembering. *Journal of Experimental Psychology: Learning, Memory, and Cognition, 23,* 1160–1175.

Werner, P. (1978). Personality and attitude-activism correspondence. *Journal of Personality and Social Psychology, 36,* 1375–1390.

West, S. G., Gunn, S. P., & Chernicky, P. (1975). Ubiquitous Watergate: An attributional analysis. *Journal of Personality and Social Psychology, 23,* 55–65.

Weston, S. B., & English, H. B. (1926). The influence of the group on psychological test scores. *American Journal of Psychology, 37,* 600–601.

Weybrew, B. B. (1963). Psychological problems of prolonged marine submergence. In J. N. Burns, R. Chambers, & E. Hendler (Eds.), *Unusual environments and human behavior.* New York: Macmillan.

Wheelan, S. A. (1994). *Group process: A developmental perspective.* Boston: Allyn & Bacon.

Wheelan, S. A., & Hochberger, J. M. (1996). Validation studies of the group development questionnaire. *Small Group Research, 27,* 143–170.

Wheelan, S. A., & McKeage, R. L. (1993). Developmental patterns in small and large groups. *Small Group Research, 24,* 60–83.

Wheeler, D. D., & Janis, I. L. (1980). *A practical guide for making decisions.* New York: The Free Press.

Wheeler, L. (1966). Toward a theory of behavioral contagion. *Psychological Review, 73,* 179–192.

Wheeler, L., & Miyake, K. (1992). Social comparison in everyday life. *Journal of Personality and Social Psychology, 62,* 760–773.

Wheeler, L., Reis, H., T., & Bond, M. H. (1989). Collectivism-individualism in everyday social life: The middle kingdom and the melting pot. *Journal of Personality and Social Psychology, 57,* 79–86.

Wheeless, L. R., Barraclough, R., & Stewart, R. (1983). Compliance-gaining and power in persuasion. *Communication Yearbook, 7,* 105–145.

White, H. C., & White, C. A. (1993). *Canvases and careers: Institutional change in the French painting world.* Chicago: University of Chicago Press.

White, R. (1990). Democracy in the research team. In S. A. Wheelan, E. A. Pepiton, & V. Abt (Eds.), *Advances in field theory* (pp. 19–26). Thousand Oaks, CA: Sage.

White, R. K. (1965). Images in the context of international conflict. In H. Kelman (Ed.), *International behavior.* New York: Holt, Rinehart & Winston.

White, R. K. (1966). Misperception and the Vietnam war. *Journal of Social Issues, 22(3),* 1–156.

White, R. K. (1969). Three not-so-obvious contributions of psychology to peace. *Journal of Social Issues, 25(4),* 23–29.

White, R. K. (1977). Misperception in the Arab-Israeli conflict. *Journal of Social Issues, 33(1),* 190–221.

White, R. K. (1990). Democracy in the research team. In S. A. Wheelan, E. A. Pepiton, & V. Abt (Eds.), *Advances in field theory* (pp. 19–22). Newbury Park, CA: Sage.

White, R. K. (1992). A personal assessment of Lewin's major contributions. *Journal of Social Issues, 48(2),* 45–50.

White, R. K., & Lippitt, R. (1960). *Autocracy and democracy.* New York: Harper & Row.

White, R. K., & Lippitt, R. (1968). Leader behavior and member reaction in three "social climates." In D. Cartwright and A. Zander (Eds.), *Group dynamics: Research and theory* (3rd ed., pp. 318–335). New York: Harper & Row.

Whitehead, T. N. (1938). *The industrial worker.* Cambridge, MA: Harvard University Press.

Whitley, B. E., Jr. (1996). *Principles of research in behavioral science.* Mountain View, CA: Mayfield.

Whitney, I., & Smith, P. K. (1993). A survey of the nature and extent of bullying in junior/middle and secondary schools. *Educational Research, 35,* 3–25.

Whitney, K., & Sagrestano, L. M., & Maslach, C. (1994). Establishing the social impact of individuation. *Journal of Personality and Social Psychology, 66,* 1140–1153.

Whyte, G. (1993). Escalating commitment in individual and group decision making: A prospect theory approach. *Organizational Behavior and Human Decision Processes, 54,* 430–455.

Whyte, W. F. (1943). *Street corner society.* Chicago: University of Chicago Press.

Whyte, W. F. (1991). *Participatory action research.* Thousand Oaks, CA: Sage.

Wicker, A. W. (1979). *An introduction to ecological psychology.* Pacific Grove, CA: Brooks/Cole.

Wicker, A. W. (1987). Behavior settings reconsidered: Temporal stages, resources, internal dynamics, context. In D. Stokols & I. Altman (Eds.), *Handbook of environmental psychology* (Vol. 1, pp. 613–653). New York: Wiley.

Wicker, A. W., & August, R. A. (1995). How far should we generalize? The case of a workload model. *Psychological Science, 6,* 39–44.

Wicker, A. W., Kirmeyer, S. L., Hanson, L., & Alexander, D. (1976). Effects of manning levels on subjective experiences, performance, and verbal interaction in groups. *Organizational Behavior and Human Performance, 17,* 251–274.

Wicklund, R. A. (1980). Group contact and self-focused attention. In P. B. Paulus (Ed.), *Psychology of group influence* (p. 189–208). Hillsdale, NJ: Erlbaum.

Widmeyer, W. N. (1990). Group composition in sport. Special issue: The group in sport and physical activity. *International Journal of Sport Psychology, 21,* 264–285.

Widmeyer, W. N., Brawley, L. R., & Carron, A. V. (1985). *The measurement of cohesion in sport teams: The Group Environment Questionnaire.* London, Ontario: Sports Dynamics.

Widmeyer, W. N., Brawley, L. R., & Carron, A. V. (1992). Group dynamics in sports. In T. S. Horn (Ed.), *Advances in sport psychology* (pp. 163–180). Champaign, IL: Human Kinetics Publishers.

Widmeyer, W. N., & McGuire, E. J. (1997). Frequency of competition and aggression in professional ice hockey. *International Journal of Sport Psychology, 28,* 57–66.

Wilder, D. A. (1977). Perception of groups, size of opposition, and social influence. *Journal of Experimental Social Psychology, 13,* 253–268.

Wilder, D. A. (1986a). Cognitive factors affecting the success of intergroup contact. In S. Worchel & W. G. Austin (Eds.), *Psychology of intergroup relations* (2nd ed., pp. 49–66). Chicago: Nelson-Hall.

Wilder, D. A. (1986b). Social categorization: Implications for creation and reduction of intergroup bias. *Advances in Experimental Social Psychology, 19,* 293–355.

Wilder, D. A., & Simon, A. F. (1998). Categorical and dynamic groups: Implications for social perception and interpersonal behavior. In C. Sedikides, J. Schopler, & C. A. Insko (Eds.), *Intergroup cognition and intergroup behavior* (pp. 27–44). Mahwah, NJ: Erlbaum.

Wilder, D. A., Simon, A. F., & Faith, M. (1996). Enhancing the impact of counterstereotypic information: Dispositional attributions for deviance. *Journal of Personality and Social Psychology, 71,* 276–287.

Wilder, D. A., & Thompson, J. E. (1980). Intergroup contact with independent manipulations of in-group and out-group interaction. *Journal of Personality and Social Psychology, 38,* 589–603.

Wilke, H. A. M. (1996). Status congruence in small groups. In E. Witte & J. H. Davis (Eds.), *Understanding group behavior: Small group processes and interpersonal relations* (Vol. 2, pp. 67–91). Mahwah, NJ: Erlbaum.

Wilkinson, I., & Kipnis, D. (1978). Interfirm use of power. *Journal of Applied Psychology, 63,* 315–320.

Williams v. Florida, 399 U.S. 78 (1970).

Williams, J. E., & Best, D. L. (1990). *Measuring sex stereotypes: A multination study.* Newbury Park, CA: Sage.

Williams, K. D., Harkins, S., & Latané, B. (1981). Identifiability as a deterrent to social loafing: Two cheering experiments. *Journal of Personality and Social Psychology, 40,* 303–311.

Williams, K. D., Jackson, J. M., & Karau, S. J. (1995). Collective hedonism: A social loafing analysis of social dilemmas. In D. A. Schroeder (Ed.), *Social dilemmas: Perspectives on individuals and groups* (pp. 117–141). Westport, CT: Praeger.

Williams, K. D., & Karau, S. J. (1991). Social loafing and social compensation: The effects of expectations of co-worker performance. *Journal of Personality and Social Psychology, 61,* 570–581.

Williams, K. D., & Sommer, K. L. (1997). Social ostracism by coworkers: Does rejection lead to loafing or compensation? *Personality and Social Psychology Bulletin, 23,* 693–706.

Willis, F. N. (1966). Initial speaking distance as a function of the speakers' relationship. *Psychonomic Science, 5,* 221–222.

Willis, R. H. (1963). Two dimensions of conformity-nonconformity. *Sociometry, 26,* 499–512.

Wills, T. A. (1991). Social comparison process in coping and health. In C. R. Snyder and D. R. Forsyth (Eds.), *Handbook of social and clinical psychology: The health perspective* (pp. 376–394). New York: Pergamon.

Wills, T. A., & Cleary, S. D. (1996). How are social support effects mediated? A test with parental support and adolescent substance use. *Journal of Personality and Social Psychology, 71,* 937–952.

Wills, T. A., & DePaulo, B. M. (1991). Interpersonal analysis of the help-seeking process. In C. R. Snyder & D. R. Forsyth (Eds.), *Handbook of social and clinical psychology: The health perspective* (pp. 350–375). New York: Pergamon.

Willsie, D. A., & Riemer, J. W. (1980). The campus bar as a "bastard" institution. *Mid-American Review of Sociology, 5,* 61–79.

Wilson, E. O. (1975). *Sociobiology: The new synthesis.* Cambridge, MA: Belknap Press.

Wilson, S. R. (1992). Face and facework in negotiation. In L. L. Putnam & M. E. Roloff (Eds.), *Communication and negotiation* (pp. 176–205). Newbury Park, CA: Sage.

Wilson, W., & Miller, N. (1961). Shifts in evaluations of participants following intergroup competition. *Journal of Abnormal and Social Psychology, 63,* 428–431.

Winquist, J. R., & Larson, J. R., Jr. (1998). Information pooling: When it impacts group decision making. *Journal of Personality and Social Psychology, 74,* 371–377.

Winstead, B. (1986). Sex differences in same sex friendships. In V. J. Derlaga & B. Winstead (Eds.), *Friendship and social interaction.* New York: Springer-Verlag.

Winter, D. G. (1973). *The power motive.* New York: The Free Press.

Wiseman, R. L., & Schenck-Hamlin, W. (1981). A multidimensional scaling validation of an inductively derived set of compliance-gaining strategies. *Communication Monographs, 48,* 251–270.

Witte, E. H. (1994). Minority influences and innovations: The search for an integrated explanation of psychological and sociological models. In S. Moscovici, A. Mucchi-Faina, & Anne Maass

(Eds.), *Minority influence* (pp. 67–93). Chicago: Nelson-Hall.

Witte, E. H., & Davis, J. H. (Eds.). (1996). *Understanding group behavior* (Vols. 1 & 2). Mahwah, NJ: Erlbaum.

Witteman, H. (1991). Group member satisfaction: A conflict-related account. *Small Group Research, 22,* 24–58.

Wittenbaum, G. M., & Stasser, G. (1996). Management of information in small groups. In J. L. Nye & A. M. Brower (Eds.), *What's social about social cognition? Research on socially shared cognitions in small groups* (pp. 3–28). Thousand Oaks, CA: Sage.

Wittenbaum, G. M., Stasser, G., & Merry, C. J. (1996). Tacit coordination in anticipation of small group task completion. *Journal of Experimental Social Psychology, 32,* 129–152.

Wittenbaum, G. M., Vaughan, S. I., & Stasser, G. (1998). Coordination in task-performing groups. In R. S. Tindale, L. Heath, J. Edwards, E. J. Posavac, F. B. Bryant, Y. Suarez-Balcazar, E. Henderson-King, & J. Myers (Eds.), *Theory and research on small groups* (pp. 177–204) New York, Plenum.

Wolf, S. (1987). Majority and minority influence: A social impact analysis. In M. P. Zanna, J. M. Olson, & C. P. Herman (Eds.), *Social influences: The Ontario Symposium* (Vol. 5, pp. 207–235). Hillsdale, NJ: Erlbaum.

Wolf, S., & Latané, B. (1983). Majority and minority influence on restaurant preferences. *Journal of Personality and Social Psychology, 45,* 282–292.

Wood, J. T. (1984). Alternative methods of group decision making: A comparative examination of consensus, negotiation, and voting. In G. M. Phillips & J. T. Wood (Eds.), *Emergent issues in human decision making* (pp. 3–18). Carbondale, IL: Southern Illinois University Press.

Wood, J. V. (1989). Theory and research concerning social comparisons of personal attributes. *Psychological Bulletin, 106,* 231–248.

Wood, J. V. (1996). What is social comparison and how should we study it? *Personality and Social Psychology Bulletin, 22,* 520–537.

Wood, J. V., Taylor, S. E., & Lichtman, R. R. (1985). Social comparison in adjustment to breast cancer. *Journal of Personality and Social Psychology, 49,* 1169–1183.

Wood, W. (1987). A meta-analytic review of sex differences in group performance. *Psychological Bulletin, 102,* 53–71.

Wood, W., & Karten, S. J. (1986). Sex differences in interaction style as a product of perceived sex differences in competence. *Journal of Personality and Social Psychology, 50,* 341–347.

Wood, W., Lundgren, S., Ouellette, J. A., Busceme, S., & Blackstone, T. (1994). Minority influence: A meta-analytic review of social influence processes. *Psychological Bulletin, 115,* 323–345.

Wood, W., Polek, D., & Aiken, C. (1985). Sex differences in group task performance. *Journal of Personality and Social Psychology, 48,* 63–71.

Wood, W., Pool, G. J., Leck, K., & Purvis, D. (1996). Self-definition, defensive processing, and influence: The normative impact of majority and minority groups. *Journal of Personality and Social Psychology, 71,* 1181–1193.

Woodman, R. W., & Sherwood, J. J. (1980). The role of team development in organizational effectiveness: A critical review. *Psychological Bulletin, 88,* 166–186.

Worchel, S. (1986). The role of cooperation in reducing intergroup conflict. In S. Worchel & W. G. Austin (Eds.), *Psychology of intergroup relations* (2nd ed., pp. 288–304). Chicago: Nelson-Hall.

Worchel, S., Andreoli, V. A., & Folger, R. (1977). Intergroup cooperation and intergroup attraction: The effect of previous interaction and outcome of combined effort. *Journal of Experimental Social Psychology, 13,* 131–140.

Worchel, S., Axsom, D., Ferris, F., Samaha, C., & Schweitzer, S. (1978). Factors determining the effect of intergroup cooperation on intergroup attraction. *Journal of Conflict Resolution, 22,* 429–439.

Worchel, S., & Brehm, J. W. (1971). Direct and implied social restoration of freedom. *Journal of Personality and Social Psychology, 18,* 294–304.

Worchel, S., Lind, E., & Kaufman, K. (1975). Evaluations of group products as a function of expectations of group longevity, outcome of competition, and publicity of evaluations. *Journal of Personality and Social Psychology, 31,* 1089–1097.

Worchel, S., & Norvell, N. (1980). Effect of perceived environmental conditions during cooperation on intergroup attraction. *Journal of Personality and Social Psychology, 38,* 764–772.

Worchel, S., & Teddlie, C. (1976). The experience of crowding: A two-factor theory. *Journal of Personality and Social Psychology, 34,* 30–40.

Worchel, S., & Yohai, S. (1979). The role of attribution in the experience of crowding. *Journal of Experimental Social Psychology, 15,* 91–104.

Worringham, C. J., & Messick, D. M. (1983). Social facilitation of running: An unobtrusive study. *Journal of Social Psychology, 121,* 23–29.

Worthington, E. L., Jr., Hight, T. L., Ripley, J. S., Perrone, K. M., Kurusu, T. A., & Jones, D. R. (1997). Strategic hope-focused relationship-enrichment counseling with individual couples. *Journal of Counseling Psychology, 44,* 381–389.

Wright, J. C., Giammarino, M., & Parad, H. W. (1986). Social status in small groups: Individual-group similarity and the social "misfit." *Journal of Personality and Social Psychology, 50,* 523–536.

Wright, P. H., & Crawford, A. C. (1971). Agreement and friendship: A close look and some second thoughts. *Representative Research in Social Psychology, 2,* 52–69.

Wright, S. C., Aron, A., McLaughlin-Volpe, T., & Ropp, S. A. (1997). The extended contact effect: Knowledge of cross-group friendships and prejudice. *Journal of Personality and Social Psychology, 73,* 73–90.

Wright, S. S., & Forsyth, D. R. (1997). Group membership and collective identity: Consequences for self-esteem. *Journal of Social and Clinical Psychology, 16,* 43–56.

Wright, T. L., Ingraham, L. J., & Blackmer, D. R. (1984). Simultaneous study of individual differences and relationship effects in attraction. *Journal of Personality and Social Psychology, 47,* 1059–1062.

Wrightsman, L. S. (1977). *Social psychology* (2nd ed.). Belmont, CA: Wadsworth.

Wrightsman, L. S., Nietzel, M. T., & Fortune, W. H. (1998). *Psychology and the legal system* (4th ed.). Pacific Grove, CA: Brooks/Cole.

Wrightsman, L. S., O'Connor, J., & Baker, N. J. (Eds.). (1972). *Cooperation and competition: Readings on mixed-motive games.* Belmont, CA: Wadsworth.

Wrong, D. (1979). *Power: Its forms, bases, and uses.* Chicago: University of Chicago Press.

Wrong, D. H. (1994). The problem of order: What unites and divides society. New York: The Free Press.

Wu, J. Z., & Axelrod, R. (1995). How to cope with noise in the iterated prisoner's dilemma. *Journal of Conflict Resolution, 39,* 183–189.

Yablonsky, L. (1959). The delinquent gang as a near group. *Social Problems, 7,* 108–117.

Yablonsky, L. (1962). *The violent gang.* New York: Macmillan.

Yalom, I. D. (1975). *The theory and practice of group psychotherapy* (2nd ed.). New York: Basic Books.

Yalom, I. D. (1985). *The theory and practice of group psychotherapy* (3rd ed.). New York: Basic Books.

Yalom, I. D. (1995). *The theory and practice of group psychotherapy* (4th ed.). New York: Basic Books.

Yalom, V. J., & Vinogradov, S. (1993). Interpersonal group psychotherapy. In H. I. Kaplan & M. J. Sadock (Eds.), *Comprehensive group psychotherapy* (3rd ed., pp. 185–195). Baltimore: Williams & Wilkins.

Yamagishi, K. (1994). Social dilemmas. In K. S. Cook, G. A. Fine, & J. S. House (Eds.), *Sociological perspectives on social psychology* (pp. 311–334). Boston: Allyn & Bacon.

Yamagishi, T. (1986). The provision of a sanctioning system as a public good. *Journal of Personality and Social Psychology, 51,* 110–116.

Yammarino, F. J., & Bass, B. M. (1990). Long-term forecasting of transformational leadership and its effects among naval officers: Some preliminary findings. In K. E. Clark & M. B. Clark (Eds.), *Measure of leadership* (pp. 151–169). West Orange, NJ: Leadership Library of America.

Yammarino, F. J., & Bass, B. M. (1991). Personal and situation views of leadership: A multiple levels of analysis approach. *Leadership Quarterly, 2,* 121–139.

Yammarino, F. J., Spangler, W. D., & Bass, B. M. (1993). Transformational leadership and performance: A longitudinal investigation. *Leadership Quarterly, 4,* 81–102.

Yang, K., & Bond, M. H. (1990). Exploring implicit personality theories with indigenous or imported constructs: The Chinese case. *Journal of Personality and Social Psychology, 58,* 1087–1095.

Yin, R. K. (1993). *Applications of case study research.* Thousand Oaks, CA: Sage.

Yin, R. K. (1994). *Case study research: Design and methods* (2nd ed.). Thousand Oaks, CA: Sage.

Youngs, G. A., Jr. (1986). Patterns of threat and punishment reciprocity in a conflict setting. *Journal of Personality and Social Psychology, 51,* 541–546.

Yukelson, D., Weinberg, R., & Jackson, A. (1984). A multidimensional group cohesion instrument for intercollegiate basketball teams. *Journal of Sport Psychology, 6,* 103–117.

Yukl, G. A. (1994). *Leadership in organizations* (3rd ed.). Englewood Cliffs, NJ: Prentice Hall.

Yukl, G., Falbe, C. M., Joo, Y. Y. (1993). Patterns of influence behavior for managers. *Group and Organization Management, 18,* 5–28.

Yukl, G., Guinan, P. J., & Sottolano, D. (1995). Influence tactics used for different objectives with subordinates, peers, and superiors. *Group and Organization Management, 20,* 272–296.

Yukl, G., Kim, H., & Falbe, C. (1996). Antecedents of influence outcomes. *Journal of Applied Psychology, 81,* 309–317.

Zaccaro, S. J. (1984). Social loafing: The role of task attractiveness. *Personality and Social Psychology Bulletin, 10,* 99–106.

Zaccaro, S. J. (1995). Leader resources and the nature of organizational problems. *Applied Psychology: An International Review, 44,* 32–36.

Zaccaro, S. J., Foti, R. J., & Kenny, D. A. (1991). Self-monitoring and trait-based variance in leadership: An investigation of leader flexibility across multiple group situations. *Journal of Applied Psychology, 76,* 308–315.

Zaccaro, S. J., Gilbert, J. A., Thor, K. K., & Mumford, M. D. (1991). Leadership and social intelligence: Linking social perspectives and behavioral flexibility to leader effectiveness. *Leadership Quarterly, 2,* 317–342.

Zaccaro, S. J., Gualtieri, J., & Minionis, D. (1995). Task cohesion as a facilitator of team decision making under temporal urgency. *Military Psychology, 7,* 77–93.

Zajac, E. J., & Westphal, J. D. (1996). Who shall succeed? How CEO/board preferences and power affect the choice of new CEOs. *Academy of Management Journal, 39,* 64–90.

Zajonc, R. B. (1965). Social facilitation. *Science, 149,* 269–274.

Zajonc, R. B. (1980). Compresence. In P. B. Paulus (Ed.), *Psychology of group influence* (pp. 35–60). Hillsdale, NJ: Erlbaum.

Zajonc, R. B., Heingartner, A., & Herman, E. M. (1969). Social enhancement and impairment of performance in the cockroach. *Journal of Personality and Social Psychology, 13,* 83–92.

Zald, M., & Ash, R. (1966). Social movement organizations: Growth, decay, and change. *Social Forces, 44,* 327–341.

Zamarripa, P. O., & Krueger, D. L. (1983). Implicit contracts regulating small group leadership. *Small Group Behavior, 14,* 187–210.

Zander, A. (1971/1996). *Motives and goals in groups.* New Brunswick, NJ: Transaction Publishers.

Zander, A. (1977). *Groups at work.* San Francisco: Jossey-Bass.

Zander, A. (1979). The psychology of group processes. *Annual Review of Psychology, 30,* 417–451.

Zander, A. (1982). *Making groups effective.* San Francisco: Jossey-Bass.

Zander, A. (1985). *The purposes of groups and organizations.* San Francisco: Jossey-Bass.

Zander, A., Cohen, A. R., & Stotland, E. (1959). Power and relations among the professions. In D. Cartwright (Ed.), *Studies in social power.* Ann Arbor, MI: Institute for Social Research.

Zander, A., & Medow, H. (1963). Individual and group levels of aspiration. *Human Relations, 16,* 89–105.

Zander, A., & Medow, H. (1965). Strength of group and desire for attainable group aspirations. *Journal of Personality, 33,* 122–139.

Zander, A., Medow, H., & Efron, R. (1965). Observers' expectations as determinants of group aspirations. *Human Relations, 18,* 273–287.

Zander, A., Stotland, E., & Wolfe, D. (1960). Unity of group, identification with group, and self-esteem of members. *Journal of Personality, 28,* 463–478.

Zelditch, M., Jr., & Walker, H. A. (1984). Legitimacy and the stability of authority. *Advances in Group Processes, 1,* 1–25.

Ziller, R. C. (1964). Individuation and socialization: A theory of assimilation in large organizations. *Human Relations, 17,* 341–360.

Zillmann, D. (1983). Arousal and aggression. In R. G. Geen & E. I. Donnerstein (Eds.), *Aggression: Theoretical and empirical reviews* (Vol. 1). New York: Academic Press.

Zillmann, D., Bryant, J., Cantor, J. R., & Day, K. D. (1975). Irrelevance of mitigating circumstances in retaliatory behavior at high levels of excitation. *Journal of Research in Personality, 9,* 282–293.

Zimbardo, P. G. (1969). The human choice: Individuation, reason, and order versus deindividuation, impulse, and chaos. In W. J. Arnold & D. Levine (Eds.), *Nebraska Symposium on Motivation* (Vol. 17, pp. 237–307). Lincoln: University of Nebraska Press.

Zimbardo, P. G. (1975). Transforming experimental research into advocacy for social change. In M. Deutsch & H. A. Hornstein (Eds.), *Applying social psychology* (pp. 33–66). Hillsdale, NJ: Erlbaum.

Zimbardo, P. G. (1977a). *Psychology and life.* Glenview, IL: Scott, Foresman.

Zimbardo, P. G. (1977b). *Shyness: What it is and what to do about it.* New York: Jones.

Zuber, J. A., Crott, H. W., & Werner, J. (1992). Choice shift and group polarization: An analysis of the status of arguments and social decision schemes. *Journal of Personality and Social Psychology, 62,* 50–61.

Zurcher, L. A., Jr. (1969). Stages of development in poverty program neighborhood action committees. *Journal of Applied Behavioral Science, 15,* 223–258.

Name Index

Abakoumkin, G., 62, 284, 290
Abbott, A. S., 317
Abel, T., 350
Abrams, D., 77–78, 86, 456
Adams, J., 352, 370
Adams, J. S., 248
Adelman, L., 399
Aditya, R. N., 348
Adler, P., 39, 65, 137, 144, 152
Adler, P. A., 39, 65, 137, 144, 152
Affleck, G., 96
Agatstein, F., 17
Aiello, J. R., 275–276, 419
Aiken, C., 280
Aiken, M., 139
Ainsworth, M. D. S., 69
Akande, A., 130
Akkermans, W., 37, 136
Albert, K. P., 430
Albright, L., 17, 49, 91
Aldag, R. J., 324, 331
Alexander, D., 417
Alexander, K. R., 413
Alicke, M. D., 238
Allen, H., 217
Allen, K. M., 274
Allen, V. L., 130, 180–181, 191–193
Alliger, G. M., 351, 353
Allison, S. T., 84, 248, 249, 391
Allport, F. H., 14, 17–18, 23, 69, 269–270
Allport, G. W., 77, 382, 386, 392, 405, 450
Altemeyer, B., 183
Altman, I., 50, 411, 419, 428–436, 438, 487
Alvares, K. M., 358
Alvaro, E. M., 185, 191

Amir, Y., 400
Anastasio, P. A., 401
Ancona, D. G., 239
Andersen, S. M., 488
Anderson, C. A., 42, 412
Anderson, C. M., 62
Anderson, L. R., 284
Andow, K., 272
Andreoli, V. A., 387, 399
Andrews, P. H., 197
Annis, A. B., 424
Ansari, M. A., 220
Anthony, T., 154, 195, 331
Appelbaum, R. P., 452
Applebaum, E., 164, 167
Appleyard, D., 413
Arcus, D. M., 93
Ardry, R., 431
Argote, L., 288, 309
Argyle, M., 421
Arizmendi, T. G., 123
Arkes, H. R., 320
Arkin, R. M., 103, 105
Arnold, D. W., 417
Aron, A., 398
Aronoff, J. R., 405
Aronson, E., 111–112, 192, 400
Arrow, H., 11, 160, 288
Asch, S. E., 175–184, 188, 202, 329
Aschenbrenner, K. M., 394
Asendorpf, J. B., 93
Ash, R., 452
Ashbrook, R. M., 105
Ashour, A. S., 359
Askling, L. R., 311
Asmus, C., 411
Aspinwall, L. G., 98
Atkin, R. S., 201

Atlas, J., 111
Atoum, A. O., 274, 275
Atthowe, J. M., Jr., 320
August, R. A., 417
Averill, J. R., 256
Avolio, B. J., 344, 369
Axelrod, R., 69, 261, 262
Axsom, D., 111, 402
Ayestaran, S., 130
Ayman, R., 368
Azuma, H., 72

Bach, G. R., 486
Bacharach, S. B., 139
Bachman, B. A., 401
Back, K. W., 11, 103, 149, 151, 153, 161, 193, 239, 451, 477, 491
Baer, R., 430
Baetz, M. L., 368
Baker, N. J., 244
Baker, S. M., 192
Baldes, J. J., 292
Bales, R. F., 8, 15, 19, 32–35, 51, 54, 66, 125–126, 128, 132, 152, 158, 160, 169, 236, 311, 346, 351, 427
Balkwell, J. W., 135
Ball, R. L., 263
Ball, S. J., 65
Bandura, A., 395, 476, 484
Banks, C., 222
Bannister, B. D., 359
Bar-Tal, D., 395
Barájas, L., 73–75
Barash, D. P., 68
Barefoot, J. C., 230
Bargal, D., 11, 24
Bargh, J. A., 77

Barker, M., 350
Barker, R. A., 343
Barker, R. G., 416
Barnard, C. I., 19, 31
Barnes, B. D., 369
Baron, R. A., 263, 411, 412
Baron, R. S., 183–184, 226, 272, 273, 275, 323
Barr, J. E., 490
Barraclough, R., 219
Barrera, M., Jr., 100–101
Barrett, D., 141
Barrick, M. R., 351
Barrow, J. C., 344
Barsaloux, J., 295, 297
Barsky, S. F., 432
Bartels, B. D., 489
Bartholomew, R. E., 451
Bartis, S., 274
Bartlett, F. C., 308
Bartol, K. M., 349
Barton, A. H., 31
Barton, W. H., 459
Basow, S. A., 95
Bass, B. M., 168, 340–344, 349, 350, 367–369, 371
Bassett, R. L., 430
Batchelor, J. P., 425
Bates, B., 490
Batson, C. D., 111
Baum, A., 411, 415, 423, 430–431, 454
Baum, C. S., 454
Baumeister, R. F., 59–63, 71, 84, 85, 95, 252, 274, 275, 432
Baumrind, D., 213
Bavelas, A., 141
Bazerman, M. H., 259
Bazzini, D. G., 62
Beaman, A. L., 224, 460–461, 463
Beck, E. M., 448
Becker, S. W., 427
Bedeian, A. G., 130
Bedell, J., 229
Bednar, R. L., 478, 487, 489–491
Beggan, J. K., 249
Belk, S. S., 219, 220
Bell, L. M., 394
Bell, P. A., 249, 411, 412
Bellack, A., 477
Bellinger, K. D., 308–309
Bem, D. J., 320, 322, 484–485
Bem, S. L., 182–183
Benford, R. D., 104

Benne, K. D., 8, 125–128, 477
Bennett, H. S., 39
Bennis, W., 162, 278, 301, 415
Bennis, W. G., 156–157, 341
Benoist, F., 379
Bergan, T., 435
Berger, J., 49–50, 52, 53, 133–135, 144
Berger, R., 82
Berger, R. E., 274
Berger, S. M., 276
Berkerle, C. A., 451
Berkowitz, L., 183, 194, 343, 445–446, 462
Berkowitz, N. H., 394
Berman, J., 422
Berman, J. J., 490
Bernard, H. S., 494
Berndt, T. J., 65
Bernthal, P. R., 331, 379
Berry, D. S., 133
Berry, P. C., 295
Best, D. L., 354
Betancourt, H., 263
Bettencourt, B. A., 401
Beutler, L. E., 123
Bickman, L., 445–446
Biddle, B. J., 124
Biederman, P. W., 162, 278, 301, 415
Bierbrauer, G., 178
Biernat, M., 78
Billig, M. G., 394
Binning, J. F., 353
Birch, L. L., 65
Birrell, P., 392
Bishop, G. D., 323
Björkqvist, K., 247
Black, T. E., 229
Blackmer, D. R., 106, 136
Blackstone, T., 185
Blaine, B., 79, 81, 83
Blair, I., 263
Blake, R. R., 359–360, 371, 378–379
Blanchard, F. A., 399
Blanchard, K. H., 359, 361–362, 371
Blaney, N., 400
Blascovich, J., 50, 257, 274, 324, 353
Blass, T., 213, 221, 233
Blatt, R., 164, 167
Blau, P. M., 47

Bledsoe, K. L., 73–75
Blegen, M. A., 216, 255
Blickensderfer, E., 165
Bliese, J. R., 111
Bloch, S., 482, 488
Block, C. H., 295
Block, C. J., 354
Blommel, J. M., 271
Bloomfield, J., 327
Blumberg, H. H., 20, 24
Blumer, H., 443–446, 454
Blumstein, P., 219, 221
Boardman, S. K., 236, 407
Bodenhausen, G. V., 398
Bogardus, E. S., 20
Bohrnstedt, G. W., 113
Bois, J. L., 97–98
Boivin, M., 139
Bollen, K. A., 150, 153
Bommer, W. H., 346
Bond, C. F., 272, 274, 275
Bond, M. H., 73, 91, 279, 350
Bond, R., 180–181, 204
Bone, E., 60
Bonevento, M., 188
Boniecki, K. A., 432
Bonner, H., 7
Bonney, M. E., 107
Bonoma, T. V., 244
Bons, P. M., 357, 358
Bonta, B. D., 247
Boone, M., 490
Booth, A., 94, 95
Borah, L. A., Jr., 255
Borden, R., 152
Borgatta, E. F., 7, 19, 158, 351
Bormann, E. G., 263
Bornstein, G., 259, 379, 381
Bornstein, R. F., 103, 183, 193
Bosley, P. J., 411
Boston, M. B., 354
Bouchard, T. J., 295, 297
Bourgeois, M. J., 188
Boutillier, R. G., 352–353
Bowers, C., 165
Bowers, C. A., 161, 278
Bowers, D. G., 168, 345, 359
Bowlby, J., 69
Boyle, M. M., 308
Bracken, B. A., 79
Braden, M., 111
Bradley, P. H., 142, 217
Bradshaw, S. D., 279, 308
Brady, J. J., Jr., 276

Bramel, D., 31
Brandes, B., 259
Brandon, A. C., 195
Brannick, M. T., 301
Branscombe, N. R., 394
Brauer, M., 324
Braun, C. C., 278
Braun, J. C., 238
Brawley, L. R., 83, 150, 151, 153
Bray, R. M., 186, 198, 201
Brazil, D., 379, 381
Brechner, K. C., 249
Breed, G. R., 250–251
Brehm, J. W., 227, 251
Brehm, S. S., 227, 251
Breiger, R. L., 35
Brenner, M., 283
Brenner, O. C., 246
Brewer, M. B., 70, 77, 82, 84, 249, 259, 378, 387, 394, 396, 400, 401, 407
Brickner, M. A., 17, 152, 291
Brief, A. P., 129–130, 213
Brief, D. E., 212, 213, 233
Brinkman, H., 421
Brinthaupt, T. M., 107
Brito, V. C. A., 39
Broadnax S., 79, 81
Brocato, R. M., 271
Brockner, J., 252, 314
Brody, R. A., 382
Bromley, D. G., 455
Brooks, D. K., 477
Brooks, G. R., 487
Brossart, D. F., 488
Brousseau, K. R., 311
Brower, A. M., 336
Brown, B. B., 65, 79, 247, 428, 433–434
Brown, C. E., 133
Brown, D. J., 242
Brown, R., 6, 24, 70, 394, 397
Brown, R. A., 152
Brown, R. C., 255
Brown, R. J., 387, 401, 407
Brown, R. W., 444–445, 448
Brown, S. M., 369
Brown, S. P., 130
Brown, V., 297
Brown, Y., 191
Browning, L., 142
Brunsman, B., 183–184
Brush, C. A., 457, 459
Bruun, S. E., 290, 292

Bryant, J., 462
Bryant, W. H., 100
Buckley, W., 208
Budescu, D., 379
Budman, S. H., 152, 490
Buehler, R., 192
Bufanio, K. A., 293, 327
Buhrmester, D., 60, 61
Bukowski, W. M., 136
Bullinger, M., 413
Bulman, R. J., 482
Bunker, B. B., 219, 220
Burger, J. M., 103, 105, 219, 220, 228
Burgoon, J. K., 421
Burke, M. J., 358, 478
Burke, P. J., 126, 352
Burlingame, G. M., 489–490, 494
Burney, C., 60
Burns, J. M., 340, 368
Burns, M. O., 482
Burnstein, E., 241, 311, 323–324
Burt, M. R., 220, 227, 229
Burwitz, L., 270
Busby, P. L., 411
Busceme, S., 185
Bushman, B. J., 42, 273, 275, 412
Buss, A. H., 62, 94
Buss, D. M., 50, 68, 219
Butler, D., 354
Butler, T., 482, 488, 489
Buttram, R. T., 213
Buunk, B. P., 98, 483
Bylsma, W. H., 98
Byme, J. A., 236, 265
Byrne, D., 92, 105, 426

Caballero, R. B., 213
Cacioppo, J. T., 101, 251, 273, 275
Cahill, S., 39
Caldwell, D. F., 219, 220, 228, 239
Calesnick, L. E., 415
Callan, V. J., 350
Callaway, M. R., 330
Callero, P. L., 124
Camacho, L. M., 291, 296
Cameron, W. B., 452
Campbell, D. T., 16–17, 123, 318, 378
Campbell, J., 99–100, 295
Campbell, J. D., 184
Campbell, R. J., 293

Campos, F. T., 246
Canary, D. J., 220
Canetti, E., 445, 448
Canfield, R. W., 107–108
Cannavale, F. J., 459, 461
Cannella, A. A., 342
Cannon-Bowers, J. A., 165, 279
Canon, L. K, 413
Cantor, J. R., 462
Cantor, N., 62
Cantril, H., 31, 451
Caplan, N., 456
Caplan, R. D., 100
Caporael, L. R., 70, 396
Cappella, J. N., 133
Carew, D. K., 361
Carli, L. C., 276
Carli, L. L., 182, 247, 276
Carlopio, J. R., 411
Carlyle, T., 347–348
Carment, D. W., 270
Carneiro, R. L., 382
Carnevale, P. J., 253, 262
Carpenter, C. R., 429
Carrell, M. R., 248
Carrere, S., 435
Carroll, J. S., 259
Carroll, J. W., 246
Carroll, S. J., 369
Carron, A. V., 149–151, 153, 294, 432
Carson, R. C., 214
Carter, L. F., 239
Cartwright, D., 5, 6, 9, 11–12, 20, 24, 29, 138, 208, 231, 328–329, 345, 486
Carvalho, E. R., 39
Carver, C. S., 275, 463
Carver, M. D., 61
Cascio, W. F., 315
Cashman, J., 367
Castell, P. J., 230
Castore, C. H., 313
Catalano, R., 100
Cattell, R. B., 20
Cavalli, L., 217
Cavanaugh, P. H., 412
Ceccarelli, R., 391
Ceplenski, P., 488
Chaiken, S., 183, 192
Chamberlain, A. S., 434
Chambliss, W. J., 452
Chanag, S., 332
Chang, S., 330

Chapman, A. J., 454
Chapman, G. C., 213
Chapple, E. D., 434
Charney, C., 315
Chase, J., 379
Chassin, L., 80–81
Cheavens, J., 98, 483
Cheek, J. M., 74, 94
Chein, I., 384
Chelladurai, P., 149
Chemers, M. M., 50, 357–359, 368, 419, 431
Chen, M. D., 94
Chen, S., 183, 192
Chen, Z., 331
Cheng, J. L., 220
Cheng, S., 450
Chernicky, P., 222, 224
Chertkoff, J. M., 449
Cherulnik, P., 433
Cheyne, J. A., 430
Chiba, S., 238
Childers, T. L., 346
Chiles, C., 191
Chilstrom, J. T., Jr., 186
Chiu, C., 72, 388
Chiu, J. S. L., 315
Choi, S., 73–75
Christensen, A., 490
Christensen, C., 307, 317
Christensen, P. N., 484
Chu, L., 91
Church, M., 62
Churchman, A. S., 411
Cialdini, R. B., 121, 152, 186–187, 223–224, 233
Cianni, M., 349
Cini, M. A., 107, 417–418
Clark, G., 448
Clark, K. B., 224
Clark, N. K., 307, 308
Clark, R. D., III, 178, 185, 186, 230–231, 323
Clark, S., 378
Clearwater, Y. A., 435
Cleary, S. D., 101
Clement, R. W., 191
Clifton, T. C., 369
Clore, G. L., 105
Coch, L., 314–315
Cody, M. J., 220
Coe, C., 107–108
Cogliser, C. C., 368
Cohen, A. R., 230

Cohen, B. P., 133, 135
Cohen, D. J., 295
Cohen, E. G., 135
Cohen, J. L., 274
Cohen, M. D., 255
Cohen, S., 50, 101, 411, 413, 423
Cohen, S. P., 54
Coie, J. D., 37, 136, 139
Cole, C. M., 224
Colligan, M. J., 451, 452
Collings, T. J., 294
Collins, B. E., 212, 213, 233, 318, 343
Collins, R. L., 98
Colman, A. M., 466
Colomy, P., 128
Conaty, J. C., 132
Condelli, L., 228–229
Condor, S., 397
Conger, J. A., 217
Connelly, M. S., 369
Conner, T. L., 133
Connolly, T., 299
Connors, M. M., 418, 435
Consentino, J., 219, 229
Constantian, C. A., 92
Contry, J. C., 449
Cook, K., 134
Cook, M., 156
Cook, M. S., 243
Cook, S. W., 398–400
Cooley, C. H., 12, 64–65, 484
Cooley, E., 167
Coon, C. S., 68
Cooper, C. L., 100
Cooper, E., 350
Cooper, H. M., 182
Cooper, V. W., 355
Cooper, W. H., 298
Cooper-Shaw, L., 150
Copper, C., 162–163
Corazzini, J. G., 486–487
Corey, G., 487
Corey, M., 487
Cornell, S. D., 142
Corsaro, W. A., 457
Coser, L. A., 157, 387–388
Costanzo, P. R., 183
Cota, A. A., 151
Cotton, J. L., 168, 243
Cottrell, L. S., Jr., 7
Cottrell, N. B., 273, 274, 299
Couch, A. S., 239, 351
Coules, J., 263

Courneya, K. S., 432
Courtright, J. A., 162, 330–331
Cousins, S. D., 72
Cowan, G., 219, 220
Cox, C., 379, 381
Cox, T. H., 279
Coyne, J. C., 100
Crago, M., 123
Crandall, C. S., 123, 457
Crano, W. D., 184–185, 191
Cratty, B. J., 294
Crawford, A. C., 105
Crawford, A. M., 150, 151
Crawley, J., 265
Cribbin, J. J., 342
Crichlow, S., 330
Crisson, J. E., 274
Croak, M. R., 401
Crocker, J., 79–83, 349
Crocker, O. L., 315
Cronshaw, S. F., 353
Crosbie, P. V., 135
Crosby, F., 456
Cross, S. E., 75, 95
Crott, H. W., 324
Crouch, E., 482
Crouch, E. C., 482, 488
Crow, W. J., 405
Crutchfield, R. S., 180, 183
Csoka, L. S., 358
Cummings, L. L., 246
Cunningham, J. D., 252
Curphy, G. J., 104, 343, 351, 371
Curran, J. P., 477
Currey, K. P., 379, 381
Curry, T. J., 105
Cutrona, C. E., 61
Cybriwsky, R., 429, 458

D'Andrea Tyson, L., 168
Dabbs, J. M., Jr., 297
Dahl, K., 379, 381
Dahl, K. R., 379
Dahlin, B., 86
Dahlke, A. E., 449
Dahrendorf, R., 156
Dailey, J. C., 297
Dakof, G. A., 98
Dale, R., 132
Dalton, B., 379
Damhorst, M. L., 133
Dane, F. C., 200
Dansereau, F., 367–368
Dardis, G. J., 379

Darley, J., 95, 222, 225, 411
Dashiell, J. F., 269
David, J. P., 238
Davidson-Podgorny, G., 401
Davies, D., 158
Davies, M. F., 20, 24
Davis, G. E., 415, 431
Davis, J. H., 135, 178, 187, 198, 201, 204, 284, 285, 292, 312, 313, 324, 336
Davis, J. R., 152
Davis, K. E., 105
Davis, M., 152
Davis, M. H., 62
Davis, W. L., 247
Davis-Stitt, C., 392
Davitz, J., 283
Dawes, R., 35, 250
Day, D. V., 367
Day, K. D., 462
Day, M., 474
Day, R. R., 358, 478
De Bruin, E. M. N., 247
De Dreu, C. K. W., 191
De Meuse, K. P., 165, 167
De Vader, C. L., 351, 353
De Vries, N. K., 191
Dean, J., 421
Dean, L. M., 421
Deaux, K., 70, 77–78, 85–86
Deci, E. L., 227
DeCotiis, T. A., 344
Defoe, D., 60
Degoey, P., 216
DeLamater, J. A., 7
Delbecq, A. L., 297–298
Dembo, T., 46, 292
Demby, A., 152, 490
Deming, W. E., 167, 315
DeNeve, K. M., 412
Dennis, A. R., 299
Denvir, B., 107
DePaulo, B. M., 100, 488
Deseran, F. A., 261
Deutsch, M., 17, 157, 190, 192, 229, 242, 245–248, 254–255, 259, 261, 264, 265, 383
Devine, D. J., 163
Devine, P. G., 402–403
DeVries, H., 214
Dewey, J., 310
Di Salvo, V. S., 318–319
Di Vesta, F. J., 184
Diamond, S. G., 426

Diamond, W. D., 383
Dickson, M. W., 166, 170
Dickson, W. J., 30, 164, 268
Diehl, M., 284, 290, 295–296
Diener, E., 460–464
Dienesch, R. M., 367
Dies, R. R., 152, 484, 487
Dietrich, D., 297
Digman, J. M., 91, 351
DiLalla, D. L., 75–76
Dillard, J. P., 219, 224
Dion, K. L., 9, 149–151, 154, 167, 388
Dipboye, R. L., 465
DiTomaso, N., 350
DiTommaso, E., 61
Ditrichs, R., 459
Dittrich, J. E., 248
Dixon, K. N., 484, 491
Dobbins, G. H., 370
Dobson, D. M., 259, 261
Dodd, D. K., 458
Dodge, K. A., 136, 139, 354
Doherty, W. J., 491
Doise, W., 322
Dollinger, S. J., 75–76
Doms, M., 186
Donaldson, S., 297
Donath, C. H., 276
Donnelly, P., 149
Donnerstein, E., 459
Donnerstein, M., 459
Doob, L., 448
Dooley, D., 100
Doosje, B., 83, 390, 394
Doreian, P., 136
Dovidio, J. F., 133, 393, 401
Downey, G., 100
Downing, L. L., 459
Downs, D. L., 63
Drauden, G., 295, 297
Drenan, S., 379, 383
Drigotas, S. M., 379, 381
Drinkard, J., 219, 220
Driskell, J., 353
Driskell, J. E., 42, 53, 134, 154, 331, 350
Druckman, D., 257
Dryer, D. C., 105
Dubé, L., 447
Dubé-Simard, L., 456
Dubinsky, A. J., 346
Dubro, A. F., 247
DuCette, J., 482

Duchon, D., 367
Duckitt, J., 394
Dudley, B. S., 276
Dukerich, J. M., 342
Duncan, B. L., 392
Dunnette, M. D., 295
Dunning, E. G., 448, 457
Duran, R. L., 152
Durand, D. E., 433
Durkheim, É., 12–13
Duval, S., 275
Dweck, C. S., 72
Dyce, J., 105
Dyer, J. L., 165
Dzindolet, M. T., 291, 297

Eagly, A. H., 182, 280, 349, 354–355, 369, 370
Earley, P. C., 324
Eckland, B. K., 113
Eden, D., 279, 370
Eder, D., 457
Edman, I., 67
Edney, J. J., 249, 420, 430, 433
Edwards, D. J. A., 421
Efran, M. G., 430
Efron, R., 293
Egido, C., 17
Ehrlich, S. B., 342
Eisenbach, R. J., 346
Eisenberg, E. M., 142
Eliot, M., 156
Ellemers, N., 83, 390, 394
Ellertson, N., 17, 153, 164
Elliot, A. J., 403
Elliott, G. C., 248
Elliott, J. D., 213
Elliott, R., 492
Elliott, T. R., 493
Ellis, D. G., 310, 336
Ellyson, S. L., 133
Elms, A. C., 210, 213
Ely, P. G., 70
Emerson, R. M., 105, 194, 215
Endicott, J., 199
Engels, F., 378
English, H. B., 270
Ennis, J. G., 35–36
Erez, M., 229, 294
Erickson, G. A., 79
Ervin, C. F., 105
Esposito, J. L., 451
Esser, A. H., 434
Esser, J. K., 330

Ethier, K. A., 70
Etzioni, A., 233, 405
Euwema, M. C., 261
Evans, C. R., 149, 151, 154
Evans, G., 423
Evans, G. W., 50, 411, 413, 415,
   419, 420, 422, 435
Evans, M., 392
Evans, N. J., 153
Ewens, W., 227
Eysenck, H., 91

Fairey, P. J., 184
Fairhurst, G. T., 220
Faith, M., 401
Falbe, C. M., 220, 227
Falbo, T., 218–220, 228
Fall, R., 276
Falloon, I. R. H., 484
Fanon, F., 224
Farrell, G. M., 8, 128
Farrell, M. P., 3, 87
Farris, K. R., 73–75
Faucheux, C., 184
Faupel, M., 133
Fazio, R. H., 190
Feld, P., 330, 332
Feldstein, M., 490
Fennell, M. L., 349
Fenzel, L. M., 354
Ference, R., 330
Ferencik, B. M., 488
Ferguson, T. J., 263, 462
Ferraris, J., 35
Ferris, F., 402
Ferris, G. R., 276
Festinger, L., 39, 46, 81, 95, 103,
   105, 111, 117, 149, 151, 153,
   193, 194, 292, 457
Fiedler, F. E., 348, 355–359, 368,
   371, 374
Field, N., 353
Field, R. H. G., 367
Fielding, K. S., 353
Filkins, J., 191, 312
Finch, J. F, 100, 242, 246
Finch, M. L., 459
Fine, G. A., 39, 150, 152
Fink, C. F., 236, 284
Finke, R., 66
Finn, J. D., 276
Firestone, I. J., 415, 421
Fischer, G. W., 389–390
Fisek, M. H., 132, 133

Fishbaugh, L., 182
Fisher, B. A., 157
Fisher, C. D., 130
Fisher, G. A., 113
Fisher, J. D., 411, 426
Fisher, M., 310, 336
Fisher, R., 257–259, 265
Fisher, R. J., 403
Fiske, S. T., 49, 230, 280, 308,
   319
Fitzpatrick, M. A., 219
Flacks, R., 43
Flores, P. J., 481, 494
Flowers, J., 476
Flowers, M. L., 331
Flynn, K., 465
Foa, E. B., 47
Foa, U. G., 47, 364
Foddy, M., 134
Fodor, E. M., 231
Folger, R., 314, 387, 399
Folk, G. E., Jr., 412
Fontaine, G., 228
Ford, C. E., 83, 152
Ford, R. S., 216, 255
Forsyth, D. R., 8, 66, 79, 80–83,
   213, 222, 250, 256, 354–355,
   457, 476, 493
Fortune, W. H., 199, 200, 202,
   204
Foschi, M., 135, 218
Foss, C., 433–434
Foss, R. D., 201
Foster-Fishman, P. G., 317
Foti, R. J., 351, 353–354
Foushee, H. C., 320
Fowlkes, J. E., 165, 279
Fox, D., 283
Fox, S., 91
Fox-Cardamone, L., 70
Foy, E., 449
Fraas, L. A., 352
Frable, D. E. S., 483
Frager, R., 181
Frank, F., 284
Frank, J. D., 486
Franke, R. H., 31
Franken, R. E., 242
Franz, T. M., 317
Fraser, N. M., 238
Fraser, S. C., 224, 460–461
Fraser, S. L., 353
Fredrickson, J. W., 238
Freedman, J. L., 224, 423, 454

Freedman, R. D., 314
Freeman, K. A., 276
Freeman, L. C., 141, 142
Freeman, S., 152
Freeze, L., 135
French, J. R. P., Jr., 162, 214–218,
   228, 232, 236, 314–315
Freud, S., 59, 78, 84, 473
Friedland, N., 227
Friedman, S., 393
Friedman, S. D., 343
Friend, R., 31
Froman, L. A., Jr., 255
Fromkin, H. L., 84
Fromm, E., 465
Frost, A. G., 48
Fry, D. P., 247
Fry, W. R., 314
Fuhriman, A., 482, 488–490, 494
Fujii, D. S., 353
Fujishin, R., 371
Fukushima, O., 238
Fulero, S., 392
Fuller, S. R., 324, 331
Fung, A. S. M., 451
Funk, W. H., 295
Futoran, G. C., 297
Futrell, D., 165, 167

Gabarro, J. J., 158
Gaelick, L., 398
Gaertner, L., 379
Gaertner, S. L., 393, 401
Gaes, G. G., 255
Gaines, S. O., Jr., 73–75, 378
Galassi, J. P., 477
Galassi, M. D., 477
Galegher, J., 17
Galen, M., 135
Galinsky, M. J., 159
Galley, D. J., 103
Gallo, P. S., Jr., 255
Gallois, C., 350
Gallup, G. H., 354
Gallupe, R. B., 298
Gamson, W. A., 224, 342, 452
Gange, J. J., 272
Gannon, T. M., 382
Garcia-Falconi, R., 219, 220
Garcia, J. E., 358
Garcia, L. T., 31
Garcia, R., 276
García, B. F., 73–75
Gardner, J. W., 341

Gardner, W., 70, 77
Garfinkel, P. E., 123
Garner, D. M., 123
Garner, K., 246
Garnier, C., 35
Gastorf, J. W., 275
Gatchel, R. J., 415
Gauvin, S., 298–299
Gavin, M. G., 220
Gazda, G. M., 20, 477
Geen, R. G., 46, 91, 272–276
Geis, F. L., 350, 354
Geis, R. G., 354
Gelgand, M. J., 73–75
Geller, D., 221
Gemmill, G., 343
Gencturk, E., 346
Genevie, L. E., 450
Gerard, H. B., 111, 190, 192, 195, 397
Gerber, G. L., 134
Gergen, K. J., 459
Gergen, M., 230
Gergen, M. M., 459
Gerhardt, G., 465
Gerrard, M., 483
Gersick, C. J. G., 160
Gerstner, C. R., 367
Gessner, T. L., 369
Giammarino, M., 139
Giannantonio, C. M., 104, 369
Gibb, C. A., 349
Gibb, J. R., 490
Gibbons, F. X., 463, 483
Gibson, C. R., 219
Giesen, M., 425
Gifford, R., 214
Gigone, D., 316
Gilbert, D. T., 411
Gilbert, J. A., 351
Gilbert, S. J., 223
Gilchrist, J. C., 107
Giles, H., 388
Gillan, P. G., 297
Gillespie, D. L., 132
Gilliland, S. W., 314
Gillmore, M. R., 39
Gilmore, R., 379, 383
Gilmore, R., 383
Gilovich, T., 273, 274
Gilroy, F. D., 354
Ginnett, R. C., 320
Ginsburg, G. P., 50, 257, 324
Giola, D. A., 83

Gist, M. E., 277
Gitelson, R., 130
Giuliano, T., 308
Giuliano, T. A., 98
Gladstein, D. L., 277
Glaessner-Bayerl, B., 392
Glaser, B. G., 31
Glaser, D., 430
Glaser, K. H., 158
Glass, D. C., 273, 274, 413
Glasser, C., 344, 346, 352, 371
Glasser, P., 159
Gleitman, H., 177
Gliner, M. D., 324
Glor, J. E., 238
Godfrey, D. K., 133
Goethals, G. R., 66, 84, 95, 193, 323–324, 425
Goetsch, G. G., 142
Goffman, E., 273
Goggin, W. C., 294
Gold, M., 11, 24, 113, 490
Goldberg, L., 382
Goldberg, L. R., 91
Goldheim, L., 344
Goldman, H. J., 246
Goldman, M., 352, 388
Goldstein, A. P., 486
Goltz, S. M., 104
Gomes, M., 219
Gomez, M. N. G., 213
Goodacre, D. M., 158
Goodman, A., 490
Goodman, G., 100, 480–481, 494–495
Goodman, P., 475
Goodman, P. S., 277, 309
Goodstadt, B. E., 229
Goodwin, S. A., 49, 308
Goore, N., 273, 274
Gordon, J., 164
Gordon, L. R., 331
Gordon, W., 297
Goto, S. G., 77
Gottlieb, A., 222
Gould, S. J., 396
Goulding, M. M., 475
Goulding, R. L., 475
Graeff, C. L., 361
Graen, G., 129, 344
Graen, G. B., 358, 367–368
Graetz, K. A., 379, 381
Grandmaison, P. S., 276
Granrose, C. S., 73–75

Grant, L., 39
Grant, P. R., 394
Graves, J., 287
Graves, L. M., 104
Graziano, W. G., 238, 242, 246
Green, L. R., 189
Green, M. L., 78
Green, S. G., 220, 367
Greenberg, C. I., 415, 417
Greenberg, J., 314
Greene, T. C., 411
Greene, T. E., 411
Greenwald, A. G., 77
Greer, D. L., 432
Gregory, D., 17, 153, 164
Greve, D. W., 475
Griffeth, R. W., 150
Griffin, D., 192
Griffin, G. W., 330
Griffith, W. I., 247
Griffitt, W., 105, 412
Grimes, A. J., 344
Groff, B. D., 275, 424
Grofman, B., 141
Groner, N., 424
Groom, R. W., 412
Gross, E., 130
Gross, S. R., 191
Grundmann, M. J., 420, 430
Gruner, L., 154, 160, 161, 486
Gualtieri, J., 161
Guerin, B., 272, 274, 275
Guerra, P., 401
Guest, T. A., 459, 461
Guetzkow, H., 238, 318
Guimond, A., 456
Guinan, P. J., 219, 220
Gulley, H. E., 318
Gully, S. M., 163
Gump, B. G., 96
Gump, P. V., 228, 417
Gunderson, E. K. E., 435
Gunn, L. K., 159
Gunn, S. P., 222, 224
Gurr, T. R., 378
Gustafson, D. H., 298
Gutek, B. A., 370
Guthman, E., 329
Guzzo, R. A., 151, 166, 170, 277, 293, 315
Gyr, J., 238

Haas, D. F., 261
Haas, S., 430

Haber, G. M., 428
Hackman, J. R., 15, 48, 161, 165, 277, 281, 300, 310, 311
Haefner, D., 239
Haga, W., 367
Hage, J., 139
Hains, S. C., 150
Hair, E. C., 238, 242, 246
Hall, C. L., 133
Hall, E. T., 419–421
Hall, R. J., 368
Hallinan, M. T., 138
Halpern, D., 411
Halpin, A. W., 345
Hamaguchi, E., 71
Hamblin, R. L., 343
Hamilton, D. L., 17, 393
Hamilton, V. L., 221, 226, 231, 232
Hamilton, W. D., 68, 69, 261
Hamner, W. C., 246
Hampton, K. L., 276
Hand, H. H., 150
Haney, C., 222
Hanks, M., 113
Hanna, C., 316
Hans, V. P., 202
Hansen, W. B., 433
Hanson, L., 417
Harary, F., 138
Hardie, E. A., 150
Hardin, G., 249
Harding, J., 384
Hardy, C., 290
Hardyck, J. A., 111
Hare, A. P., 6, 7, 19, 20, 24, 35, 39, 124, 154–155, 157–158, 161, 181, 236, 268, 427
Hare, M., 295
Hargrove, L., 219, 220
Harkins, S., 288–293
Harkins, S. G., 274
Harlow, A. F., 449
Harlow, H. F., 69
Harlow, M. K., 69
Harlow, R. E., 62
Harnett, D. L., 246
Harper, N. L., 311
Harpin, R. E., 431
Harring, K., 379
Harris, H. J., 196–197
Harris, J. R., 65
Harrison, A. A., 418, 435
Harrod, W. J., 134, 350

Hart, S. D., 218
Härtel, C. E. J., 320
Härtel, G. F., 320
Hartig, T., 411
Hartke, D. D., 358–359
Harton, H. C., 189
Hartry, A., 389
Harvey, O. J., 376–407
Harvill, R. L., 494
Haslam, A. S., 390
Haslam, S. A., 9, 81
Hass, M. A., 358–359
Hastie, R., 197–201, 204, 316
Hastorf, A. H., 31
Haupt, A. L., 64, 90
Hawkins, C., 134, 199
Hayashi, M., 290
Hayduk, L. A., 419, 421
Hays, R. B., 100, 359
Haythorn, W., 239
Haythorn, W. W., 435
Hazewinkel, A., 158
Healy, S., 92
Hearne, G., 426
Hefferline, R., 475
Heffron, M. H., 430
Heider, F., 105, 137–138, 144, 156, 239
Heifetz, R. A., 343
Heilman, M. E., 354
Heiman, R. J., 73, 85, 308
Heine, S. J., 83
Heiney, M. M., 355
Heingartner, A., 271–272
Heinicke, C. M., 158
Helgeson, V. S., 81, 96
Heller, J., 133
Heller, J. F., 424
Heller, K., 486
Heller, T., 352
Helm, B., 227
Helmreich, R., 39, 320, 343, 410, 418, 428, 435, 437, 438
Helms, J. E., 485
Heltman, K., 133
Hembroff, L. A., 135
Hemphill, J. K., 342–344
Henager, R. F., 245
Henchy, T., 273, 274
Henderson, M. C., 73–75
Hennrikus, D., 133
Henry, W. P., 91
Hensley, T. R., 330
Hepworth, J. T., 384

Herbert, T. B., 101
Herek, G., 330
Herman, E. M., 271–272
Hernandez-Sanchez, J. E., 219, 220
Herschlag, L. R., 276
Hersen, M., 477
Hersey, P., 359, 361–362, 371
Hertel, P. T., 308
Herzog, T. R., 411
Heshka, S., 421
Hewitt, J., 421
Hewstone, M., 397
Hicks, D., 73–75
Higbee, K. L., 229
Higginbotham, H. N., 476
Higgins, D. S., 219
Hight, T. L., 483
Hill, A. H., 449
Hill, C. A., 92
Hill, C. E., 485
Hill, C. T., 105
Hill, J., 392
Hill, T. E., 366–367
Hill, W. F., 154, 160, 486
Hills, H. I., 214
Hiltrop, J. M., 262
Hilty, J. A., 262
Hinkin, T. R., 219
Hinkle, S., 387, 390
Hinsz, V. B., 178, 293, 307, 320, 336
Hipel, K. W., 238
Hirokawa, R. Y., 307, 310, 311, 314
Hirt, E. R., 79
Hitch, G. J., 308
Hjelle, L. A., 229
Hoag, M. J., 490
Hochberger, J. M., 159
Hockenstein, P., 230
Hodson, G., 331
Hoey, S., 483
Hoffer, E., 217, 455
Hoffer, J. A., 160
Hoffman, L. R., 349
Hoffman, N., 354
Hoffman, S., 178
Hofstede, G., 72
Hogan, J., 104, 343, 351, 371
Hogan, R., 104, 343, 351, 371
Hogg, M. A., 9, 14, 17, 77, 81, 86, 149, 150, 152, 154, 161, 170, 353, 394

Holland, C. H., 212–213
Hollander, E. P., 168, 185–186, 193, 227, 233, 342, 344, 352
Hollander, M., 476
Hollingshead, A. B., 298, 311
Hollingworth, H. L., 446
Holmes, J. G., 246, 487
Holmes, P., 491
Holroyd, P., 482
Holsti, O. R., 382
Holt, R. W., 198, 201
Holtgraves, T., 220
Holton, B., 379
Holtzman, W. H., Jr., 219, 220
Holyfield, L., 150, 152
Holzworth, D. W., 150
Homans, G. C., 6, 7, 28, 47, 51, 152
Homma, M., 290
Hong, G., 379
Hong, G. K., 424
Hong, Y., 72
Hood, W. R., 376–407
Hooijberg, R., 350
Hook, L. H., 199, 427
Hoorens, V., 98
Hopkins, K., 94
Hoppe, M. J., 39
Hopper, C. H., 297
Horne, A. M., 487
Horner, C., 91
Horney, K., 91
Horowitz, L. M., 105
Horowitz, S. V., 236, 407
Horwitz, M., 379
Hosking, D., 359
Hottes, J., 247
Houlden, P., 262–263
Houle, C. O., 241
House, J. S., 94
House, R. J., 128, 348, 359, 367
House, R. L., 368
Houser, J. A., 142
Hovland, C., 384
Howard, J., 392
Howard, J. A., 219, 221
Howard, J. W., 392–393
Howard, M. L., 394
Howard, R. B., 419, 420
Howe, R. C., 324
Howells, L. T., 427
Hoyle, R. H., 150, 151, 153, 379, 381
Hrebec, D., 259

Hu, L., 191
Huang, J. Y., 200
Hui, C. H., 72
Hulbert, L. G., 262
Humphrey, B., 153
Humphreys, L., 31
Humphreys, P., 133
Hung-yu, L., 195
Hunt, E. B., 320
Hunt, J. G., 350, 360
Hunter, J. A., 394
Hunter, J. E., 351
Hurley, J. R., 482
Hutchinson, K. J., 81
Huth, P., 330
Hyde, M., 430
Hygge, S., 413
Hyman, H., 43
Hyman, H. M., 197

Iacobucci, D., 37
Iannaccone, L. R., 112
Ickes, W., 113, 133
Ilardi, B. C.
Ilgen, D. R., 238, 353
Ilieva, L. J., 106, 136
Indik, B. P., 153
Ingham, A. G., 287
Ingraham, L. J., 106, 136
Innes, J. M., 272, 275
Innes, J. M., 459, 463
Insel, P. M., 153
Insko, C. A., 18, 105, 288, 331, 379–381, 383, 396, 407
Instone, D., 219, 220, 352, 370
Isen, A. M., 401
Isenberg, D. J., 35–36, 324
Iverson, M. A., 107
Ivie, R. L., 328
Izraeli, D., 370
Izraeli, D. N., 370
Izumi, H., 168

Jaastad, K., 295
Jablin, F. M., 139, 142
Jackson, A., 151
Jackson, C., 189
Jackson, D. N., 180
Jackson, J. M., 179, 250, 290, 292
Jackson, P., 314
Jackson, S. E., 130, 135, 182, 279, 280
Jacobs, A., 488
Jacobs, D., 378
Jacobs, E., 494

Jacobs, J., 29, 31
Jacobs, M. K., 100, 480–481, 494
Jacobs, R. C., 123
Jacobsen, B. S., 482
Jacobson, N. S., 490
Jago, A. G., 365–367
James, R. M., 134, 199
Janis, I. L., 4, 15, 39–40, 52, 59, 161, 306, 319, 324–336
Jankowski, M. S., 457
Janowski, C. L., 352
Jarboe, S. C., 261
Jarvis, P. A., 153
Jehn, K. A., 238, 292, 311–312
Jenkins, T. B., 74
Jennings, J. R., 273, 274
Jensen, C., 392
Jensen, M. A. C., 15, 155
Jensen-Campbell, L. A., 238
Jermier, J. M., 346–347
Jetten, J., 394
Johnson, A. G., 6
Johnson, B. T., 280, 370
Johnson, C., 77, 159, 295, 296
Johnson, D., 186
Johnson, D. W., 243, 276, 400, 404
Johnson, F., 478
Johnson, M. P., 227
Johnson, N. R., 442, 449, 467, 469
Johnson, P., 388
Johnson, R., 243
Johnson, R. D., 459
Johnson, R. T., 276, 400, 404
Johnson, S., 361
Johnston, L. D., 94
Joireman, J. A., 247
Jolliff, D. L., 487
Jonas, K., 397
Jones, D. R., 483
Jones, E. E., 133, 391
Jones, E. S., 350
Jones, G. V., 386
Jones, S. C., 106
Jones, T. S., 421
Jones, W. H., 61
Joo, Y. Y., 220
Jordan-Edney, N. L., 430
Jorgensen, B. W., 105
Joseph, L., 273, 274
Josephs, R. A., 75
Jourard, S., 156
Judd, C. M., 37, 324, 389

Julian, J. W., 344
Jung, C. G., 91

Kagan, J., 93
Kagan-Moore, L., 484, 491
Kahn, A., 247, 387, 388, 425, 459, 461
Kahn, R. L., 128, 129, 344
Kallgren, C. A., 121
Kalven, H., Jr., 198, 200
Kamarck, T. W., 273, 274
Kameda, T., 189, 198, 292, 314, 324
Kandel, D. B., 105, 106, 136
Kanouse, D. E., 252
Kanter, R. M., 280
Kanungo, R. N., 217
Kanzer, M., 474
Kaplan, H. I., 474
Kaplan, K. J., 421
Kaplan, M. F., 200, 314, 324
Kaplan, R., 51
Kaplan, R. E., 478
Kaplan, S., 51
Kaplowitz, S. A., 218
Kapoor, A., 220
Kapos, M., 90
Karau, S. J., 250, 289, 291, 293–294, 297, 300, 354–355, 369
Karren, R. J., 104
Karten, S. J., 370
Karuza, J., 314
Kashima, Y., 73–75
Kashy, D. A., 91, 484
Katz, D., 129, 344
Katz, R., 311, 348
Katz, T., 259
Katzenbach, J. R., 166
Kaufman, K., 388
Kaufman-Gilliland, C. M., 259
Kaul, J. D., 31
Kaul, T., 478, 489–491
Kaul, T. J., 487
Kazaoka, K., 476
Keating, C. F., 133
Keating, J., 424
Keating, J. P., 39, 423
Keider, I., 229
Keil, L. J., 259
Kelem, R. T., 460–461
Kellehear, A., 33
Kelley, C. E., 426

Kelley, H. H., 47, 52, 107–111, 138, 156, 190, 192, 238, 246, 253, 256, 449
Kelley, J., 121
Kelley, K. N., 250
Kelly, J. R., 297
Kelly, L., 152
Kelman, H. C., 123, 225–226, 232, 404
Kelsey, R. M., 274
Kemery, E. R., 130
Kennedy, C., 79
Kennedy, J., 379, 381
Kennedy, J. F., 369, 379
Kennedy, R. F., 334
Kenney, R. A., 353
Kenny, D. A., 17, 37, 49, 91, 351, 488
Kenrick, D. T., 191
Kent, M. V., 20, 24
Kent, S., 433
Kerckhoff, A. C., 105, 451
Kerpel, L., 259
Kerr, N., 259
Kerr, N. L., 200, 201, 226, 248, 250, 253, 285, 290, 292, 307, 320
Kerr, S., 346–347, 359, 360
Keys, C. B., 317
Keyton, J., 149, 152
Keyton, J., 154
Kidder, T., 152
Kiecolt-Glaser, J. K., 101
Kieffer, S. C., 488
Kiesler, C. A., 180, 181
Kiesler, D. J., 475
Kiesler, S., 245, 420, 458
Kiesler, S. B., 180, 181
Kilham, W., 212
Kilik, L., 151
Killian, L. M., 444, 453, 456, 468
Kilmann, R. H., 31
Kilmartin, C. T., 214, 487
Kilpatrick, S., 379
Kim, H., 227
Kim, S. H., 238, 251, 265
Kim, U., 73–75
Kimberly, J. C., 135
Kimmel, A. J., 451
King, D. W., 130, 144
King, G., 187
King, G. A., 242
King, L. A., 130, 144

King, M. C., 391
King, R. G., Jr., 212
Kipnis, D., 133, 218–220, 225–230, 232
Kipper, D. A., 475
Kirby, P., 308
Kircher, J. C., 489
Kirchler, E., 135
Kirchman, C. M., 62
Kirkpatrick, S. A., 351
Kirmeyer, S. L., 417
Kirshner, B. J., 152
Kirson, D., 256
Kitayama, S., 73, 83, 85, 308
Kivlighan, D. M., Jr., 482, 485–489
Klein, K. W., 421
Klenke, K., 369, 371
Klentz, B., 224, 463
Kless, S. J., 65
Kline, N. S., 434
Klonsky, B. G., 354
Klotz, M. L., 238
Knight, D. P., 133
Knight, G. P., 247
Knight, H. C., 283
Kniveton, B., 307
Knowles, E. S., 17, 152, 273, 419, 422, 430
Koberg, C. S., 221
Kochan, T. A., 344
Koenig, K., 43
Kogan, N., 320, 322
Köhler, O., 284
Kohut, H., 59
Kolb, K. J., 276
Komorita, S. S., 245, 248, 249, 250, 256, 262, 265
Kondracki, B. A., 426
Korda, M., 434
Kounin, J. S., 227–228
Kowalski, R. M., 74, 94, 107, 117, 156
Krackhardt, D., 142
Krakauer, J., 412, 418–419
Kramer, G. P., 285, 307, 320
Kramer, M. W., 297
Kramer, R. M., 249, 290, 381
Kramer, T. J., 297
Krantz, D., 413
Kraus, L. A., 62
Krause, C. A., 4, 233
Krause, S., 92

Krauss, R. M., 254, 259, 264, 383, 388
Kraut, R. E., 17
Kravitz, D. A., 286, 288
Kreuser, B., 430
Krishnan, R., 309
Kroeck, K. G., 369
Krueger, D. L., 350
Krueger, J., 191
Kruglanski, A. W., 197, 229, 240
Kuhlman, D. M., 246
Kuhn, M. H., 86
Kulik, J. A., 96
Kulo, J., 488
Kumar, K., 135
Kunda, Z., 99
Kuo, C. L., 297
Kupersmidt, J. B., 136
Kurtz, S., 263
Kurusu, T. A., 483
Kushell, E., 370
Kushigian, R. H., 449
Kushnir, T., 159
Kutash, I. L., 474
Kutner, B., 384
Kuypers, B. C., 158
Kwan, J. L., 191
Kypri, K., 394

L'Herrou, T., 188
La Gaipa, J. J., 47
Lacoursiere, R. B., 154–155
Lafasto, F. M. J., 170
LaFrance, M., 388
Lage, E., 184
Laing, R. D., 465
Lakin, M., 477
Lal Goel, M., 95
Lalonde, R. N., 82
Lamberth, J., 105
Lamborn, S. D.
Lamm, H., 295, 322–323
Landau, J., 350
Landers, D. M., 270, 274, 294
Landry, P., 379
Landsberger, H. A., 30, 164
Lane, D. W., 248
Langan, C. J., 193
Langham, P., 239
Lanier, K., 214
Lanius, U. F., 414
Lankau, M. J., 350
Lanzetta, J. T., 311

LaPiere, R., 450
Larey, T. S., 299
Larsen, I. M., 311
Larsen, K. S., 182
Larsen, O. N., 450
Larson, C. E., 170
Larson, J. R., Jr., 307, 316–317
Larson, L. L., 360
Larson, R. W., 252
Lassegard, M., 83, 152
Latané, B., 178, 187–189, 203, 204, 222, 288–290, 460
Latham, D. R., 359
Latham, G. P., 166, 292
Latour, A., 35
LaTour, S., 262–263
Laughlin, P. R., 281, 285, 311, 317, 324
Lautenschlager, G. J., 91
Lauterbach, K., 219
Lawler, E. J., 216, 226–227, 255
Lawrence, B. S., 349
Lawson, R. B., 331
Lawton, M. P., 103
Layton, B. D., 218
Lazarfeld, P. H., 31
Le Bon, G., 12–13, 18, 453–455, 459–460, 467–469
Lea, M., 17
Leak, G. K., 487
Leary, M. R., 59–64, 74, 80, 82–85, 90, 94, 107–108, 117, 156, 222, 250, 354, 369
Leathers, D. G., 318
Leavitt, H. J., 139–142
Leck, K., 191
Leclerc, F., 447
Lee, M. T., 133
Lee, P. W. H., 451
Lee, R. M., 59
Leen, R., 133
Leffler, A., 132
Leggett, K. L., 299
Lehman, D. R., 83
Leichtentritt, J., 487
Leigh, G. K., 491
Lenk, H., 294
Lenkert, A., 397
Leo, G., 187
Leon, G. R., 435
Leonard, W. M., II, 465
Leone, D. R., 103

Lepore, S. J., 415, 423
Lepsius, M. R., 217
Lester, M. E., 491
Leung, P. W. L., 451
Levanoni, E., 128
Leve, C., 330
Leventhal, G. S., 248, 314
Levesque, M. J., 488
Levine, D. I., 168
Levine, J. M., 20, 24, 107, 110–115, 117, 123, 180, 185, 195–197, 238, 239, 265, 278, 279, 310, 412, 417–418
Levine, M., 465
Levine, S., 68
Levine, S. V., 455
LeVine, R. A., 378
Levinger, G., 105, 228, 287
Levy, A. B., 484, 491
Lewicki, R. J., 255
Lewin, K., 5, 10, 11, 14, 20, 23–24, 40–42, 46, 52, 149, 292, 363–364, 371, 473, 493
Lewin, M., 11, 24
Lewis, C. A., 394
Lewis, H. S., 340
Lewis, S. A., 193
Ley, D., 429, 458
Leyden, D. P., 309
Liang, J., 62
Liberty, H. J., 447
Lichtman, R. R., 483
Liden, R. C., 367
Lieberman, M. A., 478, 482, 483, 485, 488, 491–492
Liebowitz, S. J., 167
Lightdale, J. R., 70
Lightstone, J., 454
Likert, R., 345, 359
Limayem, M., 298–299
Lin, Y., 379
Lind, E., 388
Lind, E. A., 214, 263
Lindblom, C. E., 319
Lindeman, M., 395
Lindholm, C., 217
Lindley, P., 484
Lindskold, S., 259, 261, 404–405, 430, 459
Linkous, R. A., 271
Lintell, M., 413
Linville, P. W., 389–390, 392
Lipinski, R. M., 134, 199

Lippitt, R., 40–42, 52, 363–364, 371
Lippmann, W., 392
Lipset, S. M., 465
Lipsitz, A., 383
Litman-Adizes, T., 228
Little, B. L., 293
Littlepage, G., 48, 218, 219, 284, 308, 352
Liu, J. H., 188
Liu, X., 62
Lobb, B., 213
Lobel, M., 98, 483
Lobel, S. A., 279
Locke, E. A., 166, 277, 351
Lockwood, P., 99
Lodewijkx, H. F. M., 112
Loehlin, J. C., 65
Loewen, L. J., 415
Lofland, J., 445, 447, 467
Lofland, L. H., 120
Lohr, N., 79
Long, S., 474
Longley, J., 325, 332
Longman, R. S., 151
Lord, C. G., 133
Lord, R. G., 345–346, 351, 353–354, 368
Lorge, I., 283, 284
Lott, A. J., 150, 151
Lott, B. E., 150, 151
Lovaglia, M. J., 142
Low, L. C. K., 451
Lowe, K. B., 369
Lowery, B. J., 482
Lublin, S. C., 457, 459
Luce, R. D., 244
Lueder, D. C., 361
Luft, J., 488
Luhtanen, R., 79–83
Lundgren, S., 185
Lundin, W. A., 229
Lundy, J. L., 135
Lundy, R. M., 183
Luria, S. M., 435
Luschen, G., 294
Luthar, H. K., 355
Lutsky, N., 225
Lyall, L. M., 133
Lyde, M., 73–75
Lyman, S. M., 430

Maass, A., 186–187, 191, 204, 391

Maassen, G. H., 37, 136
Maccoby, E. E., 95
MacCoun, R., 214
MacCoun, R. J., 201, 285, 307, 320
MacCracken, M. J., 276
MacFarlane, A., 71
MacGavin, L., 219, 220
Mack, R. W., 256
MacKenzie, K. R., 486, 494
MacKenzie, S. B., 346
Mackie, D., 191
Mackie, D. M., 66
MacNeil, M. K., 15, 123
Macy, B. A., 168
Madigan, R. M., 293
Madson, L., 75, 95
Magaro, P. A., 105
Magee, J., 238
Mahar, L., 358
Maher, K. J., 353–354, 369
Mahler, H. I. M., 96
Mahrer, A. R., 482
Mai-Dalton, R. R., 350
Maier, N. R. F., 284
Major, B., 80, 98, 219, 220
Makhijani, M., 354–355, 369
Maki, J. E., 253
Malloy, T. E., 17, 49, 91, 352
Manderscheid, R. W., 485
Mang, M., 411
Manis, M., 142
Mann, F. C., 345, 364
Mann, J. H., 350
Mann, L., 90, 212, 319, 325, 328, 340, 447, 456–459, 461–463
Mann, R. D., 199, 369
Manstead, A. S. R., 394
Mantell, D. M., 222
Manuck, S. B., 273, 274
Manz, C. C., 330, 343
Manzi, J. M., 84
Maras, P., 70
Marcus, D. K., 484
Marelich, W. D., 73–75
Markham, S. E., 368
Markovitz, R. J., 488
Markovsky, B., 135
Marks, I. M., 484
Markus, H., 271, 273, 274
Markus, H. R., 73, 75, 83, 85, 308
Marriott, R. G., 330
Marrow, A. J., 11, 477

Marshall-Goodall, B. S., 273, 275
Marston, P. J., 220
Martell, R. F., 354
Martens, R., 270, 274
Martin, B., 286, 288
Martin, D. C., 349
Martin, E. D., 455
Martin, J., 213, 415
Martin, M. M., 62, 135
Martin, R., 238
Martz, J. M., 159
Maruyama, G., 243, 400
Marwell, G., 219
Marx, K., 378
Maslach, C., 74, 182–183, 466
Maslow, A. H., 465
Masson, R. L., 494
Mathes, E. W., 459, 461
Mathews, E., 413
Mathewson, G. C., 111
Matsumoto, H., 83
Matter, C. F., 273, 422
Matthews, A., 397
Matthews, R. W., 424
Mauch, D., 230
Maxmen, J., 482, 489
May, K. E., 279
Mayadas, N., 159
Mayer, T., 138
Mayo, E., 19, 30, 164, 268
Mayseless, O., 191
Mazur, A., 132, 133
McAdam, D., 452
McAdams, D. P., 92
McAndrew, F. T., 438
McArthur, L. Z., 133, 393
McAuliffe, T. G., 388
McBride, D., 17, 153, 164
McBurney, D. H., 412
McCallum, D. M., 379
McCallum, R., 424
McCanse, A. A., 359
McCarthy, B., 82
McCarthy, J. D., 452
McCauley, C., 332
McCauley, C. C., 391–392
McClaren, H. A., 425
McClelland, D. C., 92, 231
McClelland, G., 350
McCline, R. L., 213
McClintock, C. G., 246, 253, 259
McCool, M. A., Jr., 449
McCown, N. E., 354
McCranie, E. W., 135

McCusker, C., 72
McDonald, R., 484
McDougall, W., 67
McFarland, D. D., 142
McGarty, C., 9, 81
McGillicuddy, N. B., 261
McGovern, T.V., 486–487
McGrath, J. E., 6, 10–12, 20, 24, 45, 48, 240, 281, 288, 297, 298
McGrath, M. R., 360
McGraw, K. M., 327, 349
McGregor, D., 31
McGuire, C., 330, 332
McGuire, C. V., 77
McGuire, E. J., 381–382
McGuire, J. P., 487
McGuire, T. W., 458
McGuire, W. J., 77
McIntosh, B., 331
McKay, C. P., 435
McKeage, R. L., 156
McKersie, R. B., 257
McLaughlin-Volpe, T., 398
McLeod, P. L., 279
McMahon, A. M., 349
McMahon, J. T., 359
McPartland, T. S., 86
McPhail, C., 443–445, 453, 467, 469
McQueen, L. R., 248
McRoberts, C., 490
Meadow, A., 295
Medalia, N. Z., 450
Medow, H., 293
Meek, D., 201
Meeker, B. F., 248
Meeker, J. R., 246
Meerloo, J. A., 455
Meeus, W. H. J., 213, 222
Megargee, E. I., 350
Meglino, B. M., 150
Mehrabian, A., 414, 421, 426
Meier, G. H., 93
Meindl, J. R., 342
Melucci, A., 465
Mennecke, B. E., 160
Merei, F., 185
Merry, C. J., 317
Merry, J., 152
Merton, R. K., 9, 115
Messé, L. A., 245, 252
Messick, D. M., 84, 246, 248, 249, 259, 274, 381, 391
Messick, S., 180

Metcalf, J., 423
Meudell, P. R., 308
Meumann, E., 269
Meyer, C. W., III, 214
Meyer, D. J., 489
Meyer, H. J., 7
Meyer, J. P., 105
Michaels, G. Y., 252
Michaels, J. W., 271
Michaelsen, L. K., 135
Michels, R., 231
Michener, H. A., 220, 227, 229
Mickelson, K. D., 81, 96
Middlemist, R. D., 273, 422
Midgley, E. H., 249
Mikolic, J. M., 253–254
Miles, M., 485, 491–492
Miles, R. H., 129
Milesi, A., 391
Milgram, S., 18, 103, 193, 209–225, 231–233, 415, 444, 445–448, 450, 460, 466, 468
Miller, A. G., 212, 213, 233, 392
Miller, C. E., 248, 314, 324
Miller, D. L., 453
Miller, D. T., 120, 144, 224, 246
Miller, F. D., 102
Miller, F. G., 273
Miller, J. G., 47, 73
Miller, K. I., 142
Miller, N., 191, 226, 387, 400–402, 451
Miller, P., 70
Miller, R. S., 94, 178, 193, 369–370
Mills, J., 111–112
Mills, T. M., 194
Millson, M., 195
Minami, H., 430
Minionis, D., 161
Mintz, A., 449
Miranda, F. S. B., 213
Misumi, J., 345, 359
Mitchell, R. C., 491
Mitchell, T., 82
Mitchell, T. R., 238
Mitroff, I. I., 31
Mixon, D., 212
Miyake, K., 98
Mizrahi, K., 70
Mobley, W. H., 150
Modigliani, A., 223
Moede, W., 287
Moehle, D., 383

Moghaddam, F. M., 407
Molleman, E., 98
Molm, L. D., 135, 216, 227, 350
Money, W. H., 359
Monge, P. R., 142
Monroe, C., 318–319
Montanari, J. R., 330, 332
Monteith, M. J., 403
Montgomery, R. L., 123
Moore, D. L., 275
Moore, J. C., 134, 142
Moore, L. E., 197
Moore, P. J., 96
Moore, W. C., 430
Moorhead, G., 330–332
Moos, R. H., 153
Morasch, B., 424
Moreland, R. L., 20, 24, 66, 103, 107, 110–115, 117, 123, 239, 278, 279, 309, 310, 343, 417–418, 433
Moreno, J. L., 35, 37, 136, 145, 473, 475
Morgan, B. B., Jr., 161, 279
Mori, K., 245
Morrill, C., 238, 259, 260
Morrill, C., 265
Morris, C. G., 48, 281, 310
Morris, W. N., 97–98, 178, 193
Morrison, D. M., 39
Morrison, H., 228
Moscovici, S., 184–187, 203, 204, 322–323
Mosier, K., 191
Moss, M. K., 459
Mossholder, K. W., 130
Mount, M. K., 351
Mounts, N., 65
Mouton, J. S., 359–360, 371, 378–379
Mowat, F., 415
Moxley, N. F., 141
Moxley, R. L., 141
Mphuthing, T., 394
Mucchi-Faina, A., 194, 204
Mudrack, P. E., 8, 128, 149, 151, 154
Mueller, A. L., 218, 352
Mueller, J., 314
Mulac, A., 297
Mulder, M., 227, 343

Mullen, B., 7, 77, 134, 154, 162–163, 178, 188, 191, 275, 295, 296, 331, 353, 394, 448, 462
Mullison, D., 488–489
Multon, K. D., 488
Mumford, M. D., 351, 369
Mummendey, A., 390, 394
Mumpower, J. L., 399
Mungy, G., 185
Murata, K., 252
Murnighan, J. K., 256, 313
Murphy-Berman, V., 422
Murphy, C. J., 346, 359, 360
Murphy, L. R., 451, 452
Murphy, P. J., 448, 457
Murphy, S. A., 39
Murray, H. A., 91
Murrell, S. A., 101
Musante, L., 263
Myers, A. E., 161
Myers, D. E., 135
Myers, D. G., 321–324
Myers, D. J., 382, 384

Nacci, P., 227
Nadler, W. P., 482
Naffrechoux, M., 184
Nagao, D. H., 178
Nagasundaram, M., 299
Nahemow, L., 103
Nail, P. R., 180
Nash, R. F., 50, 257
Nathan, B. R., 358–359
Nathan, M. L., 358–359
Nathanson, L., 297
National Center for State Courts [NCSC], 200
Naveh, D., 39, 158
Neale, M. A., 290
Neck, C. P., 330, 332
Neider, L. L., 368
Nelson, B. N., 214
Nelson, D., 243
Nelson, R., 361
Nelson, Y., 421
Nemeth, C. J., 184–187, 191–192, 199, 279, 427
Newcomb, A. F., 136
Newcomb, T. M., 12, 17, 42–44, 52, 103–106, 116, 123, 136, 138, 175, 194, 457
Newell, J. D., 31
Newell, K. M., 270

Newman, B., 195
Newman, E., 350
Newman, O., 430
Newton, J. W., 459, 461, 463
Newton, R., 370
Nezlek, J., 227
Nicholls, J. R., 361
Nida, S., 460
Nielsen, J. M., 95, 135, 349
Nietzel, M. T., 199, 200, 202, 204
Nikkel, E., 318–319
Nixon, C. T., 219
Nixon, H. L., 294
Noel, J. G., 394
Nolan, L. L., 236, 238, 249, 260
Norasakkunkit, V., 83
Norma, E., 37
Norman, R. Z., 133
Norris, F. H., 101
North, R. C., 382
Northouse, P. G., 341, 371
Norvell, N., 81, 250, 399
Nosanchuk, T. A., 454
Nowak, A., 178, 188
Nye, J. L., 49, 336, 354, 370
Nyquist, L. V., 350
Nystrom, P. C., 360

O'Brien, R. M., 378
O'Brien, S. P., 75–76
O'Connor, B., 214
O'Connor, B. P., 105
O'Connor, C., 256
O'Connor, J., 244, 369
O'Grady, K. E., 485
O'Malley, P. M., 94
Oakes, P. J., 9, 17, 390
Offerman, L. R., 369
Offermann, L. R., 168, 219, 227, 233, 342, 344
Offner, A. K., 297
Ofshe, R., 132–133
Ohbuchi, K., 238
Ohshima, T., 272
Okun, M., 274
Okun, M. A., 100
Olian, J. D., 369
Oliver, P. E., 452, 455, 467, 469
Ones, D. S., 351
Ono, K., 198, 313
Oosterbaan, H., 379
Orbell, J., 250
Orcutt, J. D., 194

Orive, R., 190
Ormont, L. R., 487
Orne, M. T., 212–213
Orris, J. B., 358
Orth, J. E., 133
Osborn, A. F., 295, 297
Osborn, R. N., 360
Osgood, D. W., 94
Oskamp, S., 389
Ostrom, T. M., 291, 389
Otten, W., 247
Ouellette, J. A., 185
Owen, G., 141
Owen, W. F., 150
Oxley, D., 100
Oyserman, D., 448

Padawer-Singer, A. M., 201
Page, M. S., 73–75
Page, R. A., 459
Palinkas, L. A., 435
Palmer, G. J., 352
Palsane, M. N., 415
Pandey, J., 228
Pantaleo, G., 390
Panzarella, R., 222
Parad, H. W., 139
Parisi-Carew, E., 361
Park, B., 389–390, 392
Park, W., 332
Parker, J. C., 253–254
Parkinson, C. N., 319
Parks, C., 198
Parks, C. D., 20, 245, 249, 250, 256, 262, 265, 292
Parkum, K. H., 94
Parkum, V. C., 94
Parnes, S. J., 295
Parsons, H. M., 412
Parsons, T., 66, 126
Pattee, L., 136
Patterson, M. L., 133, 419–421, 426
Patton, B., 265
Paul, G. L., 492
Paulus, P. B., 291, 296–297, 299, 302, 424
Pavelshak, M. A., 113
Pearce, J. L., 256
Pearson, J. A., 97–98
Peckham, V., 287
Pelletier, L. G., 227
Pelz, D. C., 279
Pemberton, M. B., 18, 379–381

Pence, E. C., 370
Pendell, S. D., 197
Pennebaker, J. W., 413, 451, 452, 487
Pennington, N., 197–200, 204
Penrod, S., 178, 188, 197–200, 204
Pepitone, A., 12, 107, 162, 194, 457, 459, 461
Peplau, L. A., 218–220
Pepper, S., 105
Pérez, J. A., 185
Perlick, D., 454
Perls, F., 475
Perrin, S., 182
Perrone, K. M., 483
Perry, E. S., 485
Personnaz, B., 184, 186–187
Peters, L. H., 358–359
Peterson, D. R., 236
Peterson, M. F., 130, 350
Peterson, R. S., 191–192, 279, 330–332
Petty, R. E., 192, 251, 291, 293
Philipsen, G., 297
Phillips, J. S., 353
Phillips, S. T., 432
Phinney, J. S., 75
Phoon, W. H., 451
Pierce, G. R., 100
Pigors, P., 344
Pilisuk, M., 259
Pilkington, C. J., 99
Pillai, R., 343
Pinkley R. L., 379, 381
Pittard-Payne, B., 94
Platow, M.J., 394
Platt, L., 483
Platz, S. J., 370
Plous, S., 320
Podsakoff, P. M., 228, 346
Pohlmann, J. T., 358–359
Polek, D., 280
Poletes, G., 291
Polley, R. B., 35
Pollis, N. P., 123
Polzer, J. T., 290, 379
Pool, G. J., 100, 191
Porter, L. W., 142, 242, 256
Porter, N., 350
Postman, L. J., 392, 450
Postmes, T., 467
Powell, G. N., 104
Pradhan, P., 292, 311

Prapavessis, H., 150
Pratkanis, A. R., 77, 330
Pratt, J. H., 473
Preiss, J. J., 78
Prentice, D. A., 70, 120, 144
Prentice-Dunn, S., 464
Preston, L. A., 75–76
Preston, M., 224
Price, R. H., 100
Primeau, B. E., 133
Prince, C., 301
Prince, G., 297
Probasco, P., 330
Proshansky, H., 384
Prpich, W., 242
Pruitt, D. G., 238, 251, 253–254, 257, 260–261, 262, 265, 321–322, 325, 332
Pruyn, J., 98
Pugh, M. D., 135
Purvis, D., 191
Putman, V., 297, 299, 302

Quadagno, J. S., 69
Quattrone, G. A., 389, 391
Quinn, R. E., 360
Quinn, R. P., 128

Raaijmakers, Q. A. W., 213, 222
Rabbie, J., 96, 379
Radloff, R., 39, 410, 418, 428, 435, 437, 438
Ragone, G., 450
Raiffa, H., 244, 262
Ranelli, C. J., 197
Rapoport, A., 244, 245, 259, 379
Raven, B. H., 214–218, 228, 229, 323
Ravlin, E., 277
Rawlins, W. K., 314
Read, K. E., 71
Read, P. P., 3, 121, 125, 136, 143, 144
Reardon, K., 98
Reckman, R. F., 193
Reddin, W. J., 359
Reddington, K., 308, 352
Redl, F., 103
Reed, E. S., 378
Reese, H., 295
Reibstein, J., 482
Reicher, S. D., 9, 17, 465
Reichl, A. J., 394
Reichling, G., 162

Reid, A., 70, 77
Reis, H. T., 73
Reizenstein, R. M., 213
Remland, M. S., 421
Rempel, J. K., 487
Reno, R. R., 121
Reynolds, K., 150
Rhodewalt, F., 359
Rice, O. K., 382
Rice, R. W., 352, 359, 370
Rickards, T., 297
Ridgeway, C. L., 133–135, 144, 154, 280
Riecken, H. W., 39, 111, 117
Riemer, J. W., 103
Riess, M., 427
Riggiero, J., 398
Riggins, T., 379
Rim, Y., 229
Ringelmann, M., 286–289, 300
Riordan, C., 398
Ríos, D. I., 73–75
Ripley, J. S., 483
Rittle, R. H., 274
Rivera, A. N., 248, 255
Roark, A. E., 487
Robbins, S. B., 59
Robert, H. M., 241
Robertson, R. B., 369
Robison, W., 308, 352
Roby, T. B., 311
Rochat, F., 223
Rock, D. A., 276
Rodin, J., 423
Roethlisberger, F. J., 30, 164, 268
Rofé, Y., 90
Rogelberg, S. G., 280
Rogers, C., 478–479
Rogers, M. S., 311
Rogers, P. A., 107–108
Rogers, R. W., 464
Rohrbaugh, M., 489
Rojahn, K., 354
Roland, E. J., 299
Roll, S., 350
Romberger, B., 349
Romero, A. A., 288
Rook, K. S., 60
Roos, P. A., 349
Roos, P. D., 430
Ropp, S. A., 398
Rosa, E., 133
Rose, J., 61
Rose, S. D., 476

Rosenbaum, M. E., 239
Rosenbaum, W. B., 248
Rosenberg, M., 79
Rosenfeld, P., 427
Rosenfield, D., 392
Rosenholtz, S. J., 133
Rosenthal, R., 31, 53, 349
Rosenthal, R. A., 128
Rosnow, R. L., 31, 53, 450–451
Ross, J., 251
Ross, L., 178, 251, 252
Ross, M., 83
Roth, B. E., 474
Roth, C. P., 426
Roth, E. W., 487
Rothbart, M., 390, 392–393
Rothgerber, H., 384–385, 390
Rothman, A. L., 451
Rouhana, N. N., 404
Rountree, C. A., 97–98
Rourke, P. A., 273, 275
Rowe, J. S., 271
Rowe, R. R., 320
Rowe, W. G., 342
Rowland, K. M., 276
Roy, D. F., 161
Roy, M. C., 298–299
Rozell, D., 77
Rozin, P., 177
Ruback, R. B., 197, 297
Rubenstein, C. M., 60, 62
Rubin, J. Z., 238, 246, 247, 251,
    252, 257, 260, 262, 265,
    403
Rubini, M., 73
Rubner, M. B., 354
Rudin, S., 391
Ruffin, P. F., 379
Ruffin, P. P., 379
Rugel, R. P., 489
Rule, B. G., 263, 462
Rumery, S. M., 280
Runcimann, W. G., 456
Rusbult, C. E., 159, 424
Rush, M. C., 353
Rushton, J. P., 51, 69, 396
Russell, B., 208
Russell, D., 61
Russell, J. A., 414
Russell, R. J. H., 455
Russo, E. M., 180, 185
Rust, M., 401
Rust, M. C., 401
Rutan, J. S., 474

Ryen, A. H., 387, 388, 425
Ryterband, E. C., 168

Sabini, J., 177
Sacks, J. M., 475
Sadock, B. J., 474
Sadow, J. S., 276
Saegert, S., 415
Sagar, H. A., 389, 392, 399
Saks, M. J., 200–201
Salas, E., 42, 53, 154, 165, 166,
    170, 277, 279, 295, 296, 301,
    331, 353
Salazar, A. J., 8, 124
Salovey, P., 390
Saltz, E., 448
Samaha, C., 402
Samaha, G. M., 97–98
Sampson, E. E., 195
Sampson, R. V., 230
Samuelson, C. D., 248
Sandal, G. M., 435
Sandelands, L., 14–15
Sanders, G. S., 275, 323
Sanders, J., 221
Sanders, W. B., 429, 431, 438, 465
Sankowsky, D., 342
Sanna, L. J., 20, 274, 290
Santee, R. T., 74, 182
Santi, A., 259
Sapp, S. G., 350
Sarason, B. R., 100
Sarason, I. G., 100
Sarbin, T. R., 130
Sarri, R. C., 159
Sasfy, J., 274
Sattler, D. N., 253
Saul, K., 343
Saxe, L., 196–197
Sayles, M., 100
Scamahorn, S. D., 245
Scandura, T. A., 350
Scarr, H. A., 459, 461
Schachter, S., 17, 39, 96, 103, 111,
    116, 117, 153, 149, 151, 162,
    164, 192, 193–195, 203, 329,
    483
Schaefer, D., 463
Schaefer, R. E., 394
Schaerfl, L. M., 248
Schafer, M., 330
Schauer, A. H., 276
Scheier, M. F., 275, 463
Schein, E. H., 166–167, 183, 224

Schenck-Hamlin, W., 219
Schenk, C., 426
Schersching, C., 314
Scherwitz, L., 133
Scheuble, K. J., 484, 491
Schickel, R., 150, 151, 169
Schkade, J. K., 424
Schlenker, B. R., 82, 94, 112, 213,
    227, 244, 246, 250, 323, 354,
    432
Schlenker, D. R., 432
Schlesinger, A. M., Jr., 326, 327
Schmidt, D. E., 423
Schmidt, G. W., 48
Schmidt, N., 62
Schmidt, S. M., 220, 344
Schminke, M., 277
Schmitt, B. H., 273, 274, 447
Schmitt, D. P., 50
Schmitt, D. R., 219, 243
Schmitt, N., 366–367
Schneebaum, T., 71
Schneider, J., 134
Schneider, M. L., 415
Schofield, J. W., 138, 389, 392,
    397, 399, 400
Schooler, C., 64
Schopler, J., 18, 105, 218, 379–381,
    387, 390, 396, 407, 424
Schrier, P. E., 219
Schriesheim, C. A., 219, 228, 346,
    358–360, 368
Schuchart, G. E., 430
Schuler, R. S., 128–130
Schurz, G., 213
Schuster, B., 448
Schut, H., 62
Schutz, W. C., 92–93, 105–106, 116
Schwartz, B., 432
Schwartz, C. G., 29
Schwartz, H., 29, 31
Schwartz, J., 256
Schwartz, M. S., 29
Schwartz, P., 219, 221
Schwartz, S. H., 73, 222, 395
Schwartz-Kenney, B. M., 353
Schweitzer, S., 402
Scotch, N., 342
Scott, M. B., 430
Scott, R., 120
Scott, W. A., 120
Sculley, J., 236, 265
Sears, P. S., 46, 292
Sears, R., 384

Seashore, S. E., 161, 163, 168, 345, 359
Sechrest, L. B., 230–231, 311, 420, 486
Sederholm, H., 238
Sedikides, C., 379, 389, 396, 407
Seeger, J. A., 159
Seeman, M., 100
Seeman, T., 100
Segal, H. A., 224
Segal, M., 392
Segal, M. W., 103, 106, 136–137
Sekerak, G. J., 274
Seligman, M. E. P., 482, 490
Sell, J., 135, 247
Semin, G. R., 73
Senn, D. J., 105
Sensenig, J., 227
Sermat, V., 62
Service, E. R., 382
Seta, C. E., 273–275, 297
Seta, J. J., 273–275, 297, 424
Seymour, W. R., 276
Sgro, J. A., 370
Shackelford, S., 185, 354
Shah, P. P., 311–312
Shambaugh, P. W., 160
Shamir, B., 342
Shanab, M. E., 213
Shapiro, D. A., 492
Sharah, H. S., 487
Shaughnessy, P., 482
Shaver, P., 60–62, 256
Shaw, J. I., 228–229
Shaw, J. S., 84
Shaw, L. M., 161
Shaw, M. E., 6, 139–142, 161, 239, 250–251, 279, 281, 283, 490
Shea, G. P., 277, 293, 315
Sheats, P., 8, 125–128
Shechter, D., 183, 192
Shechtman, Z., 487
Sheffey, S., 191, 312
Sheinman, L., 227
Shepard, H. A., 156–157, 379
Sheppard, B. H., 261
Shepperd, J. A., 249, 291
Sheridan, C. L., 212
Sherif, C. W., 6, 122, 376–407
Sherif, M., 6, 15, 122–123, 143, 175, 192, 376–407, 456
Sherman, J., 191
Sherman, S. J., 17, 393

Sherrod, D. R., 423
Sherry, P., 482
Sherwood, J. J., 167
Shiflett, S., 285
Shils, E., 66, 126
Shiu, W. Y., 279
Shotland, R. L., 274
Shotola, R. W., 12
Showers, C. J., 432
Shrauger, J. S., 106
Shukla, R. M., 298
Shure, G. H., 246, 311
Sias, P. M., 142
Sicoly, F., 83
Sieber, J., 31, 458
Siegel, R., 238
Siegler, I. C., 91
Sikes, J., 400
Silbergeld, S., 485
Silbiger, H., 308, 352
Silver, M., 221
Silver, W. S., 293, 327
Simmel, G., 6, 378
Simon, A. F., 401, 407
Simon, B., 390, 392
Simon, R. J., 200
Simon, S., 459
Simonetta, L. G., 370
Simonton, D. K., 348, 349
Sims, H. P., 83, 330
Singelis, T. M., 73–74
Singer, A. N., 201
Singer, E., 43
Singer, J., 411
Singer, J. E., 413, 454, 457, 459
Singer, R. L. J., 201
Singh, P., 228
Sirois, F., 451
Sistrunk, F., 229
Sivacek, J. M., 245
Sivakumar, K., 195
Sivasubramaniam, N., 369
Skinner, B. F., 46–47, 476
Skon, L., 243
Skrzypek, G. J., 358
Slaten, E., 94
Slater, P. E., 128
Slavson, S. R., 474
Slim, R., 379
Sloane, L. R., 152
Smalley, B. S., 344, 346, 352, 371
Smart, R., 92
Smelser, N. J., 450
Smernou, L. E., 91

Smith, C., 394
Smith, C. M., 191, 312
Smith, D. H., 95
Smith, D. K., 166
Smith, D. M., 369
Smith, D. R., 37
Smith, J. A., 488
Smith, J. E., 488
Smith, L. F., 133
Smith, M., 99–100
Smith, M. B., 322
Smith, P. B., 130, 180–181, 204, 350, 491
Smith, P. K., 448
Smith, R. B., III, 255
Smith, S. L., 379, 381
Smith, T. G., 123
Smith, T. L., 35
Smith, V. A., 379, 381
Smithson, M., 134
Smoke, W. H., 241, 284, 313
Snapp, M., 400
Snell, W. E., Jr., 219, 220
Snidman, N., 93
Snodgrass, S. E., 349
Snoek, J. D., 128
Snow, D. A., 452, 455, 467, 469
Snow-Turek, A. L., 100
Snyder, C. R., 83, 84, 98, 152, 483
Snyder, H. N., 197
Snyder, R. C., 256
Sodikoff, C., 421
Solano, C. H., 91
Soldz, S., 152
Solem, A. R., 284
Solomon, H., 284
Solomon, M. R., 383
Solomon, S. H., 424
Solomon, S. K., 423
Somech, A., 294
Sommer, K. L., 62–63, 95
Sommer, R., 424–427, 439
Soraci, S., 82
Sorokin, P. A., 229
Sorrels, J. P., 121
Sorrentino, R. M., 187, 242, 331, 352–353
Sottolano, D., 219, 220
Soutenkijk, S., 227
Spangler, W. D., 369
Spears, R., 17, 83, 390, 394, 467
Spence, J. T., 350
Spencer, C., 388
Spencer, C. P., 182

Spiegel, S. B., 485
Spillane, R., 213
Spink, K. S., 293
Spinner, B., 61
Spira, J. L., 474
Spitzer, C. E., 187
Spivey, R. W., 464
Springston, J., 152
Sproull, L., 245, 420
Squire, S., 123
Sriram, N., 392
Sroka, K. R., 197
St. Clair, L., 14–15
Stadulis, R. E., 276
Stager, S. F., 80–81
Stahelski, A. J., 246, 253
Stahlberg, D., 391
Stangor, C., 397
Stanton & Poors, 349
Stapp, J., 74
Stark, R., 66
Starr, P. A., 252
Stasser, G., 201, 288, 309,
    316–317
Stasson, M. F., 198, 279, 292,
    308, 313, 324
Statham, A., 124
Staub, E., 221, 225, 395
Staw, B. M., 251
Steblay, N. M., 224
Stech, F. J., 259
Steers, R. M., 242
Steers, W. N., 73–75
Stein, R. T., 352
Steinberg, L., 65
Steiner, I. D., 12–13, 277,
    281–287, 300
Steininger, M., 31
Steinzor, B., 426
Stelwagen, T., 227
Stemerding, A., 343
Stephan, C., 400
Stephan, W. G., 392, 393, 397
Stephens, D., 99
Stephenson, G. M., 307, 308
Sternberg, R. J., 259, 261
Stets, J. E., 119, 220
Stevens, O. J., 246
Stevenson, W. B., 256
Stever, G. S., 91
Stewart, A. E., 20
Stewart, D., 317
Stewart, D. W., 359

Stewart, E. A., 20
Stewart, G. L., 343
Stewart, P. A., 134
Stewart, R., 219
Stiles, W. B., 133, 492
Stillwell, A., 252
Stitt, L., 392
Stockbauer, J. W., 388
Stogdill, R. M., 7, 346, 348, 350,
    351, 358–360, 364
Stokes, J. P., 62
Stokols, D., 411, 413, 421, 438
Stollak, G. E., 252
Stone, G. P., 130
Stone, P. J., 35
Stone, W., 474
Stoner, J. A. F., 320
Stones, C. R., 39
Stoop, J. R., 283
Storms, M. D., 423
Storr, A., 60, 90
Stotland, E., 17, 230
Stout, R. J., 165, 279
Stratenwerth, I., 392
Stratham, A., 370
Strauss, A. L., 31, 448
Street, M. D., 330
Streufert, S., 378, 382
Streufert, S. C., 378, 382
Stricker, L. J., 180
Strickland, D., 214
Strickland, L. H., 230
Stringer, M., 394
Strodtbeck, F. L., 134, 158, 199,
    369, 427
Stroebe, M. S., 62, 66
Stroebe, W., 62, 66, 284, 290,
    295–296, 397
Strong, S. R., 214
Strube, M. J., 358
Struch, N., 395
Stryker, S., 64, 124
Stuart, C., 370
Stull, D. E., 105
Stumpf, S. A., 314
Stuster, J., 415, 435, 438
Suedfeld, P., 60, 415, 418
Suenaga, T., 272
Sugimori, S., 189, 314
Sugisawa, H., 62
Suls, J., 85, 238, 275
Sumner, W. G., 378, 386
Sunderland, J., 394

Sundstrom, E., 165, 167, 411,
    416, 424, 434–435
Svanum, S., 463
Swaffin-Smith, C., 220
Swap, W. C., 246
Swezey, R. W., 166
Swingle, P. G., 259
Sympson, S. C., 98, 483
Syna, H., 261
Syroit, J. E. M. M., 112
Szamrej, J., 188
Szymanski, K., 274, 290, 292

't Hart, P., 330
Taber, T. D., 367
Tafarodi, R. W., 75
Tajfel, H., 9, 75, 78, 393–394, 406
Tajima, K., 290
Takahashi, Y., 73–75
Tambor, E. S., 63
Tanaka, K., 430
Tanford, S., 178, 188, 199
Tang, J., 350
Tang, S., 195
Tannenbaum, S. I., 279
Tarde, G., 454
Tarrant, C. M., 197
Tassinary, L. G., 273, 275
Tassone, J., 311
Tata, J., 195
Taylor, D. A., 436–437, 487
Taylor, D. M., 407
Taylor, D. W., 295
Taylor, F. W., 164
Taylor, H. F., 138, 239–240
Taylor, L. A., 70, 316
Taylor, M. S., 277
Taylor, S., 489
Taylor, S. E., 98, 319, 483
Teddlie, C., 422
Tedeschi, J. T., 227, 248, 255
Teger, A., 252
Tennen, H., 96
Tepper, B. J., 358
Terdal, S. K., 63
Terkel, S., 58, 63, 65, 66, 79, 80,
    84, 85
Terry, D. J., 81
Terry, R., 37
Tesser, A., 99–100, 184
Testa, M., 98
Tetlock, P. E., 327, 330, 332
Tetrault, L. A., 358

Thameling, C. L., 197
Themen, J., 482
Thew, B. D., 454
Thibaut, J. W., 47, 52, 107–111, 138, 156, 194–195, 256, 262–263, 379, 383
Thomas, E. J., 284
Thomas, G. C., 423
Thomas, J. C., 353
Thomas, K. W., 261
Thomas, L. S., 191, 312
Thomas, W. I., 15–16
Thompson, J. E., 399
Thompson, L., 238, 257, 259, 265
Thompson, L. L., 259
Thompson, M. E., 226–227
Thor, K. K., 351
Thorne, A., 152
Thorne, B., 138
Thorngate, W. B., 253
Thrasher, F. M., 429
Thune, E. S., 485
Thurman, B., 133
Tice, D. M., 63
Tichenor, V., 485
Tindale, R. S., 178, 191, 307, 312, 320, 336
Titus, L. J., 272, 274, 275
Titus, W., 316–317
Tjosvold, D., 166, 238, 242, 277
Toch, H., 444, 445, 448, 450, 466, 468
Toennies, F., 66
Toledo, R., 447
Tolnay, S. E., 448
Tolstoy, L., 347–348
Tomaka, J., 274
Torrance, E. P., 134
Touliatos, J., 130
Towler, G., 274
Trafimow, D., 77
Travis, L. E., 269–271
Triandis, H. C., 71–74, 77, 85
Triplett, N., 13, 17, 269, 272
Trommsdorff, G., 295
Troper, J. D., 276
Trost, M. R., 191
Trujillo, N., 32
Tschuschke, V., 487
Tsui, A. S., 352, 370
Tubbs, S. L., 48
Tuckman, B. W., 15, 24, 155–160, 169, 486

Turner, J. C., 6, 7, 9, 17, 70, 75, 78, 81, 393–394, 406
Turner, M., 113
Turner, M. E., 330
Turner, R. H., 128, 444, 453, 456, 468
Tushman, M., 311
Tyerman, A., 388
Tyler, T. R., 214, 216
Tziner, A., 279

Uchino, B. N., 101
Uhl-Bien, M., 344, 367–368
Uhlig, S. R., 430
Ulschak, F. L., 297
Umberson, D., 94
Urban, L. M., 402
Uris, A., 326
Ursin, H., 435
Ury, W., 257–259, 265
Utman, C. H., 277

Vaernes, R., 435
Valacich, J. S., 299
Valins, S., 430–431
Vallbona, C., 133
Vallerand, R. J., 227
van de Kragt, A., 250
van de Vliert, E., 261
van den Hove, D., 259
van der Linden, J. L., 136
van Knippenberg, A., 83, 98
van Oostrum, J., 379
Van Avermaet, E., 186
Van de Ven, A. H., 297–298
Van der Linden, J. L., 37
Van Egeren, L. F., 257
Van Kijk, R., 227
Van Lange, P. A. M., 247
Van Leeuwen, M. D., 180
Van Ryn, M., 100
Van Sell, M., 129–130
Van Zelst, R. H., 161
Vandello, J. A., 183–184
VanLeeuwen, M. D., 274, 275
Vanman, E. J., 402
Varela, J. A., 310–311
Vaughan, S. I., 309
Veach, T. L., 324
Vecchio, R. P., 358–359, 361
Veitch, J. A., 413
Veitch, R., 105, 412
Verhagen, J., 227

Vescio, T. K., 78
Vidmar, N., 202
Villaseñor, V., 4, 175, 190, 193, 204
Vinacke, W. E., 245, 246
Vinogradov, S., 482
Vinokur, A., 311, 323–324
Vinokur, A. D., 100
Vinsel, A., 433–434
Visser, L., 379
Vollrath, D. A., 178, 307, 320, 336
Volpe, C. E., 279
Von Dras, D. D., 91
Vorauer, J. D., 224
Vroom, V. H., 364–367, 371

Wachtler, J., 97–98, 185–186, 199, 427
Wack, D. L., 274
Wackenhut, J., 447
Wade, C., 182
Wade, G., 397
Wagner, D. G., 50, 133–134
Wagner, J. A., 315
Wahrman, R., 135
Walden, T., 424
Waldman, D. A., 368
Walker, C. J., 451
Walker, H. A., 133–134, 216, 349
Walker, L., 262–263
Walker, M., 152
Wall, V. D., Jr., 236, 238, 249, 260
Wallach, M. A., 320, 322
Walsh, Y., 455
Walster, G. W., 298
Walton, R. E., 257
Wang, M. A., 274
Wanlass, J., 482, 488
Wann, D. L., 394
Ward, A., 251, 252
Ware, R., 490
Warfield-Coppock, N., 350
Warncke, M., 435
Warriner, G. K., 218
Warwick, D., 43
Waters, K., 245, 420
Watkins, D., 86
Watson, C., 349
Watson, R. I., Jr., 458–459
Watson, W. E., 135
Waung, M., 133
Weaver, J. L., 161

Webb, N. M., 276
Weber, J. G., 84
Weber, M., 217, 368
Webster, D. M., 197, 240
Webster, M., Jr., 133, 350
Wegner, D. M., 308, 463
Weick, K. E., 31, 32
Weigel, R. H., 399
Weigold, M. F., 323
Weinberg, M. S., 78
Weinberg, R., 151
Weingart, L., 311
Weingart, L. R., 32, 166, 259, 292
Weinstein, N., 413
Weintraub, M. I., 451
Weiss, J. A., 311
Weiss, R. F., 273
Weiss, R. S., 61
Wekselberg, V., 294
Welch, D. A., 330
Weldon, E., 166, 292, 311
Weldon, M. S., 308–309
Wells, E. A., 39
Wells, P. A., 455
Werner, J., 324
Werner, P., 455
West, S. G., 186–187, 222, 224, 384, 476
Weston, S. B., 270
Westphal, J. D., 349
Wetherell, M. S., 9, 17
Weybrew, B. B., 435
Wheelan, S. A., 155–160, 170
Wheeler, D. D., 325, 333
Wheeler, D. S., 74
Wheeler, L., 73, 98, 436, 454
Wheeless, L. R., 219
Whisler, E. W., 48
White, B. J., 376–407
White, C. A., 117
White, H. C., 117
White, K. M., 81
White, R., 40–42, 52, 363–364, 371
White, R. K., 11, 388–389
Whitehead, T. N., 268, 269, 277–278, 293, 294, 301
Whitley, B. E., Jr., 38, 138
Whitmyre, J. W., 295
Whitney, D. J., 163
Whitney, I., 448
Whitney, K., 279
Whyte, G., 320
Whyte, W. F., 29–30, 51, 53, 429, 431–432

Wicker, A. W., 416–417
Wicklund, R. A., 275, 463
Widmeyer, W. N., 150, 151, 153, 278, 381–382
Wieselquist, J., 379, 381
Wiesenfeld, B. M., 314
Wilder, D., 407
Wilder, D. A., 179, 191–192, 280, 386, 399, 401
Wilderman, S., 433
Wilke, H., 83
Wilke, H. A. M., 134
Wilkinson, I., 219, 220
Willemsen, T. M., 354
Williams, J. A., 397
Williams, J. E., 354
Williams, J. M., 448, 457
Williams, K. D., 62–63, 250, 288–291, 293–294, 300
Williamson, S. A., 54, 160
Willis, F. N., 421, 422
Willis, R. H., 180
Wills, T. A., 85, 95, 100–101, 488
Willsie, D. A., 103
Wilpinski, C., 107
Wilson, E. O., 68, 132, 396
Wilson, J. K., 94
Wilson, J. R., 484
Wilson, M., 383
Wilson, R. K., 247
Wilson, S. R., 251
Wilson, W., 387
Winer, B. J., 345
Wingert, M. L., 239, 278, 279
Winquist, J. R., 316
Winquist, L., 17
Winstead, B., 95
Winter, D. G., 92, 231
Winter, J. P., 297
Wirtz, P. W., 369
Wiseman, R. L., 219
Witte, E. H., 184–185, 204, 336
Witteman, H., 236
Witteman, H. R., 261
Wittenbaum, G. M., 288, 309, 316–317
Wohlstein, R. R., 453
Wolf, A., 474
Wolf, S., 179, 188
Wolfe, D., 17
Wolfe, D. M., 128
Wolfe, R., 74
Wolin, S. S., 465
Wondimu, H., 86

Wood, J., 81
Wood, J. T., 312
Wood, J. V., 98, 483
Wood, W., 182, 185, 191, 279–280, 354, 370
Woodman, R. W., 167
Worchel, P., 241
Worchel, S., 97–98, 185, 227, 354, 384–385, 387, 388, 397, 399, 402, 422
Worringham, C. J., 274
Worth, L. T., 391
Worthington, E. L., Jr., 483
Wortman, C. B., 482
Wortman, P. M., 311
Wotman, S. R., 252
Wright, J. C., 139
Wright, P. H., 105
Wright, R. A., 291
Wright, S. C., 398
Wright, S. L., 97–98
Wright, S. S., 79, 355
Wright, T. L., 106, 136
Wrightsman, L. S., 181, 199, 200, 202, 204, 244
Wrong, D., 208, 216
Wrong, D. H., 59
Wu, J. Z., 262
Wulf, L. J., 426
Wyer, R. S., Jr., 398
Wynne, B. E., 160
Wysocki, J., 359

Yablonsky, L., 382, 429
Yahya, K. A., 213
Yalom, I., 485, 491–492
Yalom, I. D., 5, 161, 475–476, 482–484, 486, 495
Yalom, V. J., 482
Yamagishi, K., 249
Yamagishi, T., 246
Yamaguchi, S., 73–75
Yammarino, F. J., 368, 369
Yang, J., 220
Yang, K., 91
Yanof, D. S., 113
Yates, A., 123
Yau, J., 86
Yetton, P. W., 365–366
Yin, R. K., 39, 52
Yohai, S., 422
Yoon, C., 390
Yoon, J., 216
Yost, J. H., 451

Yost, P. R., 293
Young, R. D., 80–81
Youngs, G. A., Jr., 227, 256
Yovetich, N., 288
Yukelson, D., 151
Yuki, M., 73–75
Yukl, G. A., 219, 220, 227, 341
Yum, N., 73–75
Yurko, K., 61

Zabbini, S., 391
Zaccaro, S. J., 161, 291, 351
Zajac, E. J., 349
Zajonc, R. B., 241, 270–277, 284, 299, 313

Zald, M. N., 452
Zamarripa, P. O., 350
Zamir, S., 379
Zamorano, M. A. M., 213
Zand, D. E., 314
Zander, A., 1, 5, 6, 11–12, 17, 24, 29, 46, 53, 66, 101–102, 116, 149, 230, 231, 243, 277, 293–294, 301, 345
Zanna, M. P., 323–324, 487
Zavalloni, M., 322–323
Zeisel, H., 198, 200
Zelditch, M., Jr., 50, 53, 133–134, 144, 216
Zembrodt, I. M., 159

Zhao, L., 350
Zheng, L., 188
Zigarmi, D., 361–362
Zigarmi, P., 361–362
Ziller, R. C., 104, 457
Zillmann, D., 79, 462
Zimbardo, P. G., 94, 222, 457–463, 466, 467, 469
Zimmerman, S., 198, 313
Zimmerman, S. K., 292
Zimpfer, D. G., 490
Zuber, J. A., 324
Zurcher, L. A., Jr., 158
Zuwerink, J. R., 403

Subject Index

Action research, 20
Additive tasks, **281**–282, 286
Adjustment
   group approaches to, 472–493
   loneliness and 60–62
   and membership in radical groups, 455
   psychogenic illnesses, 451
   self-disclosure and, 487
   social comparison and, 96
   social support in groups, 100–101, 273–274
   suicide and groups, 13–14
   territory and, 433
   unhealthy group norms and, 123–124
Affiliation
   instinctive determinants of, 59–62
   introversion-extraversion and, 91
   motive (n Affiliation), 91–92
   need for intimacy and, 92
   need for power and, 92
   seating patterns and, 424
   sex differences in, 94–95
   social comparison, 95–100
Agentic state, **221**
Aggression
   deindividuation and, 458–459
   frustration and, 259
   panics, 442–443, 448–449
   reactions to queue violations, 447
   riots and mobs, 447–448
   sociometric standing and, 139
   sports spectators, 457
Alcoholics Anonymous (AA), 481, 482–483, 488
Andes survivors, 3, 120–139
Anticonformity, **182**–**183**
Apodoca v. Oregon, 201
Aristotle, 58
Arousal
   contagion in audiences, 454
   deindividuation and, 462

   in mobs, 447–448
   reactions to high density, 422–423
Artists circles, 3, 90
Attitude(s)
   Bennington study of changes in, 42–44
   correlations among group members', 189
   coercive persuasion, 224
   compliance and conversion, 225–226
   impact of groups on, 42–44
   persuasion in groups, 191–192
Attraction
   boring group members and, 107–108
   changes during intergroup conflict,
      386–387
   complementarity principle, **105**–**106**
   conflict, 239
   determinants of, 103–110
   FIRO forms of compatibility, 105–106
   leader-member exchanges, 367–368
   mere exposure and, 103
   minimax principle, **107**–**108**
   Newcomb's dormitory study of, 103–105
   personal versus social, 150
   proximity and, 102–103
   reactions to attitudinal deviants, 240–241
   reciprocity principle, **106**–**107**
   self-evaluation maintenance and, 99–100
   similarity principle, **104**–**105**
   social exchange theory of, 108–110
Attraction relations, **136**
   changes during intergroup conflict, 386–387
   determinants of standing in, 136–139
   dyadic chaining, 104
   homophily, 137
   intergroup conflict, 386–387
   maintaining balance in, 137–139
   person/group fit and, 138–139
   reciprocity in, 106–107, 136–137
   similarity and, 104–105

transitivity in, 136–137
Attributional theory of crowding, 422–423
Audiences, **446**
Authority relations, *see also* Status relations, **131**
  head-of-the-table effect and, 427
  emergence as leader, 348–353
  legitimate power and, 216
  power and, 216–217
  status differentiation, 130–135
  status generalization, 133–135
  territories and, 433–435
  verbal and nonverbal dominance, 132–133
Autokinetic effect, 122
B = f (P, E), **14**, 348
Baiting crowds, **456**–457
Balance theory, **137**–138, 239
Bay of Pigs, 4, 306
Behavior setting, **415**–418
Behaviorism, **46**–47
Belongingness hypothesis, 59–**60**
Bennington Study, 42–44
Beowolf, 340
Big five factors of personality, 91, **351**
  group affiliation and, 91
  leadership and, 350–351
Brainstorming, **295**–298
Brainwashing, 224
California vs. Juan Corona, 3–4, 174–194
Case study method, **39**
Casual crowds, 445–446
Catharsis, **487**
Charismatic leadership, 217, 368–369
Cicero, 2
Classes as groups
  coercive influence in, 227–228
  composition effects and performance, 279
  conflict in, 237
  Jigsaw method, 400–401
  noise and learning, 413
  ripple effect in, **228**
  social facilitation of performance in, 276–277
Coalitions
  conflict and, 256
  resistance to influence, 177–178
  revolutionary, **226**–227
Cognition, *see* Social cognition
Cognitive dissonance theory, 111–112
Cognitive-behavioral therapy groups, **476**–477
Coleadership, **485**
Collective
  effort model (CEM), **293**–294
  hope, 483
  identity, *see* Social identity
  information-processing model, **307**–308

inhibition, 308
  memory, **307**–309
Collective behavior, **443**–466
  characteristics of social collectives, 444
  crowds, **444**–449
  crowds-as-mad perspective, 466–467
  theoretical analyses of, 453–466
Collective movements, **449**–453
  group formation and, 101–102
  social movements, 452–453
  types of, 450–453
Collective self-esteem, **79**
Collectivism, **71**
  cultural differences in, 71–72
  group performance and, 294
  individual differences in, 73–74
  interdependents and independents, **73**
Communication
  brainstorming and, 295–298
  clustering and, 189
  cohesion and, 152
  common communication problems,
    318–319
  constraints and groupthink, 330–331
  discussion, 309–315
  discussion to consensus, 313
  during jury deliberations, 198–199
  equilibrium model of nonverbal, 420–421
  informational power, 218
  language use during intergroup conflict, 388
  measuring, 54–55
  negotiation as, 257–258
  networks, 139–142
  of intentions during conflict, 254–255, 259
  personal conflict and patterns of, 239
  pooling information through, 315–318
  power tactics and, 228
  Roberts Rules of Order, 241
  rumors, 450–451
  and seating arrangements, 426–427
  self-disclosure, 156, 487
  signaling status and authority, 132–134
  social dilemmas, 249
  when deindividuated, 459
  with subordinates, 365–366
  with a group deviant, 194–195
Communication networks, **139**
  centrality of, 141
  group efficiency and, 140–141
  hierarchical, 142
  leadership and, 142
  member satisfaction and, 141–142
  types, 139–140
Comparison level, **109**–110

Comparison level for alternatives, **109**–110
Compensation effect, **291**
Compensatory tasks, **282**–283
Competition, **242**
  between group members, 241–247
  individual differences in, 246–247
  Prisoner's Dilemma Game and, 243–248
  seating preferences during, 425–426
  sex differences in, 247
  styles of dealing with conflict, 260–261
Complementarity principle, **105**–106
Compliance, 179–180, 225–226
Compresence-arousal hypothesis, **272**–273
Computer-based groups
  electronic brainstorming, **298**–299
  electronic performance monitoring, 275–276
  flaming in, 458
Conflict, **236**
  coercive influence and, 226–227
  competition and, 241–247, 378–381
  during group development, 156–157
  and group performance, 294
  high temperatures and, 411–412
  in organizations, 239
  ripple effect, **228**
  seating preferences during, 425–426
  spirals, **255**
  types of, 238–251
  value of, 263
Conflict between groups (Intergroup conflict), **236**
  Arab/Israeli wars, 388–389
  biased ingroup-outgroup perceptions, 31–32
  deindividuation, 464–465
  escalation of, 381–385
  evolutionary foundations of, 395–396
  exclusion and, 395
  exploitation and, 382–383
  extended contact hypothesis, 398
  minimal group situation and, 393–394
  perceptual distortions during, 388–393
  realistic conflict theory, **378**–381
  reciprocity norm and, 382
  resolution of, 396–405
  Robbers Cave study of, 376–405
  scapegoat theory of, 384–385
  superordinate goals and the resolution of, 395–397
  territorial disputes, 431–432
Conflict in groups (Intragroup conflict), **236**
  anger and, 256–257, 263
  at Apple Computers, 236–237, 240–242, 263
  basic methods for dealing with, 260–261
  competition and, 241–247
  conflict spirals, **255**
  during group development, 156–157

  escalation of, 251–257
  juries, 198–202
  misperceptions and, 252–253
  personal, **238**–239
  Prisoner's Dilemma Game and, 243–246
  procedural, **241**
  reciprocity and, 255–256
  responsibility claims and, 250–251
  sex differences during, 247
  social dilemmas, 247–251
  substantive, 239–**240**
  third parties and, 262–263
  trucking game study of, 254–255
  workload and, 249–250
Conflict resolution
  cognitive approaches to, 401–403
  contact and, 396–397
  GRIT, 404–405
  Jigsaw method of, 400–401
  modes of, 259–260
  negotiation, 257–258
  third parties and, 262–263
Conformity, *see also* Social influence
  anticonformity, 182–**183**
  Asch's studies of, 175–184
  coalitions and resistance, 177–178
  cohesive groups and conformity pressures, 161–162
  compliance, **179**–180
  conformity across cultures, 181–182
  conversion (private acceptance), 186–187, 225–226
  counterconformity, 182–**183**
  Crutchfield apparatus, 180
  foot-in-the-door technique, 223
  group size and, 178–179
  groupthink and, 325–326
  idiosyncrasy credits, 185–186
  individual differences in susceptibility to, 182–183
  informational influence and, 190–192
  internalization of norms, 121–124
  interpersonal influence, 193–197
  Kelman's theory of conversion, 225–226
  Moscovici's studies of minority influence, 184–187
  normative influence, 192–193
  sex differences in, 182
  social impact theory of, 187–189
Conjunctive tasks, **284**–285
Contagion, **454**
Convergence theories of collective behavior, **455**
Cooperation, **242**
  collective (superordinate) goals and, 396–400
  conflict and, 241–246
  GRIT strategies for increasing, 404–405
  individual differences in, 246–247

intergroup conflict resolution, 396–405
Jigsaw method for increasing, 400
leadership as a form of, 344
promoting intergroup, 397–401
seating preferences during, 425–426
Corona jury, 3–4, 174–194
Correlation coefficient, **44**
Correlational methods, **43**
Counterconformity, 182–**183**
Covert observation, **31**
Crazes, **450**
Cross-cultural variations in group behavior
conformity across cultures, 181–182
contact and noncontact cultures, 421
differences in collectivism, 73–75
foreign exchange programs and conflict, 397
in social loafing, 294
in territoriality, 50, 433–432
in competitiveness, 247
in deindividuation, 458–459
and leadership, 350
social identity and, 70–73
Crowding, **422**–424 .
Crowds, **444**–449
as groups, 466–467
baiting, 456–457
street, 445
types of, 444–446
Le Bon's theory of, 12–13, 453–454
Crutchfield apparatus, 180
Cults, 452
Heaven's Gate, 452
People's Temple, 208
personality and membership in, 455
severity of initiation and, 111–112
Curative factors in change groups, 481–489
Darwin, Charles, 68
Degas, 90
Deindividuation, **457**–464
causes of, 457–459
consequences of, 462–464
self-awareness and, 462–464
Density, **421**
Density-intensity hypothesis, **423**
Dependent variables, **41**
Descriptive norms, **121**
Deviance
communication and, 194–195
reactions to, 194–196
Schachter's research on attitudinal, 194–196
Diffusion of responsibility, **222**, 459–460
Discontinuity effect, 18, **379**–381
Discretionary tasks, **284**–285
Discussion, *see also* Communication

as a means of resolving conflict in groups, 259
during jury deliberations, 198–199
polarizing effects of, 322
pooling unshared information, 315–318
stages of, 310–315
to consensus, 313
limitations of, 318–319
Disjunctive tasks, **283**–284
Diversity
conflict and, 239
group composition and, 278–280
and productivity, 279
Donne, John, 58
Downward social comparison, **98**
Dynamic social impact theory, **189**
Electronic performance monitoring (EPM), 275–276
Emergent norm theory of collective behavior, 456–457
Encounter groups, **478**–479
Entitativity, **16**–17
Entrapment, **251**–252
Environmental processes
dangerous settings, 412, 418–419
environmental load, 413–415
groups in isolation, 435–436
interpersonal zones, 419–421
leadership and dangerous settings, 343
noise, 412–413
personal space, **419**–421
reactions to high density settings, 422–424
seating arrangements, 424–427
synomorphy and behavior settings, 415–418
temperature, 411–412
territoriality, 428–435
Equilibrium model of personal space, **420**–421
Equilibrium model of group development, **160**
Ethnocentrism, **386**
Evaluation apprehension, **273**
Evolutionary theory, **50**
Expectations-states theory, 49–50, 133–135, 199
Experimental method, **41**
Fads, **450**
False consensus effect, **191**
Families, 59, 61
Fashions, **450**
Field theory, 14
Foot-in-the-door technique, **223**
Free-riding, **250**, 290
Fundamental attribution error, **224**, 252
Fundamental Interpersonal Relations Orientation (FIRO), **92**
and forms of compatibility, 105–106
measurement of, 92–34
and social motivation, 92–93

Gabor, Zsa-Zsa, 36
Gandhi, Mohandas K., 184
Gangs
    corner gangs, 29–31
    emergent norms in, 457
    territoriality and, 429, 431–432
Gestalt groups, **475**
Gestalt psychology, 14
Goals
    as a characteristic of groups, 10
    competitive, 242–243
    and performance, 292–293
    setting group, 166
    social loafing, 292
Group(s), **5**
    characteristics of, 7–11, 14–18
    congregations as, 66
    crowds as, 466–477
    exclusion from, 60–62
    functions of, 58–69, 100–101, 492–493
    history of, 2
    in exotic environments, 410–436
    interdependence in, 5
    list of definitions of, 6
    membership in stigmatized, 81–82
    open and closed, 104
    perceptions of, 15–17
    primary and secondary, 64–66
    reality of, 12–18
    types of, 2, 102, 165
Group approaches to change, 472–493
Group Attitude Scale, 153
Group attribution error, **391**
Group cohesion, **9**, 148
    alternative conceptions of, 149–154
    anonymity, 459
    as a characteristic of groups, 9
    based on commitment to the group's goals, 151
    conformity and, 161–162
    consequences of, 160–163
    group development and changes in, 154–160
    groupthink and, 328–329
    increases during intergroup conflict, 387–388
    loneliness and membership in groups, 62
    measures of, 152–154
    member satisfaction, 160–161
    performance, 162–163, 294
    primary and secondary groups, 64–66
    reactions to deviants and, 194–196
    teams, 164–168
    therapy-group effectiveness, 486
    tolerance of deviance and, 162
Group composition, **278**

    and conflict, 239
    diversity and productivity, 279
    gender heterogeneity and performance, 279–280
    leadership emergence and, 350, 269–370
    performance, 277–280
    token and performance, 280
    voir dire and juries, 202
Group decision-making, 306–324
    cognitive biases in groups, 319–320
    collective memory systems, 307–309
    commonly reported problems in groups, 318
    decisional stress and groupthink, 329–330
    defective strategies and groupthink, 328
    effectiveness of, 312
    group polarization and, 320–324
    groups as information-processors, 307–315
    groupthink, 324–334
    pooling unshared information, 315–318
    role of leaders in, 317
    social decision schemes, **312**–314, 324
    stages of, 310–315
    voting, 313–314
Group development, **15**
    changes in cohesiveness during, 157–158
    cyclical models of, 160
    dissolution stage, 158–159
    equilibrium model of group development, **160**
    in therapeutic groups, 486–487
    increased conflict during, 156–157
    measuring, 159
    phases in structured learning groups, 479–480
    and performance, 287–288, 308–309
    punctuated equilibrium, 160
    stages of, 155
    Tuckman's theory of, 15–16, 155–160
Group dynamics, **11**
    Cartwright and Zander's definition of, 11–12
    field of, 11–22
    history, 12–23
    interdisciplinary nature of, 18–19
    theoretical perspectives in, 45–51
    topics of research in, 21–22
Group formation
    attraction between members and, 103–110
    belongingness hypothesis, 59–62
    collectivism and, 73–74
    commitment and costs, 110–112
    dissolution of the group, 158–1589
    FIRO theory of, 92–93
    Freud's theory of, 59, 78
    functional theory of, 66–69
    group socialization and, 110–115
    individual differences in joining groups, 90–95

leaving the group, 83–84, 109–110, 158–159
mere exposure and, 102–103
orientation stage, 155–156
reactions to staffing, 417–418
severity of initiation and, 111–112
sex differences in, 94–95
social motivation and, 91–92
social support and, 100–101
social comparison and, 95–100
sociological view of, 64–68
spontaneous crowd formation, 445–446
task demands and, 101–102
Group Environment Scale, 153
Group Environment Questionnaire, 153
Group performance and productivity
arousal and, 273–275
audiences and coaction, **269**
brainstorming, 295–298
cohesion and, 162–164, 294
collective efficacy, **293–294**
collective effort model (CEM), 293–294
coordination losses, **287**
dominant and nondominant tasks, 270–271
effectiveness of juries, 201–202
effects of training, 309
electronic brainstorming, **298–299**
evaluation apprehension and, **273**, 289–290
goals and performance, 292–293
group composition and, 278–280
group development, 157–158
impact of leaders on, 342
interference and reactions to crowding, 424
levels of aspiration and, 47, 292–293
motivation and, **46**
noise and, 411–412
norms and productivity, 162–164
process losses, **286**
Relay test room, 268–269, 277–280, 286
Ringelmann effect, 287–288
role conflict and, 130
social facilitation, 269–277
social loafing and, 286–295
Steiner's theory of, 281–285
systems theory of, 48
task demands and, 281–285
temperature and, 411–412
Group polarization, **322**
causes of, 322–323
history of research into, 320–321
risky-shift, 320–321
Group psychotherapy, **473**, 474–477
Group socialization, **110**
changes in commitment during, 110–112

compliance with norms, 123–124
Moreland and Levine model of, 112–115
role transitions during, 113
Group structure, **8**
characteristic of groups, 8
communication networks, 139–143
development of, 120–143, 157
in juries, 201
iron law of oligarchy, 231
norms, 120–124
obedience and, 221–225
reciprocity of attraction, 106–107
roles, 124–128
sociometric structure, 136–139
status structure, 130–136
Groupmind, **13**
Group-serving bias, **82**
Groupthink, **40**
causes of, 328–330
groups that suffered from, 325
leadership and, 331
prevention, 332–334
symptoms of, 325–328
Ham v. S. Carolina, 202
Harvard Negotiation Project, 257–258
Hatfield-McCoys feud, 382
Hawthorne effect, **30**
Head-of-the-table effect, **427**
Heaven's Gate, 452
Herd instinct, 67
Heuristics, **192**
Hidden profile, **316**
Home advantage, **431–432**
Homophily, 137
Hooliganism, 448, 457
Human potential movement, 477–480
Identity, *see* Self, Social identity
Idiosyncrasy credits, **185–186**
Illusion of group productivity, 290–291
Illusory correlations, **393**
Impressionists, 3, 90–115
Independent variables, **41**
Individual mobility, 83
Individualism, **71**, *see, also,* Collectivism
Informational influence, **190–192**
in therapeutic groups, 484–486
informational power, **218**
and pooling unshared information, 317
Ingroup differentiation bias, **389–390**
Ingroup homogeneity bias, **390**
Ingroup-outgroup bias, **82**, 386–389
and deindividuation, 465
social identity and, 78–79

Injunctive norms, **121**
Interaction
    basic forms, 7–8
    measuring, 54–55
    process analysis, **32**–33, 54–55
Interdependence and independence, **73**
Interpersonal behavior
    boring varieties of, 107–108
    and poor decision making, 318–319
    seating arrangements and, 424–427
Interpersonal group psychotherapy, 475–476
Interpersonal influence, **194**
Interpersonal learning groups, **473**, 477–480
Interpersonal zones, 419–421
Interrole conflict, **129**
Intrarole conflict, **129**
Introversion-extraversion, **91**
Iroquois Theater panic, 449
Jones, James, 4, 208
Jonestown, 4, 208
Juries
    California v. Juan Corona, 3–4, 174–194
    decision rules in, 198–199
    dynamics of, 197–202
    effectiveness of, 200
    majority/minority influence in, 198–199
    size of, 200–201
    verdict- versus evidence-driven, 197–198
Kennedy, John, 4, 306, 316
Kennedy, Robert, 306
King, Jr., Martin Luther, 184
Köhler effect, **284**
KSAs, **278**–279
Ku Klux Klan (KKK), 58, 84, 459
Law of small numbers, 391
Le Bon, G., 453–454
Leader(s) and leadership, **343**, 340–370
    as an inborn trait, 342
    authority, 216–217
    brainstorming groups, 297
    charismatic, 217, 368–369
    closed and open styles, 331
    great-leader theory, 347–348
    group decision making, 317
    groupthink and, 329
    head-of-the-table effect and, 427
    in therapeutic groups, 474–478, 485–486
    in under- and overstaffed groups, 417–418
    mandate phenomenon, 230
    misconceptions about, 340–343
    power and coercion, 228–229
    power, 214–218
    prototypes about, 353–355
    sex differences in leadership style, 354, 369

    sex differences in effectiveness, 370
    substitutes for, 346
    transactional model of, 344
Leader Behavior Description Questionnaire (LBDQ),
    346
Leader categorization theory, **353**
Leader effectiveness
    contingency model of, **355**–359
    leader-member exchange, 367–368
    Leadership Grid, 359–360
    Lewin, Lippitt, and White study of, 40–42
    participation theories of leadership, 361–367, **362**
    situational leadership, **361**
    transformational leadership, **368**–369
    Vroom's normative model, **364**–367
Leader emergence, **348**, 347–353
    babble hypothesis and, 352–353
    cognitive determinants of, 353–355
    ethnicity and, 350
    gender and, 349–350
    group participation and, 352–353
    intelligence and, 349, 351
    personality traits and, 350–351
    physical characteristics and, 348–349
    sex differences, 354–355
    trait model of, 348
Leader Match, 358
Leader prototypes, **353**
Leadership Behavior Description Questionnaire, 346
Least Preferred Co-worker (LPC) Scale, **355**–356
Level of aspiration theory, **46**, 292–293
Linguistic intergroup bias, **390**
Loneliness, **60**–61
Lynch mobs, 448
Mandate phenomenon, **230**
Marx, Groucho, 36
Mass hysteria, **451**
Mcgrath's circumplex theory of group tasks, 10–11
Measurement
    assessing boringness, 107–108
    coding interaction in groups, 133
    collective self-esteem, 80
    Crutchfield apparatus, 180
    example of self-concept measure, 86
    Interaction Process Analysis, 54–55
    of group cohesion, 152–154
    of group development, 159
    operational definition, **152**
Mere exposure, **103**
Mescalero Apaches, 50
Minority influence
    cognitive impact of minorities, 186–187, 191–192
    conversion vs. compliance, 186–187
    in juries, 198–199

minority influence, 184–187
Moscovici's studies of, 184–187
social impact theory of, 187–189
Mickey Mouse, 148, 156
Minimal intergroup situation, **393**
Minimax principle, **107–108**
Mitchell/Stans Watergate conspiracy trial, 198–199
Mixed-motive situations, **243**
Mobbing, 448
Mobs, **447–448**
Monet, Claude, 90–92
National Training Laboratories (NTL), 125–126, 478
Need for power, **92**
Need for intimacy, **92**
Need for affiliation, **91**
Negotiation, distributive and integrative, 257–258
Noise, **412**
Nominal-group technique, **297–298**
Norm(s), **8**
    brainstorming and 295–298
    crowds and emergent, 456–457
    descriptive, **121**
    development of, 121–124
    equality, **248**
    equity, **248**
    group development and, 157
    injunctive, **121**
    normative influence, **192**
    of reciprocity, **246**, 255–256, 382
    productivity in groups, 162–164
    queues and, 446–447
    resource distribution and, 248–249
    Sherif's study of, 15, 122–123
    tit-for-tat, **261**
    transmission of, 123–124
Normative influence, **192**
Obedience to authority, 209–225
Observational methods, **29**, 29–35
    Hawthorne effect, **30**
    nature of, 29–35
    of group cohesion, 152
    overt versus covert, 29–**31**
    participant, **29**
    strengths and weaknesses, 35, 38–39
    structured observational methods, **32–33**
    types of, 29–35
    Whyte's use of the method, 29–31
Open and closed groups, 104
Operational definition, **152**
Optimal distinctiveness theory, 84
Organizations
    coalition formation in, 256
    conflict in, 238–239, 240–241
    contagious psychogenic illnesses in, 451

group composition and performance, 278–279
leadership in, 340–370
office size and status, 433
performance quality, 130
power and influence in, 227–228
quality circles in, 315
reactions to resource allocation in, 248–249
role conflict in, 128–130
self-directed teams, 315
social movements as, 452
status and age, 348–349
teams and performance, 164–168
types of groups in, 165
using groups to promote change, 314–315
women executives' leadership styles, 370
women leaders in, 349–350
Outgroup homogeneity bias, **389–390**
Overload, **415**
Panics, **448–449**
Participant observation, 29
People's Temple Full Gospel Church, 4
Perceived Cohesion Scale, 153
Perceptions
    biased perceptions of the outgroup, 327
    conflict, 259
    during conflict, 245–246, 252–253
    fundamental attribution error, **224**
    ingroup-outgroup bias, 386–388
    of resource allocation, 248–249
    of conflict settings, 242–243
    of leadership, 353–355
    of productivity in groups, 290–291
    outgroup homogeneity bias, 389–390
Personal identity, **70**
Personal space, **419–421**
Personality and individual differences
    group composition and, 279
    in boringness, 107–108
    in collectivism, 73–74
    in conflict modes, 260–261
    in conformity, 182–183
    in individuation, 74
    in leadership style, 355–360
    in leadership emergence, 350–351
    in negotiation styles, 257–258
    in reactions to conflict, 238
    in social participation rate, 455
    in social motivation, 91–93
    introversion-extraversion, 91
    shyness, 93
    social anxiety, 94
    and social values, 246
Persuasive-arguments theory, **323**

Philosophy of science
    basic and applied science, 19–20
    nature of a science, 28
    and the reality of groups debate, 13–15
    the role of theory, 45–51
Power, 208
    agentic state, **221**
    bases, **214–218**
    coercive, 215–216, 227
    dynamics of, 221–225
    expert, **218–219**
    exploitation of one group by another, 382–383
    foot-in-the-door technique, 223
    informational, **218**
    leadership as, 341–342
    legitimate, **216**
    metamorphic effects of, 225–231
    Milgram's studies of, 209–213
    obedience, 209–218
    referent, **217**
    reward, **214–215**
    scapegoating, 383–384
    tactics, 218–221, 253–254
Prejudice
    identity and, 58–84
    reducing racism through intergroup cooperation,
        398–399
    status allocations, 133–134
President Kennedy's advisory committee, 4, 306, 320,
        324–334
Primary groups, **12**, 64
Prisoner's Dilemma Game, **243–248**
    discontinuity effect when groups play, 379–381
    interpersonal style and choices in, 246–247
    perception of partner's motives, 245–246, 252–253
    sex differences in reactions, 247
    studying conflict using, 243–246
    tit-for-tat, **261**
Psychoanalytic group therapy, **474**
Psychodrama, **475**
Psychogenic illness, 451
Psychologie des Foules, 13
Quality circles, 315
Queues, **446–447**
Racial biases in status allocations, 134–135
Racial differences, in collectivism, 75
Reactance, **227**, 251
Reciprocity norm, **246**, 255–256, 382
Reciprocity principle, **106–107**
Reference groups, **43**
Relative deprivation, **455**
Reliability, **32**
Replacement hypothesis of groups, 59
Research methods

    advantages of each type, 28–29, 44–45, 153–154
    case studies, 39–40
    correlational, 42–44
    ethics of, 212–213
    evaluating therapeutic groups, 489–493
    experimental, 40–44
    observational methods, 29–35
    self-report measures, 35–38
Resource dilemmas, **249**
Revolutionary coalitions, **226–227**
Ringelmann effect, 287–288
Riots, 464–465
Risky-shift phenomenon, 320–**321**
Robbers Cave Experiment, **376–405**
Roberts Rules of Order, 241
Roles, **8**
    ambiguity, **128–129**
    Benne and Sheats list of, 127
    conflict, **129–130**
    definition in teams, 166
    differentiation, 124–128, **125**
    emergence of the leader role, 125–127
    examples of, 127
    power of, 222–223
    reactions to crowding, 423
    sex-roles and group membership, 95
    social identity, 70
    stress, 128–130
    task versus socioemotional, 125–127
    transitions during group socialization, 112–115
    types of, 8
Rumors, 450–451
Scapegoat theory of intergroup conflict, 384–385
Sealab, 410–436
Secondary groups, **66**
Self
    awareness, 274–275
    collective identity and, 9
    collectivism and the, 71–72
    identification and the, 78–79
    individuation, 465–466
    insight and therapeutic change, 488–489
    social identity theory of, 75–84
    "Who am I?" measure of, 86
Self-awareness, and deindividuation, 462–464
Self-disclosure, **487**
Self-esteem, **79**
    conformity and, 183
    membership in a stigmatized group and, 81–82
    outgroup rejection and, 394
    and protective biases, 79–84
    sociometer model of, 63–64
Self-evaluation maintenance model, **99–100**
Self-help groups, **473**, 480–481

Self-presentation, **273**
Self-report measures, **35**
  advantages of, 35, 38–39, 153–154
  measuring cohesion using, 152–153
  of group cohesion, 153
  of individualism-collectivism, 73–74
  sociometry as, 35–38
  therapeutic gain as measured by, 490
  types of, 35–39
Self-serving bias, **83**
Self-stereotyping, **78**
Sensitivity-training groups, **478–479**
Sex differences
  group composition and performance, 279–280
  in collectivism, 75
  in competitiveness, 247
  in conformity, 182
  in influence in juries, 199
  in leadership emergence, 349–350, 354–355
  in resource allocations, 248
  in seating preferences, 426
  in social loafing, 294
  in status allocations, 134–135
  joining groups, 94–95
  personal space, 421
Shyness, **93**
Sick building syndrome, 451
Similarity principle, 104–**105**
Size
  as a characteristic of groups, 5–7
  deindividuation, 461–462
  dynamic social impact, 189
  majority influence, 178–179
  norms of reward, 248–249
  of juries, 200–201
  primary and secondary groups, 64–66
  staffing, 417–418
  types of groups as determined by, 6
Small group ecology, 424–427
Snow White, 148, 149
Social anxiety, **94**
Social categorization
  as social cognition, 76–77
  cross-categorization, **402**
  decategorization, **401**
  in the minimal group paradigm, 394–395
  and the ingroup-outgroup bias, 386–389
  and intergroup conflict, 385–393
  recategorization, **401**
  stereotypes as, 402–403
Social cognition, 48, 78
  biased ingroup-outgroup perceptions, 31–32
  biases in calibrating resource allocations, 248–249
  cognitive biases in groups, 319–320

collective memory systems, 307–309
cross-categorization, 402
decategorization, 401
deindividuation and changes in, 465
fundamental attribution error, 224
group-serving attributional bias, 82
heuristic thought and influence, 192
in the minimal group paradigm, 394–395
information processing in groups, 48–49,
    191–192, 307–315
ingroup homogeneity bias, 390
ingroup differentiation bias, 389–390
ingroup-outgroup bias, 82, 386–388
leadership emergence, 353–355
linguistic intergroup bias, 390
misperceptions during conflict, 252–253,
    388–393
outgroup homogeneity bias, 389–390
perceiving groups, 15–17
perception of others' motives, 245–246, 252–253
recategorization, 401
self-serving attributional bias, 83
social categorization, 76–77
social facilitation, 274–275
social identity and, 78–79
social influence and, 191–192
systematic information processing, 191
stereotypes as, 402–403
verdict- versus evidence-driven juries, 197–198
Social combination theory, **277**
Social comparison, **81**
  downward, 98–99, 483
  group formation and, 95–100
  in therapeutic groups, 482–483
  risky shift, 322–324
  self-esteem, 99–100
  social influence, 190–192
  upward, 98–99, 483
  upward and downward, 98–99
Social decision schemes, **312–314**
Social dilemmas, 247–251
  communication during, 249
  free-riding, 250, 290, 292
  public goods dilemmas, 250
  resource allocations, 248–249
  social loafing, 290
  self- and group-serving responsibility claims,
    250–251
  social traps, 249
  sucker effect, 250, 290
Social exchange
  leadership as, 344
  self-disclosure, 487
  theory, 46–**47**, 109–110

Social facilitation, **269**–277
  applications in educational settings, 276–277
  electronic performance monitoring, 275–276
  theories of, 272–275
  Zajonc's analysis of, 270–271
Social identity, **9, 70**
  as a characteristic of groups, 9
  categorization-based biases, 385–393
  collective self-esteem, **79**
  components of, 70
  cultural differences in, 71–73
  deindividuation, 464–465
  ethnic identity, 75
  individual mobility and, 83–84
  individualism and collectivism, **71**–73
  ingroup-outgroup perceptions and, 78–79
  intergroup biases, 386–391
  intergroup bias and, 393–396
  personal identity and, 70
  self-esteem, 79–84
  self-stereotyping and, **78**
  social comparison and, 81–82
  territorial displays, 433
Social impact theory, **187**–189
Social influence, **175**
  attitude change and, 40–42
  brainwashing, 224
  categorization and identification, 75–79
  conformity as, 175–187
  crowd formation and, 445–446
  during conflict, 253–254
  foot-in-the-door technique, 223
  group cohesion and, 161–162
  in adolescent peer groups, 457
  in juries, 197–202
  intensification in cohesive groups, 161–162
  internalization of norms, 121–124
  Moscovici's studies of, 184–187
  nonconformity as, 184–187
  reactance and, 227
  self-esteem and, 79–84
  social identity theory and, **75**
  social impact theory of, 187–189
  sources of, 190–197
Social loafing, **288**–295
Social motivation, and group performance, 291–295
Social movements, **452**–453
  formation of, 101–102
  joining, 455–456
  types of, 452–453
Social structure, **64**
Social support, **100**–101, 273–274
Social traps, **249**
Social values, **246**

Sociobiology, **50**, 67–69
Socioemotional behavior, **8**
  leadership as, 345–346
  roles, **125**-126
  sex differences in, 95
Sociofugal seating, **424**
Sociogram, **37**
Sociometric differentiation, **136**
Sociometric structure, **136**
Sociometry, **37**–39
Sociopetal seating, **424**
Staffing theory, **416**, 415–418
Stanford University therapy group, 4–5
Status
  biases in allocation, 134–135
  differentiation, **132**
  diffuse status characteristics, **133**
  dominance, 132–133
  expectations states theory, 133–135
  generalization, **135**
  head-of-the-table effect and, 427
  influence in juries, 199
  nature of, 130–136
  personal space needs, 421
  power, 216–217
  relations, *see also* Authority relations, **131**
  resistance to influence, 185–186
  specific status characteristics, **133**
  territory and, 433–434
  women leaders in organizations, 349–350
Steinzor effect, **426**
Stereotypes, **391**
Stravinsky, I., 184
Stress, **411**–419
  environmental stressors, 412–419
  in dangerous environments, 412, 418–419
  territoriality and relief from, 430–431
Structured learning groups, **479**–480
Study groups, 276–277
Superordinate goals, **397**
SYMLOG (System of Multiple Level Observation of
  Groups), **33**–35, 152
Synectics, **297**
Synomorphy, **416**
Systems theory, **47**–48
Task(s)
  additive tasks, **281**–282, 286
  compensatory tasks, **282**–283
  conformity and task difficulty, 183–184
  conjunctive tasks, **284**–285
  demands, **281**–285
  discretionary tasks, **284**–285
  disjunctive tasks, **283**–284
  expertise and, 351–352

groups formation and, 101–102
McGrath's circumplex theory of, 10–11
roles, **125–126**
Steiner's theory of, 280–285
Task behavior
    interaction and, 7
    Interaction Process Analysis measures of, 32–33
    leadership, 345–346
    SYMLOG measures of, 33–35
    types of, 10
Team(s), *see also* Work teams
    cohesiveness and performance, 294
    group composition and performance, 279–280
    hockey, 381–382
    intergroup conflict and competition between, 381–382
    self-directed, 315
    team-building, **165**
Team building, **165**
Territoriality, **428**
    cross-cultural differences in, 433–434
    gangs and, 429, 431–432
    group spaces, 430
    home advantage, 431–432
    types of, 428–429
    within groups, 432–436
Therapeutic groups, 417–493
    Alcoholics Anonymous (AA), 481, 482–483, 488
    cognitive-behavioral therapy groups, **476–477**
    curative factors in change groups, **481–489**
    displays of cohesion in, 152
    effectiveness of, 489–491
    example of, 4–5
    Gestalt groups, **475**
    group development in, 486–487
    interpersonal learning groups, **473**, 477–480
    interpersonal group psychotherapy, **475–476**
    leadership in, 474–478, 485–486
    negative effects of, 490–491
    psychoanalytic group therapy, **474**
    psychodrama, **475**
    self-help groups, **473**, 480–481
    social learning in, 383–386
    types of, 473–481
The Rite of Spring, 184
The War of the Worlds radio program, 151
Theories
    attributional, 422–423
    balance theory, 137–138
    cognitive approaches, 48–49
    collective effort model (CEM), 293–294
    collective information-processing model, **307–308**
    collective self-esteem, 79–80
    distraction-conflict theory, 275

equilibrium model of personal space, 420–421
expectations states, 134–135
Fiedler's contingency theory, 355–359
field theory, 14
FIRO, 92–93
Freud's psychoanalysis approach to groups, 59
functional theory of groups, 66–68
idiosyncrasy credits, 185–186
implicit leader, **353**
information processing models of groups, 48–49
Kelman's theory of conversion, 225–226
leader-member exchange, 367–368
Leadership Grid, 359–360
of collective behavior, 453–466
of crowding, 422–424
of group development, 154–160
of social facilitation, 272–275
optimal distinctiveness theory, 84
participation theories of leadership, 361–367
persuasive-arguments, 323–324
realistic conflict theory, 378–381
scapegoat theory of intergroup conflict, **384**–385
selecting, 51
self-evaluation maintenance model, 99–100
situational leadership, 361
social exchange, 108–110
social identity theory, 75–84
social impact, 187–189
sociobiology, 50–51, 67–69
sociometer model, 63–64
staffing, 415–418
Steiner's social combination, 277–285
theoretical perspectives in groups dynamics, 45–51
transformational leadership, 368–369
types of, 46–51
Vroom's normative model, 364–367
Tit-for-Tat, **261**
Training groups (T-groups), 477–478
Transactive memory systems, 308
Twelve Angry Men, 198
Upward social comparison, 98
Validity, 33
van Gogh, Vincent, 90–92
Voir dire, **202**
Walt Disney Studios, 148–165
Who stampede, 442–443
Williams v. Florida, 201
Work Teams, **164**
    characteristics of, 165
    cohesion in, 151, 164–168
    defining roles in, 166
    effectiveness of, 167–168
    member satisfaction and membership in, 160–161
    team-building, **165**–167

Credits

This page constitutes an extension of the copyright page. We have made every effort to trace the ownership of all copyrighted material and to secure permission from copyright holders. In the event of any question arising as to the use of any material, we will be pleased to make the necessary corrections in future printings. Thanks are due to the following authors, publishers, and agents for permission to use the material indicated.

Chapter 2: 30: Figure 2–1 from *Street Corner Society* by W. F. Whyte. Copyright 1943 by University of Chicago. Reprinted by permission. **33:** Table 2–1 from *Personality and Interpersonal Behavior* by Robert Freed Bales. Copyright 1970 by Holt, Rinehart, and Winston, Inc. **34:** Table 2–2 Reprinted with permission of The Free Press, a Division of Simon & Schuster from *SYMLOG: A System for Multiple Level Observation of Groups* by Robert F. Bales, Stephen P. Cohen with Stephen A. Williamson. Copyright © 1979 by The Free Press. **36:** Figure 2–2: from "Perceiving Group Members: A comparison of Derived and Imposed Dimensions" by D. J. Isenberg and J. G. Ennis, *Journal of Personality and Social Psychology*, 1981, 41. Copyright © 1981 by the American Psychological Association. Reprinted with permission.

Chapter 3: 72: Table 3–4 from *Cultures and Organizations: Software of the Mind* by Geert Hofstede. Copyright McGraw-Hill © 1997. Reprinted by permission. **80:** Table 3–5 from "A collective self-esteem scale: Self-evaluation of one's social identity" by R. Luhtanen and J. Crocker, *Personality and Social Psychology Bulletin*, 18, 1992. Reprinted by permission.

Chapter 4: 93: Table 4–1 from *FIRO: A Three-Dimensional Theory of Interpersonal Behavior* by W. C. Schutz. Copyright 1958 by Holt, Rinehart & Winston, Inc. **99:** Figure 4–2 from "Friendship Choice and Performance: Self-Evaluation Maintenance in Children" by A. Tesser, J. Campbell, and M. Smith. In J. Suls and A. G. Greenwald (Eds) *Psychological Perspectives on the Self* (vol. 2). Copyright 1983 by Lawrence Erlbaum Associates, Inc. Reprinted by permission. **102:** Table 4–3 adapted from A. Zander, The Purposes of Groups and Organizations, San Francisco: Jossey-Bass, Inc., 1985, pp. 24–25. Used with permission. **108:** Table 4–4 from "Boredom in Interpersonal Encounters: Antecedents and Social Implications," by M. R. Leary, P. A. Rogers, R. W. Canfield, and C. Coe, *Journal of Personality and Social Psychology*, 1986, 51, 968–975. Copyright 1986 by the American Psychological Association. Reprinted by permission. **113:** Figure 4–5 adapted from "Socialization in Small Groups: Temporal Changes in Individual-Group Relations," by R. L. Moreland and M. J. Levine, *Advances in Experimental Social Psychology*, Vol. 15. Copyright © 1982 by Academic Press. Reprinted by permission.

Chapter 5: 122: Figure 5–1 from *The Psychology of Social Norms* by M. Sherif. Copyright 1936 by Harper & Row. Reprinted by permission of HarperCollins Publishers, Inc. **127:** Table 5–1 adapted from "Functional Roles of Group Members," by K. D. Benne and P. Sheats, *Journal of Social Issues*, 1948, 4(2), 41–49. Copyright 1948 by the Society for the Psychology of Social Issues. Reprinted by permission. **140:** Figure 5–4 from "Communication Networks," by M. E. Shaw. In L. Berkowitz (ed.), *Advances in Experimental Social Psychology*, (Vol. 1). Copyright © 1964 by Academic Press. Reprinted by permission.

Chapter 6: 159: Table 6–3 from "Validation Studies of the Group Development Questionnaire" by S. A. Wheelan and J. M. Hochberger, *Small Group Research*, 27, February 1996. Copyright © 1996 by Sage Publications, Inc. Reprinted by permission of Sage Publications, Inc.

Chapter 7: 174: Table 7–1 adapted from *Jury: The People vs. Juan Corona* by V. Villasenor. Copyright 1977 by Little, Brown, Inc. **176:** Figure 7–1 adapted from "An Experimental Investigation of Group Influence," by S. E. Asch. In *Symposium on Preventive and Social Psychiatry*, April 15–17, Walter Reed Army Institute of Research. Washington, DC: Government Printing

Office. **181:** Figure 7–3 from *Social Psychology,* by L. S. Wrightsman, Brooks/Cole Publishing Company, 1977. **195:** Figure 7–4 from "Deviance, Rejection, and Communication" by S. Schachter, *Journal of Abnormal and Social Psychology,* 1951, 46, 190–207. Copyright 1951 by the American Psychological Association. Adapted by permission. **198:** Table 7–3 from "A Computer Simulation of Jury Decision-Making," by S. Penrod and R. Hastie, *Psychological Bulletin,* 1980, 87, 133–159. Copyright 1980 by the American Psychological Association.

Chapter 8: 229: Figure 8–1 based on data from "Effects of Compliance Outcome and Basis of Power on the Powerholder-Target Relationship," by J. I. Shaw and L. Condelli, *Personality and Social Psychology Bulletin,* 1986, 12, 236–246, Sage Publications, Inc.

Chapter 9: 254: Figure 9–5 from *The Resolution of Conflict: Constructive and Destructive Processes,* by M. Deutsch. Copyright 1973 by Yale University Press. Reprinted by permission. **258:** Table 9–3 from *Getting to Yes: Negotiating Agreement without Giving In,* by R. Fisher and W. Ury. Copyright © 1981 by R. Fisher and W. Ury. Reprinted by permission of Houghton Mifflin Company.

Chapter 10: 272: Table 10–1 data from "Social Enhancement and Impairment of Performance in the Cockroach," by R. B. Zajonc, A. Heingartner, and E. M. Herman, *Journal of Personality and Social Psychology,* 1969, 13, 83–92. Copyright 1969 by the American Psychological Association. **282:** Table 10–2 Adapted from *Group Processes and Productivity* by I. D. Steiner. Copyright © 1972 by Academic Press.

Chapter 11: 331: Figure 11–5 data from "A Laboratory Investigation of Group-think," by J. A. Courtright, *Communication Monographs,* 1978, 45, 229. Reprinted by permission of Speech Communication Association.

Chapter 12: 360: Figure 12–3 from *Leadership Dilemmas—Grid Solutions,* p. 29 by Robert R. Blake and Anne Adams McCanse. Copyright 1991 © by Robert R. Blake and the Estate of Jane S. Mouton. Used with permission. All rights reserved. **364:** Figure 12–5 from *Autocracy and Democracy* by R. K. White and R. Lippitt. Copyright © 1960 by the authors. Reprinted by permission of Harper & Row, Publishers, Inc. **365:** Figure 12–6 Reprinted from *Leadership and Decision-Making,* by Victor H. Vroom and Philip W. Yetton, by permission of the University of Pittsburgh Press. © 1973 by University of Pittsburgh Press.

Chapter 13: 385: Figure 13–3 from "The view from below: Intergroup relations from the perspective of the disadvantaged group," by H. Rothgerber and S. Worchel, *Journal of Personality and Social Psychology,* 73, 1997. Reprinted by permission.

Chapter 14: 410: Figure 14–1 from *Groups Under Stress: Psychological Research in Sealab II,* by R. Radloff and R. Helmreich. Copyright 1968 by Irvington Press. **414:** Figure 14–2 from "Adaptation Levels and Affective Appraisal of Environments" by J. A. Russell and U. F. Lanius, *Journal of Environmental Psychology,* 4, 1984, pp. 119–135. Reprinted by permission of Academic Press, Ltd. London, England. **416:** Table 14–1 from *An Introduction to Ecological Psychology,* by A. W. Wicker, Brooks/Cole Publishing Company, 1979. **417:** Figure 14–3 from "Group Staffing Levels and Responses to Prospective and New Group Members" by M. A. Cini, R. L. Moreland, and J. M. Levine, *Journal of Personality and Social Psychology,* 65. Copyright © 1993 American Psychological Association. Reprinted by permission. **425: Figure 14–4 from** *Personal Space* by Robert Sommer, © 1969 by Prentice-Hall, Inc. Reprinted by permission of the author. **429:** Table 14–3 from *The Environment and Social Behavior* by Irving Altman, Brooks/Cole Publishing Company, 1976. **432:** Excerpt from *Street Corner Society* by W. F. Whyte. Copyright 1943 by University of Chicago. Reprinted by permission. **434:** Table 14.4 from "Privacy Regulation, Territorial Displays, and Effectiveness of Individual Function-

TO THE OWNER OF THIS BOOK:

I hope that you have found *Group Dynamics*, 3rd Edition, useful. So that this book can be improved in a future edition, would you take the time to complete this sheet and return it? Thank you.

School and address: _____

Department: _____

Instructor's name: _____

1. What I like most about this book is: _____

_____

_____

2. What I like least about this book is: _____

_____

_____

3. My general reaction to this book is: _____

_____

4. The name of the course in which I used this book is: _____

_____

5. Were all of the chapters of the book assigned for you to read? _____

   If not, which ones weren't? _____

6. In the space below, or on a separate sheet of paper, please write specific suggestions for improving this book and anything else you'd care to share about your experience in using the book.

_____

_____

_____

_____

_____

Optional:

Your name: _____ Date: _____

May Wadsworth quote you, either in promotion for *Group Dynamics,* 3rd Edition, or in future publishing ventures?

    Yes: _____ No: _____

    Sincerely,

    Donelson R. Forsyth

FOLD HERE

- -

BUSINESS REPLY MAIL

FIRST CLASS   PERMIT NO. 358   PACIFIC GROVE, CA

POSTAGE WILL BE PAID BY ADDRESSEE

ATT: *Donelson R. Forsyth* _____

Wadsworth Publishing Company
10 Davis Drive
Belmont, California 94002

- -

FOLD HERE